THE VISUAL ARTS:

A HISTORY

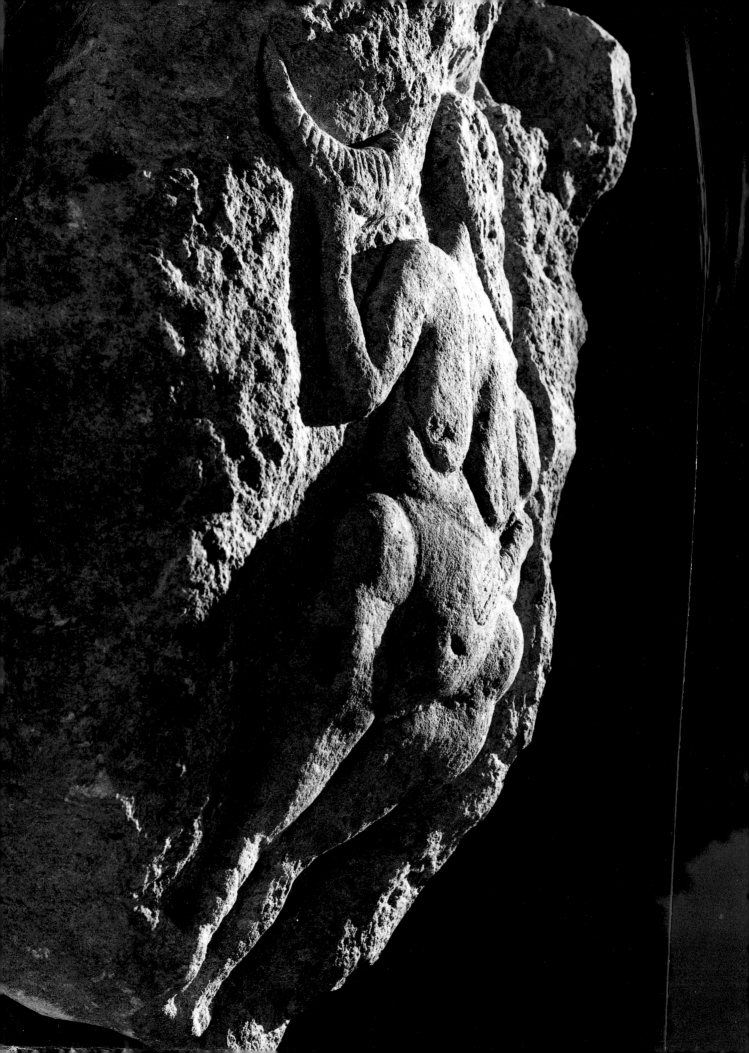

HUGH HONOUR & JOHN FLEMING

THE VISUAL ARTS: A HISTORY

FIFTH EDITION

Prentice Hall Inc., Upper Saddle River, NJ 07458

In memory of John Calmann

Copyright © 1982, 1991, 1995, 2000 Fleming-Honour Ltd.

Prentice Hall Inc.
A Division of Pearson Education
Upper Saddle River, New Jersey 07458

ISBN 0-13-095790-9

This book was designed and produced by
CALMANN & KING LTD., LONDON

Editor: Ursula Payne, Kara Hattersley-Smith
Designer: Karen Osborne, Robert Knapp
Maps: Eugene Fleury
Picture researcher: Susan Bolsom-Morris, Peter Kent
Typesetter: Tek Art Ltd, Croydon
Printed and bound in China

Frontispiece:
Mother Goddess from Laussel, Dordogne, France,
c. 22,000–19,000 BC. Stone, 18^1/$_2$ins (47cm) high.
Musée d'Aquitaine, Bordeaux

Introduction, page 11:
Frank Gehry, Guggenheim Museum, Bilbao, Spain, 1997

Front cover:
Michelangelo, *David*, detail, 1501–3. Marble, c. 18ft (5.5m).
Galleria dell'Accademia, Florence.
Leonardo da Vinci, *Mona Lisa*, detail (reversed), 1503–6.
Panel, 30^1/$_4$ins × 21ins (76.8 × 58.3cm). Louvre, Paris

Back cover:
Vase from Uruk, Iraq, detail, c. 3500–3000 BC.
Alabaster, 36 ins (91.4cm) high. Iraq Museum, Baghdad

A compromise between American and English spelling has been agreed by our publishers. In the transliteration of Greek and non-European names and terms we have adopted the most widely accepted spellings, using for Chinese the new Pinyin system but indexing also under the Wades-Giles system and cross-referencing. The Christian calendar is used throughout. Dates in brackets refer to the birth and death of artists and writers and to the reigns of rulers (emperors, kings and popes).

Acknowledgments

A number of the line drawings in this book have been specially drawn by Calmann & King Ltd. They are grateful to all who have allowed their plans and diagrams to be reproduced. Every effort has been made to contact the copyright holders, but should there be any errors or omissions, they would be pleased to insert the appropriate acknowledgement in any subsequent edition of this publication.

Foreign Languages Press, Peking: 12,60
Harcourt Brace Jovanovich, Orlando: 2,56; 4,21; 4,69; 5,38; 9,5 (Figures from *Gardner's Art Through the Ages*, Eighth Edition by Horst de la Croix and Richard S. Tansey, copyright © 1986 by Harcourt Brace Jovanovich, Inc., reprinted by permission of the publisher)
Haset Kitabevi, Istanbul: 5,22
Ministry of Culture Archeology Department, Rangoon: 6,72
Propyläen Verlag Berlin: 6,64 (H. Härtel and J. Auboyer, *Indien und Südostasien*, Berlin, 1985)
Penguin Books, London: 1,24 (W. Bray and D. Trump, *The Penguin Dictionary of Archaeology*, London 2/1982, fig. 115 copyright © Warwick Bray and David Trump, 1970); 6,7; 6,37; 6,39; 6,44 (G. Michell, *The Penguin Guide to the Monuments of India, volume 1: Buddhist, Jain, Hindu*, London 1989, illustrator K. S. Ravindran, pp. 181, 363, 169 and 470, copyright © George Michell, 1989); 6,112; 6,116; 6,117; 12,94 (R. T. Paine and A. Soper, *The Art and Architecture of Japan*, The Pelican History of Art, London, 3/1981, pp. 294, 309, 304 and 427, copyright © the Estate of Robert Paine and copyright © Alexander Soper, 1955, 1960, 1975, 1981); all reproduced by permission of Penguin Books Ltd; 7,68 (K. J. Conant, *Carolingian and Romanesque Architecture 800–1200*, The Pelican History of Art, London, 1966, fig. 280, illustrator K. J. Conant); 8,25 (R. Ettinghausen and O. Grabar, *The Art and Architecture of Islam 650–1250*, London, 1987, p. 307); reproduced by permission of Yale University Press
Royal Institute of British Architects: 5,71; 6,9; 12,30

CONTENTS

PART TWO

ART AND THE WORLD RELIGIONS

6 BUDDHISM, HINDUSIM AND FAR EASTERN ART   224

7 EARLY CHRISTIAN AND BYZANTINE ART   296

8 EARLY ISLAMIC ART   341

PART THREE

SACRED AND SECULAR ART

9 MEDIEVAL CHRISTENDOM   364

PREFACE

We have been indebted to many friends for help and encouragement in writing this book, above all to the late John Calmann, without whom we should never have had the temerity to embark on it. His death, when it was little more than half finished, deprived us of a warm friend and an outstandingly gifted publisher. Since then all possible assistance has been given to us by his sister Marianne and by his loyal staff. To Sarah Riddell's meticulous editorial skill we owe a very great deal as also to Elisabeth Ingles and Dr I. Grafe whose careful reading of the text has saved us from many errors. Susan Bolsom-Morris was indefatigable in searching for the photographs we wanted. And the book owes much to the patient cooperation and visual sensibility of the designer, Harold Bartram.

For guidance and information either on specific points or more general issues we have importuned a number of scholars, several of whom have kindly read whole chapters or sections and have given us the benefit of their specialized knowledge. They include James Ackerman, Bruce Boucher, Richard Brilliant, J. F. Cahill, Lorenz Eitner, Nicholas Gendle, Oleg Grabar, Ian Graham, Michael Grant, Francis Haskell, Howard Hibbard, Derek Hill, Robert Hillenbrand, John Dixon Hunt, Charles Jencks, Alastair Laing, Sherman E. Lee, Norbert Lynton, M. D. McLeod, Margaret Medley, Patricia Phillips, Alex Potts, Martin Robertson, Michael Rogers, Aaron Scharf, Dorota Starzecka, William Watson and Sarah Jane Whitfield. To all of them we are deeply indebted, as also to the authors of books and periodical articles, too few of whom are recorded in our necessarily very brief bibliography (p. 901), and of course to many librarians, especially those of the London Library and the Kunsthistorisches Institut in Florence.

For help in connection with photographs and other problems we are most grateful to Naomi Caplin, Peter Carson, Françoise Chiarini, John and Thekla Clark, Anne Distel, Aastrid Fischer, Michael Graves, Andreina Griseri, Anne d'Harnoncourt, John Harris, Carlos van Hasselt, John Irwin, Arata Isozaki, Margaret Keswick, Islay Lyons, Henry P. McIlhenny, Dominique de Menil, John H. Morley, John Ross, Laurence Sickman, William Kelly Simpson, Nikos Stangos, Mary Tregear, Hermione Waterfield and William Weaver. And, finally, we must also thank, most gratefully, the friends who have helped us in more personal ways – Noel and Giana Blakiston, Milton Gendel, Nicholas and Susanna Johnston, Ornella Francisci Osti, Donald Richard, Richard Sachs, Gary Schwartz and Sebastian Walker.

Hugh Honour   John Fleming
November 1981

PREFACE TO THE FIFTH EDITION

The substantial additions made to the fourth edition have now been supplemented by 'Concepts' sections and by a number of two-page discussions of urban developments and landscape architecture, from their origins to Frank Lloyd Wright and beyond. The main text has also been expanded, with new illustrations, to account for the remarkable discoveries made in the last few years, notably the paintings in the Chauvet Cave in south-west France which precede those at Lascaux by some 15,000 years; the remarkable late second-millennium BC figurative sculptures found at Sanxindui, China; and the frescoes and mosaics in the Sancta Sanctorum, Rome, the Pope's private oratory which only recently became accessible for the first time since it was completed in 1280. These paintings herald, in the most spectacular way, developments in Italian art with which Giotto and Florentine artists have, until now, been credited.

For help, information and advice in preparing the fourth and fifth editions we have been indebted to many friends whom it is a pleasure to thank by name: Eve Borsook, Bruce Boucher, Francis and Larissa Haskell, Michael Mallon, Bryan Robertson, Robert Skelton, Carl Strehlke and William Watson; for help in other ways we also wish to thank Mendes Hürgi, Margaret Daly Davis, Amanda George, Henry Hawley, Walter Kaiser, Maria Kecskesi, Ronald de Leeuw and Fiorella Superbi.

In connection with the twentieth-century chapters we owe a great deal to several friends: Michael Craig-Martin, Richard Dorment, Cornelia Grassi, Claudio Guenzani, James Hall, Gregorio Magnani, David Plante, Nikos Stangos and David Sylvester.

Throughout the work of revising and expanding the fourth edition we had the invaluable help of Vernon Hyde Minor and Ida Rigby. For errors of fact we remain, of course, alone responsible. And finally, for the enthusiastic support of Calmann & King, notably of Laurence King, Lee Ripley Greenfield, the designer Karen Osborne, the picture researcher Peter Kent and, above all, of our dedicated editors Ursula Payne for the fourth edition and Kara Hattersley-Smith for the fifth edition, we are extremely grateful.

Hugh Honour   John Fleming
January 1999

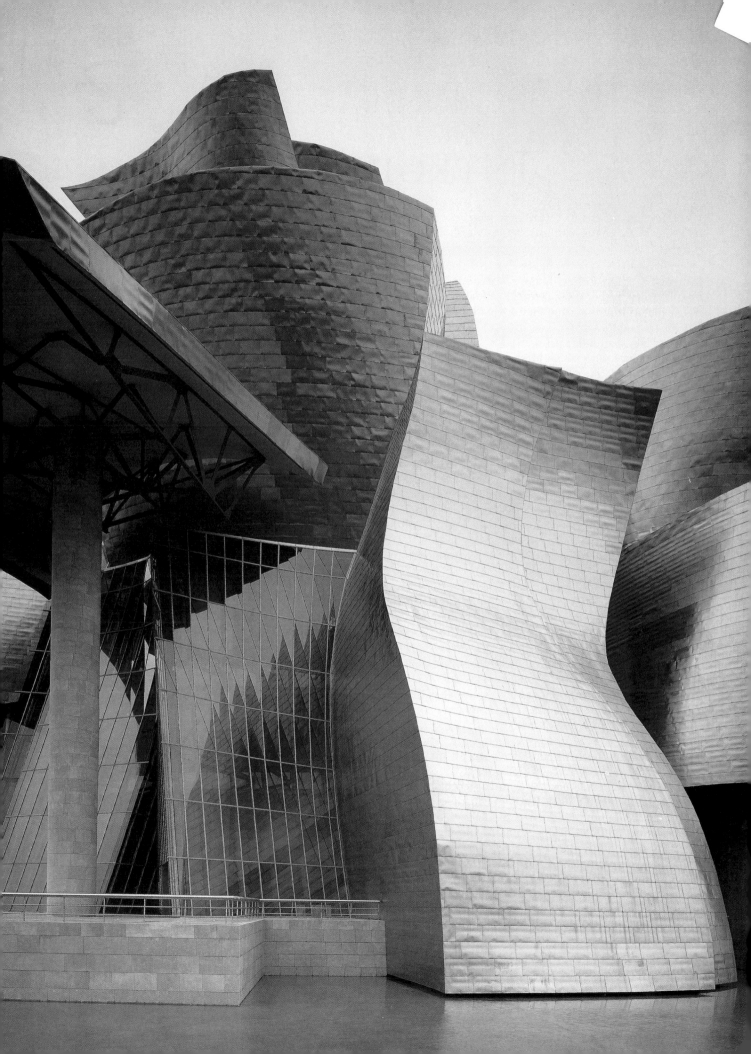

INTRODUCTION

In writing this outline history our aims have been exploratory rather than critical. We have preferred exposition to interpretation and evaluation, in so far as they are separable. And we have tried to shed assumptions about art being intended primarily for visual enjoyment, often in alliance with social prestige, assumptions determined largely by the art market and art collecting and themselves, in turn, responsible for current Western conceptions of what 'art' is. It is not always easy to bear in mind that these conceptions are peculiar to the West and, even there, relatively recent. Until the nineteenth century few, if any, great works of art were made to be seen in art galleries. Most were made in the service of religion or magic or of some secular ideal or, more rarely, to fulfil the private longings of the artist. The essential unity of aesthetic, moral and natural experience can be felt in them in varying degrees, and they sharpen our awareness of how richly it falls on the receptive consciousness. For our senses are inextricably intertwined, the religious with the aesthetic, the aesthetic with the moral, and the moral with that of order and proportion. The appeal of a great work of art is never purely visual, simply to delight the eye. So this book seeks to explore the different ways in which men and women have given visual expression to perennial human impulses and concerns – to the appetite for sensual gratification and the need for self-knowledge and self-mastery, to exalted dreams and demonic passions, to beliefs and convictions about the ends of life and about the human environment and the supernatural powers, to hopes and fears of the beyond.

Confronting so vast a horizon in both time and space, we have been obliged to focus attention on historically prominent periods and areas, which are also those of most general interest. Chapters are arranged chronologically across a wide geographical panorama in order to allow crucial events in world history (which affected artists as much as other human beings) to stand out clearly – the aggregation of hunters and gatherers into pastoral and agricultural communities, for instance, the emergence of urban cultures with stratified social structures, the expansion and dissolution of empires, the spread and transformation of world-wide religions, the rise of industrialized states – and to permit, within these and other great historical transitions, some detailed and instructive confrontations. Juxtaposition of the 'civilized' and 'barbarian' cultures of the ancient Greeks and their neighbours in the fifth century BC, or of the works of contemporaries

as dissimilar (though in some ways comparable) as Michelangelo and Koca Mimar Sinan, or of the cult of natural beauty and its expression in landscape painting in China, Japan and Europe in the sixteenth and seventeenth centuries – parallels of this kind are not only mutually illuminating but sharpen awareness of the meaning and purpose of art in general. Above all, we have tried to illustrate and discuss works of art in their original contexts, dissociating them as far as possible from the museum surroundings in which they are nowadays so often confined, without, on the other hand, trying to find in them any evolutionary pattern.

In every human society, art forms part of a complex structure of beliefs and rituals, moral and social codes, magic or science, myth or history. It stands midway between scientific knowledge and magical or mythical thought, between what is perceived and what is believed, and also between human capabilities and human aspirations. As a means of communication it is akin to language, with the aim of making statements of a didactic or morally instructive nature; but at the same time it is often a means of exerting control, akin to magic, with the aim of imposing order on the physical world, of arresting time and securing immortality. Within the social group, whether it be a single village or a vast ramifying empire, motifs, themes or subjects are drawn from a common stock. The manner of the representation is restricted by the availability of materials and tools, by the skills passed on from one generation to the next and by what can only be called 'tribal' conventions, though they are often of great sophistication. Yet art is constantly regenerated like the living organisms of social and cultural structures which are always subject to modification, as a result either of internal growth or of external pressures. In stable societies, or those that seek stability, artistic changes often take place so gradually as to be barely perceptible. Even in more dynamically expansive societies artistic change may take place at one level while continuity is maintained at another. Western ideas of 'progress' have tended to distort our view of the art of the world.

ART AS CRAFT

Art, craftsmanship and technology are three terms that have seldom had meanings as distinct as those they have acquired in the West, and only in the West, since the sixteenth century. It was at that time that painters and sculptors assumed a status superior to that of potters, furniture-makers, metalworkers, embroiderers, weavers and other practitioners of the so-called decorative arts. There is a reminder of the earlier situation, when the arts and crafts were equal, in the word 'masterpiece', which originally signified a work executed by an apprentice as a demonstration of skill in order to gain the rank of 'master' in a guild of craftsmen. Subsequently it was commonly applied to a picture or statue that seemed in some way to surpass others by the same artist or group of artists. In both senses the word implies a value judgement, but one which, until relatively recent times, was based mainly on an assessment of proficiency, or craftsmanship.

The production of any artifact is dependent on both manual skill and technical knowledge. A pottery vessel, a basket or an embroidery, no less than a temple, a painting or a statue, demands the coordination of ideas of form with dexterity of handling and a grasp of the techniques that ensure permanence. In all but the simplest utensils and buildings, however, there is a tension between ends and means, between the idea in the maker's mind and the skill needed to express it and give it form. And this tension gives art, as we understand it, a history different from that of technology. Methods of construction, carving or painting do not supersede one another in the way that a technological invention renders an older device obsolete. They often have significance apart from their function, seen most obviously in the interplay between structural and stylistic – or utilitarian and aesthetic – developments in architecture, including that of our own time.

SYSTEMS OF BUILDING

There are two basic systems of building (sometimes combined): with uprights supporting horizontal members – post and lintel, also the basis of framed construction – or with walls pierced by openings, sometimes arched. Ancient Egyptian and Greek temples, and nearly all ancient Chinese buildings, are typical examples of post-and-lintel architecture; their walls are merely fillings between uprights. Both the ancient Egyptians and the Greeks were, nevertheless, practitioners of wall architecture as well, especially for defensive purposes. Roofs to provide shelter from the elements could be supported by either system. In post-and-lintel architecture the width of the roof was limited by the length of horizontal members that could be carried by the uprights. If a building was entirely of stone the internal spaces were therefore very restricted. At an early date, and in many different places, it was discovered that a space could be completely enclosed by projecting each course of a wall slightly over that below to form a corbelled vault or dome – as in the Treasury of Atreus, Mycenae, of about 1300 BC (2,56) – though the earliest surviving example, in the Orkney Islands off the north coast of Scotland, is much earlier. It dates from about 2600 BC. The adoption of wedge-shaped stones to construct round arches and vaults, already known in ancient Egypt, was exploited by the Romans and later carried a stage further by their invention of concrete. This enabled them to span areas of an extent that was quite unprecedented and for many centuries remained unequalled. For building with concrete was abandoned in the early Christian period although other elements of Roman architecture – the columns and Classical orders and the round arch – were retained, though often in a debased and rudimentary form. In the European Middle Ages the evolution of Gothic architecture introduced a somewhat different system, with piers supporting arches and vaults of stone, as in Roman wall architecture but with the walls reduced to little more than screens, as in post-and-lintel, especially timber-framed, construction. There were radical departures from these basic systems in the twentieth century, with new developments in structural technology and the introduction of new materials, for example metal frames on which 'curtain walls' (see Glossary) can be hung, reinforced concrete shells that eliminate the distinction between walls and coverings, and 'tensile structures' with roofs of plastic webbing freely suspended on cable nets attached to masts and ground anchorages. The majority of buildings throughout the world are, however, still built in traditional ways – or designed to look as if they were.

SCULPTURAL TECHNIQUES AND MATERIALS

Sculpture also has – or had until the present century – two basic techniques: modelling and carving. As one depends on building up clay or other malleable material and the other on reducing a piece of stone or wood, they are called additive and subtractive processes. (Cast bronze sculpture usually derived from modelling, so too did the iron statues produced mainly in fifteenth- and sixteenth-century China; but iron is nowadays more usually forged and welded – see below. Such soft metals as gold, silver and copper may be either cast in a modelled mold or hammered into shape and chiselled by techniques akin to carving.) Carvers are restricted by the natural characteristics, shape and consistency of their materials and the efficiency of tools with which to fashion them. The cylinder of a tree-trunk, for example, is like an invisible cage enclosing a statue carved from a single piece of wood. The regularity of a block of stone hewn in the quarry similarly determines the form of a figure when a carver begins by drawing outlines on its four sides. Hardness or brittleness of stone dictates the degree of delicacy with which it can be worked. Iron chisels and drills, which came into use in the West in the first millennium BC, greatly lightened the carver's task and opened up new possibilities, especially in undercutting, though they resulted mainly in increased production. Some of the most finely worked statues ever created were carved without their aid from the hardest of stones in ancient Egypt. In wood, effects of the greatest intricacy and delicacy were often obtained with the simplest implements, such as flakes of stone and seashells in Melanesia (see pp. 748–9).

So far as the history of European sculpture is concerned, by far the most important development was the

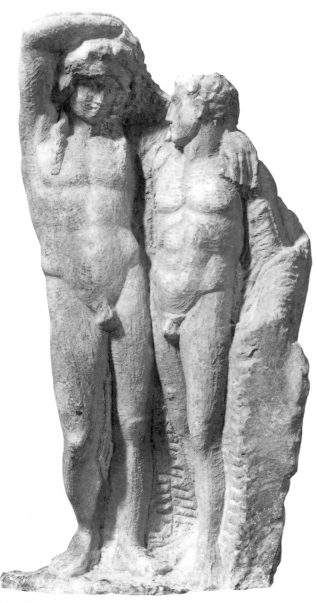

0,1 *Dionysus and Satyr*, unfinished, 2nd century AD. Marble, 28ins (71.1cm) high. National Archeological Museum, Athens.

measurements an enlarged or reduced scale version of the model could be carved. In nineteenth-century Europe this technique of working from points enabled many sculptors to confine themselves to modelling in clay and leave the arduous task of carving to assistants – in France called *practiciens*, practitioners of their craft, as distinct from creative artists.

Modellers are, however, restricted by the properties of clay, for no form extending far beyond the lump into which it naturally subsides when damp will remain standing without an interior skeleton of wood or metal. Clay figures are also impermanent unless baked hard – that is, transformed into terracotta – in an oven the heat of which must be controlled to prevent fragmentation. In the second half of the third millennium BC it was discovered in Mesopotamia (and somewhat later elsewhere) that a durable version of a clay statue could be made in bronze by a *cire perdue* or lost-wax process of casting. Two analogous procedures were later evolved. By one the figure modelled in clay was covered with wax to the thickness required for the bronze and then thickly encased in more

0,2 Francesco Carradori, *Istruzione Elementare per gli Studiosi della Scultura*, Florence, 1802. Plate IX.

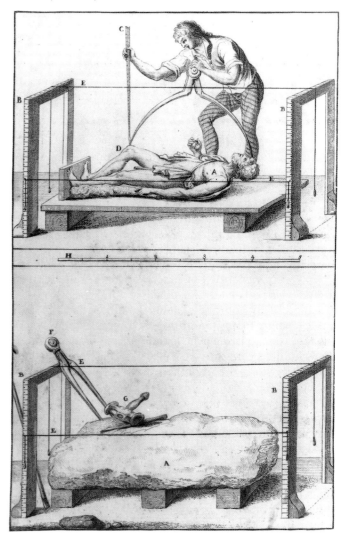

invention, probably in fifth-century BC Greece, of a technique that enabled a sculptor to carve in stone an accurate version of a model in clay, plaster or some other easily manipulated substance. The model was marked at extremities with 'points' and the distances between them and a plumb line or wooden framework were measured so that holes of equivalent depth could be drilled into a marble block at corresponding points. The material between these holes was then chiselled away to reveal a rough version of the model. An ancient Greek statue, abandoned at this stage, has by chance survived (**0,1**). This process was carried on unchanged until the early nineteenth century, as illustrated in manuals published for sculptors (**0,2**). Later, instruments were devised to measure any protuberance or cavity in the model from three fixed points and thus facilitate the finishing of the marble. By simple multiplication or division of the various

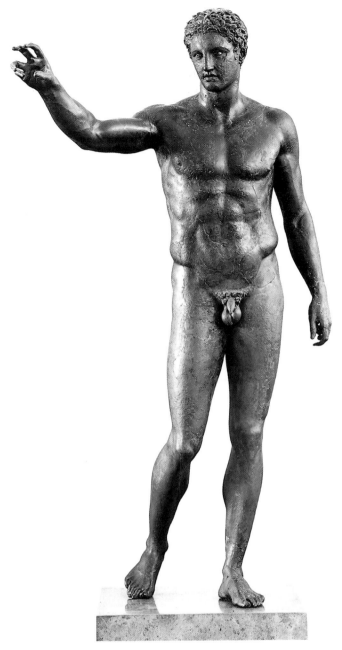

As hollow bronze statues are much lighter in weight than equivalent pieces of stone (especially marble and other close-grained stones favoured for their durability) and also have some resilience, the medium permits a wider range of formal effects. Stone sculptures must be columnar, cubic or pyramidal if they are to stand upright. The legs of a standing figure cannot be placed wide apart unless a third support is provided to prevent fracture at the ankles. Bronze figures, on the other hand, may be delicately, even precariously, balanced, giving an appearance of living, breathing movement rare in marble statues. The fourth-century BC Greek *Boy from Antikythera* is a notable example (**0,3**). When a Greek bronze statue was copied in marble in Roman times, the insertion of a third support, usually a tree-stump, was necessary and the figure lost much of its vitality as a result. (This is very obvious in copies of Myron's *Discobolus*, 4,34.)

In stone and wood, as well as clay and bronze, sculptors in many parts of the world have, nevertheless, succeeded in making images that are convincingly lifelike – more so, indeed, than casts taken from living bodies. Their production involves much more than the meticulous imitation of forms and surfaces. But this has rarely been regarded as the principal aim of sculpture, most of which has been devoted to religious and otherworldly subjects – statues of the Buddha and Hindu deities, cult figures carved in Africa and Polynesia, and masks in the American north-west. In the twentieth century verisimilitude was completely disregarded by many Western artists who conceive sculpture as the art of creating three-dimensional forms often only barely, if at all, representational in intention. Many have abandoned the long-established techniques of carving and modelling as well as such traditional materials as marble and bronze. Instead, iron has been much used as a medium, wrought by the processes of forging, hammering and welding formerly used for making weapons and utilitarian objects. It was the use of iron that made possible a great revolution in sculpture during this century: the shift away from 'closed' (solid) to 'open' (constructed) form. González's work, and in particular his collaboration with Picasso in the 1920s and 1930s, was the catalyst for this breakthrough. González himself was one of its great exponents (20,23). Later, new synthetic materials were taken up and three-dimensional works were made by 'assembling' pieces of the most miscellaneous materials. Some artists have extended 'sculpture' to include their own bodies (see p. 856).

0,3 *Boy from Antikythera*, mid-4th century BC. Bronze, 6ft 3½ins (1.92m) high. National Archeological Museum, Athens.

clay, leaving apertures in this outer coating through which molten bronze could be poured and many smaller holes through which the wax – which melted on contact – could escape. Alternatively, by the negative process of casting, hollow molds were made from the two sides of a model, their interior surfaces were covered with wax of appropriate thickness, they were then joined together and filled with a core, the bronze was poured in and the wax expelled. Whichever process was adopted, the outer casing was removed when the metal had cooled and hardened, the remains of the original model or core were then shaken out, leaving a shell of bronze which was finished by hammering and scraping away any blemishes. (For casting bronze vessels a different system was developed in China in the second millennium BC; see pp. 87–8.)

PAINTING TECHNIQUES AND MATERIALS

The only basic practical problem confronting painters was that of fixing pigments to a ground in order to preserve them (though durability has not always been desired; many paintings were and are intended to last no more than a short time). There are normally three layers to a painting: a prepared ground between a film of pigment and the support, which may be a rock-face, a wall or some transportable material such as wood, paper, canvas or other textile. Pigments are basically of two types: stains that are absorbed into the ground and colored powders (mainly of mineral substances) mixed with some adhesive binding agent and applied on to the ground. The former have been used since very early times in many parts of the world to paint on absorbent plastered walls and ceilings. They are those adopted for fresco – a term which is often given to various types of mural paintings but should be reserved for those in which the pigment is absorbed into the wall surface, notably the technique perfected in Italy towards the end of the thirteenth century by Giotto (see p. 409). For true fresco a wall or ceiling was usually covered with a fairly smooth layer of plaster which was allowed to dry before the painting was executed on another layer of plaster while it was still damp and fresh (fresco in Italian). As plaster dries quickly, no more than a section of the composition could be painted at a time, such a section being called in Italy a giornata or 'a day's work' (0,4). To avoid discontinuities between one completed section and the next – a hazard of this piecemeal manner of working – some fourteenth-century artists sketched the outlines of their compositions in a red ochre pigment (called sinopia) on to the first coat of plaster. (Some of these so-called sinopie drawings have been revealed in recent restorations.) Later the composition was sometimes drawn on paper (called a cartoon) temporarily applied to the dry plaster, which was marked through holes pricked around the main contours. (Raphael did this when painting the Stanze in the Vatican; see pp. 480–1.) The great advantage of fresco painting is that the pigments absorbed into the thickness of the plaster have great durability – with the corresponding disadvantage that no alterations or corrections can be made

0,4 Giotto, *The Nativity*, with the *giornate* marked, c. 1304–13. Fresco, 7ft 7ins × 6ft 7½ins (2.31 × 2.02m). Scrovegni Chapel, Padua.

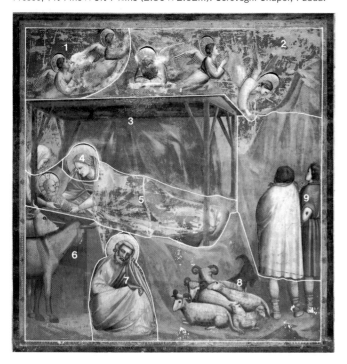

in the course of painting. Also, the range of pigments that could be used was limited. Some colors, notably blue and a few reds and greens, could be applied only after the fresco was dry (secco in Italian). In fifteenth-century Italy artists made increasing use of pigments applied a secco. But around 1500 there was a revival of pure fresco technique, which came to be regarded by art theorists as the ideal means for painting walls and ceilings, and also as the one that revealed artistic proficiency most clearly. It required, as Giorgio Vasari (see p. 473) later remarked, a hand 'dextrous, resolute and rapid', 'nimble and free'. Frescoes are large, but a somewhat similar technique was developed before the beginning of the sixteenth century for painting on small sheets of paper in watercolor. Pigments were mixed with a gum that dissolves in water and thus provides transparent stains. This, too, required rapid and free handling, for once the color had been applied and absorbed by the ground, the watercolorist, like the fresco painter, could make no changes – except by superimposing them with solid pigments or body-colors.

For painting on panels of wood, the technique generally adopted in Europe from about the twelfth century onwards was tempera: powdered pigments made workable (tempered) by egg-yolk and mixed with some form of gum. The support was covered with gesso (plaster mixed with size) on to which the composition was drawn and/or incised. If some areas were to be gilded, as they often were, they were coated with bole (a type of fine red clay) which was burnished and then covered with very thin sheets of gold leaf. Other parts were underpainted in low tones of the desired colors and finished with one layer above another of translucent tempera paint, each of which had to be completed quickly before it dried. Details could be rendered with greater delicacy than in fresco and the final work also had greater luminosity. But such effects could be more easily attained with oil paint which, in the fifteenth century, gradually superseded tempera (not to be revived until the twentieth century). Pigments had been mixed with oils for some types of painting (for example, on shields) in ancient Roman times and in the early Middle Ages. And oil painting, as the term is understood today, was not an invention, attributable to an individual at a particular moment, but a gradual, perhaps trial-and-error, development in the studios of artists some of whom mixed pigments with oils as well as egg-yolk. By the 1430s, however, Jan van Eyck and probably other painters in the Netherlands evolved mixtures that included oil (from linseed or nuts) fused with a hard resin (amber or copal) diluted with oil derived from lavender or rosemary. This was a light, fluid medium which dried easily but slowly, permitting the careful depiction of minute details. Transparent oil pigments applied in layers gave an effect of extraordinary luminosity as may be seen, for instance, in the *Ghent Altarpiece* (0,5). This type of oil medium was, however, suitable for painting only on panel or fine linen that was subsequently glued to a wooden support. A different mixture including a soft, rather than a hard, resin was developed in Italy for painting on canvas stretched over a wood frame, which became the preferred

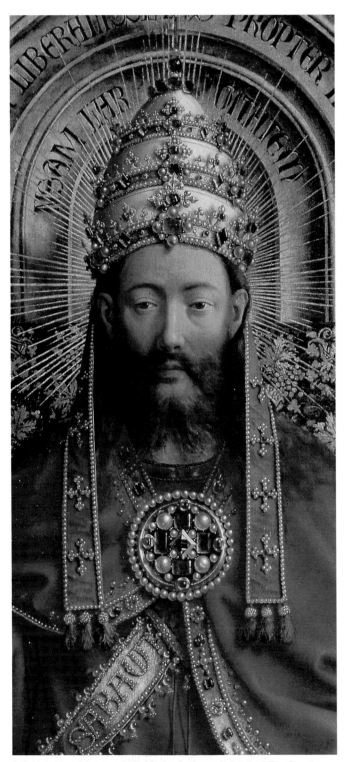

0,5 Hubert and Jan van Eyck, *Christ Enthroned*, detail of *The Ghent Altarpiece*, completed 1432. Oil on panel. St Bavo, Ghent.

type of support for all but very small oil paintings throughout Europe. It permitted much freer brushwork than tempera while also offering unlimited possibilities for shading, scumbling (applying a layer of opaque or semi-opaque pigment irregularly so that some of the color beneath remains visible), retouching and superimposing glazes (transparent films which modify underlying

colors). Painters evolved innumerable variants on the basic mixture in order to obtain not only the colors they wanted but also the consistency of the medium which might be either liquid or so thick it could be applied with a spatula if not the fingers. And in the course of time attempts were made to rediscover those found empirically – guided by experience and perhaps helped by accident – by the most famous painters, notably Titian (11,45; 46; 47; 48). Pigments that had been powdered and combined with other substances in the studios of medieval artists became, by the early sixteenth century, increasingly available ready-for-use from specialist colormen. Painters differed from one another in the pigments they used for their ground color, and still more in the mixtures they evolved to obtain the final hues. Not until the nineteenth century was the range of colors derived from natural mineral and vegetable sources expanded by the commercial production of synthetic pigments, which were similarly mixed with linseed and other oils.

Artists in the West have continued to use and exploit oil paint to the present day. There was, in fact, no other medium as satisfactory for large-scale painting on movable supports until the development in the 1960s of acrylic, a synthetic emulsion (a kind of plastic) which can be applied in the same way. Acrylic has often been adopted by artists in reaction against the mystique of oil paint (21,19) – the exaggerated prestige accorded to the medium itself, especially by connoisseurs with their admiration for bravura brushwork and their relish for the consistency of the pigments themselves, called *matière* in French with a suggestion of their luscious, juicy and other sensuously delectable qualities. (The only competitor for portraiture was pastel: painting with opaque dry chalks mixed with a little adhesive, perfected in the eighteenth century [14,18] and, after falling from favour, revived in the late nineteenth.)

The framed picture on canvas is a Western phenomenon (not imitated elsewhere before the nineteenth century) and its popularity in the West accounts for the prestige acquired by the art of painting from the sixteenth century onwards. To it is also due the distinction made between painting and the crafts. In the Middle Ages paintings on precious metals in enamel (a kind of colored glass which required great skill in handling) had been more highly prized than those in tempera which, with their gilding, were often made in emulation of them. Similarly, mosaics composed of little cubes of variously colored stones and glass, embroidered panels and woven tapestries were all more highly regarded and more costly than fresco paintings for covering walls and ceilings – not only because they required greater expenditure of time and materials. Later the relationship was reversed and oil paintings set the standard. Although tapestries remained the most expensive form of wall decoration until the late eighteenth century they were usually designed by artists distinguished as painters, and their skilful weavers ranked as subservient craftsmen. Embroidery, very often the work of women and less dependent than tapestries on models by painters, was also downgraded.

PRINT-MAKING

In the production of prints there has also been, mainly in the West and since the sixteenth century, a division of labour between designers and executants. The purpose of print-making is to produce a number of copies of a single design on sheets of paper, silk or any other material that will absorb ink. The earliest technique was that of the woodcut by which the design was drawn on a smooth block of wood, the parts that were to be white on the print were cut away, those that were to be black were left standing up in relief and covered with ink so that when the block was pressed on to paper or a textile it left an impression of the design in reverse. (This is known as a relief print.) It was first used in China in the seventh century AD for printing images of the Buddha and in Europe in the fourteenth century for Christian images. By alternative processes developed in Europe from the mid-fifteenth century, intaglio prints were made from metal plates in which the parts that are to be black and carry ink are incised by tools (engravings) or eaten away by acid (etchings). From the sixteenth century the drawing of designs and the cutting of woodblocks or the engraving of metal plates were usually separate activities. Copper-plate engravings with their fine firm lines soon superseded woodcuts for scientific illustration, anatomical, zoological, botanical and so on. For imaginative work, artists sometimes engraved copper plates but generally preferred etchings which they executed themselves, drawing with a needle on wax-coated copper plate subsequently immersed in acid which ate into the parts exposed by the needle (see p. 602). From the early nineteenth century artists also made prints by the process of lithography – drawing with an oily crayon on stone (15,18).

Woodcuts, engravings, etchings and lithographs both designed and executed by the same hand are termed 'original prints', as distinct from 'reproductive prints' executed by specialist print-makers, who copied the works of painters or draftsmen using a variety of techniques, often with the greatest skill. In the nineteenth century it was discovered that prints of very high technical quality could be made from engravings on steel-coated plates, which yielded a far greater number of copies than easily damaged copper. But artists took little interest in this process which was used mainly for illustrations – in books and periodicals – until it was superseded by photography. In the meantime Japanese artists had developed a woodcut process for making color prints which were imported into Europe and America from the 1850s and enthusiastically received by many artists who welcomed an escape from the European tradition of oil painting. In the West these prints were sometimes copied, and their effects emulated, in oil paint, as well as influencing etching and lithography (see p. 656). Early in the twentieth century several European artists reverted to print-making with woodblocks, emphasizing obviously hand-cut irregularities for expressive effect (19,15).

PHOTOGRAPHY

Photography, from the time of its invention in the 1830s, was closely allied with both painting and print-making. It had for long been known that light, if passed through a very small aperture, would project an image (in reverse) on to the side of a dark chamber – the *camera obscura* occasionally used by artists as an aid for painting townscapes and interiors in perspective. The initial purpose of photography was to fix such images, and two processes were devised simultaneously. That discovered by the French painter Louis-Jacques-Mandé Daguerre by 1837 fixed the image on a sensitized copper plate called a daguerreotype. This was a unique object, like a painting or drawing, and was much used for portraits. In England, William Henry Fox Talbot succeeded before 1839 in fixing negative images on sheets of translucent paper which could then be placed over sheets of opaque sensitized paper

0,6 Gertrude Käsebier, *Blessed Art Thou Among Women*, c. 1900. Platinum print on Japanese tissue, 9³/₈ × 5¹/₂ins (23.8 × 13.9cm). The Museum of Modern Art, New York (Gift of Mrs Hermione M. Turner).

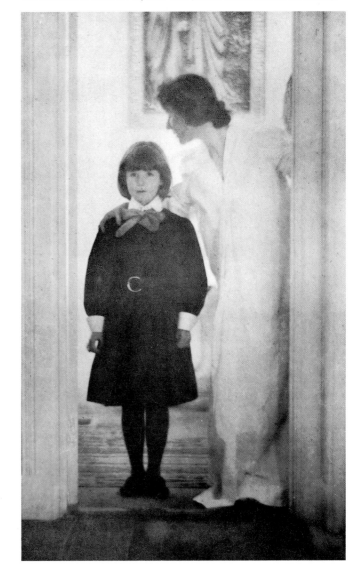

and exposed to light to make positive prints. The advantage was that many identical prints could be made from a single negative. They were, however, slightly fuzzy on account of the uneven texture of the translucent paper (15,31). The introduction of glass plates for negatives in the 1850s facilitated the production of prints as sharply defined as daguerreotypes, which they soon superseded.

Subsequent developments were mainly technical improvements, notably those that reduced the time needed for an exposure and by the 1870s made possible split-second photographs of figures in motion (15,58). Meanwhile there had been much controversy as to whether photography should or could be considered an art (see p. 668). Until the mid-century photographs were occasionally hung among lithographs in official exhibitions of art. After that they were excluded and shown only in specialized exhibitions. At about the same time, self-consciously artistic photographers began to select subjects similar to those of painters, concentrating on softly focused images of motionless figures and scenes. Sometimes the results might almost be mistaken for photographs of paintings. *Blessed Art Thou Among Women* (**0,6**) by the American photographer Gertrude Käsebier (1851–1934), for example, ranks with several notable paintings among the most compelling images of its period. Developments in the science of photography were exploited mainly by documentary photographers whose shots of street scenes (15,59) are considered nowadays to be among the finest photographs ever taken but were regarded at the time simply as photo-records, certainly not as works of art.

The cult of the unique art object led some photographers to reject the possibility of making innumerable prints from a single negative and to issue limited editions, each print being numbered and signed and slightly different from the others as a result of manipulation in the dark room. Although the process of color photography was perfected in the 1940s most of them continued, as some still do, to prefer monochrome. There is no more striking instance of unsynchronized and often contradictory developments in technology and art than that presented by the century-and-a-half history of photography. Despite the great achievements of so many photographers, it has only recently won widespread acceptance as a vehicle for artistic expression, with unique potentialities even when the very simplest equipment is used.

PICTORIAL REPRESENTATION

Throughout the world delineation, whether incised, drawn or painted, has been a means of attaining one of the prime aims of pictorial art: the isolation of an object from the array of colored patches the eye sees in nature. The earliest known paintings, in French and Spanish caves (see pp. 37–41), are profiles of animals unrelated to earth or sky or one another. Composite groups came later and the defined image field – that is to say, an enclosed area within which all the forms are interrelated – later still

with the invention of framing devices. Even in some of the most sophisticated forms of two-dimensional art, the images are all that count, the field on to which they are projected being no more than part of an undefined ground, not a background in the Western sense. In ancient Egypt it was often covered with hieroglyphic inscriptions. On Chinese scroll paintings poems are often written in the 'sky'.

Images have been drawn and painted conceptually (according to what the mind knows) or perceptually (according to what the eye sees at a particular moment). A conceptual image can, in theory, record the salient characteristics of any object by taking it apart and reassembling it – front, back and sides – so that all are visible. (The recent term 'Conceptual Art' has, of course, an entirely different meaning; see p. 850.) Perceptual images are attempts to record the truth of visual appearances, though in practice they are inevitably influenced by what painters know about not only the physical properties of a subject but also the ways in which it has previously been depicted. And they, too, may be combined in a conceptual manner. All images are to some extent both perceptual and conceptual.

PERSPECTIVE

In many, perhaps most, drawings and paintings apart from those produced in Europe between the fifteenth and twentieth centuries, differences in the size of figures signify their relative importance – a deity and worshippers, a ruler and courtiers, sometimes a man and woman – rather than their physical distance from one another and the foreground. When figures are not all ranged on a single plane like actors before a curtain, diminution may also sometimes have been intended to suggest recession in space. In an eighth-century BC Assyrian relief, for instance, three officials are very much larger than neighbouring captives and a man driving away a flock of sheep (3,28). Their arrangement in three tiers indicates distance. The artist's aim was to record an event. Much later, various techniques were devised to represent on a flat surface the appearance of such three-dimensional objects as buildings. Greek vase painters from about the fourth century BC and ancient Roman mural painters adopted a system of axial perspective by which such parallels as the walls of an interior, the beams of its ceilings or the tiles of its floor were shown converging symmetrically on a central axis.

Chinese artists evolved a logical perspective technique for representing buildings, usually from above. As they expected a horizontal scroll to be studied while it was being slowly unrolled they had no need to depict a panorama from a single viewpoint. Each group of buildings could have a perspective coherence unrelated to those on either side. Sometimes buildings in close proximity were shown as if seen from slightly different viewpoints – as in a section of an early twelfth-century scroll where one looks down on the roofs of houses but can also see the underside of the bridge (**0,7**).

European artists adopted various devices to suggest, rather than represent, three-dimensional forms during the Middle Ages. Interiors were often shown in axial

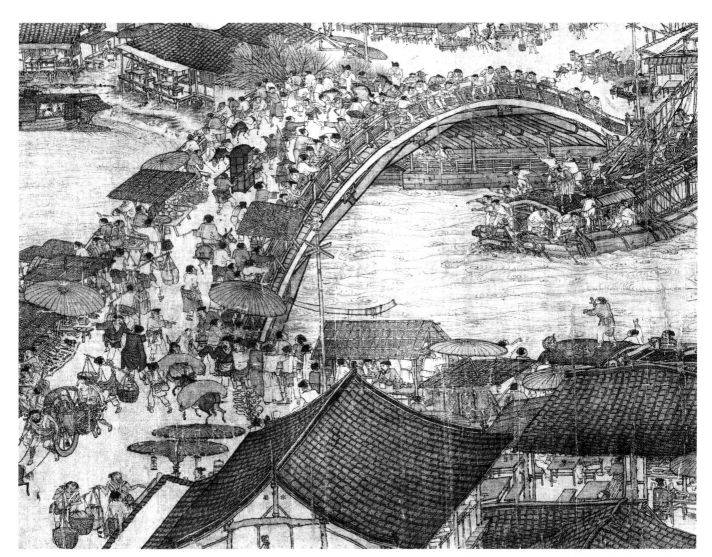

0,7 Zhang Zeduan (?), *Going Upriver at the Qing Ming Festival*, detail from hand-scroll. Watercolor on silk, 1111–26. Palace Museum, Beijing.

perspective, as in Giotto's *Marriage Feast at Cana* (9,80) where the walls of the room which seem to slant inwards were presumably intended to be understood as parallel, joining the far wall at right-angles. Not until the early fifteenth century was it noticed that all receding parallel lines at right angles to the field of vision – called orthogonals – appear to converge on a single distant vanishing-point. This was the basic assumption underlying the theory of linear perspective first used for a painting by Filippo Brunelleschi in about 1415 and codified in a treatise of 1435 by Leon Battista Alberti – both of them Florentine architects. The effect of this discovery may be clearly seen if a townscape by Ambrogio Lorenzetti of 1339 (9,83), in which each building is depicted from a separate viewpoint, is compared with the rationally ordered *An Ideal Town* (10,24) painted about a century later. In the latter the whole view is shown from a single viewpoint and the orthogonals, following the roof lines of the buildings on either side of the piazza and the lines of the pavement, converge towards a vanishing-point behind the door of the central structure. Lorenzetti gives a realistic impression

of a haphazard urban environment in which strangers might lose their way. *An Ideal Town* is depicted so precisely that accurate measured drawings could be made of its plan and of the façade of every building. Painters and also sculptors of low reliefs in Italy, mainly in Florence, soon adopted the geometric network of orthogonals to indicate the position of human figures receding into a background, as in Masaccio's *Tribute Money* (10,6). Beautiful in their logical simplicity though such one-point perspective systems were, they did not solve all the problems confronting artists in rendering space and variations had to be introduced – two or more vanishing-points, for example, might be combined, as by Donatello in his relief of *St Anthony Healing the Young Man's Foot* (**0,8**). And further, more complicated and sophisticated adjustments were made. Yet it was always recognized that these optical rules were no more than an aid to pictorial representation. Indeed they were ignored completely by Netherlandish artists until the sixteenth century. They had their own empirical means of indicating recession: there is, for instance, no single vanishing-point in Jan van

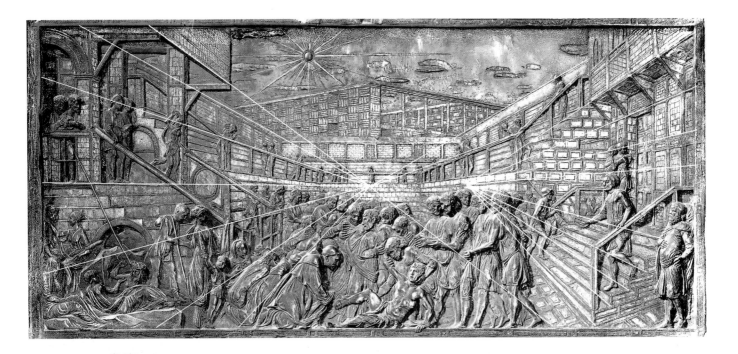

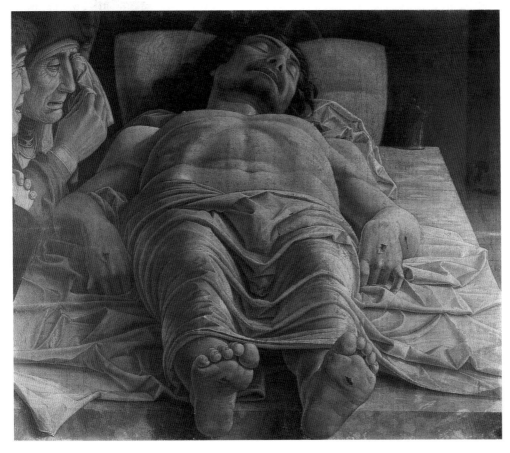

Eyck's *Madonna of Chancellor Rolin* (10,13). In Italy, Andrea Mantegna was one of several artists who mastered the principles of linear perspective well enough to depart from them when desirable. In his painting of the *Dead Christ* (**0,9**), for instance, which might almost seem to be a demonstration in the art of foreshortening, considerable liberties were taken with perspective. In a geometrical projection the feet would be very much larger and the head smaller than depicted by Mantegna.

COLOR

The development of systems of perspective coincided with the emergence of the peculiarly Western concept of a painting as a window on to a real or imaginary world, and for this color was no less necessary than drawing. Color is scientifically defined as the sensation produced on the eye by rays of light striking a surface that reflects some of them and absorbs others. This followed on Isaac Newton's demonstration in 1672 that natural light if passed through a prism is dispersed into the spectrum of chromatic rays, as is seen in a rainbow (the effect of sunlight refracted through raindrops). These rays can be separated into primary colors – red, yellow and blue – and secondary colors (i.e. green from blue and yellow) into which they merge. He believed that these colors would form a wheel with red at one end of the band merging into violet; those at opposite sides of the wheel (red-green, yellow-violet, etc.) came to be called complementary (**0,10**). Newton's explanation of the phenomenon of color was revolutionary even though it owed much to earlier theories and experiments. But it made far less impact than the invention of linear perspective on artists. They had already discovered in practice the effects that could be obtained by mixing, superimposing and contrasting pigments, few of which exactly corresponded with the colors of objects seen in nature. They had also, like Rubens, noted the colors of the rainbow.

From the earliest times, artists used colored pigments to define images by outline. Throughout the world the great majority of paintings have been executed in this linear way, with strongly marked contours which are, of course, rarely apparent in nature. Not until the late fifteenth century did European artists begin to use color to define forms without outlines, in what is nowadays called a painterly technique, facilitated by the development of oil paint. They also began to distinguish between the colors of objects seen in clear diffused daylight, called local color, and those taken on by juxtaposition, by reflection – as in the glow of the setting sun – and when seen at a distance. The value, that is to say the lightness or darkness of a color, appears to be modified by juxtaposition with one that is darker or lighter. Flesh tones look pale

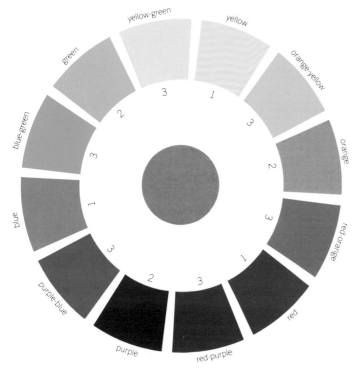

0,10 The traditional color wheel of pigment mixtures.

against a red background but reddish against yellow. The modelling of forms in *chiaroscuro* was more effectively suggested by taking reflected light into account than by shading a single color. Aerial perspective was devised in order to indicate distance in a landscape, for instance, without a network of orthogonals but by muting color contrasts and grading tones – as in the *Virgin and Child with St Anne* by Leonardo da Vinci (11,14). To emphasize aerial perspective painters often introduced a *repoussoir*, a prominent dark form in the foreground or middle distance, such as a large tree in a landscape (13,27).

Linear perspective, aerial perspective and *chiaroscuro* enabled painters to trick the viewer's eye (*trompe l'oeil*). By adopting a complex system of foreshortening, they learned to depict on ceilings figures hovering in the sky or posed on balustrades so cunningly rendered that they might at first sight seem to be part of the real three-dimensional surface of the walls. But illusionism was rarely pursued as an aim in itself. When it was, the artists intended it as a virtuoso performance of their cleverness in 'fooling the eye'. Painters in the West, from the fifteenth to the mid-nineteenth century, aimed for verisimilitude, an appearance of visual truth – an equivalent to the view through the opening in a wall or ceiling. Different degrees of verisimilitude were thought appropriate for different subjects: a religious image, a landscape, a *genre* scene recording daily life, the portrait of a ruler or that of a friend of the artist. But in general verisimilitude was sought because it enforced the message of an image by implying that what was true to visual appearances was true in other respects.

In the nineteenth century a number of artists began to question whether traditional skills in handling pigments could represent what the eye sees in nature, especially landscapes in which color fluctuates with changes of light. Determined to depict only what they saw at a particular moment, the French Impressionists (see p. 708) did their best to forget what they knew of the local color of objects and record only their optical perceptions. Painters of a younger generation, notably Georges Seurat (see p. 722), made use of discoveries in the science of optics to create as much as to record visual impressions. He devised a new process of painting with short brushstrokes of pure juxtaposed colors which fused in the eye of the spectator when seen from the right distance. The painters recognized, however, that only one of the functions of pictorial representation was served by such refined techniques for recording what the eye sees.

Colors often have a symbolic as well as a descriptive function, especially in religious art: the celestial or 'heavenly' blue robe of the Madonna, for instance. They also have expressive qualities: dark hues induce a mood of melancholy, bright pinks and pale blues gaiety; gentle gradations suggest harmony, clashing contrasts are disturbing. Such intuitively recognized qualities were more fully developed in the nineteenth century, notably by Vincent van Gogh who wrote of his painting *The Night Café* in 1888, 'I have tried to express the terrible passions of humanity by means of red and green' (17,24). The Russian painter Vassily Kandinsky, who between 1911 and 1914

0,11 Ellsworth Kelly, *Spectrum III*, 1967. Oil on canvas in 13 parts, overall 33¹/₄ × 108⁵/₈ins (84.3 × 275.7cm). The Museum of Modern Art, New York (The Sidney and Harriet Janis Collection).

gradually abandoned pictorial representation altogether, declared color to be 'a power that directly influences the soul'. The content of his paintings was, he said, 'what the spectator *lives* or *feels* while under the effect of *form and color* combinations' (see p. 784). Subsequently, forms were to be eliminated from many non-representational paintings altogether, especially in the USA after World War II.

Pure color is the subject of Ellsworth Kelly's *Spectrum III* of 1967, 13 strips of pure hues of the natural spectrum, but not merging into one another as in a rainbow, and with yellow at the two ends, red and violet in the middle (**0,11**). The painting shows the sensed but scientifically undemonstrable effects on the eye of juxtaposed colors; for although the strips are of equal width (except for those at either end) some seem wider than others, the warm reds seem to advance in space, the cool blues and greens to retract. With its reference to the theories initiated by Newton, this painting indicates the disjunction between science and art: how colors are defined scientifically and how they are experienced, not by the eye alone.

Many theoretical writings on optics were published in the eighteenth and nineteenth centuries, a few of them by artists. But painters appear to have learnt the effects of mixed and juxtaposed colors less from theories than by practice, by studying the works of others and especially by handling pigments in the studios of their teachers who imparted the manual and other skills passed on from one generation to the next. This accounts for the continuities in the history of pictorial representation – the persistance of *schemata* or visual formulae – though it has not, of course, prevented change as artists have discovered for themselves and explored new means to give expression to their individual vision.

STYLE AND INDIVIDUAL EXPRESSION

The word style is derived from *stylus*, the writing instrument of the ancient Romans, and was first used metaphorically for the various ways of public speaking appropriate for different occasions – when addressing a large popular audience, for instance, or when talking to a few highly educated people. In the history of art it is used in two somewhat deceptively similar senses both of which have analogies with writing, to the work of an individual and to that of a chronologically and geographically defined group. An individual style, akin to handwriting and similarly recognizable, is sometimes merely a set of mannerisms – quirks in the manipulation of media or in the rendering of detail, preference for a particular color scheme, and so on – hence its use in attributing unsigned pictures to named artists. But it can be very much more. It can convey or at least imply artists' whole outlook and range of response, their view of themselves and of the human condition – all can be sensed in the way a subject is rendered, sensuously or cerebrally, emotionally or dispassionately. A style, in this sense of the term, may be evolved throughout the course of an artist's life, reflecting a continual struggle with materials and meanings. The very obvious differences between early and late paintings by Titian, for instance (pp. 498–9), reveal how he developed an ever more deeply personal visual idiom or style in the course of his long career. And one artist's lonely quest for a new and more effective means of expression might inspire others and lead to a modification in the style of a whole group of artists.

The style of a group, from which that of an individual initially derives, is a visual language with a vocabulary of forms and motifs and a syntax governing their relationship. Different styles may, however, be adopted for different purposes even in a small social group, one being reserved for religious art, rather as the language of worship may differ from that otherwise spoken (Latin until recently in Catholic countries, Arabic throughout the Islamic world, Sanskrit in India). In stratified societies, different styles have been adopted in works of art made for people of different social levels: one for the upper classes, others for the rest of the population. The art made for a royal court and that for the richer citizens differed mainly in the relative costliness of materials and the expenditure of time in working with them, sometimes conditioning the development of usually only slightly different styles.

And these styles differed still more markedly from that of the often very vital, though usually conservative, so-called folk art made by and for people living in small towns and the country. Since the nineteenth century in the West, however, there has been a more striking breach between the styles favoured by the intelligentsia and those with a wide popular appeal, which many recent artists have attempted to bridge, notably in Pop Art (see p. 846). These factors and also the susceptibility of styles to change – which includes reversions to styles of earlier periods (a prominent feature in both Western and Chinese art) and the adoption of those of alien cultures – sharply distinguish the history of art from that of science or technology. Such changes were sometimes brought about by contemporary movements in thought, especially religious belief, or by political or economic circumstances. But they were effected exclusively by individuals. Styles were the creation of painters, sculptors, architects, weavers, potters, and so on. And although many of their works may be anonymous, that is to say by artists unknown to us today, they are always the unique products of the brains and hands of individual men and women, however much conditioned by shared traditions and other circumstances of time and place.

The categorization of styles has, however, been the work not of artists but of writers who have tried to impose a semblance of order on the manifold and infinitely diverse expressions of creative activity – a system akin to but without the precision of botanical classification of plants in genera, species, and so on. The names given to historical styles often have no more than a chronological significance, especially those derived from dynasties of rulers (in Egypt, India, China and Japan, for instance) or the reigns of monarchs (more usual in Europe), which subdivide and may overlap divisions by centuries. Others, applied to the history of Western art, are mainly the later inventions of writers and would seldom have been understood by the artists who created the styles, whose aims they rarely express. Several, including Gothic, Baroque, Rococo and Neo-Classical, originated as terms of abuse or disdain for the outmoded. Such labels can be useful as a means of distinguishing styles that coexist, derive from and merge into others, or are developed in one place and taken up elsewhere. They may be defined by analyzing their formal, exclusively artistic, characteristics. The distinctions between conceptual and perceptual images, linear and painterly techniques, have already been mentioned. But there are others no less helpful in the discussion of styles.

Form – that is, the configuration in bulk of an object whether drawn, painted, modelled or carved – is said to be closed or open according to whether or not it constitutes a compact mass. Sculptural forms may be frontal and closed or free-standing; intended to be seen from a single, fixed viewpoint or from all sides; monolithically static or rendered in such a way (usually an open form) as to suggest the possibility of movement. In painting, a full-face or pure profile head is usually a static image whereas a three-quarters view, though no less closed as a form, may suggest movement. A composition in which forms are juxtaposed may be said to be closed or open according to whether it isolates the subject or presents it as part of a world which the viewer is invited to enter. In the latter, forms are seen in a defined space that may cover an area of ground receding from the viewer, depicted according to some system of perspective (see pp. 19–21) which might also regulate the relative size of figures at a distance from the foreground in a naturalistic image, that is to say one that shows or purports to show objects, especially human figures, as they commonly appear.

Naturalism is a characteristic of several styles in Western art; that of Dutch seventeenth-century painters, for instance. There are, however, degrees of naturalism, notably the Realism of Gustave Courbet and other mid-nineteenth-century painters who sought to represent the harsh realities of contemporary life with uncompromising candour. Naturalism is usually contrasted with Idealism, which characterized the Neo-Classical style of the late eighteenth century, and may be defined as the representation of natural objects according to an ideal of perfection that could be discovered, it was believed, beneath the blemishes of the common face of nature. (It should be mentioned that the terms naturalism, realism and idealism have quite different meanings in philosophy.)

Idealist artists sought, above all, the perfect proportions of the human figure, that is, the relationship in size of parts of the human body to one another and the whole, derived from ancient Greek statues. This scale of proportions is not universally valid. It differs from that adopted by Egyptian artists (see p. 71). In India different scales were demanded for images of deities and those of devotees. A sense of good or harmonious proportions is probably acquired unconsciously in childhood like an ear for musical harmony, with notable differences between cultures, and often governs all artifacts including utilitarian objects made within a single culture. Sometimes, however, artists have deliberately broken with the norm of proportional ratios, not only in rendering the human figure. The relationship of height to width of a painting is often relevant, even decisive. An unusual extension of one dimension at the expense of another can be a means of expression.

A scale of architectural proportions is based on a module or unit of measurement, originally part of the human body (for example, the foot), multiplied and divided into simple fractions for all dimensions. In Classical architecture (ancient Greek and Roman temples and buildings that derive from them) a proportional system is established by the mathematical relation between the width of a column – a single module – and its height, though this was rarely worked out precisely in practice. Stylistic categorization of buildings takes into account the simplicity or complexity of their proportions, and also of their plans – that is to say the disposition of areas on a single level, though the same word is used for diagrams of them. In a plan a closed area may be centralized, as in the Pantheon in Rome (see p. 201), or axial, as in Early Christian basilicas (see p. 302). Enclosed space or volume may be so simple (cube, double cube and so on) that it can be sensed on entering, or so complex that its boundaries are difficult to discern, as in some Gothic cathedrals. The exterior form or mass of a building may indicate or disguise its volumes. Another prominent characteristic of an architectural style is the articulation of façades or interior walls, that is to say their division into parts by projections, recessions and openings (doors and windows), with or without regard to symmetry or the correspondence of parts on either side of the centre. In the ornamentation of surface, architectural styles reflect preferences that may range from the linear shapes of pure geometry (circle and rectangle) to boldly modelled organic forms.

Many of the formal terms used for stylistic categorization are based on concepts that can rarely have been present in the minds of artists or architects in the past. A preference for closed rather than open forms or compositions, for tightly integrated or asymmetrical plans, and so on, may of course have been adopted instinctively and thus indicate the ethos or distinctive character of a culture. And the study of historical styles can be illuminating when it relates diverse works of art to one another, to the literature and music and more generally to the life and thought of the time and place in which they were made.

Context: Function and Meaning

Techniques of painting and sculpture, and skills acquired for representation, were rarely employed as ends in themselves. Most large-scale works of art were created for a purpose, whether religious, social, political or, exceptionally, to express an artist's inner vision. And few objects were made by human beings without some regard for qualities that appeal to the mind as well as the senses. An almost universal demand for symmetry, patterning and color combinations can be felt in the simplest household articles dating from the earliest times. They answer two basic human urges: to impose order on nature and natural forms, and to assert individuality by marking the differences between one human being or group and another. Objects are made and decorated in accordance with preferences for certain forms and colors developed within a social group as part of its traditional way of life. Shields are a case in point. They are found in nearly all cultures throughout human history. Yet despite their simple unitary purpose, they differ far more widely in shape (round, ovoid, hexagonal, etc.) than can be explained by function or medium – modes of combat or types of material available. A particular shape of shield could, for instance, be a distinguishing mark for a group or tribe or clan. Color was often similarly used and so were figurative designs such as the coats of arms of European heraldry, especially to indicate the bearer's rank. But they often had an additional, magically protective purpose. Thus a shield shown in a sixth-century AD mosaic at Ravenna (7,29) bears a Christian symbol. The painting on a shield from the Trobriand islands in Melanesia (18,9) is, perhaps intentionally, difficult for people from elsewhere to interpret but almost certainly had some magic significance. Many other types of painting and also of sculpture were similarly apotropaic

(intended to ward off evil) – the great *lamassu* of Assyrian palaces (pp. 107–8), for instance, or the gargoyles that leer out from Gothic churches. In them art and magic are very closely integrated.

However accessible their formal qualities may be to us, however engaging their subject-matter, works of art cannot be properly or fully understood unless related to their original context – to the beliefs, hopes and fears of the people by whom and for whom they were made, which may differ widely from those prevalent nowadays in the West. In many works of art there are several superimposed levels of meaning which cannot always be recovered. For meanings have been conveyed visually in a variety of interconnected ways, from the most direct (in representations of deities and rulers) to the symbolic (by the use of conventional colors or of such non-representational signs as haloes) and the allegorical (by the personification of abstract ideas, for example a blindfold woman holding a sword and balance to represent justice). Iconography, the study of visual images, is devoted to elucidating the original meanings of works of art by reference to the literary sources of narrative compositions and by investigating the symbols and types of allegory used by artists in different places and periods.

Pictorial devices used to enforce meanings are so familiar that they can often be taken for granted, symmetry to suggest a stable order, for instance, asymmetry to convey dynamism or violent emotion. As already mentioned, scale may emphasize a figure's importance, often together with a central position, as in groups of three which recur in the art of the world. The larger central figure is normally posed frontally, looking straight ahead, while those on either side may be in profile. When symmetry is avoided, as in narrative art, and figures are scaled naturalistically, the protagonists are distinguished more subtly by placing them against a blank background, or by arranging the scene so that the spectator's eye is directed to them by the dominant lines of the composition.

Sculptors used similar devices to emphasize meaning, especially when working in low relief or high relief (that is to say, with figures at least half in the round). In ancient Egyptian art there is little distinction between wall-painting and reliefs, which were painted and colored; the same conventions were observed in both. The materials of sculpture might have significance too. Precious metals, bronze and types of hard stone that demand great expenditure of labour in carving, as well as being costly, often reflected the importance of the subject represented. Their durability was also expressive: marble statues and the 'gilded monuments of princes' were intended to last for ever. Similarly, sheer size could denote superhuman power, sculpture larger than life-size generally being reserved for religious and political imagery – closely related in ancient Egypt, imperial Rome and the Cambodia of the Khmer. The third dimension gives sculpture a tangible presence and in many cultures statues were regarded as receptacles for a human or divine spirit and thus became objects of veneration, if not worship. Hence the very strict rules that governed their forms and sometimes the process by which they were made. Hence, too, the ban placed on them by more than one religion.

Size and media are no less demonstrative in architecture. A building larger than its neighbours or raised above their level on a platform declares an importance which might be further emphasized by the use of distinguishing materials. In some places laws regulated the size of houses and their exterior decorations according to the social class of the people who lived in them. Need for shelter is no more than a point of departure for buildings and in most cultures architecture has been concerned mainly with the creation of a human environment and thus involves the manipulation of space as well as mass, answering a need for a defined spatial frame within which human actions can both literally and metaphorically 'take place'. The lay-out of a settlement corresponds to its inhabitants' conception of their relationship with one another and with exterior forces. Order is established by planning, and a grid-iron or chequer-board plan was often adopted in absolutist states where land-ownership was vested only in the ruler and portions were parcelled out among subjects (although it also came to be adopted simply as a convenience for new towns in ancient Greece and colonial North America). Strong axes or paths control movement towards a goal or outwards from a central point. Very often and in different parts of the world individual buildings and whole cities have been oriented on astronomical phenomena (sunrise and sunset or the movement of the stars) to maintain harmony between life on earth and the heavens above. The west–east axis of a Christian church has cosmic significance combined with the symbolism of the believer's path from initiation to salvation and eternal life. Such spatial organization provides, as it were, the grammar of an architectural language. Symbolic meanings are spelled out. Domed roofs, for instance, usually reserved for regal and religious structures, reflect the hemisphere of the firmament, as is often made clear by the painted or mosaic decoration of their interiors – indeed they were often understood as symbols of 'the dome of heaven', and not only in Western architecture. Articulation of mass can create such effects as those of processional movement along a horizontal path or up one of aspiring verticality. In this way a building is given architectural expression or character within the spatial field which it dominates or helps to define.

Architecture has often been employed to assist as well as signal the subjugation of one group of people by another. Muslims who conquered most of northern India in the twelfth century made their presence felt visually by building mosques which differed conspicuously in form, extent and manner of building from Hindu temples, many of which were demolished to provide material. The arch, vault and dome were so obviously associated with Islam that, despite their practical advantages, they were shunned in the Hindu-ruled southern states of India. (Muslims remained a minority of the population in China, on the other hand, and constructed mosques in local styles with minarets in the form of pagodas!) The British occupation of India was signalled architecturally by Neo-Gothic railway stations and imperial Roman administrative buildings. Wherever Western imperialism spread, buildings in European styles marked its arrival. And not only buildings. Sculptors were enrolled in the process of making colonized territory – in the words of Franz Fanon (born and brought up in French Martinique) – 'a world of statues: the statue of the general who carried out the conquest, the statue of the engineer who built the bridge; a world which is sure of itself, which crushes with stones the backs flayed with whips'. In Europe and North America also, statues of white men, rarely women, larger than life-size and raised high on pedestals, asserted the ambitions of those who commissioned them.

THE POWER OF IMAGES

Works of art always form part of a whole cultural structure being both expressions of its religious beliefs, moral codes, aesthetic preferences, and of its social system with its ranks, marginalizations and exclusions, as well as being a means of maintaining and perpetuating them. When not explicitly didactic, expounding and illustrating religious or political messages, their effect may be all the more insidious. The persistence in European art of an ancient Greek ideal of physical perfection has encouraged racial prejudice – the notion of white superiority in intellect and morals as well as physical beauty. Nor has this, along with other survivals from a male-dominated

0,12 Hieronymus Bosch, *Adoration of the Magi*, detail of central panel, c. 1490–1510. Prado, Madrid.

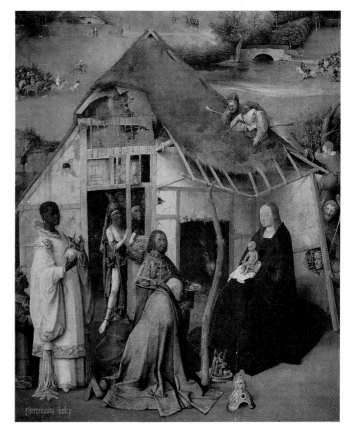

society, been without influence on the subject of gender in the visual arts of the West down to our own day. But the history of art, as of other cultural phenomena, necessarily combines that of the interplay between artists as individuals and what in modern terminology is called the 'reproduction of socio-cultural systems'. Whereas some artists have played significant and positive roles in the transformation of a culture by deepening or undermining current ideas or by widening horizons, the majority have been obliged to earn their living by tacitly supporting dominant ideologies which, on account of their education or indoctrination, they have usually come to share with their patrons. In Europe until the nineteenth century, large-scale works of art, that is, the majority of paintings and virtually all sculptures, were commissioned by patrons who chose the subjects to be represented and the artists whom they considered most likely to answer their demands. When freed from the direct control of patrons, artists still had to respect the views of potential purchasers and patrons including those who organized exhibitions and could bar the way to the main market-place. Only a few artists were prepared or able to create their own public. Those few who were could do so only because of their independent financial position which implied their membership of the bourgeoisie, even if they rebelled against it.

There are no more obvious examples of the way in which visual images can sustain cultural structures than those of blacks in Western art. A painting of about 1500 by the Dutch artist Hieronymus Bosch includes the magnificently robed, proudly erect and dignified figure of a black man, one of the three Magi or 'Wise Men' come from afar to worship the infant Christ, and given as much prominence in the composition as the Virgin herself (0,12). His facial features are characterized in such a way that Bosch would seem to have portrayed an individual, someone he knew personally. Africans had, of course, been seen in Europe since ancient times but they were never very numerous. They had occasionally been represented in art, though seldom prominently. In the religious art of the Middle Ages they appeared in a variety of roles, as saints and devils, Christian martyrs as well as torturers, despite the linguistic identification of blackness with evil and darkness, whiteness with purity and light. From the mid-fourteenth century it was by no means unusual to depict one of the three Magi as a black, often with a train of richly clad attendants, evoking myths of the riches of Africa. From the sixteenth century, upper-class portraits often included a black servant – fancily dressed page-boys were popular – to indicate the supposed superiority and emphasize the complexion of the white sitter. During this period, however, the trade in slaves from Africa to the Americas vastly increased and the word slave, derived originally from Slav (a native of eastern Europe, for centuries the main source of slaves), came to be applied mainly to blacks. The iniquity of this trade was condemned with increasing vehemence by both Christians and rationalist thinkers who in the late eighteenth century founded associations to campaign for its abolition.

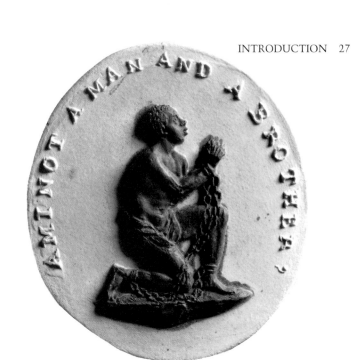

0,13 Wedgwood medallion, *Am I not a man and a brother?*, 1787. Jasper ware, $1^2/_5 \times 1^2/_5$ins (3.5 × 3.5cm). Wedgwood Museum, Barlaston, Staffordshire.

The British association adopted as its emblem, circulated in the United States and copied in France, the figure of a black man in chains kneeling in a supplicating posture, with the motto 'Am I not a man and a brother?' (0,13). Elegant little porcelain medallions of the emblem were made in England at the factory of Josiah Wedgwood, himself a leading abolitionist, set in gold mounts and worn as jewelry to further the cause and advertise their owners' philanthropy. This image of docile subservience was to be repeated time and again in large as well as small works of painting and sculpture. But in fact it betrayed rather than advanced the cause of racial justice and equality: it perpetuated the notion of the inferiority of blacks, enslaved by whites on whom they were dependent even for their liberation. Unequivocal and far more disturbing images were engraved by William Blake to illustrate the nauseating punishments meted out to slaves who had rebelled against their masters in Surinam (0,14). They portray the stoical physical and moral nobility with which their sufferings were endured. No artist of comparable ability recorded the triumph of slaves who freed themselves in Haiti even though this may have helped to form an alternative image of black men as muscular figures of overpowering strength – as in the *Death of Sardanapalus* (15,16). The degradation of slavery continued to be depicted in Britain and France (see p. 662) even after its abolition by these two countries which were, simultaneously, actively engaged in subjugating Africans by colonization.

Chattel slavery, which became an increasingly alien and distant phenomenon to Europeans, remained a domestic issue in the United States where blacks constituted a notable part of the population and many, probably the majority, were slaves. During the first three decades of the nineteenth century, however, blacks figured rarely and then only inconspicuously in paintings by American artists. When they began to appear in the 1830s they were almost invariably segregated from whites, though sometimes depicted with a sensitivity that may suggest sympathetic understanding on the part of the painter. In fact, there seems to have been a taboo on explicit references to slavery until the 1850s when its abolition was demanded by an increasing number of whites in the northern states. During these years Harriet Beecher Stowe's famous novel, *Uncle Tom's Cabin*, did much to convince whites of the evils of slavery and, like the equally well-intentioned emblem of the British abolitionists, succeeded by presenting an ambiguous but acceptable stereotype. Similarly unthreatening stereotypes conditioned the depiction of blacks, usually very young or very old, until the early twentieth century. Only in what at the time were called scenes of 'Negro Life' were robust and vigorous men and sexually attractive women allowed to appear. Yet such paintings and sculptures merely perpetuated attitudes to racial differences in a culture dominated by whites.

Another domination affected cultures through the West – that of males. Their views on gender differences were similarly reflected in and preserved by works of art. Nineteenth-century depictions of women, whether they emphasize the passivity, frailty or sexual modesty demanded of upper-class wives and daughters – the opposite of the gender characteristics ascribed to men – or the receptive sexuality of working-class women, all effectively mark the divisions of gender and social class set by men. Images of women are, of course, ubiquitous in the art of the world. The earliest known (see p. 35) are usually thought to represent a mother goddess; but as they were the products of non-literate cultures their significance cannot be known for certain. When forms of writing were invented they were limited to men closely associated with ruling groups (there were no female scribes in ancient Mesopotamia or Egypt). In early historic times female deities were worshipped (as they have been ever since in most cultures) and women sometimes gained political power; but men predominate in all records of life on earth, so often chronicling the victories of kings. And, until relatively recent times, artistic patronage has been dispensed mainly (in some places exclusively) by men of the ruling classes whose ideals of masculinity and femininity were expressed in works of art even when, exceptionally, they were executed by women.

WOMEN ARTISTS

In some communities practically every man and woman is a part-time artist. (Only the more complex stratified societies have been able to support full-time painters and sculptors.) But gender has often determined the type of work and material, according to local traditions. Among several groups of Africans south of the Sahara, for instance, cloth is made either by men or women; but where both weave they use different types of loom. Metalwork is done exclusively by men in this region, pottery is made mainly by women, partly on account of the association of clay with the earth mother or goddess. Not only simple pots for domestic use but elaborate ritual vessels – sometimes notable examples of African art – and also clay statuettes have been made by Yoruba women in Nigeria, though in other groups only men were permitted to represent the human figure. In the south-west of North America basketry was developed into a fine art by women of the indigenous cultures, the most famous being Dat So La Lee (c. 1850–1925) of the Washo tribe in Nevada (see p. 757).

The position of women in larger social groups determined their participation in artistic production. Their subjection in China from the earliest times until the revolution of 1911 (and even afterwards) is notorious. Some were, nevertheless, renowned as artists in their own day, although they tended to be ignored or downgraded by later Chinese writers about art. From at least as early as the second century AD calligraphy, sometimes regarded by the Chinese as the highest form of visual art (see p. 87), was expertly practised by women, though only by those of the educated upper class. The majority of the population was illiterate. This socio-educational distinction is important, for nowhere but in China was so much respect paid to the art produced by upper-class scholars – the so-called

0,14 William Blake, *A Negro Hung Alive by the Ribs to a Gallows*, 1792. Line engraving after a drawing, 10½ × 8ins (26.7 × 20.3cm). Illustration from John Gabriel Stedman, *Narrative of a Five Years' Expedition Against the Revolted Negros of Surinam*, London, 1796.

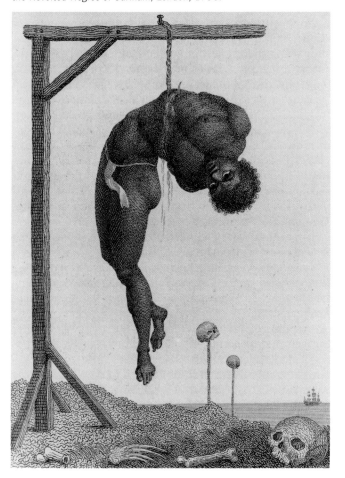

literati – who would be ranked as amateurs in the West. (In China, professionals who may have included women were classed with artisans and entertainers, beneath the attention of serious students of art, and little is recorded about them.) As education was directed towards the civil service examinations which opened the way to power and riches, it was a male province based mainly on writings ascribed to Confucius, whose attitude to women was at best paternalistic. Some women learned, however, from their fathers, brothers or husbands, and the first whose paintings won enough esteem for inclusion in the imperial collection was the thirteenth-century Guan Daosheng, well-born, highly educated and married to a still more aristocratic painter and imperial official (see p. 554). In later periods an increasing number of women, though always a minority, won recognition as *literati* painters, working in much the same way as their male contemporaries. But, with characteristic Chinese respect for tradition, they often alluded in inscriptions to their female predecessors and one, in the early nineteenth century, compiled a history of Chinese women painters.

In Japan education similarly limited the participation of women in the arts but otherwise the situation was different. From the eighth century, Chinese was the official language in the male-dominated worlds of government, Buddhist religion and scholarship. Women were expected to write only in Japanese, the language of poetry and fiction in which they excelled, using the beautiful flowing script sometimes called 'feminine hand', perhaps the purest expression of Japanese artistic genius (see pp. 293–4). This script was also used by men for poems and private letters and an analogous term applied to paintings indicated intimate, emotional subject-matter rather than the gender of the artist. Ability to compose and write out short poems came to be thought a suitable accomplishment for upper-class women, some of whom were notable calligraphers. Not until the seventeenth century do women appear in the historical record as figurative artists. Some came from the *samurai* class but most of them seem to have been the daughters of professional painters (less disdainfully treated in Japan than in China). So faithfully did they follow their masters that their work would be mistaken for that of men had they not included the equivalent of 'Miss' or 'Mrs' in their signatures.

In Persia and Mughul India, princesses and other highly placed ladies of the courts – freed from the daily tasks of humbler women – occasionally practised miniature painting (see pp. 543–4). Their names and achievements are known, however, only because of their social position. How much women may have contributed to the work of professional male painters is unrecorded, as the products of a studio were usually ascribed only to the master. But in India at a lower social and artistic folk-art level, large wall and floor compositions of religio-magic significance were and still are painted exclusively by women.

In the West, the history of women's participation in the visual arts is more amply documented. Pliny the Elder (see p. 30) named six female painters of the Hellenistic period and there must have been many more; two are shown at work in mural paintings from Pompeii. During the European Middle Ages illuminators of manuscripts included women, the earliest on record being a nun named Ende who painted scenes in a commentary by Beatus on the Apocalypse of 970 (Gerona Cathedral Treasury, Spain), perhaps the finest of all Mozarabic book illuminations. In the Rhineland in the late twelfth century another nun, Guda, included her self-portrait in one of the florid capital letters of a manuscript. But as paintings of this type were rarely signed it is seldom possible to be sure whether they were by women or men. All that is certain is that this art, and that of painting large religious pictures, was practised in convents by nuns who were, significantly, spared the bearing and rearing of children as well as the endless household tasks to which the majority of women were condemned from marriage to death. Vestments with figurative embroideries were similarly worked in convents. Aristocratic women, who led privileged lives, made very fine embroideries, probably including the famous 'Bayeux Tapestry' (see p. 377). Outside these circles, women may have taken part in the artistic work of their fathers, brothers and husbands, although they were usually excluded from the craft guilds. Women artists make their first appearance as professionals in Europe at the end of the fourteenth century. In Paris, Anastasie illuminated the borders of manuscripts (none of which has been identified) for King Charles VI and also for the ardent feminist writer Christine de Pisan (c. 1365–c. 1431) who said that no man surpassed Anastasie in this type of work. At about this time manuscripts of Giovanni Boccaccio's very popular *De claris mulieribus* (*Of Famous Women*, written in 1361) included illustrations of his account of the famous women artists of antiquity, much elaborated from the brief passage in Pliny. One shows Marcia, a Vestal Virgin whose name Boccaccio derived from a misreading, painting her self-portrait, dressed in fashionable early fifteenth-century clothing such as Anastasie must have worn (**0,15**). When women painters achieved greater prominence in the sixteenth century the accounts of their predecessors in the ancient world by Pliny and Boccaccio were often to be recalled, both by writers such as Vasari and by the artists themselves, notably Sofonisba Anguissola.

Women remained, nevertheless, a tiny minority among professional artists and those who attained distinction tended to be regarded as prodigies – hence, perhaps, the demand for self-portraits by Sofonisba Anguissola, sometimes signed *Sofonisba virgo* in emulation of Boccaccio's 'Marcia' (see pp. 507–8). In collections of artists' lives published from the mid-sixteenth century onwards (written exclusively by men, of course), greater prominence is given to their femininity than to their artistic accomplishment. Thus, Giorgio Vasari (see p. 473) remarks that the relief carving on the main portal of the church of San Petronio in Bologna, of Joseph and Potiphar's wife by Properzia de' Rossi (c. 1490–1530), was inspired by her own unrequited love for a young man – a typical myth. She was among the very few women to practise as sculptors before the nineteenth century, the

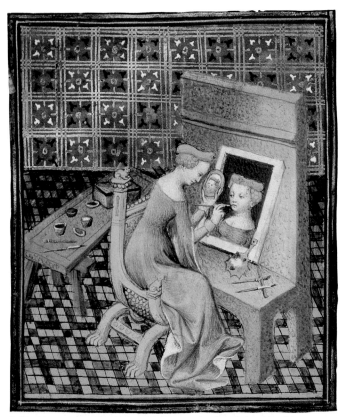

0,15 Anonymous, *Marcia*, from G. Boccaccio, *De claris mulieribus* (written 1361), early 15th century. Illumination. Bibliothèque Nationale, Paris.

strenuous work of carving being commonly believed to be beyond their physical capacity. As painters, women became more numerous. Some executed large-scale subject-pictures but they usually specialized in portraiture (see pp. 627, 633), still-life or flower painting (see p. 608). For not only were they excluded from the life-class – indispensable for the depiction of the human figure – but they were expected to display in their work those qualities of delicacy, charm, sentiment and softness, which, with a yielding conformity to convention, men supposed to be essentially feminine. Many were obliged to work mainly as copyists, originality in the visual arts (as also in music) being supposedly masculine. Despite a partial relaxation of restraints during the period of the French Revolution (see pp. 648–9), it was not until the later nineteenth century, with the breakdown of the academic system and general loosening of social conventions, that women artists were able to realize themselves fully and make vital contributions to artistic developments, in Impressionism (see p. 712), Post-Impressionism (see p. 719), non-representational art (see pp. 793–4, 797), Surrealism (see pp. 813–5), Expressionism (see pp. 780–1) and several post-World War II movements (see pp. 843, 874–7). The past four decades, in the United States especially but also elsewhere, have been notable for increasingly prominent and explicitly Feminist works of art. These are deliberately distinct from current work in styles dominated by men, of which, in fact, they often embody a critique (see p. 874). Feminists

have also initiated a major revision in the history of art by the revaluation of works by women through the ages. This has been accompanied by a fresh and attentive study of those by men to expose and lay bare their underlying assumptions about the roles assigned to women in life.

THE HISTORY OF ART

In some respects the history of art is comparable with that of literature. There is continuity and change in both, progressive improvement in neither. Both are punctuated by works that seem to transcend circumstantial limitations, with a timeless appeal independent of, and sometimes at odds with, the intentions of their creators. The history of art is, however, dependent on the physical survival of objects. And their survival has depended on a number of factors, as has their destruction. Religious images have been destroyed in order to subvert the beliefs of their devotees, by early Christians in the Roman Empire, by Muslims in India, by Spaniards in central America, by Protestants in northern Europe, by nineteenth-century missionaries in Africa and Polynesia and most recently by the Red Guards of the Cultural Revolution in China whose appalling zeal is an indication of the importance still accorded to the visual arts – for strictly non-aesthetic reasons, of course. Yet in some places, works of art have been preserved in private collections and, later, public museums, for their artistic excellence. It is no coincidence that only where this has occurred have histories of art been written. They marginalize some works and totally exclude many more in order to focus attention on the few which their authors hold up as models for later generations of artists to emulate or even in some way to improve on, thereby establishing new canons of exemplars. Such canonical works provide the skeleton for a history of art with its continuities and changes, revivals of past styles and experiments with new techniques, though what is omitted or underplayed may sometimes seem today to be of equal if not greater interest.

The earliest extant history of art, devoted to that of Greece and Rome, was written by Pliny the Elder, a Roman polymath, as part of a vast treatise on natural history completed before he died in the eruption of Vesuvius in AD 79. Pliny had, however, the benefit of some now lost Greek accounts of artists, including one of the fourth century BC, from which he derived the notion of progress towards a greater naturalism which, it was thought, had reached perfection during the writer's life-time. The earliest known treatise on Chinese painting was written in about AD 500 by Xie He: the *Classified Record of Ancient Painters*, which ranked artists according to their command of six essential principles (see p. 280) without suggesting development towards any single end. For a millennium and a half, this provided purely aesthetic criteria for the discussion of paintings; but only those by the highly educated élite known as *literati*. Dong Qichang's writings about painting in the seventeenth century are typical (see p. 562).

In Europe, after the Middle Ages when writings on art were limited mainly to technical manuals, Pliny's notion of progress was revived by the Florentine painter and architect Giorgio Vasari's *Lives of the Most Excellent Italian Architects, Painters and Sculptors*, first published in Florence in 1550. This set out to describe the 'restoration or rather the renaissance' of the arts that had been gradually achieved, according to Vasari, during the previous two-and-a-half centuries – that is to say, after their 'rise to perfection' in ancient Greece and Rome and subsequent decline. Like most historians he studied the past to explain the present. Conceiving the history of art since the fourteenth century as a series of progressive improvements, he described how Giotto had been able to suggest solidity and expressive movement, Masaccio had mastered perspective and light and shade, Leonardo da Vinci and Raphael had added grace and beauty. The hero of his story was Michelangelo, a 'genius universal in each art' – sculpture and architecture as well as painting. Although Vasari's book was devoted almost exclusively to Italian artists, giving pride of place to Florentines, it provided a model for histories of the very different art of the Netherlands and, later, of that of other nations. The pre-eminence accorded by Vasari to Michelangelo was soon contested by those who recognized that some artists had excelled him in various ways – Raphael in drawing and composition, for instance, Titian in color. None, however, had achieved that perfection in all branches of art that became the goal for further progress towards which artists were encouraged to strive.

By the second half of the eighteenth century, it was widely felt that the arts were once again in a state of decay which could be cured, according to the historian and theorist Johann Joachim Winckelmann, by a return to the true principles of Greek art. In his *History and Ancient Art* of 1764, he gave an account not so much of progress as of an organic process of birth, maturity and decadence evident also in Italian art. The arts of Greece before the fifth century BC and those of Italy before the sixteenth century were not comparable in every respect, he remarked, 'but both of them possess a simplicity and purity suitable for improvement' whereas the perfected arts already carried germs of corruption and affectation and over-sophistication which became virulent under oppressive political systems. The reassessment of the earlier arts of both Italy and northern Europe soon followed, necessitating a readjustment in historical writing. A far greater change was brought about in the early nineteenth century by the Romantics whose belief that the aim of art was to express the artist's individual feelings and perceptions underlay later developments for each of which historians traced an ancestry in the past, thereby maintaining an illusion of progress.

In the late nineteenth century when faith in the advance of Western civilization was beginning to falter, new approaches were made in the history of art, mainly in Germany and Austria where it had first been accepted as a subject for study in universities. Alois Riegl in 1893 set out to provide a purely objective study of ornament based on the notion that styles adopted in different places and periods were manifestations, albeit multifarious, of a general though somewhat nebulous 'will-to-form'; discussions of progress and decline were thus irrelevant, indeed meaningless. 'Every style aims at a faithful rendering of nature and nothing else, but each has its own conception of Nature', he later declared. In 1899 Heinrich Wölfflin in a book on *Classic Art*, a study of Italian Renaissance painting and sculpture, enunciated criteria for stylistic analysis more fully developed in his *Kunstgeschichtliche Grundbegriffe* of 1915 (translated as *The Principles of Art History* in 1932) in which he isolated tendencies in Classical and Baroque art according to contrary concepts: linear and painterly, plane and recession, closed and open form, multiplicity and unity, absolute clarity and relative clarity of subject-matter. His terminology came to be used for an almost exclusively formal analysis of paintings, whether devotional images, history paintings, still-lifes, landscapes or *genre* scenes. In this way paintings were discussed and analyzed without regard to their subject or content as if they were all non-representational. A reaction came, first in Aby Warburg's study of the survival and revival of Classical antiquity in Renaissance art and then in the study of iconography. Strictly speaking, iconography is the study and identification of subject-matter. For a broader approach to the analysis of meaning in the visual arts the term iconology has been used, notably by Erwin Panofsky. He distinguished three layers of meaning in subject-matter: its primary or obvious meaning (the image of a woman), its conventional meaning (the Virgin Mary) and its intrinsic meaning or content (the religious beliefs embedded in and conveyed by the image). The search for intrinsic meanings became the preoccupation of many subsequent art historians and has led to a much wider, more pluralistic and open-minded approach to the visual arts. It was taken up by Marxists for social histories of art and more recently and fruitfully by feminists for their critiques of male-dominated art history. They have revealed how many images represent and perpetuate – whether intentionally or not – the subjugation of women, and also how gender influences the ways in which women create and interpret art, because their experience of the world is different from that of men.

Histories of art inevitably reflect the minds and feelings of their authors, who have been almost as diverse as the artists about whom they write – as diverse and many-sided as the works of art themselves. For works of art are more than aesthetically pleasing objects, more than feats of manual skill and ingenuity: they deepen our insight into ourselves and others, they sharpen our awareness of our own and other modes of thought and religious creeds, they enlarge our comprehension of alternative and often alien ways of life – in short they help us to explore and understand our own human nature. The creation of works of art is the activity that most clearly distinguishes human beings from other animals. The history of art is an essential part of the history of the human species.

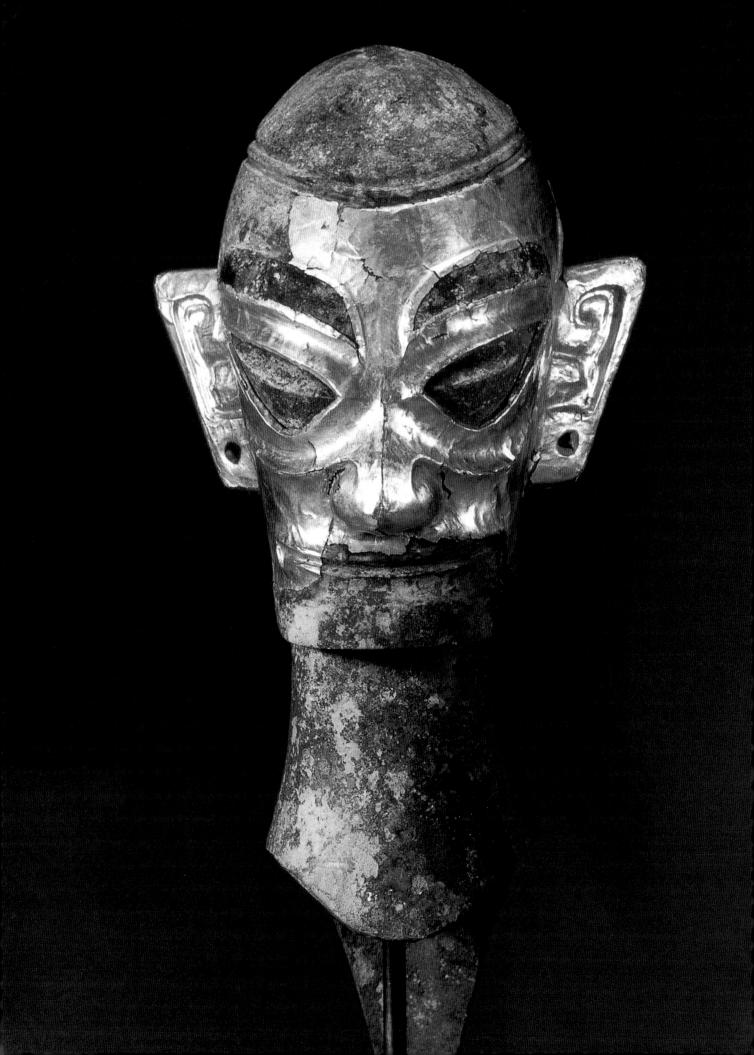

PART ONE

FOUNDATIONS OF ART

Opposite Human-like head, from Sanxingdui, China, c. 1200–1000 BC. Bronze, 14½ins (36.7cm) high. Institute of Archaeology, Sichuan province.

CHAPTER ONE

BEFORE HISTORY

The history of the manual techniques that have enabled the human race to dominate its environment began in east-central Africa more than two million years ago, when pebbles were first made into rudimentary tools by breaking off part of the surface to form a working edge. These first artifacts were made by man-like creatures, sometimes identified as *Homo habilis* (able or handy man), a species of the zoological genus of hominids. By chipping flakes from the opposite faces of a stone to give it a cutting edge, *Homo erectus* was making a more efficient tool about a million years ago in Africa and about half a million years ago in Asia and Europe. Members of this species in China had also learned the use of fire, indicating a further advance in cognitive capacity. After another quarter of a million years, choppers and multi-purpose tools called hand-axes were being flaked and smoothed into more or less regular shapes, sometimes even into roughly symmetrical shapes. Awareness of form and function and the connection between them on which tool-making depends had been heightened. In the process, the first step towards the making of art had been taken.

Neanderthal man – *Homo sapiens neanderthalensis* – who was living in Europe and west Asia from about 125,000 years ago, made a great variety of implements. Members of this sub-species colored their bodies with red ochre. Their thoughts seem to have extended beyond the immediate physical world, for they buried the dead in graves with funeral gifts of food and weapons and, in at least one instance (at La Ferrassie in France), a kind of monument – a large stone from which pairs of concave cup-like marks had been pecked out. It is impossible to be certain about this, of course, but if the markings on the stone had a commemorative, magic or at any rate non-utilitarian purpose, the second step towards the making of art had been taken. These were the millennia of the last Ice Age, broken by slightly warmer 'inter-glacial' periods, during the last of which, around 40,000 BC, Neanderthal man vanished and another sub-species, the only one to survive and that to which we belong, made its appearance in Africa, Asia and Europe: *Homo sapiens sapiens*, as we are zoologically designated. In every essential respect, including brain capacity, these people were like ourselves. Before the final stage of the Ice Age (see p. 35), they had

The visual arts

c. 30,000–25,000 BC Woman from Willendorf (1,1).
    Man from Brno (1,2)
c. 25,000–20,000 BC Mammoth from Vogelherd (1,4)
c. 25,000–17,000 BC Chauvet cave (1,6;7;8)
c. 22,000 BC Woman's head from Brassempouy (1,3)
c. 16,000–14,000 BC Lascaux paintings (1,9)
after 15,000 BC Bison from Tuc d'Audoubert (1,11)
c. 12,000 BC Spear-thrower from Montastruc (1,12)
c. 10,000 BC Coyote head from Tequixquiac (1,13)

c. 8000 BC Addaura rock engravings (1,15)
c. 8000–5000 BC Fezzan rock engravings (1,14)

c. 7000–6000 BC Plastered skull from Jericho (1,19)

c. 5800 BC Painting from Çatal Hüyük (1,20)

c. 4500–4000 BC Head from Predionica (1,21)
c. 4000–3500 BC Man from Cernavoda (1,22)
c. 2100–2000 BC Stonehenge (1,26)

Historical landmarks

c. 40,000 BC Interglacial period.
    Emergence of *Homo sapiens sapiens*

c. 18,000–15,000 BC Last Ice Age
c. 12,000 BC Human migration from Asia into America begins
c. 10,000 BC Invention of bow and arrow.
    Domestication of reindeer and dog (N. Eurasia)
c. 9000–8000 BC Domestication of wheat and barley (Near East)
c. 8000 BC Modern climate begins in Europe. Foundation of Jericho. Human settlement extends to Straits of Magellan
c. 8000–4000 BC Human population increases by 1500%
c. 7000 BC Domestication of sheep and goats (Near East). Earliest pottery (Japan)
c. 6500 BC Settlement of Çatal Hüyük
c. 6500–4000 BC Farming spreads to W. Europe
c. 6000 BC First woven woollen textiles (Near East). Rice cultivation starts in Asia
c. 5000 BC Irrigation introduced (Near East)
c. 4500 BC Copper smelting perfected (Near East)
c. 4000 BC Bronze casting begun (Near East)

carved the earliest known objects that can be called works of art.

Unfortunately, the stone carvings that survive from this remote age cannot as yet be dated with enough precision to reveal a sequence. The earliest can only be dated to within 5,000 years – a period as long as that which separates us from the beginning of history. We know nothing of the predecessors they almost certainly had in such perishable materials as wood and unbaked clay. So the curtain goes up on the history of art some time after the play has begun. Nor can we tell how far surviving carvings are typical of the culture that produced them. They have been found over an enormous area in Europe and southern Russia. And they are, of course, very rare in comparison with the tools and implements, expertly worked flints of standard form, of which a considerable number have survived.

THE ART OF THE HUNTERS

The little figure of a woman, no more than 4½ inches (11.5cm) high, found at Willendorf in Austria, is the most striking and famous of these first works of art (**1,1**). It is between 25,000 and 30,000 years old, carved out of limestone, and seems originally to have been covered with pigments, of which traces remain. The exaggerated rotundity of the body has a yielding fleshiness, felt rather than seen. The hands resting on the breasts, the arms and the lower legs are no more than sketchily indicated and the woman has no face. Tiny curls of hair cover the entire

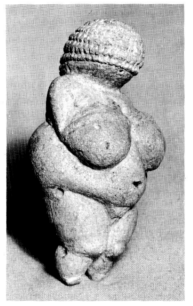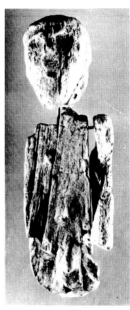

1,1 *Above left*   Woman from Willendorf, Austria, c. 30,000–25,000 BC. Limestone, 4½ins (11.5cm) high. Naturhistorisches Museum, Vienna.

1,2 *Above right*   Man from Brno, Czech Republic, c. 30,000–25,000 BC. Ivory, 8ins (20.3cm) high. Moravian Museum, Brno.

head. There can be little doubt that she was carved as an image of fertility, probably as some kind of magic charm, perhaps to be held in the hand. Other female figures which are dated slightly later (in millennial terms!) similarly emphasize the breasts, belly and buttocks, and in

Prehistoric Europe and Near East

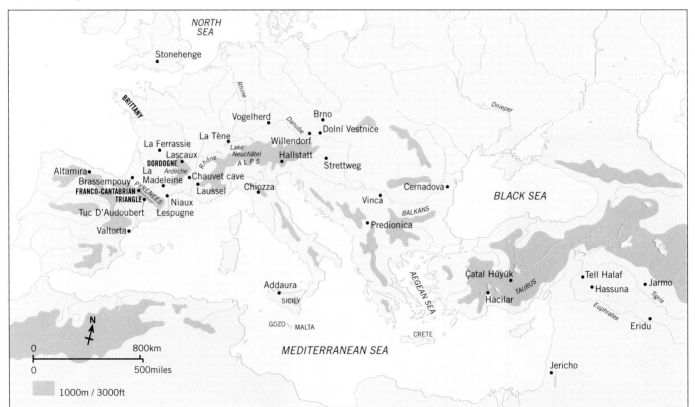

one instance, the remarkable Woman from Lespugne (Musée de l'Homme, Paris), they are almost completely abstracted into an organic geometry of cones, ovoids and spheres. Sometimes only part of the body is represented – the breasts in ivory carvings found at Dolní Věstonice in the Czech Republic (now in the Moravian Museum, Brno); well-defined belly and thighs in a stone carving from Tursac in the Dordogne, France; and numerous vulvae engraved on rock-faces in the Dordogne in about 25,000 BC. In a strange sandstone figure of about the same date, found at Chiozza in Italy, the female form, again without feet, is combined with a faceless head like the tip of a phallus as if to unite the generative organs of the two genders into a single image (Museo Civico, Reggio Emilia). Sex and art would seem to have been closely allied from the very beginning.

A badly damaged ivory statuette of a man, which seems originally to have stood some 17 inches (43cm) high, dates from the same period as the Woman from Willendorf (**1,2**). It was found at Brno in the Czech Republic in the grave of a man evidently of some importance, for he was buried wearing a head-dress or necklace made of cut and polished beads of mammoth tooth, bone roundels and some 600 pieces of shell. To judge from the present damaged state of the statuette, the body was schematically represented and the carver's attention concentrated on the naturalistically rendered head with close-cropped hair and deep-sunk eyes. Whether it was intended as a portrait, a symbol or the image of a supernatural being cannot, of course, be known. But its place of discovery reveals that it was used in a ritual of burial, which implies some form of religious belief.

The objects found with the Man from Brno were clearly used for personal adornment – another human impulse closely involved with the visual arts – though we cannot tell whether they were selected for their aesthetic or magic properties or a combination of the two. A little ivory head from Brassempouy reveals that women dressed their hair in braids even at this very remote period (**1,3**).

Other small ivory and bone carvings show signs of having been handled and worn as pendants or carried about the person in pouches, perhaps as charms. They include some remarkably well-observed animals, found with others equally fine in baked clay, in the Vogelherd Cave, near Stettin ob Lontal, Württemberg, Germany (**1,4**). Much larger, indeed very imposing, is the first true relief sculpture (**1,5**). It was found in 1911 in an open-air rock-shelter near Laussel in the Dordogne, France, not far from the caves of Lascaux (1,9). When seen in situ from slightly below eye-level, as it was when found, this remarkable sculpture is highly plastic, the outer curve of the pregnant figure following the bulging profile of the rock-face, as if the sculptor had sought to release a human form sensed within it. The head has been obliterated but seems to have been in profile looking towards the raised right hand holding up a bison's horn. The left hand rests on the belly, indicating the swelling womb. All this, and especially the bison's horn, crescent-shaped like the moon, with 13 notches perhaps indicating the phases of the moon, make her a much more complex figure than the Woman from Willendorf or other early fertility images. Hunters would almost certainly have known that the growth of horns and antlers is connected with the sexual cycle of animals and may very well have seen the horn as an embodiment of procreative powers and fertility, even if not quite a horn of plenty. That the whole figure was conceived as an image of the life-giving, nourishing and regenerative powers of nature seems likely. It may well have been intended to represent a fertility or mother goddess.

Like the Woman from Willendorf, the Woman from Brassempouy and the animals from the Vogelherd Cave, the Mother Goddess from Laussel is rendered naturalistically. This is one of the most extraordinary of all the extraordinary features of prehistoric art and it becomes even more evident in cave paintings of animals. They are visualized, not conceptualized; that is to say that, unlike children's drawings and other so-called 'primitive' attempts at visual representation, they are based on what the eye sees and not on what the mind knows. It can only be supposed that their original purpose, whatever it may have been, was in some way linked with their lifelikeness. What is still more extraordinary is that a conceptual

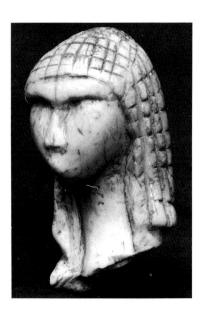

1,3 *Left* Woman's head from Brassempouy, France, c. 22,000 BC. Ivory, 1¹/₃ins (3.4cm) high. Musée des Antiquités Nationales, St-Germain-en-Laye.

1,4 *Right* Mammoth from the Vogelherd Cave, Württemberg, Germany, c. 25,000–20,000 BC. Ivory, 1⁹/₁₀ins (4.8cm) long. Institut für Urgeschichte der Universität, Tübingen.

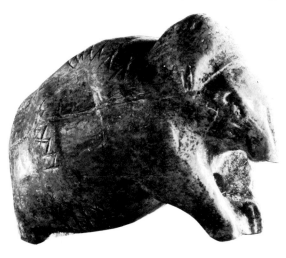

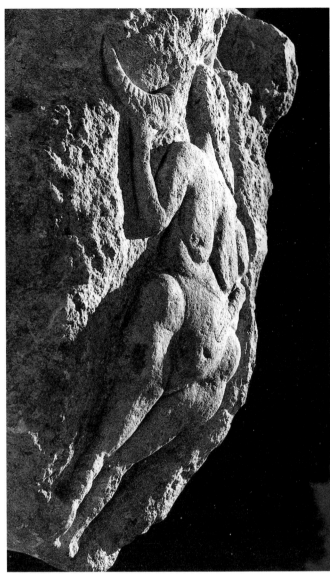

even the most ancient artifacts much more accurately. Nineteenth-century terminology is still used, none the less.

The Woman from Willendorf and the Man from Brno are products of an Upper Paleolithic culture which flourished in an area extending from present-day France to southern Russia and is called East Gravettian. Their makers lived on the edge of an ice-cap in a landscape like that of modern Greenland or the Canadian barrens. They subsisted by hunting a variety of animals – mammoths, reindeer, wolves, horses, arctic foxes, arctic hares and willow-grouse. For some part of the year, presumably the long and very cold winter, they gathered in settled communities of perhaps a hundred or slightly more people. These villages were usually sited near a spring and some were inhabited for several centuries. Huts were built of mud and other materials, including stone and mammoth bones. Each had at least one hearth, some as many as five. There were also workshops in which implements were made of stone, bone and ivory, and clay was modelled and baked – all suggesting the emergence of specialized artisans.

CAVE ART

Knowledge of prehistoric art is dependent on what has been by chance preserved and recovered. We have no means of knowing how typical or exceptional these often quite accidental survivals are; no generalizations can be made from haphazard evidence from a period about which its extraordinary length is its only certainty – an immense tract of time to be measured not in centuries but in tens of millennia. When the first examples of prehistoric paintings were discovered in 1879 – at Altamira in northern Spain – most archeologists dismissed them as a hoax perpetrated by an artist friend of the caves' owner. Few were able to believe that such vivid depictions of animals could be prehistoric (**1,10**) and not until the beginning of the twentieth century was it generally recognized and accepted that they were Paleolithic. Subsequent discoveries in the so-called Franco-Cantabrian triangle extending from the north of Spain to south-western France with its apex in the valley of the Dordogne, notably at Lascaux, enabled approximate dates to be established by scientific methods: c. 16,000–14,000 BC for Lascaux; c. 14,000 BC for Altamira; and c. 13,000–12,000 BC for Niaux. A chronology within these dates was then proposed on the presumption of a development from simple to complex forms, from animals shown in outline to those with shading, from crudely painted to more carefully finished images. All this was upset in 1994, however, by the discovery in a gorge of the Ardèche in south-eastern France of a cave with extensive paintings which can be dated by radio-carbon analysis to some 10,000 years earlier than the paintings at Lascaux – i.e. some 25,000 years ago and approximately contemporary with, if not earlier than, the Woman from Willendorf (**1,1**). These recently discovered paintings in the Chauvet cave, so called after the speleologist who found them, reveal full knowledge of the basic techniques of pictorial representation in more than 200 images of animals. A few of these are engraved but the majority are painted, some

1,5 Mother Goddess from Laussel, Dordogne, France, c. 22,000–19,000 BC. Stone, 18½ins (47cm) high. Musée d'Aquitaine, Bordeaux.

art of symbols was practised in the same area at the same time (see p. 40 below).

The period is termed Upper (or late) Paleolithic. In the nineteenth century, when people first became aware of the vast tract of time preceding the earliest written records (i.e. before the third millennium in the Near East, later elsewhere), a system already in use for classifying artifacts was applied chronologically to the early history of the human race, dividing it neatly into three: Stone Age, Bronze Age and Iron Age. The Stone Age was then subdivided into Paleolithic, Mesolithic and Neolithic (old, middle and new) and each was again split up into cultures named after places where important finds of stone implements were made. This general system based on technological criteria was also used to categorize non-literate cultures still living in Africa, Australasia and America – to the great confusion of both anthropological and prehistoric studies. For it can at best provide only a relative chronology within geographically limited areas. More recently, the radiocarbon method of dating (see Glossary) and other scientific tests have made it possible to date

being more than 6 feet (2m) long, on the walls and ceilings of natural chambers extending for some 560 yards (500m) underground. With astonishing economy of means they capture the essential 'animality' of their subjects, suggesting not only form and texture but also gait and physical presence. Near the entrance a hyena is shown in outline with spots on its head and powerful neck, as if sniffing the presence of an intruder (**1,6**). These are the earliest paintings known to us and we can only speculate on how their creators had acquired such skill, such freedom of hand and sureness of touch – shading to suggest form especially on the heads of horses (1,8) and even, it might appear, an ability to suggest perspective in the rendering of a herd of rhinoceroses (**1,7**) – perhaps on the walls of still earlier caves that have been destroyed or remain to be discovered, or perhaps on impermanent surfaces including human skin. There is no certainty that this art had its origin north of the Mediterranean. What seems certain, and is most remarkable, is that it continued in southern Europe from the time of the Chauvet cave for the following 20,000 years or more with unchanging consistency apart from slight local variations.

The Chauvet cave has many features in common with those of the Franco-Cantabrian triangle. They all extend for several hundred yards underground, with paintings mainly in their inner and deeper recesses, far beyond the entrances with natural light and other areas that might

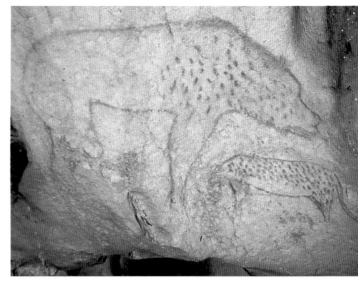

1,6 Hyena and panther, c. 25,000–17,000 BC. Pigment on limestone rock. Chauvet cave, Ardèche valley.

have been used for human habitation. At Niaux, the most elaborately painted chamber is 870 tortuously winding yards (800m) from the entrance. Visitors to the main chambers at Bédeilhac must crawl on their stomachs through a long, low, narrow passage. The pigments used in the Chauvet cave were red ochre and charcoal, the former mainly for images near the entrance, the latter for most of those in the inner chambers, notably those of horses and

1,7 Left section of the 'Lion Panel' and a herd of rhinoceroses, c. 25,000–17,000 BC. Pigment on limestone rock. Chauvet cave, Ardèche valley, France.

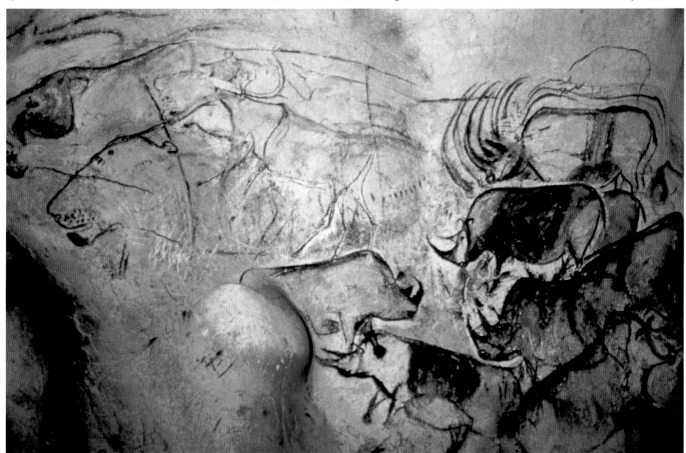

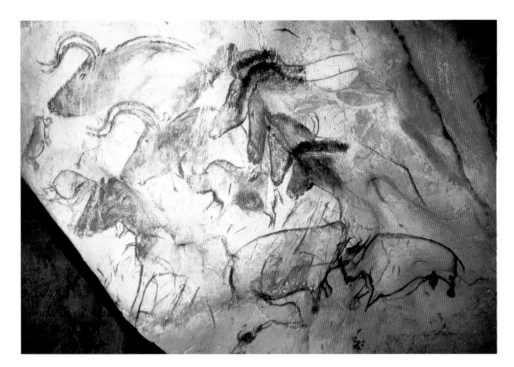

1,8 Horses, rhinoceroses and aurochs, c. 25,000–17,000 BC. Pigment on limestone rock. Chauvet cave, Ardèche valley.

lions. Sometimes lines were cut into the rock and filled with color. At Lascaux engraved images are more sharply incised, very small, and subsidiary to the paintings, and a wider range of colors was used, derived from natural minerals – reds, yellows and brown from ochre and haematite; black, dark brown and violet from types of manganese. They were ground to powder and applied directly to the damp limestone surfaces. First the outlines were either drawn with sticks of charcoal or painted – using pads of fur or moss, primitive brushes of feather or chewed stick,

or simply a finger – and then the outlines were filled in by spraying powders through bone tubes. (Such tubes with traces of color have been found in several caves.)

The natural formation of cave chambers was exploited by painters, but not at all consistently. For instance, advantage was taken of one large area about 30 feet (10m) wide in the Chauvet cave to paint a vast concourse of mixed animals, most of them facing towards the entrance to another chamber (**1,8**). Great bulls, each 16 feet (5m) long, were painted above the unusually large 'great hall' at

1,9 General view of the 'great hall' at Lascaux, France, c. 16,000–14,000 BC. Pigment on limestone rock.

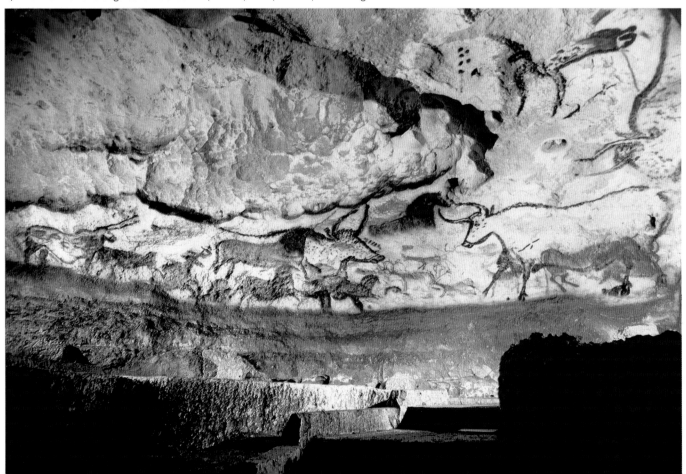

Lascaux (**1,9**). Elsewhere there are large chambers with very few paintings. The surface irregularities of the rock-face were sometimes smoothed but more usually ignored though they were occasionally exploited visually, as in the Chauvet cave, where the front paw of a bear was rendered in relief by painting over a protuberance. Whether cave painting originated in this way, in seeing animal images in the fissures and veins, the bumps and hollows of the stone surface – just as we may sometimes see pictures in the random stains on a damp wall – cannot be known. But it is tempting to speculate on the possibility that cave art began when some Stone Age hunter recognized the shape of an animal lurking as if by magic in the rock-face and then marked what he had divined so that others could see it too.

The subject-matter of cave painting is limited almost exclusively to animals. Very few men and no women appear (the contrast with Paleolithic sculpture is striking). The choice of animals is also somewhat surprising, for it was not confined to those that were hunted and eaten. Reindeer initially provided the hunters with their staple food and also with skins, antlers, bones and tendons, all of which were utilized. As they gradually moved north at the end of the last Ice Age (c. 15,000 BC) their place was taken by ibex. Reindeer appear in the Chauvet cave but are rare in the Franco-Cantabrian triangle (though they were quite often engraved on pieces of bone) and ibex are less numerous than bison and horses, which seem seldom to have been eaten. Dangerous animals – mammoths, lions, cave bears and woolly rhinoceros – have great prominence in the Chauvet cave and were also more frequently depicted elsewhere than such innocuous and commonly encountered creatures as hares, birds and fish.

That it is possible to identify all these animals – even such now extinct species as the mammoth, woolly rhinoceros and aurochs, known from surviving skeletons – testifies to the skill of the cave painters in naturalistic representation. Mammoth and rhinoceros tend to be rather summarily drawn, perhaps because they were known only by those who had seen them from a safe distance. But all the other animals are rendered with amazing fidelity to optical fact. Indeed their lifelikeness is such that one can almost hear the thunder of hooves as the bulls stampede across the ceiling of the 'great hall' at Lascaux (**1,9**). There are a very few half-animal half-human figures, one in the Chauvet cave and another at Lascaux sometimes thought to represent a shaman wearing a mask. But otherwise when cave painters depicted a human they resorted to the most rudimentary of conceptualized images – a box with sticks for legs and arms. Nor were they unaware of signs and symbols. For alongside the naturalistic depictions of animals there are often strange geometrical configurations, some of which have been interpreted as male and female sexual symbols.

The naturalism of cave painting, however, may be misleading. Paleolithic artists, like those of later ages down to our own time, worked within a conscious or unconscious set of visual conventions. They painted from memory; but

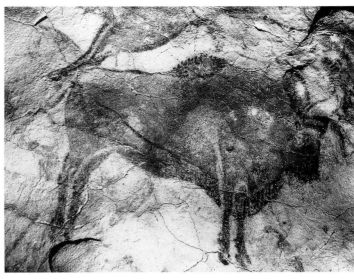

1,10 Bison, c. 14,000–10,000 BC. Pigment on limestone rock, 6ft 4³/₄ins (1.95m) long. Altamira, Spain.

their memories held both images of things and other images, and systems of representation were developed for different species of animal. Horses, mammoths and bison, for instance, are almost invariably shown in profile while deer turn their heads to look behind them or to confront the spectator. The regularity of such conventions often enables us to recognize a whole animal from a single flowing line, which defines only a part – the domed head and trunk of a mammoth, for instance, or the hump of a bison. However, our knowledge of later art, which helps us to read this kind of shorthand almost unthinkingly, probably hinders us in other respects.

The animals were painted on to the rough stone surfaces of the caves as if on to an unprepared ground, a neutral area on which images were imposed but which did not, like the backgrounds of later paintings, form part of the image. The Paleolithic artist worked on a field with no set boundaries and often an irregular surface which shows through the paintings. To this, doubtless, part of their power for us is due. We take for granted the artist's canvas, board or other defined field, forgetting how artificial it is. For it corresponds to nothing in nature or in mental imagery, where the phantoms of visual memory come up in a vague unbounded void – just as they do in cave painting. No framing devices were used by cave artists to mark off the pictorial field. There are no backgrounds, no ground lines even. We are given no clue as to whether the outstretched legs of a horse indicate that it is in a flying gallop or lying dead on the earth; nor can we assume differences in size to indicate distance – as in the juxtaposition of a hyena and much smaller panther (**1,6**). Some animals, evidently, were painted at different times, often superimposed on one another. In the Chauvet cave two rhinoceros are depicted in head-on conflict, a rare if not unique scene in Paleolithic art. Above them horses, rhinos and aurochs seem to be racing across the surface, though whether this was the intention of the artist or artists cannot be known (**1,8**). It is only too easy to read narrative meanings into these images. Their visual ambiguities are dreamlike and compelling, impossible though it is for us to see them as the people by and for whom they were painted saw them. We should bear in mind, too, that only a very limited area of wall or ceiling was ever visible at a time – only as much as could be lit by resinous torches or small stone lamps burning animal oil or fat.

Some ceilings seem at first sight to be no more than a tangle of lines and only on closer inspection do animals begin to start out of them – firmly drawn outlines of horses and bison and deer intersecting each other in higgledy-piggledy confusion. Similarly superimposed outlines appear on engraved pebbles. Various suggestions have been made to explain them, the most widely accepted being that the act of drawing an animal had some ritual or magic significance and was repeated on the same area of wall as a fire might be lit year after year, on the same hearth over past embers. Whether the superimpositions had themselves any ritualistic, seasonal significance is not known; but it has recently been demonstrated that on many bone and ivory carvings lines previously assumed to be decorative were, in fact, incised at regular intervals. Such carvings seem to have been used as tally sticks of some kind and a remarkably high proportion of them have marks corresponding with the days in the lunar month – intimating, perhaps, some concern with time for other than purely practical purposes.

Many attempts have been made to probe and uncover the meaning of Paleolithic art. It was generally assumed, at first, to have been merely decorative, made to satisfy an innate human desire for adornment. But this view was difficult to maintain after the discovery of paintings in the deepest recesses of caves unused for habitation. More elaborate theories were subsequently propounded, and support for them has been drawn from the arts and rituals of surviving tribes of hunters and gatherers in Africa, America and Australia – although perhaps the most important lesson to be learned from ethnography is that interpretations based solely on visual appearances are often very wide of the mark.

Since some, though not very many, of the bison and other animals appear to be wounded with arrows, a connection with sympathetic magic – rites to ensure successful hunting – has been suggested. However, other interpretations are possible. Bulls at Lascaux with arrow-like marks and similar paintings like those of wild horses at Niaux have been variously interpreted. One wild horse with an arrow-like mark on the side has been seen as a pregnant mare with arrows directed at it, or as a wild mare associated with a branch to indicate late spring or calving time, or as a well-fed stallion with linear signs (stylized penises) to indicate gender, and so on. Fertility symbols have been descried in the genitals of male animals and in a few apparently pregnant mares, as well as the abstract signs already mentioned. A cosmic interpretation has been based on the connection between the migration of herds and the seasons of the year. The animals have been identified as mythological beings and also as the totems of different Paleolithic clans. The caves themselves have been thought to be religious sanctuaries, temples or the locales of initiation rites. A recent analysis suggests that

cave paintings in the Franco-Cantabrian triangle may illustrate a mythology – a cultural construction of the Paleolithic hunters' relationship with the world – for a wholly unexpected consistency has been found in the placing and juxtaposition of the animals, even when repeatedly superimposed on each other, bovines being nearly always given the best locations and almost invariably accompanied by horses. In the exceptionally rich bestiary of the Chauvet cave, however, there seem to be no such clear distinctions.

The paintings owe their preservation to the very peculiar atmospheric conditions of the limestone caves in which they were sealed for thousands of years. (Many have deteriorated in the short time since their discovery and access to some, notably Lascaux, is now severely limited; it is unlikely that the general public will ever be admitted to the Chauvet cave.) Few examples of sculpture have been found in the deep galleries, the most notable being two pairs of bison, one larger than the other and each with a male following a female, modelled in clay from the floor of a chamber some 750 yards (700m) from the cave's entrance at Tuc d'Audoubert (**1,11**). They are in high relief and are rendered as naturalistically as those in the paintings. Sculpture in the cave entrances and the open air has fared less well. Here women make their appearance in reliefs, as we have seen (1,5). Two much damaged reclining nudes about life-size at the entrance to the cave at La Magdeleine, near Penne (Tarn), were discovered in 1950. Their freedom of pose and use of foreshortening, if not induced simply by their very rubbed and poor condition, are notable. They date from about 13,000 BC. There are several reliefs of animals, one of which includes a life-size horse on a limestone terrace above a river at Cap Blanc in the Dordogne. Whether these weatherbeaten

1,11 Bison, after 15,000 BC. Modelled clay, 25 and 24ins (63.5 and 61cm) long. Tuc d'Audoubert, Ariège, France.

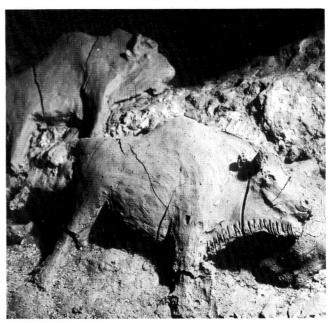

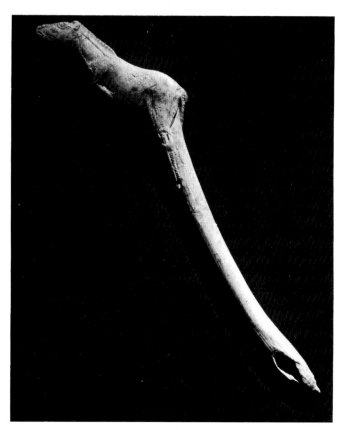

1,12 Spear-thrower carved with leaping horse, from Montastruc, France, c. 12,000 BC. Bone, 11ins (28cm) long. Bétirac Collection, Montauban.

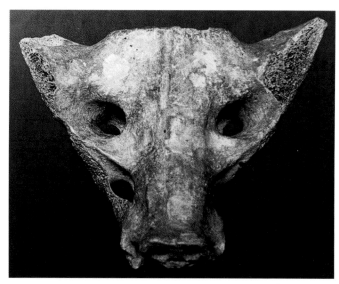

1,13 Coyote head, from Tequixquiac, Mexico, c. 10,000 BC. Bone, 7ins (17.8cm) wide. Museo Nacional de Antropologia, Mexico City.

1,14 Two giraffes and an elephant superimposed, c. 8000–5000 BC. Rock engraving. Wadi Bergiug, Fezzan, Libya.

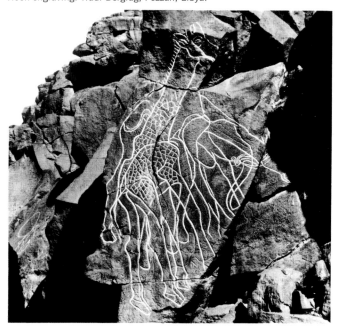

works originally had the vitality of the paintings inside the caves is hard to tell. But some small animal carvings in bone are remarkable both for their sharply observed naturalism and for an almost 'streamlined' elegance. They form part of objects generally described as spear-throwers – devices to give a hunter's arm leverage to propel his spear with additional force and steadier aim – though the most delicately curved were probably symbolic rather than utilitarian (French archeologists call them *bâtons de commandement*). One has an endearing young ibex poised on its tip, as if hesitating to take a leap, another terminates in a leaping horse (**1,12**). So perfectly is the form integrated with the medium that it is impossible to tell whether bones were carefully selected in order to carve predetermined shapes or whether the animals were suggested by the natural formations of the bones. The same could be said of the head of a coyote, of about the same date but from a very different part of the world (**1,13**). It was found in Mexico and – fashioned from the sacrum (part of the pelvis bone) of an extinct species of llama – is the earliest recorded American work of art. (Neatly chipped flint instruments testify to man's presence in America from about the thirtieth millennium.)

The coyote head is a reminder of how fragmentary our knowledge of Paleolithic art is. The little we know comes from chance survivals and discoveries. Paintings of mammoths, for instance, have recently come to light in the Kapovaya cave in the southern Urals, far to the east of Moscow. They are not unlike those in the Dordogne. Similarly, engravings of animals on rock-faces in the Sahara, including a rhinoceros more than 26 feet (8m) long and

giraffes and an elephant superimposed (**1,14**), have many of the characteristics of southern French and northern Spanish cave art. They are probably later, though they must antedate the climatic changes which transformed this area into a desert about 2000 BC. Whether there is any direct relationship between all these works remains a mystery.

A kind of unity can, however, be discerned in Paleolithic art, a generic similarity between the animals painted or engraved on stone and between the carved figures which have been found in many widely separated places. On the other hand, it is not possible to trace in them any lines of development such as may be seen in the increasingly subtle working of flint arrow-heads and hand-axes. This is perhaps significant. The magic or other, more than merely decorative or utilitarian, function of the paintings and figurative artifacts seems to have in some way immobilized, without having devitalized, the artistic impulse.

MESOLITHIC ART

A great change in climate and environment took place in Europe around 8000 BC: the ice-cap finally reached its present limit, new water-levels created many modern geographical divisions (for example, separating the British Isles from the mainland of Europe c. 6000 BC), forest spread across the continent and hindered man's mobility, and the animals on which Paleolithic hunters had preyed died out or moved to pasturage further north. This marks the beginning of the Mesolithic period, during which dogs were domesticated, bows were made for hunting and dug-out canoes for travel. So far as the arts are concerned, the most important changes took place in the Mediterranean area, which was least affected by the variation in climate.

On a rock-face at Addaura in Sicily there are outlines of animals dating from about 8000 BC or shortly after. They are not unlike those of the Paleolithic period, but they are accompanied by nude human figures, each from 10 to 15 inches (25–38cm) high, and engraved with the same degree of naturalism as the animals (1,15). These nudes are athletically lithe, firmly drawn in pure outline in such a way as to suggest both muscularity and movement. No human figures as anatomically correct or as graceful are found in earlier art and very few until the beginning of the historical period. Furthermore, three standing men wearing animal masks and two bound men at their feet are clearly related to one another in a group

1,15 Group of figures, c. 8000 BC. Engraving on rock, figures 10–15ins (25–38cm) high. Addaura, Monte Pellegrino, near Palermo, Sicily.

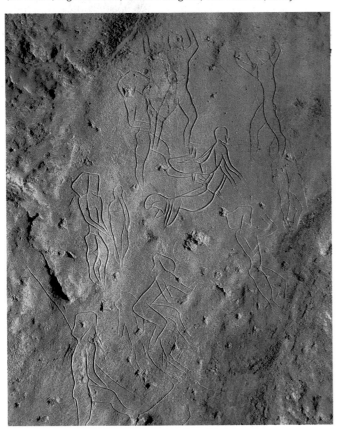

with narrative content, although we can only guess at its meaning; an initiation rite, an execution and a dance with acrobats have all been proposed.

Narrative art of a type more easily read emerged in eastern Spain by about 5000 BC. In mountainous country above the Mediterranean coast at Vallitorta, Remigia and several other neighbouring sites, paintings have been found in shallow overhung shelters lit by natural light. They differ from cave paintings not only in location but also in technique, style and subject-matter. (They are preserved under veils of stalagmite, can be clearly seen only when splashed with water and, unfortunately, cannot be satisfactorily photographed.) Animals are outnumbered by small (1–8 inches, 2.5–20cm, long) human beings busily engaged in a range of activities, mainly hunting and – a subject never depicted in earlier Paleolithic art – fighting one another. Some of the scenes which must be among the latest, though probably painted before 2000 BC, include domesticated cattle and horses led by men, testifying to a new pastoral and agricultural, rather than a hunting and gathering, way of life. Cattle also began to appear at about the same date in rock engravings in the Sahara.

THE ART OF THE FARMERS

Increasing population probably encouraged the domestication of livestock and the cultivation of cereals to supplement food obtained by hunting and foraging, and this initiated what is often called the Neolithic Revolution. The great change brought about by the introduction of agriculture, which led to land-ownership, to the formation of urban communities and eventually to states as well as to great technological advance, is certainly one of the major turning-points in the history of the human species. It is recorded in innumerable myths and folk-tales. But it took place gradually and at different periods in different parts of the world. Farming began in the middle of the eighth millennium in Palestine and western Iran, later in Egypt; in about the sixth millennium in Greece and the Balkans, early in the fifth millennium in China and also in central America but not for another one or two thousand years in northern Europe. Some tribes in Australia and central South America have survived by hunting and gathering without the need for agriculture to the present day. So Neolithic is sometimes used, rather tendentiously, as a cultural as well as a chronological term.

The adoption of agriculture was naturally accompanied by more permanent settlements, even if homesteads were often moved as soon as the land was exhausted by primitive methods of farming. The earliest known settlements of any size and permanence were at Jericho in Jordan, Çatal Hüyük in Anatolia and Jarmo in Iraq, only partially excavated. In about 8000 BC Jericho was a considerable town of oval, mud-brick dwellings on stone foundations and by about 7500 BC it was surrounded by formidable masonry fortifications of up to 12-foot-high (3.5m) walls and at least one 30-foot-high (9m) tower. Even more impressive than the fortifications are the

Çatal Hüyük

A NEOLITHIC TOWN

The discovery some 40 years ago of an unknown 8,000-year-old civilization in central Turkey – urban, agricultural, artistically sophisticated and remarkably peaceful, apparently without fortifications, weapons or wargods – very greatly increased knowledge of Neolithic life and culture. Çatal Hüyük, near present-day Konya, was one of the world's earliest towns, a human settlement of 5,000 inhabitants or more: much larger than Jericho, though unfortunately only one of its 32 acres (13 hectares) has so far been excavated. Twelve successive

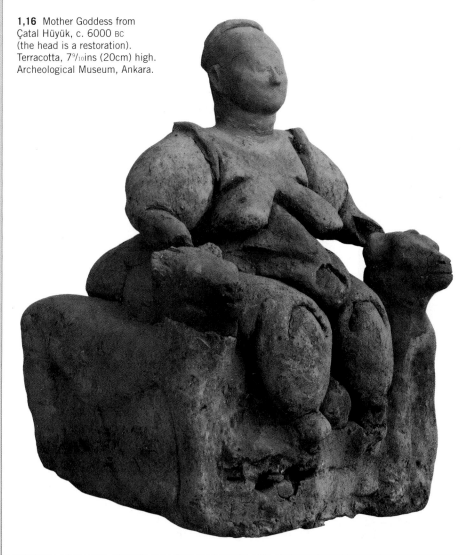

1,16 Mother Goddess from Çatal Hüyük, c. 6000 BC (the head is a restoration). Terracotta, 7⁹/₁₀ins (20cm) high. Archeological Museum, Ankara.

building levels cover a millennium from about 6500 to about 5650 BC and reveal a continuous development of economy and culture over some 800 years until the town was deserted – it is not known why – apparently without bloodshed or violence. Together with Hacilar, a smaller town about 200 miles (322km) to the west, Çatal Hüyük suggests that the central Anatolian plateau may well have been the most advanced region in the world in the sixth millennium BC. This was the age of the so-called Neolithic Revolution, of the domestication of

plants and animals and the origins of agriculture as well as of domestic crafts such as spinning, weaving, cloth dyeing, basketry, and clay and stone working. Even the smelting of copper and lead were known; Çatal Hüyük may also have been a commercial centre for goods made in obsidian, a hard volcanic stone which takes a high polish, and in other uncommon materials.

The paintings and sculptures found at Çatal Hüyük are remarkable though they raise problems in interpretation. In what context were they conceived? The *Dancing Hunter* (1,20), for example. This is one of many male figures with bows and arrows, sometimes wearing leopard skins, in a scene typical of Çatal Hüyük wall-painting in which hunting predominates. Women are rarely depicted. They appear frequently in clay figurines, however; indeed they greatly outnumber the men. Thus in one of the main dimensions of meaning discernible in these prehistoric visual images, that of the wild and the domestic, men are linked with the former just when hunting was being overtaken by agriculture. Would it be anachronistic to see them also in a context of gender difference, of changing male and female roles at this significant juncture in Neolithic life?

Many Paleolithic female figurines survive and more than one has been convincingly interpreted as a fertility or mother goddess, as we have seen (1,5). Several of the female figurines found at Çatal Hüyük can be associated with them. Quite small, from 2 to a maximum of 12 inches (5–30.5cm) high, they represent the goddess in various aspects – young, old, pregnant or in the act of giving birth. They are rendered naturalistically, the limbs and breasts being modelled sensitively, even sensuously, and sometimes the whole figure is painted with cross-like flower patterns of

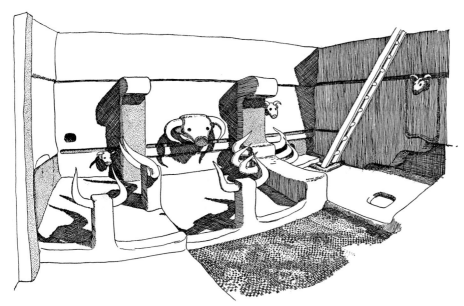

1,17 Restored view of the Third Shrine, Çatal Hüyük. Drawing by Mrs G. Huxtable.

served for work, eating, sleep and also burial after the flesh had been removed, probably by exposure to vultures, of which there are several paintings. Of the adult skeletons recovered 84 were male and 132 female. Women were found buried with obsidian mirrors, personal ornaments such as colored beads and cosmetic sets including shells filled with red ochre. Men were buried with less personal adornment but with numerous weapons such as maces, daggers, knives, arrow-heads and a few sickle blades. Little can be said about the population of Çatal Hüyük except that they were dolichocephalic (long-headed), of fair stature and thin-boned. The majority of burials are of women and children and few individuals seem to have reached middle age.

The lay-out and architecture of Çatal Hüyük are stereotyped (1,18). The shaped mud-brick houses, sometimes strengthened with wooden frames, stand on mud-brick foundations and are uniformly single-story, varying slightly in size, but are built to a standardized rectangular plan. As they were juxtaposed, access was possible only through openings in the roofs across which all movement round the town took place. The roofs varied in height as the houses rose in terraces up the slope of the mound on which they were built. There were no streets though there were occasional open spaces between one house and another, and Çatal Hüyük ended with a solid blank perimeter wall which made further defence unnecessary. From a distance it must have looked not unlike many adobe villages of today in New Mexico.

unknown significance. The most remarkable is not painted, however, and is shown sitting on a rock-like throne or chair, the first known instance of seating furniture (1,16). She is giving birth and rests her hands (now lost) upon two felines, probably leopards, which form the arm-rests of her throne. They may also indicate another of her aspects, that of tamer or ruler of wild animals. If so, she would prefigure a great sequence of mother goddesses – Inanna/Ishtar in ancient Sumeria and Babylon, Isis in ancient Egypt and Cybele in ancient Anatolia and Greece. They all walk with lions or sit upon a lion throne; Cybele even rides a chariot drawn by lions. (There are reliefs of human figures on a much bigger scale at Çatal Hüyük, but they are rendered rather schematically with arms and legs outstretched. They have been similarly interpreted, as showing the goddess giving birth, but this may be doubted as they do not show female breasts or genitalia clearly.)

The rooms in which most of the paintings and sculptures were found have been called 'shrines', perhaps misleadingly even if no more than the rituals of a fertility cult are implied. The inhabitants probably made no more distinction between ritual and domestic spheres than do small-scale societies still surviving today, such as the Nuba in Africa. However, findings in these particular rooms include wall-paintings (in natural colors, sometimes polychrome, mixed with

fat and painted with a brush on a fine white plaster ground), plaster reliefs, animal heads, bucrania (bovine skulls), bulls' horns set into stylized remodelled heads of bulls or into benches or pillars, and also numerous statuettes in clay or stone of both humans (mostly female) and animals (1,17). Nothing suggests that the bull or any other animal was regarded as a deity though the prominent bulls' horns may have been thought to ward off evil. Indeed animals are always shown as subservient to humans whenever they are depicted together.

Each room had at least two platforms, one of which was framed by wooden posts, plastered over and painted red. A raised bench stood against the wall at the far end of the main platform. These platforms

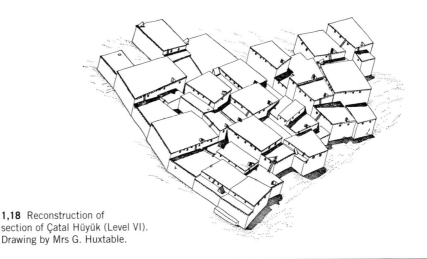

1,18 Reconstruction of section of Çatal Hüyük (Level VI). Drawing by Mrs G. Huxtable.

sculptured heads found there (**1,19**). These appear to have been placed above graves, the body being buried and the head preserved or, as it were, brought back to life in this way. For the heads were made by refashioning human skulls, the flesh being restored with tinted plaster and the eyes with seashells. The modelling is amazingly skilful and sometimes displays a most sensitive awareness of flesh and bone. So subtle, indeed, is the handling and so individual are the features (one has a painted mustache) that some conscious attempt at portraiture may perhaps be presumed, as must certainly some commemorative, if not animistic, purpose.

The sculptures and wall-paintings discovered at Çatal Hüyük are much later. This settlement was occupied from the mid-seventh millennium onwards for about 800 years by people who still hunted wild animals but also grew cereals, peas and vetches, bred sheep and cattle and traded in seashells and mirrors of polished obsidian, a hard volcanic stone. Inside many of their rectangular mud-brick dwellings, which could be entered only from the roof, were rooms with raised platforms used probably for working, eating and sleeping but also for burial, and in these rooms some remarkable paintings and sculptures have been found. One of the most notable is a large-scale composition of a deer hunt painted in strong colors in silhouette, though very naturalistically, indeed with some feeling for bodily weight and movement (**1,20**). Unlike paintings from earlier Paleolithic times, these are on a prepared ground, an evenly colored area of smoothly plastered wall, and not a natural surface. The figures are still depicted as if in a void, without ground lines, let alone a background, but a sense of enclosure within a rectangular

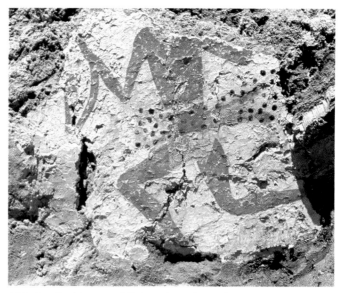

1,20 *Dancing Hunter*, c. 5800 BC. Çatal Hüyük, Turkey.

field is given by the shape of the wall. A momentous step had been taken towards the conception of a picture within a defined 'image field'. It is impossible to tell how widespread paintings of this type may have been. Çatal Hüyük is unique and its discovery in the early 1960s was a wholly unexpected revelation of Neolithic life in Asia Minor. Nothing of the kind has been found at a settlement of about the same period at Hacilar, also in Anatolia.

Apart from polished stone implements, from which the New Stone or Neolithic Age takes its name, the artifacts most closely associated with the early farmers' new way of life are pottery vessels. Clay had been modelled and baked into animal forms much earlier, as we have seen (p. 36), and rough, cord-marked (*jomon*) pots were made in pre-agricultural Japan at least as early as the seventh millennium. But pottery was not widely used until the rise of stable communities – and not always then, for

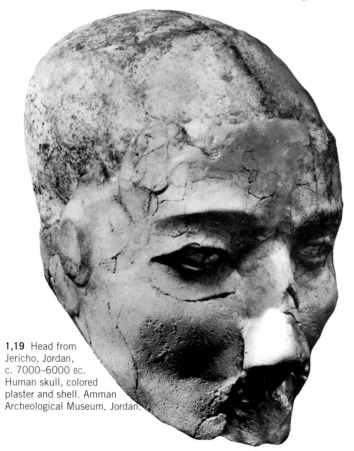

1,19 Head from Jericho, Jordan, c. 7000–6000 BC. Human skull, colored plaster and shell. Amman Archeological Museum, Jordan.

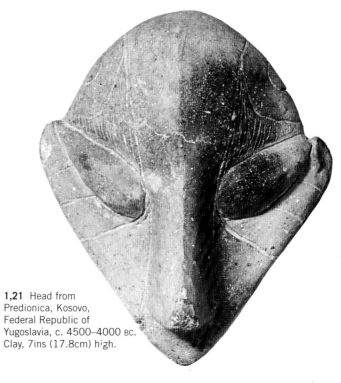

1,21 Head from Predionica, Kosovo, Federal Republic of Yugoslavia, c. 4500–4000 BC. Clay, 7ins (17.8cm) high.

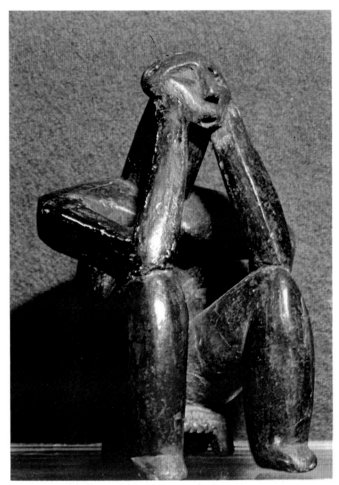

1,22 Man from Cernavoda, Romania, c. 4000–3500 BC. Clay, 4¹/₂ ins (11.5cm) high. National History Museum of Romania, Bucharest.

the first inhabitants at Jericho had vessels of stone but none of clay. Nevertheless, although not all early potters were peasants and not all early peasants were potters, it may be said that pottery first developed among agricultural communities of sedentary habit. At Jarmo in the Zagros mountains of northern Iraq, a village of some 25 households whose inhabitants grew cereals and had flocks of sheep and goats by about 6500 BC, storage pits were lined with clay baked *in situ*. Early in the sixth millennium pottery vessels and figurines of clay were also being made there and at other settlements in the same region, notably Hacilar (Anatolia) and Hassuna (Iraq) – simply shaped, thick-walled, buff-colored wares sometimes with burnished surfaces, sometimes with painted or incised geometric patterns – the earliest example known of what seems to have been a purely decorative art. Pots produced somewhat further south (called Samarra ware) were being decorated with paintings of birds, fish, animals and human beings before the beginning of the fifth millennium. Shortly after 5000 BC motifs which almost certainly had symbolical significance – a bull's head, a double axe and a Maltese cross – appear on vessels of fine thin hard ware found at Tell Halaf on the frontier of modern Turkey and Syria. It is unlikely that any of these pots were the work of whole-time potters. The clay was shaped by coiling and hand-molding and fired in small kilns, as in Neolithic China, Japan and south-east Asia. The specialist craftsman appeared with the potter's fast wheel,

that is about 3400 BC in Mesopotamia, in the course of the next thousand years in China, and not before 2400 BC in south-east Europe.

Clay continued to be used for modelling statuettes, which were baked as hard as pots and pans and have survived in far greater quantities than any earlier works of sculpture. At one site, Vinca on the Danube in Serbia, more than 1,500 statuettes dating from the fifth and early fourth millennia have been found. Most of them were in the remains of houses, not in graves. Some represent animals, domestic and wild, many are of men and women sometimes so sharply characterized that they might almost be taken to be portraits. Very different are the heads found only slightly further south at Predionica: here the features are reduced to a simple design formula – inscrutable, impersonal, with long noses and staring eyes of feline detachment (**1,21**). Yet another type appears in a pair of figures, a man and a woman, from Cernavoda on the lower Danube. Despite their small size (only 4¹/₂ inches, 11.5cm high) they have a bold monumentality and the man seated on a stool and holding his head in his hands might well be called the first 'thinker' in the history of art (**1,22**). It would be difficult to represent with greater economy and force this highly expressive pose.

NEOLITHIC ARCHITECTURE

More stable conditions of life also led to the development of architecture. Hunters and foragers had seasonally inhabited man-made as well as natural shelters from a very early period, as we have seen (p. 37), and at Jericho dwellings and fortifications were constructed to simple, regular plans. At the beginning of the fourth millennium

1,23 Entrance to temple, Mnaidra, Malta, c. 3000–2000 BC.

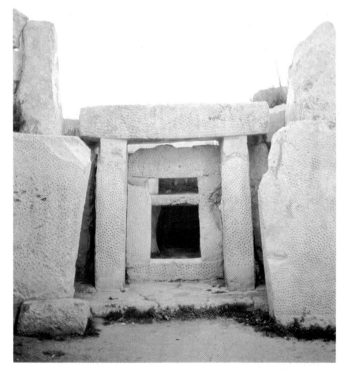

a new type of building appeared in southern Mesopotamia: the temple set apart from habitations both in siting and in form. A small shrine of this period, discovered under many subsequent layers of religious structures at Eridu, already has the internal niche in one wall and the offering table, which later became the most important elements in the temples of the Sumerians (see p. 57) and, indeed, in those of many later cultures. It was constructed of mud-brick, the only building material readily available in the area. Stone was not used either here or in Egypt until much later, after it had been used for temples on Malta and the megalithic tomb chambers of the European Atlantic coastline.

The temples on Malta and on the adjacent island of Gozo were begun before 3000 BC and abandoned by about 2000 BC. They are the earliest known free-standing buildings of stone. There are at least 16, constructed of huge blocks resting on one another without mortar. The façade of the largest, Ggantija on Gozo, has a base of fairly regularly shaped slabs of limestone, each one about 12 feet (3.5m) high, supporting smaller and rougher stones in courses, which seem originally to have risen to a total of some 50 feet (15m). Interior spaces are rounded, the most important being on a trefoil (three-leafed) plan; others are roughly oval, and some seem to have been roofed with wood. Much of the stonework is dressed (i.e. smoothed to a regular surface) and some of it decorated overall with little hammered pits, which give a mottled effect (1,23; 24). At Tarxien, the most elaborate of the temples, there are even carved spiral vine-scroll motifs of a type later found throughout the Mediterranean (1,25). Here also a fragment of a larger than life-size statue of a seated woman was discovered. The only other surviving sculptures are stone and clay statuettes of obese women rendered with considerable naturalistic skill.

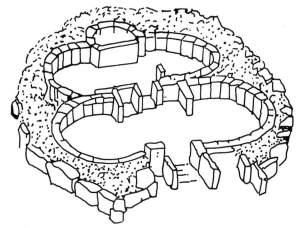

1,24 Plan of Mnaidra temple.

1,25 Vine scroll motif, Tarxien temple, Malta, c. 3000–2000 BC.

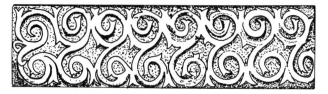

STONEHENGE

The simple post-and-lintel system used for doorways in the Maltese temples – one large horizontal stone placed on top of two uprights – had already been adopted by the builders of megalithic tombs in western and northern Europe. (The word 'megalith' simply means large stone.) Long passages were built in this way, the stones being subsequently covered with earth to form artificial hillocks. Somewhat surprisingly, some of the earliest, dating from about 4000 BC, in Brittany, are among the most elaborate technically, with their main tomb chambers roofed by placing thin slabs of stone on top of one another and slightly overlapping so that the uppermost meet to form a corbelled dome (see Glossary). Distinct types of tomb seem to have been evolved independently in different areas, conditioned mainly by the availability of materials. The rectangularity and fine corbelling of tombs in the Orkneys, for instance, are due largely to the peculiarities of a local stone which breaks neatly into straight-sided pieces. Some types of stone may, on the other hand, have acquired special significance. This would explain why in Britain, about 2100 BC, 19 large pieces of bluestone (spotted dolerite), each between 6 and 8 feet (182 and 240cm) high, were hauled from the mountains of Wales to Salisbury Plain 190 miles (300km) away to be set up in the extraordinary monument known as Stonehenge (1,26; 27).

The function of Stonehenge remains a mystery, despite numerous attempts to solve it. The most that can be said with certainty is that it was an important cult centre and that stones were carefully aligned on various points on the horizon: where the sun rose on midsummer day, where it set on midwinter day, and also the most northerly and southerly points of the moon-rise (in the second millennium BC that is to say; there has been a slight shift in the relative position of the earth and the sun since then). Such moments which marked the passage of the seasons had, no doubt, both practical and religious importance for a pastoral population. It has recently been shown that the stones could have been used for more sophisticated solar and lunar observations to predict solstices and eclipses through a 300-year cycle. Whether they were is another question. So far as the history of art is concerned, Stonehenge is notable for the quite remarkable precision, symmetry and unity of its conception and the technical abilities of its builders, despite their lack of metal tools.

To transport to the site and erect the tall 'sarsens' or Wiltshire sandstone blocks of the concentric circle at Stonehenge (a century or so after the bluestones) was an organizational, if not a technical, feat. It has been estimated that it would have taken 1,100 men 5½ years to shift them from Marlborough Downs some 20 miles (32km) away. The stones were dressed with stone hammers so that they are smoother on the inside than the outside and have outlines slightly tapering towards the top after a central bulge. The preparation of the lintels, which originally ran right round the circle, was still more

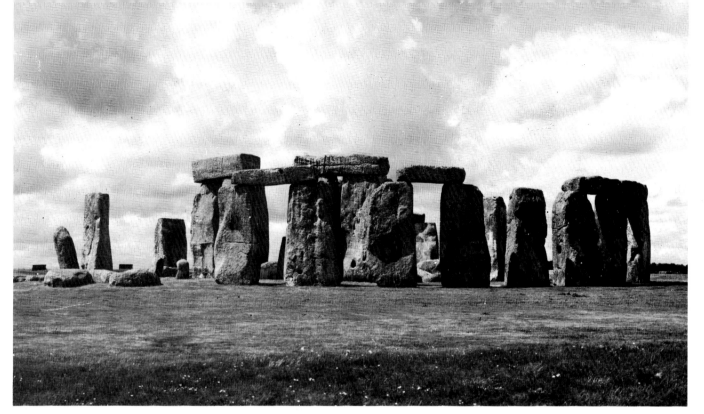

1,26 Stonehenge, Salisbury Plain, England, c. 2100–2000 BC.

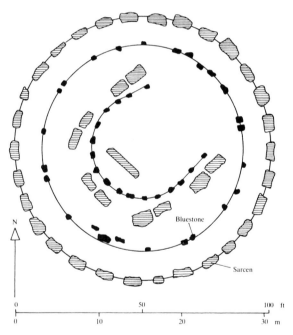

Bluestone

Sarcen

N

| 0 | | 50 | | 100 | ft |
| 0 | 10 | | 20 | 30 | m |

1,27 Plan of Stonehenge.

remarkable. Not only were holes hollowed out of them to fit exactly over projecting tenons on the uprights, but they were curved horizontally as segments of a circle and carefully levelled on top. Most extraordinary of all are the optical corrections or 'refinements', as they are called in later architecture (see p. 139) the faces of the lintels are cut so that they incline outward by about 6 inches (15cm) and thus appear to be vertical when seen from the ground. It seems possible, therefore, that the bulging profiles given to the sarsen stones were similarly intended. Small wonder that in the Middle Ages Stonehenge was believed to have been conjured up by magic. The presence of a

skilled mason from the Aegean was later invoked to account for the technical ability it displays. But radio-carbon dating has revealed that megalithic buildings (see above) were being erected in northern Europe long before the first stone structures on Crete, and Stonehenge must be understood simply as the most complex product of this northern Stone Age tradition.

The Stone Age persisted in northern Europe for some time after it had given way in the south-east and Mediter-ranean and long after it had been superseded in the Near East by the Bronze Age, during which metal implements replaced those of stone. In the Near East native copper (nuggets found on the surface of the earth) had been ham-mered into small objects before the beginning of the sixth millennium. Gold was similarly worked. As both copper and gold are softer than stone they were never used for implements. A time-lag of 3,000 years intervened before it was discovered, again in the Near East, that a much harder substance could be obtained by alloying copper with tin to make bronze. It used to be assumed that this discovery was then transmitted to China (see p. 87) and to Europe, where bronze implements make their first appearance in the Balkans about 2500 BC. There is, how-ever, a strong possibility that bronze was invented inde-pendently in both China and Europe (as was certainly the case in South America in about AD 1000). In any event, by the second millennium great skill had been attained in south-eastern Europe in both the casting and ornamenta-tion of bronze objects, which were quickly diffused to other parts of the continent. Axe-heads and swords were decorated with incised spiral motifs of a type to be elabo-rated much later in Celtic art. They mark the beginning of a new phase in European prehistory, but by then the early civilizations of the Near East, the Indus Valley, Egypt and China had already emerged.

CHAPTER TWO

THE EARLY CIVILIZATIONS

It is unfortunate that the word 'civilization' has acquired such strong qualitative overtones. For the first so-called 'civilized' cultures were not necessarily and in every way superior to those of the hunters and subsistence farmers which had preceded them. The transition from pre-civilized to civilized societies depended first of all on the production of a surplus, that is on farmers producing enough food to permit a substantial section of the population to engage exclusively in other, non-productive activities – trade, administration and, of course, warfare. The development of specialized crafts led to improved agricultural methods such as artificial irrigation and the control of floods, the use of the wheel and the plough, which, in turn, made possible the growth not only of large urban communities but also, eventually, of states. Clearly stratified social structures emerged more or less simultaneously with administrative organizations requiring permanent records, hence the invention and development of writing. New ways of paying for goods and labour by a standard medium of exchange were also introduced. Thus, a 'natural economy' based on barter was replaced by a money economy, which facilitated the storage and

manipulation of wealth. This process was repeated with only slight variations as each of the early civilizations began to evolve in different, widely separated parts of the world – in the great river basins of the Tigris and Euphrates in the Near East, of the Indus in Pakistan, of the Nile in Egypt and of the Yellow River in China.

MESOPOTAMIA

The Near East, the vast area spanning much of Asia and comprising present-day Israel, Jordan, Lebanon, Syria, Turkey, Iran and Iraq, was the cradle of the first such evolution. Neolithic cultures had flourished there, especially on the pastoral uplands around Sialk near modern Tehran, for example, as well as at Susa further south. To judge by the pottery, a high degree of technical skill was attained. The walls of some of their pots are quite amazingly thin and delicate – finer, in fact, than anything produced by their immediate successors – and the painted decorations foreshadow later developments. A beaker from Susa is painted boldly and fluently with schematic yet remarkably

The visual arts	Historical landmarks
	c. **4000** BC Emergence of Sumerian civilization
c. **3500–3000** BC Head from Uruk (2,4)	c. **3500** BC Invention of wheel and plough (Mesopotamia) and sail (Egypt)
c. **3200** BC Palette of Narmer (2,23)	c. **3200** BC Unification of Lower and Upper Egypt under Narmer
c. **3000** BC Cycladic figure (2,42)	c. **3000** BC Cuneiform script developed in Mesopotamia
c. **2685** BC Harp from Ur (2,7)	c. **2780** BC Foundation of Old Kingdom of Egypt
c. **2650** BC Sphinx and pyramid (2,30)	c. **2500** BC Domestication of the horse (central Asia)
c. **2580** BC Rahotep and Nofret (2,33)	c. **2350** BC Akkadians gain control of Sumeria
c. **2300–2200** BC *Stele* of Naramsin (2,10)	c. **2258** BC Dissolution of Old Kingdom in Egypt
c. **2300–1750** BC Bust from Mohenjo-Daro (2,17)	c. **2180** BC Dissolution of Akkadian kingdom
c. **2144–2124** BC Head of Gudea (2,11)	c. **2134** BC Middle Kingdom in Egypt begins
	c. **2050** BC Minoan civilization emerges
	c. **2000** BC Linear A script developed in Crete
c. **1760** BC *Stele* of Hammurabi (2,14)	c. **1792** BC Rise of Babylonian empire
c. **1600–1400** BC Knossos (2,43)	c. **1670** BC Hyksos from Asia gain control of Egypt
c. **1550** BC Fisherman from Akrotiri (2,45)	c. **1600** BC Hittites sack Babylon. Shang state emerges in China
c. **1500** BC Vaphio cup (2,51)	c. **1500** BC Linear B script developed in Crete and Greece
	c. **1450** BC Crete invaded from mainland
c. **1300** BC Treasury of Atreus, Mycenae (2,55)	c. **1300** BC Greece invaded from north
c. **1300–1100** BC Chinese bronze wine vessel (2,63)	c. **1200** BC Beginning of Jewish religion

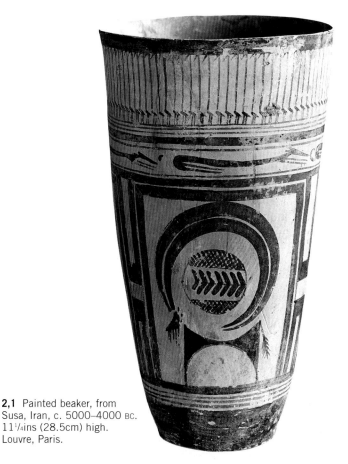

2,1 Painted beaker, from Susa, Iran, c. 5000–4000 BC. 11¼ins (28.5cm) high. Louvre, Paris.

stand on, and the dogs skim over, firmly marked ground lines, which provide the lower edges of frames enclosing regular 'image fields'. In this way the image acquires, for the first time, a definite space of its own in striking contrast to cave painting. This invention preceded that of writing, it should be noted, although its enormous possibilities for the arts of representation do not seem to have been recognized until later (see pp. 52–3).

SUMER

The civilization which developed about 4000 BC emerged not on the high plateaus favoured by the Neolithic cultures of the Near East but on the flat, low-lying plains of Mesopotamia (Greek for 'land between the rivers') formed by the Tigris and Euphrates, whose waters the new settlers learnt to control. They were able to turn the formerly unproductive and probably uninhabited flat lands into an enormous oasis, often called the 'fertile crescent', stretching some way north of the rivers' swampy confluence at the head of the Persian Gulf.

The settlers called it Sumer. Where they came from is unknown; their language is unrelated to any other known tongue. They lived in mud-brick settlements, which gradually grew to the size of towns and cities, eleven or more, including Uruk (the Biblical Erech and present-day Warka), Eridu, Ur, Larsa and the recently discovered Tell Habuba in the Upper Euphrates region. Independent and sometimes at war with each other, yet sharing one language and culture, they all held a common belief in a number or pantheon of gods personifying the creative and the destructive forces of nature. Each city was under the protection of one of these gods, to whose service its entire population was dedicated. The god was, in fact, believed to be its owner and divine sovereign, the human rulers his

lively animals in pure silhouette: a frieze of very long-necked birds at the top, a band of running dogs and, below, an ibex with huge horns (**2,1**). These animals are distorted expressively, the elongation of the dogs, for instance, suggesting speed of movement. They also imply a highly developed sense of design, with curves and straight lines echoing those of the vessel itself and integrating surface decoration with form. What is more, the birds and ibex

The ancient Near and Middle East

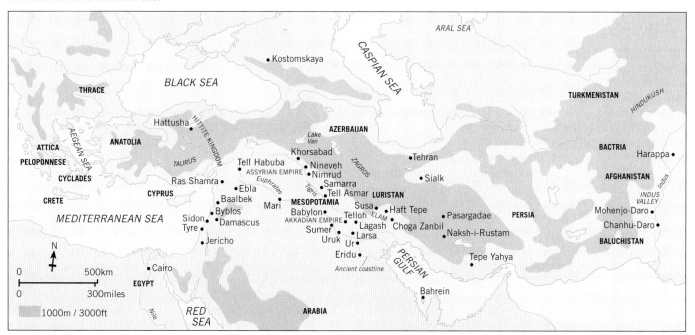

earthly stewards and priests. The form of government thus evolved has been described as 'theocratic socialism' and it certainly has elements of the welfare state. Administration was in the hands of the priests, who alone could direct the population and keep reserves of implements and draught animals. They controlled the pooling of labour for communal enterprises, such as the all-important irrigation ditches and flood channels. They also collected and distributed food to craftsmen and others not engaged on work on the land, and they stored grain against periods of famine. It was in this context that a numerical system was first evolved. Similarly, picture-signs were developed into a standardized cuneiform script, so-called from the angular, wedge-shaped form of its several hundred characters, which were impressed on clay tablets with a split reed – the oldest known writing in the world. It was used from the third to the first millennium for a number of Near Eastern languages – Sumerian, Akkadian, Elamite, Hittite and others. The earliest examples are of no later than about 3000 BC, discovered at Tepe Yahya in south-eastern Iran, a large urban centre of some complexity. Tepe Yahya, together with other widely separated urban or proto-urban sites in the Near East, has raised some as yet unsolved problems, notably that of the primacy of Sumer. Was Sumer the cradle of civilization in this area? Or was urbanization developed simultaneously and independently over a wide area? There is increasing evidence to support the latter view, i.e. that in the third millennium urban centres from Mesopotamia to the Indus Valley and from the Persian Gulf to Baluchistan and Turkmenistan were interrelated and interdependent. Development did not radiate out from one generating centre. (Similar conclusions are to be drawn from another important excavated site, Ebla [Tell Mardikh] in northern Syria, though it is of a later date. With the discovery there of more than 15,000 cuneiform tablets of 2400–2250 BC, northern Syria has been established as a cultural entity independent of Babylonia and Assyria.)

The Sumerians, however, had a literature and a literature of some quality, for it includes *The Epic of Gilgamesh* which still, after more than 4,000 years, has the power to enthral and move. It is the world's first great poem. Although it antedates the Homeric epics by 1,500 years, its heroes Gilgamesh, Enkidu and Huwawa belong to the same universe as the gods and mortals of the *Odyssey*. Nothing comparable in quality to *The Epic of Gilgamesh* has come to light as yet among the visual works of art of the Sumerians. It was a predominantly religious art and among the earliest survivals are some tall alabaster vases, about 36 inches (91.4cm) high, from the temple at Uruk. They date from what is called the Proto-literate period, i.e. the last centuries of the fourth millennium, when writing was invented. The finest records the festival of the New Year (**2,2**). On the top band of carving a man presents a basket to a woman, either the mother-goddess Inanna or her priestess, behind whom other gifts are piled up: more baskets, vases and a ram supporting clothed statuettes or figures of a man and a woman. Beneath this there

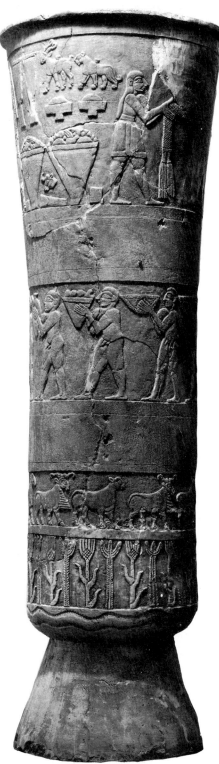

2,2 Vase from Uruk, Iraq, c. 3500–3000 BC. Alabaster, 36ins (91.4cm) high. Iraq Museum, Baghdad.

is a procession of men carrying more gifts; they are naked, as men were usually represented when approaching the gods. Alternating ewes and rams fill the lowest register above a frieze of date palms and ears of barley.

This is the earliest instance of an artist exploiting the possibilities of the defined 'image field', in which figures stand on a firm ground line in an area that could be understood as representing space. It is significant that it accompanied the invention of writing. The regularity of direction, spacing and grouping so evident in the Uruk vase corresponds to that of writing, as may also the use of

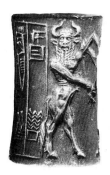

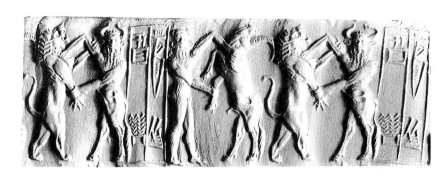

2,3 Cylinder seal and its impression, from Ur, Iraq, c. 2700 BC. Stone, about 1¹/₂ins (3.8cm) high. The Oriental Institute, University of Chicago.

parallel bands to create a tiered composition, with one row of scenes above another – a system that was to be used for the next 5,000 years, especially for narrative illustration. On the Uruk vase the sequence is hierarchical rather than chronological. Each frieze is a continuous procession without beginning or end, perhaps expressing the eternal significance of the ritual which marked the beginning of the year and the renewal of the cycle of the seasons.

The artistry displayed in the carving is akin to that of cylinder seals, little cylinders of hard stone rarely as much as 2 inches (5cm) high, incised with abstract or figurative designs so that, when one is rolled across wax or damp clay, it leaves a relief impression, usually as a mark of ownership (**2,3**). Free-standing sculpture was also being carved before the end of the fourth millennium, although only fragments survive. A life-size white marble face of a woman found at Uruk is the finest (**2,4**). The carving is of extraordinary delicacy and sensitivity, especially in the subtle, unemphatic transitions from the cheeks to the nose, upper lip, and firm, sensual mouth. The deep incision below the forehead was probably filled originally with eyebrows of lapis lazuli, the eye-sockets with some other colored material, perhaps shell for the eyeballs and obsidian for the pupils, and the head would have been covered with hair of gold or copper. Drill holes in the flat back appear to have been intended for attaching the mask to a statue, presumably a wooden cult figure.

Priests and other worshippers standing before a cult figure are the subject of several statuettes found in the temple of Abu, the god of vegetation, at Tell Asmar (**2,5**) and other similar though later figurines from Mari on the Euphrates. The group from Tell Asmar is carved in white gypsum, a soft, easily worked marble, which may partly explain the cylindrical or conical form. The hair and beards of the figures are rendered with black bituminous paint, their huge staring goggle eyes with lapis lazuli or black limestone set in white shell. Tell Asmar was a small town some way from the main Sumerian cities, and these statues are artistically inferior to the head from Uruk and to statuettes from Mari, suggesting provincial workmanship. They reveal, nevertheless, that many of the conventions of religious art in the Near East (later to be passed on to Europe and also to the Far East) were already present. All of them look straight ahead, standing or kneeling in rigidly symmetrical poses with their hands clasped just below their chests. Differences in size appear to denote differences in rank.

Inscriptions reveal that to the Sumerians a statue was not simply a representation: it was believed to have a life of its own. The god was present in the cult image, as was

2,6 *Right* Female monster, c. 3500–3000 BC. Crystalline limestone, 3¹/₂ins (8.9cm) high. Brooklyn Museum, New York (Courtesy Mr & Mrs Robin B. Martin).

2,4 Female head from Uruk, c. 3500–3000 BC. Marble, 8ins (20.3cm) high. Iraq Museum, Baghdad.

2,5 Statuette from Tell Asmar, Iraq, c. 3000 BC. Gypsum, 11¾ins (29.8cm) high. Metropolitan Museum of Art, New York (Fletcher Fund, 1940).

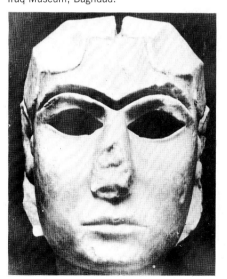

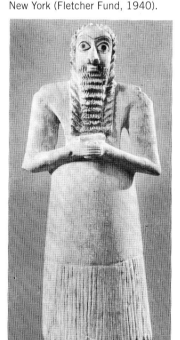

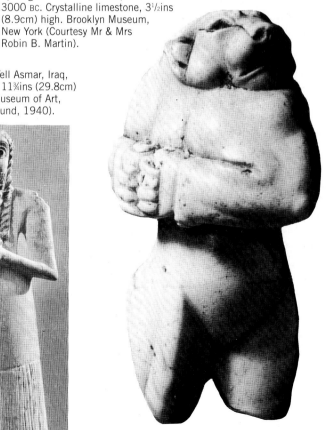

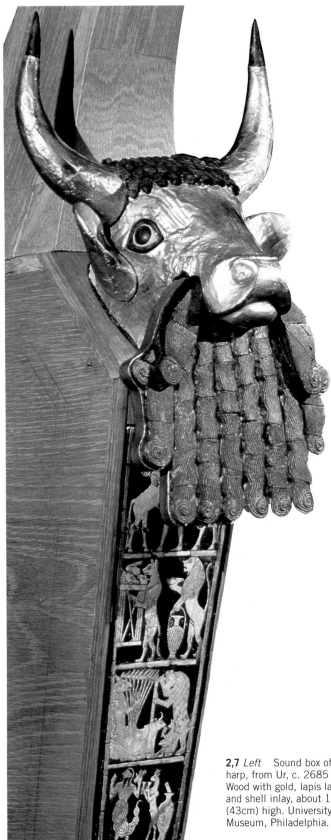

the mortal in the statuette standing in permanent awe-struck adoration before it. This primitive animistic sense is strongly felt in earlier works, even when they are on a relatively small scale, as in one of the most powerful to be unearthed so far (**2,6**). This is a tiny carving in crystalline limestone of a monstrous female creature whose powerful misshapen body and terrifying head and claws confront us with all the incomprehensibility of evil and humanity's helplessness before it in a hostile universe.

Many of the finest third-millennium works of art were discovered in the royal cemetery at Ur, where Sumerian kings and queens were buried in all the finery of their gold and jewelry, together with their attendants and courtiers, who were killed so that they could accompany them into the next world. They include palace or temple furnishings of an unprecedented and rarely equalled richness and elaboration of workmanship. A harp, for instance, has a sound box terminating in a wonderfully realistic head of a bull of carved lapis lazuli and wood with gold leaf (**2,7**). Lapis lazuli, the intensely blue stone greatly prized by the Sumerians, who imported it from its only source some 2,000 miles (3,200km) away in northern Afghanistan, was used for the bull's horn-tips, the hair between the horns, the eyelids and pupils and the human beard (presumably a ritual adornment). The panel beneath is very delicately inlaid with shell to depict four scenes, delineated with a clarity that makes the obscurity of their meaning all the more tantalizing. They are at once so sophisticated and so naive that we cannot tell how, or how seriously, these strange little pictures of animals impersonating humans were intended to be taken, or whether they illustrate myths or fables. They have the magnetizing poetry of fairytales, which suspend disbelief while they are being told. The motif of the man embracing two human-headed bulls on the top register (**2,8**) is one that recurs in the art of the ancient Near East (it is sometimes called the Gilgamesh motif, although no such scene is exactly described in the epic). His curious twisted pose, frontal above the waist but in profile below, was being used about the same time in Egypt (see pp. 70–1).

2,7 *Left* Sound box of a harp, from Ur, c. 2685 BC. Wood with gold, lapis lazuli and shell inlay, about 17ins (43cm) high. University Museum, Philadelphia.

2,8 *Right* Detail of sound box of harp, from Ur, c. 2685 BC. Wood with shell inlay, about 2ins (5cm) high. University Museum, Philadelphia.

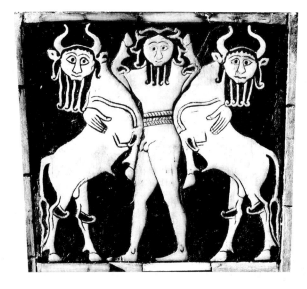

THE EARLY CIVILIZATIONS 55

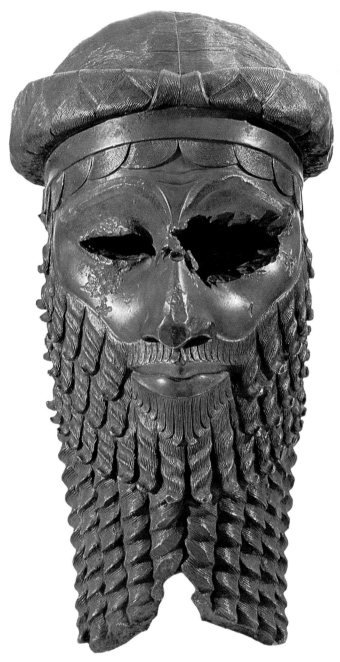

2,9 Head of an Akkadian ruler, from Nineveh, Iraq, 2300–2200 BC. Bronze, 12ins (30.5cm) high. Iraq Museum, Baghdad.

AKKADIAN ART

Towards the beginning of the third millennium, if not earlier in some places, war leaders replaced high priests as the rulers of Sumerian cities, without, however, modifying the theocratic system of government. A greater change came about 2350 BC, when Akkadians who had infiltrated the area from the north-east – they spoke a Semitic language quite different from Sumerian – gained complete control. Their first king, Sargon, incorporated the cities into a single state spreading over northern Mesopotamia and into Elam (see p. 58); his grandson Naramsin extended the realm to the west and about 2250 BC conquered Ebla (see p. 52). The expansionist policy of the Akkadians may partly account for a new

emphasis placed on the person of the ruler as an individual leader and conqueror and not simply as the servant of the local god. Life-size statues of kings were produced, and from one of them a superb bronze head with braided hair and neatly curled beard survives – displaying complete mastery of the techniques of metalwork (**2,9**). It is at once naturalistic and hieratic, the image of a ruler with a commanding aspect, which must have been intensified and made to seem almost superhuman when eyes of precious stone flashed from the now empty sockets. The Akkadian concept of godlike sovereignty could not have been more forcefully expressed.

Naramsin himself appears on a *stele* carved to celebrate a victory over an Iranian frontier tribe (**2,10**). He is shown nearly twice the size of his soldiers, as gods (here represented only by their symbols in the sky) had previously been distinguished from mortals. Perhaps to emphasize the actuality of a single moment, the sculptor abandoned the usual system of superimposed bands of

2,10 Victory *stele* of Naramsin, c. 2300–2200 BC. Pink sandstone, about 6ft 8ins (2.03m) high. Louvre, Paris.

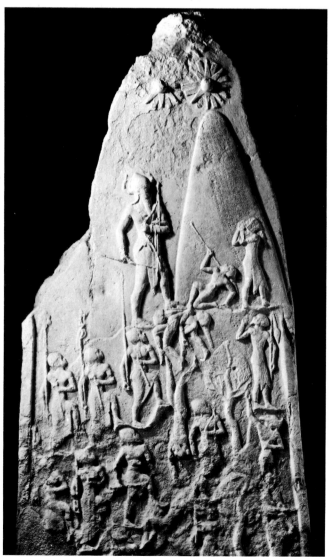

figures and treated the whole surface as a single dramatic composition. The location in mountainous country is indicated by the climbing postures of the soldiers and also by trees and a conical hill – landscape, in fact, for the first time in the history of art. Naramsin's commanding position, treading on the bodies of two slain tribesmen and with his arm poised to dispatch another, records the moment of victory. There was originally no inscription (the writing on the hill is a later addition); the meaning of the scene was expressed in purely visual terms. Every line of the composition suggests the climax of the action, with the upward movement of the Akkadians from the left balanced by the fallen and falling tribesmen and the survivors begging for mercy on the right. Naramsin stands at the top, at the dramatic peak of the composition, related to the other figures by their gestures and glances and yet isolated from them by the empty surface of stone that surrounds him. Nothing quite like this *stele* is to be found in the art of the Near East for another 1,500 years.

Akkadian rule collapsed about 2180 BC. Only one city survived, Lagash (modern Al-Hiba, Iraq), where literature and the visual arts flourished in an oasis of peace under the *ensi* or ruler Gudea. Although Gudea followed Akkadian practice and set up life-size statues of himself, they present a very different conception of kingship. He styled himself the 'faithful shepherd' of his people, the servant of Ningirsu, the god of irrigation and fertility. His clean-shaven face has a delicate, almost adolescent sensitivity, and he is always shown in a piously reflective mood (**2,11**), in one instance holding in his lap an architectural plan, probably for temple precincts. A very hard stone was used for these statues, chosen perhaps less for its rich color than its durability – its power to preserve an immutable record of royal piety.

SOURCES AND DOCUMENTS

GUDEA'S DREAM

Gudea, the ruler of Lagash (modern Al-Hiba, Iraq, formerly identified as Telloh) from about 2144 to 2124 BC, not only expended great energy and wealth on rebuilding the temple to Ningirsu but he had buried in the foundations a number of clay tablets with cuneiform inscriptions giving an account of its activities. Discovered in the late nineteenth century, these texts are very remarkable. They go beyond a factual record, which would have been remarkable enough at this date, to give some indication of Gudea's feelings and moods, even of his dreams when he slept in the temple. They convey something of the same poetic spirit that can be felt in his sculptured portraits (2,11). In the passage that follows, the god Ningirsu gives him instructions for the building of the temple:

In the dream there was a man, who was as huge as heaven, as huge as earth. As to his upper part he was a god, as to his wings he was the Imdugud bird, as to his lower part he was the hurricane. At his right and left there crouched a lion. He commanded me to build a temple, but I did not fully understand him . . . . A second hero was present. He had his arms bent and held a slab of lapis lazuli in his hands and set down thereon the ground-plan of the temple to be built. He put before me the hod, ceremonially purified, arranged the brick-mold for me, similarly purified, and fixed in it the 'brick of decision of fate'.

In another dream which finally convinces Gudea that he is called upon to build the temple, Ningirsu promises to summon a humid wind bringing life-giving rain so that prosperity will accompany the laying of the temple's foundations. The god speaks in this dream:

All the great fields will bear for thee. Dykes and canals will swell for thee; where the water is not wont to rise to high ground it will rise for thee.

The molding of the first brick was the responsibility of the king and Gudea describes how he took up the 'purified head-pad' and the brick-mold for the 'brick of decision of fate' and

. . . poured luck-bringing water into the frame of the mold;
While he did so drums were beaten.
He smeared the mold with honey, best quality oil, fine best quality oil;
He raised the holy hod, went to the mold,
Gudea worked the mud in the mold,
Performed completely the proper rites,
Splendidly brought into being the brick for the temple.

The new temple having been completed, it was consecrated, and Gudea describes how he went to the god in the temple and prayed to him:

My King, Ningirsu,
Lord who restrains the wild flood-waters,
Lord whose word is supreme beyond everything,
Son of Enlil, the hero, you have given me orders,
I have truly fulfilled them for you,
O Ningirsu, I have built your temple for you,
May you enter therein in joy.

(H. W. F. Saggs, *The Greatness that was Babylon*, London 1962, translations slightly adapted)

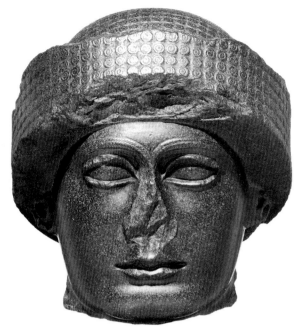

2,11 Head of Gudea, from Al-Hiba, Iraq, c. 2144–2124 BC. Diorite, 9¹/₈ins (23.2cm) high. Museum of Fine Arts, Boston (Francis Bartlett Donation of 1912).

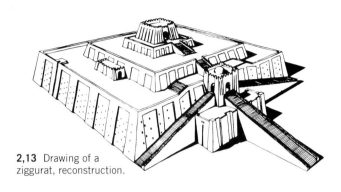

2,13 Drawing of a ziggurat, reconstruction.

ZIGGURATS

Temples had been built in Mesopotamia since the mid-fourth millennium BC (see pp. 47–8). They were small mud-brick structures and not intended for communal worship – access may well have been limited to priests and the priest-kings – but raised on platforms which gave them prominence. These platforms were soon transformed into squat stepped pyramids called ziggurats, conceived as holy mountains which brought the priests nearer to the gods, if not into their actual presence. (Moses was to climb Mount Sinai to receive the Tablets of the Law from the Lord.) For the plain-dwelling Sumerians, mountains had a further significance as the source of the waters that flowed down to the valleys, and also as a symbol of the whole earth and the life-bringing force of vegetation beneath it. They called their mother-goddess Ninhursag, 'Lady of the Mountain'. So the mountain imagery, which the Bible later spread all over the Western world, probably originated in southern Mesopotamia. According to the Book of Genesis, Abraham was a native of Ur, where the ziggurat still partially survives (**2,12**).

2,12 Ziggurat at Ur, Iraq, c. 2100 BC.

It was built shortly after the city became the capital of a revived Sumerian state in 2125 BC. The plan is oblong, oriented with its corners pointing north, south, east and west, and the walls slope inwards as they rise, their monotonously blank faces relieved by non-functional buttresses. On the north-east side, long straight staircases lead up to a gatehouse more than 40 feet (12m) above the ground. Originally there were two further stages, crowned by a temple (**2,13**).

BABYLON

A new period in Mesopotamian history began with the rise to pre-eminence of Babylon early in the second millennium BC. Under Hammurabi, who ruled from 1792 to 1750 BC, it became the capital of an empire extending from Mari and Nineveh to the Persian Gulf. Hammurabi is of great historical importance as the author of the oldest surviving code of laws. Its declared aim was to 'cause justice to prevail in the land, to destroy the wicked and the evil, that the strong might not oppress the weak', although, in fact, one of its chief concerns was to protect money-lenders from defaulting borrowers, for whom rigorous penalties were prescribed. This code is inscribed on a *stele* under a relief of Hammurabi standing before the enthroned sun god at the summit of a holy mountain or ziggurat – a perfect illustration of the semi-divine status of the priest-king, to whom the god, himself in human form, delivers the laws (**2,14**). That the stone takes the form of a phallus, an obvious symbol of male dominance, is perhaps no coincidence.

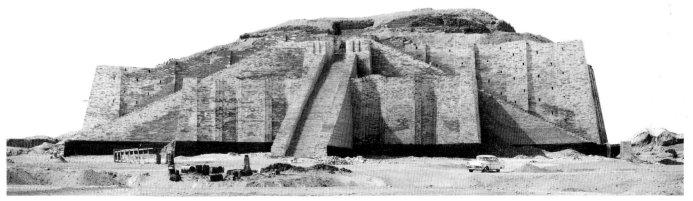

The empire ruled by Hammurabi's successors was gradually eroded and Babylon itself was sacked about 1600 BC by Hittites from Anatolia (see p. 90). Attacks came also from the opposite direction, and in the late second millennium the *stelae* of Naramsin and Hammurabi were carried off to Susa, the capital of Elam, the agriculturally productive region extending north-east from the lower Euphrates (present-day Khuzestan). The complexities of the political and artistic relationship of Elam with the cities of Mesopotamia and further east are hard to unravel. Their civilizations seem to have followed parallel courses. Well before the end of the fourth millennium, Elamites had developed a pictographic script similar to that of Sumer but adapted to their own language (tablets in proto-Elamite script of c. 3200 BC have been found at Tepe Yahya, south of Kirman). Later, cylinder seals were carved in Elam, again similar to those of Sumer, though differing in subject-matter. Among the few surviving large-scale works of Elamite sculpture there is a very fine head of cast copper (2,15), which recalls the bronze head of an Akkadian ruler (2,9). The modelling of the face is, however, softer and more sensitive and the treatment of the beard and bands round the hair broader. Elamite civilization seems to have reached its height towards the end of the second millennium. An impressive, though unfortunately headless, bronze statue of Queen Napirasu from Susa dates from about 1260 BC (Louvre, Paris). Elam's most imposing remains, only recently brought to light, are at Haft Tepe, south of Susa, where the royal tombs have some remarkably assured brick vaulting of about 1500 to 1300 BC. The ziggurat of

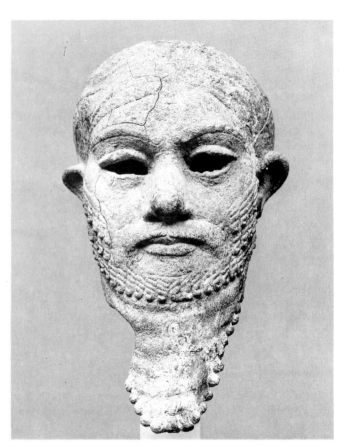

2,15 Head of an Elamite, from Azerbaijan (?), Iran, c. 2000 BC. Copper, 13½ins (34.3cm) high. Metropolitan Museum of Art, New York (Rogers Fund, 1947).

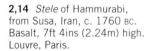

2,14 *Stele* of Hammurabi, from Susa, Iran, c. 1760 BC. Basalt, 7ft 4ins (2.24m) high. Louvre, Paris.

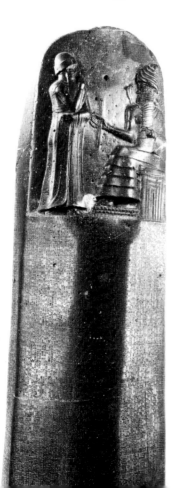

Choga Zanbil, near Haft Tepe, is larger than those of earlier Mesopotamia and differs also in other respects, being faced with green and blue bricks and incorporating three temples. Built about 1250 BC, it was originally five stories high. Elam was finally conquered by the Assyrian Assurbanipal (see p. 108) about 640 BC.

THE INDUS VALLEY

There is evidence of interchange of goods between Sumerian Mesopotamia and the cities of the Indus Valley (modern Pakistan) by way of the island of Bahrein in the Persian Gulf, and figurative carvings and other material recently discovered at Tepe Yahya in south-eastern Iran (see above) are strikingly similar to those of the Indus Valley. It seems likely, therefore, that the 'Indus Valley' or 'Harappan' civilization, which had reached its full development by about 2300 BC and began to disintegrate some five centuries later (to be totally lost and forgotten until its rediscovery in the 1920s), formed part of the great upsurge of third-millennium urbanization in Asia to which we have already referred. It could hardly have been more different from the civilization of Sumer, however, for it produced no great temples, no royal tombs, palaces or dynastic monuments of any other kind. The area it covered was much greater than that even of the Akkadian empire – about the size of western Europe, extending down the coast from the Gulf of Oman (Iran) to the Gulf of Cambay, far up into Afghanistan and the foothills of the Himalayas, and east to the region of present-day Delhi. Two of its outposts at Lothal and Rupar are more than 1,000 miles (1,600km) apart as the crow flies, and much further by passable routes skirting the mountains. But the vast majority of artifacts found at different sites and archeological levels (which indicate relative age) are so similar as to suggest a tight cultural unity lasting for more than half a millennium – even the building bricks were of the same standard size. No indication is given of any incursions from without or of disruptions within. A form of writing was in use, quite distinct from Sumerian picture-signs and from cuneiform, but it is known only from seals used to impress marks of ownership with brief inscriptions, which still remain to be deciphered. There is thus no literature to tell us of the history or the beliefs of this people. Weights and measures were standardized but, once again, according to a different system from that of the Sumerians.

So far as may be judged from the archeological record – and there is no other source of information – the Indus Valley civilization was essentially urban and mercantile. There seems to have been no dominant class of priests or warriors. Weapons were rudimentary. So, too, were the agricultural implements of the farmers, who continued to live in small rural communities, though it is known from terracotta models that they had wheeled carts (much like those still used in Sind in present-day Pakistan), presumably to transport their produce to the urban centres. The great achievement of this civilization was its cities, Harappa and Mohenjo-Daro. Nothing remotely like them had been seen before or was to be seen again for 1,000 years or more. They were regularly planned with wide

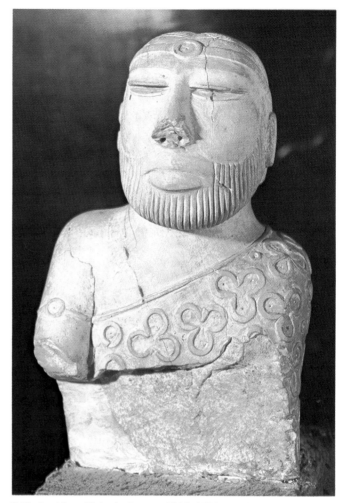

2,17 Bust from Mohenjo-Daro, c. 2300–1750 BC. Limestone, 6⁷/₈ins (17.5cm) high. National Museum of India, New Delhi.

2,16 Seals from Mohenjo-Daro, Pakistan, c. 2300–1750 BC. Steatite, about 1¹/₂ins (3.8cm) square. National Museum of India, New Delhi.

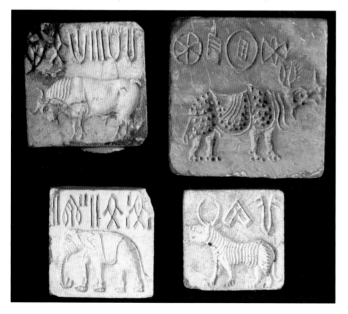

streets and thoroughfares for traffic. Various public services were systematically provided. And there were no fortifications, presumably because there was no need for them. Each had a citadel, however, raised on an artificial mound of mud-bricks, like a one-story ziggurat, and surrounded by a thick wall.

Harappa was the bigger and more important city, but its remains were largely destroyed by nineteenth-century British railway builders. More survives of Mohenjo-Daro (**2,18**). It was originally on the west bank of the Indus river (later to shift its course), into which platforms were built to control flood-waters. The large living and working area, about 1 mile (1.6km) across, was laid out on a grid plan with wide streets running from north to south to benefit from the prevailing winds. Public services included piped fresh water and drains to draw off household waste as well as rain and flood-water. Houses, workshops and merchants' stores were of much the same size. All were built of brick, fire-burnt (not sun-dried as in Mesopotamia) and regularly bonded – i.e. laid alternately with their ends and long sides on the outer face of the wall. Staircases reveal that there were upper floors of wood. No decorative features survive except narrow pointed niches in interior walls.

2,18 Plan of the citadel, Mohenjo-Daro.

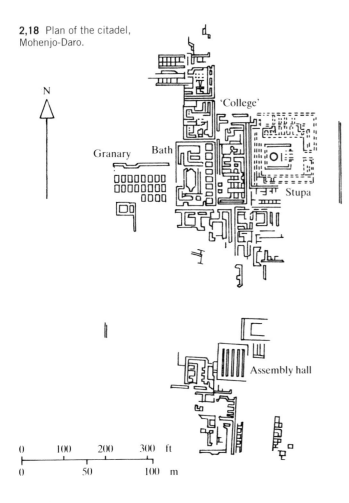

N

'College'

Granary   Bath

Stupa

Assembly hall

| 0 | 100 | 200 | 300 | ft |
| 0 | | 50 | | 100 m |

Public buildings, on the citadel, would appear to have differed from others only in size. There was a large hall or assembly place with a roof supported on many columns (a type of construction later developed in Egypt and called hypostyle by the Greeks), a vast granary, an asphalt-lined bath probably for ritual washing and, nearby, a structure with many small cells, like a college or monastery, though we can only guess at its purpose.

The inhabitants of the cities had fine but undecorated beaten copper vessels. Most of their pottery was of an equally utilitarian plainness, though some fairly large storage jars of a dignified form are decorated with geometrical and leaf motifs and an occasional animal in black on red, burnished to a high gloss. Clothing was made from patterned cotton, which was being cultivated and woven in the Indus Valley by about 2500 BC (a few centuries later than in America; it is first recorded in central Mexico c. 3000 BC). Jewelry was made of gold and silver with beads of semi-precious stones – lapis lazuli from Afghanistan, turquoise from Iran or Tibet, and jade from central Asia. There was even a bead factory in the small town of Chanhu-Daro.

All surviving works of art are small and seem to have been personal possessions. There is no trace of large-scale public art. Terracottas are numerous, ranging from rather crude figures of men and, more often, women with broad hips and emphatically marked sexual organs – probably

cult objects – to naturalistic animals and groups of models, like those of carts already mentioned, which may have been made as toys for children. Of greater artistic interest are the seals of steatite (an easily cut gray or greenish stone), which were given a lustrous surface by a gentle firing, presumably in a potter's kiln, after they had been carved (**2,16**). They are incised with figures of men, fabulous beasts and real animals on flat rectangular faces, which prevented the development of narrative effects as had been possible on the cylinder seals of Mesopotamia from the Sumerian to the Assyrian period (see p. 53). Designs reveal great feeling for the relationship between the image and the shape of the stone, and the carving has a delicate precision unsurpassed in the whole history of the gem engraver's art. Despite their small size – never more than 2 inches (5cm) square – they are packed with compressed vitality and capture the essential characteristics of the animals represented, especially the humped ox, which was a favourite subject.

Stone carvings in the round are also extremely small and are, with two notable exceptions referred to below, limited to male heads and half-figures with strange Asiatic slit eyes, flat thick lips and fringes of beard. The best is carved in a whitish limestone originally overlaid with red paste and is so imposing that, from a photograph, it might be thought to be a monumental over-life-size sculpture (**2,17**). It is, in fact, not quite 7 inches (18cm) high. The disposition of the robe over the left shoulder is distinctive and has led to the supposition that a priest or shaman is represented. In feeling it is remote from anything found in Mesopotamia despite some superficial similarities – the trefoil design on the robe, for example, the arrangement of the hair and of the beard, with shaven upper lip, and the hard mask-like smoothness of the carving. There was a deep dissimilarity between the arts of Mesopotamia and those of the Indus Valley, which can be felt more strongly in two male torsos carved in limestone, one in a dancing posture (**2,19**), the other standing upright (**2,20**), both of which have lost their heads, arms and legs.

Although barely 4 inches (10cm) high, these extraordinarily accomplished sculptures exhibit nothing of the miniature, the toy-like. The texture of firm, youthful flesh, the softness and warmth of its swelling roundness, have seldom been more sensuously suggested. Broad, convex planes melt and merge into one another so smoothly that the gently protuberant bellies and bottoms seem essential to a sculptural form intended to be seen and admired from many different viewpoints. They are conceived fully in the round. The dancing figure displays, moreover, a grasp of three-dimensional movement rare in the arts until much later periods. It is held in a sinuous three-bended twisting pose familiar from countless examples in later Indian art from the second century BC onwards and called the *tribhanga* pose (see p. 226); here it is combined with a gentle diagonal twist, which accentuates its sensuality. The figure catches the rhythm of a dance, perhaps one performed as part of a religious ritual, as in many other cultures. Both torsos treat the human figure as a living and moving organism and not, as in Mesopotamia and Egypt, the symbol of some immutable ideal of divinity or semi-divine kingship. So extraordinary are they, in fact, that their early date has been questioned. Not only the technical accomplishment, but also the sophistication in the working out of a highly contrived sculptural composition with such apparent naturalism and balance, with such freedom and ease of movement, make it difficult to believe that they were created in the third or second millennium BC. Yet both were found at Harappa, with other surviving products of the civilization

of the Indus Valley. One can do no more than speculate as to why so few and relatively small examples of the figurative arts have been recovered from these large, efficiently planned and well-built cities on the Indus. Did their culture lack those eternalizing impulses that lie behind the creation of so much of the monumental arts of Mesopotamia and Egypt? Did their religion call for no imposing cult figures and their social system demand no images of political power?

How and why this civilization disintegrated remains a mystery. Aryans, that is to say people from Iran, who were to dominate later Indian culture (they spoke an Indo-European language from which Sanskrit derived), infiltrated the area, rather than invaded it, over a period of some centuries in the second millennium. Cities were not sacked but gradually abandoned. At Daimabad, outside the main area (some 80 miles or 130km inland from Bombay), the excavation of a settlement inhabited until the end of the second millennium has brought to light a hoard of heavy bronze animals cast by the lost-wax process, probably dating from about 1500 BC – notably a chariot drawn by a pair of oxen (2,21) – similar to though rather more schematic than Indus Valley terracottas; they may have been imported but have affinities with paintings on locally-made pottery which differs from pieces found at Mohenjo-Daro. Craft techniques survived for making copper weapons and wheel-thrown pottery of two distinct types which suggest the coexistence of diverse cultures, one indigenous, the other Aryan. There is a strong line of continuity in religious thought and practice, for the earliest of the Vedas – poetic hymns in Sanskrit revered to the present day as the Psalms are in Christendom – are believed to have been composed between 1500 and 800 BC. In the archeological record, however, there is a long gap before the continuous history of Indian art begins in the third century BC (see p. 224).

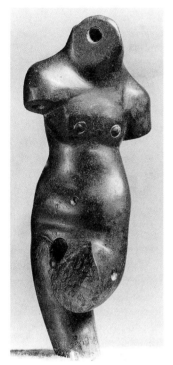
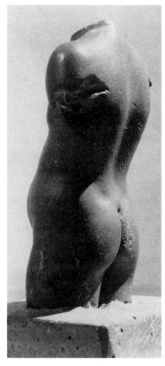

2,19 *Above left* Dancing figure from Harappa, c. 2300–1750 BC. Limestone, 3⁷/₈ins (9.8cm) high. National Museum of India, New Delhi.

2,20 *Above right* Male torso from Harappa, c. 2300–1750 BC. Limestone, 3¹/₂ins (8.9cm) high. National Museum of India, New Delhi.

2,21 Chariot from Daimabad, Maharashtra, c. 1500 BC. Bronze, 8⁵/₈ × 20¹/₂ × 6⁷/₈ins (22 × 52 × 17.5cm). The Prince of Wales Museum of Western India, Bombay.

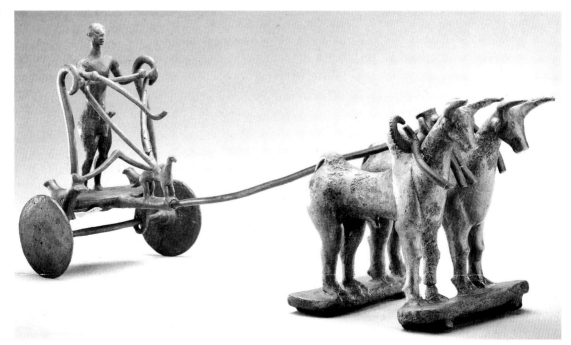

ANCIENT EGYPT

PREDYNASTIC

Ancient Egyptian civilization, like the civilizations of Sumer and the Indus Valley, grew up along a great river which provided irrigation for agriculture and also a thoroughfare for the transport of men and materials – wood, stone and, of course, agricultural produce. The pressures which brought about the great step forward from Neolithic life to that of organized communities were probably much the same here – flood control and irrigation. The impetus that they gave to communal effort must have been as crucial in Egypt as in Mesopotamia. But there were important differences. Unlike Sumer, where great cities developed in mutual rivalry and were frequently at war with one another, ancient Egypt evolved as a single, unified, far-flung rural community without any local centres and under the control of an absolute monarch. This probably came about largely through natural causes. For when the African deserts began to form in the fourth millennium, the Nile valley increasingly enjoyed the protection of these great natural barriers and the community was ever more closely bound together by the single, life-giving river that united it – and later by the central authority of the kings or pharaohs, as the Bible calls them. The Nile, together with the sun, also shaped their essential beliefs. The Nile (or rather the Nile in flood) was worshipped as the god Hapy, while the sun was

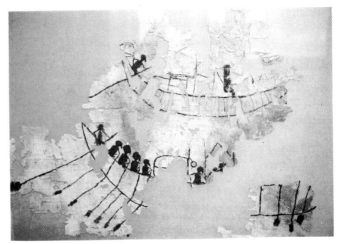

2,22 Fragment of painting from Gebelein, c. 3500–3200 BC. Linen. Museo Egizio, Turin.

revered as Re (or Ra), the father of the gods, a visible presence in Egypt, welcomed at dawn, feared at midday, honoured at dusk when he fell below the horizon.

The Nile, however, passes through two distinct environments: the narrow and sometimes cliff-confined valley of Upper (southern) Egypt and the wide alluvial plain, which opens into the huge delta of Lower (northern) Egypt. Farming began before the middle of the fifth millennium in the delta, where silt carried down by the river provided a richly fertile terrain. Upper Egypt was settled by nomads from further south and west, and was linked with the Neolithic cultures of the Sahara. This is probably the only region in the world where an unbroken thread of continuity may be traced from Stone Age rock art to the painting and sculpture of a literate people.

Animals like those engraved on rocks in the Fezzan (1,14) were painted on the pottery made in Upper Egypt in the Predynastic period (from c. 4000 to c. 3200 BC). Painted pottery seems, however, to have declined before the end of the fourth millennium. The most notable Predynastic vessels are those of marble or diorite, which already reveal great technical accomplishment in drilling, carving and polishing hard stone, even though the only metal tools available were of copper (bronze was not cast here until the beginning of the second millennium). Small figures of men and women were modelled in clay for burial with the dead. Usually they represent servants and indicate the early growth of belief in an immortality which prolonged indefinitely the pleasures of mortal life and which, in its developed form, promised a happy eternity to every good man – the belief that underlies and inspires the vast majority of surviving ancient Egyptian works of art. From about the same date paintings appear in tombs, on the wall of one at Hierakonpolis (now in the Egyptian Museum, Cairo) and on fragments of a linen cloth in another (2,22). Both depict life on the Nile: there are hippopotamus and boats with deck cabins and many oars manned by tawny figures on the linen panel. Everything is rendered in flat silhouette, floating in unbounded space,

Ancient Egypt

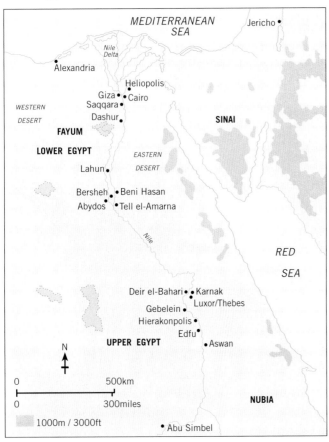

as in Paleolithic cave painting and rock art. But in subject-matter and location (tombs) they break away decisively from the prehistoric past. Thus the basic elements of ancient Egyptian culture were already nascent before Upper and Lower Egypt were united about 3200 BC by Narmer, the first king of the first dynasty.

EARLY DYNASTIC

Narmer is represented on a votive palette of carved slate (a crystalline rock) (**2,23a; 23b**). Many of the formal characteristics that were to distinguish ancient Egyptian art for the next 3,000 years make their appearance here. On the front, the entwined necks of two monsters frame a recess for the cosmetic paint used to color the eyes of a cult image in a ritual, probably to celebrate a victory (2,23a). The creatures stand on firmly marked ground lines, from which figures in ancient Egyptian paintings and relief carvings were henceforth to be allowed to stray only very rarely. They are no longer scattered images floating in an unbounded void, as on the linen fragment (2,22), nor are they rendered as flat, unarticulated silhouettes. Above them Narmer, wearing the red cobra crown of Lower Egypt, inspects the place of execution of captives, who are shown, decapitated, on the right; in the lower register his power is symbolized by a bull destroying the wall of a town above a fallen man whose stark nudity implies inferiority. The reverse side shows Narmer wearing the white crown of Upper Egypt, standing in a pose to be repeated thousands of times down the ages, his right arm raised in a ritual gesture to smite a captive (2,23b). Size denotes importance and Narmer is more than twice the height of the attendant, who carries his sandals and stands on his own detached ground line. Narmer is also distinguished by the carefully cut

musculature of his legs, probably as a sign of strength. The bird to his right is a hawk, symbol of the sky god Horus, who was also the god of Upper Egypt, holding on a tether the symbol of Lower Egypt, incorporating six heads of papyrus. Every element of the composition has a specific meaning which can be deciphered from later usage.

The tiered composition recalls the somewhat earlier vase from Uruk (2,2). On the palette, however, there is an ambivalence between realistically conceived figurative groups (the king and the captives, or the fleeing men below them) and pictorial symbols (those indicating the entrance and exit of the procession of men carrying banners, on the face, and the emblems of Upper and Lower Egypt on the reverse), an ambivalence only partly resolved by the carver's ability to unite them artistically. The palette was intended to be 'read' as a factual statement of Narmer's power to overcome his enemies. But, like so much ancient Egyptian art, it is also symbolic. The ancient Egyptians were less concerned with recording man's temporal affairs in a transitory world than with the 'eternal present', and that called for an occult language of signs and symbols.

The *stele* from the tomb of Djet the 'Serpent King', one of the early monarchs of the first dynasty, is entirely symbolic (**2,24**). It consists simply of a crisply carved falcon for the god Horus, incarnated in the person of the king, a serpent as the king's name-sign and the façade of a building, presumably his royal palace (the word 'pharaoh' originally meant great house or palace). Hieroglyphs, the signs used in picture-writing, were being systematized at about this time, mainly for inscriptions on royal monuments (not for administrative purposes, as in Sumer, where the earliest forms of writing had been evolved for temple accounts and so on). In Egypt cursive script more suitable for writing on papyrus was developed from hieroglyphs only

2,23a & 23b Palette of Narmer, from Hierakonpolis, c. 3200 BC. Slate, 25ins (63.5cm) high. Egyptian Museum, Cairo.

2,24 *Stele* of Djet, from Abydos, c. 3000 BC. Limestone, 21⅝ins (54.9cm) high. Louvre, Paris.

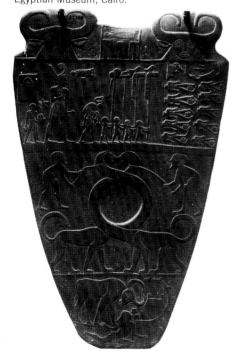
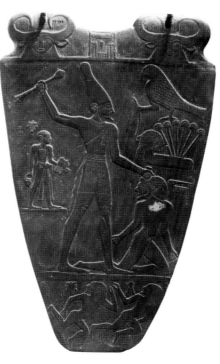
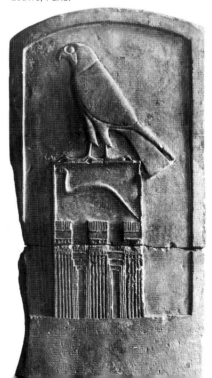

after the mid-third millennium. But hieroglyphs continued to be used for inscriptions in tombs, on monuments and in temples until ancient Egyptian religion was itself suppressed in the fourth century AD. They retained their pictorial character to the last, just as representational images retained their semantic significance.

Self-sufficiency and consistency, conservatism and an almost obsessive concern for permanence and continuity, an inflexibility quite impervious to change, these characteristics became evident very early and persisted with extraordinary tenacity throughout the entire course of ancient Egyptian art. In the fourth century BC, Plato remarked that there had been no change in Egyptian art for 10,000 years. It had not been lawful to introduce novelties, he said. These were exaggerations, of course, but only an art of a very well-marked character could have provoked them. And, despite periodic mutations and innovations, ancient Egyptian art always retained a strong and immediately recognizable flavour to a degree unmatched by that of any other civilization, except perhaps the Chinese.

Attitudes to life and death peculiar to the ancient Egyptians, and still not fully elucidated, determined the form of almost all their art from well before and until long after the pyramids. The pharaohs were regarded as gods and not, like the rulers of Sumer, merely the stewards or representatives of the gods. Yet the immortality which they, and also their faithful subjects, could attain was dependent on the preservation of their mummified mortal remains. (The practice of embalming the body and preserving its entrails separately was mastered by the mid-third millennium BC.) There is one instance, in the first dynasty, of a princess being buried with her servants, slaughtered to accompany her into the next world, a gruesome funerary custom shared by many cultures (see p. 54). But we do not know how common it was in Egypt and to what extent, if at all, the demand for sculptured and painted figures in tombs was due to it. More important for the sepulchral art of the ancient Egyptians were their notions about the relationship between the body and the spirit, notions unique to them and developed early in the Dynastic period. In general terms, it may be said that they believed there to be three distinct but closely related emanations of the spirit. The *Ka*, which was part of the life-force of the universe, accompanied the body in life and death, though its full potentialities could be realized only after death. The *Akh* was the 'effective personality' of a man and also the soul, which left the body at death to dwell in the heavens. The *Ba* was more like a ghost which could move back and forth from the dead body. The presence of these beliefs is felt not only in their sepulchral art, but behind every aspect of culture. Nothing more effectively sets ancient Egypt apart from all other civilizations. Their visual arts were largely dedicated to providing suitable dwellings for these spiritual emanations – statues were perpetual bodies for the *Ka*, or some portion of it, to inhabit for ever; reliefs depicting the pleasures of this life ensured their prolongation in the next, those depicting historical events guaranteed the everlasting power of

Egypt; even the portrayal of religious rites was intended to ensure the eternal well-being of the gods.

'The Egyptians say that their houses are only temporary lodgings, and their graves their houses', wrote the Greek historian Diodorus Siculus in the first century BC. Two distinct methods of burial had been customary in prehistoric Egypt. In the delta the dead were interred in the villages, sometimes beneath its houses, whereas in the south they were buried in graves dug in the desert (where the dry sand preserved their bodies) and provided with food, drink, clothing, weapons and implements. After Narmer's conquest of Lower Egypt, which united the two realms, the idea of building a house for the dead developed in the south. The mound of sand which had previously covered a grave was replaced by a low rectangular structure of bench-like form, nowadays called a *mastaba* (from the Arabic word for bench), built of mud-brick. With the growth of prosperity, the size of these *mastabas* and the complexity of the chambers beneath them increased. Eventually, stone was introduced, not for structural purposes but to cover floors and walls and for relief carvings – the *stele* of Djet, for instance.

OLD KINGDOM ARCHITECTURE

An ancient tradition ascribes the 'invention' of building in stone to Imhotep, a high priest of Heliopolis, who was later venerated as a god – not only the earliest but one of the very few named architects of ancient Egypt. Imhotep is a semi-mythical figure, but there are substantial remains at Saqqara of the mortuary complex he is said to have built for King Zoser, founder of the third dynasty (2780–2180 BC), which initiated the period known as the Old Kingdom. Many of its peculiarities may be due to lack of experience in the use of stone, but it set a precedent for much in later Egyptian architecture, notably the 'step pyramid'. This seems to have developed from the *mastaba*, that at Saqqara being a *mastaba* enlarged by adding units of decreasing size until it reached a height of some 200 feet (60m) and formed, in effect, a ziggurat without a temple on top. Its purpose was to mark and protect the underground tomb chamber 90 feet (27m) below.

Around the pyramid stood single-story buildings and courtyards enclosed by a 30-foot-high (9m) wall of limestone, imitating the mud-brick walls of Zoser's palace in both construction and design (**2,25; 26**). Neatly trimmed blocks of ashlar were used just as if they were mud-bricks, and the exterior was articulated with niches, like those of the buildings on the *stele* of Djet (2,24). Stone was, in fact, used throughout the complex as a substitute for less durable materials: stone columns in the form of bundles of papyrus stems, such as were used to support flimsy primitive shelters; half-columns like vast single stalks of papyrus (perhaps also symbolic). Posts and rafters were expertly carved in stone and colored to simulate wooden posts and rafters. Most extraordinary of all, in the underground chambers, there are false doors with blue-green tiles imitating rolled-up reed matting of the kind used to the present day for curtains in the Near East (**2,27**). This

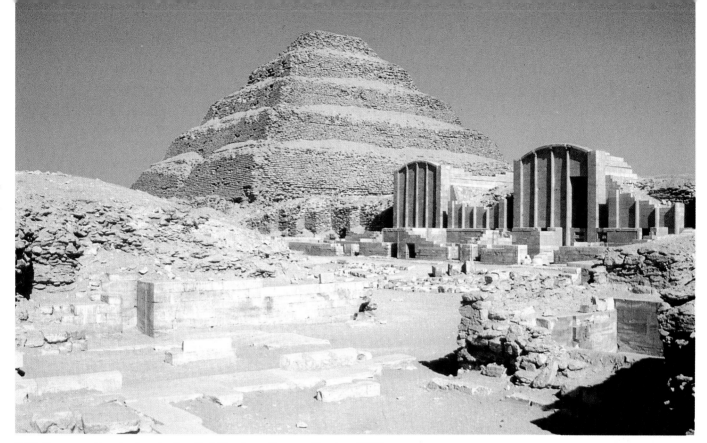

2,25 Step pyramid and palace (restored) of King Zoser, Saqqara, Egypt, c. 2770 BC.

2,26 Palace of King Zoser (restored), Saqqara.

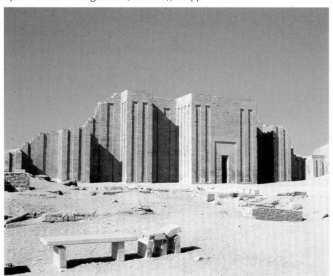

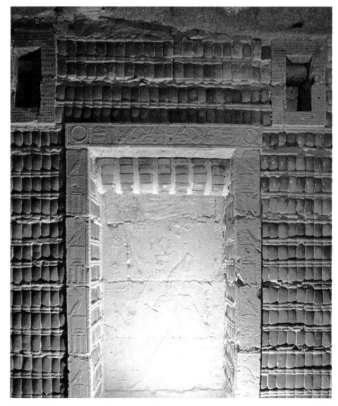

2,27 False door, south tomb of Zoser group, subterranean area, c. 2770 BC. Saqqara.

might seem to be a highly sophisticated form of illusionism or *trompe l'oeil*. But it was not intended in this sense at all. Whereas to us illusionistic art provides a deceptive image of the 'real thing', the reverse was true for the ancient Egyptians. For them the precinct of King Zoser was the 'real thing', the royal palace it imitated the ephemeral earthly substitute, subject to the laws of change and decay. Their relationship parallels that between the spirit and the mortal body. The doors in these underground chambers are of solid stone, through which the *Ba* could pass. In one of the courtyards of the precinct, 'chapels' dedicated to each of the local gods of Eygpt were no more than façades with false doors, which the mortal eye could see but only the spirit could penetrate.

False doors and stone papyrus columns recur throughout ancient Egyptian architecture. But the oblong plan and stepped form of Zoser's pyramid were gradually modified. Three pyramids built for Sneferu, founder of the fourth dynasty (c. 2680–2565 BC), had approximately square plans and one, at Dashur, comes near to the classical smooth-faced form that was finally attained by his successors Khufu (Cheops) (**2,28**) and Khafra (Chefren) for the biggest of all, at Giza just outside modern Cairo (**2,29; 30**). The form seems to have been adopted from the cult image, known as the *benben*, in the temple of the sun god at Heliopolis – a stone with a pyramidal or conical top, the ancestor of the obelisk. The pyramid also recalls the effect made by the sun shining down on the earth through a gap in the clouds – and it was on the rays of the sun that the dead king was said to mount to heaven.

The pyramid of Khufu is some 450 feet (137m) high on a square base occupying 13 acres (5.25 hectares) (it covers approximately twice the area of St Peter's in Rome), its four sides being equilateral triangles. The precision with which it was laid out is remarkable, the sides being aligned on the cardinal points of the compass to within one tenth of a degree (true north seems to have been determined by sighting a star on the northern horizon and bisecting the angle between its rising position, the point of observation and its setting position). So far as can be discovered, the stones that form the core of the pyramid were hauled up banks or ramps, which were increased

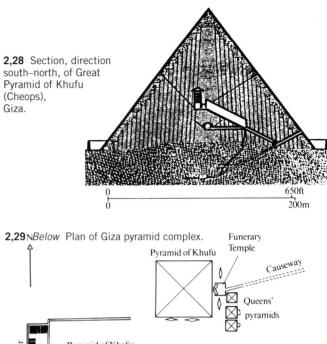

2,28 Section, direction south–north, of Great Pyramid of Khufu (Cheops), Giza.

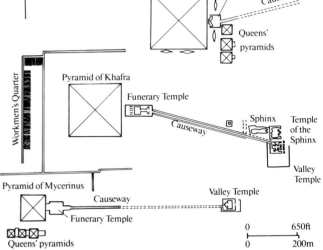

2,29 N *Below* Plan of Giza pyramid complex.

2,30 Sphinx and pyramid of Khafra (Chefren), c. 2650 BC. Giza.

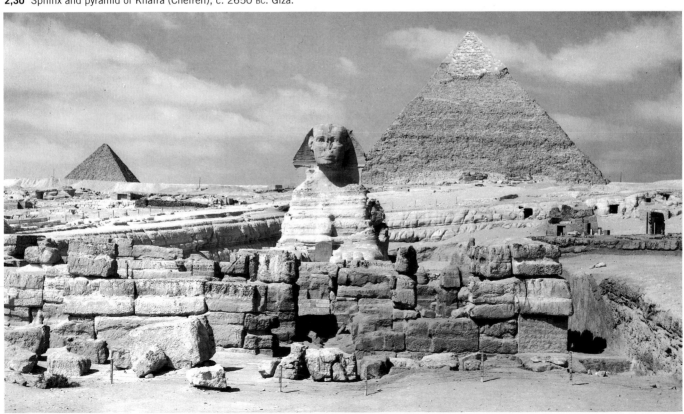

THE EARLY CIVILIZATIONS 67

in height as it rose and then were gradually demolished as the surface was covered with more finely cut stone, working from the top downwards. Skilled masons must have been employed to cut the stone lining the galleries leading to the burial chambers in the heart of the pyramid. The large work-force needed to haul the stone to the site is said to have been conscripted. It probably operated only in the period from late July to late October each year when the Nile was in flood, the land could not be cultivated and the majority of the population was idle. This was the normal period for building. The Nile flood also facilitated the transport of stone from Upper Egypt by boat. According to the fifth-century BC Greek historian Herodotus, the pyramid of Khufu took 20 years to build –

a relatively modest outlay when it is remembered that the pyramid ensured the eternal welfare of the king, on which the future prosperity of the state was believed to depend.

Later pyramids were smaller, but otherwise varied only in the arrangement of interior passages leading to the burial chambers – and others intended to mislead intruders. Each pyramid was approached through a funerary precinct laid out for ceremonies and rituals, though little survives of Old Kingdom precincts apart from the Valley Temple at the beginning of a processional way to the pyramid of Khafra at Giza – a construction of massive monolithic piers and lintels carved and placed with perfect rectangular precision. Nearby, a knoll of

---

SOURCES AND DOCUMENTS

ANCIENT EGYPTIAN PYRAMID TEXTS

The purpose and meaning of the pyramids – to ensure the eternal welfare of the king – was sometimes made explicit in hieroglyphic inscriptions of prayers and spells entirely covering the walls and ceilings of their sepulchral chambers deep inside the pyramids. The earliest known of these 'pyramid texts' are at Saqqara in the pyramid of Unas, the last king of the fifth dynasty who died in about 2345 BC. Others, more than 700 in all, are in the tombs of kings and queens of the sixth dynasty (c. 2345–c. 2184 BC). During the Middle Kingdom (c. 2134–1787 BC) similar texts were inscribed on the inside walls of wooden coffins of the nobility as well as royalty, and later, more widely and with variations and additions, on the papyri collectively known as a *Book of the Dead* (originally *Chapters of Coming-forth by Day*) enclosed in mummy cases (see p. 104).

The basic system of Egyptian hieroglyphics (see pp. 63, 72) had been discovered in 1822 by Jean-François Champollion by studying the 'Rosetta Stone' (British Museum, London), a slab of black basalt inscribed with a decree of AD 196 in hieroglyphics, demotic Egyptian (the script used in Egypt in the second century AD) and Greek. He recognized that two types of sign were combined: ideograms and phonograms. (Ideograms are conventional representations of objects signifying nouns and associated verbs such as sun, light, to rise, to shine; phonograms indicate the sounds of consonants.) Great advances were made in deciphering hieroglyphics during the following decades. But the pyramid texts first discovered in the 1880s raised special problems as the animals represented in some phonograms had been mutilated, when they could not be omitted, to prevent them from materializing and attacking the bodies of the dead. There are few clearer indications of the ancient Egyptian belief in the magical potency of visual images, especially those that were lifelike.

The pyramid texts were believed to be more effective in securing the well-being of the dead than the relief carvings of servants and animals and piles of food on the walls of outer chambers of tombs and mortuary temples. They repeated continuously the incantations recited in funeral ceremonies. Although many are similar to one another, no two are exactly the same. A typical resurrection text includes the following sentences:

O flesh of the King, do not decay, do not rot, do not smell unpleasant. Your foot will not be overpassed, your stride will not be overstridden, you shall not tread on the corruption of Osiris. You shall reach the sky as Orion, your soul shall be as effective as Sothis; have power, having power; be strong, having strength; may your soul stand among the gods as Horus who dwells in 'Irw. May the terror of you come into being in the hearts of the gods like the Nt-crown which is on the King of Lower Egypt, like the Mizwt-crown which is on the King of Upper Egypt, like the tress which is on the vertex of the Mntw-tribesmen. You shall lay hold of the hand of the Imperishable Stars, your bones shall not perish, your flesh shall not sicken, O King, your members shall not be far from you, because you are one of the gods.

In another pyramid text a prayer is addressed to the goddess of weaving, called Tait.

Hail to you, Tait, who are upon the lip of the Great Lagoon, who reconciled the god to his brother! Do you exist, or do you not? Will you exist or will you not? Guard the King's head, lest it become loose; gather together the King's bones, lest they become loose, and put the love of the King into the body of every god who shall see him.

(R. O. Faulkner, *The Ancient Egyptian Pyramid Texts*, Oxford 1969)

living rock left by the quarrying of stone for the pyramids was hacked and carved into the form of the Great Sphinx, probably to represent Khafra as the sun god at the western horizon, guarding the Gates of Sunset (2,30).

Although the pyramids of the Old Kingdom have proved the most enduring of man's large-scale monuments, they ironically failed in their main purpose of preserving the mummies, statues and furnishings of the dead who were buried beneath them. All were broken into and robbed. Devices to prevent violation were used to no avail – until much later in the New Kingdom. But the treasure from the deeply buried tomb of Queen Hetepheres I (the mother of Khufu) fortunately survives. It includes a portable pavilion supported on wooden posts covered with sheet gold, two arm-chairs, a bed, a sedan chair and caskets inlaid with gold and ebony (2,31), as well as jewelry of turquoise, lapis lazuli and carnelian set in silver (a metal rarer and more highly valued than gold in ancient Egypt). The furniture is as remarkable for the simple refinement of its design as for the exquisite precision of its craftsmanship. These pieces may have been made expressly for burial, but they resemble those shown in daily use in contemporary paintings and reliefs and thus provide some indication not only of the treasures that must have been buried in older royal tombs, but also of the elegance of the Old Kingdom palaces, of which no trace now remains.

2,31 Portable pavilion and furniture of Queen Hetepheres I, c. 2650 BC. Wood and gold leaf. Egyptian Museum, Cairo.

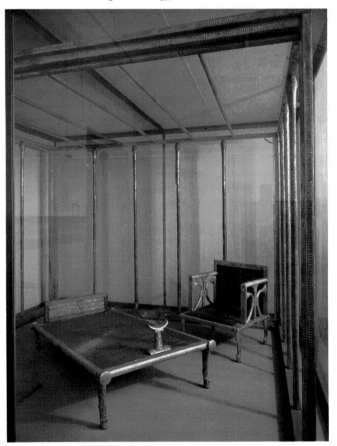

OLD KINGDOM SCULPTURE AND PAINTING

Apart from the mummy itself, the most important object in a tomb was a statue of the deceased, his 'other self', in which his *Ka* or part of it might dwell. By the beginning of the fourth dynasty, sculptors were carving such statues with a realism wholly unprecedented in the arts of the world. Several are most convincing portraits, speaking likenesses, such as those of Prince Rahotep (a son of Sneferu) and his wife Nofret, which still retain their coloring in all its original freshness (2,33). So persuasive is the rendering of the faces that the rather summary treatment of the hands, legs, thick ankles and outsize feet tends to be overlooked. The somewhat later court official portrayed as a scribe (literacy was confined to priests and government officials), with ochre-painted flesh and twinkling eyes of polished stone, is less formal and also more sensitively modelled (2,32). Although less than 2 feet (60cm) high, this figure is even more astonishingly lifelike than the statues of Rahotep and Nofret. Such illusionism was not, of course, intended as a display of technical virtuosity – it was simply the means of embodying the human spirit in stone or wood. Accuracy of portrayal was necessary if the statues were to fulfil their immortalizing function and many are inscribed as 'carved from the life'. They were no more intended to deceive than were the rolls of modelled and glazed matting over the doors in Zoser's funerary precinct. No mortal eyes would see them once they had been immured in the tombs.

2,32 Scribe, from Saqqara, c. 2600 BC. Painted limestone, 21ins (53.3cm) high. Louvre, Paris.

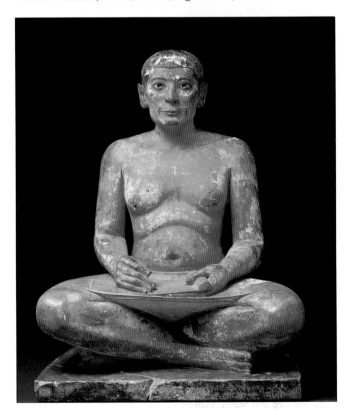

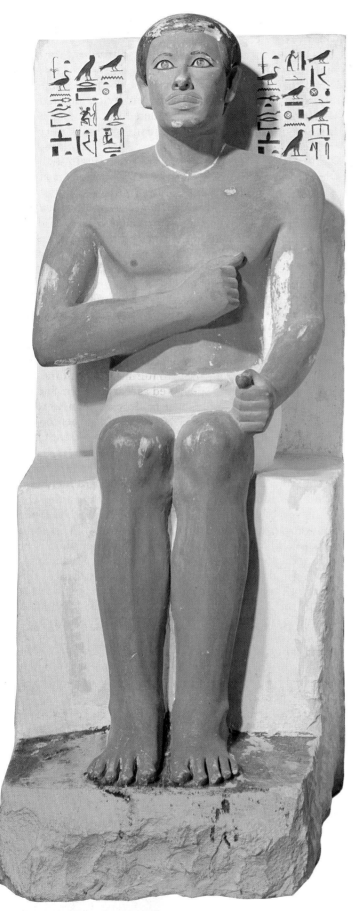 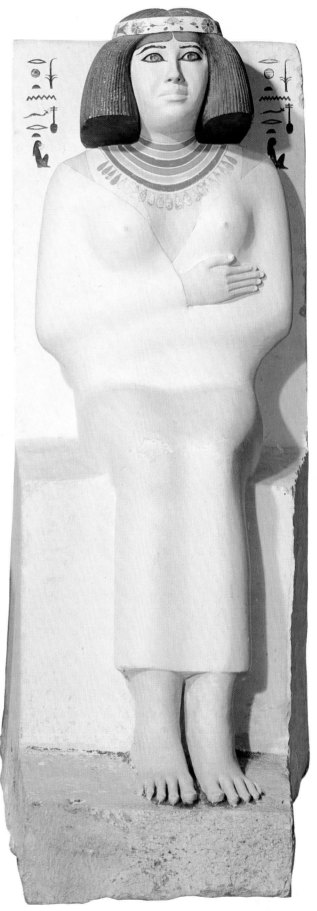

2,33 Rahotep and Nofret, from Medum, c. 2580 BC. Painted limestone, 3ft 11½ins (1.2m) high. Egyptian Museum, Cairo.

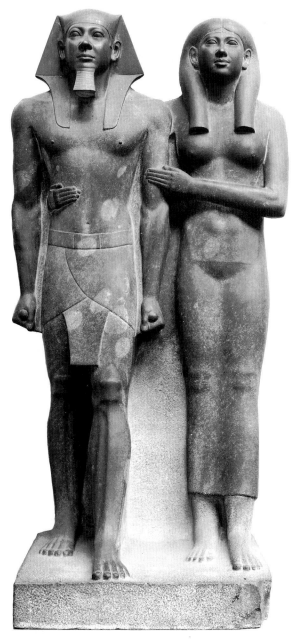

2,34 Mycerinus and his queen, from Giza, c. 2600 BC. Slate, 4ft ⅞in (1.24m) high. Museum of Fine Arts, Boston.

By no means all statues were, however, walled up in tombs. Many were carved to stand in the temples, where rites of a dead king were expected to be celebrated in perpetuity by a well-endowed priesthood. Mycerinus, the penultimate king of the fourth dynasty, commissioned a whole series (perhaps as many as 42) for the Valley Temple at the beginning of the processional way to his pyramid at Giza. In one he is accompanied by his wife Khamerernebty (**2,34**). These imposing figures are (unlike Rahotep and Nofret) integrated into a single sculptural group by the rhythmical arrangement of form (strong verticals counterbalanced by the horizontals of the king's belt and the queen's left arm, for instance), as well as by their close physical contact and the invincibly confident gaze with which they both stare into eternity. The lower part of the

group is unfinished, but this lack of finish would have been very much less apparent under the paint, of which only traces survive. All ancient Egyptian statues were painted or partly painted. (The beautiful hard stones from which they were often carved were chosen for durability rather than for their color or texture.) So, the group of Mycerinus and his wife must originally have looked very different. In its present monochrome state, however, it reveals all the more clearly the rigid framework of conventions that controlled sculpture from the time of the Old Kingdom onwards.

Statues were invariably carved and placed to be seen only from a frontal viewpoint. The range of postures was strictly limited. Figures either stand with the left leg slightly advanced or sit bolt upright – kings and queens on thrones, such court officials as scribes and physicians squatting cross-legged. (Large-scale sculpture in the round was reserved for royalty and the court.) This inflexibility has been ascribed to the peculiarities in sculptural practice, and especially to the use of rectangular blocks, which are said to have determined the four-square rigidity of the statues. The reverse might equally well be true – that it was the limited conception of sculptural form which led to the blocks being cut to rectangular shape in the quarries, so that sculptors might draw on their surfaces the outlines of the four, and never more than four, envisaged aspects of a statue: front, two sides and back (often left plain). The latter explanation seems the more likely. But whatever its ultimate origin – craft traditions or sense of form – may have been, nothing was left to chance in the carving of a statue. The sides of the block were marked with a measured grid of lines which determined the 'correct' size of every part of the body (see below). A figure could encapsulate the spirit and thus fulfil its essential purpose only if it observed established conventions.

Similar conventions which regulated the allied arts of painting and low-relief sculpture are already evident in a masterly carved wood relief of Hesira, a court official of King Zoser (**2,35**). The sensitively carved head is that of an individual, not a generalized type; the way in which the left hand clasps the staff of office could hardly be more naturalistically observed; the knees and calf muscles are lovingly, almost tenderly, defined. Yet the pose is most unnatural, if not anatomically impossible – shoulders to the front, head and legs to the right – and the figure appears to have two left feet, for only the inner side is visible of what ought to be the right – there are no little toes! The kilt is shown frontally, while the legs stride off to the right.

This strangely contrived posture is the hallmark of ancient Egyptian art and the most obvious example of its essentially intellectual or conceptual, as distinct from purely visual, nature. Ancient Egyptian artists wanted, above all, to convey what they knew and not just what they saw. They therefore laid out the human figure to show its distinguishing features as fully as possible, much as a botanist lays out and presses flat a plant or flower to display its essential parts. So the pose is no mere convention: it was most carefully devised as a means of combining in a single image all the salient features of the subject, which

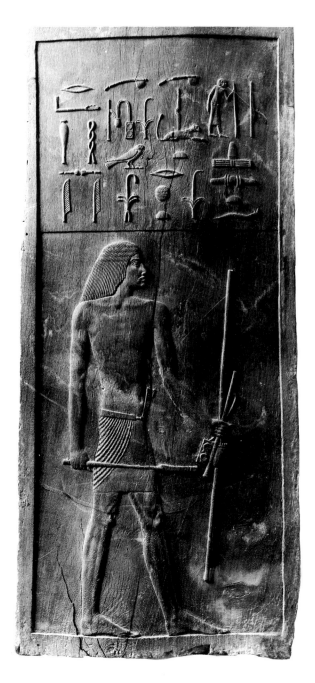

were, so to speak, taken apart and recomposed. Thus, the head shows the fullness of the eye as well as the line of the forehead, nose and chin, and the thick hair brushed back. The placing of the legs, with the one furthest from the spectator (usually the left) extended forward, was a means of displaying the sex, whether of a man or an animal, as well as the whole structure of the leg from the hip and buttocks downwards – which could not have been done frontally. (The figure is to be read as moving not to the right or the left, but out of the wall towards the spectator.) This pose very soon became accepted as the 'correct' mode for human representation. A slight deviation would have been the equivalent of a spelling mistake; a major deviation would change the meaning of the figure and transform, for instance, a court official into a peasant or a captive (for whom less strictly formalized modes were thought appropriate).

The standard Egyptian pose was intimately connected with a no less strictly observed system or canon of bodily proportions (**2,36**). Like most other people, the ancient Egyptians based measures of length on parts of the human body – their main unit, the small cubit, corresponded to the length of the arm from elbow to the thumb-tip, which equalled 6 hand-breadths or 24 finger-breadths. In nature, of course, these lengths differ from person to person, but the Egyptians noted that the relationship from one to another is almost invariable – that, for instance, the foot is three times the width of the hand (as we instinctively recognize when we measure the size of sock we need by wrapping it around a clenched fist) – and from this observation they created the canon which laid down the proportional ratios between every part of the body. To ensure its observation an Egyptian painter or relief carver drew on the surface of the wall a grid of squares, each one the size of the feet of the figure to be represented, and divided the body into units (usually 18) from the sole of the foot to the hair-line of the forehead. A fixed number of units determined the length of arms and legs, the breadth of shoulders (so clearly and measurably shown by the twisted pose in paintings), the distance between the feet and so on. Traces of several such grids survive from the Old Kingdom. Merely by altering the dimensions of the unit, figures could be enlarged or reduced without departing from the canon. Size in ancient Egyptian art always indicates the relative importance of figures and not their distance from the spectator. The system was, in fact, entirely intellectual and made no allowance for the natural muscular extension of limbs in movement, let alone the visual effects of foreshortening or perspective.

The fidelity and regularity with which the canon was observed had artistic results, perhaps unintended. To it is due much of that sense of controlled balance and repose, which can be felt throughout ancient Egyptian painting and sculpture, as well as their stately monotony, which can exert a strange, almost hypnotic charm. All these solemnly, silently gesturing figures, rank upon clean-limbed rank of narrow-waisted men and slender women delicately holding lotus flowers in their long, lean fingers, have the effect of repeated phrases in a poetic incantation. Such comments and interpretations, however, would

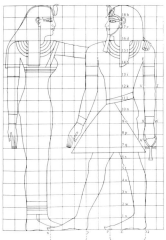

2,35 *Above* Portrait panel of Hesira, from Saqqara, c. 2770 BC. Wood, 4ft 7½ins (1.41m) high. Egyptian Museum, Cairo.

2,36 *Left* The 'canon' of ancient Egyptian art (after E. Iverson, *Canon and Proportions in Egyptian Art*).

have been considered entirely irrelevant by the ancient Egyptians – to whom, in any case, the aesthetic response of the living was of little or no importance.

Nothing more clearly reveals the intellectual rather than visual or sensual basis of ancient Egyptian art than the intermixture of hieroglyphic signs with images. On the wood relief panel of Hesira, hieroglyphs are confined to the upper section (2,35), but often they surround a figure, indicating that what we tend to regard as a background of space was conceived by the ancient Egyptian artist as a surface, on to which images were projected. Sometimes there is little or no direct connection between the meaning of the words and the explicit subject-matter of the figurative groups with which they are juxtaposed. This disjunction perhaps partly explains the inconsistency between the acutely observed naturalism of details and the extremely artificial way in which they are combined.

The function of tomb paintings and low-relief carvings was to furnish the deceased's 'eternal castle' with eternally durable effects and also to establish the status he had attained in life (fully spelt out in the inscriptions) and hoped to enjoy still more intensely in the hereafter. A funeral banquet is usually shown, together, in one royal tomb at Giza, with the cooks preparing it in the kitchen. Women appear only as wives, daughters, servants, for a

2,37 Entrance to tomb of Mereruka, c. 2400 BC. Saqqara, Egypt.

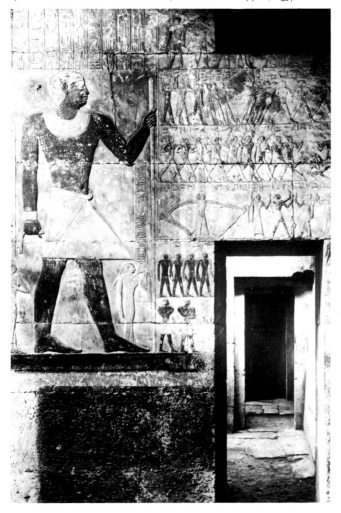

wife was regarded as a possession, 'the fruitful field of her lord' as she was sometimes termed. As the tombs not only of kings but also of courtiers grew larger, so the elaboration of their paintings increased, with the numerous records of the everyday activities of the family and servants of the deceased in one chamber after another (2,37). Under the fifth dynasty (c. 2565–c. 2420 BC) the range of subject-matter widened. Country scenes became more prominent, with the deceased enjoying boating trips through thickets of papyrus or hunting on the verge of the desert. Such pictures were intended to evoke for the dead the life-giving power of the sun god Re (or Ra). But they were outnumbered by scenes of seasonal work on the land, scenes which recorded the farms the deceased owned, and provide us with amazingly vivid glimpses of daily life in Egypt 4,000 years ago, as in those from the tomb of Ti at Saqqara which fully exemplify the principles of ancient Egyptian painting (2,38). The water of the Nile is represented by the wavy band at the bottom. Men driving a flock of sheep in the upper register are in a pose which, to indicate movement, departs slightly from the standard form, but the inferior farm-hands below, one walking beside a cow and the other bending under the weight of the calf he carries, depart further, being rendered almost as naturalistically as the wonderfully lively animals. Degrees of naturalism would seem to correspond to the strata of the social order.

MIDDLE KINGDOM

In about 2258 BC the central authority of the kings broke down, the country disintegrated into feudal states and was not reunited until Mentuhotep, ruler of Thebes, initiated the Middle Kingdom about 2134 BC. The most important outcome of the intermediary period between the Old and Middle Kingdoms was the so-called 'democratization of the hereafter'. In the Old Kingdom, only the king was destined to become a god and the afterlife of his subjects depended on his favour. Local rulers now appropriated this divine right, which was further extended to all those who could afford to have the appropriate rituals performed at their funerals and their coffins inscribed with the magic spells previously used for the royal apotheosis. This 'democratization' was accompanied by new cults (notably that of Osiris) and the questioning of old beliefs. Moral and semi-philosophical problems were taken up – including suicide in *The Dialogue of a Pessimist with his Soul* – but this outburst of intellectual activity had no parallel in the visual arts. Rather the reverse, in fact; and it was not until the Middle Kingdom that a delayed response could be discerned, especially in painting.

Essential principles remained the same in Middle Kingdom painting, but color was now used more freely and subtly, as on the outer coffin of Djehutynekht from Bersheh (2,39). Shading and other naturalistic effects were attempted here, notably on the dove's plumage rendered with delicate gray and black strokes over white, through which a suggestion of rose color permeates up from the

2,38 Cattle fording a river,
c. 2450 BC. Painted limestone,
tomb of Ti, Saqqara.

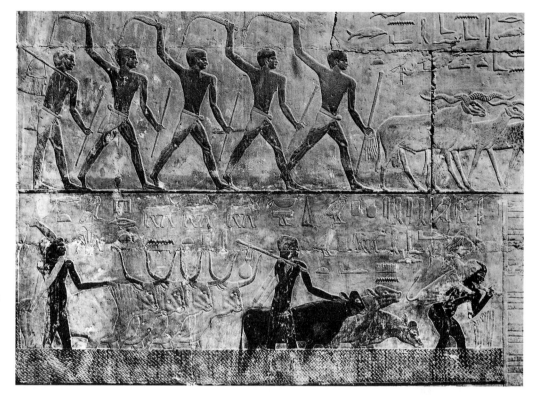

2,39 *Below*   Detail of outer coffin
of Djehutynekht from Bersheh,
c. 1870 BC. Paint on cedar wood,
total height of panel 3ft 8ins
(1.12m), width 15¾ins (40cm).
Museum of Fine Arts, Boston
(Harvard University –
Museum of Fine Arts Expedition).

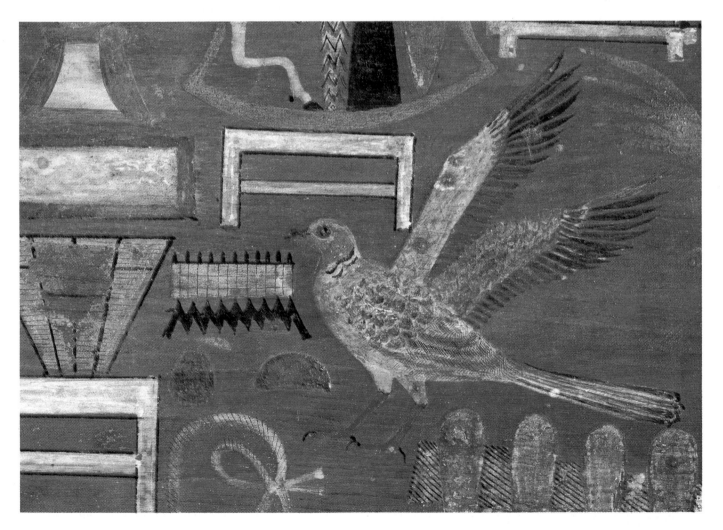

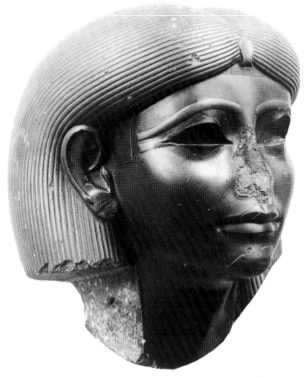

2,40 A princess, 1929–1892 BC. Green chlorite, 15⁵/₁₆ins (38.9cm) high. Brooklyn Museum, New York (Charles Edwin Wilbour Fund).

delightful is the day of hunting the hippopotamus.' It is a vivid statement of the Egyptians' love of life, implicit in their urge to perpetuate its pleasures after death – a corrective to any facile assumption that their art of the tomb was morbid. 'May I be cool under the sycamores', runs one of their prayers, 'May I bathe in my pond; May my spirit not be shut in; May I tend my acres in the field of Iaru.' Likewise, in Middle Kingdom sculpture, a new and more relaxed feeling for life can sometimes be sensed. A hint of a smile, very rare in ancient Egyptian art, hovers around the enigmatic lips of an unnamed princess, her cheeks still touched with the bloom of youth (**2,40**). Formal patterning of eyebrows and hair beautifully sets off the naturalistic rendering of meltingly smooth planes of flesh in this example of delicately subtle portraiture.

The most grandiose architectural monuments of the Middle, as of the Old, Kingdom continued, of course, to be those erected for the kings. But at Lahun in the Fayum there are remains of a whole town called Kahun built to accommodate the workers, artisans and others engaged on the pyramid of Sesostris II (1897–1878 BC). This is the earliest town of which traces survive in a country where most people lived in agricultural villages strung along the Nile. And the reason for its construction is no less significant than the rigid social stratification which its foundations demonstrate (**2,41**). It was laid out on a square grid plan (more regular than that of the earlier cities of the Indus Valley, see p. 59) about 1,300 feet (400m) across. Such a plan was probably adopted, as in later times, mainly as a convenient means of apportioning land. A stout north–south wall divided it into two parts. In the eastern part the houses of higher officials, some with as many as 50 rooms, flanked wide streets leading to the palace of the governor (perhaps used also for royal visitors) raised on an artificial platform. The much smaller

cedar-wood ground. The range of subject-matter was also expanded. Historical events were depicted, such as Mentuhotep's victory over Asians, and subsidiary figures were given more attention. Hundreds of pairs of wrestlers grapple with one another on the walls of the tombs at Beni Hasan, with an occasional (perhaps misleading) suggestion of foreshortening. Rural scenes have more of an open-air feeling. Beneath a fishing scene on the Nile hieroglyphs declare: 'Boating in the papyrus beds, the pools of wild-fowl, the marshes and the streams, spearing with the two-pronged spear he transfixes 30 fish; how

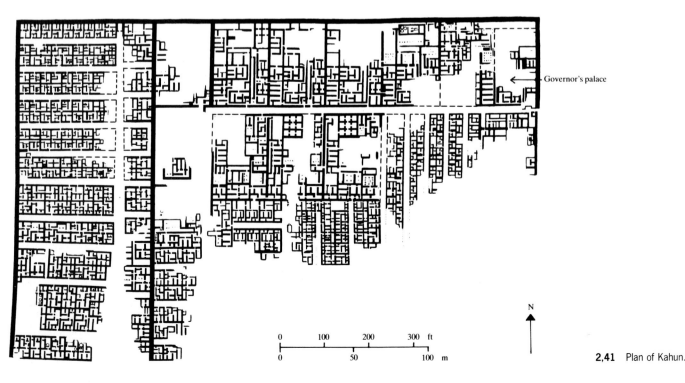

Governor's palace

| 0 | 100 | 200 | 300 ft |

| 0 | 50 | 100 m |

N

2,41 Plan of Kahun.

western part was crammed with blocks of back-to-back houses of three or four rooms apiece for the workers.

What of these workers? They took no part in the official religious cults centred on the pharaoh. The religio-political system condemned them to toil in this world and the next. They appear frequently in tomb paintings and reliefs and also as little free-standing figures called *shabti* (later *shawabti* or *ushabti*), whose role in the hereafter is made explicit in hieroglyphics, such as: 'When I am called to tend the land, then you, *shabti*, give ear and answer "Here I am".' Another reads: 'Take up your mattocks, your hoes, your yokes and your basket in your hands as any man does for his master.'

Artists and craftsmen (there was no distinction) were, of course, included among this vast body of servants of the great and as such they, too, figure on the walls of tombs. Little is known of them as individuals. Architects appear to have occupied a fairly elevated status as court officials. One named Nekhebu, who worked for a king of the fifth dynasty, stated in his epitaph (Museum of Fine Arts, Boston):

> *His majesty found me a common builder. His majesty conferred upon me the successive offices of journeyman builder, master builder, and master of a craft. Next his majesty conferred upon me the successive offices of Royal Constructor and Builder, Royal Attaché, and Royal Constructor and Architect. . . . His majesty did all this because his majesty favoured me so greatly.*

This unique glimpse into the workings and structure of the building profession in ancient Egypt unfortunately tells us nothing of the buildings Nekhebu designed. A sculptor named Iritsen, who lived in the reign of Mentuhotep, was less self-effacing in the inscription of his funerary *stele* (Louvre) – by far the earliest recorded statement by an artist. 'I was a man skilled in my art and pre-eminent in my learning', he wrote. 'I knew how to represent the walking of a man and the carriage of a woman . . . the poising of the arm to bring the hippopotamus low and the movements of a runner.' He boasted of his accomplishment in handling various, mainly precious, materials. But he clearly took most pride in his arcane knowledge of 'the secrets of the divine words', of 'the prescriptions regarding the rituals of festivals' and 'one of every kind of magic'. Though surprisingly articulate, Iritsen should not be understood as implying by these remarks any artistic independence. His claim to know 'how to represent' a human figure refers strictly to his knowledge of accepted conventions, those 'rules' which enabled an image to fulfil its ritual, religious or magic purposes and which underlay all ancient Egyptian art and architecture. So tightly were the visual arts integrated into the religio-political structure of the state that they declined sharply whenever its balance was upset, as in the first so-called Intermediate period and the much longer second Intermediate period (1786–1570 BC) after the disintegration of the Middle Kingdom. That they revived after each of these interruptions attests to the resilience and strength of their traditions. (For later developments see p. 93.)

THE AEGEAN

Late in the third millennium BC, about the time the Middle Kingdom began in Egypt (see p. 72) and Akkadian rule collapsed in Mesopotamia (see p. 56) and two or three hundred years after the foundation of the cities of the Indus Valley (see p. 58), another civilization emerged on the island of Crete in the Aegean, or eastern Mediterranean, about 350 miles (560km) north-east of the Nile delta. It had contacts with Egypt and with Mesopotamia (through intermediaries in the Levant), but was an autonomous growth, differing in many respects from the others. They were river-valley civilizations – as was to be that of China, as we shall see. This was a sea-faring, island culture. Whereas the others controlled and were sustained by vast territories, this was confined to a relatively small geographical area, Crete being only some 150 miles (240km) long and 36 miles (56km) across at its widest. The island enjoyed, however, a temperate climate, without the droughts and floods that plagued the others, and was more than self-sufficient agriculturally, producing grain, wine and enough olive oil to export – and probably enough wool as well. It was much more fertile then than it is today. The sea, which provided the means of communication for trade in raw materials and artifacts, also protected Crete from foreign invasion, though for little more than 500 years (c. 2050–1450 BC). The influence if not the power of Minoan Crete has recently been discovered in Egypt where the palace at Avaris (capital of the northern Egyptian kingdom ruled by the Hyksos from about 1670 to 1570 BC) contains frescoes depicting typical Minoan scenes and even costumes. Practically nothing is known of its history except that its buildings were destroyed about 1730 BC, probably by an earthquake, and were very

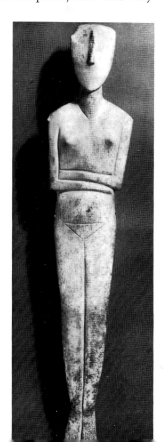

2,42 Cycladic figure from Amorgos, c. 3000 BC. Marble, 30ins (76.2cm) high. Ashmolean Museum, Oxford.

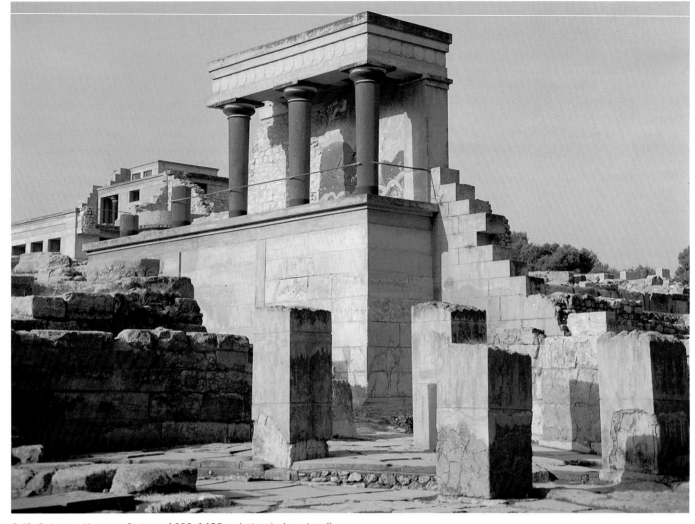

2,43 Palace at Knossos, Crete, c. 1600–1400 BC (extensively restored).

2,44 Plan of the palace at Knossos.

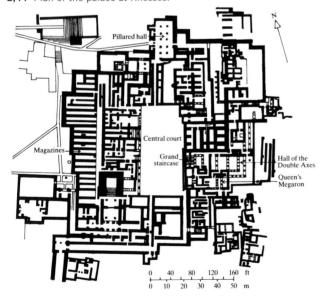

MINOAN CRETE

The origins of this Minoan civilization – so called after a mythical king Minos of Crete – are difficult to trace, however, and its emergence seems to have been as sudden as its collapse and disappearance. Recent excavations have brought to light evidence of an advanced Neolithic culture, which had merged into a Bronze Age culture by 3200 BC and extended throughout the Aegean islands, up to the east coast of Greece and as far north as Troy on the opposite shore. This seems to have provided the material background from which civilization sprang up independently of outside influence on the agriculturally rich island of Crete.

Although the Aegean culture of the third millennium used bronze implements, its only notable works of art were produced by Neolithic techniques: statuettes of hard white marble carved with obsidian blades and rubbed smooth with emery (**2,42**). They seem to have originated in the islands of the Cyclades, where these materials are readily available. Ranging in size from a few inches to almost life-size in very rare instances, they represent nude human figures, generally female and rendered with the utmost schematic simplicity. A few are in more lifelike poses with some three-dimensional feeling, though almost tubular in form. The majority are of women with strange expressionless shield-shaped faces and wedge-like

soon reconstructed. A second disaster at the beginning of the fifteenth century BC, perhaps the result of a volcanic eruption, was followed by an invasion from the mainland of Greece.

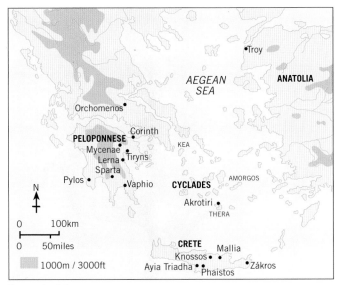

The ancient Aegean

a unified monarchy. All that is certain from archeological evidence is that Minoan Crete had a clearly stratified social structure, that the economy functioned by a process of redistribution (without money) and that government was effective enough for towns and individual buildings to do without massive fortifications. The palaces were built near the richest agricultural land and their vast storage areas reveal that they were centres for the collection and redistribution of the four main products: wool, grain, wine and olive oil (the latter used for lighting, cleansing the body and as a base for scent as well as for cooking). In a single store at Knossos there were

2,45 Fisherman, from Akrotiri, Thera (Santorini), c. 1550 BC. Wall-painting, 4ft 5ins (1.35m) high. National Archeological Museum, Athens.

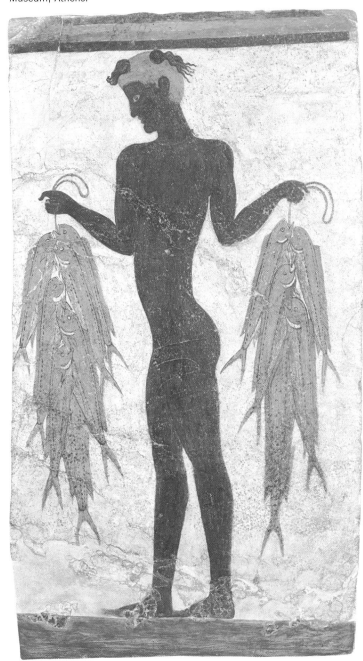

noses, tiny breasts and arms tightly folded beneath, pubic triangles sharply incised and legs held close together. Heads are tilted back and feet are extended in line with the shins so that the figures seem to be lying down (they cannot be displayed upright without a support). The human body has almost been transformed into geometric shapes (triangles, rectangles, ovals) but the stylized effect this now gives may have been less pronounced before the coloring had worn off – the eyes were painted, also various necklaces, bracelets, and other ornaments. Examples have been found mainly in tombs, but it is impossible to tell whether they were cult figures or companions of the dead (like the Egyptian *shabti*, see p. 75) – goddesses or concubines. There is something curiously innocent about them, a purity of form as if they had been washed clean of all gross matter. They make a very striking contrast with the plump fleshy images of fertility or motherhood produced by other prehistoric cultures – and also with most of the works of art found in the Cretan palaces.

Cretan civilization was centred on the palace rather than the temple (as in Sumer), the town (as in the Indus Valley) or the tomb (as in Egypt). There were no large temples; religious shrines were in domestic buildings or scattered through the countryside, in caves, by springs or on hilltops. Towns were simply unplanned conglomerations of small dwellings without fortifications such as surrounded the settlements on the Cyclades and also Troy (where the sixth of a series of towns built one on top of another is approximately contemporary with those on Crete). The Cretans buried their dead collectively in communal ossuaries. The few more elaborate tombs, like those at Knossos and Isopata which seem to have belonged to a ruling family, are stark and modest by Egyptian standards. But the palaces at Knossos, Phaistos (each of which covered between 3 and 4 acres – about 1 to 1.5 hectares), the somewhat smaller ones at Mallia, Ayia Triadha and Zákros, and the several neighbouring 'villas', lacked for nothing in richness of decoration and furnishings.

Whether these palaces belonged to different families of rulers or to a single one is not known. There may even have been a transition from a confederation of princes to

more than 400 huge pottery jars, presumably for oil, with a total capacity of some 20,000 gallons (91,000 litres). It was in this context, intermediate between barter and commerce, that Minoan writing developed for the palace accounts. Inventories of goods were inscribed on clay tablets in the later of two scripts, called Linear B. The language was a primitive form of Greek.

The palaces were curiously irregular – what today would be called 'informal' or 'open' – in plan, with rectangular rooms varying greatly in size grouped around a large, paved central courtyard (2,43; 44). Stores were on the ground floor, larger apartments and colonnaded terraces above. The centre of each palace could be reached from several directions, through a succession of spaces and along sharply turning corridors, which may well have given rise to the myth of the minotaur's labyrinth. Comfort seems to have been a factor of major importance: parts of the buildings were open to catch cool breezes in the summer; others were planned so that they could be closed and heated with braziers in the winter. Baths and latrines (with wooden seats) were provided. There was an excellent drainage system.

Decoration was evidently no less important than comfort. Façades of buildings seem to have been brightly colored, and inside the palaces and villas courtyards were paved as were rooms and other covered areas. Columns used to form colonnades and porticoes were all of wood, usually tapering towards the base. Plastered walls were painted red, blue or yellow above dados of gypsum. In the more important rooms there were also figurative paintings and occasionally stucco reliefs. Unfortunately, only fragments remain. Larger and sometimes very much better preserved wall-paintings of about 1550 BC have recently been discovered at Akrotiri on Thera (Santorini) in the southern Cyclades, a Minoan colony culturally if not politically. These wall-paintings seem to have decorated living-rooms in private houses (though a priestess is depicted in one of them) and include several human figures in what might be described as scenes from daily life – notably two boys boxing and fishermen carrying their catch ashore (2,45). They are painted in flat colors, with here and there some indications of modelling.

Perhaps the best idea of the style of wall-paintings in palaces and houses, and the general effect they originally made, can be obtained from a small sarcophagus (see Glossary) found at Ayia Triadha in Crete, even though it dates from the very end of the Minoan period and, being a tomb painting, is untypical. It is, however, complete and exceptionally well preserved. A single scene is depicted on each side, a funerary ritual on that illustrated here (2,48). At the far right the dead man stands in front of his tomb and at the other end a woman (perhaps his widow) pours a libation into an urn placed between columns topped with double axes – a symbol of unknown significance, which appeared much earlier on pottery in Mesopotamia (see p. 47) and recurs in Minoan art. As in Egyptian and Mesopotamian art, all the figures have their feet placed flat on a single ground line and their eyes are depicted frontally. The three men carrying offerings of

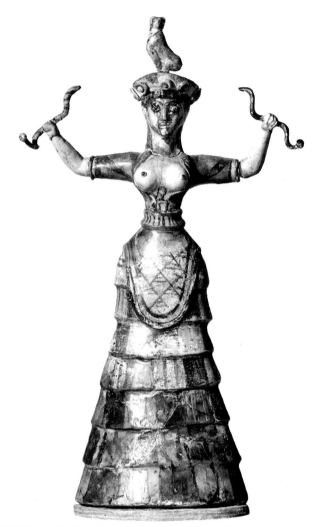

2,46 Snake Goddess, from Knossos, c. 1600 BC. 'Faience', about 13½ins (34.3cm) high. Archeological Museum, Herakleion, Crete.

animals and a boat to the tomb are in the twisted Egyptian pose. But the dead man, the lyre-player and the two women are in pure profile. There are other notable differences from Egyptian paintings. The scene is framed by bands, setting off the pictorial field, which is conceived as a shallow stage with a recessed background. There is, in fact, an attempt to catch the visual appearance of figures moving in a defined space, and this may account for some curious inconsistencies, especially in the relationship between the woman pouring the libation, the urn and the two columns. In comparison with ancient Egyptian art, the figures are crudely drawn, yet they have a suppleness and ease of movement rare in Egypt before the New Kingdom (see p. 93). It is this delight in movement and the flowing lines and free forms expressive of it that give Minoan art its air of buoyancy and vivacity.

Minoan art is seen at its best in small and usually precious objects, probably the products of palace workshops. No large-scale sculpture is known apart from some life-size and lifelike stucco reliefs of men and bulls which were combined with wall-paintings at Knossos. Unfortunately, only fragments survive, perhaps dubiously reassembled. Cult images of a bare-breasted goddess holding snakes in her hands (**2,46**) are little more than 12 inches (30cm) high, sometimes less. Two are made of the glittering, glassy substance produced by firing a mixture of sand and clay so that the surface vitrifies (invented in Egypt or Mesopotamia in the fourth millennium BC and misnamed 'faience' by archeologists). Life-size bare-breasted female figures in clay, fragments of which were discovered on the island of Kea in the Cyclades, would appear to have been not unlike the small snake goddesses in form. They were all found together in what may have been a temple, the only instance as yet discovered of such a building in the Aegean at this period.

Apart from the snake goddesses, there are few explicitly religious images in Minoan sculpture or painting. Nor is there any historical scene, nor even a single portrait which can be identified as that of a ruler. In these respects the contrast with both Mesopotamia and Egypt could hardly be more striking. The subject-matter of Minoan art was derived mainly from the natural world. The sea provided many motifs: underwater plants float and sway

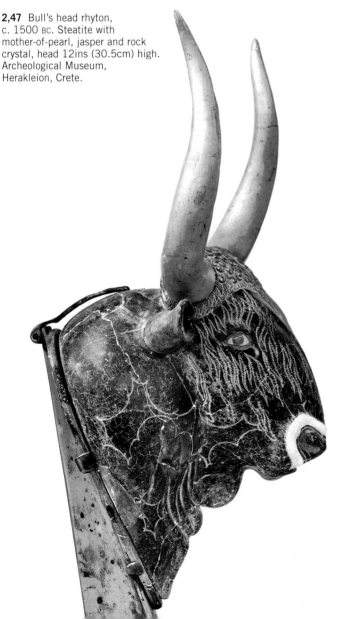

2,47 Bull's head rhyton, c. 1500 BC. Steatite with mother-of-pearl, jasper and rock crystal, head 12ins (30.5cm) high. Archeological Museum, Herakleion, Crete.

languidly, octopuses extend their tentacles with decorative rather than menacing effect, and dolphins play happily on little gold cups and large pottery vases. Birds, beasts and plants enlivened the painted walls of the palaces. On the island of Thera one house had a room entirely painted with flowers springing from hillocks and with birds flying above (**2,49**). These are the earliest pure landscapes anywhere, certainly painted before 1500 BC, although fragments suggest that there may have been others like them in the palaces and villas of Crete itself. Indeed, flowers bloom everywhere in Minoan art, on ewers and storage jars, to which they were often applied in relief, and on tiny pieces of gold jewelry together with delicately wrought insects.

The animals most prominent in Minoan art are bulls, represented in every available medium, incised on seals, modelled in clay, wrought in gold and silver, cast in bronze, carved in hard stone, painted on walls and on pottery. Rhytons – vases from which libations were poured to the dead or to the gods – often took the form of bulls' heads: one is carved of steatite with mother-of-pearl inlaid around the nostrils and also in the whites of the eyes, which have irises of red jasper and pupils of rock crystal (**2,47**). These bulls evidently had some religious significance, but precisely what remains mysterious. Though less benign than their Sumerian predecessors (2,7), they can hardly have been intended to embody dark supernatural forces. Perhaps they were connected in some way with the bull-leaping practised by youths and girls, either as a ritual or a sport or a combination of the two, of which many representations survive. Fragments of a wall-painting at Knossos show a prancing bull whose horns are held by a girl while a youth turns a somersault over its back. Acrobats also appear independently and probably without any ulterior meaning.

The sprightliness, the joyful carefree buoyancy which distinguishes the art of Minoan Crete from that of ancient Egypt or Mesopotamia is very apparent in perhaps the finest of all surviving Minoan works of art, a small stone libation vase carved with a continuous procession of farm labourers, carrying sheaves and winnowing forks, singing as they march to the sound of a rattle held aloft by an older man (**2,50**). It may well represent a ritual of some kind, though nothing could be less solemn than this exuberant celebration of uninhibited physical well-being. The broad-shouldered, wasp-waisted men are shown in the 'Egyptian' pose like those on the Ayia Triadha sarcophagus (**2,48**) – jostling one another, pulsating with spontaneous human vitality. A sense of the third dimension, of movement through space, is rendered in this small object to a degree very rare in the art of the second millennium.

Similar mastery is displayed in the exquisitely wrought repoussé (see Glossary) reliefs of bull-catching scenes on two little gold cups (**2,51**). Muscular force is vividly suggested by a youth with a rope attached to the bull's hind leg. The bull nuzzling at the cow set to decoy him displays a command of foreshortening which is unprecedented. These cups were, however, found in a

2,48 Sarcophagus from Ayia Triadha, Crete, c. 1450–1400 BC. Limestone with surface plastered and painted, total width 4ft 5ins (1.35m). Herakleion Museum, Crete.

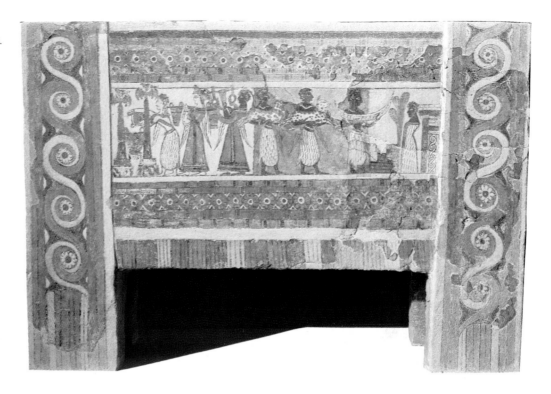

grave at Vaphio, near Sparta, in the Peloponnese, and whether they were made there or in Crete is much disputed. The same problem is raised by other pieces of metalwork found on the mainland. A bronze dagger blade from a grave at Mycenae is decorated with a lion hunt (**2,52**) and another with a leopard chasing ducks among lotus plants – an exotic scene of a type popular in Minoan painting. But nothing similar has been found in Crete, nor were the dead buried there with rich 'grave goods' until after invasions from the mainland about 1450 to 1400 BC.

MYCENAE AND THE MAINLAND

The early civilization of mainland Greece is generally called Mycenean, though this is something of a misnomer and archeologists now prefer Helladic (a term also used for the earlier prehistoric culture). It flourished in a number of small 'states' or kingdoms extending across the Peloponnese from Mycenae and nearby Tiryns in the east to Pylos on the south-west coast and included Vaphio, Orchomenos and Lerna, all of which seem to have been

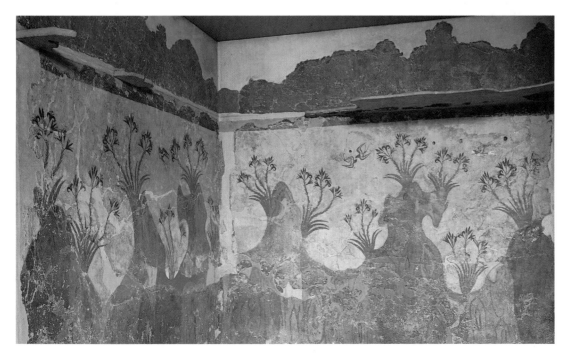

2,49 *The Springtime Fresco* from Akrotiri, Thera (Santorini), c. 1550 BC. Wall-painting, about 7ft 6ins (2.29m) high. National Archeological Museum, Athens.

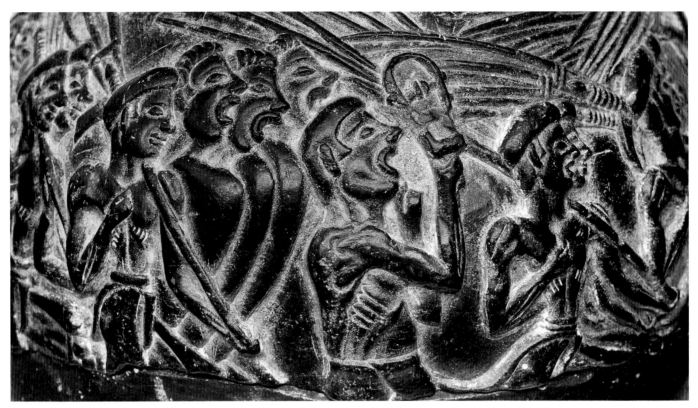

2,50 Detail of Harvester Vase, from Ayia Triadha, c. 1500 BC. Steatite, about 5ins (12.7cm) wide. Herakleion Museum, Crete.

2,51 Cup from Vaphio, c. 1500 BC. Gold, about 3½ins (8.9cm) high. National Archeological Museum, Athens.

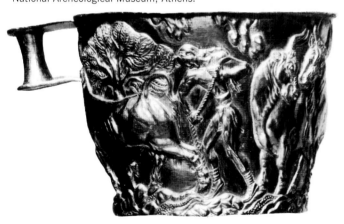

independent of, and sometimes at war with, one another. They shared, nevertheless, a common background and language (an early form of Greek, which belongs to the so-called Indo-European group), had similar buildings and weapons, and the same burial customs. There is reason to think that this civilization initially followed a path parallel to that of Minoan Crete. As bronze was increasingly used for weapons and implements, as larger and more strongly defended towns were built and the land was more productively cultivated, a redistributive economic system evolved. Helladic rulers accumulated the surplus necessary to build palaces and support artists working in such costly materials as gold from Nubia in southern Egypt, ivory from Africa or India by way of Syria, and amber all the way from the shores of the Baltic.

2,52 Dagger blade, from Mycenae, c. 1600–1500 BC. Bronze inlaid with gold and silver, about 9ins (22.8cm) long. National Archeological Museum, Athens.

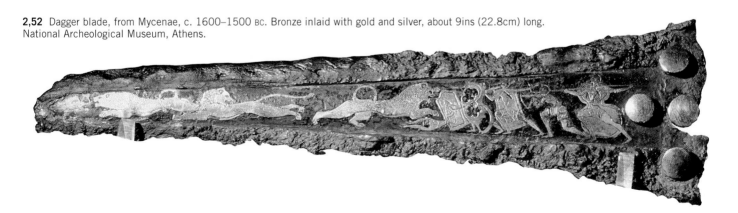

This mainland civilization differed in many respects from that of Minoan Crete. Its massive fortifications, numerous weapons and other remains suggest a fiercer and more aggressive people. Local chieftains or kings of the first half of the second millennium were buried with grave goods which, though modest in comparison with those of the kings of Ur (see p. 54) or the pharaohs of Egypt (see p. 68), are of an opulence unprecedented in the Aegean world and give some indication of their material wealth and power. There can be little doubt that by this date the Helladic states were already moving towards the stratified social system recorded in Linear B inscriptions at Pylos – a pyramid with the chieftain or king, sometimes assisted by a leader, at the top; then a 'nobility' which held land on a feudal footing in return for agricultural produce and service in war; then the artisans and land-workers, followed at the lowest level by slaves.

Little is known about the early buildings at Mycenae contemporary with the first shaft graves, which, it has recently been argued, may have been constructed as early as 1850 BC. They were probably of mud-brick and wood, not of stone. The surviving remains of the city and citadel appear to date back to about 1700 BC, with the royal palace on the hilltop isolated in the centre of a roughly triangular area enclosed by a massive stone wall following the contour of the hill (2,53). A few houses and a granary (also the shaft grave circle) lay just inside the citadel wall. The mass of the population lived below in a conglomeration of houses of varying size, simply constructed of sun-dried brick, with flat roofs and beaten earth floors. None of these houses is still standing, but unearthed fragments suggest that some of them had painted decorations. In

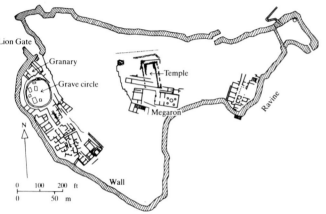

2,53 Plan of the citadel, Mycenae.

2,54 Lion Gate, Mycenae, c. 1500–1300 BC. Limestone relief, about 9ft 6ins (2.9m) high.

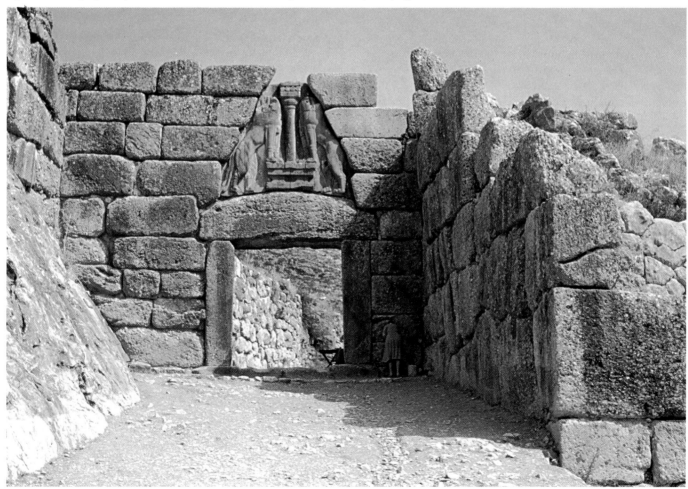

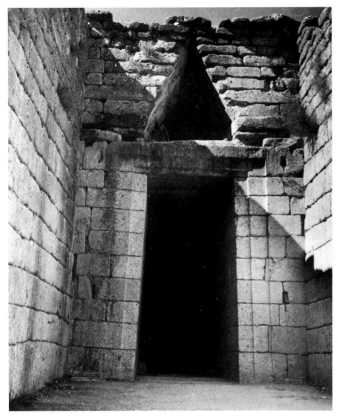

2,55 'Treasury of Atreus', Mycenae, c. 1300 BC.

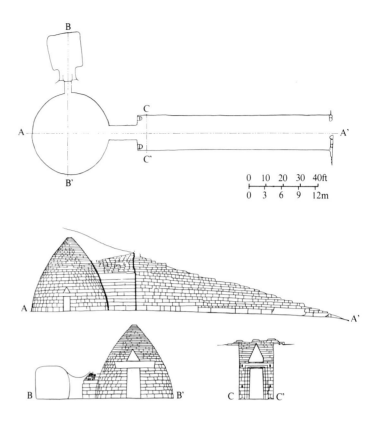

2,56 Plan and three cross-sections of the 'Treasury of Atreus', Mycenae.

times of danger the people presumably moved up to the citadel. The same general system (similar to that established earlier at Troy) was followed at Tiryns with variations conditioned by the nature of the site. The contrast between these forbidding hilltop fortresses and the very lightly defended cities and palaces of Minoan Crete could hardly be more striking. Similarities with the Hittite fortifications at Boghazköy in Anatolia, on the other hand, are quite evident (see pp. 90–1).

The citadel walls, especially, are overpoweringly impressive – obviously intended to look, as well as be, impregnable. Built of earth and rubble, they were faced with massive rough-hewn blocks later called Cyclopean because they seemed to have been set in place by the mythical one-eyed giant Cyclops. The main gate at Mycenae is constructed of three giant megaliths – i.e. a trilithon, as at Stonehenge (see p. 48) – with a carved panel filling a relieving arch above (a false arch made by corbelling the blocks of the wall to relieve the lintel stone of the trilithon from the weight of the superstructure) (2,54). As bold and forceful as the building it adorns, this carving is the most imposing example of Mycenean sculpture to survive; but its precise significance is unknown. The central column could be either a dynastic or a religious symbol, and although the two headless creatures heraldically posed on either side are usually described as lions, they may well have been sphinxes or griffins with human or bird heads of bronze, colored stone or some other medium. (The heads were attached separately.)

Originally the effect must have been much harsher than what appears today.

In comparison with the gigantic monumentality of the walls, the palaces seem small. The main room in each was a megaron, at the most 40 feet (12m) square. In Greek the word means simply 'large room', but it is now used technically to describe one of a specific form: a square or oblong chamber with a central hearth and usually four columns to support the roof, the lateral walls projecting forward beyond the entrance wall to form the sides of a porch, which is usually columned. Sometimes a second entrance wall, with a single opening like the first, is added at the back, but always within the same lateral walls. Neolithic dwellings in northern Greece were approximately of this form, but the regular megaron is first found at Troy in the middle of the third millennium. (It does not appear to have been used on Crete before the conquest of the island and the two so-called 'megarons' at Knossos are simply 'large rooms'.)

The Mycenean, or Helladic, civilization seems to have exploited Minoan art just as it did the Minoan syllabary for the Linear B script. But sometimes it did more, developing and transforming Minoan forms, most notably in tholos tombs (see Glossary). As we have seen (p. 48), tombs with corbelled roofs or 'false domes' had been built as early as the fifth millennium in northern Europe. But neither they nor the tholoi of Crete prepare one for the geometrical precision and grandeur of the royal tombs at Mycenae. This type of tomb, consisting of a passage dug

The Homeric World

When a life-size gold mask, flattened but with an air of supreme self-confidence even in death, was found at Mycenae in 1876, its discoverer Heinrich Schliemann telegraphed to the king of Greece: 'Today I have looked on the face of Agamemnon' (**2,57**). Schliemann, a retired German businessman with a passion for Homer, had convinced himself that the *Iliad* and *Odyssey* had historical origins. With the poems as his guide, he located at Hissarlik, on the Anatolian coast of Turkey, the remains of a city which he identified as Troy. Searching for the palace of Agamemnon, he then began to excavate at Mycenae in central Greece. In both places he brought to light gold and bronze artifacts which he associated with the Homeric heroes. Assisted by a trained archeologist, Wilhelm Dörpfeld, he kept careful records of stratigraphy, the layers of material culture revealed by excavation; but they were eventually to undermine his Homeric theories. The so-called mask of Agamemnon is now known to have been made in about 1500 BC; the city that he believed to have been Troy flourished around 2500–2000 BC; and a later layer identified by Dörpfeld was destroyed in about 1275 BC. Almost half a millennium of the Greek dark ages was to pass before the *Iliad* and *Odyssey* were composed for recitation; and they cannot have been written down much before 650 BC.

2,57 Mask from Mycenae, shaft grave V, c. 1500 BC. Gold, 10ins (25.4cm) high. National Museum, Athens.

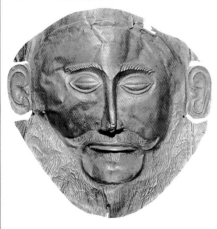

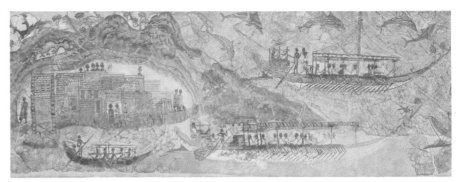

2,58 *The Flotilla*, detail of frieze, Akrotiri, Thera (Santorini), c. 1550 BC. Fresco, 17ins (43.2cm) high. National Museum, Athens.

Like most epics the *Iliad* and *Odyssey* evoke a heroic age set in a distant past but related in terms that their original audiences would have understood. Much of the life described is that of the centuries immediately before their composition; yet there are elements that seem to have been drawn from earlier epics or folk memories. However, few of the rich and superbly wrought artifacts described in the poems recall the impoverished Greece of the dark ages. Agamemnon's armour, for instance, included a breast-plate on which there were '10 bands of dark enamel and 12 of gold and 20 of tin, and serpents of dark enamel stretched up towards the neck'. The even more elaborate shield of Achilles probably owed more to poetic licence than to observation. The only surviving artifact that can be associated with anything described in the epics is 'Nestor's Cup', a simple, rather battered gold cup found at Mycenae, with doves perched on its handles as had that mentioned in the *Iliad*.

Painted decorations at Mycenae and Tiryns survive in fragments only but they have affinities with wall-paintings on Crete and the much better preserved paintings at Akrotiri. These date from shortly before 1570–1550 BC and give a unique glimpse of life in the eastern Mediterranean at this date. One frieze depicts a flotilla being rowed across a sea where dolphins play (**2,58**). It may be a trading expedition though one of the ships is so richly dressed as to suggest some ceremonial occasion, perhaps a

wedding. The human figures are small, but in other paintings they are almost life-size, as in those of the fisherman (**2,45**) and a saffron gatherer (**2,59**). It would be easy to imagine that Nausicaa, when Odysseus met her on the shores of Scheria, looked like this Theran island girl; and the ships mentioned in the *Iliad*, including the ten sent by the king of Crete, may well have been similar to those depicted at Akrotiri. But to judge from the paintings – and there is no other evidence – life at Akrotiri was very different from that evoked by the Homeric epics. They record a peaceful community of traders and fishermen far removed from the Homeric world of heroic muscular warriors and alluring strong-willed women.

2,59 *Saffron Gatherer*, detail of wall-painting, Akrotiri, c. 1550 BC. National Museum, Athens.

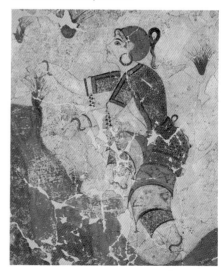

into the side of a hill and terminating in a chamber of beehive shape, was adopted from the late sixteenth century BC onwards for royal burials at Mycenae, where the remains of a dozen survive – and there are a few more elsewhere, the most notable at Orchomenos, north of the Gulf of Corinth.

The 'Treasury of Atreus' or 'Tomb of Agamemnon' at Mycenae is by far the finest. It is approached along a passage (technically called the *dromos*), the sides of which are lined with rectangular, hammer-dressed blocks of a dark-gray stone (**2,56**). An entrance slightly tapering towards the top, with a massive lintel weighing about 120 tons (122,000kg) and a relieving triangle above, leads into the tomb (**2,55**). Originally this entrance façade was decorated with engaged columns of green limestone slightly tapering downwards and crisply carved with ornament – zigzags, beading, fluting and Minoan spiral patterns. The relieving triangle was filled with carved panels of dark-red, pink and green stone. The tomb chamber is now very austere but bronze nails indicate that it, too, had some form of applied decoration. Simply as a piece of engineering this great domed space is remarkable, for each of the massive stone blocks of which it is constructed must have been very carefully shaped according to precise calculations to resist the pressure of those above and on either side as well as to provide a perfectly smooth interior surface. Measuring 47½ feet (14.5m) in diameter and 43 feet (13m) in height, it is the largest unsupported covered space built anywhere before the erection of the Pantheon in Rome about a millennium and a half later. But it is more than just a technical feat: it is a work of architecture of imposing nobility and dignity. This great monument is a reminder that the Mycenean civilization should not be dismissed – as it sometimes is – simply as a postscript to the Minoan. Whether it can be hailed as a prelude to that of Classical Greece presents a more difficult problem.

The economic system on which Mycenean civilization was based began to break down by about 1300 BC. A change in climate affecting agriculture may have been the initial cause, but before the end of the thirteenth century BC there was an invasion by people from the north, named Dorians in later literature. This was part of a major movement of population which caused havoc throughout the whole of the eastern Mediterranean, bringing about the fall of the Hittite civilization in Anatolia as well as threatening Egypt (see p. 90). A massive wall seems to have been built across the isthmus of Corinth, but this final monument of Helladic architectural engineering was unable to stem the tide of invaders and prevent the devastation of the Peloponnese. Cities were sacked, palaces destroyed. Civilization was snuffed out and with it the art of writing. But the ruins of the great Helladic citadels survived, inspiring myths and legends which have come down to us in the form of poetry, the greatest epics ever written: the *Iliad* and *Odyssey* of Homer composed in the eighth and seventh centuries BC, the *Odes* of Pindar and the supreme achievements of Classical Greek drama by Aeschylus, Sophocles and Euripides of the fifth century BC.

China

Only one of the Bronze Age civilizations – that of China – can be clearly recognized as having been the first stage in a long process of cultural evolution which has continued without a single significant break up to the present day. Chinese civilization has withstood both revolutions inside the country and invasions from outside. Time and again conquerors have found themselves engulfed and eventually overcome by it. For nearly 4,000 years Chinese art has retained its characteristic forms, its distinctive virtues and qualities and its unique and immediately recognizable flavour. This is not to suggest that it was rigidly monolithic, like that of ancient Egypt. From a very early stage it has shown great flexibility – like the bamboo that Chinese sages admired for bending without breaking (they also praised jade for breaking without bending). Tradition and innovation counterbalanced one another in an art whose history is marked by frequent revivals of past forms and by the no less frequent absorption and transformation of new and sometimes foreign styles and techniques.

The Neolithic cultures of China made fine pottery at least as early as the fourth millennium BC: rotund bowls and vases with incised or painted decorations, the latter sometimes figurative, have been found over a wide area of central China. It is comparable to the prehistoric pottery of the ancient Near East, Indus Valley, Predynastic Egypt and Japan. (Some Japanese pottery is earlier and, dating from the eighth millennium BC, possibly the earliest in

Ancient China

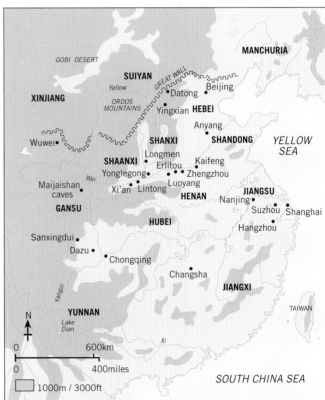

the world; a process of modelling slabs of worked clay into vessels and firing them was practised from that date.) Neolithic Chinese pieces include vessels of complex form, notably jugs resting on three bulbous feet like inverted pears. From the third millennium BC pottery was made on the fast wheel, either introduced from the West or invented independently – the device enabling a potter to shape a vessel by throwing a lump of clay on to a spinning turntable which provides the centrifugal force to raise it into a hollow form. On the east coast, south of the Yangzi river, the people of the so-called Longshan cultures made bowls and cups of extraordinarily complex shapes and of an almost paper-thin black ware, surely intended for ceremonial rather than daily use.

Jade working was also mastered in the third millennium by people living on the east coast. This is doubly remarkable as the stone is so hard that it can be shaped and decorated only by working with abrasives (not by carving); moreover, since jade is not found in China it had to be imported from central Asia or, more probably, Siberia. Prehistoric jades include axe-heads, daggers, bracelets, pendants and also two rather mysterious types of object: a tube squared on the outside, called a *zong* (**2,60**), and a disc with a large but not quite central hole, called a *bi*. The *zong* was later said to be used in worshipping Earth, the *bi* for worshipping heaven. And *bi* were to remain for millennia instruments of imperial sacrifice to heaven. The admiration for jade as a substance, which provoked an almost mystically reverent passion, later to develop into a kind of lyrical ecstasy peculiar to the Chinese, began with these Neolithic craftsmen of the fourth millennium living in village communities of farmers and landworkers whose descendants were to maintain for several thousand years the same peasant way of life and manner of work.

SHANG DYNASTY

According to the traditional history of China, as formulated by imperial chroniclers in the second century BC, dynastic rule began in the valley of the Yellow River with the Xia who were succeeded by the Shang and then by the Zhou in a linear sequence from which later rulers derived their authority. No reference was made to a contemporaneous state in the upper valley of the Yangzi though one flourished there throughout the second millennium BC with its centre at modern Sanxingdui, north of Chengdu, an area which had been incorporated into the Chinese empire by the time the first histories were written, hence its omission from them. Recent excavations at Sanxingdui have brought to light numerous imposing, expertly cast bronze sculptures dating from c. 1200–1000 BC: huge glowering masks, human-like heads (**2,61**) and a life-size

2,61 Human-like head, from Sanxingdui, China, c. 1200–1000 BC. Bronze, 14½ins (36.7cm) high. Institute of Archaeology, Sichuan province.

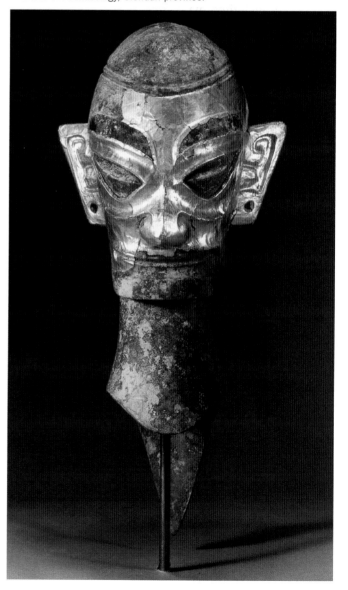

2,60 *Zong*, c. 2500 BC. Jade, 8ins (20.3cm) high. British Museum, London.

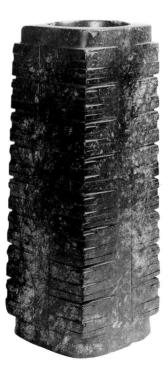

statue of a man in a delicately patterned robe – king, priest or deity – quite unlike anything known to have been produced in other parts of China, where anthropomorphic sculpture is conspicuous by its rarity until much later. They were found on the site of a large ancient city in rectangular sacrificial pits filled also with objects of jade and gold and elephant tusks, demonstrating great material wealth. But nothing is known and little can be deduced of their presumably ritual purpose and religious significance.

The Chinese Bronze Age civilization that flourished under the Shang dynasty has, on the other hand, been illuminated by a series of archeological discoveries which began in the 1920s and are still being made. Rulers who, from the accounts of ancient chroniclers, seemed to be as mythical as Homer's heroes, have now been revealed as historical figures. Two of the most notable were Ding, who enlarged his kingdom c. 1200 BC, and his consort Fu Hao, a remarkable woman who presided over important rituals, influenced political decisions, led victorious military campaigns and was buried with a hoard of valuable grave goods including many articles of personal adornment. At more than 100 sites over a wide area from north of the Yellow River to south of the Yangzi, excavations have yielded artifacts with a family resemblance to one another and some with an ancestral relationship to bronze vessels of later date, revealing a common culture and shared set of beliefs. The earliest come from Erlitou near Luoyang where there are remains of urban walls and the foundations of a large palatial or religious building dated c. 1700–1500 BC. The name of the place is now used for the initial phase of Shang art – or the last of the preceding Xia period, about which little is as yet known. The relationship between later urban complexes of the Shang period (c. 1500–1050 BC), whether they formed part of a single realm or were independent like Greek city states, is unknown. There can be little doubt, however, of the importance of the cities outside modern Zhengzhou and at Anyang – both, like Erlitou, in Henan, which was to be the heartland of the Chinese empire until the twelfth century AD.

The cities of Zhengzhou and Anyang were laid out on rectangular grid plans, oriented north, south, east and west, surrounded by walls of pisé (earth and gravel rammed between planks which could be subsequently removed), about 20 yards (18m) thick at Zhengzhou, very much less at Anyang. While Zhengzhou was more than a mile (1.6km) across, Anyang was much smaller and seems to have been less a population centre than an administrative capital. Buildings were rectangular, constructed of timber columns and beams with walls of pisé and gabled thatched roofs – unlike the almost subterranean shelters of northern China and also the houses raised on piles in the south. The more important – palaces or temples – were raised on platforms of rammed earth, symmetrically planned on a north–south axis and set apart from ordinary dwellings. At Zhengzhou the potters, jade carvers, metalworkers and other craftsmen occupied distinct quarters of the city. Royal tombs at Anyang, large pits with stairs or ramps leading down to them from the points of the compass, were opulently furnished with jewelry and precious objects of jade and bronze, as well as with the chariots, weapons and other possessions of the deceased. Human beings were slaughtered to accompany a dead ruler: the skeletons of 22 men and 24 women have been found in a single tomb together with those of 16 horses and numerous dogs, surrounded by small pits containing another 50 human skulls.

Further light is thrown on the Shang period by bones (usually ox shoulder-blades) engraved or inscribed with symbols, many of which are early forms of the Chinese script still in use to this day. These 'oracle bones', of which more than 100,000 survive either whole or in fragments, were used for divination and the sentences written on them ask questions about such topics as the health of the ruler, the weather, auspicious moments for hunting or warfare, and, perhaps most important of all, what sacrifices should be made to the ancestors, from whom the ruling class derived its authority. Thus it seems that writing was first used in China not for temple or palace accounts (as in Mesopotamia and the Aegean) nor for monumental inscriptions (as in ancient Egypt), but for communications with the other world. And this may well have influenced the later development of Chinese calligraphy as an art form, to which almost superstitious reverence was paid, another constant and distinguishing feature of Chinese civilization.

No Bronze Age civilization is more appropriately named than that of Shang China. Bronze, from which vessels were made for the rituals of ancestor-worship, had a significance both religious and social. Except for a few marble sculptures, all its finest surviving works of art are in this metal. Other materials were used and with great skill, but without the creative power concentrated on bronze. Shang tombs have also yielded jade carvings, especially ritual knives with turquoise-studded handles, woven silks known only from the impressions left on objects wrapped in them, and some very handsome glazed pottery vessels. For the most part the bronzes are ritual vessels used in sacrifices to royal ancestors and both the technical process by which they were made and the artistic forms are peculiar to China at this date.

Bronze had been made in China well before the end of the second millennium BC and although it was more extensively produced in the Near East, the Balkans and the Aegean, there is very little likelihood that the technique was transmitted across Asia. The necessary metals for the alloy (copper and tin) were readily available to the Chinese, who had also developed kilns for firing pottery and thus had the technical means at hand for smelting. Metal-workers of the West and Near East fashioned their bronzes by casting in packed sand or, for more delicate effects, by using the lost-wax or cire perdue process (see Glossary). The Chinese also developed lost-wax casting but only for small pieces. For large vessels they adopted the much more laborious method of piece-molding, in a peculiar form combining ceramic and metallurgical techniques. It was rapidly brought to an astonishing degree of refinement. From a technical point of view, no more accomplished bronze casting has ever been achieved than in Shang dynasty China. A model of the ritual vessel with the bolder forms of the desired decoration was first made, probably of clay cut and carved as if it were stone. Negative impressions of this were taken by pressing slabs of clay on to the model, piece by piece. After further and more delicate decorations had been incised on them, these piece-molds were fired, in itself a tricky undertaking if the precision of the relief was not to be lost. They were then assembled to form a whole mold, into which the molten alloy was poured. The vessel was finished by replacing the spillage of metal at the seams of the mold with vertical flanges, which also have a decorative effect.

The shapes of these vessels were basically derived from household utensils in other media, usually pottery, but elaborated to exploit the potentialities of metal. There were about 30 types ranging in size from 6 inches or so (15cm) to more than 4 feet (120cm) high and weighing up to some 2,000 pounds (900kg). Each had a specific purpose in ritual sacrifices of food and wine to ancestors. One, called a *ding*, was for food, and inscriptions on oracle bones include such proposals for sacrifice as: 'Third, in a *ding* vessel a dog. Fourth a pig', and so on. A *ding* might be either a kind of three-legged cauldron or a massive rectangular trough on four stumpy cylindrical legs. There were dishes for ritual ablutions, vases, cups and ewers for hot black millet wine. Perhaps the most remarkable in its combination of dignity with fierce, almost animal, vitality is the *jue*, a libation cup which developed from a somewhat gawky early version found at Zhengzhou into a form of wonderful poise which seems almost to dance on its three pointed feet (**2,62**).

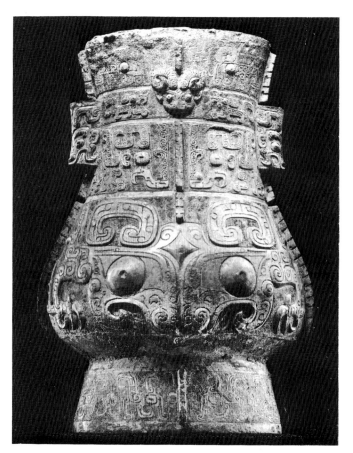

2,63 Ritual wine vessel or *hu*, c. 1300–1100 BC. Bronze, 16ins (40.6cm) high, 11ins (27.9cm) wide. Nelson-Atkins Museum of Art, Kansas City (Purchase: Nelson Trust).

2,62 Ritual goblet or *jue*, 1122–947 BC. Bronze, 9⁷/₈ins (25cm) high. Metropolitan Museum of Art, New York.

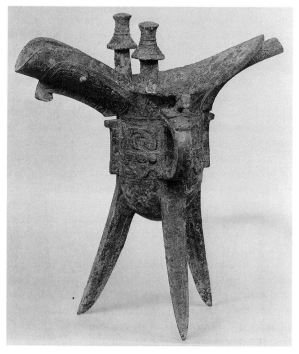

In the shape and, even more clearly, in the surface decoration of these extraordinary vessels a peculiarly Chinese, or rather Shang, sense of form is felt very strongly. Form is interpreted in terms of rounded rectangles, everything following this principle. There is complete consistency and inner coherence, as if these strange shapes had been produced by some primitive organic process such as created the regular, but never exactly repetitive, markings on the carapaces or bony shells and horny skins of certain reptiles. Flat and essentially linear, Shang forms have, nevertheless, great visual weight and solidity. They are never inert or flaccid – an inner tension is felt as if something suppressed was about to break through the surface and disrupt the solemn rhythms of the slowly unfurling patterns. As far as is known, this peculiar and very distinctive sense of form occurs nowhere but in Chinese art – and in early American art, a coincidence that may not be quite as odd as it might seem at first, as we shall see.

The decoration on these ritual vessels had a significance that has been very variously and sometimes contradictorily interpreted by Chinese writers from the third century BC onwards and by sinologists of our own time. A kind of dragon mask with two round eyes which had been incised on some Longshan jades was elaborated into a prominent motif later called a *taotie* and described variously as a storm god, a wine god, a monster who

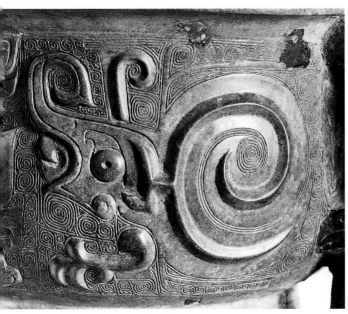

2,64 Detail of *gui*, 12th–11th century BC. Bronze.
Ashmolean Museum, Oxford.

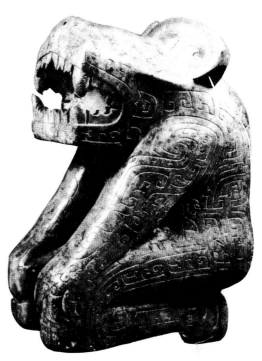

2,65 Tiger-headed monster, from Xibeigang near Anyang,
1400–1100 BC. 14³/₈ins (36.5cm) high. Academia Sinica, Taipei
(Taibei), Taiwan.

attempted to devour humankind or an emblem of fecundity – though there is no contemporary evidence for the significance of this or any other motifs on Shang bronzes. It might seem, at first, to be the face of a monster combining features of the pacific ox or water-buffalo with those of a ferocious tiger (**2,63**). Closer inspection reveals, however, that it can be read in an entirely different way: as two dragons in profile confronting one another, nose to nose, each with a single leg and clawed foot. Yet these two creatures are so perfectly symmetrical that they may alternatively be read as the two sides of a single dragon split lengthwise from head to curling tail (**2,64**). The almost uncannily similar 'fearful symmetry' of very much later carvings and paintings by the Indians of northwest America and the Maori in New Zealand are certainly to be understood in this way, as conceptual renderings of animals or animal faces in two profiles (see Chapter 18). And this coincidence, combined with the even stranger and even more striking affinities in their sense of form, mentioned above, has led to theories about some common origin or some direct contact between early China and North America.

Whatever the cause of these affinities and whatever the original significance of the Shang bronze vessels, their relief decoration reveals an astonishing ability to create forms with a life of their own. Chinese artists did not simply graft naturalistically rendered human and animal members on to one another to create compound images, like the Egyptian sphinx (p. 66) or the winged bulls of

Assyria (see pp. 107–8). They produced far more complex hybrids by integrating claws, beaks, wings, scales and fur to create what might be termed a mythozoology. Sometimes whole vessels were cast in the form of such monsters with dragons and reptiles swarming over their bodies. A wine-mixer, for instance, with eyes in the horns on its head, has linear representations of crocodiles and dragons on its sides and, on the top, the body of a snake joined to the three-dimensional head. Similar equivocal creatures carved in stone include one with tiger-like jaws and paws found in a tomb near Anyang. Despite a certain squat solidity, it has a contained muscular force, the ferocity of a real animal, although resembling none (**2,65**). This quality is no less evident in bronze and stone figures of real animals, though few date from before the end of the Shang period in the late eleventh century BC (see p. 116).

Vitality rather than verisimilitude (appearance of truth), let alone illusionism, was always to be a prime aim of Chinese artists. A myth records that a great Chinese painter drew a horse with such vigour that his drawing jumped off the paper. The story of the ancient Greek painter who depicted cherries so illusionistically that even the birds were deceived and came to peck at them neatly expresses an essential difference between attitudes to the arts in the East and West.

CHAPTER THREE

DEVELOPMENTS ACROSS THE CONTINENTS

THE HITTITES

'But, my brother, please send me a sculptor. As soon as he has finished the statues I will send him back and he will be with you again. Have I not sent back the previous sculptor? Have I not kept my word? My brother, do not deny me this sculptor.' So wrote Hattusilis III, ruler of the Hittite kingdom in Anatolia from 1275 to 1250 BC, to the Kassite king of Babylon, 1,000 miles (1,600km) away. What these sculptors did is unknown and they are as anonymous as all artists were to remain for several centuries (with a very few Egyptian exceptions). The letter is of interest for the light it throws on their position as valued royal servants and for the evidence it provides of cultural contacts in the Near East around the middle of the second millennium BC. It also implies some degree of discrimination – if only between the work of sculptors available in Anatolia and that of the Babylonians. The letter comes from a royal archive of cuneiform tablets which contains a great deal of diplomatic correspondence between the Hittite kings and their 'brothers' (as they were politely addressed), the rulers of Babylon, Assyria and Egypt.

The Hittites, a people who spoke an Indo-European language, infiltrated Anatolia from the east early in the second millennium BC. About 1600 BC a Hittite king advanced down the Euphrates and sacked Babylon (see p. 58), but then withdrew again to the rocky plateau of Anatolia. By the mid-fifteenth century BC the Hittites had become one of the major powers in the Near East, with much of Syria under their sway. After a great battle at Kadesh in 1286–1285 BC between Hittites and Egyptians a treaty was drawn up defining, in prophetically modern terms, their respective zones of influence either side of a line running through Syria.

Some of these foreign contacts were reflected in the culture of the Hittites. Although they had their own pictographic script, they took over cuneiform from Mesopotamia and, for official communications, wrote in Akkadian as the diplomatic language (rather as Latin was to be in medieval Europe). In the visual arts, influences from ancient Egypt are apparent in motifs such as the sphinx and winged solar disc (see p. 100), as well as from Babylon and neighbouring Syria. Indeed, there is some doubt as to whether some small objects are of Hittite or Syrian origin. Hittite art has a very distinctive character of its own, nevertheless.

The capital city, Hattusha, near the present-day Turkish village of Boghazköy, was founded about 1600 BC

The visual arts	Historical landmarks
c. 1480 BC Funerary temple of Queen Hatshepsut (3,11)	c. 1570 BC Beginning of New Kingdom in Egypt
1417–1379 BC Temple of Amun-Re, Luxor (3,12)	c. 1500 BC Development of loom weaving in Peru
c. 1400 BC Royal Gate, Boghazköy (3,1)	c. 1400 BC Emergence of Olmec civilization in Mesoamerica
c. 1375 BC Akhenaten (3,15)	1379–1362 BC Akhenaten king of Egypt
c. 1360 BC Nefertiti (3,16)	
c. 1340 BC Mummy-case of Tutenkhamun (3,18)	
c. 1300 BC Statuettes from Xochipala (3,45)	1285 BC Egyptians and Hittites define zones of influence
c. 1257 BC Abu Simbel (3,19)	
c. 1250–1220 BC Tudhaliyas IV relief (3,3)	
c. 1150 BC Tomb of Sennedjem (3,20)	
c. 900 BC Zhou dynasty bronze tiger (3,39). Lanzón, Chavín de Huántar (3,55)	c. 1100 BC Phoenicians develop alphabetic script
	1027 BC Beginning of Zhou dynasty rule in China
	883 BC Assurnasirpal expands Assyrian empire
c. 720 BC Lamassu from Khorsabad (3,26)	
c. 650 BC Relief from Nineveh (3,30)	612 BC Fall of Assyrian empire. Nabopolassar king of Babylon
c. 575 BC Ishtar Gate from Babylon (3,32)	550 BC Cyrus the Great king of Persia
	539 BC Babylon falls to Persia
c. 500 BC Persepolis (3,35)	525 BC Egypt falls to Persia
before 400 BC Olmec head (3,48)	490 BC Persian expedition against Greece defeated at Marathon
c. 400 BC Nok terracotta head (3,57)	c. 475 BC Beginning of Warring States period in China

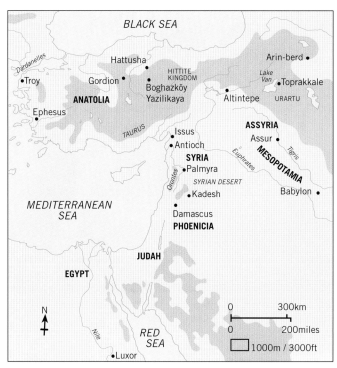

Ancient Asia Minor

over the charred ruins of an earlier, partly Assyrian, settlement destroyed about 1700 BC. From the beginning it seems to have had an axial plan and regular rectangular houses separated by paved paths. Foundations of five temples have been found. Each had an interior courtyard surrounded by many small rooms with windows on the outer walls. Their general effect must, therefore, have been very different from that of the closed and inward-looking temples of Mesopotamia and Egypt. The most impressive remains at Boghazköy and other Hittite sites are, however, the massive walls, built about 1400 BC, of coarse masonry with rubble filling and an upper level of sun-dried brick forming casemates and parapet walks. This defensive architecture is in some ways akin to that of Mycenae and Tiryns (see p. 82). At Boghazköy there was also a no less massive inner wall surrounding the citadel on a rock dominating the city. Emphasis was laid on defence and long underground passages led from the centre of the city to sally ports, from which a besieging army could be attacked. Yet the fortifications also had symbolic features.

The exterior faces of the monolithic jambs of the main entrances – themselves of an unusual parabolic or half-oval form – were carved in such a way that huge sphinxes or lions seem to be protruding out of them, in a strange combination of relief and sculpture in the round (3,1). They are far more intimately joined to the structure than

3,1 Royal Gate, Boghazköy, Turkey, c. 1400 BC.

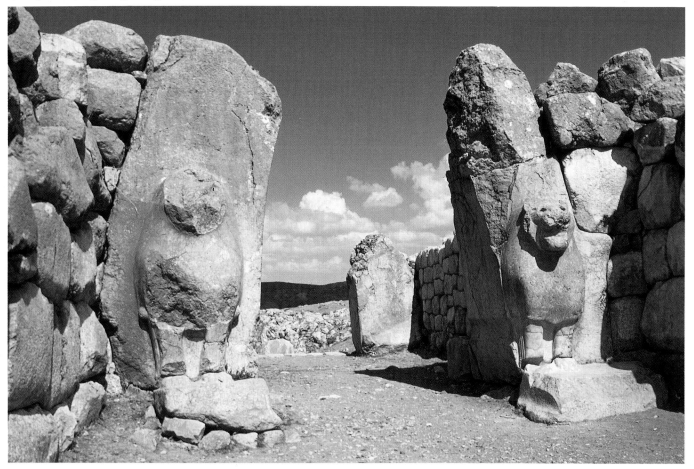

are the guardian figures in ancient Egypt and Meso-potamia. In fact, there are no precedents for these semi-engaged sculptures. And the idea of making them form part of a building, later to be taken up with great effect in Assyria, also seems to have originated with the Hittites. At Boghazköy, the outer jamb of the Royal Gate is carved in such a high relief (see Glossary) that the sturdy muscular figure of Teshub, the weather god, might well be described as a half-statue. The face is free for more than half its depth (**3,2**). Carved orthostats (slabs of stone set upright at the base of a wall) similarly made their first recorded appearance in Hittite architecture and were also later adopted and much elaborated by the Assyrians (see p. 108).

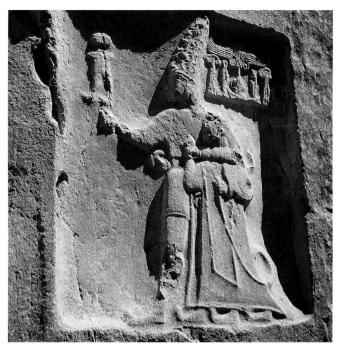

3,3 King Tudhaliyas IV protected by a god, Yazilikaya, Turkey, c. 1250–1220 BC. About 7ft (2.13m) high.

3,2 Figure of a god, Royal Gate, outer jamb, Boghazköy, Turkey, c. 1400 BC.

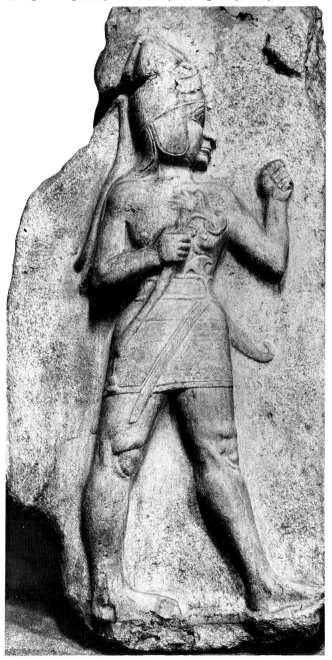

In the religious texts surviving on tablets from the royal archive, the Hittites frequently referred to their 'thousand gods', among whom the most important seems to have been the weather god or storm god – as befitted the inhabitants of this high, windswept country. Their most important shrine was less than 2 miles (3.5km) from Boghazköy, at Yazilikaya, where a natural outcrop of rock was converted into an extraordinary open-air sanctuary. There were buildings here (of which only traces remain), but they must have been dwarfed by the peaks of sur-rounding rock. The grandeur of the natural setting does not, however, diminish the power of the relatively small reliefs carved on the rock-face, which suggest, despite their being framed within reserved panels, the super-natural forces latent within. Two long rectangular panels represent gods and goddesses apparently walking in procession. One of the best preserved carvings is in a cleft or chamber of the rock and shows King Tudhaliyas IV (c. 1250–1200 BC) protected by a god wearing a long robe and tall, horned hat (**3,3**). Egyptian influence is apparent here in the winged disc which crowns the hieroglyphs meaning 'My sun, my Great King' and which, as in ancient Egypt, signified an aspect of the solar deity associated with king-ship. Both god and king stand in the so-called 'Egyptian pose', which was, of course, common throughout the Near East. (The procession of goddesses in pure profile at Yazilikaya is among the few exceptions.) Yet in its general effect this sculpture is markedly different from ancient Egyptian reliefs; it has none of their elegant linearity. In the sturdy, big-boned robustness of its forms it is much more like sculpture in the round. There is, too, a different sense of spirituality in this image of divine protection, something at once solemnly religious and almost tenderly natural in the way the god holds his arm around the neck and clasps the up-raised wrist of the king, who was also his priest. This carving in a mountain cleft, where the king's remains may have been buried, has reminded more than one modern traveller of the words of the Psalmist: 'Yea, though I walk through the valley of the shadow of death, I will fear no evil: for thou art with me; thy rod and thy staff comfort me.'

THE DISCOVERY OF IRON

With their vigorous relief sculptures and massively walled cities, the Hittites made notable contributions to the visual arts in the Near East. They also exploited bronze and the natural alloy electrum for animal statuettes. In the perspective of world history, however, these achievements are overshadowed by a technological innovation of an importance hard to exaggerate: the working of iron. Iron was being produced in Anatolia (see Map) at least as early as the fifteenth century BC. Iron differs from bronze in that it is a pure metal, not an alloy, and in that its ores are very widely distributed throughout the world. Few of the Bronze Age civilizations had large enough supplies of both copper and tin to make the alloy (bronze) without importing one or both of them. As foreign trade was a royal prerogative and mines were also monopolized by rulers, the supply of bronze implements and weapons could be controlled. But to make iron all that was needed were the ubiquitous ores, a simple charcoal furnace – and the knowledge that the spongy mass to which the ore was reduced under heat could be compacted into bars by hammering and then wrought into sickles and ploughshares, lances and swords. Armies could thus be equipped much more easily than hitherto, and those of the civilized states lost the great advantage that bronze weapons had given them. Iron also had the important military advantage of breaking less easily than bronze on impact. The Hittites do not, however, appear to have exploited the new material in the visual arts, though it made available a new range of tools for builders and sculptors. Nor did iron weapons prevent the disintegration of their empire, about 1200 BC, during the period of unrest and population movement in which Helladic civilization was snuffed out in Greece.

THE NEW KINGDOM IN ANCIENT EGYPT

In the period known as the New Kingdom (1570–1085 BC), under pharaohs of the eighteenth, nineteenth and twentieth dynasties, ancient Egypt rose to the summit of its power and wealth and the arts were more lavishly patronized than ever before, or after. It began with the expulsion of people from Asia, later called the Hyksos, who had settled in Lower Egypt during the later years of the Middle Kingdom and seized power in the delta about 1670 BC. As soon as the Hyksos had been driven out, about 1570 BC, Egypt embarked on an aggressive expansionist policy. Nubia with its gold mines was almost immediately annexed. Before 1500 BC the Egyptians advanced west into Libya and east into Asia, as far as the Euphrates on one occasion, creating an empire of tributary states even larger than that of the Hittites in the north.

Imperial expansion brought Egypt into closer contact than before with the Bronze Age civilizations of the Aegean and Near East. In the visual arts, a few foreign motifs made their appearances, notably that of horses with both forelegs in the air drawing two-wheeled chariots, as in relief carvings at Mycenae. The important innovations in the arts of the New Kingdom seem, however, to have been generated within Egypt itself, notably in tomb paintings, which now showed the deceased in scenes of daily life more freely painted than before.

Banquets were a favoured theme of the eighteenth dynasty, depicted with great liveliness and even abandon. A fragment of a painting from a tomb at Thebes shows a group of musicians and two sinuous naked girls performing a dance (**3,4**). Above there is the text of a spring-song:

> *The earth-god has implanted his beauty in every body.*
> *The Creator has done this with his two hands as*
>   *balm to his heart.*
> *The channels are filled with water anew*
> *And the land is flooded with his love.*

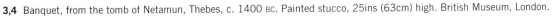

3,4 Banquet, from the tomb of Netamun, Thebes, c. 1400 BC. Painted stucco, 25ins (63cm) high. British Museum, London.

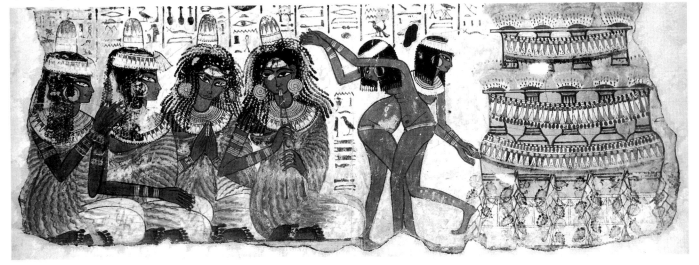

An inscription from another tomb develops the theme of awareness of death as an invitation to enjoy the pleasures of this life:

> *Follow thy desire as long as thou shalt live,*
> *Anoint thy head with myrrh and put fine linen on thee,*
> *Perfume thyself with the genuine marvels of divine oils!*
> *Enjoy thyself as much as thou canst . . .*
> *For a man cannot take his property with him*
> *For of those who depart not one comes back again.*

The mood of such texts is beautifully caught in paintings of banqueting scenes in the tomb chambers, where relatives of the deceased assembled for rituals – including anniversary banquets. Since the paintings were intended to be seen by the living, artists were free to diverge from the rules and formulae on which depended the semi-magical power of painted and carved figures made for burial with the dead (see p. 68). In the scene illustrated here, for instance, two of the musicians are full-face and we are even shown the soles of some of their feet! A sketch of a female acrobat on a flake of stone (called an ostracon – used for sketches, notes, etc. in lieu of papyrus) reveals the degree of naturalism eventually reached (**3,5**).

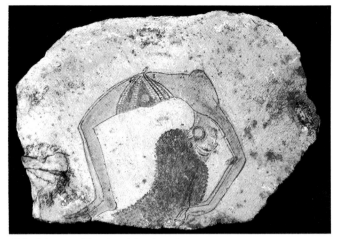

3,5 Ostracon with colored drawing of a tumbler, c. 1180 BC. Limestone, 6⅝ins (16.8cm) long. Museo Egizio, Turin.

The rather crumbly stone into which private tombs were dug in the necropolis near Thebes, the capital of the New Kingdom, was poor material for sculpture and paintings greatly outnumber relief carvings. Tombs were usually plastered to provide a surface for painting. However, the tomb of Ramose (vizier to Amenhotep III, 1417–1379 BC, and Amenhotep IV, 1379–1362 BC) was of harder rock

3,6 The brother of Ramose and his wife, c. 1370 BC. Limestone relief in the tomb of the Vizier Ramose, near Thebes.

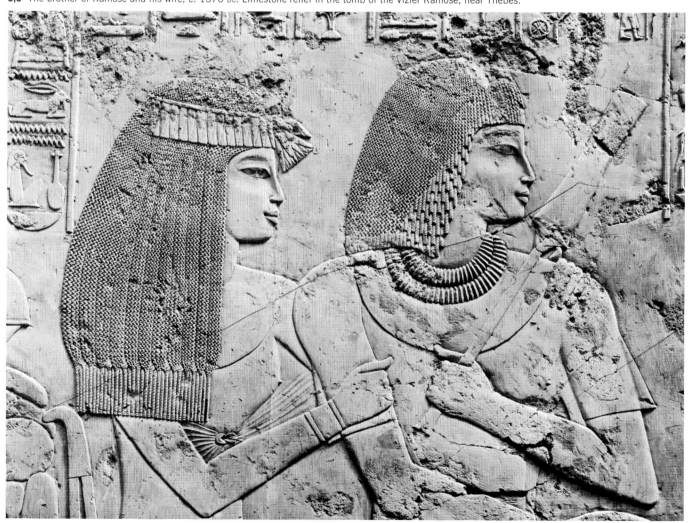

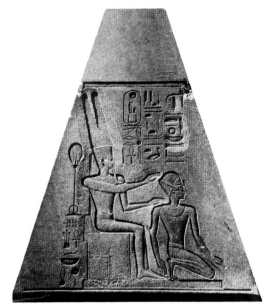

3,7 Queen Hatshepsut, c. 1480 BC. Sunk relief on fallen obelisk, Karnak.

and the ante-chamber is adorned with exceptionally fine reliefs. Ramose's brother and sister-in-law with their exquisitely modelled features are rendered with a rare combination of tenderness and sophisticated elegance

(**3,6**). The way in which the almost transparently diaphanous garments are carved to reveal the contours of the body beneath – a device that seems to have originated in the New Kingdom – suggests that the sculptor may have been influenced by paintings.

Other reliefs of the period are carved in a different technique, almost unique to ancient Egypt, which originated in the Old Kingdom – that of sunk relief. Outlines are incised in the stone and the figures cut back behind the surface so that they seem to be sunk into the block (**3,7**). Much used for large-scale architectural work intended to be seen in the open air, this technique exploited the strong shadows cast by dazzling sunlight to emphasize the image and to convert the inherent weakness of an essentially linear style of relief into its strength. For it is doubly effective – in simple bold outline when seen at a distance and with full, delicately modelled detail when seen close up. (It was also labour-saving, for it freed the sculptor from the necessity of working over the whole background to reduce it.) The combination of boldness and massive simplicity in general conception with the utmost refinement and delicacy of detail characterizes all art of the New Kingdom, in sculpture in the round as in sunk relief.

SOURCES AND DOCUMENTS

THUTMOSIS INSTRUCTS HIS VIZIER

Hieroglyphic inscriptions accompanying the reliefs in the tomb of Ramose (3,6) record his position as vizier, the highest official in the kingdom, under Amenhotep III and his successor Amenhotep IV, who changed his name to Akhenaten. Not all survive, however, and a fuller account of the duties of a vizier is found in the nearby tomb of his predecessor Rekhmire, vizier to Thutmosis III. Administration of justice was the most important function of the vizier and Rekhmire was instructed by Thutmosis not to be

. . . enraged toward a man unjustly, but be thou enraged concerning that about which one should be enraged; show forth the fear of thee; let one be afraid of thee, for a prince is a prince of whom one is afraid. Lo, the true dread of a prince is to do justice.

The vizier was also chief of police, minister of foreign affairs and, with the chief treasurer, controller of the finances of the kingdom. Architecture and the arts were also his responsibility and he even had to inspect in person the work of the royal artisans, those

. . . making all vessels for the divine limbs, multiplying vases of gold and silver in every manner of workmanship that endures for ever . . . . Bringing the Asiatic copper which his majesty captured in the victories of Retenu, in order to cast the two doors of the temple of

Amon at Karnak. Its pavement was overlaid with gold like the horizon of heaven . . . . Making chests of ivory, ebony, carob wood, meru wood and of cedar of the best.

Prisoners of war were employed on the temple of Amon at Karnak as brickmakers and bricklayers, 'building with ready fingers' according to the inscription, and Rekhmire oversaw their work:

. . . causing vigilance among the conquered who hear the saying of this official skillful in building works, giving regulations to their chiefs. They say: 'He supplies us with bread, beer and every good sort; he leads us with a loving heart for the king.' The taskmaster says to the builders: 'The rod is in my hand, be not idle.'

The not inconsiderable rewards of the office of vizier are evident in the lavishly furnished tombs of Rekhmire and especially Ramose. And there may be a note of self-justification in the inscription on the doorway to the latter.

I have arrived in peace at my tomb, possessed of the favor of the Good God. I did the pleasure of the king in my time; I did not disregard a single regulation which he commanded, I practiced no deceit against the people, in order that I might gain my tomb upon the great West of Thebes.

(J. H. Breasted, *Ancient Records of Egypt*, Chicago 1906, II)

Hatshepsut

WOMEN IN ANCIENT EGYPT

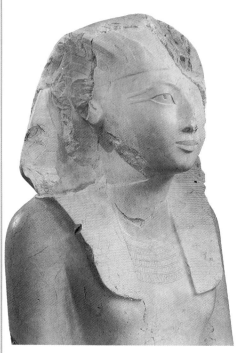

3,8 Head from a statue of Hatshepsut, before restoration, c. 1480 BC. Limestone, full seated statue 6ft 5ins (1.95m) high. Metropolitan Museum of Art, New York.

Hatshepsut was the most prominent of the several women who held positions of power in ancient Egypt. None ruled the realm for so long and no king commissioned a mortuary temple more grandiose than that at Deir el-Bahari which she built for her father Thutmosis I and herself (3,11). She raised there shrines for Amun-Re, the state god (see p. 98); Anubis, the jackal god of the necropolis; and Hathor, the cow-goddess, bringer of fertility and protector of women, whose origins may be traced back to the mother-goddesses worshipped throughout western Asia. In this way at Deir el-Bahari various strands of ancient Egyptian beliefs about divinity and divine royalty were woven into a seamless fabric

proclaiming Hatshepsut's right to rule. That the form given to the temple was innovatory may be no coincidence.

During the New Kingdom women in the royal line were given increasing importance, to judge from the rhetoric of inscriptions and representations, though the combination of pious fiction with historical fact in the former often makes their meaning far from clear. Since early times, however – probably from the beginning of the dynastic period – the roles of kings and queens, so often represented side by side in sculpture (2,33; 34), had been interdependent, as were those of gods and goddesses in creation myths. The creator god, who embodied both genders, produced by masturbation the first pair of male and female deities, those of air and moisture. Their progeny, the god and goddess of earth and sky, were the parents of the god Osiris and the goddess Isis, central figures in the ancient Egyptian pantheon. The union of Isis and Osiris was crucial to the whole Egyptian conception of cosmic harmony and it and other such marriages between divine siblings were reflected on earth by those between kings and their sisters, whether or not they were sexually consummated. Great prominence was also given to the king's mother in the rituals of court and temple, and in inscriptions she was stated to have been impregnated by the god Amun-Re. Royalty may therefore be said to have passed by matrilineal rather than patrilineal descent though this, like so much else in ancient Egypt, is open to more than one interpretation.

The complexity of the whole question of royal gender and its status in ancient Egypt is illustrated by the inscription Amosis (reigned c. 1570–1546 BC), founder of the eighteenth

dynasty and New Kingdom, had carved on a *stele* at Karnak to his mother Ahotep. This describes her as 'one who cares for Egypt. She has looked after Egypt's soldiers, she has brought back her fugitives, and collected together her deserters, she has pacified Upper Egypt, and expelled her rebels.' Though Ahotep's exercise of royal power may have been limited to her son's minority, it probably set a precedent. For Ahmose Nefertari, the principal wife and half-sister of Amosis, was accorded a role in the ritual of Amun-Re at Thebes and given the title of 'god's wife' with an endowment of land intended to be passed on from mothers to daughters.

3,9 Detail of mummy-case of Henout-oudjebou, c. 1375 BC. Wood painted and gilded, total length 6ft (1.83m). Washington University Gallery of Art, St Louis.

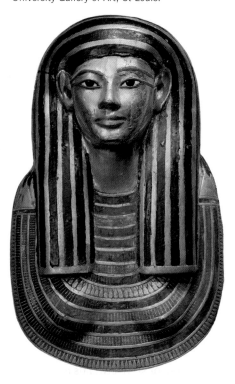

She was closely involved in the building activities of the king; and after her death she was deified and worshipped, until the end of the New Kingdom, by workmen employed on royal tombs in the Valley of the Kings. Her son became Amenophis I who had no male heir and was succeeded by Thutmosis I, the father of Hatshepsut, and the short-lived Thutmosis II. When the latter died in about 1504 BC his son succeeded as Thutmosis III but, as a chronicler of the time recorded, 'the god's wife Hatshepsut controlled the affairs of the land'.

After some seven years during which she acted as regent, Hatshepsut assumed the title of king, nominally ruling conjointly with her nephew, but for some 15 years she was the dominant partner. Described and represented as a king, she is indistinguishable outwardly, in costume and regalia, from Thutmosis III when they are represented together. Yet no attempt was made to disguise her sex or femininity. In the head that survives from a statue of her wearing male royal head-dress, her features are eminently feminine in their refinement (**3,8**). This was damaged towards the end of the long reign of Thutmosis III when images showing Hatshepsut as king (but not those in which she figured as a queen) were defaced. Sometimes the images were allowed to survive but the inscriptions were changed to eliminate her name, as on the obelisk which she had erected in the temple of Amun-Re at Karnak, where she kneels in front of Amun (3,7). Why this was done is unknown, but suspicion falls on the male priesthood's resentment at the central role in the cult having been taken over by a woman.

The role of women in ritual was circumscribed. In the Old and Middle Kingdoms upper-class women were sometimes called priestesses of Hathor but even in the cult of this goddess the prayers were read and the administration controlled by men. By the beginning of the New Kingdom, the priesthood had become as much a male preserve as the state bureaucracy and the title of priestess was no longer used. Perhaps as a gesture of compensation many of the wives and daughters of state officials and priests

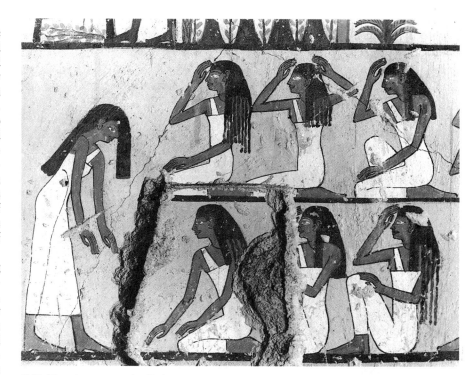

3,10 Mourning women, detail of wall-painting in the tomb of Minnakht, Thebes, c. 1480 BC.

were allowed a minor role in state and temple rituals. They were described as 'musicians', usually with the name of the deity whose cult they served. They were in charge of troupes of probably lower-class women who shook the rattles known as sistras, played tambourines and clapped their hands while the priest officiated, very much, no doubt, as is still done today at weddings in Egypt.

A very fine mummy-case of wood, painted, gilded and with encrustations of glass, was made, as the many inscriptions on it state, for Henout-oudjebou, 'musician of Amun', wife and 'mistress of the house' of the scribe Hatiay who was 'steward of the lands of the temple of Aten' (**3,9**). This combination of titles, similar to many others of the time, indicates the role of women in the higher ranks of society, dividing their time between religious rituals and domestic affairs. To judge from her elaborate mummy-case, Henout-oudjebou must have been fairly rich, probably with servants to perform the household tasks of preparing food, weaving linen, and so on, under her supervision. In scenes of everyday life on the walls of tombs such household chores, and also work on the land, are overseen by

the deceased man with his wife (if she is shown) standing demurely behind him. Women are, in fact, greatly outnumbered by men in the decoration of tombs, most of which were constructed for men. They appear most frequently in funeral rites as mourners with conventional gestures of grief (**3,10**) and in banqueting scenes as relatives or musicians, fully dressed, or as dancing girls wearing only necklaces and girdles round their slender hips (3,4). (Nakedness indicated low social status.) In these paintings, married couples are always together, husbands in front of wives (3,6). In groups, the men and women are always separated. How closely these images corresponded to the realities of social life cannot be known. There can be little if any doubt, however, that ancient Egypt was male-dominated; only men were literate and qualified for the bureaucracy. Yet religious beliefs about the interdependence of the male and female principles were to some extent reflected in everyday life. Women of all classes could inherit and own private property, for instance. In this respect, at least, they enjoyed greater autonomy in ancient Egypt than in any other early civilization.

NEW KINGDOM ARCHITECTURE

A great change came over architecture in the New Kingdom. There were no more pyramids. As security against robbers, the pharaohs were now buried in rock-cut tombs hidden away in the Valley of the Kings in the western desert behind the cliffs overlooking Thebes, sometimes tunnelled as much as 500 feet (150m) into the hillside. (The place-name Thebes, of Greek origin, covers both the ancient city of the living on the east bank of the Nile and the city of the dead on the other side, the former being now partly covered by present-day Luxor and the latter an extensive area with cult centres and tombs.) Even so, only Tutenkhamun's tomb was to survive with its contents intact (see p. 103). Mortuary temples were detached from the tombs, prominently sited as manifestations of royal power overlooking the Nile on the west bank. The largest and best preserved is that of Queen Hatshepsut, the daughter of Thutmosis I (third king of the eighteenth dynasty) and the wife of Thutmosis II, on whose death she took power, which she retained even after the male heir, her stepson, came of age. Reigning alone from 1504 to 1482 BC, she is the earliest female monarch of whom any record survives. The design of her mortuary temple is credited to her steward and adviser Senmut, formerly a soldier in her father's army, but he may well have been the general supervisor of the undertaking rather than an architect in the modern sense of the word.

Queen Hatshepsut's temple was sited almost adjoining an earlier Middle Kingdom mortuary complex of Mentuhotep I and was similarly built on terraces (**3,11**). But its sculptured decorations were richer and a still more dramatic use was made of the spectacular site beneath the cliffs behind which lies the Valley of the Kings. Indeed, the relationship between man-made and natural architecture – the one echoing the other – is very striking. Whether this was consciously intended cannot, of course, be known, but it is surely no coincidence that the temple is exactly on axis with that at Luxor, 5 miles (8km) away across the Nile (**3,12**). A monumental gateway at the edge of the valley opened into a court with a ramp flanked by painted sphinxes leading up, above a colonnade, to a large terrace planted with myrrh trees, sacred to Amun. This terrace was closed by a deep colonnade backed with walls, on which events from the life and reign of the queen were illustrated in relief carvings. (Unfortunately, these very fine carvings cannot be photographed satisfactorily.) From the first terrace a ramp led up to the second with a long portico, which originally had a statue of the queen in front of each of its columns. Behind this was a court surrounded by a double colonnade and on its far side the granite entrance to a rock-cut sanctuary of Amun. The 200 or so statues of Hatshepsut (**3,8**) which stood in various courts and chapels were removed and defaced after her death, probably by order of Thutmosis III, her stepson, nephew and son-in-law, whom she had kept from the throne.

The dramatic design of Queen Hatshepsut's temple was not repeated. But it was under the eighteenth dynasty that the ancient Egyptian temple was given its definitive form – inward-looking and enclosed within tall forbidding perimeter walls, with a processional sequence of colonnaded courts and many-columned halls, creating an architecture of inhuman, impersonal and still daunting monumentality, as, for example, in the relatively small temple of Khonsu at Karnak (**3,13**) which survives in the precincts of the much larger temple of Amun-Re. These temples had no specific funerary function. The first were dedicated to Amun (or Amon or Amen), the 'local' god of Thebes, who was united with the sun god Re and, as Amun-Re, elevated to the position of Egyptian national deity. His shrine at Karnak on the east bank of the Nile, just outside the city of Thebes, was gradually enriched, especially with the spoils of war, until it became an institution of immense wealth (by the early twelfth century BC it owned 86,486 slaves, nearly 1,000,000 head of cattle,

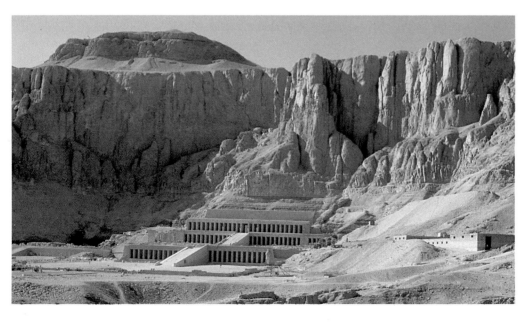

3,11 Funerary temple of Queen Hatshepsut, Deir el-Bahari, c. 1480 BC.

3,12 *Opposite* Temple of Amun-Re, Luxor, 1417–1379 BC.

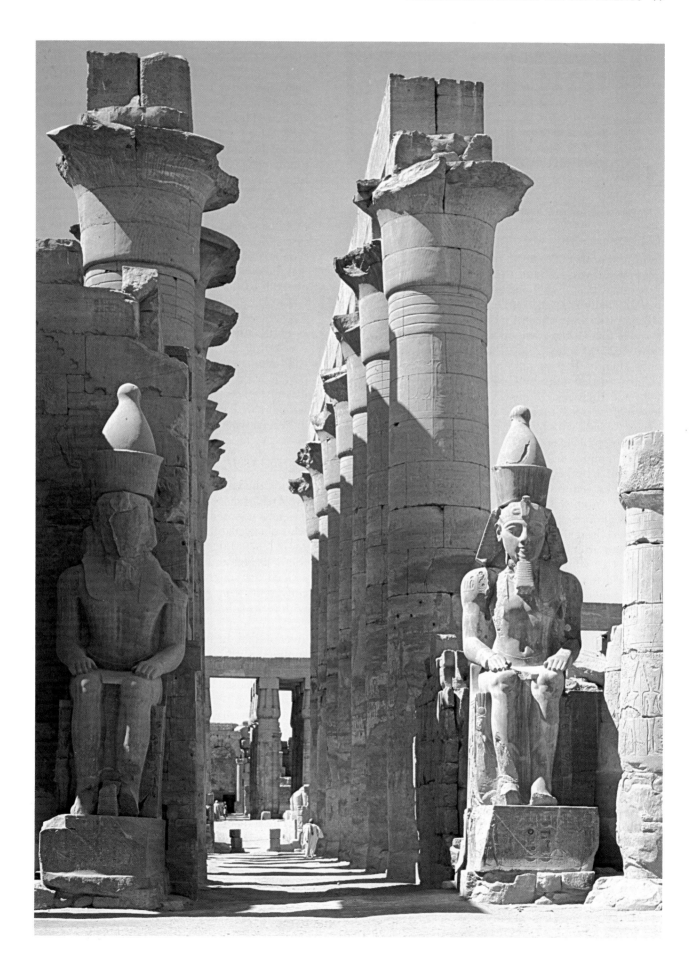

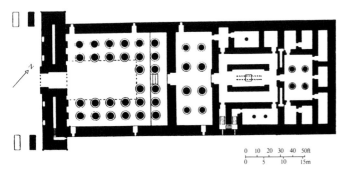

3,13 Plan of the temple of Khonsu, Karnak.

more than 500,000 acres [200,000 hectares] of land, 65 cities and towns, nine of them in Syria, not to mention vast quantities of gold and silver). The original building was gradually enlarged into one of the most imposing of all temples in the ancient world, 1,220 feet (370m) long and 338 feet (100m) wide in a sacred enclosure covering nearly 62,000 acres (25,000 hectares). A second temple, only slightly less grandiose, was built some 2 miles (3.5km) to the south at Luxor, dedicated to Amun, his wife and their son Khonsu (3,12). This was subject to fewer alterations than the temple at Karnak and the hypostyle hall, with its huge papyrus columns built under Amenhotep III (1417–1379 BC), survives almost intact.

The temples at Karnak and Luxor were joined by an avenue of sphinxes, of which hundreds are still in place, and also by water. On the god's great annual festival the image of Amun was taken by barge from Karnak to 'visit his harem' at Luxor. Like all ancient Egyptian temples, they were designed primarily as settings for ritual and the architects' attention was concentrated exclusively on the interiors to which, it should be remembered, only the privileged few had access. Exteriors present no unified view – sometimes nothing but blank walling, more than a mile (1.6km) in circumference at Karnak. The only prominent feature was the entrance through a twin-towered gateway called a pylon, which made its first appearance in stone in the New Kingdom, though the few well-preserved examples are very much later (3,22). A pylon, often called the 'horizon of heaven', was usually built with its outer face to the west so that the pharaoh could make his ceremonial appearance through the great doorway, above which the sun was seen as it rose between the towers. The temple interior was planned with strict bilateral symmetry as a succession of colonnaded courts and halls gradually ascending to the innermost chamber. To those who moved slowly up the narrow path through the progressively constricted space, with ever lower ceilings and dimmer light, the effect must have been overwhelming.

The system of construction is of the simplest post-and-lintel kind (though the few surviving ancient Egyptian brick buildings show that other techniques had been mastered: there are brick barrel vaults with a span of over 13 feet, 4m, at Thebes). Huge horizontal slabs were supported on massive columns simulating bundles of papyrus stems bulging out from the base and, as it were,

tied at the neck, or slightly tapering cylinders spreading out into palm-leaf capitals placed so closely together that they seemed to form an unbroken wall, discouraging any deviation from the straight path between them. (The entrance could be seen only from the main axis.) The structural load-bearing function of such columns was not emphasized. Indeed, it might almost seem to have been denied by horizontal bands of sunk-relief carvings and hieroglyphs. There were also reliefs on the walls, no doubt highly colored. Lavish use of gold and paint must originally have given these interiors a spectacular opulence. They were not created for the living, however, any more than the statues in tombs. Many of the carved images and inscriptions in the temples can never have been clearly seen and some must have been all but invisible, so dim was the light. Their purpose was to declare the piety of the pharaoh to the god whose incarnate son he was and on whom the prosperity of the realm depended; hence the massiveness of these great structures. Durability was essential. Amenhotep III described a temple he built as 'an everlasting fortress of fine white sandstone, wrought with gold throughout; its floor is adorned with silver, all its portals with electrum; it is made very wide and large, and established for ever. . . . Flag-staves are set up before it, wrought with electrum; the pylon resembles the horizon in heaven when Re rises therein.'

AKHENATEN

During the reign of Amenhotep III a new cult, devoted to the Aten or disc of the sun, gained in importance and was officially adopted by his son and successor Amenhotep IV, who changed his name to Akhenaten, 'pleasing to the Aten' (1379–1362 BC). Akhenaten declared the Aten to be the only god and after a clash with the priesthood proscribed the worship of Amun and other state gods. This conversion from polytheism to monotheism also brought with it the conception of a god in other than human form. For the new cult centred on the visible disc of the sun, the giver of light, heat and life. The Aten was represented as a sunburst with rays terminating in human hands. But the spirit of the cult is better reflected in hymns said to have been composed by Akhenaten himself. In at least one there are quite striking parallels, both in thought and structure, with the Hebrew Psalms composed six or seven centuries later; and some contact between Atenism and Hebrew religion has been supposed, though this can be no more than speculative. The famous *Hymn to Aten*, however, is certainly the first truly monotheistic composition in the literature of the world, its theme being the all-embracing love of god for everything he has made.

The cult of the Aten was necessarily celebrated not in dark interiors but in open-air temples, the largest of which was laid out in Akhenaten's new capital, Akhetaten, at a place now called Tell el-Amarna, more than 200 miles (320km) down the Nile from Thebes (**3,14**). Most of this huge precinct, covering more than 50 acres (20 hectares) was filled with open-air altars suitable for the worship of a solar god. Enclosed cult chambers were few. A luxuriant garden city was built around it, with an official and a residential palace for the royal family with, nearby, a smaller temple consisting of a series of courts with remarkably well-preserved mud-brick pylons giving access from one to another. There were also spacious houses for courtiers and officials. (Separate quarters on a grid plan were provided for the workers.)

There is no clearer indication of how completely subservient the arts of ancient Egypt were to the monarchy than that provided by the paintings, sculpture and architecture from the brief 17-year reign of Akhenaten. Although a tendency towards greater naturalism had been evident in the earlier art of the New Kingdom, the patronage of Akhenaten led to its speedy culmination. Portraits of the pharaoh are alone enough to demonstrate what a radical break had been made with the art of the past. The colossal statues of him, more than double life-size, from the temple of Aten at Karnak are most revealing (**3,15**). There is nothing heroic about these extraordinary royal icons. Individual features, the long lean face with thick lips, heavy-lidded eyes and protruding chin, the narrow chest and weak arms, the slack muscles, pot belly and soft, almost feminine hips, are all rendered with such realism that a medical diagnosis has been made to account for his physical peculiarities (a glandular disorder known as Fröhlich's syndrome). The thoughtful, over-refined, even effete countenance is disturbingly enigmatic, at once dreamily introspective and warmly sensual, far more expressive than the enigmatic masks of earlier – and, for that matter, later – Egyptian pharaohs, yet no less hierarchically aloof and remote from the world of ordinary mortals. For these are complex images blending

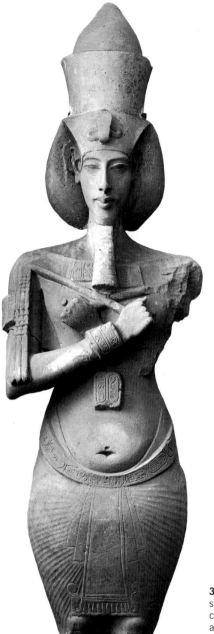

3,15 Akhenaten, colossal statue from Karnak, c. 1375 BC. Sandstone, about 13ft (3.96m) high. Egyptian Museum, Cairo.

3,14 Plan of Akhetaten.

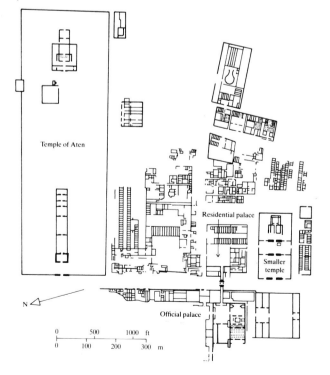

Temple of Aten

Residential palace

Smaller temple

N

Official palace

0   500   1000 ft
0   100   200   300 m

the real with the formal, psychological depth with conventional stylization. In relief carvings in tombs and on altars found at Amarna his features are almost caricatured. Sometimes he is shown in intimate groups, dandling his youngest daughter or caressing his wife Nefertiti, although always within the religious aura of the symbol of the Aten.

No less remarkable are the several sculptured portraits of members of the royal family found in the studio of Akhenaten's chief sculptor, Thutmosis, at Amarna. They include what is justly one of the most famous of all ancient Egyptian works of art, the painted limestone head of Queen Nefertiti – ideally beautiful, yet strangely naturalistic in her elegant, worldly affectation, head held regally high with lowered eyelids, skin manipulated and cosmetically colored to a uniform soft smoothness and

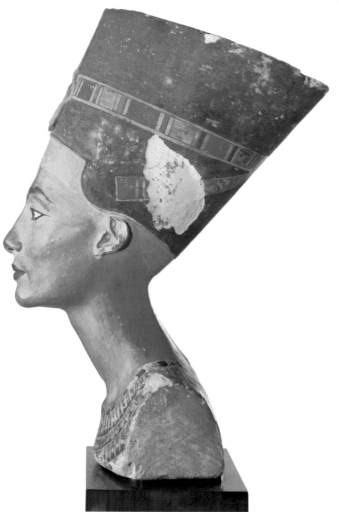

3,16 Nefertiti, c. 1360 BC. Painted limestone, about 19ins (48cm) high. Egyptian Museum, Berlin.

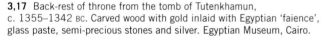

3,17 Back-rest of throne from the tomb of Tutenkhamun, c. 1355–1342 BC. Carved wood with gold inlaid with Egyptian 'faience', glass paste, semi-precious stones and silver. Egyptian Museum, Cairo.

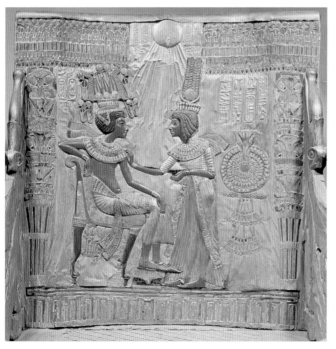

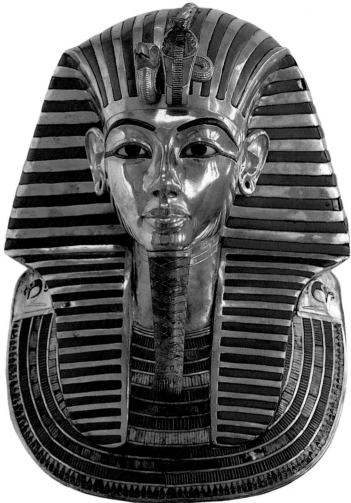

3,18 Tutenkhamun, mask from mummy-case from Thebes, c. 1340 BC. Gold inlaid with enamel and semi-precious stones, 21¼ins (54cm) high. Egyptian Museum, Cairo.

subtle pliability of flesh over bone, but with slight creases at the corners of the mouth, tell-tale indications that she had already begun to lose the first bloom of youth (**3,16**). The carving is an unusual example of sculptural form, a daring essay in 'precarious balance' with head and high-spreading head-dress perfectly poised on the slender column of the neck, reaching out obliquely from the shoulders, in such a way that it seems only momentarily to have come to rest. Yet this masterly portrait, the most immediately arresting and memorable of all images of a highly sophisticated type of untouchable female beauty, was almost certainly carved as a trial piece or model and not intended as a finished work. The final version would probably have been less naturalistic. The same studio had in it unfinished statues and heads of harder stone (including some unfinished, unpainted heads of Nefertiti), as well as models in clay and casts from life and death masks, fascinating for the light they shed on the sculptor's practice, but more than a little misleading as regards ancient Egyptian art, which always sought to transcend reality.

The pictorial style developed at Amarna may be illustrated by a wooden panel carved in very low relief and still retaining its original gilding and bright coloring (**3,17**). It shows Tutenkhamun, Akhenaten's son-in-law and successor, enthroned and anointed by his wife beneath the symbol of the Aten. Posed without the strict formality that had previously been obligatory in portrayals of the pharaohs, the two slender adolescent figures seem almost relaxed, despite their vast crowns; there is even a hint of human tenderness in their physical proximity. But the relative freedom from conventions, which permitted this increase in naturalism, was accompanied by a loosening in technique. The carving lacks the crisp precision of, for instance, the reliefs in the tomb of Ramose dating from little more than two decades earlier (3,6).

This panel forms the back-rest of the throne buried in Tutenkhamun's tomb, together with numerous other furnishings, which afford us a uniquely vivid glimpse of the luxurious splendour surrounding the pharaohs of the eighteenth dynasty. (No other pharaonic tomb has been found with its contents undisturbed.) Tutenkhamun, who succeeded to the throne in 1361 BC, was persuaded by the priests to restore the old polytheistic religion of Egypt, to take (as a mark of devotion to Amun) the name by which we know him, and to move the capital back to Thebes. The open-air temples and other buildings in Amarna were demolished. A reaction had set in. And its effect on the visual arts can be seen very clearly in, for example, his mummy-case mask, in which he has been given the attributes of the resurrected Osiris, king of the afterworld (3,18). In this impassive, almost impersonal, image of divine royalty barely a trace remains of the subtle and sensitive naturalism introduced under Akhenaten.

RAMESSIDE ART

The succeeding period witnessed a further and more radical reaction, a conscious return to the formality of pre-New Kingdom traditions. Seti I, who came to power in 1304 BC and founded the nineteenth dynasty, had reliefs of himself piously worshipping the gods carved inside the temples at Karnak and Abydos and, on the exterior at Karnak, reliefs showing him victorious in warfare, winning back territories lost in Asia while Akhenaten immersed himself in religious questions. Seti's departure for battle, scenes of the enemy fleeing in confusion at his approach, his triumphant return and dedication of spoils to Amun, are all recorded in a revived 'Old Kingdom' style. Partly as a result of Akhenaten's heresies, the pharaohs of the nineteenth and twentieth dynasties seem to have felt a need to celebrate their martial prowess in images of conquest, often carved on the outer faces of pylon gateways for all to see. For the same reason, the scale of both temples and statues increased – to assert the imperious power of an absolute monarchy.

At Abu Simbel, Ramesses II (1304–1237 BC) had a vast temple hacked out of the living rock, dedicated to Amun the god of Thebes, Re-Horakhte the sun god of Heliopolis, Ptah the creator god of Memphis – and himself. It was given the traditional temple plan, tunnelled 180 feet

3,19 Temple of Ramesses II, Abu Simbel, c. 1257 BC. The colossi are about 65ft (20m) high.

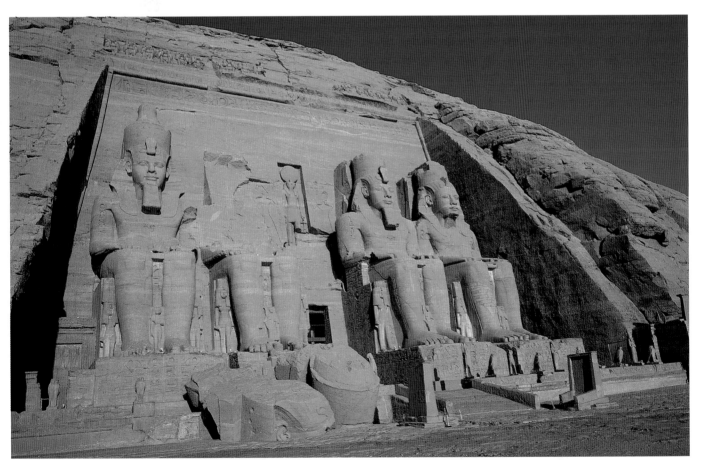

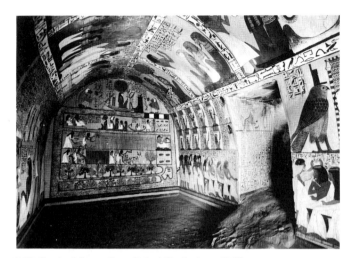

3,20 Tomb of Sennedjem, Deir el Medineh, c. 1150 BC.

(55m) into the cliff. The façade was treated as a vast pylon, the central door being flanked by four seated statues of Ramesses some 65 feet (20m) high with smaller, though still well over life-size, figures of his family standing between his gigantic legs (**3,19**). Inside there were 30-foot-high (9m) statues of Ramesses II and also reliefs recording in great detail his battle with the Hittites at Kadesh in Syria (see p. 90). The temple is, in fact, a monument to Ramesses, but since he was himself regarded as an incarnate god, no secularizing or irreligious intentions are implied by this act of self-glorification. (In 1968 the whole temple was cut out of the cliff and moved some 600 feet, 180m, up the rock-face to save it from being submerged by the new Aswan dam.)

The grandiloquence of Abu Simbel may seem a little hollow. And, indeed, before the end of the long reign of Ramesses II the power of Egypt had begun to decline. Ramesses III (1198–1166 BC) was the last pharaoh to build on a colossal scale. The only victory of which he could boast in relief carvings was that of about 1170 BC against 'peoples of the sea', who tried to invade Egypt from the north – an extension of the migratory movement that had overrun Helladic Greece (see p. 85) and wiped out the Hittite empire only a few decades earlier. Ramesses III also had to fight off invasion from Libya. Henceforth Egypt was on the defensive, a prey to marauders. This deteriorating political situation may have been reflected indirectly in tomb painting, which now lost its joyous, light-hearted spirit (3,4). The tomb of a man called Sennedjem of the late Ramesside period at Deir el Medineh (a village occupied by artists and artisans employed on the tombs in the vast nearby necropolis of Thebes) illustrates the change. No longer is the owner of the tomb the dominant figure, eternally standing and watching in serene detachment (2,37). Sennedjem and his wife are dwarfed by images of the gods, while they themselves are shown labouring in the fields of Osiris after their journey through the netherworld, during which their souls would have been weighed in the balance (**3,20**).

Collections of spells, incantations and prayers assembled to form a guide to the afterworld (called a *Book of the Dead* by scholars in the 1840s) often illustrate this scene (**3,21**), which was to reappear in Christian images of the Last Judgement millennia later. A *Book of the Dead* was inscribed on papyrus or leather and placed in a casket with a statuette of Osiris or slipped into the sarcophagus or into the mummy-wrappings of the deceased to enable him to salute the sun with hymns, identify with Osiris, conquer his personal enemies, kill the crocodile and the serpent or escape the fisherman's net. The illustrations were usually continuous, not separate images, as in later books in codex form (see p. 321). A papyrus roll might be some 30 to 35 feet (9–10.5m) long, composed of the pith of the papyrus plant, flattened, thin-shaved and glued together to form a sheet.

During many centuries of slow decline, when Egypt was conquered and subjugated by a succession of foreign

3,21 *Last Judgement before Osiris*, from the *Book of the Dead* of Hunefer, c. 1300 BC. Painted papyrus, 2³/₄ins (7cm) high. British Museum, London.

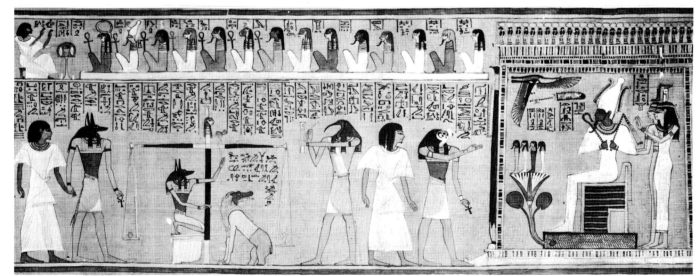

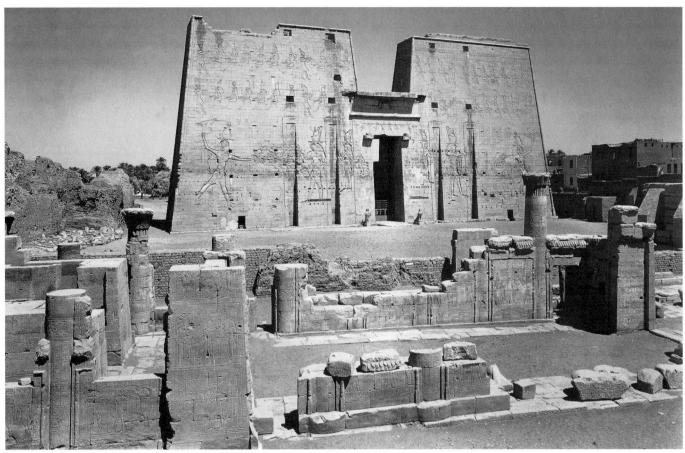

3,22 Temple of Horus, Edfu, 237–212 BC.

3,23 Plan of the temple of Horus, Edfu.

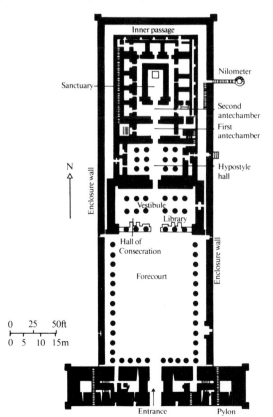

invaders – by the Assyrians in 670–664 BC, by the Persians in 525 BC and finally by Alexander the Great in 332 BC – the visual arts survived almost unchanged. Such peculiarly Egyptian forms as the cube- or block-statue, for instance, or the pylon gateway in architecture, seem to have been quite impervious to outside influence. In cube- or block-statues the figure is seated with knees drawn up to the chin, hands spread on top of them and with only the head and feet protruding from the block of stone. Their precise significance is uncertain, although they seem originally to have been associated in some way with the cult of Osiris. (Purely formal interpretations in terms of releasing the figure imprisoned within the block are mis-leading.) But they went on being made long after Egypt had been occupied. Similarly in architecture traditional forms pre-vailed. There is no better preserved example of an ancient Egyptian temple than that dedicated to Horus at Edfu (**3,22; 23**). The traditional plan with a strong longitudinal axis from the entrance, through a wide court and columned halls to the dark innermost sanctuary, was adopted intact. The pylon gateway façade is of the type developed early in the New Kingdom, and among the figures rendered in sunk relief there is one, at the left, that harks back some 3,000 years to King Narmer, founder of the first dynasty. This extraordinary longevity of artistic forms was due not simply to the persistence of the religious cults that they were largely created to serve, but to the ancient Egyptians' preoccupation with the immutable and eternal, which lay behind their whole civilization.

ASSYRIA AND BABYLON

Assyria takes its name from a Mesopotamian god, Assur or Ashur, after whom a city on the Tigris (some 60 miles, 100km, south of present-day Mosul) was also named. This city of Assur is first recorded in the third millennium BC as a frontier post of the Akkadian empire (see p. 55). But it was not until the second half of the fourteenth century BC that Assyria began to emerge as an independent power. At the end of the second millennium BC the Assyrians briefly extended their rule as far as the Mediterranean, and in a renewed effort at expansion during the reign of Assurnasirpal II (883–859 BC) they embarked on the conquest of a vast empire, which eventually stretched from the Caspian to the Nile and from the Taurus to the Persian Gulf, covering modern Iraq, Syria, Jordan, Lebanon, most of Palestine and part of southern Turkey and northern Egypt. For about 300 years – until 612 BC, when they were overrun by the combined forces of the Medes and Scythians – Assyrians were the dominant power in the Near East, with a terrorizing reputation for the brutality and ruthless efficiency of their troops armed with iron weapons. Dominant, but rarely stable or secure, they lived in a state of almost perpetual warfare and their history is that of a series of military campaigns, first to acquire and then to defend their sprawling empire.

Assyrian art was produced in these special circumstances and for a limited but related purpose: the promotion and glorification of Assyrian power and military strength. It was exclusively public, official and even, it might be said, propagandist. The figurative arts were devoted mainly to the exploits of Assyrian kings and their armies. Many of the scenes of slaughter, whether of men or animals, may seem to our eyes repetitive and degrading – but they led to the invention of the first true narrative art to be found anywhere. Earlier artists had recounted legends and recorded historical events, but they had done so in scenes that read as disconnected sentences (e.g. in New Kingdom Egypt at Beni Hasan and tombs in the Valley of the Kings). The Assyrians devised means to show how one incident led to the next, as in a well-told story – or the chronicle of a military campaign. Warfare may even have sharpened the awareness of time and space on which narrative art depends, as well as providing its subject-matter.

Many of the salient characteristics of Assyrian art appeared before the end of the second millennium BC. Much was taken over from Sumer (see p. 51), though significantly transformed. Ziggurats built at Assur differed from those in southern Mesopotamia in that they had no monumental exterior stairways, so that the upper stages, reached from the roof of a nearby temple or a special stairway building, must have seemed even more remote from the workaday world. The gods of Sumer were still worshipped, but they seem to have withdrawn themselves from mortals. On two surviving carved reliefs they are represented only by their hands reaching down from heaven. When they appear together with kings they are shown not as living beings but as statues set on pedestals.

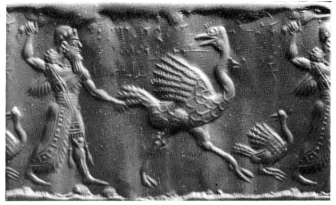

3,24 Winged demon chasing an ostrich, c. 1250 BC. Impression from cylinder seal. Pierpont Morgan Library, New York.

Assyrian literature reveals that the king alone had direct access to the gods, whose place he took, so far as the community at large was concerned. There was, however, a lesser order of supernatural beings: genii and demons, who lurked everywhere and were frequently represented on seals and protective amulets.

Seals are the most interesting as they are also, from a technical point of view, the finest Assyrian works of art of the late second millennium BC. Their compositions have a liveliness rarely found before. Sharply incised figures of men, supernatural beings and animals move briskly round the cylinders. On one, a deer skips light-hooved over the ground between two trees. A lion and a winged horse rear up on their back legs to confront each other. A winged demon in a flowing robe pursues an ostrich and its young, which turn their heads back as they run (**3,24**). A tensely muscled nude man aims his spear at a rampant lion accompanied by a bounding deer and an ostrich striding forwards. These seals date from about 1250 BC and already indicate the ability to create dramatic situations by careful disposition of the figures, as well as the talent for vigorous depiction of animals, which distinguish later and much larger relief carvings from the palaces of Assyrian kings.

Each of the major Assyrian kings of the early first millennium BC enlarged an old palace or built an entirely new

3,25 Reconstruction of Sargon II's palace, Khorsabad, Iraq.

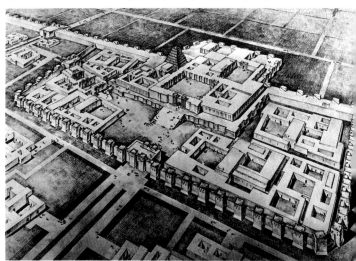

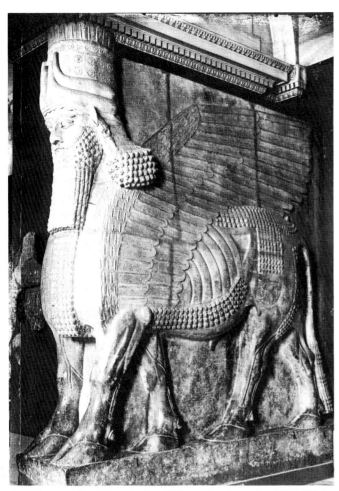

3,26 *Lamassu* from Khorsabad, c. 720 BC. Limestone, about 13ft 10ins (4.21m) high. Louvre, Paris.

one to celebrate and display his power: Assurnasirpal II (883–859 BC) at Nimrud (present-day Calah), Sargon II (721–705 BC) at Dur Sharrukin (present-day Khorsabad), Sennacherib (705–681 BC) at Nineveh (present-day Kuyunjik) and Assurbanipal (669–626 BC) also at Nineveh. That of Sargon II, completed only shortly before his death and then abandoned, has been more systematically excavated than the others (**3,25**). It stood within a citadel enclosure on the perimeter of a walled city, built at the same time and about a mile (1.6km) across. The material was mainly mud-brick, but the bases of the walls were faced with stone slabs, called orthostats, which are a distinguishing feature of Assyrian architecture. In plan the palace conformed to a peculiar system, which had appeared at Assur in the thirteenth century BC. Courts and groups of rooms were aligned not axially but diagonally, so that one monumental space succeeded another off axis. From the large, approximately 300-foot-square (90m) first court a doorway near the corner led into the corner of the second oblong court, with the throne room on the nearer of its long sides. Symmetry was, however, observed in the design of individual units, most notably monumental entrances.

Huge carvings of human-headed winged bulls called *lamassu* – genii believed to ward off evil spirits – guarded each of the entrances, through which foreign ambassadors, vassals and petitioners were obliged to pass on their way to the throne room (**3,26**). Similar *lamassu* kept

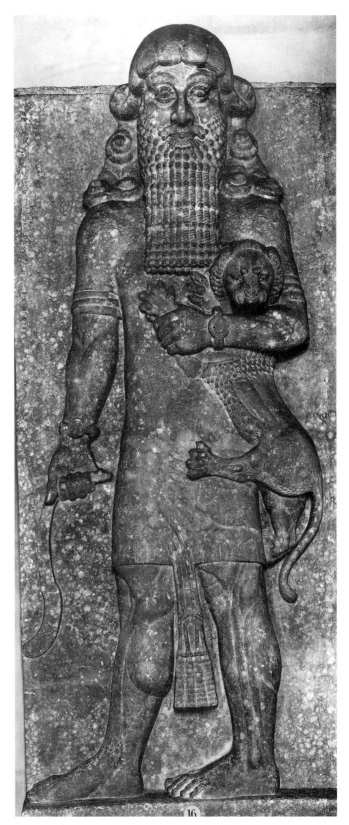

3,27 Man with lion cub, from Khorsabad, c. 720 BC. Limestone, 15ft 5ins (4.7m) high. Louvre, Paris.

stony watch on entrances to other palaces. Massively overpowering, yet carved with meticulous attention to detail – the curls of the beard, the feathers of the eagle wings and the muscles and veins of the legs – they are impressive examples of architectural sculpture. The earliest, sometimes with lion instead of bull bodies, were found at Nimrud and date from the early ninth century BC (British Museum, London). As we have already seen (p. 91), the Hittites had earlier incorporated lions and sphinxes in monumental gateways in very much this way, and they had also faced buildings with carved orthostats. Assyrian practice probably derives from them, although the archeological record is as yet so far from being complete that cross-currents of influence in the Near East at this period cannot be traced with any certainty.

Some of the Assyrian *lamassu*, however, have a striking peculiarity not found elsewhere. Seen head-on they stand stock still, seen from the side they pace slowly forward: and as an awkward consequence an oblique view reveals five legs. Clearly, they were not conceived in the round but as two reliefs joined at right-angles. High reliefs of genii carrying holy-water buckets and sprinklers or, as at Khorsabad, supermen with lion cubs, who accompany the bull-men, are ungainly in another way (**3,27**). Above their heavy beards they stare straight out of the wall and their torsos are also rendered frontally. But their stocky legs with bulging calves move disjointedly to left or right in the Egyptian way. The stiffness of their poses is emphasized by the naturalism of hands, wrists and other details, especially the lion cubs, alive in every inch from twitching tail and scratching claw to puckered muzzle, struggling to escape the brawny grasp of these brutal figures, which have sometimes been identified as the Sumerian hero Gilgamesh.

NARRATIVE RELIEF

Assyrian orthostat reliefs range in date from the reign of Assurnasirpal II (883–859 BC) to that of Assurbanipal (669–626 BC). The earliest known are from the throne room of the palace at Nimrud (now British Museum): panels of gypsum rather more than 7 feet (2m) high, some carved with large figures but the majority divided horizontally into two registers by a central band of inscriptions. These slabs provided sculptors with immensely long continuous strips, on which the king's military campaigns were recorded in an easily read continuous narrative with one episode following another. The same system was adopted in the later palaces and the subject-matter was little changed – a story of unrelieved violence, city after city besieged, stormed and sacked, prisoners slaughtered or led off to captivity, the king engaged in the ritual killing of lions and bulls. Only in a few scenes where docile vassals pay homage are there brief moments of respite from the chronicle of carnage. The general effect is not, however, monotonous; the variety and vitality of the many thousand figures are extraordinary. And in the course of two and a half centuries techniques of representation were modified.

Even in the earliest there were significant departures from the traditions of both Mesopotamia and ancient Egypt. Images were no longer projected on to the wall but seem rather to emerge out of the background, which forms an integral part of each 'picture'. Figures in a single section are of the same size, whether in the foreground or on the towers of a distant city, and the Assyrian king is no larger than his soldiers or even his foes. Difference in size ceases to indicate rank. There are even some instances of scale being used to suggest recession when one figure

3,28 *Booty from a City taken by Tiglathpileser III*, from Nimrud, Iraq, 745–727 BC. Limestone, 3ft 4ins (1.02m) high. British Museum, London.

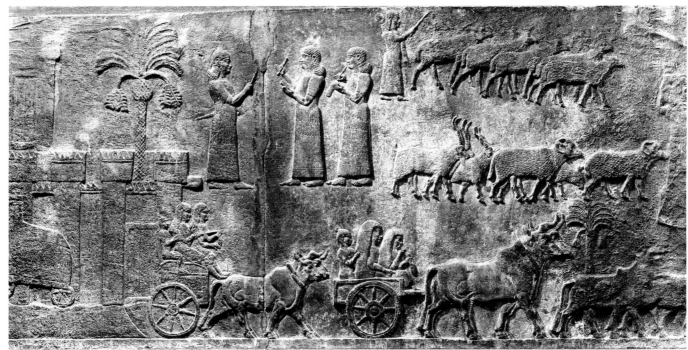

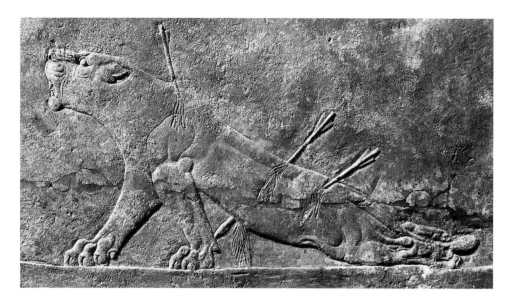

3,29 *Dying Lioness*, from Nineveh, Iraq, c. 650 BC. Limestone, about 24ins (60.9cm) high. British Museum, London.

overlaps another, that behind being slightly smaller. The importance of a figure, usually the king, was more subtly marked by his position, often at the edge of a scene towards which he looks and aims his bow, and by a blank area surrounding him and his personal attendants like an aura. Figures stand in the Egyptian pose, but in the later reliefs pure profiles become increasingly common. At the same time motifs denoting landscape settings grow less conventional and are more strongly particularized. On orthostats carved for Tiglathpileser III (745–727 BC) a nearly realistic rendering of figures in space was achieved. One shows the population of a conquered city being deported for settlement elsewhere as, according to the Second Book of Kings, Shalmaneser 'carried Israel away into Assyria' (**3,28**).

This relief should be read as a map with the officer and scribes in the centre of the composition, standing in the midst of the various activities. But the sloping ground line of the hooves of the cattle in the upper right-hand corner suggests an elementary rendering of perspective. If that was the sculptor's intention, it was unprecedented. The effect may be merely accidental. But a later, mid-seventh-century BC relief of yet another captured city clearly shows soldiers moving downhill from its gate, along a path which gradually widens as if to record a purely visual effect. Yet these experiments with perspective – if they can be so described – were to lead nowhere.

The most impressive Assyrian reliefs are, in fact, those that show figures ranged in a single plane, rather more widely apart than those in Egyptian carvings, with a suggestion of air circulating round the bodies, greater attention to naturalistically rendered detail and a heightened sense of drama. Those of Assurbanipal killing lions are perhaps the finest of all. (They should not, as they often are, be described as 'hunts', for the beasts had been captured and were then released to be slain by the king in what seems to have been partly a sport and partly a ritual display of royal power.) One panel shows the king in his chariot speeding round an arena and leaving in his wake a shambles of dead and dying animals. A dying lioness transfixed with arrows, agonizingly dragging her rear limbs, is justly famous as a fine example of animal portraiture (**3,29**). But the pity that it moves in the modern observer can too easily encourage the misapprehension that Assyrian artists shared this feeling for pathos. That they were fully conscious of the drama they depicted seems, on the other hand, beyond doubt. The lions are by no means cowed, and in some scenes the odds appear to be fairly evenly distributed between man and beast – as they had to be if royal prowess and courage were to shine forth.

Such dramatic effects would have been impossible without the invention of continuous narrative and this led to even more sophisticated developments. A culminating scene is depicted in split-second moments of

3,30 *Lion Released and Killed*, from Nineveh, c. 650 BC. Limestone, about 27ins (68.6cm) high. British Museum, London.

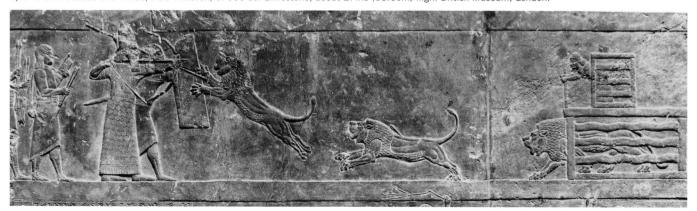

action – almost as in a film-strip – so that the excitement of watching the animal in movement is caught. Already in the thirteenth century BC the Assyrians had compressed a sequence of actions into a single pictorial space. Still earlier, Minoan and Helladic artists had sometimes shown single figures in a succession of movements (the bulls on the Vaphio cups, for instance, pp. 79–80). But Assyrian sculptors of the seventh century BC took this technique much further. A relief carved for Assurbanipal at Nineveh provides one of the clearest examples (**3,30**). It shows one lion released from a cage, hit by an arrow as it bounds forward, and then making a desperate leap towards its antagonist. The figures of the king and his attendant, holding a shield, are shown in two distinct moments in the narrative: the king draws his bow as the animal is released, the attendant begins to plunge his spear into its heart as it pounces. To read the relief correctly entails the separation, mentally, of its three sequential layers. No such effort is, however, necessary to experience the thrill of the action from the moment when the door of the cage is lifted and the snarling lion prowls out. The animal is rendered with extreme sharpness of observation and with as much feeling for its weight and muscular strength as for the texture of its pelt. It is perhaps significant that these wonderful reliefs, in which the art of pictorial narrative was brought to its height, were carved for Assurbanipal, who was also the owner of the library of cuneiform tablets that preserved the chief works of Mesopotamian literature, including the *Epic of Gilgamesh* (see p. 52).

The reliefs were almost certainly colored and the palaces that they adorned also had painted decorations (of which only fragments have been preserved) and appropriately rich furnishings. Tablets from the royal archives refer to ivory stools, beds and thrones received as tribute from Damascus and the Phoenician cities in Lebanon, on the Mediterranean coast, which formed part of the Assyrian empire from about 743 BC. Very few pieces have survived intact. A number of ivory carvings found at Nimrud and other Assyrian sites are generally believed to be of Phoenician workmanship. Some are clearly derived from Egyptian prototypes, others reflect Assyrian influence. Most notable are several carvings of animals – a cow suckling her calf, for instance – hardly less naturalistic than those on Assyrian reliefs, though very different in their sweet, almost sentimental, tone. Even violent subject-matter was treated gently and decoratively, almost playfully, as in two little reliefs of a lioness mauling a young Nubian (**3,31**). The figures are conceived more fully in the round than are those on all but the finest Assyrian reliefs, though they have none of the latter's sense of vigorous life. The emphasis is on delicacy and refinement. The background of stylized Egyptian flowers is inlaid with gold, red 'faience' and lapis lazuli, the boy's kilt is of gold leaf and his curly hair is composed of minute gilt-topped pegs of ivory. This work is of interest not only as an exquisite piece of craftsmanship but also as an example of the internationalism of its period – ivory probably from India, lapis lazuli from central Asia, Egyptian flowers, a Nubian boy, a Phoenician carver and an Assyrian patron. It dates from the beginning of the seventh century BC, when, as we shall see, Greece and Italy were being drawn into the cultural orbit of the Near Eastern civilizations. (The tendency in Phoenician art to assimilate and combine quite diverse influences made it the main intermediary, though it had a character of its own, especially in metalwork. The remarkable Phoenician chambered tombs at Ras Shamra/Ugarit in Syria are of Aegean type with excellent masonry.)

BABYLON

Assyrian power suddenly began to falter immediately after the death of Assurbanipal. Medes and Scythians, who had for some time been attacking the eastern and northern frontier, penetrated the empire and sacked Nineveh in 612 BC. They were allied with Nabopolassar, a former Assyrian army commander, who established himself as king of Babylon, which now became the capital of most of the former Assyrian territory and, once again, the centre of Mesopotamian civilization, though for little more than 70 years (until 539 BC, when Cyrus the Great of Persia took possession). Nabopolassar and the succeeding kings of Babylon called themselves the 'faithful shepherds' of the city god Marduk, but they seem to have been just as aggressive as the Assyrians – two of the tribes of Judah were taken off into captivity by Nabopolassar's more notorious son Nebuchadnezzar. The arts that flourished during this brief 'Indian summer' were marginally indebted to Assyria, yet essentially different: theocentric, static and revivalist. Sculptors adopted the pure profiles of figures in the later Assyrian reliefs, but reverted to the rather soft rounded forms and motionless

3,31 *Lioness Mauling a Nubian Boy*, from Nimrud, c. 700 BC. Ivory, gold, red 'faience' and lapis lazuli, 2³⁄₄ins (7cm) high. British Museum, London.

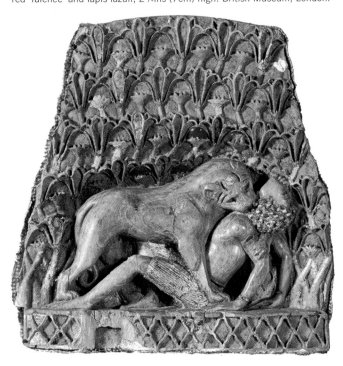

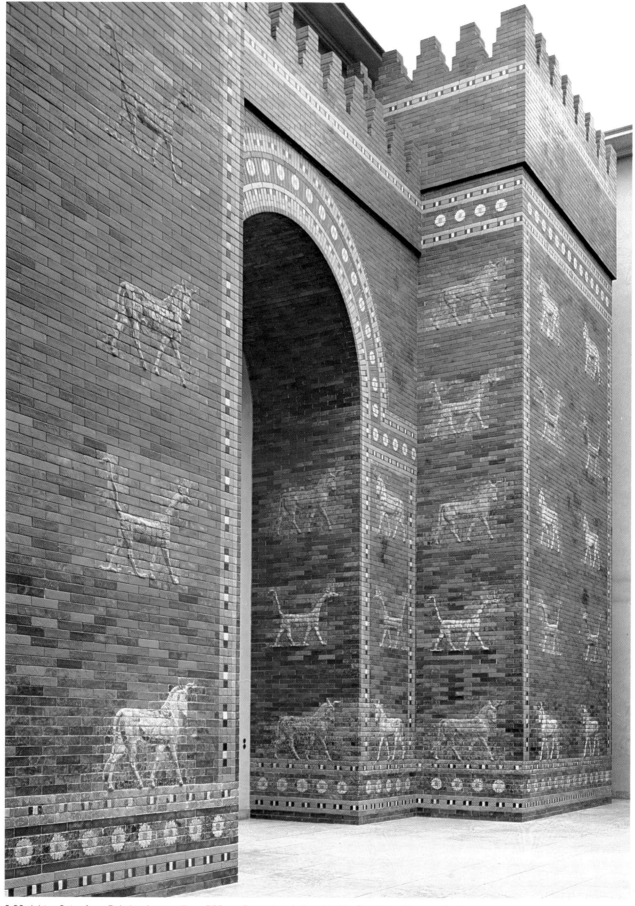

3,32 Ishtar Gate, from Babylon (restored), c. 575 BC. Colored and glazed brick. Staatliche Museen, Berlin.

compositions of the *stelae* carved for Hammurabi nearly 1,000 years earlier.

The difference between the arts of Assyria and Babylon is most clearly seen in architecture and architectural decoration, though unfortunately nothing survives of the temples and ziggurats apart from the foundations of the largest (the Biblical Tower of Babel). The royal palace in Babylon was almost as large as the Assyrian palaces, but lacked their overpowering monumentality. It consisted of numerous, relatively small rooms ranged around five courtyards and in one corner, presumably, the famous hanging gardens said to have been created by Nebuchadnezzar. There seem to have been no reliefs or other representations of royal triumphs, no vast *lamassu* glowering menacingly out from the entrances. The walls of the throne room and of the processional way leading to the Ishtar Gate were decorated with lions and monsters in raised and molded brick, colored and glazed (a technique first found in Kassite buildings of c. 1200 BC), but they are staid creatures in comparison with the beasts of Assyria. Each one is identical with all the others of its species, shown not in movement but as if frozen in the slow stride of a ritual march (**3,32**). They form, nevertheless, the most impressive surviving example of Neo-Babylonian art – long-necked dragons sacred to Marduk in white with yellow details, bulls sacred to the weather god Adad in yellow with blue hair, on backgrounds of dark blue. Rank upon rank, 575 of them in all, they covered the whole exterior of the ceremonial gateway and a further 120 white and yellow lions lined the walls of the processional way leading from it to the main group of temples.

IRAN

Mesopotamia was protected by no great natural barriers like those that had secured the integrity of Egyptian civilization for so long. It was constantly vulnerable to attack from people living in the surrounding areas, bounded on the west by the Mediterranean and on the south by the Arabian desert, but open to the north between the Black Sea and the Caspian, and to the east across the great central Asian plateau. The history of its art is that of the régimes strong enough to resist pressure from outside, usually by counter-aggression. To the north and west the civilization of Urartu flourished in the area now occupied by the Kurds and from about 825 to 750 BC challenged the military might of Assyria, while accepting its artistic influence. The principal sites, containing important architectural remains, are Van, Toprakkale and Altintepe (Turkey), Bastam (Iran) and Arin-berd (Armenia). Their metalwork is of high quality and seems, in fact, to have been (together with that of the Phoenicians) one of the main vehicles by which Assyrian and Oriental motifs were transmitted to Greece and Etruria. At about the same time bronzes of a very different kind were being produced in the area known as Luristan, in which Mesopotamian motifs are much less prominent than those derived from the prehistoric cultures of central Asia.

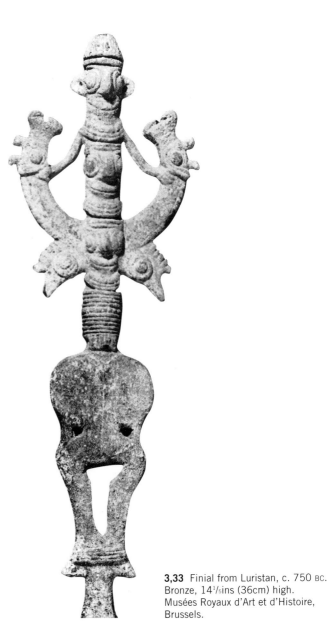

3,33 Finial from Luristan, c. 750 BC. Bronze, 14^{1}/$_{5}$ins (36cm) high. Musées Royaux d'Art et d'Histoire, Brussels.

Undecorated metal tools and weapons had been made in Luristan since the mid-third millennium BC. But these intricately wrought bronzes, cast by the *cire perdue* process, date from between the ninth and seventh centuries BC. Although most of them correspond with what has been called 'nomad's gear' – such easily portable objects as cauldrons, cups, costume ornaments, enrichments for chariots and trappings for horses – they were the work of sedentary craftsmen and made for a people whose chiefs lived in permanent dwellings on the plains of Luristan. The most interesting of these bronzes are sculptures in the round, which clearly had no utilitarian purpose and are generally called finials or standards – they have either a spike or a socket at the base (**3,33**). They may have had some supernatural function, perhaps to ward off evil spirits. The combinations of human and animal forms of which they are composed vary from piece to piece; but the top usually consists of two curving members flanking a firm vertical, sometimes a human figure, whose face with beaky nose and large round eyes is repeated below, up to three times. In the example illustrated here the figure is male, his sex being indicated beneath a second head and belt, but the legs are combined with the hindquarters of animals, which sprout dragon heads. These finials reveal an astonishing power to create seemingly organic forms merging into – or, perhaps one should say, emerging like spectres out of – one another in a kind of self-generating continuum, a morphological ferment with affinities with that which produced the earlier hybrid images of Shang China (see pp. 86–9). The culture that created the Luristan bronzes was, however, absorbed into that of Iran in the seventh century BC.

ACHAEMENID ART

Iran takes its name from a nomadic people of the steppes – Iranians or Aryans (the original meaning of this much-misused term) – who moved into the central Asian plateau shortly before the end of the second millennium BC. They spoke an Indo-European language related to Sanskrit, Greek, Latin and nearly all the modern European languages. But they did not constitute a homogeneous group. Tribes arriving independently of one another settled in vaguely delimited areas, Medes to the south of the Caspian Sea, advancing into Luristan in about 650 BC, Scythians and Cimmerians to the west and Persians further south. The Medes were the best organized and they, in alliance with the Scythians, brought about the fall of the Assyrian empire in 612 BC. Cyrus the Great (d. 530 BC) was one of their vassals until about 550 BC, when he and his Persian followers rebelled, sacked the Median capital Ecbatana (present-day Hamadan) and brought the whole of Iran under his rule, which he then extended to east and west. The empire Cyrus founded was the largest the world had yet seen: by the end of the sixth century BC it reached from the Oxus and Indus rivers to the Danube and beyond the Nile, incorporating all the former Assyrian territory, as well as all Anatolia, what is now Turkey in Europe, Bulgaria and much of northern Greece, Egypt and Libya. The Achaemenid dynasty, named after Cyrus's ancestor Achaemenes, continued to reign over most of this vast area until it was conquered by Alexander the Great in 332 BC.

In this way the Near East, or rather the whole civilized area of western Asia, came under the control of a tribe of nomadic or semi-nomadic horsemen – with the surprising result that civilization was not destroyed but enhanced. Cyrus imposed peace on kingdoms which had for centuries been at war with one another. Unlike all previous, and most later, conquerors he respected the religious and other traditions of the people he overcame. Multilingual inscriptions were used, for example. He even had the tribes of Judah repatriated from Babylonian captivity and, according to the Bible, ordered the rebuilding of the temple in Jerusalem: 'Thus saith Cyrus king of Persia, the Lord God of Heaven hath given me all the kingdoms of the earth, and he hath charged me to build him an house at Jerusalem, which is in Judea' (II Chronicles 36, 23). Thus the art of the Achaemenid empire reflected both the diversity of its subject states and the unifying ambition of its

rulers. Darius I (521–486 BC), in an inscription on his palace at Susa, itemized the provenance from various parts of his dominions of all the materials used in the buildings and went on to declare:

The stone-cutters who wrought the stone were Ionians and Sardinians. The goldsmiths who wrought the gold were Medes and Egyptians. The men who wrought the baked brick were Babylonians. The men who adorned the walls were Medes and Egyptians.

The Persians themselves are not mentioned, but it was they who effected this cosmopolitan synthesis of styles and probably contributed elements from their own tradition.

The finest artistic achievement of the Achaemenid dynasty was in architecture. The Achaemenids greatly advanced on the mud-brick architecture of the Medes, though deriving from them such prominent features as the huge, rectangular, many-columned or hypostyle hall (prefigured in eighth- to sixth-century BC Median citadels at Godin Tepe and Tepe Nushi-i Jan, near Hamadan). There were no large Achaemenid temples, for the gods were worshipped at fire altars in the open air even before the monotheistic creed of Zoroaster (628–551 BC) became the official cult of Iran (probably after the Achaemenid period). Cyrus the Great was buried in a free-standing stone-built tomb on a high stepped podium or platform at Pasargadae. Other important tombs were cut into cliffs, their fronts enriched with rock-carvings of figures and with pilasters and entablatures which are decorative and sculptural rather than functional and architectural (**3,34**). The most imposing, sometimes called the Tomb of Darius, is at Naksh-i-Rustam near Persepolis, crowned by a relief

3,34 Tomb at Naksh-i-Rustam, Iran, c. 500 BC.

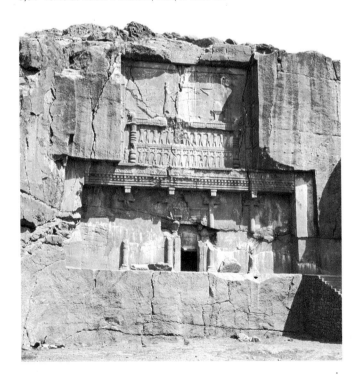

of a king standing bow in hand before a fire altar. Large-scale sculpture seems to have been limited almost exclusively to work in relief and to architectural ornament such as bull's head capitals. The free-standing and over life-size statue of Darius discovered at Susa is unique. Carved some time between 500 and 490 BC, it is unfortunately headless (Archeological Museum, Tehran).

Cyrus the Great established his capital at Pasargadae in a wide and fertile plain in the modern province of Fars. The name means 'camp of the Persians' and the palace built by Cyrus was like the encampment of a nomad chief transformed into stone, with several buildings loosely grouped and placed independently and at some distance from one another in a vast enclosure of parkland and gardens surrounded by a 13-foot-thick (4m) wall, entered through a monumental gatehouse. Much use was made of tall columns, some with lion-headed capitals in stone, both for porticoes and to support the roofs of large hypostyle halls, which may have been partly inspired by ancient Egyptian precedents (see p. 100) as well as by those of the Medes (see above), though they are square in plan, with no dominant axis in any direction. Since the columns carried beams of strong cedar-wood from the Lebanon, and not stone lintels, they could be much taller, slimmer and more widely spaced than those in Egypt, making the interiors correspondingly lighter and airier. Black and white limestone slabs were used decoratively in alternation with telling effect and with extremely precise

stereotomy (see Glossary). So the general effect must have been quite unlike that made by ancient Egyptian temples or by Mesopotamian palaces with their long, narrow rooms – even though such carved decorations as winged bulls at the entrances and reliefs of winged demons or genii were derived from Assyria.

PERSEPOLIS

Darius I, who succeeded Cyrus's son Cambyses II (the conqueror of Egypt) in 521 BC, moved the capital to the former Elamite city of Susa. The palace he erected there was apparently inspired by that of Babylon, built round large interior courtyards. Babylonian lions, bulls and griffins in molded, glazed brickwork paraded along the walls, more richly colored than in their homeland and now augmented by figures of archers from Darius's famous royal guard – the 1,000 'immortals', as they were called. Here again there was an audience-hall of grandiose proportions with 72 columns about 65 feet (20m) high. The palace was burnt down some time between 465 and 425 BC and little has survived standing. Much more remains of that at Persepolis, begun by Darius I in 518 BC and completed under his son Xerxes and grandson Artaxerxes Isome 70 years later (3,35).

The lay-out of Persepolis recalls Pasargadae, for although the buildings are closer together, they are again disposed loosely as separate entities in irregular open

3,35 Persepolis, Iran, c. 500 BC.

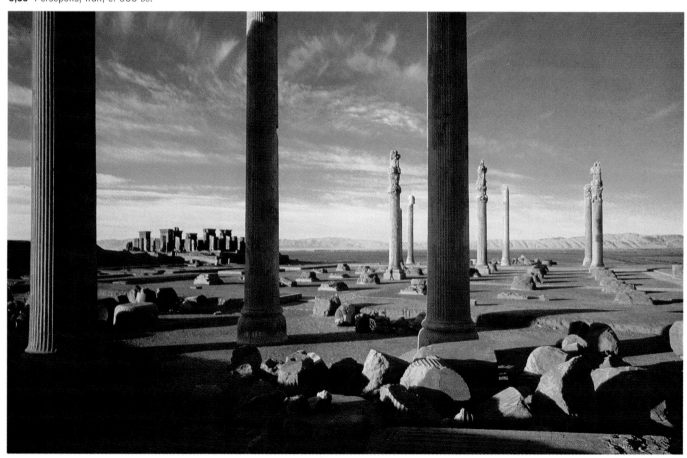

spaces as in an encampment (**3,36**). The lowest slope of a mountain behind the site was levelled and extended forwards to make a vast terrace nearly 1,500 by 1,000 feet (460 by 300m), faced by a retaining wall some 40 feet (12m) high of massive, finely cut rectangular blocks of stone. Wide flights of steps, shallow enough for horsemen to ride up them, led to the terrace where the main buildings were set on a platform approached up further flights of steps. There were two huge hypostyle halls (see Glossary), the 250-foot-square (76m) and 60-foot-high (18m) audience hall (or *apadana*) and the still larger Hall of the Hundred Columns or throne hall. The king received the Persian and Median nobles in the former, delegates of tributary states in the latter. The columns in these halls were of unique form: slightly spreading bell-shaped bases, slender fluted shafts and complex capitals with downcurving motifs somewhat like palm leaves, volutes and impost blocks (see Glossary) composed of the forequarters of two lions, bulls or human-headed bulls (**3,37**).

Even stranger than the form is the construction of the columns. Although there were mud-brick curtain walls and some brick vaulting, stone was used at Persepolis to an extent unprecedented in Asia – and it was handled in a very peculiar way. The drums of which the columns are composed, for example, are of unequal height and the joins between them do not coincide with the decorative divisions. Similarly, the windows in the residential palace were not constructed of separate vertical and horizontal elements, of posts, lintels and sills. Either a single block of stone was cut and carved to make a whole window frame in one piece; or, if two or more blocks were used, the pieces were likewise carved and then placed on top of

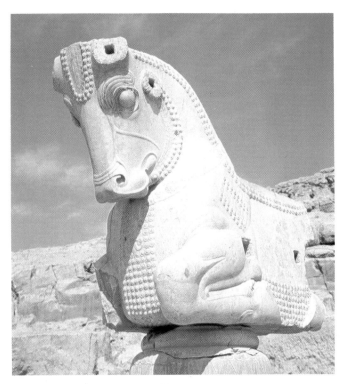

3,37 Bull capital, Persepolis, c. 500 BC.

one another rather than being joined at the angles. Flights of steps were composed not of separate slabs, one for every tread, but of large blocks, each carved to form several steps and a corresponding section of the parapet. Such a practice cannot, obviously, have derived from a tradition of timber or mud-brick construction. It may have originated in the custom of hewing flights of steps out of the living rock, as adopted at an Urartian site on Lake Van. In fact, the architect of Persepolis seems to have aimed at combining this rock-like permanence with the spacious lightness of the large tents of a nomadic chieftain's encampment.

Susa was the Achaemenid administrative capital; Persepolis was an imperial symbol, the spectacular setting for ceremonies, when tribute from every part of the empire was brought to the 'Great King, King of Kings, King of Persia' – as Darius I and his successors were titled. Architectural ornamentation symbolized the extent of his dominion – the royal winged discs of Egypt, for instance, and the human-headed winged bulls of Assyria. Every one of the hundreds of columns was composed of diverse national elements – the fluted shaft and voluted capital of the Ionian Greeks, foliage from the Nile, bulls and lions from Mesopotamia – all welded in a new imperial unity. But impressive as Persepolis is as an expression of Achaemenid imperial ambitions, it may well have had a further dimension of meaning. Various details of the sculptural decorations suggest that it was the ritual centre of the Achaemenid world, notably the repeated and prominently placed image of the lion slaying the bull, which has been connected with the conjunction of the zodiacal signs of Leo and Taurus at the vernal equinox.

3,36 Plan of Persepolis.

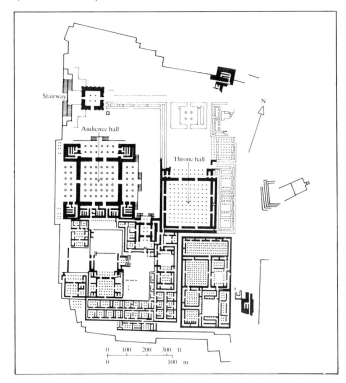

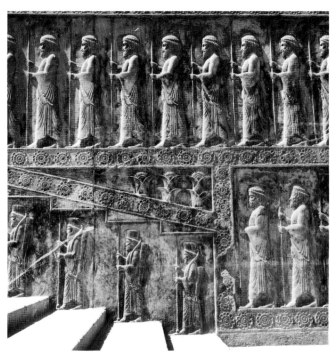

3,38 Subjects bringing gifts to the king, relief on the stairway to the audience hall, Persepolis, c. 500 BC.

Persepolis may have been conceived as a kind of sermon or prayer in stone representing and re-enacting eternally in sculpture the rites of the Persian New Year, the Now Ruz, when the world was believed to be conquered and created anew, initially by a god and later symbolically by the king. The figurative relief carvings on the terrace walls, originally colored like the glazed brickwork of Susa and Babylon, probably perpetuate the annual ceremonies performed here – line upon line of alternating Medes and Persians with their distinguishing headgear, ranks of soldiers, bevies of servants carrying dishes to the banquet preceding the enthroning of the Great King, with which the festival ended, and the long procession of representatives of subject peoples, the Bactrian with his camel, the Babylonian with a humped ox, Syrians bearing pieces of metalwork (**3,38**), in honour of the auspicious beginning of a new year and the continuance of the Achaemenid world order. All move to the same slow, regimental march, all have equally expressionless faces, all are carved in the same stylized, almost uniform, manner.

These figures follow artistic conventions established nearly 3,000 years earlier in Sumer and Egypt. Whether they are shown in pure profile or with their torsos twisted to the front, their feet are always placed in a single plane and cemented to the inflexible ground line of ancient Near Eastern art. Sometimes inspiration may have been drawn from Assyrian reliefs, though their nervous energy and dramatic intensity have been lost. That heads and heavily draped bodies are rendered with a fuller sense of three-dimensional form may be due to Ionian Greek sculptors, who are known to have been sent to the Persian court. But there could hardly be a more striking contrast than that between these regimented figures and the

athletic horsemen in the Panathenaic procession carved for the Parthenon in Athens just two decades after Persepolis was completed (4,31). Each Greek is an independent being and moves freely in a logically conceived space beyond the frontal plane. The figures at Persepolis remain bound by the rules of grammar and syntax of a visual language that the Mediterranean world had already begun to reject.

ZHOU CHINA

For some 800 years after the fall of the Shang in the eleventh century BC the greater part of China from Manchuria to south of the Yangzi – an area very much larger than that of any of the contemporary empires of the Near East – was ruled by kings of the Zhou dynasty, though no more than nominally after 771 BC (see below). The Zhou came originally from the north-west, established their capital near modern Xi'an in the early eleventh century and deposed the last Shang king in 1027 BC. As the Zhou had already been subject to Shang cultural influence for some time there was no break in continuity. Shang institutions were elaborated rather than replaced. Craftsmen seem at first to have been little affected by the dynastic change, but Chinese art gradually underwent the first of the many transmutations which were to modify, without essentially altering, its character throughout its long history.

No trace of stone sculpture of the kind that adorned Shang buildings (2,65) has as yet been found at Zhou sites and, though Zhou artists were certainly capable of modelling figures naturalistically in the round, early bronzes indicate the stylized and decorative design of their artistic sense. The bronze tiger illustrated (**3,39**) is one of a pair intended as supports (the holes in their backs are sockets for a superstructure, presumably of wood), so its function was primarily ornamental. The scrolls covering its shoulders and haunches are conceived simply as surface patterning, more elegant, more linear, more sophisticated perhaps than those on Shang bronzes, but quite without their organic vigour (2,64). They are no longer part of the object but superimposed. The harshness of Shang forms has also been smoothed out. Their aggressive jutting and jagged flanges have disappeared into evenly enriched

3,39 Tiger, 9th century BC. Bronze, 9⁷/₈ × 29⁵/₈ins (25 × 75.2cm). Freer Gallery of Art, Smithsonian Institution, Washington DC.

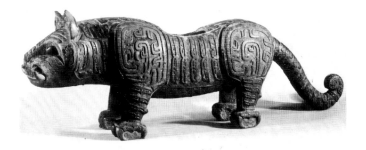

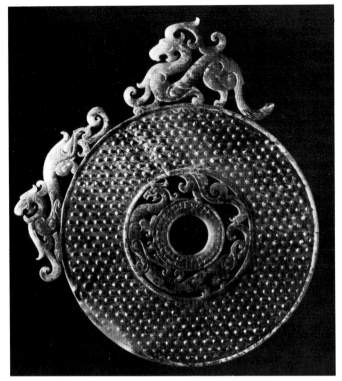

3,40 Pierced disc or *bi*, c. 400 BC. Jade, 6¹/₂ins (16.5cm) diameter. Nelson-Atkins Museum of Art, Kansas City (Purchase: Nelson Trust).

surfaces and rounded, continuous contours. A more refined art, perhaps, it is also a more purely decorative one. Even the *taotie* or dragon mask (see pp. 88–9) tended to be fragmented into separate elements and lost the sense of primitive, magical power.

The change may have been partly due to increasing secularization: indeed, the long inscriptions recording the circumstances in which ritual vessels were cast often suggest it. That on an early eighth-century BC *ding* (a type of ritual cauldron) describes in colorful detail how an official was given a royal mandate to govern a town and in commemoration commissioned vessels in which to sacrifice to the spirits of his parents 'to solicit tranquillity of heart, piety, pure blessing, steady salary and long life . . . to enjoy a myriad years and the bushy eyebrows of old age'. The cauldron was, he said, to be cherished and used by his sons and grandsons. Such bronze vessels had evidently become symbols of status for members of the ruling class.

Ancestor-worship, which encouraged conservatism in life and art, was an expression of political and social as well as religious ideas. The Zhou were a clan who claimed descent by direct male line from a single mythical ancestor, the relative importance of its members being determined by genealogical proximity to the main line of primary sons by primary wives in each generation. The king, styled 'the Son of Heaven', reigned in the capital and princes of the blood were sent to govern provinces, where they established independent lineages with ever more distant branches. Allies and court retainers were also given grants of land, which passed to their descendants. While the authority of the king remained absolute, this feudal system provided a unifying structure of government, reflected in the arts by a predominant metropolitan style. But in 771 BC people from the Ordos regions of the north

invaded and sacked the capital, killing the king, whose successor set up his court further east at Luoyang, which became the capital of the eastern Zhou kingdom. As royal power declined in the following centuries, the holders of fiefs became more independent and the country was gradually divided into warring states, after which the period from 475 BC to reunification under the first Qin emperor in 221 BC is named. (The period from 771 to 475 BC is called that of the Spring and Autumn Annals.) Yet, somewhat surprisingly, this turbulent period was one of rapid economic, technological and social advance – notably in irrigation, agriculture and metallurgy. Similarly in art, a proliferation of regional styles in the eighth and seventh centuries BC, sometimes influenced by the nomads of central Asia (see p. 159), was followed during the Warring States period by a flowering of Chinese inventive genius in decorative works of the highest artistic order. Conventionalized natural forms usually become decorative formulae, but these remain intensely, tremulously alive. No other artists have been able to bring artistic forms to such a pitch of stylistic generalization and abstraction without loss of energy or vitality. It was during this troubled period, also, that scholars and philosophers first acquired the influence they were to exert throughout subsequent Chinese history. The founders of the two great philosophies Confucianism and Daoism (see p. 263) lived at this time.

Jade had been prized in China from a very early date, decorated mainly with incised linear designs. Now the exacting art of shaping it in subtle relief by grinding away the hard and brittle stone was perfected. Some jade ritual objects are remarkable, both for their technical virtuosity and for their controlled vitality in design (**3,40**). The regularity of the surface decoration balances the free, but always supremely elegant, forms of the dragons along

3,41 Lacquer box, c. 400 BC. Diameter about 8ins (20cm). John Hadley Cox Collection, Washington DC.

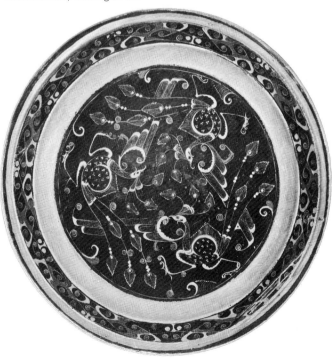

its edge. It is precisely this held tension between the designer's intellectual control and the artist's more instinctual responses that gives Zhou art its peculiar and very powerful quality. This can be seen at its finest in lacquer, a new medium which calls for as much technical dexterity as jade. The sap of the lac tree – *Rhus verniciflua* – had previously been used for waterproofing clothes and also possibly for inlays on bronze vessels. About the fifth century BC it was discovered that brilliantly colored caskets and plates, resistant to damp and heat, could be made by applying successive coats of lacquer to a wooden or cloth core. The process was extremely laborious as each coat had to be left to harden before the next was applied, and designs painted in lacquer colored with other substances had to be repeated at each stage. Decorative effects of the greatest sophistication were achieved, however, as on the lid of a casket with peacocks in shades of vermilion red on a lustrous black ground (3,41). The strutting birds, each one with its tail feathers overlapping the wing of the next, make a pattern of perfectly integrated

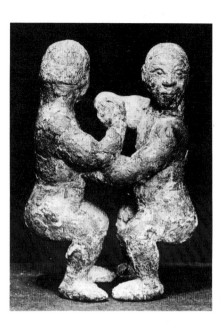

3,43 Acrobats or wrestlers, c. 400 BC. Bronze, 6ins (15.2cm) high. British Museum, London.

3,42 Mask and handle from Yixian, Hopei, c. 400 BC. Bronze, mask and retaining bar 18ins (45.5cm) long. China.

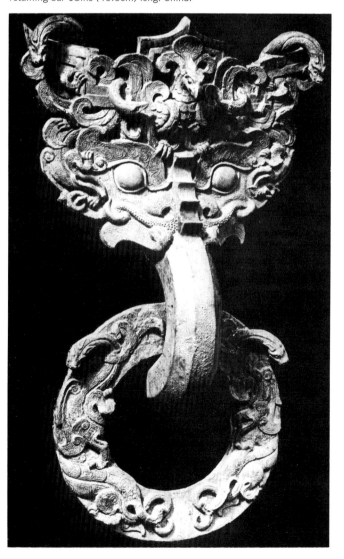

intricacy set off by the abstract decoration of the outer rim, which echoes the spacing, rhythm and accents of the central medallion.

Iron came into use in China in the fifth century BC, long after its revolutionary effect had been assimilated in the West (p. 93), but probably as a result of an independent discovery. (Implements were forged in the West and not cast until the fourteenth century AD: the sequence was reversed in China.) On the other hand, the lost-wax or *cire perdue* process of casting bronze used in the late Zhou period to supplement the traditional and peculiarly Chinese technique of casting from piece-molds (p. 87) may have been transmitted across Asia. A mask and handle with many undercut projections could have been cast in no other way (3,42). It was found in a tomb, where it had probably been attached to a door, to ward off evil spirits as well as to demonstrate the wealth and status of the deceased. On the mask there is a reminiscence of the *taotie*, but elaborated into bold complexity by the addition of lifelike serpents, dragons with scaly bodies and a central phoenix. Supple forms seem to be in perpetual motion, writhing smoothly in and out of one another within the tight symmetrical pattern. On the suspended ring, dragons arch back their heads like those on the upper corners of the mask, visually uniting the two parts.

Alongside this purely decorative art a number of late Zhou (or Warring States period) sculptures manifest an extraordinary naturalism new to China and of a kind not to be reached (or perhaps attempted) for several centuries in painting. Statuettes of stocky horses and vessels in the form of rhinoceroses would seem to have been modelled from life. Human figures are usually rendered with less vitality, but a small group of acrobats or wrestlers, knees bent as if about to leap into action, is in every way exceptional (3,43). The figures are entertainers and the group seems to have been intended quite simply to give visual pleasure (i.e. it had no ritual function nor was it intended for burial with the dead). But few works better exemplify

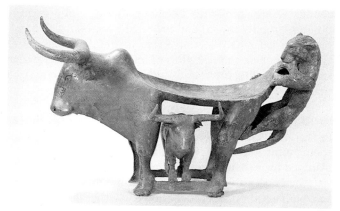

3,44 Dian culture, offering table, 6th to 5th century BC. Bronze, 17ins (43cm) high. National Museum, Kunmin, Yunnan.

the rigorous co-ordination of parts into a single artistic unity, which characterizes all Chinese art of this time. Like the finest works of Zhou decorative art, it derives its force from a tension between free visual rhythms and the controlling intelligence which gives structural unity. Expressive rather than descriptive, an embodiment of energy rather than thought, and in no way an idealization of the human form, it makes a striking contrast with the statues of athletes which, as we shall see, were being produced in Greece at exactly the same moment.

Between the areas in which the Greek and Chinese civilizations evolved, the vast plains of central Asia were peopled mainly by tribes of nomads whom the Greeks regarded as 'barbarians' (see p. 159) though the Chinese were less, if at all, contemptuous of them at this period. On the south-west border of territory contested by the Chinese 'Warring States', a people with an independent culture were settled round Lake Dian (in present-day Yunnan province bordering Burma, Laos and Vietnam). They were not to be mentioned in Chinese chronicles until after they had been incorporated in the Han empire in 109 BC. But their tombs, which began to be excavated in the 1950s, have brought to light the remains of a structured society that had been able to support skilled artists and craftsmen. A bronze offering table (**3,44**) dating from the sixth to fifth century BC is among the earliest of their works of art that have so far been found; it is also among the most accomplished both technically and artistically. It differs strikingly from Shang and early Zhou bronzes both in the way it was cast (in pieces but not from ceramic molds) and in the extraordinary naturalism of the head of the large bull, the smaller one standing under it and the tiger attacking the hind-quarters. Among other relics of this 'Dian culture' some have links with the Animal style of central Asia (see p. 160), others with the art of south-east Asia, notably drum-shaped containers for cowrie shells topped by groups of lively little figures fighting or taking part in rituals. They are of interest for themselves and also as examples of forms of artistic expression rejected by the Chinese though they shared a common language and, despite regional diversities, various formal artistic affinities.

THE AMERICAS

There are arresting similarities between the arts of the Americas and those of China and the ancient Near East – artificial mounds like ziggurats in Mexico, carvings that recall the reliefs on Shang dynasty bronzes in Peru – but quite as many, more fundamental, differences reflecting attitudes to life at variance with those of the rest of the world. Early stages of social evolution were much the same. In about the seventh millennium hunting and foraging were supplemented by the cultivation of maize, which gradually became, and still remains, the staple food of Mesoamerica (i.e. present-day Mexico, Belize, Guatemala and Honduras). By about 1500 BC there were settled agricultural villages in the uplands of Mexico, and before the end of the second millennium these had been aggregated into some form of state with large cult or ceremonial centres, which presuppose organized religion and a ruling class of priests. Improvement in the quality of domesticated maize by a process of selection seems to have had an effect akin to that of irrigation in Mesopotamia, providing the surplus of food necessary to support a social superstructure. But no cities were built until a thousand years later (Teotihuacán appears to have been the first; see Chapter 12), and the economic developments that usually accompany urbanization hardly took place at all. Priests acquired the mathematical ability to calculate in millions, discovered and understood the concept of zero and learned how to measure the length of the solar year with scientific precision; but no standard system of weights, measures and currency was devised. The people who laid out vast temple precincts and produced some of the world's most imposing monumental sculpture were slow to develop metallurgy and never grasped the principle of the wheel, on which so much technology is based.

A gap of some 8,000 years in the archeological record intervenes between the prehistoric carved coyote head from Tequixquiac (1,13) and the beginning of a recoverable sequence of works of art. Near Xochipala, some 60 miles (100km) inland from the Pacific coast in the modern

Ancient Mesoamerica

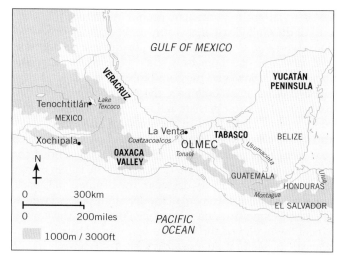

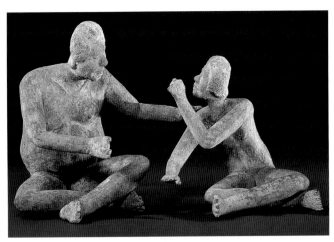

3,45 Statuettes from near Xochipala, Mexico, c. 1300 BC. Terracotta, 5⅓ and 4⅓ins (13.5 and 11cm) high. Art Museum, Princeton University.

Mexican province of Guerrero, a number of clay statuettes have been found dating from about 1300 BC, but modelled with a sureness of hand, a sensitivity to three-dimensional form and a liveliness that suggest a well-established tradition (**3,45**). Two of them form a group, earnestly engaged in conversation, seated in easy poses, with expressive faces and eloquent gestures, the middle-aged corpulence of the one almost touchingly contrasted with the adolescent slenderness of the other. Like many later Mesoamerican figures, they are of puzzlingly indeterminate sex. Others are of youths dressed for the ball-game – a religious ritual as well as a sport (like ancient Greek athletics). These Xochipala figures are the earliest works of art that can be associated with the Olmecs, whose formative influence on the first civilizations of the Americas is comparable with that of the Sumerians in the ancient Near East.

The Olmecs

The great Olmec sites are on the opposite coast of Mexico in the provinces of Veracruz and Tabasco, where occupation can be dated back to before 1200 BC. (The word Olmec means 'dweller in the land of rubber' and was originally given to an entirely different people inhabiting the same area of the Gulf Coast at the time of the Spanish conquest.) Most works of art found in the region are stone sculptures and cannot be dated precisely since stone resists scientific dating tests. However, they are probably much later than the figures found at Xochipala, though the remarkable naturalism of the latter persists and is, indeed, brought to a far more sophisticated level in the finest of all Olmec sculptures, the bearded athlete known as the Wrestler, which may well be a portrait (**3,46**). (Beards are rare among the indigenous people of the Americas.) Controlled inner energy is felt to an extraordinary degree in the firmness of muscle and slow, flexing movement of the spiralling pose, as well as the steady concentration of the face. Moreover, the continuous flow of curved surfaces can be fully appreciated only when it is seen, as it must have been conceived, in the

round. Other surviving Olmec sculptures are entirely different, rigidly frontal and rigorously symmetrical. Small pieces in jade – a material prized in the Americas, as in China – include many figures of infants with the growling snouts of jaguars, their heads fully carved in a schematized manner, their bodies often no more than indicated by incised lines (**3,47**). There are also colossal stone heads, up to 12 feet (3.5m) high, of which 16 have been discovered at various Olmec ceremonial centres (**3,48**). Most of them wear hemispherical, often helmet-like head-gear clamped over their brows and have similarly puffy cheeks, flattened noses and thick lips, the ethnic traits of a master-race perhaps, though it is not known whether they represent gods or hierarchs (chief priests). Differences in their head-gear suggest the possibility of individual portraiture or at least of specialized regalia. These heads were placed facing outwards from a ceremonial precinct, perhaps to ward off evil (like Assyrian *lamassu*).

3,46 *Right* Wrestler, from S Maria Uxpanapan, before 400 BC. Basalt, 26ins (66cm) high. Museo Nacional de Antropologia, Mexico City.

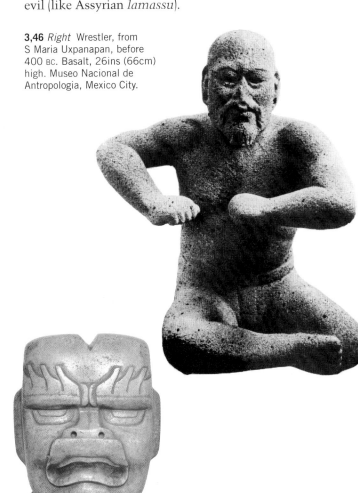

3,47 *Left* Stone knife or celt, before 600 BC. Jade, about 12ins (30.5cm) high. British Museum, London.

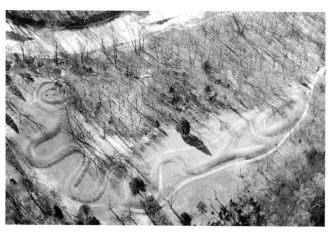

3,49 Great Serpent Mound, Adams County, Ohio, c. 300 BC–c. AD 400.

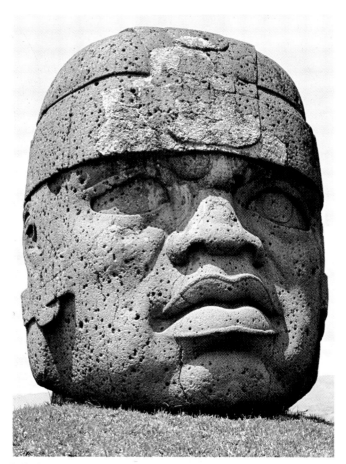

3,48 Colossal monolithic head from S Lorenzo, Tenochtitlán, before 400 BC. Basalt, 5ft 10ins (1.8m) high. Museo Regional de Veracruz, Jalapa, Mexico.

Olmec ceremonial centres were not in the maize-growing lands that supported them, but in the tropical rain forests, and were permanently inhabited by no more than a few hierarchs and their retainers (probably including sculptors). The materials of which they were constructed and also the huge stone heads were brought from far away. The most important, La Venta on an island on the Tonalá river, had a fluted conical mound 420 feet (130m) across and more than 100 feet (30m) high, a long court flanked by platforms and a smaller court surrounded by thickly set basalt columns, on a south–north axis. A deep rectangular pit in the smaller court was filled with layer upon layer of small blocks of serpentine marble presumably brought as offerings – the nearest source is 350 miles (560km) away by water. It was topped with a jaguar mask, reduced to the point of geometrical abstraction, apparently covered up as soon as it was completed – the act of making it being of greater importance than its visual effect. The Olmecs seem to have initiated the practice of ritual construction, destruction and reconstruction of religious buildings, which was observed by later civilizations of Mesoamerica in accordance with 52-year cycles of the calendar. (In Japan, also, Shinto temples were to be destroyed and rebuilt at regular prescribed intervals, see p. 285.)

The plan of the mounds and courts at La Venta resembles a jaguar mask. Symbols of such a size that their imagery can be recognized only when seen from far above were created in other widely separated parts of the Americas. In the north, between about 500 BC and AD 500,

earth-works called 'effigy mounds' were raised in the form of snakes and birds, presumably as ceremonial centres for the farming communities which supplemented agriculture with hunting and gathering. The Great Serpent in Adams County, Ohio, USA, an undulating bank of earth some 6 yards (5.5m) wide and more than 400 yards (365m) long, testifies to the mound-builders' ability in planning on a grand scale and in organizing a large workforce in order to honour or propitiate supernatural powers (**3,49**). In southern Peru, probably some centuries later, the barren plateau between the Palpa and Ingenio rivers was used as a field for a gigantic network of inflexibly straight lines many miles long, zigzags and 'drawings' of animals made by removing surface stones to expose the yellow soil – the largest work of art in the world (**3,50**). The lines

3,50 Marking on the pampa above the Palpa river, Peru, first millennium BC.

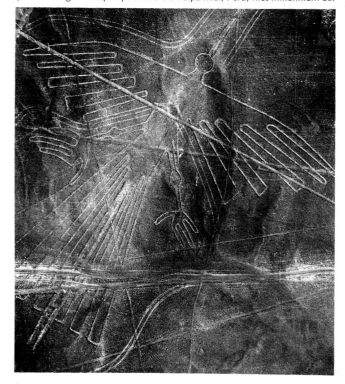

seem to have been determined by astronomical observation and were perhaps permanent records of rituals with cosmic significance, transforming an area of several hundred square miles into a temple without walls, an architecture of two-dimensional space, of diagram and relation of lines rather than of mass.

PERU

There would seem to have been parallel developments of civilization in Mesoamerica and some 2,000 miles (3,200km) away in the valleys leading down from the Andes to the Pacific, where the adoption of agriculture and a settled way of life was accompanied by the construction of religious buildings even before the introduction of pottery. At Aspero (about 100 miles – 160km – north of modern Lima) there are substantial remains of large stone-faced platforms which supported temples, dating from the beginning of the third millennium – contemporary with the ziggurats of Mesopotamia and the great pyramids of Egypt. The sheer size of these early Peruvian monuments is astonishing. At El Paraiso on the central coast an area of more than 140 acres (57 hectares) was laid out around 2000 BC, incorporating two rectangular stone structures, each about 135 feet (41m) wide. At Sechin Alto a truncated pyramid 115 feet (35m) high built in about 1200 BC dominates a series of plazas and sunken courts extending for nearly a mile (1.6km) in front

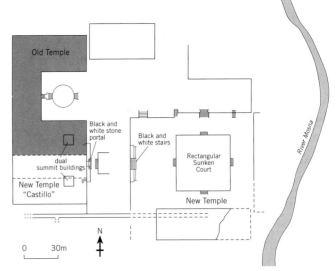

3,51 *Above* Plan of Chavín de Huántar, Ancash, Peru, 900–500 BC.

Right The Old Temple.

1 Gallery of the Madman
2 Gallery of the Offerings
3 Field Camp Gallery
4 Gallery of the Bats
5 Gallery of the Snails
6 Gallery of the Labyrinths
7 Alecenas Gallery
8 Gallery of the Staircases

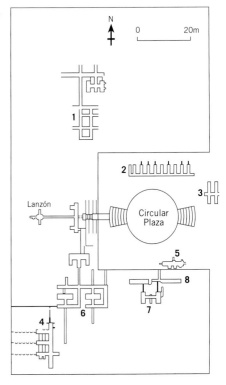

Ancient Peru

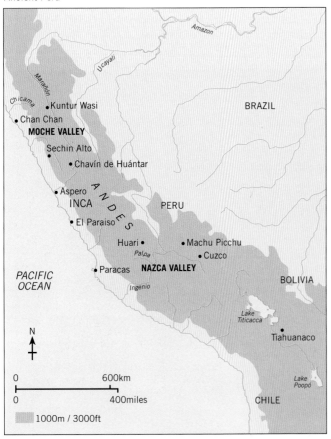

of it. At Kuntur Wasi, high up in the Andes, a natural peak was levelled towards the end of the second millennium to form a quadrangular platform of about 32 acres (13 hectares), approached up wide stone staircases.

Chavín de Huántar, begun about 900 BC and enlarged some 400 years later, seems to have been one of the most important of these early religious complexes. The original structure, a U-shaped block with the two arms of different heights (**3,51**), faced with well-cut stone, embraced a square court and sunken circular plaza lined with flat slabs on which figures of jaguars and mythological creatures were carved in very low relief. The block, the highest section of which rises to 52 feet (16m), is windowless but encloses three stories of narrow galleries linked by stairs and ingeniously ventilated by air-shafts. In its central parts a white granite monolith some 15 feet

Chavín de Huántar

RELIGION AND SOCIETY IN ANCIENT PERU

Chavín de Huántar is high up in the Andes, some 10,300 feet (3,140m) above sea level, on the eastern side of the Cordillera Blanca at the point where two rivers join to flow down towards the Marañon and Amazon, approximately half way between the arid Pacific coast and the tropical forests. It is also at a junction of old trade routes. The local population, dispersed in hamlets, lived by high-altitude farming and the herding of indigenous llamas. How they succeeded in constructing such a large and elaborate monument as the temple at Chavín in about 900–500 BC is something of a mystery. There is no trace of a ruling caste of warriors or priests: no burials have been found with grave goods indicating wealth or power. And the same may be said of earlier religious complexes elsewhere in Peru, where the work of assembling materials seems to have been co-operative.

The religious beliefs to which the vast temple complexes at Chavín and elsewhere remain as witnesses, survived for 2,000 years and neither the Incas (see pp. 522–4) nor the Spanish conquistadors were able to eradicate them entirely. Though flourishing in the climatically very diverse environments of the Pacific littoral, the Andean highlands and the lush valley of the tropical Marañon river, all shared a common cosmology and worshipped and propitiated common deities who, to judge from their images, were none too beneficent. The temple complexes all have high platforms with steeply battered sides, often on U-shaped plans, as at Chavín, with one arm of the U higher and wider than the other. But there are as many differences as similarities between their architectural forms and, especially, their sculptural enrichments.

The platform at Chavín de Huántar opens to the east with no habitations between it and the river and the distant mountains rising above the valley beyond. Its orientation seems to have been determined by a western axis taken from the point of sunset at the winter solstice. From the courts this would have been seen glowing above the snow-clad peak of Huánstan, a sacred mountain. The approach to the temple was from the west. Visitors were there confronted with a vast blank wall from which stone heads, about three times life-size, stared out (**3,52; 53; 54**). They had to walk down from there to the river and then climb back up again by stone-faced terraces to the court with its sunken circular plaza, which could hold some 500 people. It seems likely that rituals of some kind were performed on top of the great platform though they could have been seen only from below. The 'priests' would have emerged from, and may even have lived in, the windowless interior. The recurrence in carvings at Chavín of the San Pedro cactus, source of mescalin, and the presence of mortars of the kind used for grinding vilca seeds, indicates that hallucinogenic drugs were used to induce shamanistic trances. Sequences of the giant heads originally on the west wall of the platform vividly suggest the transmutation of a human face into a fanged semi-animal and then into an entirely animal form such as would have been achieved by a shaman during the passage to the world of spirits (3,52; 53; 54). In a state of trance an initiate could also become an oracle conveying the wishes of the gods. And oracles were still greatly respected by the Inca rulers when the Spanish invaded Peru.

The discovery at Chavín of pottery vessels made in distant places and of precious seashells from the Pacific – presumably temple offerings – reveals the presence of pilgrims before 500 BC. They may have helped to finance the enlargement of the temple platform at about that date and the creation of a new sunken rectangular plaza capable of holding more than 1,500 people. But by this time the patterns of life were changing. Old religious beliefs survived but were no longer the main bond between the populations of the coast and the mountains. Chavín became no more than a minor cult centre and it was a ruin by the time a Spaniard went there in 1616.

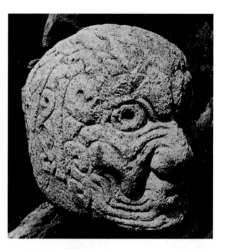

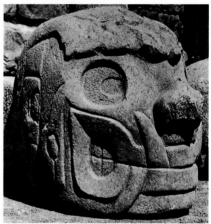

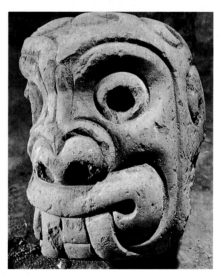

3,52; 53; 54 Three heads from the west wall of the temple, 900–500 BC. Sandstone, about 34½ins (87.6cm) high. Chavín de Huántar.

(4.5m) high, called the *Lanzón* (lance) (**3,55**), is fixed between the floor and ceiling of the central chamber. This cult image is carved in very low relief to represent a standing man with a tusked feline face, curls of hair which terminate in snake heads and, above, curving lines suggestive of more eyes and teeth and snarling lips. It differs as much from the great rounded stone heads and even the jaguar-faced infants of the Olmecs as does the tightly planned complex of buildings at Chavín from the widely spaced masses of the sanctuaries in Mesoamerica. The double meanings of individual elements (snakes and hair), the device of splitting a head so that two profiles share a single mouth, and the aggressive, though rounded, rectangles are all reminiscent of Shang dynasty bronzes (2,64). Such similarities are as striking as they are difficult to

explain. Forms and motifs still closer to those of early Chinese art occur again in stone vases carved in the Ula valley of Honduras some 2,000 years later. One can only speculate as to whether the inhabitants of the lands on either side of the Pacific inherited from their remote common ancestry not only physical traits but also aesthetic preferences, handed on from generation to generation and expressed only in such impermanent media as body-painting or drawing in the sand.

There is little possibility of direct contact having brought artistic motifs from Asia to America. Had there been direct contact, such fundamental inventions as that of the wheel would have reached America. In fact, many manual techniques developed quite independently in the Americas; that of weaving, for example, was far in

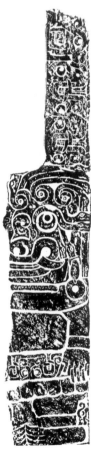

3,55 *Above* Rubbing of upper part of the *Lanzon* in the Old Temple, Chavín de Huántar, after 900 BC. White granite, total height about 15ft (4.57m).

3,56 *Right* Mantle from Paracas, Peru, detail, about 200 BC. Wool. Museum für Völkerkunde, Munich.

advance of the rest of the world. The cotton plant was domesticated and the processes of preparing, dyeing and twining its fibres into fabrics were mastered in Peru before 3000 BC (rather earlier than in the Indus Valley, p. 58). Wool from the llama, alpaca and vicuna was subsequently treated in the same way. A form of heddle-loom was invented by about 1500 BC and nearly all the pre-industrial textile techniques of the world with threads dyed in nearly 200 different colors were in use before the first century AD.

Great mantles from tombs on the Paracas peninsula, where they were preserved in the exceptionally dry climate and soil, display as much virtuosity in design as in technique. Motifs embroidered on finely woven panels are robustly delineated – human beings, birds, beasts, fish and various monsters – every shape being endowed with vivacious intensity. On one mantle the figure of a man with head thrown back, as if in an ecstatic dance, is repeated to form a pattern of bare simplicity, but enlivened throughout with minute variations in color and inflections of form, so that a rippling sense of unity without uniformity is created (3,56). Such garments wrapped round the dead (naturally desiccated, not mummified in the ancient Egyptian manner) were found in tombs of two types: one a bottle-shaped underground chamber; the other, which is later (from c. 200 BC), a rectangular chamber with stone walls. They were made to be worn by members of an élite dwelling not on the coast but in fertile country at least 20 miles (32km) inland, where they evidently had commercial contact with the highlands, the source of the wool used to weave most Paracas textiles. The Paracas peninsula was presumably chosen as a burial place because of its unusual aridity, to preserve the bodies of the dead. The textiles, which were found buried together with fine painted pottery vessels, give a vivid impression of a style of life achieved by a civilization that had developed without the aid of – or perhaps one should say without the need for – writing to record its history and its religious beliefs.

AFRICA: NOK CULTURE

In Africa, too, an accomplished artistic style was created by a non-literate people in the course of the first millennium BC. They were farmers occupying the extensive area of the Jos plateau in northern Nigeria, and at least as early as 400 BC they acquired the technology of iron smelting, possibly diffused across the continent from the upper Nile. But their art appears to have been an indigenous growth wholly independent of contemporary developments in north Africa and the Near East. More than 150 works of sculpture have come to light in recent years, the first discovered near the village of Nok, after which 'Nok culture' has been named. All are in boldly modelled and skilfully fired terracotta. Some are naturalistic representations of animals – an elephant, monkeys, snakes and even a giant tick. There are also human figures and large, sometimes nearly life-size heads, which seem to have

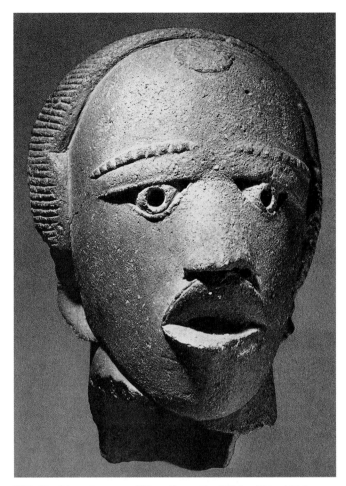

3,57 Head from Jemaa, c. 400 BC. Terracotta, 9¹³/₁₆ins (25cm) high. National Museum, Lagos.

formed part of whole-length statues (3,57). Although these generally spherical, conical or cylindrical heads are slightly stylized with flattened noses, pierced nostrils and eyes with segmental lower lids and pierced pupils, they are also strongly individualized. Each has a different personality marked by facial expression and a variety of hairstyles. It is this unusual combination of human individuality and artistic stylization that gives them their peculiar power. They are commanding presences, probably portraits of ancestors of the ruling group (several wear an abundance of beads and bangles indicating status). The technique of modelling with sharp incisions suggests an earlier tradition of wood-carving, about which nothing is known, and it seems likely that terracotta was adopted for its almost indestructible quality – to ensure the permanence of the images for their magic properties (not for artistic reasons). After about the third century AD the Nok culture vanishes from the archeological record, but it seems to have exerted a formative influence on the art of the whole area (west Africa) for centuries to come – as did that of the contemporary Olmecs in Mexico and the Chavín culture in Peru on later pre-Columbian art in America, not to mention that of the Greeks during these centuries on later art in Europe.

CHAPTER FOUR

THE GREEKS AND THEIR NEIGHBOURS

Greek civilization differed in nearly every respect from the civilizations of Egypt and the ancient Near East, however much it may have owed to them. It occupied no clearly defined geographical area but spread across the Greek peninsula, over the Aegean islands and along the coast of Anatolia, with important outposts on the shores of the Black Sea, in Sicily and southern Italy, on the south coast of France and as far west as Spain. Dispersed, not centralized, maritime and linked only by the sea, not territorial and closely integrated, it lacked any political unity and even a common system of government. The Hellenic world was composed of numerous, small autonomous states often at war with one another and ruled at various moments by single individuals, by small groups or by a majority of the community – tyranny, oligarchy or democracy (we owe these terms to the Greeks, of course, as also the word 'politics' itself, from *polis* or 'the self-governing state'). Yet the Greeks, or Hellenes as they called themselves, were highly conscious of

possessing a single culture – what Herodotus called in the fifth century BC 'our being of the same stock and the same speech, our common shrines of the gods and rituals, our similar customs'. He might well have added 'the visual arts', for anyone travelling round the northern Mediterranean in his time would have encountered temples, statues, paintings, pottery vessels, jewelry, arms and armour, all in much the same style in every Greek city.

Hellenes called those who did not speak Greek as their native language barbarians – because their speech was unintelligible and seemed to them to be little more than a succession of grunts, 'bar-bar-bar'. Many Greeks thought themselves to be not only different from, but superior to, the rest of mankind – including the highly civilized Egyptians, Mesopotamians and Persians as well as the less sophisticated, but by no means uncouth, nomadic tribes of Thracians and Scythians, whom they encountered on the borders of their states. Such was the thrust of their self-confidence that they even managed to

The visual arts	Historical landmarks
c. 800–500 BC Sardinian bronze (4,62)	c. 850–800 BC Homer
c. 700 BC *Helmet-maker* (4,2)	c. 800 BC Hesiod
c. 700–600 BC Strettweg cult-wagon (4,57)	c. 800–700 BC Etruscan civilization begins
c. 650 BC Goddess from Delos (4,6)	c. 733 BC Greek colony founded at Syracuse (Sicily)
c. 600 BC Scythian plaque (4,52).	c. 654 BC Greek colony founded in S. Russia
Head from Olympia (4,7)	c. 612 BC Sappho born
c. 570 BC *Kouros* from Tenea (4,9)	c. 594 BC Solon's reforms at Athens
c. 550–500 BC Vix krater (4,58)	c. 550 BC La Tène culture in central Europe
c. 500 BC Etruscan *She-Wolf* (4,63)	c. 546 BC Persian conquest of Asia Minor
	c. 518–438 BC Pindar
c. 480 BC *Kritios Boy* (4,10)	509 BC First Roman republic
c. 478 or 474 BC Delphi *Charioteer* (4,23)	490 BC Persians repulsed by Greeks at Marathon
468–460 BC Olympian *Apollo* (4,24)	480 BC Persians defeated at Thermopylae and Salamis
c. 450 BC Riace *Warrior* (4,36)	c. 462 BC Rise of Pericles
447–438 BC Parthenon (4,15)	458 BC Aeschylus, *Oresteia*
	431–404 BC Peloponnesian war
c. 400 BC Head of a man (4,61)	429 BC Death of Pericles. Euripides, *Medea*
c. 400–350 BC *Mars of Todi* (4,72).	423 BC Aristophanes, *Clouds*
Basse-Yutz flagon (4,59)	399 BC Death of Socrates
	396 BC Etruscan city of Veii destroyed by Rome
c. 350 BC Epidaurus theatre (4,44)	347 BC Death of Plato
c. 340 BC *Hermes and Dionysus* (4,38)	338 BC Greek Confederacy under Philip of Macedon
c. 340–300 BC *Boy* from Marathon (4,37)	336 BC Death of Philip of Macedon
c. 300 BC *Brutus* (4,74)	

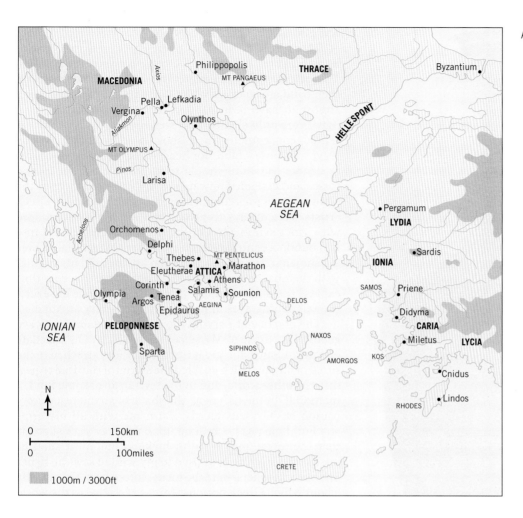

Ancient Greece

impose this view on others. Romans and later inheritors of the Greek tradition came to believe that a standard of excellence, to which all art should aspire, had been set by Greek 'canonical' works. But with their emphasis on simplicity and structural clarity in architecture, their preoccupation with visual appearances in painting and with the convincing rendering of an idealized male nude in sculpture, the canon of beauty the Greeks created was very peculiar, much more peculiar than Europeans were subsequently able to realize.

ARCHAIC GREECE

The period after the destruction of the Helladic palaces in about 1300 BC by invaders from the north (see p. 85) is generally called the Dark Age. The country lapsed into total illiteracy until about 800 BC, when an entirely different script was developed from the Phoenician alphabet. Nor was there any architecture, painting or large-scale sculpture until about the same date. Only two arts survived from the Helladic past: those of the bronze-worker and potter, the former engaged for the most part in producing weapons and the latter mainly simple utilitarian wares, roughly decorated, if at all, with motifs handed down from an earlier period. (Of some 70 Helladic vase forms only ten continued to be made.)

In the archeological record, which is our only source of information, signs of recovery start to appear about the beginning of the first millennium BC with the introduction of iron technology. The most interesting artifacts of this period are pottery vases made in Athens – then a small town which had had a citadel on the Acropolis in Helladic times but only now began to gain a leading position. The word 'vases' is perhaps misleading, for they were all strictly utilitarian – cups, jugs and mixing-bowls for wine and water – and never intended for ornamental purposes, though they were sometimes placed over graves. Technically they are as fine in quality as any previously made in Greece or Crete, wheel-thrown, boldly and symmetrically shaped with an even surface texture. But the lively free-hand painted decoration of natural forms and scrolls on earlier vessels has given way to very severe patterns of lustrous black bands and lines and concentric circles on a buff ground; the bands and lines were painted by holding a brush against the surface while the vessel was rotated on a wheel, the circles by brushes attached to a pair of compasses. Decoration thus echoes both the form of the pot and the process by which it had been made – hinting at a precocious development of that rationalizing mentality later to be expressed in the words inscribed on the entrance to Plato's Academy: 'Let no one enter here who is ignorant of geometry.'

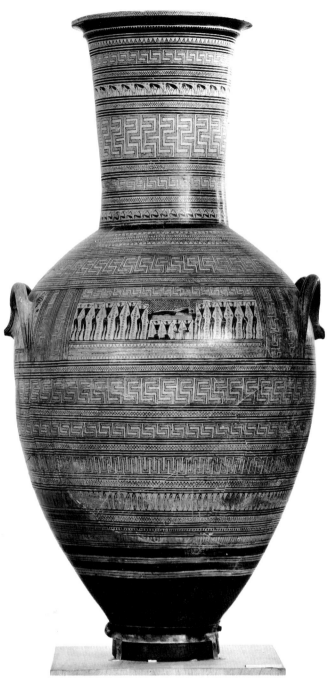

4,1 *Dipylon Vase*, Attic Geometric amphora, 8th century BC. 4ft 11ins (1.5m) high. National Archeological Museum, Athens.

(see Glossary) of grazing deer just below the top, another of seated deer at the base of the neck and panels with human figures encircling the belly between the handles. The animals are schematically rendered and those on each band are so exactly like one another that they seem almost to have been painted through a stencil. Human figures are only slightly less stereotyped. They are represented conceptually in a short-hand reduction of the 'Egyptian' pose – blobs for heads with slight excrescences to denote the chin, simple triangles filled in for frontal torsos and extended upwards to indicate arms bent at the elbow. The figures conform to the regularity which Greek artists were always to favour and are likewise arranged with strict symmetry. On the front they mourn a corpse laid out on a central bier: on the other side similar figures are shown in the same traditional attitude of lamentation with their hands on their heads. The figurative scenes thus express the purpose of the vase, which was one of several used to mark graves in the Dipylon cemetery at Athens.

The practice of burying the dead with elaborate 'grave goods', like those of Mycenae (see p. 82), had by this date been abandoned. But great importance was attached to the ritual of burial, which enabled the spirits of the dead to pass into the other world, and to the setting up of some kind of memorial. In the *Odyssey*, the shade of an unburied companion of Odysseus pleads: 'Burn me with all my arms and build me a grave mound upon the gray sea's shore so that the future may learn of luckless me; on it shall be raised the towering oar I used to ply while I saw the light.' Similarly in funerary art the focus shifted from the afterlife (about which Greek notions were very vague) to the world of the living. Greek religion and philosophy henceforth were to concentrate on the here and now – how to confront death rather than what might happen afterwards.

Geometric pottery was not exclusively funerary: nor was art confined to pottery. Bronze statuettes of stiffly posed men, wearing nothing but very tight belts, and equally wasp-waisted centaurs and horses survive from the eighth century BC, moulded versions of the men and animals on Geometric vases. The bronze figure of a helmet-maker is in a different class aesthetically – no less remarkable as the image of a craftsman wholly absorbed

Such vases are called 'Proto-geometric' and precede the much more elaborately painted 'Geometric' vessels found at Athens and elsewhere on the Greek mainland and the Aegean islands. On Geometric pottery the spaces between the horizontal bands are filled with lozenges, checkers, chevrons, the squared scroll of the Greek fret pattern (later used extensively in architectural decoration) and sometimes men and animals. The finest example is nearly 5 feet (1.5m) high – a virtuoso display of ceramic craftsmanship, for so large a vase had to be constructed in horizontal sections and fitted together (**4,1**). It has a frieze

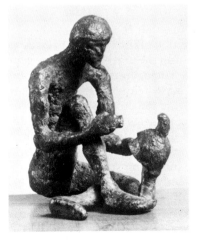

4,2 *Helmet-maker*, c. 700 BC. Bronze, 2ins (5.1cm) high. Metropolitan Museum of Art, New York (Fletcher Fund, 1942).

over the misty sea'. Significantly, because shortly before the end of the eighth century BC luxury articles made in the Assyrian empire, then at the height of its power, began to exert an animating influence on Greek art; and thus Greece was drawn briefly into a Near Eastern current.

Motifs derived from the Near East had occasionally been incorporated into the decorations on Geometric pottery – the two friezes of deer on the funerary vase illustrated on page 128, for instance (4,1). But in the seventh century BC they predominate on vessels in what has, as a result, been termed the Orientalizing style. This is especially evident on pottery made at Corinth, which now emerged as a rival to Athens in pottery production. A jug painted with monstrous beasts of Oriental breed is typical (4,3). It differs from Geometric pieces on account not only of the Oriental motifs but also of the red, black and buff color scheme, the greater size of the animals in relation to the vessel and the use of incised lines to suggest the form and texture of their bodies. No pottery exactly like this is known to have been made in the Near East, and the Corinthian painter must have taken his motifs from Near Eastern works in other media, probably metal and perhaps also textiles.

Influences from the East are also apparent in carvings of the human figure, but here they are more complex and seem to have been more quickly assimilated into a new and unmistakably Greek idiom. An ivory carving of a kneeling boy found on the Aegean island of Samos – originally perhaps part of the decoration of a lyre – seems to be Syrian or Phoenician in its refinement of carving and minute elaboration of detail, but not in the boy's nakedness, which is accentuated by the intricate belt, the carefully dressed hair and the head-band (4,4; 5). Male nudity is rare in Near Eastern art. Its peculiar appeal and

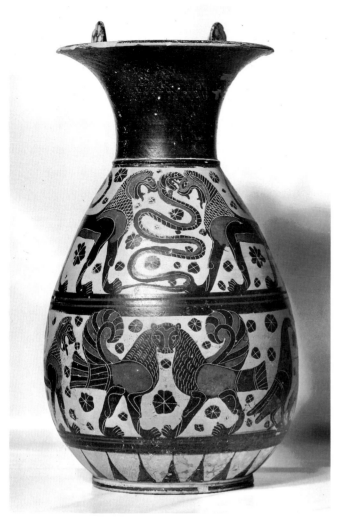

4,3 Early Corinthian *olpe*, c. 600 BC. 11⁷/₁₆ins (29cm) high. British Museum, London.

in his work than as a representation of the human figure in an entirely natural, unconventional and uncontrived pose of great three-dimensional subtlety (4,2). That metalwork was the most highly regarded form of art or craft (the Greeks did not distinguish between the two) is evident from descriptions in the Homeric epics, which were given their final form at this time, notably the famous description of Achilles' shield. This is almost certainly fanciful, but that of Agamemnon's may correspond with one Homer had actually seen: 'Big enough to hide a man, intricately worked, mighty, a beautiful shield; around it there were ten circles of bronze, and on it were 20 raised bosses of white tin, in the middle of which was one of dark enamel. And wreathed around in the very centre was the grim face of the Gorgon, glaring terribly, and around it were Terror and Fear.' The few surviving examples of eighth-century BC armour are a good deal less extravagant. Significantly, perhaps, a silver vase said in the *Iliad* to have 'surpassed all others on earth by far' was made at Sidon on the coast of the Lebanon – 'skilled Sidonians had wrought it well, and Phoenicians had carried it

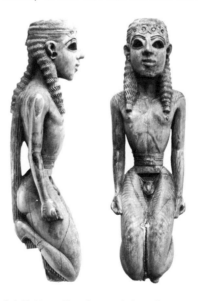
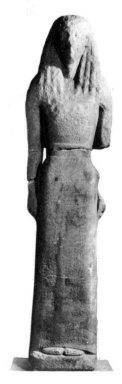

4,4; 5 *Above* Kneeling youth from Samos, side and front views, c. 600 BC. Ivory, 5ins (14.6cm) high. Vathy Museum, Samos.

4,6 *Right* Goddess from the Artemision of Delos, c. 650 BC. Stone, 5ft 8⁷/₈ins (1.75m) high. National Archeological Museum, Athens.

significance for the ancient Greeks – and the enormous effect this was to have on the visual arts – will be discussed later. It was, however, connected in some no less mysterious way with their avoidance of female nudity until well into the fourth century BC. The Phoenician mother-goddess and goddess of fertility, Astarte, usually nude in her homeland, was clothed by the Greeks when they transformed her into Aphrodite. A marble goddess from the island of Delos, influenced by the images of Astarte, is one of the earliest large-scale Greek statues to survive, carved in the rudimentary style called Daedalic (after Daedalus, the legendary founder of the art of sculpture, who was said to have worked in Crete) (**4,6**).

Despite its battered condition and the loss of coloring, which would no doubt have helped to articulate the flat drapery, this statue from Delos has a dignified presence. A larger than life-size (and probably slightly later, early sixth-century) limestone head of a woman from Olympia, with an enigmatic smile on her lips, is still more imposing (**4,7**). Whether it comes from a sphinx or, as some archeologists believe, a statue of Hera, wife of Zeus, the most powerful of the gods, it represents a figure apart from the

4,7 Head from Olympia, c. 600 BC. Limestone, 20½ins (52cm) high. Archeological Museum, Olympia.

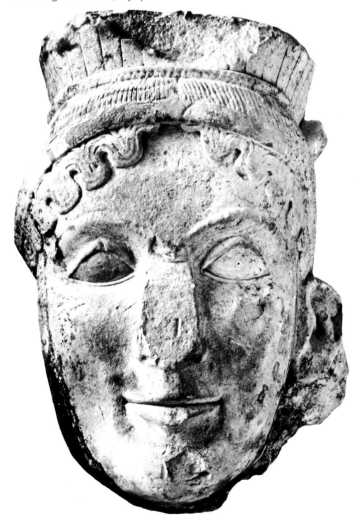

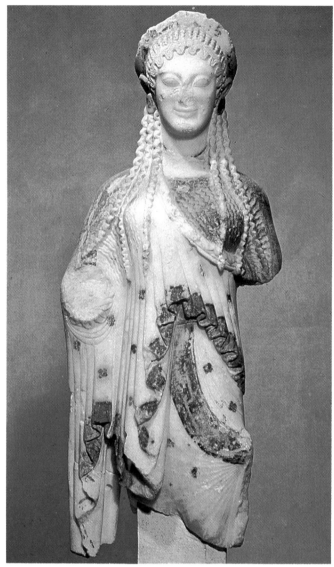

4,8 *Kore*, c. 510 BC. Marble, 21½ins (54.6cm) high. Acropolis Museum, Athens.

ordinary world of mortals. She has, rather, the air of some Eastern goddess or queen. The way in which the hair on the forehead is carved persisted in marble statues of *korai* (usually translated as 'maidens') for about 100 years (**4,8**). But everything else changed in the so-called Archaic style. This term is used to distinguish works of the late seventh to early fifth centuries BC from those of the succeeding period known as the Classical period. These Archaic *korai* are at once more delicate and more human than any earlier statues. Jewelry and neatly pleated dresses give them an almost modish elegance, not entirely uninfluenced perhaps by such luxury objects as ivory carvings from the Near East. All this finery is, however, worn with an air of happy innocence, lending the statues a tender poignancy as new to art as that of Sappho's epigrammatic poems to young brides (written c. 600 BC) had been to literature:

*Like the wild hyacinth flower, which on the hills is
     found,
Which the passing feet of the shepherds for ever tear
     and wound,
Until the purple blossom is trodden into the ground.*

From an early stage the Greeks had a trading station on
the Syrian coast at Al Mina (in present-day Turkey). In the
mid-seventh century BC they established another in the
delta of the Nile. Syria provided a repertory of exotic
motifs, but Egypt may have contributed a stronger stimulus to the independent development of Greek art. In
Egypt the Greeks encountered monumental sculpture and
architecture in stone, and although they copied neither in
detail, they seem to have learned from both. They almost
certainly took over Egyptian techniques of working in
hard stone – a trickier process than that of carving wood
or even limestone – and adapted them to their native
types of marble. In these they were extraordinarily fortunate, for Parian marble and that from other Aegean
islands and from Mount Hymettus and Mount Pentelicus
near Athens are most beautiful, almost golden in color
and gently luminous.

The Egyptian method of preparing a block by drawing
the outlines of the statue on its faces (see p. 70) also seems
to have been taken over. Archaic Greek sculpture has the
same limited number of viewpoints – sometimes only
two, front and back. Archaic statues are posed with their
weight distributed equally on two legs, one of which is
slightly advanced. Of the many that survive, however,
only one conforms to the strict Egyptian canon of proportion, which was based on an abstract numerical system.
From the beginning Greek sculptors seem to have preferred a more empirical approach to the human figure, and
since the disparity between the Egyptian canon and a normally proportioned body becomes more obvious when the
figure is completely undressed – which it seldom was in
ancient Egypt – this may well have resulted from the
Greek demand for male nudes.

THE MALE NUDE

The overwhelming majority of free-standing Archaic
statues are of nude youths, generally known as *kouroi*,
which quite simply means 'youths'. More than a hundred
survive, either whole or in large fragments, ranging in
height from an average 5 feet (1.5m) or so to an exceptional 11 feet (3.35m) (the *kouros* of Sounion, National
Archeological Museum, Athens). Examples have been
found in most parts of the Hellenic world, but mainly in
Greece itself. All stand in the same stiff attitude, head
held high, eyes to the front, arms hanging down with fists
clenched. Emphasis is placed on breadth of shoulders,
athletic development of pectoral and calf muscles,
narrowness of waist, hardness of knee, roundness of
thigh and buttock. Facial expressions vary from an impassive, rather loutish, stare to a conventionalized and to
our eyes all too knowing, and sometimes slightly pert,
alertness (**4,9**).

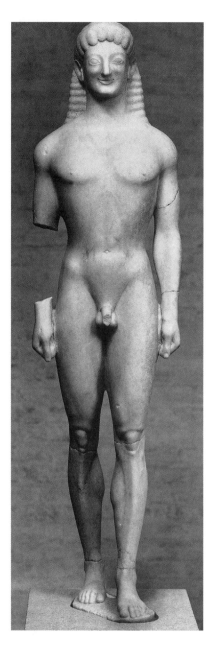

4,9 *Kouros* from
Tenea, c. 570 BC.
Marble, about 5ft (1.52m)
high. Staatliche
Antikensammlungen und
Glyptothek, Munich.

Two such statues, slightly over life-size and perhaps
among the earliest, are known to record the legend of the
dutiful brothers Cleobis and Biton, who died in their sleep
after their mother – a priestess whose chariot they had
drawn to a religious festival – prayed that they might be
rewarded with what was best for mortals. The original
significance of the other *kouroi* is, rather surprisingly,
obscure. Many were placed in sanctuaries as votive offerings, beside their fully clothed female equivalents, the
korai; others served as funerary monuments, and not
necessarily for those who died young. They have been
described as images either of the youthful god Apollo or of
mortal athletes (though obviously not intended as portraits). To give them, however, such precise meaning is
perhaps to misunderstand them. Greeks never distinguished between the physical features of men and gods.
Nor did they (like the Mesopotamians and Egyptians)

4,10 *Kritios Boy*, c. 480 BC.
Marble, c. 34ins (86cm) high.
Acropolis Museum, Athens.

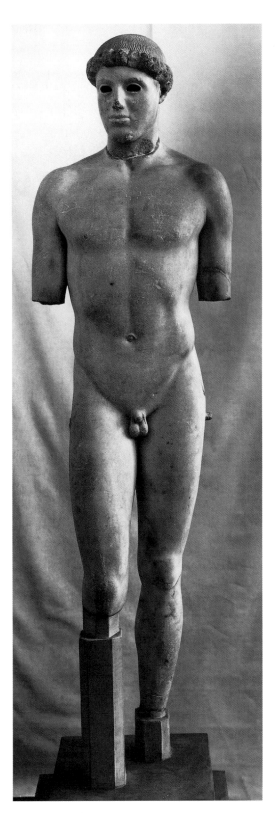
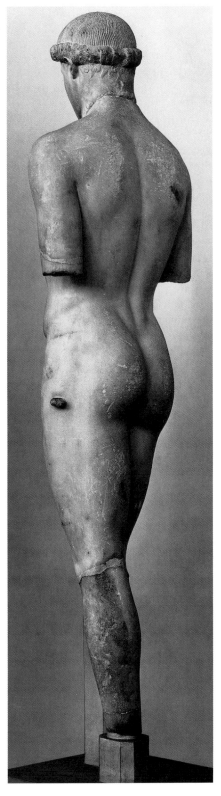

invest statues of either with the spirits of those whom they represented; there is nothing animistic about Greek sculpture. *Kouroi* and *korai*, caught at the moment when the body is just on the point of reaching maturity, in their first bloom of that youthfulness which mortals possess briefly and only the gods enjoy eternally, are at once human and divine. And this duality may account for the increasing care devoted to the rendering of anatomy. It may also, paradoxically, underlie the tendency to avoid characterization by deriving from individuals a highest common factor of physique – in other words, it may contribute to that unique combination of naturalism and idealism which became, when fully developed in the Classical period, the great and enormously influential contribution of the Greeks to Western art. *Kouroi* may thus have been intended as images both of the gods and of their human worshippers – those naked athletes who took part in the games at Olympia and elsewhere, which were, of course, primarily religious festivals of a type wholly peculiar to Greece.

To explain their practice of disporting themselves naked in the games – which has always seemed odd to members of other civilizations – the Greeks told the story of a runner at Olympia who dropped his loincloth and won the race. Its true origin probably lies deeper, somewhere between the earlier association of nudity with the act of worship (as in Sumer, see p. 52) and later symbolism of the naked soul as a body divested of its earthly trappings. The athletes were also soldiers, it should be remembered, and belonged to a superior caste on whom the safety of their *polis* or state depended. They came from the richer or upper ranks of citizens who were bound to serve in the infantry (as hoplites) or, if they were very well-to-do, in the cavalry. The work-force consisted of second-class citizens and slaves who left these favoured young men free to devote themselves to athletic training when they were not fighting. The *kouroi* thus reflect a distinctly élitist view of youth. Their air of blithe self-confidence, their obvious pride in the bodies they so freely display, form part of it. They symbolize the upper echelon of a male-dominated society which relegated women to the home, smiled on pederasty and seems never to have doubted the superiority of men, in beauty as well as in strength.

Kouroi and *korai* vary greatly in anatomical accuracy and attempts have been made to date them almost by decade on the assumption that their sculptors were constantly striving towards greater naturalism. Regardless of whether this attempt at a chronological classification is sound, a more naturalistic style does seem to have begun to emerge in the early fifth century BC. This can be seen from the statuary that was pulled down when the Persians, under Xerxes, sacked the Athenian Acropolis in 480 BC. These statues (later buried in new foundations and thus preserved) include a number of Archaic pieces and also the greater part of a statue in an entirely different style, which seems to have been carved not very long before the disaster: the *Kritios Boy* (so-called because of its similarities with statues by Kritios, the fifth-century Athenian sculptor, whose works are unfortunately known only from later copies). The rigidity of the Archaic *kouros* is relaxed in this outstandingly beautiful and calmly passionate tribute to the Greek cult of the youthful male nude (4,10). The right leg is slightly bent at the knee, the boy's weight being shifted mainly to the left, while his head – which originally had eyes of glass or colored stone – is turned to the right, very slightly but just enough to send a current of animation through the whole figure. What is perhaps still more notable is that the torso is no longer conceived as a kind of chart or diagram of separate anatomical parts (as in most Archaic *kouroi*), but as a single, organic form in which muscular rhythms find their natural balance. It is carved with a controlled sensuality which gives the marble something of the quality of firm young flesh. Even in its damaged state, the statue seems so amazingly alive that one hardly notices the liberties the sculptor has taken to avoid the deadness of a simulacrum. The ripple of muscle over the pelvis, for instance, is exaggerated partly to link the thighs with the

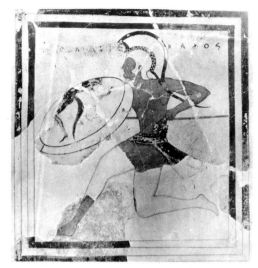

4,11 Warrior, late 6th century BC. Painting on terracotta, 16 × 15ins (40.6 × 38cm). Acropolis Museum, Athens.

torso and effect a smooth transition from the front to the back of the figure – a device used by nearly all Greek sculptors and their imitators in subsequent periods. Emphasizing the shift in balance, these muscles lead the eye round the figure so that the four main viewpoints begin to merge fluidly into one another and the figure itself acquires the potential of movement.

Sculpture was normally colored and thus more closely related to painting than is nowadays apparent; indeed, there seems to have been a symbiotic relationship between the two arts. Until later in the sixth century BC painters continued to render figures in the conceptual Egyptian manner. A terracotta panel (see Glossary), probably torn down when the Persians sacked the Acropolis, depicts a warrior exactly according to the Egyptian convention: the spear in his left hand seems to pass behind his back, so that prominence is given to what is most important (4,11). Much more attention was paid to visual appearances by the carver of reliefs of boys shown wrestling and playing various games. A passionate delight in the human body, in watching the play of muscle beneath the skin, in catching the fleeting rhythms as it passes from one position to another, inspired this notable example of early Greek art. So enthralled was the sculptor by the beauty of what he saw that he tried to present the human body from every angle – back, front and sides – and in order to show it as it actually appeared he confronted the problem of foreshortening. The left foot of the boy on the right (4,12) is seen frontally and not aligned with the base, as it would have been in Egypt or the ancient Near East. It is a small detail. But the difference between the way in which the Greek artist rendered it and the visual convention previously accepted by artists is a crucial one.

A similar process can be observed in vase painting. The same delight in bodily movement is evident from many sixth-century vases, on which figures run and leap, dance and fight, ride horses and drive chariots. On a vase probably painted about 540 BC, Ajax and Achilles are

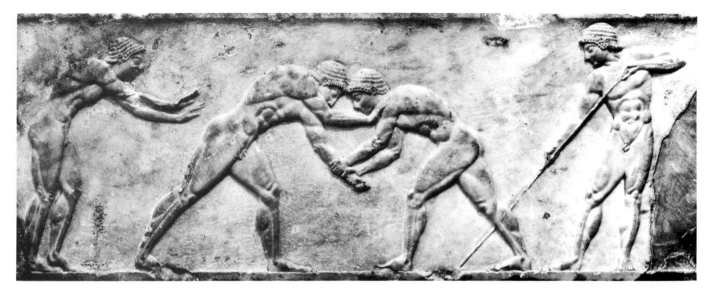

4,12 Wrestlers, from a statue base, c. 500 BC. Marble, 12½ins (31.8cm) high. National Archeological Museum, Athens.

4,13 Exekias, amphora from Vulci, 540–530 BC. 24ins (60.7cm) high. Vatican Museums, Rome.

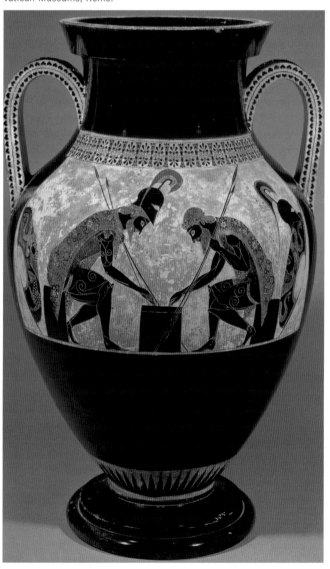

shown at rest, concentrating on a table-game, but with a great animation and sense of drama (**4,13**). Here the practice of arranging scenes in strips has been abandoned and a single moment in the story, very economically delineated, fills the whole area available for figurative painting. The composition is delicately balanced on a central axis with just enough deviation from bilateral symmetry to give it life – the helmet worn by Achilles, for instance, is counterpoised by that hung up over the shield behind Ajax. No attention was, however, paid to the relationship between the painting and the curvature of the vessel. The composition seems to have been worked out on a flat surface, although whether it was derived from a larger painting, on a panel or wall, cannot be known.

Behind Ajax an inscription reads *Onetorides kalos* 'Onetorides is beautiful' – referring to the youth who was presumably given the vase by an admirer. Such 'love-names', nearly always male, appear on numerous cups and vases of this period, some of which are decorated with paintings of handsome young athletes (**4,14**), and others are still more explicitly homo-erotic. They are of interest for the light they shed on a prominent aspect of life in ancient Greece. But there are other inscriptions on the Achilles and Ajax vase. One around the mouth records: 'Exekias painted me and made me', and Exekias also wrote his name in the background of the figurative panel. Such signatures appear quite frequently, though by no means consistently, on vases made in Athens – rarely elsewhere – during a limited period from the mid-sixth to the mid-fifth century. Why only these should have been signed is a mystery.

Artists' signatures have been found on a few earlier Egyptian relief carvings but on no works of art outside the Hellenic world until much later periods (in about the eighth century AD in China). Already in the seventh century BC a Greek sculptor, of whom nothing else is known, signed the base of a statue in the sanctuary of Apollo on Delos: 'Euthykartides the Naxian made and dedicated me.' Later sculptors often signed the statues that their

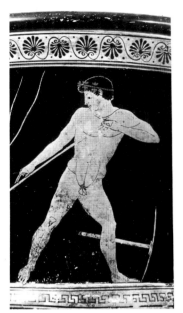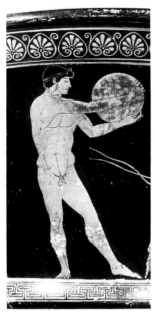

4,14 Kleophrades Painter, details from a calyx-krater, 500–490 BC. 17³/₄ins (45cm) high. Museo Nazionale Tarquiniese, Tarquinia.

patrons dedicated to the gods. Greek painters are known to have signed their works, though none survives; also engravers of gems and dies for coins. Yet the significance of these signatures has never been satisfactorily explained. Were they expressions of pride in artistry or simply a means of advertisement? Were they applied with the consent, or at the bidding, of patrons? Is it a mere coincidence that they make their sudden appearance at the moment when artists were beginning to assert their individuality? And has this anything to do with Greek democracy? These questions must remain unanswered; but it is significant that they can be asked. They simply do not arise in connection with the products of any earlier civilization.

THE *Polis*

The distinctive characteristics of Greek art became evident at about the same time as did those of the no less distinctly Greek political unit: the *polis* or self-governing state. Before the end of the Dark Age, kings or hereditary chieftains had been eliminated from the various communities of the Greek mainland (apart from Sparta, which remained the exception) and power passed into the hands of leading families. In other words, monarchy gave way to aristocracy – a word that originally meant rule by the 'best' people in terms of riches and birth. The same system of aristocratic government was initially adopted in the Hellenic cities, which, from the mid-eighth century BC, were established in Italy, Sicily and elsewhere overseas, partly for trade but much more to relieve population pressure at home (it is misleading to call them colonies, for they were wholly independent of the states from which their founders had emigrated). Subsequent developments varied from place to place. In Athens, a city of

the greatest importance in the history of the arts, the famous constitution drawn up by Solon at the beginning of the sixth century created a status hierarchy based on wealth – reckoned in terms of agricultural produce – and for the first time gave a role in government, albeit a minor one, to a middle class of fairly prosperous farmers, merchants, shippers and craftsmen. Despite a period of tyranny from 545 to 510 BC – which was, in fact, more like constitutional monarchy than the word tyranny suggests nowadays – this system survived to become the basis of a democratic state in which all free citizens could participate directly in government.

The Athenian *polis* was a very small state by modern standards. It occupied an area of some 1,000 square miles (1,600sq km) – the size of the Grand Duchy of Luxembourg today and rather less than Rhode Island in the USA – with a population which rose at its height in the mid-fifth century BC to no more than a quarter of a million people, about a third of whom lived in the city itself. Other *poleis* were still smaller: Corinth seems to have had a population of around 90,000, Argos about half that, and many had 5,000 or less, yet contrived to remain independent. Both the proliferation and the small size of these 'city-states' (misleadingly so-called, for most were, in fact, agricultural communities) may well have conditioned artistic developments more than the various political systems they adopted – aristocracies and tyrannies being more usual than democracies. Each one had its temples decorated with sculpture and paintings, and each had a comparatively rich and leisured upper class. Artists (like poets) were free to travel from one to another in search of patronage. Their products, especially metalwork and pottery, were also exported to the Greek cities overseas, whence they might be traded with Etruscans in Italy and Scythians in southern Russia (see p. 159).

The potential market for works of art in the Hellenic world may thus have been larger than in the incomparably vaster empires of ancient Egypt, Assyria and Iran, for in them patronage was concentrated at the top of a single social pyramid. But if the patrons of Greek artists were more numerous, they were much less wealthy. They could afford to give few opportunities for work on the grand scale. Significantly, the largest and showiest of Greek temples were built by tyrants, on the island of Samos and at Syracuse in Sicily. The main demand seems to have been for statues rarely more than life-size, for panel paintings rather than great decorative schemes, for small pieces of finely wrought gold jewelry and for pottery vases, which were, of course, of slight intrinsic value. A premium was thus set on artistry. Artistic experiment was quite evidently not discouraged and the artists themselves, perhaps for the first time in history, seem to have competed with one another in attempts to improve on their predecessors' efforts. Competition was a great feature of Greek life, not only in athletics: the fifth-century BC Greek tragedies were first performed in poetical competitions. Perhaps artists were also fired by that love of independence which enabled the Greeks to defeat the massive Persian invasion of 480 BC.

THE CLASSICAL PERIOD

Two historical events, the Persian war of the early fifth century BC and the temporary unification of Greece by Philip II of Macedon in 338 BC, stand at either end of what has for long been called the Classical period of Greek civilization. In 490 BC a Persian invasion of Greece – as a reprisal for Athenian support of an insurrection of Greek cities in Asia Minor which had been absorbed into the empire of Darius I (see p. 114) – was repulsed on the plain of Marathon. A second invasion in which Athens was taken and sacked was initially more successful, but the Persian fleet was destroyed at the battle of Salamis in 480 BC and their army routed at Plataea in the following year. Nothing could have more effectively convinced the Greeks of their superiority to 'barbarians', however numerous and well-equipped. The final victory was achieved by a very exceptional co-operation between Greek states. But Athens, which with Sparta had played a leading part in the war, took most of the credit and all of the profit, immediately emerging as the dominant power in the Aegean, where the islands were virtually reduced to the status of colonies.

The Athenian hegemony was not uncontested. Only a brief spell of peace followed the defeat of the Persians; thereafter Athens was almost constantly fighting with one or other of her neighbours and in 404 BC was herself defeated by Sparta at the end of the disastrous 27-year-long Peloponnesian War. Nor were the following decades any less disturbed by dissensions between the Greek states. Yet the period was marked by the most extraordinary flowering of artistic and intellectual activity the world had ever seen. From fifth-century Athens date the tragedies of Aeschylus, Sophocles and Euripides, which explore and express in sublime poetry the depths of human passion, the comedies of Aristophanes, which expose with no less sublime ridicule the absurdities of human behaviour, and the teachings of Socrates, which probe the complexities of man's predicament and revealed for the first time the full capacity of the brain for abstract reasoning. All retain their vital force undimmed to the present day, after nearly 2,500 years. The visual arts also flourished and were similarly focused on human concerns, but time has treated them less well.

It is more than likely that the fifth-century works of literature which have been preserved are those which were most highly regarded in their own time. The reverse could be said of the visual arts. The large statues of ivory and gold which were believed by the ancient Greeks to be their greatest works of sculpture have all vanished. Buildings survive but in ruins and they have lost most, and sometimes all, of the decorations for which they were renowned. Bronzes were melted down; marbles were burnt and converted into lime; of the vast number of bronze and marble statues described by ancient writers only a very few still exist. Rather oddly, more Greek sculpture remains from the Archaic than from later periods. Thus our knowledge of the most famous fifth-century works of art comes largely from written descriptions and Roman copies – made sometimes as much as seven centuries later – whose fidelity to the originals cannot be assessed. It is as if, to revert to a literary parallel, we knew Shakespeare's plays only from the comments of critics and French nineteenth-century translations! Enough survives, nevertheless, of architecture to justify the claim that the visual arts of the fifth century BC were comparable with its literature. It was a Classical period in the sense that its products belonged to a superior class (the original meaning of the Latin word *classis*) and provided models of excellence, free equally from the artless simplicity of earlier and the sophisticated over-elaboration of later works – although all this could not, of course, be recognized until long afterwards.

THE PARTHENON

Of surviving monuments, none characterizes this Classical moment in Greek art better than the Parthenon, which still dominates the city of Athens and the surrounding country for many miles (**4,15**). Bold in outline, delicate in detail, majestically imposing, yet built to a scale of proportion so carefully regulated by the physical and mental capacities of humanity that it is not at all overpowering, the Parthenon is so designed that all the parts are intimately adjusted in scale and size to one another and to the whole. It is a product of that rare combination of abstract thought and sensual feeling which typifies the Greek achievement. Though sadly damaged (mainly by the explosion of a Turkish powder-magazine in 1687) and robbed of most of its sculpture (now in the British Museum), it still retains the timeless quality which Plutarch ascribed to the buildings on the Acropolis (**4,16**) some 500 years after their erection. 'They were created in a short time for all time', he wrote. 'Each in its fineness was even then at once age-old; but in the freshness of its vigour it is, even to the present day, recent and newly wrought.' The significance of this extraordinary group of buildings cannot, however, be fully understood without reference to the circumstances in which they were erected and the earlier history of Greek architecture.

The first temple of the goddess Athena on the Acropolis seems to have been built between 570 and 560 BC. But even before the Persians demolished it another more grandiose temple had been begun on an artificial platform raised above the summit of the hill. After the defeat of the Persians the first building task for the Athenians was, naturally, the repair and reconstruction of dwelling-houses and the city's fortifications. Nothing is known as to what efforts were made to repair the damage to the Acropolis and although it is possible that work was resumed on the Parthenon in the 460s, the building we know today was not begun until 447 BC. Its structure was completed in 438 BC and the sculpture set in place in the pediments in 432 BC. Two architects are recorded: Callicrates and Ictinus (author of a long-lost book about the building). Phidias, who created the colossal chryselephantine – i.e. gold and ivory – statue of Athena placed inside the temple, is said to have supervised all the sculptural work.

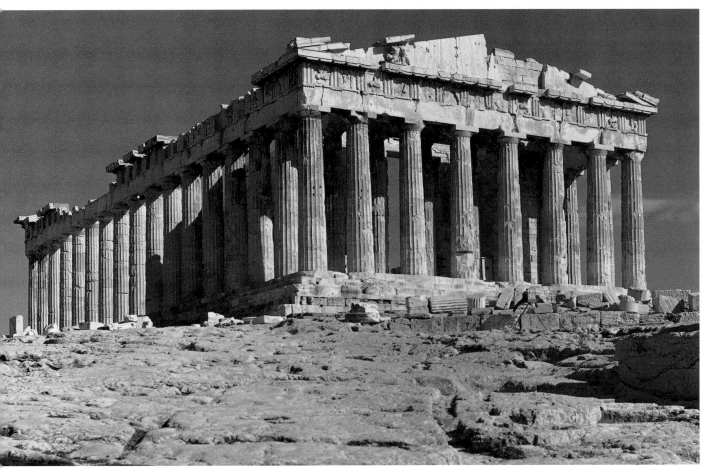

4,15 Parthenon, Athens, from the north-west, 447–438 BC.

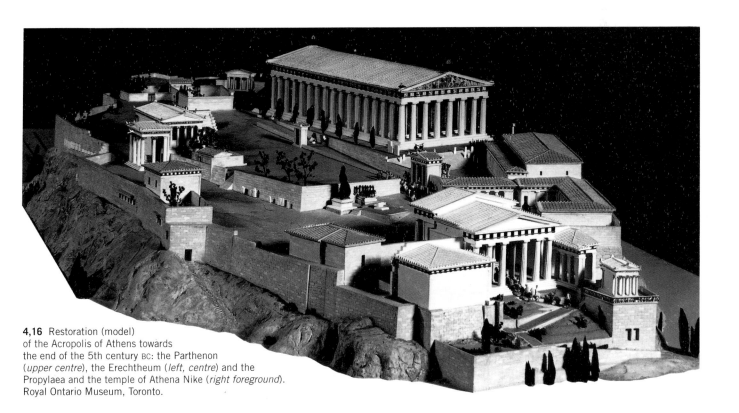

4,16 Restoration (model)
of the Acropolis of Athens towards
the end of the 5th century BC: the Parthenon
(*upper centre*), the Erechtheum (*left, centre*) and the
Propylaea and the temple of Athena Nike (*right foreground*).
Royal Ontario Museum, Toronto.

PAUSANIAS ON THE PARTHENON

For Plutarch (c. AD 46–c. 127), the Greek biographer and essayist who has already been quoted (p. 136), the Parthenon was above all a technical feat. The builders and artists all competed with each other not only in skill but in speed. Each of Pericles' projects would have normally taken several generations to finish, but they had all been completed within his life-time. Thus, Plutarch remarks,

. . . there is a certain bloom of newness . . . and an appearance of being untouched by the wear of time. It is as if some ever-glowing life and unaging spirit had been infused into the creation of these works.

The Greek traveller and antiquarian Pausanias (fl. AD 150–70) wrote slightly later than Plutarch and was more pedestrian but his first-hand descriptions are meticulous. Almost every important building and monument in Athens was still standing when he wrote. He saw the temples, paintings and sculptures on the Acropolis shining with all their gold and ivory and painted and bejewelled embellishments. Going right round the Parthenon to the entrance at the east end, he follows the route of the Panathenaic processions sculpted on the frieze above him (4,31) though he does not mention it. It was barely visible from the ground. Inside, however, he describes the great statue of Athene, which no longer survives, as being:

. . . of ivory and gold. She has a sphinx on the middle of her helmet, and griffins worked on either side of it . . . the statue of Athene stands upright in an ankle-length tunic with the head of Medusa carved in ivory on her breast. She has a Victory about 8 feet high, and a spear in her hand and a shield at her feet, and a snake beside the shield; this snake might be Erichthonios. The plinth of the statue is carved with the birth of Pandora. Hesiod and others say Pandora was the first woman ever born, and the female sex did not exist before her birth . . . . In addition a bronze statue of Athene by Phidias also stood on the Acropolis. The spear-tip and helmet-crest of this Athene can be seen as you come in by sea from Sounion.

(Pausanias, *Guide to Greece*, tr. P. Levi, London–New York 1971)

The promoter of the whole undertaking was Pericles, an aristocrat by birth who won the support of the poorer classes, gave Athenian democracy its definitive form and led the state from 460 until his death in 429 BC. His ostensible and closely related aims were to glorify the city of Athens and to honour its divine protectress. The birth of Athena and her struggle with Poseidon for the land of Attica were the subjects of sculpture in the pediments. On the metopes carvings of combats between gods and giants, men against centaurs and Amazons – the civilized versus the savage or barbarian – may well have been intended as an allegory of the Greek war with the Persians. To finance it he diverted funds subscribed by the allies and subject-states to Athens for mutual defence against further Persian aggression. This was denounced at the time as dishonest, especially as the Parthenon was one of a number of public works initiated by Pericles as a means of providing well-paid employment for the class on which he relied for political support – the *demos* or free citizens. It is, however, likely that some of the men were slaves hired out by their owners.

The Parthenon is the supreme example of the Doric temple, a type of building evolved in the course of the preceding two centuries – and one made so familiar by later imitations throughout the Western world that its original purpose and peculiarities are too often overlooked. Greek temples were not designed for ritual. Religious ritual was focused on the open-air altar where sacrifices were made to the gods, not on the temple which stood behind it. Other altars proliferated in public and private places, in town and in the country. The temple was built to enshrine the statue of the deity to whom it was dedicated – a statue which could be seen through its open doors and was sometimes carried outside. Essentially a show-piece, the temple testified to the piety, and also to the wealth and power, of the city which lavished funds on it – Greek writers record the great importance attached to the mundane value of objects dedicated to the gods. It was a static type of architecture: the visitor passed round and into, not through, a Greek temple. Emphasis was placed on its exterior rather than – as in Egypt – its interior.

Greeks learned the technique of building with posts and lintels, or rather stone columns and entablatures, from Egypt. But to answer their own needs they turned the Egyptian temple inside out, using columns mainly to support the outer framework of the roof, which was also carried by the walls of the chamber or cella, with further columns inside only when necessitated by width. (In form it may possibly have derived from the megaron, see p. 83.) The sequence in which a Greek temple was built is instructive. First a stepped platform of stone was laid out, then the columns (composed of drums held together by central pegs) were erected and the blocks of the entablature set on top of them. Only then did work begin on the walls of the cella.

The origin of the embellishments of the Doric order is

more than a little obscure. In Roman times it was stated that they were derived from the tradition of building in wood, that the tapering column followed the natural shape of a tree-trunk and the concave grooves of fluting repeated its rough shaping with an adze, that the triglyphs of the frieze represented the ends of planks bound together to serve as rafters, and that the guttae beneath them acted as pegs to keep them in place (see Glossary under Order). In fact, however, there is no evidence that wooden columns were roughly fluted with an adze; triglyphs do not appear in a Doric temple where rafters would end in a wooden building, nor indeed is it conceivable that beams would ever have been cut into planks and then joined together again. Nevertheless, these elements of a Doric temple were obviously derived in some way from carpentry, and it seems likely that they were used quite deliberately to give visual intelligibility and an appearance of structural soundness and coherence to buildings in what was, for Greece, a new medium. For Doric is quintessentially stone architecture, conditioned by the potentialities and limitations of blocks resting on one another without mortar (concealed metal clamps were used to resist lateral thrusts). The decorative elements have only an apparent functional significance, though they soon became the distinguishing features of the style.

Little survives of the earliest known Doric temples built about 540 BC, at Corinth, but that at Paestum in southern Italy of about the same date shows how robust and massive they were (**4,17**). By the early fifth century BC a more athletically trim version had been developed in Attica, facilitated perhaps by the fine local marble which needed no stucco coating to give a smooth, sharp finish but permitted effects of great delicacy and precision. Much of the beauty of the Parthenon derives from the wonderful bloom and texture of the marble, though it

must have looked rather different when the moldings were brightly painted.

The Doric temple, especially when seen obliquely – the lay-out of sanctuaries reveals that the oblique view was that envisaged by the architect – appears to be perfectly rectilinear and regular (4,15). This is a carefully contrived illusion. The lines are not straight nor are the columns equally spaced. Appreciating that true verticals appear to slope and true horizontals to sag in the middle, Greek architects introduced what are called 'optical refinements' to compensate for what might have been disturbing visual effects (though doubts have been expressed as to the precise intentions of the architects). The optical refinements of the Parthenon are so effective that they pass unnoticed until they are pointed out. The whole platform, for example, is very gently curved down from the centre – like the tip of a vast dome. The sides of the platform and the steps beneath are concave curves (the centre of each long side is about 4ins, 10cm, higher than its ends). This line is repeated, but with the curve slightly reduced, in the entablature. The columns all slope inwards, though by no more than 2 inches (6cm); those at the angles are also a couple of inches thicker than the others to allow for apparent diminution when silhouetted against the sky. To compensate for another optical illusion the columns are shaped on the principle of *entasis* (see Glossary) so that they do not taper directly to the top but bulge out very slightly (by ⅔ of an inch, 1.7cm) about two-fifths of the way up the shaft. Above them the entablature slants slightly inwards. The columns also appear to be spaced regularly, but the three at each corner are closer together than the rest and the six in the centre of the front and back are wider apart than those down the sides.

These optical refinements are by no means peculiar to the Parthenon: they were employed with variations only in degree in all Greek temples of the fifth century BC.

4,17 The 'Basilica', c. 540 BC. Paestum, Italy.

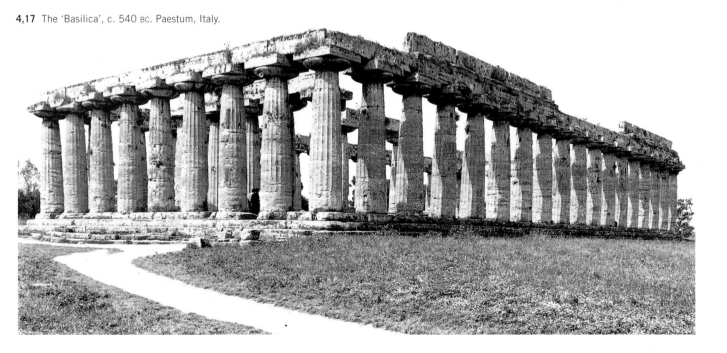

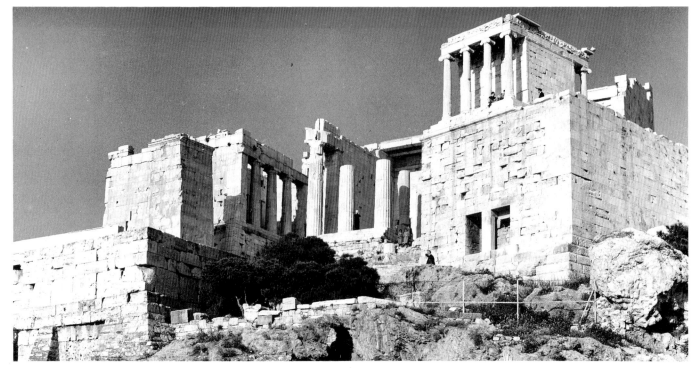

4,18 The Propylaea, Athens, from the west, 437–432 BC.

They do not, however, seem initially to have been worked out, as it were, on the drawing-board. (It is not known, of course, how Greek temples and other buildings were designed, but plans and sections and elevations must have been drawn in some way, either on papyrus or other material or in a sand-tray.) The stages by which a temple was erected allowed a fairly wide margin for improvisation while the work was in progress. And this may account for variations from regularity which can hardly have been accidental, which cannot have been intended to correct optical illusions, but do, in fact, give the Parthenon an elasticity, a vitality, the very slightest shimmer of movement, conspicuously lacking in its imitations. There is a free-hand element in the building, as in the sculptures that adorn it. The main proportions are very simple and the entirely satisfying relationship in size between the various parts seems to have been determined not by mathematics but by rule of thumb – or rather, rule of eye. A theorist of the first century AD, Heliodorus of Larisa, may have reflected the attitude of Ictinus and his contemporaries when he remarked:

> *The aim of the architect is to give his work a semblance of being well-proportioned and to devise means of protection against optical illusion so far as possible, with the object, not of factual, but of apparent equality of measurements and proportion.*

(Heliodorus, *Optica*, tr. A. W. Lawrence)

As soon as the structure of the Parthenon was complete a ceremonial entrance-way, the Propylaea, to the sanctuary on the Acropolis was begun, but never finished as work was interrupted by the Peloponnesian War. For an awkward sloping site the architect Mnesicles devised a complex building with two Doric façades like the fronts of temples linked by an Ionic colonnade (**4,18**). Two later buildings on the Acropolis were wholly Ionic – the exquisite little temple of Athena Nike or Victory (**4,19**) and the Erechtheum (**4,20**). As its name suggests, the Ionic style originated in the Greek cities on the coast of Asia Minor and the islands of the eastern Aegean which came under their cultural influence. Greek civilization owed much to this area. It was much richer in natural resources than mainland Greece and this may be reflected in an architecture less austere than the Doric and characterized

4,19 Athena Nike temple, Athens, 427–424 BC.

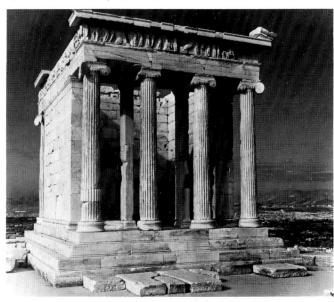

4,20 The Erechtheum, Athens, 421–405 BC.

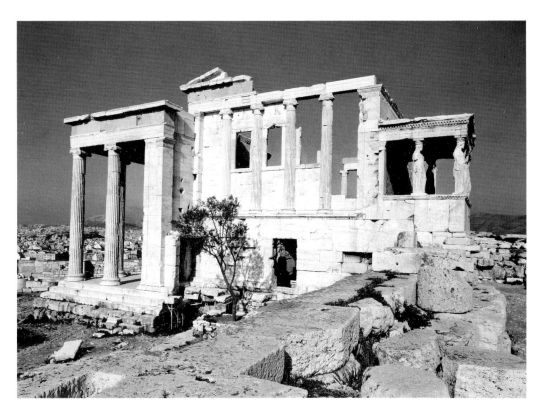

by delicately carved moldings, slender columns and volute capitals (**4,21**). Doric was regarded by mainland or Dorian Greeks as their 'national' style and seems to have been associated with moral and especially with manly virtues. The first buildings in the Peloponnese with Ionic features were little treasuries constructed by eastern Greeks at the sanctuaries of Olympia and Delphi. The presence of temples with Ionic columns beneath the Doric Parthenon on the Acropolis may therefore have had

a political significance, to suggest the unity of the Greek world led by Athens against the Persians.

Little is known about the earliest Greek temples in Ionia. But some eighth- or seventh-century BC capitals found at Larisa and elsewhere in Anatolia are of the so-called 'Aeolic' type, composed of curling members or volutes. Similar capitals were carved for Persepolis about 500 BC by craftsmen from Ionia, which was then part of the Persian empire (see pp. 115–6). By this time the Ionic

4,21 Doric and Ionic orders (after Grinnell).

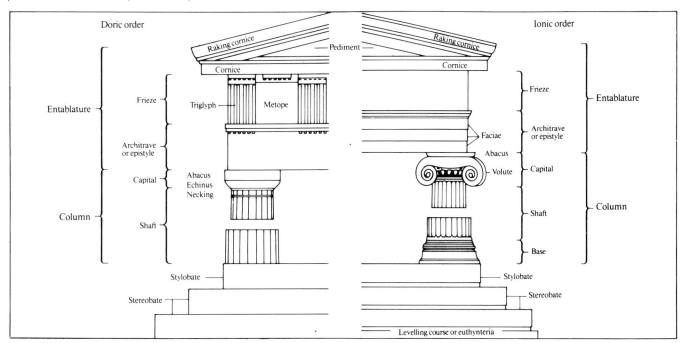

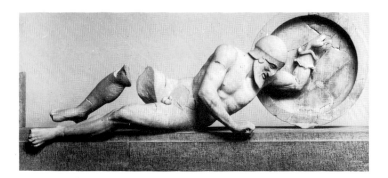

4,22 *Left Fallen Warrior*, from the Temple of Aphaia, Aegina, early 5th century BC. Marble, 5ft2¹/₂ins (1.59m) long. Staatliche Antikensammlungen und Glyptothek, Munich.

4,23 *Below Charioteer*, from the Sanctuary of Apollo, Delphi, c. 478 or 474 BC. Bronze, life-size. Archeological Museum, Delphi.

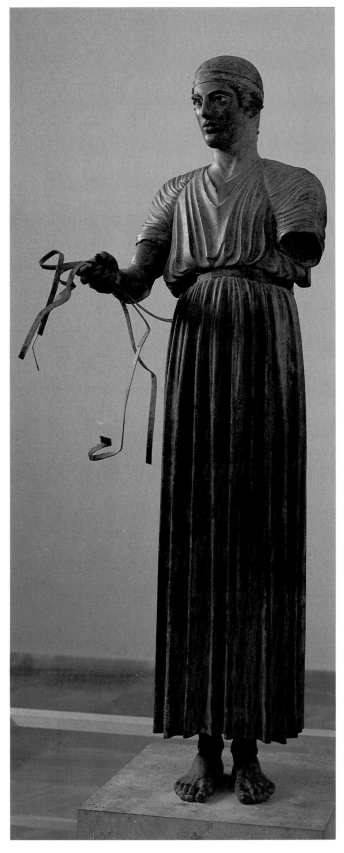

capital, which may derive from the 'Aeolic' (the point is disputed), had already been given its definitive form. Despite their decorative effect, both these types of capital are more truly functional than the square slab of the Doric order, for they spread the bearing surface of the column in line with the horizontal member of its supports (see Glossary under Order). In Ionic architecture the emphasis is, however, on ornament which elaborates structure. The frieze, uninterrupted by triglyphs, provided the field for a continuous band of figurative relief, as in the temple of Athena Nike. Sometimes columns were replaced by statues, as on the Siphnian Treasury at Delphi and the Erechtheum on the Athenian Acropolis. In Doric temples, on the other hand, sculpture seems to have been applied to, rather than to have formed part of, the structure – for example, rectangular reliefs in the metopes and groups of figures in very high relief or carved in the round to fill the pediments. As all this sculpture was placed far above eye-level it called for treatment entirely different from that of Egyptian, Assyrian and Persian reliefs.

The earliest substantial groups of pedimental sculpture come from the temple of Aphaia on the island of Aegina near Athens. They date from two periods, before and after the Persian invasion of 480 BC. Both groups represent Homeric battle scenes with figures in similar poses – much more varied than in any other sculpture of the time – but markedly different in handling. A fallen warrior from the earlier pediment has the stiffness of a *kouros* who has been toppled over, while his opposite number is shown in a far less awkwardly contrived manner (**4,22**). Similarly, the body of the former is schematically rendered and retains a kind of stoniness; that of the latter seems almost to be of flesh and blood. Moreover, an expressiveness in the face of the second warrior, a suggestion of thought and feeling, links him with the world of the great fifth-century BC tragedies.

The second of the Aegina pediments probably dates from the same years as the bronze *Charioteer* at Delphi, cast to record a victory in the games of 474 or 478 BC – one of the finest and best preserved of all Greek statues and one of the very few which can be firmly dated (**4,23**). Here there is no violent movement and the boy's regularly handsome face seems at first to be almost expressionless; yet the figure has an animating inner vitality; an ideal of moderation or the 'golden mean' – 'nothing in excess', the famous saying inscribed in the temple at Delphi –

was surely the guiding principle of the creator of the *Charioteer*. The statue reveals its breathing life in only very slight deviations from regularity. The folds of the lower part of the tunic, which at first sight might seem as rigid as the fluting of a Doric column, are ruffled by a gentle tremor; creases in the clinging drapery of the sleeves are nearly, but not quite, symmetrical; though looking straight ahead, the upper part of the charioteer's body and his head are turned just a little to the right. Again, although the figure's stance is motionless, the spectator feels drawn to move round it. From every angle it reveals a different but equally clear-cut outline, a pattern

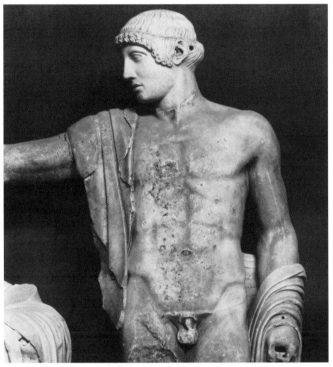

4,24 *Apollo* from the temple of Zeus, Olympia, 468–460 BC. Marble, over-life-size. Archeological Museum, Olympia.

4,25 Reconstruction of the west pediment of the temple of Zeus at Olympia, 468–460 BC. About 91ft (27.7m) wide.

of three-dimensional forms modelled with such an acutely developed appreciation of the effects of light and shade that nothing is blurred and nothing over-emphasized. (The same could be said of a Greek temple.) Once it has been seen from a succession of viewpoints, the face also takes on intensity and depth, a look of concentrated thought with the eyes unself-consciously trained on the horses.

The subtlety of the modelling of the *Charioteer*, the extreme refinement and sensitivity of his strong, highly-bred hands and feet would all have been lost in a statue placed high up in a pediment. The heroic-scale *Apollo*, which originally stood some 50 feet (15m) above ground level on the temple of Zeus at Olympia, for instance, was carved to be seen from a distance and from only a limited number of viewpoints (**4,24**). The subtleties of the *Charioteer* would have been out of place here. The gesture is bold, the turn of the head emphatic, the body is rendered in broad flat planes. Standing in the centre of the pediment (**4,25**), quelling a struggle between drunken centaurs and lapiths (members of a mythological Thessalian tribe) raging on either side, this Apollo seems to symbolize divine order – the triumph of light over darkness and, perhaps, culture over savagery. Victory is gained simply by his radiant presence as a perfect embodiment of the Greek ideal of physical beauty at its simplest and severest. The figure has all the sublime imperturbability, the remote aloofness and arrogant self-assurance that we associate with the word Olympian.

The statues from the pediments at Olympia are carved in what has been called the 'severe style' (or 'transitional' or 'early Classical'), with which the Delphi *Charioteer* and other sculptures of these years (now known only from copies) are associated. The draperies of the stern-faced female figures, for instance – quite unlike the light and ornamented clothing of earlier *korai* – seem to be made of thick, heavy material which falls in regular folds (though coloring may originally have made them look less austere). All these statues retain traces, nevertheless, of an Archaic hardness of form and rigidity of pose which were eliminated from sculptures carved little more than two

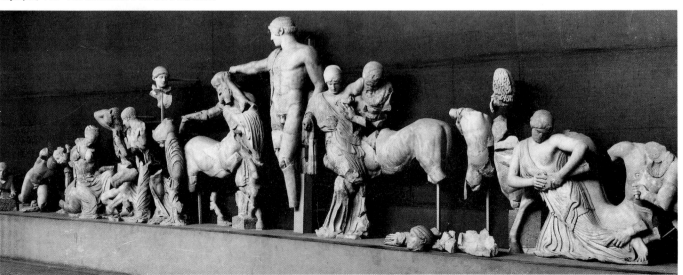

The Delphi Charioteer

ANCIENT GREEK RELIGION

AND ATHLETICS

This life-size bronze figure (4,23) was made for the Sanctuary of Apollo at Delphi, one of the most sacred places in ancient Greece, believed to be the centre of the world. Backed by bare cliffs on the steep, south-western slope of Mount Parnassus with a dizzying view down to the Gulf of Corinth 2,000 feet (610m) below, the site inspires awe even today. The main temple (of which little remains) bore the famous admonitory inscriptions that encapsulate ancient Greek belief in reason and moderation: 'know thyself' and 'nothing in excess' – remember that you are a mortal and don't overreach yourself. But Delphi was also famous for its oracle which reflects another, alternative aspect of the Greek genius: awareness of the irrational and acknowledgement of its power. For a fee, an appropriate sacrifice and ritual purification, an oracle called Pythia – the only woman admitted to the sanctuary – would sit on a tripod above a smoking pit and, in a state of shamanistic delirium, would shriek her incoherent but divine utterances in answer to her petitioners' prayers.

The Pythian Games, similar to the Olympic Games, were called after her. They were athletic contests which from the early sixth century BC accompanied the musical competitions held at Delphi in honour of Apollo at regular festivals. These festivals attracted devotees from all over the Greek world, from the coast of Turkey to Sicily and southern Italy, partly because of their appeal to that competitive spirit which was so marked a feature of ancient Greek life – notably in drama, rhetoric, poetry and music as well as sports and games – but also because of their religious significance, the nature of which has never been fully understood by later civilizations. The only prizes given were crowns of laurel leaves sacred to Apollo. But winners also gained *kudos* or public esteem in return for which they made gifts to the

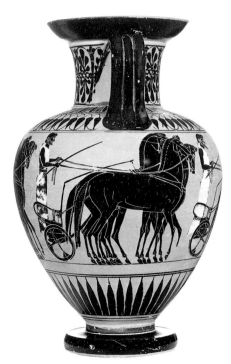

4,26 Amphora, late 6th century BC. 16½ins (41.9cm) high. Staatliche Antikensammlungen und Glyptothek, Munich.

sanctuary. The *Charioteer* was one of these. It joined and was later joined by many others, in gold, silver, ivory, bronze and terracotta, nearly all of which were later destroyed or broken up for the value of their materials. The *Charioteer* survived by chance. It was buried under a rockfall and was only discovered in 1896.

Originally it stood in a small two-wheeled racing chariot drawn by four horses, shown at rest (as surviving fragments reveal). This type of chariot was often depicted on vases (**4,26**) and the horses were probably similar to the one represented in a bronze statuette from Olympia (**4,27**). The *Charioteer* has lost his whip, his left forearm, the copper inlays on his lips and most of his silver eye-lashes (like those of the Riace *Warrior*, 4,36), and no more than a trace remains of an inlaid silver key-pattern on his head-band. But otherwise he is quite remarkably well preserved.

As we have seen (pp. 142–3), the *Charioteer* is a superlative work of art but it is hardly less remarkable as a technical feat in bronze casting by the ancient 'lost-wax' or *cire perdue* process (see Glossary). The figure was cast from hollow molds in seven sections: head, two arms, the garment above and below the belt, and the two ankles and feet. The original model may have been of clay with a metal armature or of wood – the treatment of the drapery and other features

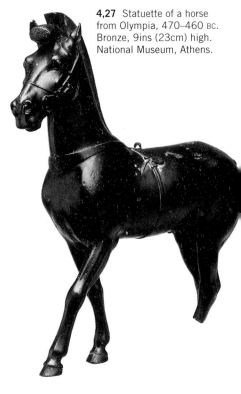

4,27 Statuette of a horse from Olympia, 470–460 BC. Bronze, 9ins (23cm) high. National Museum, Athens.

suggests that it was of wood. When all the pieces had been satisfactorily cast they were soldered together. It is not known where the *Charioteer* was made. Athens was one of the main centres for bronze-working and a painting on an early-fifth-century BC Attic cup shows a sculptor's studio with statues being cast in sections by the method used for the *Charioteer* (**4,28**). Bronze casting was, however,

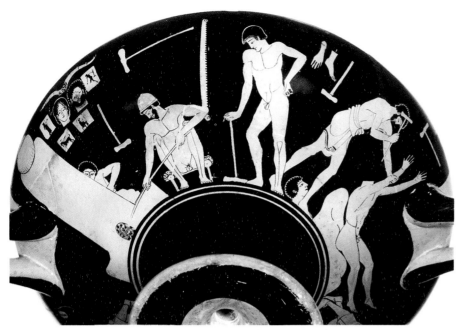

4,28 Cup from Vulci, detail, early 5th century BC. 15⁴/₅ins (40.2cm) diameter. Charlottenburg Museum, Berlin.

practised elsewhere in Greece, Asia Minor, Italy (by Etruscans as well as Greeks) and Sicily.

A racing chariot with its driver and team of horses might nowadays seem to be a secular rather than a religious subject. But it would not have occurred to anyone in ancient Delphi to make such a distinction. Certainly, its dedication to a sanctuary was as much a religious act as the sacrifice of a bull. That it was a very expensive object no doubt made it particularly acceptable to Apollo's priests. No private individual could have afforded to pay for it or, for that matter, to have engaged in chariot racing. An inscription reveals that it was dedicated by 'Polyzalos, tyrant of Gela' (478– c. 470 BC) whose team must therefore have won the race at the quadriennial festival in either 478 or 474 BC. Gela was a small but agriculturally rich Greek colony on the southern coast of Sicily near Syracuse, and Polyzalos had only recently become its tyrant – a word then meaning simply a ruler who had gained power by his own efforts and not, like a king, by birthright. Tyrants often overthrew aristocracies and supported the common people, thus unwittingly preparing the way for democracy in some places, for example in Athens and for a brief period in Syracuse. In Sicily some were generous patrons of literature and the arts. The great tragedian

Aeschylus spent several years at the court of Hiero, tyrant of Syracuse and brother of Polyzalos. Pindar wrote an ode congratulating Hiero on his team's victory in another chariot race at Delphi.

Polyzalos was the owner, not the driver, of the chariot and horses. The charioteer was his subject or servant, possibly his slave, and is shown dressed for the race in a tunic tightly belted at the waist and with cords tied over the shoulders and under the armpits to prevent it from catching the wind. This completely covers his body and limbs, setting him apart from the *kouroi* (4,9; 10) whose nude bodies display an ideal of youthful beauty. Male figures were rarely clad in Greek art of this period even when engaged in activities for which some clothing would have been desirable and must normally have been worn – the central figure in the sculptor's studio, for example (4,28). It might be suggested that clothing ranked the charioteer with the tyrant's other household slaves who were usually female and therefore always depicted fully clad. Yet the almost too regularly featured head (**4,29**) with its perfect Greek profile and the amazingly refined and delicate feet and surviving hand indicate some idealization. Polyzalos would not have wished to dedicate to Apollo anything but thoroughbred horses and an equally beautiful charioteer.

4,29 *Charioteer*, from the Sanctuary of Apollo, Delphi, detail, c. 478 or 474 BC. Bronze, life-size. Archeological Museum, Delphi.

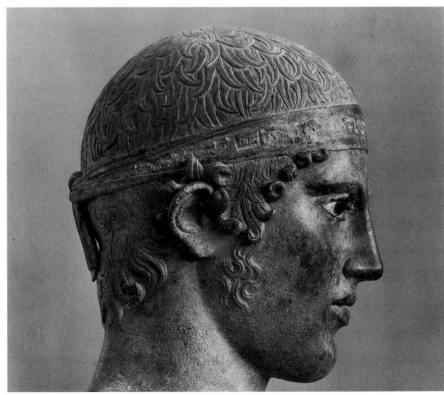

decades later for the Athenian Parthenon. A few are still in place, but the majority, often called the 'Elgin Marbles', were removed in 1799 by the Earl of Elgin and sold to the British Museum in 1816. Comprising free-standing statues from the pediments, several high-relief metopes and a long low-relief frieze, from the exterior of the cella, this group of work illustrates the mastery attained by Attic carvers. In conception and style they seem to reflect a single artistic personality and Phidias, the leading Attic sculptor of the time, has been named, but without evidence. Whether the figures are shown in action or at rest they are all at ease – too much so, perhaps, in the metopes where lapiths battle against centaurs, gods against giants, Greeks against Amazons, without overstraining a muscle or ever falling into an inelegant posture (**4,30**).

The frieze depicts the Great Panathenaia, the most important Athenian religious festival, celebrated in July every fourth year with a great procession from the city to the Parthenon. Here it is commemorated as an eternal, rather than a temporal, event in the living presence of the gods, who are represented over the main entrance. Originally 524 feet (160m) long (of which about a fifth has perished), the frieze includes several hundred figures, all idealized, yet quite as individual in their poses as in the variety of their clothing or lack of it. (Comparison with the only very slightly earlier processions in low relief [see Glossary] at Persepolis is revealing; see p. 116.) There are no exact repetitions throughout the whole length of the frieze. The vast composition is rhythmically composed with a quiet beginning at the west end of the building,

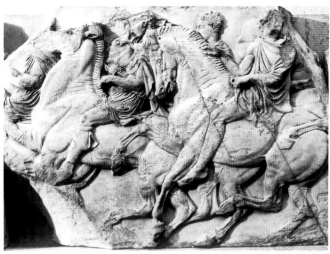

4,31 Parthenon frieze, detail, 447–432 BC. Marble, about 3ft 7ins (1.09m) high. British Museum, London.

where men are shown preparing to set off, rather more movement rising to crescendos along the side walls and a slow, solemn finale above the entrance at the east end. The figures seem to determine the pattern, to create rather than follow the rise and fall of this great composition (**4,31**). Prominent among them are young men in perfect control of the spirited horses they ride, recalling lines from the *Oedipus at Colonus* of Sophocles:

Every bridle flashes
And each man gives his horse its rein, as onward
The whole troop surges, servants of Athena,
Mistress of horses. . . .

4,30 Lapith and centaur, metope from the Parthenon, c. 438–432 BC. Marble, 4ft 8ins (1.42m) high. British Museum, London.

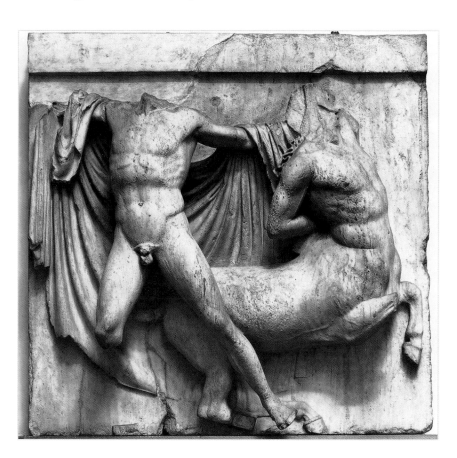

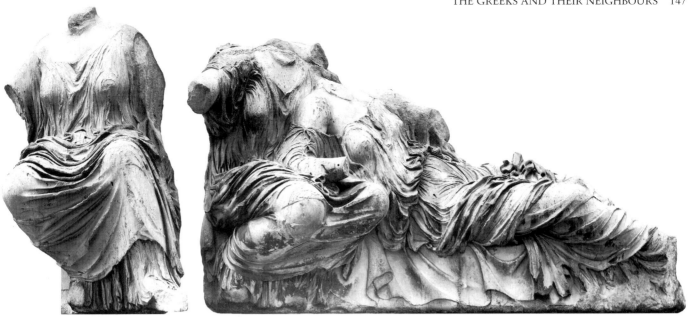

4,32 *The Fates*, from the east pediment of the Parthenon, c. 438–431 BC. Marble, over-life-size. British Museum, London.

4,33 Paeonius of Mende, *Nike* from Olympia, c. 420 BC. Marble, 7ft 1in (2.16m) high including base. Archeological Museum, Olympia.

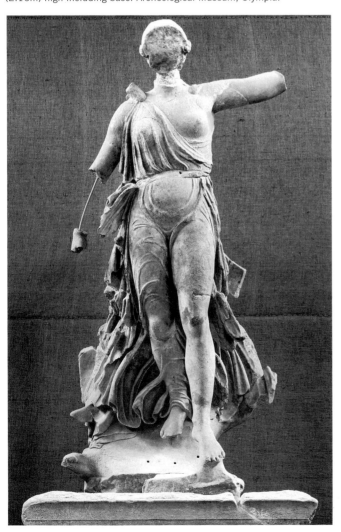

The technical problems involved in the naturalistic representation of men and animals in movement on a shallow stage, with one overlapping the other, have been completely mastered even when complicated, as they were here, by optical distortions due to the siting. The spectator's angle of vision, looking up from the colonnade, had to be taken into account and compensation made for it in the carving. The heads, for instance, are cut in higher relief than the feet and the backgrounds slant inwards. The imposing figures from the pediments were similarly designed to be seen from below, though in much brighter light. As a means of heightening their plastic expressiveness – their tactile sense of form – the sculptors developed a new technique for the carving of drapery, using what are now called 'modelling lines'.

Whereas the cloak over the shoulder and round the left forearm of the *Apollo* at Olympia looks as if it had been ironed flat, the garments of the Parthenon statues are carved in ridges and deep furrows, which catch the light and hold the shade. No cloth naturally rumples in this way. The effect is entirely artificial. These gossamer-like draperies must have given the pediments a shimmering vitality and – what was far more important – they revealed, rather than concealed, the forms of the bodies beneath them. In the group of *The Fates* (**4,32**) the soft fullness of the breasts is emphasized by gently swirling lines, the firm roundness of the arms by tight gatherings across them, the robustness of the thighs by the broad diagonals of deeper folds. Sometimes the concentric lines describe forms almost with the precision of a volumetric diagram. Greek sculptors now realized also that drapery running counter to the direction of the body could indicate movement as well as form. The torso of Iris from the Parthenon is an early instance of this, but a slightly later statue of Nike at Olympia illustrates better their quickly attained mastery of the technique (**4,33**). The goddess of victory is seen in flight with her dress swirling out behind her and the drapery pressed close to her front so that those parts which it covers seem fuller and rounder than those left naked.

NATURALISM AND IDEALIZATION

The use of modelling lines was no mere trick of the trade. It marks a turning-point in the history of European sculpture comparable with that of foreshortening in two-dimensional art (see p. 133). A new attitude to the statue, as a visual equivalent and not a reduplication of its subject, had emerged out of attempts to invest marbles and bronzes with the appearance of life. Socrates (d. 399 BC) is reported as saying of statues that 'the quality of seeming alive has the strongest visual appeal'. But shortly before the middle of the fourth century BC his follower Plato (?427–347 BC) condemned further developments towards naturalism, drawing a distinction between 'the art of producing a likeness and the art of producing an appearance', with a reactionary preference for the former. 'Artists nowadays care nothing for truth', he complained; 'they incorporate into their images not proportions that really are beautiful, but those that appear to be so.' In another passage he praised the Egyptians, who did not allow painters and sculptors 'to make innovations or to create forms other than the traditional ones'.

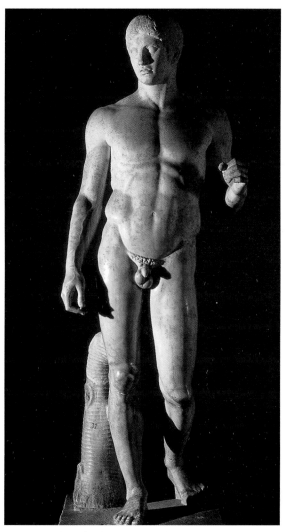

4,35 *Doryphorus*, Imperial Roman copy. Marble, 6ft 6ins (1.98m) high. Museo Archeologico Nazionale, Naples.

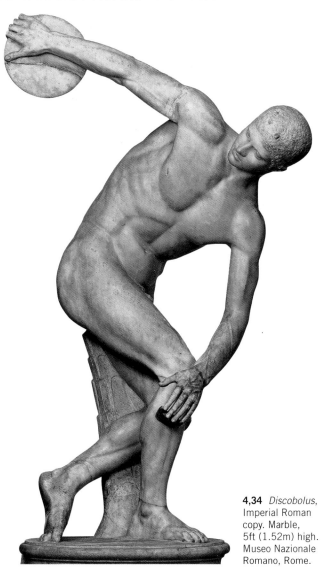

4,34 *Discobolus*, Imperial Roman copy. Marble, 5ft (1.52m) high. Museo Nazionale Romano, Rome.

The *Nike* at Olympia is by Paeonius of Mende, but he does not seem to have been very highly regarded by his contemporaries. It is, however, the only surviving fifth-century BC statue by a named sculptor. The works of the more famous artists are known to us only from descriptions, some of which may have been written towards the end of the fourth century BC, although the form in which we have them dates from the first century AD. It is, to say the least, difficult even to imagine the appearance of Phidias' *Athena* and his still more celebrated *Zeus* at Olympia, some 40 feet (12m) high, covered with ivory, gold and colored glass, and incorporating a great deal of ingeniously wrought figurative relief work on the throne and robe. Copies of less famous statues by other fifth- and fourth-century BC sculptors have, however, been identified from descriptions in later literature, notably the earliest extant account of Greek art which Pliny the Elder (d. AD 79) appended to a work on natural history, and a fascinating guide to Greece written by Pausanias in the second century AD (see p. 138). These copies were made between the first century BC and the third century AD, mainly for Roman patrons, whose tastes they must to some extent reflect. Many are marble versions of bronze statues and although some have considerable artistic merit, they probably give little more than a general idea of the originals, in

THE IDEAL: IDEALISM, PROPORTION AND THE 'CANON'

As an artistic concept, the 'ideal' is based on the belief that sculptors and painters might transcend everyday appearances by idealization, that is by selecting only the best models and eliminating all apparent flaws. A need to create images of physical perfection emerged in fifth-century BC Greece. Artists sought to create human forms that embodied their notion of beauty, sexually and socially conditioned though invested also with moral qualities. It was in this intellectual climate that Plato developed his metaphysical theory of 'Ideas' as universals or abstractions existing in a realm of timeless essences, quite distinct from anything that might exemplify them. He argued that all perceptible objects are imperfect copies approximating to imperceptible ideas, ideas that can be apprehended only by reason, and hence all visual images are no more than copies of copies. It followed that the more closely paintings and sculptures imitated visual appearances, the more deceptive and corrupting they were. So all imitative art, including poetry, was banned from his *Republic*. Nevertheless, Plato's theories allowed the possibility that artists might intuitively see beyond sensory appearances and in this way his concept of the 'ideal' was to have a lasting influence on European aesthetic theory. In practice, however, the more down-to-earth process of idealization as described in Greek and Latin literature was to have a greater effect.

Xenophon recounts that Socrates remarked to the painter Parrhasius, 'When you are painting figures, as it isn't easy to come across one single model who is beyond criticism in every detail, you combine the best features of every one of a number of models and so convey the appearance of entirely beautiful bodies.' Much later, Cicero (BC 106–44), who must have derived the story from a Greek source, told how the fifth-century painter Zeuxis had employed five different young women as models for a single picture of Helen, 'for he did not believe that it was possible to find in one body all the things he looked for in beauty, for nature has not refined to perfection any single object in all its parts.' The urge to idealize was, nevertheless, held in check by the need for verisimilitude and it is significant that the same two artists should have been celebrated also for their illusionistic skill. According to Pliny the Elder,

who had access to Greek sources lost to us, Zeuxis 'painted some grapes with such success that birds flew up to them' and Parrhasius 'depicted a linen curtain with such truth' that Zeuxis asked for it to be drawn aside.

The ideal could not be represented, however, simply by a kind of identikit combination of features, no matter how well selected. Proportional relationships, called by the Greeks *symmetria*, were of fundamental importance, especially for statues. The fifth-century sculptor Polyclitus wrote a treatise on the subject and to illustrate it made a statue now known only from later copies (4, 35). The treatise or *Canon* (meaning rule or law in Greek) is lost, but the Roman physician Galen or Claudius Galenus (c. AD 130–20) wrote that according to the *Canon* the beauty or perfection of a human figure 'arises not in the commensurability or *symmetria* of its constituent elements but in the commensurability of the parts such as that of finger to finger, and of all the fingers to the palm and wrist, and of these to the forearm, and of the forearm to the upper arm, and, in fact of everything to everything else.' To display these relationships a statue was necessarily nude, and in fifth-century Greece, male. It could also have cosmic significance, 'man the measure of all things' in the often quoted words of the Stoic philosopher Protagoras (c. BC 480–410). Polyclitus declared that 'perfection arises from the minute calculation of many numbers' which suggests the influence of sixth-century BC Pythagorean philosophers who developed a theory of cosmic proportions derived from the discovery of the relationship between the measurable lengths of the chords of a lyre and audible harmony.

The idealized statues modelled and carved in ancient Greece, much copied in the Roman empire and rediscovered in fifteenth-century Italy, became part of the western artistic canon – to use the word in a different sense, derived from the canonical books of the Bible and now adopted for an accepted body of supposedly major works of art and literature. They also established a criterion of human beauty that has insidiously conditioned the attitudes of Europeans to themselves and to others, encouraging belief in 'the eternal law that first in beauty should be first in might', as John Keats put it in *Hyperion* (1818).

many cases little more than the pose. So they may confuse as much as they illuminate the history of Greek sculpture.

Several Roman versions survive of a lost *Discobolus* or discus-thrower by Myron of Eleutherae, who is said to have worked in the mid-fifth century BC (**4,34**). The differences between them indicate how far they all depart from the original, for example in the rendering of muscles and bones, especially the ribs. They reveal, nevertheless, that Myron's statue – in bronze and without the tree-stump that supports the figure and spoils the effect in the marble copies – must have been an outstanding example of the

compositional quality that the Greeks called *rhythmos*, with the limbs balancing one another in a complex pattern of forms. It is an essay in equilibrium, for the figure is shown not in movement but eternally poised between two actions. According to modern athletes the attitude is not one that would naturally be adopted by a man throwing a discus. Yet it vividly suggests both the winding and unwinding torsion of the body, as well as the trajectory of the discus. Movement – or rather the idea of movement – has rarely been more effectively expressed in static terms. And the original statue in polished bronze with colored

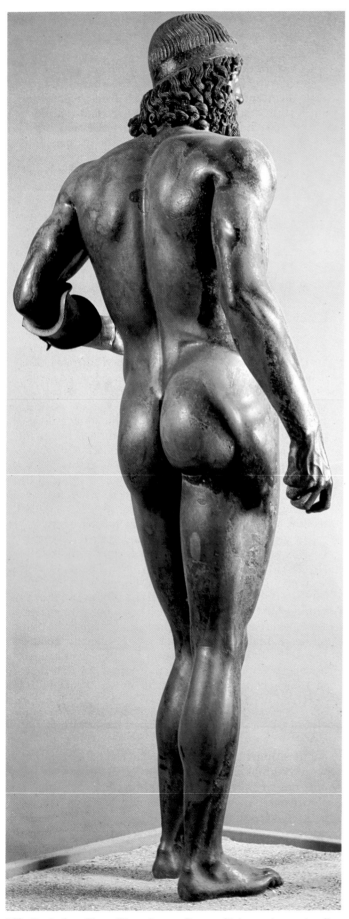 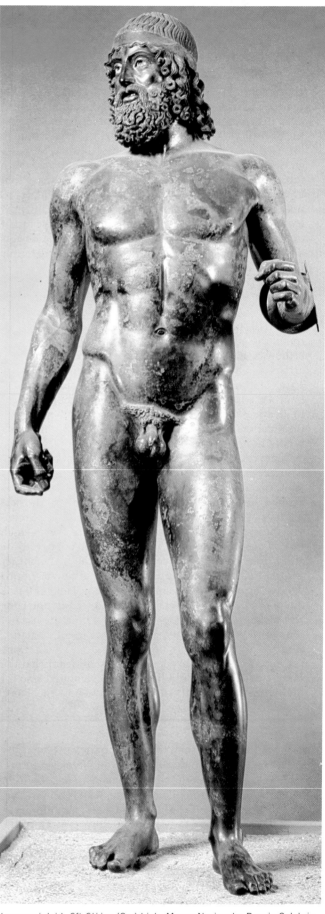

4,36 *Warrior* from Riace, 5th century BC. Bronze with bone, glass paste, silver and copper inlaid, 6ft 6⁴/₅ins (2m) high. Museo Nazionale, Reggio Calabria.

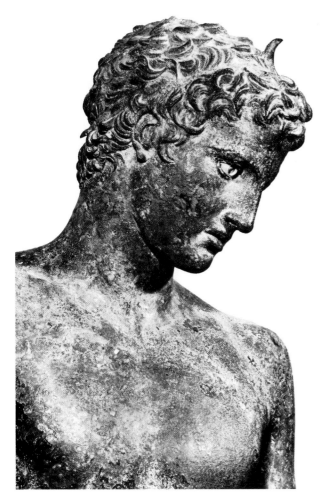

4,37 *Boy* from the Bay of Marathon, detail, c. 340–300 BC. Bronze, full height 4ft 3¼ins (1.3m). National Archeological Museum, Athens.

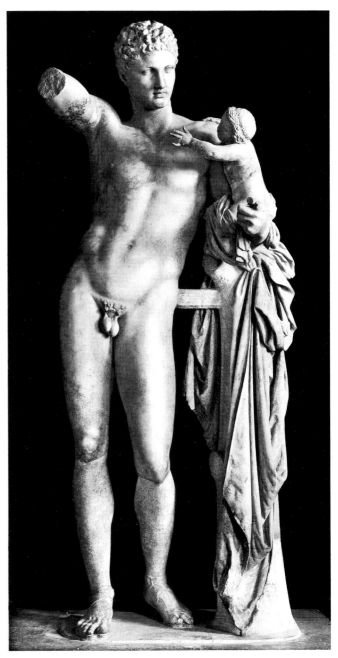

4,38 *Hermes and Dionysus*, c. 340 BC. Marble, about 7ft (2.13m) high. Archeological Museum, Olympia.

eyes must have looked almost startlingly alive, especially when it was seen in the company of the more usual types of athlete statues standing upright. Myron was famed in antiquity for his naturalism, and there are no fewer than 36 surviving neatly turned Greek epigrams devoted to the unpromising subject of his deceptively lifelike bronze statue of a cow (of which no copy or other record survives).

The composition of the *Discobolus* is confined to a single plane, as if it had been conceived as a high relief. Polyclitus of Argos, on the other hand, who worked between 452 and 417 BC, took account of multiple viewpoints. His statues are similarly known only from Roman marble copies of varying quality after the bronze originals. The most famous is the *Doryphorus* or spearbearer, striding slowly forward with his weight almost entirely on his right leg, his left arm holding a spear, his head turned slightly to the right – changes in direction that send a tremor of life through the figure (**4,35**). This statue is said to have been modelled to illustrate the sculptor's theories about bodily proportions and it became very influential in Roman times when it was called and had the authority of the 'Canon'.

These copies are of interest mainly as records of the poses invented by fifth-century sculptors. They show very little of the subtlety of modelling and amazing naturalism in handling and in the treatment of detail that characterize the very few surviving contemporary bronze statues (none of which can be securely attributed to a

named artist). One dredged from the sea off southern Italy near Riace in 1972 has eyes of bone and glass paste, eyelashes, lips and nipples of copper and bared teeth of silver (**4,36**). The hair is rendered with the most minute delicacy. And yet, the general effect could hardly be more different from that of in some ways comparable Egyptian figures (**2,33**). Greek sculptors appreciated that the human figure cannot be simply 'reproduced', as if in a cast from a living model: they saw that it must be, as it were, 'translated' not only into marble or bronze but also into the medium of art and the tension held between idealization and naturalism in a delicately balanced equilibrium – those creative life-giving qualities lost in marble copies. The muscular bronze warrior is at once an ideal male figure and a wholly convincing image of a man in the prime of life. Another bronze (found in the sea near Marathon) is of later date and the balance between idealization and naturalism has been tipped towards the former to catch that mood of adolescent dreamy melancholy which first appears in Greek art in the fourth century BC (**4,37**). It is the product of a world quite different from that of heroic extrovert *kouroi*, athletes and stalwart warriors.

The sturdiness and air of serene detachment so marked in Classical Greek sculpture began to give way to stylish elegance of form in the mid-fourth century. The sculptor mainly associated with this was Praxiteles (fl. 375–330 BC), of whom very little is known. Classical archeologists disagree as to whether the famous statue of *Hermes* at Olympia is his original or a very good copy (**4,38**). Certainly, it has a subtlety of soft modelling conspicuously lacking in the 49 surviving copies of his most famous statue, that of Aphrodite (whom the Romans called Venus) carved for the city of Cnidus on the coast of Asia Minor (**4,39**). None has more than a hint of the sensual quality ascribed to the original by poets and other writers of the first two centuries AD. They all lauded it as the perfect embodiment of female beauty, supremely and deceptively lifelike. One visitor was so overcome that he leaped on to the plinth (see Glossary) to embrace her.

Surprising as it may seem, in view of the innumerable nude male statues, the *Aphrodite of Cnidus* is the first completely nude female in ancient Greek sculpture. (Literary sources mention none earlier, and the supposed pre-fourth-century BC origin of two known from Roman copies, in the Louvre and the Museo dei Conservatori in Rome, is by no means certain.) As we have already seen, when the Greeks adopted the Syrian fertility goddess Astarte and renamed her Aphrodite, they immediately clothed her naked form (4,6). The proximity of Cnidus to Syria may partly account for the nudity of the statue carved by Praxiteles, but for no more. For with this figure he virtually created the classic Western image of the beautiful female nude, an image which was to appear again and again in the art of Europe and which also encapsulates some of the fundamental differences between European and other cultures. As in the nude male statues that proliferated in ancient Greece, naturalism and idealism are combined. Moreover, the stance is in effect an adaptation in reverse of that used for statues of young athletes – Aphrodite's weight being on her right leg, with left knee slightly advanced and left foot withdrawn. The only significant modification is in the thighs, held tightly together, and in the general emphasis given to the dimpling roundness and softness of the limbs. Unlike the brazen male nudes, however, she seems slightly shy of her nakedness. Her eyes are averted and the gesture with which Astarte had boldly pointed to her sex has been transformed by a slight shift of the hand into one of protective concealment. By raising the other arm in front of the breasts, in a statue of about 300 BC, an anonymous sculptor effected the most significant change made to the image, creating one of the great prototypes in European

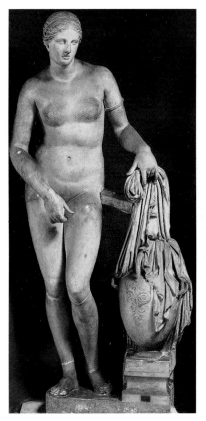
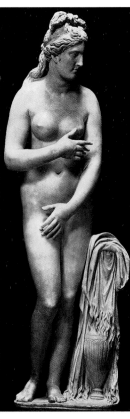

4,39 *Above left Aphrodite of Cnidus*, Imperial Roman copy. Marble, 6ft 8ins (2.03m) high. Vatican Museums, Rome.

4,40 *Above right Capitoline Aphrodite*, Imperial Roman copy. Marble, 6ft 1½ins (1.87m) high. Museo Capitolino, Rome.

art with a long subsequent history, when it was known as the 'pudic Venus' or Venus of modesty – a figure whose erotic attraction was, of course, enhanced by her modest gesture (**4,40**).

A conjunction of social and aesthetic concerns may account for the rarity of female nudes in the earlier periods of Greek art, as well as the particular form they took when they eventually appeared in the fourth century. Few civilized societies have been so completely male-dominated as that of ancient Greece. Laws make this abundantly clear: adultery, for example, was defined one-sidedly as intercourse between a married woman and a man who was not her husband, rape as an offence against a woman's husband, father or guardian, not herself. Regarded and guarded as possessions, upper-class wives were kept at home and confined to child-rearing and household maintenance, while their husbands sought emotional, physical and intellectual stimulus elsewhere, either with members of their own sex or among the *hetairai* or *porne* (common prostitutes). The latter were depicted naked, in a variety of seductive poses, on sixth- and fifth-century vases, usually in brothel scenes, which are pornographic in the strictest meaning of the word. To have included a nude female among the statues of male athletes which crowded the sanctuaries would therefore have seemed extremely odd.

There can be little doubt that it was the Greek painters of the Classical period who developed both the ideas and the techniques that were to differentiate the arts of Europe from those of all other civilizations – their predominant naturalism, above all. The painters were, it must be remembered, just as famous in their own day as the sculptors. But whereas we know something about the work of the sculptors, even if only at second- or third-hand, we know absolutely nothing about the work of the great ancient Greek painters. Descriptions, however, testify to their naturalistic skills in representing spatial recession and movement. Socrates, according to Xenophon, urged artists to go beyond mere representation and express character and emotion at their finest and noblest. Aristotle, writing in the fourth century BC, suggests that already by that date painters had evolved what we could call idealization, caricature and realism ('Polygnotus represented men as better, Pauson represented them as worse, and Dionysius represented them as they are'). How far any of them succeeded cannot, of course, be known since all the works of the great Greek painters whose names are known have vanished. Not a scrap remains of those that hung in a building attached to the Propylaea on the Acropolis at Athens, of the hundreds in other Greek sanctuaries and the many taken to Rome. The painted tomb of c. 470 BC discovered in 1968 at Paestum, Italy, is probably Greek work but provincial and so also are the recently discovered fourth- and third-century BC Macedonian painted tombs at Lefkadia and Vergina, all of which necessarily give only a partial impression of ancient Greek painting, remarkable though the paintings at Vergina are even in their damaged state (5,7).

VASE PAINTING

Paintings of the Classical period are known to have been copied in Italy and probably provided models for scenes depicted on the walls of houses at Pompeii (see p. 189). But there is no means of telling how faithful the copyists were or whether their work gives more than a very general impression of the original compositions. The only other visual evidence we have is that provided by the decorations on Greek pottery. These naturally differ from wall and panel paintings in several important respects, notably in scale. But they illustrate the development of those techniques of representation to which the literary sources refer.

Most Greek pottery painting is on useful wares (made for the toilet or for drinking parties, etc.), although some vases were intended for funerary or ceremonial purposes (e.g. for presentation at the Panathenaic games). They were, of course, less highly valued than metal vessels, few of which survive, for, unlike pottery, bronze and silver can be only too easily recycled. Yet great skill and artistry were lavished on them. Basic shapes both elegant and practical had been devised by the sixth century BC for the tall two-handled *amphora* with swelling body for wine, the three-handled *hydria* or water jug, the wide-mouthed *krater*, in which wine and water are mixed (as was customary), the

4,41 Meidias, vase, detail, c. 410 BC. British Museum, London.

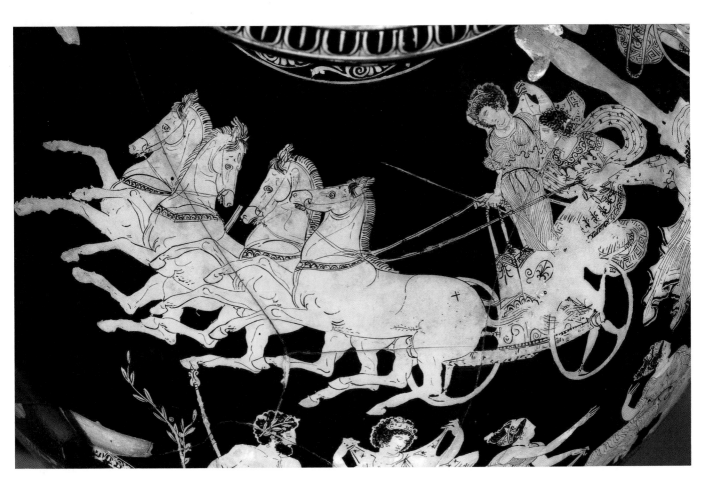

small jug called an *oinoche* for pouring the mixture, and the wide, shallow cups, *kylix* and *kantharos*, from which it was drunk. The subject-matter of the figurative scenes depicted on them was usually mythological – very similar, in fact, to that of contemporary dramatic poetry and of such large-scale paintings as are recorded. A preference for stories about men and fabulous beasts rather than the immortals on Olympus is evident, although Dionysus, the god of wine, with his female followers the maenads attacked by lascivious satyrs, appears quite frequently. Also depicted are numerous scenes from daily life: artists and craftsmen at work, women engaged in household chores, athletes exercising in the gymnasium, drinking parties and theatrical performances. Love-making both heterosexual and homosexual is represented with extreme candour. Indeed, these vases reflect more clearly than any other surviving works of art the Greeks' preoccupation with their own world, the here and now.

In the sixth century BC figures were usually shown in black on a light orange-red ground. This so-called 'black-figure' process was a Greek invention which called for great technical skill. After a vessel had been formed (on a fast wheel by hand), allowed to dry and then burnished smooth, it was brushed over with a very thin coat of refined and diluted clay known as 'slip' (sometimes misleadingly called a glaze). When dry, it provided the ground on which decorations were painted, also in slip. The chemical properties of the clay used for the slip were such that when the pot was fired, and the heat of the kiln carefully controlled in three stages, the undercoat took on an orange-red color and the decorations a glossy black. Before the beginning of the fifth century BC the reversed 'red-figure' process was introduced as an alternative. The background of the composition was painted in with black slip, which was also used for adding details on the figures 'reserved' on the red undercoat. As the same type of local clay and the same method of firing were used in both processes, some potters 'showed off' by painting one side of a vase in black-figure, the other in red-figure. Red-figure gradually replaced black-figure, which, from the early fifth century onwards, was used only for certain traditional types of vessel, notably those filled with oil and awarded to the winners in the Panathenaic games.

Black-figure was essentially an art of silhouette. The details that indicate the modelling of the body are picked out in red lines (or rather are incised through the black slip to the ground color) and make little visual effect. The red-figure process had to be used in order to transform these shadowy forms into light-illuminated figures and this led, in turn, to a departure from the purely conceptual image. On black-figure vases eyes, for instance, had to be shown frontally, even when the head was in profile, as it almost invariably was (the silhouette of a full face being insignificant). Foreshortening appears for the first time on red-figure vases.

It is more than likely that the development of red-figure was inspired by a desire to emulate the effects achieved by painters working on a large scale and with a much less restricted palette. Red-figure vase painters

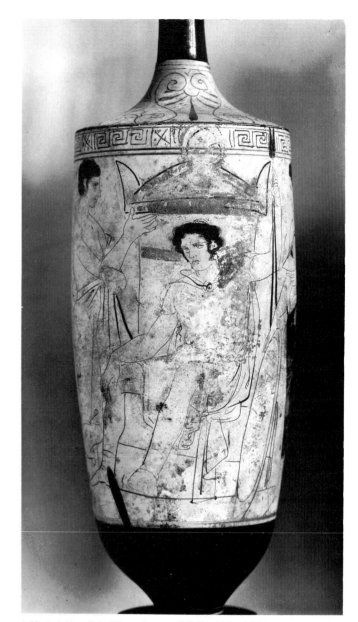

4,42 *Lekythos*, late 5th century BC. 19¼ins (49cm) high. National Archeological Museum, Athens.

could delineate figures in a far wider range of postures than before; they could indicate (if not quite express) emotion and character in their features; they could even suggest recession in space. The influence of Polygnotus has been detected in a vase made (and perhaps also painted) by Meidias (**4,41**). Draperies are agitated, horses turn their heads as they canter along, Hilaeiria, who is carried off in the chariot of Polydeuces, has an expression of almost caricatured despair on her face, some wispy branches of olive hint at a landscape setting. The potentialities of finely drawn lines to suggest form as well as movement have been brilliantly exploited. This vase is, indeed, a virtuoso performance, though one that betrays signs of striving after effects that could be fully realized only on a much larger scale by mural or panel painters.

The achievements of such artists as Parrhasius and Zeuxis may be more faithfully reflected on vessels decorated by a process closer to that of panel painting: the white-ground *lekythoi*. These relatively small jugs of supremely elegant form were made to hold oil for cleansing the body and many were specifically intended for use in burial rites and subsequent interment with the dead. They were entirely covered with white slip and after firing were decorated in tempera colors (see Glossary), which would soon have rubbed off vessels in frequent use. Indeed, they have all but vanished from most that survive. The figure drawings that remain, however, are no less astonishingly free than they are expressive (**4,42**). Nothing quite like them is to be found in European art for another 2,000 years. A few bold lines suffice to indicate a limb or a garment, a broad splash a shock of hair, two or three slight brush-strokes give emotional expression to a mouth or an eye. What is even more remarkable is that outline is used not merely to define silhouette, as in black-figure and red-figure vases, but to indicate volume. It is a kind of visual shorthand that can be employed only by an artist who has already solved the problems of graphic representation, and one that can be 'read' only by those familiar with its conventions.

Several of the finest *lekythoi* – including the one illustrated here – were buried with Athenians who fell in the Peloponnesian War. Few memorials of the dead are simpler or more poignant. Two figures, probably friends or relations, stand on either side of a soldier, who is seated before his tomb with eyes open as if to catch a last lingering look at the 'warm precincts of the cheerful day'. There are no heroic gestures, the mourners strike no attitudes of grief and the soldier seems to confront the inevitability of extinction with a mixture of resolution and regret. Love of life counterbalances the fatalistic outlook summed up in the famous saying 'Call no man happy ere he die, he is at best but fortunate' (attributed by Herodotus to the law-maker Solon, but also used by Sophocles).

Stelae

Graves were often marked by stone monuments – that is, by stone 'reminders' or 'memorials' – without the religious or magic properties that invested the sepulchral art of most other civilizations. Greek monuments emphasized life rather than death – the memory of the dead in the minds of the living. They were usually upright slabs called *stelae* carved in relief. Earlier examples rarely had more than one figure, but the type devised in the mid- or late fifth century BC shows two or more framed by a kind of pedimented porch. The relationship between the figures gives these works a sombre dramatic power, all the more effective for being underplayed. A husband takes leave of his wife, tenderly but without any demonstration of emotion; similarly a son says farewell to his aged father, and a father to a son who died in youth. More than one *stele* shows a pensive seated woman, the subject of the monument, with a standing woman – a slave or daughter – holding a casket (**4,43**). Repetitions make it clear that these cannot have been portraits (though portraits of distinguished men had begun to appear in Greek art by the early fourth century BC).

Not only the rich were commemorated by such *stelae*. Several record humble craftsmen with their tools. At least one is of a slave girl, presumably set up by her master or mistress. None has the grandiose pretensions of monuments to rulers such as were then being created on the fringes of the Hellenic world in Asia Minor (e.g. that of Mausolus of Caria, from whom the word 'mausoleum' derives). Fear of the dire consequences of *hubris* or arrogance may partly account for this. Similarly, they make no reference to an afterlife; they have no 'magic' function. Because of their scale and simple human subject-matter, they are perhaps more directly and immediately appealing than statues and reliefs of divinities behind which there always lurk those irrational beliefs prominent in Greek literature, but which nowadays seem remote and difficult to comprehend.

In the ancient world *stelae* were not regarded as major works of art. The Romans seem rarely to have robbed them or to have had them copied. Pliny and Pausanias passed them by. Yet, doubtful though it is whether any are by leading sculptors, they sometimes possess in the

4,43 Grave *stele* of Hegeso, c. 410–400 BC.
Marble, 4ft 11ins (1.5m) high. National Archeological Museum, Athens.

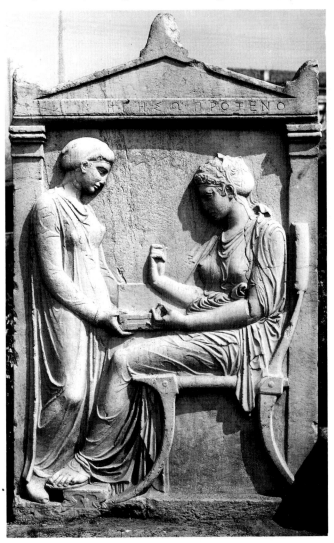

sensitivity of their carvings the very qualities that are lacking in the copies by which the work of celebrated sculptors is known. The majority, however, seem to have been almost mass-produced. The similarities between some examples are so close as to suggest that they had been roughed out with the help of some kind of pointing apparatus (see Glossary) from a single model: and in them and others we can follow the development of such techniques of working in marble as that of the running drill to cut deep furrows (introduced in the early fourth century BC). *Stelae* also reflect the main stylistic trends in Greek sculpture from the severity of the early Classical period, in the years immediately after the Persian wars, to the serenity of the mid-fifth century and the more highly worked elegance and greater expressiveness of the fourth. As very few are dated, this stylistic sequence can, of course, provide no more than a rough chronological framework. Some sculptors of the fourth century BC – and vase painters too – may well have harked back to earlier styles in response to those who, like Plato, distrusted change in art as in politics. Tradition played as important a part as innovation in Greek art and, especially, in architecture.

THE LATE CLASSICAL PERIOD

The fourth century BC is often described as a period of artistic decline; it was certainly one of change. New tendencies in architecture are most clearly apparent in two buildings at Epidaurus: the theatre and the *tholos*, a circular structure of unknown function. Both are in the sanctuary of Asclepius, the god of healing who was also credited with the power of resurrecting the dead and whose cult became very popular in the fourth century. Offerings from many devotees who sought his protection provided the funds for the buildings. The theatre is among the most spectacular of all ancient Greek constructions and one that seems to crystallize an ideal of architecture

as pure geometrical form (**4,44**). It could hardly be simpler – a vast auditorium 387 feet (118m) in diameter, composed of 55 tiers of marble benches rising round rather more than half the circular orchestra platform or dancing space for the chorus (not for musicians), beyond which there was a long, narrow structure for the stage. The form regularized and embellished the earliest type of theatre, which had been simply a natural hollow in a hill adapted for rituals connected with the cult of Dionysus. It was out of these rituals that drama as we know it evolved. In Athens the theatre where tragedies and comedies were first performed in the fifth century BC had been a fairly simple affair in a cleft of the rock below the Acropolis, with wooden benches in an auditorium hemmed in by buildings on either side. (The extant remains date from a later remodelling.) At Epidaurus space was unlimited in the open country and the theatre could therefore take its 'natural' geometrical shape, which also enabled some 14,000 spectators to see and hear the performers – a feat of acoustics that still amazes audiences today. The theatre was, however, built after the great creative period of Greek drama had come to an end. Whereas in fifth-century Athens only new works had been given – three tragedies (each in three parts) and five comedies each year – now there were revivals of the most popular of those 'classics' from which Aristotle was soon to draw the rules of dramatic poetry. It was not only the architectural form of the theatre but Greek drama itself that had been regularized.

The *tholos* at Epidaurus is said to have been designed by the same architect as the theatre, Polyclitus (not to be confused with the slightly earlier sculptor of the *Doryphorus*), but it was strikingly different in style, with much carved decoration. Corinthian capitals, first devised in Athens in the fifth century but little used before the middle of the fourth, are prominent and characterize a new tendency in Greek architecture (**4,45**). With their curling tendrils and acanthus leaves they were not only

4,44 Theatre, Epidaurus, begun c. 350 BC.

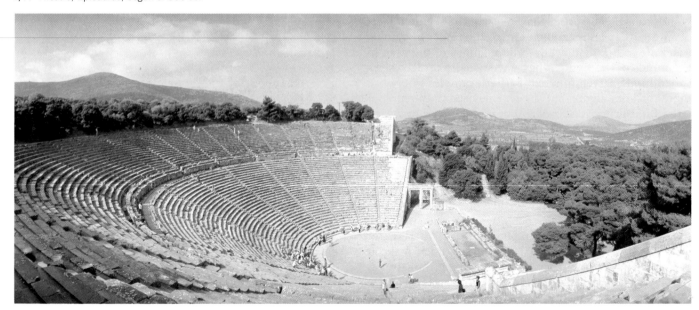

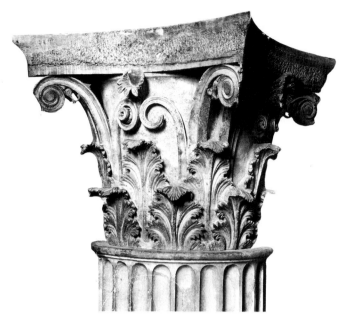

4,45 Corinthian capital from the *tholos* at Epidaurus, c. 350 BC. Archeological Museum, Epidaurus.

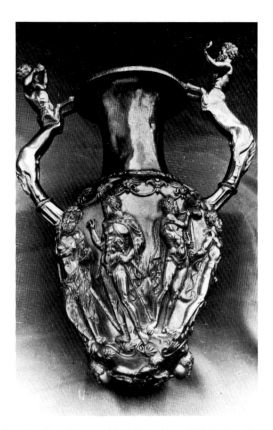

4,46 Amphora from Panagyurishte, Bulgaria, c. 350–300 BC. Gold, 10ins (25.4cm) high. Archeological Museum, Plovdiv.

more decorative than Ionic capitals but also, since all four faces were alike, avoided the awkward effect which the latter made when seen from the side (as at the angle of a building) but were used almost exclusively inside temples. They perfectly answered new demands for both embellishment and regularization.

Similar tendencies were apparent also in domestic architecture. Demosthenes (b. c. 384 BC), the great orator and leading opponent of Philip II of Macedon (see p. 175), declared that luxurious houses had made their first appearance in Athens in his life-time. There is an interesting signed floor mosaic in a house in Athens, but little else survives. At Olynthos near the coast of Thrace in north-east Greece – a town laid out about 430 BC and destroyed in 348 BC – excavations have revealed that the larger houses already had figurative mosaic pavements in the main room (the *andron* used for entertaining male guests). A magnificent though slightly later example survives from a house in Pella, some way inland from Olynthos (5,8). Olynthos was built on a regular grid, a type of planning not used in central and southern Greece, except for the rebuilding of the Athenian port of Piraeus (c. 460–445 BC) to the design of Hippodamus of Miletus, who was called in by Pericles. Athens itself was a maze of narrow winding streets and alleys. Its centre of daily life, market-place and meeting place, the *agora* (literally 'field'), remained an irregular space with a simple *stoa* or long portico to provide shelter from the weather, until order was imposed on it in the second century BC (see pp. 184–5).

Further evidence of a taste for luxury indulged by the ruling classes in northern Greece is provided by gold vases found in a tomb near Philippopolis (present-day Plovdiv in Bulgaria), the capital founded by Philip II of Macedon (**4,46**). They are of an extraordinarily sophisticated elegance. Figures which had become either tired or over-wrought on painted pottery vases in the south here exude a new vigour. Contact with 'barbarians' may have been

responsible. The handles have the same animal vitality as the ibexes that serve the same function on Achaemenid vessels, although here they have been metamorphosed into lively young Greek centaurs.

Some of the finest examples of ancient Greek goldsmiths' work were, in fact, made for the Scythians of southern Russia. No gold ornament of any period or country is more exquisitely wrought than a pectoral intended to be worn on the breast of some nomadic chief and buried with him near the Dnieper river (**4,47**). Animals are rendered with a vitality and naturalism that makes the griffins of the lower register no less credible than the extremely sharply observed horses, cattle, sheep, dogs, hares and even a couple of grasshoppers. Four men are incorporated, one milking a ewe, another holding an amphora and two in the centre stitching a shirt out of animal skin. The contrast between the simple pastoral way of life represented by these figures and the highly developed technical accomplishment of the goldsmith who made them is not, however, stressed. The Scythians are neither caricatured nor idealized. Not until much later, in Roman times, did these people come to be regarded as 'noble savages', preserving the innocence and moral qualities that 'civilized' man had lost.

Before the end of the Classical period numerous examples of Greek artistry had found their way far beyond the frontiers of the Hellenic world: gold ornaments, bronze vessels, painted pottery vases and, much more widely, coins. The idea of fashioning precious metals into small

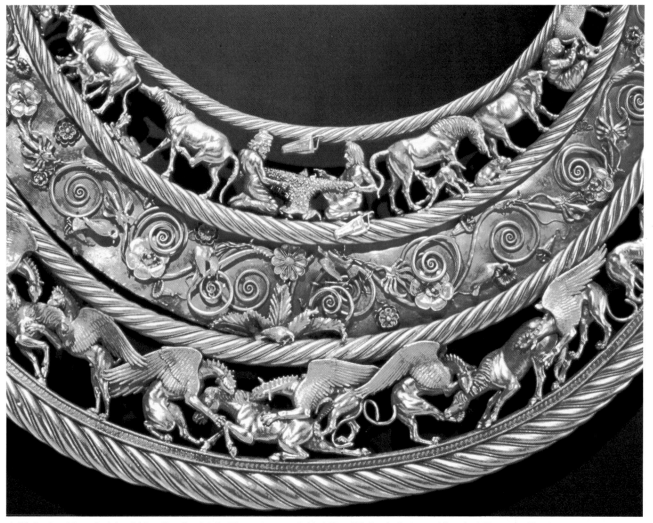

4,47 Pectoral from Ordzhonikidze, Russia, detail, 4th century BC. Gold, 12ins (30.6cm) diameter. Historical Museum, Kiev.

pieces of uniform size, weight and value originated, like so much else, in Asia Minor. Bean-shaped lumps of electrum stamped with devices were minted in Lydia shortly after the middle of the seventh century BC. But within 100 years the Greeks had regularized the shape to a disc modelled in relief with the emblem of the city that issued it – at Athens, for instance, the head of Athena on the front and the owl sacred to her on the back (**4,48**). As their designs were frequently modified and changed, coins provide a miniature history of Greek art from the Archaic to the Hellenistic period. On the earliest, profile heads have frontal eyes and animals are schematized. Later they reflect the naturalistic ideals of the Classical period, none more beautifully than those of Syracuse in Sicily, which bear the firmly modelled head of Arethusa surrounded by dolphins (**4,49**), and in the later fourth century BC a tendency towards greater delicacy and intricacy becomes apparent (**4,50**).

The most widely diffused coins were those issued by Philip II of Macedon after 356 BC, when he acquired the gold mines of Mount Pangaeus in Thrace. The gold *stater* (a piece weighing 8.6 grams) became an item of international currency and continued to be issued in Macedonia for a long time. It was subsequently imitated by central and northern Europeans ignorant of the significance of its emblematic designs. The process by which such designs

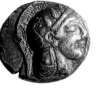

4,48 Attic tetradrachm with head of Athena and owl, c. 479 BC. Silver, 1in (2.5cm) diameter. British Museum, London.

4,49 *Below* Decadrachm from Syracuse, 413–357 BC. Silver, 1³/₈in (3.5cm) diameter. British Museum, London.

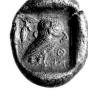

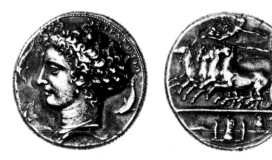

4,50 Didrachm from Heraclea in Lucania, 370–281 BC. Silver, ⁷/₈in (2.2cm) diameter. British Museum, London.

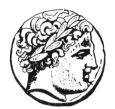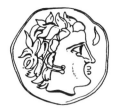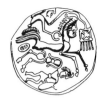

4,51 Progressive stylization of imagery in 2nd century BC. Celtic coins, imitating the gold *stater* of Philip II of Macedon. Drawings.

were slowly denaturalized and transformed into non-figurative patterns is very instructive. The head of Apollo, for instance, was gradually reduced to an assembly of disjointed facial features, and the two-horse chariot on the reverse of this coin – which probably referred to Philip's racing victories in the Olympic games – was completely dissolved into abstraction (**4,51**). The power of Greek art to reassert itself is forcefully demonstrated by the coins we use today with their idealized heads and naturalistically rendered symbols. Coins provide a chain – the only one that has never been broken – linking the arts of the modern world with those of ancient Greece.

BARBARIAN ALTERNATIVES: SCYTHIANS AND THE ANIMAL STYLE

Herodotus, who, in the mid-fifth century BC, went to Olbia on the northern shore of the Black Sea to gather information about the Scythians, noted that they were 'a people without fortified towns, living in wagons which they take wherever they go, accustomed, one and all, to fight on horseback with bows and arrows, and dependent for their food not upon agriculture, but upon their cattle'. He set down what he could find about their origins, believing them to have come from further east, described their customs and gave a vivid account of the gruesome rites performed for the burial of a dead king. Although he did not admire them, he was bound to admit that 'they have managed one thing, and that the most important in human affairs, better than anyone else on the face of the earth: I mean that no one who invades their country can escape destruction, and if they wish to avoid engaging with an enemy, that enemy cannot by any possibility come to grips with them' (*The Histories, IV*). They are hardly less elusive, in a different way, to the modern observer. Numerous Scythian artifacts have been dug up in various parts of Russia – fascinating, beautiful but baffling. Archeologists have been continually foiled in attempting to reconstruct their history.

The Scythians are the most prominent of a number of groups of mounted nomads with related cultures who thinly populated the vast area of steppe or treeless grassland stretching from the Danube to the Gobi desert in Mongolia – a distance roughly double that from one coast to the other of north America. All that is known about these peoples derives from their artifacts, almost invariably found in tombs, and from the records of the neighbouring literate societies of the Mediterranean, the Near East and China, to whom they were an ever-present menace from the second millennium BC until well into the European Middle Ages. The Great Wall of China was begun in the late third century BC to keep them out.

The territory occupied by these nomads lay between the great northern forests, inhabited by hunters and fishers, and the temperate fertile regions, where agriculture was highly developed and cities had been established. They have often been described as living in a state of arrested development between the two. But this is to misunderstand them. Nomadism sprang not directly from Stone Age hunting and gathering but from mixed farming – with the domestication of horses – as a means of obtaining the maximum yield of food from land that was unsuitable for permanent pastoral or agricultural settlement. It was based on the careful breeding of different species of animals to make the most of grazing possibilities: cattle that graze well on long grass, sheep and goats that crop close. Climatic conditions necessitated constant movement from wide areas that provided fodder in spring and summer to the more restricted pastures, where the flocks could survive the winter. Nomads exploited for their own purposes the technologies developed in the cities: the working of bronze and then of iron, the use of wheeled vehicles. They created a form of society that was to outlive the ancient civilizations of the Near East and the Classical world (which, indeed, they helped to destroy). Their way of life was, in fact, a parallel development to that of urban civilization: an alternative with its own set of values. The art conditioned by it similarly provides an alternative to that evolved in the Mediterranean, and the conflict between the two determined much of the subsequent history of painting and sculpture in Europe.

As we have seen, Scythians clearly valued Greek craftsmanship. Many of the finest examples of Greek goldsmiths' work were preserved in the tombs of their kings (**4,47**). So too were bronze and pottery vessels, including a fifth-century BC amphora, which had originally been made as a prize for a victor in the Panathenaic games. Egyptian artifacts have also been found in these tombs. Fine objects from Achaemenid Persia and Zhou dynasty China were buried with nomads of the eastern steppes and Altai mountains. But the so-called 'Animal' style developed by the cultures of the steppes differs

4,52 Recumbent stag, shield plaque, from Kostromskaya, south Russia, late 7th to early 6th century BC. Gold, 12½ins (31.7cm) long. State Hermitage, St Petersburg.

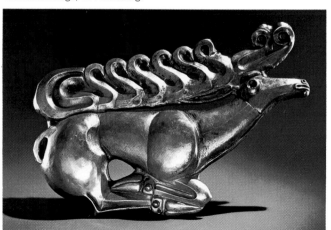

almost as much from Persian and Chinese art as from ancient Egyptian and Greek. A gold plaque of a stag wrought to decorate an iron shield or breast-plate is a characteristic example (4,52), modelled in relief but with extraordinary feeling for full-bodied form, simplified, schematized and contracted into a tight pattern, yet mysteriously alive with animal vitality.

The origins of the Animal style are obscure. So too are those of the Scythians, who established themselves to the west of the Volga and on the northern shores of the Black Sea in about the eighth century BC, displacing another group of nomads known to the Greeks as Cimmerians (who retreated into Asia Minor and sacked Greek cities on the coast). Excavations have revealed traces of a succession of pre-Scythian cultures in the southern Caucasus – a famous tomb dating from the late second millennium at Maikop and several tombs of the early first millennium have yielded some notable bronzes of animals, but these are closer to the arts of Assyria and Anatolia than to that of the Scythians. A more likely connection would be with the bronzes of Luristan (see p. 112). But the latter include numerous human figures, which are very rare in Scythian art. Also the animals of Luristan often merge into one another by what is known as the 'zoomorphic juncture' – the tail of one creature being fashioned like the head of another of different species – a device which does not seem to have been adopted by Scythian craftsmen until a relatively late period. The arts of the Shang and Zhou China (see pp. 86–9, 116–9), at the other end of the steppes, probably contributed to the formation of the Animal style, but here influences seem to have been reciprocal and are, therefore, very hard to disentangle. Works in perishable materials, of which we now know very little or nothing at all, may also have played a part – not least the tattoos with which the nomads decorated their bodies.

Whatever its origins, the Animal style as we know it seems to have first emerged on the western steppes in the seventh century BC. It is found almost exclusively on small objects, mainly metal – bronze or, quite often, gold enriched with colored glass paste – to be attached to clothing, arms and armour, chariots and the harnesses of horses. The animals from which it takes its name were wild (not those bred by the nomads), usually various species of deer, wolves and large felines although fabulous monsters also

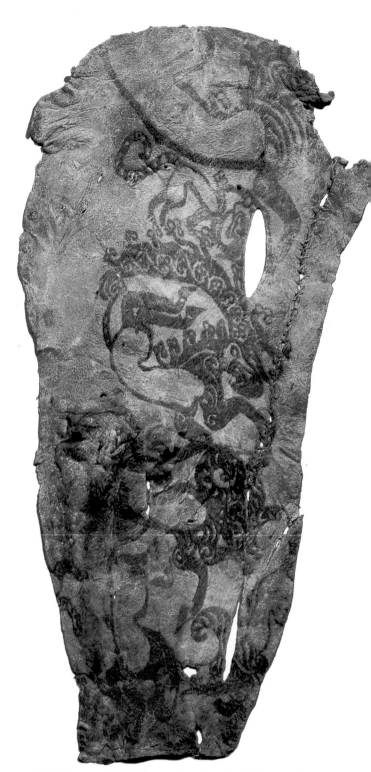

4,54 Tattoo on a chieftain's arm, from Pazyryk, Altai region, Russia, 5th century BC. Human skin, 23^{7}/$_{10}$ins (60cm) long. State Hermitage, St Petersburg.

appear. Single animals are rendered with a sharp-edged compactness that gives them an almost monumental quality, despite their small size. A stag's antlers are rendered as a series of scrolls running the length of the back; the legs folded together beneath it (4,52). The slim body of a feline, probably a snow-leopard, is coiled into a circle, schematized with ruthless concision but given a tensely flexed muscular vitality. But what do they signify? They can be read in more than one way. Is the stag bound for sacrifice and, therefore, a symbol of man's mastery of the

4,53 Panther, shield or breast-plate plaque, from Kelermes, south Russia, late 7th to early 6th century BC. Gold with inlays, 12^{13}/$_{16}$ins (32.6cm) long. State Hermitage, St Petersburg.

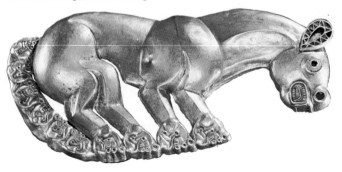

animal world – or was the reverse intended? Is the stag in full flight, escaping capture by its fleetness and superior muscular force, wound up like a hard metal spring?

Another animal, usually identified as a panther, is shown on the prowl (4,53). Its paws are fashioned like curled felines, which are repeated along the tail, a device probably intended to compress the force of many animals within a single image. Similar superimpositions occur on many other pieces, including bronze finials for poles. The significance of the animals themselves remains, none the less, mysterious. Clearly they are more than merely decorative in intent. But their 'meaning' remains obscure, just as their form resists analysis. It is impossible to say more than that the extraordinary contortions and involutions of this art sprang from a culture and sense of form totally distinct from that of the Mediterranean world.

Numerous attempts have, of course, been made to explain or interpret these works of art. They have been associated with the rites of hunting magic, for the nomads are known to have hunted wild beasts as well as bred the tame. They may have represented supernatural beings. Later peoples of the steppes are known to have believed that stags transported the dead to the other world. They have also been explained as totems venerated by the various clans of nomads as ancestors. Their transformation into clan symbols would have followed naturally and easily. The heraldic beasts of medieval chivalry, which include many deer and felines like those on the British royal coat of arms, may certainly be traced back to emblematic devices of later barbarian tribes from central Asia.

Animal style art was essentially aristocratic, intended for the adornment of the person and possessions of the rulers, their families and perhaps some of the more important mounted warriors. (Kingship seems to have been hereditary among the royal Scythians of the west.) The vast majority of examples come from tombs in which the riches and power of the deceased are very clearly displayed. Herodotus described in chilling detail how a dead king was embalmed and taken in a chariot around his dominions, accompanied by an increasing crowd of mourners, to the burial place. There the corpse was placed in a pit together with a selection of royal treasures. One of his wives, his butler, cook, groom, steward and chamberlain were strangled and buried with him, as were a number of horses which had been clubbed to death. A mound of earth was heaped over the tomb and a year later 50 youths and 50 of the finest horses were killed, stuffed with straw and stationed round it. Several tombs excavated in the Kuban region to the east of the Black Sea have confirmed the substantial accuracy of this account, notably one at Kostromskaya, containing the dead man's armour, a gold plaque of a stag (4,52), leather quivers, bronze arrow-heads, copper and iron horsebits. Thirteen human skeletons without any adornments lay in the compacted earth above. Outside the main area the remains of 22 horses were found, apparently buried in pairs.

A still more extraordinary group of tombs, rather more elaborate than those of the Scythians and constructed partly of stone, is located far to the east at Pazyryk in the Altai mountains of Mongolia (near the present-day frontier between Russia and China). Here the peculiar climatic conditions preserved their contents deep-frozen in solid ice, allowing us a unique close-up glimpse of the lifestyle and art of the nomads of the steppes some 2,400 years ago. The body of a king or chieftain has been found, strongly marked with tattooing in the Animal style – a tantalizing indication of the role that decorations on the human skin, now totally lost and unknown to us except for this one chance survival, may well have played in the development of drawing and painting from a very early period (4,54). Also deep-frozen were fabrics with their colors still bright and fresh, including a magnificent Persian pile carpet (the earliest known), delicate Chinese silks and panels of *appliqué* work in felt, which were presumably local products. A particularly fine saddle-cover is decorated with dragon masks and fighting griffins and goats, motifs derived respectively from Chinese ritual bronze vessels and the arts of the ancient Near East, but transformed and incorporated into a richly luxuriant version of the Animal style of the steppes (4,55). Such objects as pole-tops made of wood and leather reveal a mastery of

4,55 Saddle-cover from Pazyryk, Altai region, 5th century BC. Felt, leather, fur, hair and gold, 3ft 10⅞ins (1.19m) long. State Hermitage, St Petersburg.

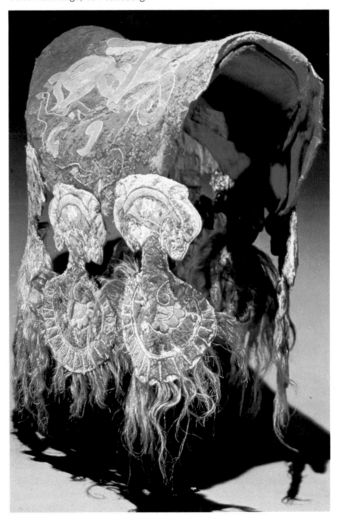

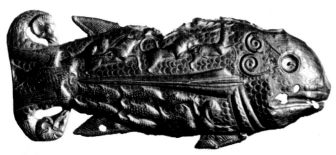

4,56 Fish, from Vettersfelde, Germany, early 5th century BC. Electrum, 16¹/₈ins (41cm) long. Antikenmuseum Staatliche Museen Preussischer Kulturbesitz, Berlin.

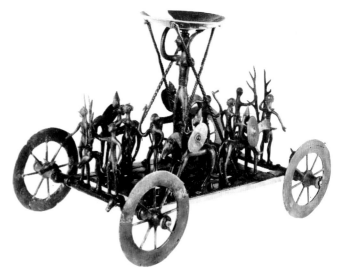

4,57 Cult-wagon from Strettweg, Austria, 7th century BC. Bronze, goddess 8³/₄ins (22.2cm) high. Steiermärkisches Landesmuseum, Johanneum, Graz.

complex three-dimensional form: one is fashioned like the head of a plumed griffin holding a deer's head in its jaws, another as a deer with antlers of exaggerated magnificence. That nothing quite like these pieces has been found at the western end of the steppes may well be due simply to climatic conditions less favourable to survival.

There are other related cultures of the steppes, notably that of the Sarmatians, a nomadic people from south Russia who moved into Scythian territory in about the third century BC and then pressed on towards Europe. Sarmatian art reveals contacts with both China and Persia and is notable mainly for metalwork, especially gold and the early development of *cloisonné* enamelling (see Glossary). The Sarmatians were eventually absorbed into the 'empire' of the Huns from central Asia, whose art forms yet another variant of the Animal style.

Examples of Animal style art may well have reached central and northern Europe long before the mounted nomads from Asia. One of the finest of all, probably dating from the fifth century BC, was found in a hoard of treasure at Vettersfelde in Germany (some 50 miles, 80km, from Berlin); how it got there remains a mystery. This is a relatively large electrum plaque in the form of a fish embossed with a shoal of fish on its belly and animals on its back, with its tail terminating in rams' heads – a good example of the zoomorphic juncture (**4,56**). An electrum plaque of a stag, of about the same period, in exactly the same pose as the stag from Kostromskaya (**4,52**), was found in Hungary on the frontier between the nomadic world of the steppes and agrarian Europe. How far work in the Animal style influenced European art at this time is, however, impossible to determine.

HALLSTATT AND LA TÈNE

The history of art in Iron Age Europe of the first millennium BC is divided by archeologists into two overlapping phases, the earlier named Hallstatt after a lakeside village near Salzburg in Austria, the later (beginning in the second half of the sixth century BC) called La Tène after the place where a group of votive objects was found at the east end of Lake Neuchâtel in Switzerland. In the course of the first period the peoples later known as Illyrians, Celts and Germans settled, respectively, in the south-eastern, central and northern regions of Europe, from

which they were to make their first appearance in written history. They were farmers with an upper, warrior class. Burials suggest a change in the social structure in about the seventh century BC. The so-called Urnfield cultures (those of people who placed the ashes of the dead in pottery vessels and interred them in communal cemeteries) gave way to those in which individuals were, like the Scythians, buried in tombs richly furnished with bronze arms and armour, articles of personal adornment and riding equipment. A sixth-century BC king or chieftain was buried in a cave in Moravia with his chariot, jewelry, table-wares and some 46 companions – a rare instance in Europe of the Eastern practice of immolating the living to accompany the dead.

Hallstatt Iron Age culture anticipated by many centuries the confrontation of northern with southern (Mediterranean) art which marks the much more accomplished Scythian work, especially in gold. By far the most remarkable instance of this at Hallstatt is a seventh-century BC bronze group usually called a 'cult-wagon' or 'ritual car' – though its original significance is unknown –

4,58 Krater from Vix, France, detail, c. 550–500 BC. Bronze, 5ft 4¹/₂ins (1.64m) high. Musée Archéologique, Châtillon-sur-Seine, France.

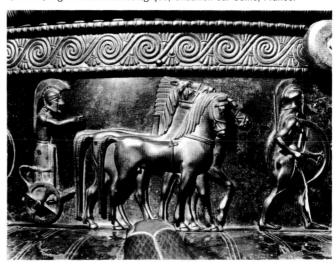

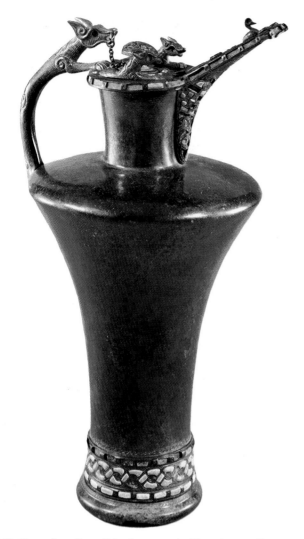

4,59 Flagon from Basse-Yutz, France, early 4th century BC. Bronze, coral and enamel, 15¼ins (38.7cm) high. British Museum, London.

central France. There is reason to believe that it was made in the Peloponnese and intended for export; the frieze round its top represents Greek soldiers, chariots and horses in the best style of mid-sixth century BC Archaic sculpture (**4,58**). Many other Greek works have been found in northern graves, even cups which still retained traces of resinated southern wine, as if they had just been emptied and put down after the funeral feast. One chieftain at Heuneburg on the Upper Danube employed southern engineers to fortify his citadel in the Greek fashion (but only on the side facing a friendly settlement, whose inhabitants he evidently wished to impress).

La Tène art might seem, nevertheless, to have been only marginally influenced by the Greeks, as also by the Scythians – only marginally because these influences were completely assimilated. Decorative elements on the magnificent pair of bronze ewers unearthed in a tomb at Basse-Yutz in Lorraine can be traced to both eastern and southern sources (**4,59**). The lithe wolf-like animal which serves as a handle and the two animals seated on the lid have a recognizable Asian ancestry. Their ears are drawn, rather than modelled, with continuous scrolled lines and their joints are rendered by spirals as in some wood-carvings from the Altai mountains. The idea of making a handle in the form of an animal, on the other hand, probably derives from Iran by way of Greece and Etruria. The form of the vessel is basically Greco-Etruscan, although it has been given greater angularity and a more elongated elegance. Just above the base a Greek wave pattern (later called Vitruvian scroll, see Glossary) is neatly incised in the bronze. The plaited pattern around the foot is also of Greek origin (technically called a *guilloche*, see Glossary) and the decoration beneath the spout seems to derive from Greek motifs, but the geometricality of the prototypes has been lost in the process of rendering them with insets of enamel and pieces of coral. The ewer is as typically Celtic in its coiling linearity and nicely balanced asymmetry as in the very distinctive use of color and the schematization of the spout, which merges into a bearded human face with goggle-eyes of coral.

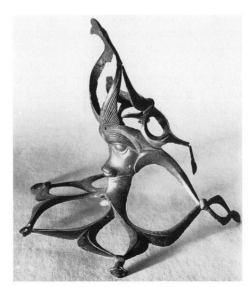

4,60 Openwork ornament from Brno-Malomeřice, Czech Republic, 3rd century BC. Bronze, animal head 2⅓ins (6cm) high. Moravian Museum, Brno.

found in a tomb at Strettweg near Graz in Austria (**4,57**). A female figure, probably a goddess, stands in the centre holding a bowl on her head. She is surrounded by four warriors on horseback, a woman and a man with erect penis wielding an axe and, at either end of the chariot, two stags flanked by naked, but curiously sexless, figures. They are all uniformly schematized to a degree that is best appreciated by comparing the stags – rigid, spiky, antlered – with the much more vital, compact, supple creatures of the Scythians.

Like the central goddess, the warriors and especially the horses, these stags are much closer to the Geometric art of ancient Greece. The piece may well have been made by a bronze-worker who had learned his craft in Greece, if not by a Greek. For although the general effect is distinctly northern, with possible antecedents in Scandinavia, the Strettweg chariot is perhaps best understood as the product of a European Iron Age culture, from which Greece was only just beginning to diverge at this moment.

Celtic chieftains of the La Tène period evidently valued Greek art no less than did the Scythians. By far the largest extant Greek bronze vessel, a sixth-century krater more than 5 feet (1.5m) high, was found in the tomb of a princess or priestess at Vix, near Châtillon-sur-Seine in

Celts rejected as much as they took from the arts of other cultures, and the motifs they adopted tended to be increasingly broken down into linear patterns of scrolls and flourishes. Their art is at once non-representational and yet organic. Many of its qualities are evident in a bronze openwork ornament found in the Czech Republic (**4,60**). No explanation of the original purpose of this extraordinary piece is entirely convincing and it may owe some of its strange effect to its separation from the object, probably of wood or leather, of which it originally formed part. A head with curiously sad human eyes and an animal snout peers out of an intricate network of curves flowing naturally into a highly complex three-dimensional pattern. Although the lines cannot have been geometrically determined, their twisting and counter-twisting is rigorously controlled so that they echo and balance one another in a perfectly self-contained composition. Like the Basse-Yutz flagon and many other examples of La Tène art, this bronze has a refinement of craftsmanship and elegance of form hard to reconcile with what is known of the tribal society for which it was created.

Celtic tribes swept down the Italian peninsula and burnt Rome in about 390 BC, Rome being then only one of several small city-states in Italy which had grown up alongside those of the Etruscans (see p. 165). Other Celtic tribes made periodic raids into Greece and in 279 BC sacked Delphi. In the course of the following centuries they were gradually driven back and most of their territories were eventually occupied by the Romans. But the art that made its first appearance in the La Tène period had an enduring vitality and survived, as we shall see (p. 329).

IBERIA AND SARDINIA

There were several other European cultures of the first millennium which the Greeks dismissed as barbarian and which the Romans were to suppress by force. At the far western end of the Mediterranean, on the south coast of Spain, the Iberian civilization developed from the mid-sixth century BC under Phoenician as well as Greek influence. It had a literate class using a script derived mainly from Greek, but their language has so far resisted translation. Several of its cities are known to have been extensive, although little remains of them. But a number of sculptures have survived, mainly small stone, terracotta and bronze figures of women with elaborate coiffures, apparently votive offerings to deities who remain none the less mysterious. Large stone carvings, though damaged and fragmentary, are more impressive (though the authenticity of one supposedly ancient Iberian work in a remarkably good state of preservation is now questioned). Smaller but very striking are several heads, notably that of a man with short hair whose bulging eyes, protuberant ears and determined chin lend it a rugged individuality (**4,61**). Whether or not it is a portrait cannot, of course, be known; but it differs markedly from the idealized heads of Greek statues – or perhaps one should say, realizes a different ideal. For the ability to carve a

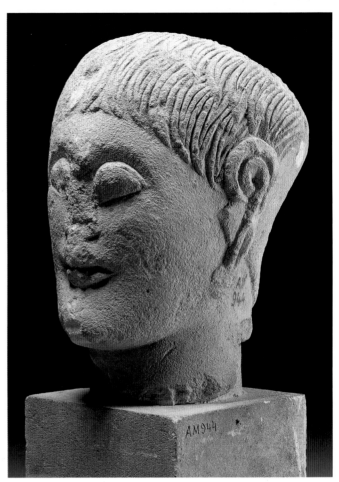

4,61 Head of a man, 5th to 3rd century BC. Stone, 18ins (46cm) high. Musée des Antiquités Nationales, Saint-Germain-en-Laye, France.

lifelike three-dimensional form seems to have been derived, if indirectly, from Greece.

The relationship of another Mediterranean culture, that of Sardinia, with the civilization of Greece and the Near East is difficult to define. Its most conspicuous relics are the defensive round towers called *nuraghi*, of which there are some 6,000 remains. The earliest date from the mid-thirteenth century BC, and they continued to be built until the Romans conquered the island 1,000 years later. Of cyclopean masonry, sometimes with mortar, they form truncated cones two or more stories high. The rooms inside them had corbelled false domes (see Glossary). Sometimes a number of towers are connected by walls and corbelled passages in their thickness. Underground chambers are built on the same principle around wells and springs, which evidently had some religious significance. Houses were built in a similar fashion, and the foundations of a whole village have been unearthed around the *nuraghi* of Barumini. It is generally assumed that the technique of construction was learned from Minoan Crete or Helladic Greece. However, unlike the *tholoi* of Mycenae, the *nuraghi* of Sardinia towered above ground level as free-standing buildings.

Their small-scale sculpture was equally distinctive. Several hundred bronze statuettes, mainly of human figures, survive and are believed to have been made between the eighth and sixth centuries BC. The lost-wax process (see Glossary) by which they were cast must surely have

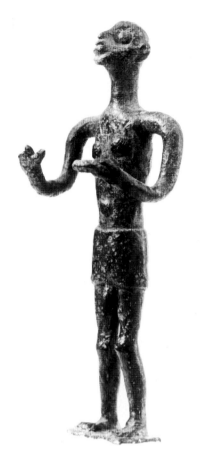

4,62 Man from Sardinia, c. 800–500 BC. Bronze, 7¼ins (18.4cm) high. Museo Nazionale, Cagliari.

THE ETRUSCANS

Soon after the Greeks founded their first colonies in southern Italy in the mid-eighth century BC they encountered an Iron Age culture not so very different from their own: that of the people who called themselves Rasenna, but were later known as Etruscans. The Etruscans were beginning to transform their small agricultural settlements into cities and were becoming the best organized inhabitants of the peninsula, the only ones who were to be a match for the Greek invaders. During the next hundred years or so their materially rich civilization rivalled that of Archaic Greece. Their language, preserved in many thousand inscriptions, was not of the Indo-European group and is still little understood. It set them apart from the other people of Italy, who spoke dialects closely related to one another, including a primitive form of Latin. It has been suggested that they were themselves relatively recent arrivals in Italy, probably from west Asia, as Herodotus stated, but this can neither be proved nor disproved.

Although they shared a common language and religion, the Etruscans were not a political unit. Their independent city-states (traditionally said to be 12), at first monarchical and later republican, were somewhat similar to the Greek *poleis*, though much less frequently at war among themselves. From cities on the coastal plain between the Tiber and the Arno, they expanded inland as far as the Apennines, occupying the area of modern Tuscany and Umbria, rich in minerals which they exploited. Later they spread north into the fertile valley of the Po and south nearly as far as Naples. Rome itself was ruled by Etruscan kings until 510 BC. Their influence stretched further and by the end of the sixth century BC they seem to have dominated the whole peninsula apart from the areas colonized by the Greeks. Their fleet, perhaps the most powerful in the Mediterranean, protected their widespread commercial interests.

Cultural relations between Etruscans and Greeks were complex. Before the end of the eighth century BC the

been transmitted from the eastern Mediterranean at about the same time that it was taken up by the Greeks. Subjects include warriors, women with flowing robes who might represent goddesses, musicians playing double-pipes, a shepherd carrying a sheep on his shoulders, wrestlers and so on, many of them probably made as votive objects to be placed in shrines. Typical is a small male figure, rudimentarily schematized and with arms reduced to simple bent rods, yet vividly alive (**4,62**). He speaks or shouts as he gesticulates. This little bronze captures the character as well as the appearance of a well-known and happily still flourishing Mediterranean type.

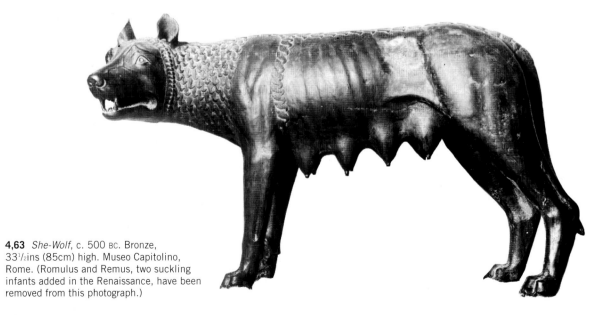

4,63 *She-Wolf*, c. 500 BC. Bronze, 33½ins (85cm) high. Museo Capitolino, Rome. (Romulus and Remus, two suckling infants added in the Renaissance, have been removed from this photograph.)

Etruscans adopted an alphabet like that of the Greeks (though an independent derivation from the Phoenician has been proposed), but they wrote from right to left. They bought Greek artifacts on a large scale, notably pottery painted with scenes from Greek myths and legends and statues of Greek deities, some of whom they adopted, for example, Apollo and Artemis. From the seventh century BC onwards Greek artists are known to have been working in Etruscan cities. Yet Etruscan culture was not simply an offshoot from that of Greece. It sprang quite independently from similar Iron Age origins. Significantly, the Greeks and later the Hellenized Romans regarded the Etruscans as people apart.

The Etruscans left no literature from which we might gain some insight into their thought, feelings, way of life or their history. We know them only from the probably biased comments of Greek and Latin writers and from the material remains of their culture, found mainly in tombs and susceptible to a bewildering range of interpretations. They have been described by ancient and modern authors as a people obsessed by death and as one wholly devoted to the pleasures of living, as deeply religious and as amorally dissolute. Their art has been condemned for its lack of originality and praised for its vital spontaneity. Etruscan bronze work is known to have been prized in Athens in the fifth century BC, that is at the height of the Greek Classical period. At least one surviving work fully justifies this estimate – the famous *She-Wolf* of the Capitol (**4,63**), for centuries the totem of the city of Rome which was traditionally founded by Romulus and Remus, who had been suckled by a she-wolf. This is a superb example of bronze casting and chasing. It is also, of course, quite unlike any Greek animal sculpture. The extraordinary realism of the tense, watchful stance – ears pricked, brow furrowed, jaws snarling, hackles rising – epitomizes at its finest and most vividly factual the unidealized, down-to-earth quality of Etruscan art.

The frontier between the arts of the Greeks and the Etruscans is less easily defined than that between the arts of the Greeks and the Scythians, Celts and Iberians. Controversy among archeologists and scholars has raged around the numerous objects found in the cities and cemeteries of Etruria. There are literally thousands of Etruscan tombs with painted and sculptured decorations, cinerary urns, sarcophagi and 'grave goods' ranging from the simplest household equipment to lavish and even sophisticated works of art. Yet much remains obscure. The objects themselves have been variously attributed to Greek or Etruscan artists, all too often by highly subjective criteria. It is for this reason rather more difficult to define the art than the artistic taste of the Etruscans.

Greek 'Geometric' pottery (see p. 128) of the early eighth century BC has been found in tombs at Veii (a few miles north-west of Rome). But the majority of imported objects in Etruscan tombs of the eighth and seventh centuries are in Near Eastern styles: pieces of 'faience' from Egypt, Phoenician bronze-work and ivory carvings and also Greek 'Orientalizing' bronzes and painted vases. They provide evidence of a substantial luxury-loving

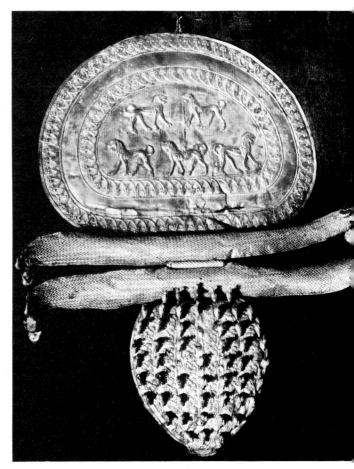

4,64 Fibula, 7th century BC. Gold, 12⁵/₈ins (32cm) long. Vatican Museums, Rome.

upper class in each of the main Etruscan cities. It was for their own use or pleasure, it should be noted, that rich Etruscans bought bronze cauldrons of a type made by the Greeks exclusively for dedication to the gods.

Among the many objects in 'Orientalizing' styles there are some which are generally agreed to have been made in Italy, presumably by Etruscan craftsmen. They include ivory arms with long-fingered hands, probably handles for mirrors or fans, their sleeves decorated with prowling lions, which no inhabitant of Italy at this date is likely to have seen for himself and which must have derived ultimately from Assyrian art. Lions also appear prominently on one of the finest examples of Etruscan gold jewelry, a large fibula or clasp from a very rich and perhaps royal tomb at Caere (modern Cerveteri) (**4,64**). The maker of this piece derived from the Near East not only decorative motifs but also techniques of working gold which he elaborated into a feat of virtuoso craftsmanship. The five lions on the upper part are cut out and applied to the ground. Lines indicating their manes are composed of minute granules of gold; so, too, are the lines of the wreaths that surround them and the zigzags on the bars joining the two parts of the fibula, soldered to the surface by an exceptionally tricky process. On the lower part six rows of winged lions are outlined by granulation and here there are also tiny ducks modelled in the round. Etruscans clearly loved such work, on which wealth was conspicuously displayed both by the precious nature of the material and, still more, by the lavish expenditure of time and skill.

The 'Orientalizing' style of the seventh century BC drew the Etruscan cities on to the periphery of a cultural world that had its centre in Assyria, then the dominant power in the Middle East (see p. 106). It was carried throughout the Mediterranean not only by Greeks but also by Phoenicians. This great maritime trading nation had settled in the Lebanon and about 800 BC established at Carthage a colony that became their new capital, from which they gradually expanded along the coasts of north Africa and southern Spain. The Etruscans were to be closely involved with the Phoenicians, or Carthaginians as they came to be called, until both were conquered by Rome. In the sixth century BC they were allied against the Greek cities of the western Mediterranean. It was, none the less, to the Hellenic world that the Etruscans turned for works of art.

The Archaic Greek style which, as we have seen (p. 130), followed the 'Orientalizing' style in sixth-century Greece, was introduced to Etruria by imports and also by Greek artists many of whom were probably refugees from Asia Minor after the Persian conquest of Ionia in 548–547 BC. Most of the more notable surviving works of art made for the Etruscans – whether by Greek or local artists – are in this style. A magnificent and unusually well-preserved bronze-covered processional chariot found in a tomb near Spoleto is a case in point (4,65). Both the subject-matter and the style of the decorations are Hellenic. On the front Achilles receives his armour, a helmet and a shield with grimacing gorgon mask, from his mother Thetis. One of the side panels shows Achilles battling with Memnon, the other the apotheosis of Achilles. Scenes from the story of the Trojan War as recounted by Homer were, of course, often painted on Greek pottery at this period, sometimes with great narrative ability. But here the compositions are so crowded

4,65 Chariot from Monteleone di Spoleto, Italy, 550–540 BC. Bronze and wood, 4ft 3½ins (1.31m) high. Metropolitan Museum of Art, New York (Rogers Fund, 1903).

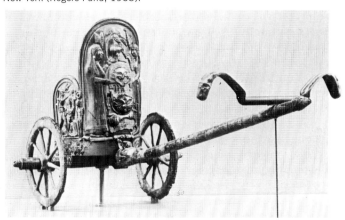

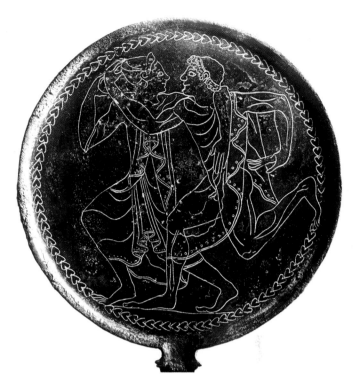

4,66 Engraved mirror, c. 500 BC. Bronze, 5¾ins (14.6cm) diameter. Staatliche Antikensammlungen und Glyptothek, Munich.

that the artist's aim seems to have been merely one of enrichment.

Etruscan love of adornment found its most striking expression in bronze mirrors and caskets engraved with figurative designs of great vivacity and elegance. An early example shows an embracing couple animated in a jerky dance (4,66). Comparison with contemporary Greek vase decoration is illuminating. On an Archaic Greek vase the figures are depicted with the utmost clarity, almost as if they were a frieze of silhouettes (4,13). Here they are placed together in such a way that the design is at first sight difficult to 'read'. They are to be understood as facing one another, with the youth's right arm around the girl's shoulders. Apparent similarities between the arts of the Greeks and Etruscans are often deceptive. They overlie differences which go much deeper. For instance, a Greek statue of the late sixth or early fifth century BC, like those of the warriors on the temple at Aegina (4,22), may have provided the model for the figure of a youth on the cover of an urn found at Caere (4,67). But there is a world of difference between them. The heroic idealization of the Greeks has been brought down to earth. The Etruscan figure is much more descriptive, much more factual – almost the portrait of an individual caught in a casual moment, a banqueter resting his elbow on a cushion, with a cloth thrown lightly over his loins.

A different kind of deviation from the Greek ideal is apparent in the *Apollo of Veii*. This famous Etruscan statue has the face, the braided hair and even the enigmatic smile of a *kouros* (4,68). The motif on the pier which serves as a support between the legs is lifted

SOURCES AND DOCUMENTS

PLINY ON

ETRUSCAN SCULPTURE

Pliny the Elder (c. AD 23–79) was a Roman polymath who died in the eruption of Vesuvius which he had gone to see. He wrote, among much else, the single most valuable ancient literary account of Greek and Roman art. His remarks on Etruscan sculpture are of great interest although he assigns Vulca's work in Rome to an earlier period than archeological evidence now supports.

Varro [Marcus Terentius Varro, 116–27 BC, scholar and antiquarian] *records further that this art* [modelling in clay] *was well developed in Italy and especially in Etruria; that Vulca, the artist to whom Tarquinius Priscus awarded the contract to make the image of Jupiter which was to be dedicated on the Capitoline, was summoned from Veii; that this image was of terracotta, for which reason, as is usual, it was colored red; that there were terracotta quadrigas, of which we have spoken often, on the peak of the temple; and that the Hercules, which even today in the city retains the name of the material* [from which it was made], *was also done by this artist. For these were the most praiseworthy images of deities of that era; nor do we feel dissatisfied with those* [earlier] *men who worshipped such images; for it was not their habit to make gold and silver images, not even for gods. Images of this sort have survived in many places today; they survive, in fact, even on a great many rooves of temples in Rome and in the municipal towns – images which are to be marveled at for their surface detail and artistry and for their stolidity, more revered than gold, and certainly more innocent.*

(Pliny, *Natural History* XXXV, 157, tr. J. J. Pollitt, *The Art of Rome*, Englewood Cliffs 1966)

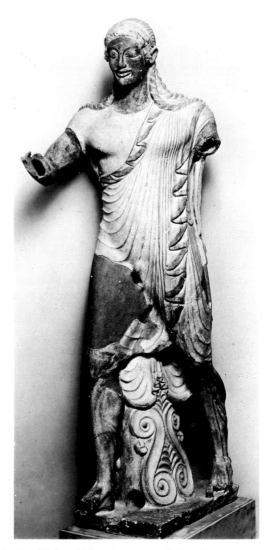

4,68 *Apollo of Veii*, c. 500 BC. Terracotta, 5ft 9ins (1.75m) high. Museo Nazionale di Villa Giulia, Rome.

straight from Greek architectural ornament. The drapery which seems to have been ironed into pleats and folds is also Greek, though imitated from a *kore* since male figures in Greek sculpture were usually nude. But this Apollo with his heavy limbs and somewhat lumbering gait has none of the poised elegance of Greek statues. And it differs still further from the Greek in two other respects. It is of molded terracotta, not of marble, which was very rarely used for sculpture in Etruria (not until much later did the Romans exploit the quarries at Carrara; see p. 198). And it was one of a group of figures which stood outlined against the sky along the roof ridge of a temple, giving the latter a very different aspect to that of its Greek prototype.

The earliest Etruscan temples seem to have been simple rectangular huts built of timber and mud-brick with decorations of molded and painted terracotta. Although the building materials remained the same, this basic form was amplified under Greek influence before the end of the sixth century, when temples began to be set on high plinths or podia and provided with columns, pitched roofs

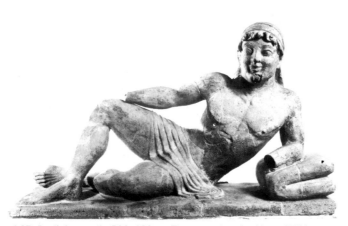

4,67 Reclining youth, 500–480 BC. Terracotta, length of base 35½ins (90cm). Museo Nazionale Cerite, Cerveteri.

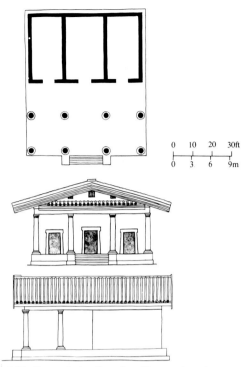

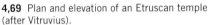

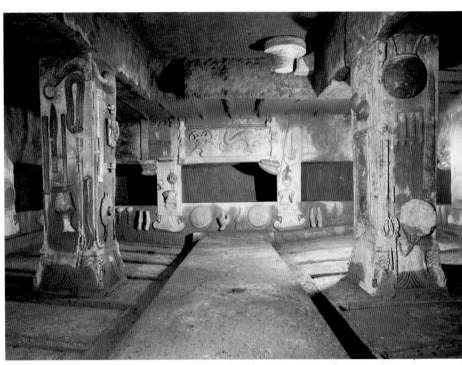

4,69 Plan and elevation of an Etruscan temple (after Vitruvius).

4,70 Interior of the *Tomb of the Reliefs*, Cerveteri, Italy, c. 300 BC.

and triangular pediments, later filled with sculpture. Very little survives apart from foundations and fragments of terracotta, but the descriptions by Roman writers enable us to reconstruct their general form (which was to influence later Roman architecture; see p. 195). In contrast to Greek temples, the cella was often divided into three compartments for different cult figures and seems never to have been completely surrounded by columns (**4,69**). There was a deep porch in front and sometimes colonnades on either flank, but not at the back. The podium had steps only at the front. Thus, whereas the Greek temple was intended to be seen from an angle, the Etruscan was designed to be approached along its axis and this determined the symmetrical plan of its forecourt. Etruscan temples were much smaller than the great Doric structures of the Greeks but very much more richly decorated – with figurative acroteria on the pediments, antefixes along the eaves, as well as statues on the roof ridge. Painted terracotta was extensively used both to protect the impermanent building materials and for ornamental effect.

Symmetrical planning and rich decoration similarly marked their domestic architecture. Our knowledge comes mainly from tombs, which were conceived as habitations for the dead (like those of ancient Egypt) and reproduce the interior architecture and even the furniture and furnishings of the now vanished cities. The wooden columns, door-posts, lintels and decorative details of Etruscan houses are simulated in roughly carved tufa (**4,70**). Foundations show that the larger houses, though built only of mud-brick and timber, had spacious rooms and often a central courtyard or atrium open to the sky. By Athenian standards they were luxurious. Figurative paintings on the tomb walls, larger than any that survive from

Greece, similarly reflect their interior decoration. The earliest known, in a tomb at Veii, date from the second quarter of the seventh century BC and are of ducks painted directly on the tufa without a prepared ground. They were followed slightly later by paintings of creatures from the semi-fabulous bestiary of 'Orientalizing' art. Shortly after the mid-sixth century BC human figures made their appearance in the tombs of Tarquinia, painted on a prepared ground of clay plaster. (Most of the surviving tomb paintings are at Tarquinia.)

The Archaic Greek style of these Tarquinian tomb paintings is so similar to that of recently discovered paintings of about the same date in Asia Minor (notably at Gordion and in Lycian tombs) that there can be little doubt of its having been introduced by Ionian artists. Subjects include hunting and fishing scenes, athletic contests, riding exercises, wild ecstatic dancing and occasional illustrations of Greek myths and legends. A decorative scheme or program, often repeated from about 500 BC, shows banqueters reclining on one wall of a tomb chamber and, on the other three, musicians and dancers in an outdoor setting amongst trees and birds (**4,71**). Whether these depict funeral banquets, as in Egypt, is hard to say. Much in Etruscan tomb paintings is foreign to Italy. But as indications of the wealth of the families who commissioned them they are certainly effective. They vividly reflect the worldly pleasures of members of a moneyed upper class, who loll on their couches listening to the music of lyre and pipes while watching the elegant motions and postures of dancers and the contortions of acrobats. The Etruscans appear, in fact, as spectators and not as participants in the Dionysiac dances and athletic sports with which the Greeks honoured the gods.

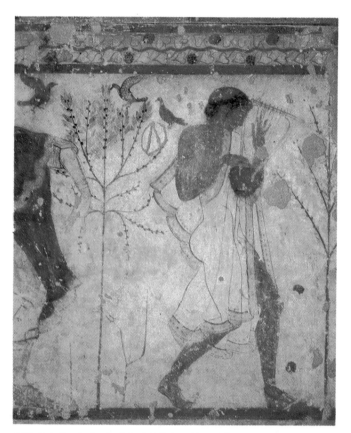

4,71 Painting in Tomb of the Triclinium, Tarquinia, Italy, c. 500 BC.

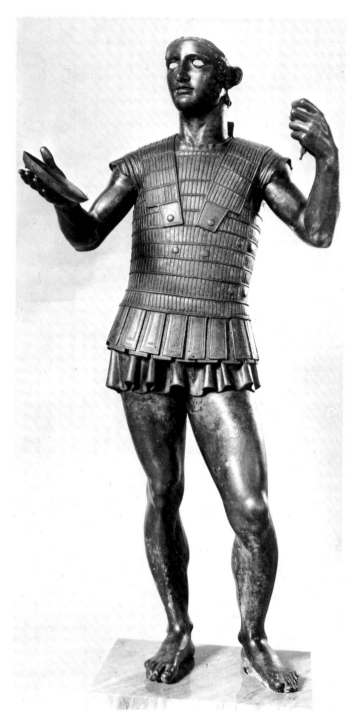

4,72 *Mars of Todi*, early 4th century BC. Bronze, 4ft 7¹/₈ins (1.4m) high. Vatican Museums, Rome.

It seems likely that Greek art had in Etruria the value of what would now be called a status symbol. This may partly account for the persistence there of the Archaic Greek style, which had been introduced when the Etruscan cities were at the height of their wealth and power. Schematically drawn figures in a limited number of poses, with heads and legs in profile and frontally rendered torsos, went on being painted on the walls of Etruscan tombs long after they had been superseded by more naturalistic representations on Greek pottery. Often they have great linear grace and convey a sense of exuberant, rhythmical movement. The youthful lyre-player illustrated here is a good example, his body drawn nude, partly covered with the drapery that Etruscans demanded and the outline then filled in with bright color without any modelling (4,71). No attempt seems to have been made to follow the Greeks along the path towards greater naturalism. Indeed, any departure from well-established conventions seems to have met with disapproval from Etruscan patrons. Similarly in architecture, once the form of the temple (adapted from Greece, as we have seen) was established it remained unchanged until Etruria was swallowed up by Rome.

In sculpture, too, the Greek Archaic style lived on, barely influenced by fifth-century developments in Greece. The closest approximation to the Classical style is seen in the famous life-size statue known as the *Mars of Todi* (4,72); but this is in every way an exceptional work, the only surviving large-scale bronze of Etruscan workman-

ship dating from before the second century BC. It was found, carefully buried in a sarcophagus, in the ruins of a temple at Todi, just outside the territory of the Etruscan cities. An inscription written in a mixture of Etruscan and Latin characters records that it was dedicated by a man named Ahal Trutitis. As on many Greek bronze statues, the lips were originally inlaid with copper and the eyes filled with colored material (a helmet, which is lost, was cast separately and attached to the head). In craftsmanship it is as skilful as the best Hellenic work of the same late fifth- or early fourth-century date. Yet it could hardly be mistaken for a Greek statue. The slightly awkward pose as well as the armour which conceals the torso set the *Mars of Todi* apart. His features are idealized, but according to an ideal altogether different from that of the Greeks: burly rather than athletic, with an expression of blunt assertion rather than inward self-confidence. There is, furthermore, a disturbing incongruity between the delicacy of the hands, the feet and the undergarment (especially its ruffled collar) and the lack of articulation in the thick neck and gross, swollen, rather than muscular, thighs. As in so many other Etruscan works, the naked flesh is treated summarily without any hint of that obsessive attention to the underlying structure of bone and muscle which marks the art of Greece. Nudity is rare in Etruscan art, in sculpture as in painting, where it usually indicates the inferior status of paid performers, servants or slaves.

Etruscan art was focused less on images of the gods or of men displaying godlike physique with the bloom of eternal youth than on mortals. Even in the tomb the emphasis was on the here and now (at any rate until a late period). Their funerary art is, therefore, bafflingly paradoxical. The dead were normally cremated and cremation suggests a distinction between spirit and body. Yet belief in a material link between the two is implied by the Etruscan practice of providing the dead, whether cremated or buried, with the necessities and luxuries of the living. These apparently contradictory ideas lie behind the peculiar form taken by the containers in which the remains of the dead were placed.

Cinerary urns of the seventh century BC, found mainly in the cemetery of Clusium (modern Chiusi), have covers in the form of heads, sometimes with torsos and arms as well. They seem to have been evolved by a process of reification – the opposite of abstraction – from urns with helmet-shaped lids made for ashes by the early Iron Age people who preceded the Etruscans in north-central Italy (called Villanovans after an archeological site near Bologna). The impassive countenances with tightly closed lips and, usually, lowered eyelids are too alike to be described as portraits, although they were presumably intended as representations of the dead. In the tombs they were placed on chairs and later the whole urn was sometimes fashioned like an enthroned figure. For bodies which were inhumed, rather than cremated, a type of sarcophagus was developed in the sixth century BC in the form of a rectangular couch, on which a figure (or a couple) reclines (**4,73**). This was probably inspired by Carthaginian sarcophagi, which combined the mummy-case of ancient Egypt with the rectangular coffin of the Near East. The same general form was adopted also for cinerary urns. Stylistically the figures derive from Archaic Greece and, as we have already seen, at least one of them is a distant relative of the warriors from Aegina.

What is new and distinctive about Etruscan sarcophagi and urns is that the figures are shown alive and apparently enjoying the pleasures of the table. From the fourth

4,73 Sarcophagus from Caere (Cerveteri), c. 520 BC. Terracotta, about 6ft 7ins (2m) long. Museo Nazionale di Villa Giulia, Rome.

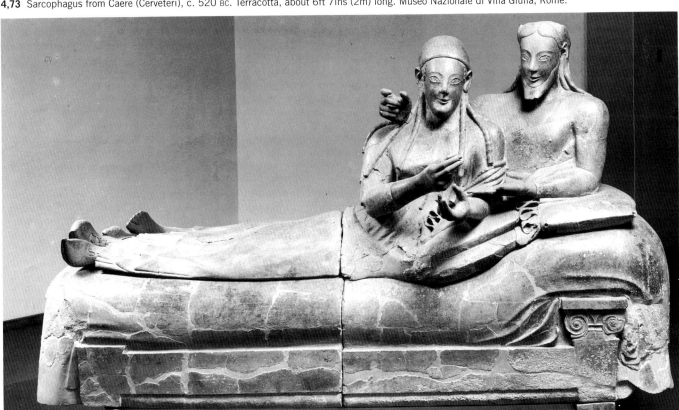

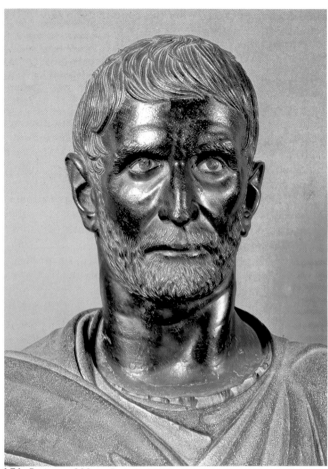

4,74 *Brutus*, c. 300 BC. Bronze, 12⅝ins (32cm) high.
Palazzo dei Conservatori, Rome.

A similar, if more restrained, naturalism is apparent in bronze heads. The finest, probably from a whole-length statue, is that traditionally said to portray Lucius Junius Brutus (fl. 509 BC), the supposed founder of the republic, who roused his fellow Romans to expel the last Etruscan king, Tarquinius Superbus, from their city (**4,74**). Whether or not the identification is correct, this rugged face with piercing eyes, aquiline nose and sternly set jaw surely records an individual, and one with an unbending sense of purpose. Hair and short beard are rendered with all the accomplishment for which Etruscan bronze-workers were renowned. As an example of skill in casting and chasing, it surpasses the *She-Wolf* of the Capitol (4,63) and confirms the survival of these skills into a later period. (The drapery below the neck is part of a later, probably sixteenth-century, addition.)

The Etruscans, although they had shown themselves so strangely impervious to later developments of the Greek Classical style, were drawn into the cultural orbit of the Hellenistic world towards the end of the fourth century BC. So, too, were the Romans, soon to become the dominant power in the Italian peninsula. One by one the cities of Etruria fell to Rome and by the beginning of the first century BC the Etruscans had been absorbed into the composite population of Italy. Before long, the Roman poet Propertius was to write his famous lament:

> *Veii, thou hadst a royal crown of old,*
> *And in thy forum stood a throne of gold.*
> *Thy walls now echo but the shepherd's horn,*
> *And o'er thine ashes waves the summer corn.*

(Propertius IV, X, 27, tr. G. Dennis)

century onwards they were also modelled with almost caricatured individuality as if to preserve their physical identity. Curiously, however, the introduction of this more realistic style of representation coincided with a sharp increase in references to a terrifying dark afterworld – in tomb paintings as well as in sarcophagi and urns. Two figures with strongly characterized faces and attenuated bodies on an urn from Velathri (modern Volterra) may represent either a none too happily married couple or a man accompanied by a demon of death.

But enough survived above ground for other Roman writers, notably the architectural theorist Vitruvius, to record and discuss. One Etruscan temple built about 500 BC, with a cult statue of Jupiter by Vulca of Veii, the only named Etruscan sculptor, survived in the heart of Rome itself until 83 BC. It was then burnt down. Only the plan was preserved in the rebuilding. Otherwise the new temple was completely Hellenistic in style. It neatly illustrates the complementary legacies of Etruscan and Hellenistic culture in the formation of the art of the Roman empire.

CHAPTER FIVE

HELLENISTIC AND ROMAN ART

Asumptuously sculptured and colored sarcophagus found at Sidon, the former Phoenician city on the coast of present-day Lebanon, is a feat of technical accomplishment in the handling of marble (**5,1**). The workmanship is Greek and the amazing skill with which the material is chiselled, undercut, drilled and finished to present varying surfaces of subtly contrasted textures testifies to a long tradition of carving, gradually and laboriously refined since the beginning of the Classical period (see p. 136). Figures, especially the athletic nudes, the riders and their horses, lucidly arranged on a shallow stage, recall those on the frieze of the Parthenon, and not only as ideal 'types'. They all have that organic unity of structure which was fundamental to Greek art and its naturalistic bent. And yet, the work as a whole differs radically from anything previously produced in the Hellenic world.

Sarcophagi had rarely been made in Greece, least of all in Athens, where the dead were either cremated or buried in simple, unpretentious receptacles and commemorated by laconic, though often very beautiful, *stelae* (4,43). Greek attitudes to the afterlife and aversion to any idea of personal apotheosis were unfavourable to the development of sculptural glorifications of the dead. As an art form the sarcophagus had Oriental, ancient Egyptian and Etruscan antecedents. Often shaped like a house with a pitched roof, it provided a dwelling-place for the deceased and implied beliefs about the hereafter rather different from those held by the Greeks. But it was to become the predominant art form in funerary sculpture from the late fourth century BC throughout the Hellenistic and Roman eras right down to early Christian times.

In the example illustrated here, the so-called *Alexander Sarcophagus*, the reliefs show Greeks and Persians. On the front, they are fighting one another. On the back they join in a hunt in one of the big-game preserves which were a Persian speciality, the lion recalling those on Assyrian reliefs (**5,2**). Not only the form of the sarcophagus itself, therefore, but also iconographical and other elements reflecting attitudes to the afterlife, mark the re-entry into Greek art of influences from other cultures, which had been rare since the much earlier Orientalizing period. By the time this sarcophagus was carved, Greek civilization was, in fact, no longer limited to the shores of the

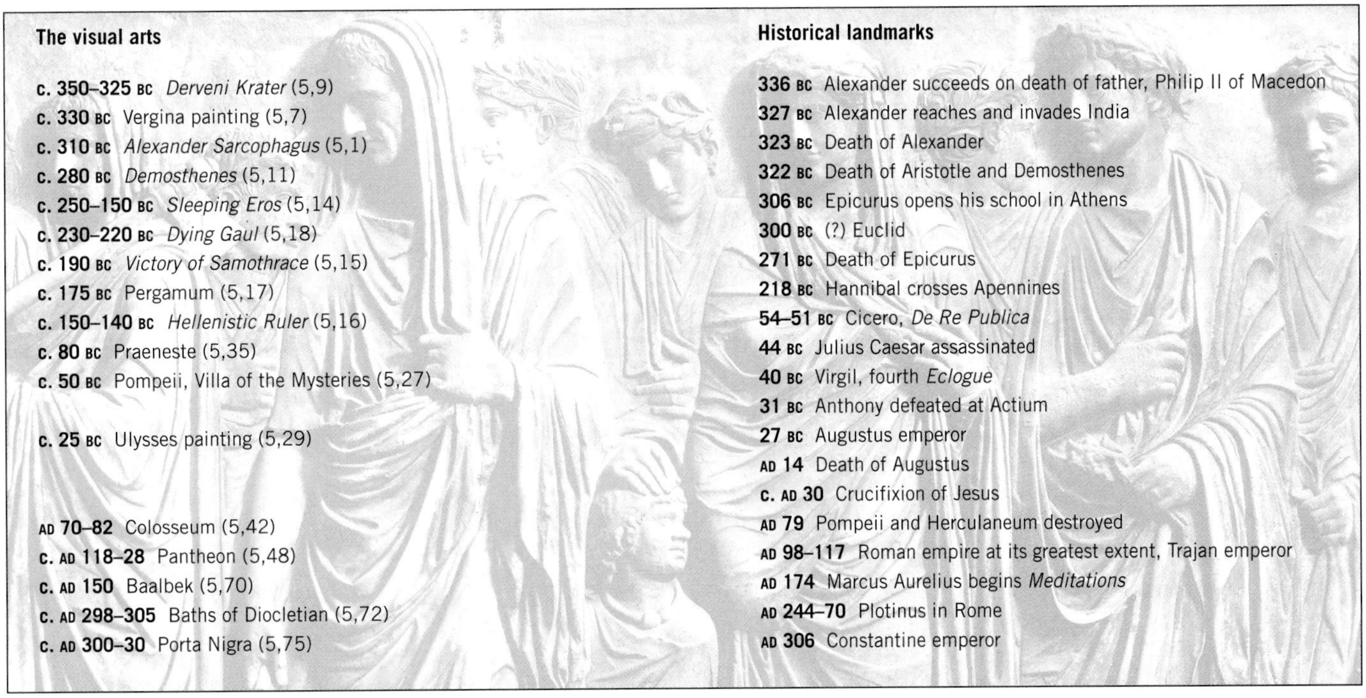

The visual arts	Historical landmarks
c. 350–325 BC *Derveni Krater* (5,9)	336 BC Alexander succeeds on death of father, Philip II of Macedon
c. 330 BC Vergina painting (5,7)	327 BC Alexander reaches and invades India
c. 310 BC *Alexander Sarcophagus* (5,1)	323 BC Death of Alexander
c. 280 BC *Demosthenes* (5,11)	322 BC Death of Aristotle and Demosthenes
c. 250–150 BC *Sleeping Eros* (5,14)	306 BC Epicurus opens his school in Athens
c. 230–220 BC *Dying Gaul* (5,18)	300 BC (?) Euclid
c. 190 BC *Victory of Samothrace* (5,15)	271 BC Death of Epicurus
c. 175 BC Pergamum (5,17)	218 BC Hannibal crosses Apennines
c. 150–140 BC *Hellenistic Ruler* (5,16)	54–51 BC Cicero, *De Re Publica*
c. 80 BC Praeneste (5,35)	44 BC Julius Caesar assassinated
c. 50 BC Pompeii, Villa of the Mysteries (5,27)	40 BC Virgil, fourth *Eclogue*
	31 BC Anthony defeated at Actium
c. 25 BC Ulysses painting (5,29)	27 BC Augustus emperor
	AD 14 Death of Augustus
	c. AD 30 Crucifixion of Jesus
AD 70–82 Colosseum (5,42)	AD 79 Pompeii and Herculaneum destroyed
c. AD 118–28 Pantheon (5,48)	AD 98–117 Roman empire at its greatest extent, Trajan emperor
c. AD 150 Baalbek (5,70)	AD 174 Marcus Aurelius begins *Meditations*
c. AD 298–305 Baths of Diocletian (5,72)	AD 244–70 Plotinus in Rome
c. AD 300–30 Porta Nigra (5,75)	AD 306 Constantine emperor

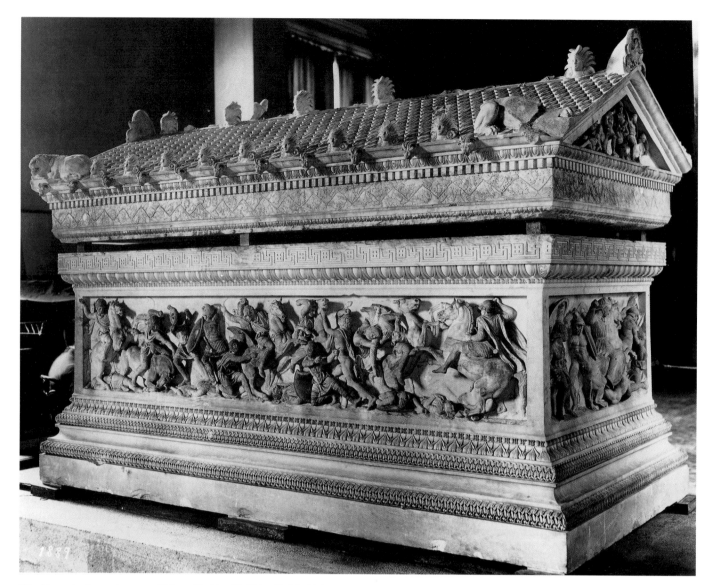

5,1 *Alexander Sarcophagus*, c. 310 BC. Marble, 6ft 4½ins (1.94m) high. Archeological Museum, Istanbul.

5,2 *Alexander Sarcophagus*, detail.

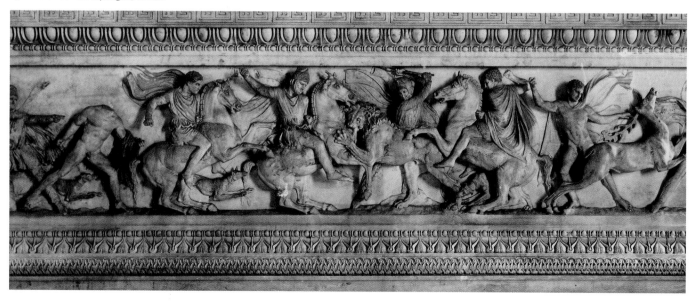

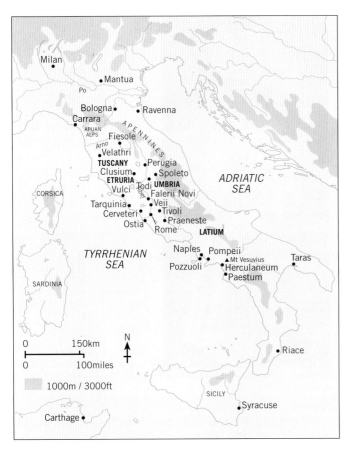

Etruscan and Roman Italy

Mediterranean. Philip II of Macedon (c. 359–336 BC), who united the city-states of Greece and robbed them of their independence, was succeeded by his 20-year-old son Alexander the Great (336–323 BC). As soon as he had firmly established control of the Greek mainland, Alexander led his army across the Hellespont into Asia. The Persians, the traditional enemies of the Greeks, were soon defeated and with astonishing speed Alexander made himself master of their entire empire and more. He conquered all Asia Minor, Syria, Egypt, Iran, Bactria and then passed beyond the Indus into the Indian sub-continent.

The battle on the front of the *Alexander Sarcophagus* records one of his first victories, possibly that over the Persian king Darius at Issus in 333 BC. Alexander is shown on the far left, clearly recognizable from his facial features as portrayed on coins (**5,3**). Near him in each scene there is the same much older figure in Persian costume, almost certainly the man for whom the sarcophagus was carved – the satrap of Sidon, who had prudently surrendered to

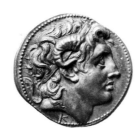

5,3 Silver tetradrachm of Lysimachus of Thrace, 306–281 BC. 1¹⁄₅ins (3cm) diameter. British Museum, London.

Alexander and became his vassal. Portraiture had rarely been practised by the Greeks, but became increasingly important from the fourth century BC onwards. Alexander is not simply portrayed, however; he is all but deified by the emblems he wears on his head – the lion-skin of the deified hero Hercules, with whom he was often compared, and the horn of the Egyptian ram god Amun, whose 'son' he was claimed to be after his conquest of Egypt. He thus appears as the first in a long line of European emperors and kings who – like Oriental monarchs – were accorded the worship that the Greeks had hitherto paid only to the gods.

The meeting and intermingling of different cultures, so clearly visible in the *Alexander Sarcophagus*, is one of the essential aspects of both Hellenistic and Roman art. The interpenetration of Oriental and Occidental, of primitive and advanced ideas from East (Persia) and West (Etruria) reanimated and made more fluid the Greek inheritance and thus brought about the creation of a great new art for the enormously expanded, cosmopolitan world of the succeeding era.

THE HELLENISTIC PERIOD

The term 'Hellenistic' which originally had a mainly linguistic significance, distinguishing speakers of Greek from others in the empire founded by Alexander the Great, is now taken to refer to the period of some three centuries from Alexander's death in 323 BC. Babylon was to have been the capital of Alexander's vast Hellenized Near Eastern empire, but when he died, aged only 32, his conquests devolved upon his generals, known as the *diadochi* or successors, who set themselves up as absolute monarchs. Ptolemy took over Egypt and southern Syria, including Judea. The rest of the empire in Asia fell to Seleucus; Macedon was taken by the successors of Antigonus; other Hellenistic kingdoms were smaller. In Greece and the Aegean islands the city-states recovered some of their independence during the third and second centuries BC, but they had lost their power and importance; and Athens was now little more than a centre of culture and learning. The end of the Hellenistic period cannot be as precisely dated as its beginning. In the mid-third century BC the Seleucids were driven out of Iran by Parthian nomads from the steppes, who pressed on to occupy Mesopotamia in 141 BC. During these same years the Roman republic (see p. 186) became the dominant power in the Italian peninsula and eventually in the whole Mediterranean area (see p. 193).

The rulers of the Hellenistic kingdoms were of Greek (strictly Macedonian) descent, and so, too, were most of their administrators. The official language was a form of Greek called *koiné* – the Greek of the New Testament – spoken and written from Sicily to the Hindu Kush, from the shores of the Black Sea and the Caspian to the cataracts of the Nile. Greek culture spread over the same area. What had previously been confined to a few, relatively small independent communities now became the artistic language of half the civilized world. Cities were

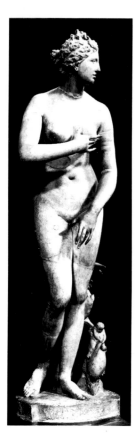
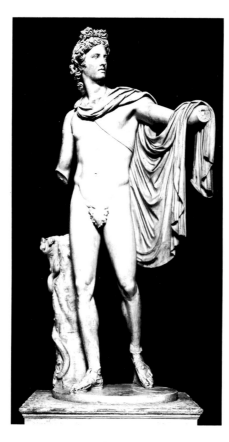
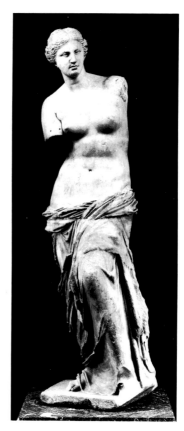

built or rebuilt on the pattern of the Greek *polis*, each with its temple, assembly hall, theatre, gymnasium, stoa and agora all conforming to the Greek orders of architecture and adorned with sculptures embodying the Greek ideal of the beautiful human form. The capital cities grew into large and wealthy centres of trade, industry, learning and artistic activity: Alexandria in Egypt, Seleucia on the Tigris, Antioch near the coast of Syria and, later, Pergamum in Asia Minor. And their influence extended to the Greek cities of the western Mediterranean, to Etruria and to Rome.

Small, tightly knit, heroically competitive societies had given way to vast, amorphous, cosmopolitan urban centres, predominantly commercial and manufacturing. Their history has sometimes been described, and often dismissed, as a confused and unhappy epilogue or degenerate sequel to the Classical age. But they made important contributions to civilization. The two most widely influential philosophies of life in the ancient world were Hellenistic: Stoicism, which held virtue to be its own reward, and Epicureanism, with its belief in virtue as the prerequisite of happiness. Both were philosophies of withdrawal, reflecting a shift in emphasis from problems of human relations – man is by nature a 'political animal' in Aristotle's famous definition, i.e. a citizen of a free *polis* – to those of the inner life of the individual.

Aristotle (384–322 BC), who had been tutor to Alexander, began his long domination of scientific thought and method, and nearly all the major achievements of the ancient world in science and mathematics date from the Hellenistic period: Euclid's *Elements*, the discovery of specific gravity and the invention of the water-pump by Archimedes, the calculation of the diameter of the earth to within a few hundred miles of the correct figure by Eratosthenes.

In the visual arts the influence of the Hellenistic world was to be equally pervasive. The Greek sculptures admired and collected by the Romans included such Hellenistic works as the *Medici Venus* and *Apollo Belvedere* (**5,4; 5**). The *Medici Venus* is the best of 33 surviving copies or versions of a lost original presumed to be of the third or second century BC. It owes a debt to the *Aphrodite of Cnidus* by Praxiteles (4,39), but the rendering is less idealized – softer and more fleshy – and there is a hint of self-conscious coquetry in the turn of the head and almost alluringly defensive gesture. The arms held in front of the body also emphasize the third dimension and lend the whole figure a gyrating movement. The *Apollo Belvedere* is a second-century AD Roman copy or version of a lost original usually presumed to have been a late fourth-century BC bronze, although it is at least equally likely that the statue was based on more than one original and is a pastiche. With its almost dancing posture, effeminate physique, elaborately dressed hair and heartlessly beautiful face, the *Apollo Belvedere* makes a very striking contrast with surviving male statues from fifth-century BC Athens. Although neither the *Medici Venus* nor the *Apollo Belvedere* was as famous in its own time as it became when rediscovered 1,000 or more years later (in the late fifteenth and mid-sixteenth century respectively), they illustrate very well certain formal tendencies of the period. Sensuous delight in the handling of marble, equally characteristic of Hellenistic sculpture, can be seen in the *Venus de Milo* (**5,6**). The material here might almost seem to have been caressed rather than chiselled and rasped into the texture of soft, warm flesh, complementing an air of rather precious worldly elegance and sophisticated self-awareness.

PLATO, ARISTOTLE AND THE ARTS

It was in late fourth- or early third-century BC Alexandria that the first histories of art (as distinct from criticism and aesthetic theory) seem to have been written. They have all perished, as have most Hellenistic prose writings, but passages survive, sometimes as direct quotations, embedded in the works of such later writers as the elder Pliny and Pausanias. From these fragments it can be deduced that they were conceived in terms of a linear progression from crude beginnings in the distant past to a high point of achievement in the later fourth century BC – neatly coinciding with the rise to power of the Macedonian dynasty. Praxiteles and Lysippus, Alexander's court sculptor, were claimed to have excelled all their predecessors, and Alexander's court painter, Apelles, was said by Pliny to have 'surpassed all those who were born before him and all those who came later'.

The notion of a 'norm' towards which art aspires was first put about in this way by Hellenistic writers. To them also is due the idea of a 'Classical moment' or high point, when the summit of achievement is reached and after which it declines. They located this apogee in the late fourth century BC, it should be noted, and not in the fifth century BC. (The idea that Greek art and culture reached its height under Pericles came later.)

Artists were, for the first time, placed in history and came to see themselves as living in the aftermath of a great period. Hence the strong, conservative 'Classicistic' tendency in Hellenistic art, for which a philosophical rationale could be found in Plato's contention that works of art should, like everything else, ideally conform to some absolute standard. As we have already seen, he praised the Egyptians for permitting no artistic innovations. His theory was, however, criticized by Aristotle, who propounded a more commonsensical and relativist doctrine (see below). Whereas Plato believed the works of man to be at best but pale imitations of heavenly prototypes or 'Ideas', Aristotle approached the problem empirically and tried to identify the various 'causes' governing the generation of any man-made object and thus giving it its form. The form an object took depended, according to him, not on some fixed 'Idea' to which it approximated but on who made it, what it was made of and, above all, on its purpose or 'final cause'. In this way began one of the great debates in the history of Western aesthetics – and to it the expanding range of Hellenistic art was largely due.

For Aristotle's teaching opened the door (in theory at any rate) to expressiveness and the cultivation of the artist's individuality, even to eclecticism and to the notion that an artistic style might be appropriate in certain circumstances and not in others. His relativism in this sense is most explicit in his discussion of rhetoric. A speech in the public assembly should, he said, be like *skiagraphia* or shadow-painting (probably a style of painting using strong contrasts of light and shade to give an illusion of the third dimension). Bold outlines and broad handling were therefore desirable. In the law-courts, on the other hand, a finer and more intricately and subtly constructed speech would be appropriate. By analogy, styles in the visual arts might be regarded like literary genres – epic, tragic, comic, lyric, elegiac – each with its own rules, laid down in Aristotle's *Poetics*.

The emergence of such ideas signals a profound change in attitudes to the arts. Statues, paintings and even temples gradually came to be thought of as 'works of art' rather than as images, whether animistic or merely ritualistic. Increasingly they were seen as the creations of individual artists, working for individual patrons. And this process of secularization was taken a stage further with the rise of art-collecting in the Hellenistic period, leading to the 'promotion' of famous artists. That the first histories of art should have appeared at the same time was no coincidence, more especially as they seem to have been written by practising artists. But other, non-artistic factors may also have been involved. Propagandist overtones may be detected occasionally in the praise accorded to artists of Alexander's time. How far the motivating impulses for this entire intellectual structure were political, and how far aesthetic, is by no means clear. There can, however, be little doubt that the artistic style of the late fourth century acquired political significance, visually associating Hellenistic rulers with Alexander and his legacy of prestige and power.

This was obviously the intention of the satrap of Sidon in commissioning his sarcophagus (5,1). Here Alexander appears as the superhuman victor and hero, taking the place of a god watching over the fate of men in earlier Greek battle reliefs or paintings. The sculptor clearly intended Alexander to be symbolic – but also a portrait. The youthful clean-shaven face (Alexander drove beards out of fashion) is recognizably that of the same person in several other representations which probably go back to contemporary likenesses. And this naturalism extends to the other figures, whose heads are so strongly individualized as to suggest that they, too, are portraits. The costumes and physiognomy of the Persians are recorded as in the generically similar Alexander mosaic (5,24), with an ethnographic fidelity rare in Greek art except occasionally in vase paintings of Africans and, more notably, the fourth-century pectoral made for a Scythian chief (4,47). In the sarcophagus naturalism is combined with symbolism to generalize and give eternal significance to historical events. Thus some of the Greeks are heroically nude, perhaps to symbolize the triumph of Greek intelligence over barbarian brute force, which enabled Alexander to rout armies greatly outnumbering his own. The composition is complex enough to give an impression of action and yet sufficiently formal to suggest that order is being brought out of confusion. The figures are posed to echo and counterbalance one another within a carefully devised pattern of diagonals.

The carving is still as sharp and crisp as it was when the sarcophagus was placed in the tomb chamber which protected it from the elements for over 2,000 years. It even retains some of the pigments with which it was painted, enough to show that the colors were naturalistic and not, as on Archaic Greek sculpture, conventional.

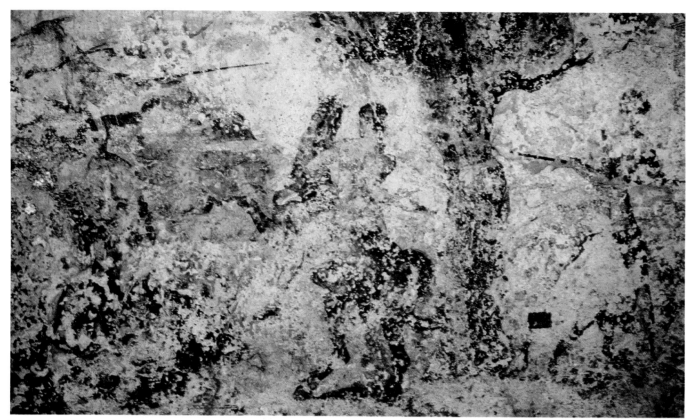

5,7 Painted frieze, detail, c. 330 BC, on the Great Tomb at Vergina, Greece.

Flesh was given a yellow wash, slightly darker for the Persians than for the Greeks, and hair, eyes, lips and garments were picked out in shades of brown, red, violet and blue. Because of its almost unique state of preservation there are very few other works in marble with which the *Alexander Sarcophagus* can be compared. But the same sophisticated taste for virtuoso displays of craftsmanship is apparent in the recently discovered paintings on the tomb at Vergina in northern Greece, thought to have been that of Alexander's father, Philip II of Macedon (**5,7**), and in the slightly later pebble-mosaics from Pella, where Alexander was born (**5,8**). The extraordinary technical accomplishment so evident, despite considerable damage, in the Vergina paintings illustrates their mastery of a naturalistic style in which feats in the representation of torsion and recession seem to have been effortlessly achieved. Similarly in the decorative arts – notably in metalwork – the most subtle and sensitive handling of the medium is displayed. On a magnificent krater found at Derveni in Macedonia – a technical feat of bronze casting, chasing and repoussé hammering (**5,9**) – Dionysus is shown in a wonderfully relaxed, yet elegant, pose of erotic abandon, resting his right thigh on the lap of Ariadne. With this sexually symbolic gesture of casual dalliance the grand passions of the ancient gods are tamed and refined. (The krater was found in a tomb but it seems unlikely, in view of its voluptuous subject, that it was made as a funerary offering. The pensive figures around the neck are solid cast and could have been added to adapt it to its mortuary function.)

Statuettes of bronze and other materials had, of course, been produced in Greece for centuries, usually, it seems, as votive offerings; only now did they begin to appear as independent decorative works of art. One of the finest is a statuette of a dancer, apparently a professional mimer (**5,10**), quite clearly not the Muse of Dancing nor one of the worshippers of Dionysus who had appeared in ecstatic poses in so many early vase paintings. Clutching at drapery tightly drawn across her body, her right foot slipping out from beneath her long dress, she seemingly sways to some slow rhythm. Both the structure and the movement of the form beneath the clothing are rendered with a naturalism that could have been achieved only by close observation. The figure is also a *tour de force* of three-dimensional form which demands to be examined from every viewpoint and seems to have been modelled quite simply in order to be admired. A whole series of complicated changes of direction are beautifully contrasted and balanced and held together in a continuous sweeping but subtly restrained rhythmic phrase. But statuettes of much less attractive subjects were also produced: grimacing dwarfs, emaciated youths, crippled hunchbacks begging for alms. Whether such images of lower-class poverty and misery had already acquired the sinister charm that they later held for rich upper-class art-lovers it is impossible to say.

According to Aristotle, an imitation is in itself pleasurable, and looking at it delights the eye. Things that repel in everyday life may please when represented in art, he wrote. This is diametrically opposed to Plato's

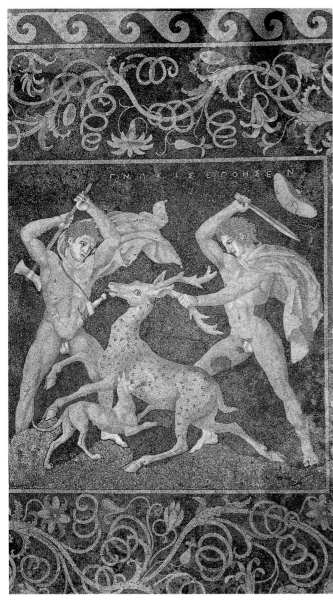

5,8 Stag Hunt, floor mosaic from Pella, c. 300 BC. Pebble mosaic, central area 10ft 4ins sq (3.1m²). Archeological Museum, Pella, Greece.

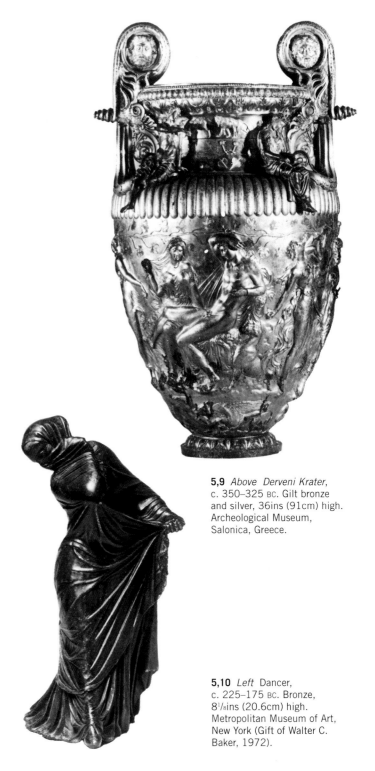

5,9 *Above Derveni Krater*, c. 350–325 BC. Gilt bronze and silver, 36ins (91cm) high. Archeological Museum, Salonica, Greece.

5,10 *Left* Dancer, c. 225–175 BC. Bronze, 8¹⁄₈ins (20.6cm) high. Metropolitan Museum of Art, New York (Gift of Walter C. Baker, 1972).

contention that all imitations are false and therefore morally harmful as it is to Socrates' demand that artists should concentrate on representing the 'good' and 'beautiful', terms that are interchangeable in ancient Greek. Little distinction was made by the Greeks between physical and moral beauty: all Homer's heroes are handsome, all his villains ugly or deformed; the fat men occasionally depicted on vases are invariably figures of fun. But Socrates, himself snub-nosed and short of stature, had begun to evolve a more subtle and profound conception of the outer and inner man and the relationship between them. This and similar currents in Greek thought, coinciding with the rise of naturalism in the visual arts, modified very notably the traditional Greek conception of beauty. Nobility, if not beauty, of soul might now be discerned within an unprepossessing exterior. No longer was the clean-limbed young athlete the sole and exclusive

ideal. (By this date, prize athletes were no longer aristocratic amateurs but professional performers, and this may not be irrelevant.) This modification was to have enormous and profound consequences for the visual arts and was felt immediately in the sudden development of lifelike portraiture in the last decades of the fourth century and first of the third.

The contrast between weakness of body and strength of soul was very clearly expressed in a statue of Demosthenes – that vociferous opponent of both Philip II of

Macedon and Alexander – and also in the words inscribed on its base: 'If your strength had equalled your resolution, Demosthenes, the Macedonian war-god would never have ruled the Greeks.' Surviving copies reveal how the frail, lean body was animated and ennobled by the indomitable spirit shining through the stern, forthright expression on his face (**5,11**). It was a posthumous portrait set up by the Athenians in 280 BC and there may be a touch of idealization in his head. But there is none whatever in the several images of Socrates and later philosophers (again known only from copies), which might almost be thought to emphasize their physical peculiarities. One of the few which can be dated to the third century BC is perhaps of Hermarchus, the chief follower of Epicurus, an unflattering but none the less endearing figure of an old man, bearded head slightly bent, loose flesh on his chest, toga gathered around a pot-belly, and shrunk shanks held rather wide apart (**5,12**). Even the rulers of the Hellenistic world were portrayed with surprising frankness – Philetaerus of Pergamum, who had been accidentally castrated in childhood, is shown on coins with the heavy bloated features of a eunuch, and Euthydemus, who usurped the Bactrian throne in 230 BC, might almost seem to have gloried in his bottle-nosed brutality (**5,13**).

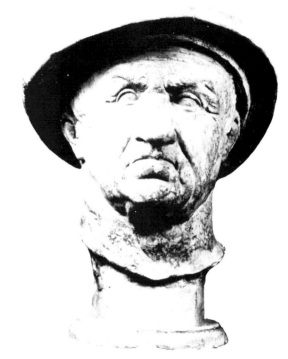

5,13 *Euthydemus of Bactria*, c. 200 BC. Marble, 13¾ins (35cm) high. Villa Torlonia, Rome.

5,11 *Right Demosthenes*, Roman copy of an original, probably by Polyeuctes, c. 280 BC. Marble, life-size. Vatican, Rome.

5,12 *Far right Hermarchus* (?), mid-3rd century BC. Bronze, 10⅜ins (35cm) high. Metropolitan Museum of Art, New York (Rogers Fund, 1910).

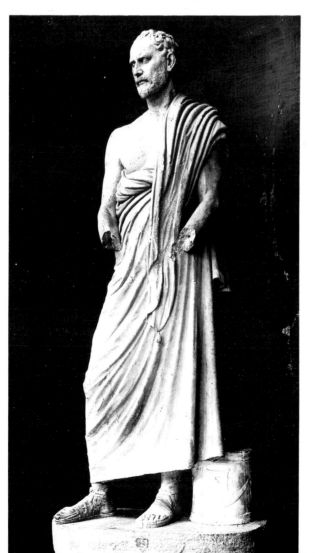

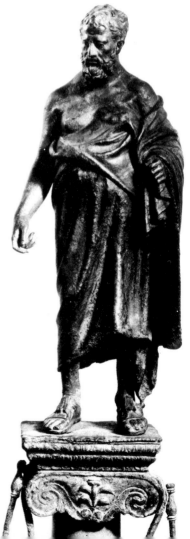

ALLEGORY

Sleeping figures appear for the first time in Hellenistic sculpture, notably a famous Ariadne and a sleeping faun slouched back in sensuous indolence, both expressive in their uncontrolled movements and gestures of a new awareness of man's instinctual nature. Their unconscious bodily responses betray a temporary disjunction of body and mind. An exceptionally fine bronze beautifully catches the complete relaxation of a tired child in deep sleep, legs apart, one arm thrown across the body, and faithfully renders the appearance of loose, dimpled infantile flesh (**5,14**). As the wings with ruffled feathers reveal, however, this is no ordinary child. He is usually identified as the god of love, Eros, son of Aphrodite, though why he should be sleeping is something of a mystery. (Deities were usually shown in characteristic attitudes and actions.) Does he represent the tranquillity attained, so the Stoics believed, when desires are laid to rest? Is he one of the brothers Hypnos and Thanatos – sleep and death – who were visualized as winged children? Is he some other personification reflecting that shift in emphasis, to which we have already alluded in connection with Hellenistic thought, towards the inner life and introspection and philosophies of withdrawal? Or is he simply a decorative figure? It is impossible to give a certain answer: but it is indicative of the expanding range of Hellenistic art that such questions should arise.

It is in this context that allegory, which means literally 'saying something else', first occurs in European art. By the second century BC the Greek gods had lost much of their credibility as inhabitants of a superior world influencing the life of mankind below. In Hellenistic art they tend increasingly to become personifications – of love, death, wisdom, courage, and even of such abstractions as opportunity, luck, strife and forgetfulness, which had not been previously deified. Lysippus carved a statue of *Opportunity*, running on tip-toe with winged feet, a razor

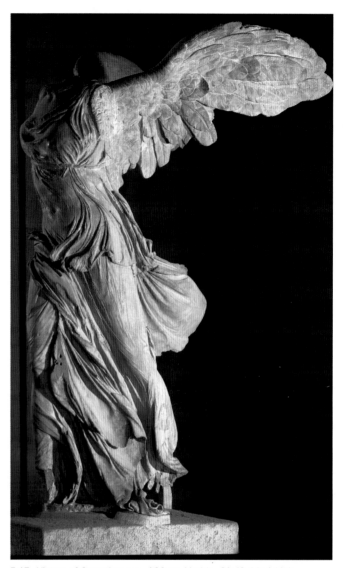

5,15 *Victory of Samothrace*, c. 190 BC. Marble, 8ft (2.44m) high. Louvre, Paris.

5,14 *Sleeping Eros*, c. 250–150 BC. Bronze on marble, 33¾ × 30¾ins (85.7 × 78cm). Metropolitan Museum of Art, New York (Rogers Fund, 1943).

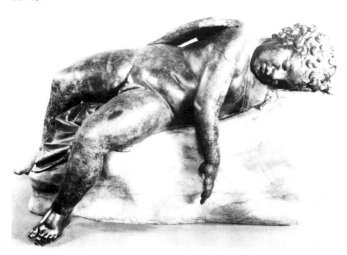

in the right hand, the proverbial forelock in front of the face, the back of the head bald to indicate that he cannot be caught from behind. Such statues were intended to be 'read'.

A Greek statue of a deity, hero or athlete had been self-sufficient, a thing in itself. In the Hellenistic world such figures might acquire allegorical significance from their contexts. One of the most famous examples of Hellenistic art is a case in point: the *Nike* or 'Victory' set up about 190 BC by the inhabitants of the small north Aegean island of Samothrace to commemorate a naval victory (**5,15**). Here the context redefined the meaning of an old image and so reanimated it, as comparison with the late fifth-century *Nike* at Olympia reveals (4,33). Whereas the earlier figure flutters atop a high column, the *Nike of Samothrace* lightly 'touches down' as if in a sudden gust of wind on the prow of a ship, which was originally set in a fountain with boulders emerging from the water in the foreground. Although both were made in connection with historical events, the former is generalized, with the goddess

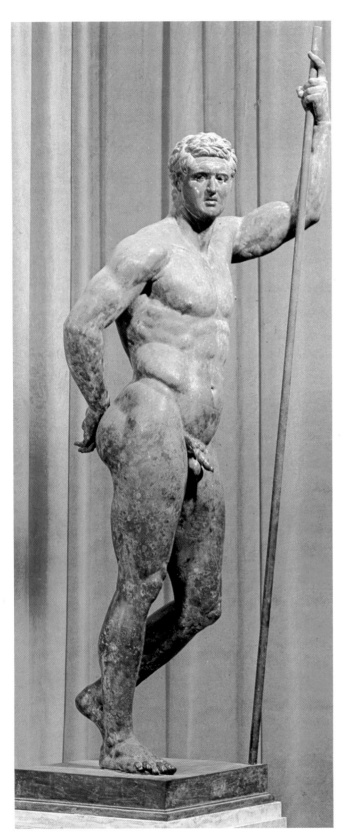

5,16 *Hellenistic Ruler*, c. 150–140 BC. Bronze, 7ft 3³/₈ins (2.22m) high. Museo Nazionale Romano, Rome.

Victory shown as if ready to descend where she will, while the latter is quite specific in representing the victory off the coast of Samothrace. The difference in meaning is reflected in the form, even in the handling of the marble. On the *Nike of Samothrace* drapery is rendered as thick wind-swept cloth rather than as a diaphanous, almost insubstantial membrane. The structure of her well-built form is, none the less, apparent beneath the rich folds and furrows of billowing material, which, with complex rhythms of light and shadow, heightens the figure's dramatic impact.

A taste for the small and exquisite was combined with a love of the vast and grandiose, both extremes becoming typical of Hellenistic art and contrasting very strongly with the aims of fifth-century Greek artists and their ideal of the 'golden mean' (see p. 142). Lysippus was renowned for his ability to work on either scale. One of his sculptures is said to have been a little bronze Hercules he made to stand on Alexander's table, another was a colossal bronze Hercules some 58 feet (18m) tall set up in the Greek city of Taras (present-day Taranto) in southern Italy. His pupil, Chares of Lindos, nearly doubled this height in his famous Colossus of Rhodes.

The over-life-size figure poses problems of structure and also of proportions, for it cannot be simply a mathematical enlargement. The optical distortions, due to the spectator's viewpoint, would make any simple enlargement appear grotesque. It may well have been in this context that Lysippus is said to have boasted that where his predecessors had represented men 'as they really were', he represented them 'as they appeared to be'. He is credited with a complete revision of the Polyclitan canon of proportions (see pp. 149–51), which had been based on actual measurements of the human form. Although none of his reputed 1,500 works survives, and very few are known even from copies, numerous Hellenistic statues are based on the scale of proportions associated with him, which involved mainly a slight reduction in the size of the head and a corresponding extension of the limbs, thus producing an appearance of greater height.

One of the finest of the Lysippic statues is a slightly more than life-size male nude, an original Hellenistic bronze variously dated between the early third and the late second century BC (**5,16**). There is a characteristically Hellenistic combination of naturalism and rhetorical allegory in this work. The traditional walking posture is given a more vivid sense of lively movement by the wider spacing of the feet and the placing of the arms in a bold spiral curve. Somewhat overdeveloped broad-shouldered muscularity conforms to a new ideal of physical vigour, which stresses strength and weight rather than the nimble, light-foot agility of earlier Greek athletes. Yet the face is anything but idealized and would seem to be that of an individual, a portrait head, in fact. This type of portrait statue – the 'ruler portrait', as it is called, with only the head as a likeness – was a Hellenistic invention. The physical perfection which, in Archaic and Classical Greece, athletes had shared with the gods was now attributed to the ruler, to whom divine honours were paid.

5,17 *Altar of Zeus*, from
Pergamum, c. 175 BC. Marble,
reconstructed and restored.
Staatliche Museen, Berlin.

HELLENISTIC ARCHITECTURE

Many of the qualities that differentiate Hellenistic from
Classical Greek art reach their apogee in the great *Altar of
Zeus* from Pergamum in north-western Asia Minor (**5,17**).
It was by far the largest sculptural complex created in the
ancient world, a work so grandiose and imposing that the
author of the Biblical Book of Revelation later called it
'Satan's seat'. Erected as a memorial to the war which,
ironically, established Rome as the dominant power in
the eastern Mediterranean, it commemorates in more
ways than one the beginning of the end of the Hellenic
world. Pergamum had been a kingdom of minor importance until 230 BC, when its king Attalus I defeated an
invading force of Gauls from the north and briefly made
himself master of Asia Minor. The event was celebrated
in a series of statues of dead or dying Gauls, now known
only from later copies (**5,18**), which reveal the emergence
of a distinctive Pergamene style responsive to the highly
'civilized' demands of its patrons. For in this remarkable
sculpture the defeated is endowed with dignity, even
nobility, and those introspective, spiritualizing trends in
Hellenistic thought, which held that the body is the
prison of the soul, found their classic expression. The
spirit persists while life slowly drains away from the body
of the *Dying Gaul*. Comparison between him and the
Fallen Warrior from Aegina (4,22) shows how much had

been gained in expressiveness – and how much lost in
purely sculptural power.

The *Altar of Zeus* was erected some 50 years later. It
stood on a 20-foot-high (6m) platform, surrounded by an
Ionic colonnade. The approach was from the back, so that
only after a walk round the building did the great flight of
steps leading up to the altar come into view. Running
round the base was a sculptural frieze (which only partly
survives) some 7½ feet (2.3m) high and, in all, more than

5,18 *Dying Gaul*, Roman copy of a bronze original of c. 230–220 BC.
Marble, life-size. Museo Capitolino, Rome.

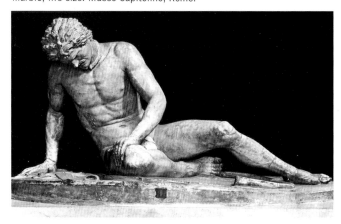

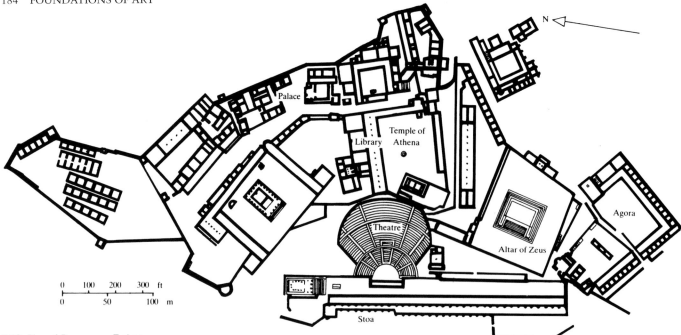

5,19 Plan of Pergamum, Turkey.

300 feet (90m) long. On the interior wall of the colonnade at the level of the altar a second frieze, of which a good deal less has been preserved, runs for some 240 feet (73m); it is about 5 feet (1.5m) high. (The remains of the building were dismantled after excavation in the late nineteenth century and re-erected in the Berlin Museum in about 1900.) The first and larger frieze is devoted to a battle between gods and giants, the gods being the full height of the relief slabs and the giants even bigger, only their huge menacing torsos being visible. Muscles swell in great hard knots, eyes bulge beneath puckered brows, teeth are clenched in agony. The writhing, overpowering figures seem contorted, stretched, almost racked, into an apparently endless, uncontrolled (in fact, very carefully calculated) variety of strenuous, coiling postures to which the dynamic integration of the whole composition is due. Rhythmic sense is felt very strongly – a plastic rhythm so compelling that the individual figures and complex groups are all fused into a single system of correspondences throughout the whole design. Deep cutting and under-cutting produce strong contrasts of light and dark which heighten the drama and seem to echo in abstract terms the great cosmic conflict between Olympians and earth-bound giants. The effect, in fact, is painterly rather than sculptural in its dramatic use of *chiaroscuro* – the stone is carved so that effects of light and shade suggest forms without describing them in full – and in its extreme naturalism, which is taken to such lengths that some of the figures break out of their architectural frame altogether and into the spectator's space. One of the giants leans out to kneel on the steps leading up to the altar. The upper frieze is quite different, with figures smaller than life, subtly carved in low relief and intended to be examined closely – a contrast recalling Aristotle's description of the various contrasting oratorical styles (p. 177).

Likewise, in the structure as a whole, a sculptural conception of architecture as mass in space – rather than space regulated by mass – was taken to its furthest extreme. Yet the classic virtue of a clear relationship of parts to the whole might be said to have culminated here. For the continuous band of sculpture makes a wonderfully rich, almost a color contrast with the base below and colonnade above, giving by its complexity a peculiar value to the cool lucidity and elegance of the Ionic columns. The interior – always of less importance than the exterior in ancient Greece – has been eliminated altogether. The whole building is nothing but a façade.

In urban planning, too, some very significant departures were made at Pergamum from former Greek practice. On its rocky acropolis the *Altar of Zeus* was only one of several structures, including a temple of Athena, a library, large theatre, royal palace and stoa, all visually related to one another and placed so as to take full advantage of the terraced hilltop site (**5,19**). Such an interest in the monumental effects obtained by careful siting, grouping and the creation of vistas first becomes apparent only in Hellenistic times. In Athens itself at the end of the fourth century BC, the agora was still simply an irregular open space bordered by a number of detached and unrelated buildings. All this was changed in the second century BC

5,20 Temple of the Olympian Zeus, Athens, 174 BC–c. AD 130.

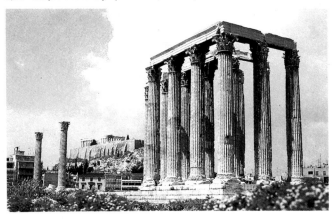

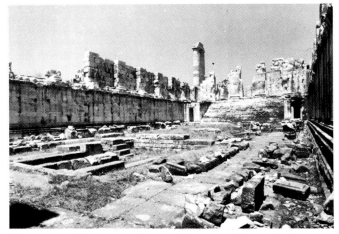

5,21 Interior of the temple of Apollo, Didyma, near Miletus, Turkey, begun 313 BC.

5,22 Plan of the temple of Apollo, Didyma.

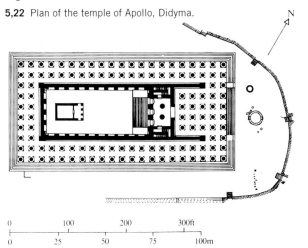

by, significantly enough, Attalus II of Pergamum. Two long stoas were built on the south and east sides, thus creating a united spatial composition out of the previously amorphous area.

The history of Hellenistic architecture is, however, hard to trace. We know less about it than about earlier, Classical Greek architecture, for much less has survived. Nothing remains in the three great capital cities: Alexandria and Antioch were both entirely rebuilt by later inhabitants; Seleucia on the Tigris was deserted and left to crumble away after the Parthian occupation. The *Altar of Zeus* from Pergamum (5,17) and the huge Corinthian temple of Olympian Zeus at Athens, begun in 174 BC but not completed until about AD 130 (5,20), are almost the only major buildings of which more than the foundations are visible, although enough survives at Didyma on the west coast of present-day Turkey to indicate the dramatic effects sometimes achieved in planning (5,21; 22). The central doorway of this great dipteral temple, approached through gigantic Corinthian columns over 64 feet (19.5m) high, led from an antechamber to a great flight of steps descending into an open, sunlit interior court, where an elegant small Ionic temple contained the cult statue. Similarly inventive planning has been revealed by excavations in temple precincts (sanctuary of Asclepius on the island of Kos, third century BC) and in whole urban areas (e.g. Priene) (5,23); but our knowledge of ancient urbanism is very limited. (The name of Hippodamus, the fifth-century BC Milesian architect credited by Aristotle with the systematization of regular street patterns of the

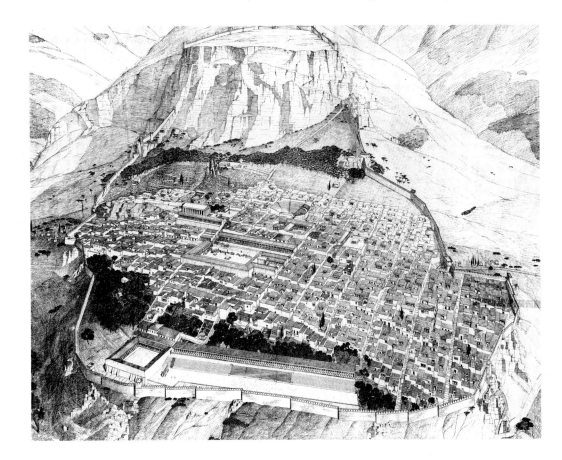

5,23 Reconstructed view of Priene, Turkey.

gridiron type, has been associated with Priene; and regular, usually rectangular, street-planning goes back to the seventh century BC in the Aegean and much further in ancient Egypt, Mesopotamia and the Indus Valley; see pp. 74, 59.) However, excavations show the new importance given in Hellenistic cities not only to prominent civic buildings but to monumental effects in their disposition – and to an increase in the size and decorative richness of private houses with painted walls and elaborate pebble-mosaic pavements, as at Pella in Macedonia, the birth-place of Alexander (5,8), and on the island of Delos, an important centre for trade in slaves. If little remains from the period itself, it seems almost certain that the opulent architectural style elaborated in Asia Minor and Syria under Roman rule, especially at Baalbek (5,70) and Palmyra, derived from Hellenistic prototypes and reflects Hellenistic aspirations and achievements.

HELLENISTIC AND ROMAN PAINTING AND MOSAICS

Wall-paintings and floor mosaics which decorated town and country houses in Italy in the last two centuries BC and the first AD are mainly in the pictorial style developed in the Hellenistic kingdoms, and some were the work of artists from the eastern Mediterranean. They are geographically, rather than culturally, Italian – like much of the earlier pottery, metalwork and paintings in Etruscan tombs (see p. 169). But they date from the period when Rome had already gained control of a large part of the Hellenistic world and also of territories to the north and west. By the beginning of the second century BC, the Romans had made themselves masters not only of the

whole Italian peninsula, Sicily, Sardinia and Corsica, but also of the former Carthaginian colonies in the south of France and Spain. They subdued Carthage and its north African territories in 151 BC, annexed Greece three years later and the kingdom of Pergamum in 131 BC. The Ptolemaic kingdom of Egypt came under Roman 'protection' early in the first century BC and was constituted a Roman province in 30 BC. Roman power and influence were, however, military, political and economic. The Roman upper class had absorbed Hellenistic culture. As Horace (65–8 BC) put it, 'When Greece had been enslaved she made a slave of her rough conqueror and introduced the arts into an uncultivated Latium [the province of Rome, present-day Lazio].' The territories amassed by the Roman republic were more tightly organized under the Emperor Augustus (27 BC–AD 14), whose reign initiated a century and a half of peace – the *Pax Romana* – throughout the whole Mediterranean area. The Roman empire grew still larger under Augustus's immediate successors, the Julio-Claudian emperors and the Flavian dynasty (69–98), reaching its greatest extent – from the Euphrates to the Atlantic, north Africa to Scotland – under Trajan (98–117) and the Antonines (139–92). This vast expansion of the empire geographically, ethnically and in other ways raises almost insuperable problems in defining Roman art (see p. 204).

The sculpture, paintings, mosaics and other works of art from Pompeii and Herculaneum, smothered under lava and ashes from Vesuvius in August AD 79 and not uncovered until the eighteenth century, illustrate the problem. The most impressive of the mosaics represents Alexander's victory over the Persians, the battle of Issus, and is as Hellenistic in style as in subject-matter (5,24). Its composition is almost certainly derived from a late fourth-century BC painting, perhaps by Philoxenus of Eretria,

5,24 *Battle of Issus*, 2nd to 1st century BC. Mosaic, 8ft 11ins × 16ft 9½ins (2.72 × 5.13m). Museo Archeologico Nazionale, Naples.

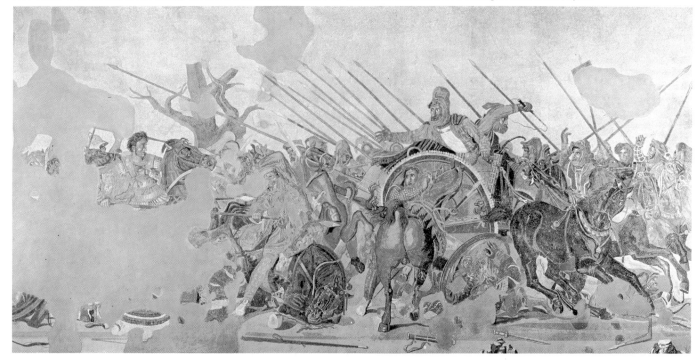

Roman Luxury

SILVER AND CAMEO GLASS

Roman moralists extolled the austere life-style of the founders of the republic and condemned luxury and conspicuous expense. The historian Livy (59 BC–AD 17), for example, traced the origin of 'foreign luxury' to soldiers returning from a successful campaign against the Hellenistic kingdom of Antiochus III in Syria in 186 BC. These men 'first brought to Rome bronze couches, precious coverings, curtains and other textiles, and also what they considered magnificent furniture in those days'. He quoted Cato (234–149 BC), the republican general and *censor* (a magistrate who supervised the morals and conduct of citizens), complaining how 'the state suffers from two diverse vices, avarice and luxury, those pests which have overturned all great empires'. Pliny the Elder (see p. 148) said that victories over the Hellenistic kingdoms had done less harm to the defeated than to the Romans, who 'learned not just to admire foreign opulence but actually to love it'. They became, he said, 'not only mad for silver in great quantity, but perhaps even crazier for it in the form of works of art'. In contrast, he recalled a patrician in the time of the republic who had bought for an extravagant sum two cups by a famous Greek artist, 'but from a sense of shame he never dared to use them'. Later, with the expanding empire and its large and increasingly rich upper-class, the taste for ostentatious splendour and the luxury objects with which to express it also increased and was indulged with fewer inhibitions. Admonitions from disapproving moralists continued and were to be taken up by Christians, though without any noticeable effect.

Silver vessels graced the tables of relatively modest houses in the provincial city of Pompeii and magnificent, even sumptuous, pieces of Roman silver have been found on the frontiers of the empire. Some of the finest were dug up (in 1868) at Hildesheim in northern Germany, though

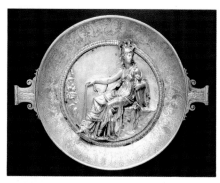

5,25 Dish with relief of Athene, c. 50 BC–c. AD 50. Silver, partly gilt, 12⁷/₁₀ins (32.3cm) wide including handles. Staatliche Museen, Berlin.

how they came to be buried there is a mystery. They appear to date from the time of Augustus and were made in Italy (as Latin inscriptions recording their weights reveal), perhaps by some immigrant artist from the Near East. The high relief of the goddess Athene on a partly gilded silver dish is a miniature work of sculpture in the Hellenistic tradition (**5,25**). The Classical balance and form of the figure and the high quality of its execution reflected the owner's cultivated taste just as its weight in silver and gold indicated his wealth. The association of luxury with the 'perfumed East' may account for the persistence of motifs derived from Hellenistic art on Roman silver as late as the fourth century.

Other luxury objects prized by rich Romans were carvings in such semi-precious hard stones as onyx (**5,57**). The very ancient art of engraving hard stones to serve as seals (see p. 53 and 2,3; p. 60 and 2,16) had been practised with great refinement in ancient Greece where such gems, as they are usually called, were incised so that impressions would show the designs in relief. Cameos carved in relief – not for use as seals but as independent works of art – were an invention of the Hellenistic period. They were normally carved from pieces of onyx, which have strata of contrasting colors; one was used for the background, the others

for figures in relief. Numerous examples dating from the last years of the republic and from the empire period are signed by their engravers, whose names were almost invariably Greek. A similar technique was used for the decoration of glass by carving the outer surface of a vessel blown by a tricky technique from molten glass of two different colors, called cased or cameo glass. The process of glass-blowing originated in Syria in the mid-first century BC and soon afterwards Syrian glass-workers settled in Italy where the finest surviving examples of cameo glass were made, probably during the reign of Augustus. The *Portland Vase* (**5,26**) is among the finest, a *tour-de-force* of the glass carver's skill. It is decorated with a mythological scene which may have alluded to Augustus but was rendered in the most artificially mannered of Hellenistic styles. Its exquisite refinement combined with its sumptuous physicality must have impressed as well as delighted its owner's guests as, of course, it was intended to do.

5,26 *Portland Vase*, c. 27 BC–AD 14. Blue and white cameo glass, 9³/₄ins (24.8cm) high. British Museum, London.

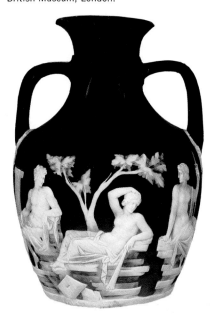

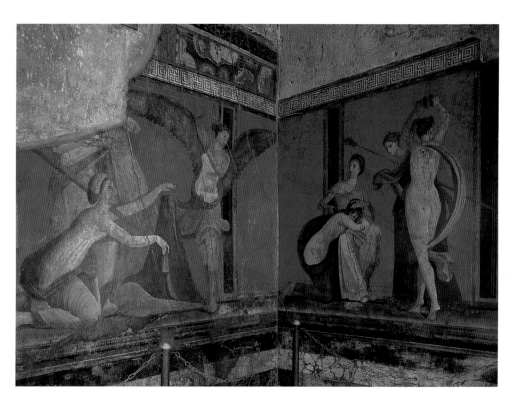

5,27 *Dionysiac Mystery Cult*,
c. 50 BC. Wall-painting,
5ft 3³/₄ins (1.62m) high.
Villa of the Mysteries, Pompeii.

whom Pliny credits with such a scene – and whose name has been mentioned in connection with the c. 330 BC paintings discovered at Vergina (5,7). There is also a tantalizing reference to a picture of this subject by Helen, daughter of an Egyptian named Timon, one of several women artists mentioned as working in the Hellenistic period. (They were the first women artists, or at any rate, the first professional women artists, so far as is known. None is recorded in Classical Greece.) The mosaic is carried out in the limited range of four colors – black, white, red and yellow with their intermediate tones – to which some Greek painters of the fifth and fourth centuries are known to have restricted their palettes.

As we have already seen, the battle of Issus is possibly represented on the *Alexander Sarcophagus* (5,1). In the relief the subject is elevated to universal significance by generalization – the warriors are all given equal prominence, though three Greeks, each with an expiring Persian at his feet, stand out in the mêlée – whereas in the mosaic everything is particularized. The artist concentrated on the vividness of the scene, which is shown as it was thought to have really happened. An actual incident appears to be depicted, the vital moment when the battle turned into a rout as the Persians took to their heels, though, of course, this is an imaginary reconstruction. A bare-headed Greek youth, Alexander, advancing from the left and spearing a cavalryman, faces the Persian King of Kings Darius, who turns towards him with a helpless gesture and expression while his charioteer raises his whip to lash his horses into a galloping retreat. There are no nudes or symbolical elements, except perhaps for the blasted tree, which balances the head of the defeated Darius. Emphasis is laid on the drama of the moment, registered by the movement of the ranked spears – a brilliantly effective visual device.

Figures in the mosaic are robustly modelled with shading to give them weight and substance; they move through clearly lit space, casting shadows on the ground. Indeed, light is rendered as in no surviving earlier work except those at Vergina, with reflections and highlights glancing off bared swords and glittering on armour. All the pictorial devices learned in the Classical period (so the ancient literary sources tell us) have here been exploited to give an appearance of movement in three dimensions. Figures are shown in a great variety of natural attitudes and from as many viewpoints – the head of one is turned away and his terrified face reflected in a polished shield. Rearing, shying, bolting horses are delineated with complete command of foreshortening, notably that to the right of centre, seen from behind and held by a Persian groom, who gazes apprehensively towards Alexander.

So skilful is the execution of this mosaic that some impression of the fluid brushwork of the original painting can even be recaptured in the mind's eye. The picture is built up from tiny *tesserae* or cubes of carefully graded naturally colored stone, by a technique that seems to have been invented in the third century BC – previously figurative mosaics had been composed of small pebbles, as at Pella (5,8). Small mosaic pictures, called *emblemata*, were produced as works of art independently of the usually less subtly colored and more broadly treated ornamental mosaics set in floors and wall surfaces. Their origin is unknown. They may have been imported ready-made from the eastern Mediterranean. All that is certain is that they reflect artistic tastes which upper-class Romans shared with the upper class of the Hellenistic kingdoms.

Pompeii and Herculaneum were provincial cities and not major centres of wealth and artistic patronage in any way comparable with Alexandria or Rome. They may, therefore, give a somewhat misleading impression of Hellenistic and Roman painting, though we necessarily depend on them for much of our visual knowledge of it. Very rarely do paintings from Pompeii and Herculaneum equal the technical accomplishment of the battle of Issus mosaic. Relatively few rise above the level of rapidly daubed hack-work. A painted room in a large country house known as the Villa of the Mysteries, just outside Pompeii, is altogether exceptional (**5,27**). There has been much discussion about its authorship (Greek or south Italian) and also whether it was copied from an earlier prototype. For although the composition is so carefully adapted to the size and shape of the room that it might seem to have been determined by it, individual figures are in poses that occur in Hellenistic sculpture.

The subject of this painting – still not completely elucidated – seems to be some form of initiation. Prominent are the ritual flagellation of a woman and the toilet of a bride under the gaze of a seated priestess, perhaps the mistress of the villa. One wall is given up to immortals with Ariadne reclining in the lap of Dionysus, symbol of the eternal bliss of the initiate who espoused the god. Dionysus, son of Zeus, was a god of the fertility of nature, a suffering god who died and came to life again; he was also the god of wine who inspired music, dance and drama. His cult had been introduced from the Near East to Greece and thence to Italy (where he was called Bacchus) as had other, more esoteric cults in the westward migration of Oriental spiritualism during the last two centuries before Christ.

There is nothing orgiastic about this painting, none of the delirious intoxicated frenzy of the devotees of Dionysus as depicted on Greek vases. Both mortals and immortals look distinctly cool and collected – apart from one apparently terrorized figure, though even she maintains her statuesque deportment. They are represented a little less than life-size, standing on a simulated stage or platform which runs round the room so that they seem to move in a shallow extension of the real space, giving the impression almost of a *tableau vivant*. Furthermore, they look across the real space of the room, with some rather complicated and sophisticated results, as when the flagellator raises her whip to strike the woman kneeling on the adjoining wall. Anyone coming into the room is given an embarrassingly vivid sensation of having intruded into a religious ceremony, of interrupting some solemn and arcane ritual.

If the ritual scene in the Villa of the Mysteries is a unique survivor, the illusionism of the architectural framework in which it is set is characteristic of painting in Italy of this period. Ambitious – spatial and not flat – decorative schemes appeared early in the first century BC, visually enlarging the space of rooms with columns, entablatures and other architectural elements. Figurative scenes were often incorporated, as if they were panel pictures hanging on or set in the walls. Later, a further step was taken by visually opening the wall, sometimes completely, sometimes with make-believe windows, to disclose vistas of colonnades stretching into the far distance. In the first century AD this imaginary architecture was treated with increasing fantasy to conjure up buildings of a more insubstantial elegance than any that could be erected on earth. Recession was indicated by a perspective system apparently devised for theatrical scenery,

probably in the Hellenistic East, though it may have had Italian origins as well, with orthogonals or lines of perspective projection slanting towards a central axis (not towards a single vanishing-point, see p. 425).

These various types of painting are usually categorized as the Pompeiian Styles I, II, III and IV, though there is, of course, no reason to suppose that they followed one another in strict sequence. The development was additive, not sequential. Nor did they originate at Pompeii, though by far the largest number of examples have survived there. One room in the house of evidently prosperous merchants combines all four illusionistic systems or styles – a dado of simulated panels of rare marbles; pictures hung on or set in the wall and surrounded by frames which seem to project forwards; windows opening on to views of airy structures; and, above, statues placed on top of the wall, beyond which fanciful buildings may be glimpsed in space (**5,28**). Sometimes the 'pictures' were of fruit, dead fish and game and glass vessels half full of water (the earliest known still lifes), themselves exercises in eye-deceiving illusionism or *trompe l'oeil*, creating a complex and sophisticated play with levels of reality – illusionistic paintings of *trompe l'oeil* pictures set in walls which were given the appearance of having relief decorations and also openings on to the world beyond! Deception in art is pleasurable, wrote the late Roman man of letters Philostratus the Younger about AD 300. For, he asked rhetorically, 'to confront objects which do not exist as though they existed and to be influenced by them, to believe that they do exist, is not this, since no harm can come of it, a suitable and irreproachable means of providing entertainment?' Mythological scenes such as those

5,28 Ixion Room, House of the Vettii, Pompeii, 1st century AD.

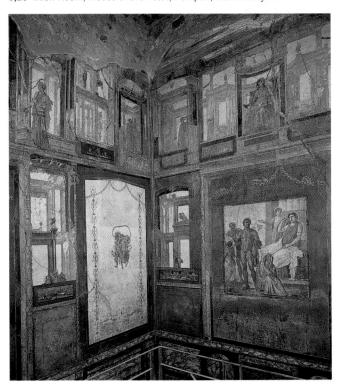

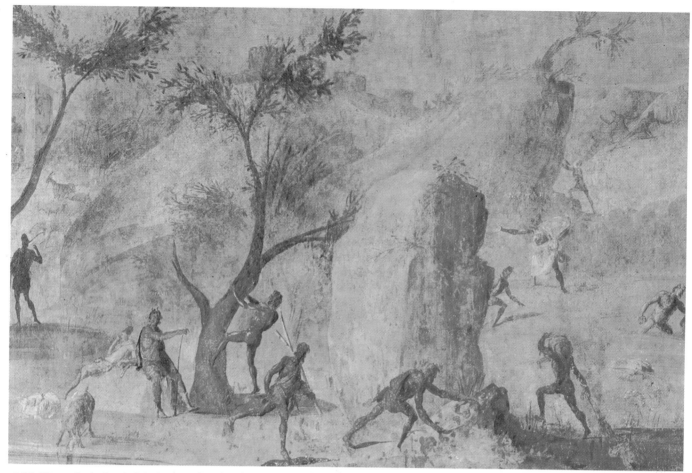

5,29 *Ulysses in the Land of the Lestrygonians*, late 1st century BC. Wall-painting from a house on the Esquiline Hill, Rome, about 5ft (1.52m) high. Vatican Museums, Rome.

in the House of the Vettii (5,28) may, however, have had for those who commissioned them greater significance than meets the modern eye. The Roman house was a shrine and place of sacrifice as well as a human habitation. Its main living rooms were under the protection of different deities, who might be represented on their walls: Bacchus in the *triclinium* or dining-room, Venus in the *cubiculum* or bedroom. Paintings might also indicate cultural and social status: Greek subject-matter for educated upper-class taste, decorative profusion and opulence for the newly rich – an appearance of wealth, sometimes a doubly deceptive one. Accelerated social mobility in the Italian cities of the first century BC had created an increasingly complex social structure, which made visible indications of social standing desirable. But aesthetic factors must also have been involved. Decorations on walls and ceilings were by no means limited to paintings and mosaics. Some of the most elegantly refined of all are in stucco.

5,30 Wall-painting from the Villa Livia, Rome, detail, late 1st century BC. About 9ft (2.74m) wide. Museo Nazionale Romano, Rome.

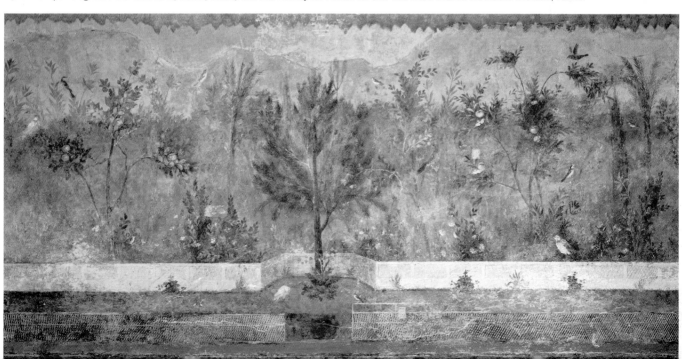

Landscapes, or rather figurative compositions in land-scape settings – airy little country scenes with trees, rustic buildings, a few pensive figures and sometimes a herm – were often incorporated in decorative schemes. The finest surviving examples, from a house in Rome, illustrate eight scenes from the *Odyssey*, framed by simulated pilasters (**5,29**). Their artist created evocative atmospheric effects of cool Mediterranean water and warm still air with the headlands of a bay shimmering in a slight haze. Distance is suggested and the forms of boats and rocks only vaguely defined, but the painting opens the wall surface on to the crystalline dream-world of poetry. Some of the energetic little figures are labelled with their names in (not always correct) Greek lettering and it is assumed that the artist was of Greek origin, though it is impossible to say for certain whether his work was orig-inal or copied from an earlier composition, a painting on the inner wall of a stoa, perhaps, or even an illustrated manuscript. But here we stand on the frontier, or rather the overlap, of Hellenistic and Roman art.

Pliny ascribed to an artist of the Augustan period named Studius Ludius or Spurius Tadius – the manuscripts give different readings, but he must have been Italian if not strictly Roman – 'that most delightful way of painting walls with representations of villas, porticoes [see Glos-sary] and landscape gardens, woods, groves, hills, ponds, channels, rivers and shores – any scene in short that took the fancy'. The same artist, he wrote, painted the walls of open galleries with views of seaside towns 'producing a charming effect at minimal cost'. A room in the villa out-side Rome believed to have belonged to Livia, wife of the Emperor Augustus, might illustrate this style of work (**5,30**). Flowering plants and trees of several types with

5,31 Wall-painting from the Temple of Isis, Pompeii, detail, 1st century AD. Museo Archeologico Nazionale, Naples.

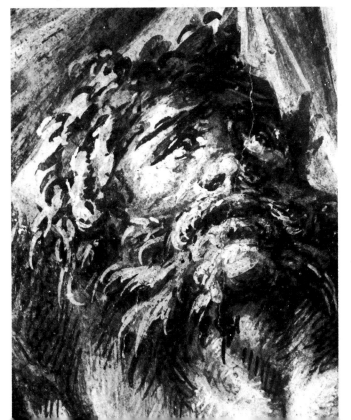

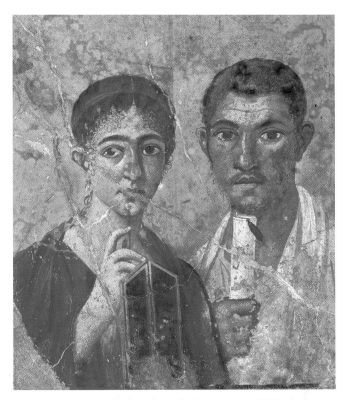

5,32 *Baker and his Wife*, from Pompeii, 1st century AD. Wall-painting, 19¼ × 16⅛ins (48.9 × 41cm). Museo Archeologico Nazionale, Naples.

brightly feathered birds perching on their branches com-pletely encircle it, bringing permanently indoors a luxu-riant garden of the type that was frequently integrated into the planning of larger Roman palaces and villas (**5,33; 34**). Beyond a narrow strip of grass, which visually extends the real space of the room, the world of nature is tantaliz-ingly fenced off – as if to suggest the paradise of the 'Islands of the Blessed', where eternal summer reigned, as described by Horace in a poem written about this time.

Freshness and freedom of handling distinguish the finest of these Pompeiian and Roman decorative paintings. This can best be appreciated in isolated details, which often display quite extraordinary mastery and bravura (**5,31**). Such sophisticated delight in dexterity is much less evi-dent in portraiture, however, an art form greatly culti-vated by the Romans, especially in sculpture (see pp. 207–10). Pliny refers to lifelike portrayals of gladiators as having been 'for many generations the highest ambition of painting'. His remark may be sarcastic, but, in fact, por-traits of relatively humble sitters are among the most arresting of the many paintings found at Pompeii. One, from the wall of a shop, is of a man and woman tradition-ally called the *Baker and his Wife* and probably a wed-ding picture (**5,32**). The features of the swarthy man are anything but patrician: he seems to be an ordinary tradesman (though he has been identified with Terentius Neo, a law student). The woman with her carefully dressed hair and pale complexion might seem to have higher social ambitions, the writing tablet and the stylus which she presses against her chin perhaps indicating literary interests. In the gesture of her hand there is a touch of

VITRUVIUS ON ROMAN PAINTING

Vitruvius Pollio was a military architect in the service of Julius Caesar and later Augustus. In his old age he wrote, for Augustus, a book on architecture which is the only treatise by an ancient artist or architect to survive. His account of Roman painting sheds some light on taste in the age of Augustus.

. . . For other apartments, that is, those used for spring, autumn, and summer, and also in atriums and peristyles, clearly defined principles for depicting objects were derived by the ancients from prototypes which really existed in nature. For a picture is an image of something which either really exists or at least can exist – for instance, men, buildings, ships, and other things from whose clearly-defined and actually existent physical forms pictorial representations are derived by copying. Following this principle, the ancients, who first undertook to use polished wall surfaces, began by imitating different varieties of marble revetments in different positions, and then went on to imitate cornices, hard stones, and wedges arranged in various ways with relation to one another.

Later they became so proficient that they would imitate the forms even of buildings and the way columns and gables stood out as they projected from the background; and in open spaces, such as exedrae, because of the extensiveness of the walls, they depicted stage façades in the tragic, comic, or satyric style. Their walls, because of the extended length of the wall space, they decorated with landscapes of various sorts, modeling these images on the features of actual places. In these are painted harbors, promontories, coastlines, rivers, springs, straits, sanctuaries, groves, mountains, flocks, and shepherds. In places there are some designs done in the megalographic style representing images of the gods or narrating episodes from mythology, or, no less often, scenes from the Trojan war, or the wanderings of Odysseus over the landscape backgrounds, and other subjects, which are produced on the basis of similar principles from nature as it really is.

But these, which were representations derived from reality, are now scorned by the undiscriminating tastes of the present. For now there are monstrosities painted on stuccoed walls rather than true-to-life images based on actual things – instead of columns the structural elements are striated reeds; instead of gables there are ribbed appendages with curled leaves and volutes. Candelabra are seen supporting figures of small shrines, and, above the gables of these, many tender stalks with volutes grow up from their roots and have, without it making any sense whatsoever, little seated figures upon them. Not only that, but there are slender stalks which have little half-figures, some with human heads and some with beasts' heads.

Such things do not exist, nor could they exist, nor have they ever existed. Consequently it is the new tastes which have brought about a condition in which bad judges who deal with incompetent art have the power to condemn real excellence in the arts.

(Vitruvius, *de Architectura*, tr. M. H. Morgan, *Vitruvius: The Ten Books of Architecture*, Cambridge, Mass. 1914)

---

affectation made more obvious by the plain, candid style of the painting itself. This and other equally direct and vivid portraits, some scenes of contemporary life – a riot in the amphitheatre, for instance – and grotesquely erotic caricatures on the walls of a brothel suggest that a vigorous popular art coexisted with the upper-class and rather high-flown paintings in the richer houses and public buildings.

Pompeii and Herculaneum show that by AD 79 every type of painting (every *genre* as they were later to be called) was being practised and patronized – history-painting, figure-painting, portraiture, landscape and still life. A system of perspective had been devised to give a sometimes illusionistic appearance of recession in space. Various pictorial styles had also been developed, ranging from hard linearity with flat areas of color to an impressionistic rendering of form with rapid flicks of the brush. When Pompeii and Herculaneum were at their heyday, however, Roman writers were already lamenting that the art of painting was in a bad way. The architectural theorist Vitruvius (fl. 46–32 BC) and later Pliny thought painting a 'dying art'; it was said to be 'completely dead' by Petronius, arbiter of elegance at the Emperor Nero's court and author of the brilliant bawdy novel *Satyricon*, in which a 'picture gallery with a marvellous collection of all kinds of painting' consisted exclusively of Greek and Hellenistic works:

I saw a work by the hand of Zeuxis which was not yet worn away with the injuries of age, and I beheld not without a certain awe the sketches of Protogenes which were so real that they vied with nature herself. And when I came upon the work of Apelles . . . I actually worshipped it. For the outlines of the figures gave a rendering of natural appearances with such subtlety that you might even believe their souls had been painted. . . .

(Petronius, *Satyricon*, AD 83, tr. J. J. Pollitt)

It was, perhaps, to give the effect of such a collection that rooms like that in the House of the Vettii at Pompeii were painted.

Livy, the great historian of the Roman republic, declared that paintings robbed from the temples of Sicily in 211 BC initiated 'the craze for works of Greek art'. Such paintings were at first placed in public buildings as trophies of conquest. But private collectors appeared on the scene in the first century BC. One paid for a single fourth-century BC picture as much as 36,000 *denarii*, an enormous sum at a time when a capable slave cost 500 and a free labourer was paid around 250 a year. This collecting of

Greek and Hellenistic 'old masters' by very rich Romans stimulated a demand for copies to grace the walls of those who could not obtain originals. Only now, significantly enough, did the conception of an 'original' and its corollary, a 'copy', first arise. Once it had, the copy was despised. The influential Stoic philosopher Seneca made a point of distinguishing between the divinely inspired artist of the past and the artisan copyists of his own day. Such views might be justified philosophically; yet one may question how far they were the cause and how far the effect of the high commercial value then being placed on originals in the 'old master' market.

Art collecting may also have played a part in transforming attitudes to artists and their work in other ways. Pictures that had been dedicated to the gods in a Greek sanctuary necessarily lost much, if not all, of their religious significance once they were removed to private residences in Italy. They were transformed into collectors' pieces, objects of luxury and status symbols. As a result, the rather occult aura which seems to have surrounded artists in earlier times was dimmed. Both Cicero and Seneca excluded painting from the 'liberal arts', the latter classifying painters simply as 'agents of extravagance'. That Nero dabbled in painting was often mentioned, but not as one of his virtues.

In the vast body of Latin literature there are few references to, and fewer words of praise for, contemporary painters. Not even their names would be known were it not for Pliny, and his remarks are extremely brief. (They end before AD 79, for he died while watching the fatal eruption of Vesuvius.) Although Romans were fascinated to the point of obsession by their political history, they wrote no histories of their visual arts. Very little is recorded about the artists who worked in Rome itself, let alone those in the provincial cities. It is not known whether they were of Italian or eastern Mediterranean origin, freemen or slaves. They were classed simply as artisans, beneath the attention of writers. In ancient Greece, disdain had sometimes been expressed for *banausoi*, a word that originally meant 'blacksmiths' but came to include all who worked with their hands, and this attitude hardened in Rome. Sculptors were as little regarded as painters or, for that matter, carpenters. The versatile writer Lucian (c. AD 120–200) described a sculptor as 'no more than a workman, doing hard physical labour . . . obscure, earning a small wage, a man of low esteem, classed as worthless by public opinion, neither courted by friends, feared by enemies, nor envied by fellow citizens, but just a common workman, a craftsman, a face in a crowd, one who makes his living with his hands' (*Dream* 9 [13]). This may be an exaggeration, but even the greatest artists of the past were downgraded by the Romans, despite the prices and the praises commanded by their works. 'No gifted young man upon seeing the Zeus of Phidias at Olympia ever wanted to be Phidias', wrote the great moralist and biographer Plutarch (c. AD 46–120). 'For it does not necessarily follow that, if a work is delightful because of its gracefulness, the man who made it is worthy of our serious regard.'

Unlike painting and sculpture, architecture was regarded by Cicero as one of the liberal arts, that is to say one in which a free man (*liberalis*) might engage without loss of status. Vitruvius, himself a practising architect as well as a theorist, declared that 'persons can justly claim to be architects only if they have from boyhood mounted by the steps of their studies and, being trained generally in the knowledge of arts and sciences, have reached the temple of architecture at the top.' An architect, he demanded, 'should be a man of letters, a skilful draftsman, a mathematician, familiar with scientific thought, a diligent student of philosophy, acquainted with music, not ignorant of medicine, knowledgeable about the opinions of jurists, and familiar with astronomy and the theory of the heavens'. How often these requirements were fulfilled is, of course, impossible to say. But there can be no doubt that the buildings which were to be Rome's greatest and most enduring contribution to the visual arts of the West were designed by men who not only combined artistic sensibility with great expertise in engineering, but also had the freedom of mind to break away from traditional methods of construction and accepted canons of judgement. They created an entirely new concept of architectural mass and space.

ROMAN ARCHITECTURE

The Romans' artistic genius was most fully expressed in architecture, the art in which their extraordinary gifts for organization and planning could find a natural outlet. They excelled in urban design and in new systematized construction methods, which facilitated large-scale programs for utilitarian and civic structures – roads, drainage systems, bridges, aqueducts, vast apartment blocks and public buildings of various kinds (see pp. 196–7). Temples and other religious edifices, so prominent hitherto in the history of architecture, now became relatively unimportant. It was essentially the same practical, managerial gifts which, in other fields, enabled the Romans to make their finest contributions to Western civilization: first Roman Law, that supreme expression of ancient probity from which Western legal codes derive; and secondly the *Pax Romana*, that century and a half's display of continuously expert and energetically efficient administration initiated by Augustus, which brought stability and peace to an empire covering the whole of Europe as far north as Scotland, the whole Mediterranean area and much of the Near East. The phenomenon was to be unique in world history.

DOMESTIC ARCHITECTURE

Pompeii provides a copious record of an ancient city as a living organism conditioned by and conditioning the daily life of its inhabitants. Nearly all the various types of ancient Roman buildings and all the methods of construction from mud-brick wall and post-and-lintel to concrete vaulting are represented at Pompeii (Herculaneum has been only partially disinterred). A covered market, a warehouse or granary, a triumphal arch, a *comitium* where municipal elections took place, and a *basilica* – the most characteristic building type developed by the Romans, comprising a covered hall with aisles and usually, though not at Pompeii, an apse, and used for the transaction of business and the administration of justice – all stand round the forum, which was the rigidly rectangular, axially planned heart of this as of every other Roman city. There are also three public baths, two *palaestrae* for gymnastic exercises and sports, two theatres, an amphitheatre for gladiatorial combats and other spectacles (the earliest example known), barracks for gladiators, and so on. Remains of similar structures survive elsewhere, of course, scattered over the whole vast area ruled by Rome, and many of them have greater architectural merit. But it is rarely possible to see so clearly as at Pompeii the urban texture, the relationship of public buildings to each other and to private dwellings, built for single families of varying degrees of wealth and social standing, which cover the greater part of the ground within the city walls.

The building history of Pompeii and Herculaneum came to its catastrophic end at the very moment when Rome and the major provincial cities of Italy were in the throes of urban renewal. The single-family house or *domus* was everywhere being torn down and replaced by many-storied tenement blocks or *insulae*, which were needed to accommodate a steadily increasing middle- and lower-class population, the latter flocking to the cities as landowners went over to farming with slaves (imported in quantity as prizes of colonial wars). Simultaneously, the richer families were moving out of the congested areas to live in suburban or country villas. Had the fatal eruption of Vesuvius been delayed for a few decades, it is more than likely that much of Pompeii and Herculaneum would also have consisted of huge regular overcrowded *insulae* uniformly built of concrete faced with brick and stucco, similar to those whose foundations have been found elsewhere, notably at Ostia. Eventually, by the fourth century, almost 90 per cent of the population of Rome was to be housed in *insulae*, built to the maximum legal height of five stories (about 70 feet [20m] high) with communal latrines and other facilities. Some of the larger houses in Pompeii had already been converted into such apartments by AD 79. But the city still contained a wide variety of domestic architecture with the homes of bankers, merchants, tradesmen and artisans in close proximity to inns, brothels, bakeries or evil-smelling dye-works, perhaps reflecting a looser social structure than that which was to follow in later imperial times.

The Pompeiian house was inward-looking with an unimpressive exterior often given over to single-room shops (*tabernae*), which had no connection with the rest of the building (**5,33**). From the street a narrow passage led into the main interior space called the atrium, a courtyard surrounded by small rooms, which were covered with tiled roofing sloping inwards to a rectangular opening. The word atrium is of Etruscan origin and the type of house planned round it seems to have been peculiar to Italy. In the earliest and simplest the owner's bedroom

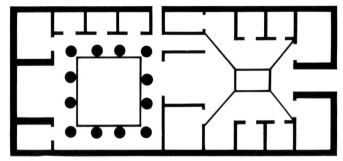

5,33 Plan of a Pompeiian house.

was in the centre of the side opposite the entrance and beyond it lay a small high-walled garden. Later in larger houses the garden was sometimes extended and surrounded by a covered colonnade called a peristyle – a Greek word, recalling its Hellenistic origin.

From this combination of Etruscan and Hellenistic elements a new type of domestic architecture evolved in Italy. Planned with a regard for axial symmetry, unusual in the Hellenistic East, one space flows harmoniously into the next in orderly sequence. From the outside a Pompeiian house is a featureless, solid block; but its interior reveals that preoccupation with the molding of space – also expressed in the illusionistic wall-paintings – which distinguishes Roman from Greek architecture. Contrasts of light and shade were often exploited, as in the house illustrated here, with its dim cool atrium (the roof has been restored so that the original effect can be recaptured) giving on to a sun-drenched peristyle garden, where there were flowering plants, statues and fountains (**5,34**).

Suburban and country villas were sited to take full advantage of prevailing breezes and wide views over land and, sometimes, water, but also to be seen, to make an

5,34 Atrium and peristyle, House of the Silver Wedding, Pompeii, mainly 1st century AD.

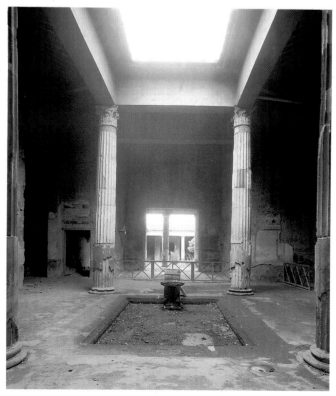

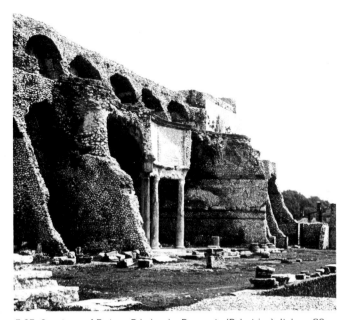

5,35 Sanctuary of Fortuna Primigenia, Praeneste (Palestrina), Italy, c. 80 BC.

5,36 Model of the reconstructed Sanctuary of Fortuna Primigenia. Museo Archeologico Nazionale, Palestrina.

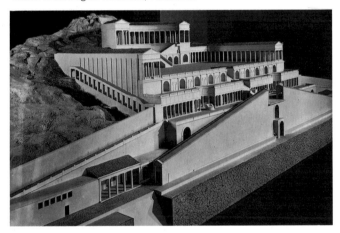

impression of many-columned opulence. A portico was an essential feature; one type of villa resembled a Hellenistic stoa and consisted simply of a single row of rooms behind a long colonnade. Others had more elaborate plans, including that in Tuscany owned by Pliny the Younger (AD 61/2–c. 113), whose description of it in a letter vividly conveys the highly civilized taste for which the architects of such luxurious houses had to cater. Besides dwelling lovingly on its many rooms, interior courtyards, terrace and formal garden, Pliny describes the south-facing colonnade, which caught the full strength of the sun, and such features as the pool beneath his bedroom window, 'a pleasure both to see and hear, with its water falling from a height and foaming white as it strikes the marble'. Outside the formal gardens there were meadows no less 'well worth seeing for natural beauty', he wrote; 'then fields and many more meadows and woods'. His dining-room looked on to a terrace, 'the adjacent meadows and the open country beyond' – a great spreading plain 'ringed round by mountains, their summits crowned by ancient woods of tall trees'. Ornamental gardens had been laid out much earlier in Egypt, but the park merging into the natural landscape seems to have been a Roman invention.

TEMPLES AND PUBLIC WORKS

Although the siting of Roman temples and sanctuaries was determined by religious rather than aesthetic considerations, as in Greece, a heightened sense of the relationship between architecture and landscape is also evident in their design. That dedicated to Fortuna or fate at Praeneste (present-day Palestrina, south-east of Rome) must have been the most impressive by far, with seven wide terraces steeply rising, one above the other, to a theatre framed by a semicircular colonnade and crowned by a round temple (**5,35**). The acropolis at Pergamum (a Roman possession from 133 BC) provided a recent precedent for the use of colonnaded terraces on a rocky site (see p. 184). But whereas the temples and other buildings simply crown the hilltop at Pergamum and are informally related to one another, at Praeneste the whole hillside was transformed into architecture. This molding of space into a unified composition of strict axial symmetry – combined with massive scale and boldness of conception – marks Praeneste as one of the first major works of specifically Roman architecture (**5,36**).

As we have already seen (pp. 168–9), the Etruscans had modified the Doric temple by heightening the base and by doing away with the steps on three of its sides, pushing the cella back at the same time to make way for a deep frontal porch. The Roman temple, like the Roman house, evolved by skilful and inventive blending of Etruscan and later Greek elements. The Maison Carré at Nîmes (Roman Nemausus) in the south of France, which is the finest surviving example, might at first sight be taken for a peripteral temple set on a high Etruscan podium (**5,37**). It is, in fact, a new and typically Roman invention, partly dependent for its effect on illusionism – hence its technical description 'pseudoperipteral' – for the columns along the flanks are not free-standing, as they might seem to be, but engaged. They are purely decorative and have no supporting function. In this way Greek post-and-lintel construction was harmoniously combined with the wall

5,37 Maison Carré, Nîmes, France, 1st century BC.

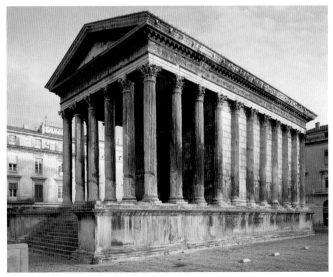

From Jericho to Imperial Rome

GRID PLANNING AND ORGANIC GROWTH

The essential elements of urban design are: boundaries, paths or streets, open spaces, and districts designated for different types of habitation, work or ceremony. Boundaries came first, either natural – an escarpment or river – or artificial, usually a combination of the two. By about 7500 BC, Jericho (Jordan) was surrounded by massive stone walls about 12 feet (3.5m) high, but the dwellings within them were clustered in an unplanned conglomeration, as at Çatal Hüyük (1,18). Paths between approximately rectangular and equal sized plots for housing appear in the fourth millennium at Ur (Iraq). Planning within a regular orthogonal grid of streets, the simplest means of apportioning land for building, was developed in the Indus Valley (India and Pakistan) c. 2,300–1750 BC (2,18) and practised in Egypt (2,41) and China in the second millennium –

later, so far as is known, in America. A grid could be intersected by wider streets separating districts and joined to an area set apart for palaces or temples as at Khorsabad (Iraq) in c. 700 BC (3,25). And the grid remained the basic system of urban design, worldwide, until the late nineteenth century, though the vast majority of cities grew organically without any predetermined planning.

The earliest known attempt to construct a theory of urban design was made by Hippodamus of Miletus (c. 500–440 BC) after whom grid planning is sometimes misleadingly called Hippodamian. According to Aristotle, he devised an ideal city for a population of 10,000 inhabitants divided into three classes (soldiers, artisans and husbandmen) with the site also divided into three areas (sacred, public and private), apparently assuming that each area would

be laid out on a grid. He seems to have been the first to appreciate that a town plan might formally embody, clarify and perpetuate a rational social order. The town of Miletus (Turkey) destroyed by the Persians in 479 BC is said to have been rebuilt on his plan, with three grids on a promontory. The Athenian port of Piraeus, apparently the earliest example of grid planning on the Greek mainland, is also ascribed to him. But his fame derives less from his practice than his ideas, transmitted to posterity by Aristotle and inspiring later projects that combined social engineering with urban design.

Inflexible grid planning could be used only for such new or completely reconstructed towns as mid-fourth century BC Priene (Turkey) (5,23). Where property rights had been established, as in Athens, urban design was inhibited. In fifth-century BC Athens prominent and architecturally notable public buildings were informally related to one another. The agora, the administrative and commercial heart of the city was a rough trapezoid space until it was regularized by the construction of two stoas (financed by King Attalus II of Pergamum). By this time new approaches to urban design had been developed for the royal and sacred areas of Hellenistic capitals, most notably at Pergamum where from 240 BC, under a dynasty of rich, cultivated and ambitious kings, a hilltop site had been exploited to lay out a complex of buildings – temples, palace, library, theatre, agora and stoas – ingeniously grouped for monumental effect (5,19).

The kingdom of Pergamum became a province of the Roman republic in 133 BC. But Rome itself was still a sprawl of timber and mudbrick buildings within walls of rugged local tufa. And so it would have remained if republican moralists had had their way: they prized simplicity, despised the opulence of Hellenistic kingdoms and deplored their autocratic governments. A change was initiated in 53 BC when Julius Caesar had a new

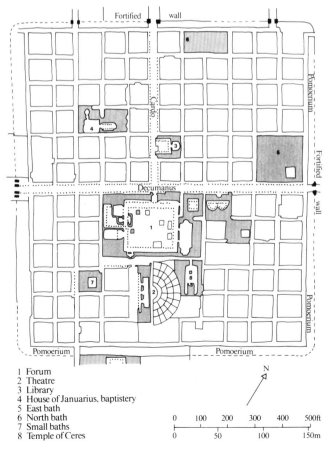

5,38 Plan of Timgad, Algeria, founded c. AD 100.

1 Forum
2 Theatre
3 Library
4 House of Januarius, baptistery
5 East bath
6 North bath
7 Small baths
8 Temple of Ceres

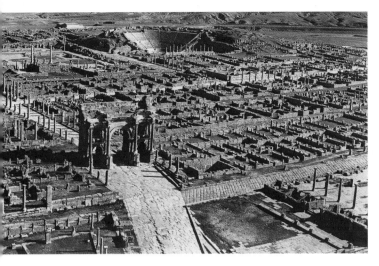

(called the *decumanus*), and the forum, colonnaded and closed to traffic, was sited just off the crossing. The four quarters were subdivided into square blocks and all structures and open spaces were fitted into these areas or their multiples, as may still be seen at Timgad, Algeria, a town founded c. 100 AD (**5,38; 39**). The strict uniformity of this planning was a result and expression of Roman administrative efficiency, while also embodying the equality of all Roman citizens under the emperor. Yet the general effect at Timgad and other cities, notably Pompeii, is of homogeneity rather than monotony. For the public buildings were distributed throughout the city, among the private dwellings, rather than confined to a single district as had formerly been usual. The forum was only one, albeit the most important, of several focal points in the urban plan. From each of the gateways in the walls, visitors passed along colonnaded streets, through triumphal arches and past the entrances to public baths, temples and an amphitheatre or theatre, buildings of different heights creating a varied skyline. But the profusion of Corinthian and Composite columns which gave homogeneity to the urban fabric, was also a ubiquitous reminder of Roman rule, especially on the frontiers where such towns were in striking contrast to the settlements of the indigenous population.

strictly rectangular forum flanked by stoas built near the irregular Forum Romanum which had for centuries been the civic centre of the republic with its Senate housed in a simple brick-built hall. Under his great-nephew Augustus (see p. 186), Rome was transformed from a republican to an imperial capital, both politically and visually, with fine new marble-clad buildings of unprecedented size and magnificence for public use – the Colosseum (5,42; 43), Trajan's Forum with its great market (5,46) and later the Baths of Diocletian and Caracalla (5,72; 73). These great buildings were, however, simply inserted in the urban fabric that had grown up over the centuries. The result was a fortuitous mixture of grandiose public buildings

and plain or nondescript privately owned tenement blocks on narrow streets where the mass of the population lived (5,40).

Only in the provinces where new towns could be founded were Roman urban designers able to develop their ideas, with remarkable results. Indeed, the centralised power and unity of the Roman empire was nowhere more strongly felt. Whether in Italy, north Africa, Palestine, France, the Rhineland or Britain, their settlements were laid out in the same regular manner based on that of a military encampment (or *castrum*) – a square divided into equal quarters by two main streets crossing at right angles in the centre. One ran north-south (called the *cardo*), the other east-west

5,40 Reconstruction model of ancient Rome. Museo della Civiltà Romana, Rome.

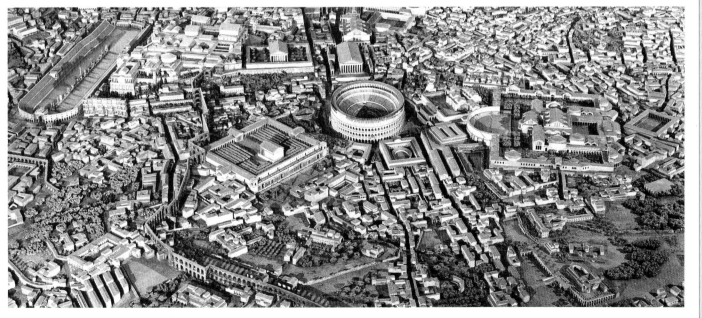

architecture developed by the Romans. So perfect was the join that hardly any variations were introduced, except for increasing refinement of the non-figurative carved ornament, from the late second century BC (Temple of Fortuna Virilis, Rome) until Roman religion itself was suppressed.

In Roman architecture, however, the temple was much less conspicuous than in the architecture of Greece or even of the Hellenistic kingdoms. Temples were not invariably the largest structures in a Roman city. Despite the Romans' love of magnitude, none of the temples they built before the second century AD exceeded in size the largest raised by the Greeks in the fifth and fourth centuries BC. Even so, Cicero questioned the expenditure of public funds on them rather than on utilitarian structures – harbours, aqueducts or some other of 'those works which are of service to the community'. The remark is a complete denial of the belief cherished by all earlier civilizations that no work could be of greater service to the community than a temple to its gods.

Politics played a greater part than religion in the development of Roman architecture. Rome of the early republic had been little more than a conglomeration of villages among the seven hills, rebuilt without plan after it had been sacked by the Gauls in the early fourth century BC. At the beginning of the second century the city itself was still a confused mass of mud-brick buildings divided by narrow winding streets, its forum an irregular space surrounded by both private and public buildings. In about 200 BC, so the historian Livy tells us, visitors from Macedon were shocked by its squalid appearance, for 'it was not yet made beautiful in either its public or its private quarters'. This began only in the first century BC with the greater public works and building programs initiated partly, if not mainly, for propaganda purposes by the succession of ambitious men (notably Sulla and Julius Caesar) who made bids for absolute power, plunging the republic into civil war, and then by Augustus and the early emperors. Julius Caesar planned a complete reorganization of the heart of the city and some new buildings were begun in his time (49–44 BC). But the transformation of Rome into a monumental imperial capital was left to his great-nephew and adopted son Octavius, who in 30 BC restored peace after 14 years of civil war. In 27 BC he was hailed by the Senate as Augustus (a word implying both divine appointment and individual ability) and thus became the first Roman emperor, ruling with undisputed authority until his death at the age of 76 in AD 14.

Augustus carried through the building program initiated by Julius Caesar and in addition gave Rome another new forum, several temples and other imposing buildings (5,40). Public works of a more utilitarian kind – such as a huge new warehouse, aqueducts and sewers – were sponsored by Augustus' right-hand man and, so to speak, political manager Marcus Agrippa, who also built a pantheon (see p. 201), a basilica and the first of the magnificent *thermae* or public baths, which were to be perhaps the most splendid and lavishly equipped of all the great public building types invented by the Romans. Even the poorest citizens could frequent them and enjoy their luxurious

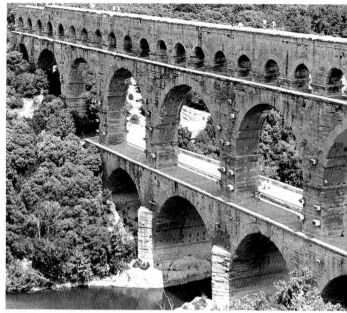

5,41 Pont du Gard, near Nîmes, France, 1st century BC.

'facilities' – cold baths, warm baths, hot baths, steam baths, dressing-rooms, recreation rooms, lecture halls, restaurants, libraries, gymnasiums and gardens.

Towards the end of his life Augustus claimed to have 'found Rome a city of brick and left it a city of marble'. For the Romans, marble was a symbol of magnificence. Vitruvius, who had been employed by Julius Caesar and dedicated his architectural treatise to Augustus, wrote of an early first-century temple in Rome: 'If it had been of marble, so that besides the refinement of art it had possessed the dignity which comes from magnificence and great outlay, it would be reckoned among the first and greatest works of architecture.' Extensive use of marble was made possible by the opening of quarries in the Apuan Alps a few miles inland on the north-west coast of Italy (near present-day Carrara), whence it could be easily transported by sea to Rome or indeed to any part of the empire. Colored types of marble imported from the colonies in Asia Minor, Egypt and north Africa were also used for the first time in Rome. Employed mainly for cladding and decorative purposes, to give a smooth clean surface to buildings constructed of concrete or brick, they transformed the drab, predominantly mud-brick and terracotta face of Rome. Nearly all this marble facing vanished during the Middle Ages and later. The interior of the Colosseum, for instance, was clad throughout in marble, none of which survives. In fact, the only large-scale surviving example is the interior of the Pantheon (see p. 202).

Far more important than marble, however, was concrete. The development of this building material by the Romans and especially their use of it in conjunction with the arch and vault revolutionized architecture. Neither concrete nor the arch and vault were Roman inventions. Numerous ancient Egyptian prototype arches and vaults in brick were available and it might seem rather surprising that the true arch (constructed of wedge-shaped stone voussoirs) was not developed earlier. It first appears in the fifth or fourth century BC. Etruscan arched city gateways, dating from shortly after 300 BC, survive at Perugia and Volterra and a few decades later the Romans were building neatly constructed semicircular arches, for example, the gateways in the city walls at Falerii Novi (present-day Maria di Falleri). The potentialities of arched construction were soon realized and put to use in causeways, bridges and aqueducts, of which none is more impressive than the Pont du Gard in the south of France (5,41), commissioned by Marcus Agrippa to carry water some 30 miles (48km) across the plain and valley of the river Gardon to Nîmes. Built entirely of dressed stone, it is a remarkable feat of engineering by any standards ancient or modern, and has proved astonishingly durable. The graceful proportions of its seemingly light structure are eminently simple, the width of the arches at the top being multiplied six times for the total height, four times for the span of the great central arches, three times for those at either end. Its majestic simplicity is also due partly to the systematized construction methods adopted by the Romans. The Pont du Gard was substantially prefabricated, the huge voussoirs of the arches being fully dressed before erection, and it was to facilitate this that all measurements were made standard and all profiles strictly semicircular. (The voussoirs were laid out on the ground as a preliminary check and lettered and numbered, some of these markings still being visible.)

THE COLOSSEUM AND THE INVENTION OF CONCRETE

The arch became the essential element in Roman architecture, emphasizing the strength and massiveness of the masonry structure as if to symbolize the sustaining power of the empire itself – most obviously in the triumphal arches erected in honour of emperors (see pp. 210–2). Arches enframed by engaged columns and entablatures – used from early in the first century BC – were a dominant motif in the imperial period. The exterior of the great Flavian amphitheatre, known since the eighth century as the Colosseum, is entirely composed of them in arcades which integrate the units of the design by rhythmic

5,42 Colosseum, Rome, c. AD 70–82. Aerial view.

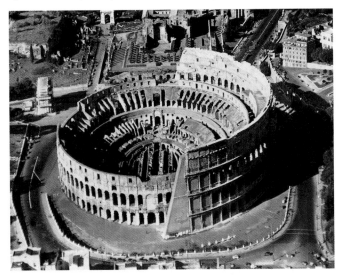

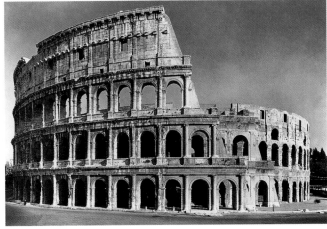

5,43 Colosseum. Exterior view.

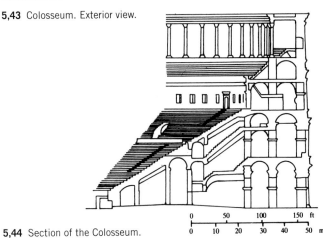

5,44 Section of the Colosseum.

horizontal and vertical repetition (5,42; 43). The orders follow the ascending sequence established by the Romans for multi-story buildings – Doric-Ionic-Corinthian. (The sequence is purely aesthetic, the Doric being visually the heaviest and strongest and the Corinthian the lightest.) Although several such permanent arenas for gladiatorial combats and other spectacles had been built elsewhere, somewhat surprisingly this was the first in the city of Rome, where 'games' had previously been held in the forum or in temporary structures. With a seating capacity estimated between 45,000 and 55,000, the rapid entrance–exit problem for filling and emptying the vast seating space was formidable. It was brilliantly solved by an ingenious arrangement of stairways and corridors all leading down to the continuous ground-floor arched openings (5,44). The Colosseum was begun as a shrewd bid for popularity by Vespasian, the first emperor of the Flavian family, who came to power in AD 69 as the result of a mass uprising against Nero, the last of the dynasty established by Augustus. To fulfil its purpose it had to be built quickly: the enormous structure, which is on an elliptical plan measuring 615 by 510 feet (188 by 155m) externally and 159 feet (48m) high, was completed in no more than a decade. Various materials were used: concrete for the 25-foot-deep (7.5m) foundations, travertine (a fine local limestone lighter in weight and less strong than marble, easily cut when first quarried, but hardening with exposure to air) for the framework of load-bearing piers, tufa and brick-faced concrete for radial walls between the piers, travertine for the exposed dry-jointed stonework held together by metal clamps (most of which have gone) and marble (of which no trace remains today) for the interior. A giant awning to protect spectators from the sun was supported on wooden poles projecting inwards from the top and manipulated by ropes tied to bollards on the pavement surrounding the building.

The Colosseum is an outstanding work of Roman engineering as well as of architecture. In both design and structure it was, however, conservative. Concrete was used simply for foundations and walls, as it had been in many earlier buildings, including, for example, the sanctuary at Praeneste. Roman concrete (*opus caementicum*) was a combination of mortar and pieces of aggregate (*caementa*) laid in courses – unlike modern concrete, which can be mixed and poured. Its unique strength and durability derived from the binding agent, a mortar made of lime and volcanic sand, first found at Pozzuoli near Naples and thus called *pozzolano*, used as early as the third century BC. Exposed walls of this concrete were usually faced with another material, an irregular patchwork or neatly squared pattern of stone and later, under the empire, brickwork. The full potentialities of the material were, however, only gradually discovered. In early examples the cement dried out quickly so that each layer formed a single horizontal band like an enormous stone slab. But the development, about the time of Augustus, of a slow-drying mortar, probably made with volcanic sand found near Rome, produced a concrete core that hardened into an inert homogeneous mass. This revolutionized architecture for, when combined with the arch and vault, it enabled the Romans to cover, without any interior support, spaces far larger and of far greater flexibility of form than had ever been possible before. Ancient Egyptian, Mesopotamian and Greek architecture had been essentially an art of composition in mass. Space was simply what was left over or left between the solids. This negative conception was now replaced by that of an architecture of space. A building was conceived as a shell molding space into whatever shape the architect or his patron desired.

The earliest building in which the possibilities of using concrete for this new 'spatial' conception of architecture are known to have been explored is the Golden House designed for the Emperor Nero (AD 54–68) by an architect named Severus. Of the parts that remain, the most interesting is a group of rooms which, although divested of all their surface decorations apart from some traces of delicate stucco-work, reveal a truly revolutionary originality (**5,45**). An octagonal space covered by a rather shallow dome is surrounded on five sides by rectangular vaulted rooms, one of which terminated in an ornamental cascade of water. Lighting, unusually bright and even for a Roman interior, was provided by a circular opening or *oculus* in the centre of the dome and, very ingeniously, by clerestory windows high up on the walls of the radial rooms. The inner surface of the dome was probably decorated with mosaics, which must have given

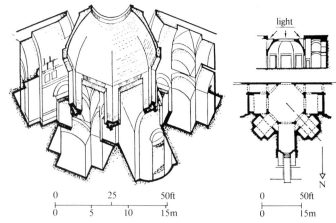

5,45 Nero's Golden House, Rome. Octagonal hall: axonometric view from below, section and plan.

an almost magically insubstantial effect. And the views through the wide square openings of the octagon from one room to another and on to the garden to the south may well have seemed to realize architectural prospects of the type that Pompeiian painters had feigned. For here the walls really had been broken and bent to permit free spatial flow and to give the appearance of an unending series of opulent chambers. From no single point would it have been possible to grasp and resolve the visual complexities and ambiguities of this highly sophisticated interior.

The surviving ruins are no more than a small part of the Golden House, in which, Nero remarked, he could 'at last begin to live like a human being'. His biographer Suetonius (AD 69–140) described the main banqueting hall, which 'constantly revolved, day and night, like the heavens'. The remark is tantalizingly brief, but it is usually assumed that the ceiling – not the room itself – revolved and was constructed in the form of a vast wooden dome decorated with stars or astral symbols, a kind of planetarium beneath which the emperor entertained his guests at the very centre of the cosmos, as it were. The idea of placing such a cosmic canopy over a ruler with pretensions to universal authority probably derived from the royal tents and canopies of Achaemenid Persia. It would certainly have appealed to Nero; and it may well lie behind the domes that became such a prominent feature of imperial Roman architecture. The development of the concrete dome may even have been stimulated by the symbolism of the textile or wooden cosmic canopies of the East.

The Emperor Domitian (AD 81–96), whose palace on the Palatine Hill in Rome exhibits similar flexibility of planning, used the new technology to provide an appropriate setting for his imperial rule. Trajan (AD 98–117), who ruled for the 20 years during which the Roman empire reached the peak of its power and its greatest extent, was more concerned with public works. The most notable were public baths, of which unfortunately little survives, and a new commercial quarter known as Trajan's Market, created by cutting away the slope of the Quirinal Hill. Trajan's Market is one of the most fascinating of all surviving Roman structures, at once logical and complex, utilitarian but possessing an austere monumental beauty. One hundred and fifty or more shops and

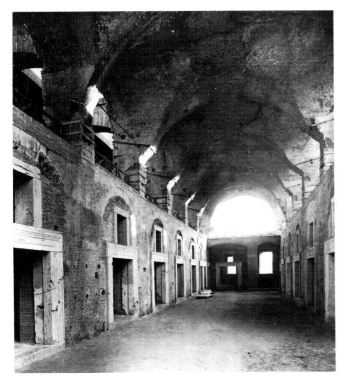

5,46 *Above* Trajan's Market,
Rome, c. AD 98–117.

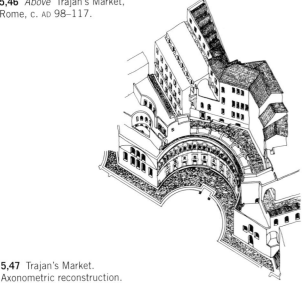

5,47 Trajan's Market.
Axonometric reconstruction.

stairways. (Concrete was made compulsory for floors and stairways after the great fire of AD 64.) Great ingenuity was applied to the planning. The architect's aim was eminently practical: to provide the maximum space, well lit and aired, for the various activities connected with buying and selling within a limited area on an extremely awkward sloping site. The result is a rare achievement of volumetric organization, an autonomous structure of interlocking curved corridors, straight streets and passages, and vaulted rooms of different sizes (5,47). Nowhere else – except in the Pantheon – can the characteristically Roman genius for molding space be better experienced.

THE PANTHEON

The Pantheon was built under Trajan's successor, the Emperor Hadrian (AD 117–38), on the site of an earlier temple, which had been of an entirely different design but similarly dedicated to all the gods by Marcus Agrippa (see p. 198), whose name is boldly recorded on the façade (5,48; 49). It consists of two parts, a traditional rectangular temple-front portico with massive granite columns, and

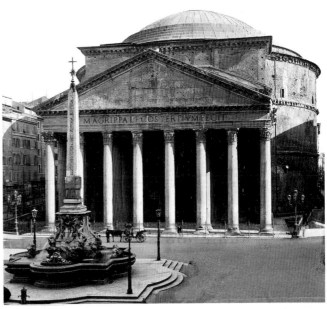

5,48 Pantheon, Rome, c. AD 118–28.

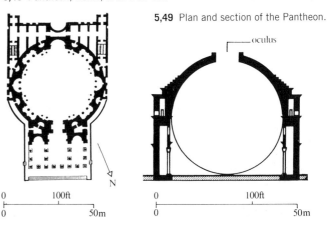

5,49 Plan and section of the Pantheon.

offices on three different levels connected by streets and steps are combined with a great covered market hall (5,46). Built for a city most of whose inhabitants were engaged exclusively in working for, buying from and selling to one another, it had a social importance hard to exaggerate. The concave main façade was articulated with pilasters, but the rest of the exterior and the interiors were severely simple, of brick-faced concrete with travertine surrounds to rectangular doors and windows. A better idea can be obtained from them than from the numerous but much less well preserved remains at Ostia and elsewhere of the architectural form and appearance of Roman multi-story construction. At street level there are shops with small windows above giving light and air to timber-floored mezzanines or garrets approached from within the shops by timber ladders. The main horizontal divisions, however, are concrete barrel vaults between the party walls, and access to the upper stories is by concrete

an enormous domed rotunda of a size made possible by the development of slow-drying concrete. The awkwardness of the join between these two parts would have been much less evident originally, when the building was not free-standing as it is today, but was approached on axis through a colonnaded forecourt, which screened all but the portico. The ground level was much lower also, so that five wide marble steps had to be mounted to reach floor level. Yet the contrast – or unresolved conflict – between the rectangularity of the portico and the circularity of the rotunda, between the exterior architecture of mass and the interior architecture of space, must have been even sharper because largely concealed, and the visual excitement and feeling of sudden elation experienced on passing through the door must have been even more overwhelming. One passes from a world of hard confining angular forms into one of spherical infinity, which seems almost to have been created by the column of light pouring through the circular eye or *oculus* of the dome and slowly, yet perceptibly, moving round the building with the diurnal motion of the earth (**5,50**).

This exhilarating space is composed, as Vitruvius had recommended for a rotunda, of a drum the height of its own radius and a hemispherical dome above – diagrammatically a sphere half enclosed in a cylinder, the total height of 144 feet (44m) equal to the dome's diameter. The effect is not, however, that of geometrical solids. The lower part of the drum wall is pierced by niches which suggest continuity of space beyond; the columns

5,50 Pantheon, interior, dome.

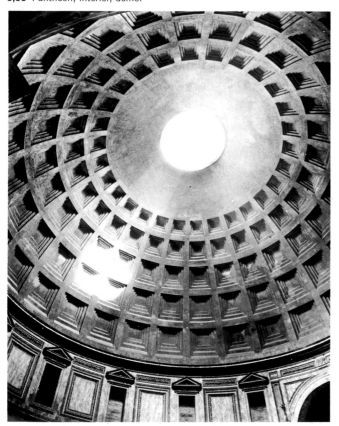

screening them have lost even the appearance of being structural supports: they seem more like ropes tying down the dome, which floats above. The surface of the dome is broken by five rings of coffers very ingeniously molded to give the illusion that they are rectangular and that, although they diminish in area, all are of equal depth. To achieve this effect, account had to be taken of the dome's curvature – which presented a tricky geometrical problem, for no straight line can be drawn on it – as well as of the shadows cast by light from above and of the spectator's angle of vision from the ground. Originally, these coffers probably had gilded moldings around their edges and enclosed gilt bronze rosettes.

Minor changes were made to the interior in about 609, when, as the reigning Pope Boniface IV put it, 'the pagan filth was removed' and the temple converted into a Christian church – to which, of course, its extraordinary and unique preservation is due. In the 1740s the attic zone (i.e. the band of wall immediately beneath the dome), which had fallen into disrepair, was insensitively stuccoed and provided with overlarge false windows. Otherwise the interior is substantially intact. The various types of marble, mainly imported from the eastern Mediterranean and used for the pattern of squares and circles on the pavement, for the columns and the sheathing of the walls – white veined with blue and purple (*pavonazzo*), yellowish-orange (*giallo antico*), porphyry (see Glossary) and so on – still reflect and color the light that fills the whole building.

That the Pantheon should eventually have been made into a place of worship for monotheistic Christians was not wholly inappropriate. It was built at a moment of religious speculation and exploration, when faith in traditional beliefs was giving way increasingly to Eastern mystery cults, and its design marks a break with the traditional form of Roman temple, which, as we have seen, harked back to Etruscan and Greek prototypes (p. 195). Less than a century after its completion the historian Dio Cassius (c. 155–c. 235) pondered its significance, remarking that it was called the Pantheon 'perhaps because it received among the images which decorate it the statues of many deities, including Mars and Venus; but my opinion of the name is that, because of its vaulted roof, it resembles the heavens'. He appreciated that the images of individual gods were of less importance than the building itself, within which the supreme god, so often associated with the sun, was immanent, visible yet intangible in the light streaming through the *oculus* and moving over the surface of the dome. It was, in fact, not so much the temple of a specific religious cult as an attempt to express the very idea of religion, of the relationship between the seen and the unseen, between mortals and the inscrutable powers beyond their ken. Domes had previously been decorated to symbolize the heavens, but no single building embodied this idea more effectively and on a grander scale than the Pantheon. Nor did any exert greater influence on subsequent developments in the religious architecture of the West. Domes and half-domes as symbols of heaven had become essential features of Christian churches long before the Pantheon itself was converted into one.

ROMAN SCULPTURE

The Pantheon is quintessentially Roman. But the Emperor Hadrian, to whom its design has sometimes been attributed, displayed more eclectic tastes in his enormous, rambling imperial residence outside Rome – Hadrian's Villa near Tivoli. A philhellene who spoke Greek better than Latin and preferred Athens to Rome, Hadrian furnished the villa throughout with Greek statues. Several hundred, perhaps as many as 1,000, survive in fragments now scattered among the museums of the world. They are mainly copies or variants of Classical Greek or Hellenistic figures or groups. The only original works seem to have been portraits of Hadrian himself and his favourite Antinous, a youth from Asia Minor who was mysteriously drowned in the Nile in AD 130 and promptly numbered among the gods. Images of Antinous, set up all over the empire, were, however, more often than not pastiches in which earlier statues of Hermes, Dionysus or other gods were combined with heads portraying the youth's sultry and often rather sulky good looks (**5,51**).

In his obsession with Greek sculpture Hadrian followed a long and well-established tradition. Romans had begun to collect Greek statues before the end of the third century BC, and after Greece was absorbed into the Roman empire as the province of Achaia in 146 BC the flow of Greek sculptures westwards was continuous. The sanctuary at Delphi alone is said to have been robbed of some 500 statues. Even so, the demand in Rome far exceeded

5,51 *Antinous*, AD 130–8. Marble, 3ft 4ins (1.02m) high. Villa Albani, Rome.

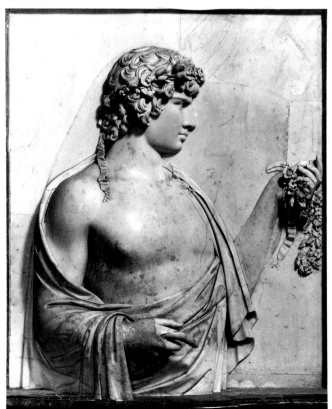

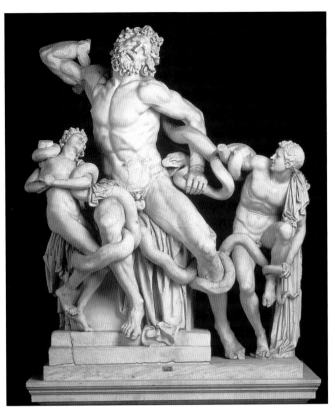

5,52 Hagesandrus, Polydorus and Athenodorus, *Laocoön and his Two Sons*, 1st century AD. Marble, 8ft (2.44m) high. Vatican Museums, Rome.

the supply. In letter after letter Cicero, for example, implored a friend who was living in Athens to procure sculpture for him. He was building a country house near present-day Frascati, a few miles outside Rome, and needed some sculpture to adorn it. A great deal of sculpture was bought in this way as 'furniture pieces' and was doubtless produced specifically for this market – hence the proliferation of copies and imitations and their usually rather poor quality. (It is on these shaky foundations, it should be remembered, that much of our knowledge of Classical Greek sculpture rests.) They were mostly produced in Greece – either in Athens itself, the Greek islands or the Greek cities on the coast of Asia Minor – or by immigrant Greek artists in Rome. Sometimes these sculptors seem to have worked from casts with the aid of pointing apparatus (see Glossary). But they had no respect for either medium or scale. Bronzes were reproduced in marble, with the addition of unsightly supports as a result, and scale was adjusted arbitrarily to suit the decorative demands of the purchasers. Statues were even copied in reverse to make up pairs. A mid-fourth-century BC statue by Skopas, which, Pliny tells us, was 'worshipped with extremely sacred ceremonies at Samothrace', was duplicated in this way to fill balancing niches in a Roman house of the imperial period. There could hardly be a more telling instance of the transformation of a Greek devotional image into a luxury ornament.

It is seldom known how faithfully a marble of the imperial period reproduces an earlier original (the caryatids from Hadrian's Villa and from the Forum of Augustus are the only Roman copies that can be compared with the still surviving originals), and there is reason to believe that some were essays in earlier styles rather than copies – including two of the most famous of all, the *Apollo Belvedere* (5,5) and the *Laocoön* (**5,52**). The latter derives stylistically from the relief of similarly straining muscular figures with tortured faces on the frieze of the *Altar of Zeus* from Pergamum (5,17) and was for long regarded as a copy after a lost work of that period. That it is an original work of the first century AD is strongly suggested by the recent discovery (at Sperlonga, south of Rome) of very similar groups signed by the three sculptors to whom Pliny attributed the *Laocoön*, and almost certainly carved expressly for a grotto used as a banqueting hall by the Emperor Tiberius (AD 14–37). The incident represented by the *Laocoön* is not recorded in Greek literature in just this form; the earliest known source for it is the greatest of all Latin poems, Virgil's patriotically Roman *Aeneid* (written c. 27–20 BC), where Laocoön appears as the Trojan priest who warned his fellow countrymen against admitting the wooden horse of the Greeks into their city. While he was sacrificing a bull to Poseidon, Virgil relates, two serpents swam out of the sea, coiled round him and his sons and killed them. As the Romans believed themselves to be descended from the Trojans, the heroic suffering of Laocoön had special significance for them. The priest and his sons are at once figures from the mythical prehistory of Rome and symbols of human fortitude in a struggle against malign, incomprehensible supernatural forces. In turning to Hellenistic art for inspiration, however, the three sculptors, who came from Rhodes, introduced a declamatory sensationalism, both technical and emotional, which ill accords with the dignity, restraint and gravity of the *Aeneid*.

If Roman cultural dependence on Greece was evident even in a major original work like the *Laocoön*, which stood in the imperial palace when Pliny saw it, it became quite blatant in the practice of making full-length portrait statues by the simple expedient of adding a portrait head to a body copied direct from a Greek original. The bodies were produced independently and could be bought, as it were, from stock. A variety of poses and types and sizes were available to choose from, each with a socket in the neck so that a portrait head could be attached. How prevalent the practice was – and how indifferent the Romans were to its demeaning implications – is shown by its use for prominent imperial portraits, though sometimes, it is true, with such latitude that the resulting image has the force of an original conception. The statue of Augustus, which originally stood outside the imperial villa at Primaporta near Rome, is the best known of these (**5,55**). For it the famous *Doryphorus* (4,35), an accepted exemplar of ideal male proportions, was treated more freely than usual, almost, in fact, as if it were a tailor's dummy. Not only the portrait head but a Roman general's costume was added as well, including the cuirass crisply carved with allegorical figures probably alluding to the

diplomatic victory over the Parthians in 20 BC. Adjustments were also made to the pose, notably by raising the right arm to a speaking gesture. By these means a highly idealized statue of an anonymous nude athlete was transformed into an image of imperial power personified by Augustus, a Greek model into what seems to be a characteristically Roman work of propagandist art – though it may well have been carved by a sculptor of Greek origin.

TOWARDS A DEFINITION OF ROMAN ART

This statue raises the peculiar and peculiarly complex problem of how to define Roman art. What criteria should be applied? – geographical? chronological? ethnic? stylistic? None is very satisfactory. It is sometimes suggested that the Romans leaned so heavily on the figurative arts of earlier times that their own has no definable identity – that they produced no body of works in the visual arts (except in architecture) comparable with their literature. Roman literature, though most of it was written by men who were not strictly speaking Roman, can be defined linguistically. Moreover, the Latin language was itself the creation and vehicle of a culture to so marked a degree that its use alone conferred distinctive 'Latin' or 'Roman' qualities, even on imitations and translations from the Greek (e.g. the plays of Terence, a slave of Libyan stock). A comparable unifying visual language is lacking in Roman art, especially in the imperial period, when Rome was the capital of an ethnically mixed empire, including Greece and the eastern Mediterranean, where Hellenistic traditions survived almost intact. The term Roman may, of course, be used for all works of art produced in territory under Roman rule, but such a geographical definition would necessarily embrace very diverse and stylistically heterogeneous works. Attempts at an ethnic definition founder on our ignorance of the artists and their origins. In the fluid conditions prevailing in so vast a multi-racial empire the identification of any supposedly national tendencies (Italic or Greek) must be very speculative. The *Pax Romana* permitted great mobility to artists and their works: statues carved in Greece and the eastern Mediterranean were shipped to Rome, imperial portraits were diffused from Rome to the furthest corners of the empire. Nor can any consistent process of artistic development be traced, though there were many and important changes in direction during these centuries. Political history provides no more than a series of convenient date brackets, of dubious stylistic significance, for periods named after the emperors. Markedly different styles, ranging from a crude realism to a refined Greek Classicism, were practised simultaneously or recurrently revived, usually to accord with subject-matter and to satisfy ideas of appropriateness or 'decorum'.

Yet certain characteristics or qualities commonly associated with ancient Rome can be recognized in major works of art and in many others as well, as the mention of so essentially Roman a concept as that of 'decorum' already suggests. A funerary portrait of an upper-class couple of the late republican period, for example,

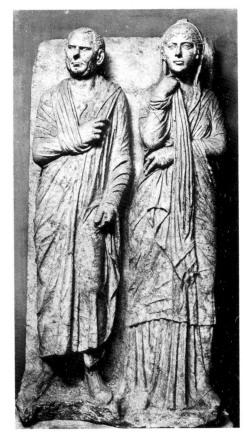

5,53 Roman husband and wife, 1st century BC. Marble, 6ft ⅞in (1.85m) high. Museo Capitolino, Rome.

5,54 *Below Ara Pacis Augustae*, 13–9 BC. Marble, outer wall c. 34ft 5ins × 38ft × 23ft (10.5 × 11.6 × 7m). Rome.

epitomizes the straightforward republican virtues so eloquently extolled by Cicero (**5,53**). The woman with her distinctly superior expression recalls, no doubt intentionally, statues of Pudicitia, personifying female modesty. Her grim unsmiling husband is every inch a Roman, the embodiment of dignity, moral rectitude and gravity. Many other portraits of the same period are of elderly men with equally stern, heavily wrinkled, businesslike countenances, quite unassuming in their ordinariness and plainness. None could be described as amiable. Yet the marks of age may not have been thought unsightly. To Romans, especially of the republic, fullness of years implied success in life. The patrician became not simply an old man but an honoured elder, as well as a *pater familias*, the sovereign ruler of his unmarried daughters, sons, grandsons and their wives, and the sole legal owner of all his family's property.

Figures on the *Ara Pacis Augustae* – the altar of Augustan peace (**5,54**) – are equally stern and grave and no less realistic, though carved with greater refinement and set in a structure of complex allegory. The *Ara Pacis* was set up to mark the return of Augustus to Rome in 13 BC, after a lengthy absence in the western provinces, and also to celebrate the peace that followed the civil wars, which had convulsed the dying republic. Its form – an altar on a podium surrounded by a rectangular walled enclosure – is Greek, probably derived from the fifth-century BC Altar of Pity in the Athenian agora. On the outer walls, above

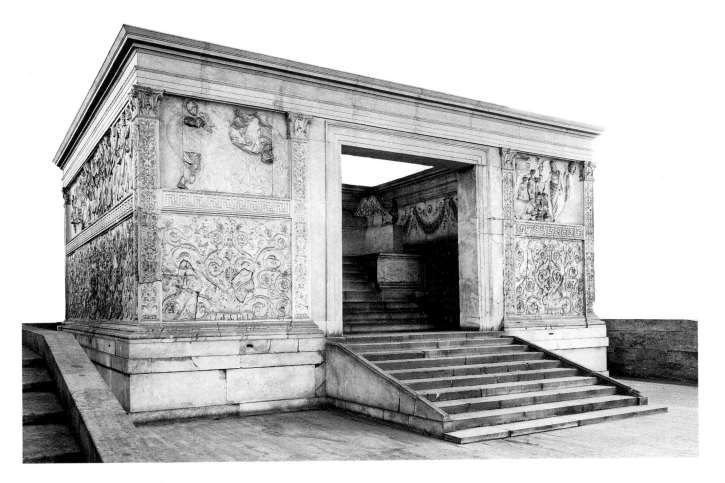

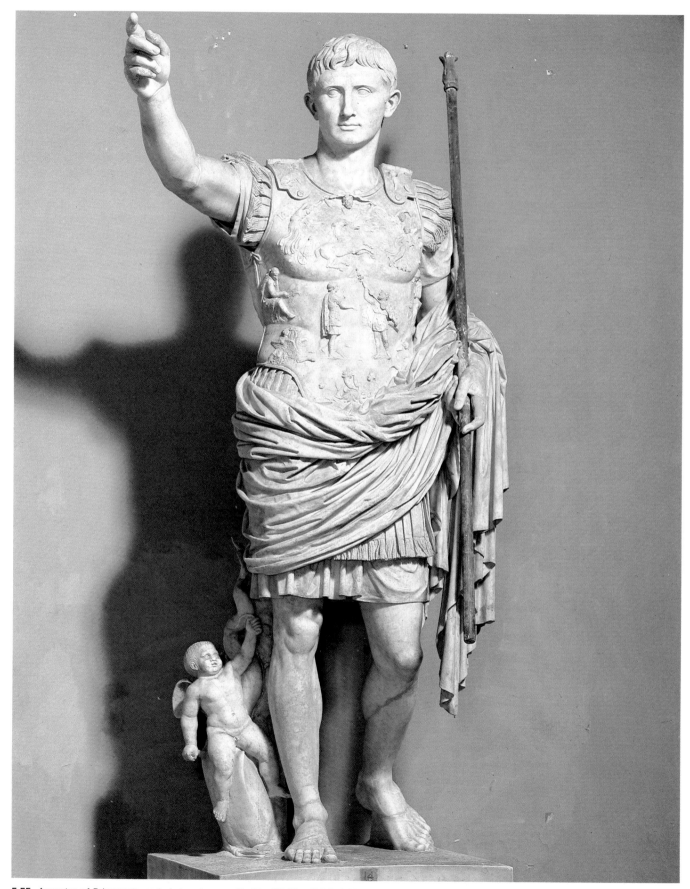

5.55 *Augustus of Primaporta*, early 1st century AD. Marble, 6ft 8ins (2.03m) high. Vatican Museums, Rome.

exquisitely chiselled panels of foliage ornament, there are figurative reliefs of mythological subjects (Tellus, the Roman earth goddess, and Aeneas, the legendary founder of Rome and ancestor of Augustus) and two long processions, one of senators, the other of Augustus's family (5,56). These processional reliefs differ as much from those on the Parthenon (4,31) as from those at Persepolis (3,38), being neither of idealized youths nor of expressionless, regimented types all marching in step. Informally grouped, they appear, from their glances, to be in quiet, civilized conversation with each other and they are all recognizably portraits. Augustus (unfortunately damaged) leads as high priest and *pater familias* of his own family and, by implication, of the entire Roman empire. The prominent man in the centre of our illustration is probably Agrippa, his son-in-law and right-hand man. Unlike earlier processional reliefs, those on the *Ara Pacis* record and commemorate a specific moment in time, the dedication of the altar itself. And this emphasis on actuality reinforces the cool realism of the carving and hence the truth of the propagandistic claims it makes for the beneficence of the new Augustan régime.

If the message of the *Ara Pacis* is emphatically Roman, the visual language in which it is expressed remains Hellenistic. The same can be said of a cameo known as the *Gemma Augustea*, whose carver almost certainly came from the Hellenistic East, where the exacting technique of working semi-precious stones to exploit their natural veins of color had been developed into a fine art by the second century BC (5,57). Romans greatly prized such virtuoso feats of craftsmanship – technical accomplishment was, indeed, the only artistic quality of which they wrote. But the *Gemma Augustea* is more than merely decorative. On the upper register Augustus is shown deified with the personification of Oikoumene (the whole inhabited earth)

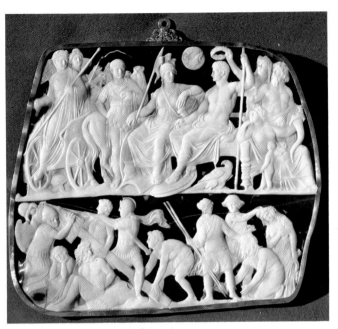

5,57 *Gemma Augustea*, early 1st century AD. Onyx, 7¹/₂ × 9ins (19 × 23cm). Kunsthistorisches Museum, Vienna.

placing a crown on his head and the goddess Roma enthroned beside him; the youthful figure descending from a chariot on the far left is probably Tiberius, who succeeded him as emperor. Below, Roman soldiers are setting up a trophy of captured arms after a victory over barbarians, four of whom are shown as prisoners awaiting their fate. Such a mingling of allegorical and historical figures, abstract ideas and hard facts, is a recurrent feature in the official art of the empire.

It was their preoccupation with actuality, above all, that enabled Roman artists to enlarge their range, as can be seen very clearly in portraiture. A high degree of verisimilitude had been attained by Etruscan and Italic sculptors (4,74) and there are equally vivid and penetrating characterizations in Hellenistic portraiture – sometimes extremely matter-of-fact in a 'warts-and-all' style (5,13). But the finest Roman portraits surpass them in unflattering directness. A wide cross-section of society is represented, from craftsmen and tradesmen to government officials and courtiers, whose features, unique even in their ordinariness, speak for single individuals caught at a single moment.

The portrait bust was the most notable Roman contribution to sculptural form. Until now portraits had been either full-length statues, detached heads or herms (square pillars terminating in heads originally of Hermes but later of famous men). The portrait bust, comprising head, neck and a portion of the torso, was introduced by the Romans as an offshoot of their practice, dating back to very early republican times, of making wax masks of their ancestors. This was a jealously guarded privilege of the patrician class – indeed it was restricted by law to them alone. The wax portraits were piously preserved in the atria of aristocratic homes, to be brought out for family funerals (see p. 208). Most surviving busts are, however, in marble or bronze.

5,56 Frieze of the *Ara Pacis Augustae*, detail. About 5ft 3ins (1.6m) high.

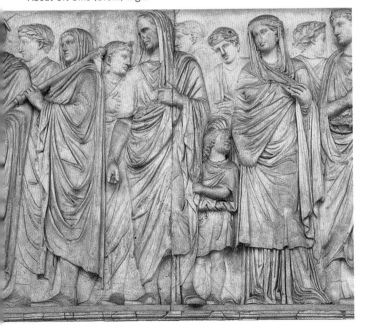

Family Piety

THE ROMAN PORTRAIT BUST

A life-size statue of an ancient Roman patrician carrying two portrait heads of his ancestors (**5,58**) illustrates a feature of Roman republican life that was to have notable repercussions in sculpture. Family feeling among the ancient Romans was so strong as to amount almost to a form of ancestor worship. However, the right to make portraits of ancestors was restricted by law to patricians only. They had realistic wax heads made from death-masks and displayed them at family funerals and other public ceremonies. The two being carried by the patrician in our illustration are recognizably relations with a marked family likeness to one another, that in his right hand dating from about 50–40 BC and that in his left hand from about 20–15 BC. (The patrician's own head is missing and was recently replaced by an unrelated one of about 40 BC.) Normally such heads of ancestors were kept in a special recess or shrine which had a central position in patrician homes. There they were also associated with the *lares* (spirits of dead ancestors) and *penates* (household gods) around which the ancient Roman household revolved. As such they also had a place, in spirit, at the hearth on which a fire was kept burning permanently in their honour, and likewise at the family table which was kept furnished for them with a salt-cellar and fresh fruit at every season.

None of the original wax heads has survived, presumably because of the impermanence of the material. The earliest account of them dates from the mid-second century BC. This is by a Greek writer, Polybios (202–120 BC), who had been taken to Rome in about 168 BC as a hostage. How long the custom had been in existence before this time is unknown. It may have gone back to the Etruscans, who placed terracotta heads of the deceased on their cinerary urns. Polybios recounts that when a prominent Roman died he was taken, in the

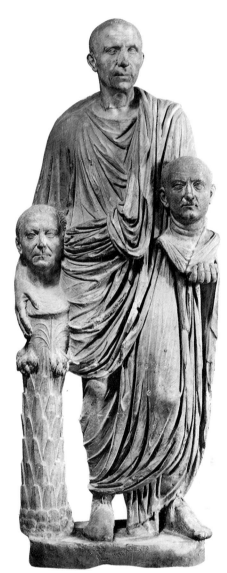

5,58 *Patrician carrying two portrait heads of ancestors*, c. AD 15. Marble, life-size. Museo Capitolino, Rome.

course of his funeral procession, to the forum where a son or other relative gave an oration on his virtues; afterwards, having buried him and performed the funeral rites, the relative returned to the family home and placed his portrait in the atrium or main hall where it was enclosed in a wooden aedicular shrine or miniature temple. 'The portrait is a mask', Polybios writes, 'wrought with the utmost

attention being paid to preserving a likeness in regard both to its shape and its contour.' These masks were later displayed at public sacrifices, and when a prominent member of the family died they were carried in the funeral procession by those who most resembled the ancestors in size and build and could impersonate them by wearing the masks. To further the illusion, ancestral togas and other robes and official insignia were also worn by them. 'One could not easily find a sight finer than this for a young man who was in love with fame and goodness', Polybios writes. 'Is there anyone who would not be edified by seeing these portraits of men who were renowned for their excellence and by having them present as if they were living and breathing? Is there any sight which would be more ennobling than this?'

Two hundred years later this ancestral custom may not have been extinct but it had become a relic of the past, of that noble and austere republican past which was recalled with nostalgia by such writers as Pliny the Elder (see pp. 148, 187). He remarked, apropos the lack of appreciation of portraiture in his own day, that things were different in times gone by when patrician houses were filled with family portraits. 'Wax impressions of the face were set out on separate chests, so that they might serve as portraits to be carried in family funeral processions, and thus when anyone died the entire roll of his ancestors, all who ever existed, was present.' Genealogical lines of descent were drawn to form family trees, with portraits and not heraldic devices as became usual in later periods. The family archive rooms were filled with scrolls and other records commemorating the family and if the house was sold the purchaser was not allowed by law to remove certain family relics of the original owner.

The connection between this

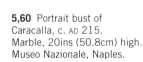

aristocratic family tradition and portrait sculpture need not be stressed. Strikingly realistic portrait heads had been made in Etruscan and Hellenistic times (4,74; 5,13). But the *genre* was to be developed by the Romans – both republican and imperial – into one of their most significant and innovative contributions to the visual arts. An arresting marble head of an unknown citizen of the Roman republic (**5,59**) would seem indeed to have been made direct from an ancestor mask in wax, for there was originally no back to the head. The uncompromising realism of this stern portrait of a quite homely man in late middle age is in keeping with the high standards of honesty and unpretentious simplicity maintained in all walks of life during the republic, as we have seen (5,53). His cheeks are slashed by deep folds of leathery skin, his thin lips are set in a slightly scornful expression of cautious doubt, his high, protruding cheekbones and deeply sunken temples frame half-closed eyes below a gently creased forehead and balding head of close-cropped hair.

Such unflinching honesty gave way during the early imperial period to more subtle but still candid character studies, often in the form of busts rather than just heads. The bust, as an artistic and expressive form, was introduced and perhaps invented at this time. That of a high-born Roman lady is one of the most notable (5,61). Her eminently polite if ever so slightly haughty character is vividly caught in the way she holds her head with its heavy and elaborate hairdo and by the whole poise of head and shoulders. This could not have been conveyed by a head alone; it was made possible only by exploiting the possibilities of the bust form. The development of the bust form was due partly to its use in the imperial cult, when hundreds of busts of the emperor were distributed all over the empire (see p. 210). As a result a remarkable series of imperial busts survives, culminating artistically in that of Caracalla, a monster of brutality who ruled from AD 211 to 217 (**5,60**). To portray this coarse and cruel man the sculptor made subtle use of the bust form to suggest abrupt and forceful movement. Draperies sweep vigorously to the left, emphasizing the emperor's arrogant turn of the head and his cold indifference to the spectator.

5,59 Portrait head, late 1st century BC. Stone, 10⁴/₅ins (27.4cm) high. Museo di Antichità, Turin.

5,60 Portrait bust of Caracalla, c. AD 215. Marble, 20ins (50.8cm) high. Museo Nazionale, Naples.

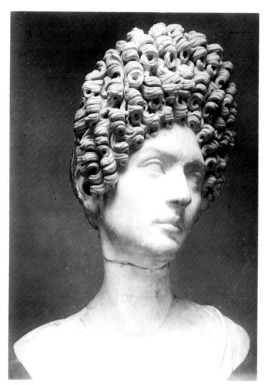

5,61 Portrait bust of a Roman lady, c. AD 90.
Marble, life-size. Museo Capitolino, Rome.

One of the finest is of an unknown but clearly very fashionable and high-ranking lady of the court (**5,61**). From this period onwards the form was, as it were, canonized by its prominent use in the imperial cult. Busts of the emperors were made in large numbers for distribution throughout the empire and were set up in public places to be looked on with religious awe. Every Roman citizen had to burn incense in front of the emperor's bust in token of his loyalty and allegiance. It was partly because of their refusal to do this that the persecution of the early Christians began.

There can be little doubt that behind these customs lay some residue of the ancient belief that the likeness preserves the spirit – a belief already encountered in ancient Egypt and Etruria and, of course, the more lifelike the portrait, the more effective the icon. However, the imperial image transmitted throughout the Roman world in busts and statues and, of course, on coins had to be both a recognizable likeness and a symbol of the head of state. Thus, Augustus was always portrayed as a man in the prime of life with a serious open expression, large frank eyes and a serene, unfurrowed brow, which makes him seem almost boyish. His is the unageing face of the man who made himself master of the Roman world when no more than 33 years old. He is shown in his various roles, as military commander (*Imperator*), first citizen of Rome (*Princeps*) and chief priest (*Pontifex Maximus*) – never as an absolute ruler, as were the Hellenistic kings. The image may originally have been intended to mark the new epoch of peace and prosperity he brought, but it persisted unchanged throughout his long reign. His short-back-and-

sides hairstyle set a model for later imperial portraits, including those of the bald Caligula. Only Nero broke away to have himself portrayed with a charioteer's or gladiator's fringe – 'he did not take the least trouble to look as an emperor should', the historian Suetonius caustically remarked.

Hadrian was the first Roman emperor to make a radical break with tradition and have himself portrayed with neatly curled hair and a beard in Greek fashion. He may have done this partly to indicate his Hellenism, but he must also have been influenced by Roman theories of physiognomy, which gave great importance to hair and hairstyles as an indication of character. A rich profusion of hair on the head and face marks the Antonine emperors, who succeeded Hadrian, notably the Stoic philosopher emperor Marcus Aurelius (161–80), of whom the most famous portrait is that formerly on the Capitoline Hill in Rome (**5,62**), now in the adjacent Museo Capitolino. It is the only survivor of more than 20 bronze equestrian figures of various emperors and generals to be seen in the city at the end of the imperial period. The naturalism evident in both the rider and the horse, with its bulging eyes and loose skin creased at the neck, is such that one is hardly aware of the completely artificial discrepancy in scale between them. An impression of calm authority and magnanimity is powerfully conveyed – an impression that may well have been even more compelling originally, when the figure of a captive barbarian chieftain (now lost) cowered beneath the horse's raised hoof. (Recent restoration has revealed that the horse and rider were cast separately; they may well have been intended originally for different monuments, for the rider is not in scale with the horse.)

Similar messages were spelt out by many other works of art. The most frequently used vehicle for visual propaganda was the triumphal arch – another Roman invention – half sculpture, half architecture. The origin of these structures, which were set up in all parts of the empire, is surprisingly obscure. Monumental entrances to cities, temple precincts and palaces had, of course, been embellished with sculpture by the Hittites, Assyrians, Babylonians and Mycenaans. In Egypt, as we have seen (p. 63), entrances to temples sometimes bore hieroglyphic inscriptions and carved reliefs referring to the pharaohs who commissioned them. Etruscans, too, built monumental gateways to their cities, of which one survives from the second century BC at Perugia. But the Roman triumphal arch is essentially different. It is free-standing and purely ornamental. Its only function was to carry and display visual propaganda. It might also serve as a monumental entrance to a forum or a city; but it was not necessarily the entrance to anything. Usually it stood across a thoroughfare – one type, the *quadrifrons* arch, spanned a crossroad and was designed as part of a regulated traffic flow, to be passed through, not round.

The earliest surviving triumphal arches date from the time of Augustus. The first recorded was built in Rome at the beginning of the second century BC with spoils from the war against the Carthaginians. Their precise

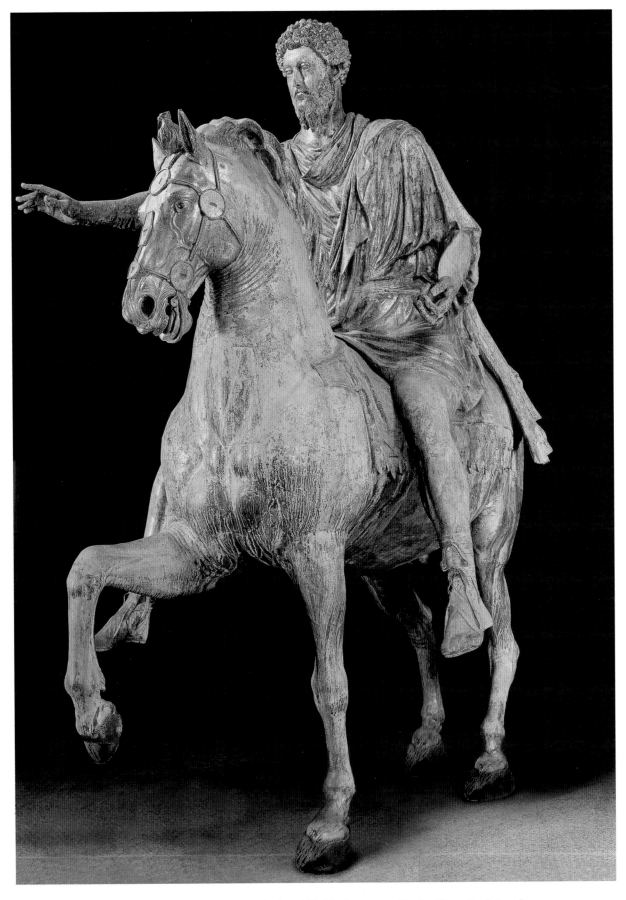

5,62 Equestrian statue of Marcus Aurelius (after restoration), AD 161–80. Bronze, over-life-size. Museo Capitolino, Rome.

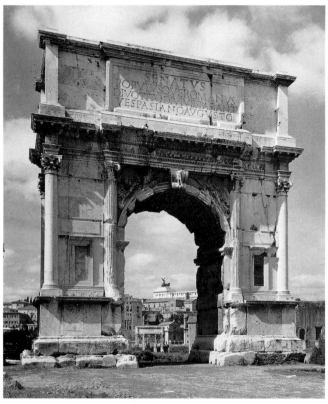

5,63 Arch of Titus, Rome, AD 81, restored and partly rebuilt 1818–24.

5,64 Spoils from the temple in Jerusalem, from the Arch of Titus, Rome. Marble relief, about 7ft 10ins (2.39m) high.

connection with the triumphal processions with which victorious generals were honoured is unknown, but the bronze groups that originally crowned them were of figures riding in chariots drawn by two or four horses, as in a procession. Coins show such a group above the arch erected in the Forum Romanum in 19 BC to celebrate Augustus's purely diplomatic victory over the Parthians – that seems to have set the pattern for subsequent imperial arches: a rectangular block with a round-headed opening framed by pilasters and entablature with a large panel for an inscription above.

The Arch of Titus in Rome is one of the finest examples, built of concrete faced with honey-colored marble from Mount Pentelicus in Greece (**5,63**). Its columns are of the Composite order, combining Corinthian and Ionic elements, invented by Augustan architects. Winged figures of Victory, descended from those of Greece, hover in the spandrels. But the Roman preoccupation with actuality asserts itself in the reliefs on either side of the passageway. These represent the triumph that Titus shared with his father Vespasian in AD 71, when, to celebrate the suppression of a Jewish revolt, treasures looted from the temple in Jerusalem were paraded through Rome (**5,64**). Even in their damaged state these reliefs convey an astonishingly vivid illusion of space and movement – the men and horses eternally accompany whoever passes through the arch. Titus had died (AD 81) before the work was completed, and his apotheosis is shown in the centre of the vault, borne up to heaven on the back of an eagle.

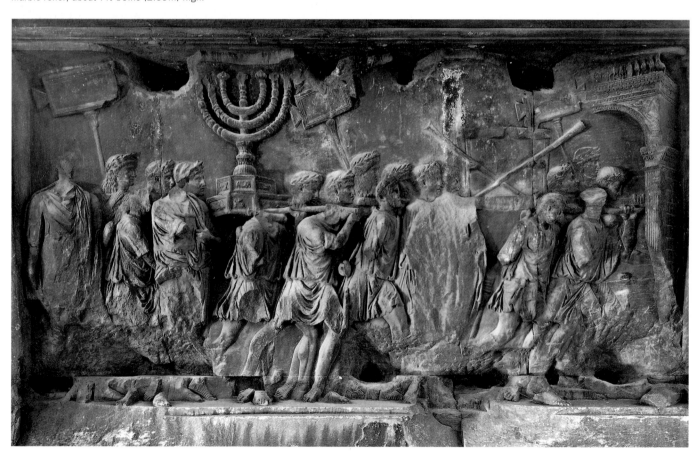

In the attic an inscription in very finely cut, originally gilded letters reads: 'The Roman Senate and People to Deified Titus, Vespasian Augustus, son of Deified Vespasian'. Romans placed enormous importance on such monumental inscriptions. They were the first to discover their artistic possibilities. Clear and simple lettering, in which the form of every letter and the equally important spacing between them was made to conform to the laws of architectural structure, thereby enhancing the authority and dignity of the words, was one of the greatest Roman inventions. It was certainly the Romans' most influential and lasting contribution to the arts, for it has never been excelled and remains the basis of all our lettering, including that in which this book is printed (but see also p. 333). In its boldness, clarity and compactness, in its total rejection of any kind of decorative flourish, it perfectly reflects the Roman sense of dignified restraint and disciplined order. Most ancient Greek inscriptions are quite formless in comparison.

If triumphal arches were conceived as historical statements, so, too, were the tall commemorative columns set up in Rome – another and even more peculiar Roman invention than the triumphal arch. The first was Trajan's Column (**5,65**), entirely covered by a marble band of figurative carving winding up its shaft and originally topped by a gilded statue of the emperor (replaced in 1588 by a statue of St Peter). It commemorates his campaigns in Dacia (present-day Romania) in AD 101 and 105–6, the main events of which are depicted in chronological sequence from bottom to top. As the column originally stood between two libraries founded by Trajan, it has been suggested that the cylindrical helix of the carving was inspired by the scrolls on which all books were then written. To read this figurative history from end to end, however, is not as simple a matter as unrolling a papyrus or parchment scroll. The reader must walk round the column no less than 23 times with eyes straining ever further upwards! The scale increases slightly towards the top, but the upper registers are hard to see and impossible to appreciate and must always have been so, even when the figures were picked out in bright colors and gilding. Evidently, the artist's concern was with a very generalized conception of posterity.

The entire strip of carving, more than 600 feet (183m) long if it could be unfurled and including some 2,500 figures, was composed as a continuous narrative, a manner of visual story-telling which had first appeared in Assyria and later in Egypt and on the upper frieze of the *Altar of Zeus* at Pergamum. There are 150 episodes, each merging into the next without any vertical break to interrupt the flow of the composition and the sequence of events – save for an allegory of history marking the interval between the two campaigns. Trajan's victory over the Dacians is thus presented as an irresistible historical process, but one rendered less in the style of a dry chronicle than in that of an epic poem with much colorful detail. The many different scenes of warfare could, however, be accommodated and represented legibly only by renouncing the spatial logic of such earlier reliefs as those on the *Ara*

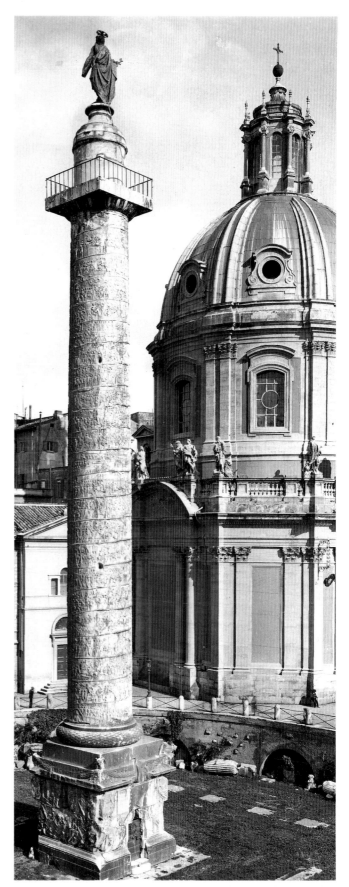

5,65 Trajan's Column, Rome, AD 113.

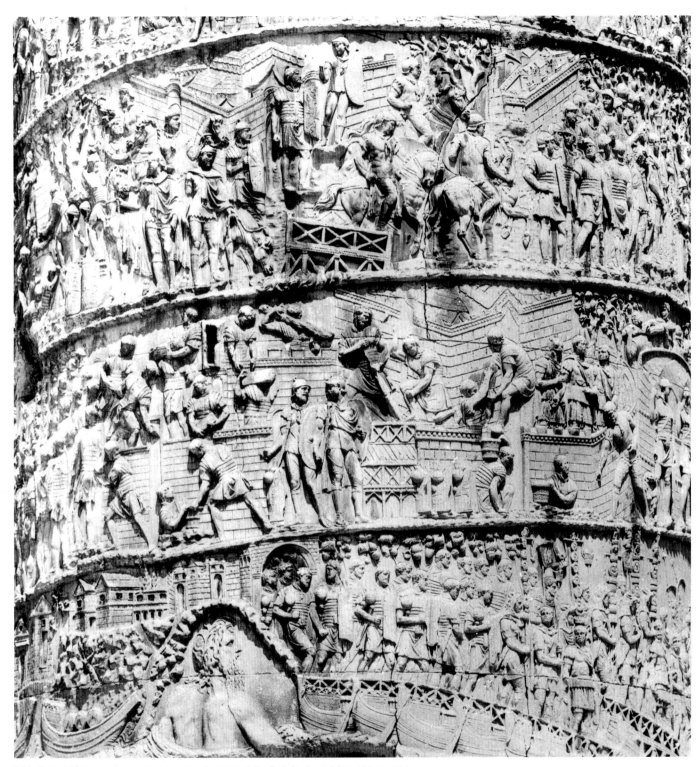

5,66 Trajan's Column, Rome, lower bands of spiral reliefs. Reliefs about 36ins (91cm) high.

Pacis (5,56) and on the Arch of Titus (5,64). On Trajan's Column the ground is tilted and space is rendered schematically almost as on a map; realistic scale is similarly abandoned so that distant figures stand above but are no smaller than those in the foreground. Men are larger than the horses they ride, the boats in which they cross the Danube and even the citadels they build and storm (**5,66**).

Narrative relief was further developed on a similar column set up some 65 years later to commemorate the victories of Marcus Aurelius over the Germans and other barbarian tribes on the north-eastern frontiers of the empire (**5,67**). Its designer – for it must, like Trajan's Column, have been conceived by a single mind, even if it was executed by several hands – attained greater legibility by reducing the number of scenes and figures in them and

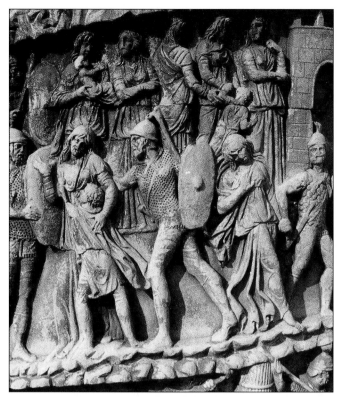

5,67 Captive women and children, relief on the Column of Marcus Aurelius, Rome, c. AD 181.

by cutting away the background more deeply to give higher relief. Stronger emphasis is placed on the emperor, easily distinguished by his central position in every scene in which he appears and also by the frontal pose, which had by this date come to be reserved for gods and incipiently divine rulers (as yet the emperors were not deified before they died). Other figures are vividly characterized, with ruthless determination on the faces of the Roman soldiers, terror on those of the barbarians, who are being butchered or herded off to slavery. The forms seem to have been brusquely hacked out. In the process of carving, too, drills were more extensively and obviously used than before, leaving dark pits and channels which play as important a part in the composition as highlighted surfaces. Voids were, in fact, used pictorially to suggest substances as well as space – a technique known as 'negative modelling', much exploited in later Roman sculpture.

The carvings on the Column of Marcus Aurelius have a harsh realism which sometimes recalls the unflattering portraits of the republican period (5,53) and even Etruscan tomb effigies. A native Italic tradition of sculpture had, perhaps, begun to reassert itself. The column signals the coming renunciation of Greek and Hellenistic ideals with their emphasis on logical clarity, physical beauty and elegant urbanity. It was erected at the close of the golden age of the Antonines and the *Pax Romana*. Yet intimations of the hieratic, schematized and often illogical art that emerged in the subsequent period, reflecting the aspirations and fears of a new era, are already felt in this last monumental expression of Roman imperial power.

LATE ANTIQUE ART

A large carving on a rock-face at Naksh-i-Rustam in Iran is a kind of 'barbarian' reply to such pieces of Roman propaganda as the Columns of Trajan and Marcus Aurelius (5,68). It shows the Sassanian king Shapur I triumphing over two Roman emperors, who had vainly fought against him – Philip the Arabian (244–9), who had been obliged to buy Shapur off with money, kneels in homage, and Valerian (253–60), who ended his days in captivity, is forcibly held by the hand. Lest there be any mistake about the meaning of this and other reliefs of the same subject (one at Nishapur in Iran includes the Emperor Gordian III lying dead beneath the hoofs of Shapur's horse), Shapur had trilingual inscriptions carved nearby, giving an account of the war significantly different from (and perhaps more accurate than) those by Roman historians. The narrative technique, by which three distinct events – with 16 years between the first and last – are condensed into a single image, derives from an ancient tradition going back to the palette of Narmer. And yet the carving, with its suggestion of spatial depth, albeit shallow, and its sense of harmonious human proportions, clearly owes a debt to Roman sculpture, whose influence, by this date, could be felt far beyond the frontiers of the empire – as far as India, as we shall see.

Cracks had begun to appear in the fabric of the Roman empire before the death of Marcus Aurelius in AD 180. With the benefit of hindsight we can see that the three-centuries-long process of Rome's declining power had already begun, but whether there was any immediate reflection of it in the visual arts is questionable. There is certainly no hint of any lack of confidence or sense of ebbing authority in the architecture of the late second and third centuries, either in Rome or the provinces. Many of

5,68 Triumph of Shapur I, Naksh-i-Rustam, Iran, late 3rd century AD.

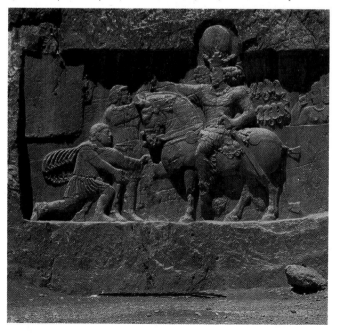

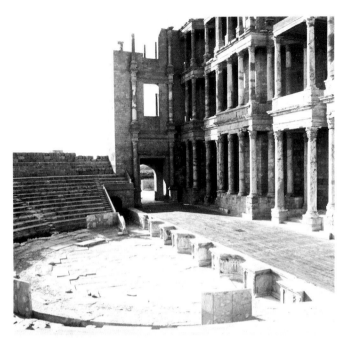

5,69 Theatre (largely restored), Sabratha, Libya, late 2nd century AD.

flanked portico of the propylaea, giving access to the effectively constricted space of a hexagonal court, from which the worshippers entered a wide colonnaded court-yard in front of the temple (5,71). Magnitude was further enhanced by richness, the dramatic management of space by spectacular elaboration of surfaces. In the interior of the nearby temple of Bacchus, which is better preserved, Corinthian columns alternate with pedimented and arched niches, somewhat oppressively compounding the columnar architecture of Greece with the wall architecture of Rome (5,70; 71). Concrete, the great liberating invention of Roman engineers and architects, was seldom used in the eastern provinces of the empire. Columns continued to reign supreme there – literally thousands of

the largest and, originally, most richly ornamented of all Roman buildings date from this period. The theatre at Sabratha on the coast of Tripolitania (present-day Libya), for instance, still gives an overwhelming impression of the magnificence of a prosperous, but not very large, provincial city, not even a provincial capital (5,69). It also demonstrates how the logical and straightforward Greek language of architecture had been elaborated by the Romans into a richly articulated vocabulary for decorative display. On the *scaenae frons* or permanent stage set, Corinthian columns of various types of marble, some plain-shafted, others fluted, a few with spiral fluting, are used without any structural function, apart from that of supporting entablatures to carry yet more columns. Advancing and receding, they provide an openwork screen in front of the great sustaining wall, originally marble-clad, which is itself hollowed out into three semi-circular apses.

Similarly opulent buildings with grossly inflated decorations rose up all over the vast empire, but especially in the eastern Mediterranean – in Egypt, Syria and Asia Minor – where Hellenistic architectural forms were reorganized according to Roman ideals of axial symmetry and logical sequence. Individual buildings, temples, basilicas, public baths and long colonnaded streets at Baalbek and Palmyra have far closer affinities with Pergamum than with Rome, although the way in which they are deployed is Roman in its formal monumentality. At Baalbek the huge peripteral temple of Jupiter – the Near Eastern storm god Ba'al had been equated with the presiding deity of the Romans – set on a massive 44-foot-high (13m) podium, was begun in the mid-first century AD and was provided some 200 years later with a daunting system of approaches, which made it appear still larger. A flight of steps about 100 yards (90m) wide led up to the tower-

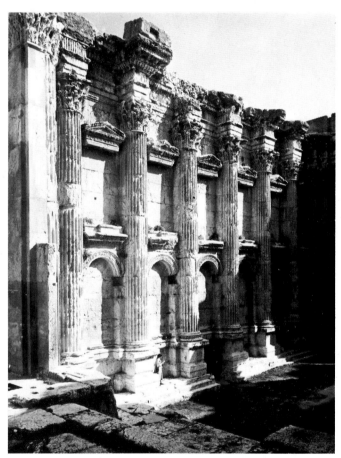

5,70 Temple of Bacchus, mid-2nd century AD. Baalbek, Lebanon.

5,71 Plan of temples of Jupiter and Bacchus, Baalbek.

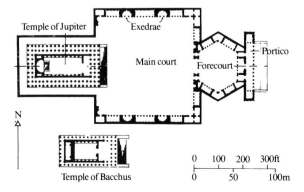

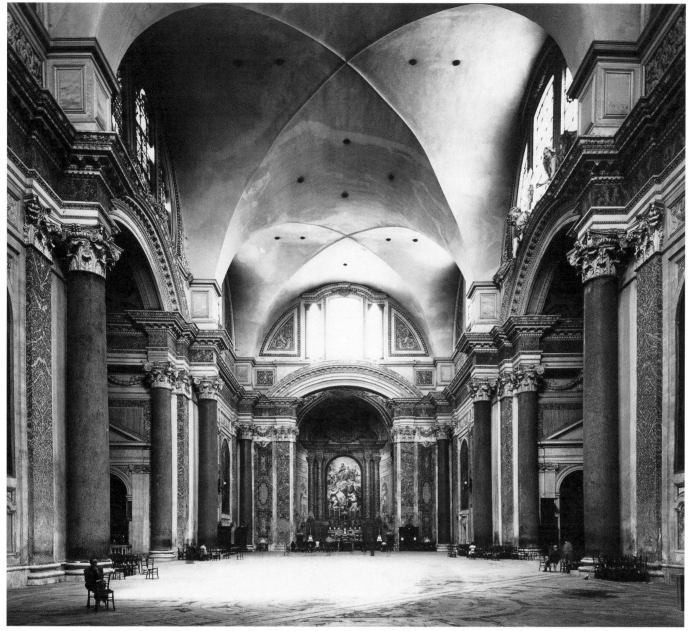

5,72 *Frigidarium* of the Baths of Diocletian, Rome, c. AD 298–305. (Converted by Michelangelo and others into the church of S Maria degli Angeli.)

them at Palmyra, where they still stand like sentinels of a rearguard in the desert.

Although the centre of gravity, both politically and economically, had begun to shift towards the East, the emperors continued to promote their most lavish building projects in Rome itself. The Baths of Caracalla (AD 212–16), for example, dwarfed all earlier *thermae*. The main building alone covered more than 5 acres (2 hectares) within a 50-acre (20-hectare) enclosure. Decorations were of unprecedented lavishness. There were numerous free-standing statues, some appropriately colossal – the 10-foot-high (3m) *Farnese Hercules* being one of them (now Museo Nazionale, Naples). Floors were paved with black and white marble in both figurative and geometrical designs, walls veneered with colored marble,

vaults lined with painted stucco or mosaics. Within a tight symmetrical plan the architect ingeniously integrated rooms of all the different shapes and sizes made possible by the development of concrete construction – rooms covered by barrel vaults, groin vaults, domes and half-domes (**5,73**). Even among the ruins of the concrete core stripped bare of its marble cladding and carved enrichments, it is still just possible to experience some of its spatial effects, to glimpse views from one enormous enclosed space into another and to sense the contrasts in cubic volume, which must have been hardly less exhilarating and relaxing than the differences in temperature between the lofty rectangular *frigidarium* (cold room), the much lower and narrow *tepidarium* (warm room) and the circular domed *caldarium* (hot room).

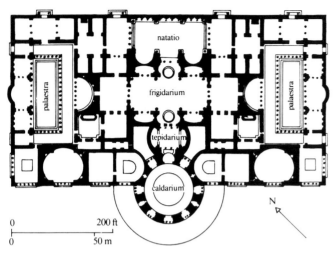

5,73 Plan of the Baths of Caracalla, Rome, AD 212–16.

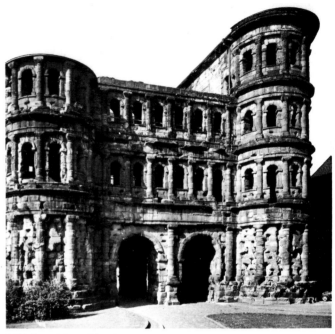

5,75 Porta Nigra, Trier, Germany, early 4th century AD.

A better impression of the grandiose monumentality of the *thermae* may be gained from the *frigidarium* of the later, larger (nearly double the size), but similarly planned Baths of Diocletian (**5,72**). The proportions of this vast hall were spoiled by raising the floor some 7 feet (2m) after it was converted into a church; the wall and ceiling decorations of marble and mosaic, which originally reflected and colored the light pouring through the high windows, were also largely replaced by paint and plaster; and the great openings which afforded vistas of magnificence into adjacent rooms were closed. But the great vault spanning an area of some 200 feet by 80 feet (60 by 24m) remains: three bays of equal size visually upheld by 50-foot-high (15m) monolithic columns of Egyptian granite. It rests, in fact, on eight huge concrete piers. Like the Pantheon and the similar and equally massive Basilica of Maxentius completed by Constantine (306–13), the last great Roman building in Rome (**5,74**), it powerfully displays not merely engineering skill but unquestioning self-confidence in the Roman's ability to shape and organize his environment, in Roman power to order the world. And, indeed, the Baths

5,74 Basilica of Maxentius, Rome, AD 307–12, completed by Constantine after 312.

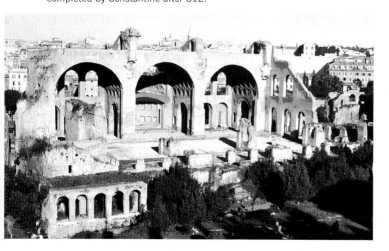

of Diocletian were built partly to demonstrate that a strong-minded man had restored imperial authority after a period of near-anarchy.

In the half-century between the assassination of the last of the Severans in 235 and the advent of Diocletian in 284, no fewer than 21 men had borne the title of emperor; less than three years was the average duration of a reign. They were no longer elected by the senate, but proclaimed by the army, usually some provincial army of barbarian troops. Indeed, they were often barbarians themselves. None had the time, let alone the taste or resources, to indulge in artistic patronage. Instability within the empire was accompanied by repeated attacks from without. Significantly, the most notable architectural undertaking of these years was a 10-mile-long (16km) fortified wall round the city of Rome itself, built under Aurelian (270–5) after barbarians from the north had invaded Italy and penetrated as far as the Po valley. The Roman empire had been put on the defensive. Fortifications, especially city gates, were none the less designed to overawe as well as to repel assailants. The Porta Nigra at Trier (ancient Augusta Treverorum) – the city in western Germany that was for a while the administrative capital of the empire – is the best preserved survivor (**5,75**).

Verisimilitude in portraiture and narrative clarity in relief carving had been the prime aims of Roman sculptors – or the demands of their patrons – ever since republican times. But in the third century emphasis began to shift from outward appearances to inner thoughts and feelings, from the body to the soul and from actions to reactions. On sarcophagi the pagan gods and their votaries – uninhibited devotees of Bacchus revelling in the pleasures of the flesh (**5,76**) – give way to more intellectual, more spiritually dignified, sometimes nervously introspective

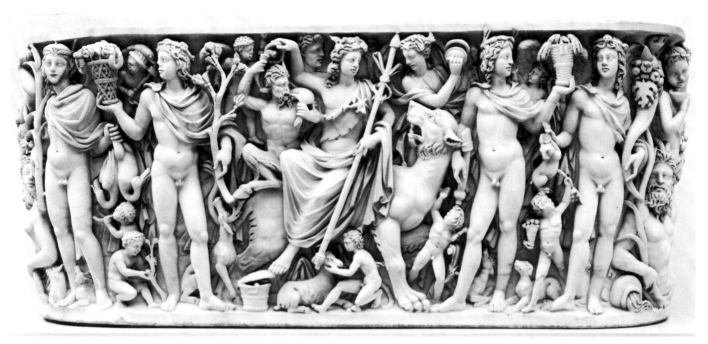

5,76 *Seasons Sarcophagus*, C. AD 220–30. Marble, 35½ins (90cm) high. Metropolitan Museum of Art, New York (Joseph Pulitzer Bequest, 1955).

5,77 Sarcophagus from Acilia, C. AD 250. Marble, about 5ft (1.52m) high. Museo Nazionale Romano, Rome.

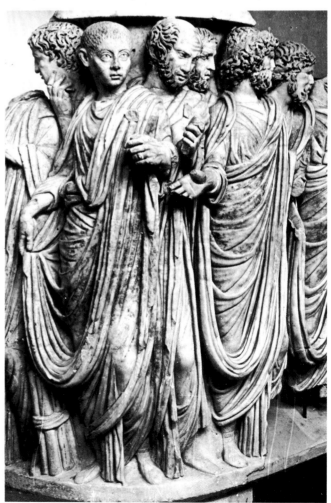

figures. Pagan myths (of Orpheus and Eurydice or Alcestis, for example) and such images as that of Aion (personifying the cycle of cosmic time) are drawn on to symbolize the passage from life to death and the translation of the soul, sometimes even suggesting, it might also seem, the concept of eternity. Others, with figures of philosophers or Muses draped and holding scrolls, symbolize a virtuous, disinterested life, which rises beyond the world to a higher realm of values. In this way educated Romans sought to evade oblivion by being remembered as devotees of philosophy or poetry, and perhaps comforted themselves with the thought of an afterlife with lofty spirits who had cultivated the undying truths of the mind. One of the finest examples was probably made for Gordian II, emperor for no more than 22 days in AD 238 (**5,77**). A delicate youth with a poignant expression of anxiety on his large-eyed, beardless face – perhaps Gordian III, who succeeded at the age of 13 and was murdered six years later – is surrounded by older men who look like philosophers, though they may be senators. One points towards him but they all turn their heads away, sunk in their own thoughts and suggesting the utter loneliness of individuals confronting death. Bodies are swathed in voluminous togas, creating a slow rhythmical pattern of folds, behind which it is difficult to distinguish one from another; only the pensive heads are differentiated, only their incorporeal thoughts seem to matter. We have moved into a world as far away from that of the *Ara Pacis*, where each figure was a self-confident physical presence, engaged in a public, religious ritual (5,56), as from that of republican tomb effigies, who stare at us with such hard-headed self-assurance in their own materialistic values (5,53).

Amid the disasters afflicting the empire in the third century, the more thoughtful Romans averted their minds from harsh mundane realities in order to contemplate the purer realms of thought. Increasing numbers of converts were drawn either to Neoplatonism or to Christianity. Plotinus (204–70), the founder of Neoplatonism, was the last great philosopher of the ancient world. A Greek-speaking native of Upper Egypt, he studied in Alexandria under the same teacher as the Christian theologian Origen (c. 185–c. 254), joined an expedition of Gordian III against the Persians in the hope of learning something of Oriental thought, and in about 245 settled in Rome, where he expounded a mystical philosophy to a circle that included the emperor Gallienus (260–8). His dialec-

tical method and many of his ideas derived from Plato and Aristotle, but he showed no interest whatever in their political theories or in Aristotle's scientific writings. He was exclusively concerned with fundamentals, with the source of all existence and values, which he identified as 'the One' and 'the Good'. All modes of being, material and mental, temporal and eternal, were, according to Plotinus, an expansion or 'overflow' of this immaterial and impersonal force, of which beauty also was an emanation. From these premises he originated a new aesthetic.

Plotinus rejected the then current definition of beauty as 'proportional correspondence of parts to each other and to the whole coupled with pleasing color', since this implied that only measurable compounds and no

5,78 Reliefs from the Arch of Constantine, Rome. Medallions AD 117–38, frieze early 4th century AD. Marble, frieze about 3ft 4ins (1.02m) high.

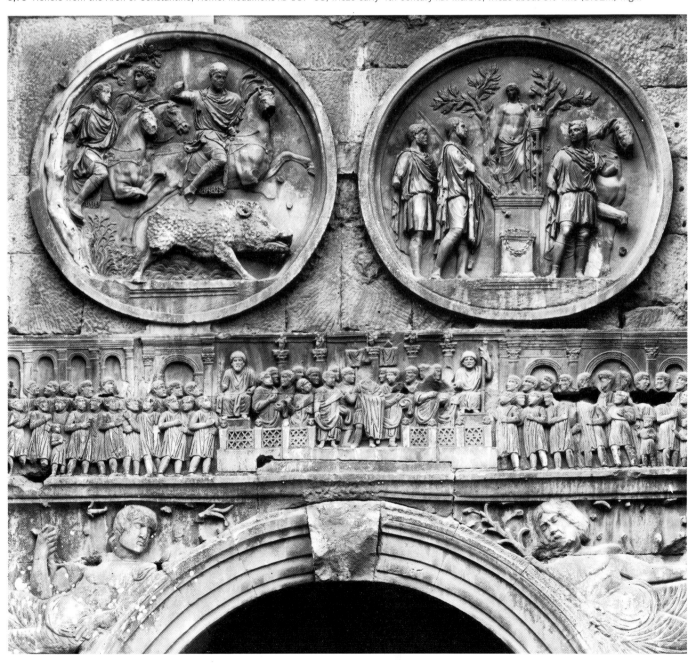

incommensurable single entities (sunlight, for instance) could be beautiful. In his view progression from unity to plurality involved a decline from the perfect to the imperfect. He also denied that art was necessarily limited to imitation of the visible, material world.

> *When someone looks down upon the arts because they are concerned with imitating nature, it must first be replied that also the things of nature, too, imitate other things; then you must know that artists do not simply reproduce the visible, but they go back to the principles in which nature itself had found its origin; and further, that they on their part achieve and add much, whenever something is missing [for perfection], for they are in possession of beauty. Phidias produced his Zeus according to nothing visible, but he made him such as Zeus himself would appear should he wish to reveal himself to our eyes.*
>
> (Enneads, V,8,1, tr. E. Panofsky)

Thus the artistic 'Idea' acquired a completely new importance and lost the rigidity of Plato's conception of it. The Idea beheld by the mind became the living 'vision' of the artist. This did not, however, lead Plotinus to revalue the visual arts – rather the reverse. For, he argued, the artist's vision or idea of beauty, imparted from 'the One' to the artist's soul, could never be more than imperfectly expressed in material which was inherently ugly and evil. Although works of art might, like nature, afford glimpses of an unrealizable 'intellectual beauty', they hindered true enlightenment in so far as they persuaded a spectator to mistake the earthly illusion for the heavenly reality – as Narcissus was beguiled by his own reflection in the water. Plotinus is said to have been ashamed of his own body and refused to sit for a portrait. It could be no more than an image of an image, he thought.

The contemporary renown of Plotinus as a teacher is enough to indicate how well his philosophy answered the spiritual needs of intellectual Romans as well as of students who flocked from Egypt, Syria and Arabia to sit at his feet. What, if any, immediate impact his aesthetics had on artistic practice is, of course, impossible to determine. (His later influence, after Neoplatonism had been absorbed into Christian theology, is easier to trace, as we shall see, p. 385.) The sculpture of the late third and early fourth centuries tends, however, to discard or disregard Classical Greek notions of physical beauty, the accepted 'canon' of bodily proportions. Yet how far this was deliberate and consciously willed and how far it was due to extraneous factors, to what extent the Classical tradition was renounced in order to create a new style expressive of the spiritual turmoil of the time, may be questioned. The problem is posed in very clear terms by the reliefs on the Arch of Constantine erected in Rome in 313–15 to commemorate Constantine's assumption of sole imperial power in 312 – which was immediately followed by the Edict of Milan, proclaiming the toleration of Christianity.

The Arch of Constantine might almost have been designed to stand as an epilogue to the 600-year-long history of Hellenistic and Roman art. The structure is of traditional, characteristically Roman, triumphal arch form, but its lavish sculptural decoration is a patchwork of old and new. This is unprecedented; and whatever the cause may have been, the effect is to emphasize by contrast the radical change that had come over Roman sculpture in the late third century. In one panel, for instance, two Hadrianic roundels representing a boar hunt and a sacrifice to Apollo are inset above the frieze of Constantine delivering a public oration, one of several similar Constantinian reliefs on the arch (5,78). The roundels are elegantly suave examples of the Hellenized art favoured by the Emperor Hadrian, delicately cut, naturalistic, vivacious and graceful. In comparison, the relief of Constantine is crude in its simplicity, as if it were a throwback to a less civilized, less highly skilled level of culture. All the hard-won technical knowledge for creating spatial depth and other naturalistic illusions has been abandoned. There is no foreshortening, no indication of movement: space is flattened, scale is ignored and gestures and poses are repeated without variation, almost mechanically. Uniformly squat and sturdy figures, with heavy oversize heads of regular unvarying features, stand in rows – all in profile except for those of the statues of Hadrian and Marcus Aurelius at either end of the rostrum and that (now missing) of Constantine himself, frontally posed and looking straight ahead.

Ever since republican times a popular Italic style, sometimes termed plebeian, though it was patronized by the middle, rather than the lower, classes (pp. 191–3), had coexisted with that favoured by the more highly educated and consequently more strongly Hellenized patricians. The relief of Constantine belongs to this popular Italic tradition. But the blunt simplicity and directness characteristic of the style are accompanied here by a new consistency in conception – a consistency and thoughtfulness also evident in the choice of earlier sculptures for use on the arch. They were all taken from monuments erected by the 'good' emperors with whom Constantine wished to associate himself: Trajan, Hadrian and Marcus Aurelius. Their new function and new meaning arise simply from the architect's act of choice. In this way the idea behind the work of art acquired greater importance than the work itself; and all the naturalistic skills cultivated in Classical Greece, the Hellenistic kingdoms and the Roman empire came to seem irrelevant to the main purpose of art. The sculptor or sculptors of the Constantinian reliefs must almost certainly have carved sarcophagi for Christians – patrons for whom 'meaning' rather than 'form' was always foremost and who demanded a richly symbolic art to express their otherworldly ideals.

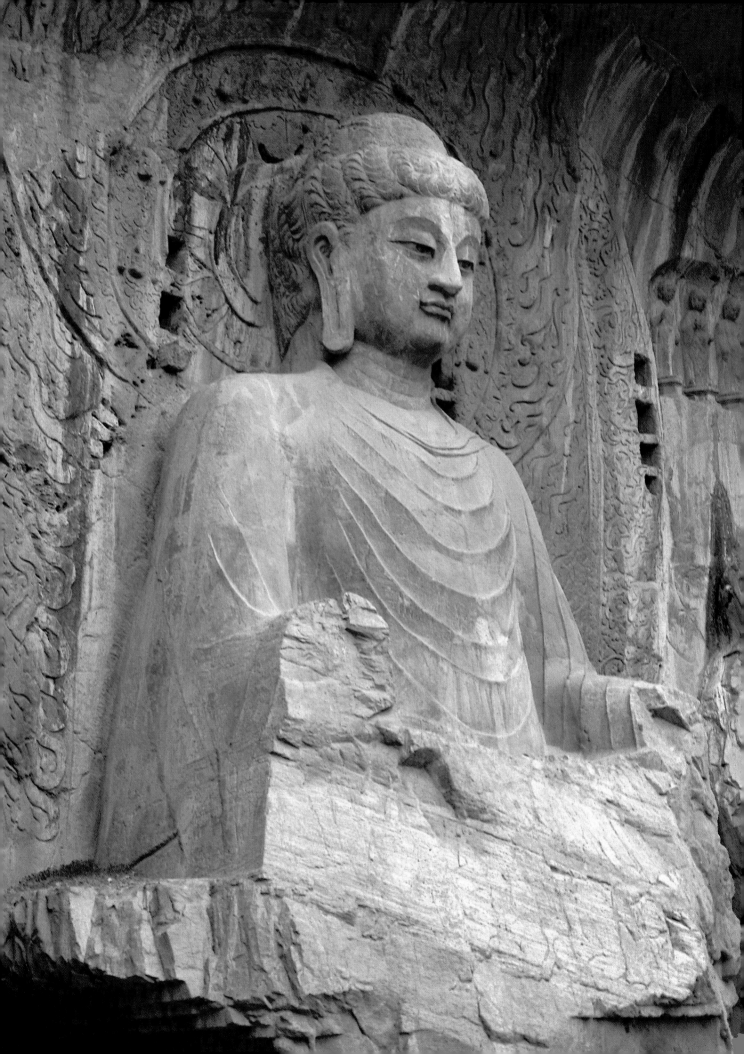

PART TWO

ART AND THE WORLD RELIGIONS

Opposite Vairocana Buddha, Longmen, near Luoyang, Henan, China, AD 672–5. Natural rock, about 49ft (15m) high.

CHAPTER SIX

BUDDHISM, HINDUISM AND FAR EASTERN ART

Aslender 34-foot-high (10m) smooth-shafted mono-lithic column, crowned by a crouching lion in sandstone, which stands near the village of Lauriya Nandangarh on the vast plain of the Ganges in north-eastern India, is a monument of manifold artistic, political and religious significance (6,1). At first sight it might seem to have strayed from Persepolis, more than 2,000 miles (3,200km) to the west (3,37). Both its capital, in the form of a lotus flower, and the lion on top recall Achaemenid sculpture. It is, in fact, some two and a half centuries later. The inscription on the shaft declares that it was set up by Asoka (272–232 BC), grandson of the founder of the Mauryan dynasty, who had begun to build the first Indian empire. Asoka had several such columns erected in various parts of his empire (6,2), which extended over most of the Indian sub-continent from the Himalayas to the Deccan mountains in the south (covering all present-day Pakistan, Bangladesh and most of the Republic of India). They may owe their origin partly to the columns that had an ancient religious significance in India as symbols of the cosmic pillar or axis of the universe, and partly to the inscribed stones that from a very early period had recorded the conquests and territorial claims of west Asian rulers, such as the *stele* of Naramsin (2,10). The message of Asoka's inscriptions was, however, entirely unprecedented: a declaration of non-violence and adherence to the teaching of the Buddha. On one column he stated that he had been moved to remorse, had 'felt profound sorrow and regret because the conquest of a people previously unconquered involves slaughter, death and deportation' and that he had learned from the Buddha to consider 'moral conquest the only true conquest'. Another records that Asoka had sent missionaries to preach Buddha's pacific doctrine to all the Hellenistic rulers in the West, 'to where the Greek king Antiochus dwells, and beyond that Antiochus to where dwell the four kings severally named Ptolemy, Antigonus, Magas and Alexander'.

There is no reference to these emissaries in Classical sources, but Buddhist missionaries certainly reached the West and went on doing so – they are known to have been active in Alexandria around the first century AD – though it is unlikely that much heed was paid to them. Links

The visual arts	Historical landmarks
	c. 800–500 BC Upanishads
	c. 570 BC Birth of Lao Zi
	c. 563 BC Birth of Siddhartha Gautama, the Buddha
	c. 550 BC Birth of Confucius
	c. 500 BC *Bhagavad Gita*
	273–232 BC Buddhism promoted by Mauryan emperor Asoka in India
243 BC Asokan lion column (6,1)	**c. 242 BC** Buddhism introduced into Sri Lanka (traditional date)
c. 221–209 BC Tomb of Qin Shihuangdi (6,73)	**221 BC** Qin Shihuangdi, first Chinese emperor
c. 150–50 BC Sanchi stupa (6,6)	**207 BC** Han dynasty begins in China
c. AD 120 Karli (6,8)	**c. 100 BC** Basic text of *Mahayana* Buddhism compiled in India
c. AD 100 One of the earliest Gandharan Buddhas (6,16)	**c. AD 65** First recorded Buddhist community in China
c. AD 150 Mathura Buddha (6,18)	**AD 78–101** *Mahayana* Buddhism promoted by Kushan emperor Kanishka I throughout India
c. AD 400–500 Yungang Buddha (6,88). Sarnath Buddha (6,21)	**c. AD 300** Tantric Buddhism developed
	AD 320 Chandragupta establishes the Gupta dynasty in N. India
AD 670 Horyuji, Nara (6,113)	**AD 420** Buddhism state religion in N. China (Wei dynasty)
AD 672–5 Longmen Buddha (6,91)	**c. AD 550** Buddhism introduced into Japan; adopted by ruling family in AD 588
c. AD 600–700 Ajanta Bodhisattva (6,24)	
c. AD 840 Borobudur (6,52)	**c. AD 700** *Mahayana* Buddhism introduced into Java
c. AD 900–1000 Guanyin from Dunhuang (6,94)	**AD 845** Buddhism proscribed in China for a period
c. AD 950 Li Cheng scroll (6,104)	
c. AD 1000–1200 Byodoin temple, Uji (6,122)	**AD 1022** Murasaki completed *The Tales of Genji*

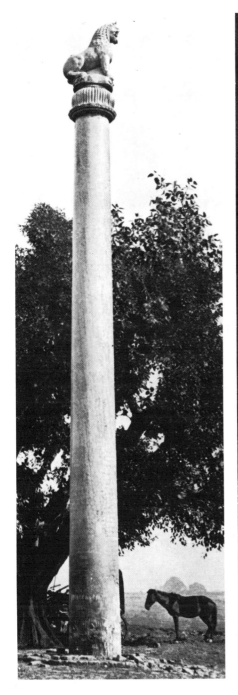

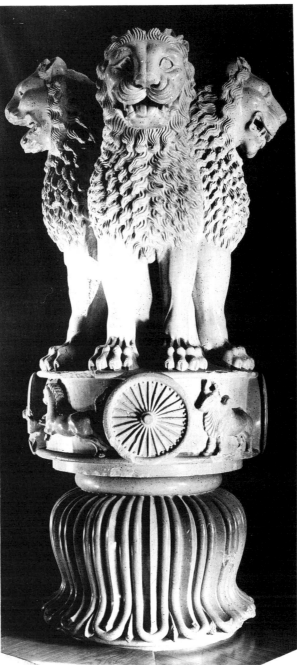

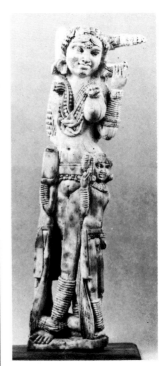

6,1 *Far left* Lion column at Lauriya Nandangarh, India, 243 BC. 34ft (10.36m) high.

6,2 *Left* Lion capital, from an Asokan column, India, 3rd century BC. Sandstone, 7ft (2.14m) high. Sarnath Museum.

6,3 *Above* Andhran female figure, pre-AD 79. Ivory, 9⁷/₈ins (25cm) high. Museo Nazionale, Naples.

between India, the Hellenistic kingdoms and, later, the Roman empire were mainly commercial. Works of art passed along the trade routes, perhaps more frequently from west to east than the other way though Chinese textiles were being imported into the Mediterranean world in Classical times. The art of India and the ideas it expressed were, however, deeply foreign to Europeans.

An ivory carving, which had reached Pompeii before the city was destroyed in AD 79, is an isolated example of Indian art in Roman Europe (**6,3**). The minutely detailed workmanship reveals considerable technical skill in handling the medium, certainly the equal of any comparable Roman work, though lacking the extraordinary accomplishment and exquisite sensuality of second–third century AD Indian ivory carving (**6,4**). The proportions of the figure from Pompeii, with her overlarge head, and the two attendants on either side, no taller than her hips, indicate the East's indifference to any ideals of human beauty of the kind evolved by the Greeks. Dressed only in jewelry, which frames and sets off the sexual organs, she displays just those parts of the body that the gesture of the *Venus pudica* hides (**4,40**). Yet this ivory has none of the grossness of the many erotic Pompeiian sculptures and paintings.

The ivory served originally as some kind of support, probably of a small table, and the subject is usually identified as a courtesan. She is closer, however, to a *yakshi* or

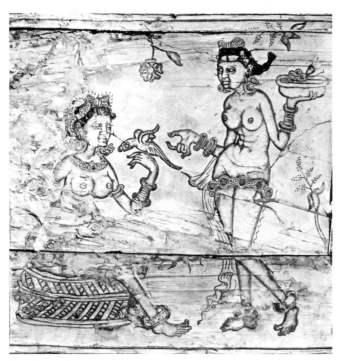

6,4 Detail of Kushan plaque from Begram, Afghanistan, pre-AD 241. Ivory. Kabul Museum, Afghanistan.

nature spirit such as that carved on a gate to the Great Stupa at Sanchi, in a similarly alluring state of bejewelled undress with a necklace hanging down between her large and sexually provocative breasts, a belt round her hips and bangles on her arms and legs (**6,5**). Holding on to the branches of a banyan tree, the *yakshi* sways with rhythmical *déhanchement* – there is no English word for this bending of the body from the hips – in the Indian *tribhanga* (literally 'three bends') pose which obsessed Indian artists for centuries and provided the sinuous three-dimensional curves that pervade their sculpture, even when it is purely decorative and non-representational. The figure seems to be composed entirely of soft malleable flesh without any hard bone structure. Yet this gives it, paradoxically, a strangely ethereal quality, exemplifying the combination of sensuality and spirituality that distinguishes the arts of India from those of all other civilizations. It forms part of the exterior of one of the holiest shrines dedicated to the Buddha, who taught that the pains and sorrows of existence stemmed from desire, attachment to self and to the ephemeral pleasures of the senses.

Yakshis belonged to the complex religious beliefs that preceded, coexisted with and were destined to outlast Buddhism in India. As spirits of the trees and streams they were worshipped by the Dravidians, who had peopled India before Aryan invaders arrived from the North in the second millennium BC. Aryans brought with them a pantheon of 'higher' deities not unlike those of the Greeks, personifying the great elemental forces worshipped without images or temples, notably Indra, god of the atmosphere and thunder, and Surya, the sun god – cousins, as it were, of Zeus and Apollo. These gods were celebrated in the

famous Vedic hymns, composed between about 1500 and 800 BC in Sanskrit, a language akin to the dialects of the Greek, Celtic and German peoples who moved into Europe also in the second millennium BC. Both Dravidian and Aryan beliefs contributed to the religion, or rather to the group of magic practices, religious cults and philosophies of life known in the West as 'Hinduism', a word with no precise equivalent in the Indian languages. The metaphysic expounded in the early *Upanishads*, composed between about 800 and 600 BC as commentaries on the Vedic hymns, was focused, however, less on easily visualized anthropomorphic deities than on elusive abstract ideas: *Brahman* the universal spirit or world soul, *Atman* one eternal human soul, *Maya* the cosmic flux which animates all things. The aim of religious exercises was not, as in other contemporary civilizations, to propitiate or coerce the supernatural powers but to achieve the absorption of the *Atman* into the *Brahman* and thus liberate the soul from the retributive principle known as *Karma*, the endless succession of reincarnations in human and animal form determined by conduct.

Belief in *Karma* had social as well as ethical significance. For it was generally held to justify the caste system, which provided a structure of classes: Brahmins or priests, Kshatriyas or warriors, Vaisayas or cultivators, and Sudras or serfs. Brahmins alone were credited with the power to escape from the cycle of rebirth by means of asceticism and by sacrifices according to a ritual known only to them. (Others could hope to attain this goal by leading exemplary lives and practising self-denial, which might be rewarded by reincarnation as a Brahmin.) Their absolute spiritual and temporal authority was questioned by the founders of Jainism and Buddhism, the two great

6,5 *Yakshi*, detail of east gate, Great Stupa, Sanchi, India, 1st century BC.

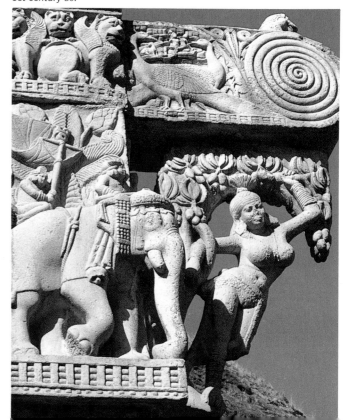

religious movements that emerged in the sixth century BC. The former was destined to remain a relatively small sect confined to India. But Buddhism revolutionized the thought and art of the whole of east Asia.

BUDDHIST ART IN INDIA

The word 'Buddha' signifies 'the enlightened one', and the aim of Buddhism is release from the sufferings of existence not by ritual sacrifice and extreme asceticism, but through enlightenment attained by the obliteration of all desires and, finally, of the self through concentrated meditation or yoga. Buddhism opened the way to salvation to all who followed the Eightfold Path of right knowlege or understanding, right motive, right speech, right deeds, right way of life, right effort, right self-mastery and right meditation. Its founder, Siddhartha Gautama (c. 563–483 BC), was born into the warrior caste as a prince of the Sakya family – he was often called Sakyamuni, 'Sage of the Sakyas' – on the border of Nepal in north India. He withdrew from the world, studied under Brahmins who advocated self-mortification, but renounced their asceticism and achieved the enlightened cosmic consciousness known as Buddhahood as the result of meditations under the Bodhi Tree or Tree of Wisdom at Bodhgaya, Bihar. The rest of his life was devoted to preaching his message to members of all castes in northern India. After he died or, in Buddhist terminology, attained *Nirvana* (which originally meant extinction), his work was carried on by an ever-increasing band of followers. In the mid-third century BC, as we have seen, Buddhism was adopted by Asoka as the official religion of the greater part of India.

The early development of religious art in India is a direct consequence of the spread of Buddhism. Brahmins had had no need for temples and little desire for images to make the mysteries of religion accessible to the laity. Although images were almost certainly made in perishable media for the cults of the non-Aryan population, there are no sculptures or paintings to set beside the works of religious literature composed in the millennium after the disappearance of the Indus Valley civilization (see pp. 58–61). The first great Buddhist ruler, Asoka, was also the first major patron of the arts in India. In addition to setting up inscribed columns (6,1), he is known to have had mounds or artificial hills, called stupas, built to enshrine the bodily relics of the Buddha, which he distributed to the principal cities of his empire as a means of 'moral conquest'. No stupa of his time survives, but the essential form – derived initially from the mounds raised over the dead, especially Brahmins and members of ruling families – is preserved in the Great Stupa at Sanchi in central India (6,6). Although it dates mainly from the second and first centuries BC, it is probably an enlargement of a stupa founded by Asoka.

This is a symbolic structure, at once a visible manifestation of the Buddha – the contemplation of his natural remains enabling the worshipper to think of the Buddha as an immanent reality – and an architectural diagram of the cosmos, precisely oriented and designed according to

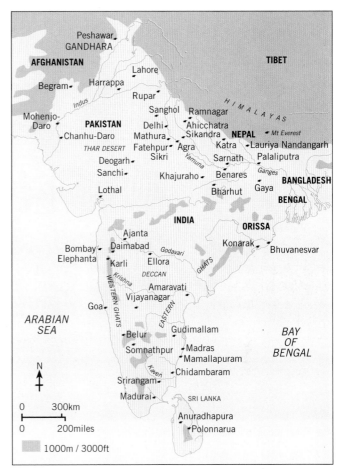

India

an elaborate system of proportional relationships with mystical significance. It consists of a solid hemisphere, typifying the dome of heaven, levelled at the top to carry a square superstructure with a central mast to represent the world axis extending from the infra-cosmic waters to the skies. On the mast three parasol-like forms called *chattras* signify the heavens of the gods, with that of Brahma at the top, and perhaps also the Three Jewels of Buddhism – the community of monks, the Law and the Buddha. From their resemblance to the parasols carried over the heads of earthly potentates, they also declare the Buddha to be the universal ruler.

A palisade more than 10 feet (3.2m) high encircles the mound; it is built of stone but in the form of a wooden fence or railing. Carefully dressed stones were fitted together as if they were stout posts and thick bars. The four gateways called *toranas* are similarly constructed in stone to simulate wood with their horizontal beams carved so that they appear to pass through the uprights – the spirals at their ends suggesting the rings in the section of a tree-trunk and perhaps symbolizing the vegetative stem of life. Why wooden prototypes should have been followed so closely despite the technical difficulty of treating heavy stone in such a way is a mystery – the same phenomenon is found in other cultures, for example, ancient Egypt, Greece and, less obviously, in imperial

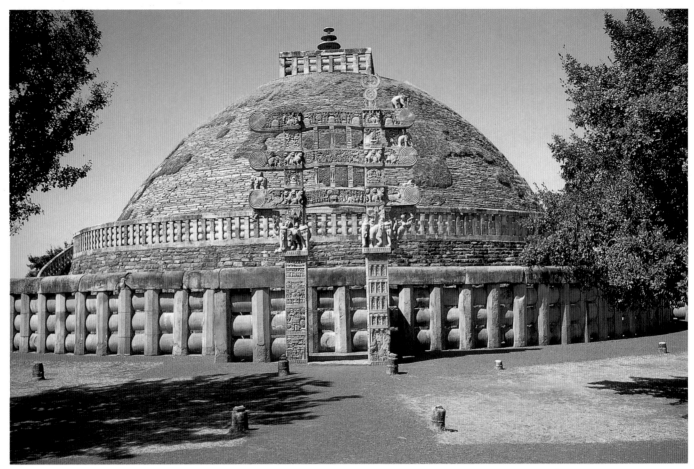

6,6 Great Stupa, Sanchi, 2nd and 1st century BC.

6,7 Plan of Stupa 1, Sanchi.

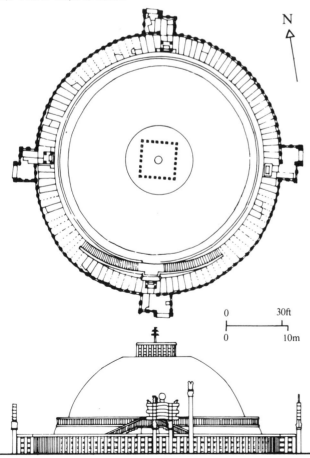

Rome (see p. 139). There can be no doubt that the form of the railing at Sanchi, especially of the gates, had some earlier symbolical significance perhaps connected with the temporary open-air fire-altars on which the sacrificial ritual of the Brahmins was centred. Railings seem also to have been placed round trees venerated in the nature cults of the indigenous population. The very careful orientation of the gates to the cardinal points of the compass, and the walls behind them obliging visitors to turn left on entering and thus walk round the stupa following the course of the sun (**6,7**), certainly reflected the Brahmins' cosmological preoccupations. But on all Brahminical sacrificial implements ornamentation was – and still is – avoided. The *toranas* at Sanchi and other stupas, on the other hand, are entirely covered with carvings. There are animals and Dravidian *yakshis* (6,5) as well as symbols of the Hindu gods and scenes from the Buddha's life on earth – though without his image. (The anthropomorphic Buddha image was not created until later, see p. 232.)

Whatever their previous significance may have been, the *toranas* acquired a special meaning for Buddhists. As they passed through the gate and walked round the stupa, contemplating the holy relic buried at its heart, they moved from the world of the senses to that of the spirit, from the temporal to the eternal, approaching the enlightenment of cosmic consciousness. They also passed from the diverse beliefs of the earlier religions of India to the all-embracing unity of Buddhism. As a whole the Great Stupa at Sanchi thus demonstrates how a new art emerged

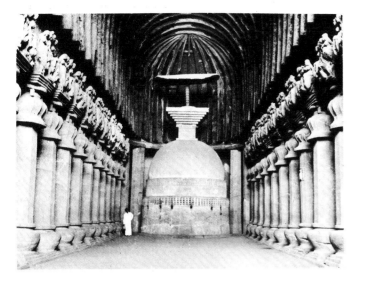

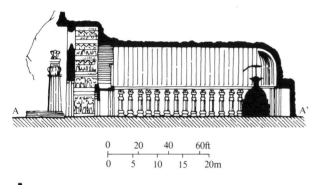

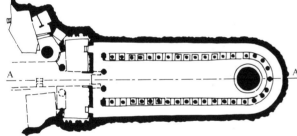

6,9 Plan and section of *chaitya*-hall, Karli.

out of the Buddhist integration of the metaphysical content of the *Vedas* and *Upanishads* with animistic pre-Aryan beliefs, which had remained the religion of the masses.

Emphasis placed by the Buddha on the supreme importance of the contemplative life encouraged an increasing number of his followers to withdraw into monasteries, called *viharas*. They seem to have lived at first in very simple buildings of wood or thatch or, like earlier holy hermits of India, in natural caves. From the third century BC more elaborate groups of cells and halls were cut into the living rock of hillsides or gorges. One of the largest and most impressive of these is the *chaitya*-hall (the word *chaitya* means 'place of worship') at Karli (**6,8**). Its façade, with a huge ogee arch (see Glossary) like the gable of a thatched roof, is carved to imitate the elements of wooden structures. So, too, is the interior, divided into a nave and aisles by rows of closely set columns (**6,9**). Strictly speaking, this is sculpture rather than architecture; it is not constructed but excavated and carved. A passage was first tunnelled into the rock-face, the ceiling with its sim-

ulated beams was then carved, without any need for scaffolding, and work proceeded downwards until the space around the columns and the small stupa in the apse at the end of the hall was cut away and the floor smoothed.

The hall provided a setting for the stupa which the devout could approach directly or, more usually, walk round by passing along the passage between the columns and wall, thus performing the rite of *pradaksina* or circumambulation. Light, filtering through a large window above the main door, is focused on the stupa. Glimpsed from the dark aisles, through the narrow gaps between the columns, the interior appears to be radiant with ethereal light emanating from the stupa. Seen from the nave, the stupa seems to be the only reality in an infinite void of primal darkness, held back by the half-lit columns along either side. Decoration is restricted to these columns, each with a base carved like a water-jar (perhaps an allusion to the waters beneath the cosmos), a 16-sided shaft, a bell-shaped capital and, above, a pair of elephants bearing male and female figures looking into the nave, and paired horses facing the aisles. There is much more figure sculpture on the façade, including reliefs of *yakshis* and their male equivalents *yakshas*. But a clearer impression of the entrance to a rock-cut temple is given by a later and richer example at Ajanta (**6,10**). Here, however, the carvings include images of the Buddha, which had made their first appearance in the first or early second century AD.

6,10 Exterior of cave temple at Ajanta, India, 4th century AD.

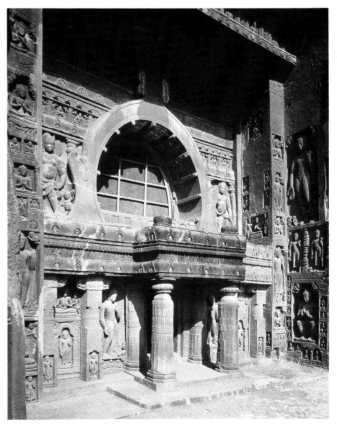

The Life of the Buddha

SCRIPTURES AND IMAGES

Although Buddhist scriptures are more voluminous than those of any other religion, they include no single text with the fundamental authority that the New Testament has for Christians and the Koran for Muslims. They are closer to the Hindu *Vedas* and *Upanishads* from which, however, they differ in one important respect: they report the life and teachings of a historical figure who made no claim to divinity or even to association with deities. They also permit, almost encourage, a wide variety of interpretations in accordance with the Buddha's final message to his followers: they must all work out their own salvation by themselves in solitary meditation – though he also said that one cannot attain enlightenment (that state of perfect selflessness and freedom from all desires and consequent sufferings) through contemplation alone. After his death or *Parinirvana* (final entry to *Nirvana*) his words were transmitted orally. Nothing appears to have been written down for some 400–500 years, that is, until shortly before the beginning of the Christian era; and by that time the historical Buddha, Sakyamuni, was already shrouded with an aura of myth and legend. He must have spoken in Maghadi, the language of eastern India in his life-time, but the earliest surviving scriptures are written in literary languages, Pali and Sanskrit. The Pali canon is believed to be the earliest and it remains the essential scripture for *Theravada* Buddhists in Sri Lanka and south-east Asia. Consisting of three parts – the Buddha's sermons (*sutras*), his rule for monks and nuns, and early commentaries – a recent edition filled 45 large volumes. Before these Pali texts were written, however, numerous additions had been made to the oral tradition by followers of the *Mahayana* school of Buddhist thought (see p. 254) and they were incorporated in the Sanskrit canon.

The Buddha himself was as uninterested in images as he was in ritual. However, one late text reports him prescribing meditation on his own painted likeness and Buddhist images certainly preceded written records. The earliest known date from the second century BC (6,14) and they reveal abilities in Buddhist narrative representation and symbolism that must have been developed even earlier. Paintings on cloth were no doubt also made for use as aids in religious instruction, similar to those that are known to have been displayed in the second century BC by itinerant 'picture showmen' reciting the Hindu epics – as they were to do until the present century. The Buddha's message had been addressed to all people irrespective of caste and level of education and artists began by illustrating those aspects of the master's life and teaching that could most easily be understood, derived of course from oral sources. Traditional

6,11 *Maya's Dream and the Birth of the Buddha*, drum slab from stupa at Amaravati, India, c. AD 200. White marble, 63 × 38½ins (160 × 97.8cm). British Museum, London.

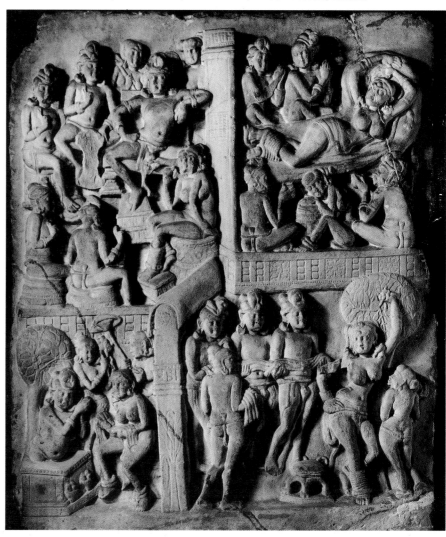

beliefs about the Buddha's life were first assembled in the *Buddhacarita*, a Sanskrit poem by Ashvaghota of the first century AD; no extensive account of it was given in either the Pali or Sanskrit canon.

The story of his birth was often illustrated. A relief from the Amaravati stupa of about the second century AD (**6,11**) shows his mother Maya dreaming that she has been penetrated by a white elephant (top right). In the adjoining scene she and her husband, seated just above her, consult seers who interpret the dream. Realizing that she is about to give birth, Maya goes to a grove dedicated to the mother goddess Lumbini and while she holds a branch of a flowering tree (an ancient symbol of fertility) the child emerges from her right hip (lower right) and she presents him to the *yaksha*, the tutelary nature spirit of the Sakya clan. In neither of these scenes is the child represented: the cloth held out before the *yaksha* is empty. Attention is focused on Maya, whose name in Sanskrit also signifies the illusory phenomenal world. Her full-breasted, wide-hipped figure is rendered with the same soft sensuality as the female nature spirit at Sanchi (6,5).

Ashvaghota's account of the youth of Siddhartha – as the Buddha was called at this stage in his life – tells how female attendants 'entertained him with soft words, tremulous calls, wanton swayings, sweet laughter, butterfly kisses and seductive glances. Thus he became a captive of these women who were well versed in the subject of sensuous enjoyment and indefatigable in sexual pleasure.' His spiritual awakening began when he went out of his family's palace and saw for the first time an old man, a sick man and a corpse, which troubled him as pointers to the impermanence of all things in this world. But it was his fourth encounter with a begging ascetic or hermit sage that won him over and weaned him away from sensual indulgence. He escaped from his family's palace, gave away his rich clothes and jewelry, cut off his hair (6,58) and went to join the ascetic hermits in the forest, adopting their austere way of life, giving himself up to meditation and starving himself until his body was emaciated. But 'wasted

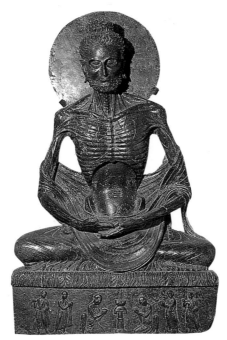

6,12 *Fasting Siddhartha*, late 1st century BC to 2nd century AD. Schist, 33ins (83.8cm) high. Lahore Museum, Lahore.

away though he was, his glory and majesty remained unimpaired, and his sight gladdened the eyes of those who looked upon him. It was as welcome to them as the full moon in autumn to the white lotuses that bloom then.' Several sculptures show his emaciated body, protruding ribs, fleshless arms, hollow abdomen, and eyes sunk deeply in his skull but nevertheless retaining an expression of serene intensity (**6,12**). They were carved in Gandhara where the influence of Hellenistic art was strong, though it is difficult to imagine even the most naturalistic Greek-trained artist representing the human body in such a way. But Indian aesthetics have always demanded the subordination of beauty to the evocation of the sacred, of the numinous. To a Buddhist the beautiful had value only in so far as it embodied a religious idea. After six years of ascetic practices, however, Siddhartha realized that he could not attain enlightenment through self-mortification, effective though it might be as a means of renouncing egoistic attachment to self. And later, in his first sermon, he expounded the doctrine of the middle way, avoiding extremes of self-denial and self-indulgence.

Accounts of the Buddha's life exemplify his teaching. They are no more susceptible to Western notions of historical objectivity than the

Jataka stories, that is to say, accounts of his previous avatars or manifestations on earth, in both human and animal forms, many of which were included in the Pali canon and were frequently illustrated. One that recounts his avatar as the chief of a troupe of monkeys appears as early as the second century BC at Bharhut in north-central India (**6,13**). He is shown painfully stretching his body from one tree to another so that it could serve as a bridge on which the smaller monkeys might escape from soldiers sent by a king to gather the best fruit in the forest. The king was so impressed that he questioned the monkey chief, whose back had been broken but who told him: 'Those always prompt to act up to my orders charged me with the burden of being their ruler. And I, for my part, bound with the affection of a father for his children, engaged myself to bear it.' A later version in Sanskrit of about AD 200 adds at the end that the story should be told when discoursing on compassion, on gratitude and especially when instructing princes. Such simple moral tales and their illustrations presented the practical aspects of Buddhism as a rule of life in ways that were easily understood. The more elevated and abstruse metaphysical doctrines, developed by the *Mahayana* school of Buddhist thought, found expression later, and sometimes in sublime form, in China and Japan.

6,13 *The Great Monkey Jataka*, pillar medallion on railing of Bharhut stupa, India, early 2nd century BC. Red sandstone, 18⁹/₁₀ins (48cm) high. Indian Museum, Calcutta.

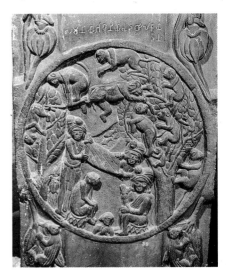

THE IMAGE OF THE BUDDHA

The early Buddhists revered Sakyamuni as a mortal teacher who attained enlightenment and finally *Nirvana* – the release of the spirit from its incarnations. This consummation could for them be expressed visually only by abstract forms, such as that of the stupa. There was no means by which his person could be represented. 'For him who (like the sun) has set, there is no longer anything with which he can be compared', declares one of the earliest Buddhist texts. But a religion with the steadily growing popular appeal of Buddhism called for icons as visual aids to doctrine, and stupa gateways were carved with reliefs illustrating his life as early as the late second or early first century BC. A fine example from the stupa at Bharhut depicts the visit paid to the Buddha by a king (**6,14**). It is a strange mixture of the conceptual and the naturalistic, for while some figures are taller than the columns of buildings by which they stand, elsewhere a remarkable degree of illusionistic skill in carving is displayed – as in the two oxen which trot forwards drawing the royal chariot on the right and are shown head on; and in the hind-quarters of a horse passing through a *chaitya*-arch gateway on the left and, above, a mahout trying to prevent his elephant from pulling down the branch of a mango tree. Altogether a surprising amount of descriptive detail is given. Yet the Buddha himself is represented only symbolically, by a wheel above his flower-strewn throne. The wheel, which had been associated in west Asia with the solar disc, the supreme deity and knowledge, acquired in India additional significance as the multiple symbol of birth, maturity and death and of the great cosmic revolutions in the unending cycle of reincarnations. It also had a more specific Buddhist meaning as the *Dharmacakra*,

6,14 King Prasenajit visits the Buddha, detail of a relief from the Bharhut stupa, early 2nd century BC. Red sandstone, 18⅞ins (47.9cm) high. Freer Gallery of Art, Smithsonian Institution, Washington DC.

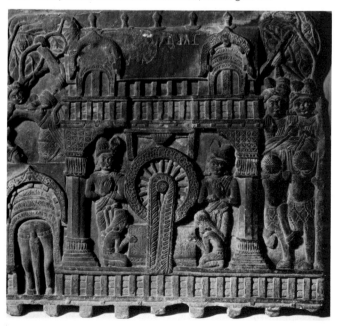

the Wheel of the Law (or Doctrine) set in motion when the newly enlightened Buddha preached his first sermon, which, like the wheel of the sun, illuminated all quarters of the earth, giving spiritual light to all beings. In other early relief carvings the Buddha's ineffable presence is indicated by a horse he rode when he made the great renunciation and left his father's house, or by the Bodhi Tree beneath which he meditated, or by his footprints or simply by an empty seat as in the example illustrated here (6,14). The same symbol is later found in Byzantine and Early Christian art (7,3). Emphasis was placed not on the person of the Buddha Sakyamuni but on his teachings which included the accounts he gave of previous incarnations through which he rose to the potentiality of Buddhahood – each one a kind of parable.

A momentous change came about with a new school of Buddhist thought called by its adherents the *Mahayana* or Great Vehicle (of Salvation) to distinguish it from the earlier form which they dismissed as *Hinayana* or Small Vehicle, later to be named by its followers as *Theravada*, the 'way of the elders'. Early Buddhism had been a literally atheistic philosophy derived from the Buddha's teaching and especially his final injunction that his disciples should work out their own salvation for themselves. It encouraged withdrawal and the contemplative life of a monastery. The *Mahayana*, however, conceived the Buddha not as a mortal teacher whose precepts and example were to be followed, but as a god who had existed eternally, like Brahma (the creator god, not to be confused with *Brahman*), without beginning or end. In this form Buddhism became more easily reconcilable with other religious beliefs both in India and, as we shall see, China and Japan. From a transcendental viewpoint, the historical Buddha came to be seen as an illusion in an illusory world; this paradoxically permitted him to be represented by images, for all images are illusory too. At a lower intellectual level the *Mahayana* opened the door to the worship of a Buddhist pantheon of deities visualized anthropomorphically like, and sometimes together with, the deities of other religions. Most important among them were the Bodhisattvas or Buddhas-in-the-making, who, for the salvation of humanity, renounced the *Nirvana* they were capable of attaining.

An image of the Buddha in human form appears on coins issued by Kanishka I, a follower of the *Mahayana*, who, probably in AD 78, became ruler of the Kushan empire, which extended from the Aral Sea through Afghanistan and south-eastwards as far as Benares on the Ganges (**6,15**). This tiny figure incorporates many of the distinguishing features of later Buddha images, for instance the *ushnisha*, a cranial protuberance indicating superior spiritual knowledge, ear-lobes greatly elongated by the heavy jewelry he had worn in his gilded youth as a prince, right hand raised in a gesture of reassurance or benediction, a monastic robe, and haloes of sanctity behind his head and body. There must surely have been precedents for these features, either in sculpture or painting. But none of the early surviving Buddhas can be more than approximately dated. They are in two distinct styles, one developed at Gandhara in the north (around Peshawar in present-day Pakistan), the other at the southern extremity of the Kushan empire at Mathura (some 90 miles, 140km, south of Delhi).

Artistically, though not geographically, Gandhara was some way to the west of India. This central Asian frontier region had been opened up to Greek influence in the Hellenistic period, when it formed part of the kingdom of Bactria, ruled over by a succession of Greeks, including the bottle-nosed Euthydemus (5,13). By the time it had become part of the Kushan empire it was separated from the Mediterranean world by the Parthians (see p. 175), but this did not interrupt the flow of works of art and, almost certainly, of artists as well from Rome's eastern provinces. The result was an art owing as much or more to Rome as to India, an interbreeding of two deeply antipathetic ideals. Yet it was from this strange artistic cross-fertilization that the first great Buddha images were to come, some of the most serene and spiritual of all works of art. To express the idea of divinity in human form Gandharan sculptors turned to statues of Greek and Roman gods, as artists were to do some two centuries later when Christians demanded visual images of Christ (see p. 305). The haloes placed behind the heads of both the Buddha and Christ probably share a common origin (see p. 309). But the sculptors of Gandhara derived more than iconographical devices from the West.

One of the earliest Gandharan Buddhas is also among the most Classical, in a European sense (6,16). Drapery hanging in loose folds, but indicating the form and movement of the body beneath, is like that on contemporary statues of deified Roman emperors or, more appropriately, of the Muses, who brought to humanity the purifying

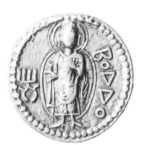

6,15 *Above* Gold coin of Kanishka showing the Buddha, late 1st to early 2nd century AD. Formerly Museum of Fine Arts, Boston (Seth K. Sweetser Fund).

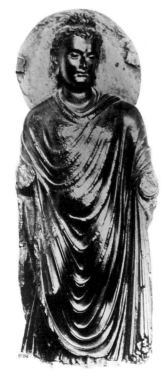

6,16 Standing Buddha from Hoti-Mardan, Pakistan, 1st to 2nd century AD. Formerly Guides' Mess, Hoti-Mardan (present location unknown).

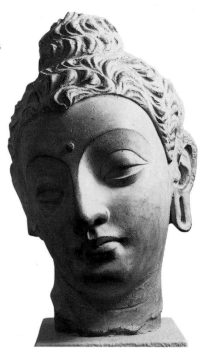

6,17 Head of Buddha from Gandhara, 3rd century AD. Lime composition, 16¹/₁₀ins (41cm) high. Victoria & Albert Museum, London.

power of poetry and divine wisdom (5,55; 5,77). The pose has an enlivening twist typical of Late Antique sculpture and the head recalls a Greek Apollo. Wavy hair conceals the *ushnisha*, and only the *urna*, a tuft of hair between the brows, and elongated ear-lobes remain as distinguishing marks of the Buddha. For the elevated but gentle expression of a heart at peace so eloquently conveyed by this noble figure there was, however, no precedent in the art of the West. In another, probably later, Buddha head (6,17) Greek symmetry, balance and repose are again combined with the peculiarly sensual spirituality of India to create a sublime image of Eastern serenity, an Orientalized Apollo. The meeting of East and West in the art of Gandhara brought forth a new type of human beauty, which was to haunt not only the Indian image of the Buddha but also, and perhaps more strongly, the Chinese.

In contrast, the Mathura Buddha images are purely Indian, as exemplified by an imposing high relief in the red sandstone of the region (6,18). Here the Buddha, or rather, as the inscription reveals, Sakyamuni before he achieved enlightenment, sits in the cross-legged yoga posture beneath the Bodhi Tree. Royal status is indicated by the lion throne and the two attendants with fly-whisks, spiritual power by the heavenly beings hovering above and by the distinguishing marks on his body, including wheels incised on the palm of his hand and the soles of his feet. The torso with distended skin has the same somewhat pneumatic quality of the *yakshis* at Sanchi (6,5) or even of the very much earlier Indus Valley statuettes (2,19; 20). The same may be said of the very different – extremely virile and forceful, monumental despite its small size – standing figure identified by an inscription as Maitreya, the Buddha of the future, wearing the jewelry normal on Bodhisattvas and with his virility clearly indicated beneath his clinging garment (6,19).

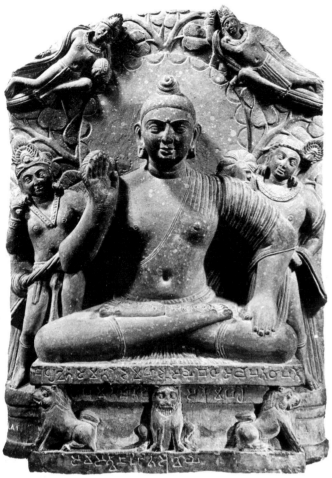

6,18 Seated Buddha from Katra, Mathura, India, 2nd century AD. Red sandstone, 27¼ins (69.2cm) high. Government Museum, Mathura.

Images of this type influenced the sculptors of Gandhara. They appear, for instance, on a Gandharan frieze (**6,20**) surrounded by figures which would not look out of place on a Roman sarcophagus of about the same date – one man appears to be wearing a toga and another, Classically posed beside him, is in a state of stark nudity rare in Indian art even in the most uninhibited erotic scenes. But the sculptor had evident difficulty with the Indian yoga pose, for which the arts of the West provided no model. (The folded legs look like a bolster beneath the torso and the upturned right foot has been transformed into a swirl.) The frieze depicts the Buddha's birth, his meditation under the Bodhi Tree and, in the part illustrated here, his first sermon in the Deer Park (symbolized by the wheel between the two deer on the throne) and his death, with the last disciple meditating in front of the bed. Difference in scale indicates relative importance. The Buddha on the Mathura relief also is much larger than his attendants; they are no more than shadowy presences beside the living teacher, who bends forwards slightly with a compassionate expression on his face, as if to address the spectator. On the Gandhara frieze, the small subsidiary figures are full of vitality and jostling movement, while the Buddha is withdrawn in static detached monumentality, like a heroic-scale statue surrounded by living worshippers. He is represented as a god, far removed from the joys and sorrows of humanity, as he was to be in later Buddhist art.

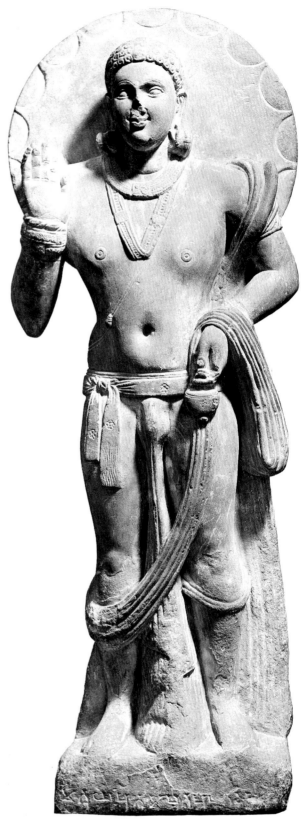

6,19 Maitreya from Ramnagar (Ahicchatra), India, 2nd century AD. Red sandstone, 26ins (66cm) high. National Museum of India, New Delhi.

The arts of both Gandhara and Mathura contributed to the formation of what is generally called the 'Classical' style in Indian art. It reached maturity in the three-century-long Gupta period named after Chandra Gupta I, who was crowned king of kings in the old Mauryan capital

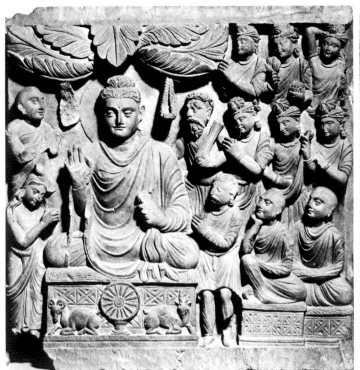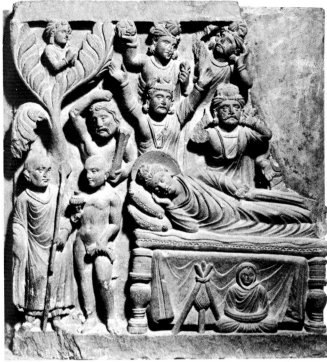

6,20 Relief from Gandhara showing the First Sermon in the Deer Park and the Death of the Buddha, Kushan, details, late 2nd to early 3rd century AD. Dark gray-blue slate, 26³/₈ins (67cm) high. Freer Gallery of Art, Smithsonian Institution, Washington DC.

of Pataliputra in AD 320. A high relief of the Buddha preaching his first sermon is among the finest examples of this style and, indeed, of the religious art of the world (**6,21**). The superb technical accomplishment of the carving may perhaps derive from Gandharan practice, but has been further refined by an exquisite precision of detail and by a sensuously subtle definition of form unlike anything in the West.

Gandharan sculptors had represented the Buddha as an anthropomorphic god, almost as in the West. In the Gupta statue he appears as a divine essence, pure spirit purged of all earthly matter, light without heat. Such a figure seems to be a product of the meditation it was intended to stimulate, transcending the senses among which Indians include the intellect. Essential symbols from earlier representations of the subject have been assimilated and subjected to the general effect – the heavenly beings, the wheel, the deer (sadly damaged) and the disciples. The Buddha's exquisitely expressive hands, in one of the *mudras* or gestures which constitute an esoteric sign language, turn the Wheel of Doctrine, the *Dharmacakra*. Yet the statue derives its silencing religious aura, the spiritual potency of non-violence, as much from its form as from its symbolism. Otherworldly serenity is suggested by perfect symmetrical equilibrium and is the combination of the simplest and most self-contained of geometrical figures. The great circles of the halo are echoed in the lines that indicate the creases of the neck, the waist and the drapery beneath the legs. Two triangles intersect, one enclosing the body from the crown of the head to the knees, the other expanding along the lines of the narrow-waisted, broad-shouldered torso to the heavenly beings who hover on the edge of the halo. The head is oval, an allusion maybe to the Indian idea of the egg-shaped

cosmos, and the sharply cut lines of eyebrows and eyelids repeat its curves. It is a mark of the sculptor's genius that so severely abstract a configuration could be fused so apparently naturally and effortlessly with an image of such gentle humanity, one which is supernatural without being in any way unnatural.

Like many Indian statues, the figure is under life-size. In pursuing an inner spiritual reality, a pursuit that immunized them from the Western obsession with naturalism and the lifelike, Indian sculptors often, and perhaps most effectively, worked on a small scale, though they occasionally went to the opposite colossal extreme. They also evolved a canon of bodily proportions designed to give heroic stature even to small-scale figures, but based on mathematical ratios and thus more closely akin to that of ancient Egypt than to that derived from visual appearances in Classical Greece. (The distance between the chin and the top of the forehead provided the module, multiplied nine times for a full-length figure.) Careful observance of this intellectually conceived canon did not, however, preclude sensuous handling when the subject-matter demanded it – to indicate, for instance, the nature of a Bodhisattva. Physical beauty attracted the eye but also disposed the mind to meditate beyond the range of the senses and the intellect. A red sandstone torso, probably later than the Gupta period but maintaining the same high standard of technical accomplishment, illustrates the extreme sensitivity with which the velvet-soft but firm flesh of a lithe athletic youth could be rendered, bulging slightly above the belt and set off by sharply cut jewelry and the scarf of antelope skin (**6,22**). Here again, as at Sanchi (**6,5**), full-blooded life and provocatively swaying movement are suggested by the *tribhanga* pose. A relief at Ajanta of the Naga king – the serpent deity who

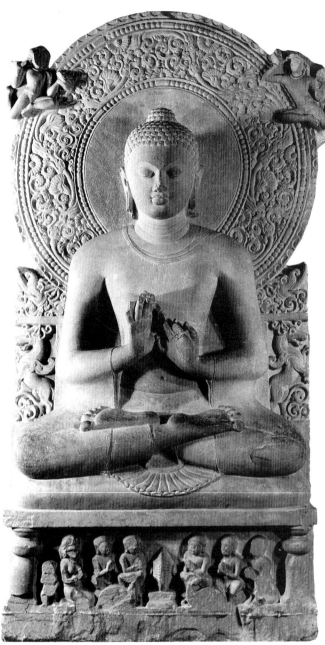

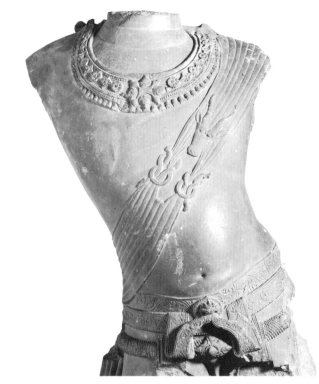

6,22 Torso of Bodhisattva from Sanchi, post-Gupta (?), 5th century AD. Sandstone, 34¼ins (87cm) high. Victoria & Albert Museum, London.

6,23 Nagaraja and his wives, Cave 19, Ajanta, India, late 5th century AD.

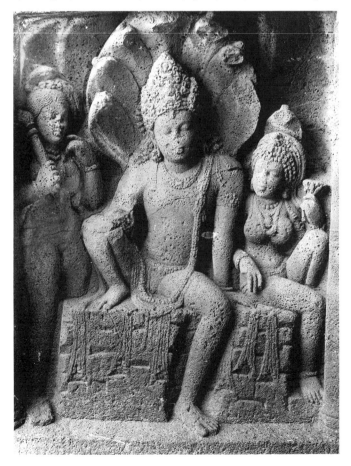

6,21 Teaching Buddha from Sarnath, India, Gupta, 5th century AD. Sandstone, 5ft 2ins (1.58m) high. Sarnath Museum.

had come to be regarded by Buddhists as a protector – seated in the pose of royal ease with his two wives, is rendered with still greater naturalism (**6,23**).

That pictorial art was as highly developed as sculpture in the Gupta period is demonstrated by wall-paintings in the rock-cut temples known as the Ajanta caves, very poorly preserved though they are. One of the most impressive, and least badly damaged, is of a Bodhisattva rather larger than life-size and very much larger than the numerous figures around him (**6,24**). In technique it is akin to fresco: the rock-face was covered with a mixture of clay and other materials, this was coated with lime which was kept moist to absorb pigment, outlines were

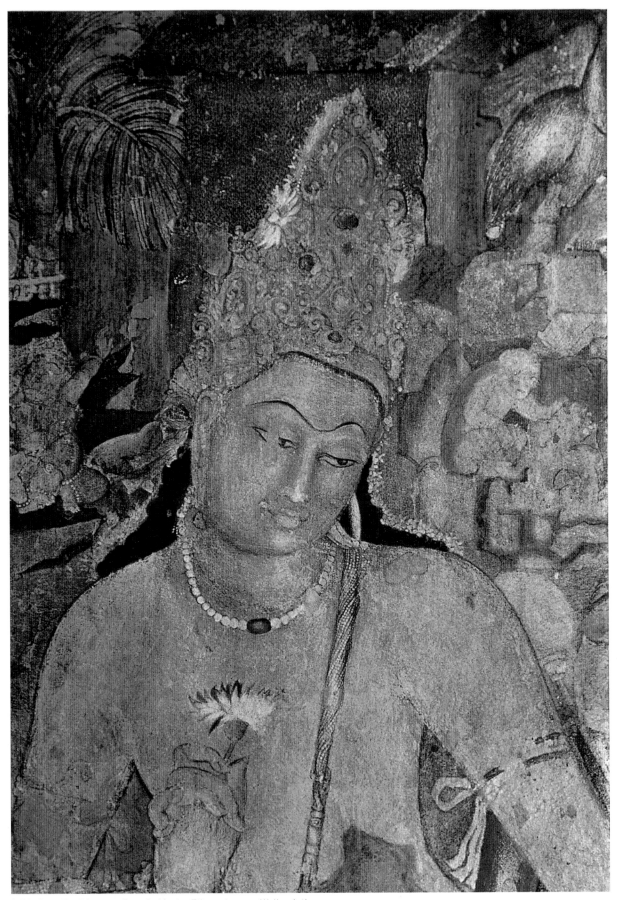

6,24 Great Bodhisattva, Cave 1, Ajanta, 7th century AD. Wall-painting.

painted in red then filled in with color and the whole surface was finally burnished to a lustrous gloss. Outlines define forms with an occasional use of shadows and highlights to suggest solid modelling, not to record the effect of light (the bridge of the Bodhisattva's nose is paler than the rest of his skin and there are shadows on both sides of it).

A visionary harmony, a sense of universal well-being, pervades this great painting. Although it teems with figures, they are all so much at their ease that there is not the slightest sense of overcrowding. It suggests not so much *horror vacui* (dislike of emptiness) as a positive delight in fullness. An amorous couple, royal or divine, reclines to the left of the Bodhisattva; a dark-skinned woman with richly jewelled head-dress stands on the other side. There are monkeys, peacocks and fabulous creatures among the trees in the background, or rather at the top of the wall, for the painting should not be 'read' in a Western way as an illusion of figures in space. The figures, immersed in their own intimate thoughts, must be examined individually by a similarly meditative spectator. They look straight out of the wall, since Indian artists avoided the profile almost as studiously as did the Egyptians and Greeks the full face. There is no composition in the European sense, no comprehensive controlling pattern to which the parts relate. Forms seem to have drifted together like clouds, giving the work its visionary or dreamlike quality. It differs as profoundly from European painting as does Indian from Western music.

The Bodhisattva stands in the *tribhanga* pose, gazing with an expression of thoughtful tenderness. His features recall, no doubt intentionally, the similes by which supernatural beauty was evoked in Buddhist literature – brows curving like an Indian bow, eyes like lotus petals and so on. A jewelled tiara, a pearl necklace with sapphire clasp, and the strand that Brahmins wear across their chests woven of seed pearls all indicate princely status. The symbolically blue lotus flower in his hand identifies him as Avalokitesvara ('the being capable of enlightened insight') Padmapani, one of the most important figures in *Mahayana* Buddhism, who was to be worshipped in China as Guanyin and in Japan as Kwannon (see pp. 276, 289). He is the potential Buddha, eternally teaching the doctrine of enlightenment to all creatures on earth. His regalia refer to his role as a heavenly prince and also to the historical Buddha's youth as an earthly prince. As a personification of divine mercy and compassion for humanity, he satisfied devotional and emotional needs better than the remote figure who had attained *Nirvana* and had come to be seen less as a teacher than a symbol of the redemptive power latent in every soul. He was also much more like the ever-present deities of traditional Indian religious cults. His lotus links him with the pre-Aryan Lakshmi, and also with Vishnu and Brahma.

By the seventh century, when this painting was executed at Ajanta, *Mahayana* beliefs were, in fact, beginning to draw Buddhism in India back to its origins. After the Islamic invasion, which began in the early eleventh century, it was entirely eradicated in the north (hence the scarcity of surviving monuments) and completely re-assimilated into Hinduism in the south, where the Buddha was eventually regarded as an avatar or incarnation of Vishnu. The subsequent history of Buddhist art thus lies mainly outside India (see pp. 252–95).

HINDU ART IN INDIA

During the first millennium of the Christian era Buddhism, Jainism and Hinduism developed side by side without friction, submitting to the same influences, exchanging ideas and insights. This is clearly evident in sculpture. Buddhists and Jains may not always have practised the non-violence they preached any more than Christians did. But they did not persecute, nor were they persecuted by, adherents of the manifold and undogmatic religious and philosophical beliefs that comprise Hinduism. The arts inspired by these religions, therefore, differ less in style than in iconography. Images of the Jain *tirthankaras* – the 24 men who had over the ages attained perfect knowledge, also called *jinas* or conquerors – seated in the yoga pose are completely naked but otherwise barely distinguishable from Buddhas who are always clad. (Their tight-fitting robes were originally painted and were thus rather more conspicuous than they are now.) *Yakshis* (see p. 226) figure in the scriptures of all three religious groups, though the most notable representations of them come from the outer railings of Buddhist stupas, including a whole voluptuous series found at Sanghol – one with swaying hips and a provocative smile carries a toilet tray beneath the gaze of a boy peering over a fence (**6,25**). Hinduism has remained to this day the religion of the vast majority of Indians, and its artistic heritage is incomparably richer than that of Indian Buddhism or of Jainism (which has always been a relatively small sect). Its iconography is also much more complex, incorporating numerous figures with multiple significance.

Images of Hindu gods, known to have been carved at least as early as the first century BC, seem to have been still more ruthlessly destroyed by Muslim iconoclasts (destroyers of images) than those of the Buddha. One has been preserved, however, in south-east India at Gudimallam, near Madras, where it is still venerated and anointed each day with clarified butter – hence its shiny surface (**6,26**). Carved with much greater naturalism than any Buddhist image, it represents Shiva or, rather, his prototype Rudra-Agni, the wild hunter and god of fire mentioned in the most ancient and sacred of Sanskrit scriptures, the *Rig Veda*, holding a dead antelope in one hand, a vase and weapon in the other, standing on the shoulders of a dwarf. The gigantic phallus behind him has a different origin in earlier indigenous fertility cults. Numerous little terracotta phalluses survive from the period of the Indus Valley civilization and the *Rig Veda* alludes contemptuously to people who made the penis their god. Indigenous and Aryan religious beliefs were, however, combined in Hinduism.

Nearly all the main members of the Hindu pantheon are gathered together in a fine relief of the Gupta period on a temple at Deogarh in central India (**6,27**). Vishnu, to

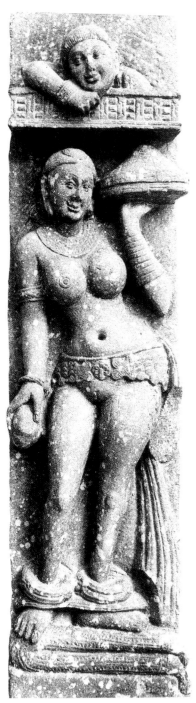

6,25 Railing pillar from Sanghol, India, 2nd century AD. Red sandstone, 3ft 4ins (1.01m) high.

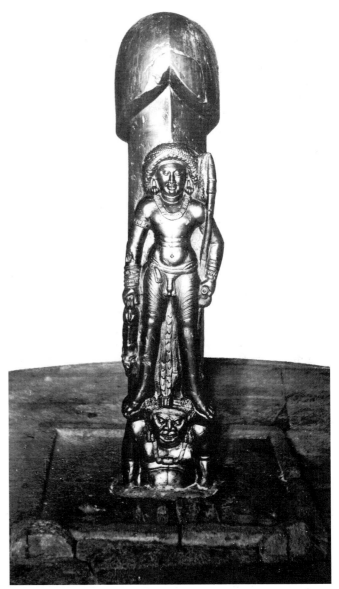

6,26 *Linga* with Shiva, Gudimallam, India, 1st century BC. Stone, 4ft 11¼ins (1.5m) high.

whom the temple is dedicated, has pride of place. The world and all its creatures are often referred to as figments in the dream, or nightmare, of Vishnu. He is here shown asleep, resting on the coils of the giant serpent called Ananta (endless), who dwells in the cosmic waters which give life to all beings, divine as well as terrestrial. The god and the serpent, which raises its nine heads to form a canopy over him, are both manifestations of the single divine cosmic substance – the energy underlying and inhabiting all forms of life. Vishnu's right leg is held and caressed by his wife Lakshmi, goddess of fortune and mediator between the devotee and the god, in origin one of the nature spirits worshipped by the pre-Aryan

inhabitants of India. (The serpent may also be connected with Dravidian water-spirits called *nagas*.) In the centre of the upper register a figure in the yoga posture might be mistaken for the Buddha were it not for his three faces, which reveal him to be Brahma. He is enthroned on a lotus blossom said to grow from Vishnu's navel (though this is not directly indicated in the carving at Deogarh). Flanking him on the left is Indra riding his elephant; on the right Shiva and his consort are mounted on a bull. Five men and one woman at the base of the relief, in busy attitudes which contrast with the atmosphere of eternal somnolence above, are terrestrial incarnations of other gods. Their story is associated with Vishnu's avatar or individual manifestation as Krishna, related in the *Bhagavad Gita*, the enormously influential religious poem that was composed in about 200 BC and marks the emergence of popular theistic Hinduism out of the esoteric Vedic religion of the Brahmins. In the context of Indian religious

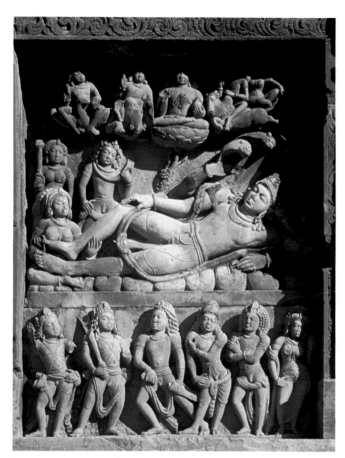

6,27 Vishnu on Ananta, Vishnu temple, Deogarh, India, 5th century AD.

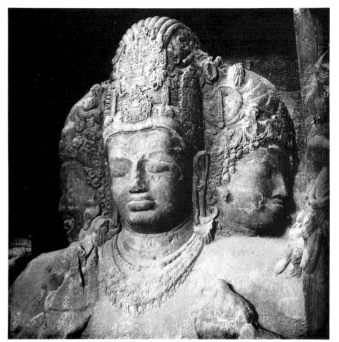

6,28 Shiva Mahadeva, Shiva temple, Elephanta, India, mid-6th century AD. Stone, 17ft 10ins (5.44m) high.

6,29 *Linga*, Shiva temple, Elephanta, mid-6th century.

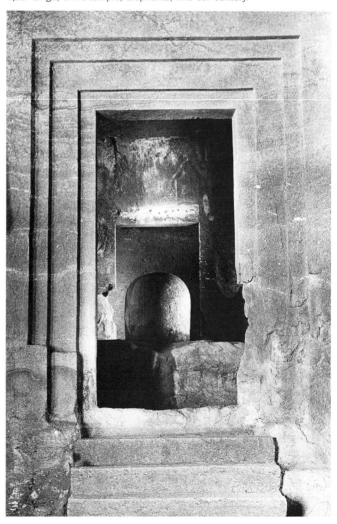

history, it is interesting to note that the relief at Deogarh gives second place to Brahma but only alludes to Krishna, whose cult later became, as it still remains, the most widespread in India.

The orthodox Hindu trinity is composed of Brahma, the creator of the universe, Vishnu, its preserver and supporter and Shiva, its destroyer. But as they are identical in substance, their roles are interchangeable and each may be credited with those of all three. Shiva is shown as a trinity himself in the rock-cut temple dedicated to him on the island of Elephanta, some 6 miles (9.6km) out from Bombay harbour. A more than 17-foot-high (5m) bust with the three heads seemingly rises out of the ground within a dark recess opposite the entrance (6,28). A stern virile mustached profile crowned with a cobra and death's head on the left is balanced, on the other side, by that of a female counterpart, softly modelled with voluptuous lips and delicately dressed hair. They indicate respectively the male and female, destructive and creative, principles that proceed from the divine essence or Absolute represented by a sublimely aloof androgynous central countenance. As a whole this overpowering image – so different from the simply conceived and, one might say, naively anthropomorphic deities of the ancient West – gives concrete form to the mystery of the unfolding of the Absolute into the dualities of phenomenal existence. It was not, however, the main object of worship in the temple. An inner

THE DIVINE: FROM APOLLO TO VISHNU

The concept of Divinity as a power above humanity and beyond full human comprehension, intangible but none the less vividly experienced intuitively, has been a major source of inspiration for the visual arts. It prompted, over the millennia, emanations of the spiritual that were often great and memorable works of art. Aspects of the divine could be represented in diverse ways ranging from abstract symbols to images in human, animal or combined human and animal forms. The ancient Greeks conceived their gods and goddesses in idealized human forms with attributes to indicate their divinity – as Aphrodite or Apollo, for instance – and this practice was taken over by the Christians for their saints. The prohibition of graven images in the Second Commandment, however, prevented them using it as regards God the Father except in narrative scenes where the image could not be mistaken for an idol to be worshipped. Muslims also abominated idolatry and were as rigorous as the Christians in their respect for the prohibition and even more so in destroying the religious art of the countries they overran, notably in the Indian sub-continent. Yet nowhere have the possibilities of giving concrete form to the abstract concept of divinity been more subtly explored than in Hindu sculpture.

The earliest Indian scriptures, the *Vedas* (c. BC 1300–600) and the *Upanishads* (c. BC 800–500), embody lofty metaphysical doctrines that could be fully understood only by the initiated. They make no concessions to the common human demand for divinities that can be visualized. In the later and more accessible *Bhagavad Gita* of the second century BC, however, the warrior Arjuna asks Krishna, avatar of Vishnu, god of gods, to show himself in his Supreme Being: he was vouchsafed:

. . . countless visions of wonder: eyes from innumerable faces, numerous celestial ornaments; celestial garlands and vestures, forms anointed with heavenly perfumes. The infinite divinity was facing all sides, all marvels in him containing. If the light of a thousand suns rose in the sky that splendour might be compared to the radiance of the Supreme Spirit. And Arjuna saw in that radiance the whole universe in its variety, standing in a vast unity in the body of the god of gods. Trembling with awe and wonder, Arjuna bowed his head, and joining his hands in adoration he thus spoke to his god: 'I see in thee all the gods, O my God, and the infinity of the beings of thy creation . . . All around I behold they infinity; the power of thy innumerable arms, the visions from thy innumerable eyes . . . I rejoice in exultation, and yet my heart trembles with fear. Have mercy on me Lord of gods, Refuge of the whole universe, show me again thine own human form. I yearn to see thee again in thine own four-armed form, thou of arms infinite'. The god of all gave peace to his fears and showed himself in this peaceful beauty.

The *Bhagavad Gita* is the earliest Indian text in which the idea of a personal relationship between a mortal and a god is found. The first images of Hindu gods appear to have been carved at about the same time. Their distinguishing features were presumably determined initially by priests and knowledge of them handed down from one generation of sculptors to another. By the sixth century AD they were codified in such treatises as the *Manasara Silpasastra* which ruled that, for instance, an image of Shiva 'should be furnished with four arms, three eyes and be crowned with matted hair . . . the upper right hand should be in the refuge offering pose, the upper left hand in the boon giving pose; the other left and right hand should hold the antelope and the drum respectively . . . Saravati [consort of Brama and goddess of learning] should be placed on a lotus pedestal and seated in the cross-legged posture . . .' Similarly, rules were also laid down for a scale of bodily proportions, distinguishing deities from mortals. It was assumed, though not stated, that more than two arms were necessary to express divine omnipotence, and more than two eyes to suggest all-seeing omniscience.

Such sculptures were easily misunderstood as objects of worship in themselves, rather than representations that could be consecrated or charged with divine spirit by ritual. According to the eighth-century AD philosopher and mystic Shankara, 'the Supreme Lord may if he wishes assume a corporeal form as a favour to his devout worshippers'. Theologians interpreted the popular cult of statues of Vishnu as proof of the god's compassion in manifesting himself to devotees and allowing himself to be perceived by the senses even at the risk of being transformed into an idol and of being confused with the material objects he had sanctified with his presence. For Hindus, truth lies beyond the world of appearances and their images of deities are thus illusory manifestations of a single ultimate reality.

shrine with four entrances encloses a simple monolithic cylinder with a domed top – the *linga*, literally 'sign', but particularly the sign of male sex as a manifestation of Shiva (**6,29**). Such a shrine is found in every temple dedicated to Shiva. By the fifth century the *linga* had been given a form less explicitly phallic than it has at Gudimallam (6,26) to indicate a far wider significance. While continuing to express the creative energy of Shiva, it also symbolizes the transmutation of sexual into mental power, the ascent from a sentient to a transcendental plane achieved through the practice of yogic meditation. It is often placed on a circular *yoni*, the symbol of the female generative organ, so that together they express the unity within the duality of the cosmos. The simple swelling phallus of ancient fertility cults had now been given austere, almost geometrical, form and been invested with transcendentally supranatural significance, purged of all trace of erotic sensuality. Abstraction could be taken only one step further: the faithful go to a temple at Chidambaram, south of Madras, to worship the *Akasalinga*, an invisible *linga* of ether.

To the Western mind the idea of an invisible symbol is contradictory. But neither Indian art nor the religious philosophy with which it is so closely integrated is susceptible to rational analysis. Both are suprarational. A work of Indian sculpture is not an illusory imitation – in the Platonic or Aristotelian sense (see p. 177) – but part of a visible world which is itself entirely illusory. No distinction is made between the real and the ideal, the naturalistic and the symbolic.

Nor is any distinction drawn between what the West calls space and solid matter. According to Indian cosmology our visible world is composed of an all-pervading radiant substance, *akasa* or ether, a small part of which condensed to form air. By a similar process fire was formed from air, water from fire and solid earth from water. Air is as much a substance as the other elements, there is no empty space in the cosmos and thus the problem of creating an illusion of space in reliefs (or paintings), which perplexed and obsessed European artists for so many centuries, simply did not arise. The Indian sculptor shaped figures, often out of the living rock, by a process analogous to that by which ether condensed into tangible substance under the creative influence of the supreme divine being.

The force of these ideas and their effect on the forms taken by Indian art can be seen quite clearly in an extraordinary carving on a huge granite boulder at Mamallapuram, south of Madras on the east coast (6,30). The subject has been variously interpreted as either the myth of the descent of the river Ganges to earth through the locks of Shiva's hair or as an incident in the great south Indian epic, the *Mahabharata*, in which Arjuna obtains by ascetic austerities the aid of Shiva in war – and there is even a possibility that these two subjects were combined.

6,30 *Descent of the Ganges*, Mamallapuram, India, 6th to 7th century AD.

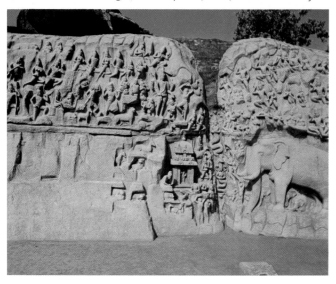

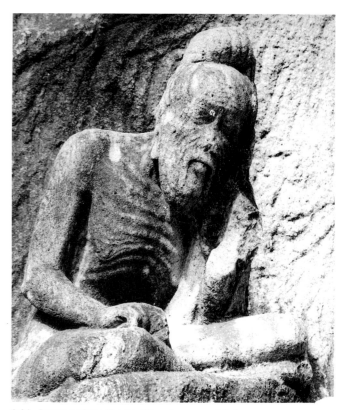

6,31 *Descent of the Ganges*, Mamallapuram, detail, 6th to 7th century AD.

More than 100 large figures of deities, humans, half-humans and animals, including life-size elephants, stand on either side of a natural cleft, up which the king and queen of the *nagas* float. The whole surface, some 20 feet (6m) high and 80 feet (24m) long, seethes with life as if it were fermenting and this effect must have been heightened when, on special occasions, sparkling water flowed down the fissure from a cistern above. Individual figures, especially the animals, suggest that the relief depicts a single episode in the myth: the moment when the Ganges descends from the heavens to make the earth fertile. But earlier events are also recorded, meshed into the composition rather than strung out in narrative sequence. Two yogis meditating by a temple just to the left of the cleft belong to the very beginning of the story (6,31). Two Brahmins, immediately beneath them, are figures who seem to come from the sculptor's own world and time; one dries himself after bathing in the sacred stream which washes away sin. The descent of the Ganges to water the north-east Indian plain is a perpetually miraculous phenomenon, and different episodes in the myth can therefore be shown simultaneously. The art that ignored Western ideas of space also transcended time. There is no sense of continuity or sequence. All time is eternally present in this carving, for – to quote T. S. Eliot – 'the end and the beginning were always there before the beginning and after the end'.

This Indian conception of eternity, or of an eternal moment, is implicit in such sculptures as the relief carving inside a nearby cave temple of a woman mounted on a lion and accompanied by an army of dwarfs riding into battle against a buffalo-headed man (6,32). She is one of the personifications of the supreme goddess, the

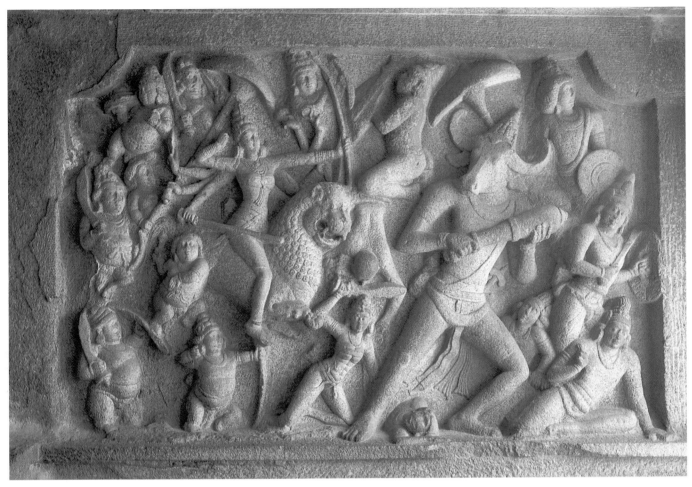

6,32 Durga and the demon, Mahisasaramardini cave, Mamallapuram, 7th century.

6,33 The Bhima Ratha and Dharmaraja Ratha, Mamallapuram, AD 630–70.

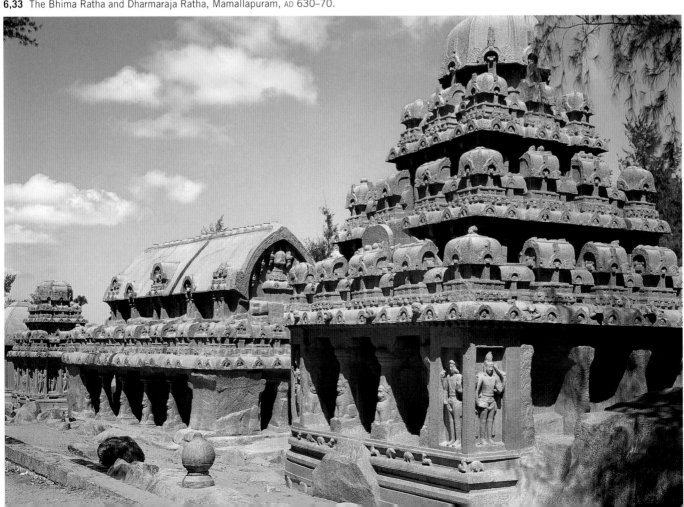

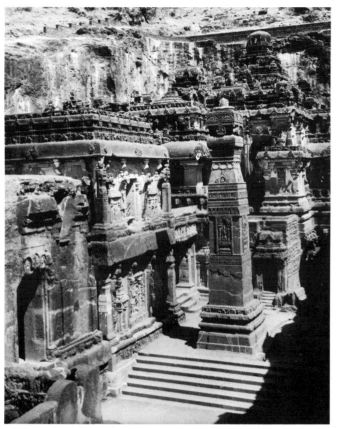

6,34 Kailasa temple, Ellora, India, c. AD 750–850. Volcanic rock.

surviving Indian temples and monasteries were burrowed into cliffs. But temples were also cut in the round out of the living rock by a complementary process of separating and molding the elements of earth and air. The most impressive is at Ellora, a place of immemorial sanctity where both Buddhist monks and Brahmin ascetics lived and worshipped. An entire slope was excavated to leave a richly sculptural shrine measuring nearly 100 feet (30m) from base to cupola-shaped crown, dedicated to Shiva as the Lord of Kailasa, a mountain in northern India regarded as the earthly counterpart of Mount Meru, believed to be the vertical axis of the universe (**6,34**). Originally it was painted white, like a snow-covered Himalayan peak, in shimmering contrast to the gray rock that surrounds it. The whole surface is enlivened with figurative reliefs which not only seem to materialize out of the stone (**6,35**) but are in fact part of the fabric (rather than applied to it as in Europe and the West), like such architectural elements as pilasters and lintels which here have, of course, no structural function. And as in the caves, many features are derived from buildings of wood and thatch. This is more obvious at Mamallapuram where the upper part of the Dharmaraja Ratha is adorned with numerous little model temples akin to the nearby Bhima Ratha with its simulated thatched roof. The immediate predecessors of these rock-cut shrines were, however, stone-built temples similarly decorated with motifs taken from constructions

6,35 Kailasa temple, Ellora, detail, c. AD 750–850. Volcanic rock.

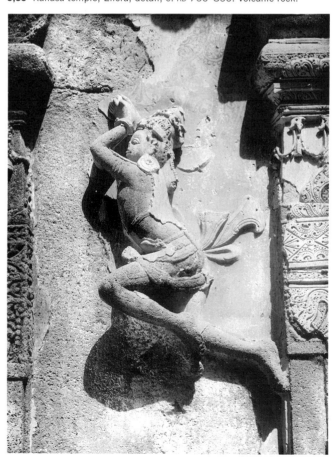

mother of all, whose nature is so complex that she is given different names according to her various interconnected roles, ranging from that of Parvati, consort and energizing female counterpart of Shiva whose passive, benevolent, philosophical aspects she may also embody, to that of the fearful Kali who symbolizes the power of death. Here she is shown as Durga, the embodiment of energy, created by the gods and equipped with weapons to destroy the buffalo demon whose power was greater than theirs. The eternal conflict between good and evil is the burden of the story illustrated and Durga's victory is to be understood as a metaphor for religious attainment though, as shown here, it is still to be completed; her bow in the centre of the composition neatly separates the two elemental forces, the demon and his retainers having only just begun to retreat. The wider, human relevance of the story is emphasized by the naturalism of the figures not only in pose – the one tumbling forwards just in front of the lion's head, for instance – but also in scale. The slender Durga, although the most important, is much smaller than the demon and his followers for this is the narrative of a myth to be pondered, rather than an icon to be adored, like many images of the goddess with the demon dead at her feet.

Three natural boulders at Mamallapuram were carved into free-standing statues of animals – elephant, lion and bull – and five outcrops of granite into monolithic sanctuaries somewhat misleadingly called rathas, or 'chariots' (**6,33**). As we have already seen (p. 229), the earliest

Ellora

AN ARCHITECT-SCULPTOR'S SUMMIT

The surfaces of exterior and interior walls of the Kailasa temple complex at Ellora (6,34) are alive with figures seated in meditative contemplation of the infinite, standing in attitudes of ease or of divine majesty, fighting, making love, ecstatically dancing and flying through the air (6,35). They make the hard volcanic rock pulsate. A narrative scene with the main figures carved in such high relief that they might be free-standing is the most spectacularly dramatic (6,36). It shows Ravana, the many-headed many-armed evil demon, shaking the mountain where Shiva is resting with his consort Parvati, who clings to his arm in fright while her female attendant runs away. In the sky deities have come together to witness an event that was intended to be quite literally earth-shattering. But two guardian figures are quietly seated on either side and Shiva, by the pressure of a foot (some accounts say one toe) overpowers Ravana, condemning him to perpetual imprisonment beneath the earth. Despite the rhythmic movement of individual figures, the almost geometrically

controlled composition with its fine balance of projecting mass against receding void emphasizes the moral of the story: that the forces of evil cannot prevail against the power of the god.

This relief was created by the so-called subtractive sculptural process (see p. 13), cutting away unwanted material as opposed to building up a form in a malleable medium. So too was the whole temple. It was hacked out from a slope of volcanic rock, from the tip of the spire down to the pavement. This process is the exact opposite of normal construction from a ground-plan upwards, but the architect-sculptor's genius was in no way hampered. And the whole elaborate temple complex at Ellora should be seen first in the context of this peculiarly Indian conception of 'carved' architecture, complementing the no less elaborate and infinitely ramifying complexities of the Hindu mythologies it celebrates.

To the outside world the precinct is closed by a wall of rock which is richly carved but gives no inkling of what lies within. Visitors coming from the bare open plain, sun-parched and sun-drenched with only occasional scrub to give shade, pass through a gatehouse and are then confronted, to their amazement, by a vast open court nearly 300 feet (91.4m) long and 150 feet (45.7m) wide enclosing 'buildings' of two stories, tall free-standing columns and carved elephants as large as, if not larger than, life, with abundant space for movement around them. (The plan at first floor level, 6,37, indicates the buildings' spatial distribution.) Oriented on a strict east–west axis these massive forms, as well as the southern cliff-face itself, cast welcome, slowly moving shadows. Rippling light and shade animate the two long sides where porticoes at two levels set off the darkness of temples cut horizontally into the rock.

Ritual circumambulation of the main temple, as practised by devout

Hindus, discloses an ever-changing sequence of vistas, punctuated by reliefs such as that of Ravana carved into the base of the temple, which is itself an evocation of Mount Kailasa (see p. 244). At ground level the central blocks are solid. Interiors are hollowed out above and are reached by stairways in the gatehouse leading to a stone bridge connecting it with the pavilion of Nandi, the bull that Shiva rides. Another bridge leads on to the main temple with a sanctuary for the sacred *linga* (see p. 241) in its innermost recess. The temples cut into the cliff-face are also on the upper level, that to the north dedicated to Lakeshvara (a local name for Shiva), that on the south to the seven mothers of gods.

As an architectural group the temple complex is of great intricacy. But the various elements are so ingeniously related to one another on the two levels that it resolves itself into an animated harmony. An anonymous writer of the eighth century declared that the 'immortals who ride in celestial chariots, struck with astonishment, say this temple of Shiva is self-existent: such beauty is not seen in anything made by art', and the architect himself was 'suddenly struck with astonishment, saying "Oh, how was it that I built it!"'

6,36 *Shiva and Parvati on Kailasa*, Kailasa temple, Ellora, c. AD 750–850. Volcanic rock, about 12ft (3.66m) high.

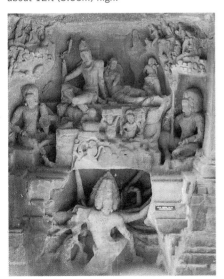

6,37 Plan of Kailasa temple, Ellora.

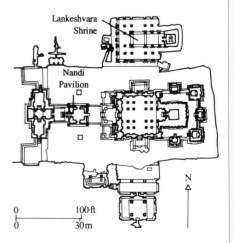

Lankeshvara
Shrine

Nandi
Pavilion

0   100 ft
0   30 m

N

in impermanent materials, and similarly giving an impression of sculptured mass that is not inert but alive.

The earliest surviving free-standing Hindu temples were built during the Gupta period (c. 300–500). They are relatively small but sufficient for their purpose: to house the image of a deity or a *linga*, with space for a priest to celebrate ritual on behalf of the community. As there was no congregational worship, this space, reserved exclusively for the priest, always remained limited and temples were enlarged around, in front of and above it. In this way it came to be enclosed within the building as a sanctuary – called *garbhagria* or 'womb-chamber' – with a passage round it for the rite of circumambulation, as important in Hinduism as in Buddhism. A porch or veranda in front of the simplest type of temple was extended to form one or more halls (called *mandapas*) on axis with the sanctuary which can be dimly seen from the entrance so that worshippers may experience *darshana* (auspicious viewing) as they move towards the cult image, sometimes through a succession of doorways marking degrees of sanctity. Externally the sanctuary is marked by the tall *sikhara* or tower directly above it and projecting its sacredness upwards. Whereas interiors are almost invariably dark with little sculpture to distract attention from the cult image, exteriors are often exuberantly covered with carvings in relief to be seen in the bright light of the Indian day by worshippers who take in their message as they circumambulate before entering.

Temples were built at places that already had some religious significance and were usually sited with a precisely calculated east–west axis of the rising and setting sun. The various stages of their design and construction were determined astronomically or astrologically – undifferentiated in Indian thought – and the first account of their form appears in a treatise on astronomy dating from the Gupta period (see p. 248). Thus the temple of the sun god Surya at Konarak (6,42) was completed and dedicated in 1258 on a particularly auspicious day, the god's birthday which coincides with the Aryan Sunday only once in every seven years. A Hindu temple is associated also with the formal structure of the universe being, in fact, a microcosm with every measurement determined by a very elaborate scale of proportions derived from the mystical numerical basis of the cosmos as shown diagrammatically in a *mandala*, an aid to meditation on abstract concepts. By these means it could become the dwelling place of a deity – Shiva or one of the goddesses who are no less important – whose presence could be invoked by ritual. Infinitely richer than the palace of any mortal ruler and constructed with the durable materials generally reserved for religious buildings, the temple was decorated with motifs derived from mundane architecture but multiplied *ad infinitum*. Lintel is piled upon lintel, roof upon roof in seemingly endless succession; even the basic form of the building is repeated again and again and sometimes whole façades are tiered one above another. Numbers have always fascinated Indians. A single incarnation of Indra, king of the gods, is said to last 306,720,000 human years, that of Brahma 1,103,760 times

longer, according to popular doctrine. The human soul can, however, transcend this temporality and escape the cycle of birth and rebirth, to which even the gods are subject, by attaining union with the Absolute. And this potentiality is symbolized by the crowning member of the *sikhara*, sometimes shaped like a bubble which bursts into non-being or like a lotus bud which opens to release pure essence.

Techniques of construction, on the other hand, were determined by conservative craft traditions. Stone temples were built without mortar and only rarely with the aid of iron clamps. Pillars, cross-beams and lintels are held together by their sheer weight, hence the powerful impression of massiveness. Although the principle of the arch and vault was known at a fairly early date it was not exploited for Hindu or Jain temples (the true arch and dome were to be characteristics of Muslim architecture in India from the thirteenth century). Openings were spanned by monolithic lintels, sometimes carved into arch-like shapes. Interiors were usually covered by horizontal slabs, occasionally by overlapping stone courses to

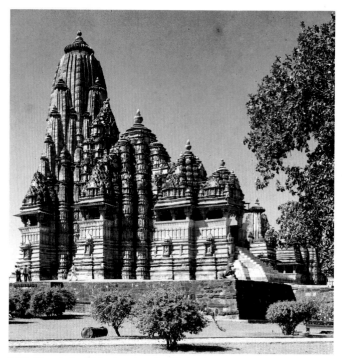

6,38 Khandariya Mahadeva temple, Khajuraho, India, c. AD 1000.

6,39 Plan of Khandariya Mahadeva temple, Khajuraho.

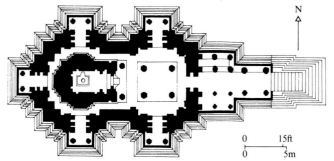

N

0   15ft
0   5m

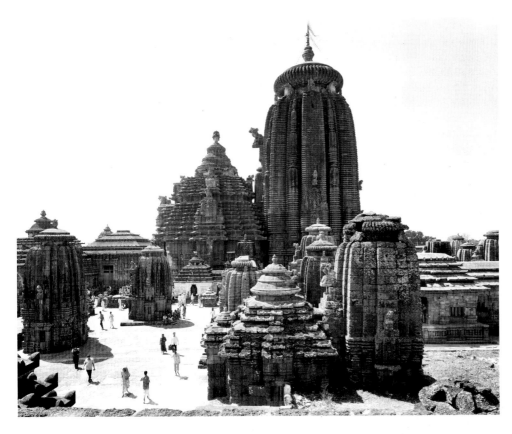

6,40 Lingaraja temple, Bhuvanesvar, India, c. 1100.

create dome-like spaces. Huge *sikharas* were raised with hollow corbelled interiors.

There are, nevertheless, stylistic differences from one region and period to another over an area as vast as the Indian subcontinent and during some ten centuries (or more in the south). Every major temple is, in fact, a unique creation, the work of an architect and teams of masons and sculptors under the direction of priests. Yet it is rare for any name to be recorded save that of the ruler who financed it as a means of earning merit for himself and prosperity for his subjects. 'Let him who wishes to enter the worlds that are reached by meritorious deeds of piety and charity build a temple to the gods', a writer of the Gupta period advised. And as patrons wished to improve on the work of their predecessors a premium was set on the inventiveness and structural daring of architects, as well as on sheer size and richness of sculpture. Many of the most ambitious projects date from that moment when a dynasty had reached the peak of its power, just before economic decline set in – a relapse to which the expense of temple building had not infrequently contributed.

At Khajuraho, the capital of a small central Indian kingdom ruled by the Chandella family, the Khandariya Mahadeva temple is the latest and richest of three temples in the same style and one of the most perfect expressions of the Hindu conception of architecture (**6,38; 39**). It is set on a platform from which a flight of steps leads up to a porch preceding the great hall with the sanctuary surrounded by an ambulatory at its end. Worshippers thus pass from daylight into the shade of the porch and thence

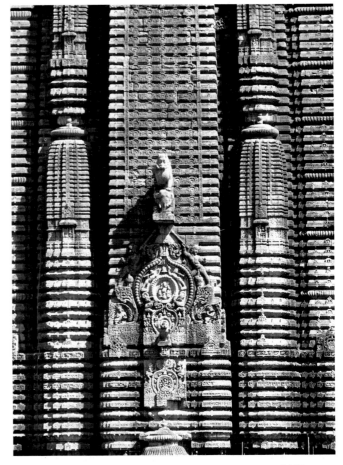

6,41 Lingaraja temple, Bhuvanesvar, detail of the *sikhara*, c. 1100.

from the dimly lit interior to the darkness of the shrine. The relative importance of these spaces is marked externally by three superstructures of increasing size and the magnificent *sikhara* soaring like a mountain peak some 100 feet (30m) above the platform. The whole structure has a remarkable organic unity, a sense of tumescent upward growth.

The Lingaraja temple at Bhuvanesvar, built about AD 1100 with some later additions, gives the impression of a whole mountain landscape. Its *sikhara* is the finest example of a type developed in this region, Orissa, in the course of some 400 years (**6,40**). Verticality, emphasized by deep recessions, is interrupted at the top by lions carrying the crowning member and balanced by the horizontal lines of the carved decoration. On the sides there are reliefs of the *sikhara* itself, one above another, between bands each of which is carved with motifs derived from the windows of *chaitya*-halls (**6,41**). There is no better example of the obsessive Indian delight in multiplication, the repetition of motifs having here the same hypnotic power as the reiterated phrases in a sacred chant.

The forms of the Lingaraja temple were enlarged for the temple of Surya at Konarak, not far away, where the superstructure of the shrine has gone but that of the

SOURCES AND DOCUMENTS

KONARAK TEMPLE BUILDING ACCOUNTS

More is known about the construction of the vast thirteenth-century sun temple at Konarak than about any other building of its time in India, or anywhere else. The original building accounts, copied in a seventeenth-century palm-leaf manuscript (discovered at Puri near Konarak in the 1960s by the American scholar Alice Boner), provide a detailed chronicle of its planning and construction. There are frequent mentions of the male and female builders and artisans employed, the wages they received and their occasional misconduct, bringing vividly to life the human endeavour that went into what might seem to have been an almost super-human undertaking.

The temple was commissioned by Raja Narasimha I of the Ganga dynasty, ruler of most of Orissa in eastern India (c. 1238–64), and financed initially from booty taken in his military campaigns against neighbouring Muslim states. Six years and three months were devoted to its planning, twelve years and ten months to its construction and the carving of innumerable statues and reliefs, before it was completed on an auspicious day in 1258, the birthday of the sun god Surya. The palm-leaf manuscript begins with the appointment of the chief architect, a Brahmin priest called Sadaskva Samantaraya Mahaputra, who appointed the executive architect, the superintendent of works, the chief image-maker, the head stone-mason, the maker of the scaffolding, the plasterers, and so on. The ground of the enclosure in which the temple was to stand was then ritually purified, the ground-plan marked out and materials were assigned to the various groups of workers. Three different types of stone – none found in the vicinity – were quarried, placed on wooden rollers and hauled to the site by elephants. As the height of the temple increased the roughly shaped stone blocks were lifted into place by pulleys and a system of leverage. For one lintel, for example,

. . . four wooden posts with six iron pulleys were set up and six ropes were tied round the stone . . . . The mahouts

brought two elephants and shouting 'Haribol' had them press down the ends of the planks with their fore-legs.

There were accidents, however, as when the image of Surya was being lifted from the scaffolding to its position on the west side of the temple. Seventeen labourers were employed and during the operation:

. . . the workman Damajana fell down on his head and gave up the ghost. His son Raghua was given a life-sustaining sum of 30 madha [gold coins] *and 10* guntha *of land* [about 1,090 square feet or 100m²].

There were problems with quarrelling labourers and with absentees – a woman was made pregnant by one of the workmen, both ran away and a guard was sent to bring them back.

Many entries in the building accounts refer to carvings. For instance: . . . *to make six* banda-murtis [love images] *Rama Mahaputra, Nila Mahaputra, Gopi Mahaputra and Ganga Mahaputra have jointly a contract of 5* madha *and received down payment.* Contemporary attitudes to religious images are reflected in disputes about them with the sculptors.

When Visi Mahaputra supplied three female figures, Narayana Mahaputra objected to one of them saying that it was the portrait of Visi's wife and therefore could not be placed on the temple. Therefore the image was rejected and only two images accepted for which he received 4 madha. *But Ganga Mahaputra intervened and said that the image had been carved on a lotus pedestal like that of a goddess and therefore should not be objected to. Visi received again 2* madha. *These images were set up on the* mandapa [dance pavilion].

Much of the information contained in the accounts for Konarak may be taken as typical. However no building accounts for other Hindu temples have as yet been traced.

(A. Boner and S. R. Sarma, *New Light on the Sun Temple of Konarak*, Varanasi 1962)

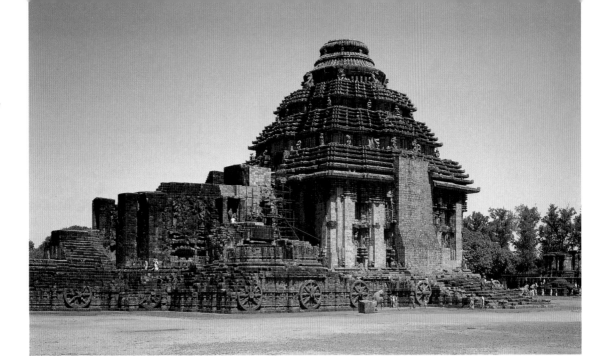

6,42 Temple of Surya, Konarak, India, completed 1258.

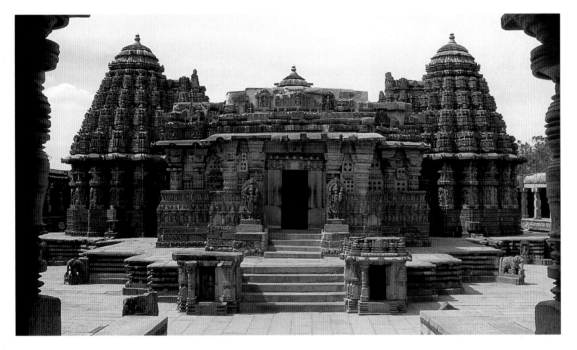

6,43 *Left* Keshava temple, Somnathpur, India, begun 1268.

6,44 *Below* Plan of Keshava temple, Somnathpur.

mandapa remains (**6,42**). It was built to resemble the chariot on which the god traverses the sky, with huge wheels carved on its plinth and sculptured horses prancing in front. The nearly contemporary Keshava temple at Somnathpur in southern India, begun in 1268, could hardly be more different in its squat horizontal emphasis and complex plan with three star-shaped shrines leading out of the rectangular *mandapa* (**6,43; 44**). This is the finest of a number of temples built under the rule of the Hoysala dynasty, and the most ornate anywhere in the subcontinent. It seems to have been conceived as a work of sculpture as much as architecture, and seldom have the two arts been more intimately fused though the general impression is of sculptured mass rather than tectonic form. Carvings that seethe over every surface of the many-faceted walls also form part of the structural framework of pilasters and lintels. Here, as in other Hoysala temples like that at Belur, figures on the exterior and also inside,

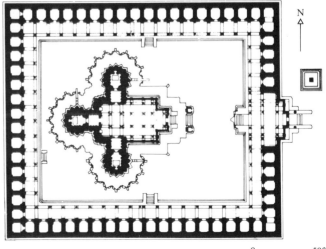

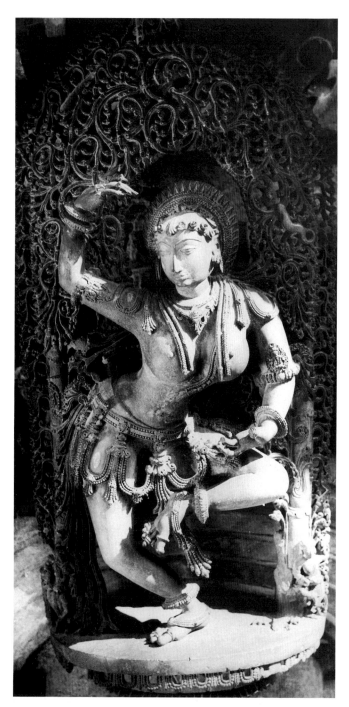

6,45 Bracket figure, Chennakeshava temple, Belur, India, c. 1117.

in the north, most notably at Khajuraho and Konarak, whole surfaces of exterior walls are alive with couples in every posture of love-making, twisting lithe limbs round one another in delirious abandon (**6,46**). There are few if any temple carvings dating from later than the thirteenth century as overtly erotic as those at Khajuraho and Konarak and since no religious or other early texts refer to them directly their original significance, though much discussed, remains mysterious. They have been described as metaphors for the ecstasy of the human soul united with the divine. They have been associated with Tantric teaching that the female principle is the dominant force in the universe without which the male force cannot be stimulated to action – a doctrine that emerged in the seventh century, influencing Buddhism as well as Hinduism and encouraging meditation to resolve the sexual duality within the microcosmic soul. It has also been suggested that the carvings at Konarak illustrate orgiastic rites actually performed in the temple and later suppressed by orthodox Brahmins. But, whatever their original significance and purpose, they are peculiarly Indian. No other civilization in the world has given such prominence to overt eroticism – nor, paradoxically, laid greater stress on ascetic spirituality. As that extraordinarily frank and curiously unprurient account of the art of love, the *Kama sutra* (written in Sanskrit some time between the fourth and seventh centuries BC), is alone enough to demonstrate, Hinduism was far from denying the pleasures of the flesh. In Indian religious art, however, sensuality becomes a vehicle for spiritual ideas.

6,46 Khandariya Mahadeva temple, Khajuraho, detail of exterior, c. AD 1000.

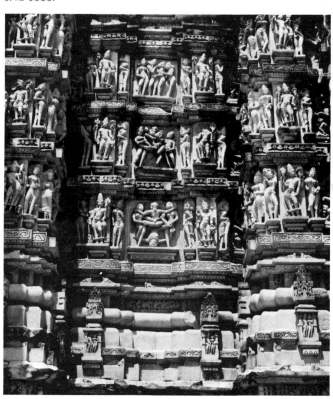

carved from a hard local stone, boldly modelled with much undercutting and miniaturist refinement of detail, have the sharp definition of intricately wrought metalwork (**6,45**). Exceptionally in India, but perhaps significantly, many of these virtuoso feats are signed by their sculptors.

Sculptures on Hindu temples are never merely decorative. But they include, in addition to images of deities, many figures who seem to spring from a lower world of the physical senses. There are innumerable carvings of richly bejewelled nude or lightly clad women displaying their full breasts and swaying their wide hips provocatively as they dance or play musical instruments. Mainly

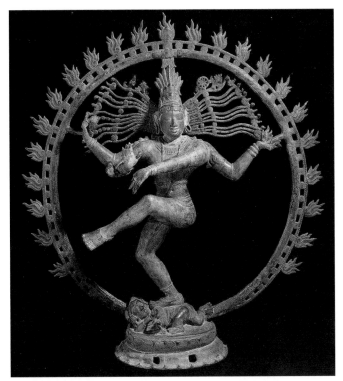

6,47 Shiva Nataraja, Chola, 11th to 12th century. Bronze, 32¼ins (82cm) high. Museum Rietberg, Zürich.

Representations of deities, though more strictly governed than other works of sculpture by iconographic precedents, realized the same ideals of youthful physical perfection (there are no aged gods and goddesses in Indian art). 'The divinity draws near if images are beautiful', a Hindu text declares. A cult image through which a deity is worshipped gives form to the formless, bridging the gulf between the physical and spiritual realms, the yogi and the object of his meditation. It had, therefore, to incorporate the multifarious aspects of divinity present in a single, individual manifestation or 'avatar', the relationship between the image and the god being the same as that between the god and the Absolute.

Four arms are necessary to express the manifold powers and attributes of Shiva Nataraja – Shiva as Lord of the Dance – one of the most popular subjects for bronze statuettes made in southern India especially during the Chola period (ninth to thirteenth centuries) (**6,47**). The symbolism goes beyond the legend of the dance of Shiva (*nadanta*) to express the whole Indian concept of life as an eternal becoming. In the cycles of creation, according to Hindu cosmogony, nothing ever ends or is ever lost or can be lost; all things are interchangeable. Shiva personifies the forces and powers of the cosmic system, the universal flux of energy, the dynamic process of perpetual disintegration and renewal. In his upper right hand he holds a small drum to connote sound, associated with the ether from which all other elements are created; in his upper left hand there is a tongue of flame for the fire with which the universe will be destroyed. Creative and destructive powers are thus balanced. His lower right hand is in a gesture which means 'fear not'. It is addressed to the devout, whose attention is drawn by the lower left hand to the upraised foot which symbolizes escape from the illusions of the world embodied in the demon crushed

beneath Shiva's other foot. His long hair, an attribute of asceticism, streams out on either side of his head enclosing on the left a little figure of Ganges (see p. 242). The encompassing ring of flames is said to signify the vital processes of the universe in the dance of nature, the informing energy of all matter, and, simultaneously, the light of transcendental wisdom. There is neither arrest nor movement in this wonderful composition, or perhaps one should say there are both – with the impassive face of the god at the still point to which the worshipper aspires, where past and future are gathered.

An Indian cult image was the product of ecstatic meditation similar to that which it was intended to assist. 'Let the imager establish images in temples by meditation on the deities who are the objects of his devotion', one of the many Indian craft treatises stipulates. 'For the successful achievement of this yoga the lineaments of the images are described in books, which are to be dwelt upon in detail. By no other means, not even by the direct or immediate vision of an actual object, is it possible to be so absorbed in contemplation as by this meditation in the making of images.' The artist's individual vision of both the natural and supernatural was thus directed and circumscribed by tradition. Individuality was, and still is, alien to Hindu thought except in so far as it refers to the individual manifestation or avatar of a god – Shiva as Lord of the Dance, for instance, or Vishnu appearing on earth as Krishna. Human beings were regarded as types of their caste, occupation, sex or age. Artists were no exception. Their vocation and training were entirely hereditary and they constituted a kind of sub-caste with its own immemorial and carefully maintained traditions of craft practice as well as imagery. Hence the strong sense of continuity in Indian art from at least the time of Asoka and possibly from the Indus Valley civilization more than a millennium earlier. For artists seem to have preserved some of the aura surrounding the shaman or magician. Craft treatises enjoined them to work 'in solitude or with another artist present, never before a layman'. They were the agents of the deity from whom the mystical power of an image is derived.

Indian art is almost exclusively religious – very few secular works from before the sixteenth century survive. Its history, therefore, follows very closely that of religion: the development of Buddhism, the interactions between Buddhism and Hinduism, the spread of Tantric teaching and the periodic re-emergence of indigenous pre-Aryan cults. Numerous works of sculpture and architecture and the few paintings that have been preserved seem to reflect something of that intensity and profundity of Indian religious thought which has never ceased to pervade Indian life. There was, however, a marked decline in artistic quality from the thirteenth century. This was due mainly to the invasions of Muslims, who penetrated as far as Delhi where they founded a Sultanate in 1206. Though they rarely persecuted Hindus they destroyed many of their monuments, and brought the building of temples to a halt in northern and central India. It continued in the kingdoms of the far south which never came under Islam.

BUDDHIST AND HINDU ART IN SRI LANKA AND JAVA

Indian artistic styles spread to south-east Asia and to the Indonesian islands in the wake of Indian religious beliefs. Buddhism was the first proselytizing religion, the first to offer salvation to all mankind and to break away from the worship of local and tribal deities. As we have already seen (p. 224), the emperor Asoka sent missionaries to preach its pacific doctrine to the Hellenistic kingdoms of the West. With much greater success, he dispatched his son to propagate Buddhism in Ceylon (modern Sri Lanka), where it was soon accepted as the established faith in the early *Theravada* form (see p. 232) which has been maintained there to the present day, no more than marginally influenced by *Mahayana* beliefs. Stupas, locally called *dagabas*, were founded from the third century BC onwards and, like that at Sanchi (see pp. 227–8), were often enlarged in later periods, the greatly venerated Mahathupa Ruvvanveliseya in the first capital of the kingdom, Anuradhapura, eventually reaching a height of 300 feet (91.5m) (**6,48**). Kings sought to outdo their predecessors by having *dagabas* built on an ever grander scale until in the fourth century another at Anuradhapura was nearly 400 feet (122m) high, now a mountain of bricks overgrown with tropical vegetation. And their construction has never ceased. They have an austere beauty symbolizing the purity of *Theravada* Buddhist doctrine, notably the idea of liberation from the lusts of the flesh, the lust for life, the love of the present world and from all desire and its concomitant suffering. Shapes vary only slightly in the outline of the cupola – from a hemisphere to the shape of a bubble or a bell – set on a triple ringed plinth and crowned by a spire rising from a square block. Some

South-east Asia

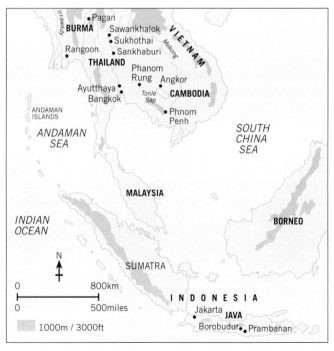

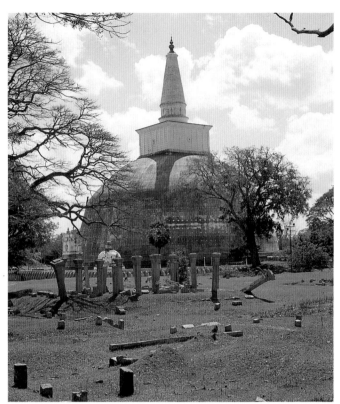

6,48 Mahathupa Ruvvanveliseya *dagaba*, Anuradhapura, Sri Lanka, begun 2nd century BC.

6,49 *Vatadage*, Medirigiriya, Sri Lanka, late 11th century.

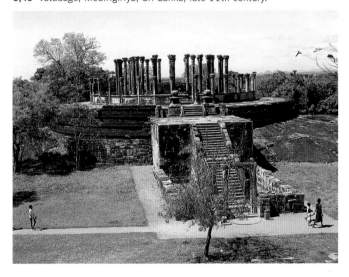

were originally surrounded by monolithic columns carrying wooden roofs beneath which the faithful could circumambulate. And by the eighth century a type of monument peculiar to Sri Lanka, the *vatadage*, had been evolved – a circular platform with two or more rings of columns surrounding a small *dagaba* against which four statues of the meditating Buddha were placed, exemplars of detachment from the world and the self. The most impressive, at Medirigiriya near Polonnarua, dates from the late eleventh century and enshrines earlier statues and *dagaba* (**6,49**).

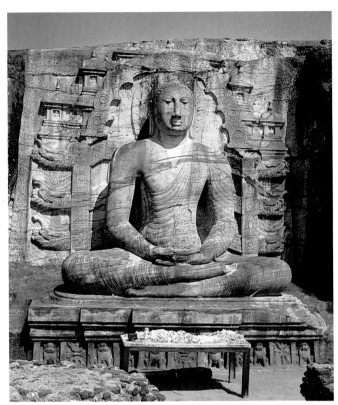

The earliest surviving Buddhist images in Sri Lanka were carved in about the third century AD following Indian precedents but without any of the fleshiness of Mathura sculpture. Later statues of the Buddha tend to be similarly unsensuous and static, even though great naturalistic liveliness was achieved in other carvings on Buddhist buildings – reliefs of guardian figures, cavorting dwarfs and processions of such symbolic creatures as geese and elephants. The Buddha was shown more often meditating with folded hands than gesturing and stripped of all ornament in order not to distract attention from his teaching. These inward-looking figures present the face of *Nirvana*. Three statues of gigantic proportions cut from the living rock at Polonnarua – Buddha in meditation, his death or *Parinirvana* and his favourite disciple Ananda (**6,50; 51**) – date from the late twelfth century but have a stylistic archaism that was surely intentional. There is a very striking contrast between them and sculptures of Shiva Nataraja (6,47) and other Hindu deities, some of which were executed in Sri Lanka when the island was under the rule of the south Indian Chola dynasty (933–1070) – just as there is between clean-lined *dagabas* and luxuriantly sculptured Hindu temples.

Theravada Buddhism, the 'way of the elders', encouraged conservatism in the arts and restricted iconography to subjects directly associated with the historical Buddha

6,50 Buddha in meditation, Gal Vihara, Polonnarua, Sri Lanka, late 12th century. About 25ft (7.6m) high.

6,51 Ananda and Parinirvana Buddha, Gal Vihara, Polonnarua, late 12th century. About 50ft (15.2m) long.

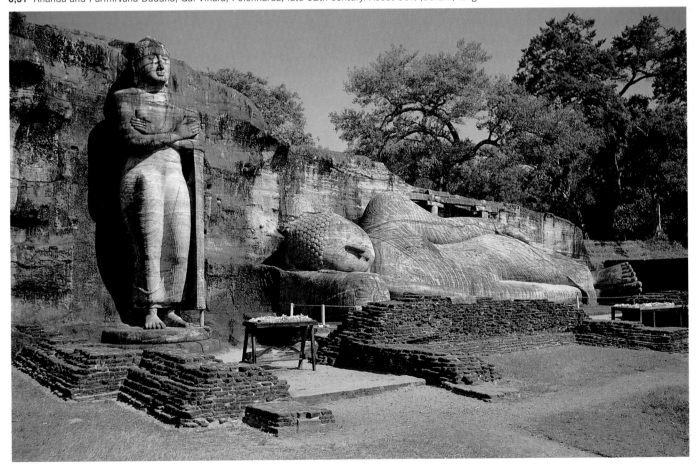

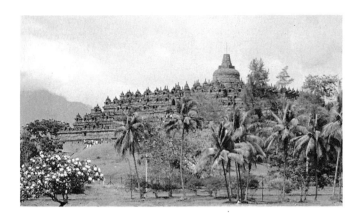

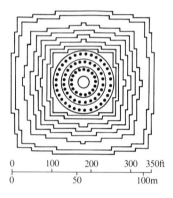

6,52 *Above* Borobudur, Java, completed c. AD 840.

6,53 Plan of Borobudur temple.

completed c. 840. It is a holy mountain of nine terraces built round the solid core of a natural hill and has no 'interior' apart from a sealed chamber at the very top, originally enclosing a statue of the Buddha (6,52). For the only rite performed here was that of circumambulation. Borobudur measures about 360 feet (100m) across the base and is 115 feet (35m) high, but emphasis was placed less on grandeur of scale than on intricacy of detail. The form of a Buddhist stupa was multiplied rather than magnified. There are 72 small bell-shaped stupas encircling the main one on the upper terraces; and lower down there are still more, some cut in half to provide niches. All contained statues of the Buddha seated in the yoga pose and differing from one another only in the *mudras* or significant gestures of the hands – teaching, turning the wheel of the law, casting down evil or simply meditating. Indeed, the name Borobudur (or Baraburdur) probably means 'mountain of Buddhas'.

The plan of the building, composed of four concentric circles inscribed within squares which break forward in the centre of each side, resembles a *mandala* or diagram used in meditation (6,53). Its form, essentially a truncated pyramid crowned by a cone, combines the symbolism of Mount Meru (the centre of Buddhist and Hindu cosmology) with that of the stupa – earth and heaven, existence and *Nirvana*. Relief carvings which line the walls of the rectangular terraces are more simply or overtly didactic, providing a kind of Buddhist pilgrim's progress from the illusory world of the senses to the ultimate transcendental reality. Those at the lowest level illustrate scenes from human life subject to *Karma*, the cycle of birth and rebirth. They were, however, completely closed from view by a massive outer wall (now removed in one corner) probably built as a last minute structural reinforcement for the upper terraces and not, as is sometimes claimed, to symbolize the 'underworld'. Scenes of uninhibited sensuality (6,54) were perhaps not unwillingly sacrificed as they had served as no more than a contrast to the spiritual subjects represented above. In the first gallery the reliefs are devoted to the Buddha Sakyamuni's several incarnations, illustrating his spiritual and active

Sakyamuni. But the boldly speculative, constantly developing sects or schools of the *Mahayana*, with their belief in Bodhisattvas and their heavens, their esoteric rituals and Tantric practices, inspired a wider range of works of art, comparable with those of Hindu cults, in a religious as well as aesthetic sense. This is most clearly evident in Java where both Buddhism and Hinduism were introduced from India at about the same time and promoted by the rulers of the island. Here the earliest surviving buildings are small temples dedicated to Shiva in the seventh century AD. But Borobudur, begun c. 775–80 probably as a Hindu monument, was enlarged and elaborated by stages into one of the greatest achievements of Buddhist art,

6,54 Scenes from Earthly Life, Borobudur, c. 780. Relief carving in andesite.

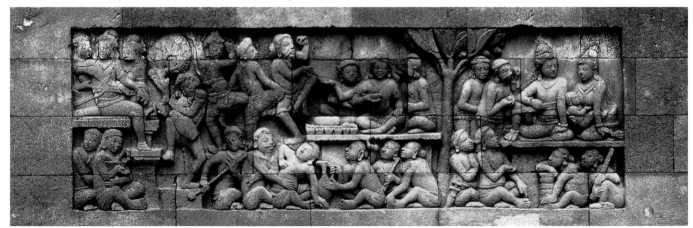

6,55 Scenes from the Legend of the Buddha, Siddhartha bathing (*above*) and Hiru landing on Hiruka (*below*), Borobudur, c. 780–90. Relief carvings in andesite, 9ft (2.74m) wide.

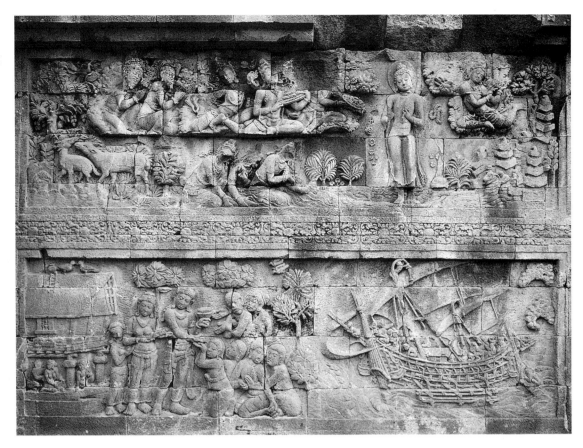

6,56 Scenes from the Legend of the Buddha, Sudhana with a Bodhisattva, Borobudur, c. 780–90. Relief carving in andesite, about 4ft 6ins (1.26m) high.

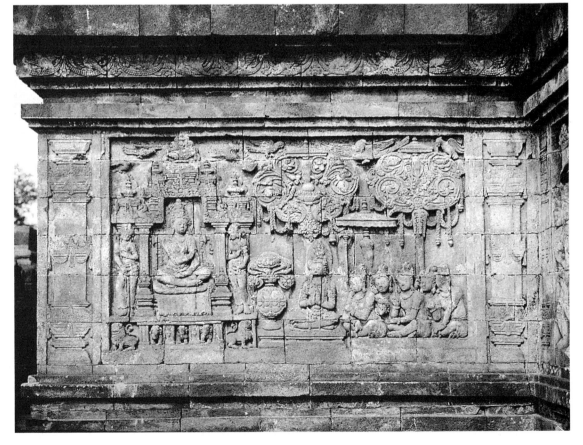

life in two registers – he is, for instance, shown bathing in a river, an act of purification which preceded his struggle with the forces of evil, in a scene above one that shows his earlier avatar as Hiru landing on the island of Hiruka (6,55). As pilgrims climbed the steep stairs they entered the realm of the *Mahayana* which inspired the reliefs on the upper three galleries. This doctrine is illustrated by the spiritual quest of Sudhana, a rich merchant's son who some time after the *Parinirvana* of the historical Buddha sought enlightenment and encountered the Bodhisattvas including Maitreya, the Buddha of the future who will eventually descend to earth (6,56). This exemplary story prepares the devout for ascent to the eternal sphere of the symbolically circular upper terraces, where ethereal Dhyani Buddhas, or transcendental saviours, sit in sublimely composed meditation beneath perforated stupas, one of which has been removed (6,57).

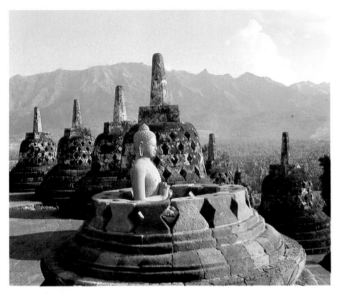

6,57 Dhyani Buddha, upper terrace, Borobudur, c. 810. Andesite, about 4ft (1.2m) high.

Despite the Indian origin of their subject-matter, their symbolism and some of their forms, the carvings at Borobudur could hardly be mistaken for Indian work. Javanese facial features alone would set them apart. But differences that are more than skin-deep are apparent in such a panel as that of the young Buddha cutting his hair in preparation for the ascetic life (6,58) – as the *Jataka* recounts: 'He thought, These locks of mine are not suited to a monk; but there is no one fit to cut off the hair of a Future Buddha, so I will cut them off myself with my sword. Grasping a scimitar with his right hand, he seized his top-knot with his left hand, and cut it off, together with the diadem.' He should, of course, be called Siddhartha at this stage of his life, and he is shown in the relief as a slender youth, not as an ageless sage. But the scene has been conceived imaginatively rather than 'transcendentally' and rendered not so much symbolically as sacramentally. The incident has been formalized into a ritual, attendants have been included, to carry the tiara and shorn curls, as well as four spectators with hands clasped in prayer (the *Jataka* text mentions only the horse on which the Siddhartha left his father's house and the heavenly beings who carried away his hair and head-dress). The composition is logical. Figures are consistent in size and, furthermore, rendered as three-dimensional forms in space rather than as manifestations of the *Maya* bursting out of the stone (see p. 226). The relief that shows Siddhartha bathing in the river is similar although his figure is more idealized, perhaps to indicate progress on the way to enlightenment or Buddhahood (6,55). But in the one below two scenes – to be 'read' from right to left, a ship at sea and Hiru surrounded by men and women on land – are rendered naturalistically, with perspectival diminution on the left for the distant house (of a type still inhabited in some parts of Indonesia). Visual appearances mirrored in these glimpses of the illusory temporal world were, however, ignored in the relief showing Sudhana in mystical communion with a Bodhisattva (6,56).

At about the time that Borobudur was being completed (c. 840), work began not far away on a magnificent group

6,58 Scene from the Legend of the Buddha, Siddhartha cutting his hair, Borobudur, c. 780–90. Relief carving in andesite, 9ft (2.74m) wide.

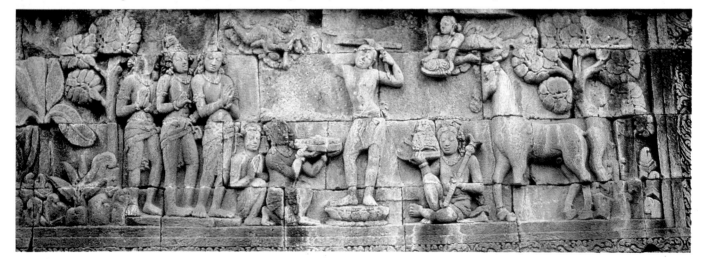

sculptors. In one, the central figure might be mistaken for a Bodhisattva were it not for his trident and lotus crowned by a skull which identify him as Shiva. And the figures on either side seem to have been similarly converted from Buddhism to Hinduism with ease – no doubt like many Javanese who changed their religious practices to conform to those of their rulers (6,60). Borobudur had been erected under the Buddhist kings of the Sailandra dynasty; the temples near Prambanan were founded by the first king of the Sanja dynasty which ruled Java from 832 and promoted Hindu cults without, however, attempting to suppress Buddhism. To finance large-scale building in stone, royal patronage was necessary in Java as in India. And, although Hinduism and Buddhism flourished side by side, royal favour might change with each succeeding dynasty. In the early thirteenth century Queen Dedes – an important historical figure as the mother of the first king of the Singosari dynasty which ruled eastern Java 1222–93 – is traditionally said to have been portrayed in one of the finest of all south-east Asian sculptures, that of Prajnaparamita, the Buddhist personification of transcendental wisdom, turning the wheel of the law (6,61). Meanwhile, in Cambodia the process of identifying rulers with the deities they worshipped had already been taken much further.

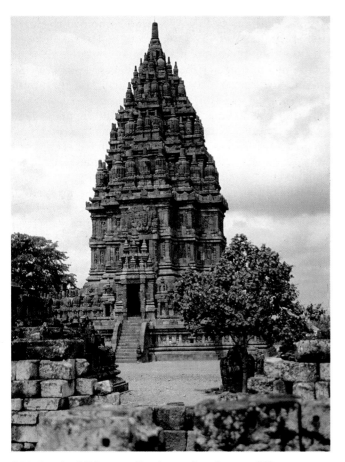

6,59 Temple of Shiva, near Prambanan, Java, begun c. 835.

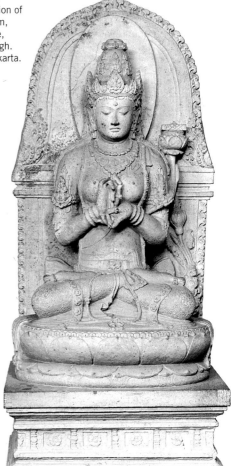

6,61 Prajnaparamita, Buddhist personification of transcendental wisdom, c. 1280–90. Andesite, 4ft 1½ins (1.26m) high. National Museum, Jakarta.

of temples dedicated to Shiva, Vishnu and Brahma (near the present-day village of Prambanan) (6,59). Architecturally they are quite different, with a very strong vertical emphasis. Each was conceived as a holy mountain, but one to be contemplated from ground level rather than ascended slowly as at Borobudur. And they all have interior shrines for images of deities. However, their numerous relief carvings are very similar to those at Borobudur and some may even have been by the same

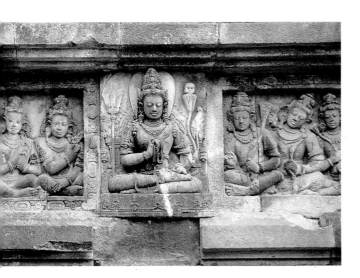

6,60 *Left* Shiva and attendants, temple of Shiva, near Prambanan, c. 850. Relief carving in andesite.

BUDDHIST AND HINDU ART ON THE SOUTH-EAST ASIAN MAINLAND

Pilgrims and merchants on the trade route between India and China appear to have introduced Buddhism to the area of present-day Cambodia. In about the fifth century AD the cult of Shiva was also being propagated by a group of Indian ascetics who won over the rulers of its several warring kingdoms. Shiva's power could, it was believed, be transmitted to the people and the soil by the ritual acts of the ruler, hence the erection of temples and the carving of images. Indian models of the Gupta period were followed at first. By the seventh century, however, a strongly individual style of sculpture had been evolved, as in the

6,62 *Harihara* from Prasat Andet, Cambodia, 7th century. 6ft 4¹/₂ins (1.95m) high. Museum, Phnom Penh.

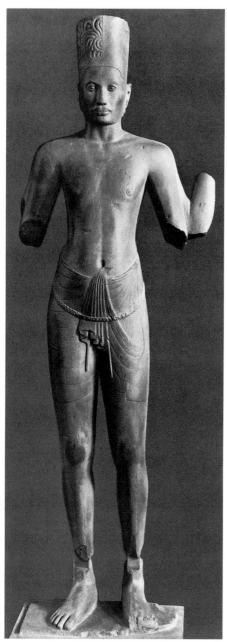

statue of Harihara (**6,62**), a god who combined the attributes and potency of Shiva with those of Vishnu. Beneath the smoothly modelled flesh, set off by the delicate carving of the drapery, there is a suggestion of concentrated energy, of resilient inner vitality. And the physiognomy is characteristically Cambodian, associating the god with his worshippers. This extraordinary naturalism is perhaps more apparent to us today than it would have been originally when the figure was entirely enclosed within a partly detached oval stone frame. The head, hands and base would have been attached to this frame, as in other similar Khmer sculptures of the same period, giving the figure a superhuman, omniscient, even a numinous presence as does, in Western art, an aureole, which the oval frame resembled in form.

In the early ninth century the Khmer speaking people living near the Tonle Sap or Great Lake (about 150 miles, 240km, north-west of Phnom Penh) gradually gained control over the whole of Cambodia under Jayavarman II who in 802 proclaimed himself a 'universal monarch' in a ritual that united religion with politics – the cult of the *Devaraja*, a Sanskrit word meaning 'king of the gods' though it came to signify for the Khmer 'deified king' – a concept alien to Indian thought. The empire he founded soon became the dominant power in south-east Asia, expanding both east and west into the area of present-day Vietnam and Thailand, leaving a rich legacy of architecture and sculpture.

The major artistic achievements of the Khmer were the great stone temples erected by a succession of rulers from the ninth to the twelfth century. They originally towered above cities built of perishable materials, now vanished without trace in the depths of the jungle. Angkor Wat (the name means 'temple of the capital') is the grandest of them and probably the largest temple in the world, a mountain of carved stone rising to a height of some 200 feet (60m), surrounded by covered passageways and a moat nearly 2 miles (4km) in circumference (**6,63**). It was begun in the reign of Suryavarman II (1112–c. 1150) as a tomb for himself and a temple dedicated to Vishnu. No building has ever been more methodically devised as a cosmic symbol, in lay-out, orientation, dimensions, form and in the iconographical program of its sculpture. The axially symmetrical plan consists of crosses within rectangles oriented towards the west (as was usual for mortuary temples in many parts of the world) (**6,64**). A high platform, approached up steep flights of steps, supports the central shrine – originally enclosing a metal statue of Vishnu – and four smaller shrines, all crowned by spires derived from the Indian *sikhara*, to symbolize the five peaks of Mount Meru, originally repeated in diminishing scale at the corners of the two enclosures. Surrounded by its moat, the temple thus illustrated the Hindu cosmological system with Mount Meru at the centre of concentric continents bounded by the ocean. Indian tendencies towards multiplication of single elements were extended as far as they would stretch and the whole massive construction was designed with a logical coherence rare in India – entirely lacking, indeed, in such

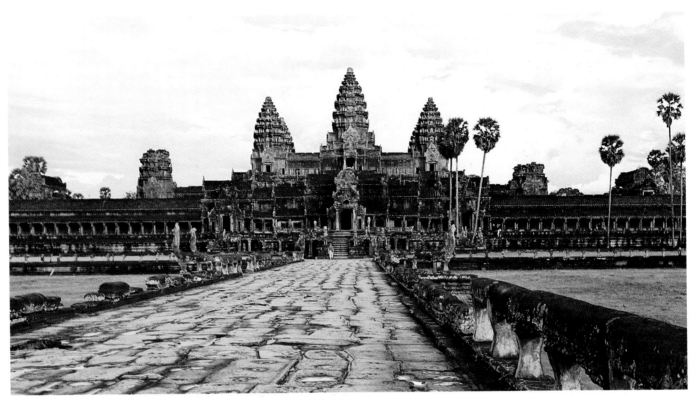

6,63 Angkor Wat, Cambodia, c. 1120–50.

6,64 *Right* Plan of Angkor Wat.

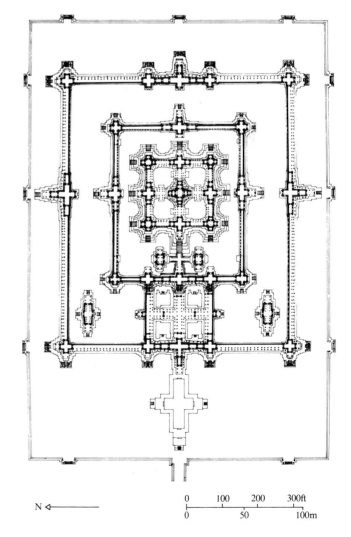

a major temple as that of the Lingaraja at Bhuvanesvar (6,40). Nor was this all. Angkor Wat was sited so that from outside the western entrance the sun could be seen rising above the central spire on 21 June, the beginning of the solar year according to Indian astronomy, as was appropriate for the monument to Suryavarman whose name means 'protected by the sun'. And the distance from this entrance to the central shrine is 1,728 *hat* (the Khmer unit of measurement), corresponding with the 1,728 years of the first 'golden' age of the universe according to Hindu reckoning.

Angkor Wat was built of vast slabs of limestone held together by iron clamps without mortar. Roofs were corbelled, as in India, not vaulted. The width of the long galleries was thus restricted, but their walls were carved with reliefs of uniformly high quality and sometimes great delicacy. Regimentation is one of the hallmarks of Khmer art. Identical figures were carved by the hundred. Rank upon rank of marching soldiers appear in some reliefs. *Apsarases* – spirits of the sky and members of Indra's seraglio – were made to dance in unison. One relief catches a group of them in frantic movement (**6,65**). Twisting their supple bodies into erotic postures, they have all the sensual allure, if none of the spirituality, of Indian *yakshis*.

That the whole vast mass of Angkor Wat should have been not only erected but also adorned with so much sculpture in no more than three decades is astonishing. Several smaller though no less richly sculptured temples

N ◄

| 0 | 100 | 200 | 300ft |
| 0 | | 50 | 100m |

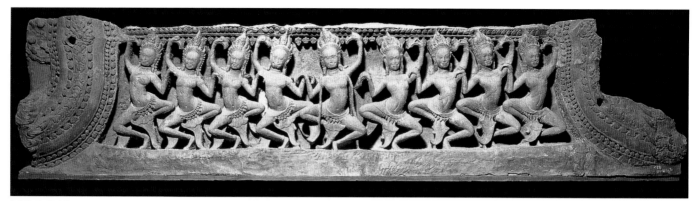

6,65 Relief from Angkor Wat, c. 1120–50. 23³/₅ins (60cm) high. Musée Guimet, Paris.

were built at about the same time elsewhere in the Khmer empire. One of the most impressive, Phanom Rung (in present-day Thailand) is set on a hilltop site above a wide plain stretching east towards Angkor, a commanding symbol of the power of Khmer rule under – one might almost say on behalf of – the gods. It is approached up a monumental stairway flanked by balustrades from which

6,66 Prasat Phanom Rung, Thailand, early 12th century.

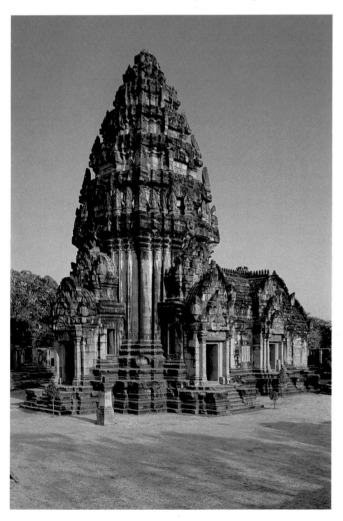

nagas raise their many cobra-heads. The sanctuary, set in the centre of a rectangular galleried enclosure, has an exterior alive with relief sculpture, repeated architectural and foliage motifs with figurative scenes over the doors, all crisply and most sensitively carved in the Khmer style (**6,66**).

The Khmer rulers were not all Hindus. Several were Buddhist followers of the *Mahayana*, most notably the last of historical importance, Jayavarman VII (c. 1175–c. 1220), who in 1178 reunited the empire which had fallen apart after the death of Suryavarman II, and made his presence felt in architecture as well as political control. He was styled not a *Devaraja* but a *Buddharaja* – the incarnation of a Bodhisattva as ruler – and he did his best to impose Buddhism as the national religion. The capital city had been sacked by invaders from Vietnam, so he founded a new one nearby, Angkor Thom, laid out on a square grid plan, as well as many temples both at Angkor and elsewhere in his kingdom. His numerous public works included roads, rest-houses along them, reservoirs and hospitals as well as temples. He seems, in fact, to have created a kind of theocratic welfare state: an inscription in one of the hospitals declares, 'Filled with a deep sympathy for the good of the world, the king swore this oath: "All the beings who are plunged in the ocean of existence, may I draw them out by this good work. And may the kings of Cambodia who come after me attain with their wives, dignitaries and friends, the place of deliverance where there is no more illness."' At the centre of Angkor Thom he raised the temple mountain known as the Bayon (literally 'ancestor *yantra*', a *yantra* being a magical Tantric diagram) – only slightly less enormous than Angkor Wat with a similar plan of concentric galleried enclosures. From its many spires a face, probably that of the king himself with the attributes of the Bodhisattva Lokesvara, eyes half-closed and lips half-smiling, looks out to the four points of the compass (**6,67**). The idea of divine beauty – of the holiness of beauty – present in Gandharan sculpture of the first century AD (see p. 233) survives in these gigantic yet strangely gentle countenances. Similar heads appear on the gateways to Angkor Thom, and Jayavarman VII is also represented in more than one of the reliefs at the Bayon illustrating his campaigns in Champa. Two statues and two heads resemble these so closely that they are believed to be portraits. In the finest of them, a slightly over-life-size statue now in Phnom Penh (**6,68**), he is sitting cross-legged in peaceful contemplation. He is posed like the Buddha, and had not the arms been lost they would no doubt have borne out this interpretation, with the hands making one of the Buddhist *mudra* gestures. (There is no trace of the hands having rested on the knees or thighs in the traditional contemplative position.) His broad strong body, reminiscent of a wrestler or prize-fighter, his head bowed with his hair pulled tight to form a little chignon at the back, his eyes closed and his lips mysteriously smiling all convey a sense of controlled power and inner spiritual calm. Inscriptions on a *stele* at Ta Prohm, one of his new temples near Angkor, describe him as a fervent Buddhist honouring 'the high path which leads to supreme enlightenment, the unique doctrine without obstacle to attain a

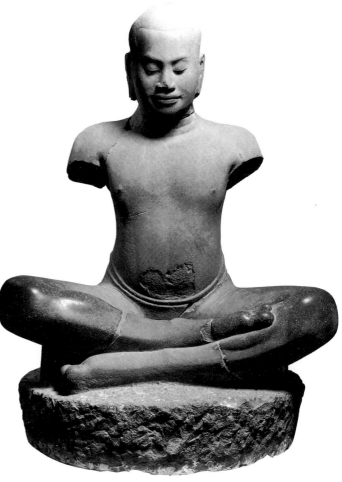

6,68 *Jayavarman VII*, from Angkor Thom, c. 1200. Slightly over-life-size. Museum, Phnom Penh.

6,67 Bayon, Angkor Thom, Cambodia, c. 1190–1220

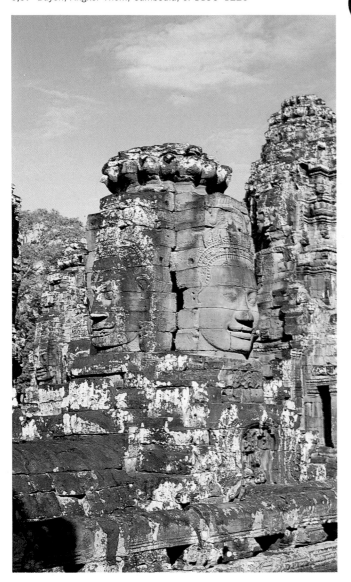

comprehension of reality, the law which the immortal honour in the three worlds, the sword which destroys the jungle of the passions'. He had, according to the same inscription, 'found his satisfaction in the nectar which is the religion of Sakyamuni', Buddhism of the Greater Vehicle, centred in the worship of Lokesvara.

However, the design of the Bayon owes less to Buddhist than to Hindu precedents, as do also much of its other relief sculptures and statues. Nowhere, indeed, was *Mahayana* Buddhism's syncretic capacity for incorporating Hindu cults more clearly manifested than here. But the temple is mainly a monument to an ideal of divine monarchy in which there was no distinction between the temporal and spiritual realms. For the entire population was in the service of the Buddharaja – the soldiers who fought his battles, the no less large armies of masons and sculptors employed on his buildings and the farmers who provided the food for the vast temple population – an inscription reveals that one temple owned 3,140 villages which supported 18 high priests, 2,740 officiating priests, 2,202 assistants and 615 temple dancers.

The sculptural program of the Bayon was never completed. After the death of Jayavarman VII in about 1220 the Khmer empire began to contract. And throughout the area *Mahayana* Buddhism gave way to *Theravada* Buddhism with notable consequences for the arts – a restricted iconography and architectural emphasis on stupas rather than temples. To the west, in present day Thailand, powerful reminiscences of Khmer sculpture survived in images of the Buddha – for example, a magnificent bronze head from Sankhaburi, the site of an ancient city in one of the small states that emerged in the thirteenth century (6,69), notably at Sukhothai. But the Thais (originally emigrants from southern China) also evolved independent and, one might almost say, anti-Khmer, styles. Statues of the Buddha with expressions of meditative beneficence are graceful and receptive rather than commanding, as in a Sukhothai bronze Buddha calling the earth to witness (6,70). Such images represent transcendental sanctity in conformity with an ideal of human beauty described in ancient Indian treatises on the theory and practice of the arts – an egg-shaped head, hair resembling the stings of scorpions, nose like a parrot's beak, eyebrows forming drawn bows, chin in the shape of a mango stone. The skill in manipulating a fluid medium displayed in such bronzes may have been employed also in the fourteenth century, as well as much later, in the use of stucco finely modelled and painted to coat buildings and large-scale statues of laterite – a very hard, coarse, ferruginous natural substance used as the main building

6,69 Head from a statue of the Buddha, from Sankhaburi, Thailand, c. 1300. Bronze, 12ins (30cm) high. National Museum, Bangkok.

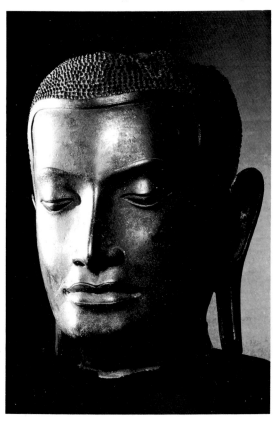

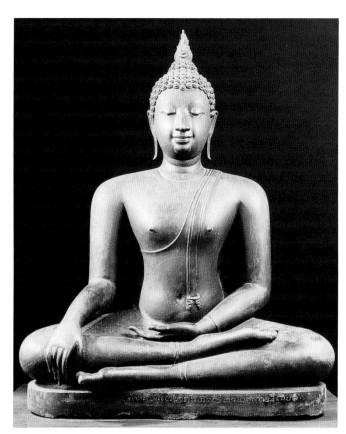

6,70 *Buddha calling the Earth to Witness*, from Sawankhalok near Sukhothai, Thailand, 14th century. Bronze with red lacquer and gold leaf, 18(?)ins (38.5cm) high. National Museum, Bangkok.

6,71 Ananda temple, Pagan, Burma, begun 1091.

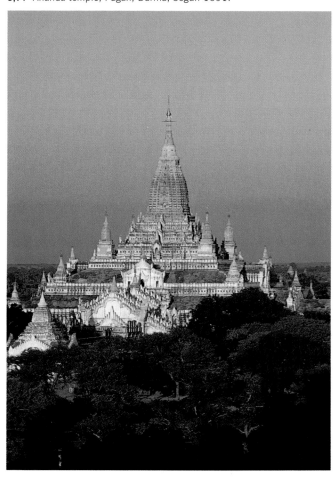

material for religious structures (all others were of wood). Stucco was, of course, much less durable than stone and surfaces inevitably decayed in the tropical climate even if they were not destroyed in the wars that periodically devastated the cities of south-east Asia. And although the characteristic forms of Thai architecture – the elegant spire-crowned stupa, the tall reliquary tower called a *prang* in Thai, and the large lofty monastic halls for the display of images, communal prayer and ordinations – may have been evolved at Sukhothai, the most important city flourishing in the centre of the country from the thirteenth century, none of the many buildings that survive there as ruins can be securely dated to that period (16,15).

More remains of the twelfth to thirteenth century architecture in Burma (Myanmar). Buddhism had been introduced from India at an early date and, according to tradition, the great stupa known as the Shwedagon Pagoda in Rangoon was founded in the fifth century BC though what is seen today is the result of the last, eighteenth-century, enlargement and later embellishment. Various sects coexisted but *Theravada* gradually emerged as that with the widest following. There are remains of no less than 2,000 Buddhist structures built between the early eleventh and late thirteenth centuries at Pagan, a capital city that originally covered 16 square miles (41 square km) in a bend of the Irrawady river. One of the best preserved is the Ananda temple, symbolizing the Buddha's endless wisdom (Ananta Panna) but later named after his favourite disciple (6,71). Its exterior bristles with spirelets mounting up to a central peak like a *sikhara* which, however, surmounts not a shrine (as it would in a Hindu temple) but a solid block of masonry. At the base of the walls and surrounding the entrances there are glazed terracotta plaques illustrating the *Jataka* stories. The plan is in the form of a Greek cross with each of the four arms serving as a hall for teaching and an entrance to two concentric corridors, with figurative reliefs of doctrinal significance on their walls, for circumambulation of the central block against which there are four colossal

6,72 Plan of Ananda temple.

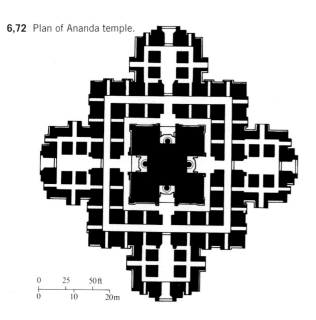

standing Buddhas 33 feet (10m) high (6,72). It is essentially a didactic structure similar in some ways to Borobudur but expounding only the *Theravada* doctrine.

In 1287 Pagan was despoiled by the Mongols under Kubilai Khan (who had recently made himself emperor of China, see p. 551). The kingdom disintegrated and many centuries were to pass before there was any revival of the arts. But *Theravada* Buddhism survived and has remained to the present day the predominant religious faith of Burma.

CONFUCIAN, DAOIST AND BUDDHIST ART IN CHINA

HAN DYNASTY

The teaching of the Buddha reached China in the first century AD, at a moment of great prosperity and national self-confidence hardly propitious for the introduction of a religion both otherworldly and alien. After a long period of internal warfare which followed the disintegration of the Zhou empire (see p. 116), the country had been reunited with ruthless efficiency during the brief reign of the first emperor of the Qin dynasty (c. 221–209 BC). Under the succeeding Han dynasty, which ruled from 209 BC to AD 220, China enjoyed one of the most brilliant epochs of its history. Peace was maintained throughout the land and barbarian tribes were steadily driven back from the frontiers until the empire extended from the Pacific to the Pamirs, from Korea to south-east Asia. Looking back, the Chinese of later times were often to call themselves the 'Sons of Han'. It was during the next four centuries of instability, when much of northern China once more came under foreign rule, between the fall of the Han dynasty and the rise of the Tang in 617, that Buddhism began to win widespread acceptance, though not without rivalry from Confucianism and Daoism.

Confucius (551–479 BC), the founder of Chinese philosophy, was an almost exact contemporary of the historical Buddha (563–480 BC). Several centuries passed, however, before the sayings of Confucius were formulated into a consistent philosophy as Confucianism. This was a product of the Han period and, despite shifts in emphasis, it has endured as an underlying structure for Chinese thought ever since. From the Han period onwards, Chinese education was almost exclusively Confucian and had the explicit aim of preparing young men for the competitive written examinations (already established in the mid-second century BC) that opened the door to government service. Confucianism as a philosophical system might almost be said to have exalted the virtues of the conscientious civil servant into a moral code. Deeply concerned with conduct and the interrelated duties of ruler and ruled, parents and children, old and young, employers and employees, it stressed conformity and tradition. The social order was conceived as a reflection of the moral order of the universe. Virtue was understood by Confucians simply as the right and proper way of doing things and thus provided a comprehensive rule of life – and of art. As a ninth-century writer declared, 'Painting promotes

0   25   50 ft

0   10   20m

6,73 Tomb of Emperor Qin Shihuangdi, c. 221–209 BC. Terracotta, life-size figures. Lintong, near Xi'an, Shaanxi, China.

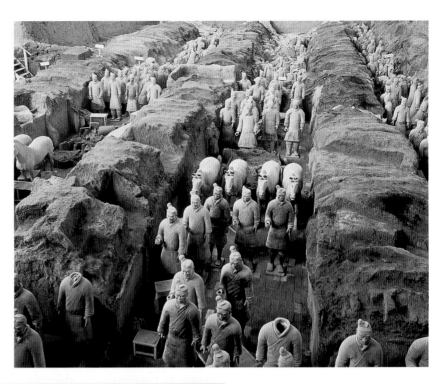

6,74 *Below* Four horse chariot and driver from the tomb of Emperor Qin Shihuangdi, c. 210 BC. Bronze, partly gilt and gold, 10ft 6ins (3.28m) long and 3ft 2ins (1.04m) high. Lintong.

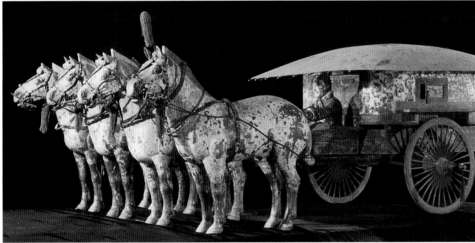

culture and strengthens the principles of right conduct. It penetrates completely all the aspects of the universal spirit.' Painting (but not sculpture or architecture, which, like the crafts, were too closely associated with manual skills) and the closely allied art of calligraphy formed part of the official education program, which thus trained the largest class of amateurs of the arts produced by any civilization. Every educated person was a connoisseur of painting and calligraphy, and many were very able practitioners, including several emperors.

Confucianism was not a religion, although it encouraged from the beginning the piety towards spirits of ancestors that was traditional in China. Daoism was much more deeply concerned with the spiritual and the supernatural. Also formulated in the Han period, Daoism derived mainly from the teaching of Lao Zi, an elusive mystical philospher who is said to have lived in the sixth century BC. But it took over popular beliefs in dragons, celestial and infernal spirits, and the power of magicians. However, Daoism – like Hinduism and Buddhism – was accessible at more than one intellectual level. The *Dao*, as

understood by Daoists, is an irrational life-force beyond the grasp of the conscious human mind and submission to it means the liberation of natural instincts without regard for social conventions or even moral imperatives. The ultimate attainment is an Inward Vision (*ming*), in which all distinctions between 'self' and 'things', between 'inside' and 'outside' are lost in a lyric, almost ecstatic, acceptance of the universal laws of nature. Daoists looked back to a golden age when man lived in absolute harmony with his surroundings, when life was as effortless as the passage of the seasons and the two vital, female and male, principles of nature – the Yin and Yang – worked together and not in opposition. Their ideal was the recluse who abandoned all worldly ambition to cultivate inner powers and inner happiness.

Confucianism encouraged conformity, moderation, logical thought; Daoism individuality, passion, imagination. Yet the two are not so much antithetical as complementary. 'We are socially Confucian and individually Daoist', the modern Chinese writer Lin Tung-chi (Lin Tongji) has remarked. Buddhism introduced an altogether different

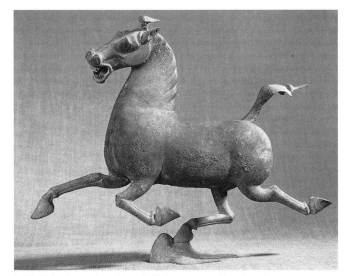

6,75 Flying horse from Wuwei, China, eastern Han dynasty, 2nd century AD. Bronze, 13½ × 17¾ins (34.3 × 45cm).

system of intellectual and spiritual values, focused on a belief in salvation which looked beyond the life of men and women in society, with which the Confucians were mainly concerned, and the Daoist preoccupation with the interior life of the individual. A monk living in a religious community exemplifies Buddhist ideals. Buddhism reached China as a fully developed religious system with its holy scriptures, priests, monks, images and rituals. In the course of time it was influenced by and marginally influenced Confucianism and Daoism, yet always remained somewhat alien to China, despite the following it gathered between the fifth and twelfth centuries and the many great works of art it inspired.

In the tombs from which our knowledge of Han art is almost entirely derived, Daoist and Confucian elements appear side by side. Indeed, a meeting between Confucius and Lao Zi is shown in one relief carving. Entrances are guarded by fabulous beasts endowed with the power to ward off evil spirits. Figures from the traditional and Daoist pantheon appear in the decorations of burial chambers and the adjacent rooms in which offerings to the spirit of the occupant were placed by his pious descendants. Little models of buildings and statuettes of attendants and animals hark back to the ancient practice of immolating the living to accompany the dead into the afterlife. The megalomaniac first Qin emperor, an implacable enemy of the Confucians, had been buried in 209 BC with a vast bodyguard of clay warriors, of which more than 500 with 24 horses were brought to light in 1974, when one of the gateway chambers of his tomb at Lintong, Shaanxi, was excavated (**6,73**). Partly cast and partly modelled – the detachable heads and hands were modelled individually – these life-size figures in unglazed terracotta stand at the beginning of a long tradition of human and animal tomb art. In their emphasis on human personality rather than on human form they typify perennial Chinese concepts and attitudes. But greater artistry was displayed in the astonishing gilt bronze chariot with driver and four richly caparisoned horses, discovered in 1980 near the first Qin emperor's tomb (**6,74**), and smaller, and considerably later, figures from Han tombs, such as the bronze 'flying horse' found at Wuwei in Gansu (**6,75**).

Perfectly balanced on the one hoof which rests without pressure on a flying swallow, it is a remarkable example of three-dimensional form and of animal portraiture with the head vividly expressing mettlesome vigour. The horse belongs, in fact, to the 'celestial' or 'blood-sweating' breed which had been introduced into China from Ferghana in central Asia about 100 BC and became a kind of status symbol. The same tomb contained many other statuettes of horses of this prized breed, a clear indication of the high standing of the provincial governor with whom they were interred.

Worldly importance is stressed in most tombs of the Han period. Government officials and their retinues were a favourite subject for paintings, the figures moving with the decorous solemnity on which Confucius had insisted. Other subjects are specifically moral in a Confucian sense, including illustrations to such collections of improving stories as the *Gallery of Devoted Sons* (written 79–78 BC). Some were engraved on stone in a technique peculiar to Han China, whereby the silhouettes of the figures were polished smooth and the background hatched. Tiles either painted or modelled in relief also adorned the walls of tomb- and offering-chambers. Two officials on one of the tiles exemplify a Confucian ideal of courtesy maintained even in argument. The scene records the thwarting of a palace revolution in 180 BC, when the man on the right persuaded the other to support the imperial clan against the machinations of an empress (**6,76**). They

6,76 *Two Officials*, detail from lintel and pediment of a tomb, late 1st century BC to early 1st century AD. Hollow ceramic tiles, total 29 × 80½ins (73.8 × 204.7cm). Museum of Fine Arts, Boston (Denman Waldo Ross Collection).

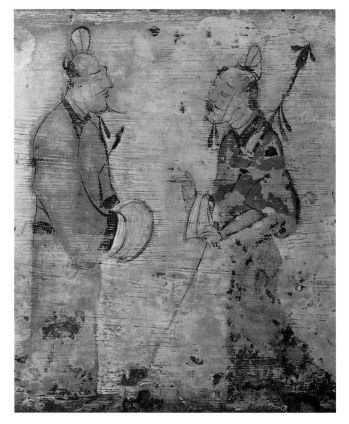

Confucius

HAN RELIEF CARVING

The most direct expressions of Confucian ideas and ideals in early Chinese art are in shrines or offering chambers adjoining tombs dating from the period of the Eastern Han dynasty (AD 25–220), some 300 years later than that of the anti-Confucian Qin emperor. The Confucian message is conveyed as much by the purity and simplicity of the strictly linear style of these reliefs – in striking contrast to the looser and more technically advanced naturalism of the earlier Qin tomb sculptures (6,73; 74), which the followers of Confucius would seem to have renounced – as by the inscriptions recording the Confucian virtues of the deceased. Commissioned at the expense of descendants, they are enduring testimonies to that filial piety on which Confucius laid such great stress as the most intimate of the virtues that ensured harmony, not only socially but within oneself. Intended to be seen by the living who crowded to funerals, they would also reassure future members of the family who performed the rite of venerating ancestors. Nowhere is the austerely sceptical, unrelentingly conscientious, totally disinterested code of behaviour taught by Confucius brought so close to us. No rewards, no consolations, no hopes for the future are offered. Unlike the vast majority of tombs in other civilizations they barely even refer to the possibility of an afterlife.

A group of three shrines for members of the Wu family, in the Jiaxiang district of Shandong province in north-eastern China, is notable for the thematic richness of the stone slabs carved in relief-silhouette. This was a technique that had just been perfected: the silhouettes were polished smooth and the background hatched. (Such reliefs are very difficult to read from photographs and are here reproduced from rubbings made by beating damp paper on to the surface of the stone and dabbing the parts in relief with a silk pad soaked in ink, as practised in China from at least as early as the first century AD to the present day). A memorial inscription records that one of these shrines was made for Wu Liang who died in AD 151, distinguished for his virtues, his loyalty and filial piety, his upright bearing and his intelligence. He had mastered all the literary classics and instructed others. Although offered an official position he refused, preferring to live modestly and simply and devote himself to his studies and the pursuit of truth. The inscription goes on to relate that his two sons and grandson followed his example of filial duty and spent all they had on his shrine. 'From south of the southern mountains they chose excellent stones without flaws or yellow color. . . . The clever workman Wei Gai engraved the texts and carved the designs, putting everything in its proper place and giving full rein to his skill. The work will be transmitted to posterity and endure for ten thousand generations', on whom Wu Liang's wisdom will fall 'like the scent of an orchid. Although his body has perished, his renown lives.'

The carvings, with men in billowing robes, and horses with proudly arched necks, muscular rumps and delicate hoofs, pulling two-wheeled

6,77 Wei Gai, *Allegorical Scene*, c. AD 151.
Ink rubbing from stone relief in the Wu family shrines, 27½ × 61 ins (70 × 155cm). Jiaxiang, Shandong, China.

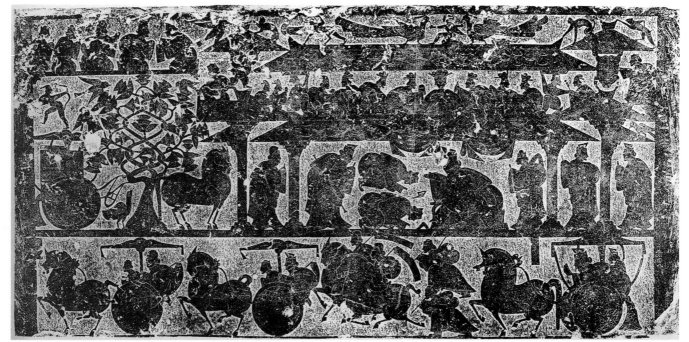

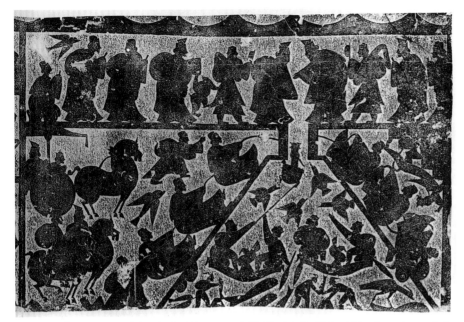

6,78 *The First Emperor raising the Cauldron*, c. AD 147–67. Detail of ink rubbing from stone relief in the Wu family shrines.

chariots, might appear at first sight to be no more than *genre* scenes. They are indeed of great interest nowadays for the information they provide about architecture, costume and other aspects of daily life in Han China. Their function was, however, didactic and their visual message would originally have been easily understood. One of them is a kind of allegory of good government (**6,77**). Inside a pavilion two men make the kow-tow to an enthroned figure, probably the founder of the Han dynasty, the emperor Gaozu who seized power in the civil war after the death of the first Qin emperor (see p. 263). In what might seem to be the upper story of the pavilion, the Queen of the Immortals – a figure from ancient Chinese mythology – presides over her court and, by inference, life in the worldly court below. On the roof there are long-tailed phoenixes of good omen which were believed to descend from the skies only when China was well governed. To the left the cult hero Yi, another figure from traditional mythology, shoots at crows representing the nine extra suns that would otherwise scorch the earth. On the lowest register armed men on horseback and in carriages hurry away, presumably in pursuit of brigands.

Another relief (**6,78**) illustrates a story about the Qin emperor whose memory was reviled by followers of Confucius. In an attempt to legitimize his tyrannical rule the emperor tried to retrieve the bronze vessels with which rulers of the ancient Zhou dynasty had sacrificed to their ancestors. A cauldron was found in a river but while it was being dredged up a dragon emerged and snapped the rope. It was a story dear to the hearts of all followers of Confucius and is represented in several shrines. A bad ruler figures in another scene which was similarly recurrent (**6,79**): Duke Liang, who resented the criticism of his dissolute life from one of his officials, Zhao Dun, released a dog to kill him during an audience. Zhao was saved by the palace cook whom he had once helped, and spread the tale as an example of the baseness to which a tyrant could stoop.

When these relief silhouettes were being carved Confucianism was official state policy. Entry to the civil service was by examination in the mainly Confucian classics, promotion was achieved by a virtuous reputation.

Wu Liang's sons and grandson may perhaps have hoped to gain some esteem by their display of filial piety, that pre-eminently Confucian virtue that was joined with loyalty to the emperor in the chain of relationships that bound the life of the Han nation together. But true followers of Confucius believed that they should also be unbending in the condemnation of corruption or any abuse of correct behaviour, even by the emperor. And in the mid-second century there were reasons for complaint as eunuchs, originally employed simply to guard the women of the palace, played an increasingly important part in imperial affairs, enriched their relatives in the merchant class and came into conflict with the Confucianists in the civil service. The vulgar artistic taste of the eunuchs and their dependants, their grandiose buildings with towers and pavilions, were deplored. There may thus be an element of protest in the stylistic restraint and sobriety of the carvings in the Wu family shrines. The narratives are illustrated economically, without any superfluous decorative flourishes. Figures are stylized, rendered flat in silhouette without a hint of modelling or foreshortening, which were known and used elsewhere in Han China (6,76; 80). This emphasis on contour combined with the format and subjects might suggest that they derive from some earlier tradition of drawing on scrolls, none of which survives. Other carvings of similar Confucian subjects from tombs of the same period and area are even simpler, sometimes almost crude in their simplicity, as if to suggest the virtuous poverty of those who commissioned them. For Confucianism taught people to despise the money it prevented them from amassing.

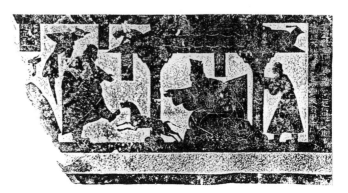

6,79 *Duke Liang and Zhao Dun*, c. AD 147–67. Detail of ink rubbing from stone relief in the Wu family shrines.

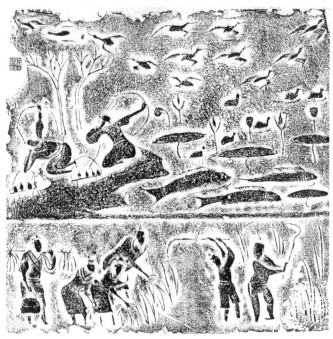

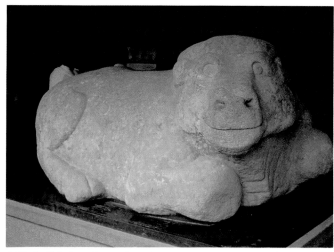

6,81 Buffalo from the tomb probably of Huo Qubing, Xingping, China, c. 117 BC.

6,80 *Above* Duck-shooting and rice-reaping, 2nd century AD. Rubbing of a tomb tile, 16½ins (42cm) high. Museum Chongqing, China (from R. C. Rudolph, *Han Tomb Art of West China*, 1951).

6,82 *Below* Admonitions of the Instructress to the Court Ladies, detail, 10th-century copy probably after Gu Kaizhi. Horizontal scroll, ink and color on silk, 9¾ins (24.8cm) high. British Museum, London.

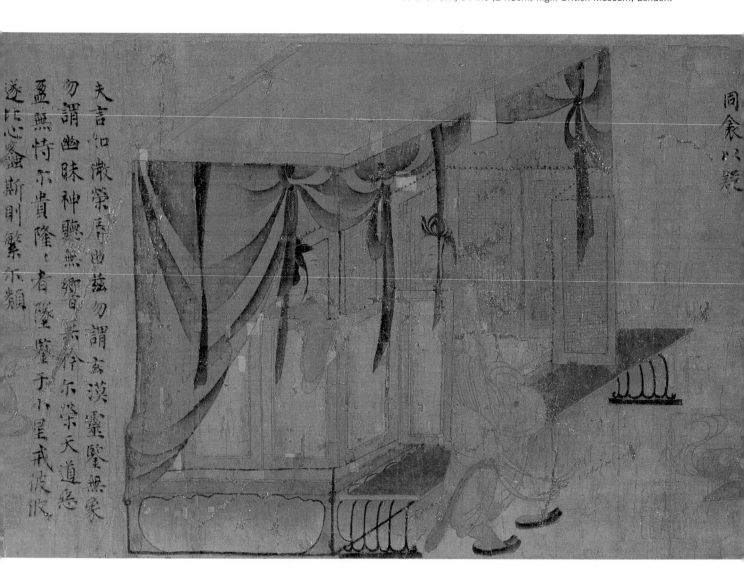

are rendered in outline with some color but no shading, yet a sense of three-dimensional form is vividly conveyed, as well as of character. Unlike the sharp outlines of Greek vase painting or of Indian painting (at Ajanta, for instance), the assured, flexible Chinese brush-strokes modulate in response to the weight and consistency and movement of the forms they describe – now thick and fat, now sharp and tight, now trembling with the lightest possible flick of the brush. They have the same highly expressive quality as Chinese calligraphy. On relief tiles, form is shown in silhouette. In one (**6,80**) the varied attitudes of the figures – reapers in the lower part and archers above – imply close study of the human figure in movement. Fish are depicted rather schematically, as if on the surface of the water, but the leaves of the lotus and their seed-pods are rendered with a sensitivity to actual appearance, which distinguishes them from the symbols of the same plant in Indian art. Although they are the work of provincial craftsmen, such tiles probably reflect the art of the imperial capital, none of which survives, for the fondness of the Han emperors for paintings had the unfortunate result that all the treasures they assembled were destroyed in AD 190, when their capital was sacked.

Some works of art of the Han period that have been brought to light by recent excavations seem isolated, like mountain peaks emerging from the mists that still conceal connecting ranges. Large carvings of animals that stand apart from all other known sculptures of the time were unearthed in 1957 at Xingping near Xi'an, in a tomb probably of General Huo Qubing who died in 117 BC, notably a recumbent water-buffalo shaped from a boulder to suggest a latent power that is no more than temporarily somnolent and given an extraordinary, unnerving presence (**6,81**). The earliest paintings on silk – by 1,000 or more years – were found in 1973 in tombs of the second century BC at Mawangdui near Changsha (Hunan). They are, however, the products of a southern provincial culture expressing religious beliefs that probably date back to the Shang period in an artistic style of which they are the only surviving examples. And their possible relationship with the paintings collected by the Han emperors (now all lost) is unknown.

The early history of painting on scrolls that the Chinese regarded as the highest form of figurative art can be traced only from literary sources and later copies which are in themselves evidence of that respect for the past which was to condition all subsequent developments. (In this the study of ancient Chinese painting is similar to that of ancient Greek painting, most of which is also lost.) A tenth-century hand-scroll entitled *Admonitions of the Instructress to the Court Ladies* is believed to be a copy after Gu Kaizhi (c. 344–406) who worked at the court of Nanjing, which became the cultural centre of China where Confucianism survived after the dismemberment of the Han empire. It consists of a series of figurative scenes separated from one another by columns of edifying text (**6,82**). A bedroom scene illustrates the passage: 'If the words you utter are good, all men for a thousand leagues around will make response to you. But if you depart from this principle, even your bedfellow will distrust you.' Presumably, the man is an emperor and the woman a concubine, but the confrontation of the three-quarter face and the profile suggests some complex psychological relationship. Gu Kaizhi was renowned as a portrait painter able to catch not merely the appearance but also the character and spirit of his subjects. He is known to have been a Daoist who cultivated eccentricity and perhaps had some reservations about the worldly Confucian morality of the poem illustrated. But the scenes depicted are no more important than the columns of words between them written in the characters that had been evolved from the angular inscriptions on oracle bones and bronze vessels. The Chinese had begun by writing with a stylus which gives a line of uniform thickness; but by the fourth century they had developed calligraphy with a flexible brush not simply as a means of verbal communication but also as a form of visual expression which may interpret as well as record a text (rather as a musician interprets a score) by the softness or strength with which the individual characters are drawn and the way they are related to one another. It was of course an art of the élite, limited to a literate minority though practised by all its members. Several emperors were distinguished as calligraphers and their statements as written by their own hand were often reproduced on stone *stelae* so that both what and how they wrote could

6,83 *Portraits of the Emperors*, detail, 10th-century copy probably after Yan Liben. Horizontal scroll, ink and color on silk, 20ins (51.3cm) high. Museum of Fine Arts, Boston (Denman Waldo Ross Collection).

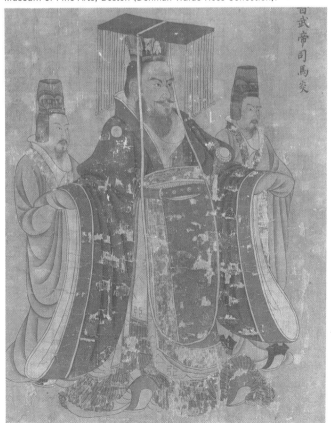

be preserved. Similarly the Chinese classics were engraved on *stelae* with due respect to the brushwork of a master, as exemplars of, equally, uplifting thought, verbal or literary refinement and visual, calligraphic expression. (A complete series of 114 of these *stelae* engraved in 837 is now in the Historical Museum at Xi'an.)

Another tenth-century scroll portraying notable emperors is probably a faithful copy after Yan Liben (c. 600–73), the most celebrated artist of his time at the Tang court (**6,83**). The art of defining volume by line without shading has been mastered to give the figures substance and an imperturbable self-assurance. Despite their small scale, the compositions are monumental and the whole scroll, as it is unrolled, reveals a pageant of imperial pomp. Early eighth-century paintings on the walls of the recently excavated tomb near Xi'an of a prince, Zhang Huai, record lighter aspects of life at the Tang court – men hunting and playing polo, women idling in the garden – rendered with great economy of line and sureness of touch to catch the most fleeting of moments (**6,84**). They were, however, probably the work of artists regarded as no more than craftsmen, as distinct from the likes of Yan Liben who held a succession of important posts in the bureaucracy (perhaps sinecures) and was one of the first of the long line of Chinese artists who were also scholars and civil servants.

Styles of painting, sculpture and architecture foreign to China were introduced with Buddhism by way of the great trans-Asian caravan trails – the so-called Silk Road – along which an ever-increasing quantity of Chinese silk was borne in the opposite direction to India, Iran and Europe. Beginning at Dunhuang, these routes passed through what is now Xinjiang, the vast western province of the People's Republic of China bordered in the north by Kazakhstan and in the south by Tibet. In the first century AD it was an area peopled mainly by nomadic tribes but with a number of city-states under the cultural influence of India and the West. There was a last outpost of Gandharan art (see p. 233) at Miran, only 300 miles (480km) west of Dunhuang, where second- or third-century paintings of Buddhist subjects were signed by an artist whose name, Tita or Titus, suggests that he came from one of Rome's

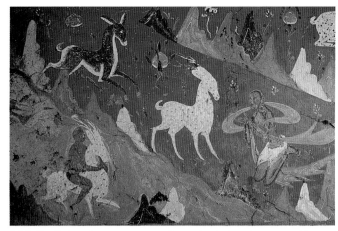

6,85 The Buddha's avatar as a gazelle, wall-painting, Dunhuang, China, 5th century AD.

eastern provinces. To the north-east the small state of Kuqa on the Tarim river became an important Buddhist centre in about the fourth century with extensive free-standing and rock-cut temples and monasteries. The splendours of this and other central Asian cities were celebrated by Chinese travellers from the fifth to the seventh century. All were destroyed and Buddhism was wiped out as a result of the Muslim invasions of the eleventh century. But the cave temples cut into a cliff-face at Dunhuang, an oasis in the Gobi desert, survive – nearly 500 of them, more than half with paintings on walls and ceilings, ranging in date from the fifth century to the eleventh and many preserved in astonishing freshness. The earliest are in a style transmitted from India and their most important figures of the Buddha and Bodhisattvas were probably the work of central Asian painters who attempted to give substance to their stiffly posed figures by somewhat rough modelling. But *Apsarases* – see Glossary – swooping across the ceilings, and the small *Jataka* stories depicted on the walls, show the influence of Chinese art which gradually predominated. In a painting of the Buddha's avatar as a golden gazelle (**6,85**) the animals seem to have strayed from Iran but the mountains and especially the kneeling figure with floating drapery have their origins in China, recalling the linear elegance of clouds and dragons on Zhou dynasty lacquer (3,41) and the figures on Han reliefs (6,80). On the other hand, the anthropomorphic devotional image introduced by Buddhists was wholly without precedent in China. As the message of the Buddha was addressed to all classes of society there was a need for visual images to illustrate texts that only a minority could read. Hence the adaptation of *stelae* from calligraphic to representational art – instead of being inscribed with texts they were carved in relief with didactic or narrative scenes – as on one of the many dating from the early sixth century with figures of the Buddha one above the other and framed with scenes from his life on either side (**6,86**).

The most notable early Chinese Buddhist images that survive (apart from wall-paintings, the vast majority of which are at Dunhuang) are in sculpture – an art excluded from the Confucian syllabus. A small bronze inscribed with a date equivalent to AD 338 is the earliest (Asia Art Museum, San Francisco). Few others survived a violent

6,84 Wall-painting from the tomb of Prince Zhang Huai, near Xi'an, China, early 8th century. Shaanxi Provincial Museum, Xi'an.

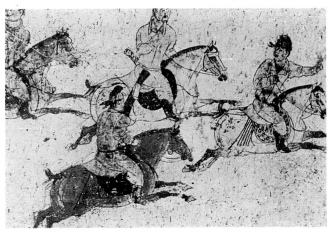

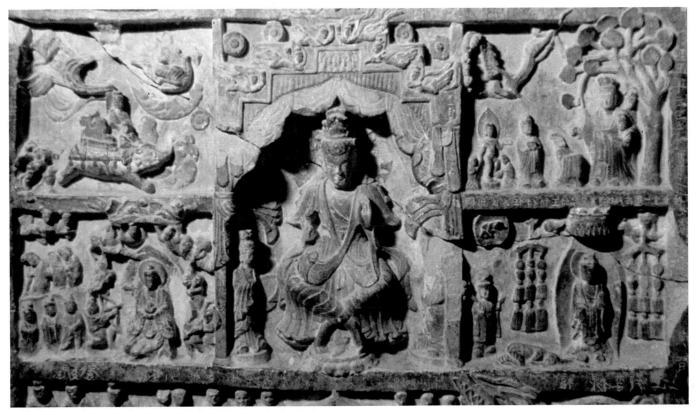

6,86 Buddhist *stele*, early 6th century. Maijaishan caves, Gansu, China.

6,87 Interior of Cave VI, late 5th century AD, Yungang, Shanxi, China.

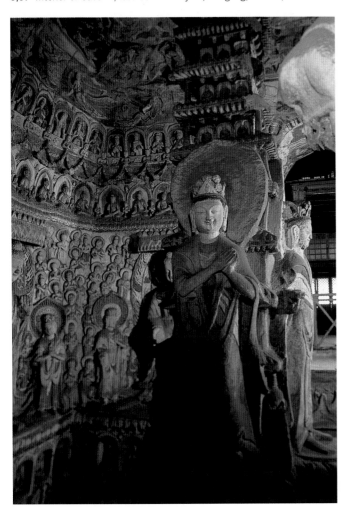

persecution of the Buddhists and wholesale destruction of their temples in AD 444. A period of intense artistic activity was, however, initiated in 452 on the succession of a Buddhist to the throne of the northern Wei 'empire' (one of the three realms into which the country was divided at this date). Between 460 and 494 a sandstone cliff at Yungang in Shanxi, not far from the Great Wall, was transformed into one of the most spectacular of all groups of rock-cut temples, lined with images large and small similarly carved from the living rock (**6,87**). These extraordinary man-made caves must have been inspired by the *viharas* and *chaitya*-halls of India, and their colossal figures of the Buddha by two famous statues 120 and 175 feet (37 and 53m) high, hewn out of a cliff at Bamiyan, Afghanistan, between the second and fifth centuries AD. By their huge dimensions such statues symbolized the more-than-mortal nature of the universal Buddha, the equivalent to the cosmos itself. The rich intricacy of the interiors and style of sculpture seem, however, to derive more immediately from Kuqa. One of the temple façades has fallen away to reveal a 45-foot-high (13.7m) statue of the Buddha, originally flanked by two Bodhisattvas forming a trinity which must have looked still more mysteriously overwhelming when it could be seen only at uncomfortably close quarters in a dimly lit cavern (**6,88**). Pose and robe recall the preaching Buddha from Mathura (6,18), but all naturalism has been eliminated from the colossus at Yungang. The face has become an inscrutably smiling mask. The *ushnisha* and the elongated ear-lobes have been so conventionalized that they look like detachable pieces of regalia. Small-scale carvings – on the walls of the cave (6,87) and the *stele* illustrated here (6,86) – often show the Buddha seated, with legs crossed at the ankles and wearing a high crown, a

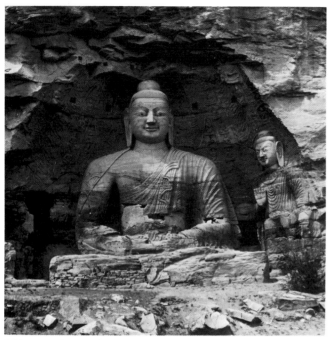

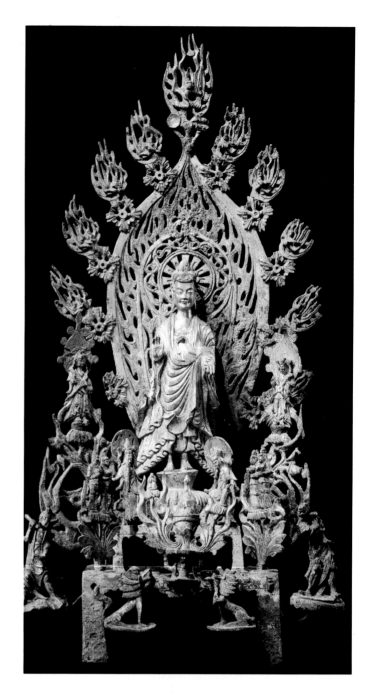

6,88 *Above* Colossal Buddha, 5th century, Yungang.
Natural rock, 45ft (13.7m) high.

6,89 *Top right* Altar with Maitreya Buddha, AD 524. Gilt bronze,
30¼ins (76.8cm) high. Metropolitan Museum of Art, New York.

6,90 *Bottom right* Empress as Donor with Attendants, from the Binyang
cave chapel at Longmen, Henan, c. AD 522. Limestone with traces of
color, 6ft 4ins × 9ft 1in (1.93 × 2.76m). Nelson-Atkins Museum of Art,
Kansas City (Purchase: Nelson Trust).

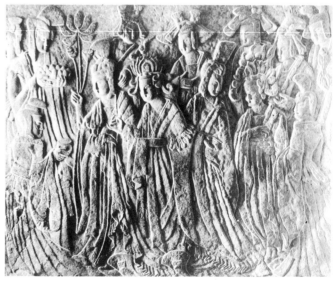

regal pose which associates religion with the rule of the
northern Wei emperors.

Small images were made in bronze. As we have already
seen, the art of bronze casting had been mastered in China
at a very early period; but a shrine made in 524 (**6,89**) could
hardly be further in feeling from either Shang ritual vessels, with mysterious dragon forms lurking on their surfaces (2,63), or the much more recent, vividly naturalistic
figures of animals from the Han dynasty tombs (6,81). The
central figure of the Buddha, the tiny Bodhisattvas below
his feet and the *Apsarases* – see Glossary – fluttering their
draperies on the edge of the halo all derive from Indian
models. These elements have, however, been skilfully
worked into a cogent linear composition. The whole piece
flickers with life, recalling the legend that Sakyamuni's
body emerged unburnt from his funeral pyre and metaphorically suggesting the elevation of the spirit. Symbols
have, in fact, been integrated into a devotional image of
more profound significance than the sum of its parts.

Sculptors and painters of devotional images of all cults
are usually bound by iconographical rules to ensure religious efficacy. In the representation of devotees, however,
Buddhist artists were allowed a freer hand, as the relief of
a pious empress and her attendants demonstrates (**6,90**).
In contrast to the static, almost geometrically solid Buddhas
and Bodhisattvas – some on a colossal scale – which
remain in the cave at Longmen from which this relief came,
the figures are at once naturalistic and insubstantial,

intentionally so perhaps to mark the distinction between eternal verities and transient illusory appearances. Clad in garments which fall naturally from their shoulders, the wraith-like empress and her ladies are grouped informally, with a suggestion of recession in space, and they move as if drifting on the lightest of breezes. The ability of Han dynasty painters to create form by a few deft brush-strokes, which also develop a rhythmically linear pattern with a life of its own, has here been transferred to sculpture without any loss of subtlety or delicacy and infused with the emotional spirituality that Buddhism had brought to China.

TANG DYNASTY AND THE FIVE DYNASTIES

Under the first emperors of the Tang dynasty (618–906) a reunited China enjoyed another period of peace at home and prestige abroad. The arts flourished as never before during the reign of Minghuang (713–56), founder of the Imperial Academy of Letters, which still survives under a new name. In 715, however, Chinese Turkestan was lost to Muslims advancing from the west and an internal rebellion followed, weakening the imperial administration. A period of decline set in. By this date a Chinese version of *Mahayana* Buddhism had become almost if not quite the national faith and it was blamed by Confucians

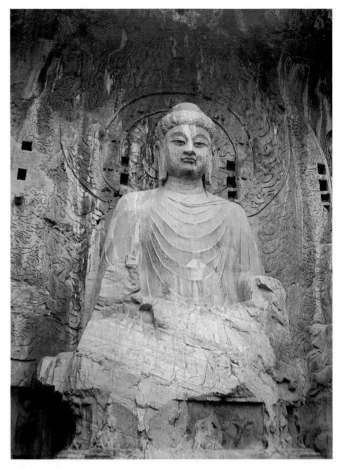

6,91 *Right* Vairocana Buddha, AD 672–5.
Natural rock, about 49ft (15m) high. Longmen, Henan.

6,92 *Below* Buddha and Bodhisattvas, 7th to 8th century.
Painted stucco, restored. Cave 45, Dunhuang.

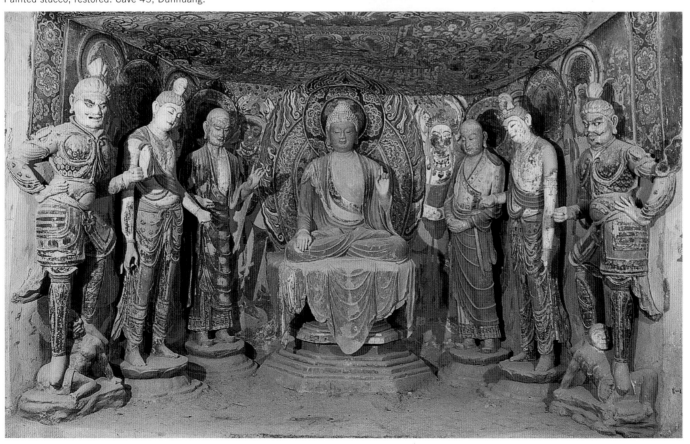

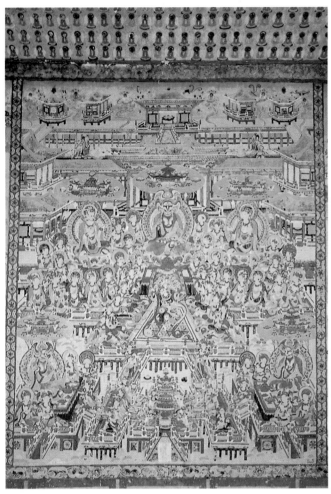

6,93 Buddhist paradise, late 9th century. Wall-painting. Cave 12, Dunhuang.

Buddha, each one containing a hundred million other Buddhist worlds. Longmen is just outside the city of Luoyang, one of the two capitals of the Tang empire, but artistic styles developed there spread out as far as Dunhuang where whole cave temples still preserve their original paintings and statues from this period. As no stone suitable for carving was available in this remote desert oasis, figures were modelled in a kind of stucco, a fragile material which required periodic restoration and repainting. This medium facilitated greater naturalism, as in the figures of Bodhisattvas and especially those of armed guardians, flanking an idealized Buddha (**6,92**). The walls are painted from floor to ceiling with representations of the Mahayanist heavens as described in the *sutras* but visualized as an imperial palace with its several symmetrically disposed buildings and gardens (**6,93**). The eighth-century painter and poet Wang Wei had, indeed, likened the emperor's garden outside Luoyang to the gardens of the immortals in their nine heavens – water flowed everywhere in the Luoyang imperial gardens, with 'laughter of girls in the painted summer-houses and the red pavilions, gold and jade flutes which sadden the stroller, walls of banners reaching as far as the Jian river, mandarin orange flowers in bloom'.

In this later phase of Chinese Buddhism a figure who answered emotional rather than intellectual needs came to the fore: Guanyin, the Bodhisattva of Mercy. He had

6,94 *Guanyin as the Guide of Souls*, from Dunhuang, 10th century. Painting on silk, 31½ × 21ins (80 × 53.3cm). British Museum, London.

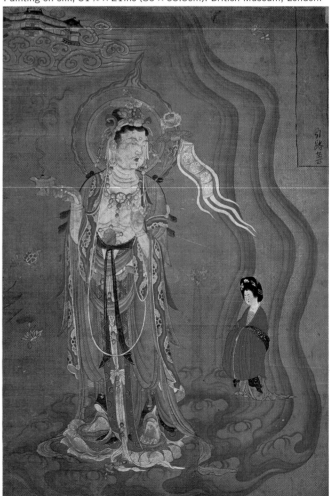

and Daoists for the drain of wealth to temples and of manpower to the unproductive celibate life of monasteries. In 845 the reigning emperor proscribed all 'foreign' religions, especially Buddhism. Some 4,600 temples and 40,000 shrines were destroyed and 200,000 monks sent back to work on the land. The ban was later relaxed and, in fact, there was a Buddhist revival not long afterwards. But there was no economic or political recovery and in 907 China disintegrated into a state of confusion known as the period of the Five Dynasties.

One of the finest examples of Tang sculpture – and one of the most impressive religious images in the whole world – dominates a cliff-face at Longmen (**6,91** and p. 272) where it was originally enclosed by a wooden temple. The contrast between this gigantic but serene image with its extreme refinement of carving and the earlier and equally large Buddha in the Yungang cave (6,88) is striking. It embodies a more advanced and complex conception for it represents Vairocana who, unlike the historical Buddha, is not a saviour but the personification of a philosophical concept of the original creative spirit that embraces Buddhist law and the cosmos. He sits on a lotus throne (now destroyed) representing that described as bearing 1,000 petals each of which is a universe with its

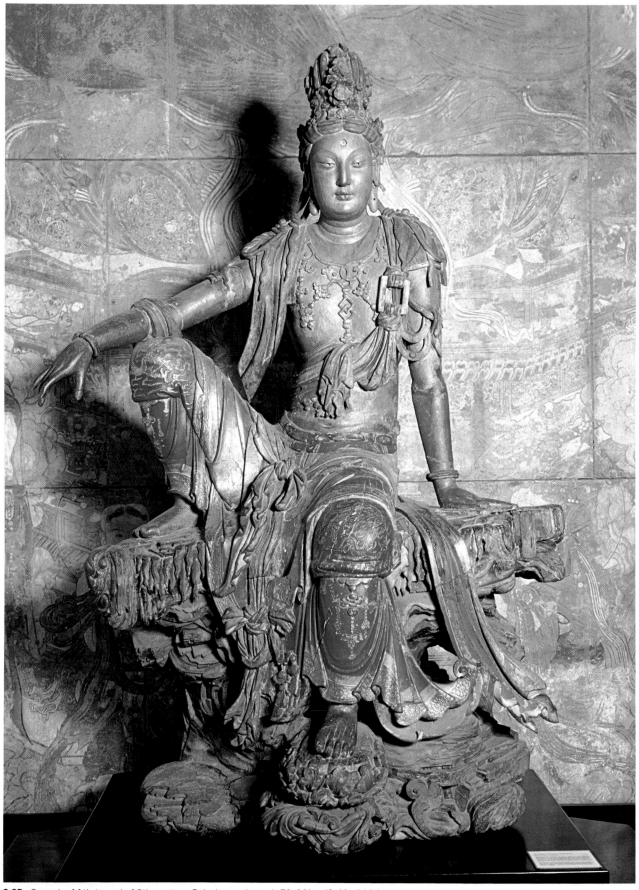

6,95 *Guanyin*, 11th to early 12th century. Polychromed wood, 7ft 11ins (2.41m) high.
Nelson-Atkins Museum of Art, Kansas City (Purchase: Nelson Trust).

been called Avalokitesvara in India (see p. 238), but no trace of an Indian origin survives in such a painting as that of the tenth century from Dunhuang in which he manifests himself swathed in the finest, lightest, most delicately patterned of Chinese silks (6,94). Invoked by an exquisite little lady, presumably the donor of this votive image, he has floated down from the celestial mansion in the upper left corner, one of the several humanly desirable heavens which had all but replaced the remote ideal of *Nirvana*. Distinctions between the divine and the human have been blurred and Guanyin is represented, larger in size but no less naturalistically than his devotee, as if he were an earthly prince. What theologians might regard as a naive conception of divinity is, nevertheless, rendered with the utmost sophistication, and the whole composition with its softly curving lines and gently vibrant colors is pervaded by an atmosphere of compassionate tenderness. Guanyin, who is here depicted with a mustache and imperial beard, was later to be transformed into a female figure associated with the traditional Chinese mothergoddess. Bodhisattvas are sexless (like angels), possessing the spiritual virtues of both men and women and able to manifest themselves in either form. The fusion is vividly suggested in a carved wood statue of the Song period (6,95). The sexual organs and other physical features, which the Greeks had combined in their hermaphrodites, have here been ignored in order to create an image of

androgynous love which transcends sexuality. The idea of the pure distilled spirit of humanity is embodied in this sensuously carved figure. The ornaments, drapery and fluttering scarves play a major part in the composition of delicately molded forms, no less subtle than intricate, with asymmetry enhancing the impression of life and movement.

SONG DYNASTY

The Song came to power in 960 and within 20 years reunited China. Under their rule the upper classes, living in the cities on the income of their estates, no longer engaged in such violent sports as hunting or polo playing (in which the Tang aristocracy had indulged) nor in the martial arts (defence being entrusted to mercenaries). Instead, cultivating literature, music and painting, they created an ideal of civilized life to which educated Chinese of later periods were to aspire, as many do even today. Unfortunately, however, the Song were eventually unable to resist the 'barbarians'. In the north the Khitan tribes established the Liao empire which spread from Manchuria and Mongolia to south of the Great Wall taking Beijing (in Pinyin spelling, the Chinese word for northern capital; the Khitan named it Nanjing, southern capital) and from 1004 obliging the Song to pay an annual tribute. Worse was to follow: the Jurchen Turks, who

6,96 *Torments of Hell*, 12th to 13th century. Painted rock carving. Dazu, Sichuan, China.

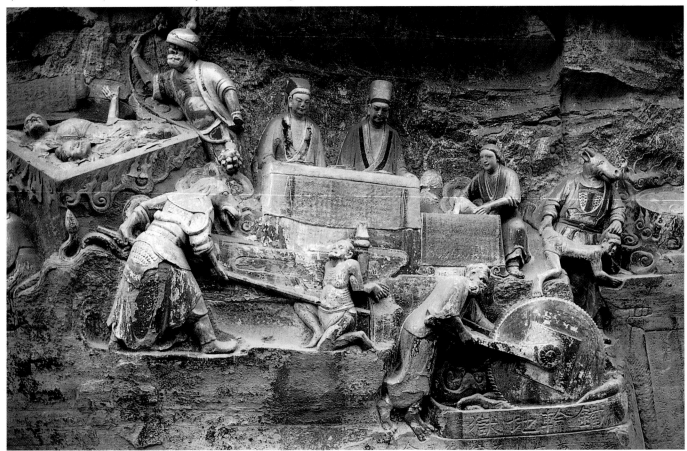

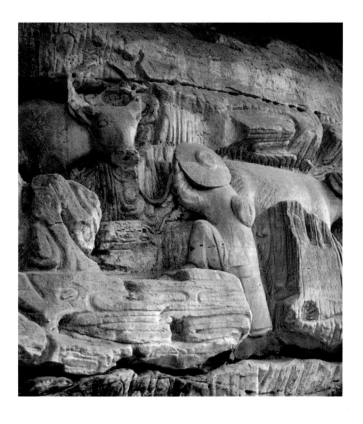

6,97 Pastoral scene, 12th to 13th century. Rock carving. Dazu, Sichuan.

elsewhere in south-east Asia – is carved naturalistically with a bold and weighty assurance appropriate to the cow-shed and paddy-field.

Outside Song territory in north-west China a less plebeian but equally naturalistic style of sculpture was developed in the Liao empire where Buddhism was promoted by the régime. Painted clay statues of Bodhisattvas dating from the early eleventh century in the Huayan monastery at Datong (**6,98**) are at once more elegant and more naturalistic than the Tang sculptures at Dunhuang from which they partly derive (6,92), serenely meditative yet animated by the rustling loops and folds of flowing draperies. Even more naturalistic is a Liao glazed pottery statue (**6,99**). With all the vividness of portraiture from the life, it represents one of the *luohans* or *Theravada* Buddhist monks who had achieved enlightenment by

6,98 Bodhisattva, early 11th century. Painted plaster. Huayan monastery, Datong, China.

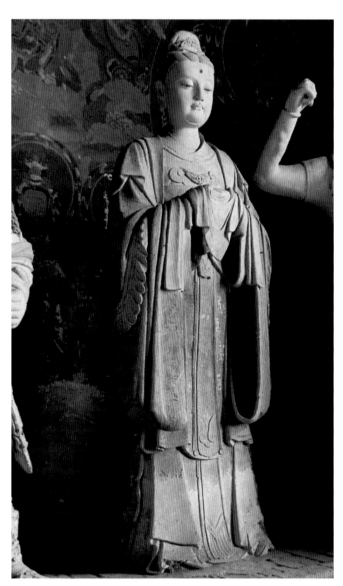

named their dynasty Jin, advanced steadily from central Asia and in 1127 raided the Song capital Kaifeng, taking prisoner the emperor and most of his court. A young prince fled beyond the Yangzi river and settled with the remaining officials at Hangzhou, which became the capital of the southern Song empire until it fell to the Mongols a century and a half later.

At the Song court the dominant doctrine was Neo-Confucianism, a highly intellectual synthesis reconciling Confucian moral principles with Daoist metaphysics in a typically Buddhist spirit of contemplative self-cultivation. *Mahayana* Buddhism with its Bodhisattvas and paradise gardens had become a popular, indeed plebeian, religion – hence, no doubt, the directness and vigour, the blunt simplicity and lack of *finesse* in its more memorable artistic manifestations. At Dazu, for instance, in the upper Yangzi valley beyond Chongqing, some 930 miles (1,500km) inland from the sea, an extraordinary series of popular scenes, including several everyday low-life ones, was carved on a cliff-face between 1179 and 1249. Some illustrate the evils of alcohol, others the torments of sinners in hell (**6,96**). One section is an allegory of submission to the teaching of the Buddha, symbolized by the taming and tending of cattle but realized as a vast pastoral *genre* scene – a vivid record of life on the land which survives unchanged by the passing of dynasties (**6,97**). The figure of a man wearing baggy trousers and a huge straw hat – such as are still to be seen in this region and

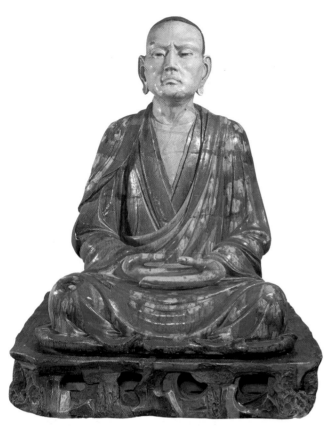

6,99 *Luohan*, 10th to 13th century. Three-colored glazed pottery, 3ft 4ins (1.02m) high. Nelson-Atkins Museum of Art, Kansas City (Purchase: Nelson Trust).

meditation and their own strength of mind without super-natural aid. Yet it is far from being a mere simulacrum. In this carefully composed sculptural form even the folds of the robes are arranged to express physical and mental con-centration. The figure was originally part of a group (made for some monastic building but now dispersed) differing from one another in drapery, the position of the hands and physiognomy but all conveying intensity of thought emu-lated by monks who strove to free themselves from desire. That such realistic characterization should be used to express the idea of abnegation of the self and of the world might seem paradoxical; but it was surely intentional, suggesting that every believer might, despite individu-ality, find the true way.

This statue is also a demonstration of ceramic tech-nique in modelling, glazing and firing. But it stands at the end of a tradition. Naturalistic pottery sculpture had first appeared in the Qin period in tomb figures (6,73) and was further developed in the Han and Tang periods, when it was sometimes wholly or partly covered with colored glazes (similar to those used on domestic wares). A large number of Tang statuettes survive, but they give a mis-leading impression of Tang art and of Chinese ceramics in general. Statuettes were never rated highly by the Chinese. The pure forms and smooth cool jade-like tex-tures of bowls, vases and other vessels in porcelain, first made in the Tang period and brought to perfection under the Song, were preferred (**6,100**). Nor was large-scale

figure sculpture to be prominent in the later art of China; it was limited to repetitive statues often of impermanent materials covered with textiles and its artistic quality declined as the Buddhist faith that had introduced it lost intellectual prestige.

The popularization of Buddhism had already, however, had a consequence of revolutionary importance, or rather, potentiality: the invention of woodblock printing, first fully exploited in the periods of the Five Dynasties and the Song empire. Tantric doctrines, with their emphasis on esoteric rituals and magic spells, having infiltrated from Tibet and direct from India in the seventh century, had created a demand for huge numbers of amulets and images. And this was met by impressing ink-impregnated woodblocks on woven silk or paper (also Chinese inven-tions dating from the Shang and Han periods respec-tively). The next step, towards the printing of illustrated texts, was taken well before 868, the date of the earliest surviving dated printed scroll (the *Diamond Sutra*, a Bud-dhist text found at Dunhuang and now in the British Library, London). In the following century woodblock printing was used for the publication of imperial decrees and for the first paper money. And the laborious task of printing books, each page from a carved wooden block, began: the Confucian classics and the Daoist texts as well as the Buddhist scriptures or *Tripitaka* (260,000 pages) – assisting Neo-Confucianists in their search for a religio-philosophical synthesis. By the twelfth century, printed

6,100 Ru ware vase with copper rim, Song dynasty, 12th century. Porcelain, 9¾ins (25cm) high. Percival David Foundation of Chinese Art, London.

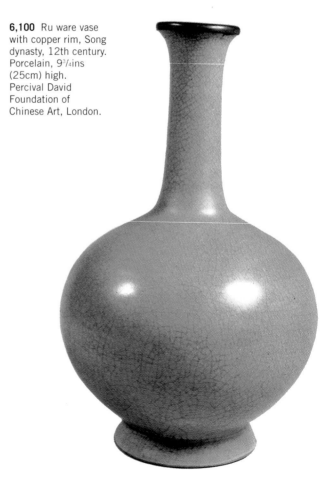

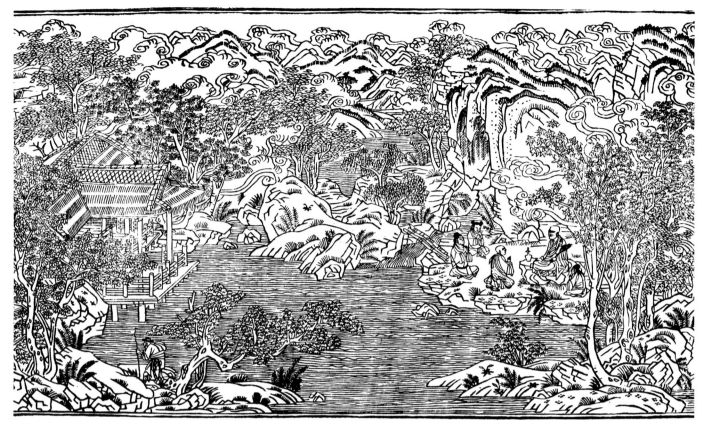

6,101 Landscape with Buddhist sages surrounded by disciples, printed 1108. Woodblock printed handscroll, 12³/₈ × 20¹⁵/₁₆ins (31.3 × 53.2cm) maximum, Arthur M. Sackler Museum, Harvard University Art Museums, Cambridge, Mass. (Louise H. Daly, anonymous and Alpheus Hyatt Funds).

books included encyclopedias, dynastic histories and also such illustrated works as a *Materia medica* and catalogues of art collections. And yet printing made a far less forceful impact on China than it was to on Europe when it was introduced or re-invented there several centuries later. The nature of Chinese script with some 20,000 different characters greatly limited the exploitation of movable type, which was to enable European printers to produce books that were infinitely cheaper than manuscripts. (Movable Chinese characters were introduced in about 1050, but many thousands were needed, and most Chinese books continued to be printed from woodblocks cut for every page until the sixteenth century.) Moreover, the Chinese preoccupation with the artist's touch discouraged recognition of the figurative woodcut as an art form in its own right. One of a set of four prints of landscapes with Buddhist sages surrounded by disciples reveals the possibilities of the medium (**6,101**). But they were not exploited. The majority of prints produced before the sixteenth century were either technical diagrams or popular religious images which circulated only among the lower strata of society.

Another development in Buddhism had a more direct influence on the arts: the emergence of the Chan sect (known as Zen in Japan; see p. 295), founded in 520–7 but achieving little prominence before the ninth century. Its members declared that there was no Buddha save the Buddha in man's own nature, that all rituals, acts of worship and study of texts were worthless. They strove in

6,102 Muqi, *Six Persimmons*, Chan sect, Japan, 13th century. Ink on paper, 14¹/₄ × 15ins (36.2 × 38.1cm). Daitokuji, Tokyo.

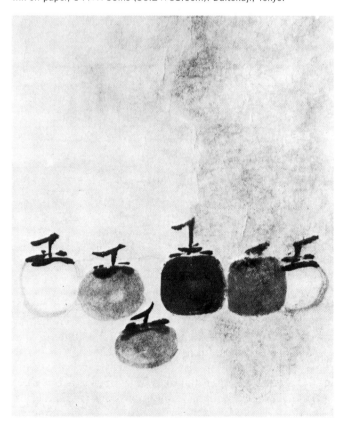

inspiration Liang Kai (c. 1140–1210), who called himself 'Liang the Fool', summoned up the spirit of the bibulous, free-living eighth-century poet Li Bai (**6,103**). An almost uniquely aniconic religious art was thus created – that is to say, without any devotional function (see pp. 565–6). But Chan ideas are remarkably close to those of Daoists, who found in landscape painting a means of expressing their apprehension of the workings of the cosmic spirit. And as Neo-Confucian philosophy, founded in the Song period, developed in the same direction towards an intuitive communion with the natural world, the art of landscape painting acquired in China an importance it has been given by no other civilization.

LANDSCAPE PAINTING

Buddhist art was essentially public; images made for domestic shrines were small-scale versions of those displayed in temples. But Chinese landscape painting is deeply private and, furthermore, an élitist art – an art made by a few highly cultivated artists, especially gentlemen amateurs (professionals were less highly regarded) for an intimate circle of congenial spirits. Only initiates could fully understand the six enigmatic principles distinguishing a 'good painting' – indeed they can be no more than very roughly translated: (i) animation through spirit consonance; (ii) structural method in the use of the brush; (iii) fidelity to the object in portraying forms; (iv) conformity to kind in applying colors; (v) proper planning; (vi) transmission of the experience of the past in making copies. Enunciated by Xie He in the early sixth century, these principles constitute the foundation of Chinese art theory. Significantly, the first refers to a quality unattainable by mere technical skill or by rational analysis. The last alludes to that respect for 'old masters' and the practice of copying them which gives such consistency to Chinese painting over nearly a millennium and a half – as well as bedevilling its study by Westerners.

In early Chinese literature there are many references to Tang landscape painters, including some extreme individualists who adopted unorthodox procedures. One is said to have applied ink with worn-out brushes and his bare fingers; when asked how he learned this technique he replied: 'Outwardly, nature has been my teacher, but inwardly I follow the springs of inspiration in my heart.' These stories were to influence later generations of artists (see Chapter 12), but no examples of such paintings survive. Indeed, very few Tang landscapes are known at all, even from copies. The earliest surviving paintings that to some extent reflect Tang ideas date from the tenth century. One of the finest is a hanging scroll, *Buddhist Temple in the Hills after Rain*, which was in the Song imperial collection (**6,104**). It has been attributed to, and is almost certainly in the style of, Li Cheng (fl. 940–67), a prime representative of the Chinese ideal of the artist: a man of good family, well educated, wholly devoted to painting and scorning the nobles and careerist officials who clamoured for his work. An eleventh-century biographer records that his only ambition was to lead a quiet

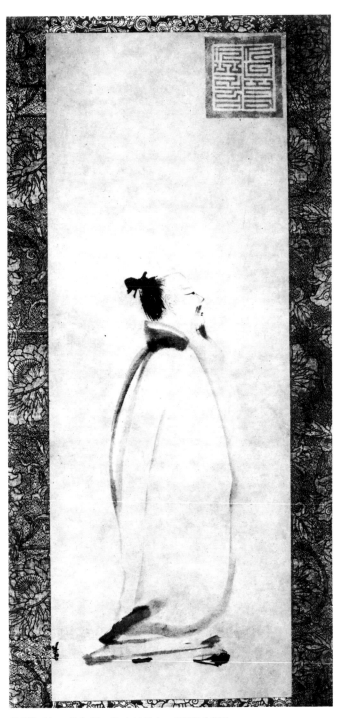

6,103 Liang Kai, *The Poet Li Bai*, c. 1200–1210. Ink on paper, 42⅞ × 13ins (78 × 33cm). Tokyo National Museum.

meditation for communion with the Absolute or First Principle – a communion vouchsafed in rare flashes of blinding illumination. This transcendental experience could never be described in words but might be evoked by a work of art, by a painting – of a plant, a wild landscape or just six persimmons (**6,102**) – which expressed the inner life of things and which could, in turn, assist the viewer's quest for enlightenment. Imaginary portraits, not necessarily of holy men, were among the favoured subjects. With a dozen rapid brush-strokes of spontaneous

life and that, as an artist, 'his inspired versatility was the quintessence of the spiritual, very far beyond normal human capacities'. The scene is imaginary, as are most Chinese landscape paintings, but rendered with an intimate understanding of nature such as comes only from observation as sharp-eyed as it is loving. Artists roamed the countryside; many of them are known to have

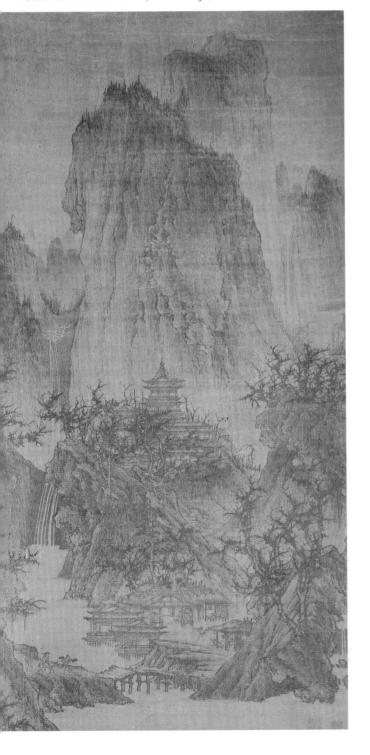

6,104 Li Cheng, *Buddhist Temple in the Hills after Rain*, c. AD 950. Hanging scroll, ink and slight color on silk, 44 × 22ins (111.8 × 55.9cm). Nelson-Atkins Museum of Art, Kansas City (Purchase: Nelson Trust).

sketched what they saw, and their landscapes thus bear a strong likeness to the real scenery, though only a generic one, for they were painted indoors and were intended to represent the essence of nature and not simply views of natural beauty. A landscape is called in Chinese *shanshui*, a 'mountain-water' picture, and *Buddhist Temple in the Hills after Rain* exploits the relationship of the two elements spiritually as well as visually. 'The wise men find pleasure in waters; the virtuous find pleasure in mountains', Confucius had remarked. For Daoists water had a special significance exemplifying the *Dao*, and their basic text celebrated the place where streams from the mountain are gathered.

Buddhist Temple in the Hills after Rain is painted on silk in black ink with only a few touches of color. Such artists as Li Cheng shunned the bright colors favoured by ungentlemanly and unscholarly professionals for merely decorative work. They preferred the ink used for calligraphy (generally regarded in China as the highest form of art, though it is the least accessible to Westerners) and thus bound landscape painting in technique as well as subject-matter to the learned literary tradition. It was from the practice of calligraphy, which demanded vitality of line, structural strength in each character and firm control over the composition of the whole page, that these artists derived much of their skill and sensibility. The effect is not, however, linear in a Western sense: washes and dabs of ink are freely used and long brush-strokes have no hard confining uniformity. Nor is there any composition in the Western sense: no framing devices enclose the view. Li Cheng's painting has a strong vertical axis, or rather three, ascending in height and receding in depth from left to right almost like three long-drawn-out musical chords. Distance is indicated by clearly defined planes separated by banks of mist, against which the nearer objects are silhouetted. Unlike the hand-scrolls, which gradually revealed landscapes as they were unfurled inch by enthralling inch, this hanging scroll was intended to be seen as a whole, but to be pored over no less minutely. The viewer's eye is invited to wander with the pilgrim in the left foreground, across the bridge to the rustic huts and pavilions where people are eating, drinking and talking, to climb up among the autumnal trees to the temple and to scan the remoter distances. But the eye is simultaneously held on the surface of the painting by the amazing delicacy and deftness of the brush-strokes indicating texture as well as form, and by the expressive dabs of ink with which the rocks are modelled.

Why are landscapes painted? The question was asked by Guo Xi (c. 1020–90), for more than 60 years a member of the Song imperial academy, at the beginning of his *Advice on Landscape Painting*. No man of high principle, he thought, could evade his responsibility to family and society by retiring to live as a recluse in the mountains. But 'the longing for forests and streams, the companionship of mists and vapours' need not be satisfied only in dreams and denied to the waking senses. Paintings of such scenes could enable the city dweller to sit to his heart's

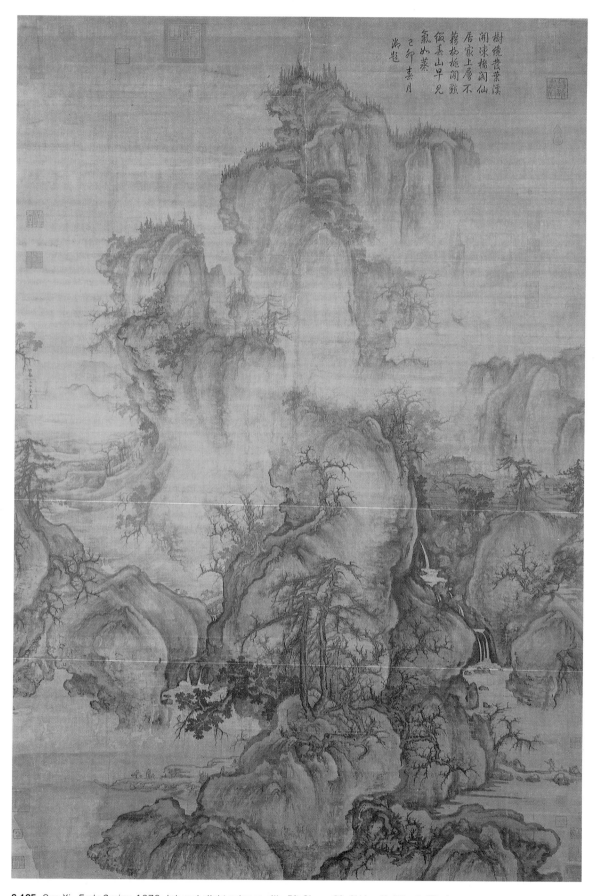

樹繞荔葉溪
澗凍檐閱仙
居家上層不
蘚枘枢間窈
微喜山早見
氣如蒸
已卯春月
尚题

6,105 Guo Xi, *Early Spring*, 1072. Ink and slight color on silk, 5ft 2ins × 3ft 6½ins (1.58 × 1.08m).
National Palace Museum, Taipei (Taibei), Taiwan.

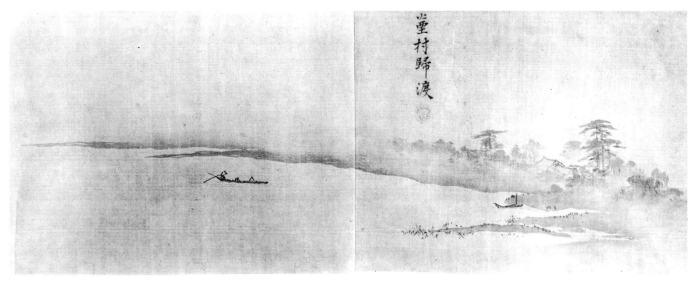

6,106 Xia Gui, *Twelve Views from a Thatched Cottage*, detail, c. 1200–30. Hand-scroll, ink on silk, 11ins (28cm) high. Nelson-Atkins Museum of Art, Kansas City (Purchase: Nelson Trust).

content among streams and valleys. This, Guo Xi declared, 'is the ultimate meaning behind the honour the world accords to landscape painting'. The same idea underlay the creation of the artificially 'natural' in private gardens. It should not, however, be supposed that this attitude to wild scenery was either purely aesthetic or 'sentimental' – like that to be developed in Europe many centuries later. Guo Xi regarded landscape painting as a means of conveying a sense of the totality of the natural order – of the cosmos itself. This is perfectly exemplified in his *Early Spring* (**6,105**), an imaginary view based, none the less, on close study of trees and rocks and streams, composed in such a way that the eye is led from the tiny figures in the foreground to a temple in a cleft on the right and up through the mist to the rocky heights, or far away on the left through a valley to distant mountain peaks. 'The spring mountain is wrapped in an unbroken stretch of dreamy haze and mist, and the men are joyful', he wrote.

A later, southern Song landscape is in a different style, softer and more atmospheric (**6,106**). It is part of a long scroll entitled *Twelve Views from a Thatched Cottage* by Xia Gui (c. 1180–1230), painter-in-attendance to the emperor. Unrolled, from right to left of course, it reveals a mountain range and then a wide lake with boats on the water and fishing nets on the shore. Inscriptions entitle successive sections, such as: 'Distant Mountains and Wild Geese', 'The Ferry Returns to the Village in the Mist', 'Fisherman Playing the Flute in the Quiet Dusk', 'Anchoring at Evening on the Misty Bank', as well as many others. Time as well as space is taken into account in this scroll, which moves from far to near, from misty daylight to dusk. And the effect of scanning it is akin to that of listening to music or reading a poem – one passage lingers in the memory and reverberates there as the eye passes on to the next. Transitions are so subtle that they are hardly noticed until they are gone. Although the mood is one of uninterrupted reverie, monotony is avoided by

subtle transitions from soft washes to firm brush-strokes, from diaphanous suggestions of form to sharply focused details. Much of the silk is left blank. Only a gentle diagonal (a device often used) indicates how the lake widens out and the far shore vanishes from view. A few perfectly placed blobs and lines of jet-black ink suffice to conjure up a boat and also the expanse of still water on which it floats. The art of pictorial suggestion could hardly be taken further.

In China, a landscape painting was understood as a depiction of reality. Wholly fantastic scenes were ruled out and merely conventional views were despised. But it was also – and this was more important – a reality in its own right, as a manifestation of the cosmic spirit working through the hand of the artist and in perfect harmony with it. Li Cheng was, in fact, criticized by a contemporary for giving too great importance to visual appearances and especially for painting buildings from a single viewpoint and not 'from the angle of totality'. Objects should be correctly delineated but their 'essence' could be lost in overparticularization.

The building in the centre of *Buddhist Temple in the Hills after Rain* (6,104) is of great interest now, however, in that it records a type of structure known from very few surviving examples of the period in China. Buddhism had introduced not only the rock-cut temple but also free-standing stone architecture. A few early stone or brick temple towers, known in the West as pagodas (from a Portuguese word of uncertain origin), survive. One at Xi'an (formerly Chang'an) was erected for the abbot of a monastery who had made a pilgrimage to India, but it owes almost as much to Han dynasty watch-towers (known from pottery tomb-models) as to any Indian structure (6,107). Its eaves are supported on brick corbels simulating the wooden brackets normal in China. Wood was the main Chinese building material for both secular and religious structures, stone and brick being used mainly for

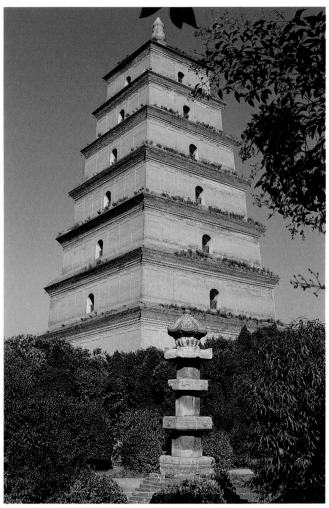

6,107 Dayanta pagoda, Xi'an, China, AD 647.

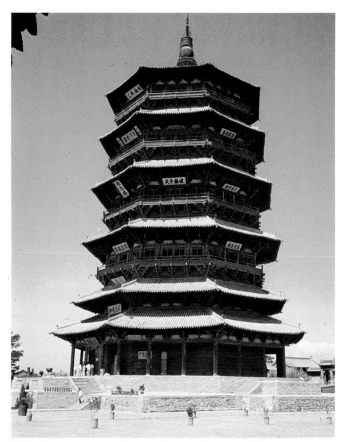

6,108 Fogongai pagoda, Yingxian, Shanxi, China, AD 1058.

fortifications. Pagodas were normally built of wood, though very few survive, the earliest being that erected under Liao rule in 1058 at Yingxian – a tower 216 feet (66m) high of nine stories, four of which have windows and contain statues of the Buddha and Bodhisattvas (**6,108**).

The pagoda is the only exclusively religious building type evolved by the Chinese. A purely symbolical structure, a signal of faith in the greatness of the Buddha, towering above the sacred relics buried in its foundations, it distinguished a Buddhist monastery from the temples of other religious cults and also from palaces. For there was otherwise no external distinction between palatial and religious complexes. (Those shown in the paradise painting at Dunhuang, 6,93, could be either.) Both consisted of detached buildings laid out in the same axially symmetrical way, the largest and richest being the south-facing throne room of a palace and the temple in which the most impressive statue of the Buddha was enthroned in a monastery – for an early surviving example of the latter one must, however, turn to Japan (6,115). The pagoda at Yingxian was, so to speak, composed by extending a pavilion vertically, raising one basic element

on top of another. The architecture of Buddhism was naturalized much more quickly than its sculpture and completely transformed in the process of adaptation to Chinese methods of construction in wood. A new style was evolved, far more remote from Indian architecture than the latter had been from its own wooden prototypes.

Chinese architecture is quite different from that of the West in that the roof is given the major visual importance that Egyptians and Assyrians had given to the walls and the Greeks to columns. Drawings and reliefs reveal that this began at least as early as the Han period and had been

6,109 Drawing of the Chinese beam-frame system.

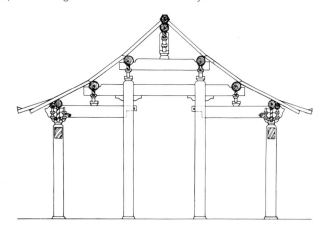

perfected by the sixth century. The basic principle of Chinese roof construction is that of post and lintel, but the horizontal members or beams are tenoned into or pass through the tops of the posts (**6,109**). The joins are reinforced both structurally and visually by brackets often of an ingenious complexity, which take the place of the capitals in a European Classical order, but appear to be functional rather than symbolic or ornamental. The length of available timbers conditions the distance between uprights, but the width of a building could be increased by a simple process of repetition (the entrance is beneath the slope of the roof on the long side and not at the gable end as in a Greek temple). To increase depth and height further pairs of taller columns in the interior are needed. The roof covering of shingles, or of tiles for the grander buildings, is supported on purlins (see Glossary) carried by the beams, and can thus be given the concave profile that is such a distinguishing feature. Eaves are wide, originally intended no doubt to protect the walls from torrential rain and to provide shade, though turned up at the corners of hipped roofs for aesthetic as much as practical reasons. To support them elaborately carpentered brackets are cantilevered out from the columns. Beneath these great roofs there are no load-bearing walls, only partitions. Buildings are held together by their vertical and horizontal timbers. This system of construction was adopted for palatial and religious buildings throughout east and south-east Asia. Its earliest surviving examples are in Japan where Chinese or Korean craftsmen were initially employed to erect Buddhist monasteries in the late sixth century.

SHINTO AND BUDDHIST ART IN JAPAN

Although separated from the Asian mainland by little more than 94 miles (150km), Japan for long remained immune to Chinese cultural influence, despite contacts by way of Korea. Techniques of working bronze and iron were learned probably from Koreans in the third century BC. Han dynasty objects, notably bronze mirrors, were imported. But not until the sixth century AD was this isolation disturbed. Then Buddhism, writing, painting and sculpture as well as a new manner of building were all introduced together from China and almost immediately accepted. That this cultural invasion came about without territorial colonization is an indication that Japanese civilization, though non-literate, was already sufficiently advanced and mature to assimilate foreign influence of a highly sophisticated kind. Indeed, neither at this date nor later were Chinese ideas and attitudes imposed on the arts of Japan, except by the Japanese themselves, usually by members of the ruling families. They were grafted on to a rootstock that continued to thrive.

The indigenous Japanese religion, Shinto, or the 'Way of the Gods', was a polytheistic nature cult without dogmas, scriptures or images. As a result little is known of its early development apart from what may be deduced from burials. In the Kofun period (c. 300–600) huge earthworks were raised over the graves of rulers and surrounded by moats: one near Osaka covers some 277 acres (111 hectares) and rises to a height of 110 feet (35m). Tombs were surrounded by *haniwa*, terracotta tubes usually about 24 inches (61cm) high, surmounted by human heads, whole-length human figures or animals (**6,110**). They are peculiar to Japan, smoothly modelled, with slits for eyes and mouth, expressionless yet curiously expressive. Tradition holds that they were substitutes for the living beings who had previously been slaughtered at the funeral of a chieftain – like Tang tomb figures in China.

The first places of Shinto worship were probably simple open-air enclosures. But at least as early as the seventh century AD shrines were constructed of timber with posts sunk into the ground, raised floors, plank walls and pitched roofs of thatch supported by a network of intersecting spars and ridge-pole. They symbolically resembled communal village granaries for the storage of rice – the staff of life, a product of the beneficent forces of nature and the annually recurring miracle of growth and regeneration. The original form of the most famous, at Ise, has been preserved by the perennial Japanese custom of building, every 20 years, a new shrine next to and exactly like the old one, which was subsequently demolished – a religious ritual in itself and also a means of maintaining pristine purity (**6,111**). Depending for their effect on the logical simplicity of structure and materials – thatch and wood carefully selected for its grain which remains visible – these shrines already intimate that love of rusticity which was eventually developed by the Japanese into the most sophisticated of aesthetic cults. Shintoism was to be

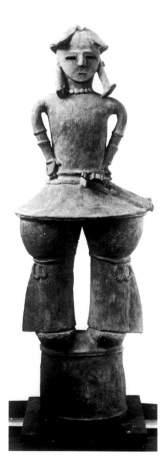

6,110 *Haniwa* figure, c. AD 300–600. Terracotta, about 24ins (61cm) high. Musée Guimet, Paris.

SOURCES AND DOCUMENTS

THE NIHONGI ON THE FIRST BUDDHIST IMAGES IN JAPAN

The *Nihongi* history of Japan was compiled by members of the imperial court between AD 714 and 720. It provides a year-by-year chronicle of notable events including the introduction of Buddhism, revealing incidentally the importance of the arts in the propagation of the faith. In 552, for example, the emperor is recorded as receiving from the king of Paekche (Korea) an image of the Buddha in gold and copper, several Buddhist flags and volumes of *sutras* (sacred texts).

The countenance of this Buddha is of a severe dignity such as we have never seen before, he told his ministers and then asked them: *Ought it to be worshipped or not?*

Most of the ministers objected that it would excite the wrath of the national (that is, Shinto) gods. Only one was in favour of acceptance. The image was given to him and he transformed part of his house into the first Buddhist shrine in Japan. But soon afterwards a plague broke out and was blamed on the Buddha; the image was thrown into a river and the house burnt down. Although the date has been questioned (538 is more probable), in outline the story is thought to be historical. The *Nihongi* goes on to state that in 578 the king of Paekche sent a new emperor:

. . . . a number of volumes of religious books, with an ascetic, a meditative monk, a nun, a reciter of mantras, a maker of Buddhist images and a temple architect.

Once again there was resistance from Shinto devotees but as further Korean missionaries arrived bringing Buddhist images with them, the number of Japanese converts increased.

The emperor Yomei, who came to the throne in 586, 'believed in the Law of the Buddha and reverenced the Way of the Gods', thus initiating the combination of Buddhism and Shinto that was to become imperial policy. Two years later the king of Paekche sent him further Buddhist relics with a priest, three ascetics, two 'temple carpenters', a metal worker, 'men learned in pottery' and a painter. These men were presumably engaged to plan and construct the first two large-scale Buddhist monasteries in Japan, the Shitennoji at Osaka and the Hokoji at Asuka, the capital at that time. Progress on the Hokoji is regularly recorded up to 596 when the temple was finished and monks took up residence. (The buildings of the Shitennoji were to be destroyed and rebuilt many times, but always on the original platforms which survive. Excavations have revealed the plan of the Hokoji, centred on a pagoda.)

In 593 the empress Suiko began her 34-year reign and with her nephew, the Prince Imperial Shotoku Taishi, secured the acceptance of Buddhism. Thirty years later, less than a century after the arrival of the first image of the Buddha,

. . . there was an inspection of the temples, priests and nuns . . . . There were at this time 46 temples, 816 priests and 596 nuns.

(W. G. Aston, *Nihongi,* Transactions and Proceedings of the Japan Society, London 1896; Aston's wording has been retained although 'temples' and 'priests' should be rendered as 'monasteries' and 'monks')

---

modified by Buddhism and vice versa, for the two religions were not always antagonistic and both were to remain living forces in Japan (much more so than Buddhism and Daoism in China).

The earliest surviving example of Buddhist architecture in Japan is the monastery called Horyuji (the suffix -ji meaning 'temple'), near Nara in the south of Honshu, the main island of the archipelago. Founded in 607, it appears to have had an axially symmetrical plan like other monasteries of which only the foundations survive, notably the much larger Hokoji completed in 596 (**6,112**). But when it was rebuilt after a fire in 670 a very remarkable change was made at Horyuji by setting the pagoda and *kondo*, or 'golden hall' for statues, side by side rather than one behind the other, and by placing the entrance gateway slightly off centre so that it balances the void between the two buildings of unequal plan. As a result, a far more interesting composition of solids in space was

created – one that seems, with the benefit of hindsight, to be already characteristically Japanese (**6,113**). The three buildings which have been preserved intact (though doubtless continually renewed, and sometimes radically restored as was the *kondo* after a fire in 1949) are of Chinese design, roofed with ceramic tiles rather than the thatch normal in Japan. So too is the eighth-century octagonal *yumedono* or 'hall of dreams' in another part of the monastery (**6,114**). But the *kodo*, or lecture hall on the north side of the main court, is a tenth-century addition and has a Japanese-style roof with a ridge nearly as long as the whole building – unlike Chinese hipped roofs – giving an accent of horizontality that nicely sets off the verticality of the *kondo* and pagoda, enriching without disrupting the architectural composition.

The Horyuji *kondo* appears from outside to have two stories but, in fact, has only one; the function of the elaborately constructed upper part is to indicate the

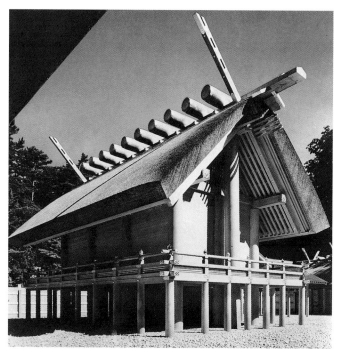

6,111 *Shoden*, main building of Ise shrine, Japan, rebuilt 1973.

6,113 Horyuji, near Nara, Japan, AD 670.

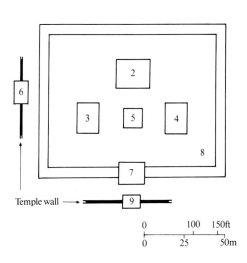

6,112 Plan of Hokoji, Asuka, Japan.
1 *Kodo* (lecture hall) **2** *Kondo* **3** Western *kondo*
4 Eastern *kondo* **5** Pagoda **6** Western gate
7 *Chumon* (central gate) **8** *Kairo* (peristyle)
9 Southern gate (front gate)

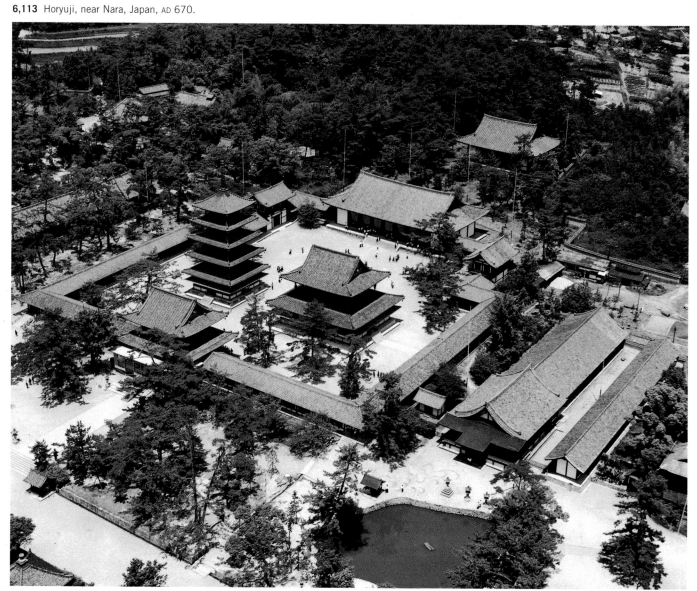

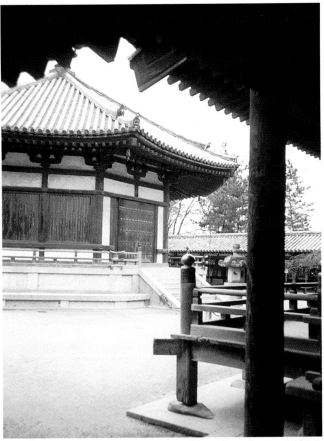

6,114 *Yumedono*, Horyuji, near Nara, AD 739 and later. Courtyard 13th to 14th century.

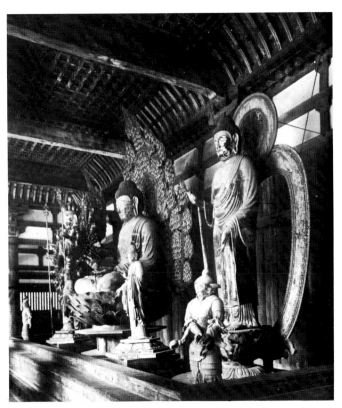

6,115 *Kondo* at Toshodaiji, near Nara, AD 759 (interior from the east).

building's importance. Inside, statues facing the four cardinal points to suggest the cosmic centrality of the Buddha are placed on a raised platform surrounded by a narrow ambulatory so that the faithful could make their circumambulation as round the stupa in an Indian *chaitya*-hall (see p. 229). This plan was presumably that of the earlier, seventh-century building. But in the *kondo* of another monastery near Nara, the Toshodaiji, founded by a Chinese missionary in 759 and said to have been designed by a Chinese architect-monk, the statues of the Buddha and Bodhisattvas are placed in front of a screen facing south, like a throned emperor flanked by his courtiers (**6,115**). The carved wooden ceiling above them is partly suspended from the hipped roof, the main feature of the exterior which was, however, heightened at a later period with a still more complex system of supports (**6,116**).

By the beginning of the eighth century Buddhism had become the dominant religion of the Japanese empire while Confucianism, introduced at the same time, provided a model for the reorganization of its government on Chinese lines. Both were promoted by the imperial family. When the city of Nara was founded as a permanent capital in 710 (breaking the Shinto tradition of moving the capital after the death of each emperor to avoid spiritual pollution) it was laid out on a grid plan in emulation of

Tang dynasty Chang'an in China. And the same amount of space was given to the palace and to the main monastery, Todaiji, which was made the administrative centre for all Japanese monasteries. (Nuneries were administered from the Hokkeji founded by an empress.)

The Japanese were as orthodox architecturally as theologically and strictly followed Chinese precedents in design if not in scale. Todaiji was laid out on a symmetrical plan, more extensive than any monastery in China, with twin pagodas and, in the centre, the 'great Buddha

6,116 Drawing of original roof (right) and present roof (left), Toshodaiji *kondo*.

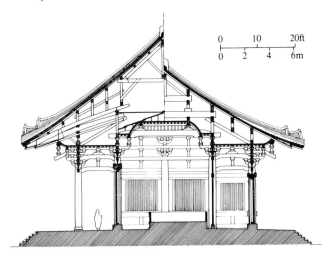

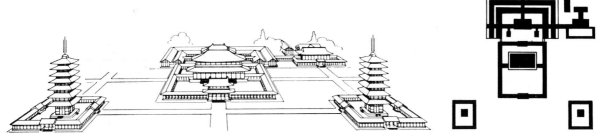

6,117 Plan of *daibutsuden*, Todaiji, Nara, Japan.

hall' or *daibutsuden* erected to house a 53-foot (15m) high bronze statue commissioned by the emperor Shomu in 743 (**6,117**). The eighth-century buildings were later destroyed but the statue survived (it is rather harshly restored but still impressive seen *in situ*, as one gazes up from the floor of the dimly lit temple). The *daibutsuden* itself was rebuilt on a slightly reduced plan but following the original design, with a massiveness unusual in Japanese architecture: it is still the largest wooden building in the world (**6,118**). The scale was determined by the height of the statue covered by a hipped roof with wide-spreading eaves which, with those of the lower roof over the ambulatory, give a sense of buoyancy to the building. The roofs seem to float above rather than bear down on the structure.

In the eighth century Japanese architects began, nevertheless, to experiment and take liberties with Chinese precedents, thus evolving a style of their own as in the east pagoda of the Yakushiji, Nara (**6,119**), which differs very obviously from that of the Horyuji. Originally one of a pair, this building has its tower set on a wider base and roofs of alternating size which lend it an almost calligraphic character. Great importance is given to the brackets supporting eaves and balconies, composed of blocks and bars of cleanly cut wood locked together, apparently with as much regard for abstract three-dimensional form as for function. (Both the west pagoda and *kondo* of the Yakushiji were reconstructed, in 1976 and 1980 respectively.)

The early history of Buddhist sculpture in Japan is similar to that of architecture, iconographical patterns and

techniques being introduced from China by way of southern Korea. Not only Korean sculptures and paintings but also Korean artists are known to have arrived in the mid-sixth century and the first notable Japanese-born sculptor, Tori Busshi (fl. 600–30), was the grandson of an immigrant metalworker. But as so few Chinese and still fewer Korean large-scale sculptures survive from this period it is impossible to tell how far early Japanese works were dependent on them. The famous seventh-century camphor wood sculpture of Kwannon (as Guanyin is called in Japan) in the Horyuji (**6,120**) is called the Kudara Kwannon after the Korean kingdom of Paekche or Kudara but is generally thought to have been of Japanese workmanship. Certainly there is no extant seventh-century Korean sculpture of equal technical accomplishment or

6,119 East pagoda of Yakushiji, Nara, 8th century.

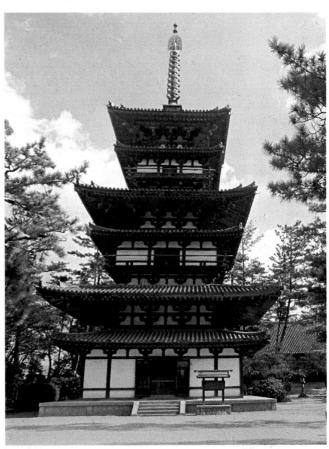

6,118 *Daibutsuden*, Todaiji, Nara, 8th century, rebuilt c. 1700.

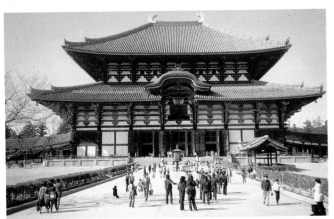

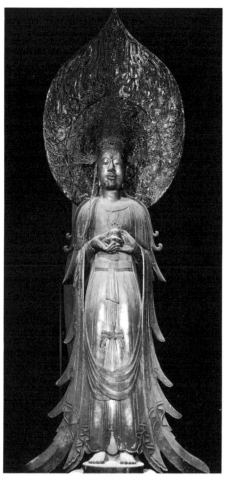

6,120 *Kwannon*, AD 623. Gilded camphor wood,
6ft 5¹/₂ins (1.97m) high. Horyuji, near Nara.

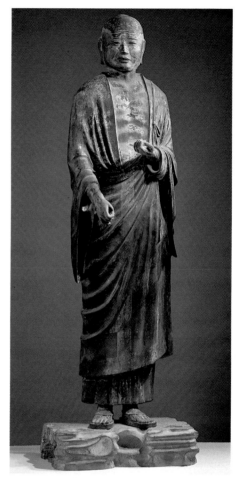

6,121 *Furuna*, c. 734. Painted dry lacquer,
4ft 10¹/₂ins (1.49m) high. Kofukuji, Nara.

artistic refinement. The pierced copper crown and the flame-like halo are of extreme refinement and delicate craftsmanship. And the fluent carving of the bands of drapery lends the figure a sense of levitation as if it were slowly ascending to the heavens.

Likewise the triad of statues in the Toshodaiji (6,115) have that ambiguous character of early Japanese sculpture made under Chinese or Korean influence – the names inscribed on the plinths are of Japanese craftsmen though the temple chronicle ascribed them to Chinese artists brought to Japan, presumably, by Jianzhen, the famous Buddhist teacher who founded the monastery. These imposing, over-life-size sculptures – the central Rukana Buddha (the Japanese name for Vairocana Buddha, see p. 274) is 11 feet (3.4m) high – are made of hollow dry lacquer, a process invented in China (see p. 118) but brought to technical perfection in Japan at this period, probably as a substitute for bronze (the country's entire copper supply having been exhausted in casting the great Buddha for the Todaiji). Dry lacquer must be supported on an armature of wood or basketwork which necessitates vertical balance and rigidity of posture while permitting great delicacy of detail, as in a figure of Furuna (called Purna in India), the eldest of the Buddha's ten Great Disciples, represented as

a monk with shaved head, wrinkled brow and an expression of somewhat anxious benevolence (6,121). The normal material for sculpture in Japan at this date and later was, however, wood which is less durable than lacquer and seldom survives, though the small guardian figures at the angles of the enclosure of the triad at the Toshodaiji are of wood.

THE HEIAN, FUJIWARA AND KAMAKURA PERIODS (794–1333)

The alliance between religion and the state, between Buddhism and a system of government based on Confucian principles, was shortlived. In the second half of the eighth century the influence of monks at the imperial court became increasingly oppressive to the laity. To escape their meddling the emperor Kammu left Nara (which remained a religious centre as it still is today) and in 794 founded a new capital some 25 miles (40km) to the north which he called Heian-Kyo, 'Capital of Peace and Tranquillity'. This city, the present-day Kyoto, was to remain for more than a millennium the seat of the imperial court – though only intermittently the centre of power. From the late ninth century the role of the emperor was little more than ceremonial; rival clans struggled for political control which was eventually seized by members of the Fujiwara family (after whom the period 895–1185 has been named) and in 1192 by the first of the Shoguns or supreme generals who established their administrative centre at Kamakura, 200 miles (320km) to the north on the east coast, not far from present-day Tokyo.

During the Fujiwara period the arts developed a stronger Japanese character than before. At its beginning the breakdown of the close religious, diplomatic and commercial relations with China cut Japanese artists off from developments on the mainland during the late Tang and early, troubled decades of the Five Dynasties. Contacts were resumed in the eleventh century but were never to be as close as in the Nara period. In the interim, specifically Japanese religious sects, influenced by the Tantric Buddhism of Tibet but incorporating Shinto elements, began to flourish, inspiring a mysteriously meditative art while, simultaneously, a sudden flowering of secular art reflected the nationalistic and hedonistic tone of the Japanese court. The first great – indeed the greatest – work of Japanese fiction was written at this time: *The Tale of Genji* by the Lady Murasaki (c. 980–c. 1030), as was also that other great Japanese literary achievement, the *Pillow Book* by Sei Shonagon (b. 965). Both describe in vivid detail the extreme urbanity and sophistication of a dominant upper class that cultivated literature, music and the arts without, as Lady Murasaki reveals, losing touch with simple humanity.

The palaces and court buildings in which her stories are set have vanished but a fair amount is known about them from other sources. China provided the model for the imperial administration and its buildings but the private apartments at the imperial palace at Kyoto depart from Chinese precedent in ignoring symmetrical planning in favour of convenience. Indoors, spaces were divided by sliding screens painted with landscapes. There were no raised stone platforms as in China: floors were of wood covered with matting and everyone sat on them. Externally palaces were similar to temples of the same period of which the finest example, built for a Fujiwara prince in 1052, is the *hoodo* ('phoenix hall') of the Byodoin temple at Uji near Kyoto (**6,122**). Despite an almost dandified elegance, it retains a mood of dreamy quietude. Roofs with dashingly uplifted corners seem to float above the horizontal lines, giving the whole fabric a mirage-like quality, as if it were no more substantial than its own reflection in the still waters of the lake. Nor was this effect accidental. The temple was built to enshrine an image of the Buddha Amida, Lord of Boundless Light. By faith in Amida and repetition of his name, devotees of the Pure Land sect believed that they would be admitted to the western paradise with its jewelled trees, lotus ponds and palaces of celestial beauty, which the *hoodo* prefigures. With its 'Easy Way' to salvation this Buddhist

6,122 *Hoodo*, Byodoin temple, Uji, near Kyoto, 1052.

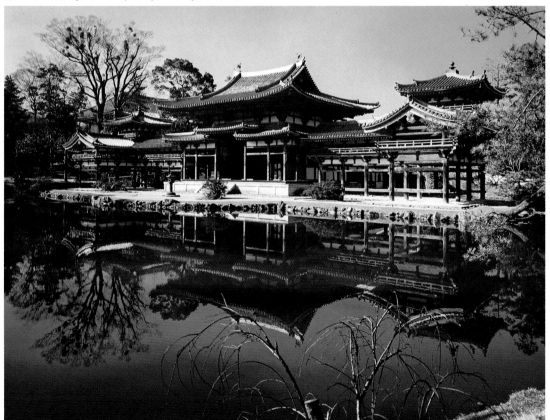

sect had a strong appeal for pleasure-loving courtiers in Japan and inspired some of the most exquisite, if least spiritual, of Buddhist works of art. It also promised salvation to women who, according to stricter Buddhist doctrines, could hope to attain *Nirvana* only after a male reincarnation.

Sculpture no less than architecture reflects the sophisticated tone of Kamakura society. A small, brightly painted statue of the goddess of felicity Kichijoten – the Indian Lakshmi absorbed into Mahayanist Buddhism – is a notable example (**6,123**). Comparison with the nearly contemporary Chinese statue of Guanyin (6,95) reveals how different Japanese aesthetic ideals had become. There is no sense of the ideal and unattainable – or of the ambiguous – about the buxom Kichijoten. She is a very solid down-to-earth manifestation of a goddess, clad not in fluttering gauze-like draperies but in a robe as rich as it is heavy. Were it not for her lotus pedestal, she might easily be mistaken for a very superior lady of the court, such as Lady Murasaki could so well have described.

Other aspects of Fujiwara art and religion appear in a number of fans printed from woodblocks with passages from the Buddhist *sutras* and the outlines of *genre* scenes colored by hand and further decorated with little squares and specks of gold (**6,124**). The combination of sacred text with a wittily drawn glimpse of everyday life in a composition of highly sophisticated elegance is uniquely Japanese. These fans are among the earliest manifestations of the Japanese genius for purely decorative design and also for secular narrative painting (see p. 564). Many were presented to a temple in Osaka, the Shitennoji (one of the first Buddhist foundations in Japan), some way from the court at Kyoto – and this may perhaps explain the

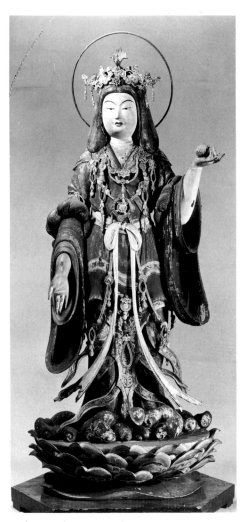

6,123 *Kichijoten*, 12th century. Polychromed wood, 34⁷/₈ins (88.6cm) high. Joruriji, Kyoto.

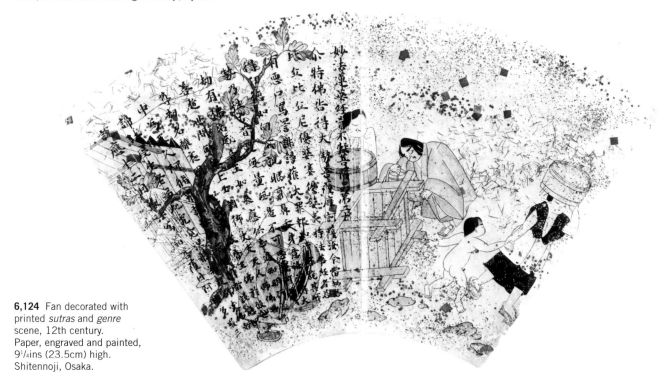

6,124 Fan decorated with printed *sutras* and *genre* scene, 12th century. Paper, engraved and painted, 9¹/₄ins (23.5cm) high. Shitennoji, Osaka.

preference they show for working-class rather than aristocratic subjects. These scenes, curiously, have no apparent connection with the words of the *sutra* in Chinese characters which could be read only by the educated minority of the population.

Ability to read and write Chinese had already become, as it was to remain, the distinguishing mark of educated Japanese. (There is a striking analogy in the European retention of Latin as the language of religion and state bureaucracy and the basis of upper-class education; nor is this the only similarity between the attitudes of the Japanese to Chinese culture, and of Europeans to Greek

SOURCES AND DOCUMENTS

LADY MURASAKI ON CALLIGRAPHY

Murasaki Shikibu (c. 980–c. 1030), the great Japanese novelist, belonged to the powerful Fujiwara family who ruled Japan in the name of successive emperors throughout most of the Heian period. She lived in Kyoto, married and had a daughter, and after her husband died became a lady at the court of the empress Akiko at which most, if not all, of her outstanding novel *The Tale of Genji* was written. Her account of calligraphy and Japanese appreciation of it is among the most vivid to survive. In the passage that follows Genji is preparing his daughter's library which contains many outstanding works by calligraphers of an earlier day – much finer, Genji thought, than anything by his contemporaries.

'We live in a degenerate age', said Genji. 'Almost nothing but the "ladies' hand" seems really good. In that we do excel. The old styles have a sameness about them. They seem to have followed the copybooks and allowed little room for original talent. We have been blessed in our own day with large numbers of fine calligraphers. Back when I was myself a student of the "ladies' hand" I put together a rather distinguished collection. The finest specimens in it, quite incomparable, I thought, were some informal jottings by the mother of the present empress. I thought that I had never seen anything so fine. I was so completely under their spell that I behaved in a manner which I fear did damage to her name. Though the last thing I wanted to do was hurt her, she became very angry with me. But she was a lady of great understanding, and I somehow feel that she is watching us from the grave and knows that I am trying to make amends by being of service to her daughter. As for the empress herself, she writes a subtle hand, but' – and he lowered his voice – 'it may sometimes seem a little weak and wanting in substance.

'Fujitsubo's was another remarkable hand, remarkable and yet perhaps just a little uncertain, and without the richest overtones. Oborozukiyo is too clever, one may think, and somewhat given to mannerism; but among the ladies still here to please us she has only two rivals, Princess Asagao and you yourself, my dear.'

'The thought of being admitted to such company overwhelms me', said Murasaki.

'You are too modest. Your writing manages to be gentle and intimate without ever losing its assurance. It is always a pleasant surprise when someone who writes well in the Chinese style moves over to the Japanese and writes that just as well.'

He himself had had a hand in designing the jackets and bindings for several booklets which still awaited calligraphers. Prince Hotaru must copy down something in one of them, he said, and another was for a certain guards commander, and he himself would see to putting something down in one or two others.

'They are justly proud of their skills, but I doubt that they will leave me any great distance behind.'

Selecting the finest inks and brushes, he sent out invitations to all his ladies to join in the endeavour. Some at first declined, thinking the challenge too much for them. Nor were the 'young men of taste', as he called them, to be left out. Yugiri, Murasaki's oldest brother, and Kashiwagi, among others, were supplied with fine Korean papers of the most delicate hues.

'Do whatever you feel like doing, reed work [a highly mannered style in which the calligraphic strokes merge into a landscape painting] or illustrations for poems or whatever.'

The competition was intense. Genji secluded himself as before in the main hall. The cherry blossoms had fallen and the skies were soft. Letting his mind run quietly through the anthologies, he tried several styles with fine results, formal and cursive Chinese and the more radically cursive Japanese 'ladies' hand'. He had with him only two or three women whom he could count on for interesting comments. They ground ink for him and selected poems from the more admired anthologies. Having raised the blinds to let the breezes pass, he sat out near the veranda with a booklet spread before him, and as he took a brush meditatively between his teeth the women thought that they could gaze at him for ages on end and not tire. His brush poised over papers of clear, plain reds and whites, he would collect himself for the effort of writing, and no one of reasonable sensitivity could have failed to admire the picture of serene concentration which he presented.

(Murasaki Shikibu, *The Tale of Genji*, tr. E. G. Seidensticker, London 1976; Harmondsworth 1981)

and Roman antiquity.) The Japanese had, however, been faced with a major difficulty in transcribing their own polysyllabic and agglutinative language, with many suffixes for verbs and adjectives, in characters that had been evolved for monosyllabic and non-inflected Chinese. In the ninth century they adapted simplified Chinese characters for the sound values of syllables, using a somewhat angular script for official writings and a cursive form, much better adapted to Japanese, called *hiragana*, for personal communications and for stories and poetry. As women were generally excluded from education in Chinese, they wrote in Japanese using *hiragana* which came to be called *onnade* or 'ladies' hand' though it was no less extensively used by men. This script was perfected in the Fujiwara period, and nothing more clearly differentiates Japanese from Chinese culture. Chinese calligraphy remained boxed-in, almost regimented, conditioned by their obsessive regard for masters of the past despite subtle variations in the way each element of a character might be brushed; its merits are strength, clarity and balance (12,62; 63). *Hiragana* flows over the page with apparent freedom and spontaneity, with an apparently effortless natural grace like that of a ballet dancer,

achieved only after gruelling practice. Colored papers, sometimes with decorative motifs in gold or silver, were carefully selected so that the ground is combined with the calligraphy and the meaning of the words to create a unique work of art which appeals as much to the eye as to the mind. An album leaf inscribed in the early twelfth century with two poems by Ki no Tsurayuki (872–c. 946) is a notable example (**6,125**). The three columns on the right read in translation: 'One whom I met / Until yesterday / Is gone today / Swept away / Like mountain clouds.' This is a type of poem composed of 31 syllables, permitting a range of expressive possibilities within formal limits that might seem loose and unconstraining – like the *hiragana* calligraphy itself.

The aesthetic ideas developed in the rarefied atmosphere of aristocratic court life at Kyoto survived the civil wars at the close of the Fujiwara period when many works of art and architecture were destroyed. After the transfer of the administrative centre of government from Kyoto to Kamakura, the rule of a few immensely rich, highly cultivated and pleasure-loving families gave way to a more broadly based feudal regime of Daimyo or barons among whom vigorous, virile simplicity was the

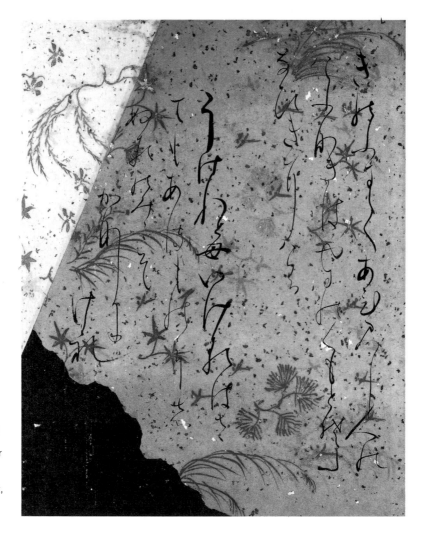

6,125 Calligraphy attributed to Fujiwara no Sadanobu, early 12th century. Ink, silver and gold on assembled dyed paper, 8 × 6⁵/₁₆ins (20.3 × 16.1cm). Freer Gallery of Art, Smithsonian Institution, Washington DC.

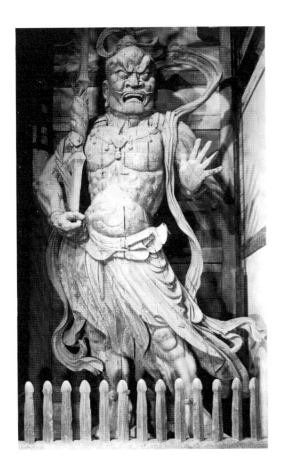

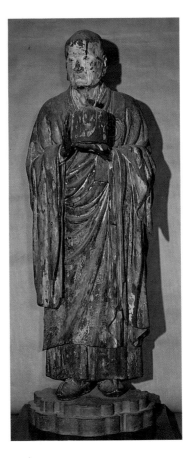

6,126 *Far left* Unkei, *Nio*,
1203. Wood, 26ft 6ins
(8m) high. Todaiji, Nara.

6,127 *Left* Unkei, *Mujaku*,
1208. Wood, 6ft 3½ins
(1.92m) high. Kofukuji, Nara.

order of the day. No artist expressed this more forcibly than the leading sculptor Unkei (d. 1223) whose most famous work is the pair of colossal wooden statues of Buddhist guardian figures in the gateway to the Todaiji at Nara, built in 1199 as part of the reconstruction of the monastery after the civil war and following the revival of Buddhism at Nara promoted by the Shogun (**6,126**). With fiercely glowering eyes, tensed muscles and swirling draperies, these guardians are gigantically demonic to the tips of their extended fingers. Despite their huge scale – and also the number of different sculptors or carvers who worked on them under Unkei's direction – they have an almost unique intensity of vigour, as of some explosive volcanic force.

Unkei's genius was not confined to images of violence, however. He was one of the most deeply human of all artists and his most tender and penetrating insights were conveyed in portraits or imaginary portraits. That of Mujaku, one of the ancient *Mahayana* Buddhist teachers, called Assanga in India, is a profound work of religious sculpture – the figure of a man of unexceptional physical appearance, set apart from others by no esoteric symbolism, and yet endowed with extraordinary spirituality. Holiness is made visible in his serene countenance (**6,127**). This image of a great religious teacher is rendered with far greater naturalism than was the earlier dry lacquer statue of Furuna (6,121) – one foot slightly advanced, as if moving towards the spectator, the head turned a little to the right and a suggestion of the weight and preciousness of the vessel carried in the left hand. It is indeed a declaration of faith in the belief that every human being has the power of soul to transcend the human condition, the doctrine that was first enunciated by the Buddha and transformed every aspect of life throughout Asia. But Unkei's are perhaps the last great works of Japanese religious art. For although Buddhism has never ceased to be a living force in Japan, its power to inspire artists declined after the thirteenth century – with the notable exception of the Zen sect which dispensed with conventional religious imagery (see pp. 565–9). The subsequent history of art in Japan was to be predominantly secular.

CHAPTER SEVEN

EARLY CHRISTIAN AND BYZANTINE ART

In the opening years of the second century AD, the great Roman historian Tacitus referred to:

A class of persons hated for their vices, whom the crowd called Christians. Christus, after whom they were named, had undergone the death penalty in the reign of Tiberius, by sentence of the procurator Pontius Pilate, and the pernicious superstition was checked for a moment only to break out once more, not only in Judea, the home of the disease, but in the capital itself, where everything horrible or shameful in the world gathers and becomes fashionable.

(*Annales*, xv, 44)

Such was the view of a prominent senator, consul and colonial governor. At this date Christianity was as yet no more than a fairly small and scattered sect composed mainly of the underprivileged, so far as we can tell – small shopkeepers, artisans and so on. To an outsider it might well have seemed to differ little from other Oriental mystery cults, which held out hopes and promises of a life beyond the grave. But there were features that sharply differentiated Christianity from all other religious beliefs then current and made it potentially dangerous to the Roman moral order – that complex structure of ancient pieties, traditional customs and social hierarchies.

Christianity emerged out of Judaism (as had Buddhism out of the religion of the Brahmins), with worship of the same creator-God, acceptance of the same scriptures and observance of the same ten commandments, but broke away so decisively that Christians were persecuted in the Roman empire while Jews were tolerated, despite their periodical revolts in Palestine. The break with Judaism was brought about by the Christian belief that Jesus Christ was the Son of the (Jewish) creator-God, had been born of a virgin, performed miracles, suffered death on the cross as atonement for the sins of all humankind, rose from the dead and ascended into heaven. His teaching had much in common with Jewish thought and, especially as expounded in the Epistles of St Paul, with Greek philosophical ethics. But it also introduced ideas that were startlingly new – that thought could be as sinful as deed ('whoever looketh on a woman to lust after her hath committed adultery with her already in his heart') or the injunction to 'love your enemies'. Humility, regarded by the Romans as weakness of character, was extolled as a virtue, with the incarnation and suffering of Christ as the supreme example. His life was the model for Christian behaviour. And whereas Romans generally separated ethics from religion (though most philosophers encouraged traditional pieties), and conduct from the performance of cults, Christians made no distinctions whatsoever: their religion encompassed all aspects of being, thinking and believing. Supernatural beliefs of the Christians were based on faith, ranked by Greek and Roman philosophers as the lowest cognitive faculty. But they were unlike those of the mystery cults which derived mainly from oral traditions harking back to an immeasurably distant past. For the life of Jesus Christ from which they were inseparable was a historical event, and a recent one precisely dated by reference to the emperors Augustus and Tiberius in the Gospel according to St Luke and to Pontius Pilate in the Apostles' Creed.

By the second century, however, numerous written accounts of the life and teaching of Christ were in circulation, arousing controversy as to which was authentic. Those that were to be included in the New Testament were accepted by the group of Christians who began to exert a dominating influence and established what they declared to be the only true faith summarized in a creed, dismissing all who disagreed as heretics (from the Greek word *hairesis* which originally signified no more than a school of thought). Pagans, as Christians came to call them, had never been troubled by such matters. Nor did they believe – any more than did the devotees of different Hindu deities – that one cult was superior to or inconsistent with another. Roman religion in fact embraced numerous diverse local cults and could and would have accommodated Christianity among them quite comfortably. But the main body of Christians soon began to constitute a unified community held together physically by letters and other writings that passed from one end of the empire to the other, and spiritually by the idea of the Church as the assembly of the people of God throughout the world and in heaven – a great source of strength to themselves and a prime cause of the anxiety felt by their fellow Roman citizens.

Christianity spread during the stable eras of the *Pax Romana* and the age of the Antonine emperors (see p. 186), while pagan cults remained strong, as the imposing ruins of their temples demonstrate. Though widely dispersed it was still numerically a very small sect which seems to have aroused no more than local hostility where such disasters as fires, plagues, droughts, and famines were ascribed to its followers' refusal to honour and appease the old gods. By the early third century, however, the frontiers of the empire were being eroded, its social structure was changing as barbarians in the army gained control, its administration was faltering and its economy was in steep decline. In December AD 249 a new emperor, Decius, bent on restoring the old order, issued an edict requiring every citizen to sacrifice to the gods. Only

the Jews were exempted by Roman respect for ancient traditions. The aim of the edict was quite simply to reinforce religious practices on which the political well-being of the empire was believed to rest. Its effect was to launch the first official and widespread persecution of Christians. For they refused to comply, even by sacrificing to the cult of the living emperor, and refusal to make obeisance to imperial images was tantamount to treason. They preferred martyrdom (another new concept) with its promise of eternal life.

Christianity, by being based on historical fact – or recorded events – held out the prospect of theological certainties which were conspicuously lacking in current philosophical systems and religious cults. And so, despite intermittent persecution, the faith spread not only across the empire but up its hierarchy. The discovery that the army had been infiltrated prompted the last and cruellest persecution under another reforming emperor, Diocletian (see p. 218), who decreed in 303 that Christians were to lose all the privileges of citizens, their churches were to be destroyed and scriptures burned. But this was no more than a decade before Christianity was legalized by Constantine's Edict of Milan (313) and began to attract a steadily increasing number of converts of all social classes.

THE BEGINNINGS OF CHRISTIAN ART

Ironically, a caricature roughly scratched on a wall of the house of the imperial pages in Rome in the second century may be the earliest surviving visual image of Christ's death on the cross. It shows a man gazing at a crucified figure with an ass's head and is inscribed in Greek: 'Alessameno worships god'. Christians themselves adopted the sign of the cross, but for long avoided explicit representations of the Crucifixion – the humiliating punishment meted out to common criminals. They also hesitated to depict Christ directly until the late third or early fourth century (though there were exceptions). The central doctrine of the Incarnation, that God became Christ, raised the problem of the desirability, and even the

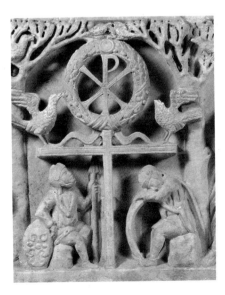

7,1 *Chi-Rho* monogram, detail of a sarcophagus, c. AD 340. Museo Pio Cristiano, Vatican.

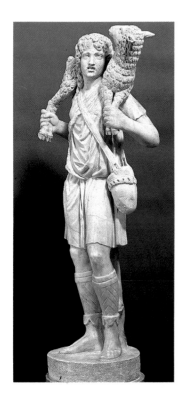

7,2 *Left The Good Shepherd*,
c. AD 300. Marble, 36ins (92cm) high.
Vatican Museums, Rome.
(The legs are restored.)

7,3 *Right* The Throne of God as a
Trinitarian image, probably
Constantinopolitan c. AD 400.
Marble, 65⅔ × 33ins (167 × 84cm).
Stiftung Preussisches Kulturbesitz,
Berlin-Dahlem.

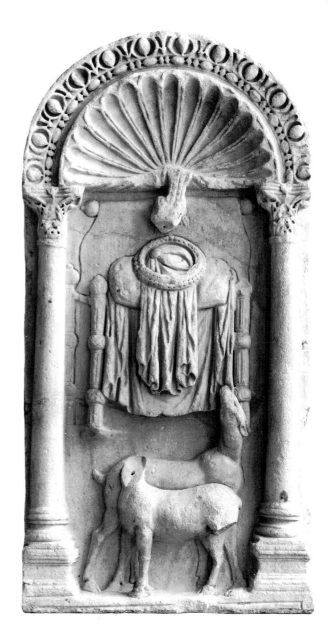

possibility, of his portrayal, which was argued with mounting vehemence during the next 500 years.

Initially, the natural prudence of a persecuted sect may also have encouraged the creation of an arcane imagery intelligible only to the initiated. The first symbols invented by the early Christians were semantic rather than representational and some were purely verbal – for the word outlives the flesh and thus pertains to eternity. The *Chi-Rho* monogram, for example, was simply a combination of the first two letters of *Christos* – XP – in Greek, the language of early Christianity (**7,1**). A fish was adopted as a rebus for Christ's name because the word fish in Greek provided the initials for the formula: 'Jesus Christ Son of God Saviour'. Other symbols were based on literary metaphors; the lamb, for instance, on St John the Baptist's description of Christ as 'the Lamb of God, which taketh away the sins of the world'. Christ's own words, 'I am the shepherd: the good shepherd giveth his life for the sheep', lent particular significance to a figure that had been used to symbolize benevolence or philanthropy in pagan Classical art (**7,2**). Such figures acquired new meaning only from their context (Christian tombs). They were not supposed to represent Christ. As we have seen (p. 232), the development of Buddhist imagery had run a similar course, early Buddhist images being no less arcanely symbolic than early Christian ones and representations of the Buddha in human form being evolved several centuries later, as were those of Christ. Indeed, there are some striking parallels between early Buddhist and early Christian symbols, e.g. the empty throne (6,14 and **7,3**), which in early Christian art often stood for God the Father in Trinitarian images, as in the example illustrated here, which is among the earliest known representations

of the Trinity. The Son is indicated by the diadem and *chlamys* (cloak) and the Spirit by the dove. The deer stands for the faithful (i.e. the Church).

The earliest Christian symbols appear among the paintings in Roman catacombs. These underground cemeteries, running up to five galleries deep beneath the cheap land outside the city, were adopted possibly as early as the second century by Christians (also by Jews and others), who shunned burial places dedicated to pagan deities. Because of their belief in the resurrection of the body, the early Christians insisted on burial and objected to cremation, the norm for the lower classes in Rome. Their symbolism referred primarily to salvation from death – crosses, *Chi-Rho* monograms, fish, anchors of hope and figures of the Good Shepherd – all painted on the low ceilings and the very limited wall spaces between recesses for coffins in these subterranean corridors and chambers.

Some of these paintings seem to have been deliberately left open to more than one interpretation, so that they have multiple layers of meaning. That of men and women at table with bread and wine might be understood simply as an *agape* or early Christian 'love-feast' (**7,4**). On

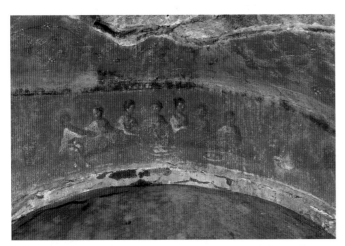

7,4 *The Breaking of Bread*, late 2nd century AD. Wall-painting in the catacomb of Priscilla, Rome.

Noah, Abraham sacrificing Isaac, Jonah and the whale, the three Hebrew children in the fiery furnace and Daniel in the lions' den. To the initiated they were a reminder of how the New Testament fulfilled the Old. Greek and Roman mythology also provided subjects if they could be given a Christian interpretation – Cupid and Psyche as an allegory of body and soul, for instance. The best of these paintings were clearly by professional artists, not necessarily Christian, who were otherwise engaged in enlivening the walls of private houses with briskly sketched figures of gods, fauns and nymphs of the kind seen at Pompeii. Catacomb paintings were rarely as vivid and they mark no new stylistic departure. In Rome Christians took over the artistic, as well as the literary, language of pagans, changing only the meanings with which they invested its images.

Christian paintings, in a different style and on a larger scale than was possible in the cramped conditions of the catacombs, have been found in Syria at Dura Europos, a trading station and frontier town garrisoned by the Romans from 165 to 256, when it was abandoned. The Good Shepherd, Adam and Eve in the Garden of Eden, David slaying Goliath and two of Christ's miracles (walking on the water and healing the paralytic man) were depicted. They are too badly damaged to be legible in reproduction but are similar stylistically to the better preserved wall-paintings in the nearby and much larger synagogue of the Jewish community (**7,5**).

the other hand, it could refer to two of Christ's miracles, the transformation of water into wine at the wedding feast at Cana and the feeding of the 5,000 with five loaves and two fishes, with, in addition, an allusion to the Last Supper and its commemoration in the simplest form of the sacrament of the Eucharist and perhaps also to the reunion or banquet of the faithful in heaven. Incidents from the Gospels are, however, greatly outnumbered by Old Testament subjects prefiguring Christian salvation:

7,5 Synagogue from Dura Europos, Syria, view of north-west corner, c. AD 250. National Museum, Damascus.

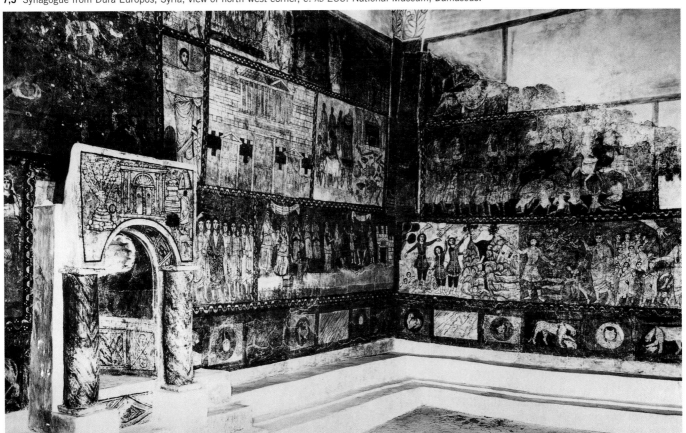

The Catacombs

EARLY CHRISTIAN ART

Ancient Roman funeral customs did not suit the early Christians for several reasons, cremation especially being abhorrent to them. Their belief in the resurrection of the body made burial essential. So from at least as early as AD 200 they avoided Roman cemeteries or *columbaria* (dovecotes), as they were called, with urns for ashes stacked in niches or shelves on every wall, although they were open to all regardless of religious belief. Instead, the Christians sought burial places for their own exclusive use, uncontaminated with paganism. The solution was found in underground cemeteries or catacombs just outside Rome where excavation was easy in the soft, porous *tufa* rock underneath the open country surrounding the city. Similar conditions led to the excavation of catacombs near Naples and elsewhere. Begun in the late second or early third century and constantly enlarged, they date mainly from the time of the great Christian persecutions, notably those of AD 250 and 257–60. The catacombs were not, however, used as a refuge during the persecutions. They were used only for burial, including memorial services or love-feasts such as may have been depicted in the catacomb of Priscilla (7,4).

Starting sometimes from a disused quarry or an abandoned pagan tomb chamber, the Roman catacombs ramify some 24 to 26 feet (7–8m) underground into a dark and unsavoury maze of narrow tunnels or corridors (no more than 36 inches – 91cm – wide and 8 feet – 2.4m – high) hacked out of the granular *tufa* rock on a gridiron plan which allowed endless extensions. As they grew they expanded both horizontally with intersecting corridors and also vertically downwards to two, three or four stories underground, connected by narrow ramps or stairs – not unlike present-day underground car-parks though of course very much less spacious. Eventually this subterranean network stretched for between 60 and 90 miles (96–145km) of tunnels or corridors in which as many as four million Christians may have been buried. The corridor walls are perforated with narrow slits or shelf-tombs called *loculi* into which the bodies were slid with a layer of lime between their winding sheets (7,6). These *loculi* were then sealed with marble slabs or tiles bearing the name of the deceased and a blessing. Sometimes a coin or medal or a glass medallion portrait might be embedded in the mortar for remembrance. Some of these glass medallions with engraved gold-leaf on the back are among the most vivid portraits to survive from early Christian times. They stare out at us still with an extraordinary stern and melancholy intensity (7,7).

Branching off at intervals from the corridors are square or polygonal chambers called *cubicula* made for affluent individuals or families; their walls and ceilings are decorated with fresco paintings. The earliest of these

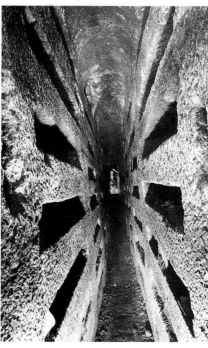
7,6 Corridor in catacomb of Pamphilus, Rome, 3rd to 4th century AD.

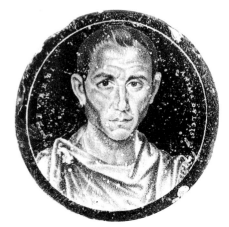
7,7 Portrait medallion, 3rd to 4th century AD. Gold on glass, 1½ins (3.8cm) diameter. Vatican Library, Rome.

are in the Callisto catacomb, named after one of the great organizers of the early church, St Callixtus (d. 222), who was deacon in charge until he became pope in 217. They are notable for being entirely without any Christian content. Instead they faithfully follow the current fashion in pagan Rome for architectural decorative schemes forming light and airy trellis-work patterns over walls and ceilings. In fact, there is no evidence for a specifically Christian art – that is, an art with Christian content – until the late second century. It seems likely that the cause was not, as has been thought, the Old Testament commandment against graven images (see p. 302) so much as a natural association in the early Christian mind of images and image-making with pagan religion and the whole pagan way of life. Already by the mid-third century, however, there is evidence in Christian literature of changing attitudes and by the next century religiously meaningful paintings began to occur in Christian contexts, thus making a clear break with what had until then been a taboo.

A fourth-century ceiling in the catacomb of Saints Peter and Marcellinus combines the linear architectural style of pagan Rome with

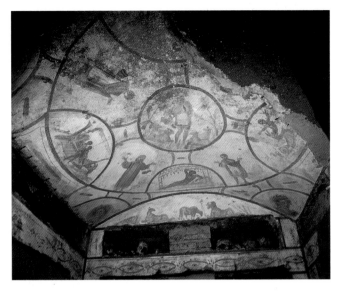

7,8 Ceiling in catacomb of Saints Peter and Marcellinus, Rome, c. AD 340.

Eve, Daniel in the lions' den, Noah and the ark. They are united only by their common message: the Messianic idea allied to the Christian hope of salvation. Of course the catacombs were so dark that it must have been difficult to see them. However, the extreme simplification of the images to create a language of signs is striking.

The New Testament is rarely drawn on except symbolically as, for example, the Good Shepherd who is not, however, intended to portray Jesus himself, as we have seen (p. 298). For this reason it is unlikely that the paintings of a mother and child that occasionally appear in the catacombs were intended to represent the Virgin and Child (7,9). Mary's importance in the doctrines of the Church did not come to the fore until the fourth century (p. 326). An Old Testament interpretation of such catacomb paintings is therefore much more probable, for example as illustrating the prophecy of Isaiah (7:14): 'Behold, a virgin shall conceive and bear a son and shall call his name Immanuel.'

Christian symbols rendered in the free, sketchy manner of Late Antique painting though drastically simplified (7,8). A low saucer dome, like that of the Pantheon, is inscribed with the cross which, as it were, embraces the Dome of Heaven such structures were thought to symbolize. The *oculus* or central opening to the sky here encloses the Good Shepherd flanked by resting sheep while the four arms of the cross end in semicircles or lunettes, one of which is lost. They all tell in simple imagery the story of Jonah, tossed from his ship on the left, being swallowed by the whale on the right and reclining below the gourd vine in the middle – his apparent death and miraculous deliverance prefiguring the crucifixion and resurrection of Christ. Between the arms of the cross are figures making the open-armed *orant* gesture of prayer inherited from the pagan world and still used today by the celebrant in the Mass. At the four corners were Classical heads symbolizing the four seasons of the year. The whole scheme is typical of catacomb painting and the beginnings of Christian art, not so much in its combination of the pagan and the Christian as in the way the images were intended to function.

Simplified, indeed almost schematic, they point beyond themselves to an unusual degree, indicating only the minimum necessary to call to the viewer's mind the Biblical themes illustrated. Often they are no more than ciphers or pictographs. And the

Biblical texts also were abridged so that only essentials had to be represented. No narrative or other thread links them, whether they be pagan motifs such as Orpheus or the luxuriant vine of Dionysus which could be given Christian interpretations, or whether they be Christian such as the Old Testament stories of Adam and

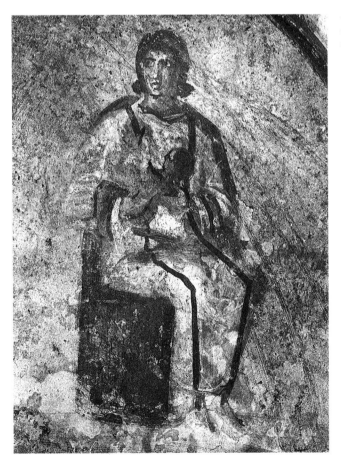

7,9 *Mother and Child*, wall-painting in catacomb of Priscilla, Rome, mid-3rd century AD.

At this time the Mosaic prohibition of 'any likeness of any thing that is in the heavens above, or that is in the earth beneath' was freely interpreted (only the image of God being totally banned) and the scriptures were illustrated also in Hebrew manuscripts, which Christian artists were soon to use as models.

The painters of the Dura Europos synagogue disregarded all the naturalistic techniques developed by Hellenistic and Roman artists. No attempt was made to break the surface of the wall or to create an artificial space. Scenes are arranged without any visual relationship to one another or to the design of the room as a whole. Figures are flatly painted without modelling or shadows, frontally posed and placed motionlessly side by side. They have no reality, only significance. Wall-paintings in other buildings at Dura Europos are similarly schematic – the temples of Zeus, the Persian god Mithras (whose cult was widespread in the Roman army) and the Mesopotamian god Bel (worshipped since Sumerian times). It is impossible to know whether painters in this provincial outpost of the empire ignored illusionism because of their non-materialistic, religious ideals or simply because they had been trained in a schematic tradition more closely allied to Persia or even further east than to Rome and the West. In this small town there were no fewer than 16 different cult buildings, erected mainly for Roman troops – vivid testimony to the spiritual turmoil of the late second and third centuries.

From *Domus Ecclesiae* to the Christian Basilica

The Christians' place of worship at Dura Europos – the earliest to survive anywhere – was not built as such. It was an ordinary private house in a poor district. A central courtyard was surrounded by rooms, two of which had been united to make an assembly hall for some 50 people, and another – with mural paintings – was provided with a large basin or font, surmounted by a canopy, for the all-important initiatory rite of baptism. There may have been a room for the celebration of the Eucharist on the upper floor. During the centuries of persecution Christians normally congregated in such a building. It was called a *domus ecclesiae* from the Latin word for a private house and the Greek for an assembly. Churches built after the

legalization of Christianity in 313 kept the external plainness of their predecessors (the only architectural feature to be retained being the atrium [see p. 194] enlarged to serve as a forecourt), but for the increasingly large congregations spacious interiors were needed. The traditional Roman temple rarely allowed much space for communal worship in its cella, which was reserved for cult statues, and for this reason, and to mark a decisive break with paganism, its form was not taken over by Christians. Prototypes for the first great churches built under the patronage of Constantine were found in public secular architecture (i.e. basilicas) mainly, no doubt, for practical reasons, but also in order to symbolize the alliance he had forged between Christianity and the empire.

The promotion of Christianity by Constantine (c. 274–337) invites comparison with that of Buddhism by Asoka in India more than five centuries earlier (see p. 224). Irrespective of their personal convictions, both found religion to be a most effective aid to political unification. This was the main aim of Constantine's career. He succeeded his father as ruler of the north-western provinces in 306, obtained control of Italy in 312 and in 324 subdued the rich eastern provinces, where he founded his new capital Constantinople. Long before he came to power the ideological base of the empire had begun to disintegrate. The old Roman religion, of which the emperor was high priest, had lost its appeal to a variety of 'foreign' cults including Christianity, and during the political upheavals of the second century the idea of the 'god-emperor' had become irretrievably tarnished. Christians refused to pay it so much as lip-service. But their objections were removed at a stroke by Constantine, when he placed himself at the head of their Church as the vice-regent of Christ, whose *Chi-Rho* monogram was inscribed on his standards. Although he was not baptized until shortly before his death, he felt himself to be the 'servant of God' in a special sense and strove throughout the Arian controversy for unity, presiding at Church councils, including that which promulgated the Nicene Creed – still the basic declaration of faith of most Christians today. (A united empire needed a united Church to support it.) The position he had assumed and passed on to his successors was neatly summarized in a fourth-century military manual, written after Christianity had become the one official religion of the empire: 'When the emperor has received the name Augustus, loyalty and obedience are due to him as to a present and incarnate deity. For in peace and in war it is a service to God to adhere loyally to him who rules at God's ordinance.' By a complementary process, the simple rites of the early Church were elaborated into ceremonies resembling those of the imperial court – with momentous consequences for Christian art.

In 313 Constantine gave the Christian community in Rome an imperial palace for its bishop and a piece of land on which to erect a church. Foundations of the latter, beneath S Giovanni in Laterano, which is still the cathedral of Rome (i.e. the church containing the bishop's throne or *cathedra*), reveal that it was a type of building called in Latin a *basilica* (p. 194) (**7,10**). The Roman

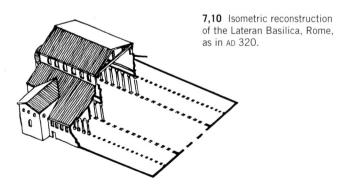

7,10 Isometric reconstruction of the Lateran Basilica, Rome, as in AD 320.

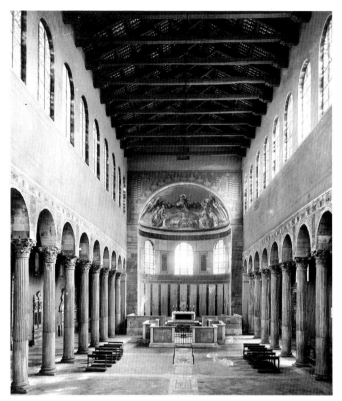

7,11 S Sabina, Rome, AD 423–32.

basilica varied quite considerably both in function and form. It might be an imperial throne-room, a court of justice or simply a covered market, money-exchange or drill-hall. Usually it took the form of a large hall with aisles, and sometimes galleries above them, flanking a central space, covered with concrete vaults or timber roofs. One wall was generally broken by a semicircular or rectangular apse. Its public character was indicated by a statue or bust of the emperor, before which oaths were taken. From this variety of building types the architect of the church at the Lateran selected the elements that were to make up the Christian basilica: an oblong timber-roofed hall divided by columns into a nave, well lit from large clerestory (see Glossary) windows, and flanking aisles giving a strong longitudinal axis from the entrance door to the apse. In a Roman throne-room or law-court the apse contained the emperor's or magistrate's throne flanked by seats for courtiers or assessors, and this

7,12 Plan of Old St Peter's, Rome.

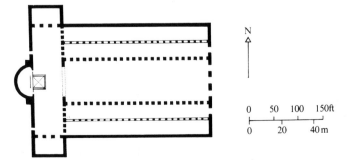

became the apse with bishop's throne and benches for celebrating clergy (the *synthronon*), as in S Sabina in Rome, one of the best-preserved early examples of a Christian basilica (**7,11**). (The columns and capitals are Roman, probably from a pagan temple.)

A variation of the basilican plan was adopted for the much larger church dedicated to St Peter, which was built on the Vatican hill in Rome in the 320s with funds supplied by Constantine (**7,12**). Excavations under present-day St Peter's have revealed that the rear wall of the basilican hall, with its central apse, had been moved back to create a transverse space or transept (see Glossary) to accommodate large congregations of pilgrims. The interior was, in fact, divided into two parts marked off at the end of the nave by a huge arch. On this there was a mosaic of Constantine accompanied by St Peter presenting a model of the church to Christ with the inscription: 'Because under Thy leadership the world rose up triumphant to the skies, Constantine, himself victorious, has founded this hall in Thy honour.' The division indicated this church's special and dual purpose of *martyrium* and burial-place. St Peter's was primarily a *martyrium* (i.e. a church built on a site bearing witness to the Christian faith, in this instance the shrine which had long been venerated as the tomb of St Peter). It was also a covered cemetery, where Christians could be buried near the shrine, with the customary rituals of the period including funerary feasts. The transept was reserved for the shrine; nave and aisles provided a burial-place.

The shrine was the focal point of St Peter's, backed by the apse and, when seen from the entrance, framed by the arch – a very ancient architectural symbol of heaven and perhaps also recalling the triumphal arches of imperial Rome. A *ciborium* or canopy, similar to those held over imperial thrones, was placed above it, supported on spiralling 'barley-sugar' columns sent from Greece by Constantine, but later believed to have come from Solomon's temple. It was to St Peter that Christ had said: 'Thou art Peter, and upon this rock I will build my church.' He was the founder of the Christian community in Rome and its first bishop, from whom all subsequent bishops of Rome derived their authority – as popes – over not only the city but all Christendom. The plan of the church that Constantine had built in his honour therefore acquired symbolic significance.

Constantine also founded churches in his new capital at Constantinople and in the Holy Land. Very little survives of them, but it is known that the Holy Sepulchre outside Jerusalem, where Christ's body was believed to have been placed after the Crucifixion, was enshrined in a circular building with a dome supported on 12 pairs of columns (corresponding to the number of the apostles). The circle was a religious symbol of immemorial antiquity in many cultures. As we have seen, the hemispherical Buddhist stupa symbolized the cosmos (see p. 227); Greeks and Romans also built round temples for their gods and a centralized (often circular) plan had been usual for tombs and shrines of deified or semideified heroes (mortals who had become immortal by their deeds). The form now

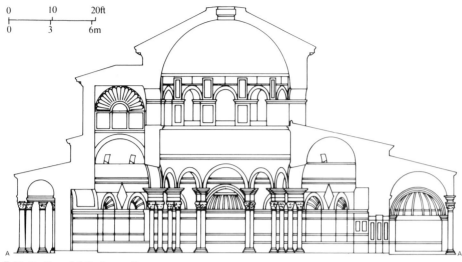

7,13 Section of S Costanza, Rome.

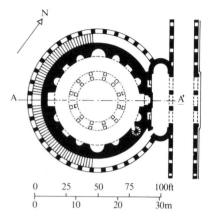

7,15 Plan of S Costanza.

7,14 S Costanza, c. AD 350.

7,16 S Costanza, exterior.

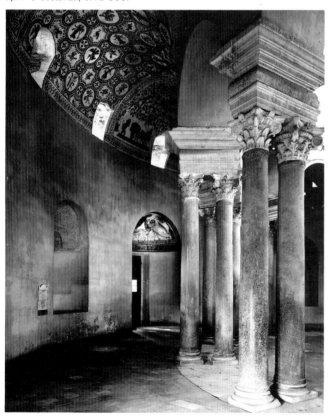

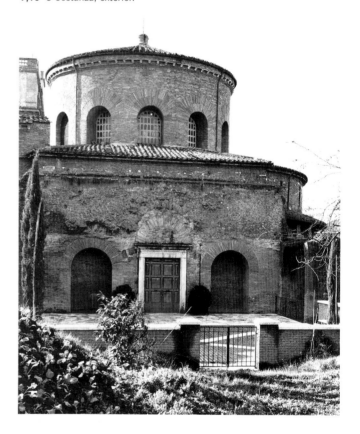

entered Christian architecture as a *martyrium*, the building on a site that was either hallowed by an event in Christ's life or the tomb of a Christian who had borne witness to the faith (the meaning of the word 'martyr'). It was used for the Holy Sepulchre in Jerusalem, for the tomb of Constantine's daughter Constantia in Rome, now the church of S Costanza (**7,13; 14; 15; 16**), and, later, for St Simeon the Stylite at Qal'at Si'man in Syria (7,37).

The terms 'Late Antique' and 'Early Christian', as applied to the art of the fourth and fifth centuries, are both equally appropriate for the church of S Costanza, which beautifully illustrates how pagan form coalesced with Christian meaning. Its dome rises from 12 pairs of granite columns with crisp composite capitals (see Glossary), almost certainly removed from some earlier pagan building. On the vault of the ambulatory surrounding the central space there are mosaics which might also seem to have come from some ancient Roman palace or temple – geometrical designs above the entrance and then, on either side, panels of rambling vines with children joyfully engaged in the vintage. They may derive from earlier mosaics, but have Christian significance as a metaphorical symbol of Christ's saying: 'I am the true vine and my Father is the husbandman.'

In the bay opposite the door, above the niche in which stood Constantia's richly carved imperial porphyry sarcophagus (now in the Vatican Museum), there was originally a mosaic of paradise with the apostles symbolized as lambs, and in the dome Old Testament scenes separated from one another by gilded caryatids with panthers at their feet. All this has now vanished. The effect must have been one of bejewelled opulence in sharp contrast with the roughly painted tomb chambers in the catacombs only half a century or so earlier.

THE IMAGE OF CHRIST

When Christianity ceased to be an underground religion the need arose not only for a new architecture with a richness of decoration to reflect its imperially sponsored status, but also for a new visual language – a language less cryptic and allusive than that of the catacombs. Large Biblical scenes painted on the walls of the church at the Lateran and in St Peter's were probably the first attempts to answer this need. Unfortunately, little is known of their appearance and it would be hazardous to suppose there were any parallels between them and the paintings in the church and synagogue at Dura Europos (7,5). Relief carvings on sarcophagi provide the best surviving evidence of the first steps in the creation of a specifically Christian art. The earliest are so similar to the friezes on

the Arch of Constantine that they might seem to have been products of the same workshops. Soon afterwards there was a reversion to older and more Classical types of sarcophagus – to those that had, in fact, assisted the sculptors of Gandhara in their quest for a visual language of Buddhism some 200 years before (see p. 233). Several figures on the Early Christian sarcophagus of the 'Two Brothers', for instance, were directly copied from Classical prototypes of this kind, most obviously an athletic male nude (7,17). But they are huddled together on two registers to illustrate a number of incidents, juxtaposed without divisions in no narrative sequence, unlike the traditional sarcophagus with one frieze devoted to a single scene. In the upper register, for instance, Christ raises Lazarus from the dead and prophesies that St Peter will deny him, Abraham prepares to sacrifice Isaac, and Pontius Pilate washes his hands. Below, St Peter is apprehended by Roman soldiers, who stand next to Daniel in the lions' den.

The sarcophagus of Junius Bassus, a prefect of the city of Rome who died in 359, is a more elaborate and accomplished work with figures well proportioned and delicately carved in the Classical spirit (7,18). But the same need to say as much as possible in a limited space is evident. Even the spandrels of the lower arcade are filled with lambs enacting such scenes as the Hebrew children in the fiery furnace, the baptism of Christ and the raising of Lazarus. Here again the scenes follow no narrative sequence but are set on separate stages, flanked by colonnettes so that attention can be focused on each in turn, and arranged in thematic relationship to one another. At

7,17 Sarcophagus of the 'Two Brothers', c. AD 330–50. Museo Pio Cristiano, Vatican.

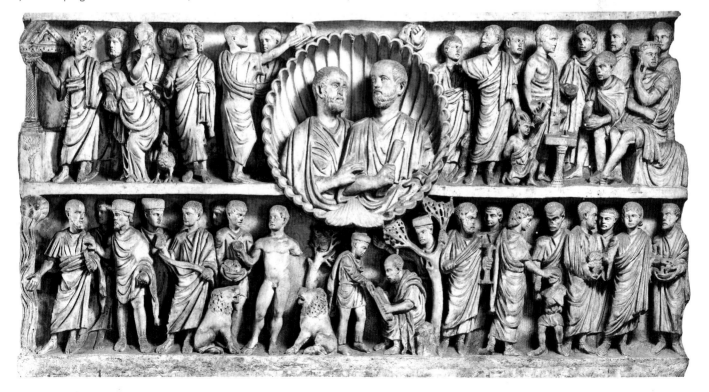

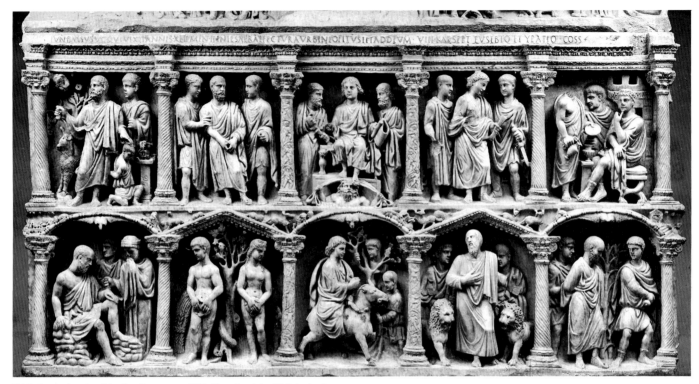

7,18 Sarcophagus of Junius Bassus, AD 359. New Sacristy, St Peter's, Rome.

7,19 *The Miracle of the Loaves and Fishes*, c. AD 504. Mosaic in S Apollinare Nuovo, Ravenna.

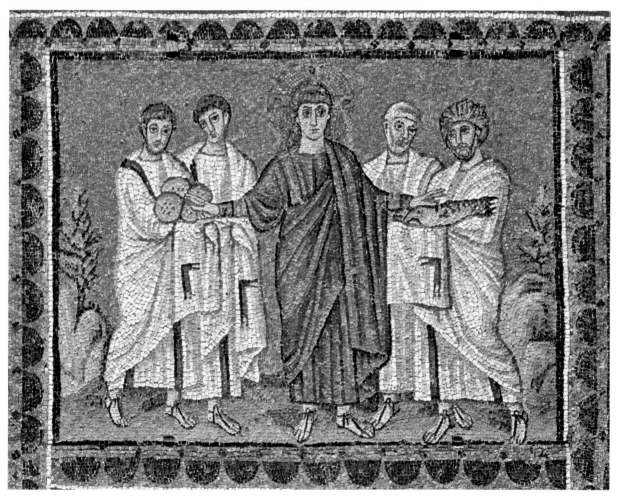

either end of the lower register, for instance, the afflicted Job and St Paul led off to martyrdom are parallel instances of redemption through suffering, which also allude to Christ's humiliating flagellation and Crucifixion – neither of which was directly represented at this time. Christ is, moreover, no longer a figure barely distinguishable from the others (as on the sarcophagus of the 'Two Brothers'), but is given the central place in the composition as in the doctrine of redemption, which it illustrates. He is shown in the middle of the lower register riding into Jerusalem on Palm Sunday – his moment of triumph on earth – and, immediately above, enthroned between St Peter and St Paul. The seated figure flanked by two standing attendants is an image of authority, which was taken over from imperial Roman art and also occurs in Buddhist art (the Buddha between Bodhisattvas). Christ's feet rest on a canopy supported by the Roman sky god Coelus to indicate that he is enthroned above the firmament, 'ascended into the heavens'.

On the sarcophagus of Junius Bassus, Christ is dressed not in a Roman toga but the Greek pallium, which in Italy had come to be associated with philosophers and teachers. He is not, however, bearded like a philosopher but has a fresh adolescent face. The sculptor seems to have taken a youthful Apollo as his model. This image of eternal youth recurs in Early Christian art, but gradually takes on a more ritualistic cast. In a mosaic at Ravenna the beardless Christ, wearing a pallium of imperial purple cloth, stands with arms outstretched to bless the loaves and fishes, carried by symbolically shorter disciples, whose hands are covered, as was usual at this time for subjects bringing tribute to their ruler (**7,19**). (A priest celebrating a Catholic mass still makes the gesture of Christ as in this mosaic and, until very recently, the deacon carried the paten for the consecrated bread in veiled hands.) This youthful Emmanuel ('God with us') figure continued to be used for Christ until well into the Middle Ages.

An entirely different image of Christ, lean-faced, long-haired and bearded, first appears in a fourth-century catacomb painting. He is shown in this way (**7,20**) on a sarcophagus probably carved about 390 in Milan, then an important centre of Christianity and the western capital of the Roman empire. Here Christ stands with the apostles (also symbolized by sheep below) before the entrance to the heavenly Jerusalem, confiding the New Law to St Peter, as God had handed down the tablets of the ten commandments to Moses. Clearly, a more mature appearance than that of a beardless youth had been thought appropriate for Christ the law-giver, one that associated him with God the Father. The artist had, therefore, looked to the father of the pagan gods, Zeus or Jupiter, for inspiration. A still more authoritative, awe-inspiring image was evolved and given canonic form in such mosaics as that in S Pudenziana (**7,21**) or that of the early sixth century in SS Cosma e Damiano in Rome. The bearded image was, of course, the one destined to become familiar throughout Christendom, although several centuries were to pass before it was invested with the pathos of the Man of Sorrows. At this early date Christ was represented almost exclusively as either the miracle-working healer, or the great teacher, or the law-giver. Scenes of his Passion always stopped short of depicting his humiliation and the Crucifixion was generally avoided, as in the earliest surviving cycle of Gospel subjects of c. 490 in S Apollinare Nuovo, Ravenna. The cross was rendered as a symbol not of suffering and death but of triumph and resurrection, sometimes fashioned in gold and studded with precious stones.

7,20 Sarcophagus, detail, c. AD 390. S Ambrogio, Milan.

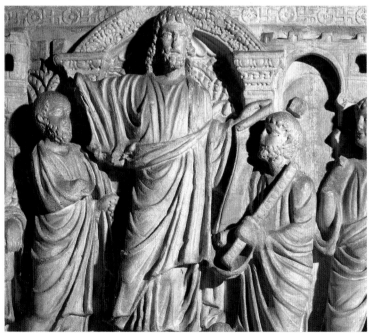

7,21 Apse mosaic, detail, AD 402–17. S Pudenziana, Rome.

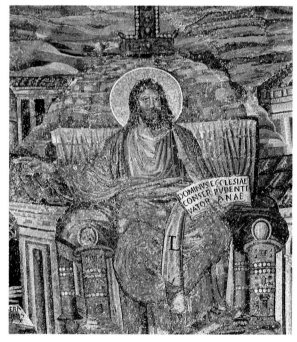

SOURCES AND DOCUMENTS

AGNELLUS ON S APOLLINARE NUOVO

Agnellus or Andrea Agnello (late 8th century to after 841) was born in Ravenna and spent his life there as a priest and, for a time, as abbot of a small monastery. He was an ardent defender of the Church and its autonomy, even from Rome so far as discipline and administration were concerned. This inspired his *Liber Pontificalis ecclesiae Ravennatis* (first printed in 1708). In the extract that follows, from the life of Bishop Agnellus (b. 487), he recounts how the bishop took over S Apollinare Nuovo and:

. . . decorated the tribunal and both walls with mosaic images of martyrs and virgins walking in procession. He also affixed panels of stucco [metala gipsea] which he covered with gold, and he reveted the walls with different kinds of marble and made a wonderful pavement of inlaid stone [lithostratis]. If you look at the inside of the front wall, you will find portraits of Justinian Augustus and bishop Agnellus decorated with golden mosaic cubes. No other church or building is like this one with regard to ceiling panels [laquearia] and beams. After he had consecrated the church, he gave a banquet at the Confessor's episcopal palace. Now, if you look carefully in the tribunal, you will find above the windows the following inscription in stone letters: 'King Theodoric built this church from the foundations in the name of Our Lord Jesus Christ.' . . . This, too, you may see on the wall. As I have said, two cities are represented there. On the men's side, the martyrs are proceeding out of Ravenna and going towards Christ, while the virgins are proceeding out of Classis towards the holy Virgin, and in front of them walk the Magi offering gifts. Why is it, however, that they are depicted in different garments, and not all in the same kind? Because the painter has followed divine Scripture. Now, Caspar is offering gold and wears a blue [iacintino] garment, and by his garment he denotes matrimony. Balthasar is offering frankincense and wears a yellow garment, and by his garment he denotes virginity. Melchior is offering myrrh and wears a variegated garment, and by his garment he denotes penitence. He who was before all time is dressed in a purple robe and by this He signifies that He was born a King and that He suffered. The one who is offering a gift to the newborn in a variegated robe signifies at the same time that Christ heals all those that are sick, and that He is to be flagellated by the Jews with various insults and lashes. For it is written of Him: 'He hath borne our infirmities and carried our sorrows, yet we did esteem Him as if he were a leper,' etc. And further down: 'He was wounded for our transgressions and affixed for our iniquities.' He who makes his offering in a white garment signifies that after the resurrection he will dwell in divine light. Just as these three precious gifts contain a divine mystery, i.e. that by gold is meant kingly wealth, by frankincense the priestly form, by myrrh death, so by all of these it is shown that He is the one who has taken men's iniquities upon Himself, namely Christ; thus also, as I have said, these three gifts are contained in their garments. Why is it that just three came from the East, and not four, or six, or two? That they may signify the perfect plenitude of the entire Trinity.

(Agnellus, *Liber Pontificalis ecclesiae Ravennatis*, tr. C. Mango, *The Art of the Byzantine Empire 312–1453*, Englewood Cliffs 1972)

The two entirely different images of Christ that coexisted in the minds of early Christians were evolved against a background of theological questioning. Hatred of pagan idolatry, which Christians shared with Jews, led some to a total condemnation of representational art. The writer and polemicist Tertullian (c. 160–c. 225) claimed that the devil created 'sculptors, painters and producers of all kinds of portraits'. The absolute Mosaic ban on images of God was strictly observed – not until the twelfth century was he to be represented by more than a hand reaching down from heaven (7,46; 7,73) – and sometimes extended to Christ. When the sister of the emperor Constantine applied to a bishop for a portrait of Christ she was said to have been sharply rebuked for displaying a tendency towards idolatry. And before the end of the fourth century Epiphanius (d. 403), bishop of Salamis, in a letter to the emperor Theodosius, asked: 'Which of the ancient Fathers ever painted an image of Christ and deposited it in a church or private house? Which ancient bishop ever dishonoured Christ by painting him on door curtains?' Images of saints were equally objectionable, he went on, since painters habitually 'lied' by depicting them 'according to the whim' sometimes as old men, sometimes as youths and so on. 'Wherefore', Epiphanius entreated the emperor to have all such paintings removed or whitewashed over and 'let no one paint in this manner henceforth. For our fathers delineated nothing except the salutary sign of Christ both on their doors and everywhere else.'

Nevertheless, theological support could be found for the widespread desire for images. The original version of the Nicene Creed, formulated in 325, had stated that Christ was 'of one substance with the Father' and 'for us men and our salvation came down and was made of flesh, and became man'. It followed that he could be represented as a man and, indeed, to deny it implied adherence to a heresy prevalent among Gnostics of the third century – that

Christ's appearance on earth was visionary. Thus the image of Christ eventually came to be seen as an affirmation of orthodoxy, especially later in connection with the fifth-century heresy of the Monophysites, who held that the divine nature of Christ overwhelmed the human. Images made explicit the doctrine defined at the Council of Chalcedon in 451 that Christ was 'of one Substance with the Father as regards his Godhead, and at the same time of one substance with us as regards his manhood; like us in all respects, apart from sin'.

The imperial Roman art on which Christians drew for their sacred images continued to furnish models for secular work as well. There are figures from pagan mythology – cupids not yet converted into angels – on a magnificent silver plate made in 388 to celebrate the tenth anniversary of the accession of the emperor Theodosius (7,22). But the general effect is most un-Classical. The emphasis has shifted. The corporeal has given way to the incorporeal, verisimilitude to symbolism. Theodosius is enthroned in front of a pedimented arch of a peculiar form, which had acquired symbolic significance from its imperial use. His head, an idealized portrait, is surrounded by a halo, which probably derives from Sassanian and Hellenistic images of sacred monarchy but later came to indicate the divine aura – of the Buddha (6,15) and of Christ and his saints. Without so much as a glance towards the official to whom he hands a document, Theodosius stares straight ahead, his eyes fixed on the source of his divine power in heaven. Scale indicates status, descending from Theodosius to his co-emperors and the dwarfed soldiers of his bodyguard. Christ was frequently depicted in exactly the same way, at the centre of a symmetrical composition. Thus secular and religious meanings interfused with and reinforced each other in the art of an empire governed by a divinely appointed Christian ruler.

7,22 *Missorium* of the emperor Theodosius, AD 388. Silver, 29ins (73.4cm) diameter. Real Academia de la Historia, Madrid.

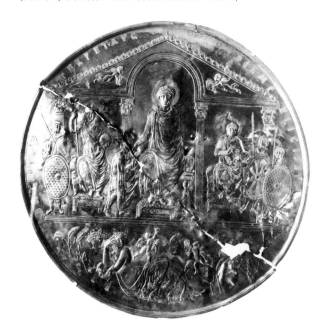

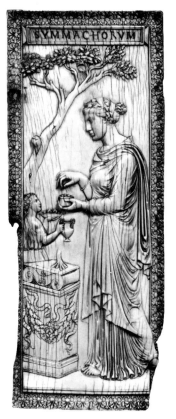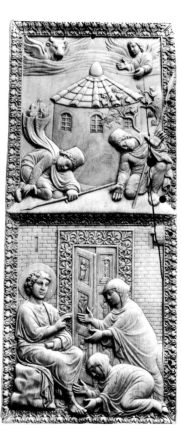

7,23 *Above left Priestess performing Pagan Rites*, c. AD 400. Ivory, 11¾ × 4¾ins (29.5 × 12cm). Victoria & Albert Museum, London.

7,24 *Above right Holy Women at the Tomb*, c. AD 400. Ivory, 14⅖ × 5³⁄₁₀ins (37 × 13.5cm). Castello Sforzesco, Milan.

Many upper-class citizens, however, clung tenaciously to the old gods, even after Theodosius proscribed all non-Christian cults in 392. There were artists who went on working for pagan as well as Christian patrons – sometimes in a style that must at this date have been self-consciously 'Classicizing'. Two late fourth-century ivory panels, for example, one pagan and one Christian in subject, quite clearly came from the same workshop, probably in Rome. The border ornamentation of palmettes is identical on both (7,23; 24). In one, carved for a member of an ancient senatorial family called Symmachi, who were promoters of a pagan revival, a distinctly patrician priestess sacrifices to Bacchus or Jupiter. The other panel shows the holy women visiting Christ's sepulchre on the morning of the Resurrection and originally formed part of a diptych (two hinged leaves with blank inner sides on which to write the names of those for whom prayers were to be said at the Eucharist). It differs from the pagan panel by illustrating not a single scene but two successive incidents. Above, the guards are stunned by the angel arriving to remove the stone from the sepulchre. Below, the angel tells the holy women that Christ has risen from the dead. Symbols of two of the evangelists who recorded the event are placed in the upper corners. The panel is, nevertheless, carved with as much delicate precision as that of the pagan priestess, the same attention to the natural fall of draperies and to the build and flexibility of the bodies beneath them, and the same feeling for form and space. The lucid and also sensuous language of the Classical tradition has been most tactfully and sensitively adapted to express a Christian message. It was about this time, it should be noted, that St Augustine (354–430) was forging out of Cicero's precise and elegant Latin a literary style in which to expound the intricacies of Christian theology – hitherto written mainly in Greek – and St Jerome (c. 348–420) was translating the Bible into a plainer style of Latin, closer to common speech, a style which was to become the unifying language of Western Christendom for more than a millennium, and of the Roman Catholic liturgy until the mid-twentieth century.

After the death of Theodosius in 395 the rift that had begun to open between the eastern and western parts of the empire was deepened by their political division between his two sons. The Eastern empire remained prosperous and intact, but the Western, already impoverished, began to disintegrate under attack from the people of central and northern Europe. Rome was sacked by the Visigoths in 410 – three days of mourning were ordered in Constantinople but nothing more was done. It was sacked again and more seriously by the Vandals in 455. In 476 it came, with the rest of Italy, under the rule of a barbarian king, Odoacer, later overthrown by Theodoric (d. 526), king of the Ostrogoths.

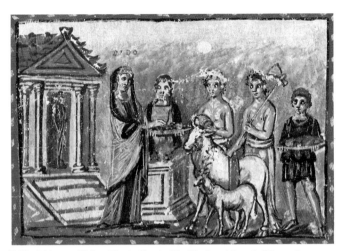

7,26 *Dido sacrificing*, illustration to Virgil's *Aeneid*, early 5th century AD. Parchment, page 13ins (33.2cm) wide. Biblioteca Apostolica, Vatican. (MS lat. 3225. fol. 33 v).

Yet, surprisingly, the visual arts flourished throughout this troubled period. Church building was promoted in Rome in the fifth century as never again until the seventeenth. The standard form of Christian basilica was finally established (e.g. S Sabina, 7,11), and at S Maria Maggiore, completed in 440, the Roman Church began to aspire to the splendour of the city's imperial past (7,25). The bishops of Rome, who now called themselves 'popes', put forward claims to universal authority. Sixtus III, the

7,25 S Maria Maggiore, Rome, c. AD 432–40. Nave.

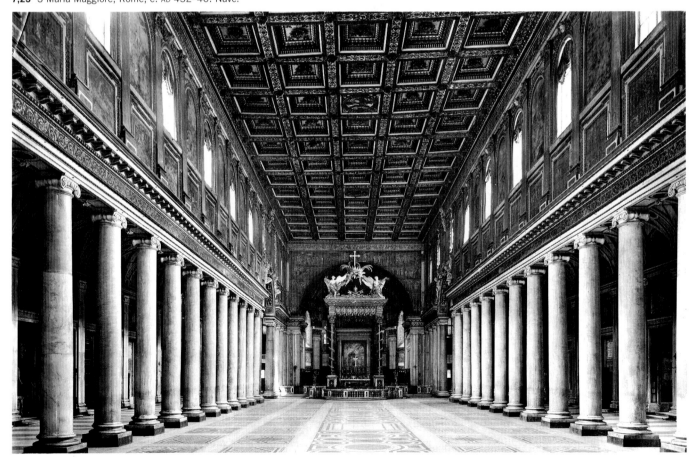

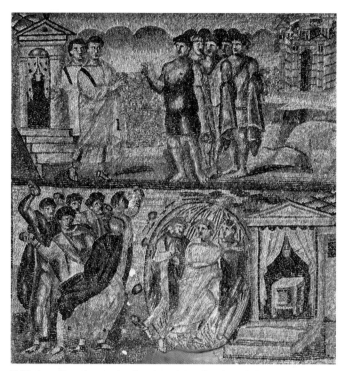

7,27 *Israelites threatening Revolt* and *The Stoning of Moses, Aaron and Joshua*, AD 432–40. Mosaic in the nave of S Maria Maggiore, Rome.

founder of S Maria Maggiore, is described in the bold dedicatory inscription above the apse as *episcopus plebi dei* – bishop of God's people. Nearby, in a mosaic, Solomon's temple was given the form of the ancient *Templum urbis* in the Forum, dedicated to the goddess Roma, as if to suggest that Rome was the new Jerusalem.

There are many reminiscences of ancient Roman art in the mosaics at S Maria Maggiore. Their designers were evidently as familiar with second-century Roman narrative relief sculpture as with more recent sculpture and painting, notably that in illustrated Bibles and Classical texts (**7,26**). One of the panels beneath the clerestory windows depicts the children of Israel on their way to the Promised Land threatening revolt against Moses and then, below, stoning Moses, Aaron and Joshua, who are protected in a cloud sent by the Lord (**7,27**). The story is told dramatically, much as on the Column of Marcus Aurelius (**5,67**), with a similar disregard for scale and concentration on emphatic expressions and gestures.

RAVENNA

The walls of the earliest churches in Rome had been covered with paintings. The more durable medium of mosaic was more expensive and so less often used. The technique of making decorative patterns and figurative scenes or *emblemata*, as mosaic pictures were called (the origin of our word 'emblem'), out of small tesserae of stone had been highly developed in Hellenistic times, mainly for pavements (see p. 186). About the first century AD the introduction of lightweight squares of glass together with that of a new type of cement, in which they could be fixed,

greatly facilitated the use of mosaics on walls and ceilings. Glass also increased the color range and could be made to reflect the light with gold-leaf backings. By setting the pieces at a slight angle to the surface a shimmering effect could be created. Design did not, however, keep pace with these technical advances. Mosaics went on being conceived as pavements, so that those in the ambulatory of S Costanza, for example, look rather like carpets laid out over the ceilings (**7,14**). Not until the fifth century was the medium fully exploited for wall and vault decoration in churches in Rome, Milan and, most notably, Ravenna, the most important city in Italy from 402 until the mid-eighth century (capital of the western emperors until 455, then of the Ostrogothic conquerors and the Romanized court of Theodoric and finally the see of Byzantine viceroys after the reconquest of Italy by Justinian's armies in the sixth century).

The so-called Mausoleum of Galla Placidia is the earliest building in Ravenna to preserve its full complement of mosaics. It was originally attached to a church founded by Galla Placidia, daughter of Theodosius and, as mother of the emperor Valentinian III, empress of the West from 425 until her death in 450. It follows a cruciform plan which had recently been recommended as symbolically ideal for a church by St Ambrose, the great theologian and bishop of Milan. Over the main door a mosaic lunette shows the Good Shepherd in a landscape strongly reminiscent of Pompeiian paintings (**7,28**). Schematic rocks at the front place the scene beyond the frame and provide a solid base. Spatial recession is indicated by the foreshortened sheep, the twisting pose of the Good Shepherd and the pale-blue sky gently darkening towards the zenith. Conceived in the tradition of *emblemata*, it is so placed as to suggest an opening on to the exterior from inside a tent or awning of imperial richness. Above the crossing the vault is transformed into a starry night sky with a gold cross gleaming at its centre, symbolizing the kingdom of heaven in which the souls of the victorious faithful would shine like stars. But the illusionistic devices of Hellenistic and Roman painting, so brilliantly put to Christian use in this building, were soon to be renounced. Figures have already begun to lose their solidity, standing against plain gold backgrounds in ambiguous spatial relationships, in the sumptuous mosaic decorations of S Apollinare Nuovo, built on a basilican plan around 490 as the palace church of the Ostrogothic king Theodoric. Gospel scenes – the earliest extant cycle – are here rendered not as parts of a narrative but as static ritual moments symmetrically composed (**7,19**).

Emblemata gave way to emblems a century later, when the chancel of the church of S Vitale was encrusted with some of the most beautiful of all mosaics. Every square inch sparkles with color, green and gold predominating, cool blues, occasional touches of scarlet and purple, and very telling use of white. The designs, intricate but never fussy, are so perfectly integrated with the structure of the building that the mosaics and architecture, surfaces and forms, seem to have been conceived together. The general effect is of great, though controlled and unostentatious,

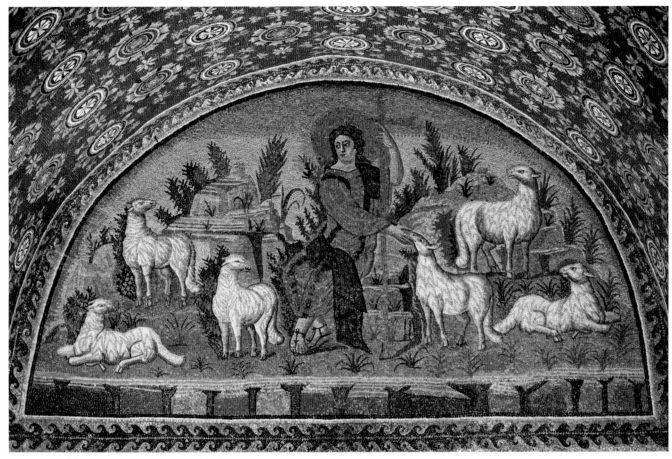

7,28 *The Good Shepherd*, c. AD 425. Mosaic in Mausoleum of Galla Placidia, Ravenna.

7,29 *Justinian and his Retinue*, c. AD 547. Mosaic in apse of S Vitale, Ravenna.

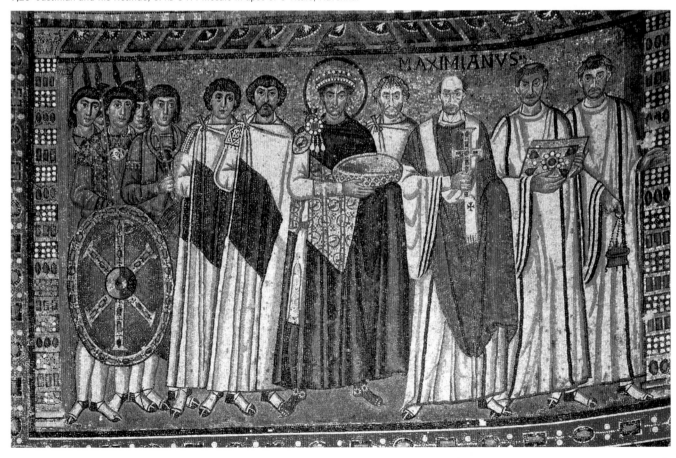

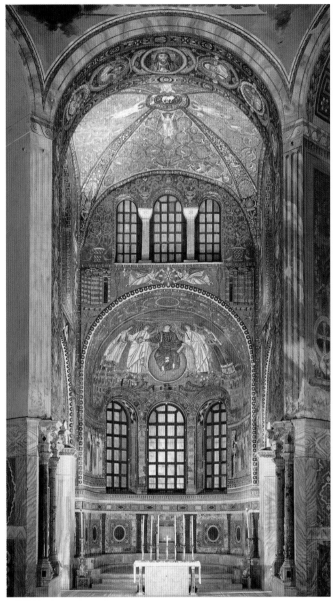

7,30 S Vitale, Ravenna, c. AD 540–7.

diploma to an official (7,22). All the figures are posed frontally, looking directly at the spectator and communicating with each other only by gestures.

On the lower walls of the apse we move from the court of heaven to that of the Byzantine emperor Justinian (527–65) and his empress Theodora, depicted with attendants carrying offerings to the altar. Justinian, with a halo, is accompanied by his bodyguard, carrying a shield with the *Chi-Rho* monogram, officials and three ecclesiastics including Maximianus (identified by name), bishop of Ravenna when the church was completed (7,29). The vivid characterization of the heads suggests portraiture from the life. And, at first sight, the panel might seem to be a straightforward representation of visual appearances in the tradition of *emblemata*. But the illusion of figures standing in space was created only to be denied. Justinian's feet are behind, but his cloak is in front of, the bishop. Although all the figures stare straight ahead, the gesture of the acolyte carrying a censer reveals that they should be read as moving in procession to the right, towards the centre of the apse.

Shortly after the completion of S Vitale, the apse of the church of S Apollinare in Classe (at the port of Ravenna) was decorated with mosaics hardly less fine (7,33). Here illusionistic devices were retained only for the bishops of Ravenna standing in curtained niches between the windows, in what constitutes the terrestrial zone of this great cosmic conception. In the lower part of the conch the garden of paradise, its little trees planted so carefully that they never overlap one another, is depicted quite flat, without any suggestion of recession, for in this eternal sphere where there is no time there can be no space. St Apollinaris, the first bishop of Ravenna, his hands raised in the traditional gesture of prayer (*orans*) and wearing the

magnificence. Yet S Vitale was not intended simply to charm the eye. Every motif is symbolic – vines of Christ, peacocks and doves of the immortal soul and so on. For the figurative scenes, the eucharistic sacrifice provides the unifying theme, with the Lamb of God in the centre of the vault. These wonderful mosaics were executed shortly after 540, when Ravenna with the rest of Italy was won back from Theodoric and they have perhaps political overtones.

In the centre of the half-dome or conch of the apse, a youthful and beardless Christ is flanked by angels. On the far right stands Bishop Ecclesius, founder of the church of S Vitale, of which he holds a model (7,30). St Vitalis is on the far left. The scene is set in the flowery meadows of paradise with its four rivers, issuing like twists of blue hair just beneath Christ, and its golden sky. Christ is, however, seated on the orb of the world, suspended in space. He is dressed in the purple robe of an emperor and hands a crown to St Vitalis without so much as a turn of the head – just as Theodosius was shown handing a

7,31 Plan of S Vitale, Ravenna.

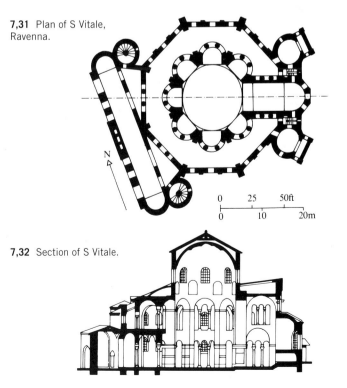

7,32 Section of S Vitale.

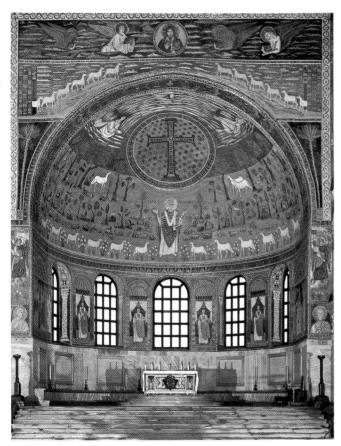

7,33 S Apollinare in Classe, Ravenna, c. AD 549.

eucharistic chasuble of an officiating priest, stands in the centre, with six sheep on either side, representing the 12 apostles. Three more sheep are placed at the top of the landscape to symbolize St Peter and the brothers St John and St James witnessing the Transfiguration. The Gospel according to St Matthew states that Christ took them up to a high mountain 'and was transfigured before them: and his face did shine as the sun, and his raiment was white as the light. And, behold, there appeared unto them Moses and Elias talking with him.' In the mosaic the two prophets are shown emerging from the clouds and the blinding glory of Christ is symbolized by a jewelled cross set in a dark-blue star-studded disc. At the very top of the apse the hand of God the Father reaches down through the clouds. Iconographically the whole scheme is quite unprecedented, nor was it to have any successors.

S Apollinare in Classe and S Vitale were both begun during the reign of Theodoric, with funds donated by a local banker, but neither was completed until after 540. Columns and carved capitals for both were imported from the eastern Mediterranean. But whereas S Apollinare in Classe is a basilica of the Early Christian type – one of the best preserved examples – S Vitale is in a new style developed in the East. It is possible that Bishop Ecclesius, who went on an embassy to Constantinople shortly before 525, brought back plans for S Vitale, or even an architect. The central octagon with upper galleries (for women) may perhaps have been derived from the chapel of the emperor's

palace at Constantinople (**7,31; 32**). In any event, the simple clarity of the basilica or of the circular or cruciform plans used by Early Christian builders was renounced in favour of a design which, by the subtle interplay of solids and voids, of brightly lit and shadowy spaces, creates in S Vitale a sense of mystery and awe. In this, its affinities with contemporary buildings in Constantinople are so evident that it may be regarded as Byzantine. In this way, too, it reflects the changed political situation. For after the reconquest by Justinian's armies, Italy became no more than a province in an empire whose ruler resided at Constantinople and no longer spoke Latin.

BYZANTINE ART

The foundation of Constantinople in 330, on the site of the old Greek city of Byzantium, had far-reaching consequences (see pp. 316–7). Constantine's intention had not, however, been to divide the empire; rather the reverse. Constantinople, overlooking the narrow waterway that separates Europe from Asia, was at the empire's centre of economic gravity. Nor was his move the decisive gesture it was later to seem. It had been said much earlier that 'where the emperor is, there is Rome', and from the beginning of the third century this was rarely Rome itself. Imperial residences and administrative centres were established under Diocletian in various strategically placed garrison cities: Milan, Trier and Nicomedia in Asia Minor. None of these cities was as populous and prosperous as Rome or, in the East, as Antioch and Alexandria, which were also commercial and cultural centres of great importance. But when, in the course of the fourth century, Constantinople became the emperor's usual place of residence it swiftly grew into the richest city in the empire and the main centre of artistic patronage.

ECCLESIASTICAL ARCHITECTURE

Hardly any traces survive of the buildings erected for Constantine in Constantinople, and eye-witness descriptions which praise their magnificence are imprecise. One church seems to have been a basilica. Another, dedicated to the holy apostles and intended as the emperor's mausoleum, was more original, having a large central space for the imperial sarcophagus and four naves – a combination of a centrally planned *martyrium* and a cruciform church. Foundations of two late fourth- or early fifth-century palaces have been unearthed, both with concave semicircular façades and rooms of varied shapes, either circular or indented with large niches. This use of deep niches had the effect of masking or concealing the structure – a feature that became characteristic of Byzantine architecture.

Substantial ruins of fifth-century churches have survived elsewhere in the Eastern empire. The most imposing are at Qal'at Si'man in northern Syria, where the famous ascetic St Simeon the Stylite (c. 390–459) spent the last decades of his life on a platform atop a 60-foot-high (18m) column, from which he gave spiritual instruction to people

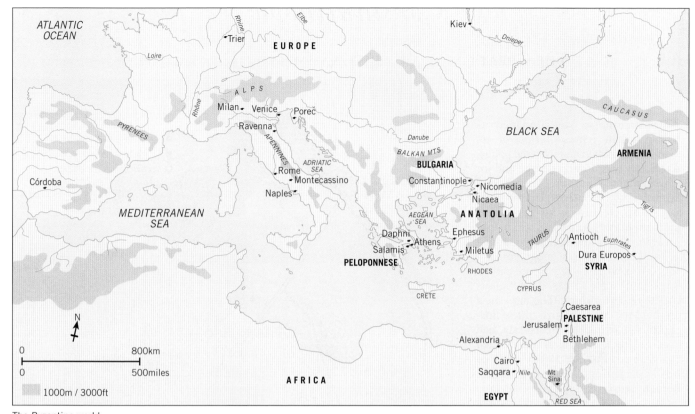

The Byzantine world

who came from far and wide to consult him. After his death pilgrims continued to crowd to the place in large numbers and the column was enshrined in the octagonal centre of a vast cruciform church (**7,37**). Other buildings extended over several acres. (Groups of hermits had begun to form monastic communities in Egypt and Palestine in the fourth century, but this is one of the earliest surviving complexes of monastic buildings.) Finely dressed ashlar, which had never been displaced by Roman concrete in the East, was used for walling, and timber for the roofing of the church. Decorative details were derived from the Classical repertory of ornament with only such variations as had been made in the eastern Mediterranean since Hellenistic times. Bold string courses divided the walls horizontally and framed windows and doors. Interior spaces were clearly defined and marked off from one another with the four arms of the cross as double-aisled basilicas, that at the east terminating in three apses. Over the central octagon there may perhaps have been a dome of wood sheathed in metal, a type of dome that originated in the Near East and was later used extensively in Byzantine architecture as a manifold symbol of the cosmos, the heavens, death and resurrection. Indeed, the whole conception of the church of St Simeon the Stylite, like that of the Holy Apostles in Constantinople, to some extent foreshadowed in embryonic form the 'quincunx' or cross-in-square plan of fully developed Byzantine architecture (see p. 328).

One of the first indications of the new direction Byzantine architecture was to take is provided by the capitals of columns. Builders of early churches in Rome had been able to obtain these costly items ready-made from abandoned pagan temples (see p. 303). When new capitals had to be carved, especially in the East, those of the Corinthian order, traditionally reserved for important public buildings, were usually copied with variations that became increasingly pronounced. Stiffly curving leaves of acanthus were ruffled, volutes were replaced by human and animal heads, Christian symbols were sometimes incorporated. A sequence of such capitals would illustrate the disintegration of Classical form as the naturalistic elements used by the Greeks were gradually schematized and deprived of their visual logic (see pp. 156–7). The Classical ideal of regularity and uniformity was modified. A new type of capital was evolved and perfected by the early sixth century – a type which allowed great variation in detail. For diversity was now prized, as in the carving of intricate patterns of stylized spiky leaves. The function of the capital was masked – in a way that was to be very typical of Byzantine architecture generally. The richly carved three-dimensional acanthus foliage of a Corinthian capital has been replaced by flat lacy open-work patterns, deeply undercut by drilling, so that the sustaining core is left darkly indeterminate. The effect of these so-called 'basket capitals' is of an almost weightless piece of starched lace veiling the structurally all-important join between vertical and horizontal. They provide an almost exact counterpart in decoration of the spatial effects Byzantine architects were to achieve with structure. The mysterious and insubstantial have taken the place of the self-explicit and sustainingly solid.

Constantinople

THE CREATION OF A CHRISTIAN IMPERIAL CAPITAL CITY

Constantinople was designed as an urban representation of its founder's Christian and imperial policy. As such it was unprecedented and for long remained unique. The Second Rome that Emperor Constantine aspired to create was to be no less monumentally imposing than the first but clearly and logically planned as a single organism, scenographically conceived with a great processional route and open spaces for religious and state ceremonies. The site, on a promontary at the mouth of the Bosphorus where Europe meets Asia, had been a Greek trading station called Byzantium until AD 193–6 when it was besieged and destroyed by the Roman emperor Septimius Severus (AD 193–211). He rebuilt it with three temples on its acropolis, a hippodrome, theatre and pubic baths. In 324 Constantine, immediately after defeating his co-emperor Licinius, a pagan, on the Asian side of the Bosphorus, chose it for his new capital.

7,34 Christopher Buondelmonti, map of Constantinople, 1420. Ink on parchment. Biblioteca Marciana, Venice (Cod. Marc. lat. xiv, 45 (= 4595)).

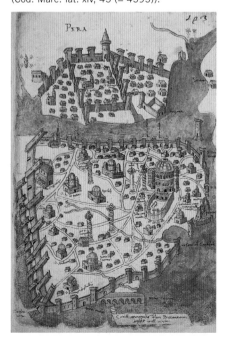

7,35 Plan of early Byzantine and medieval Constantinople.

He was now master of the whole Roman empire, with Christianity as its privileged religion. But its economic centre had moved from the West to the East, hence the need for a new capital city. The landward boundary was marked by a wall from the Golden Horn to the Sea of Marmara and the city was solemnly dedicated to the Christian god and martyrs in 330. Within a century and a half the population grew from about 20,000 to nearly half a million, the inhabited area being extended to ten times that of the original Byzantium, covering seven hills, as did Rome, within a new wall built under Emperor Theodosius II in 412–3 which still largely survives. The basic plan of the city laid out for Constantine, with its streets and squares, also survives beneath the surface of modern Istanbul although there are few traces of it above ground (7, 36).

Although the pagan temples were left untouched by Constantine, public sacrifices in them were discouraged and eventually banned. The new alliance between imperial rule and Christianity was manifested in the main group of new and refurbished buildings at the apex of the approximately triangular site (7, 35). A palace called the Daphne was built adjoining the hippodrome which was enlarged as a setting for imperial ceremonies as well as popular entertainments. Beside it a square was laid out, named the Augustaeum in honour of Constantine's mother, Empress Helena Augusta (c. 255–c. 330) who had followed him into the Christian fold and was later to be canonised as St Helen. A statue of her was set on top of a porphyry column in the centre of the square. On one side of the square was a basilica for the Senate – a ceremonial body, as in

Rome. To the north, a church was dedicated to Christ and Hagia Eirene (Holy Peace) and a residence provided for the bishop. On a plot of land perhaps intentionally left vacant, the first church dedicated to Hagia Sophia (Holy Wisdom) was to be built by Constantine's son and successor Constantius II (337–61). Churches thus formed a prominent part of the administrative nucleus, whereas in Rome those founded by Constantine had been on the periphery, far from the Palatine.

Above all, the difference between Rome and the new capital was marked by the great processional way, the Mese, a dramatically straight street some 25 yards (23m) wide and flanked by marble porticoes, which led through a triumphal arch to a circular forum with a still surviving central column bearing a bronze statue of Constantine (now lost) with rays flaring out of his head, like Helios the sun god at the centre of the universe. Leading uphill and down, the Mese passed through a four-faced

or *quadrifons* arch over a crossway to a point of bifurcation where there were more commemorative columns, one crowned by a statue of Constantine, another by a cross like that he had seen in the vision that prompted his conversion, and the third by a statue of his mother. Here there was also a porphyry high relief of his four prospective heirs embracing one another, as an optimistic augury for the future of his dynasty. (Looted in 1204, it was attached to the façade of S Marco, Venice, where it survives.)

The Mese branched north-west to the gate on the road to Adrianople (modern Edirne) and south-west to join the Via Egnatia that led across the Balkans to the Adriatic sea. Just inside the northern gate on the highest of the city's hills a church intended for Constantine's mausoleum was dedicated to the Holy Apostles, later destroyed. In a cemetery outside the other gate a church enshrined the relics of St Mokios who had been martyred in Byzantium. Emanating from the palace complex and linking the

three churches founded by Constantine, the Mese was not only the city's main channel of communication but also the route for religious and imperial processions, in every sense its spinal cord. It was extended on axis when the outer wall was built under Theodosius II. In the meantime some thirty churches had been built and two forums added to those on the Mese, each with a column like that of Trajan in Rome (5, 65; 66) with a spiral of narrative reliefs.

A fire which destroyed much of the city in 465 was followed by more than half a century of riots that wrought further destruction. Peace was restored by Justinian I (527–65) for whom the great church of Hagia Sophia was built and outside it a column bearing an equestrian statue that showed him holding a cross. (This is visible in Buondelmonte's schematic plan of 1420, **7, 34**). Further troubles followed Justinian's reign, but shortly after the beginning of the ninth century, in a period of increasing prosperity from trade, Constantinople began to acquire a medieval character submerging that envisaged by Constantine and his successors. More churches were built, plain externally but rich inside, also monasteries, and palaces for the wealthier merchants. Pera or Galata on the other side of the Golden Horn was also developed. The hippodrome remained the scene of chariot races and imperial displays – though also the epicentre of riots – the commemorative columns stood as landmarks, but the forums around them were degraded to market places, the porticoes lining the Mese were converted into shops and houses, the baths ceased to function and the temples on the acropolis were allowed to fall into ruin.

Constantinople remained the largest and most prosperous city in Europe – Muslim Córdoba (Spain) being its only rival – until it was sacked by the Crusaders in 1204. There was a revival of the arts in the fourteenth century (9, 70) but no further urban development. The capital of the eastern empire and Orthodox Christianity was reduced to a cluster of villages before it was conquered in 1451 by the Ottoman Turks who superimposed the Islamic city of Istanbul on the Constantinian urban fabric.

7,36 Aerial view of Istanbul.

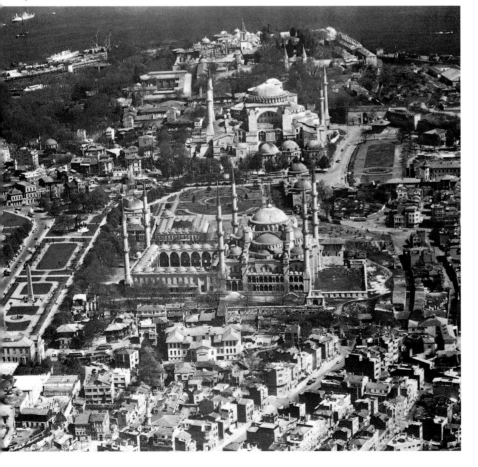

7,37 S Simeon Stylites, Qal'at
Si'man, Syria, south façade,
c. AD 480–90.

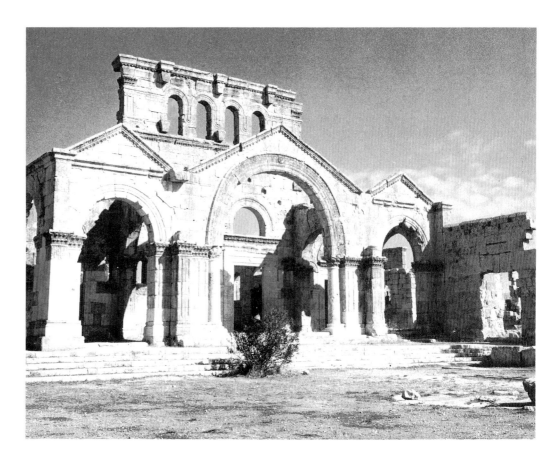

HAGIA SOPHIA

What has been called a 'dialectical principle of statement and denial' underlies much Byzantine architecture. It is most notable in the design of its greatest monument, the church of Holy Wisdom, Hagia Sophia, in Constantinople (**7,38; 39; 41**). 'Through the harmony of its measurements it is distinguished by indescribable beauty', wrote Justinian's court historian Procopius, who witnessed its erection. 'A spherical shaped tholos standing upon a circle makes it exceedingly beautiful.' Mathematics was at the time regarded as the highest of the sciences and the two architects of Hagia Sophia, Anthemius of Tralles and Isidorus of Miletus, were known primarily as mathematicians. The former described architecture as the 'application of geometry to solid matter'. And the impression given by Hagia Sophia is that it was applied to conceal the solidity of matter. In this vast and inspiring space the eye cannot assess the niceties of its geometrically calculated proportions or penetrate to the defining boundaries of the plan. Volumes are not clearly marked off, as in the Pantheon, for instance, but interpenetrate one another. The air of mystery and splendour must have been further enhanced originally when the dome, brightly lit by the windows around its circumference, was inlaid with a plain gold mosaic. 'It abounds exceedingly in gleaming sunlight', wrote Procopius: 'You might say that the space is not illuminated by the sun from the outside, but that the radiance is generated within.' Another contemporary, Justinian's court poet, Paul the Silentiary, described in

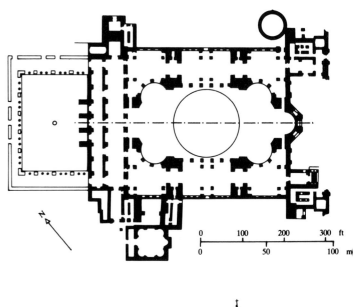

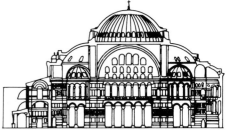

7,38 Plan and section of Hagia Sophia.

563 how 'to the east there open the triple spaces of circles cut in half, and above, upon the upright collar of the walls, springs up the fourth part of a sphere; even so, above his tripled-crested head and back does a peacock raise his many-eyed feathers.'

Hagia Sophia was built at the command of the emperor Justinian with the specific aim of outshining all other religious buildings. When it was consecrated in 537, only five years after the foundations had been laid, he is said to have remarked: 'Solomon, I have outdone thee.' It was very much bigger than any church in Rome and remained for many centuries by far the largest church in Christendom. The moment was propitious for such an ambitious under-taking, politically as well as artistically. Justinian was set on reviving the glory of the empire and establishing his own autocratic power – he had savagely put down the popular insurrection in which an earlier church of Hagia Sophia (the second on the site) was destroyed. At his instigation a new code of laws had been drawn up and an all but incor-ruptible civil service created. A strengthened army under the command of brilliant generals such as Belisarius had begun to win back western territory lost to the barbarians in the previous century. That a new architecture should have been brought to sudden maturity at the same moment is hardly a coincidence. And the two architects of Hagia Sophia, who came from quite outside the tradition of Roman master-builders, had the courage as well as the inventive genius to design a structure of unprecedented form.

The plan is surprisingly simple: a large rectangle enclosing a square space, at the corners of which there are huge piers to carry the dome. It looks as if the halves of a church with a central octagon (like S Vitale at Ravenna) had been pulled apart and a domed area placed between them. The dome is, however, the dominant feature of the whole structure. Of a type originated in the Near East, it rests not on a drum (like that of the Pantheon) but on four

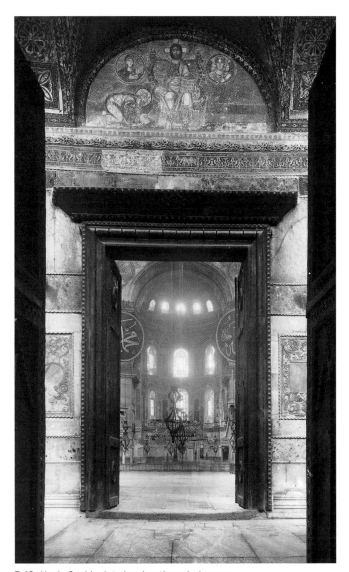

7,40 Hagia Sophia, interior view through doorway.

spherical triangles or pendentives, which rise from the piers and are structurally the skeletal remains of a lower and larger dome, from which the crown and four semicir-cular arches have been notionally cut away. (The origins of the pendentive dome have been variously traced to Armenia and Iran, but this method of covering a very large space was perfected by Byzantine architects and consti-tutes their main contribution to structural engineering.) To the (liturgical) east and west of the central dome, swelling out from the great arches, there are half-domes of the same diameter, and below them smaller half-domes.

In materials as well as in form Hagia Sophia differs from the concrete domed structures of ancient Rome. The piers are of ashlar; walls and vaults are of rather thin brick set in mortar. The use of brick for roofing such a vast area was a daring innovation, rather too daring as it turned out. The dome collapsed in 558 and had to be replaced by one slightly higher, completed in 563. Other alterations had to be made to steady the structure at the same time and also later. The exterior of Hagia Sophia is, in fact, the product

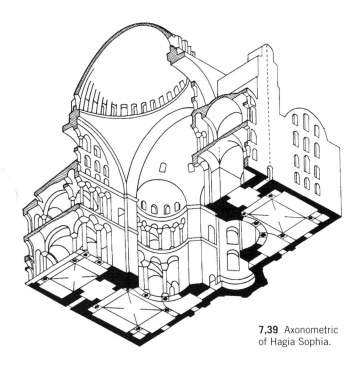

7,39 Axonometric of Hagia Sophia.

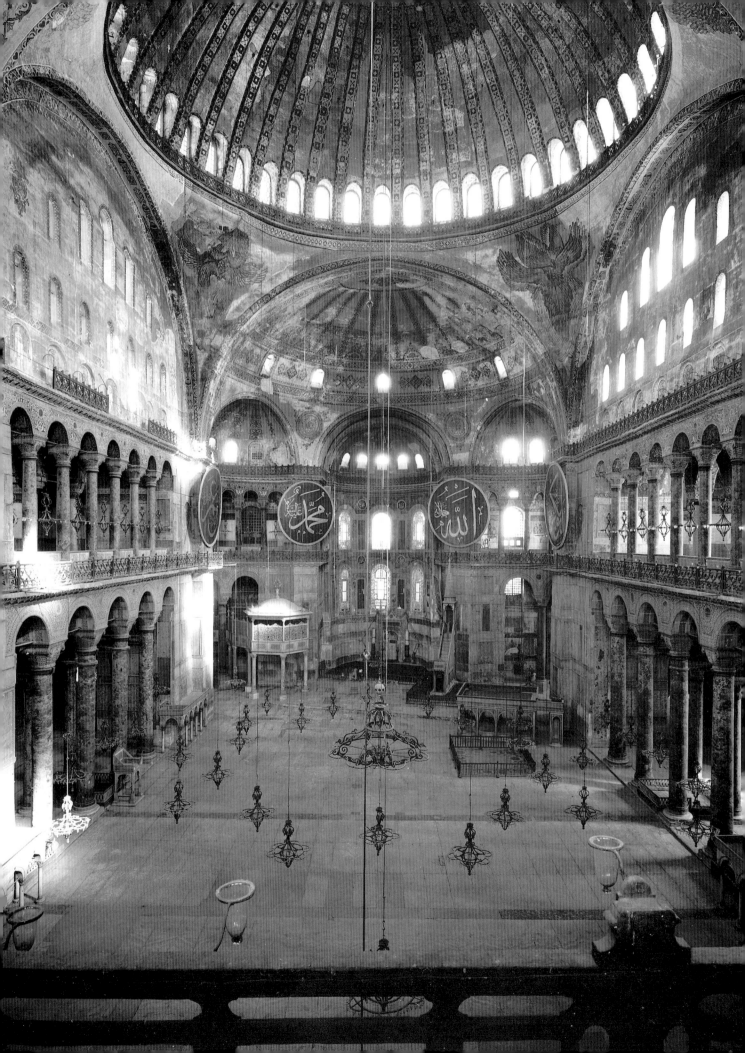

of a long succession of expedients to buttress the dome rather than of architectural design.

Hagia Sophia is a building without a façade, in the usual sense of the word; it is the skyline, not the entrance front, that commands attention. Here again, the difference from Italian practice is very striking. Domes had been given very little prominence in the architecture of pagan Rome – that of the Pantheon was barely visible behind the pediment of the façade. On Early Christian churches they were boxed in and concealed behind brick walls, being intended only for their interior effect (7,13). They symbolized the dome of heaven. But in Asia, from Syria to Buddhist India (see p. 227), the hemispherical exterior was equally important as a symbol of the cosmos.

Hagia Sophia, built on a high ridge, crowned the city of Constantinople and its dome could be seen from far away. Few people were allowed to see any more of it. The breathtaking view that greets the modern visitor walking through the central door was for the privileged few only (7,40). Hagia Sophia was the church of the imperial court. It was not like the Early Christian basilicas in Rome and elsewhere, intended for ordinary communal worship, but as a setting for rituals of quintessentially Byzantine complexity. The great nave under the dome and half-domes was a processional space, through which the clergy passed to the chancel and the emperor and his court to their enclosure in the south aisle. The congregation, accommodated in the aisles and galleries, men on one side and women on the other, could see only parts of the church and of the rite, most of which was celebrated in the chancel. It was, however, in the most prominent place, beneath the eastern rim of the dome, that patriarch and emperor exchanged the kiss of peace immediately after the eucharistic consecration. At this solemn moment the two earthly representatives of God stood together as if in an aura of divine light. The theocratic basis of the Byzantine empire could not have been more clearly displayed.

THE CLASSICAL TRADITION

Justinian's patronage of architecture was a direct expression of his ambition to create a monolithic state with one set of laws, one religious creed and one ruler, the earthly representative of the one almighty God. Procopius, probably at his command, devoted an entire volume to the religious and other buildings that he founded, rebuilt, restored or embellished. They were scattered throughout the empire to demonstrate his far-reaching power, in the Balkans, Palestine, north Africa and Italy, even on the barren slopes of Mount Sinai.

The church he built there is of interest mainly for its exceptionally well preserved mosaics, among the finest of their period and probably the work of artists and craftsmen from Constantinople (7,42). In the conch of the apse medallion heads of the apostles, 16 prophets and King David frame a representation of the Transfiguration – Christ transformed in glory and conversing with Moses

7,41 *Opposite* Hagia Sophia.

and Elias. The subject was particularly appropriate for the place as it was here that the God of the Old Testament had appeared in a burning bush to Moses, an incident illustrated on the arch above the niche and commemorated in an open-air *martyrium* beyond the apse. Two epiphanies, or manifestations, of the one God were thus combined.

As we have already seen, the Transfiguration was also represented at about the same time in the apse of S Apollinare in Classe (7,33). On Sinai, however, Christ and three disciples are depicted as men, not as symbols. They and the two prophets are, indeed, quite substantial, boldly modelled forms, though they seem to hover above, rather than stand on, the strip of ground reduced to three bands of dark green, light green and yellow, which merge into the gold background. Landscape has been eliminated and the figures appear as real, but remote, presences, quite literally out of this world and also isolated from one another in the golden glow of the heaven above the heavens, infinite and eternal. In the centre, Christ is clad, as the Gospels say, in raiment 'white as the light', accentuated by the almond-shaped aureole or mandorla in four shades of blue, darkest in the centre like the sky. From the cross that crowns the niche a ray of light bearing the hand of God shines down and seems to be refracted into the seven beams emanating from Christ, flickering across the mandorla and the gold vault, filling the whole composition with divine radiance.

A huge floor mosaic laid in the imperial palace in Constantinople at about the same time is in an entirely different style (7,43). Pastoral scenes with naturalistically posed men and animals, trees and small buildings are depicted in gradations of color as subtle as had ever been achieved in the medium. Without any apparent symbolical significance, they maintain Classical traditions, kept alive in Constantinople in a secular art no less sumptuously sensuous than that produced in the Hellenistic kingdoms at their height (5,29). Satyrs and nymphs continued to dance and the old Greek gods to display their athletic figures on silver vessels until well into the seventh century. Both the art and the bucolic poetry of ancient Greece and Rome were evoked, sometimes with a gravely retrospective note, as in a magnificent silver plate delicately wrought with the figure of a shepherd or, rather, goat-herd – emphatically not the Good Shepherd (7,44).

Most works of art that survive from the reign of Justinian are, however, religious. Many of the finest are on a small scale, including exquisitely carved ivories and illuminated manuscripts. It was during this period that miniature painting – book illustration so called from minium, a red pigment used to outline figures – first became an important art form. The book or codex, consisting of single sheets of parchment or vellum bound together and protected by a cover, had been introduced towards the end of the first century AD and gradually superseded the scroll. A codex was very much easier to read and less easily damaged than a scroll (usually some 30 feet, 9m, long). Its flat pages also provided a better ground for paintings, as we have seen (7,26). The importance of the book to Christians, who set such store by the Holy Scriptures and

322 ART AND THE WORLD RELIGIONS

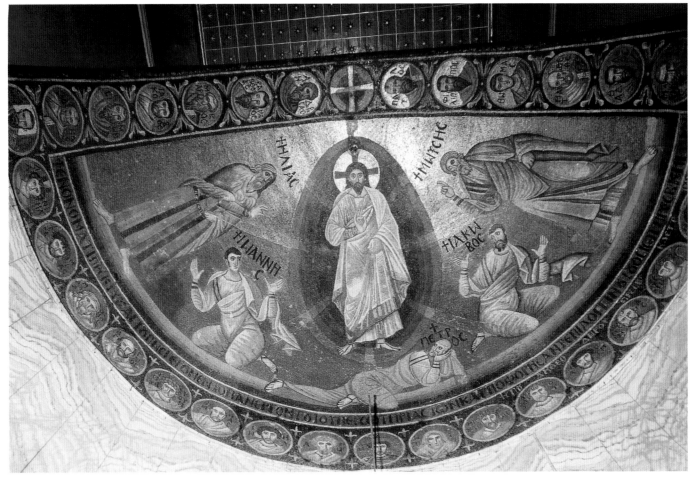

7,42 *The Transfiguration*, c. AD 550–65. Apse mosaic in the Church of the Monastery, Mount Sinai, Egypt.

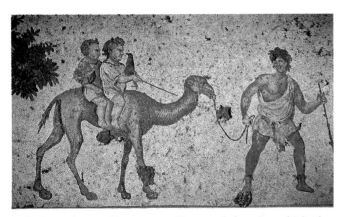

7,43 *Pastoral scene*, 6th century AD. Floor mosaic from the peristyle of the imperial palace, Istanbul.

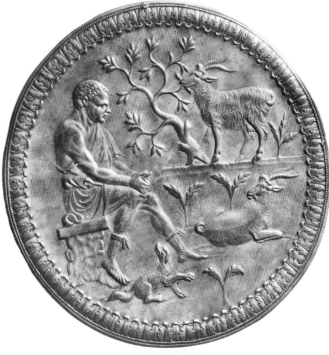

7,44 *Seated Goat-Herd*, AD 527–65. Silver plate. State Hermitage, St Petersburg.

included readings from the Gospels and Epistles in their liturgy, need not be stressed. To call Christianity a 'religion of the book' is no mere figure of speech.

Fragments of three magnificent sixth-century examples survive: two Gospels and one Genesis. Their texts are written in gold and silver letters on parchment, colored with the purple dye that was reserved for imperial use and indicates that they were made for presentation by the emperor. Illustrations delicately painted in bright colors

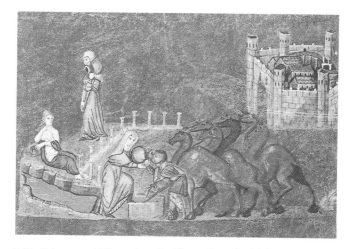

7,45 *Rebecca and Eliezer*, from the *Vienna Genesis*, detail, 6th century AD. Pigment on parchment, page 13¼ × 9⅞ins (33.5 × 25cm). Österreichische Nationalbibliothek, Vienna.

have great prominence. On one page of the Genesis manuscript the story of Rebecca and Eliezer, the servant of Abraham who was sent to find a wife for Isaac, is told verbally and pictorially (**7,45**). Rebecca 'very fair to look upon' is shown twice, on her way to the well and then giving water to Eliezer. Heads of ten camels (numbered in the Bible) are clearly indicated, but with only a few bodies and legs. Both the walled city and the fountain nymph symbolizing the well seem to have been copied from Classical sources – neither would look out of place on the Column of Trajan. But the relationship between text and illustration has been reversed. Here the words explain the image, which was intended as an aid to meditation on the all-important inner meaning of the story. Rebecca, the wife of Isaac and mother of Esau and Jacob, was seen as a precursor of the Virgin Mary, and her meeting with Eliezer was construed as an Old Testament parallel to the angel's annunciation to Mary that she was to be the mother of Jesus.

ICONS AND ICONOCLASTS

The distinction between an image that was an aid to thought or prayer and one that was in itself an object of veneration was somewhat blurred in the course of the sixth and seventh centuries. Small portable pictures of Christ, the Virgin and Child or the saints, nowadays called icons (from a Greek word which originally signified a much wider variety of 'likenesses' or 'images') were increasingly demanded throughout the Byzantine world. They had a stronger emotional appeal than the intellectually conceived symbols and doctrinal allegories of earlier Christian art. In 692 this move away from symbolism was officially sanctioned by the Trullan Council of the Church, which ordained that 'the human figure of Christ our God, the Lamb, who took on the sins of the world, be set up even in the images instead of the ancient lamb. Through this figure we realize the height of the humiliation of God the Word and are led to remember His life in the flesh, His suffering and His saving death and the redemption ensuing from it for the world.' To achieve this aim painters reverted to a more naturalistic style, as in a panel painting of the Virgin and Child flanked by two saints and

two angels with the hand of God reaching down from the top (**7,46**). The heads of the two angels are foreshortened with the skill of a Hellenistic painter, the Virgin and Child have substance and weight, the two saints, especially the lean St Theodore on the left, might almost be portraits of ascetics. The picture is composed hierarchically, but the figures staring straight at the spectator seem to have been intended as more than aids to meditation. They invite a face-to-face meeting with the holy persons depicted. And devotion was paid to such icons as if they were themselves holy relics. This example is among the few to escape the fury of the Iconoclasts, which broke loose in the early eighth century against the, as they thought, idolatrous tendencies such icons were arousing.

An edict issued by the emperor Leo III in 730 ordered the destruction of all images that showed Christ, the Virgin Mary, saints or angels in human form. It brought into the open a smouldering conflict which raged for the next 113 years between Iconoclasts (image-breakers) and, as they styled their opponents, Iconodules (venerators of images) throughout the Byzantine empire. (The edict was repudiated by the Pope in Rome and by Western Christendom.) No controversy about works of art has ever aroused such violent passions, polarizing sentiments on

7,46 *The Virgin and Child enthroned between St Theodore and St George*, 6th century AD. Panel painting, 27 × 18⅞ins (68.6 × 47.9cm). Monastery of St Catherine, Mount Sinai, Egypt.

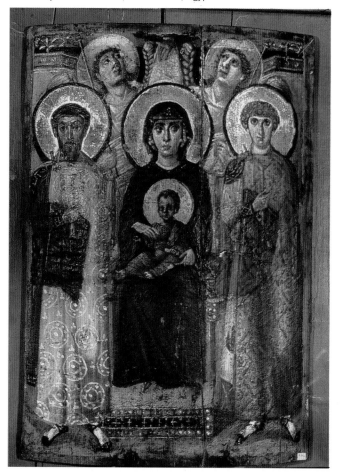

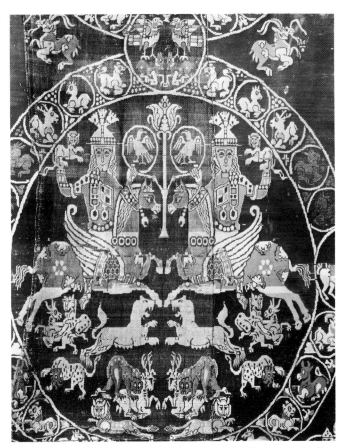

7,47 *Emperors hunting*, late 8th or 9th century AD. Silk compound twill. Staatliche Museen, Berlin.

other religious, political, social and economic issues as well. Any Iconodule discovered harbouring an icon could be punished by flogging, branding, mutilation or blinding. Religious images survived openly only in those parts of the earlier Byzantine empire that had been overrun by 'barbarians' – the word is poignant in this context.

Iconoclasts were not, however, opposed to art as such. While they were in control, churches were richly adorned with mosaics of jewelled crosses and leafy gardens of paradise (e.g. the Blachernae Palace church in Constantinople known from descriptions). Palaces were still more opulently decorated. Ambassadors from the court of Tang China to Constantinople noted with admiration the abundance of wrought glass, crystal, gold, ivory and rare woods, as well as 'a human figure of gold which marks the hours by striking bells'. They also admired ingenious devices to keep rooms cool in summer. None of these wonders has survived, though some examples of Byzantine silks of this period have, finely woven with heraldically stylized patterns of men and beasts (**7,47**). Their designs are strongly influenced by Persian textiles, a reminder that Byzantium had by now become more Asian than European, even though all the eastern territories of the empire, save Asia Minor, had been lost to the forces of Islam (see p. 341). It should be mentioned, however, that there seems to be no direct connection between Iconoclasm and Islamic abhorrence of religious images.

THE TRIUMPH OF ORTHODOXY

The defeat of Iconoclasm was officially proclaimed in 843, on the first Sunday in Lent, which is still celebrated in the Eastern Church as the festival of the Triumph of Orthodoxy. From this time onwards orthodoxy was to be the key concept in Byzantine art – though the doctrinal differences between the Orthodox Church of Constantinople and the Catholic Church of Rome did not develop into a schism until the eleventh century. So far as the arts are concerned, the most important outcome of the controversy was the formulation of a doctrinal statement on the value of images of Christ, the saints and angels. They were recommended:

> *For the more frequently they are seen by means of painted representation the more those who behold them are aroused to remember and to desire the prototypes and to give them greeting and worship-of-honour, but not the true worship of our faith, which befits only the Divine Nature.*

> (Mansi, *Concilia*, XIII, 377 B-E, 397 C)

7,48 *Virgin and Child*, AD 867. Detail of apse mosaic, Hagia Sophia, Istanbul.

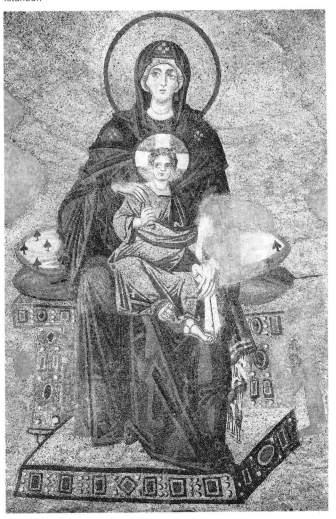

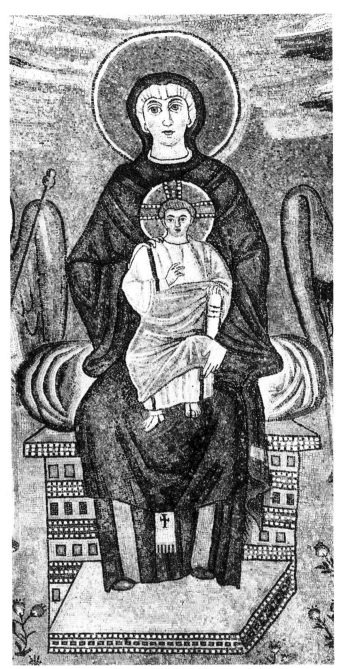

7,49 *Virgin and Child*, c. AD 550. Detail of apse mosaic, Poreč Cathedral, Croatia.

new mosaics is not surprising, for the mystery of the Incarnation was, as we have seen (pp. 308–9), the main theological justification for images of Christ.

The Virgin had gained increasing importance in Christian thought since 431, when the Council of Ephesus declared her to be the Mother of God. She came to be regarded as the great intercessor for mankind and, from the sixth century, was sometimes given the prominence hitherto reserved for Christ alone by being represented with the Child in the conch above the high altar. The earliest surviving example is of c. 550 at Poreč, Croatia (**7,49**). After the Iconoclastic period this became normal in Byzantine churches. Similarly, the tradition was established of placing the image of Christ *Pantocrator* (ruler of all things) in the central dome, 'looking down from the rim of heaven', as a Byzantine writer described him. The largest, set in the previously plain gold dome of Hagia Sophia in the late ninth century, was destroyed when the church was converted into a mosque. But one of the most impressive examples still dominates the little monastic church at Daphni near Athens, as humbling an image of divine omnipotence as has ever been depicted (**7,50**). He is the ruler and judge. The Virgin in the apse is the intercessor, represented as the Queen of Heaven enthroned on the cushions of Byzantine royalty.

7,50 *Christ Pantocrator*, c. AD 1020. Mosaic in dome of church at Daphni, near Athens.

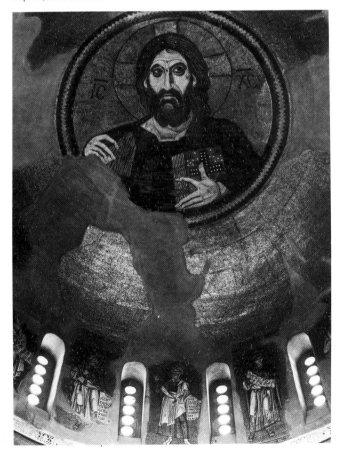

Elsewhere in this document mosaics as well as paintings are specified, but not statues, which were never to be approved by the Eastern Church. Byzantine sculpture is practically non-existent.

For a century after the triumph of Orthodoxy, in a period of uninterrupted political and economic stability, mosaicists were engaged on the slow work of covering the vaults of the larger churches with figurative compositions. In a sermon preached in Hagia Sophia in 867 Photius, patriarch of Constantinople, was able to extol the recently finished mosaic of the Virgin and Child above the apse (**7,48**). That this should have been the first of the

The Virgin

THE FIRST IMAGES

It is highly probable that women outnumbered men in the early Christian churches. Some of them came from high-ranking families, unlike the men, and chastity was valued by them as a supremely Christian ideal which set them apart from the pagan world. There may even have been nuns before there were monks, as early as the third century. It is against this background and that of the Councils of Nicaea (AD 315) and Ephesus (AD 431), which defined the Virgin Mary's divine maternity and declared her to be the Mother of God, that early images of the Virgin should be seen.

Even in pagan Rome chastity had been acknowledged as a virtue: the Vestal Virgins, for example, enjoyed legal and other privileges. But when ancient philosophers wrote about it they did so as part of a wider discussion concerning self-control and the passions, the mastery of the soul over the body. Early Christian teachers conceived the matter differently. They saw it in the context of the Fall

and original sin, of the guilt of Eve. It was through the Virgin Mary, theologians declared, that the fall of Eve might be reversed. Formerly women had been the 'gateway to the Devil'; now, by maintaining their virginity, they could be redeemed. In heaven the rewards of a virgin were 60 times greater than those of an ordinary Christian; only martyrs were more favoured. Eventually the Church itself came to be thought of as a virgin, the bride of Christ, pure, unblemished and uncorrupted and, at the same time, a mother – the mother of all she brought to Christ.

Though virginity was a universal virtue and Christians were addressed generally when theologians and teachers wrote about it, it was women they usually had in mind. Indeed such early Christian authors as Tertullian and Cyprian wrote specifically of female virgins. Had they unconscious motives? Were early Christian tracts on the virtue of virginity tinged with misogyny? Women were barred from

the Church's leadership and although they could serve as deaconesses they were not allowed to teach. They were relegated to the back of the congregation in church, isolated from the men. However, chastity was urged on men as well as women, on married couples as well as individuals, and it would be an exaggeration to interpret it simply and solely as a means of suppressing women.

Mary's virginity was central to Christian doctrine from the fourth century onwards for without it there could be no 'Son of God' and Jesus would have been a man like other men. The Councils that defined the special nature of the Virgin Mary were held at Nicaea and Ephesus where she was declared to have been not just 'Christ bearer' but 'God bearer' or *Theotokos*, the Mother of God. In this way the question of Christ's dual nature was resolved. Ephesus was the supposed burial place of Mary and also, equally if not more significantly, the place where the great temple of

7,51 *Annunciation*, AD 432–40. Detail of mosaic on triumphal arch over the high altar, S Maria Maggiore, Rome.

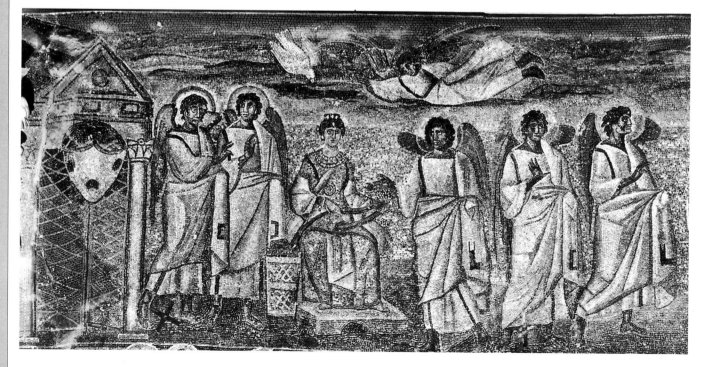

Artemis or Diana, as she was known in Rome, had stood for many centuries. The cult of Artemis had only recently been officially suppressed but still survived in practice, which prompts the question as to whether the incipient cult of the Virgin Mary was an instance of the recurrence of an ancient archetype to which Artemis–Diana, Cybele and other manifestations of the immemorial mother-goddess all belong. Early Christianity with its 'feminine' ideals of compassion and non-violence would have made such a recurrence all the more readily acceptable amid the turmoil and bloodshed of fifth-century Rome, which was more than once sacked during these years by the Vandals.

It was only after the Council of Ephesus that images of the Virgin began to proliferate. Earlier paintings are very doubtfully identified as depicting the Virgin and Child even when they occur in a Christian context as, for example, those in the Roman catacombs (p. 301). But when Sixtus III founded his great new church in Rome in the year following the Council of Ephesus he dedicated it to the Virgin, S Maria Maggiore, and great prominence was given to her in its decoration. Sixtus III's intention of glorifying her as the Virgin Mary and Mother of God are clearly shown in the mosaics on the arch over the high altar. At the Annunciation she appears enthroned and dressed in the robes of a Byzantine princess with diadem and jewels, almost as if giving an imperial audience (**7,51**). She is attended by four white-robed angels (not mentioned in the Bible). Gabriel, like a Roman symbolical figure of Victory, flies above her and the dove, symbolizing the Holy Spirit, descends on her. It is the moment of the Incarnation. On the left an aedicule with closed gate probably symbolizes her virginity. By this time the social upgrading of Mary the carpenter's wife had already taken place in written accounts. In them she was usually given rich and well-born parents and was even said, sometimes, to have been learned and well-read. Unfortunately the great apse mosaic of the Coronation of the Virgin in S Maria Maggiore was replaced in 1288–92 but it probably showed the Virgin with the Child on her knees while a hand emerged from

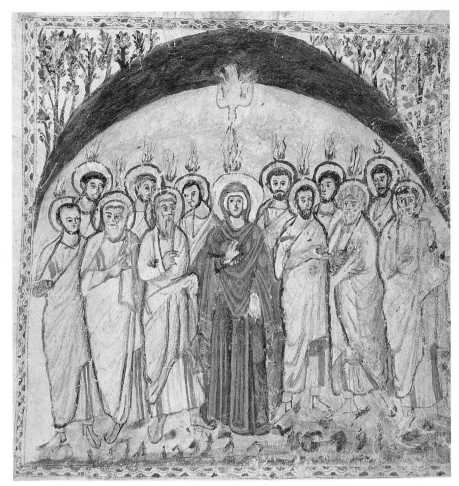

7,52 *Pentecost*, from the Rabbula Gospels (fol. 14v), AD 586. Vellum, page 13¼ × 10⅖ins (33.6 × 26.6cm). Biblioteca Medicea Laurenziana, Florence.

heaven above and held a crown over her head, as in the earliest surviving apse mosaic of only about 100 years later (**7,49**).

In AD 586 the Virgin was depicted in a set of Syriac gospels written at the monastery of St John at Zagba in Mesopotamia. Though not called for by the Bible texts she is shown in both the Ascension and Pentecost scenes very prominently, again as a dignified upper-class Roman lady, dressed in dark blue which distinguishes her from the other figures (**7,52**). In the latter scene she stands as if blessing with her right hand, surrounded by the apostles who are standing and not, as was normal, seated in a semicircle. At about the same time a similarly imposing and dignified representation of her appeared in a devotional image at Mount Sinai. She is shown with the Child as well as St Theodore and St George and two angels (**7,46**). Her role as intercessor is here made quite explicit.

The Virgin was not always shown in such an imposing way, however, although fewer examples of her other aspects are known. One of the earliest is a sixth- to seventh-century AD wall-painting from the Coptic monastery of Jeremias at Saqqara near Cairo, Egypt, in which she is depicted breast-feeding the Child. She holds her breast with her left hand while supporting the Child on her knee. The intimate humanity, even homeliness, of such paintings was much more approachable and probably had a much greater popular appeal than the learned and sophisticated mosaics and manuscript paintings mentioned above. Indeed it may well be for this reason that so few examples have survived. However, the Virgin breast-feeding the Child, or *Maria lactans* as it was known in the Church, was certainly being represented in sculpture as early as the late fourth century AD in Constantinople.

The emperor was the living symbol of divine power, Christ's viceregent on earth. A mosaic over the central door of Hagia Sophia shows Leo VI (886–912) prostrate before Christ (7,40), and a poet of the time imagined an emperor in this position saying: 'It is Thou who hast appointed me lord of Thy creatures and master of my fellow slaves, but having proved to be the slave of sin, I tremble before thy scourge, O Lord and Judge' (Joannes Mavropous, *Poems*, tr. C. Mango). All who approached the emperor were required to prostrate themselves in this way, and when they looked up they might see his throne elevated by a mechanical contrivance (Liutprand, bishop of Cremona, described this astonishing spectacle in 949). The sacred status of the ruler was displayed to a wider public by the coinage. Justinian II (685–95, 705–11) had Christ's head stamped on one side of coins and his own image holding a cross on the other (7,53). The practice was abandoned during the Iconoclastic period but was resumed immediately afterwards. A slightly later coin showed the emperor Basil I and his son holding a patriarchal cross on the front and Christ enthroned on the reverse (7,54). Emperors might, nevertheless, be regarded as no more than symbols, to be discarded and mutilated without damage to the idea they represented. In Byzantine life, as in art, divine ideas were far more important than earthly realities.

In accordance with the concept of orthodoxy, Byzantine artists of the post-Iconoclastic period began by looking back for models to the sixth century. And orthodoxy governed the subsequent development of Byzantine art, which is insistently symbolic and regulated by strict conventions. The figure of a saint had to face the spectator in order to act as a channel for prayer to his or her prototype in heaven. Biblical scenes had to conform to established iconographical norms. Gestures and perhaps even colors acquired fixed meanings. In centuries of declining wealth the size of new churches was greatly reduced, leading to the quincunx or cross-in-square plan with a small central dome and sometimes four subsidiary ones over the corners. But a uniform system of decoration was evolved to express a Byzantine church's threefold significance: as a microcosm of the celestial and terrestrial worlds, as a setting for Christ's life on earth and for the sequence of festivals in the Christian year. The conch of the apse usually signified the cave of the Nativity in Bethlehem and thus bore an image of the Virgin *Theotokos* (Mother of God). The *Pantocrator*, as we have seen, looked down from the central dome.

This art exerted continuing influence throughout Christendom. The full iconographic program was, however, limited to those regions which looked to Constantinople rather than to Rome for doctrinal authority. Orthodox Christianity became the official state religion of Bulgaria in 864 and of Russia in 988. Vladimir, prince of Kiev (980–1015), who formed his Russian kingdom on the model of the Byzantine empire, sent to Constantinople for priests to teach and baptize his subjects and for architects, mosaicists and painters to build and decorate churches. A local variant of the Byzantine style was subsequently developed in Kiev, and others emerged in the Balkans and the outlying regions of the empire itself. Despite the rigidity of its iconographical conventions and its essentially self-generating character – from an unbroken tradition stretching back to the Classical world – Byzantine art continued to develop, with a great final flowering in the late thirteenth and early fourteenth centuries (see p. 404). Constantinople held its position as a metropolis of Christian scholarship and of the arts throughout the European Middle Ages and remained the greatest and most magnificent city on the continent until, and even after, it fell to the Turks in 1453.

CHRISTIAN ART IN NORTHERN EUROPE

In the depths of the so-called 'Dark Ages' of western Europe – the 500 years or so of confusion as migrant peoples from the East swept across the continent after the collapse of Roman power in the early fifth century – there was a sudden flowering of Christian art in Ireland and in various remote and isolated islands off the coasts of north Britain. Although its origins can be traced in the history of religion and of art, nothing quite prepares us for the brilliance and suddenness of this phenomenon on the outer fringe of the world known to the Greeks and Romans. The style that was created has been called Celtic, Irish and Hiberno-Saxon, but the more general term 'Insular', which also suggests its isolation, may be preferred. Its most notable surviving products are illuminated manuscripts, among the most intricately beautiful ever painted, with a unique quality summed up by the twelfth-century writer Giraldus de Barri, who was shown one of them in Ireland, perhaps the *Book of Kells* (7,55). 'Examine it carefully and you will penetrate to the very shrine of art', he wrote. 'You will make out intricacies so delicate and subtle, so concise and compact, so full of knots and links, with colors so fresh and vivid, that you might think all this was the work of an angel, not a man.'

Christianity, which had been introduced into England during the Roman occupation, did not long survive the withdrawal of the last legions in 407 and the subsequent invasions by Angles, Saxons, Jutes and Frisians across the North Sea. About the same time, however, the conversion of Ireland began and was largely effected before the death of the great missionary St Patrick (the traditional date is 461). Christianity was spread among a large rural

7,53 Solidus of Justinian II (first reign AD 685–95). British Museum, London.

7,54 Solidus of Basil I (AD 869–79). British Museum, London.

population from monastic communities in the open country, like those of Syria and Egypt, on which they may have been modelled. In the sixth century similar monasteries were established by Irish monks elsewhere as missionary stations, from the island of Iona off the west coast of Scotland, right across Europe to Bobbio in Italy. In 634 monks from Iona were given the island of Lindisfarne, which was to become one of the most important centres of religious thought and art in Britain.

In the meantime a mission sent direct from Rome in 597 had begun work in the Anglo-Saxon south of England, and gradually moved towards the north. Since the Irish Church had developed practices different from those of Rome, a clash was inevitable when the two groups of missionaries met. The schism was resolved at the Synod of Whitby (644), after which all England came under the spiritual rule of Rome, and the effect on every aspect of monastic life, including art and architecture, was soon felt. St Benedict Biscop, who founded two monasteries at Jarrow and Wearmouth in County Durham in 674 and 682, called in stone-masons from France 'to build him a church of stone after the Roman fashion which he always loved' – as his pupil the Venerable Bede tells us. Parts of both buildings survive with massive walls and small round-headed windows set rather high. Bede also records that Biscop brought back many paintings from Rome, 'in order that all men who entered the church, even if they might not read, should either look (whatsoever way they turned) upon the gracious countenance of Christ and His Saints, though it were but in a picture; or might call to mind a more lively sense of the blessing of the Lord's Incarnation'. However, this Mediterranean Classical influence did not penetrate very deeply; the *Codex Amiatinus* illuminated at Jarrow (**7,56**) is the only surviving example. Native artistic traditions were too strong. Indeed, they took on a new lease of exuberant life in the great Insular style illuminated manuscripts, the first of which were produced in the late seventh century.

INTERLACE AND ILLUMINATION

When St Columba was asked whether Irish poets should be allowed to go on composing ballads in the vernacular, he agreed that they should. Similar licence seems to have been given to metal-workers, the most notable artists of the time, who went on using ornamental motifs which had formerly been – and perhaps still were – credited with supernatural powers. A local variant of the Celtic 'La Tène' style (see p. 162) lived on in Ireland. A latchet for fastening clothes, cast in bronze and originally inlaid with enamels, illustrates the skill of Irish craftsmen (**7,57**). The main motif on the disc is one much favoured in Celtic art, a *triskele*: three 'legs' issuing from a single point, each one curling round and dividing into spirals, the larger of which terminates in a bird's head, the smaller in a kind of comma. Similar spiralling lines, sometimes ending in animal heads, embellish the capital letters of the earliest known Irish manuscripts dating from about 600 (e.g. the *Cathach of Saint Columba*, Royal Irish Academy, Dublin). They

also appear in more elaborate manuscripts in the mature Insular style, such as the *Lindisfarne Gospels* (**7,58**). On the page illustrated here the border is composed of strange birds knotted together by ribbons, which pass from the wing feathers of one to the neck of the next. More knots are within the frame, each in a square compartment, also arrangements of squares and panels in a stepped pattern. In the lay-out of this page there may be some reminiscence of the mosaic pavements in Romano-British villas, some of which incorporated crosses and other Christian symbols in their designs. But the general effect is closer to jewelry made for the migrant peoples who flooded into Europe from the east as the Roman troops withdrew. A gold bracelet inlaid with garnets (from India) and colored glass (perhaps from Syria) has, like the pages of the *Lindisfarne Gospels*, panels of rectangular stepped patterns surrounded by intertwined creatures, which seem, in turn, to be remotely derived from the prehistoric Animal style of central Asia (see p. 159) (**7,59**). This remarkable object was found at Sutton Hoo on the east coast of England, in a ship buried under a mound as a memorial to some East Anglian king of the mid-seventh century. Gold coins minted by the Merovingian kings of Gaul and many pieces of silver including a large Byzantine bowl were also found at Sutton Hoo – an indication that northern Europe was by no means cut off from the rest of the world at this date. In a burial of the same period at Helg in Sweden a bronze statuette of the Buddha was found (Historical Museum, Stockholm)!

Various origins have been proposed for the knotwork or interlace pattern which fills so many pages of the *Lindisfarne Gospels* and other Insular manuscripts. Similar devices are found in the arts of Coptic (i.e. Christian) Egypt from the fifth to the ninth century, and there may well have been a direct connection. (Bowls made in Alexandria were buried in non-Christian graves in England: and Irish monks seem to have had direct contacts with Egyptian monasteries.) But interlace occurs in the arts of many cultures, especially in the North, where it was as pervasive as leaf ornament in the Mediterranean. In Scandinavia, patterns of plaited and coiled ropes and thongs were applied to grave-stones, jewelry, weapons and the carved prows of the ships from which the Vikings – 'people of the inlets' – harried the coasts of northern Europe from the eighth to the eleventh century (**7,60**). The contrast between the interlace pattern and the form it decorates is often very striking, as here or when carved on stone crosses set up in Ireland, Scotland and the north of England, e.g. Bewcastle (**7,61**). Whether interlace had any meaning is not known; it has been suggested that it may have been a charm against evil spirits credited with a human desire to unravel the knots. Nowhere was it used to better artistic effect, however, than in Insular manuscripts. A single strand may be followed as it winds its way backwards and forwards all round a page of the *Lindisfarne Gospels*, weaving a kind of seamless fabric with no loose ends. To paint such a design, clearly indicating at each of several thousand points the over-and-under passage of the thread, was an exercise in patience as demanding as

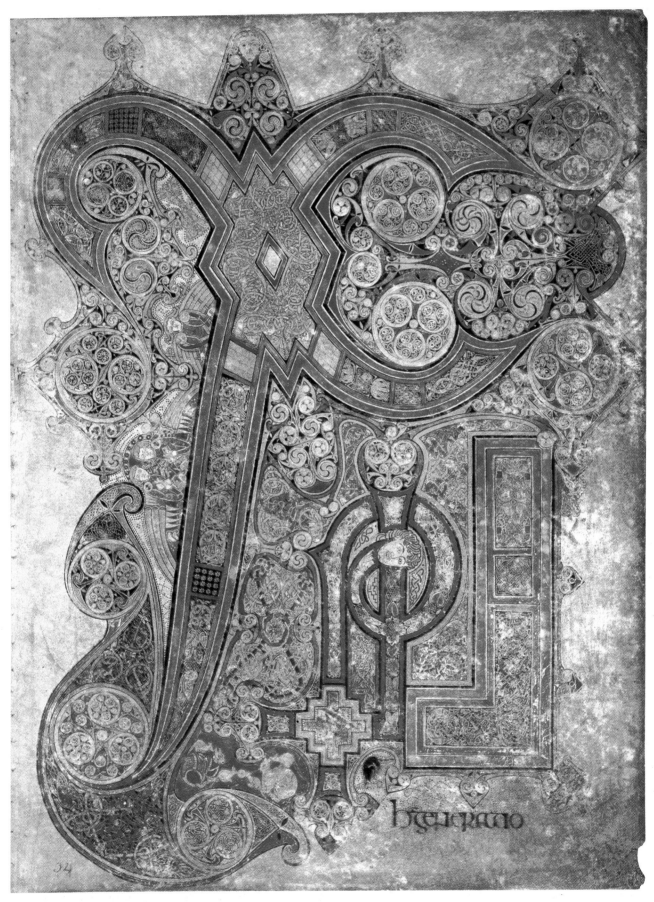

7,55 Incarnation initial from the *Book of Kells* (fol. 34), early 9th century AD. Vellum, 13 × 10ins (33 × 25cm). Trinity College Library, Dublin.

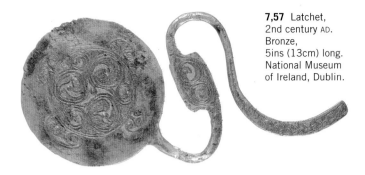

7,57 Latchet, 2nd century AD. Bronze, 5ins (13cm) long. National Museum of Ireland, Dublin.

7,58 *Below* Carpet-page with cross, from the *Lindisfarne Gospels* (fol. 2v), before AD 698. Vellum, 13½ × 9¾ins (34.3 × 24.8cm). British Library, London.

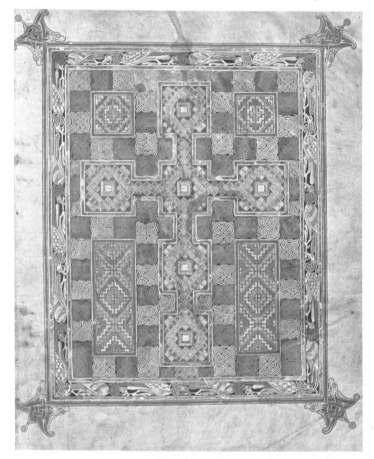

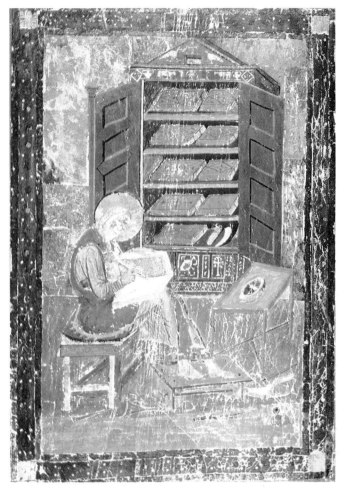

7,56 *The Prophet Ezra rewriting the Sacred Records*, from the *Codex Amiatinus* (fol. Vr), Jarrow, early 8th century. Vellum, about 14 × 10ins (35.6 × 25.4cm). Biblioteca Medicea Laurenziana, Florence.

the more physically strenuous feats of endurance that monks imposed on themselves for the mortification of the flesh and the benefit of the soul. The immense expenditure of time and skill on each decorated page and on the meticulous copying of the Gospel text was an act of service to God.

The scribe and illuminator of the *Lindisfarne Gospels*, Eadfrith, bishop of Lindisfarne (698–721), must have taken his text from an Italian manuscript illustrated with images of the evangelists similar to those so carefully copied at Jarrow (7,56). But Eadfrith ignored all the illusionistic devices of these pictures when he came to his evangelist portrait pages, reducing his figures schematically almost to patterns of flat colors. He lavished attention on the abstract decoration of the so-called carpet-pages placed before each Gospel (7,58). These pages, on which the sign of the cross is elaborated and set in a no less rich background with all the convolutions and near repetitions of a Gregorian chant, are peculiar to Insular manuscripts. The earliest known are those in the *Book of Durrow* dating from about 680 (Trinity College Library, Dublin). They are not illustrations but, like bookbindings embellished with precious materials, earthly

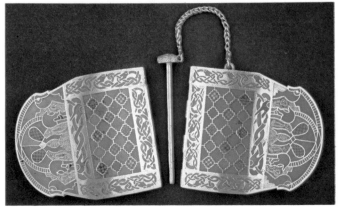

7,59 Hinged clasp from the Sutton Hoo ship burial, 7th century AD. Gold decorated with garnets, mosaic, glass and filigree. British Museum, London.

pointers to the otherworldly, spiritual beauty and significance of the text.

The other innovation made by Insular manuscript illuminators was the elaboration of capital letters into configurations of labyrinthine complexity, which culminated in the *Book of Kells*, inscribed and decorated by monks of the Iona community very shortly before the island was sacked by Vikings in 807 or immediately after they found refuge in central Ireland. An enriched capital letter marks the beginning of each brief passage of the four Gospels, setting off one or more verses for meditation and study. There are more than 2,000 in all, differing widely in the ways they are formed, colored, gilded and filled with interlace. At the opening of St Matthew's account of the Nativity a whole page is devoted to the *Chi-Rho* monogram (7,55). This is a far cry from the austere symbol of Early Christian art (7,1). It appeals to the eye and to the senses as well as the intellect, whereas the other had engaged the mind alone. The eye is enthralled by the impenetrable subtleties of tight scrolls, intricate knots and whirling *triskeles* within the expansively sweeping curves of the design. The attention is caught by angels on the outer face of the great X, by a man's head in the P, and surprised by vividly depicted animals at the base: an otter with a salmon and a group of cats and mice. The page celebrates the Incarnation with a painting as rich as the finest goldsmiths' work, perhaps conceived as the artist's

7,60 Animal head from the Oseberg ship burial, c. AD 825. Wood, about 5ins (12.7cm) high. Universitetets Oldsaksamling, Oslo.

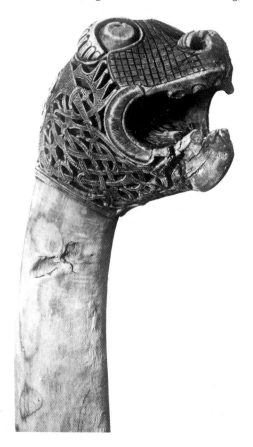

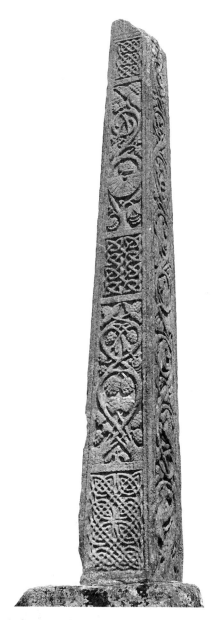

7,61 Bewcastle Cross, late 7th century AD. Stone, 14ft 6ins (4.42m) high above the pedestal. Bewcastle, Cumbria, England.

equivalent to the precious gifts brought to the Christ Child by the Wise Men from the East. There is, indeed, something almost Orientally luxuriant about it. Yet it is essentially Northern, a supreme example of a style that provided a valid alternative to the Classical still being promoted by the Church in Rome.

CHRISTIAN ART IN WESTERN EUROPE

Christian art in continental Europe had remained bound to its Classical origins. The art of the Teutonic peoples who swept across the former Western empire in the Migration Period – as the fifth and sixth centuries are sometimes called – adopted Italian and Byzantine prototypes after they settled and were converted to Christianity. Under the Franks, who occupied Gaul (later called France after them), the style established for church-building in

Roman times was continued without a break, fostered no doubt by the many ecclesiastics who were descended from the old imperial aristocracy; similarly in Spain, under the Visigoths, who ruled Spain from the early sixth century until they were overcome by the Arabs in 711 (see p.344). In Italy local traditions persisted, though often modified by influence from Byzantium. As we have already seen (p. 311), some of the finest buildings at Ravenna date from the years when the city was the capital of the Ostrogothic king, Theodoric. The peninsula was won back for the Eastern empire between 535 and 563 but was again invaded in 568 by the Lombards, another Germanic people, who set up a kingdom with its capital at Pavia in the Po valley, not far from Milan. Churches continued to be built under their rule, but they were small in size, for here, as in the rest of Europe, funds were limited. Decorations were, perforce, executed in stucco and paint rather than the more expensive and durable media of marble and mosaic. Only because it was walled up for centuries has a stucco frieze been preserved intact in the little church of S Maria in Valle, Cividale, probably built between 762 and 776 (though later dates have sometimes been proposed). Six larger than life-size figures of female saints of a truly Classical serenity and a severe elegance flank an arch springing from debased Corinthian columns and decorated with interlace (**7,62**). They are lonely

7,62 Three saints, c. AD 770. Stucco reliefs, over-life-size. S Maria in Valle, Cividale.

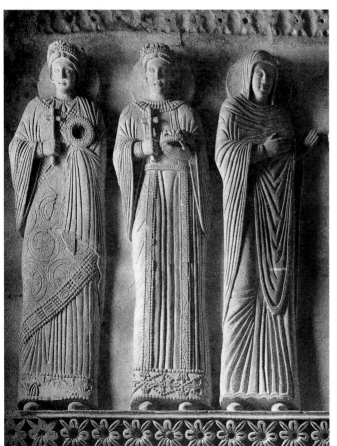

survivors from the Dark Ages in Italy. How far they were typical is impossible to say. Recently discovered frescoes at Castelseprio, near Milan, may date from as early as the eighth century and are Byzantinizing in style (**7,63**).

The survival of a basically Classical language of Christian art was, perhaps, connected with the retention of Latin as the language of the liturgy and theological writing, even though it became increasingly foreign to the vast majority of Christians north of the Alps. In the course of more than three centuries the corruption of Latin was aggravated and not until after Charlemagne (c. 771–814) had become king of the Franks in 771 was any serious effort for reform initiated.

THE CAROLINGIAN *RENOVATIO*

Charlemagne inherited a realm which covered, in modern terms, much of Germany, most of the Netherlands, the whole of Belgium and Switzerland and nearly all France. To this he added the Lombard kingdom of Italy, as far south as Rome, further territory in Germany and Austria, and rather less on the borders of Islamic Spain. Essentially a man of action, Charlemagne nevertheless patronized scholarship and the arts on a lavish scale unprecedented in northern Europe. Although his native language was German, he recognized the value of Latin for official as well as for religious use throughout his dominions, and he learned to speak it fluently. He also came to appreciate the value of literacy. He tried to learn to write, his friend and adviser Einhard tells us: 'He tried very hard, but had begun too late in life and made little progress.' From Italy and elsewhere he gathered to his court many of the most learned men of the day with the main purpose of schooling a civil service of clerics – priests and monks, who were also clerks in the modern sense. At his instigation they restored Latin as a literary language, purged it of barbarous usages, revised its spelling and devised a beautifully clear script in which official documents could be written. This involved the study and copying of Classical texts and it is to the Carolingian scribes that we owe the preservation of a very large proportion of Latin poetry and prose, including Vitruvius' treatise on architecture (see p. 192). When the manuscripts were rediscovered some six centuries later (i.e. in the early Renaissance), the script in which they were written, technically known as Carolingian minuscule, was revised and adopted by printers for lower-case letters – the lower-case type that we still use to this day, as in this book. (The ancient Roman alphabet had consisted of capital letters only.)

The restoration of Latin to its Classical clarity and elegance was accompanied by an attempt to reform the visual arts. This is often described as a renaissance of Classical antiquity; but the word used in Charlemagne's circle, *renovatio*, implied the renovation of a surviving tradition rather than the rebirth of one that had died out. Thus it was S Vitale in Ravenna, with its domed octagonal central space, that seems to have provided the model for the Palatine (imperial palace) Chapel at Aachen, Charlemagne's favourite residence in his later years (**7,64; 65;**

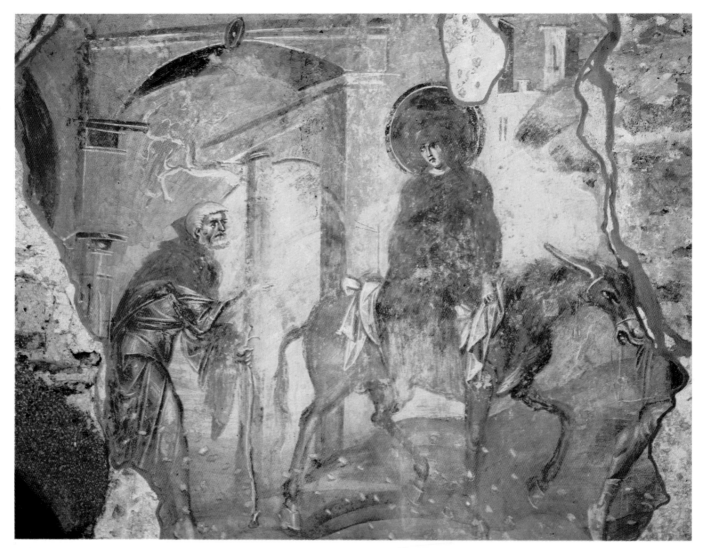

7,63 *The Virgin Mary and St Joseph on the Way to Bethlehem*, detail of fresco, 8th to 10th century AD. S Maria Foris Portas, Castelseprio.

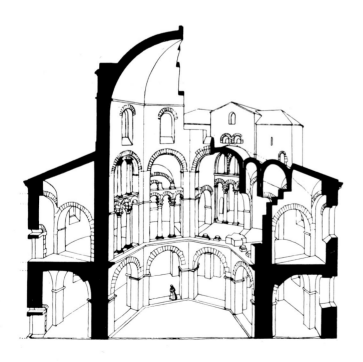

7,64 *Left* Axonometric reconstruction of Palatine Chapel, Aachen, Germany.

7,65 Plan of Palatine Chapel.

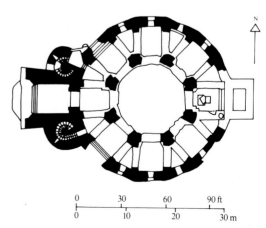

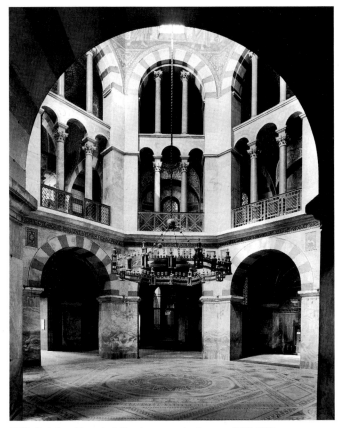

7,66 Palatine Chapel of Charlemagne, Aachen, AD 792–805.

7,67 Monastery gateway, AD 768–74. Lorsch, Germany.

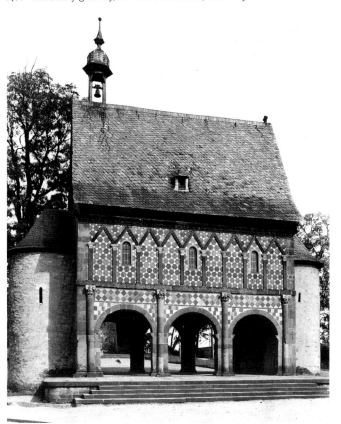

SOURCES AND DOCUMENTS

EINHARD ON THE PALATINE CHAPEL

Einhard (c. 771–840) was sent to Aachen by the bishop of Fulda when he was about 20 and became an influential member of Charlemagne's court. He was entrusted with the emperor's buildings, including the Palatine Chapel, and other works. His portrait of Charlemagne in his *Vita Karoli Magni* is outstanding among medieval biographies.

The Christian religion, in which he had been brought up from infancy, was held by Karl [Charlemagne] as most sacred and he worshipped in it with the greatest piety. For this reason he built at Aachen a most beautiful church, which he enriched with gold and silver and candlesticks, and also with lattices and doors of solid brass. When columns and marbles for the building could not be obtained from elsewhere, he had them brought from Rome and Ravenna.

As long as his health permitted, he was most regular in attending the church at matins and evensong, and also during the night, and at the time of the Sacrifice; and he took especial care that all the services of the church should be performed in the most fitting manner possible, frequently cautioning the sacristans not to allow anything improper or unseemly to be brought into, or left in, the building.

He provided for the church an abundance of sacred vessels of gold and silver and priestly vestments, so that when the service was celebrated, it was not necessary even for the doorkeepers, who are the lowest order of ecclesiastics, to perform their duties in private dress. He carefully revised the order of reading and singing, being well skilled in both, though he did not read in public, nor sing, except in a low voice and only in the chorus.

(Einhard, *Life of Emperor Karl the Great*, tr. W. Glaister, London 1877)

66). Polished granite and marble columns with finely carved Corinthian capitals were brought to Aachen from Italy, some of them from Ravenna. Yet there are some striking differences between the two buildings.

The Palatine Chapel, designed by a Frankish architect, Odo of Metz, has little of S Vitale's spatial subtlety and air of mystery. It is more massive; space is constricted and the vertical axis is felt more strongly than the horizontal. The sturdiness of the piers supporting the dome is emphasized and columns are used decoratively rather than structurally (most obviously those fitted rather awkwardly into the openings of the upper gallery), as they are on the exterior of the gatehouse or guesthouse of one of Charlemagne's favourite monasteries, Lorsch in the Rhineland

Monasticism

EAST AND WEST

Christian monasticism, which culminated architecturally in such imposing buildings as the abbeys of St Gall and Cluny, began in the fourth century. But it had been preceded by many centuries in India where a deeply religious inner compulsion for self-denial, still seen today in the Indian *fakir*, was evident among Brahmin ascetics of the Vedic period (1500–800 BC). The Buddha's search for enlightenment began with his joining such ascetics and he left instructions for his followers who wanted to become monks or nuns. The earliest surviving Buddhist monasteries are rock-cut, as at Bhaja (c. 250 BC) and Karli (6,8; 9). From India monasticism spread north to central Asia and China where monasteries are often misleadingly called grottoes or caves; many of them are outstanding for their paintings and sculptures.

Christian monasticism originated in Egypt. It had its roots in the Gospels and St Paul's teaching on celibacy which, with fasting, prayer and poverty, was essential for an ascetic Christian life. Egyptian monks were hermits living in huts or caves in the desert, but early in the fourth century some moved together to share a communal church and refectory, without abandoning their individual huts. Such monks are called coenobites and by the mid-fourth century there were coenobitic monasteries for both monks and nuns all over the eastern part of the Roman empire. Soon they spread to Italy and later further west and north. But up to the time of St Benedict, monasticism remained an eastern importation, marked by the austerities of its desert origin.

In about 520 St Benedict of Nursia (c. 480–c. 547) founded a monastery at Montecassino, north of Naples – a highly successful religious house which still stands despite periodic destruction, the last time by the Allies in 1944 (rebuilt 1950–7). Western monasticism and its architecture developed as an expression of the Rule of St Benedict, which he

wrote to regulate life at Montecassino. The plan for St Gall made by a cleric of Cologne in about 820 is the prime example (7,69). Here we have all the main elements: a clearly defined axial lay-out with regular placement and coordination of buildings within a walled enclosure. The dormitory for sleeping and refectory for meals are alongside the cloister and form a nucleus with the abbey church and chapter house which often occupied a ground floor with dormitory above. The abbot or prior usually had his quarters at the west; the infirmary was to the east; and there would be several other buildings – guesthouse, kitchen, brewhouse, bakery, smithy, library and *scriptorium* for the copying of books, printing not having been as yet introduced in the West. This plan was followed approximately at Montecassino when abbot Desiderius carried out his great building program in 1066–75 and although nothing remains it can be reliably reconstructed on paper (7,68). The main difference between it and St Gall would seem to have been the church; that at Montecassino was taken from Old St Peter's in Rome with its monumental stairs, atrium or forecourt and T-shaped basilica with a single aisle on each side. The Benedictines were the most active builders in the eleventh to twelfth century and the rich decorations they introduced into their abbeys towards the end of that period gave sculpture its first strong impetus since late antiquity

as, for example, at Autun with Gislebertus (9,26).

St Benedict's strictly hierarchical system, so well reflected in architecture, regulated every hour of a monk's or nun's life, beginning at 2 o'clock in the morning with the chanting of psalms. Monks and nuns took vows of obedience, chastity and poverty and under St Benedict's Rule could not leave one monastery for another, each monastery being self-governing and self-contained. They were bound together into a permanent family, united by bonds that lasted for life. Religious observance with seven daily services was the centre of Benedictine life but it occupied only a third of the day; the rest was taken up with meals, sleep and recreation and, for the remaining third, work. This was at first manual labour in the fields but might also include work in the *scriptorium* where the great Benedictine illuminated manuscripts were made, for example the *Montecassino Homilies* by the eleventh-century monk Leo which are still in the library at Montecassino.

However, the Benedictine monasteries tended to become lax and corrupt as they expanded over central Europe and accumulated property, especially land. Around 1200 they had about 1,500 establishments. In 1098 the Cistercian Order was founded to reform Cluny (see pp. 374–8), and there were to be many further attempts to return to the simplicity of St Benedict's Rule.

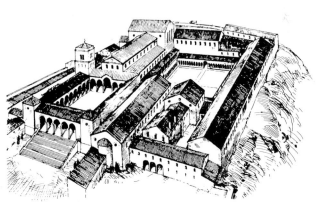

7,68 Montecassino Abbey, restoration study as in 1075 (K. J. Conant).

(7,67). Some of the differences between the two buildings are due simply to the technique of construction: rubble faced with marble for the piers and solid stone for the vaults instead of the light brick and terracotta used at Ravenna. Others were determined by function. Charlemagne's throne was placed in the first gallery above the door and looked down across the central space to the main altar in a small square apse (later replaced by a Gothic choir). This part of the building was strongly marked externally by what is called a westwork, a porch at ground level surmounted by the large recessed windows of a chapel, open towards the nave inside, and flanked by towers enclosing staircases for access to the galleries. The westwork, one of the most influential innovations in Carolingian church architecture, perhaps derived from Roman city gateways, which had come to symbolize imperial authority – e.g. Trier less than 100 miles (160km) south of Aachen (5,75). An example of 873–85 survives in relatively well-preserved form at Corvey-on-the-Weser and another at St Pantaleon, Cologne, of about 980 (9,4).

The Palatine Chapel is the only great Carolingian building to have been preserved, but the important developments made to the basilican form in Charlemagne's monastic foundations are known from descriptions and other records, notably those of the abbey church of Centula (St Riquier, France) of 790–9. This was a revolutionary building in both plan and elevation, having a westwork, nave and aisle, transepts, a chancel and an apse, with towers over the west and east crossings flanked by round towers, some impression of which can be obtained only from later buildings such as the late eleventh-century abbey church at Maria Laach (9,32). A plan of about 820 for the monastery of St Gall, Switzerland, followed the basilican innovations at Centula, but is of greater significance for the systematic and orderly manner in which

the monastic buildings are laid out according to St Benedict's rule (7,69) – very different from the higgledy-piggledy arrangements at earlier monasteries in Egypt and Ireland. It was to be very influential.

While the Palatine Chapel was being built Charlemagne was crowned emperor by Pope Leo III in St Peter's in Rome, on Christmas Day 800. He was recorded in lists of emperors as the 68th in succession from Augustus. (Not until much later was he to be seen as the first ruler of a new Holy Roman Empire.) He assumed the guardianship of the Roman Church and, on at least one occasion, intervened in the controversies of the Eastern Church. When in 787, during a lull in the Iconoclastic controversy (see p. 323), a council summoned by the Byzantine emperor and the patriarch at Nicaea worked out a guarded formula permitting images to be honoured, Charlemagne protested at what had been 'arrogantly done in Greece'. His theologians were instructed to draw up a counter-statement, the 'Caroline Books', denying that images could be more than reminders 'of things that have happened'.

DEVELOPMENTS IN CHRISTIAN IMAGERY

Of several manuscripts contemporary with Charlemagne, the most interesting is the *Coronation Gospels* – so-called because it was used from the eleventh century onwards at the coronation of Holy Roman Emperors. The text is written in gold and silver on parchment colored with the purple dye reserved for imperial use in the East. A Greek name, possibly that of the scribe or illuminator, appears in one of the margins; but the four 'portraits' of evangelists, which are its only figurative decorations, have little in common with Byzantine art. The artist responsible for the St John (7,70) had clearly studied illustrated manuscripts like the early fifth-century Virgil (7,26) or the sixth-century original of the *Codex Amiatinus* (7,56). He even indulged in a little illusionistic trick, projecting the footstool in front of the substantially modelled frame.

Were it not for his halo, St John might be mistaken for some staid Roman writer pondering his next periphrastic sentence. An entirely different impression is given by the image of St Mark in a Gospel manuscript made for Ebbo, imperial librarian and, from 816 to 835, archbishop of Reims (7,71). The furniture is more obviously Roman, with a lion monopod support for the throne, but it has been wrenched out of all semblance of perspective. The head is fully modelled with effective use of shade and highlights, but the expression is ecstatic. As he dips his pen in an inkwell, the evangelist gazes anxiously towards his symbol, tense with emotion that makes his hair bristle and vibrates through the trembling folds of his clothing. Behind him the landscape heaves up as if in sympathy. The solid and tranquil Classical ideals so eloquently expressed in the *Coronation Gospels* have been completely abandoned in the quest for a more vividly expressive visual language. The so-called *Utrecht Psalter* of c. 820–32, also by artists associated with Reims, was probably based on a fifth-century model; the lettering is stolidly Roman too, but the agitated little figures drawn

7,69 Plan of the monastery of St Gall, Switzerland, c. AD 820.

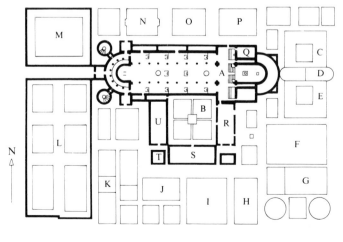

A Church	H Barn	O School
B Cloister	I Workshops	P Abbot's House
C Infirmary	J Brewery and Bakery	Q Scriptorium and Library
D Chapel	K Stables	R Dormitory
E Novitiate	L Animal Pens	S Refectory
F Orchard/Cemetery	M Hostel	T Kitchens
G Garden	N Guest House	U Cellars

with flickering pen-strokes have a highly-strung nervous energy that is unprecedented (**7,72**). Similar tendencies were noted in literature. In the 830s Lupus of Ferrières, one of the greatest Classical scholars of the time, lamented to Einhard that writers had begun to 'stray from that dignity of Cicero and the other classics which the best of Christian writers sought to imitate'.

The *Coronation Gospels* illustrate Carolingian art at its most Classical. But perhaps the clearest indication of the desire to recapture the purity of Early Christian art is provided by ivory carvings modelled on those of the late fourth century, which (as we have seen, p. 309) reverted to the style of earlier pagan art just when St Augustine was striving to emulate the gravity of Ciceronian prose. Because of this there has been much controversy as to whether certain ivories date from the late fourth or the late eighth century. An exceptionally large panel inset in a book-binding (**7,73**) is framed by bands of acanthus ornament as delicate and crisp as any carved in ancient Roman times; but the subject-matter and the expressiveness of the figures indicate a later date. At the top the hand of God reaches down from heaven between Apollo and Diana in their chariots symbolizing the sun and moon. The Crucifixion is shown below, then the visit of the holy women to the sepulchre, and in the lowest register the resurrection of the saints, which, according to St Matthew, followed the Crucifixion – 'and the graves were opened and many bodies of the saints which slept arose'.

7,70 *Saint John*, from the *Coronation Gospels* (fol. 178v), late 8th century AD. Parchment, 12¾ × 10ins (32.4 × 24.9cm). Weltliche Schatzkammer, Vienna.

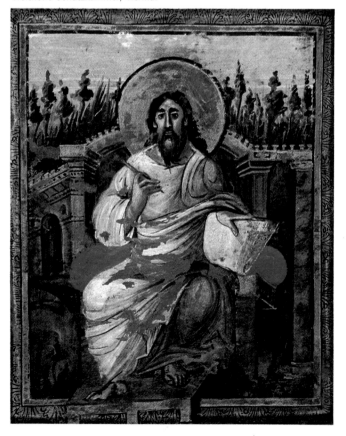

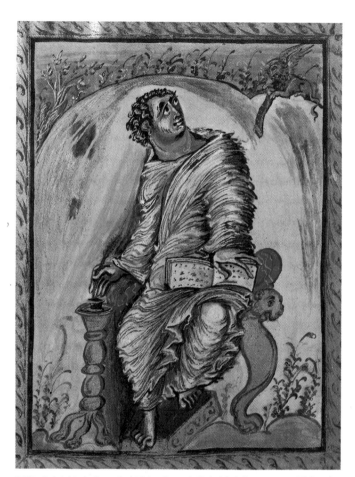

7,71 *Saint Mark*, from the *Ebbo Gospels* (fol. 18v), between AD 816 and 835. Parchment, about 10 × 8ins (25.4 × 20.3cm). Bibliothèque Municipal, Epernay.

The Crucifixion, which had been rare in Early Christian art, dominates this panel and others of the period. Why it now assumed the importance that it was to have in later European art is a question that permits no simple answer. In the earliest known examples (e.g. on the wooden door of S Sabina, Rome, 432–40) Christ's head is erect and his eyes are open. There is no suggestion of agony, or even of death. On the Carolingian ivory, on the other hand, the body is racked and the head slumped on one shoulder. These two types coexisted, the one emphasizing Christ's victory over death, which had dominated the thought of the early Christians, the other his suffering for the sins of humankind, which gradually acquired equal importance, especially in the Western Church, where the fear of sin overshadowed that of death. In the East images of the suffering Christ were always to be more ritualistic than those in the West, due to differences between Eastern and Western attitudes to religious art. Pope Gregory I (590–604) wrote to a bishop who had destroyed images to prevent them from being worshipped idolatrously: 'To adore images is one thing; to teach with their help what should be adored is another.' And he went on: 'What scripture is to the educated, images are to the ignorant, who see through them what they must accept; they read in them what they cannot read in books.' His

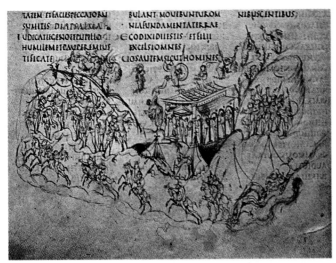

7,72 *Angels of the Lord smiting the Enemies of the Israelites*, from the *Utrecht Psalter*, c. AD 820–32. Illumination 4¾ins (12cm) wide. University Library, Utrecht, The Netherlands (MS 32 fol. 48v).

letter, which was frequently quoted in later periods and underlies the 'Caroline Books', provided the basis of a predominantly didactic theory of religious art in the West distinct from the beliefs of both the Iconodules and the Iconoclasts in the East. Western art thus became increasingly illustrative. The aim of such an ivory as that of the Crucifixion was to assist the believer in visualizing the event. Surrounding figures vividly express the tragic pathos of the scene, and below we sense the wonder of the holy women learning of Christ's resurrection, the joy of the saved leaping from the grave. In the eleventh century the relief was set in the book-binding and surrounded with Byzantine enamel plaques of Christ and the apostles staring straight ahead to act as intermediaries between their heavenly prototype and the worshipper. The two entirely different purposes of Christian images, illustrative and devotional, Carolingian and Byzantine, are here combined, almost as if in deliberate contrast.

The need for reminders, rather than objects of devotion, set a premium on narrative. Visual storytelling had, of course, an additional importance for a laity that was almost entirely illiterate (unlike that of Byzantium or the early Church in Italy). Charlemagne is known to have

7,73 *The Crucifixion, Visit of the Holy Women to the Sepulchre, and Resurrection of the Saints*, c. 820–30. Ivory on book-cover of the *Pericopes* of Henry II, early 11th century AD. Gold, enamels, gems and pearls, 16⅔ × 12½ins (42.3 × 31.5cm). Bayerische Staatsbibliothek, Munich (MS Clm. 4452).

7,74 Scenes from the *Life of St Ambrose*, c. AD 850. Silver, partly gilt, whole panel 33½ × 86½ins (85 × 220cm). S Ambrogio, Milan.

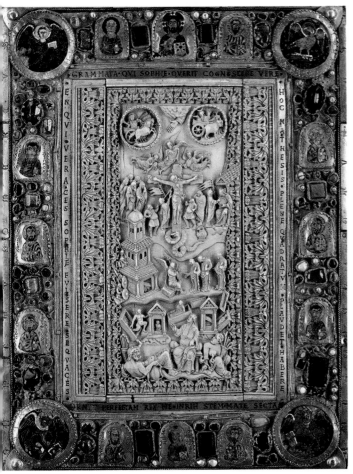

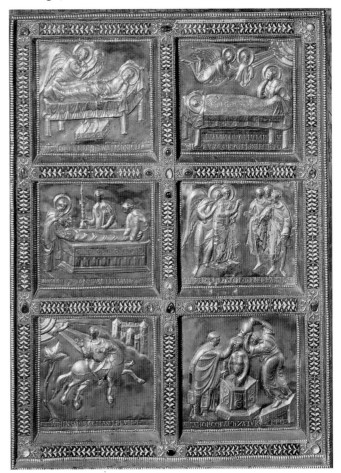

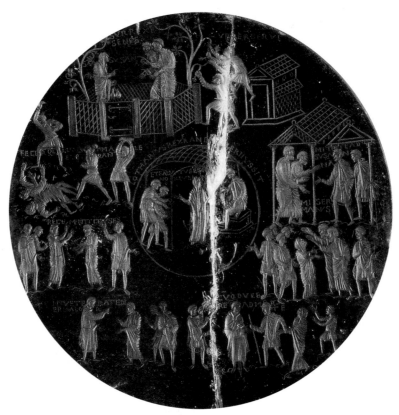

7,75 The Lothar Crystal, AD 865(?). Rock-crystal, 4⅛ins (10.5cm) diameter. British Museum, London.

encouraged the painting of Biblical scenes in churches for didactic purposes, though only a few damaged fragments survive. Narrative illustrations were given increasing prominence in Bibles. They were included even in a manuscript of the Psalms, which themselves have no narrative content (7,72). They were executed in all available media. The Biblical story of Susanna falsely accused and finally vindicated was illustrated with tiny, vivaciously gesturing figures engraved on a disc of rock-crystal for King Lothar II of Lotharingia (modern Lorraine in France) (**7,75**). Nor was the subject-matter of religious art any longer limited to the Old and New Testaments. Scenes from the lives of more recent saints were also represented, the earliest surviving example of a complete cycle being that devoted to St Ambrose on the back of the magnificent gold and silver altar in S Ambrogio in Milan (**7,74**).

In the course of the ninth century, however, artists began to abandon the logical construction of their Classical models in favour of a new pictorial language of gestures and poses, one that gave greater importance to inner emotions and permitted the expression of profound spiritual ideas within a formal or decorative idiom. This was to be their major contribution to the later art of western Europe. In the feverish penmanship of the *Ebbo Gospels* (7,71), the *Utrecht Psalter* (7,72) and the exquisite engraving on the Lothar Crystal (7,75) the solid forms of Classical art almost seem to be dissolving into the intricate abstract embellishments of Insular manuscripts. But this spiritualizing tendency did not find release in great works of art on a large scale until after Europe had emerged from another century of conflict, which marked the end of the Dark Ages.

In the great hall of the Palace at Ingelheim, completed for Charlemagne's son Louis the Pious, one wall was painted with images of Cyrus, emperor of Persia, Romulus and Remus, founders of Rome, Alexander the Great and Hannibal. On the other side, so a description of 835–6 tells us, were the emperors Constantine, Theodosius, and Charlemagne with his father and grandfather. It is in this context that Charlemagne is best understood, as the last great ruler of the ancient world. The empire he built was less like the Holy Roman Empire it was to become in the later Middle Ages, with its elaborate structure of vassalage, than that of Alexander – and it fell apart nearly as quickly. In the history of art the Carolingian period similarly marks the end of the ancient world, the swansong of the Classical tradition. But Charlemagne had succeeded in shifting the centre of Western culture and civilization from the Mediterranean to the triangle bounded by the Rhine, the Loire and the North Sea – where it was to remain for the next 600 years, until the Italian Renaissance.

CHAPTER EIGHT

EARLY ISLAMIC ART

The Arabic words from which 'Islam' and 'Muslim' are derived mean 'submission' and 'one who has submitted' – to the will of Allah, the One and Only God, as revealed by the Prophet Muhammad (d. 632) in the *Qur'an*, or Koran as it is usually rendered in English. To the inhabitants of the Near East and the southern shores of the Mediterranean in the seventh century, Islam also meant submission to the armies that had precipitately burst out of the Arabian peninsula – an area less barren in prehistoric times but now an enormous desert – and from there conquered with amazing rapidity a very large section of the Hellenized Orient. Architects, painters and craftsmen in this huge area, formerly part of the Roman, Byzantine and Sassanian empires, were obliged to submit to the demands of Arab patrons, for whom a new artistic style was gradually evolved out of conflicting Near Eastern, Hellenistic and Roman traditions.

Early Muslim attitudes to the visual arts were indeterminate, conditioned as much by opposition to those of other religious faiths as by any positive desire to find artistic forms to embody their own beliefs. In contrast to all others, theirs was to be a religious art entirely without holy images. Even visual symbols were avoided – the crescent moon was a very late introduction, a heraldic device adopted by the Turks in the sixteenth century, which only later acquired religious significance, mainly in the eyes of non-Muslims. The only specifically religious elements in Islamic art are inscriptions, and Islamic art became, partly for this reason, essentially an art of signs and not of symbols or images. Calligraphy itself was more highly cultivated in Islam than anywhere outside China and Japan, and it determined more than just the fluid linearity of Islamic decoration. Yet the inscribed texts, which appear on buildings and all manner of objects in metalwork, ivory, glass, pottery and textiles as well as in manuscripts of the holy book itself (**8,1**), constantly remind the faithful that the word of God is the only reality in an ephemeral world and, by implication, that all the works of man, including works of art, are vain.

Islam has been described by the French anthropologist Claude Lévi-Strauss as the third of mankind's 'major religious attempts to free itself from persecution by the dead, the malevolence of the beyond and the anguish of magic'. Like Buddhism and Christianity in their early stages, it

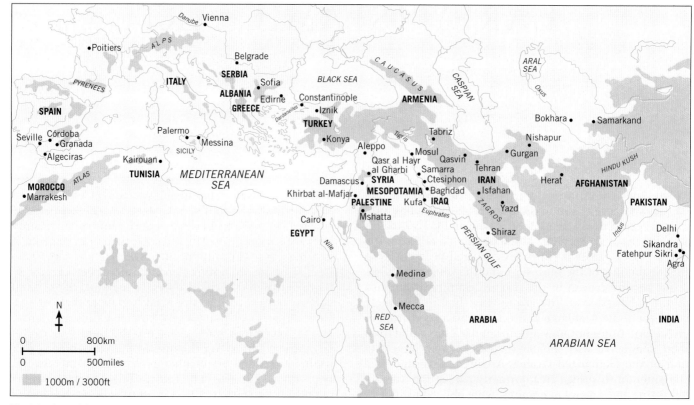

The Islamic world

was a great liberating force. Each of these religions transformed a body of locally held beliefs and customs into a coherent spiritual and ethical system with a promise of salvation. Buddhism was the least, and Islam the most, strictly codified. To this day there are fewer essential differences between the various sects of Muslims than between those of Buddhists and Christians. A complete and comprehensive guide for the inner and outer life of the individual and also for the 'constitution' of the Islamic state is provided by the Koran, which Muslims believe to have been dictated by God to the Prophet. The Koran was given canonical form immediately after Muhammad's death and has never been altered (no translations or paraphrases were officially permitted until fairly recently).

Muhammad made no claim to be divine – in this respect, if in no other, he was like the Buddha. His mission was to save his fellow men – at first his compatriots, later all mankind – from eternal damnation by recalling them to the worship of the One God – the God of Abraham, from whom he and other Arabs believed themselves to be descended. Muhammad was born about 570 into an impoverished branch of the main merchant family in the trading city of Mecca, an important junction of caravan routes, along which products of the Arabian peninsula, especially incense, were carried to the Mediterranean. At this time Arabia was occupied by fiercely independent groups of nomads on the heights, agriculturalists in the valleys and merchants in the few scattered towns. A variety of local religious beliefs were held, ranging from animism and ancestor-worship to a form of monotheism around holy leaders called *hanifs* or *hunafa*. Foreign religions also found adherents in Arabia. In the north there were followers of the Persian Zoroaster. Elsewhere colonies of Jews, whose ancestors had fled from Palestine, were settled in several towns. There were also many Christians both orthodox and heretical – Monophysites, who believed that there was only one 'nature' in the person of Christ, and Nestorians, who maintained that he united two distinct 'persons', human and divine, in one

8,1 Koran page written in Kufic script, Iraq or Syria, 8th or 9th century. Parchment, 8½ × 13ins (21.6 × 32.5cm). Museum für Islamische Kunst, Berlin.

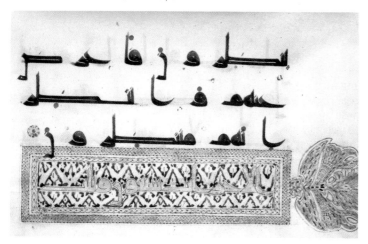

body. All these people had, in Muhammad's view, strayed from the true path. Although he never doubted the authority of the Pentateuch (the first books of the Bible) and accepted both John the Baptist and 'Jesus Son of Mary' as divinely inspired prophets, he questioned Jewish practices and completely rejected the complexities of Christian doctrine, especially the doctrine of the Trinity. His teaching was dominated by the concept of a last judgement, which would determine eternal salvation or damnation – heaven or hell – for every individual. No religion is more exclusively monotheistic than Islam, based as it is on the direct relationship between the individual and God without the intercession of saints in heaven or the mediation of priests on earth. Every individual stands alone before God. As there is no priesthood, so there is virtually no ritual in Islamic worship to distract from the prayers that the faithful are bound to say five times a day and that are usually said alone, except on Fridays. The duties of Muslims are simple: prayer, fasting during the month of Ramadan, abstinence at all times from strong drink and some foods (notably pork, but not all the others forbidden to Jews), almsgiving, a once-in-a-lifetime pilgrimage to Mecca – and, of course, faithful observance of the moral code contained in the Koran.

Muhammad was a social, as well as a religious, reformer. All believers were equal, he declared. The idea of a brotherhood of the faithful, which is still very strongly felt to this day, began with him. The injustice and materialistic greed of the upper merchant class of Mecca – especially their practice of usury – fell under his censure, and the hostility this aroused led to his *hegira* (exodus or emigration) with his family and a few followers in 622, the year that was to mark the beginning of the Muslim calendar. Settling some 300 miles (480km) to the north in the town of Yathrib, later called Medina – the City (of the Prophet) – he took on the dual role of political and military leader which most strikingly distinguishes him from the founders of Buddhism and Christianity. Within a decade he had united the greater part of Arabia under his spiritual and temporal leadership. In Medina he initiated the practice of praying while facing towards Mecca, which fell to his army only after stubborn resistance. And in the last year of his life, 632, he led the first Islamic pilgrimage (*hajj*) to the Ka'ba in Mecca, the ancient shrine associated with Abraham.

Muhammad himself lived and worshipped in surroundings of extreme simplicity. His house at Medina was built of mud-brick, palm trunks for columns and palm leaves coated with mud for partitions and roofing. It consisted of a number of small rooms opening on to a partly shaded courtyard with a shelter for his poorest followers at one end. He seems to have been sublimely indifferent to his surroundings and is said to have declared that 'nothing so much wastes the substance of a believer as architecture'. Another statement attributed to him is that 'the angels will not enter a house in which there is a picture or a dog', and this has always been interpreted by some groups of Muslims as an outright condemnation of figurative painting. However, these remarks come not

from the Koran but from the Hadith, a collection of traditional sayings which have less authority. Apart from calling idols 'an abomination', the Koran mentions neither sculpture nor painting. So the arts have been regulated less by the letter than by the spirit of Islam.

Muslim prayers can be said anywhere – in the home, in the fields or in the workshop – even for the weekly act of communal worship on Fridays, when the faithful are addressed by their *imam* or leader, no more is strictly necessary than space in which all can prostrate themselves together. As there are neither rituals nor priests there are neither ritual vessels nor vestments. Teaching is based exclusively on the word of God, not on the life of the Prophet, hence no didactic images are needed (another contrast with Christianity, which has laid such stress on the life of Christ and the saints). Nor were elaborate ceremonial manuscripts of the Koran required, for the holy words were learnt and recited by heart. In fact, art seems to have been regarded as at best an embellishment, at worst a mere distraction, and it is hardly surprising that early Islam evolved no aesthetic theory.

Long before the birth of the Prophet, however, Arabia had been open to artistic as well as religious influence from neighbouring civilizations. Remains of pre-Islamic architecture and sculpture in provincial versions of Hellenistic, Byzantine, Iranian, Ethiopian and other styles of 'the age of ignorance', as Muslims later referred to it, survived in various parts of the peninsula. After Islam began to expand under the caliphs, who succeeded Muhammad as temporal and spiritual leaders, Arabs were confronted with not only far more but far more sophisticated works. In Palestine and Syria they found magnificent stone-built Early Christian and Byzantine churches. In Mesopotamia and Iran they saw the spectacular structures erected under the Sassanian dynasty, who had ruled the area since the third century. The palace at Ctesiphon near Baghdad, probably dating from the fourth to mid-sixth century, is the most impressive of those that still partly survive today (**8,2**). With its huge *iwan* or hall opening beneath a gently pointed arch and its stucco panels of flower and leaf motifs (**8,3**), this building was to exert great influence

8,2 Palace of Chosroes, Ctesiphon, near Baghdad, Iraq, 4th to mid-6th century. (From a 19th-century photograph; much less survives today.)

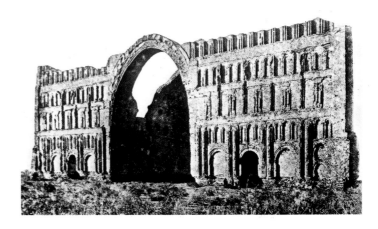

8,3 Sassanian relief ornament from Ctesiphon, 6th century. Stucco, 3ft 4ins × 3ft 4½ ins (1.02 × 1.03m). Museum für Islamische Kunst, Berlin.

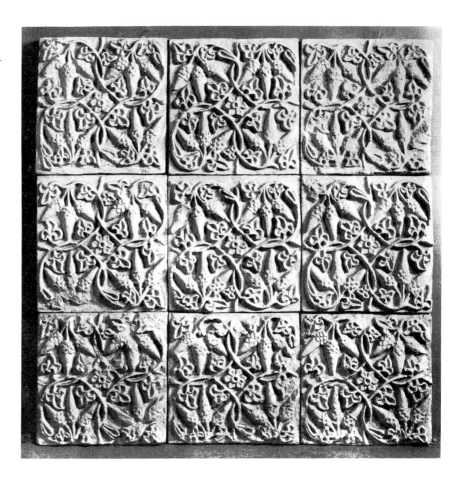

on the development of Islamic architecture and decoration – though not for a century or more after the Muslim annexation of Mesopotamia in 640.

The Islamic state expanded with a rapidity that has never ceased to astonish. By 647 its armies had conquered Iraq, Palestine, Syria, Egypt, Iran, Cyrenaica and Tripolitania. Two years later they had reached the Indus in present-day Pakistan. North-west Africa fell to them in 670. In 710 they crossed into Europe, conquered the Visigothic kingdoms of Spain and passed over the Pyrenees as far as Poitiers in France, where they were finally checked in 732 by Charles Martel (grandfather of Charlemagne). For places of worship in all these lands Muslims took over whatever buildings were conveniently available, whether Christian churches or Zoroastrian temples. So long as it contained no idol, any building could become a mosque, a word derived from the Arabic *masjid*, which means simply 'a place where one prostrates oneself'.

UMAYYAD ART AND ARCHITECTURE

In the early years of Islamic expansion mosques were built or laid out only where, as in new garrison towns, no existing structure was large enough to be taken over and used. The earliest were not even roofed: a space surrounded by a fence sufficed. At Kufa in Iraq in 638 a large square was marked off by a ditch, and two rows of columns taken from nearby buildings were set up to form a covered colonnade on its south side – i.e. that facing towards Mecca. In Jerusalem, which fell to the Arabs in 637, no more elaborate mosque was erected than that still in use some 30 years later, when a Christian pilgrim described it as a 'quadrangular place of Prayer, which they have built rudely, constructing it by setting great beams on some remains of ruins: this house can, it is said, hold 3,000 men at once.' Not until about 685 did work begin on the first major monument of Islamic architecture, the Dome of the Rock in Jerusalem (**8,5**), built near the site of Solomon's temple at the command of the caliph Abd al-Malik of the first dynasty of Islam – the Umayyads, who were descended from a companion of the Prophet. It was, however, conceived as a special sanctuary, not as an ordinary place of worship. Its design – an octagon with two concentric ambulatories surrounding a central space covered by a dome – was derived from Early Christian *martyria*, of which the most famous was that enshrining the Holy Sepulchre on the other side of Jerusalem.

The natural outcrop that the Dome of the Rock surrounds had been venerated by the Jews as the tomb of Adam and also as the place where Abraham prepared to sacrifice Isaac. According to Muslim tradition, it was the place from which Muhammad ascended into heaven on the night journey described in the Koran, though it is not known to have been identified as such until after the Dome was built. The rock itself seems to have provided little more than a pretext for this spectacular departure from earlier Islamic architectural practice or non-practice. A tenth-century writer declared that Caliph Abd al-Malik, 'seeing the greatness of the *martyrium* of the Holy Sepulchre and its magnificence was moved lest it should dazzle the minds of the Muslim and hence erected above the Rock the Dome, which is now seen there'. The caliph's aim was to create a prominent monument which would outshine the Christian churches of the city and even, perhaps, the Ka'ba in Mecca, then in the hands of a rival caliph. It is unlikely that he was inspired by, or even aware of, the ancient cosmic symbolism of the dome.

Although the brilliant spectacle that greets the modern visitor to Jerusalem is largely the result of later redecorations (notably the glazed pottery tiles replacing exterior mosaics), the original effect made by the building must have been very similar and no less arresting, with mosaics in gold and many colors glittering on the walls beneath the gilded dome. Much of the seventh-century decoration survives inside: panels of variously colored marble cladding piers and walls, sheets of gilded metal worked in relief and mosaics of glass and mother-of-pearl with flower and leaf motifs surrounding vases and crowns (**8,7**). Here there are also long inscriptions of passages from the Koran addressed specifically to Christians. 'O ye People of the Book', one of them begins. 'The Messiah Jesus Son of Mary is only an apostle of God, and His Word which he conveyed into Mary, and a Spirit proceeding from Him. Believe therefore in God and his apostles and say not Three. It will be better for you. God is only one God. Far be it from his glory that He should have a son.'

The Dome of the Rock was clearly intended to 'dazzle the eyes' of Christians as well as to distract those of Muslims from the splendour of Christian churches. So, too, was the Great Mosque, built between 706 and 715 by Abd al-Malik's son and successor Caliph al-Walid in Damascus, then the capital of Islam. This is the earliest mosque of which a substantial part survives (even though it has been sacked several times and all but burnt down) and also the first known to have had any pretensions to grandeur in form or decoration (**8,6**). It exerted great influence on nascent Islamic architecture. Artists and craftsmen employed on it were, however, predominantly non-Arab and probably non-Muslim; and a considerable element of improvisation entered into its creation.

The site was the rectangular walled *temenos* or precinct of a pagan temple, which had been converted into a Christian church in the late fourth century. When the Muslims took Damascus in 635 they adopted part of the *temenos* as an open-air mosque, which served their needs for some 70 years. In 705 al-Walid acquired the church, demolished it and set about building the largest mosque in Islam. All that was allowed to survive of the original fabric was the Roman wall with its four corner towers, which were converted into minarets from which the faithful could be called to prayer – the first in the history of Islam. Columns and capitals of various types (mostly Corinthian) were taken from earlier buildings to support an arcade running round three sides of the *sahn* or courtyard. The fourth side of the *temenos* was filled by the

sanctuary or prayer hall, a covered structure deriving from a Christian basilica with three equal naves divided by arcades. The effect, however, on entering is unlike that of a Christian church, one of indeterminate breadth rather than length. Just as there is no altar to provide a focal point, so there is no strong axis from one end to the other. This plan enabled the maximum number of men (women were relegated to a separate place) to pray, shoulder to shoulder, immediately facing the *qibla* wall (i.e. that on the side facing Mecca), the importance of which was marked by three shallow niches called *mihrabs*. Whereas the Christian basilica reflects the hierarchical structure of the Church – laity, priests, a bishop enthroned in the apse – the mosque no less clearly expresses the Islamic conception of the brotherhood of believers, all equal before God, to whom each has direct and equal access through prayer.

Early accounts of the Great Mosque of Damascus attest to the splendour of its decorations, most of which have perished by sack or by fire (the last and most serious in 1893). Few traces remain of the colored marble panelling that encased the piers and lower walls. But six windows still have their marble grilles (**8,4**), carved probably by Egyptian craftsmen with interlace designs strikingly similar to the carpet-pages of manuscripts, which were being painted at exactly the same time far away in the north-west of Europe (7,58). Both derived, in all probability, from the same Coptic sources. Fragments of the mosaics that glittered in the courtyard – in the spandrels of the arcades, on the undersides of the arches and on the upper parts of the walls – have also been

8,4 Marble window grille, Great Mosque, Damascus, c. 715.

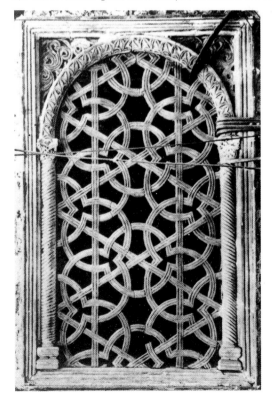

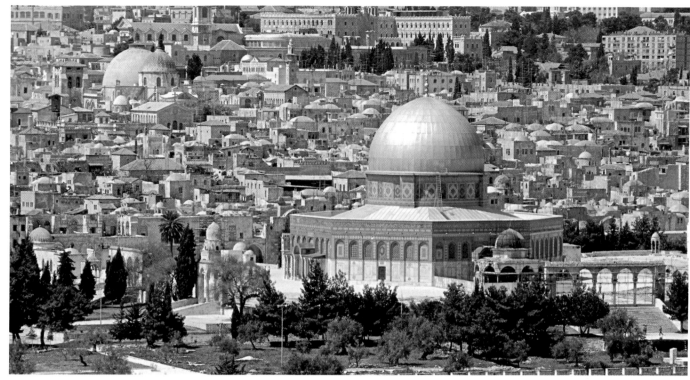

8,5 Dome of the Rock, Jerusalem, late 7th century.

8,6 Great Mosque, Damascus. Courtyard looking west, c. 715.

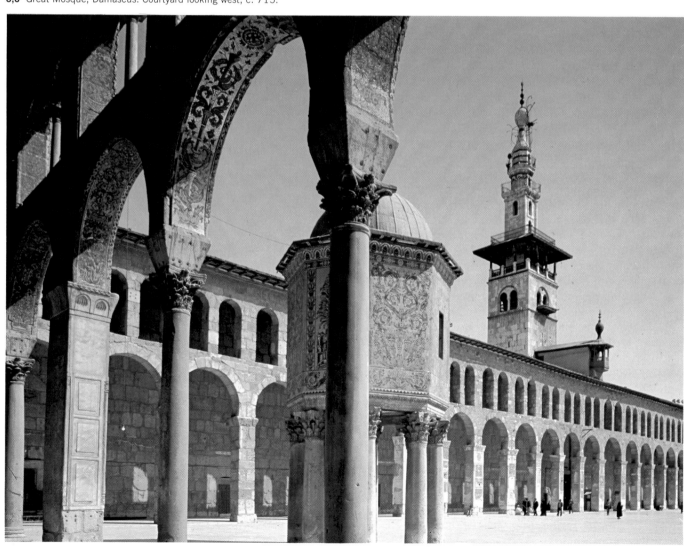

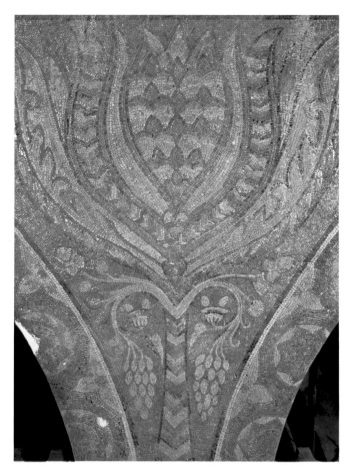

preserved (8,6; **8,8; 9**). Among the most accomplished of all mosaics, they are almost certainly the work of Byzantine craftsmen. The panoramic views especially, like that illustrated here, with numerous buildings rendered in the Hellenistic landscape tradition, recall mural decorations painted some seven centuries earlier at Pompeii and Rome. Only in one respect do they differ: the palaces, houses and gardens at Damascus are all eerily uninhabited. There has been much discussion as to the possible symbolical meaning of these mosaics and whether they

8,9 Great Mosque, Damascus, detail of mosaic decoration, c. 715.

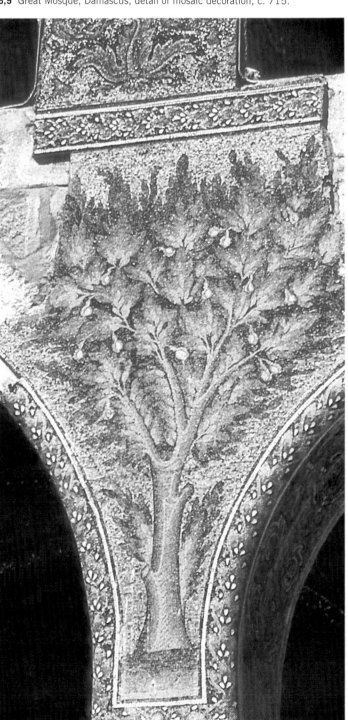

8,7 Dome of the Rock, Jerusalem, detail of mosaic decoration, 691–2.

8,8 Great Mosque, Damascus, detail of mosaic decoration, c. 715.

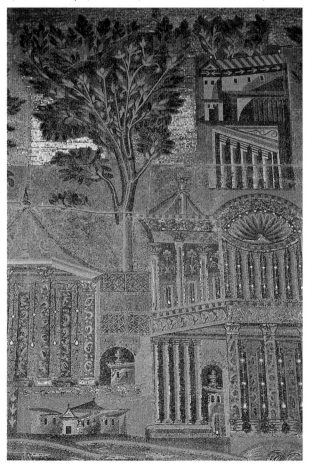

might have been intended to represent a specific place (the environs of Damascus), the vision of a peaceful Islamic world, or paradise. But it seems rather more likely, in view of the negative and somewhat cursory way in which Western artistic conventions were adapted, that they were conceived simply as decorative backgrounds, as palatial and opulent settings for life in the courtyard of the Great Mosque.

Mosaics in a similar style have been found on the floors of palaces built in the open country for the Umayyad family and their supporters, who had been granted lands vacated by Christians. Here there were also figurative paintings, both on walls and floors, confirming the absence of an absolute ban on images outside a religious context. Most of these paintings derive, like the mosaics, from Hellenistic prototypes. But one of the most spirited, with figures of musicians standing under arches and a mounted horseman hunting gazelles, recalls Sassanian art and may well have been inspired by an Iranian model (8,10). On stone reliefs from the most famous of the Umayyad palaces, that at Mshatta in Jordan, lions, birds and fabulous beasts from Sassanian and earlier Near Eastern art are entangled in luxuriant growths of vine, which can be traced back to Coptic Egypt (8,11). The general effect is, nevertheless, quite new and this great band of carving, which went right across the façade of the

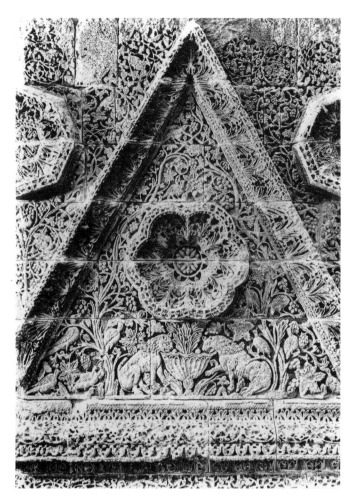

8,11 Frieze from Umayyad palace at Mshatta, Jordan, detail, c. 743. Limestone, about 9ft 6ins (2.9m) high. Staatliche Museen, Berlin.

8,10 Floor painting from Qasr al-Hayr al Gharbi, Syria, c. 730. Fresco. National Museum, Damascus.

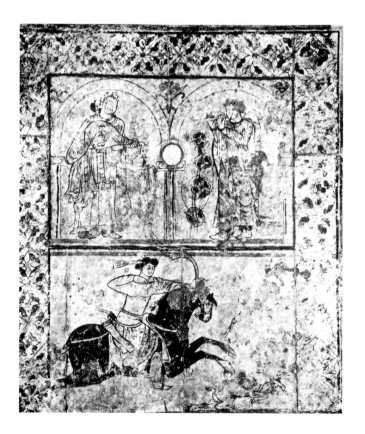

palace just above eye level – a zigzag forming triangles each with a huge rosette in the centre – may be thought to be the earliest example of an art distinctively Islamic, derivative though every individual motif may be. It is purely ornamental and unrelated to the structure of the building (from which it was removed in the nineteenth century) and seems to have no symbolical or other meaning whatever. It was merely a sign indicating the grandeur and importance of the palace. In design each triangle is so tightly integrated that neither the foliage nor the animal motifs dominate. Geometrical and organic forms are combined and balanced. Motifs recur from one triangle to another and, although they are subtly varied, an effect of rhythmical repetition prevails, as in later Islamic decorative art and also in Arabic music and literature.

Mshatta, which was left unfinished in about 744, was the last of the great Umayyad palaces. Traces of some 50 others survive (notably at Khirbat al-Mafjar in Jordan), sited far from cities, not, as is sometimes thought, to satisfy nostalgia for the wide open spaces, but in order to be at the centre of farmland and hunting country (now all desert). In their splendour and luxury they seem a world apart from the tents of the central Arabian nomads and also from the simple mud-brick courtyard house in which the Prophet had lived and died at Medina, little more than a century earlier. The larger Umayyad palaces were symmetrically planned and each was provided with a mosque, an audience hall and numerous private apartments, latrines (at Mshatta they were in the towers, which had no defensive purpose) and hot baths of the Roman type, later called Turkish. These great palaces mark the end of the first stage in the history of Islamic architecture, and also the end of a single unified Islamic state.

The empire ruled from Damascus by the Umayyad caliphs extended from central India to the Atlantic, covering most of the countries which have remained Islamic to the present day. Its spread had been effected not only by the force of arms. Muslims proved to be tolerant overlords and in the course of two or three generations very large numbers of the conquered peoples adopted the religion of their masters, either out of conviction or to avoid paying a poll-tax imposed on non-Muslims. Many Christians responded to the uncomplicated theology of the Koran. But in due course discontent arose among converts and their descendants, who tended to be treated, in defiance of the Koran, as second-class Muslims in an empire ruled by and for an Arab élite. From 661 the Arabs were divided among themselves by a dispute over the succession to the caliphate, which widened into a schism between orthodox Muslims or Sunnites and the more mystical and philosophical Shi'ites. The schism polarized doctrinal issues, and has continued to split Islam. In the 740s, the Shi'ites joined with other malcontents in a revolt that broke out in Iran and in 750 overthrew the reigning Umayyad caliph in Damascus, whose relatives were massacred with the exception of one who escaped to Spain. He became the emir of Córdoba and from that date the western part of the empire developed independently (see pp. 353–6).

ABBASID ART AND ARCHITECTURE

The Abbasid dynasty of caliphs, who succeeded the Umayyads, was descended from Abbas, an uncle of the Prophet. Arabic remained the legal as well as the religious language throughout Islam (necessarily, as translation of the Koran was prohibited), but power began gradually to pass out of the hands of Arabs and into those of officials of other ethnic origins. At the same time the empire evolved into independent states, which rarely acknowledged the caliphs as more than spiritual leaders, while its eastern territories were slowly eroded by the advance of the Mongols, who finally, in 1259, drove the Abbasids out of Asia altogether. They retreated to Egypt. The 500-year-long Abbasid period is, nevertheless, generally regarded as the 'Classical' age of Islamic culture. The court of the reigning caliph was a brilliant centre of luxury, poetry and learning. The most famous was that of Harun al-Rashid (d. 809), a contemporary of Charlemagne, with whom he corresponded, well known in legend from *The Thousand and One Nights*. The visual arts, music and literature all

flourished. So, too, did the sciences, in which Islamic men of learning made a major contribution by reanimating Greek ideas and preserving Greek texts – it was the Muslims, not the Christians, who were the direct inheritors of those parts of the Greek tradition which the Eastern empire had kept alive. In addition, they developed algebra from India, chemistry and alchemy from China and initiated the scientific study of optics and astronomy. Above all, their culture was unified and well-integrated. Omar Khayyam (fl. c. 1100) was both poet and mathematician. It is instructive to consider some of the words we owe to Arabic – algebra, zero, alkali, azimuth, zenith – and to remember that it is to Islam that we are indebted for the transmission from India of what are called 'Arabic' numerals, the numerals we still use (as in this book) and without which the advance of mathematics and all related and dependent sciences would have been impossible.

In 762 the second Abbasid caliph, al-Mansur, transferred his capital from Damascus to the banks of the Tigris, where he founded Madinat as-Salam – the City of Peace, known better as Baghdad. It was a decisive shift away from the Mediterranean world – preceding by only a few decades Charlemagne's establishment of a new centre of power in northern Europe. Perhaps significantly, Baghdad was laid out not on the rectangular grid, ubiquitous throughout the Roman empire, but on a circular plan which had a long history in the ancient Near East. Astrologers determined the date on which the foundations should be laid, and the whole concept may reflect the influence of Persian cosmology and indicate that the new city was the hub of the universe. A simple scale of proportions was used throughout: bricks one cubit (about 15 inches, 38cm) square, the outer wall with a total circumference of 16,000 cubits (rather more than 5 miles, 8km), the palace 400 cubits square, the mosque 200 cubits square, and so on. The throne-room of the palace was in the very centre, a cube (20 cubits) with a domed ceiling, surmounted by another room of the same size crowned by the famous Green Dome, which dominated the city. It was approached through an *iwan* as at Ctesiphon (8,2), another instance of the increasing Iranian influence, which also determined court ritual under the Abbasid caliphs. The palace, the large mosque attached to it and the administrative buildings were all in a vast enclosure more than a mile (1.5km) across, a city within the city, encircled by a massive wall with four gates, from which vaulted galleries about 300 yards (275m) long led to monumental gateways in the outer wall, each with an audience hall covered by a gilded dome over the entrance. The ordinary population of the city was crammed into this narrow ring – only 300 yards (275m) across but some 5 miles (8km) long. The inconvenience to the inhabitants of such an arrangement is a striking instance of how Abbasid Baghdad embodied the Islamic ideal of submission to one absolute spiritual and temporal ruler, successor to the Prophet of the one God. Early accounts state that engineers, craftsmen and artists from all parts of the Islamic world were assembled to build and decorate the new capital.

However, Baghdad soon burst out of its tight, ideal, circular plan to grow and sprawl into one of the richest, most densely populous and famous cities in the world, celebrated in the reports of travellers from East and West and, of course, in a whole series of stories in *The Thousand and One Nights*. The palace enclosure was a 'paradise' in the ancient Persian sense of the word: a game reserve, in which gardens surrounded numerous pavilions. Affluent court officials built only slightly less magnificent palaces in the suburbs, which spread far beyond the walls. In contrast to the rigid formality of the original city plan, these buildings seem to have been informally related to one another, establishing a precedent for later Islamic palace architecture – the Alhambra at Granada, for example, and Topkapi Saray at Istanbul. It seems likely that they kept alive Sassanian architectural forms and methods of decoration, which were to re-emerge so brilliantly in later buildings in Iran (see p. 532). Similarly, their settings among lawns and canals and circular pools, flowers and fruit trees maintained a tradition of garden design probably derived from ancient Roman villas and palaces but invested with the imagery of the Islamic paradise and later passed on to Iran and Mughal India (see pp. 544–5). But the extent of their influence is impossible to estimate, for practically no visible trace of the city of the Abbasids survived its remorseless destruction in 1258, when the last of the Abbasid caliphs was put to death by the Mongols, along with 800,000 of the inhabitants of Baghdad. The loss is irreparable and our knowledge of Islamic art necessarily incomplete as a result.

At Samarra, a little more than 60 miles (96km) up the Tigris from Baghdad, excavations have revealed the remains of a second Abbasid capital with a vast palace, which was built in 836–8 by a son of Harun al-Rashid. Here, too, artists from all parts of the Islamic world were employed and some of their signatures have been found, written in Greek, Syriac and Arabic characters. Fragments of abstract stucco decoration (**8,12**) and figurative wall-paintings reveal the influence of Chinese and European as well as Persian art, and the general effect must have been, perhaps intentionally, cosmopolitan. The richest and finest of them appear to have been reserved for the harem,

---

SOURCES AND DOCUMENTS

THE BYZANTINE AMBASSADORS VISIT BAGHDAD

A contemporary account of the reception of Byzantine ambassadors in Baghdad in 917 describes vividly the magnificence of the caliph's palace and also makes clear its flexibility as an architectural setting, a notable feature of Islamic domestic design. The palace consisted of numerous pavilions loosely arranged like a bedouin encampment at some desert oasis. Their various halls and chambers had been specially arranged for the ambassadors' visit, being as adaptable as stage-sets which could be modified at short notice to suit the occasion and provide appropriate backgrounds for the sumptuous carpets and other textiles. On arrival, however, the ambassadors were surprised to find no armed guards, only eunuchs and black page-boys – 7,000 eunuchs and 4,000 black page-boys! (Doubtless an exaggeration permitted by 'poetic licence'.) As they moved in stately procession from one pavilion to another through formal and sometimes informal gardens, accompanied by the sounds of fountains and pools and chained wild animals, they realized that the caliph's treasures had all been brought out of storage for them. There were 38,000 hangings, including:

. . . curtains of gold – of brocade embroidered with gold – all magnificently figured with representations of drinking-vessels and with elephants and horses, camels, lions and birds . . . . The number of carpets and mats of the kinds made at Jahram and Darabgird and Ad-Dawrak was 22,000 pieces; these were laid in corridors and courts, being spread under the feet of the nobles, and the Byzantine envoys walked over such carpets all the way from the main gate right to the presence of the Caliph – but this number did not include the fine rugs in the chambers and halls of assembly, spread over the other carpets, and these were not to be trodden with the feet . . . . Then they came to a palace where there were 100 lions, 50 to the right-hand and 50 to the left, every lion being held in by the hand of its keeper, and about its head and neck were iron chains.

After passing through a garden with lawns and palm-trees protected with teak-wood fences bound with gilt copper rings, they found themselves by a large pool with a gold and silver tree standing in the middle, every branch having numerous twigs on which sat all kinds of gold and silver birds.

The leaves of the tree move as the wind blows, while the birds pipe and sing.

At last, after seeing 22 pavilions, the ambassadors were ushered into the presence of the Caliph Muktadir and his five sons. The caliph was arrayed in gold embroidered silk and sat on an ebony throne. The ambassadors halted before him and stood in the posture of humility, with their arms crossed.

(Al-Khatir's account of the Byzantine ambassadors' visit to Baghdad in 917, *Journal of the Royal Asiatic Society*, 1897, tr. G. Le Strange, adapted)

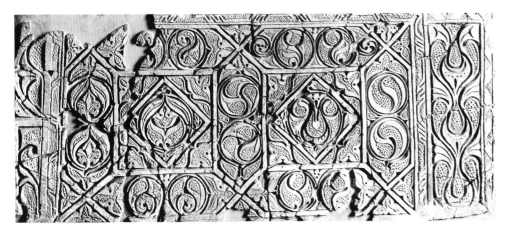

8,12a & 12b Fragments of stucco decoration from Samarra Palace, Iraq, 836–8. Staatliche Museen, Berlin.

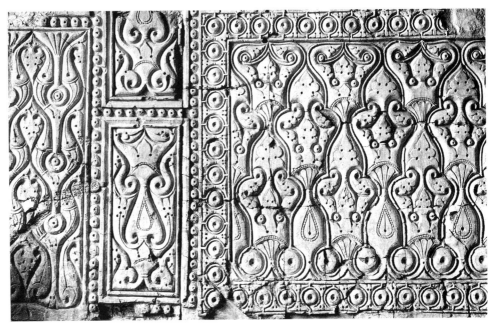

for the exclusive enjoyment of the caliph and his wives. Here a desire for art as an embellishment of aristocratic life was reconciled with the religious conception of art as vanity – albeit accompanied by a salutary awareness of life's transience. In Muslim palaces, as at Samarra, the pleasure pavilions were always most highly prized and often seem to have been deliberately fragile structures with a kind of built-in evanescence, owing much of their effect to the precious objects and richly colored and patterned textiles displayed temporarily, just for the occasion.

Very different indeed in its conception was the mosque. That at Samarra was the largest in the world, 784 by 512 feet (240 by 156m) and capable of accommodating 100,000 people. Of the vast prayer-hall, reminiscent of the hypostyle halls of Persepolis (see pp. 114–5), barely a trace survives of the 216 square brick piers that supported the roof. But the minaret still stands (**8,13**), recalling even more directly the spiral towers of Iran.

The main factor conditioning the structural development of the mosque was the need to provide sufficient free space, at least partly under cover, for the whole male population of an area when they assembled for communal prayers on Fridays. The relatively small enclosures, which had sufficed for the conquering Arabs in the early decades of Islamic expansion, were quite inadequate for the more settled populations of their descendants, let alone the growing number of converts. Increased space was

8,13 Minaret and Great Mosque of al-Mutawakkil, Samarra, Iraq, c. 848–52.

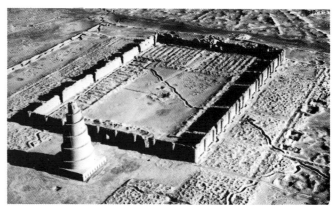

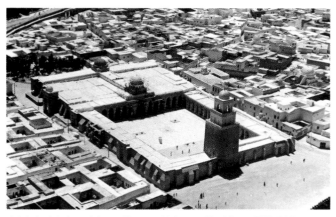

8,14 Aerial view of Great Mosque, Kairouan, Tunisia, c. 772–863.

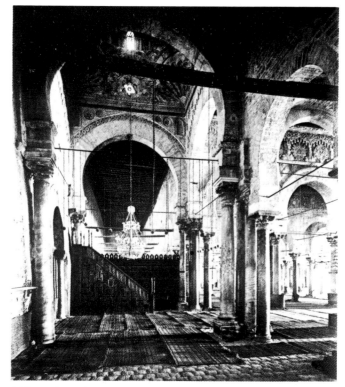

8,15 Interior of Great Mosque, Kairouan, Tunisia, c. 862–3.

obtained either by piecemeal additions or by wholesale demolition and rebuilding, yet almost invariably with conservative respect for pre-Islamic local traditions. The Great Mosque at Kairouan (**8,14**), for instance, was begun about 724, when the governor of the city obtained the caliph's permission to enlarge an early mosque by expanding into an adjacent garden and adding a sturdy, square minaret. All but the minaret was demolished and rebuilt in 772–4 and again in 836. Alterations were made in 862–3, when a wooden dome was raised over the bay in front of the *mihrab*, reserved for the governor. At the same time the *mihrab* was redecorated with lustred faience tiles imported from Iraq and beside it was placed a wooden *minbar* – the pulpit from which the *imam* addresses the faithful and leads the Friday prayers (**8,15**). A decade or so later the prayer-hall was extended on one side and towards the courtyard, where a second dome was placed over the central entrance. Although Kairouan was sacked and deserted after the massacre of its population by the Berbers in 1054–5, enough survived of the mosque for it to be restored with only minor modifications in the late thirteenth century. It is a remarkable record of tenacious adaptability and artistic conservatism. A Christian church would never, during these centuries, have been enlarged and rebuilt again and again with such unchanging stylistic consistency.

As it stands today, the Great Mosque of Kairouan is thus the work of many periods and the typological history of its various parts goes back to pre-Islamic times. The basic unit of construction is a round arch slightly compressed to swell out into a horseshoe shape, first found in fifth-century Christian churches in Syria, and resting on columns with capitals of Corinthian type. There are seven of these arches in each of the 16 arcades running in the direction of the *qibla* wall. Monotony was avoided, perhaps fortuitously, by using columns of greatly varying size and type of marble, some with bases to bring them up to uniform height, others without, and all presumably removed from earlier buildings, either Christian or ancient Roman. Yet no adaptation was attempted. No modifications in style were introduced to disturb the atmosphere of harmony needed for prayer. Despite its long building history, the whole mosque is remarkably

homogeneous and, despite the disparate origins of the elements used in its construction, it remains quintessentially Islamic.

The enlargement of an existing mosque did not always provide a solution to the problem of space for the Friday prayers, however. New mosques had to be built as well. And perhaps the finest of all mosques, that of Ibn Tulun in Cairo, was one of these. Designed and built between about 877 and 879 and never subsequently enlarged or altered, it is a rare instance of the completely realized architectural conception in early Islamic architecture. Its patron was Ahmed Ibn Tulun, born at Samarra in 835, the son of a Turki slave taken there from Bokhara. He attracted the attention of the caliph, who had him

8,16 Arcade of Mosque of Ibn Tulun, Cairo, c. 877–9.

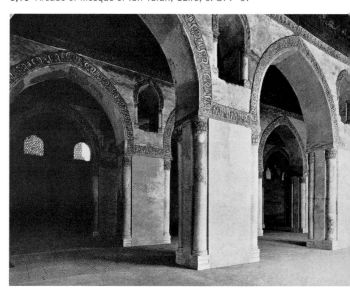

educated, and swiftly rose in the service of the caliphate, always open to talent. In 869 he was appointed governor of Egypt, which he and his descendants ruled as a semi-independent state until 907. His mosque was built with brick piers instead of columns, perhaps because of shortage of materials and, according to legend, because of his refusal to rob Christian churches of the 300 or so columns needed for the very large building he envisaged (the quarrying of marble had long since ceased in Egypt). He may also have wished to emulate the Great Mosque at Samarra (8,13), which he had known as a boy. The minaret (later rebuilt in its present form) seems to have been inspired by that at Samarra. The piers in both mosques have simulated columns at their corners, those in the mosque of Ibn Tulun emphasizing visually their massive strength and lending the great arcades a grandeur and gravity fully equal to that of the finest ancient Roman buildings. If ever a building could be called 'big-boned', it is the mosque of Ibn Tulun (8,16).

At Samarra the piers had directly supported a flat ceiling; at Cairo, however, they carry arches. Furthermore, the arches are pointed, not round or horseshoe-shaped. Gently pointed arches had been used much earlier in Christian and Islamic buildings in Syria, but those in the mosque of Ibn Tulun are much bolder and their form is accentuated by bands of relief decoration. They are also repeated in the 'windows' above each pier, an unusual feature, inserted, it has been suggested, to save building material, to lessen the load on the piers, or simply to allow more light to pass through the interior.

ISLAMIC SPAIN

It may have been partly for the same reason – to increase the light in a wide prayer-hall – that the architect of the mosque in Córdoba devised a unique system of double arches. The columns available for use were of various types, smooth and fluted, varying from 14 to 17 inches (36 to 43cm) in diameter, and some can have been no taller than the 9 feet 9 inches (3m) to which the others were reduced. Had they been used to support simple arcades in the normal way, the effect would have been murkily cavernous. Impost blocks (see Glossary) were, therefore, set on the capitals to carry arches (constructed of red bricks alternating with stone voussoirs) and also the 6-foot-high (1.82m) stone piers, from which the segmental upper

8,17 Interior of Great Mosque, Córdoba, begun 786.

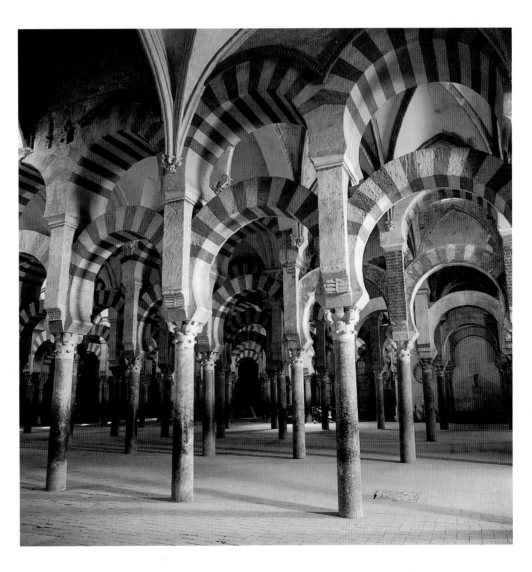

arches spring. This device, introduced at Córdoba with the earliest part of the mosque in 786, was so successful that it was repeated with only slight variations as the prayer-hall was gradually enlarged by piecemeal addition of one block of aisles after another until, in 987–9, it reached its present enormous extent, some four times its original area (8,17).

Córdoba – originally a Roman city – had been chosen as the Islamic capital of Spain after the Arab conquest of the peninsula in 710–11. Here in 755 one of the Umayyads, who had escaped the general massacre of his family in Syria (see p. 349), found refuge and was accepted by the Muslim population as emir or military governor. The title was retained by his descendants until the early tenth century, when they began to style themselves caliphs, in open rivalry with the Abbasids in the east and the Fatimids, descendants of the Prophet's daughter, who had established a second caliphate in north Africa. Under the despotic, but generally benevolent, rule of the Umayyads, Córdoba grew to be by far the most prosperous city in western Europe, second only to Baghdad in Islam. There are said to have been no fewer than 3,000 mosques and 300 public baths within its walls. The mosque that survives was the most important, attached to the palace by a bridge across a street so that the caliph could enter it without passing through the congregation. It was, in fact, a kind of Islamic equivalent to the great court churches of Christendom – Hagia Sophia in Constantinople (7,41) and the Palatine Chapel in Aachen (7,66) – though the Great Mosque at Córdoba is much larger, even, than Hagia Sophia. Great attention was lavished on its decoration, especially of the *qibla* wall and the area in front of it, which date from the 960s. The *mihrab* is unique in that it consists of a small, domed chamber entered through an arched doorway of the pronounced horseshoe shape that the Muslims of Spain particularly favoured (8,19). Around the opening there are bands of carving in stone, as delicate as work in ivory, as well as mosaic patterns of leaves and, above, inscriptions from the Koran in gold and colored-glass mosaic executed by craftsmen from Constantinople (and presumably, therefore, Christian). The area in front of the *mihrab* is divided off from the rest of the prayer-hall by columns supporting arches which burst into multi-lobed life, crossing one another in intricate, regular patterns created as if by some complicated process of multiplication and division (8,18). Above there is the richest of the mosque's three domes (8,19), similar feats of Islamic skill and precision in geometry. Each dome is constructed on eight intersecting arches. By this date there were two main methods of erecting masonry domes over rectangular bases: one with arches, technically called squinches, across and projecting over the corners; the other with spherical triangles or pendentives, like those at Hagia Sophia. The former method was adopted by Islamic architects, who developed it in conjunction with a framework of ribs of the kind used to reinforce ancient Roman concrete domes. But whereas the Romans had concealed the framework inside the fabric, Islamic architects displayed the whole structural system and its complex patterns of

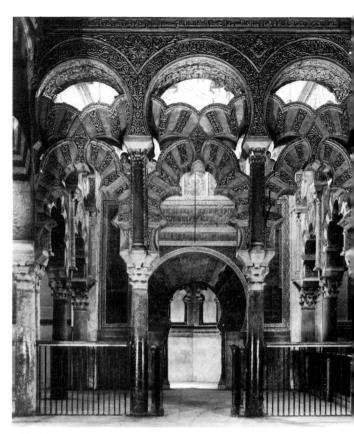

8,18 *Mihrab* in the Great Mosque, Córdoba, c. 961–76.

symmetrical arcs – regular geometric patterns and linear grids of a kind that greatly appealed to Muslims with their interest in mathematics and astronomy. Indeed, it was probably at least partly for this reason that squinches with ribs were introduced, for they are of an intricacy that is quite often gratuitous structurally. Islamic domes are seldom of any great span and could have been constructed by simpler methods long in common use.

Basic differences in aesthetic attitudes are revealed by a comparison between the vaulting systems at Hagia Sophia (7,41) and the Great Mosque at Córdoba (8,19). The former conceals its structure, at enormous cost in labour and technical ingenuity for, ultimately, transcendental reasons; the latter exposes it partly as a display of technical virtuosity, partly just for the intricate decorative beauty of the geometric interlaces it forms. Moreover, early Islamic architects did not exploit their technical feats. Nor did they go on to vault large areas with a structural system of vaults. That was left for Christian architects to do some centuries later, quite independently (see p. 381). It was as if early Islamic architects, having mastered and perfected a vaulting system and having demonstrated the extreme structural and decorative elegance that could be attained in it, were quite content to leave its practical exploitation to others, just as they did with the pointed arch. Their interest in structural problems would seem to have been primarily intellectual, their appreciation of architecture focused on the decorative and ornamental.

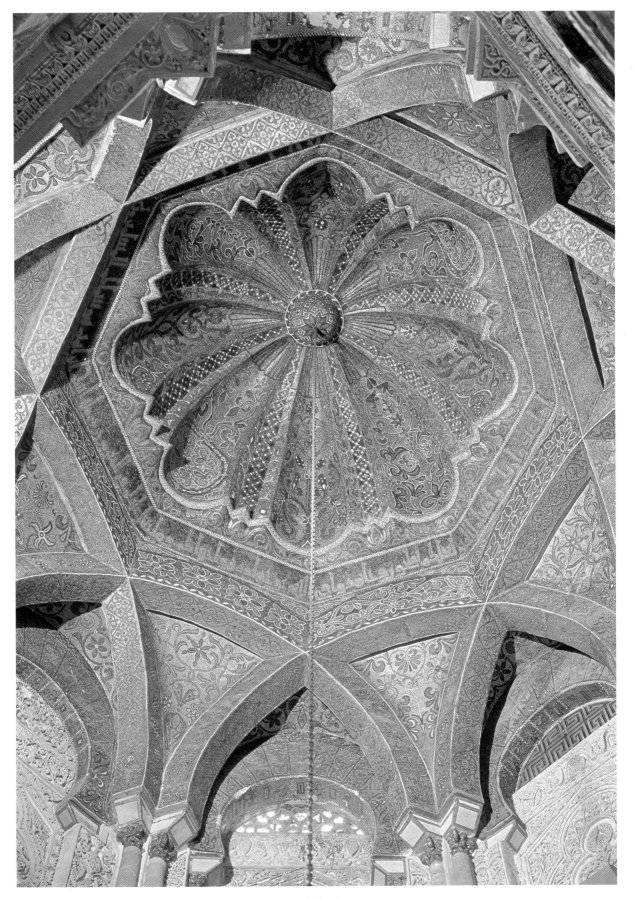

8,19 Dome above the *mihrab*, Great Mosque, Córdoba, Spain, c. 961–76.

8,20 Minaret of Kutubiya Mosque, Marrakesh, Morocco, 1196.

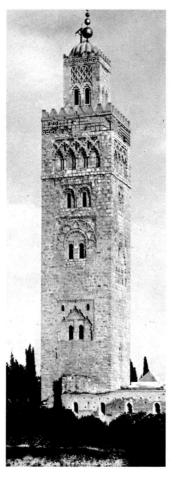

Height was hardly necessary for 'a place where one prostrates oneself', and early mosques emphasized the horizontal. A vertical accent was supplied externally by the minaret. As we have already seen, the first minarets were those of the Great Mosque at Damascus, originally towers at the corners of the pagan temple *temenos* from which it was adapted. Of minarets built as such, the earliest survivor is that of Kairouan, 103 feet (31m) high (**8,14**). Its ostensible purpose was, of course, to provide a place from which the *muezzin* could call the faithful to prayer. But, above a certain point, height begins to diminish rather than increase the range of the human voice, and the function of the tall minaret must have been as much, if not more, visual than auditory – to mark the location of the mosque in a crowded city. Tall towers had similarly been erected on or alongside Christian churches, sometimes, but not always, as bell-towers. The Kairouan minaret derived from this source and in turn provided the model followed throughout north Africa and Spain. There is a very handsome twelfth-century example at Marrakesh in Morocco, decorated with panels of arcading carved to such an elaboration of texture that they look like fabrics hung on its walls (**8,20**). A similar minaret was built at about the same time in Seville and needed little alteration when it was transformed into the bell-tower of the cathedral after the Christian conquest of the city – a rare example of a structure being returned to its typological origin!

SAMANID AND SELJUK ARCHITECTURE

Meanwhile, an architectural variant was being developed contemporaneously at the other end of the Islamic world, in the vast plains on either side of the river Oxus in central Asia (now Turkmenistan and Uzbekistan). Its patrons were members of an ancient Iranian aristocratic family, the Samanids, who had been converted from Zoroastrianism to Islam in the eighth century and ruled from 874 to 999 as emirs virtually independent of the caliphate. A mausoleum erected at Bokhara for one of these emirs – perhaps Isma'il, who died in 907 – is its most notable surviving monument and, despite its small scale (only 36 feet, 11m, wide), one of the most remarkable buildings of its time anywhere (**8,21**). The form is probably derived from a Zoroastrian fire temple with four columns supporting a domed roof, but its decorative elaboration seems to have had no precedents. Brick was the material used for both construction and, with the addition of a few panels of terracotta, decoration. An extraordinary variety of surface patterns was created by laying the bricks vertically, diagonally and in circles as well as horizontally. Structure and ornament were, in fact, completely integrated, but in a most unusual way, for the former was not expressed by the latter. The columns at the corners have no structural function – not even visually, like those engaged in the piers of the mosque of Ibn Tulun (**8,16**). The impression given is not that of a solid, weighty mass of brick and mortar so much as of a temporary pavilion woven out of wickerwork and draped with fabric. Some of the interwoven

8,21 Samanid Mausoleum, Bokhara, Uzbekistan, pre-943.

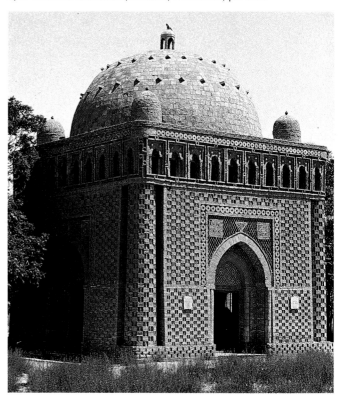

patterns are, in fact, taken from basketry. Unlike most funerary monuments, from the pyramids onwards, this mausoleum suggests transience and impermanence, perhaps reflecting in this way Muslim attitudes to death.

The Koran prescribed that the dead should be buried with the greatest simplicity, and the Hadith attributed to Muhammad a ban on buildings over graves. But the impulse to commemorate and perpetuate was too deeply rooted, especially in ruling families, to be resisted for long. Abbasid caliphs succumbed before the Samanids. More prominent monuments were built by the Seljuks, a dynasty of rulers of a Turkish people from the eastern steppes, who were converted to Islam, took over Iran and spread into Mesopotamia, where, in 1055, the Abbasid caliph surrendered most of his temporal power to their leader – retaining only his spiritual authority. Thus, the Seljuks became the first sultans to have more than regional authority. Seljuk tombs were given the form of lofty towers dominating the landscape for miles around, lasting testimonies to Seljuk power. One of the earliest and most imposing tomb towers, the Gunbad-i-Qabus (tomb of Qabus, a prince who died in 1012), near Gurgan in north-eastern Iran, tapers to a height of 190 feet (58m) (8,22). It is a masterly composition of contrasting sharp-edged and smoothly rounded forms. The ten pointed buttresses have the clean-cut elegance of a polished steel instrument. There is no ornamentation or decoration of any kind, apart from two slender bands of lettering.

But brickwork patterns, reminiscent of those on the Samanid mausoleum at Bokhara, were to be much used on later Seljuk architecture, which soon lost its original

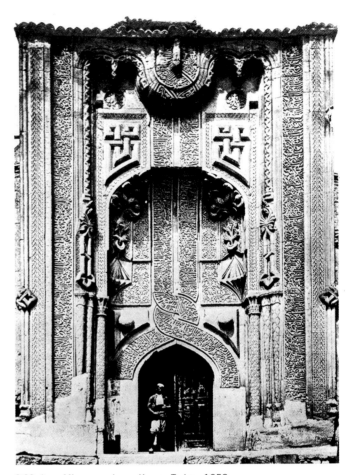

8,23 Ince Minare madrasa, Konya, Turkey, 1258.

austerity. Later buildings are exuberantly decorated, especially in Anatolia, where the Seljuks established the sultanate of Rum on territory won from Byzantium in the eleventh century. No more opulent example survives than the façade of the Ince Minare (slender minaret) madrasa (a college for related religious and legal studies) in their capital at Konya (8,23). Here the basic design follows that of the entrance to a Christian church, with a doorway recessed in a tall niche and flanked by engaged columns, but it has been elaborated almost out of recognition. The effect is, in fact, of a structure swathed in very thick and very heavy textiles. At the top the stone seems to be gathered up into a kind of valance, from the centre of which two bands of inscriptions fall and are twisted into a knot over the door. To trace this style back to the tents of nomads is, perhaps, no more than fanciful, for it did not mature until its patrons had long since been urbanized. But the crafts of weaving had been expertly practised by the peoples of central Asia since prehistoric times (see p. 60), and the Seljuks initiated the production of knotted carpets in Anatolia – the source of the world-famous Turkish carpet of later times. The prominent rectilinear knots above the niche on the Ince Minare madrasa façade are very reminiscent of motifs that recur on carpets. This building also takes to its logical – or illogical – extreme that tendency to overlay, almost to hang, panels of ornament like pieces of fabric on wall surfaces, a tendency already evident at Mshatta five centuries earlier (8,11).

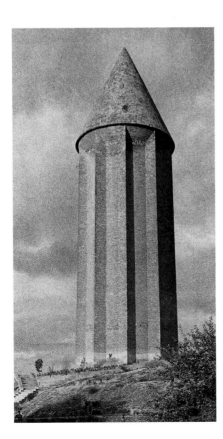

8,22 Tomb of Qabus near Gurgan, Iran, c. 1012.

The Madrasa

ARCHITECTURE FOR EDUCATION

The Ince Minare madrasa was founded by the vizier of a Seljuk sultan in 1258 (8,23). The architect Keluk ben Abdulla, whose name appears among the inscriptions on the façade, is said to have been a convert from Christianity. It was one of 24 such colleges built in the twelfth and thirteenth centuries in Konya, capital of the Seljuk Sultanate of Rum which covered most of Anatolia (wrested from the Byzantine empire in the eleventh century). There are substantial remains of some 50 Anatolian madrasas, differing from one another in size, plan and richness or severity of decoration. In Islamic architecture and intellectual life of this period the madrasa had an importance second only to the mosque.

From the beginning, great stress was laid on education in Islam and literacy soon became more widespread than in medieval Christendom. As the Koran and Hadith (see pp. 341–3) were believed to hold the keys to all knowledge, not simply theology, instruction was given in mosques to which full-time teachers were sometimes attached. But in Baghdad (see pp. 349–50) in the eighth century the caliph al-Mansur founded an academy whose members translated Persian, Sanskrit and Greek texts into Arabic, opening the way to philosophical speculations contrary to the Koran. In Cairo in 970 a mosque with accommodation for paid or aided students was founded to teach doctrines derived from the Shi'ite sect (see p. 349). The Seljuks, on the other hand, were staunchly Sunnite and the madrasas they founded were law schools for teaching the orthodox practices and beliefs that gave authority to their régime.

The madrasa was a residential institution rather like an Oxford college or the University of Virginia but smaller, with a master and rarely more than about 20 students who led a communal, almost monastic, life. In a four-year course students learnt the Koran and parts of the Hadith by heart, were instructed in the interpretation of civil law and engaged in carefully regulated debates or 'disputations'. Afterwards the most promising passed to higher studies and acquired licences to teach and give legal opinions.

The architectural origins of the madrasa lie buried in central Asia. Literary sources reveal that some were built in the early tenth century in the far east of Iran, and it seems likely that their plans were derived from Buddhist monasteries which had flourished in the region before the Muslim conquest. Although the earliest survivors, dating from the twelfth century, are in Syria they are in styles that derive from further east. The plan always included a central court, either covered by a dome or left open with an *iwan* (vaulted porch) on at least one side. An oratory, lecture hall and small cells for the students were adjacent. The Firdaws (paradise) madrasa in Aleppo is one of the most spacious and finest examples (8,24; 25). It was founded in 1235–6 by the niece and daughter-in-law of the sultan of Egypt, Salah ad-Din, known as Saladin in Europe, who was an indefatigable founder of madrasas, a militant upholder of Sunnite orthodoxy and as formidable an opponent of the Shi'ites as of the Crusaders whom he expelled from Palestine. (In Cairo he converted the Shi'ite mosque into the Sunnite university of al-Azhar, which still survives as the main centre of orthodox Islamic learning.)

Madrasas were founded and endowed by individuals who sometimes arranged to be buried in them. Although by no means secular, they were outside the jurisdiction of caliphs, the spiritual leaders of Islam who appointed the *imams* of congregational mosques. They could thus have a political role within a sultanate, securing for their founders the support of the professors they appointed and generations of students. The Ince Minare madrasa was founded by a vizier, a precarious position in courts where intrigues were rife. Manifesting wealth as well as piety, the madrasas also enhanced the prestige of their founders. Hence perhaps their remarkably individualistic variety as architecture. The façade of the Ince Minare madrasa is unique.

8,24 Court of the Firdaws madrasa, Aleppo, founded 1235–6.

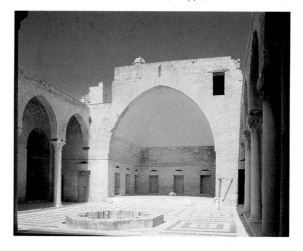

8,25 Plan of the Firdaws madrasa, Aleppo.

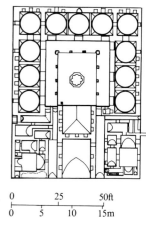

```
0        25        50ft
0    5    10    15m
```

ISLAMIC DECORATION

Although Islam's major contribution to the arts of the world was in architecture, Islamic buildings are seldom very original structurally, despite the ingenuity and inventiveness of Islamic architects, for example, in vault construction. A distinctively Islamic style is more evident in ornament and surface decoration, widely and quickly diffused by itinerant craftsmen and by trade in such luxury objects as metal vessels and panels of silk. Yet, even in ornament, many motifs were derivative and the initial impact of Islam was negative, marked by the absence of religious symbols and, in religious art, of animal and human figures. The first explicitly Islamic feature was Kufic lettering.

Calligraphy was the art most highly regarded by Muslims, and its practitioners – both professional scribes and amateurs, the latter including several viziers or ministers of state – are practically the only artists to be named in early literary sources. Kufic (so-called from an erroneous belief that it originated at Kufa in Iraq) was a ceremonial script. It was not used for day-to-day business but was developed mainly for manuscripts of the Koran, which, since illustrations were out of the question, could be given appropriate dignity only by fine penmanship and an occasional panel of abstract ornament (8,1). The page illustrated here begins: 'On the Day of Judgement, the faith of those who shall have disbelieved shall not avail them.' As these early Korans were intended to be pored over by several of the faithful at a time their pages are wide with few boldly written lines only – they were not intended, as were the Christian Gospels, for the eyes of priests alone. The same style, thick and heavy but rapier-sharp, was used extensively for monumental inscriptions usually in long frieze-like bands, where its strong visual rhythm – so different from that of Roman lettering – was either adapted to, or inspired by, the foliage ornament that

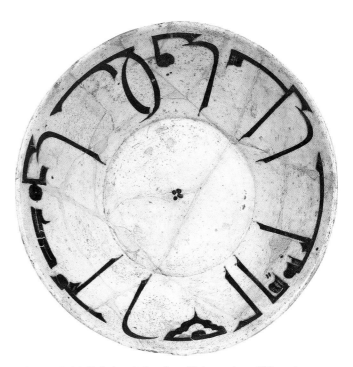

8,27 Bowl with Kufic inscription, from Nishapur, Iran, 10th century. Glazed earthenware, 3ins (7.2cm) high, 9¾ins (25.1cm) diameter. Khalili Collection.

often accompanied it, as on the *mihrab* arch in the Great Mosque at Córdoba.

Kufic inscriptions were also prominent in the decoration of such luxury objects as ivory caskets. The inscription on one made near Córdoba reads: 'The sight I offer is the fairest, the firm breast of a delicate girl. Beauty has invested me with splendid raiment, which makes a display of jewels. I am a receptacle for musk, camphor and ambergris' (**8,26**). In striking contrast with this 'vanity-box' are pottery plates of an austere beauty which have no decoration other than inscriptions of pious wishes and such wise saws as 'generosity is the disposition of the dwellers of Paradise' (**8,27**). Here the decorative potentiality of Kufic was fully exploited – to such a degree that it was often imitated and used as abstract ornament by artists unable to read it.

These plates, dating from the ninth and tenth centuries, are of interest from another point of view, as the earliest surviving examples of Islamic art clearly intended neither for the mosque nor the palace. Pottery had long been regarded, in the Near East as in Europe, as a 'humble' medium suitable for common utensils. In China, of course, a different attitude prevailed and artists of the Tang period (see p. 273) had refined pottery into a substance of exquisite beauty, a kind of proto-porcelain. Slightly later, true porcelain was invented. It was importations of Chinese stoneware and porcelain into Iran and Iraq in the Abbasid period that sparked off the sudden development of Islamic ceramics.

Since the type of clay (kaolin) essential for making true porcelain was unavailable in the Near East, a new type of pottery was invented, probably in Baghdad – tin-glazed

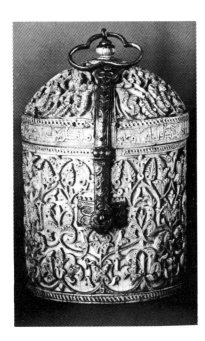

8,26 Ivory casket made in the workshop of Khalaf, Madinat az-Zahra, near Córdoba, c. 965–70. 6½ins (16cm) high. Hispanic Society of America, New York.

earthenware (also called faience or maiolica) with an equally glossy pure white surface, which provides an excellent ground for painted decorations in color. It was also discovered that this pottery could be given a wonderfully iridescent metallic surface by coating it before a second firing with lustre pigments (invented a little earlier in Egypt for use on glass). These developments were to transform not only household utensils and table-wares but also architecture. As we have already remarked, the *mihrab* of the Great Mosque at Kairouan was adorned with lustred tiles in 862–3 (they are, in fact, the earliest datable examples). Subsequently, tiles with inscriptions, geometrical patterns and leaf ornament in a range of cool colors – black, white, various blues and greens – were to become as much a distinguishing feature of Islamic architecture as are the orders of Classical architecture or the roof-carpentry of Chinese and Japanese. In the sixteenth century they replaced mosaics on the exterior of the Dome of the Rock.

Officially, the making of solid gold or silver vessels was prohibited; and although the ban (like that on

8,28 Griffin, 11th to 12th century. Bronze, about 3ft 4ins (1.02m) high. Museo dell'Opera della Primaziale, Pisa.

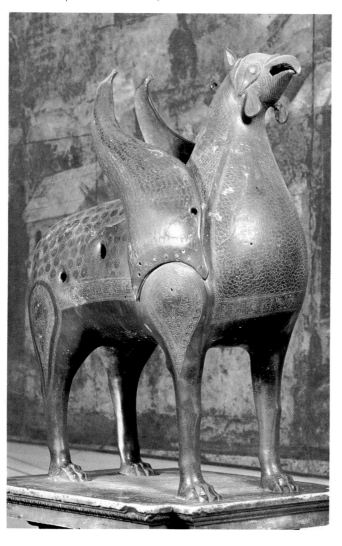

figurative representations) was often violated, it stimulated refinement of craftsmanship in base metals. Here again, as with the invention of tin-glazed earthenware, it was probably Muslims of the merchant or middle class who were the instigating patrons, rather than the upper-class élite of viziers and court officials, who could probably obtain porcelain from China and also gold and silver. The most famous centres of production were Herat (Afghanistan) and Mosul (now northern Iraq), where, from the Seljuk period until the late fifteenth century, magnificent ewers and basins for ablutions at home and in the mosque, handsome bronze candlesticks and other decorative objects were made of bronze or brass, often inlaid or partly coated with gold or silver. Surfaces were entirely covered with delicately incised ornament – geometrical, plant and animal motifs in addition to the ubiquitous Kufic inscriptions. Equally fine work was produced in Egypt especially under the Fatimid caliphs (990–1171) and in Spain. The finest surviving example is a bronze griffin said to have been taken to Italy by the crusader king of Jerusalem, Amalric I (1162–73). It comes as near as any Muslim artist ever went towards sculpture in the round (**8,28**).

Islamic art was appreciated and admired in Christian Europe almost from its beginning, and pottery, silks and metalwork were imported from all the main centres of the Islamic world. Commercial relations were never seriously interrupted – neither by the wars in Spain, for example, nor by the Crusades, which regained the Holy Land for Christians in 1099 and held it for nearly two centuries. Since no religious symbols were used in their decoration, Islamic artifacts were as acceptable to Christians as to Muslims. In Sicily, for instance, Muslim craftsmen went on working in their own style long after Messina had been conquered by the Normans in 1061. The finest surviving example of Islamic textile art was, in fact, produced in Palermo for King Roger II: a mantle of scarlet silk embroidered with gold thread and pearls (**8,29**). A lion attacking a camel, a motif that goes back to the very beginning of art in the Near East, is duplicated on either side of a Persian tree of life. Around the edge an Arabic inscription in Kufic lettering expresses fulsome good wishes to the wearer and is dated, according to the Muslim calendar, 528 (i.e. AD 1133–4). This superb robe was used from the sixteenth century onwards as the coronation mantle of the Holy Roman Emperors.

Islamic art raises a number of general questions about the nature of art, and in particular it poses the problem of artistic style and its causes. As we have seen, a consistent, well-marked and easily recognizable 'Islamic style' can be felt almost from the beginning – even in works which, as is not infrequent during the early centuries of Islam, can be shown to be largely composed of heterogeneous elements drawn from other cultures and civilizations. No one, for instance, could fail to identify the Dome of the Rock as a Muslim building, even though it derives quite directly in structure and form from a Christian prototype. This phenomenon is evident all over the Islamic world,

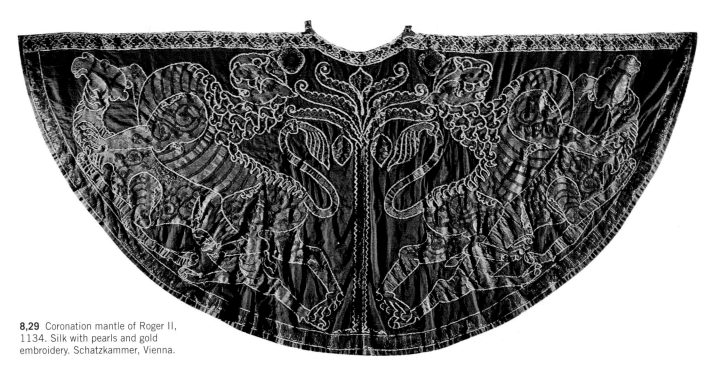

8,29 Coronation mantle of Roger II, 1134. Silk with pearls and gold embroidery. Schatzkammer, Vienna.

covering a tremendous range in time and space – from Spain to India for a period of more than 1,000 years – involving many different peoples of varying cultural and ethnic origins. Geographical and racial traditions are, therefore, inadequate as explanations and unilluminating generally in this context. Islamic art is not comparable to, say, Mexican art or Spanish art or Eskimo art. Religion, too, must be discounted as an explanation or cause in any simple, direct sense; for many Islamic works of art have quite obviously little or nothing to do with the faith which was, in any case, unconcerned with the visual arts, except negatively. Moreover, many typically Islamic works of art are known to have been made either by or for non-Muslims, as for instance the mantle of Roger II. To this extent, therefore, it would be as unhelpful and misleading to compare Islamic art with Buddhist or Christian art as it is to compare it with any of the national styles. Nevertheless, a few salient features distinguishing

Islamic art – notably its non-figurative and non-symbolic nature – arise directly or by implication from the Koran or the Hadith. And, more positively, the basic impulse behind Islamic artistic creativity may be traced, if not to the Prophet's teaching, then to his message in a wider and perhaps deeper sense. A ninth-century Muslim mystic described the tones of a flute as 'the voice of Satan crying over the world because he wants to make it outlive destruction; he cries over things that pass; he wants to reanimate them, while God only remains. Satan has been condemned to hold to things that pass and this is why he cries.' To the Muslim, God is the only reality. The world of the senses – of sight and touch – is transient and vain. Its beauty is evanescent, but, for that reason, all the more poignant and exquisite and desirable, all the more passionately to be cultivated and enjoyed. It might be said that Islam inspired no religious art – only an art that just stopped short of being irreligious.

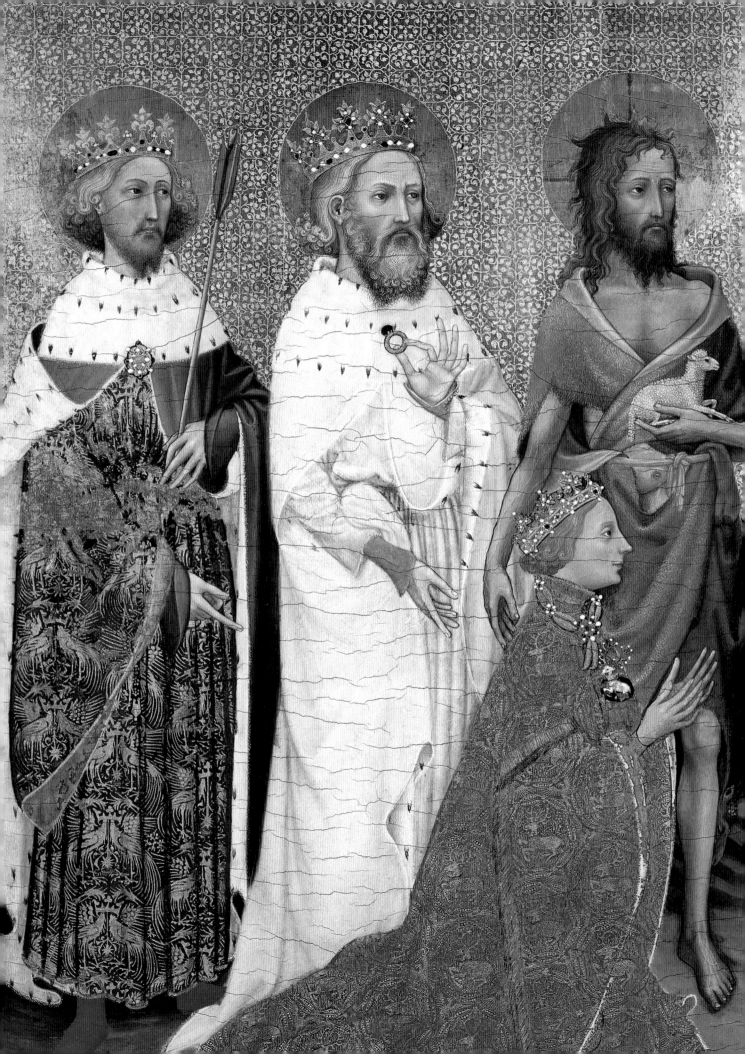

PART THREE

SACRED AND
SECULAR ART

Opposite The Wilton Diptych, detail, c. 1395. Egg tempera and gold leaf on oak panels, each 18 × 11½ins (45.7 × 29.2cm). National Gallery, London.

CHAPTER NINE

MEDIEVAL CHRISTENDOM

A crucifix in Cologne Cathedral (9,1) dates from about the same decade of the tenth century as the *mihrab* in the Great Mosque at Córdoba (8,18). Nothing could be further removed from the ideals of Islam or, indeed, of any of the other great religions of the world than this harrowing image. The degraded, humiliated, suffering god in human form is a peculiarly Christian conception. It reflects aspects of Christian thought which did not, however, become central until the Middle Ages. The early Christians had depicted Christ as healer, teacher, law-giver or judge (7,19; 20; 21). For them, the cross was a symbol of triumph over death, and the Crucifixion was seldom represented even in cycles of New Testament subjects (see p. 307). Byzantine artists sometimes depicted it after the Iconoclastic period, but always with a restrained and dignified, often rather ceremonial, remoteness stressing its sacramental significance rather than the painful actuality. Nor did they depart very far from Greek ideals of physical beauty in representing the incarnate deity.

There is no precedent for the stark and anything but idealized figure in Cologne Cathedral, a Christ exhausted by physical pain and torment, chest strained to the limits of endurance, stomach bulging, head slumped forward with eyes closed and mouth very slightly open. It was carved for Gero, archbishop of Cologne (969–76), and is the earliest known instance of that preoccupation with Christ's agony which originated in northern Europe and was to become a distinguishing feature of Western Catholic, as opposed to Eastern Orthodox, Christianity. No image other than that of Christ on the cross was appropriate for a church, Bernard of Angers declared in about 1020. Only in the West was it believed that the miraculous reproduction of the stigmata – the five wounds in Christ's hands, feet and side – on the body of a living man or woman was a gift of divine grace. They were received by St Francis of Assisi in 1224 (see p. 401) and later, with the pain but without the visible signs, by St Catherine of Siena. Only in the West did lay confraternities of flagellants whip themselves in public, so that, according to an early thirteenth-century writer, onlookers 'shed floods of tears as if they saw before their own eyes the very Passion of the Saviour'. To present events of the Gospel story, and especially the Passion, so vividly that spectators might feel they were participants was to be one

The visual arts		Historical landmarks	
969–76	Cross of Gero (9,1)	**c. 910**	Cluniac Order founded
c. 980	St Pantaleon, Cologne (9,4)	**962**	Otto I crowned Holy Roman Emperor
c. 1000	Cross of Lothar (9,2)	**1066**	Norman invasion of England
1063	S Marco, Venice, begun (9,14)	**1095–99**	First Crusade
c. 1073–83	Bayeux Tapestry (9,24)	**1098**	Cistercian Order founded
c. 1120	Cathedral of Santiago de Compostela (9,23)	**1204**	Crusaders take Constantinople
1128	Durham Cathedral begun (9,33)	**1216**	Dominican Order founded
1140–4	St-Denis (9,35)	**1225**	*Roman de la Rose*
1194–1220	Chartres Cathedral (9,48)	**1226**	Death of St Francis of Assisi
c. 1220–36	Amiens Cathedral (9,43)	**1274**	Death of St Thomas Aquinas
1228–53	Assisi (9,65)	**1290**	Spectacles invented (Italy)
1260	Nicola Pisano, Pisa pulpit (9,73)	**1291**	Fall of Acre: end of Christian rule in Near East
c. 1280–90	Cimabue, *Madonna* (9,71)	**1309**	Papacy moves to Avignon
c. 1304–13	Scrovegni Chapel (9,79)	**c. 1309–20**	Dante, *The Divine Comedy*
1308–11	Duccio, *Maestà* (9,76)	**1337**	Beginning of Hundred Years' War between England and France
1339	Lorenzetti, *Allegory of Peace* (9,83)	**1348**	Beginning of Black Death
c. 1345	Doges' Palace, Venice, begun (9,85)	**1353**	Turks invade Europe. Boccaccio, *Decameron*
c. 1395	The *Wilton Diptych* (9,86)	**1374**	Death of Petrarch
1395–1403	Sluter, *Moses Fountain* (9,90)	**1387**	Chaucer begins *The Canterbury Tales*

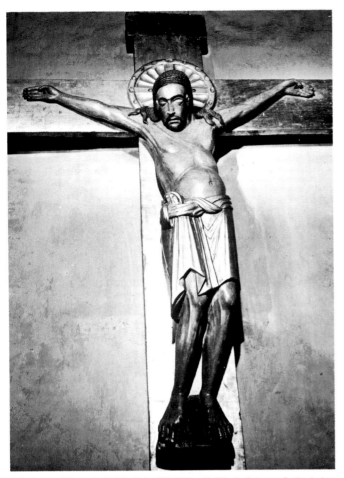

9,1 Cross of Gero, 969-76. Oak, 6ft 1⅝ins (1.87m). Cologne Cathedral, Germany.

of the prime aims of western European artists throughout the Middle Ages, setting their imagery ever further apart from that of Byzantium.

A different image of Christ appears on a large boulder carved between 965 and 985 at Jelling in Denmark (**9,3**). He is here shown bound in toils of interlace. Such patterns of twisted and knotted ropes and thongs had been painted on Insular manuscripts two centuries earlier (see p. 329), but at Jelling they seem to evoke a Christ already absorbed into a Nordic world of elemental gods and magic charms. The stone was carved at the command of King Harold Bluetooth, who, so the runic inscription claims, 'conquered all Denmark and Norway and made the Danes Christians'. For more than 100 years these people – called Danes and Norsemen in England, Normans in France – had been feared as remorseless pagans in Christian Europe. 'From the fury of the Norsemen, Good Lord deliver us' was a phrase inserted into many ninth-century litanies. Harold Bluetooth's attempt to impose Christianity on his subjects was a failure and led to his deposition. The conversion of Denmark and Norway was not effected for another century, and Sweden held out still longer. But northern artistic traditions of intricate flat patterning were to contribute much to the creation of medieval art in Western Christendom.

Very different in spirit and significance, though only a little later in date, is a magnificent gold cross in the Palatine Chapel at Aachen, studded with emeralds, amethysts, rubies and pearls in exquisite gold filigree

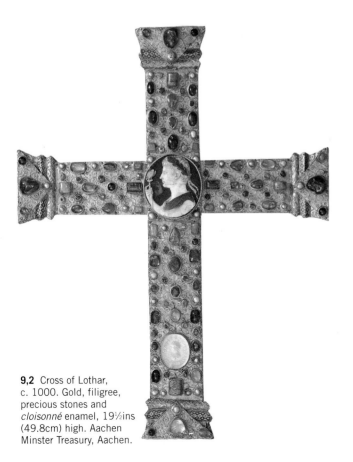

9,2 Cross of Lothar, c. 1000. Gold, filigree, precious stones and *cloisonné* enamel, 19½ins (49.8cm) high. Aachen Minster Treasury, Aachen.

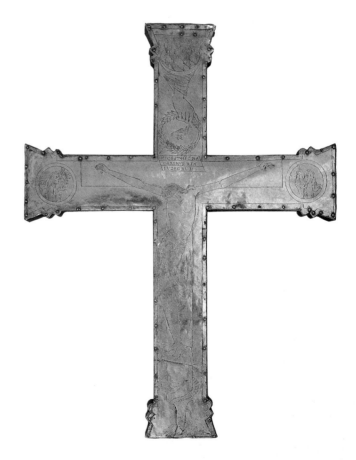

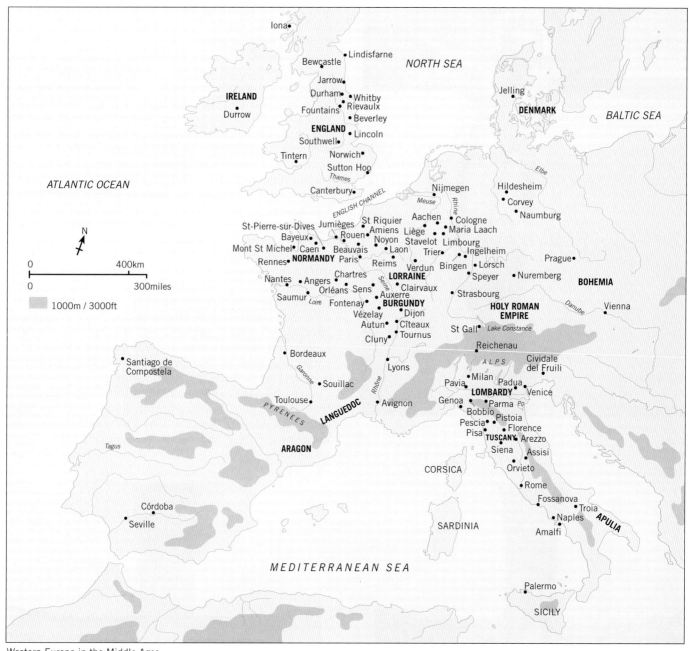

Western Europe in the Middle Ages

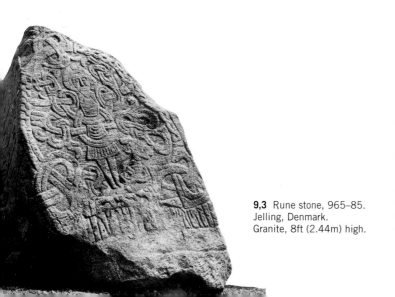

9,3 Rune stone, 965–85.
Jelling, Denmark.
Granite, 8ft (2.44m) high.

mounts (**9,2**). Whenever funds permitted, crosses, liturgical vessels and reliquaries were encrusted at this period with precious stones, like those of which, according to the Apocalypse, the heavenly Jerusalem will be built. Sometimes antique gems were used, despite the pagan subjects incised on them. One, of the three Graces, is set on its side in the cross at Aachen. But the most prominent gems were chosen carefully and with intent: in the centre an ancient Roman cameo of Augustus with imperial insignia and, lower down, a rock-crystal intaglio with the head and title of Lothar II, king of Lorraine (855–69), a great-grandson of Charlemagne (see p. 339). The idea of such a *crux gemmata* or jewelled cross goes back to the emblem adopted by Constantine, the first Christian emperor. And this spectacular example was made for the Holy Roman

Emperor Otto III (983–1002), who was possessed by the ambition to recreate the empire in the West. The victory of Christ – *Christus triumphans* – is symbolized by the imperial Classical imagery. On the reverse side, however, there is an engraving of the dying or dead Christ, closer to Byzantine formality than to Archbishop Gero's crucifix, with the hand of God the Father reaching down from above and holding a wreath which encloses the dove of the Holy Spirit – so that the three Persons of the Trinity are represented. When displayed in the ritual of imperial coronations, this side faced the clergy, the other the emperor. In this way the cross as a whole symbolized the union of Church and state under an emperor anointed and crowned by the Pope, a union passionately sought throughout the Middle Ages but rarely achieved.

The complexities of early medieval civilization – of which the cross of Lothar is so eloquent an emblem – reflect its origin in the turbulent centuries following the death of Charlemagne in 814. His empire had begun to crumble internally a decade before then and very quickly disintegrated into anarchy within the three areas nominally ruled by his descendants – roughly corresponding with present-day Germany, France and a central strip running from the Netherlands to Switzerland. It also came under constant attack from outside. Muslims from Spain marauded southern and central France in search of loot and slaves. Vikings harried the northern and western coastlands, and sailed up the rivers to the interior – Cologne, Rouen, Nantes, Orléans and Bordeaux had all fallen to them before 888. Then a new menace appeared: Magyars from central Asia swept into Europe, penetrating as far as Pavia in Italy by 899 and southern France by 917. Not until 924 were they forced to withdraw to Hungary and lead a more settled life.

In 911 the king of the western Franks granted territorial rights to a Viking band who had settled in what was later called after them Normandy, their leader being titled a duke and baptized a Christian the next year. The Normans were to play a very important part in medieval Europe, especially in the long struggle between popes and Holy Roman Emperors. By 1053 a group of Norman adventurers had moved into southern Italy, where they took possession of the last Byzantine colony in the west and went on to oust the Muslims from Sicily, while Duke William effected the conquest of England in 1066.

If the century that followed the death of Charlemagne was perhaps the most turbulent in the history of Europe, it was also the period in which the foundations of its medieval civilization were laid. Germany and France began to take shape under their own ruling houses and to develop individual cultures. Within them new social structures were built up from the complex relationships binding vassal to lord, in chains which extended from peasant to king – what is now called 'the feudal system', though there were several kinds of feudalism and none was systematic. Similarly, monasticism developed organically, gradually acquiring the importance of a supranational force. But not until the tenth century did the arts begin to revive.

OTTONIAN ART

Recovery from the century of terror came first in Germany with the re-establishment of stable government by King Henry (919–36), consolidated by his son Otto I (936–73), who was crowned by the Pope in Rome in 962 as the first of a new line of Holy Roman Emperors. Ottonian art, named after Otto I and his descendants who ruled Germany and northern Italy until 1056, was in some respects a conscious revival of the Carolingian style, with strong imperialist overtones. The abbey church of St Pantaleon in Cologne, financed by Archbishop Bruno, youngest brother of Otto I, harked back in plan to Carolingian churches (e.g. St Riquier; see p. 337), with a westwork that remained little altered when the rest of the church was reconstructed in later centuries (**9,4**).

Imposing westworks, such as that at St Pantaleon, are typically Ottonian – not least in being Carolingian in origin, the interior incorporating an upper-floor chapel looking down the nave to the high altar at the other end, as did Charlemagne's throne in the Palatine Chapel. But although Ottonian art, like the Ottonian *imperium*, derived inspiration from Carolingian precedents, it was by no means backward-looking. There is a new boldness in the massing of solids in the westwork of St Pantaleon and a new feeling for interior space at, for instance, St

9,4 St Pantaleon, Cologne, c. 980.

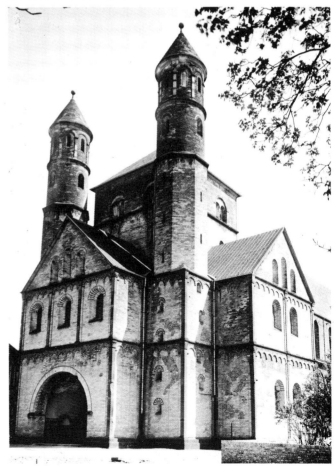

Michael, Hildesheim. St Michael's has two chancels, two transepts and two apses, that at the west being raised above a semi-basement chapel or crypt (**9,5**). Different areas are thus clearly articulated, yet held together by a controlling mathematical scheme based on equal squares. The nave consists of three squares with piers at the corners and columns in between, a system of alternating supports for arcades which was to be widely followed in Germany for a century or more. It is a complex plan and breaks decisively away from the Early Christian basilica's monotonous procession of columns on either side of the straight path from west door to apse. At St Michael's the interior was conceived as an encompassing space (**9,6**) and the main entrances were placed in the south flank so that the aisles into which they opened served as a narthex at right angles to the main axis with its balanced focal points. (The church was all but destroyed in the Second World War and has been rebuilt.)

The patron and, almost certainly, the architect of the church was the bishop of Hildesheim, St Bernward (c. 960–1022, canonized 1193), formerly tutor to Otto III (grandson of Otto I), whom he accompanied to Rome in

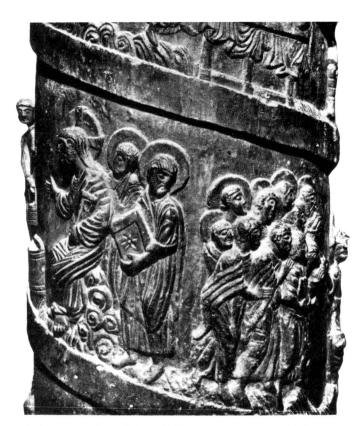

9,7 Column, detail of reliefs, c. 1015. Bronze, about 21ins (53.3cm) diameter. Hildesheim Cathedral.

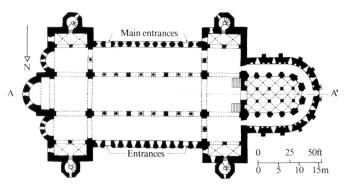

9,5 Plan of St Michael, Hildesheim.

9,6 Interior of St Michael, Hildesheim, Germany, c. 1001–31 (photograph pre-1938).

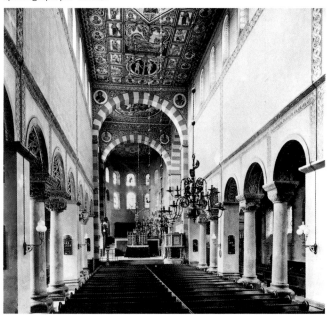

1001 – which suggests that the departure from the basilican plan must have been quite deliberate. His contemporary biographer described him as 'foremost in writing, experienced in painting, excellent in the science and art of bronze founding and in all architectural work'. He may, therefore, have done more than merely commission the great works in bronze for St Michael's (now in the cathedral). One is a 12-foot-high (3.65m) column with a spiral band of relief (**9,7**) inspired by the columns of Trajan and Marcus Aurelius in Rome (see pp. 213–5), but illustrating the life of Christ and originally surmounted by a large crucifix (destroyed in 1544). A pair of bronze doors survives intact, about 15 feet (4.5m) high, each apparently cast in a single piece with figures in bold relief, some heads being almost in the round (**9,8**). There are eight scenes on each door, from the Book of Genesis on the left reading down from the top, from the Gospels on the right reading in the reverse direction. This arrangement made it possible to confront subjects from the Old and New Testaments: the temptation of Adam and Eve is paired with the Crucifixion, for instance, to contrast the fall with the redemption of mankind. These subjects, though often depicted before in manuscript illustrations, which the designer probably consulted, had never been rendered with such common humanity and dramatic expressiveness. The sharpness of focus is such that each incident appears as if freshly imprinted on the artist's mind in a sudden flash of vision. Naked figures owe little or nothing to the Classical tradition of heroic nudity. They have a kind of natural gaucherie, a heaviness of trunk and weakness of limb suggestive of the frailty of the spirit within the flesh. Adam and Eve, meeting one another for the first time,

festivals of the liturgical year, were depicted instead. Inspiration for them was initially derived from Byzantium (close connections between the Ottonian court and Constantinople were cemented by the marriage in 972 of Otto II to a Byzantine princess). But distinctive styles were soon evolved.

A group of outstandingly fine manuscripts has been associated with the Abbey of Reichenau (on an island in Lake Constance), though there is no evidence that they were produced there. An illustration from the Gospel Book of Otto III epitomizes the style (**9,9**). It represents Christ preparing to wash the feet of the disciples, an act of humility annually commemorated in Constantinople by the Byzantine emperor and in Rome by the Pope (who, to this day, ceremonially washes the feet of 12 men the day before Good Friday). Here there are elements derived from Classical antiquity by way of Byzantium but used out of context, almost like the engraved gems embedded in a reliquary or cross. A Hellenistic statue of an athlete provided the distant model for the disciple undoing his sandal on the right. The figure of Christ, beardless as in Early Christian art, harks back to still earlier Roman relief carvings of a physician healing a patient, here replaced by St Peter. Christ and St Peter are hierarchically larger than the other figures; Christ's right arm is greatly lengthened

9,9 *Christ washing the Apostles' Feet*, from the Gospel Book of Otto III, c. 1000. Bayerische Staatsbibliothek, Munich.

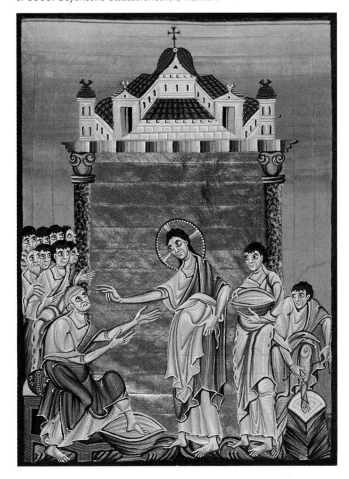

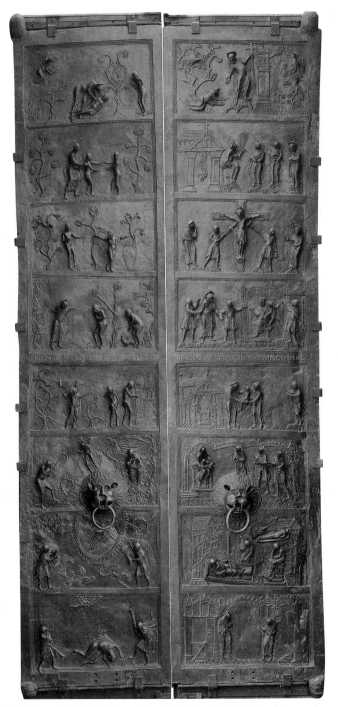

9,8 Bronze doors, with scenes from the Old and New Testaments, c. 1015. Hildesheim Cathedral.

seem tremulously shy. They gain self-confidence in the scene of the temptation, but after they have eaten the forbidden fruit and God points an accusing finger, they cringe with shame, Adam passing the blame on to Eve, who points to the dragon-like serpent at her feet.

Similarly in painting, a desire for greater emotional expressiveness is now increasingly felt and found an outlet in a new type of liturgical book which came into use during the Ottonian period, the *Pericope*. In this texts were cut up and arranged according to liturgical usage. There was no place for 'portraits' of evangelists, which had prefaced each Gospel in Carolingian manuscripts, and incidents from the life of Christ, commemorated in the

to emphasize the gesture of benediction, while St Peter similarly speaks with his hands in the dumb-show soon to be conventionalized as a visual language throughout medieval Europe. The buildings at the top also have a Roman origin in stage scenery and mural paintings (5,28), but the sense of perspective recession has been lost and they have all been flattened into a symmetrical motif crowning a frame filled with gold. They should be read as the earthly Jerusalem in front of, not above, the pure gold space of heaven within the frame, distinguished from the atmospheric mundane space in which the disciples move.

In this characteristically Ottonian miniature all sense of Classical rationalism has been lost. Instead a solemn monumentality is combined with a vibrant inwardness, an unworldly, visionary quality with sharp attention to actuality, surface patterns of flowing lines and rich bright colors with passionate emotionalism. Such conjunctions and syntheses typify the art of the Ottonian period and of the centuries that immediately followed. With the crucifix in Cologne Cathedral and the bronze doors at Hildesheim, this miniature signals the beginning of a new period in the history of European art.

ROMANESQUE ARCHITECTURE IN ITALY

By 961–2 Otto I had moved into Italy and restored relative political stability after more than 100 years of internal anarchy, aggravated by the attacks of the Magyars and the Saracens (as Muslims from north Africa were known in Italy, from the late Latin name for Arabs). This created conditions propitious not only for economic recovery but also for the rise of the communes or city-republics – the most important event in Italian history since the fall of the Roman empire and one that was to affect every aspect of political and cultural life in the peninsula for centuries.

About the year 1000, so the monk Raoul Glaber wrote a few decades later, 'it befell almost throughout the world, but especially in Italy and Gaul, that the fabrics of churches were rebuilt, although many were still seemly and needed no such care; but every nation in Christendom rivalled with the other, which should worship in the seemliest buildings. So it was as though the very world had shaken itself and cast off her old age, and was clothing herself everywhere in a white garment of churches.' In Italy this outburst of church building and rebuilding in the late tenth and early eleventh centuries led to no immediate change in style. Conservatism was the order of the day. Early Christian plans and decorative schemes were revived, especially in Rome, where one church, S Clemente, completely rebuilt after 1084, was later mistaken for a fourth-century basilica. Church builders in Lombardy reverted to a style of brick architecture, with brick and rubble vaulting, which had been first introduced about 800 (there is still much doubt about the date of some churches in and around Milan, variously assigned to the early ninth or the eleventh century). In Tuscany, too,

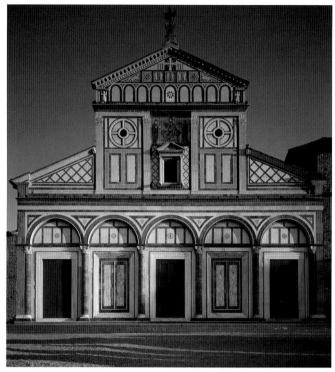

9,10 S Miniato al Monte, Florence, begun 1018.

they adhered to traditional plans but evolved a distinctive Classicizing style for the exterior elevations, most notably in Pisa and Florence. It is sometimes called the Tuscan 'Proto-Renaissance'.

The church of S Miniato al Monte overlooking Florence is probably the earliest surviving example, begun in 1018 (**9,10**). In general outline, the façade emphasizes the basilican form of the interior with a tall nave flanked by aisles. But its lower register (probably completed by 1062) is a shallow arcade with Corinthian columns framing three real and, for symmetry, two false doorways. The later (twelfth-century) upper part was designed as a Classical temple front, with the un-Classical insertion of a simulated arcade between the entablature and the pediment. The whole surface is clad in white and green marble in geometrical patterns of taut, clean elegance, lending it the dignified restraint and intellectual sharpness characteristic of later Tuscan art. The same style was adopted for the exterior of the most important religious building in Florence itself, the Baptistery, dedicated to the city's patron St John the Baptist (**9,11**). Both buildings date from the years when Florence was winning its way to acceptance as an independent republic.

At Pisa, on the coast only 50 miles (80km) west of Florence, churches were built on similarly traditional plans, but decorated externally in an increasingly divergent style. The monk Raoul Glaber's remark about the 'white garment of churches' is nowhere more vividly brought to mind than in the Piazza del Duomo or Cathedral Square of Pisa (**9,12**). Clad in white marble with thin horizontal lines of black, which give a gently shimmering effect, the cathedral, the Baptistery, the leaning tower or campanile,

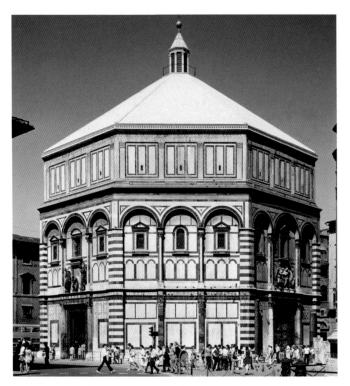

9,11 Baptistery, Florence, begun 1152.

and the walled cemetery still have a brilliance that is almost blinding on a sunny day. The cathedral was begun in 1063 to the design of an architect whose sarcophagus is embedded in the wall and inscribed in Latin: 'Unequalled is the temple of snowy marble which was in very truth

made by the talent of Buscheto'. Buscheto must have been responsible for the remarkable decorative scheme of very shallow, elegantly attenuated arcading, with windows and lozenges of colored marbles alternating in the arches, which was maintained when the nave was extended to the west and the present façade for the 'ground floor' of the Baptistery (begun 1152) and the campanile (begun 1173) – the famous leaning tower, whose foundations began to shift in the course of construction.

The idea of sheathing buildings in marble came, of course, from ancient Rome (see p. 197), and Pisans were able to obtain the material from nearby quarries used since the time of Augustus. Marble dignifies a building, as do columns; and at Pisa columns were used equally lavishly, no longer attached to the wall but free-standing and supporting open galleries or loggias on the cathedral façade, apse and campanile (**9,13**). The profusion of columns, rank above rank, on church fronts became the hallmark of a style which spread inland (though not as far as Florence) and appeared wherever Pisan influence was felt, in Sardinia and Corsica and the far south of Italy (e.g. at Troia in Apulia).

Pisa, formerly an important imperial Roman naval base, so prospered from trade with the eastern Mediterranean that at the beginning of the eleventh century it was recognized as a free republic. In alliance with the Genoese and later the Normans in southern Italy, the Pisans waged war on the Muslims, and it was loot from Muslim ships, taken at a battle in the bay of Palermo in 1062, that provided the funds to begin Pisa Cathedral. According to a contemporary chronicler, the Pisans 'declared with unanimous consent that a splendid temple

9,12 Baptistery, cathedral and campanile, Pisa, 1063–1272.

9,13 Plan of Baptistery, cathedral and campanile, Pisa.

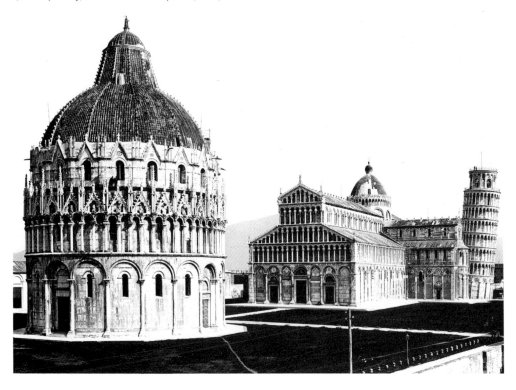

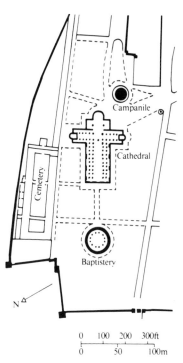

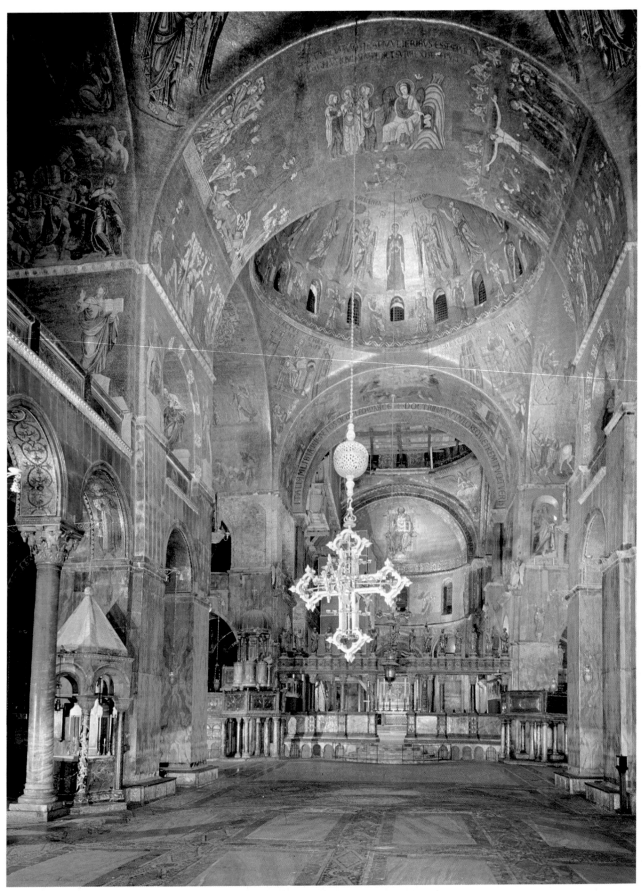

9,14 S Marco, Venice, begun 1063.

should be erected worthy of the Divine Majesty, and also such as to command universal admiration'. Ninety years later they celebrated a victory over Amalfi, a rival (Christian) maritime republic in southern Italy, by building the Baptistery. These great buildings in the Piazza del Duomo are, therefore, direct reflections of the thrusting expansion and prosperity of the Pisans, much increased at the beginning of the twelfth century, when they were shipping crusaders to the Holy Land at considerable profit. They are, in a sense, both civic and religious, rather as ancient Greek temples had been – monuments of a proud republic. Perhaps significantly, at a time when it was usual to state that a building had been erected 'by' the patron who commissioned it – the emperor, king, pope or bishop – the Pisans recorded the names of the individual architects in the inscriptions on the fabric: Buscheto, Rainaldo, who began the cathedral façade, Diotisalvi, who designed the Baptistery.

These buildings at Pisa, and also S Miniato al Monte and the Baptistery at Florence, are usually called 'Romanesque'. Originally meaning 'debased Roman', the term was invented in the early nineteenth century to categorize medieval architecture which retained the column and round arch, before the adoption of the pointed Gothic arch. It thus embraces architectural styles (and by extension painting and sculpture) still more widely divergent than the Pisan and Florentine – those of the great abbey churches of Germany and France, for instance, and the buildings of Norman Sicily, which owe as much to Islam as to Rome. But early medieval Venetian architecture is generally excluded.

S Marco in Venice is essentially Byzantine, designed by a Greek architect about 1063 and closely modelled on the Church of the Holy Apostles in Constantinople (tenth century, but destroyed 1469), with five domes, one over the centre and one over each of the arms (**9,14; 15; 16**). It

was built as a chapel attached to the palace of the Doges, the elected leaders of the Venetian republic, and had functions akin to those of Hagia Sophia in Constantinople and the Palatine Chapel in Aachen. As such, it was, still more obviously than Pisa Cathedral, a monument to the power of the state. Although few church interiors create a more deeply spiritual atmosphere than this, with its dim light, mysterious spaces and the lean faces of ascetic saints staring out of the gleaming gold mosaics on wall and roof, none was more inspired by temporal, non-religious ideals.

Venice was founded in the fifth century and soon came under the rule of the eastern (Byzantine) empire, to which it long remained attached – though only nominally after the end of the ninth century, when it became a virtually independent state (called a republic, but oligarchic rather than democratic) and grew rich from trade between northern Europe and the Near East. Venetians acknowledged their dependence on Constantinople only when it suited them, but S Marco was built between 1063 and 1094 under three pro-Byzantine doges, one of whom was married to a sister of the Byzantine emperor. Shortly after its completion, the Pala d'Oro – the gold altarpiece on the high altar – was enlarged by the addition of *cloisonné* enamel plaques (see Glossary) either imported from Constantinople or made by Byzantine artists in Venice (**9,17**). These panels are among the finest Byzantine works of art of their time, of a superbly sophisticated elegance of line and color.

Much of the present appearance of S Marco (and its Pala d'Oro) is the result of later workmanship and of later events in Venetian history. In 1204 the Venetians turned the tables on Byzantium by diverting a crusade from fighting the Muslims and leading it instead to sack Constantinople, after which they became for a time rulers of the eastern empire. In the following centuries, as Venice grew still richer by supplying Eastern merchandise to

9,15 Plan of S Marco, Venice.

9,16 S Marco, Venice.

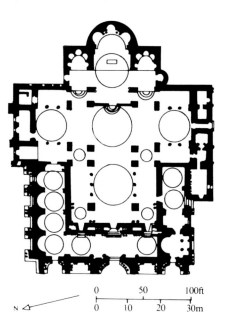

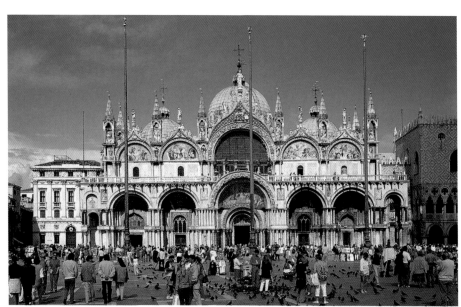

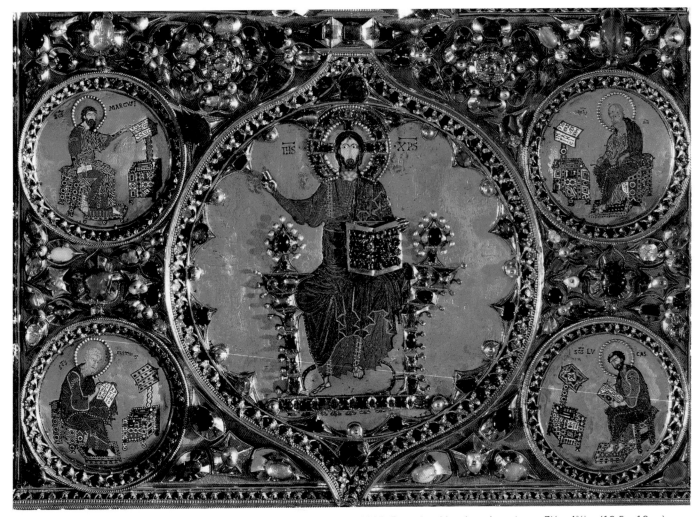

9,17 *Christ in Judgement and the Four Evangelists*, detail from the Pala d'Oro, 1105. Enamel, gold and precious stones, 7½ × 4¾ins (19.5 × 12cm). S Marco, Venice.

northern Europe, the interior of S Marco was gradually transformed with mosaics in non-Byzantine styles. Windows were filled in to provide additional wall space, thus dimming the light to which Byzantine architects gave such importance (see p. 318). S Marco symbolizes the rise of the Venetian republic to international importance and, by implication, its independence even from the Papacy. In fact, the bishop's church, the Cathedral of Venice, is a quite modest structure in comparison to S Marco and stands in a part of the city remote from the Doges' Palace and the centre of power.

ROMANESQUE ART AND ARCHITECTURE IN NORTHERN EUROPE

The flowering of Romanesque art and architecture in late eleventh-century France came after a long, bleak period. France suffered more from the disintegration of Charlemagne's empire than Germany; many towns had been devastated by Vikings, Muslims and Magyars, and recovery was slow. In 987 the west Frankish nobles (they

can hardly be called French as yet), who ruled a patchwork of independent duchies and counties, elected as king the undistinguished Hugh Capet. But the territories under his direct control and that of his immediate successors, in the Île de France around Paris, were poorer and less extensive than those of his more important nominal vassals – including the dukes of Normandy, who became kings of England in 1066 and ruled an exceptionally well organized state on both sides of the Channel. The Church, which held more land than any single lay ruler, was the only unifying institution, overlying and touching at many points the secular structure. Some bishops were, in fact, great feudal lords, and many bishops and abbots were members of the ruling families. It was, nevertheless, from French monasteries – first Cluny, then Cîteaux – that two major movements for religious reform radiated out to the rest of western Christendom, with momentous consequences in the visual arts, especially architecture expressing both temporal and spiritual authority.

In 910 the duke of Aquitaine bequeathed a large tract of land to establish a monastery at Cluny, with the unusual condition that it should be exempt from ecclesiastical, as well as secular, interference. This differentiated it from many monastic houses in France which had come under lay control (to the detriment and sometimes extinction of contemplative religious life), and also from those in Germany, which Otto I had made into imperial foundations. Benefiting from his unique situation, the second abbot of Cluny, St Odo (879–942), founded a kind of monastic empire by uniting under his authority a number of houses, from which a reformed Catholicism generated the militancy of the Church in the eleventh century. (Pope Gregory VII, who humbled the German emperor Henry IV at Canossa in 1077, and Pope Urban II, who summoned Europe to the first crusade in 1095, both began as monks at Cluny.) The first monastery at Cluny was already proving too small by 955, when work began on a new church vaulted with stone and surrounded with cloisters, dormitories, refectory, farm buildings and so on, all laid out on a clear rectangular plan. Before the end of the century more buildings were needed and a third and greater church was begun in c. 1085. It remained for long the largest in the world (**9,18**). Only the southern end of the transept survived destruction in 1810 (**9,19**).

The Cluniac Order set new standards for religious life and monastic organization, and also for churches whether of their own or other orders – large fabrics of imposing magnificence, boldly planned, solidly constructed with great stone vaults. It did not, however, initiate a new architectural style so much as accelerate developments that had already begun elsewhere at about the time of the Order's foundation. St-Sernin, Toulouse, contemporary with the third church at Cluny, though much smaller, derives from the same origins and its form was determined by similar structural possibilities, functional needs and spiritual ideals (**9,20; 21; 22**). Proportions were conditioned by the use of stone vaulting – a single great tunnel vault along the nave, strengthened with diaphragm arches – instead of the flat timber ceiling with which church naves had been covered during the earlier Middle Ages and often still were, as at Pisa. Many French churches with wooden roofs had been burnt out in the troubles of the ninth and early tenth centuries; but it was not solely in order to lessen the risk of fire – a hazard even in times of peace – that efforts were now being made to recover the ancient Roman art of large vault construction. Stone gave a nobler and more solemn effect and also provided better acoustics for the sonorous Gregorian chant, which had become an essential part of religious services, especially in monastic churches.

Externally the emphasis at St-Sernin is placed firmly on the east end, enclosing the choir and the high altar (the west end with its twin towers is unfinished). From the large apse and also from the east walls of the transept small apses project, presenting a bold grouping of rounded masses crowned by the great octagonal tower rising above the crossing (heightened in the thirteenth century by the addition of two upper stages). St-Sernin was the church of a house of Augustinian canons (priests who lived a communal life according to a rule less strenuous than that St Benedict had prescribed for monks; see p. 336). The little apses enclose chapels with altars so that several priests could say mass at the same time. Church plans of this type, incorporating numerous small chapels into a unified organic structure, had been evolved in the course of the previous 100 years or so in response to the relatively new

9,18 *Below* Elevation and plan of third abbey church, Cluny, France, c. 1085–1100 (from an 18th-century engraving).

9,19 *Right* South arm of transept, third abbey church, Cluny, c. 1085–1100.

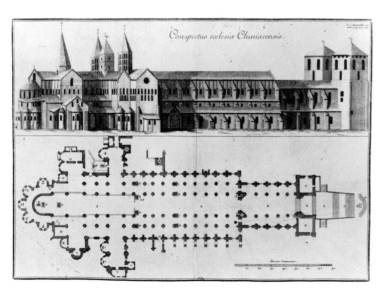

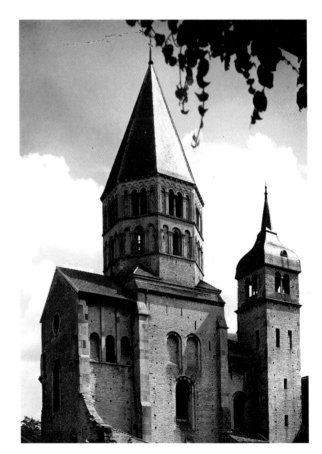

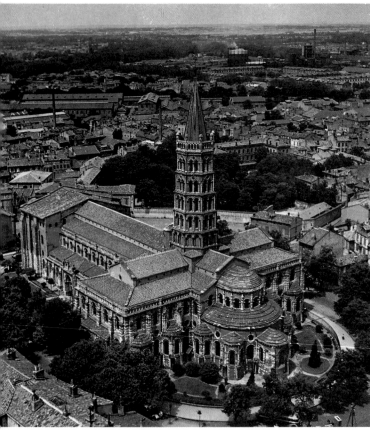

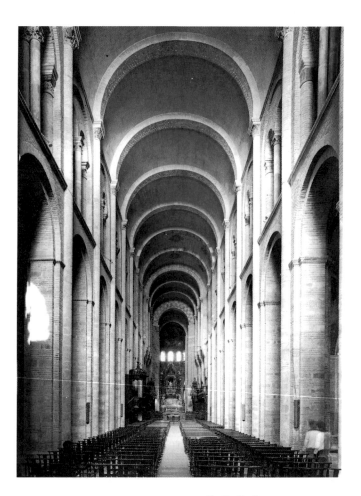

9,20 St-Sernin, Toulouse, France, c. 1080–1120.
(The top part of the tower was added in the 13th century.)

9,21 *Right, top* Interior of St-Sernin, Toulouse, c. 1080–1120.

9,22 *Right* Plan of St-Sernin, Toulouse.

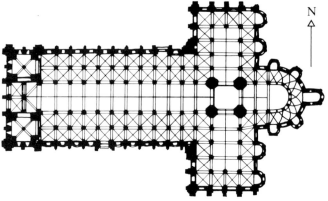

practice of daily celebration of the mass by every priest. The daily mass and the increased number of priests in monastic houses were among the more conspicuous results of the great religious reform movement of the mid-tenth century. But the apsidal chapels in St-Sernin were also used to display relics, which could be seen from the ambulatory dividing them off from the choir. The long nave and wide transepts with galleries above the aisles were intended to accommodate pilgrims. For St-Sernin was one of the many 'pilgrimage churches' built on the roads leading across France to the shrine of St James at Santiago de Compostela, in the north-western corner of Spain.

The cathedral of Santiago de Compostela is more grandiose than St-Sernin, with perhaps the most impressive of all Romanesque interiors (**9,23**). An enormous tunnel vault is supported on square stone piers with four attached half-column shafts, which divide the space into its component parts and, visually as well as structurally, bind it into a coherent whole. One shaft is extended the entire 68 feet (21m) height of the nave to carry a transverse arch, that on the other side carrying an arch of the aisle. The other two support the stilted round-headed arcade and seem to be continued within the stonework to re-emerge in the double arcade of the gallery. Lighting in

the nave is indirect, filtered from the outer windows of the aisles and galleries, but at the crossing it is direct and floods the central area with sunlight, emphasizing the stable bulk of walls and piers. Masses of almost unbroken masonry, squared and rounded blocks of brown granite, define the geometrically simple volumes of this great interior space. Solid, dignified, inflexibly self-assured, it exemplifies the Romanesque style. Here can be felt, more strongly than anywhere else, the style's origins, not so much in ancient Roman basilicas and temples as in Roman engineering and utilitarian architecture. In grave serenity it rises above the tumults of the Middle Ages, recalling the words of the Lord to Zachariah: 'Turn you to the stronghold, ye prisoners of hope.'

'The word pilgrim may be understood in a broad and a narrow sense', wrote Dante Alighieri in *La Vita Nuova* ('The New Life', c. 1292). 'In the broad sense anyone is a pilgrim who is outside his fatherland: in the narrow sense only the man who travels to or from the sanctuary of St James.' From the beginning of the eleventh century increasing crowds of men and women trudged sometimes more than 1,000 miles (1,600km) along the roads of France and through the unfriendly landscape of northern Spain to Santiago de Compostela. Why it should have attracted more pilgrims than any other shrine is difficult to say; relative inaccessibility may, paradoxically, have been in its favour at a time when Jerusalem was too remote and the road to Rome seemed almost too easy. Pilgrimages to Compostela were, in any event, aided by the Augustinian and other religious orders, whose houses became hostels along the way and sometimes profited greatly from offerings. People went for a variety of reasons – in thanksgiving for divine favours received, to benefit from prayer at the end of the journey, and often as acts of penitence, to relieve the sense of sin that permeated religious thought in western Europe (see p. 338). Pilgrimages were a binding force in medieval life, bringing together clergy and laity, rich and poor, of different regions and languages, and quickening the diffusion of secular, as well as religious, culture.

Secular, almost as much as religious, art and culture depended on Church patronage. Leading churchmen used the knowlege of Classical Latin acquired in the cloister to write not only pious hymns and lives of saints but also poems in the manner of Ovid, recalling with simulated regret the pleasures of wanton youth, when, as one recalled, 'my mind did stray, loving with hot desire'. At the same time, however, French vernacular poetry began to blossom in the charming *chansons de toile*, love songs for ladies to sing as they sewed, and the epic *chansons de geste* recounting the deeds of chivalry. The latter poems have a visual counterpart with a similar narrative structure in the Bayeux Tapestry (not a true tapestry with a woven design, but a 240-foot-long, 73m, strip of linen embroidered in colored wools), almost certainly worked by women – traditionally by the 'court ladies' of Matilda, the wife of William the Conqueror. In words and pictures it records the events leading up to the Norman Conquest of England in a sequence of separate scenes, each dominated by a few figures (**9,24**). Emphasis is placed on actions and abrupt, stiff-limbed, but expressive, gestures and close attention to details of contemporary costume, armour, arms, horse-trappings, carts and boats. Although much is conventionalized, rudimentary naturalistic effects were attempted: figures in each group are approximately the same size and not scaled according to rank; boats in the distance are appreciably smaller than those in the foreground. Other figurative hangings are known to have been made about the same time, but none has been preserved. Nor are there many surviving examples of the secular works of art which are recorded as decorating the lodgings of abbots and priors, as well as feudal castles in the eleventh century.

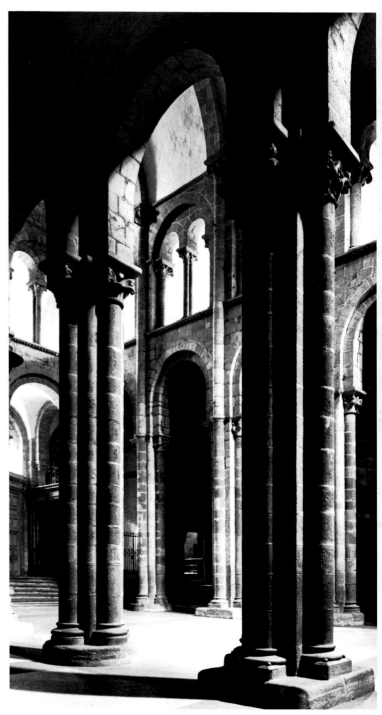

9,23 Cathedral of Santiago de Compostela, Spain, c. 1120.

The growing riches of the monasteries, especially Cluny, and the increasingly luxurious way of life adopted by abbots and priors, prompted a new call for monastic reform. In 1098 the stricter Cistercian Order was founded at Cîteaux some 15 miles (24km) south of Dijon. Here, as the old rule of St Benedict prescribed, the waking hours of the monks were divided between work and prayer. Work included the illumination of manuscripts (see Glossary), sometimes with scenes from daily life as well as religious imagery. Two of the brethren in ragged habits, indicating

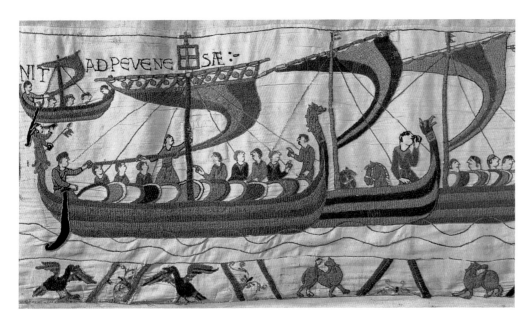

9,24 *The Fleet Sails*, detail from the Bayeux Tapestry, c. 1073–83. Wool embroidery on linen, 20ins (50.8cm) high. Bayeux Tapestry Museum, by special permission of the city of Bayeux.

their avowed poverty, are, for instance, shown splitting a tree-trunk and composing the letter Q in a commentary on the Book of Job (**9,25**). But even such innocent irrelevancies were frowned on by St Bernard of Clairvaux (1090–1153), the severest critic of monastic abuses who took command of the Cistercian Order in 1134. In a letter of 1127 denouncing the secular tone that had crept into monasteries, especially those of the Cluniac Order, he provided the most vivid description ever written of their carved decorations:

In the cloisters, under the eyes of the brethren engaged in reading, what business has there that ridiculous monstrosity, that amazing mis-shapen shapeliness and shapely mis-shapenness? Those unclean monkeys? Those fierce lions? Those fighting warriors? Those huntsmen blowing their horns? Here you behold several bodies beneath one head: there again several heads upon one body. Here you see a quadruped with the tail of a serpent; there a fish with the head of a quadruped. There an animal suggests a horse in front and half a goat behind; here a horned beast exhibits the rear part of a horse. In fine, on all sides there appears so rich and so amazing a variety of forms that it is more delightful to read the marbles than the manuscripts, and to spend the whole day in admiring these things, piece by piece, rather than in meditating on the Law of God.

(St Bernard of Clairvaux, *Apologia ad Willelmum Abbatem Sancti Theodorici*, tr. E. Panofsky)

When St Bernard wrote this denunciation the art of French Romanesque sculpture was at its height. Large-scale carving in stone had been little practised anywhere in Europe since the fall of the Roman empire; now several different local styles developed almost simultaneously in central and southern France, like a spontaneous flowering after a long winter. It was limited almost exclusively to the capitals of columns and the main exterior entrances to

churches. The Romanesque portal, consisting of a large semicircular tympanum carved in relief and resting on a lintel above the doorway, which usually had further carvings on its jambs, was given its characteristic form by about 1100. Christ was almost always shown in the centre, dwarfing all the other figures, and the favourite subject was the Last Judgement. The worshipper entered the church under the stern gaze of the all-seeing judge. That above the west door of Autun Cathedral in central France (**9,26**) is prominently signed by Gislebertus, one of the few named Romanesque sculptors whose work has survived and master of a style which combines sophisticated delicacy of line with great dramatic intensity. On Christ's left hand, the souls of the dead are shown as they are weighed in the balance – a scene which had been depicted in ancient Egyptian art (3,21). Little figures hide behind and clutch at the immaculately pleated robes of ethereally slender angels with faces and gestures of the utmost gentleness, while demons, open-jawed, claim the souls of the damned. In another part of the huge composition there are pilgrims among the saved, one wearing a

9,25 Initial Q from St Gregory's *Moralia in Job*, detail, 1111. Parchment. Bibliothèque Municipale, Dijon (MS 170, fol. 41).

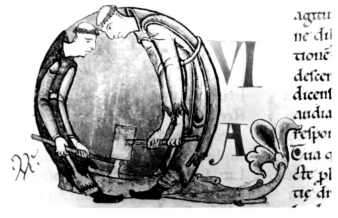

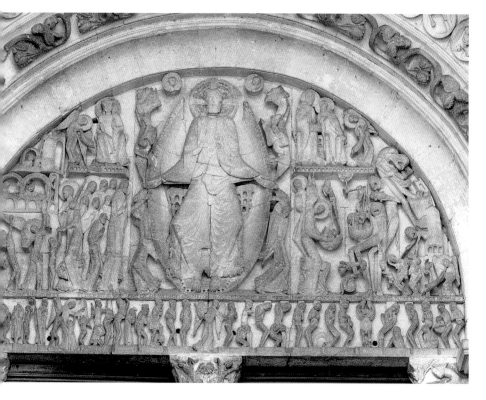

9,26 Gislebertus, tympanum, Autun Cathedral, France, c. 1130.

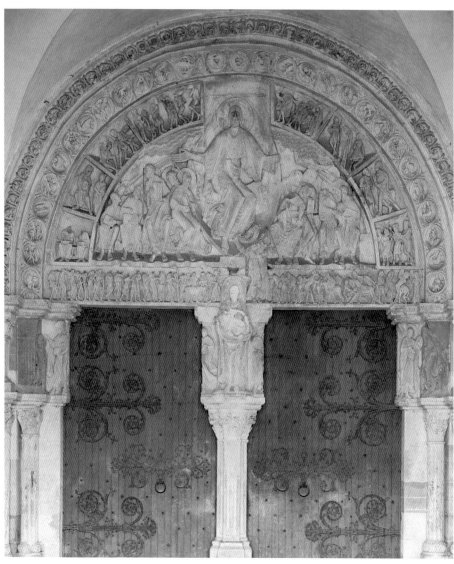

9,27 *Below, left* Central portal of La Madeleine, Vézelay, France, c. 1120–32.

9,28 *Below, right* Trumeau of the portal, abbey church, Souillac, Périgord, France, c. 1125.

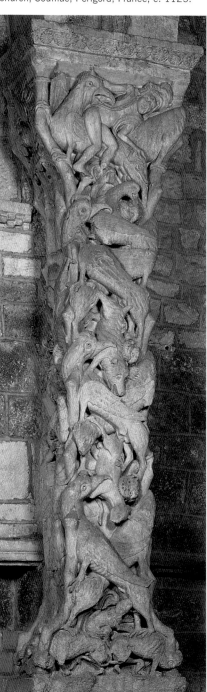

cockle-shell badge (symbol of St James) to show that he has been redeemed by a visit to Santiago de Compostela, another wearing a cross to indicate the benefit of a visit to Jerusalem. Equally significant is the miser among the damned – a victim of the deadly sin of avarice, which inhibited gifts to the Church.

More robustly carved are the sculptures over the entrance from the narthex to the nave of the Cluniac abbey and pilgrimage church at Vézelay (9,27). Christ is seated in majesty in the centre, sending the apostles forth on their mission to convert the heathen, heal the sick and cast out devils from the possessed – all of whom are shown on the lintel and inner archivolt (see Glossary). On the semicircle of the outer archivolt there are figures of men engaged in the 'Labours of the Months' and also the signs of the zodiac, in which the pagan gods lived on throughout the Middle Ages, here signifying Christ's rule over the cycle of the year. At the very top a man has twisted his body into a perfect circle – an image of uncertain significance and great antiquity going back to Minoan gems. Among the many small figures there are men with the heads of dogs (to the left of Christ's head) and men with huge wing-like ears (at the right of the lintel), dwellers in distant lands, who had been described by Pliny and entered the medieval imagination through the encyclopedic writings of the seventh-century archbishop, Isidore of Seville. Here, however, they seem to illustrate a passage in Isaiah, which had come to be read as a prophecy of the apostolic mission and also, in the early twelfth century, of the 'liberation' of the Holy Land by the crusaders (in 1099). The integration of Old Testament, New Testament and topical concerns is very characteristic of medieval art and thought.

The sculptor of this great tympanum obviously learnt much from manuscript illuminations – the calligraphic swirl of drapery on Christ's left knee, for instance – yet the figures have considerable three-dimensional substance. The manuscript illuminator's conventional seated posture with knees bent has been adapted in such a way that Christ seems to be materializing out of the stone. His head breaks the inner archivolt, just as that of St John the Baptist standing on the trumeau breaks through the lintel. The semicircle of the arch conditioned, without confining, the composition of the tympanum so that it remains part of the fabric of the building visually, though it has, in fact, no structural purpose or function. (It needs a special central member, the trumeau, to support it.) A tympanum exists solely in order to provide a field for relief sculpture, its only precedents being the painted or mosaic lunettes and conches of apses in Byzantine churches (7,29; 42). The similarity of effect must have been striking when tympana still retained their painted surfaces, for they were brightly colored as were all medieval carvings. Like a Byzantine apse mosaic, the tympanum presents an image of heaven, linking the building with its prototype in the celestial Jerusalem. The idea of carving it in stone and placing it on the exterior to draw the attention of pilgrims and other visitors seems to have been conceived in France.

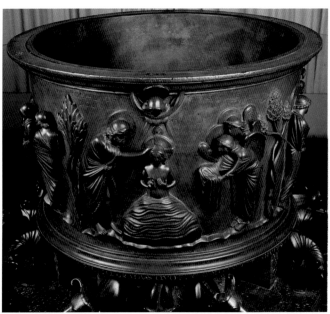

9,29 Rainer of Huy, Christ's baptism by St John, baptismal font, 1107-18. Bronze, 25ins (63.5cm) high. St Barthélémy, Liège, Belgium.

The trumeau supporting the lintel of the tympanum was also richly carved, never more strangely than at Souillac in south-western France (9,28). Monstrous birds with heads twisted back, their huge beaks grabbing at suspended animals, clamber over one another to the top of the column, where one attacks a naked man. They are fiercer than the creatures in the margins of Insular manuscripts (7,58), and personify the evil spirits which prey on human souls, as described by Marbod, bishop of Rennes (c. 1035–1123). It was carving of this kind, on the capitals of columns in churches throughout southern France, that aroused St Bernard's disapproval (p. 378).

An entirely different type of sculpture made a sudden appearance about the same time on a bronze font cast at Liège (Belgium) in the prosperous valley of the Meuse, then on the north-eastern frontier of the Holy Roman Empire (9,29). The font was inspired by Biblical accounts of the forecourt of Solomon's temple in Jerusalem, where a huge basin described as a 'molten sea' was supported on 12 oxen. Christ's baptism by St John and four other baptismal scenes are shown with figures so fully conceived in the round that they seem like statuettes detachable from the surface. In bodily proportions, poses, gestures and garments, they recall Classical models far beyond Byzantine, Carolingian or even Early Christian art. Their partly nude bodies have the sleek athletic flesh and even the hairstyle of ancient Greek youths. The contrast between them and the nude Adam on the doors at Hildesheim (9,8) or the figures in French Romanesque tympana is very striking. It would seem extremely likely that the sculptor of the Liège font, traditionally identified as Rainer of Huy, had seen ancient Greek statues. Perhaps he was among the many crusaders from the Mosan region in Godfrey of Bouillon's army, which passed through Constantinople in 1096 on its way to the Holy Land. Constantinople was the

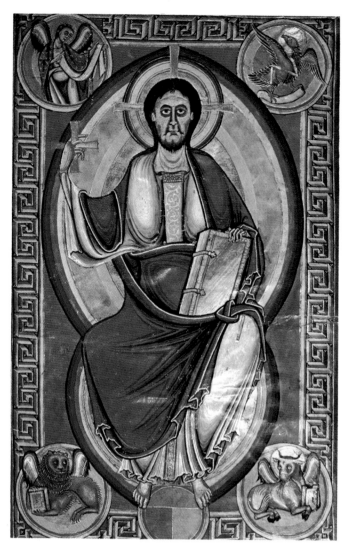

9,30 *Christ in Majesty*, page from the Stavelot Bible, 1093-7. Parchment, 22½ × 14½ins (57.5 × 37cm). British Library, London.

one place where numerous examples of ancient Greek sculpture were still to be seen. (Very few remained above ground in Rome by this date.) The almost literal Classicism of his figures is unique in early medieval art.

Although there is nothing comparable in manuscript illumination of about this date in the Mosan region, a similar tendency towards monumentality is sometimes evident, as in the miniature of Christ in Majesty in a Bible from the rich and important monastery of Stavelot (Belgium) (**9,30**). Modelling is bolder, lines are more firmly drawn than before with nervous touches only on the ruffled hem of the robe. Moreover, Christ seems to project beyond the frame, overlapping the roundels with symbols of evangelists that partly cover the sharper rectilinear fret of the border. The design is made up of separate elements, like plaques of embossed or enamelled metal superimposed on the ground. And it may well owe a debt to the metalwork, especially *champlevé* enamelling (see Glossary), for which the Mosan region was renowned at this date.

INNOVATIONS IN ROMANESQUE ARCHITECTURE

Architectural developments of great importance, which took place at the end of the eleventh century in both Germany and France, were at least partly inspired by similar demands for greater unity of effect. The technical knowledge and skill required for stone-vaulting on a large scale had been recovered by the mid-century, as we have seen (pp. 375–6), naves of churches being covered with simple tunnel vaults or with a series of tunnel vaults placed transversely. The transverse system, an ingenious alternative, survives at St Philibert, Tournus, vaulted shortly after 1066 with such a variety of different types that it might almost seem to have been an experimental workshop. It was probably in the course of developing these two main systems, the tunnel and the transverse, that the potential advantage of the groin vault – half one and half the other – became apparent (see Glossary). In a groin vault the weight is carried by the four corner points instead of by the whole wall – hence the greater difficulty in construction. Groin vaults were first used to span a wide nave at Speyer in the Rhineland, where the great, gaunt imperial cathedral, begun about 1030 with a flat timber ceiling, was remodelled between 1082 and 1106 (**9,31**). The nave is 45 feet (14m) wide and 107 feet (33m) high – i.e. wider and higher than Cluny (40 feet, 12m, wide

9,31 Interior of Speyer Cathedral, Germany, c. 1082–1106.

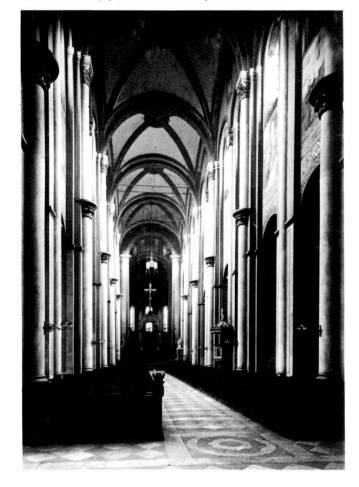

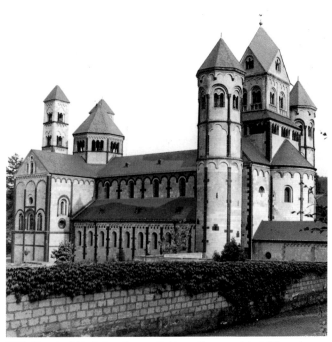

9,32 Church of Maria Laach, near Coblenz, Germany, late 11th century.

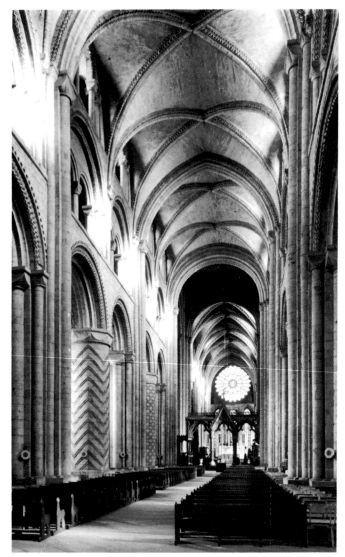

9,33 Nave of Durham Cathedral, England, 1093–c. 1130.

and 98 feet, 30m, high) and a little short of the highest Gothic nave, at Beauvais. Grand and austere, as befitted the dynastic pantheon of the Franconian emperors, Speyer has all the defiance and assurance of German Romanesque. Lining the nave are huge piers with alternate engaged shafts forming blind arcades very reminiscent in their stern solemnity of a Roman aqueduct. They probably derive from the exterior elevation of the Roman basilica at Trier, less than 100 miles (160km) away. Unfortunately, the exterior of Speyer Cathedral has been much altered, but its originally splendid display of towers – octagonal, round and square – of double transepts and double chancels can still be seen on a smaller scale at the contemporary abbey church of Maria Laach, near Coblenz (**9,32**).

Although the great vaults at Speyer were not formed by a true interpenetration of tunnel vaults, substantial transverse arches being needed to strengthen them, a very significant step had been taken. Even more significantly, projecting diagonal ribs – that is ribs constructed before filling in the intervening triangular webs and not embedded in them, as ancient Roman ribs had been – followed only a few years later in widely separated locations in England, Italy and France. At Durham Cathedral they seem to have been intended from the start (1093); they were completed by about 1095 in the chancel aisles, by about 1104 in the chancel and by 1130 in the nave (**9,33**). At S Ambrogio, Milan, they were probably built shortly after 1117 and St-Etienne, Caen, between 1115 and 1120, but here they were rebuilt in the seventeenth century (**9,34**).

The introduction of ribbed groin vaults brought the medieval architect's quest for lofty, well-lit, fire-proof and aesthetically unified interior spaces close to a solution. And it raises the question of how far the evolution of vaulting was determined by aesthetic preferences. The

notion that its development was due simply to the need for improved technical means for spanning wide naves now seems a nineteenth-century misinterpretation, important though structural considerations clearly were. Aesthetic motives must have been involved as well, as we have seen (p. 375); indeed, they were inseparable, except in retrospect.

Tunnel vaults were unsatisfactory, not only because the massive stone piers and thick, unbroken walls needed to take their weight and outward thrust were both costly and cumbersome, but also because they accounted for much of the characteristic heaviness of Romanesque architecture. In addition, they tended to exclude light. Light could reach the chancel and nave only through the tribunes and galleries above the aisles, as at Santiago de Compostela (**9,23**). Groin vaults, by spreading their weight, allowed space for clerestory windows above the tribunes; but groin vaults were difficult to form, required a great deal of woodwork for centering to support them while they were being built, and sometimes produced

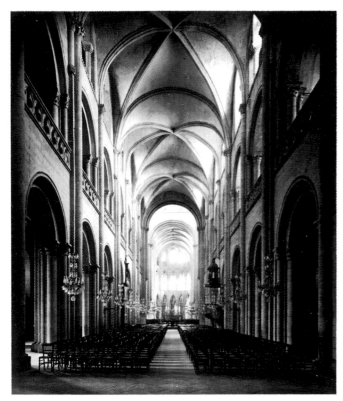

9,34 Interior of the abbey church of St-Etienne, Caen, France, early 12th century (restored 1616).

disturbing effects of double curvature. Rib vaults had the practical advantage that the ribs formed the supports and were built first, the webs between them being filled in later with lighter stone or other material, thus removing the need for the gigantic wooden frameworks formerly used during construction. No less important, however, was the visual effect. The ribs integrated each bay (or double bay) into clearly defined units, while creating a firm rhythm that binds them all together and gives the whole interior space a lighter, less stern and forbidding appearance. Indeed, ribs may have been introduced initially for aesthetic rather than structural reasons, as their predecessors in the Islamic world had been. In Islamic architecture projecting ribs had been used from at least as early as the tenth century in domes and domical vaults where there was no real structural need for them at all, as in the Great Mosque at Córdoba (8,17).

The rib vault was the most important structural device by which the inert masses of Romanesque architecture were gradually reduced and lightened, both in fact and in appearance. Its visual effect was emphasized, however, by combination with tall, thin shafts attached to the piers. These shafts, found separately at Notre-Dame, Jumièges (1037–66), rise from ground level up to the roof, and at Speyer, Durham, Caen and elsewhere appear to fan out across the vault as ribs, drawing the eye upwards so that it tends to overlook the solidity of wall and roof. At Caen a further and more daring refinement appeared for the first time, the sexpartite vault (9,34). Created by adding a second transverse rib, cutting across the vault

from side to side and splitting it into six compartments, the sexpartite vault greatly increased the unified effect of the interior space, especially when, as at Caen, it was used with a double-bay vaulting system. At Durham there was a third and perhaps more important innovation, the combination of rib vaults with pointed arches (9,33). This might almost seem to herald Gothic effects of aspiration and upward growth. But Durham remains essentially Romanesque. The great bare round arches, block capitals and moldings of uniformly blunt simplicity, the sheer size of the massive piers with their deeply cut zigzags and other bold geometrical ornamentation, convey an overwhelming impression of absolute power and authority. Durham is the most forceful of all the noble expressions of that proud moment in medieval Christianity at the end of the eleventh century, when reform had triumphed at Rome and initiated the last great flowering of monasticism at Cîteaux, when the supremacy of the papal tiara over the imperial crown had been asserted at Canossa with the humiliation of the Emperor Henry IV by Pope Gregory VII and the knights of Europe set out to recover the Holy Land in the first crusade (1095).

GOTHIC ART AND ARCHITECTURE

The ambulatory of the abbey church of St-Denis, now a northern suburb of Paris, holds a position of unique importance in the history of European architecture (**9,35; 36**). It is all that remains of the *chevet*, or east end, completed after only four years of work in 1144 as the first major part of any building in the Gothic style (the choir which it originally surrounded was replaced a century later). The ancestry of every subsequent Gothic church in the world – including the Episcopalian Cathedral recently completed in Washington DC – can be traced back to it. Whether the builders realized the import of what they had done is, however, very doubtful. There is no hint that they did in either of the two detailed accounts of its construction and decoration written by Suger (1081–1151), abbot of St-Denis, who initiated and directed the whole enterprise. Nor is the architect responsible for the epoch-making design named, though one must certainly have been employed.

No individual element in St-Denis was, in fact, completely new. Apses with radial chapels had been built much earlier, as at St-Sernin (9,22), though they had not been planned so that space could flow round them uninterrupted by walls. Pointed arches and ribbed vaults – the most obvious characteristics of a Gothic interior – had also been used before, but not so consistently as to transform a Romanesque architecture of massive load-bearing walls into another (Gothic) one of slender supports with no inert matter, only active, thrusting energy. The architectural revolution effected at St-Denis was one of structural relationships rather than forms. It is in many ways analogous to the developing intellectual movement known as Scholasticism, which, without introducing original ideas, created a new and enduring structure of thought from a systematically dialectical reconciliation

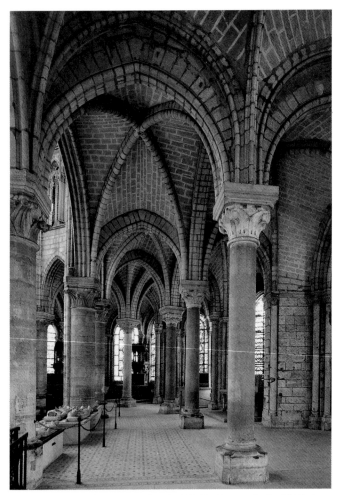

9,35 Ambulatory of the abbey church of St-Denis, near Paris, 1140–4.

9,36 Plan of the *chevet* of St-Denis.

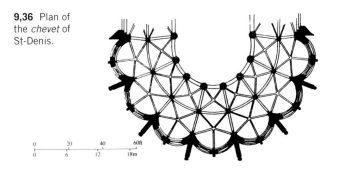

of the truths of reason and faith, philosophy and theology, Aristotle and the Bible. What was new, and strikingly so, at St-Denis was the way in which well-established techniques of construction were combined to create an interior of wholly unprecedented clarity. As Suger himself remarked, by virtue of the ambulatory chapels the whole church shone 'with the wonderful and uninterrupted light of most luminous windows, pervading the interior beauty'.

Although Suger wrote, and may have understood, little of architectural practice, his writings abound in remarks which reveal his purpose and suggest the crucial role he played as patron. In his account of the consecration of the *chevet* on 11 June 1144, for instance, he recorded how five archbishops and 14 bishops celebrated mass at the new

ABBOT SUGER FINDS COLUMNS
AND BEAMS FOR ST-DENIS

Abbot Suger's determination and practicality, as well as his close personal participation in the work at St-Denis, is illustrated by two incidents. Having failed to get marble columns from Rome, where he had seen 'wonderful ones' in the Baths of Diocletian, the 'Almighty revealed to the astonishment of all' that there was a good quarry nearby, used for millstones. Suger had columns quarried there and hauled up by ropes.

Both our own people and the pious neighbours, nobles and common folk alike, would tie their arms and chests and shoulders to the ropes and, acting as draft animals, draw the columns up.

Similarly, when he was told that no timber for beams was available nearer than Auxerre, nearly 200 miles (320km) away, he decided in bed one morning, after Matins, to go himself and find what was needed in a forest nearby belonging to the abbey. The foresters told him that all suitable timber had just been felled. Suger wrote:

We however – scorning whatever they might say – began, with the courage of our faith as it were, to search through the woods; and towards the first hour we found timber adequate to the measure. Why say more? By the ninth hour we had, through the thickets, the depths of the forests and the dense, thorny tangles, marked down 12 timbers (for so many were necessary), to the astonishment of all, especially those on the spot.

He had them felled and carried to the abbey where they were placed: . . . *with exultation upon the ceiling of the new structure, to the praise and glory of our Lord Jesus.*

(*Abbot Suger on the Abbey Church of St-Denis and its Art Treasures*, ed., tr. and annotated by E. Panofsky, Princeton 1979)

altars in the choir, ambulatory and crypt beneath:

. . . *so festively, so solemnly, so diversely and yet so concordantly, and so joyfully that their song, delightful by its consonance and unified harmony, was deemed a symphony angelic rather than human; and that all exclaimed with heart and mouth: 'Blessed be the glory of the Lord from His place, Blessed and worthy of praise and exalted above all be Thy name, Lord Jesus Christ . . . . Thou uniformly conjoinest the material with the immaterial, the corporeal with the spiritual, the human with the Divine . . . .*

(*Abbot Suger on the Abbey Church of St-Denis and its Art Treasures*, ed., tr. and annotated by E. Panofsky, Princeton 1979)

The last words in particular might equally well refer to Gothic architecture. Indeed, they indicate its essence most succinctly.

One source of Suger's inspiration for St-Denis is known. The monastic library owned a manuscript of writings attributed to 'Dionysius' (later called the pseudo-Areopagite), an important theologian who lived in Syria about 500 but was mistakenly identified with St Dionysius or Denis (the French form of the name), believed to have evangelized France. However, confusion could not have been more happily confounded. From Dionysius, who had fused the philosophy of Plotinus (see pp. 220–1) with Christian theology, Suger derived the idea of God as the 'superessential light' reflected in 'harmony and radiance' on earth. The new *chevet*, 'pervaded by the new light', as Suger wrote, was thus designed to illustrate the Neoplatonic theology of the saint to whom it was dedicated. The brightly colored gems with which Suger had the high altar, the great cross and liturgical vessels encrusted (**9,37**) also reflected divine light 'transferring that which is material to that which is immaterial' and, he declared, transporting him 'from this inferior to that higher world in an anagogical manner'.

But the church had a political as well as a religious role. St-Denis was a royal abbey which enshrined the relics of the patron saint of France and, from Hugh Capet onwards, had been the burial-place of French kings. Suger himself had close ties to the royal house and was perhaps more active in the political than in the religious sphere. When he was elected abbot of St-Denis in 1122, the fabric

9,37 Chalice, c. 1140. Agate and silver gilt. 7½ins (19cm) high. National Gallery of Art, Washington DC (Widener Collection).

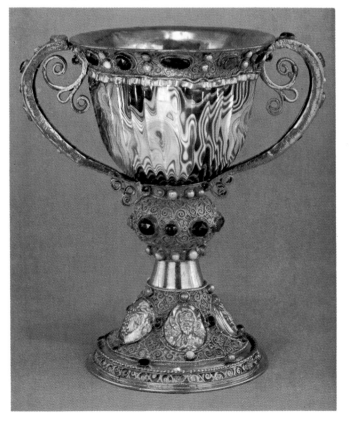

was in a sad state of disrepair, the monastery's extensive estates were mismanaged and the morals of its monks were said to be lax. A contemporary called it a 'synagogue of Satan'. Suger was to reform all this. He began to raise funds for rebuilding in 1124 and continued while he was promoting the re-establishment of royal power in France as first minister to Louis VI (1108–37).

St Bernard of Clairvaux (see p. 378), a sharp critic of the monastery at the time of Suger's election, felt bound to congratulate the abbot on its reformation five years later. It is impossible to say how far, if at all, he inspired the design of the new church. But, about 1130, the archbishop of Sens, who had come under his spell, began to rebuild the *chevet* of Sens Cathedral with piers for vaulting similar to that at St-Denis (begun later but finished sooner). Ascetic, high-born, high-minded St Bernard was quite unlike the humbly born but rather worldly Suger with his devotion to royalty, his love of pomp and ceremony, his infectious delight in objects made of precious substances. Yet both contributed to the creation of the emerging Gothic style.

Like Suger, St Bernard was deeply influenced by Neoplatonism, but in a very different way. In a typically Neoplatonic image he described the union of the soul with God as 'immersion in the infinite ocean of luminous eternity'. This spiritual, indeed mystical, view led him to join his voice to the mounting criticism of the mundane splendour of Cluniac churches, their vast size, their 'costly polishings, the curious carvings and paintings which attract the worshipper's gaze and hinder his attention'. Monks should, he thought, renounce 'all precious and beautiful things for Christ's sake . . . all things fair to see or soothing to hear, sweet to smell, delightful to taste, or pleasant to touch'. The abbey of Fontenay (1139–47), built while he was abbot, reflects his views – it is in a kind of expurgated Romanesque (**9,38**). In this way the Cistercians

9,38 View from the chapter-house into the cloister, Fontenay Abbey, France, c. 1147.

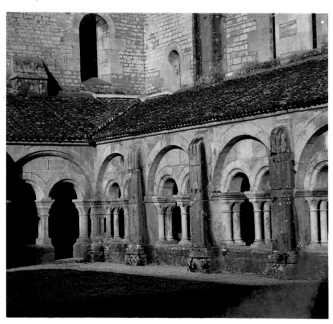

The Gothic Cathedral

THE NEW JERUSALEM

The great Gothic cathedrals, with their towers and spires soaring above even the tallest modern buildings in many European cities, seem to epitomize medieval civilization. They seem to reflect, as comprehensively and accurately as in a mirror, the beliefs and lives of the people by whom and for whom they were created. Angels and saints and devils, kings and queens, noblemen and their ladies, merchants, artisans and peasants all figure in their numerous carvings and stained glass windows. And they were indeed often the outcome of local communal effort and thus became the expression of regional

9,39 *Assumption of the Virgin*, from the Glasgow Psalter, c. 1170. Illumination on vellum, 6½ × 5⁹⁄₁₀ins (16.5 × 15cm). Hunterian Library, Glasgow (MS U.3.2, fol. 5, 3v).

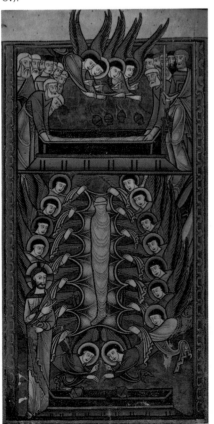

life. A cathedral, by definition a church containing the bishop's throne (*cathedra*), was a centre of temporal power as well as of spiritual authority.

But for those who built and created them, the Gothic cathedrals were above all great symbols, ever-present emblems and pointers to heaven. Their secular significance was no more than a corollary of their transcendental religious meaning in a world where the hierarchies of Church and state were believed to be no less divinely ordained than that of heaven. It was as a new Temple of Jerusalem, or rather as a New Jerusalem or City of God, that they were often conceived. Their symbolism was based not on any simple one-to-one relationship of image to idea, as in allegory, so much as on anagogy or a mystical interpretation which leads the mind upwards from the material to the divine. Abbot Suger (see p. 383) relates that when contemplating the beauty of precious stones set in the altar of St-Denis he was led to reflect on the sacred virtues: 'Then it seems to me that I see myself dwelling, as it were, in some strange region of the universe which exists neither entirely in the slime of the earth, nor entirely in the purity of Heaven; and that, by the grace of God, I can be transported from this inferior to that higher world in an anagogical [mystical] manner'.

Biblical accounts of the temple of Jerusalem, built by Solomon and destroyed by the pagan Romans, were a source of inspiration in this spiritual quest. Sometimes elements were emulated quite literally, for example by Rainer of Huy (9,29). Similarly at the abbey of Cluny there was a large bronze candelabrum with seven branches like that which had been stolen from the Temple of Jerusalem by Titus and brought back in triumph to Rome (5,64). St Bernard of Clairvaux (p. 378), however, condemned Clu-

niac churches with their rich decoration and lavish use of gold which reminded him, he wrote, of the 'old rites of the Jews'. The Temple in Jerusalem was not a model to be followed in every respect. Its Holy of Holies was enclosed, for 'the Lord said he would dwell in the thick darkness', and the Ark of the Covenant was concealed behind the curtain that was rent from top to bottom at the moment of Christ's death on the cross. But the sanctuaries of Gothic churches, unlike their Romanesque predecessors, were bathed in mysterious light transmitted through the predominant blues and reds of stained glass windows. As Abbot Suger writes, 'bright is the noble edifice which is pervaded by a new light' – the *lux nova* contrasted with the darkness of the old dispensation.

'The church in which the people come together to praise God signifies the Holy Catholic Church which is built in Heaven of living stones', wrote the theologian Hugh of St Victor (1097–1141) who was named after an abbey in northern France, between Amiens and Rouen, where the great Gothic cathedrals were to be built. The Gothic church looked to the future – to the 'holy city, new Jerusalem' described in the Revelation of St John the Divine as 'coming down from God in heaven, prepared as a bride adorned for her husband'. It had a 'wall great and high' with three gates in each of its four sides, 'And the building of the wall was of jasper; and the city was pure gold like unto clear glass. And the foundations of the wall of the city were garnished with all manner of precious stones. The first foundation was jasper, the second sapphire; the third chalcedony . . . .'

The portals with three doors on the north, south and west fronts of Chartres cathedral may have been intended to evoke this passage. Stained glass windows bring to mind

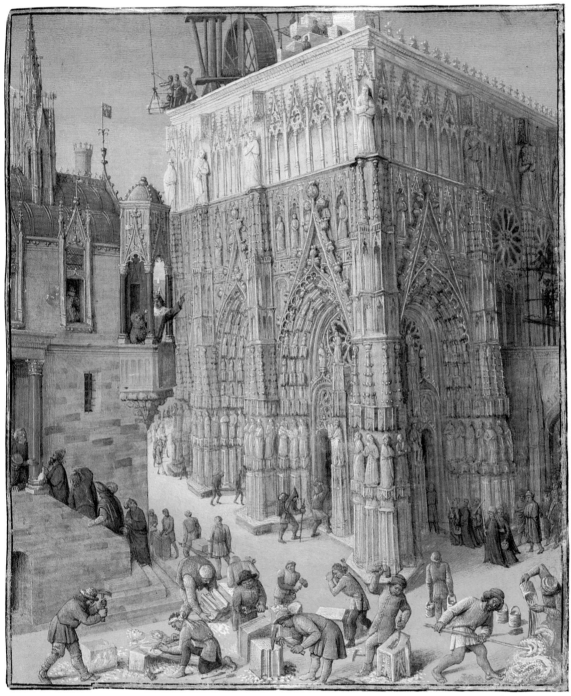

9,40 Jean Fouquet, *Building the Temple of Jerusalem*, from Josephus's *Antiquities and Wars of the Jews*, c. 1475. Illumination on vellum, 15⅜ × 11½ins (39 × 29.2cm). Bibliothèque Nationale, Paris (fr. 247, fol. 163).

the colors of translucent semi-precious stones such as were, indeed, carved into liturgical vessels (9,37). In a mystical sense, however, the New Jerusalem was associated with the Virgin Mary as the 'bride' mentioned by St John. And a late twelfth-century English miniature shows her shrouded body borne up to heaven in a canopy held by angels, resembling a Gothic ribbed vault (9,39). The anagogical or mystical interpretation of Gothic

could not be more explicitly expressed.

Solomon's Temple was by no means forgotten by the builders of Gothic cathedrals or indeed by architects of later centuries who believed that its measurements, recorded in the books of Kings and Chronicles, provided a scale of ideal proportions. But artists depicted it in the architectural styles of their own times. In an illustration to Josephus's *Antiquities and Wars of the Jews*, for instance, the

French painter Jean Fouquet (c. 1420–82) showed it as a structure in the elaborate Gothic style of fifteenth-century France (9,40), with an abundance of statues and crockets, giving also a vivid glimpse of masons at work carving stones and hoisting them into place under the eyes of Solomon himself. Like so many Gothic cathedrals, however, this building has a porch with the three gates that link it with the Heavenly Jerusalem.

created a version of the Gothic style that expressed their ascetic ideals. And they made it mandatory for all their houses – 525, including nunneries, by 1200. Their churches with flat-ended choirs (no apses), slender Gothic windows and inspiring lofty vaults rely for effect solely on the well-cut precision of masonry and perfect balance of simple proportions. The many that survive (if only as ruins like Rievaulx, Fountains and Tintern in England) remind us that the effect of St Bernard's attack on Cluniac architecture was not negative. It directed attention away from ornament and decoration to form and structure.

The aim of Cistercian and other contemporary movements for monastic reform was a return to primal simplicity and purity, and this may partly account for some striking analogies between the essential principles of Gothic architecture and ancient traditions of timber construction. In northern Europe wood was plentiful and had always been the normal building material – as stone was in the south and mud-brick in the Near East. The basic unit of construction was that of the great barns on country estates: four upright posts joined at their tops by beams, which also support the sloping rafters of a pitched roof (in section a rectangle inscribed in a triangle). There can be little doubt that this skeleton was the origin of the 'bay system', which divides a nave into a sequence of equal compartments and distinguishes such northern churches as St Michael's, Hildesheim (see p. 368) or Santiago de Compostela (see p. 376) from Italianate basilicas. Clearer reminiscences of the primitive wooden skeleton reassert themselves in Gothic architecture, which, significantly, originated in the Île de France, where timber construction was in general use.

Within two decades of the consecration of St-Denis, three great Gothic cathedrals were begun in the Île de France: those of Noyon (c. 1150), Laon (c. 1160) and Notre-Dame in Paris (1163). Soon afterwards the Gothic style is found elsewhere. When the choir of the monastic and cathedral church of Canterbury was burnt out in 1174 the monks engaged an architect, whom they called 'William', from Sens (9,41). One of the Canterbury brethren, Gervase, who chronicled the rebuilding, summed up the merits of the new style in what is the only known contemporary comparison of 'Romanesque' and 'Gothic':

The pillars of the old and new work are alike in form and thickness but different in length. For the new pillars were elongated by almost twelve feet. In the old capitals the work was plain, in the new one exquisite in sculpture. There the circuit of the choir had twenty-two pillars, here are twenty-eight. There the arches and everything else was plain, or sculptured with an axe and not with a chisel. But here almost throughout is appropriate sculpture. No marble columns were there, but here are innumerable ones. There, in the ambulatory, the vaults were plain, but here they are arch-ribbed and have keystones. There a wall set upon pillars divided the crosses from the choir, but here the crosses are separated from the choir by no such partition and converge together in one keystone, which is placed in the middle of the great vault which rests on the four principal pillars. There, there was a ceiling of wood decorated with excellent painting, but here is a vault beautifully constructed of stone and light tufa.

(R. Willis, *The Architectural History of Canterbury Cathedral*, London 1845)

HIGH GOTHIC

The amazing achievement of French architects in the early twelfth century was to create a system in which structure, construction and visually expressive form became indistinguishable in the Gothic cathedral – the building-as-symbol of an all-embracing religious faith. The system was, moreover, so flexible that it not only permitted variations in planning but also seems to have stimulated dynamic evolution as detail and carved decoration quickly reassumed importance. The early Gothic of St-Denis and Sens matured extremely quickly into what is called 'High Gothic' in three still more imposing cathedrals of northern France: Chartres, begun in 1194 and completed 1220; Reims, begun in 1212, and Amiens, begun in 1220. Jean d'Orbais (fl. 1212–29), the architect of Reims, had clearly learned much from the anonymous master of Chartres; and Robert de Luzarches, who designed the nave of Amiens Cathedral, was indebted to both. Masons and master-masons or architects travelled widely and it is more than likely that many made drawings of features of buildings that caught their attention. Villard de Honnecourt (fl. 1225–35), author of the only surviving architect's sketchbook of this period, drew

9,41 The choir, Canterbury Cathedral, begun 1175.

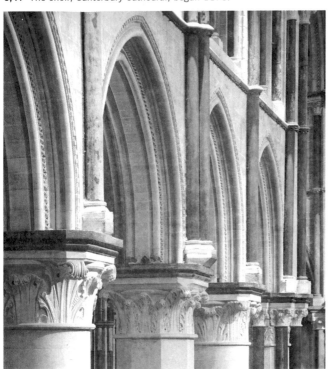

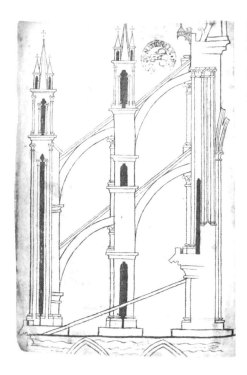

9,42 Villard de Honnecourt, page from notebook, c. 1235. Ink on vellum, 9½ × 6⅓ins (24 × 16cm). Bibliothèque Nationale, Paris.

combines with the new and insistent verticality to direct the eye and mind heavenward, ever onward and upward. An exhilarating sensation of ascent is induced, as well as of propulsion along the nave, by the rapid succession of aspiring arches. And it is the precarious balance between these two axes that gives the interior its vibrant life and almost elastic tension, held together visually by lines as taut as the strings of a well-tuned musical instrument.

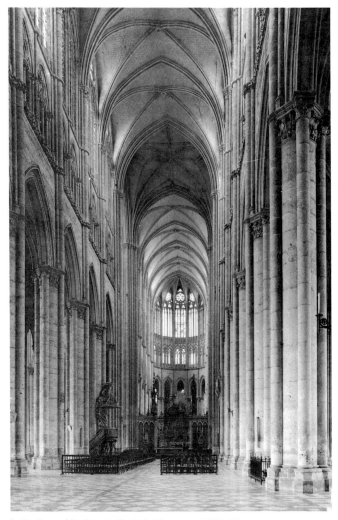

9,43 Nave of Amiens Cathedral, France, c. 1220–36.

9,44 Plan of Amiens Cathedral.

details of plans, structures and decorations at Laon, Chartres (**9,42**), Reims and elsewhere, as far afield as Hungary.

The High Gothic interior reached its apogee at Amiens (**9,43; 44**). All reminiscences of Romanesque mass and weight have been obliterated in this huge, soaring interior space, three times as high as it is wide. In plan, too, it goes beyond its predecessors. The nave and chancel with an almost centrally placed transept, as at Notre-Dame in Paris and at Chartres, create a wonderfully smooth and clear spatial rhythm. It is no longer split up, as in Romanesque churches, into numerous separate units which must be combined visually in order to grasp the totality, but is concentrated into a few, in fact, only three units – the transept acting as the centre of the balance. But the general and compelling momentum is vertical – one of long, upward, finely ruled lines yielding at their summit to the reserved grace of Gothic arches and weaving, as it were, the whole spatial envelope into a seamless garment of stone. Piers are no longer conceived as isolated supports like Classical columns, punctuating and therefore interrupting the horizontal flow, but rather as bundles of circular shafts, with those on the inner side reaching right up to the clerestory, where they branch out into the ribs of the vaults. Bays of vaulting are no longer square (and static) but oblong. The arches of the arcade are narrower than before and separated from tall clerestory windows only by a low triforium – an arched screen in front of a narrow passage – so there is nothing to hinder the eye's upward flight. In this way the impetus of the nave piers is accelerated vertically. It is also quickened horizontally in the apse, where the arcade becomes narrower, the arches more acute and the wall behind the triforium is replaced by windows, thus greatly strengthening the traditional axis from west to east, from entrance door to altar. This

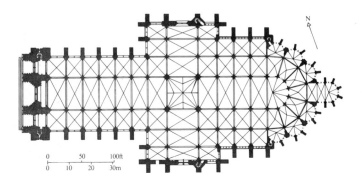

STAINED GLASS AND FLYING BUTTRESSES

The interior of Amiens Cathedral beautifully exemplifies the lucidity of Gothic architecture, in which all the parts are related to each other and to the whole, both in form and proportions. This visual logic was originally raised to an even higher, transcendental plane by the unearthly light filtered through stained glass windows and suffusing the whole space with immaterial color. Church windows had often been filled with colored glass since the fourth century (no crystal-clear glass was made until much later) and early theologians had endowed it with Neoplatonic significance. At least as early as the eleventh century the window sometimes incorporated figures composed like translucent mosaics from pieces of variously colored glass overpainted in black to indicate details. It was at St-Denis that figurative stained glass windows (only fragments of which survive) were first given the importance they were

to retain for some four centuries in northern Europe. Suger saw in them a double symbolism, that of their subject-matter irradiated by the *lux nova*, or new light, of the Gospel. 'Miraculous' was the word he used for the light admitted by these 'most sacred windows'.

Chartres Cathedral still preserves most of its original stained glass, conceived as the source of both spiritual and physical illumination. Figures in each window or group of windows are theologically related to one another and to the doctrines illustrated in the whole series. Many are devoted to the cult of the Virgin Mary, centred on Chartres Cathedral, which cherished as its holiest relic the tunic she was believed to have worn when she gave birth. The Virgin with the Christ Child on her knee is in the centre of the great rose window of the north transept (**9,45**). Around her, panels are arranged in symbolical twelves: angels, archangels and four white doves representing both the Holy Spirit and the Gospels, then in

9,45 Rose window, north transept, Chartres Cathedral, France, c. 1230. Stained glass, 42ft 8ins (13m) diameter.

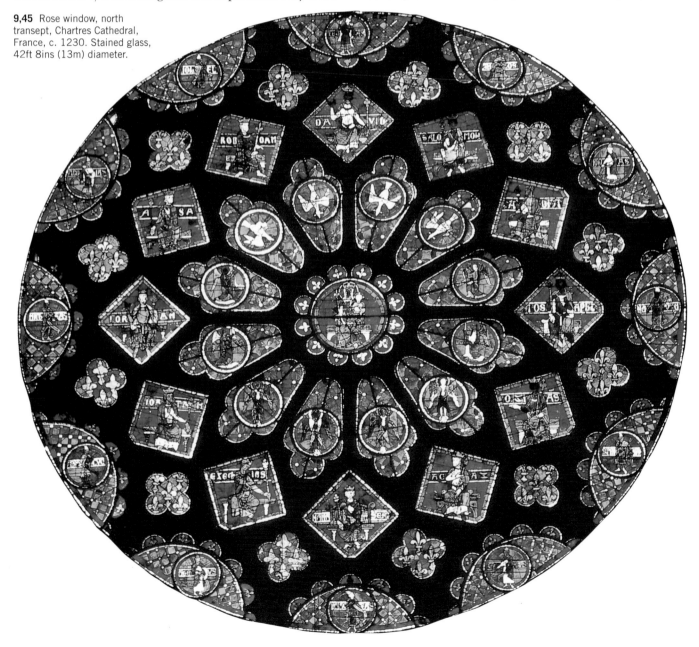

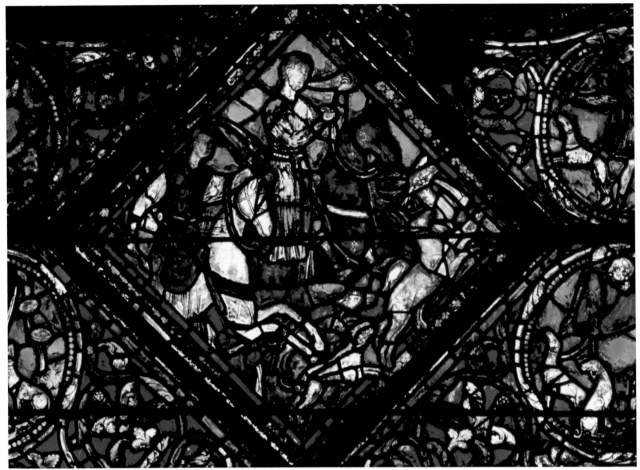

9,46 Scene from the life of St Eustace, north aisle, Chartres Cathedral, c. 1210. Detail of stained glass.

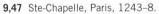
9,47 Ste-Chapelle, Paris, 1243–8.

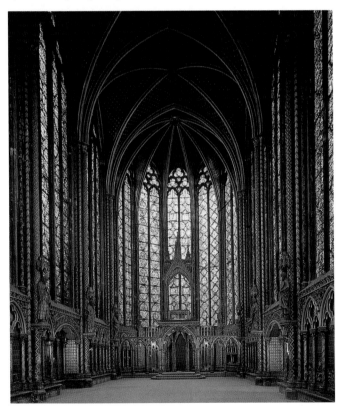

squares, the kings of Israel named by St Matthew as the ancestors of St Joseph, with prophets on the outer rim. Every element of the design points towards the Virgin and Child in an intricate network binding the Old Testament to the New. Other windows at Chartres illustrate scenes from the lives of saints (**9,46**), reflecting a less strenuously intellectual and more popularly accessible tendency in religious thought, which was soon to inspire Jacobus de Voragine (c. 1230–98) to collect all the colorful stories of saints into the *Legenda Aurea* or Golden Legend.

It is often said that windows such as those at Chartres constituted the 'Bible' of the poor and illiterate, although whether they could ever have been understood without the aid of the inscriptions identifying the figures seems doubtful. The mystical significance of the light they transmit may well have been equally difficult for the unlettered layman to comprehend, but the essential meaning of these jewel-like windows could hardly be missed. They create an atmosphere far removed from that of the everyday world outside. From the predominant blues and reds the light takes on a violet tone, which floods into the church from every side and diffuses softly an unearthly glow and glimmer. It is, however, of low intensity, and very large areas of stained glass were needed. As Gothic architecture developed, masonry walls were gradually replaced by windows filling the spaces between ever more slender supports. Eventually, in such buildings as the Ste-Chapelle in Paris, the chapel of the kings of France, the interior becomes one single tall space with, except for a low dado zone, walls entirely of glass (**9,47**). The stonework

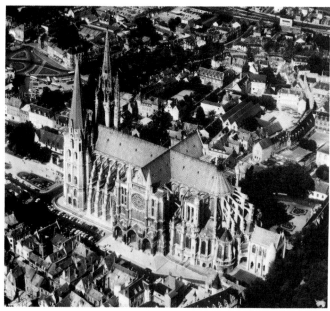

9,48 Chartres Cathedral, aerial view, mainly 1194–1220.

dividing one panel of glass from another (still fairly prominent at Chartres) is reduced to a lacy mesh of tracery more conspicuous from the outside than from within. (Tracery was a Gothic invention and its development towards ever greater dissolution of the wall – from 'bar tracery' to 'plate tracery' – can be followed stage by stage from Chartres to Reims and from Reims to Amiens and beyond.) The desire for light and immateriality complemented the Gothic quest for ever greater height. Clerestory windows grew steadily taller, pushing up the vaults to 120 feet (37m) at Chartres, 125 feet (38m) at Reims, 140 feet (43m) at Amiens and a dizzying 157 feet (48m) at Beauvais (1230–40). But at Beauvais the architect overreached himself. Only the apse survived the collapse of the choir in 1284 and, although the choir was rebuilt, the nave was never even begun.

These lofty vaults required external support and this led to another Gothic invention, 'flying buttresses' as at Chartres, where they completely surround the apse (**9,48**). Their structural purpose is well illustrated in a drawing by Villard de Honnecourt which shows how their arms stretch out to resist the outward thrust of the vaulting (9,42). A similar system of buttressing had been used in Romanesque architecture, but was concealed beneath the roofs to the tribune galleries above the aisles. To admit more light, Gothic architects did away with the tribune galleries, exposed the buttresses and pared them down to slender skeletal supports no less aesthetically satisfying than functional. They also had them carved and topped with little spires so that they contribute to the general upward force of the building, entirely concealing, indeed contradicting visually, their structural function of resisting the building's lateral spread. Flying buttresses help, in this way, to integrate the interior and exterior of a High Gothic church into an organic whole. The same can be said of the main façades, which repeat the horizontal divisions (arcade, triforium, clerestory) of the interior elevations of

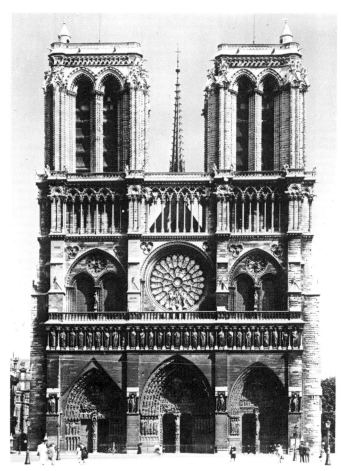

9,49 Façade of Notre-Dame, Paris, 1210–5.

9,50 Façade of Reims Cathedral, France, 1255–60.

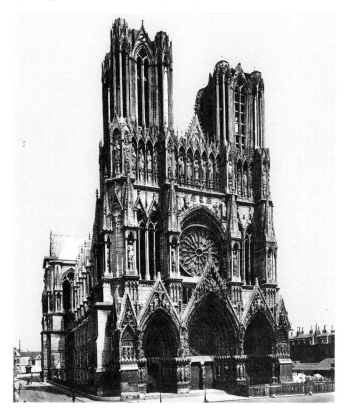

the nave. That of the Cathedral of Notre-Dame in Paris also states very clearly the geometrical system on which the design of the whole building was based (**9,49**). This is a rationalization of the still Romanesque façade of St-Etienne, Caen, and St-Denis, which already had what seems to have been the first rose window in its centre. Later, at Amiens and Reims (**9,50**), the residual Romanesque horizontality of Notre-Dame was muted, much greater emphasis being placed on verticals.

ECONOMICS AND THEOLOGY

None of the High Gothic cathedrals has its full complement of towers and spires as envisaged by the architects. Chartres was to have had eight. (Of its two existing towers, one predates the 1194 fire and the other is a sixteenth-century addition.) Building work at a cathedral normally began with the choir, moved along the nave and then up the façades, which were rarely finished before money ran out. For the building of cathedrals was a major financial undertaking and, according to some historians, seriously affected the economic stability of France. Funds were raised from a variety of sources, sometimes by popular appeals which could lead to 'happenings' such as the so-called 'Cult of the Carts' at Chartres. This was an extraordinary outburst of religious enthusiasm. Crowds of more than 1,000 were reported to have dragged carts and wagons for the building of the cathedral, moving slowly and painfully forwards in utter silence broken only by spasmodic cries, confessing guilt and imploring divine mercy, sometimes even grovelling half-naked on the ground in penitence. Such phenomena were rather exceptional, however, and the cathedral authorities relied on more normal methods to finance the great works in hand.

SOURCES AND DOCUMENTS

ABBOT HAYMO AND THE 'CULT OF THE CARTS' AT CHARTRES

In about 1145 a new religious cult was observed at Chartres and more than one church dignitary remarked on it. Archbishop Hugo of Rouen wrote in a letter of about that year to the bishop of Amiens that at Chartres:

. . . men began in their humility to drag carts and wagons for the building of the cathedral, and their humility was even illuminated by miracles.

Similarly, Robert of Torigni, abbot of Mont St-Michel, wrote in his chronicle that:

In that year [1145] men at Chartres began to drag carts, harnessed to their own shoulders, laden with stones and wood, corn and other provisions, needed for the new church, whose towers were being built at this time.

A more circumstantial account was given by Haymo, abbot of Saint-Pierre-sur-Dives in Normandy, who presented it as a revivalist movement affecting all classes of society. It had produced:

. . . new and unheard-of methods of returning to Christ. Whoever saw, whoever heard, in all the generations past, that powerful princes of the world, that men brought up in honor and in wealth, that nobles, men and women, have bent their proud and haughty necks to the harness of carts, and that, like beasts of burden, they have dragged to the abode of Christ these waggons, loaded with wines, grains, oil, stone, wood, and all that is necessary for the wants of life, or for the construction of the church? But while they draw these burdens, there is one thing admirable to observe; it is that often when a thousand persons and more are attached to the chariots – so great is the difficulty – yet they march in such silence that not a murmur is heard, and truly if one did not see the thing with one's eyes, one might believe that among such a multitude there was hardly a person present. When they halt on the road, nothing is heard but the confession of sins, and pure and suppliant prayer to God to obtain pardon. At the voice of the priests who exhort their hearts to peace, they forget all hatred, discord is thrown far aside, debts are remitted, the unity of hearts is established.

But if any one is so far advanced in evil as to be unwilling to pardon an offender, or if he rejects the counsel of the priest who has piously advised him, his offering is instantly thrown from the waggon as impure, and he himself ignominiously and shamefully excluded from the society of the holy. There one sees the priests who preside over each chariot exhort every one to penitence, to confession of faults, to the resolution of better life! There one sees old people, young people, little children, calling on the Lord with a suppliant voice, and uttering to Him, from the depth of the heart, sobs and sighs with words of glory and praise! After the people, warned by the sound of trumpets and the sight of banners, have resumed their road, the march is made with such ease that no obstacle can retard it . . . . When they have reached the church they arrange the waggons about it like a spiritual camp, and during the whole night they celebrate the watch by hymns and canticle. On each waggon they light tapers and lamps; they place there the infirm and sick, and bring them the precious relics of the Saints for their relief. Afterwards the priests and clerics close the ceremony by processions which the people follow with devout heart, imploring the clemency of the Lord and of his Blessed Mother for the recovery of the sick . . . .

(Tr. H. Adams, *Mont Saint-Michel and Chartres*, Boston 1904)

Revenues from the vast agricultural estates owned by the Church and the taxes levied by bishops as temporal lords naturally provided considerable sums. Suger set aside annually a proportion of the St-Denis estate income to meet the cost of building. At Chartres the canons of the cathedral (its governing body) are said to have foregone their stipends for three years from 1194 so that reconstruction work could begin after a fire. Offerings made by pilgrims and the local population contributed much, especially for adornment of the fabric – probably more than donations from kings and noblemen. The wealthy seem, in fact, to have preferred to subscribe to specific undertakings to which their names could be attached, e.g. stained glass. The north transept windows at Chartres (9,45), for instance, were given by Queen Blanche, mother of the sainted crusader Louis IX. Others were the gift of guilds, the associations which regulated the religious and social as well as the working lives of medieval craftsmen and tradesmen. Butchers, bakers and other local guilds donated the great windows in the *chevet*, the most important of all. In fact, whether directly by gift or indirectly through taxes, the inhabitants of Chartres, though they numbered no more than 10,000, contributed a large proportion of the funds to build the cathedral, which dominated, and still to this day dominates, the town. Their lives revolved around it. Justice was administered at its door. The great fairs or markets, on which the mercantile prosperity of the town depended, took place in neighbouring streets and squares owned by and under the jurisdiction of the cathedral chapter. Wine-sellers were even allowed to transact business in the crypt. So the cathedral became almost as much a civic as a religious building. And it was a great financial asset to the town in that it attracted a constant flow of pilgrims. For these reasons, perhaps, the thirteenth-century citizens of Strasbourg shouldered the financial responsibility for constructing the nave and façade of their cathedral, taking it out of the hands of the bishop and chapter, with whom they were at loggerheads.

The architects who designed and directed these great undertakings are often recorded by name, but very little else is known about them. As personalities, Robert de Luzarches at Amiens and Jean d'Orbais at Reims are no less shadowy than the three anonymous masters whose individual touch can be detected in successive stages of the building at Chartres. Like other medieval architects each had doubtless risen from the ranks of masons after having served an apprenticeship in a quarry, where stone was cut, and having earned the title of 'master' by carrying out some technically difficult piece of work or 'masterpiece'. His expert knowledge of construction, architectural draftsmanship, geometry and the rules of proportion were acquired through the jealously guarded traditions of the masons, handed down from one master to another in the 'lodges' or workshops, which often became permanent fixtures at the great cathedrals in order to maintain the fabric. Work was, however, always carried out in close consultation with the bishop, who initiated the project, or with one or more members of the chapter, who administered the finances.

In view of the architect's training as a mason, it is hardly surprising that carved stonework should be so prominent in Gothic buildings. Moldings become steadily more complex in section, and figure sculptures proliferate (at Chartres there are some 1,800), yet carved decorations have greater uniformity in early and High Gothic than in Romanesque churches. Already in the ambulatory of St-Denis (9,35) capitals of the type condemned by St Bernard are replaced by sharply carved wreaths of naturalistic leaves, which set a pattern later followed over the whole of northern Europe. They are similar to one another but, significantly, not identical. The design of a Gothic church left room for variation in details and it was this that invested the intellectual geometry of its conception with throbbing yet disciplined life.

St Thomas Aquinas (c. 1225–74), or a close follower, defined beauty as 'a certain consonance of diverging elements'. He was the greatest theologian of the Middle Ages, author of the *Summa theologica*, which set out to provide a systematic exposition of all Christian doctrine but was left unfinished – in this respect, as in others, like the great Gothic cathedrals. For in the closely woven fabric of medieval thought a church was a microcosm of the all-embracing Catholic Church, personified by the Virgin Mary, to whom the cathedrals of Chartres, Paris, Reims and many others were dedicated. With its spires, which strove to pierce what an English mystic called 'the cloud of unknowing', its stained glass windows radiant with divine light shining through them as the Holy Spirit penetrated the body of the Virgin and illuminated the Church, the Gothic cathedral was at once a symbol and an exposition of Christian faith. One translucent layer of meaning was superimposed on another. Vine leaves or oak leaves might be specific symbols; but they also declared that, in the words of the 24th Psalm, 'The earth is the Lord's and all that therein is: the compass of the world and they that dwell therein.' Every detail in these great buildings proclaimed the glory of God and the wonder of his creation (9,51). The worst heresy of the period – that of the Albigenses or Cathars, who were ruthlessly persecuted in

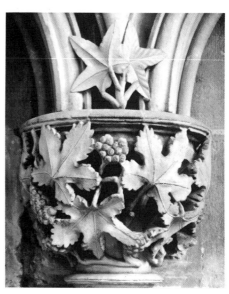

9,51 Vine-leaf capital in chapter-house of Southwell Minster, England, c. 1290.

the early thirteenth century – was the dualistic belief that all matter was evil and only spirit good. So a cathedral was not only a *Summa theologica* but also an encyclopedia of divinely ordered creation.

SCULPTURE AND PAINTING

As all things came to be seen as a manifestation of the divine, a great impetus was given to naturalism in the figurative arts, especially sculpture. On the west or royal portal of Chartres, which was carved in the 1140s and survived the fire of 1194, columns are still decorated with geometrical patterns, while the Old Testament kings and queens, attenuated and columnar, have already begun to separate themselves from the architectural background (**9,52; 53**). On the south transept portal of about 1215–20 they are projected further forwards and given more strongly marked individuality. The process was completed on the west portal of Reims, carved about 1225–45, where heroic-scale saints and angels are wholly detached from the building and conceived not as reliefs but as statues in the round (**9,54**). Despite their grandiose scale and withdrawn expressions and poses, either sunk in meditation or in silent commune with one another, they are essentially human figures occupying the same space and apparently breathing the same air as the spectator.

9,52 West portal of Chartres Cathedral, c. 1145–70.

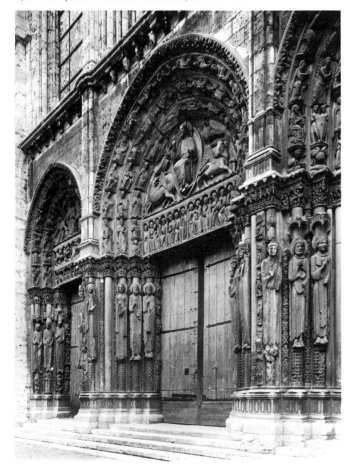

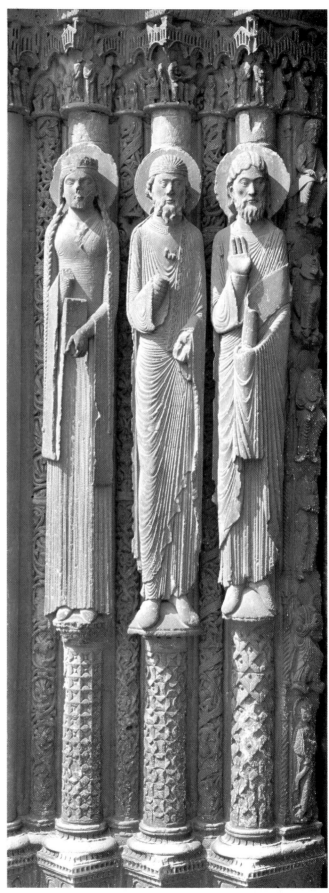

9,53 Detail of jamb figures, west portal, Chartres Cathedral, c. 1145–70.

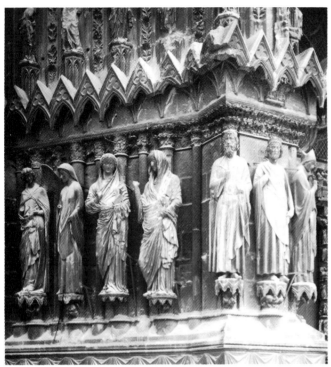

9,54 Detail of west portal, Reims Cathedral, c. 1225–55.

9,55 *Visitation*, west portal, Reims Cathedral, c. 1225–55.

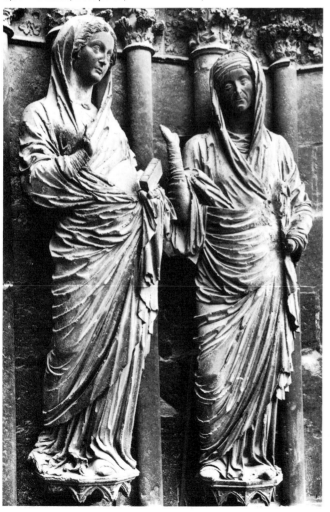

The *Visitation* at Reims (**9,55**) may be interpreted as a quiet colloquy between the gravely dignified expectant mothers of Jesus and St John the Baptist. Weight, both physical and moral, is suggested by the substantial gathered folds of their garments. Like Nicholas of Verdun, a few decades earlier and not far away (see p. 399), the sculptor at Reims must have known and studied ancient Roman statues, for the draperies are carved in a technique not known to have been practised for some 900 years. The pose of each figure, with one knee bent, also harks back to the Classical past. But the sculptor took all this over from antiquity in the same spirit as Scholastic theologians adopted arguments or 'modes of reasoning' from Aristotle. He used it afresh for his own purposes. His statues have a new warmth and a new human sympathy.

The Virgin in the group to the left of the *Visitation* was carved by another sculptor in a slightly different, though no less remarkable way, with draperies apparently studied from life, falling smoothly and clearly revealing the form of her firm young breasts. The smiling angel on the far left is the work of a third hand and was probably placed originally on another part of the façade. It may be a little later in date. Here the draperies are clearly realized as quite independent of the body beneath, but they are arranged with great attention to decorative effect. And the pose of the Visitation figures has been both anatomically corrected and eased into the gentle spiral which recurs in later Gothic art – in an exquisite ivory statuette of the Virgin and Child, which was for long in the Ste-Chapelle

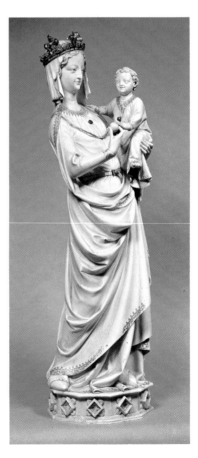

9,56 *Virgin and Child*, c. 1300. Ivory with some gilding, 16ins (40.6cm) high. Louvre, Paris.

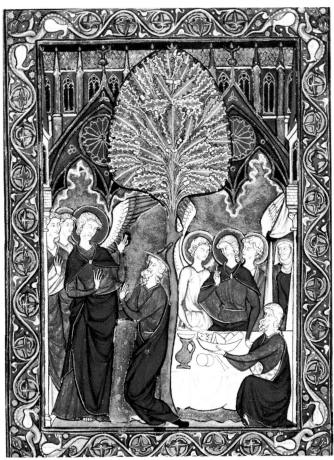

9,57 *Abraham and the Three Angels*, page from the *St Louis Psalter*, 1253–70. Parchment, 8½ × 5½ins (21 × 14.5cm). Bibliothèque Nationale, Paris.

in Paris, for instance (**9,56**). The three sculptors at Reims had moved as far from Romanesque conventions as the architect of the cathedral façade on which they stand. Their naturalism complements his structural lucidity.

All visual arts were involved in the construction and decoration of the great cathedrals of the late twelfth and thirteenth centuries, and Gothic was soon established as the norm not only for architecture. On a page in the *St Louis Psalter* an edifice with pinnacled buttresses, pointed arches and rose windows forms the background for Abraham receiving the three angels and (in the right half) entertaining them under a tree while his wimpled wife Sara, who has prepared the meal, peeps out from his tent – according to the story told in the Book of Genesis 18 (**9,57**). The whole page is rendered with the same strong outlines and broad areas of glowing color as a stained glass window. The angel on the left, furthermore, bears a family resemblance to the statue on the west front of Reims Cathedral (**9,54**). Behind both there lies that desire to visualize the scene in human terms which so sharply differentiates Gothic from Romanesque art. The allegorical significance, which had formerly been stressed, remains important but now takes second place to dramatic presentation.

ENGLISH AND GERMAN GOTHIC

As we have already seen, the style was transmitted in its formative stage to England. Here, even before the twelfth century was out, local variations were introduced and further developed at the very moment when a sense of national identity was beginning to grow (English was first used as an official language in a mid-thirteenth-century document). In the vaulting of the nave of Lincoln Cathedral, for instance, ribs are multiplied by running one along the centre and splaying out subsidiary ribs to join it, creating a pattern of stars which wilfully sacrifices logic to decorative effect (**9,58**). The so-called 'Decorated Style', with much use of double-curving ogee arches and bars of window tracery twisted and turned into intricate networks of stone, was developed in England in the later thirteenth century, long before the equivalent 'Flamboyant Style' appeared in France (**9,59**). The same delight in fantasy and elaborate curvilinear ornament is felt in the richly elaborate vestments, which were among the finest works of art produced in England at this time (**9,60**). Embroidery was an English specialty and was prized all over Europe, where it was known as *opus Anglicanum* (English work).

Until the end of the twelfth century Germany clung to the Romanesque style so closely associated with the Holy Roman Empire, and intimations of a coming change are

9,58 Nave vault, Lincoln Cathedral, England, c. 1240–50.

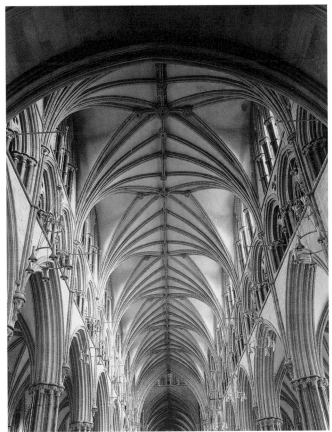

SOURCES AND DOCUMENTS

PIERS PLOWMAN ON STAINED GLASS AND *OPUS ANGLICANUM*

Very little is known about William Langland or Langley (c. 1331–99?), the author of *Piers Plowman* (begun 1362). A deeply religious poem, it consists of 11 dream visions but is also remarkable for its vivid pictures of contemporary life. When Piers is asked, 'What should we women work at?' he replies that some should sew sacks for grain but others:

> . . . ye lovely ladies,
> With your long fingers,
> That you have silks and fine stuffs
> To sew, when time is;
> Chasubles for chaplains,
> Churches to honor.

The poem contains, however, a good deal of criticism of worldliness and lavish church decoration, especially of the Mendicant Orders, that is, the Franciscans and Dominicans. They are associated with such personifications of worldliness as Lady Mede, who is told by a Franciscan friar:

> We have a window to be wrought
> It would suit us full well
> Wouldst thou glaze that gable
> And grave therein thy name,
> Surely will thy soul reach heaven.

She replies that she will gladly decorate the whole church. Piers remarks that windows engraved with the names of donors are displays of pride and 'pomp of the world', forbidden by God.

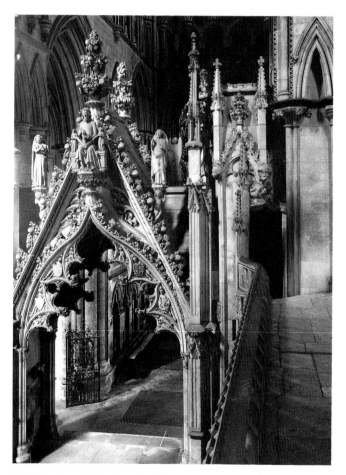

9,59 The Percy Tomb, Beverley Minster, after 1339.

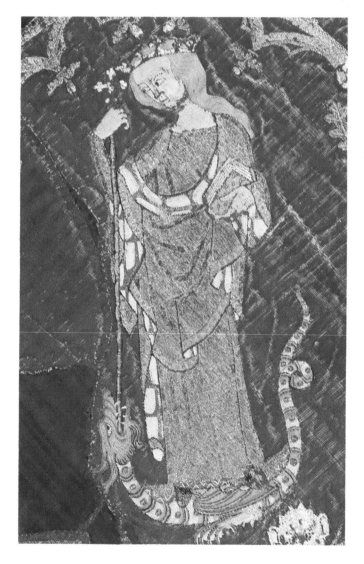

9,60 *Right* Butler-Bowdon Cope, detail, 1335–6. Embroidery in silver and silver-gilt thread and silks on red velvet, with pearls, green beads and gold rings, full width 11ft 4ins (3.45m). Victoria & Albert Museum, London.

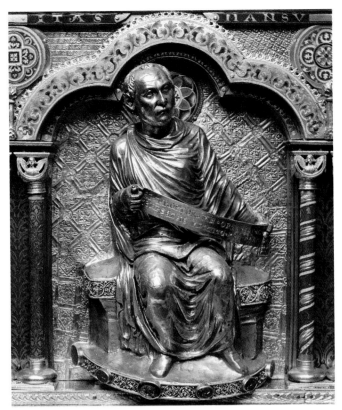

felt first in small-scale works. The Shrine of the Three Magi made by Nicholas of Verdun (c. 1140–c. 1216) for Cologne is architecturally Romanesque in its round arches and short columns (9,61), but the high-relief figures anticipate by some two decades the statues on the cathedral at Reims less than 200 miles (320km) away (9,55). The pliant loose draperies of the silver figures, following both the form and the movement of the body beneath, resume a style which had passed from Greece to Rome, while their strongly characterized thoughtful heads have the spirituality of Gothic sculpture. The naturalism of such works was taken to its furthest extreme in Germany, most notably in two of the quite extraordinarily lifelike statues of the founders of Naumburg Cathedral – the burly Margrave Ekkehart, hand on sword, and his elegant, worldly wife Uta, drawing the collar of her cloak across her cheek (9,62). When Gothic architecture was introduced into Germany it expanded in both scale and richness. Cologne Cathedral, probably inspired by Reims, was begun in 1248 as the tallest and longest of all Gothic churches – though it was not to be completed until the nineteenth century and is substantially a nineteenth-century building (9,63).

9,61 *Above* Nicholas of Verdun, *Prophet Jonah*, detail from the Shrine of the Three Magi, c. 1182–90. Gold, enamel and precious stones. Cologne Cathedral.

9,62 *Below left Ekkehart and Uta*, c. 1250–60. Naumburg Cathedral, Germany.

9,63 *Below right* Cologne Cathedral, begun 1248, completed 1880.

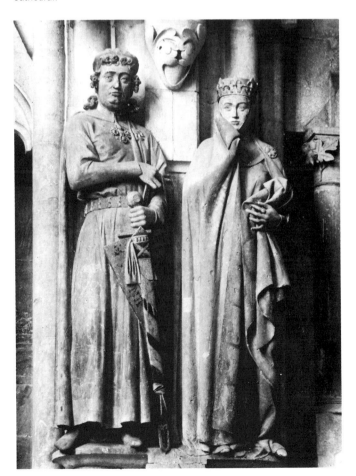

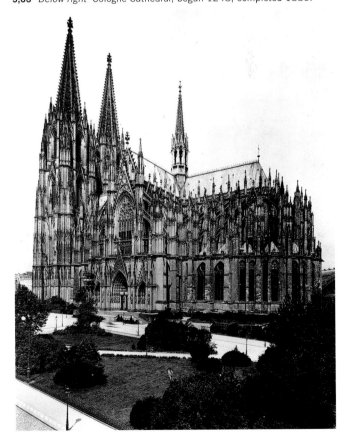

ITALIAN GOTHIC

Gothic architecture was introduced into Italy by the Cistercians, whose abbey churches, e.g. Fossanova, south of Rome (**9,64**), look as if they had been bodily transported from France. S Francesco at Assisi, begun in 1228 when St Francis was canonized, substantially completed by 1239 and consecrated in 1253, is quite different (**9,65**). Although there are curious and unexplained affinities with early Gothic churches built in western France nearly a century before, all it has in common with the great High Gothic cathedrals are rib vaults and pointed traceried windows. The aims of its architect were not only different from, but almost contrary to, those of his French contemporaries. Their soaring ecstasies of yearning for the infinite are replaced by something equally noble, if less rarefied. The plan is of emphatically rectilinear simplicity: a Latin cross with a five-sided apse (**9,66**). Horizontals and verticals are exactly balanced, creating a wonderfully self-confident and self-contained effect in the upper church (the exceptionally high crypt below is called the lower church). The broad and aisleless nave, evenly lit and airy, is a clearly defined space unassertively articulated into bays by attenuated columns bunched into piers that cling to the walls. There are no carvings apart from inconspicuous capitals. Surfaces are uniformly smooth, emphasizing the massiveness of the walls. The whole church has a solidity and volumetric clarity typical in medieval Italy, as we shall see, not only of architecture but of painting and sculpture as well.

S Francesco was a new type of church, designed to meet the needs of a religious order founded by St Francis

9,64 Nave of abbey church, Fossanova, Italy, 1187–1208.

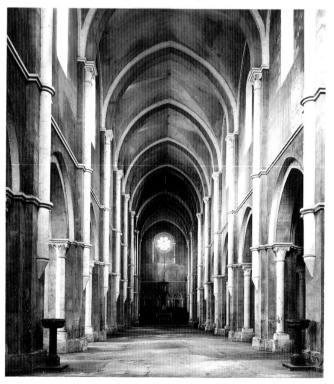

of Assisi (c. 1181–1226) to recall people of all conditions to faith and penitence. Its dimensions and form were determined by the size of the congregations which flocked to hear Franciscan sermons, its decoration by the demand for a direct, non-allegorical exposition of Christian doctrine focused on the life of Christ and the Christ-like founder of the order. St Francis renounced all worldly goods to 'wed Lady Poverty', as he put it, and, although he was not a priest, he and 11 companions obtained in 1211 papal sanction to be wandering preachers. These first friars, who called themselves *Fratri minori* or lesser brethren, practising the humility they preached, soon attracted a large following of men and women – including St Clare (c. 1194–1253) (9,68), founder of the sister order of nuns – similarly vowed to absolute poverty and subsisting on what they could obtain by menial work or begging for alms. St Francis intended that they should not own even corporate property, though this restriction was relaxed to enable them to build churches and communal houses, as at Assisi. But he attacked the worldliness of the Church only by example – he was not censorious. (Arnold of Brescia, less than a century earlier, had been outspoken about 'priests who have estates, bishops who hold fiefs, and monks who possess property'. He was burnt at the stake.) Yet St Francis's views on otherworldly monks who lived in richly endowed seclusion were obvious enough to provoke reaction from the Cistercians, who did their damnedest to have the Franciscans suppressed.

Another order of mendicant preachers was founded at the same time by the Spaniard St Dominic (1170–1221) as a task-force to battle against the heresy of the Albigenses (see p. 394–5). Dominicans later staffed the dreaded Holy Office or Inquisition. Like St Francis – and unlike St Bernard of Clairvaux – St Dominic was primarily concerned with the spiritual life of the laity, and nearly all the most learned men of the thirteenth century were drawn to one or other of the two orders, Dominican (Black Friars) or Franciscan (Gray Friars). Albertus Magnus (1206–80), for instance, and his pupil St Thomas Aquinas (see p. 394) were Dominicans; Duns Scotus (c. 1265–1308), who opposed reliance on deductive reasoning, was a Franciscan.

Both orders had houses in all the main university cities. But however influential among the educated laity, they were even more active among the unlettered and poor. Their sermons were given in a plain, vigorous, unerudite style which all could understand and were full of lively, topical descriptions, especially of incidents from the lives of saints held up as exemplars. In Italy, where Latin remained the written language, these sermons in the language of common speech stimulated the growth of a vernacular literature, which blossomed astonishingly quickly in the work of one of the greatest European poets, Dante Alighieri (1251–1321). The influence of their sermons on the visual arts was no less strong. They created a demand for vivid and easily read imagery.

Italian literature virtually begins with St Francis's *Cantico delle creature* (Canticle of all created things), a hymn which owes its poignancy to the unaffected directness of its invocations and the concrete simplicity of its

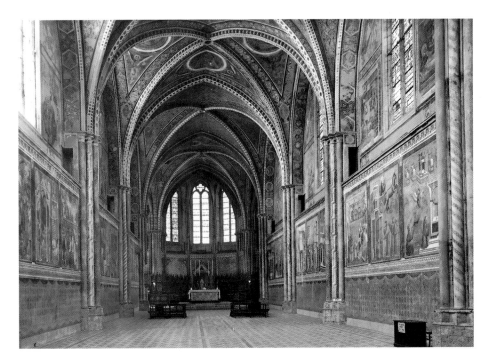

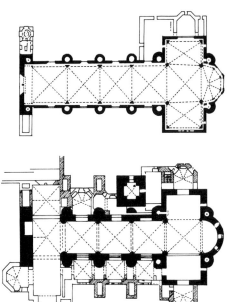

images. God is praised for brother sun and sister moon, for sister water, 'greatly useful and humble and precious and chaste', brother fire, 'beautiful and joyful and vigorous and strong', our sister, mother earth, who 'brings forth diverse fruits and colored flowers and grass' and finally for 'our sister bodily death, from whom no living man can escape'. Similarly in the visual arts, it might almost be said that Italian painting – as distinct from late Roman and Byzantine – begins in S Francesco at Assisi with frescoes ascribed to Cimabue (on the upper walls) and, less certainly, to Giotto (see pp. 409–11).

A painting of St Francis by Bonaventura Berlinghieri (fl. 1228–35) dates from only nine years after the saint's death and may well record memories of his actual appearance (**9,67**). But, despite its spiritual force, this image is not a portrait so much as a kind of identikit assemblage of remembered characteristics – coarse, gray-brown habit and rope girdle with three knots symbolizing poverty, chastity and obedience, hands and feet marked with the stigmata, lean, ascetic, lightly bearded face and tonsured head. Six little scenes on either side are similarly informative rather than expressive, telling or reminding the spectator how St Francis received the stigmata (upper left), preached to the birds who 'rejoiced in wondrous fashion', ministered to the poor and ailing, and (lower right) rid the city of Arezzo of evil spirits. The panel was painted as an altarpiece to rise from the back of an altar – a type of picture peculiar to Catholic Europe. (Altarpieces came into being as the result of a liturgical change at about this date, when priests celebrated the mass with their backs to the congregation.) Figures and architectural backgrounds are, nevertheless, depicted according to time-honoured Byzantine conventions. Indeed, one of the artist's aims seems to have been to integrate the recently canonized saint into the Eastern icon tradition.

9,65 *Above left* Nave of S Francesco, Assisi, Italy, 1228–53, pre-1997 earthquake which seriously damaged the vaults.

9,66 *Above right* Plan of upper and lower churches, S Francesco, Assisi.

9,67 Bonaventura Berlinghieri, *St Francis*, 1235. Panel, about 5ft × 3ft 6ins (1.52 × 1.07m). S Francesco, Pescia.

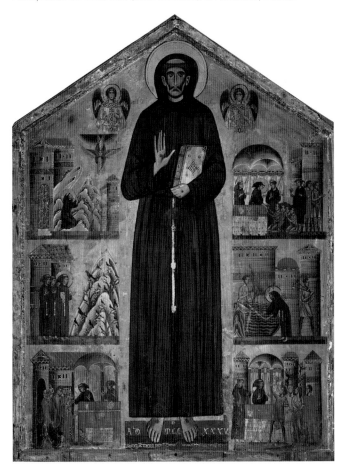

St Francis and St Clare

Some 50 years after St Francis had been depicted by Bonaventura Berlinghieri (9,67) a similar image was painted of his first female disciple, St Clare (**9,68**). In the meantime he had been the subject of numerous paintings which show him renouncing all his worldly goods including his clothes, espousing 'lady poverty', preaching to the birds and to the Muslim Salah ad-Din (Saladin to the crusader), miraculously visiting his followers in France and receiving the stigmata – the wounds of the crucified Christ – in his hands, feet and chest. And these subjects were to be painted again and again for centuries, commissioned by rich patrons whose admiration for St Francis was, however, tempered by caution as regards his literal interpretation of Christ's injunction to 'go and sell that thou hast, and give to the poor'.

St Clare was very much less often depicted partly, no doubt, because her cult had little appeal for men who predominated as patrons of the arts. Her cult was maintained by nuns who led strictly cloistered lives in the very simple houses of the religious order she founded. They adhered more closely to the rule of poverty than did the Franciscans who soon possessed large friaries and churches. The earliest image of her is also the most distinguished, indeed it is one of the finest late thirteenth-century paintings on panel. It was not an altarpiece but intended to be placed on a screen dividing the nave of the church from the chancel, beside a painting of Christ on the cross and balanced by a (now lost) image of the Virgin. The future of St Clare is rather more substantial and removed from the Eastern tradition of icon painting than Berlinghieri's *St Francis*. And the scenes on either side record events from her life with less emphasis on the supernatural.

St Clare (Chiara in Italian), born in 1193 the daughter of a noble family in Assisi, was 12 years younger than St Francis. In 1211, the year after he and his followers obtained permission from the Pope to travel about the country as penniless preachers, she resolved to withdraw from the world and in church on Palm Sunday the bishop of Assisi handed her a palm branch to indicate his approval (bottom left in the painting). The following night she escaped from her home and met St Francis who cut off her hair to consecrate her as a nun and arranged for her temporary residence in a Benedictine convent from which her parents tried to reclaim her (top left). She was joined by her sister Agnes (top right) and, with other upper-class women of Assisi including her mother, formed a community living in seclusion according to a rule provided for them by St Francis. As they had renounced all possessions but could not, like the Franciscans, work on the land or gather alms in the streets, they had difficulty in supporting themselves. On one occasion St Clare is said to have multiplied their few loaves by a miracle – the only one attributed to her – which may also symbolize the multiplication of communities living under the same rule (the first founded in Florence in 1219 by her sister Agnes). This is depicted in the second scene from the top right, above those recording her vision of the Virgin as she lay dying, and her funeral. She died in 1253 and was declared a saint two years later. Agnes died a few months later but was not to be canonized until 1751.

St Clare remained throughout her life a disciple of St Francis who gave her spiritual advice and on one occasion stayed in her convent, where he wrote the *Cantico delle creature* (see p. 400). After his death in 1226 she struggled to maintain his teaching although the papal authorities questioned his glorification of poverty and opposed his insistence that his followers, the *fratri minori*, should own not even communal property. It was for this reason that papal approval of her conventual rule, adapted from the Franciscan model and the strictest laid down for any female order, was withheld until shortly before her death. By this time, however, it was observed in convents in Spain, France and Germany as well as Italy where there were nearly 70, each with at least 30 members. The nuns were called 'poor ladies' (*Clarisse* or 'Poor Clares') only after her canonization and they seem to have come almost invariably from the upper classes. The abbess of one of these convents was a daughter of the king of Bohemia, Agnes (later venerated as the blessed Agnes of Prague), with whom St Clare corresponded, remarking in one letter that asceticism should not be exaggerated, 'for our bodies are not made of brass'.

Contemporary writers referred to nuns finding shelter from the 'storms of the world'. This was no merely poetic figure of speech. While St Clare was abbess Assisi was twice attacked and the convent threatened by soldiers in the service of the Emperor Frederick II. The conventual life produced women with an alternative, often the only alternative to arranged, loveless marriages and frequent child-bearing. But the convent was not simply a refuge from a male-dominated world. Women became nuns to devote themselves to prayer and meditation. Some of the most profound and mystical writings of the Middle Ages were by nuns, notably by St Hildegard of Bingen and Julian of Norwich.

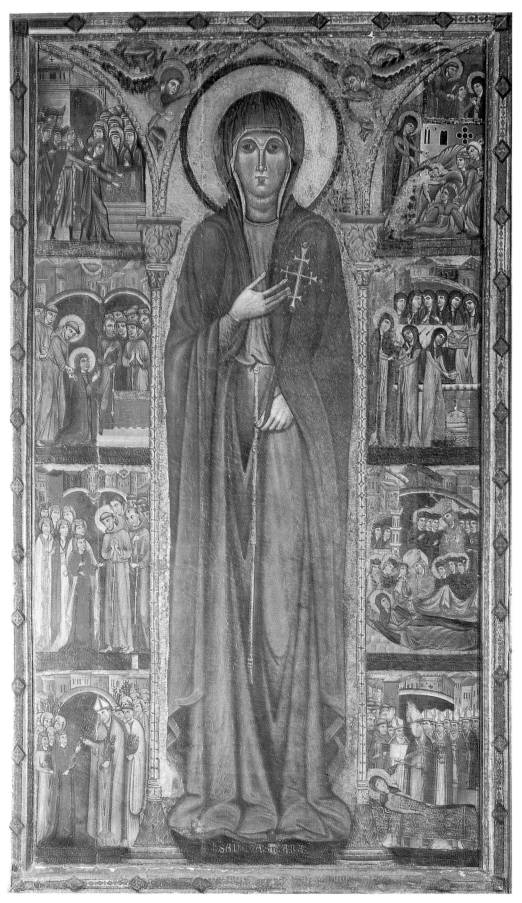

9,68 Anonymous, *St Clare*, 1283. Panel, 9ft 1in × 5ft ⅔in (2.77 × 1.53m). S Chiara, Assisi.

This was the 'Greek style' (*maniera greca*) from which, as Renaissance writers were to claim, Giotto liberated Italian art. In fact, Byzantine artists had preceded him in relinquishing their ancient hieratically stiff manner. During the second half of the twelfth century compositions became more complex, figures more dynamic, and draperies more agitated, in the great decorative schemes carried out by Greek mosaicists not only in the eastern Mediterranean but also in Italy (mainly in Venice) and in Norman Sicily. A further change took place in wall-painting during the thirteenth century. Boldly modelled figures, outlined by sweeping brush-strokes and richly colored, were set in front of landscape or architectural backgrounds in which a new feeling for solidity of form and hollowness of space is felt. The apostles painted in the monastic church of Sopočani in Serbia seem like giants and express gigantic grief as they cluster round the bed of the dying Virgin Mary, their forceful heads and bodies animated and yet controlled as if by vast reserves of interior energy (**9,69**).

The use of wall-paintings to supplement the far more expensive mosaics was probably due to the sharp economic decline during the half century after 1204, when the crusaders sacked Constantinople, placed a puppet Latin emperor on the throne and carved up the eastern empire among themselves. In the following period of partial recovery and cultural revival, sponsored by the Greek emperors of the Paleologan dynasty, the greater freedom of handling and the expressiveness developed by painters was transferred back to mosaics. The finest of these are in the church of St Saviour in Chora (or Kariye Djami), Constantinople (present-day Istanbul). Still more remarkable, how-

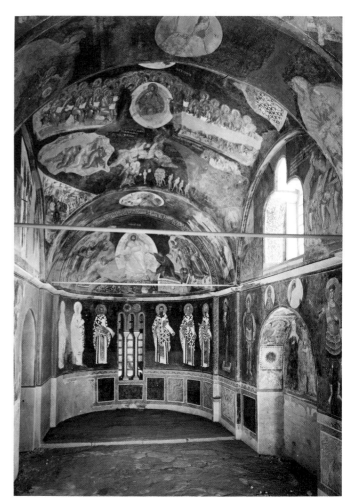

9,70 Funerary chapel, St Saviour in Chora, Istanbul, c. 1303–20.

ever, are the paintings in the attached funerary chapel (**9,70**). Here the old Byzantine style survives only in the saints, posted like sentries around the walls and constrained by heavy vestments. On the ceiling, figures are charged with energetic life, especially in the *Anastasis* or Harrowing of Hell depicted in the conch of the apse, where Christ drags Adam and Eve from their tombs in limbo. That paintings of a similarly dramatic intensity began to be produced in Italy at the same time is more than a coincidence.

It is perhaps significant that the only documented work by Cimabue (fl. 1272–1302), revered as the founder of the Italian school of painting, should be in mosaic (apse of Pisa Cathedral, 1301–2) – the medium most closely associated with Byzantium. But his reputation rests, ironically, on a stanza in Dante's *Purgatorio* – written in about 1315 as the second part of the Divine Comedy – where he is mentioned as an instance of the vanity of all human endeavour:

> *Of painters, Cimabue deemed his name*
> *Unrivalled once; now Giotto is in fashion;*
> *And has eclipsed his predecessor's fame.*

(Tr. I. Grafe)

No specific works were, however, attributed to Cimabue

9,69 *Dormition of the Virgin*, detail, 1258–64. Fresco, Church of the Trinity, Sopočani, Federal Republic of Yugoslavia.

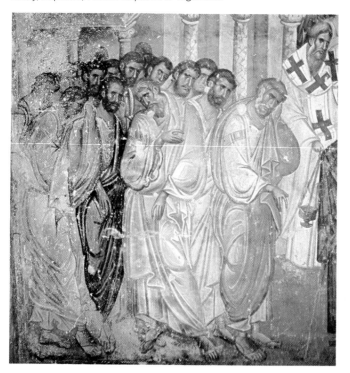

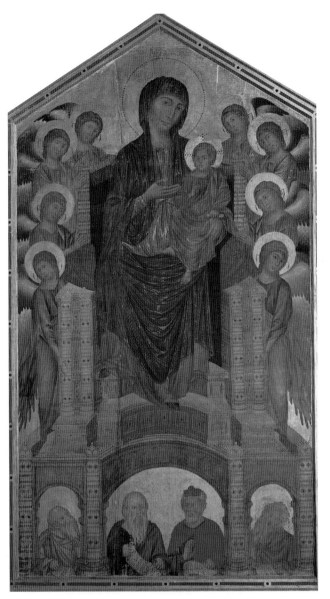

until some 200 years after his death. His name is, in fact, little more than a convenient label for a closely related group of panel and wall-paintings.

Of the paintings assigned to Cimabue by modern scholars the most impressive is an unusually tall altarpiece with a larger than life-size image of the Virgin and Child (**9,71**). It is no more than 50 years later than Bonaventura Berlinghieri's *St Francis* (9,67), but marks a radical change in style. The composition is tightly controlled in form and color, the all-over symmetry being broken only by the Christ Child, who thus immediately attracts attention. Figures, held in tense immobility, have incisive contours and are modelled in soft gradations of tone giving some sense of corporeality – the two foremost angels and the Virgin have their feet flat on the platforms of the throne (not suspended in space like those of St Francis). Recession is indicated by the architecture of the throne rising up in stages and surrounded, not merely flanked, by angels. Everything is immersed in the golden light of heaven, which flickers along the folds of drapery and glistens on the haloes. The four half-length prophets below are bound into the composition by color and expression, but the artist's inability to render space is revealed all too clearly in the arches – are they three arches, or two arches and an indentation?

The Virgin Mary, known in Italy as the Madonna (My Lady), had been venerated throughout Christendom since the fourth century, and in the thirteenth she began to occupy in the minds of the faithful a position almost equal to that of Christ himself. In the West her cult was greatly encouraged by the Franciscans. Duns Scotus formulated the doctrine that she was free from original sin, which was to be given

9,71 *Left* Cimabue, *Madonna Enthroned with Angels and Prophets*, c. 1280–90. Tempera on wood, 12ft 7ins × 7ft 4ins (3.84 × 2.24m). Uffizi, Florence.

9,72 Benedetto Antelami, *Deposition*, 1178. Relief, total width 7ft 6½ins (2.3m). Parma Cathedral.

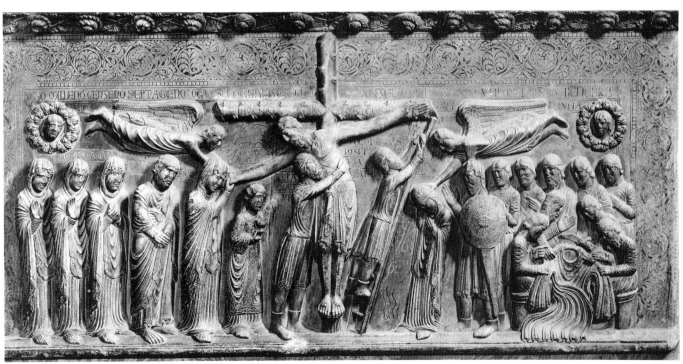

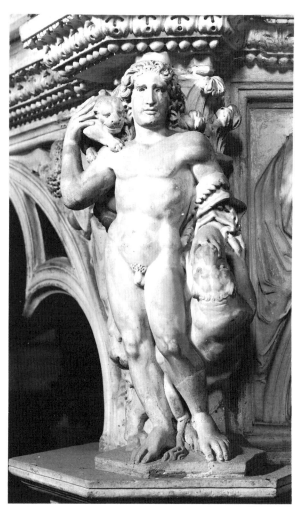

9,73 Nicola Pisano, *Allegory of Strength*, 1260. Marble, 22ins (56cm) high. Baptistery pulpit, Pisa.

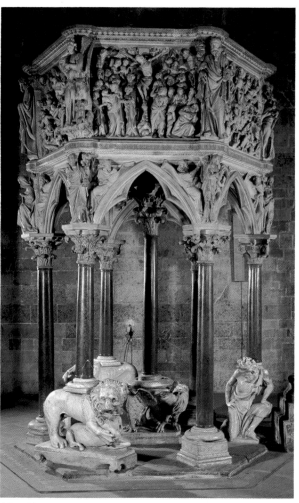

9,74 Giovanni Pisano, Pulpit, begun 1297. Marble, Sant' Andrea, Pistoia.

9,75 Lorenzo Maitani, *The Damned*, detail from the *Last Judgement* relief, 1310–30. Marble, Orvieto Cathedral.

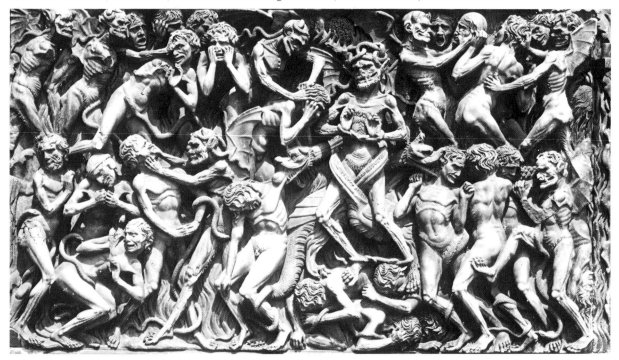

official recognition by a Franciscan Pope, Sixtus IV, in the fifteenth century, but not promulgated as the dogma of the Immaculate Conception until 1854. It was a thirteenth-century Franciscan who wrote what was to become one of the most popular of all hymns to the Virgin, beginning 'Stabat mater dolorosa / Juxta crucem lacrimosa' – the sorrowful mother stood weeping beside the cross – and emphasizing the need to visualize. 'Who would not weep', it goes on, 'if he were to see the Mother of Christ in such great suffering?' Such poems were a challenge as well as an inspiration to sculptors and painters, as may be seen by comparing two reliefs of Christ's Passion, both great works of art but separated by almost exactly 100 years (**9,72; 74**).

The *Deposition* by Benedetto Antelami (fl. 1178–96) is a carving of great restraint and makes a solemn impact akin to that of the slow rhythm of Gregorian chant. Emotion is contained by the austere geometry of the composition and its sequence of dignified figures, among whom the Virgin takes her appointed place. The effect is sacramental. A human tragedy of agony and loss has become a solemn rite and symbol of atonement. Very different indeed is the Crucifixion panel on the pulpit by Giovanni Pisano (fl. 1265–1314). The emphasis here is on vivid visualization of the actual events – as in the *Stabat Mater* and, probably, the sermons preached from this and many other pulpits at that time. Christ's emaciated body, abdomen contracted, rib-cage bursting, hangs on the cross, his arms forming a V, which has the effect of a loud cry to heaven – 'My God, my God, why hast thou forsaken me?' And the eye is caught and finally held by the figures on earth: St John, to the left of the cross, bursting into tears, the men on the right cowering in terror and, above all, the Virgin collapsing in a convulsive faint.

Giovanni Pisano's father, Nicola Pisano (fl. 1258–78), had absorbed Classical culture at the court of the Holy Roman Emperor Frederick II Hohenstaufen (1212–50), who lived mainly in the south and in Sicily. From a close study of antique sculpture he evolved what might be called a sculptural 'proto-Renaissance' style with numerous direct quotations from Roman sarcophagi, including the male nude, as on his pulpit in the Baptistery, Pisa (**9,73**). Giovanni, who is first recorded in 1265 as assisting his father on the magnificent pulpit in Siena Cathedral, acquired his technical mastery from him but also came under the spell of northern art. The Gothic arches supporting Giovanni's Pistoia pulpit are distinctly French and the tall figures standing between the reliefs have the graceful *contrapposto* of statues on the façade of Reims Cathedral, though there is no precedent in France or anywhere else for the dramatic intensity of the reliefs themselves (**9,74**). He proudly, if somewhat boastfully, signed it with an inscription describing himself as the 'son of Nicola and blessed with higher skill'. He had created a new visual language in which to express the religious ideals of the day.

The influence of Giovanni Pisano was pervasive throughout the early fourteenth century in central Italy, for instance in the reliefs by Lorenzo Maitani (c. 1275–1330) on the façade of Orvieto Cathedral. The damned are rendered so vividly that they arouse our compassion, like the sinners in Dante's *Inferno* – whatever the intention of either the poet or the sculptor may have been (**9,75**). The new visual language created by the Pisani helped painters as well as sculptors, and Nicola's Classicism may have contributed as much as Byzantine art to the monumentality of Cimabue's altarpiece (**9,71**). The same could be said of the main panel of the *Maestà* (or Virgin and Child

9,76 Duccio, *Virgin and Child Enthroned in Majesty*, main panel of the *Maestà* altarpiece, 1308–11. Panel, 7 × 13ft (2.13 × 3.96m). Museo dell'Opera del Duomo, Siena.

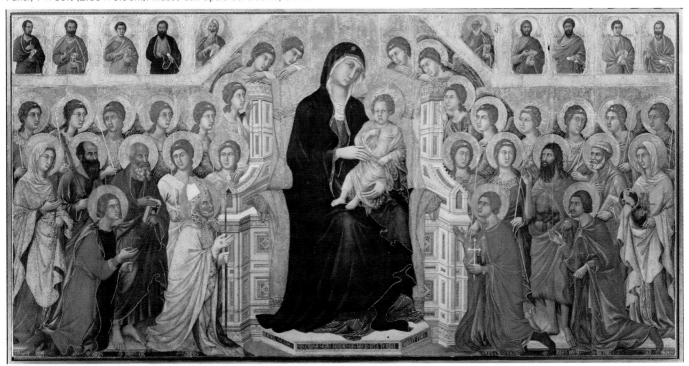

Enthroned in Majesty) painted by Duccio di Buoninsegna (fl. 1278–1318) for the high altar of the cathedral in his native Siena (**9,76**). Here the statuesque, centrally placed Virgin towers above angels and saints hierarchically ranked on either side of her. The small scenes originally above and below and on the back of the altarpiece are less rigid (it consisted of some 70 panels, several of which were lost when it was dismembered in the eighteenth century). There are reflections of the latest developments in Byzantine art here, and individual figures are so close to those in the mosaics of St Saviour in Chora, Constantinople (see p. 404), that they must surely derive from some common source. But Duccio's narrative ability and sharpened sense of space owe more to Giovanni Pisano, who worked in Siena from 1285 to 1297.

In one of the Passion scenes from the back of the altarpiece the old convention of showing an interior by removing one wall is maintained (**9,77**). The room is, however, a clearly defined cubic space and, despite the rudimentary perspective, provides a visually effective stage-like setting for the religious drama. It is the third of the panels in which Duccio illustrated with increasing tension the last verses of the 26th chapter of the Gospel according to St Matthew. Blindfold but dignified, Christ stands in the centre, mocked by the men who crowd round him. On the right the high priest and elders darkly plot his fate. But the eye is drawn to St Peter, who, like the spectator, stands outside the room and exemplifies the

predicament of every Christian torn between denial and affirmation of the faith.

When the great altarpiece was completed in June 1311, it was carried in procession through Siena to the sound of trumpets, pipes, and castanets and the ringing of church bells. Duccio signed his name on the base of the Virgin's throne. Yet, despite all this, he had been hired by the Cathedral authorities as a wage labourer. They supplied the paints and other materials and paid him by the day. And he was soon all but forgotten.

Painters active in late thirteenth-century Rome were treated no better and were soon forgotten, apart from Pietro Cavallini (fl. 1273–1309), though few of his works survived. Nothing whatever is known, for example, of the authors of the remarkable and important cycle of frescoes that have recently been restored and made accessible for the first time since they were completed in 1280 in the Sancta Sanctorum (Holy of Holies) in Rome. The Sancta Sanctorum was a private oratory in which the Pope could celebrate the Mass alone at an altar enclosing some of the most sacred relics in Christendom. The chapel itself – a cube some 25 feet (7.5m) across covered by a Gothic vault and with a shallow rectangular apse – was originally attached to the Lateran Palace and had been built for Nicholas III during his brief pontificate (1277–80), when he promoted a revival of the arts as part of his campaign to re-establish the power and prestige of the Papacy. An inscription declares that there is no holier place in the

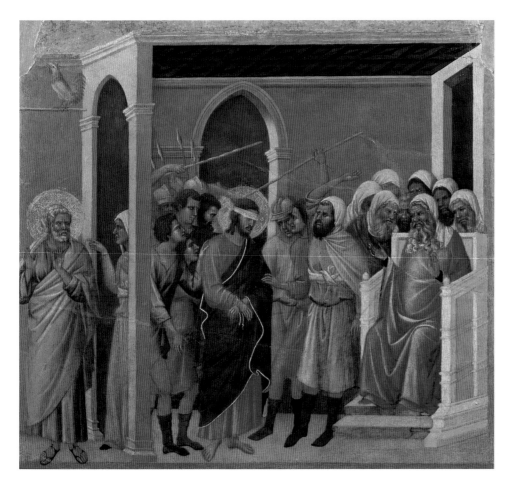

9,77 Duccio, *The Third Denial*, from the *Maestà*, 1308–11. Panel, about 19½ × 21¼ins (49.5 × 54cm). Museo dell'Opera del Duomo, Siena.

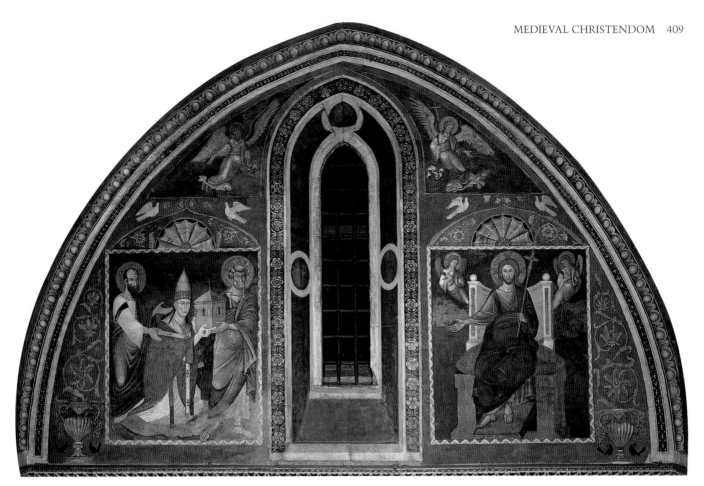

9,78 Lunette in the Sancta Sanctorum, Rome, 1277–80. Fresco and gold leaf, approximately 23ft (7m) wide.

world, and it was embellished with appropriately concentrated splendour – as if it were itself a holy reliquary turned outside-in – with mosaics glittering above the apse, much use of gold and of porphyry and other rare types of precious stone on the pavement and walls, under the direction of 'Magister Cosmatus' whose name is inscribed at the entrance. (Intricate inlays of stone executed in Rome at this period are called Cosmati work after him.) On the upper walls, between the spandrels of the vault, the effect of opulence is maintained by paintings in fresco, regarded at the time as inferior to mosaic but already beginning to be exploited as a medium of greater subtlety and expressive power.

Each of the lancet windows, with simulated porphyry embrasure, is flanked by two rectangular scenes which appear to be attached like embroideries (their slender surrounds have a textile pattern) to a glowing red ground enlivened with motifs derived from Late Antique and Early Christian wall decorations. In the most important position, above the apse, Nicholas III backed by St Paul hands a model of the oratory to St Peter as the mediator with Christ enthroned on the other side of the window – a clear declaration of the source of papal authority (**9,78**). The heads of Christ and the two saints follow inconographic patterns long established in Rome but their bodies, well indicated beneath naturally falling draperies, have a new solidity and potentiality for movement. The Pope was almost certainly, if very unusually at this period, portrayed from life and the model he holds is an

accurate perspectival representation of the exterior of the Sancta Sanctorum. These frescoes seem, indeed, to herald the new developments in Italian painting with which the Florentine Giotti di Bondone (c. 1267–1337) has traditionally been credited.

GIOTTO

That Giotto's fame was to overshadow his contemporaries in Siena and Rome was due partly, perhaps largely, to the local patriotism of Florentines who wrote the first histories of Italian art. There can, however, be no doubt that he was, in every sense, a success. Documents record his financial prosperity, his houses in Florence and Rome, his agricultural estates and his hiring out of looms – a method of investing money to yield as much as 120 per cent per annum without infringing the Church's ban on usury. Not for him the asceticism and self-denial of St Francis. As for his contemporary renown as a painter, we have already mentioned Dante's testimony and before the mid-fourteenth century an historian of Florence listed him as the only artist among the great men of the city. But only one work by him is mentioned, a mosaic in St Peter's in Rome, of which very little now survives. Paradoxically, he has been obscured by his own fame. He became the subject of fables previously told about ancient Greek artists. Writers eulogized him with phrases copied out of Pliny. And, of course, his name was attached to a large number of heterogeneous paintings. In his life-time Assisi

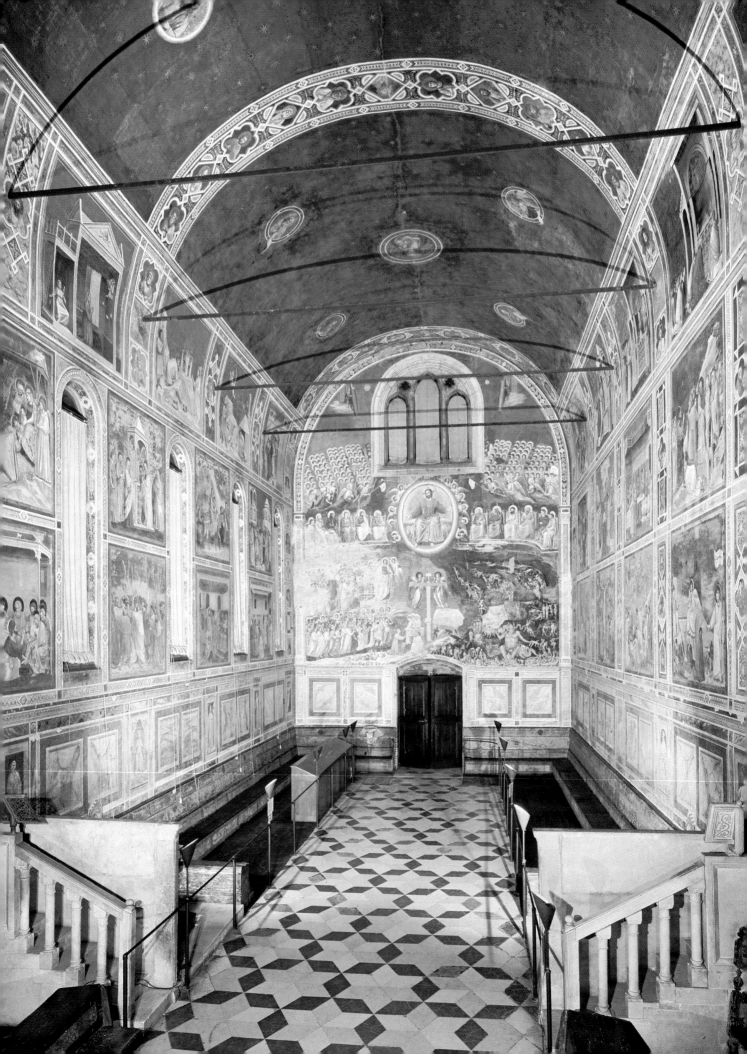

THE MONKS IN PADUA COMPLAIN
ABOUT THE SCROVEGNI CHAPEL

On 9 January 1305 the prior and monks of the Eremitani monastery in Padua complained to their bishop about the 'grave scandal' of the new Scrovegni Chapel bell-tower and its huge new bells, just a stone's throw from their church. However they were probably offended less by the proximity of the bell-tower and the noise of the bells than by what they thought the excessive pomp and splendour of the new chapel's decoration (9,79), about which they go on to remark in their submission to the bishop, that:

. . . there ought not to be a huge church in the Arena, but a small one with one altar in the manner of an oratory, and not with many altars, and further it ought to be without bells and without a bell tower according to the manner and form ascertained and contained in the document of the concession made of the aforementioned Lord Enrico [Scrovegni] by the then Lord bishop of Padua. The form and manner of the concession is as follows:

That Lord Enrico will be allowed to construct in the Arena, or in that place which is called the Arena, without prejudice to the rights of others, a small church, almost in the manner of an oratory, for himself, his wife, his mother and his family, and that people ought not to be allowed to frequent this church. He should not have built a large church there and the many other things which have been made there more for pomp, vainglory and wealth than for praise, glory and honor of God. And again, these things have been done counter to the form and tenor of the concession of the Lord Bishop, whereby the aforementioned Prior in the name of the aforementioned Bishop begged you, according to the due power of your offices, to think us worthy to restrain the aforementioned and to let us see the document by which the concession of the Lord Bishop was made to the aforementioned Lord Enrico, that is, the document made or written by Lord Bartolommeo the notary, and diligently examine the tenor of this same document or concession and compel the aforementioned Enrico, by ecclesiastical censure, to observe the tenor of this document or concession and the pacts, conditions and manner contained or inserted in it and cause to be given to the above-mentioned Prior the aforementioned document or a copy thereof.

(Convento degli Eremitani vol. 62 in Archivio Communale di Padova, tr. J. Stubblebine, *Giotto: The Arena Chapel Frescoes*, New York 1969).

was mentioned as a place where he had worked and a century later he was said to be the author of the scenes from the life of St Francis in S Francesco – whether he did paint them or not is still disputed. No surviving work nowadays attributed to him is fully documented.

His authorship of the frescoes in the Scrovegni (or Arena) Chapel in Padua, however, need not be doubted; and they mark a turning point in the history of Western art and of artistic patronage. Hitherto major works of religious art had been commissioned by rulers, churchmen and civic authorities. Enrico Scrovegni, who had this chapel built next to his grandiose palace (demolished, but originally on the site of the ancient Roman arena), was a private citizen, albeit one of the wealthiest in the republican city-state of Padua, the son of a money-lender so notorious that Dante placed him in the *Inferno*. Scrovegni declared that he built the chapel 'in honour of the cult of the Virgin Mother of God and to honour and adorn the good city-state and commune of Padua'. The honour of his own family was also involved, for the chapel was decorated with a lavishness quite unprecedented for a private foundation and, as the paintings reveal, he sought thereby to expiate the sins of his father. In Giotto's large *Last Judgement* over the entrance door damned usurers are balanced by the very prominent figure of Enrico Scrovegni presenting a model of the chapel to the Virgin (**9,79**). There are three registers of figurative paintings on the other walls, of scenes from the life of the Virgin and of Christ. Below them is a dado with single grisaille figures of virtues and vices, where, it is worth noting, Avarice, the sin of the rich, is omitted to make room for Envy, a failing ascribed mainly to the poor! As a whole, the cycle of paintings answers to the demands of Bishop Sicardo (c. 1155–1215), who wrote in a treatise on the liturgy that images should not merely be suitable as decorations for a church, but should serve to remind the laity of 'things past (stories and visions) and direct their minds to those of the present (virtues and vices) and the future (punishments and rewards)'.

The paintings in the Scrovegni Chapel are the earliest securely attributed to Giotto. They are, nevertheless, the work of a fully mature artist who had completely assimilated influences from Cimabue, Early Christian art in Rome, Roman painting of the late thirteenth century and the Pisani (Giovanni Pisano carved a statue of the Virgin and Child for the chapel). Although Giotto borrowed iconographical patterns from earlier art, he revised them almost out of recognition, omitting irrelevancies so as to give each scene a compelling and totally coherent simplicity. Indeed, he carried the elimination of everything inessential to the furthest point attainable. Those reproduced here represent the Marriage Feast at Cana, where Christ miraculously changed water into wine, the Raising of Lazarus, the Lamentation of the dead Christ, and *Noli me tangere* (**9,80**). So clearly are the Gospel stories presented that there is no need for demonstrative emphasis, for contorted features or violent gestures, to stress their meaning. It emerges quite naturally. With only the gentlest movement of the hand the risen Christ says to St

9,79 *Opposite* Scrovegni Chapel, Padua, with *The Last Judgement* by Giotto over the door, c. 1304–13.

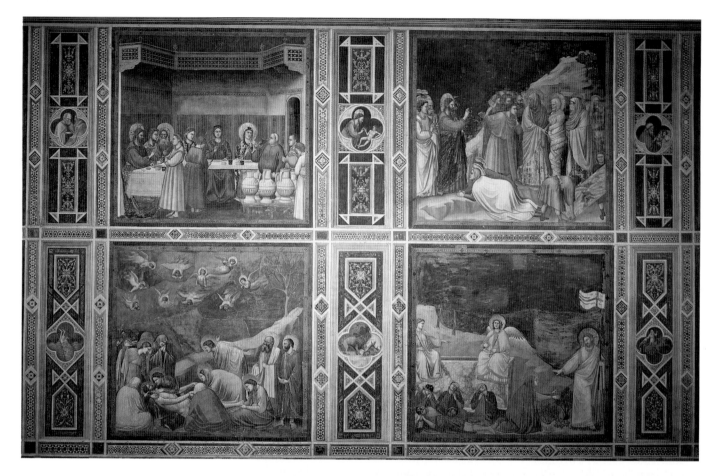

9,80 Giotto, *Marriage Feast at Cana, Raising of Lazarus, Lamentation* and *Noli me tangere*, details of fresco decoration, c. 1304–13. Scrovegni Chapel, Padua.

9,81 Giotto, *Lamentation*, detail of fig. 9,80. Fresco, 7ft 7ins × 6ft 7½ins (2.31 × 2.02m).

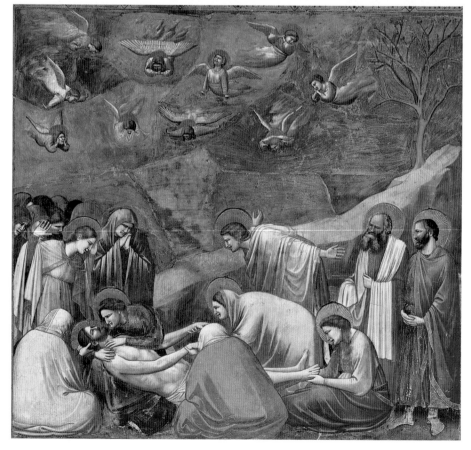

Mary Magdalen: 'Touch me not' (*Noli me tangere*). Every figure is similarly expressive, even those squatting on the ground with their backs to the spectator in the Lamentation. All are solemnly posed, yet seemingly endowed with the capability of motion within the space that surrounds them. Draperies fall in natural folds according to their different textures, all carefully rendered, and contribute to the disciplined formal construction that gives to the whole conception of the chapel's decoration so extraordinary a sense of gravity and weight and eternal stillness. The unity of the whole is felt in every part. Individual scenes are related to one another not only thematically, as hitherto, but also compositionally, the *Raising of Lazarus* being linked directly with the *Noli me tangere* and also diagonally by the line of the hill with the *Lamentation*. Above them all there is the same cloudless blue sky, which also spreads across the vault of the chapel and binds the scheme together – just as the doctrine of the Redemption unites the various subjects.

Each group stands on a shallow but logically constructed stage. Interiors are depicted according to the ancient Roman tradition of 'wide-angle' perspective, which Giotto used more systematically than Duccio. But the aims of both artists were the same. Both transformed the flat picture-plane, from which solidly modelled figures projected, as in low relief, into a kind of transparent window, beyond which scenes from the Gospel are brought vividly to life. Some figures are partly cut off by the frame; the risen Christ is shown as if about to move out of the spectator's field of vision altogether. Giotto was, however, quite as much concerned with inner states of mind as with outward appearances. In the *Lamentation*, where each figure is individually and uniquely expressive, the Virgin clasps her dead son and gazes at his closed eyes, creating an unforgettable image of the desolation of bereavement, made all the more poignant by the rigorous, one might almost say Stoic, control with which it is rendered (**9,81**).

There are, however, two levels of reality – or unreality – in the Scrovegni Chapel: religious and mundane, or poetic and prosaic. While the narrative scenes elevate the mind, their frames trick the eye with simulated inlays of porphyry, lapis lazuli and other semi-precious stones, and the dado (see Glossary) imitates marble panelling with inset carvings. Paint was, in fact, being used here as a *trompe l'œil* substitute for more expensive materials. Up to this period figurative wall-painting had usually been regarded as an inferior alternative to mosaic, which was both costly and slow to execute (18 men worked for ten months without completing the apse mosaic in Pisa Cathedral). Venice seems to have been the only Italian city rich enough to afford extensive schemes of mosaic decoration (**9,14**) and, doubtless for this reason, was almost the only one to produce no school of mural painters in the Middle Ages. Franciscans preferred painting partly because it *was* a humbler medium – no mosaics and only a very limited quantity of stained glass were permitted in their churches – and for this reason S Francesco, Assisi, has very extensive painted decoration (**9,65**).

True frescoes – the word fresco is often misused for all forms of mural painting – are almost as durable as mosaics. They were painted on fresh (*fresco*) damp plaster, with which the soluble earth pigments unite chemically as it dries, fixing the colors and lending them a unique transparency. Pigments which could not be absorbed into the plaster in this way but had to be mixed with an adhesive could be added *a secco* after the surface had dried, though only for finishing touches in the Scrovegni Chapel. These pigments were the same as those used for such panel paintings as Duccio's *Maestà* (**9,76**), applied in layer after layer on the dry gesso (a kind of plaster) ground with which the wood panel was coated. Whether painting on walls or on panels, artists at this period normally worked with groups of assistants. But the difficult fresco technique set a premium on the virtuosity of the master, demanding great swiftness and sureness of hand as well as a grasp of the total composition, which had to be finished patch by patch. No more plaster was laid at a time than the artist could paint in one session. This might vary, of course. In the Scrovegni Chapel Giotto sometimes painted a whole group of figures in a single session, sometimes only a head. His increasing reliance on assistants for his later wall-paintings (in S Croce, Florence) was, significantly, accompanied by more extensive use of pigments applied *a secco*.

The poet Petrarch (1304–74) wrote of a *Virgin and Child* by Giotto, which he owned, that its beauty would not be understood by the ignorant but would astound all those with knowledge of the arts. Some years were to pass, however, before any painter took the full measure of Giotto's genius (see p. 426). His immediate followers in Florence, including those who probably began their careers as his assistants, like Taddeo Gaddi (fl. 1330–63), did little more than imitate aspects of his work. The most interesting Italian painters of the next generation were Sienese, notably Simone Martini (fl. 1315-44), a personal acquaintance of Petrarch, who commemorated him in two of his exquisitely phrased and delicately cadenced sonnets. But with Simone we move out of the austere world of Dante and Giotto into a more courtly ambience.

SECULAR AND INTERNATIONAL GOTHIC

Within a century of the death of St Francis of Assisi the fervent but simple pieties of the early friars were being overlaid and sometimes compromised by concessions to secular demands. A large altarpiece painted in 1317 by Simone Martini for the French (Angevin) king Robert of Naples might almost be read as an illustration of this process, for the rough brown Franciscan habit of the saint is sheathed and all but concealed by richly embroidered vestments (**9,82**). St Louis of Toulouse, the king's elder brother, had joined the 'Spiritual' branch of the Franciscan Order, which strictly observed the founder's rule of poverty, chastity and obedience, unlike the larger 'Conventual' branch, whose members were often said to be too lax in observing their vows. In 1296, the year before he died, Louis had reluctantly accepted the archbishopric of Toulouse.

Two angels bearing a heavenly crown hover above St Louis while he holds a smaller but otherwise identical earthly crown over the strongly characterized head of his brother Robert, in whose favour he had renounced the Neapolitan kingdom. Scenes from his life and a miracle he had worked after his death are depicted in the predella. King Robert commissioned the picture in the year of St Louis's canonization, which he had eagerly promoted to endorse his own divine right to the throne and as a move in a complicated political game to establish Angevin supremacy in central Italy. Heraldic lilies, the French royal emblem, are prominent on the frame as well as on the 'heavenly' gold background of the main panel. Beneath its serene surface, therefore, Simone Martini's altarpiece attempts to reconcile religious and political, eternal and temporal, concerns that might well seem discordant if not irreconcilable.

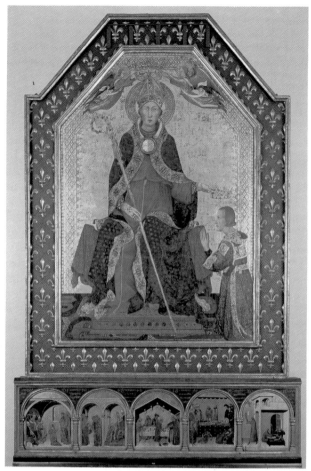

9,82 Simone Martini, *St Louis of Toulouse crowning Robert of Anjou King of Naples*, 1317. Panel 6ft 6¾ins × 4ft 6¼ins (2 × 1.38m), predella 19¾ × 68¾ins (50 × 174.6cm). Museo di Capodimonte, Naples.

9,83 *Below* Ambrogio Lorenzetti, *Allegory of Peace*, 1339. Fresco. Palazzo Pubblico, Siena.

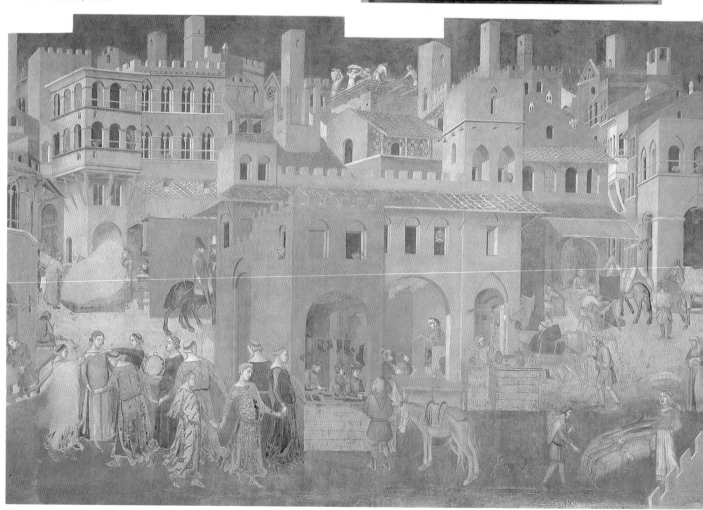

There are reminiscences of courtly Byzantine art in the hierarchically scaled and ceremonially posed figures. Just so, the emperor Theodosius had been shown handing down a scroll to an official more than 900 years before (7,22). The painting has an Eastern opulence, which must originally have been heightened by the glitter of precious stones (now lost) set in the surface. But the textiles, which contribute so much to the rich effect, are painted in a wholly un-Byzantine manner. Velvets, brocaded silks, embroideries with gold thread, and a knotted carpet – evidently of Turkish or Persian manufacture – are rendered almost illusionistically. And despite the rigid formality of their full-face and profile poses, the figures have three-dimensional substance and are placed in a space clearly defined by the foreshortened pattern of the carpet. Still more remarkable are the five scenes in the predella, with their architecture depicted in perspective from a single central viewpoint so that we see only the left part of the vault above the scene on the left, the right wall of the house of that on the right. In this logical organization of space from a precisely determined viewpoint, Simone Martini completely rejected the *maniera greca* of Bonaventura Berlinghieri (9,67) and went some way beyond Cimabue (9,71) and even his own master, Duccio (9,76).

Another Sienese artist, Ambrogio Lorenzetti (fl. 1319–47), made a further advance towards a naturalistic vision in his large mural paintings in the town hall in his native city (**9,83**). Emphasis is firmly placed on the here and now in this enormous panoramic view of town and country, based on Siena and its surrounding hills – perhaps the first convincing cityscape ever painted and one of the first monumental secular paintings in Western art since antiquity, reflecting a notable shift in patronage, which was no longer exclusively ecclesiastical. Buildings of many types are shown, shops with open fronts, palaces of the rich (with masons still at work on one), some with towers for defence which had been erected in earlier times of civil war. They are clearly detached from one another, and men and animals pass in the space that flows between them. Trade prospers and a note of happy harmony is struck by a group of girls in the foreground, dancing rather sedately to the tinkle of a tambourine, their silk dresses rustling as they gyrate. The right half of the painting depicts a well cultivated agricultural landscape. Peasants till the soil in the foreground while farmers with their produce make their way up the hill to the city whence elegantly dressed and mounted figures ride out. The vineyards and olive groves in the middle distance draw the spectator's eye into a degree of spatial depth unknown since the decline of the Roman empire. Above this tranquil scene floats an allegorical figure of Security. She holds a scroll indicating the blessings of peace under her aegis, with a similar visual message above. Swinging from a rope on the gallows is a criminal executed for violating the laws of good government.

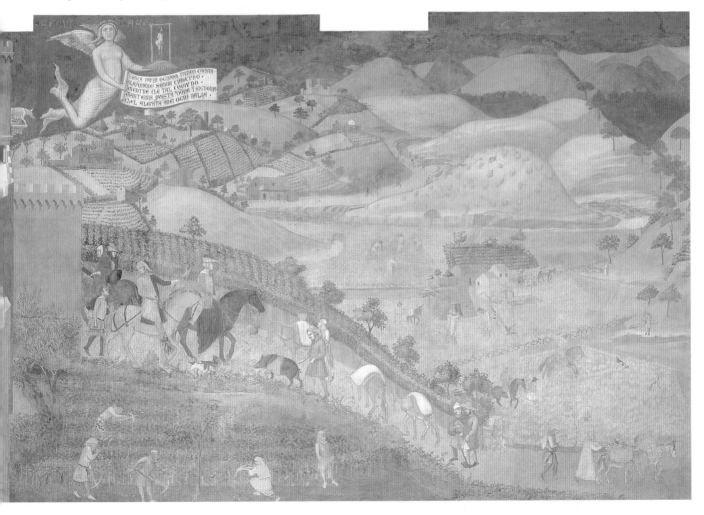

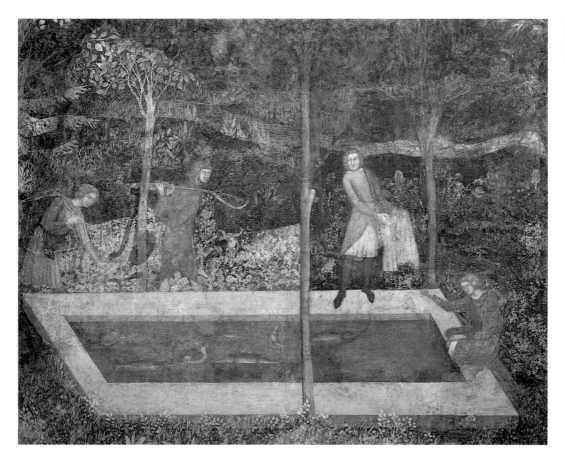

9,84 *Bird-Catchers*, 1343. Fresco. Chambre des cerfs, Papal Palace, Avignon, France.

Facing this peaceful vision, on the opposite side of the room, there is (or rather was, for little survives) another view of the same city and landscape devastated by war. Personifications of justice, wisdom, peace, the Christian virtues and the Sienese commune itself, holding a shield with an image of the Virgin and Child, are painted on the third wall, facing that with windows opening on to the real landscape. It was in this room that the nine magistrates who governed Siena from 1292 to 1355 held their meetings – surrounded by the paintings which were originally entitled 'Peace' and 'War' (not 'Allegories of Good and Bad Government'), visual reminders of a political theology specifically directed to maintaining peaceful stability.

Ambrogio Lorenzetti presented a realistic, not to say materialistic, view of the Tuscan countryside, which provided his home town with food and the raw materials for manufacture (Siena was a centre of the cloth trade). In the Palace of the Popes at Avignon, on the other hand, a woodland scene becomes an idyllic but totally unproductive setting for elegantly mannered sportsmen (**9,84**). A whole room was transformed into the likeness of a forest glade, with streams, many different trees and singing birds, of a type described by Virgil and Ovid in phrases that had inspired poets throughout the Middle Ages, thus linking the decoration across the centuries with that of similar painted rooms in ancient Rome (5,30). The papal court had moved out of Rome, mainly for political reasons, and in 1309 settled at Avignon in the south of France (on ter-ritory of the Angevin king of Naples), remaining there until 1376. Several Italian artists went there, notably Simone Martini, and the unknown painter of the frescoed room was probably one of them. It forms part of the palace built and decorated for Clement VI (1342–52), a French aristocrat who had spent most of his career in royal service in Paris and became the most luxury-loving of the popes who ruled from Avignon.

In 1348 Europe suffered the greatest natural calamity in its history: the bubonic plague known as the Black Death, which many contemporaries believed to have been sent as divine punishment for the profligacy of the Church and especially the papal court. At least a third of the population died in a single summer. The long-term effects of the disaster are, however, hard to estimate and often seem contradictory. Many changes that had gradually been taking place, most notably in the feudal structures of obligation (service in return for protection), were abruptly brought to a head. No longer was there a shortage of land and food, or a surplus of manpower; but attempts to exploit the scarcity of labour were suppressed so that wealth came to be more than ever concentrated in the hands of increasingly exclusive land-owning and mercantile classes. There was a wave of popular religious fervour, marked by heightened emotionalism and public acts of penitence, for example by flagellants who scourged their backs as they walked in processions. But the proximity of death could, and often did, sharpen the appetite for earthly pleasures.

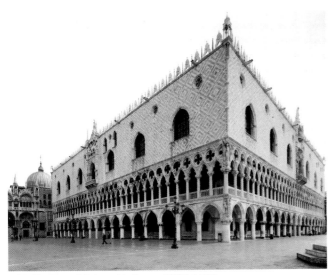

9,85 The Doges' Palace, Venice, c. 1345–1438.

Although many artists must have died in the plague (Ambrogio Lorenzetti probably among them), there was no more than a brief hiatus in artistic activity in Italy. Major building projects were carried forward without any change in plan or in style. In Venice, for instance, work continued almost uninterrupted on the Doges' Palace, which had been begun in the 1340s (**9,85**). Its main function was to provide a vast hall for the *Maggior Consiglio*, the elective assembly of the republic as constituted in 1297, when an oligarchic system was adopted – a system destined to endure for five centuries. Whereas the civic buildings of Florence and Siena were fortresses designed to protect the administrators, the Doges' Palace has an openness which reflects the tranquillity of Venice. The two rows of loggias and damask-like brickwork above give it an almost insubstantial appearance. The style is a uniquely Venetian version of Gothic, somewhat influenced by Islamic architecture and developed mainly for the palaces of its powerfully rich merchant class.

Venetians were none the less susceptible to the charm of the paintings and sculpture in a late Gothic style evolved around 1400 mainly by artists working for the interrelated but jealously competitive ruling families of Europe. This style has been called International Gothic, which is something of a misnomer in so far as it implies a unified current of artistic taste and intention. The ease and rapidity with which illuminated manuscripts and textiles circulated at that date certainly facilitated artistic cross-fertilization. But artists in different places developed out of their local traditions styles that were strikingly individual despite their sharing in general tendencies. The intricate elaboration and enrichment of surface patterning, and the more detailed naturalism with which animals, flowers and, especially, fashionable costumes were depicted, all combined with an accentuation of distinctly Gothic elegance in the representation of figures, both human and divine, to suggest sometimes an ascetic spirituality though always, in their well-mannered gestures and poise, with a courtly air.

The *Wilton Diptych*, named after the English country-house in which it belonged until it passed to the National Gallery in London, is a well-marked, indeed an almost paradigmatical, example of this courtly art (**9,86**). It shows King Richard II presented to the Virgin by his three patron saints, St Edmund, St Edward the Confessor – both former kings of England – and St John the Baptist. Richard wears an exquisitely woven robe brocaded in gold thread with crouching hart (male deer), which were his personal badge, shown also in the enamel medallion on his breast. Around his neck he wears a collar of gold pods of broom like one given to him in 1396 by his father-in-law, Charles VI of France, who had adopted it as an emblem, though the broom plant, *planta genista*, was also the punning device of the royal Plantagenet family to which Richard belonged. The angels surrounding the Virgin have crowns of roses, necklaces of broom-pods and wear the white hart badge. One of them holds a flag with a red cross on a white ground (the banner of England and St George and also a symbol of the Resurrection) and the gesture of the Christ Child indicates that he is either about to receive it from or have it passed to Richard whose long-fingered hands are open. Despite the superabundance of royal heraldry, the painting has an otherworldly visionary aura and in this way seems to reflect the combination of pride, hedonism and mysticism in the personality of Richard himself.

An unstable ruler, Richard is remembered today as the martyr-victim of Shakespeare's play. In 1377 at the age of ten he succeeded his grandfather as king of England, assuming autocratic power 12 years later. He married a daughter of the Holy Roman Emperor in 1382 and after her death a daughter of the king of France. His court was more internationally cultivated than that of any previous king of England. Geoffrey Chaucer, one of his civil servants, influenced by both French and Italian literature, transformed English into a literary language during his reign. His household included a band of musicians and a number of artists; his wardrobe was stocked with garments of the most precious materials, rare furs with silk brocades, and in his treasury there were examples of French and Spanish goldsmiths' work enamelled and set with jewels, none of which survives. But his extravagance was one of the factors that led to his deposition in 1399 and death the following year (though it is not known whether he was murdered as in Shakespeare's play). The *Wilton Diptych* may well have been painted for him to express his idea of divinely instituted kingship, at a moment when his authority was being undermined, for although its date is uncertain the heraldry reveals that it must be after 1395. Its authorship is also problematic. The artist may have been either English or French. Cultural contacts were strong during the reigns of Richard II in England and the peace-loving Charles V and his mentally unbalanced son Charles VI in France, which marked a brief interval in the wars between the two realms. But no surviving English painting of the period is as technically accomplished, not to mention its poetry, its combination of the visionary and the exquisite. Nor is there any known French work quite like it.

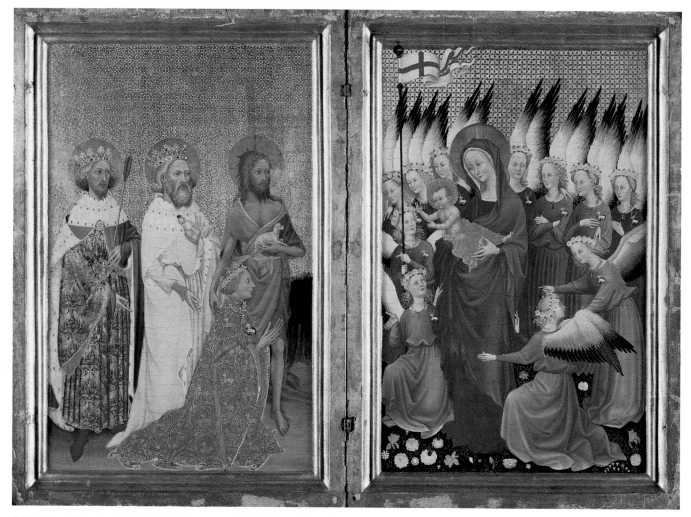

9,86 *Wilton Diptych*, after 1395. Egg tempera and gold leaf on oak panels, each 18 × 11½ins (45.7 × 29.2cm). National Gallery, London.

The *Wilton Diptych* has, nevertheless, the elegance of line, delicacy of color and jewel-like sharpness prized by patrons in France. Pol de Limbourg (fl. 1400–16) and his brothers, Herman and Jean, were among its most accomplished practitioners. Born at Nijmegen (then in the Duchy of Burgundy), and working in France, they drew much inspiration from Italian art – one of their works derives from a fresco in Florence by Giotto's pupil Taddeo Gaddi. Their main achievement is the *Très Riches Heures* (the Very Rich Book of Hours) illuminated for John, duke of Berry, a younger brother of Charles V and uncle of Charles VI.

The *Très Riches Heures* opens with 12 calendar pages, one for each month with an appropriate scene and the signs of the zodiac in a semicircle above. Thus, *September* shows the vintage in front of the duke's castle of Saumur on the Loire (**9,87**). Although the perspective is anything but scientific, the precision with which every separate detail is represented lends the whole scene a poetic truth which suspends disbelief. It is, of course, a highly idealized vision of peace and plenty. It was, in fact, painted in the midst of the Hundred Years' War, which devastated northern France. Moreover, it is a view not only of but, as

it were, from a castle, both literally and metaphorically looking down on the peasants. As ungainly as they are natural, these are among the first of the semi-comic 'rustics' who figure as foils to courtly elegance in European paintings, and in literature as well. For the *Très Riches Heures* is, above all, an essay in the exquisite and the refined. There is, significantly enough, no reference whatever to religion: the vines, for instance, are not symbolic, as they had always been in earlier medieval art.

A Book of Hours was a prayer-book containing the devotions for the seven canonical hours (matins, vespers, etc.), arranged to be read by the laity through the year – hence the prefatory calendar. One may question whether the duke of Berry was as interested in the text as he was in the Limbourgs' calendar. He was perhaps the most notable art collector of his time, the owner of Italian paintings, antique coins and engraved gems (including the *Gemma Augustea*, 5,57), and a passionate bibliophile. The *Très Riches Heures* is one of the very few great medieval works of art made for a private patron's delectation. Many devotional images and other religious works of art were, of course, created for private patrons throughout the Middle Ages, for example Giotto's

Delight in jewelled richness of colors and textures, closely observed and meticulously recorded naturalistic detail and intricacy of composition, typical of late Gothic painting in the courtly style, were never more fully expressed than in this altarpiece. Indeed the religious significance of the subject was almost taken for granted and the scene given the appearance of a pageant still more splendid than those staged in any European court. The Magi are represented as crowned kings, elderly, middle-aged and youthful, and everyone is dressed in their best. Among the hundreds of men and boys there are only three women – the Virgin and her two attendants; there is, however, an ample gathering of livestock – horses, dogs, monkeys, cheetahs, doves, a falcon, a hare and a stag, as well as the ox and the ass of the Bethlehem stable. And although these may have had or could have been given symbolical significance, they seem to have been included in the altarpiece simply to celebrate the abundance of the natural world, and perhaps to display the artist's skill. They are rendered with the same sharp precision as the human figures which are shown in a variety of attitudes, turning their heads or gazing upwards, one crouching as he removes the spurs of the young king standing in the centre. Foreshortening and the play of light and shade (especially in the *Nativity* in the left panel of the predella) are effectively suggested. But the story of the three Magi, as told in the Gospel according to St Matthew, is depicted in the manner of multiple narrative adopted by earlier medieval illuminators: at the top of the painting, under the arch on the left, they sight the star; in the centre they ride uphill through a Tuscan landscape to Herod's palace in Jerusalem; and on the right they proceed towards Bethlehem. These little scenes beneath the arches are strikingly like miniatures by the Limbourg brothers and just as delicately painted, although they can never have been very clearly visible when the painting was in the place originally intended for it above the altar in the church of S Trinità. Recession in space is suggested rather than defined by the diminution of figures. In the lower part there is hardly any suggestion of space at all. The figures are simply piled up, one head above another; those at the back of the group are no smaller than the Magi in the foreground. The idea that a picture should represent a single pregnant moment from a single viewpoint according to the laws of linear perspective was, however, to be evolved in Florence very soon after Gentile da Fabriano painted the *Adoration of the Magi*. With its technical accomplishment in the rendering of form and textures and its precision in the depiction of animal and human physiognomy, based on direct observation, combined with a conception of pictorial space that is still in the medieval tradition, this painting seems to bestride·two epochs in the history of art.

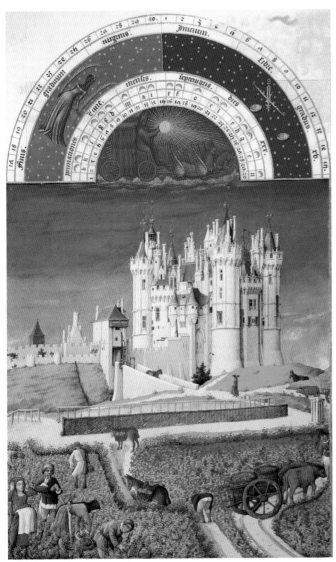

9,87 The Limbourg Brothers, *September*, page from the *Très Riches Heures du Duc de Berry*, 1413–16. Illumination on parchment, about 8½ × 5½ins (21.6 × 14cm). Musée Condé, Chantilly.

Scrovegni Chapel (9,79; 80), but in them the artistic intent is not the same. The large altarpiece of the *Adoration of the Magi* by Gentile da Fabriano (c. 1370–1427), painted in Florence in 1423, is another notable example (**9,88**). Rather surprisingly for so eminently late Gothic a work, it was commissioned by one of the leading Florentine humanists, Palla Strozzi, who had learnt and studied ancient Greek and collected manuscripts of Classical authors with the intention of founding a public library. He was the richest man in Florence, the head of a bank with international connections, and was eventually to arouse the jealousy of the Medici, who had him expelled in 1427. But Gentile da Fabriano was the most highly esteemed and sought after painter in Italy at this date which no doubt counted in Palla Strozzi's eye. Gentile had been official painter to Pope Martin V since 1419 and was to receive the most important commission of the time, to fresco the interior of S Giovanni in Laterano in Rome (destroyed in the seventeenth century).

Some of the last great medieval works of religious art were commissioned by the duke of Berry's younger brother, Philip the Bold of Burgundy. The dukes of Burgundy were probably the most powerful rulers in northern Europe around 1400 and it was for the monastery Philip founded at Champmol, just outside his capital city of

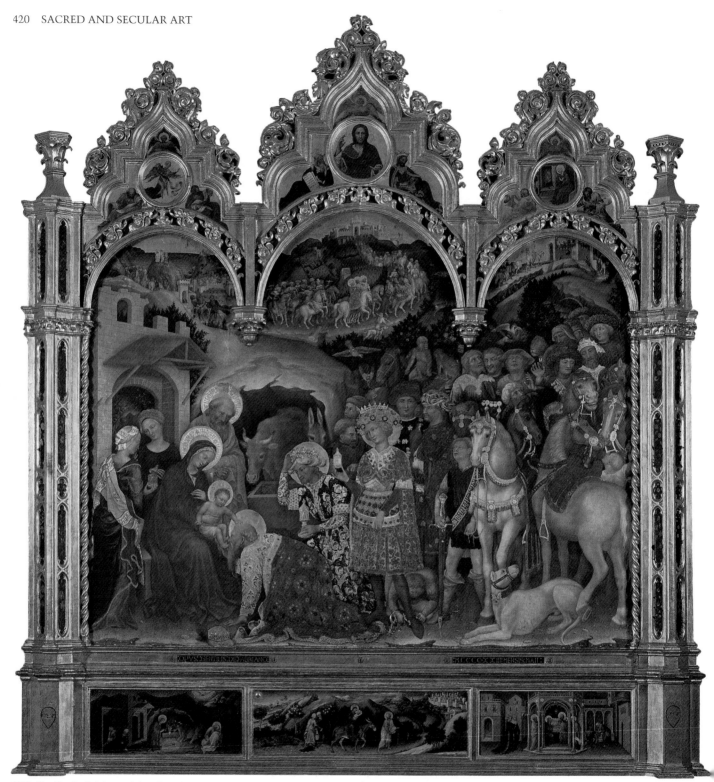

9,88 Gentile da Fabriano, *Adoration of the Magi*, 1423. Panel, 9ft 10⅛ins × 9ft 3ins (3 × 2.82m). Uffizi, Florence.

Dijon, that the Netherlandish sculptor Claus Sluter (fl. 1379–1404) created his greatest work, the *Moses Fountain*. Only the base survives intact (**9,89**). The Crucifixion group which it supported is now known only from fragments (**9,90**). That the central mystery of the Christian faith should have formed, or rather should have been made to form, part of a fountain is a conceit typical of the period – the sacrifice of Christ as the fountain of life. But the sense of human dignity and tragic intensity which

Sluter brought to the conception and execution of this great work raises it far above all other examples of International Gothic, however exquisite and sophisticated some of them may be. Moreover, the personality of the artist is now very strongly felt, as of a sovereign master. Little more than a decade, it should be remembered, divides Sluter's fountain from the early works of Donatello (see pp. 439–40).

Old Testament prophets – the six men whose words,

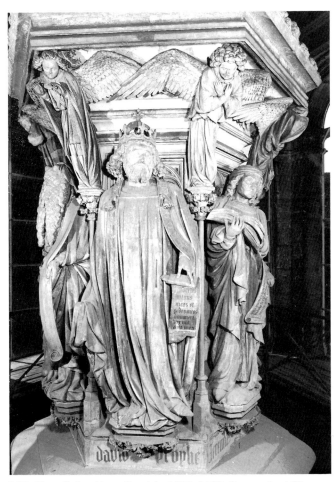

9,89 Claus Sluter, *Moses Fountain*, 1395–1403. Figures about 6ft (1.83m) high. Chartreuse de Champmol, Dijon, France.

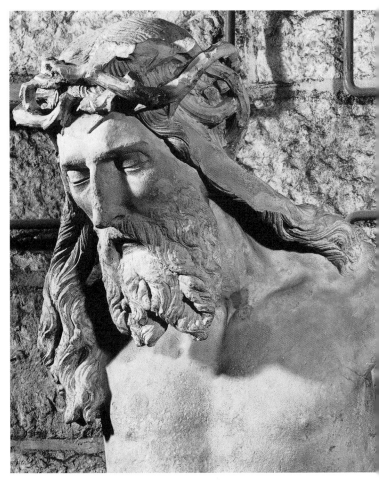

9,90 Claus Sluter, *Head of Christ* from the *Moses Fountain*, 1395–1403. Wood with traces of polychrome, 24ins (61.2cm) high. Musée Archéologique, Dijon.

inscribed on the scrolls they carry, had predicted the Passion – meditate on the meaning of that terrible event (9,89). Their life-size figures recall the sculptures on Gothic portals (9,52; 53; 54) but go beyond them in their boldly realistic rendering of detail and in their sheer corporeality. The heads are so sensitively carved that they might well be mistaken for portraits; and so overpowering is the sense of weight and bulk of their great forms under the swelling draperies that they seem to expand into the surrounding space. They must have been almost unnervingly lifelike when they still had all their original coloring (partly by Jean Malouel, uncle of the Limbourg brothers). Jeremiah wore brass spectacles made by a Dijon gold-smith. But Sluter's fascination with the specific and the tangible would seem, from the surviving fragments, to have given way to something much more impressive in the main group. The head of Christ, torn with pain and still bearing the twisted crown of thorns in which he had been mocked and humiliated, is an entirely new image, as noble and tragic in its humanity as it is sublime in its withheld divinity. Remote both from the idealized Christs of Byzantium (7,50) and the abject images of suffering of the early Middle Ages (9,1), this great work combines the spirituality and the realism, the mysticism and the logic that had inspired, in varying degrees, all the greatest works of Gothic art and architecture.

CHAPTER TEN

THE FIFTEENTH CENTURY IN EUROPE

Gothic artists did not know that they were Gothic, or even medieval, but the Renaissance artist was well aware that he was different. No previous movement in Western art had been so self-conscious. The whole idea of a Renaissance or 'rebirth' of Classical culture, with dark Middle Ages intervening between it and the fall of the Roman empire, was largely a myth propagated in the late fourteenth and fifteenth centuries by Italian Classical scholars – humanists in the original meaning of the word. 'When the darkness breaks, the generations to come may contrive to find their way back to the clear splendour of the ancient past', wrote the poet Petrarch (1304–74) shortly before the middle of the fourteenth century. Less than 100 years later the architect Leon Battista Alberti (1404–72) recognized among his Florentine contemporaries several artists who were 'not to be ranked below any who was ancient' – he named Brunelleschi, Donatello, Ghiberti, Luca della Robbia and Masaccio. Soon afterwards a Roman humanist, Lorenzo Valla (1405–57), somewhat complacently remarked that he did not know why the arts 'had been so greatly in decline and had almost died out altogether; nor why they have revived in this age, and so many good artists and writers have appeared and flourished.' This, in a nutshell, was how the Renaissance saw itself.

In fact, as we have seen, the Classical heritage survived throughout the Middle Ages. Greek as well as Latin literature continued to be read. There were many medieval artists who were neither blind to the beauty of Classical art nor indifferent to Classical legends and history. But the humanists of the Renaissance differed from medieval theologians and others who had studied Aristotle, Cicero and the Neoplatonists. The humanists found in Classical antiquity absolute standards by which cultural and, indeed, all human activities could be judged. They created, or recreated, a structure of values different from that on which medieval ideals of chivalry and nobility were based – one in which birth, for example, counted for less than individual prowess and intellectual ability. Humanism was nurtured in the Italian city-states, which could trace their history back to ancient Roman times and, with their republican (not clerical or aristocratic) governments, epitomized the new ideals of self-reliance and civic virtue – civic and mundane, not chivalric or contemplative.

The visual arts	Historical landmarks
c. 1415–17 Donatello, *St George* (10,26)	**1415** Battle of Agincourt: England resumes attack on France
1424–52 Ghiberti, *Porta del Paradiso* (10,8)	
1425 Masaccio, *Holy Trinity* (10,5)	
1432 van Eyck, *Ghent Altarpiece* completed (10,15)	**1431** Joan of Arc executed
1440 Brunelleschi, Pazzi Chapel begun (10,1)	**1434–64** Cosimo de' Medici rules Florence
c. 1440–5 Fra Angelico, *Annunciation* (10,38)	
1443–51 House of Jacques Coeur (10,22)	
1444 Michelozzo, Palazzo Medici-Riccardi begun (10,20)	**1445** Gutenberg prints first book in Europe
c. 1445 Piero della Francesca, *Baptism of Christ* (10,40)	
c. 1445–7 Uccello, *The Flood* (10,39)	
1450 Alberti, S Francesco begun (10,23)	**1452** Habsburg rule of Holy Roman Empire begins
c. 1460 Mantegna, *St Sebastian* (10,48)	**1453** End of Hundred Years' War
1460–6 Donatello, *Lamentation over the Dead Christ* (10,28)	**1453** Fall of Constantinople: Turks end Byzantine empire
1469–70 Cossa, *Month of March* (10,46)	**1469–92** Lorenzo de' Medici rules Florence
c. 1470–80 Verrocchio, *Madonna and Child* (10,35)	**1482** Ficino's translations of Plato printed
c. 1478 Botticelli, *La Primavera* (10,44)	**1485** Alberti's *On Painting, On Architecture* printed
c. 1485 Bellini, *S Giobbe Altarpiece* (10,49)	**1492** Fall of Granada: Arabs and Jews expelled from Spain
	1492 Columbus lands in West Indies
	1497 Josquin des Prez, *Nymphes des Bois*
	1498 Vasco da Gama sails to India; Columbus lands in South America; Savonarola executed
1500 Dürer, *Self-Portrait* (10,58)	

THE FIFTEENTH CENTURY IN EUROPE 423

The growth and spread of humanism is pre-eminent in the intellectual history of the fifteenth century; but its relationship with the visual arts is complex and sometimes ambiguous. Although humanists were not initially anti-clerical, still less anti-Christian, they were preoccupied by problems of the here and now rather than of the hereafter. The visual arts, on the other hand, remained largely religious both in Italy and northern Europe. For the fifteenth century was the golden age of Flemish as well as Florentine painting, and only towards its end did Italian art acquire international prestige – at least partly because of its association with humanist thought.

THE BEGINNINGS OF THE ITALIAN RENAISSANCE

The Pazzi Chapel in Florence (**10,1; 2**) and the choir of St Lorenz in Nuremberg (**10,3**) are almost exactly contemporary, though they might seem to belong to different worlds and different centuries. The difference is not due solely, or even mainly, to the fluted pilasters with Corinthian capitals of the one and the hexagonal piers and pointed arches of the other; it is more profound. The architects of the choir of St Lorenz developed the High

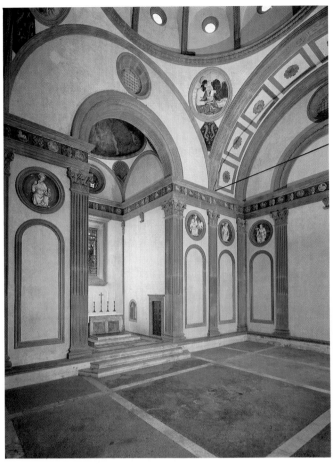

10,1 Filippo Brunelleschi, Pazzi Chapel, S Croce, Florence, begun 1440.

10,2 Sectional diagram of the Pazzi Chapel.

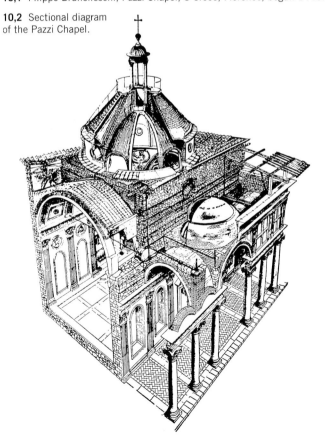

10,3 K. Heinzelmann and K. Roritzer, choir of St Lorenz, Nuremberg, Germany, begun 1439.

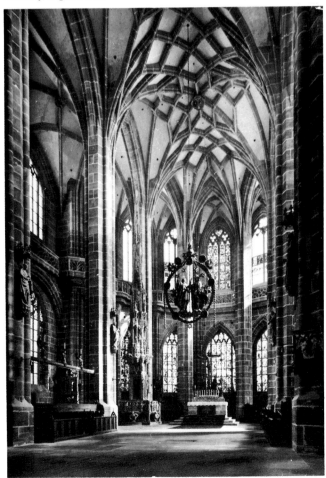

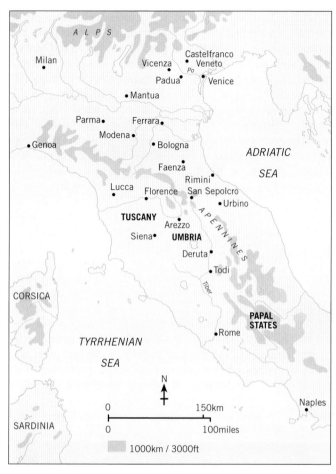

Renaissance Italy

Gothic style of, for instance, Amiens Cathedral (9,43) to create a space of great complexity and apparent freedom, one that is by no means easy to comprehend. Although the plan is symmetrical and mathematically determined, a series of subtly differing patterns of lines soaring up to the intricate tracery of the vault is presented from every viewpoint. In the Pazzi Chapel there are no mysterious depths or soaring heights, no sense of the beyond. Space is precisely defined in cubes, half-cubes and hemispheres. Horizontal and vertical axes are held in balance and the effect is supremely simple, lucid and static. It is almost severely tectonic, a construct without any suggestions of organic growth. Human figures in the glazed terracotta reliefs by Luca della Robbia are confined within circles so that temporal life seems to be set in the pure and eternal geometry of the spheres. (A curiously different, visionary effect is made by the later Annunciation group suspended in St Lorenz, the work of Veit Stoss; see p. 470.)

Renaissance churches are sometimes thought to be unspiritual. But the attitude to Christianity which they embodied was no less intensely devout for being predominantly cerebral. Divinity is revealed in them by equilibrium and the harmonious relationship of the parts to one another and to the whole – as in the human body, created by God in his own likeness – rather than by mystery and aspiration towards the otherworldly. The Pazzi Chapel is

ascetic and spiritual in its renunciation of superfluous ornament and in its concentration on the purity of geometrical volumes. Simple proportional relationships, mathematically determined and emphasized by the articulation of the walls and even the grid of the inlaid marble floor, have metaphysical significance, reflecting the perfection of God and the divinely ordered cosmos. As one of Brunelleschi's Florentine contemporaries, Gianozzo Manetti (1396–1459), declared, the truths of the Christian religion are as self-evident as the laws of mathematics.

BRUNELLESCHI

A finite expression of infinity, the Pazzi Chapel also answers to the definition of beauty which Alberti derived from Vitruvius (see p. 193) – 'a harmony and concord of all the parts achieved in such a manner that nothing could be added or taken away or altered except for the worse'. Such perfection could, of course, be realized only by an exceptional architect, and the Pazzi Chapel has, since the late fifteenth century, been ascribed to Filippo Brunelleschi (1377–1446). In 1429 Andrea Pazzi, the head of a noble Florentine family enriched by trade and banking, commissioned Brunelleschi to design an addition (chapterhouse and family chapel combined) to the monastery of S Croce. Relatively little had been constructed before Brunelleschi died, however, and the intervention of another hand has been suggested, especially for the exterior. The chapel thus raises a problem of attribution of a type seldom encountered in medieval architecture, a problem created by the new (Renaissance) attitude to architecture and the distinction drawn between artist and craftsman, between architect and builder. For although the two architects responsible for the choir of St Lorenz are recorded – Konrad Heinzelmann (d. 1454) and Konrad Roritzer (d. c. 1475) – it would not be possible to attribute parts of the building to them on stylistic grounds. They are little more than names. Brunelleschi's character and accomplishments, on the other hand, are well known to us.

Brunelleschi was the first of a new type of architect, one who had served no apprenticeship in a masons' lodge (see p. 394). The son of a well-to-do Florentine notary, he was given a liberal education. In 1418 he and the sculptor Lorenzo Ghiberti (see pp. 427–9) jointly provided a model for the construction of the dome of Florence Cathedral by an ingenious engineering system which did away with centering (see Glossary), an amazing technical feat. Before work on the cathedral was under way, however, he was commissioned in 1419 to design the Foundling Hospital in Florence, usually cited as the first Renaissance building (**10,4**), and in 1421 he began the sacristy of S Lorenzo, Florence. With its Corinthian pilasters and pure geometrical space (a cube surmounted by a hemispherical dome with pendentives, a Byzantine form in origin), this prefigured the design of the Pazzi Chapel and of later Renaissance buildings on centralized plans.

Brunelleschi was praised in the fifteenth century both for his engineering skill and his revival of antique architectural forms. The architect and theorist Filarete (Antonio

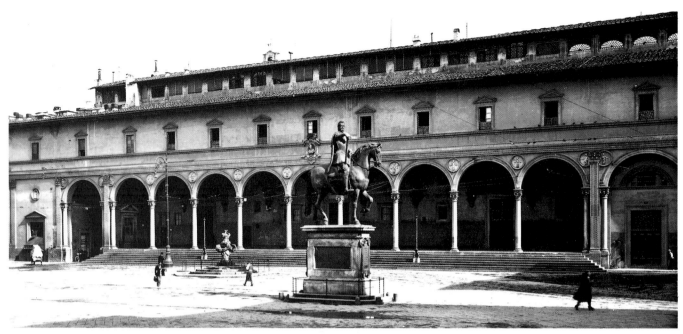

10,4 Brunelleschi, Foundling Hospital, Florence, designed 1419, built 1421–44.

Averlino, c. 1400–69) 'blessed' him for reviving 'in our city of Florence the ancient style of building in such a way that today in churches and private buildings no other style is used'. But why did this occur? Filarete suggests that it was quite simply because the ancient style was 'correct' and an architect who adopted it did 'exactly the same thing as a man of letters who strives to reproduce the classical style of Cicero and Virgil'. Brunelleschi is said to have visited Rome and if he did he was probably the first architect or artist since ancient times to go there to study its ancient monuments. However, the causes leading to the fifteenth-century revival of antique forms and motifs may have been more diverse than Filarete supposed – as were its sources. (Brunelleschi, for instance, found in Tuscan Romanesque architecture a system for making the structural skeleton visible on the surface of the building.)

The Gothic style was associated with the north and at the very beginning of the century the independence of the Florentine republic had been threatened from the north by the Milanese Giangaleazzo Visconti, an ally of the Holy Roman Emperor in Germany. His death in 1402 not only removed the peril of conquest, but also enabled the Florentine republic to expand to the Mediterranean coast and transform itself from a city-state to a region-state. At this buoyant moment Florentines looked back with pride to their supposed origin as a colony of republican Rome. 'I believe that this is why it has been and is true that of all peoples the Florentines appreciate liberty most and are the greatest enemies of tyrants', wrote the humanist and historian Leonardo Bruni (c. 1370–1444). 'Other peoples were founded by fugitives or exiles or peasants or obscure strangers', he went on. 'But your founder is the Roman people, conqueror and lord of all the world' (*Laudatio flo-*

rentinae urbis, c. 1403–4). Northern European royalty and nobility might trace their lineage to the Gothic chiefs who had vanquished Rome; the leaders of the mercantile republic of Florence found nobler ancestry in ancient Rome itself. In this context Brunelleschi's rejection of Gothic and his return to the Roman column, the round arch and the rectangular window have more than just an aesthetic significance.

Brunelleschi's contemporaries credited him with another achievement of equally great and far-reaching effect: the invention of linear perspective. Various devices had previously been used to suggest distance in pictures and drawings, but Brunelleschi worked out a system by which it could be rendered in a scientifically measurable way. Assuming that visual rays are straight lines subject to the laws of geometry, he seems to have been the first to realize that if a picture is regarded as a window between the viewer and what he sees, the objects on it can be made to obey the same laws. The key to his system lay in the observation that all parallel lines running into space at right angles to the 'window' will seem to converge on a central vanishing-point at the viewer's eye-level. These lines, called orthogonals, provide a geometrical network defining pictorial space. Brunelleschi demonstrated his system in two paintings (now lost), but his friend Alberti codified and probably elaborated on it in his treatise on painting (1435). The enthusiasm with which Brunelleschi's discovery was greeted can hardly be exaggerated. At a stroke it had raised the art of painting to a science. It opened the door – not to say window – to the idea of a picture as an illusionistic representation of objects in space seen from a fixed viewpoint. More important, it seemed to impose order – a rational order – on the visible world.

MASACCIO

The architectural style and the system of perspective developed by Brunelleschi were very quickly taken up by other artists, notably by Masaccio (1401–28) in his fresco of the Holy Trinity, commissioned as a memorial to a prominent Florentine family (**10,5**). In the foreground a skeleton lies on a tomb beneath the inscription: 'I was what you are, and what I am you shall be'. Above, the painting's donor in the scarlet costume of a *gonfaloniere* (the highest civic office of the republic) kneels with his wife at the entrance to a chapel in which the Virgin and St John stand on either side of a crucifix supported from behind by God the Father. In a medieval painting the donors would have been much smaller than the sacred figures. Here they are slightly larger. For with the aid of the new system of perspective Masaccio painted all the figures to scale and set them within a single unified space. Thus the tomb is 'read' as a projection into the church, and the chapel as a view through the wall. The chapel with its coffered vault is depicted with such care that a measured ground plan can be drawn of it. Otherwise, however, the perspective system is rather less simple than it may at first appear.

The Virgin and St John are foreshortened to show that they stand beyond the two columns, and the Virgin gazes down on the spectator, whose attention she directs with a gesture to the figure of Christ. But the Trinity is depicted from a much higher, literally supernatural viewpoint, without any foreshortening. Two levels of reality, temporal and eternal, are thus indicated; and in the temporal sphere past and present are visually detached yet spiritually linked with one another and with the world without end.

10,5 *Right* Masaccio, *Holy Trinity*, 1425. Fresco, 21ft 9ins × 9ft 4ins (6.67 × 3.17m). S Maria Novella, Florence.

10,6 Masaccio, *Tribute Money*, c. 1427. Fresco (after restoration 1989), 8ft 4ins × 19ft 8ins (2.54 × 5.9m). Brancacci Chapel, S Maria del Carmine, Florence.

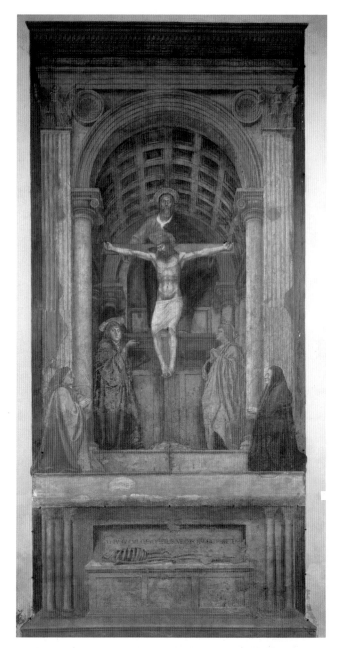

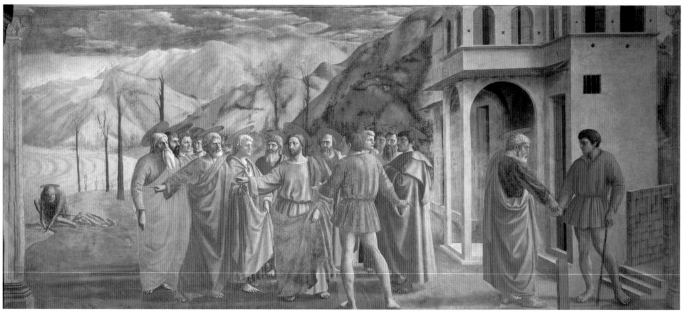

Masaccio's major achievement, however, was to revitalize the human figure with the robustness it had had in the frescoes of Giotto (9,80) and to create an illusion of tangibility by means of *chiaroscuro* (the manipulation of light and shade). Although he died when only 27, Masaccio completed one great cycle of frescoes in which this tangibility endows the figures not only with solidity and weight, but also with a new sense of dignity and independence, of flesh-and-blood vitality. Recently cleaned, these great paintings cover the upper walls of the Brancacci Chapel in S Maria del Carmine, Florence, and reveal with astonishing force Masaccio's power to create a wholly convincing illusion of mass in space. In the *Tribute Money* (10,6) the figures are arranged in depth around Christ in a spacious landscape – not, as in Giotto's frescoes, forming a screen across a confined stage space. Whereas the weight and bulk of Giotto's figures are conveyed by generalized modelling and a flat, neutral light from an unspecified source, Masaccio's are strongly lit from a source outside the picture as if, in fact, from the chapel window located to the right. The light strikes them at an angle, casting shadows on the ground and playing over their forms so as to reveal some sharply and conceal others. Great importance and solemnity are given in this way to a rather trivial episode in the Gospel story – in the centre Christ tells St Peter that he will find a coin in the mouth of a fish (shown on the left) with which to pay the tax collector (on the right) – the narrative being conveyed by a few emphatic gestures and intense, significant glances between the figures which remain rather static. However, Masaccio's ability to animate them is seen in the *Expulsion from Eden* (10,7) where Adam and Eve stumble blindly but compulsively, with an almost audible sense of anguish and despair, towards an uncertain dawn.

'PROGRESS' IN SCULPTURE

Mastery of perspective was assumed to be evidence of progress and thus set the new men of the early fifteenth century apart from their immediate predecessors. The idea of artistic 'progress', implicit in Pliny's account of the history of art (see p. 177), was both revived and revised during the Renaissance, influencing artists as well as historians and encouraging painters and sculptors to vie with one another. The Florentine Baptistery doors illustrate the effect this notion of progress had in practice.

Andrea Pisano (c. 1290–1348) had made for the Baptistery a pair of bronze doors with gilded figures in relief, still distinctly Gothic in style, in 1300–30. In 1401 sculptors were invited to compete in making trial reliefs for a second pair of doors. (This seems to have been the first public competition of the kind in the history of art.) The winner was Lorenzo Ghiberti (1378–1455), who maintained Andrea Pisano's scheme of 28 Gothic quatrefoils enclosing narrative scenes or single figures. But he gave greater depth, both real and apparent, to the individual scenes, and in the process of modelling them seems gradually to have abandoned Gothic grace in the pursuit of a

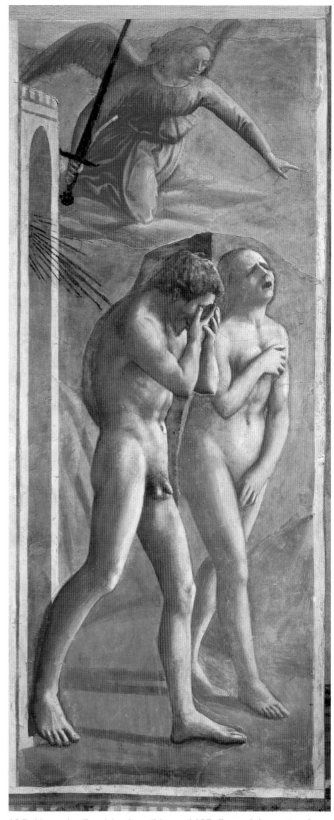

10,7 Masaccio, *Expulsion from Eden*, c. 1427. Fresco (after restoration 1989). Brancacci Chapel, S Maria del Carmine, Florence.

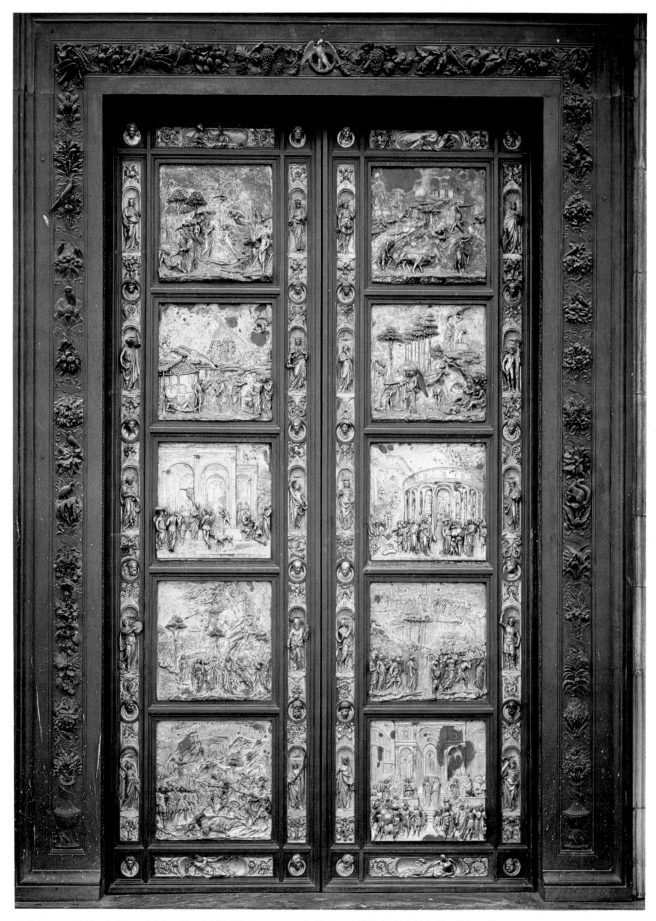

10,8 Lorenzo Ghiberti, *Porta del Paradiso*, 1424–52. Bronze parcel-gilt, about 17ft (5.2m) high. Baptistery, Florence.

more robust naturalism and a more dramatic narrative. On completing these doors in 1424 Ghiberti was promptly commissioned to make another pair for a third portal. He had improved on Andrea Pisano and now set out to surpass himself – as Florentines of the day agreed he had succeeded in doing when his second pair of doors was completed in 1452 and given the place of honour in the portal facing the Cathedral – known as the *Porta del Paradiso* (**10,8**).

On Ghiberti's second pair of doors the reliefs are fewer, larger and gilded overall. A single scale of proportions is used throughout so that the foreground figures are of the same size in all the scenes. Leonardo Bruni (see p. 425) had worked out the program, though Ghiberti himself may have modified it in the course of the work. Ghiberti certainly exploited the Old Testament subjects to display not only his skill as a craftsman, in the exquisitely refined modelling and finishing of every detail, but also as an artist in the representation of human figures – whether nude or elaborately clad, at rest or caught in gently lilting movement – as well as in the use of linear perspective (**10,9**). In the two central scenes, indeed, he seems to have incorporated buildings, one on a rectangular and the other on a circular plan, just to show how well he could represent them. 'I strove to imitate nature as clearly as I could, and with all the perspective I could produce, to have excellent compositions with many figures', Ghiberti wrote.

In his *Commentaries* (c. 1450–55), Ghiberti included both a history of ancient art, derived from Vitruvius and Pliny, and an account of art in Tuscany from the time of Giotto to the mid-fifteenth century. The idea of 'renaissance' is nowhere more clearly expressed than in his parallel description of the birth and rebirth of painting and sculpture. An enthusiastic student and collector of ancient Roman art, Ghiberti was on friendly terms with the Florentine humanists who were studying Classical texts. But his account of the revival of the arts, elaborated by later writers (notably Giorgio Vasari, see p. 473) into the history of a movement originating in Florence and gradually spreading to the rest of Italy – rather as Christianity had spread from Jerusalem – is misleading. Italian Renaissance art is multifarious, if only because it was the product of individuals (patrons as well as artists) more acutely conscious than ever before of their individuality.

The work of the Sienese sculptor Jacopo della Quercia (c. 1374–1438) provides an antidote to the Florentine version of the Renaissance. Little if at all influenced by the humanists, hardly affected by Brunelleschi's rationalization of pictorial space, no more than marginally interested in antique art, della Quercia evolved a new style intuitively. Yet it has all the steady poise and controlled naturalism of the new age. Even when set in Gothic niches, his saints seem to be unaware of them, so deeply are they immersed in themselves (**10,10**). Though not, in fact, free-standing, they appear to be detached in both senses of the

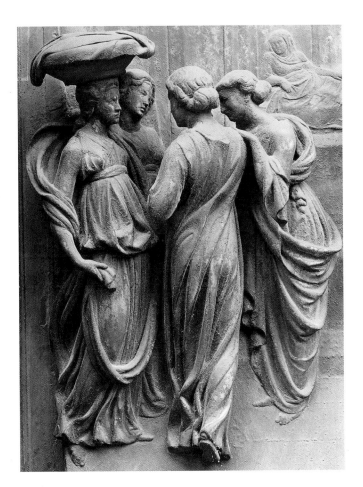

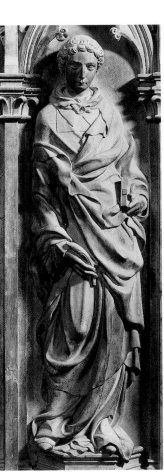

10,9 *Far left* Lorenzo Ghiberti, detail of the *Story of Jacob and Esau*, centre-left panel, *Porta del Paradiso*, 1424–52. Bronze, parcel-gilt, 15⅓ × 10½ins (39 × 26cm). Baptistery, Florence.

10,10 Jacopo della Quercia, *St Lawrence*, detail of Trenta altar, 1416–22. Figure 3ft 9¾ins (1.16m) high. S Frediano, Lucca.

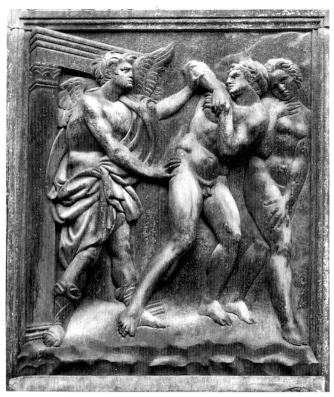

10,11 Jacopo della Quercia, *Expulsion from Paradise*, c. 1430. Istrian stone, 34 × 27ins (86.4 × 68.6cm). Detail of main portal, S Petronio, Bologna.

word. Della Quercia's attention focused on the human figure, sometimes to the exclusion of almost all else, as in the reliefs he carved on two pilasters (see Glossary) flanking the main doorway of S Petronio in Bologna (**10,11**). In the *Expulsion from Paradise* three figures fill the entire panel, which has a tragic intensity lacking in Ghiberti's conception of the same subject. As in Masaccio's *Expulsion* (10,7), Eve derives her pudic gesture ultimately from an antique statue of Venus (4,40), but della Quercia's and Masaccio's distraught figures express an internal anguish quite foreign to ancient art. And della Quercia's Adam is still more remarkable, a powerful image of man's nobility in defeat, defiantly confronting the archangel with a twist of his muscular torso as he struggles to resist divine judgement.

A New Style in Flanders

By the mid-fifteenth century Italy and Flanders – the two most densely urbanized areas in Europe – had emerged as the two great centres of European art. There were both economic and cultural links between them and although Florence was nominally a republic, while Ghent, Bruges and Ypres, the three leading Flemish cities of the time, formed part of the duchy of Burgundy (which was to pass by marriage to the Austrian Habsburg monarchy in 1477), this difference was not as great as the political labels might suggest. Both areas were prosperous, though they suffered from the general economic depression of fifteenth-century Europe.

While the Florentines were working out theories and systematic rules for the representation of three-dimensional space, the Flemish discovered linear perspective by trial and error and went on to experiment in the same empirical spirit with aerial perspective (the subtle gradation of tones suggesting distance in a landscape). This distinction is fundamental. Flemish artists were not of a theorizing turn of mind. But, despite this and their lack of interest in antiquity, the break they made with their immediate predecessors was no less strongly marked.

In Flanders, of course, there had previously been little if any large-scale painting. There were magnificent, richly glowing stained glass windows. But the great contribution Flemish painters were to make to Western art – the development of easel or panel painting – owed more to the tradition of manuscript illumination. And to obtain on panels effects as bright and lustrous as those of the Limbourg brothers (9,87), for instance, called for a medium more luminous than tempera. It was in this context that oil painting was developed.

From at least as early as the tenth century various oils had occasionally been used as media to bind powdered pigments. (In tempera painting the pigments are bound with egg yolk.) Not until early in the fifteenth century and in Flanders, however, did artists begin to exploit the potentialities of pigments mixed with oil (usually linseed) in applying translucent films of paint over opaque colors to give an appearance of depth beneath a hard enamel-like surface. Whereas artists using tempera, which dries in a matter of minutes, were obliged to work quickly across the surface of a panel, piece by swiftly painted piece, those using oil could build up a picture slowly. The new process permitted and encouraged the great precision of detail which is perhaps the most immediately appealing feature of fifteenth-century Flemish painting. (Of course, media were often mixed, e.g. oil colors applied over tempera.)

Van Eyck and van der Weyden

Flemish artists who developed this technique which revolutionized the art of painting in Europe and, together with linear and aerial perspective, led it ever further away from that of the rest of the world, are shadowy figures. No biographies were written of them nor were their works so much as listed by contemporaries. Only in Italy were artists deemed worthy to appear in collections of lives of famous men and, significantly, the earliest account of Jan van Eyck (c. 1390–1441) – to whom the 'invention' of oil painting was for long ascribed – was written in 1455–6 at the court of the king of Naples, who owned a triptych by him. Its author, Bartolommeo Fazio, called him 'the leading painter of our time' for his technical accomplishment, his truth to nature and – here speaks the Renaissance humanist – his rediscovery of pigments known to Pliny and other ancient authors. Van Eyck's skill in handling oil paint is indeed extraordinary. The transparency of the pigments gives his paintings a unique jewel-like quality to which no reproduction can do justice. They seem to emit light from within. He developed the medium to give form the palpable solidity of, for example, the *Adam and Eve* on the great altarpiece in Ghent Cathedral (begun by his brother Hubert [d. 1426]). These almost disturbingly life-like figures owe their impact also to his mastery of perspectival foreshortening – they are seen as if from below, the under-side of Adam's toes being visible, and his right foot seems to stick out over the edge of the frame (**10,12**). Strikingly naturalistic, they are nevertheless quite uninfluenced by Classical sculpture, to which Italians habitually turned when painting nude figures. Their warm, breathing, flesh-and-blood quality is contrasted by van Eyck with the simulated relief carvings of the sacrifice and murder of Abel directly above them.

Jan van Eyck also rivalled his Italian contemporaries in rendering space. In the *Madonna of Chancellor Rolin* (**10,13**) both the volume of the room and the extent of the view through the triple arches at its end are convincing. The landscape is indeed so convincing that attempts have been made to identify it. The room might also seem to be in a real building, though the architecture is of a type (basically Romanesque with Gothic details) developed by van Eyck to depict the New Jerusalem. For this is a celestial audience-chamber in which the Queen of Heaven receives the chancellor of Philip the Good, duke of Burgundy. Practically every one of the exquisitely painted details has a symbolic meaning. Yet all the learned symbolism remains unobtrusive. For the more naturalistically van Eyck and other Flemish painters depicted the visible world, the more intensely did they saturate it with spiritual significance. Their naturalism was far from being profane, since to them everything could be a symbol.

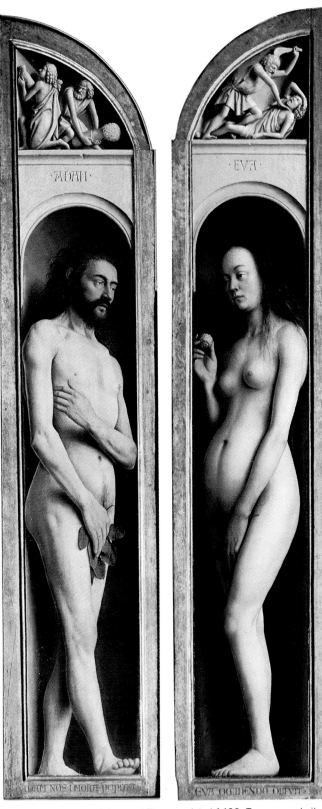

10,12 Jan van Eyck, *Adam and Eve*, completed 1432. Tempera and oil on panel, each panel 80 × 18ins (204 × 32cm). St Bavo, Ghent, Belgium.

10,13 *Right* Jan van Eyck, *Madonna of Chancellor Rolin*, c. 1433–4. Oil on panel, 26 × 24⅜ins (66 × 61.9cm). Louvre, Paris.

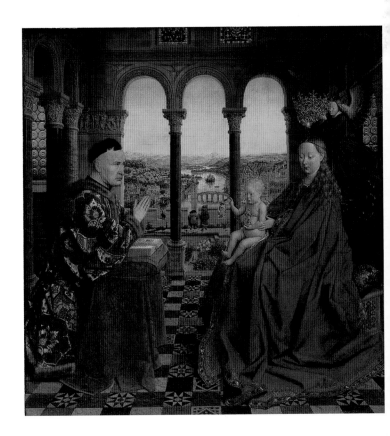

The Ghent Altarpiece

JAN VAN EYCK AND HIS PATRONS

The altarpiece of the *Lamb of God* by the brothers Hubert and Jan van Eyck is one of the few large fifteenth-century polyptychs (multi-panelled paintings) that can be seen today in its original location (St Bavo, Ghent), though recently moved from the chapel for which it was painted to a 'special environment'. It was commissioned by Joos Vijd (d. 1439) and his wife Elisabeth Borluut (d. 1443) who paid for the construction of the chapel, where daily masses were to be said for them and their ancestors in what was then their parish church, dedicated to St John the Baptist, whose emblem is a lamb. The chapel itself, with high windows and a vault in the Gothic style, differs from others in the apse only by inconspicuous carvings of the Vijd and Borluut coats of arms. But the altarpiece, begun before 1426 and finished in 1432, is in every way exceptional; it is one of the earliest, finest and largest examples of fifteenth-century Flemish painting. Every detail contributes to its religious meaning as an exposition of the doctrine of Redemption. Everything has a symbolic significance although being rendered with the vivid naturalism that the development of oil paint had just then made possible (see p. 430). The shadows of the figures and framing devices seemed to be cast by the natural light falling from the windows in the chapel. In this way the spiritual truth of the Christian doctrine was corroborated by the tangible fidelity with which the visible world was represented.

The altarpiece consists of 20 panels, 16 of them mounted on the doors which, when closed, cover the central four. Originally there was a predella beneath, representing the hell or limbo into which Christ descended to redeem the virtuous. On the outside of the doors the donors are portrayed life-size, kneeling before simulated stone statues painted in *grisaille* (see Glossary) of St John the Evangelist and St John the Baptist (**10,14**). Above them the archangel Gabriel is shown announcing to the Virgin that she is to give birth to the Redeemer, as foretold by the

two prophets and two sibyls who appear in the top register. The windows of the Virgin's room open on to a townscape of typically Flemish buildings.

When the doors are opened a more brilliantly colored celestial vision is revealed (**10,15**). In the centre of the top register Christ (sometimes mistaken for God the Father), more than life-size, is enthroned as 'King of Kings and Lord of Lords' (the inscription embroidered on the hem of his robe), wearing the papal crown, raising his right hand in benediction and holding a sceptre in his left, with a jewel-encrusted royal crown at his feet (0,5). He is flanked by the Virgin and St John the Baptist, with angels singing and making music on either side of them. Adam and Eve, depicted in the end panels in niches beneath simulated stone reliefs of Cain and Abel, seem to have been placed there to record the origin of sin that necessitated redemption. Inscriptions state 'Adam thrusts us into death' and 'Eve has afflicted us with death'. The beautifully painted flesh of their bodies, frail but living, Adam's sunburn on hands and wrists and above the neck, is a reminder of mortal weakness and transience (10,12). (He was evidently painted from a model normally clothed, whereas Adam lived in a state of nature.)

The lower register has a unified background, a panorama of wooded hills surrounding a lush meadow bright with flowers of all seasons. There are trees that grow in different parts of Europe, including the palms, cypresses, stone-pines, pomegranates, olives and oranges of the Mediterranean region. Swallows and other small birds soar and swoop in the clear summer sky. This is a vision of paradise where all the most beautiful plants flourish; and they are depicted with such precision that they may be botanically identified. Towers and spires rising above the horizon include those of Utrecht Cathedral and the church of St Nicholas in Ghent; they symbolize the heavenly Jerusalem (see p. 307) where the whole community of the

redeemed, the 'ransomed of the Lord', will be united in worship. The meadow is approached over rough ground in the other panels by Just Judges, Christian warriors, hermits and a giant St Christopher leading pilgrims. Patriarchs and prophets (including Virgil); popes, bishops and other clergy are in the foreground of the main panel, as well as confessors who avowed the Christian faith despite persecution, and an endless procession of female saints beyond them. In the centre beneath the dove of the Holy Spirit, the Lamb of God stands on an altar, blood flowing from his breast into a chalice. A fountain in the foreground is inscribed: 'This is the fountain of the water of life proceeding out of the throne of God'.

The meaning of the open altarpiece would have been explicit when it was seen above the head of a priest celebrating the Mass and, after the consecration of bread and wine, reciting the *Agnus Dei*, 'Lamb of God who takest away the sins of the world, have

10,14 Hubert and Jan van Eyck, *Ghent Altarpiece* (closed), completed 1432. Tempera and oil on panel, about 11ft × 7ft 6ins (3.35 × 2.29m). St Bavo, Ghent.

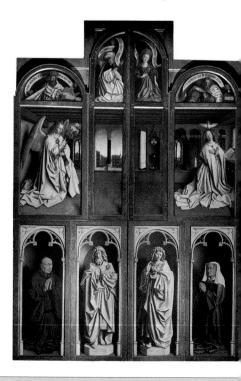

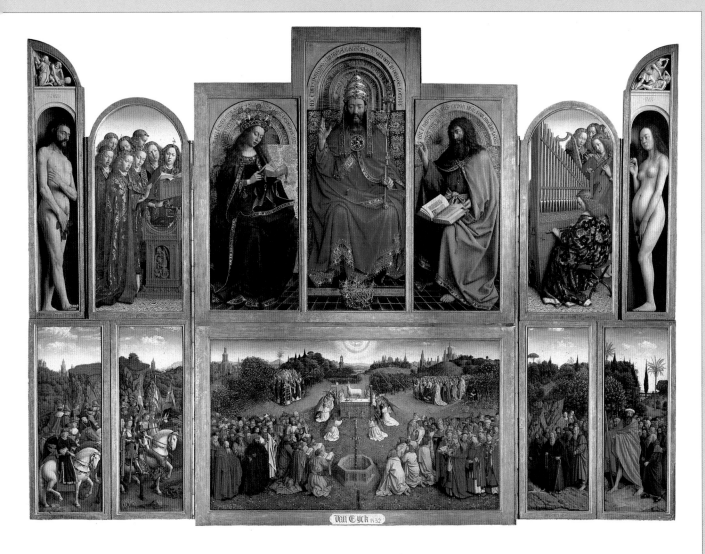

10,15 Hubert and Jan van Eyck, *Ghent Altarpiece* (open), completed 1432. Tempera and oil on panel, about 11 × 15ft (3.35 × 4.57m). St Bavo, Ghent.

mercy on us'. But the iconographical program of the whole polyptych is complex, inspired by various medieval writings and presumably drawn up by the donors in consultation with an erudite priest who selected the Biblical texts for the numerous inscriptions. No fewer than 18 manuscript volumes are depicted, and the words in some of them are legible. The impression made by the painting is, nevertheless, visionary. The van Eycks succeeded in translating what must have been an abstruse theological discourse, propounded by the donors and their priestly advisers, into a pellucid visual language.

On the outer frame of the doors a dedicatory inscription in Latin verse states that 'Hubert van Eyck, than whom none was greater' began the altarpiece and his brother Jan, 'second in art', completed it at the request of Joos Vijd on 6 May 1432. This is the only contemporary record of the work's authorship and has given rise to much discussion. Hubert is an obscure figure, occasionally mentioned in the civic archives of Ghent where he died and was buried in St John's Church (now the cathedral of St Bavo) in 1426. A sister named Margaret, also a painter, probably worked with him and is said to have been buried beside him. By 1432, however, Jan was already embarked on the career that was to win him international renown, although no work from his hand earlier than the Ghent altarpiece survives. Ten years earlier he had been taken into the service of Duke John of Bavaria, Count of Holland, at The Hague where he executed wall-paintings. Three years later he was appointed court painter to Philip the Good, Duke of Burgundy and ruler of most of Flanders, who entrusted him also with secret missions as far afield as Portugal.

Philip the Good was the grandson of Philip the Bold who had employed Claus Sluter at Dijon (9,89; 90) and great-nephew of the Duke of Berry who had commissioned the *Très Riches Heures* from the Limbourg brothers (see p. 418). Employment by a member of this family of distinguished patrons helps to set the work of Jan van Eyck, emerging from the so-called International Gothic style, in its social and art historical contexts. For although Joos Vijd was a burgher, serving from 1395 intermittently on the Ghent city council, he was a member of the minor nobility and a landowner. As such he had sometimes attended the court of Philip the Good. His wife Elisabeth Borluut came from a patrician family of Ghent that had included knights and abbots. However, their wealth probably came from wool on which the prosperity of Ghent was founded and so, for them, the Lamb of God – which had appeared on the city's seal since the thirteenth century – must have had a mundane as well as a spiritual significance.

God is diffused in all visible objects, which are, to quote St Thomas Aquinas, 'corporeal metaphors for things spiritual'. So total a sanctification of the visible world is now difficult to comprehend and often these religious paintings seem to be no more than scenes from contemporary life in a Flemish town. The simplest everyday household furnishings could have meaning in a universe which shone with 'the radiance of delightful allegories' – a candlestick symbolizing Our Lady, a brass ewer her purity, and so on. In the *Madonna of Chancellor Rolin* the river might be the Meuse – or the 'pure river of the water of life, clear as crystal', described in the Book of Revelation. The garden is such as might be found adjoining a palace – but it is planted with roses, lilies and irises, attributes of the Virgin, and so becomes the Garden of Paradise. The earthly and the heavenly are fused in this painting, where the Virgin, over whose head an angel hovers with a crown, and the Child with the creased skin of a mortal baby are no less vividly perceived and depicted than the rock-faced, proud and unscrupulous Nicholas Rolin kneeling before them.

Jan van Eyck was one of the first great European painters of portraits, descriptive rather than interpretative

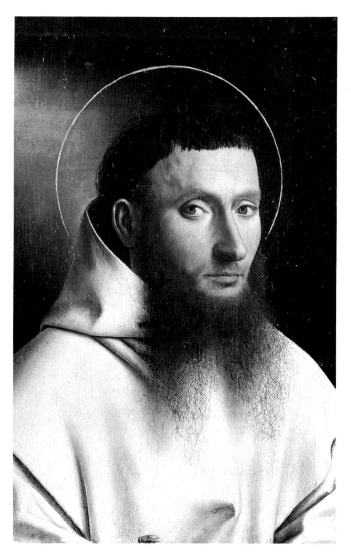

10,17 Petrus Christus, *Portrait of a Carthusian*, 1446. Tempera and oil on panel, 11½ × 8ins (29.2 × 20.3cm). Metropolitan Museum of Art, New York.

10,16 Rogier van der Weyden, *Portrait of a Lady*, c. 1455. Oil on panel, 14½ × 10¾ins (36.8 × 27.3cm). National Gallery of Art, Washington DC (Andrew W. Mellon Collection).

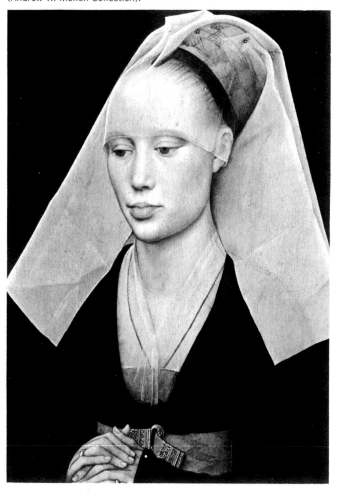

in their sharp concentration on physical individuality. The slightly younger Rogier van der Weyden (1399/1400–64) approached his sitters with less attention to detail than to general effect. The refinement of his delicate modelling and gently felt contours gives to nearly all his sitters an aristocratic air. The unknown young lady in one of his best portraits is very obviously well born to the tips of her exquisitely manicured fingers (**10,16**). Her eyes are demurely cast down so that she avoids our gaze, but the fullness of the lips and the tenderness of the delicate clasped hands beautifully convey nervous sensitivity. She is depicted in the three-quarter view which Rogier van der Weyden and other fifteenth-century Flemish artists preferred. This pose introduces a sense of movement, the sitter turning and, as it were, advancing from the pictorial space into the real space occupied by the spectator, with whom a *rapport* is thus established.

SOURCES AND DOCUMENTS

BARTOLOMMEO FAZIO ON JAN VAN EYCK

Bartolommeo Fazio (Bartholomaeus Facius, fl. mid-fifteenth century), a humanist scholar from Genoa, was employed at the court of Alfonso V of Aragon at Naples from 1444. He was one of the first to admire and write about northern painters and in his book *de Viris Illus-tribus* (*Of Famous Men*), written in 1456, he included both Jan van Eyck and Rogier van der Weyden, who was still alive at the time. Gentile da Fabriano and Pisanello were the only other painters he discussed. Jan van Eyck (called Jan of Gaul by Fazio) is praised for his scholarly and scientific accomplishments, especially his technical innovations, although Fazio ascribed their origin to Pliny. All the works by Jan van Eyck he saw in Naples have now been lost.

Jan of Gaul has been judged the leading painter of our time. He was not unlettered, particularly in geometry and such arts as contribute to the enrichment of painting, and he is thought for this reason to have dis-covered many things about the properties of colours recorded by the ancients and learned by him from reading of Pliny and other authors. His is a remarkable picture in the private apartments of King Alfonso, in which there is a Virgin Mary notable for its grace and modesty, with an Angel Gabriel, of exceptional beauty and with hair surpassing reality, announcing that the Son of God will be born of her; and a John the Baptist that declares the wonderful sanctity and austerity of his life, and Jerome like a living being in a library done with rare art: for if you move away from it a little it seems that it recedes inwards and that it has complete books laid open in it, while if you go near it is evident that there is only a summary of these. On the outer side of the same picture is painted Battista Lomellini, whose picture it was – you would judge he lacked only a voice – and the woman whom he loved, of outstanding beauty; and she too is portrayed exactly as she was. Between them, as if through a chink of the wall, falls a ray of sun that you would take to be real sunlight. His is a circular representation of the world, which he painted for Philip, Prince of the Belgians, and it is thought that no work has been done more perfectly in our time; you may distinguish in it not only places and the lie of continents but also, by measurement, the dis-tances between places. There are also fine paintings of his in the possession of that distinguished man, Otta-viano della Carda: women of uncommon beauty emerging from the bath, the more intimate parts of the body being with excellent modesty veiled in fine linen, and of one of them he has shown only the face and breast but has then represented the hind parts of her body in a mirror painted on the wall opposite, so that you may see her back as well as her breast. In the same picture there is a lantern in the bath chamber, just like one lit, and an old woman seemingly sweating, a puppy lapping up water, and also horses, minute figures of men, mountains, groves, hamlets and castles carried out with such skill you would believe one was 50 miles distant from another. But almost nothing is more won-derful in this work than the mirror painted in the pic-ture, in which you see whatever is represented as in a real mirror. He is said to have done many other works, but of these I have been able to obtain no complete knowledge.

(Bartholomaeus Facius, *de Viris Illustribus*, tr. M. Baxandall from a fifteenth-century manuscript in the Vatican Library. *Journal of the Warburg and Courtauld Institutes* XXVII, 1964)

Jan van Eyck and, still more, Rogier van der Weyden set the pattern for north European painting until the first decades of the sixteenth century. They created standards rarely achieved and never excelled by their immediate successors in the Low Countries, many of whom were art-ists of great ability – Petrus Christus (d. 1472/3), painter of quiet religious scenes and shy portraits (**10,17**); Dirc Bouts (c. 1415–75), whose sad figures stand in landscapes of exquisite beauty (**10,18**); the more dramatic and mystical Hugo van der Goes (d. 1482), whose largest work, the *Porti-nari Altarpiece* (**10,19**), was to influence Italian painters after it arrived in Florence in the 1470s (see p. 448). During this period Flemish art was exported to all parts of Europe: to Germany, England, Scotland, France, Spain, Portugal and Italy, where it was valued by Italian patrons and painters until late in the fifteenth century. Then the current of influence from north to south began to turn. Flemish painters were, however, always admired mainly for their technical accomplishment in the exploitation of oil paint. The arts of the two countries came closest to one another in portraiture. Even here, however, there are as many differences as similarities. Italians favoured pure profiles, which dissociate the subject from the spectator and were reminiscent of heads on antique coins. Even at its most naturalistic, Italian fifteenth-century art was more conceptual than that of Flanders. Artists of both countries claimed to imitate nature but, to use a distinction of the period, the Flemish were preoccupied largely with *natura naturata* (the created world), the Italians with *natura nat-urans* (the creative force behind it). And in the north the new artistic impulse found an outlet only in painting; sculpture was little affected and architecture not at all.

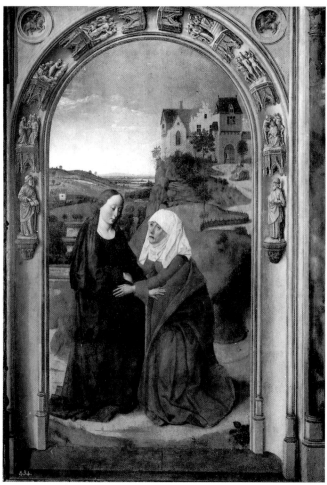

10,18 Dirc Bouts, *Visitation*, c. 1445–50. Panel 31⅖ × 22ins (80 × 56cm). Prado, Madrid.

10,19 Hugo van der Goes, *Portinari Altarpiece* (open): the *Nativity between the Donors and their Patron Saints*, c. 1476. Panel, centre, 8ft 3½ins × 10ft (2.53 × 3.04m), wings 8ft 3½ins × 4ft 7½ins (2.53 × 1.41m). Uffizi, Florence.

ARCHITECTURE IN ITALY

Palazzo Medici, which set a pattern for Florentine townhouses, is sober and severe, even a little forbidding. On the exterior, windows are simple and regular and the design makes its effect largely by very carefully adjusted variations in texture, massive blocks for the ground floor, smooth rustication (see Glossary) above and a flat wall-surface on top, overshadowed by a massive spreading cornice (**10,20**). There is a greater elegance, but little more ornamentation, in the interior courtyard's composite columns supporting round arches with circular reliefs above (**10,21**). All is rigidly integrated and controlled – in striking contrast to the house of another wealthy financier being built in France during the same years (**10,22**). Although similarly ranged round a central courtyard, Jacques Coeur's house sprawls with rooms of varying shape added to one another horizontally and vertically according to function or fancy. Similarly in decoration, one is gravely Classical and solemnly decorous, while the other is lavishly Gothic with whimsical touches (illusionistic figures leaning out of simulated windows, innumerable carvings alluding to the owner's name).

Both patrons must have played a role in determining the designs, Jacques Coeur's house giving an impression of extravagant opulence, Cosimo de' Medici's one of ample, solid wealth. Head of the Medici bank and the richest man in Florence, Cosimo was the first citizen of the republic and took his civic responsibilities seriously. His palace was intended to be both a dwelling and an ornament to his city, a model of 'decorum', which implied more than good taste. He is said to have rejected a design by Brunelleschi because it was too ostentatious and turned to Michelozzo di Bartolommeo (1396–1472), whose art and, if we are to believe Vasari, life were regulated by prudent economy. This may well have recommended him to Cosimo. Significantly, the name of Jacques Coeur's

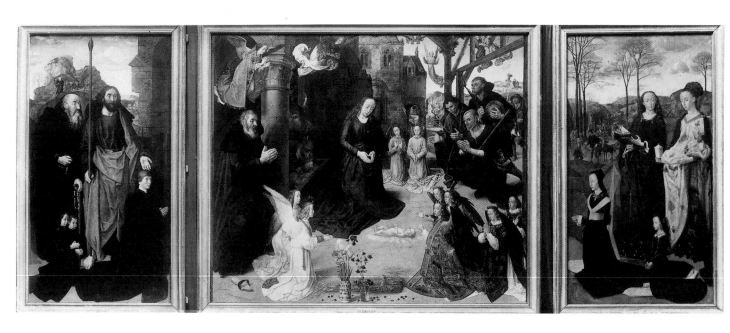

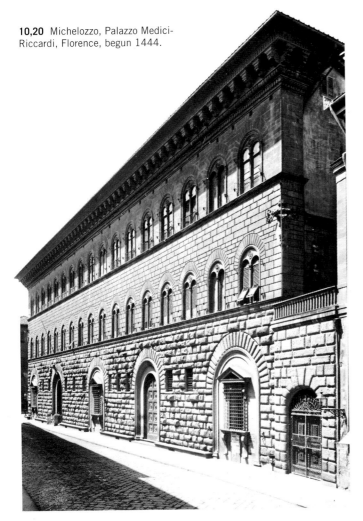

10,20 Michelozzo, Palazzo Medici-Riccardi, Florence, begun 1444.

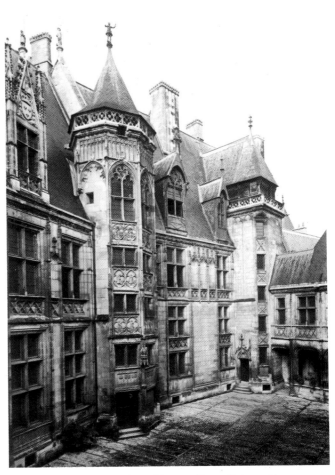

10,22 Interior courtyard, house of Jacques Coeur, Bourges, France, 1443–51.

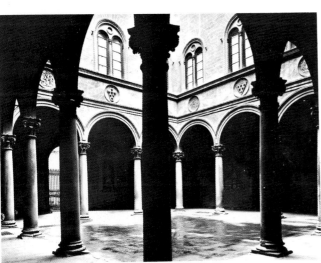

10,21 Michelozzo, Cortile of Palazzo Medici-Riccardi, Florence.

architect is not recorded. Not that an architect was any less important for a Gothic building than for one in the Renaissance style, but in fifteenth-century Florence the role of the architect underwent a fundamental change (as already mentioned, p. 424), due almost entirely to one man: Leon Battista Alberti (1404–72).

ALBERTI

Alberti might be said to have created the ideal of the complete man of the Renaissance in his own image. Moralist, lawyer, poet, playwright, musician, mathematician, scientist, painter, sculptor, architect and aesthetic theorist, his range was extraordinary and his knowledge profound. No one did more to enhance the status of the visual arts and, consequently, of artists. To him we owe the basic idea of an all-embracing Renaissance style. In his treatises on painting (1435, published 1540), on architecture (1452, published 1485) and on sculpture (c. 1464–70, published 1568), he developed a rational theory of beauty based on the practice of the ancients and what he called the 'laws of nature'.

The illegitimate son of a noble family exiled from Florence, Alberti was given a classical education and began to develop an interest in architecture only after joining the papal civil service in Rome in 1431. Inspired by antiquity, he evolved a style more massively plastic than that of Brunelleschi and also more archeologically correct. Although his columns, for example, are often used decoratively rather than structurally, they are always combined with architraves, not arches. One of his greatest and most influential achievements was, in fact, to adapt the

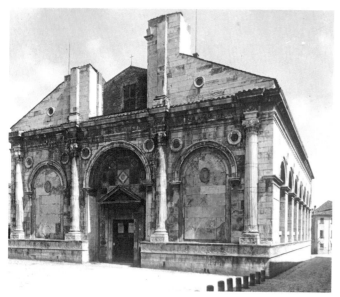

10,23 Leon Battista Alberti, S Francesco, Rimini, begun 1450.

intended for poets and philosophers (one contains the bones of a Byzantine Neoplatonist, Gemistos Plethon, snatched from Mistra in the Peloponnese as if they were the relics of a saint). Here the early Renaissance style in architecture came of age. There are no reminiscences of Romanesque (as in so many Florentine buildings); all is magnificently Roman, yet derived from no specific ancient building. So perfectly had Alberti mastered the Classical language of architecture that he was able to compose in it with original imaginative potency. But like other Renaissance projects, initiated by those whose ambitions outran their means, it was never completed. It lacks the intended dome and in its unfinished state fortuitously resembles a ruin. Although the finely chiselled half-columns, the beautiful clean lettering of the inscription and the wreaths of bay which encircle the windows all hark back to ancient Rome, this building is the reverse of a ruin; it is rather a symbol of aspirations towards a new ideal, of faith in the future as much as veneration for the past.

A townscape painted a decade or so later neatly expresses the ideal towards which Italian architects and their patrons aspired (**10,24**). A circular building stands in the centre of a marble-paved piazza surrounded by buildings of varying size and character, yet all designed with the logical geometry as well as the Classical detailing of the early Renaissance style. Order is not so much imposed as accepted in a framework which permits individuality so long as it is kept within the limits of decorum. The airy lightness and spaciousness, which differentiate this view from that of a medieval city (9,83), make it a symbol also of the Renaissance ideal of civic humanism.

The unknown painter was obviously influenced by Piero della Francesca (see p. 446), who worked for both Sigismondo Malatesta at Rimini and for his great antagonist Federigo da Montefeltro at Urbino, and it may well have been painted for the latter. Federigo, lord of the tiny dukedom of Urbino, was another condottiere and discerning patron of both artists and Classical scholars. His architectural activities were concentrated on the palace built to house his court, which became a curious combi-

elements of the Classical post-and-lintel temple, in which the wall is conceived as no more than a filling between upright supports, to an architecture of walls pierced by openings. Another innovation was his self-promotion to professional status. He took no part in construction, but limited himself exclusively to design.

One of the first to ask Alberti for designs was Sigismondo Malatesta, the prototypical Renaissance prince, who at the age of 14 seized the lordship of Rimini from his uncle and his brothers and soon emerged as a daring military commander, a ruthless ruler and a patron both of humanist scholars and of artists. In 1450 he decided to transform the medieval church of S Francesco into a monument to his own glory as the burial-place for himself, his mistress Isotta degli Atti and various luminaries of his court. It was subsequently called the Tempio Malatestiano (**10,23**). Alberti designed a marble case for the old church, the front freely based on a Roman triumphal arch symbolizing triumph over death, the side walls pierced by deep arched niches containing austerely plain sarcophagi

10,24 Circle of Piero della Francesca, *An Ideal Town*, mid-15th century. Panel painting, 23½ × 79ins (59.7 × 200.6cm). Galleria Nazionale delle Marche, Urbino.

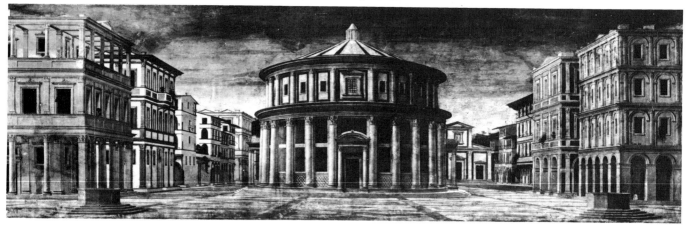

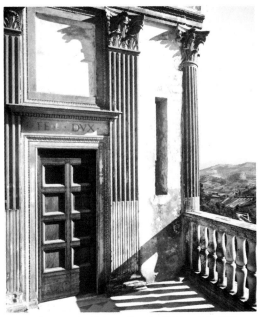

10,25 The Loggia, Palazzo Ducale, Urbino, late 15th century.

10,26 Donatello, *St George*, c. 1415–17. Marble, about 6ft 10ins (2.08m) high. Orsanmichele, Florence.

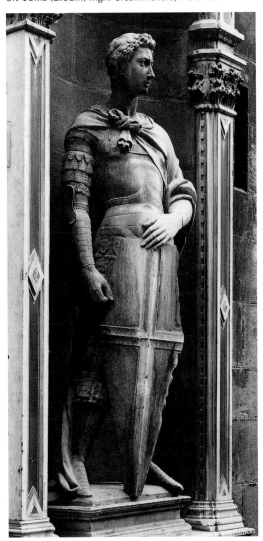

nation of military academy and institute of Classical studies. The vast building was erected slowly, probably as money became available, to the designs of a succession of architects. Throughout, the emphasis is on the delicate adjustments of proportions and the refinement rather than the prodigality of carved decorations even more exquisite than those of the slightly earlier Palazzo Medici in Florence; they were limited mainly to corbels and the surrounds of doors and fireplaces, sharply carved with Classical ornament.

The richest room must always have been Federigo's *studiolo*. But this study and the adjoining loggia, both intimate in scale, were intended not for public display but for the duke's personal delectation (**10,25**). From the loggia he could survey the rugged countryside; in the privacy of the *studiolo* he kept his most precious possessions, his library of manuscripts, many of them written out by the 20 or 40 scribes he employed, comprising numerous theological works, all the medical treatises then available, Greek texts including the plays of Sophocles and the poems of Pindar, a section devoted to Dante, Boccaccio and other Italian writers, not to mention original works and translations by contemporary humanists. The manuscripts are now in the Vatican but the room is still lined with the cupboards which contained them, richly decorated with *intarsia* work, tiny segments of wood skilfully inlaid to form pictures. Above this inlaid woodwork were painted portraits of famous men and allegories of the liberal arts. If the ideal townscape symbolizes one of the aspirations of the early Renaissance, this room and its loggia epitomize some of its human achievements.

SCULPTURE IN ITALY

DONATELLO

Passion for antiquity inspired sculptors as well as architects, and none more so than Donatello (Donato Bardi, c. 1386–1466). He began as an assistant on Ghiberti's first bronze doors for the Florentine Baptistery and very soon emerged as an independent artist, one who revitalized almost every form of sculpture from free-standing monuments to the low relief. His first statues were, like those of medieval sculptors, intended for architectural settings, usually for niches. But the Gothic niche he designed for his *St George* is so shallow that it projects the figure forward away from the building and into the spectator's world (**10,26**). It is, in effect, almost a free-standing figure – and has been exhibited as such since the late nineteenth century, when it was removed to a museum and its place taken by a copy.

Because of the cost of materials, a sculptor was necessarily limited to the commissions he received, and those for large free-standing figures were rare in early fifteenth-century Italy. So there can be little doubt that Donatello welcomed the commission for a bronze equestrian monument in Padua which gave him a chance to rival the famous antique statue of Marcus Aurelius in Rome (5,62). Its subject was to be the condottiere Erasmo da Narni, nicknamed Gattamelata, who died in 1443 after serving the Venetian republic for many years as captain-general of its armies. In modelling the horse Donatello seems to have kept in mind that ridden by Marcus Aurelius and also the four even earlier bronze horses on the façade of S Marco in Venice, though he gave to his charger a new sense of controlled vigour (**10,27**). Gattamelata wears a Roman breastplate, but is otherwise dressed in contemporary costume with a long sword, armour on his legs and his feet in stirrups (unknown in ancient Rome). Donatello made other innovations. The head of Gattamelata is not modelled (like that of Marcus Aurelius) to be seen at eye-level. The features are daringly distorted to make the maximum effect when the statue on its high plinth is seen from the ground. The work is, in fact, an attempt to surpass antiquity.

Likewise in the reliefs modelled for the church of S Antonio, beside which the Gattamelata monument stands, Donatello vied with antiquity by displaying his mastery of linear perspective (conspicuously lacking in antique reliefs) and of pictorial narrative as prescribed in Alberti's treatise on painting (see 0,8 and p. 437). In his last reliefs, however, modelled for the two pulpits in the

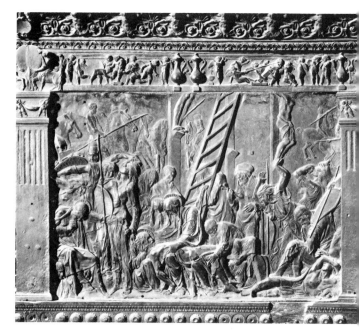

10,28 Donatello, *Lamentation over the Dead Christ*, 1460–6. Bronze, about 4ft 7ins (1.4m) wide. S Lorenzo, Florence.

10,27 Donatello, *Equestrian Monument to Gattamelata*, 1445–50. Bronze, about 11 × 13ft (3.4 × 4m). Piazza del Santo, Padua.

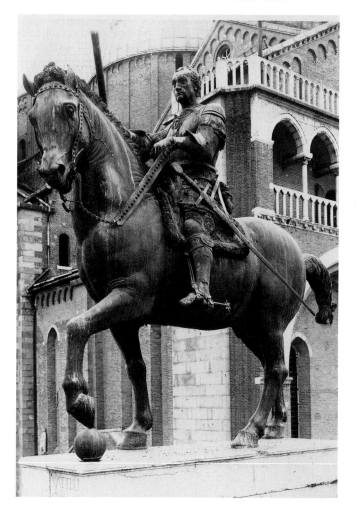

church of S Lorenzo in Florence, all technical accomplishment was subordinated to the expression of fervently felt religious convictions. There is emotional violence in these profoundly moving scenes from the Passion. They convey a spiritual message with an almost brutally physical realism. In that of the *Lamentation* (**10,28**) the distraught grief of Christ's mother and followers is felt not only in expressive features and gestures, but also in the composition as a whole, in the absence of logic, in the agonized confusion of the group of mourners, in the strange way in which the sharp diagonal of the ladder and the bodies of the two thieves are severed by the frame. Foreshortening devices and distortions which enable the scene to be 'read' from below are so effective as to be unobtrusive. Similarly, borrowings from antiquity – such as the Maenad-like dress of the figure below the right cross, the nude horseman in the left background – have been assimilated fully, but again quite unobtrusively. Only the relief of cupids in the frieze owes an obvious debt to antiquity.

NEW DEPARTURES

This frieze is largely by Donatello's pupil and assistant Bertoldo di Giovanni (c. 1420–91), later to be the master of Michelangelo (see p. 482) and thus the link between the two greatest Renaissance sculptors. His independent works are on a small scale, notably medals and bronze statuettes. However, it is in such works that Renaissance ideals can be most clearly seen in concentrated form. Medals went back directly to the imperial coinage of ancient Rome ('medal' originally signifying a coin out of circulation); but like the portrait bust, which had a similar ancestry in ancient Roman art and reappeared in the fifteenth century (10,34), they are examples of rebirth

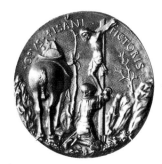

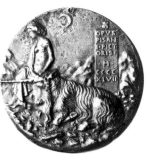

10,29 Pisanello, Domenico Malatesta Novello medal, c. 1445. Bronze, 3⅜ins (8.5cm) diameter. Victoria & Albert Museum, London.

10,30 Pisanello, Leonello marriage medal, 1444. Bronze, 4ins (10.2cm) diameter. Victoria & Albert Museum, London.

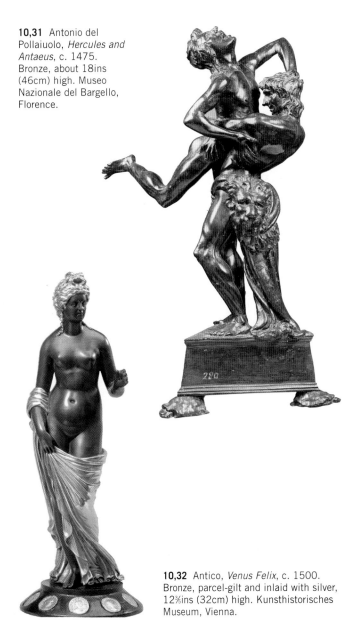

10,31 Antonio del Pollaiuolo, *Hercules and Antaeus*, c. 1475. Bronze, about 18ins (46cm) high. Museo Nazionale del Bargello, Florence.

10,32 Antico, *Venus Felix*, c. 1500. Bronze, parcel-gilt and inlaid with silver, 12⅝ins (32cm) high. Kunsthistorisches Museum, Vienna.

rather than revival. Pisanello (Antonio di Puccio Pisano, before 1395–1455), a distinguished painter and exquisite draftsman, was the first artist to make a specialty of them and created a virtually new art form. Each of his medals has on the front a profile portrait, more strongly characterized and also more boldly modelled than the heads of emperors on ancient coins. Usually there is an allegorical device on the back. That of Domenico Malatesta Novello (younger brother of Sigismondo Malatesta, see p. 438), for instance, has on its reverse a scene incorporating an armoured knight kneeling before a crucifix and a horse, the latter represented with amazing economy of means (**10,29**). Another, commemorating the marriage of Leonello d'Este to Maria of Aragon, has the charming device of Cupid teaching a lion (Leonello) to sing (**10,30**). Medals became increasingly popular in humanist circles as vehicles for transmitting personal fame with delicately contrived devices, often ingeniously abstruse. Intensely private works of art, which could be fully understood only by an erudite élite, they were intended to stimulate philosophical thought, just as religious images inspired devotion.

Bronze statuettes are also essentially private and reflect even more clearly the same secular tastes, being intended purely as works of art. Whereas medieval statuettes had been devotional (9,56), these were often quite overtly pagan. Their appearance in fifteenth-century Italy was prompted partly by descriptions in Latin literature. 'What precision of touch, what daring imagination the cunning master had, to model a table ornament, yet to conceive such mighty forms', the first-century AD poet Statius (a writer popular with humanists) had remarked of a statuette of Hercules. The same words could be applied to a group of Hercules and Antaeus by Antonio del Pollaiuolo (1433–98), in which not only an antique form but an antique aesthetic attitude was reborn (**10,31**). Formal artistic problems to which Alberti had alluded in his treatise on sculpture, in connection specifically with Hercules and Antaeus, were brilliantly solved by Pollaiuolo. The bronze must be handled and turned round so that it can be seen from multiple viewpoints, being centrifugally composed and at the same time perfectly balanced. The energy of the male nude in action, which Pollaiuolo extolled in paintings and in an engraving of a

battle between naked men, is here condensed into an image of dramatic intensity.

The bronze may, nevertheless, have had an allegorical significance (see p. 181) for its original owner, probably Lorenzo de' Medici (the Magnificent). He would have been aware of the medieval conception of Hercules as a prototype of the Christian knight and how, by restoring him to his pagan context, the humanists had transformed him into a symbol of 'Renaissance Man', the mortal who achieves immortality by his own efforts. Further philosophical meaning could be read into the story of his overcoming Antaeus, a giant who remained invincible only as long as he was in contact with the earth. But bronze statuettes were, of course, also prized simply as highly sophisticated and exquisitely refined works of art and some of the finest, for instance those by Piero Jacopo Alari Bonacolsi appropriately named Antico (d. 1528), had no ulterior meaning or purpose at all (**10,32**). The mercurial hedonism of such works seems almost provocative when,

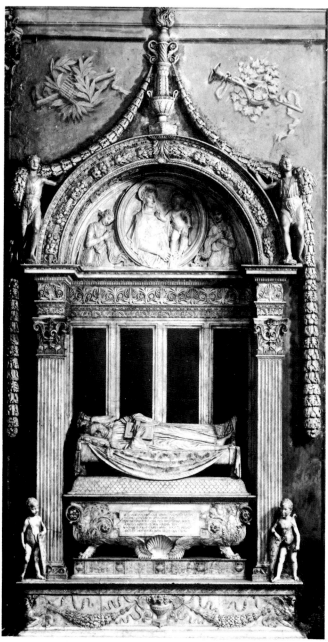

10,33 Desiderio da Settignano, *Monument to Carlo Marsuppini*, begun c. 1453. Marble, 19ft 9ins × 11ft 9ins (6.01 × 3.58m). S Croce, Florence.

as sometimes happened, the same 'antique' skills were lavished on figures of Christ and the saints.

There is a dichotomy rather than a conflict in Renaissance thought between Christianity and the humanism which encouraged the enhanced view of the dignity of man and the beauty of the physical world implicit in such works of art. This becomes evident in humanist tombs, such as the monument by Desiderio da Settignano (c. 1430–64) to Carlo Marsuppini, a Classical scholar, the first translator of Homer into Italian verse and, from 1444 until his death, state chancellor of Florence (**10,33**). Marsuppini is shown lying in state with a book under his lifeless hands, probably as at his funeral, which was one of

unprecedented pomp. Beneath him there is a sarcophagus standing on a plinth, both carved with Classical ornaments which combine springing vitality with incisive precision. On either side stand slender naked boys carrying shields, winged but very obviously mortal children rather than angels. The Latin inscription on the sarcophagus reads: 'Stay and see the marbles which enshrine a great sage, one for whose mind there was not world enough. Carlo, the great glory of his age, knew all that nature, the heavens and human conduct have to tell. O Roman and Greek Muses, now unloose your hair. Alas, the fame and splendour of your choir is dead.' There is not so much as a hint in all this of Christian beliefs or even of Christian virtues. The monument is, however, crowned by a relief of the Virgin and Child flanked by angels, as beautifully carved as the rest. Christianity and humanism are thus visually detached from one another, yet each has its appropriate place within a framework of early Renaissance architecture.

The head of Marsuppini with high brow and prominent cheekbones was probably a likeness, not a generalized image of the kind usual on medieval tombs. Significantly, Desiderio da Settignano is known to have been one of the Florentine sculptors who carved the first portrait busts since ancient Roman times. It was the idea rather than the form of these busts that derived from antiquity, much more of the chest and arms being shown than in ancient Roman examples. Some, of local notabilities whose names are inscribed on them, are products of that cult of fame which found expression also in medals (see p. 440–1). Several, including one of the finest, variously attributed to Antonio Rossellino (1427–79) and Desiderio, represent the daughters of Florentine patricians and appear to have been commissioned simply for personal and aesthetic reasons as enduring records of individual beauty (**10,34**). But portrait busts were rare in comparison to other types of sculpture.

10,34 Desiderio da Settignano, *Bust of a Lady*, c. 1460–4. Marble, 20⅝ins (52.5cm) high. Staatliche Museen, Berlin.

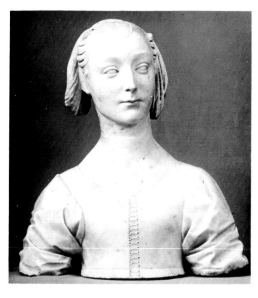

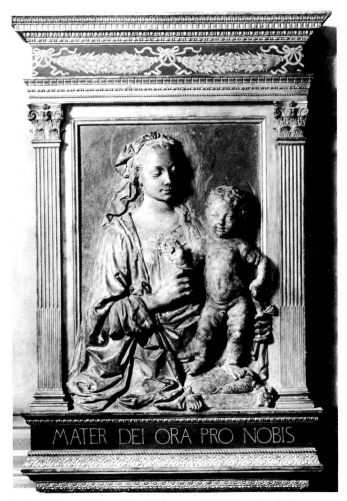

10,35 Andrea del Verrocchio, *Madonna and Child*, c. 1470–80. Terracotta partially painted, 33⅘ × 26ins (86 × 66cm). Museo Nazionale del Bargello, Florence.

Reliefs of the Virgin and Child were also made in what was a new medium for sculpture, terracotta coated with colored enamel glazes (previously used only for plates, jugs and other domestic utensils), first developed by Luca della Robbia (1399/1400–82) and exploited by his nephew Andrea (1435–1525), whose sons continued to use it until after the mid-sixteenth century. One of the select band of artists praised by Alberti in 1435 (see p. 422), Luca della Robbia was a highly accomplished sculptor who had worked in marble and bronze before he turned to glazed terracotta in about 1440. This new medium seems to have been taken up partly as a cheap alternative to marble and bronze, partly for its texture and color.

The roundels in the Pazzi Chapel (10,1) have the effect of painted rather than sculptured elements, but the later *Madonna and Child* (**10,36**) combines what were at the time regarded as the chief merits of sculpture and painting – form and color. Luca della Robbia did not strive after illusionism. The meditative serenity which emanates from his reliefs is achieved by a uniquely simple idealization. Colors are often limited to a background of beautiful sky-blue, to flowering plants and fruits, the figures with their Classically modelled draperies being left white so that they diffuse a celestial radiance.

There was, however, a tendency towards the illusionistic in much fifteenth-century Italian sculpture outside

10,36 Luca della Robbia, *Madonna and Child*, c. 1455–60. Enamelled terracotta, about 6ft (1.83m) in diameter. Orsanmichele, Florence.

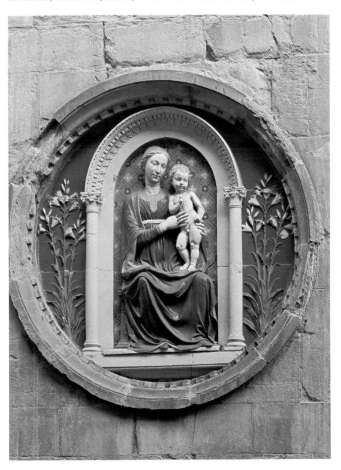

Reliefs of the Virgin and Child were the stock-in-trade of Florentine sculptors in the mid- and late fifteenth century. (In painting the demand was so great that a special class of painter called *madonnieri* arose to satisfy it.) Many are still to be seen in Florence, in churches, civic buildings, private houses and, enshrined in tabernacles, in the streets; others are now scattered among the art collections of the world (the Victoria and Albert Museum, London, alone has more than 60). They are usually rectangular, though sometimes circular, and show the Virgin half-length, often life-size. They derive from paintings rather than sculptures, and, as they were almost invariably colored, suggest a demand for images more lifelike than had previously been available. The majority of surviving examples are in stucco, apparently molded from terracotta or marble originals, and were probably within the reach of buyers who could not afford works in marble or bronze. A rare documented example in painted terracotta is by Andrea del Verrocchio (1435–88), the master of Leonardo da Vinci, a work as remarkable for tenderness in feeling as for its boldness and plasticity in modelling (**10,35**).

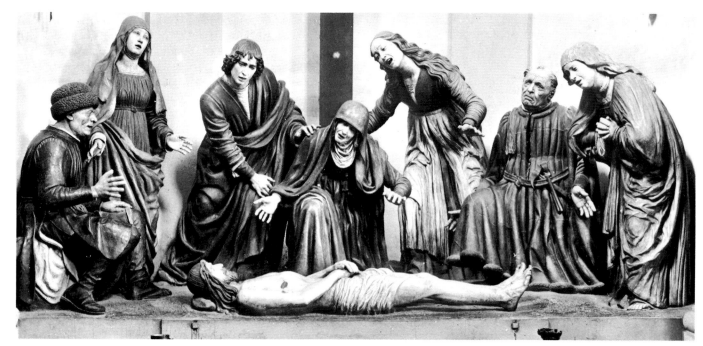

10,37 Guido Mazzoni, *Lamentation*, 1477–80. Terracotta, life-size. S Giovanni Battista, Modena.

Florence. Guido Mazzoni (d. 1518) of Modena was one of the first and most gifted of a number of sculptors who modelled life-size and disturbingly lifelike figures enacting scenes from the Gospels – usually groups of the Nativity and the Lamentation (**10,37**). The figures are dressed in contemporary costume and must resemble quite closely the actors who took part in the sacred dramas, which, like the miracle plays of medieval England, were performed in the open air at religious festivals and were intended to bring home the meaning of the Bible story to large and mainly illiterate audiences. Their extreme naturalism gives them the same sense of actuality as these dramatic performances must have had. But whereas the miracle plays, and the Gothic manuscript illuminations related to them, often indulged in a strain of grotesquerie, all inessentials have been eliminated in Mazzoni's groups.

ITALIAN PAINTING AND THE CHURCH

There were three reasons why religious images were introduced into churches, a popular Franciscan preacher remarked in the mid-fifteenth century:

> First, on account of the ignorance of simple people, so that those who are not able to read the scriptures can yet learn by seeing in pictures the sacraments of our salvation and faith . . . . Second, on account of our emotional sluggishness; so that men who are not aroused to devotion when they hear about the histories of the Saints may at least be moved when they see them, as if actually present in pictures. For our feelings are aroused by things seen more than by things heard . . . . Third. Images were introduced because many people cannot retain in their memories what they hear, but they do remember if they see images.

> (Fra Michele da Carcano, *Sermones Quadragesimales*, 1492, tr. M. Baxandall)

This is an elaboration of a passage in a thirteenth-century theological dictionary which similarly provides both a justification and a program for religious paintings, intermittently under attack for their lack of reverence in the depiction of sacred subjects. In 1450 the pious archbishop of Florence condemned such apocryphal matter in pictures as 'midwives at the Nativity' and all 'things that do not serve to arouse devotion but laughter and vain thoughts – monkeys, and dogs chasing hares and so on, or gratuitously elaborate costumes'. He clearly looked askance at much Gothic art.

FRA ANGELICO, UCCELLO AND PIERO DELLA FRANCESCA

The fifteenth century was a period of reform movements within the Church – reformations before the Protestant Reformation – led mainly by ascetic monks and friars who tightened up the rules of their own orders and never ceased to exhort the laity to more intense devotion. It was to culminate in the 1490s with Savonarola, the Dominican preacher who denounced the Medici and their artists, poets and philosophers in a spirit of extreme puritanism. But before Savonarola, a new note of austerity had been struck in Italian religious art, counterbalancing yet also complementing the contemporary revival of antique forms.

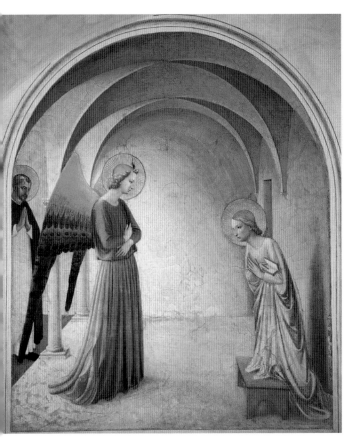

10,38 Fra Angelico, *Annunciation*, c. 1440-5. Fresco, 6ft 1½ins × 5ft 1½ins (1.87 × 1.57m). S Marco, Florence.

In each of these little square rooms a fairly large fresco (usually about 6 feet, 1.8m, high) was painted beside the window, so that the wall seems to have two openings, one to the spiritual and one to the physical world. That of the Annunciation is one of the most beautiful and revealing in its extreme simplicity (**10,38**). The scene is set in a cloister with columns of the kind beloved by Brunelleschi and Michelozzo, but the ornamental capitals are almost entirely obscured by the angel's wings, the only highly colored part of the painting. In other paintings of the same subject Angelico showed the Virgin reflecting on the angelic salutation; here she kneels in submission, a sublime model of humility and obedience for the friar who lived in the cell. All the technical developments which enabled painters to give logical cogency to depictions of the physical world are here applied to an austerely spiritual end. The figures are shown 'as if actually present', just beyond the cell's wall.

Paolo Uccello (1397–1475) seems to have been more concerned with visual realities than with their spiritual significance. *The Flood*, painted as a lunette below the vaulted ceiling of the cloister of S Maria Novella, Florence, vividly expresses the horror of the Biblical cataclysm with figures struggling for survival (**10,39**). Two young horsemen in the left foreground brandish weapons at one another, though their mounts are almost submerged. One man clings to the ark, another tries to break into it. Two figures swim frantically, others find temporary refuge with wolves and dogs on a tiny island of dry land. There are also such gruesome details as a drowned baby with distended stomach and a crow picking the eyes out of a corpse. In the tradition of continuous narrative, the lunette embraces two incidents: on the left the ark is floating and on the right has come to rest, with Noah looking out of the window. The two moments in time are, however, united in space by the strong compositional pattern and also by an unusual system of perspective, which gives the painting much of its mysterious power.

The demand for religious paintings both memorably clear and emotionally and spiritually stimulating was answered by Fra Angelico (Guido di Pietro, d. 1455). He entered the Dominican Order before 1423. All his work is religious, much of it painted for the Dominican friary at Fiesole, of which he was prior for three years, and its daughter house, the friary of S Marco in Florence, where, with a number of assistants, he frescoed the walls of the cloister, the chapter-house, the corridor on the upper floor and 41 cells.

10,39 Paolo Uccello, *The Flood*, c. 1445–7. Fresco, 49ft 6ins (15.1m) wide. Chiostro Verde, S Maria Novella, Florence.

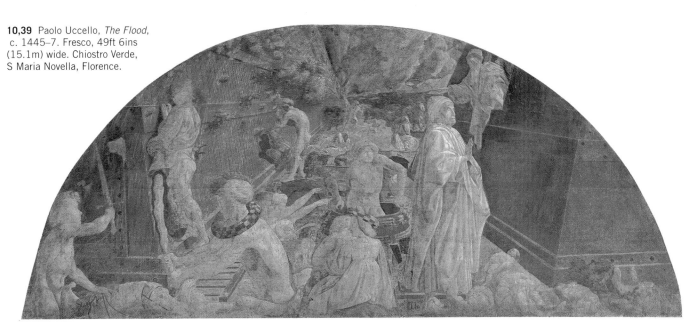

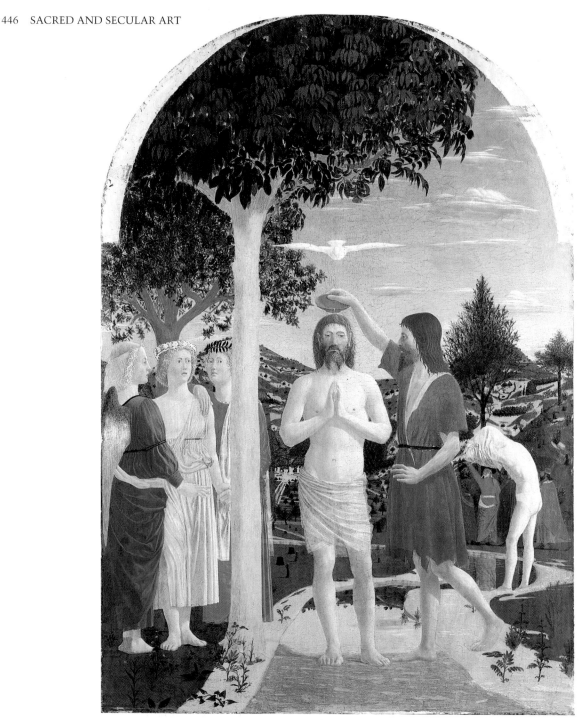

10,40 Piero della Francesca, *Baptism of Christ*, c. 1445. Panel painting, 5ft 6ins × 3ft 9¾ins (1.68 × 1.16m). National Gallery, London.

Uccello was obsessed by the problem of representing solids in space. The strange objects on the head of the seated girl in the foreground and around the neck of the youth beside her are *mazzocchi* (multi-faceted rings of wood or wicker used as foundations for a type of head-dress), which were so difficult to draw accurately that they were used as tests in perspective exercises. In *The Flood* they prominently display the scientific precision with which Uccello rendered every element of the composition, despite the contradictory scale of the foreground figures. Dissatisfied with Brunelleschi's and Alberti's simple scheme of pictorial perspective, based on a single vanishing-point, Uccello experimented with a more

elaborate system. In *The Flood* he used it to imaginative and expressive, rather than illusionistic, effect.

Uccello's fascination with such geometrical problems was very typical of fifteenth-century artists – and not only of those, like Uccello, of an experimental turn of mind. One of the most poetic, Piero della Francesca (c. 1420–92), devoted much of his intellectual energy to them. He composed treatises on geometrical bodies (cube, sphere, cone, cylinder and polyhedron) and on perspective and even wrote a mathematical handbook on the abacus for merchants, with rules for assessing the cubic capacity of barrels and so on. Thus he covered the abstract, the pictorial and the practical application of geometry and mathematics.

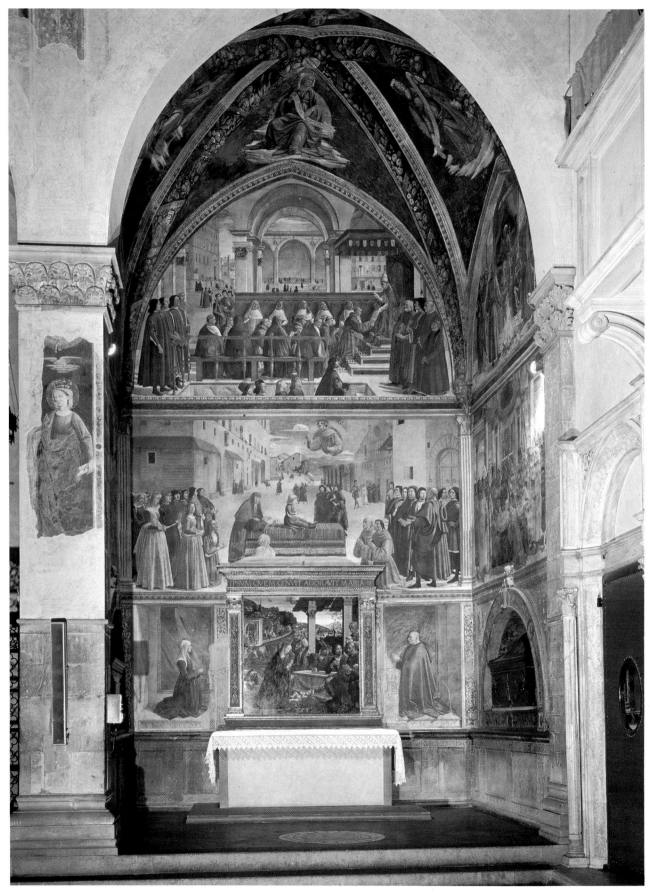

10,41 Domenico Ghirlandaio, Sassetti family chapel, 1479–86. S Trinità, Florence.

But numbers also had a religious, quasi-mystical significance. Hence the preoccupation of his time with the 'golden section', supposed to provide the key to the harmony of the heavens – a line divided in such a way that the smaller part is to the greater as the greater is to the whole, which sounds simple enough but cannot, in fact, be worked out mathematically as a numerical ratio.

Piero della Francesca's mathematical interests may well have sprung from his practice as a painter and his attempts to plumb the divine order beneath the surface of visual appearances. Even such a relatively early work as the *Baptism* (**10,40**) seems to have been geometrically based on a grid of three equidistant horizontals and four verticals, against which the slightest movements vibrate like the gently struck strings of a musical instrument. His interest in optics is revealed by the reflection of the landscape and of the robes of the priests in the clear river, which also induces a mood of stillness and tranquillity. In later paintings Piero was to record architectural space and mass with scientific precision; but in the *Baptism* a sense of clear, clean air circulating between the figures is conveyed without the aid of emphatic guidelines. His whole art is fastidiously unemphatic; light is so evenly diffused that shadows are barely perceptible, and there are no strident contrasts between the beautiful, slightly powdery colors, which make the palettes of most other painters seem garish. Piero's unique color harmonies enabled him to fuse the pattern on the surface of the panel with the representation of forms in the third dimension. In this way his work is not so much dependent on as analogous to the more mystical theories of mathematicians who found in numbers and geometrical diagrams a means of comprehending unity in the diversity of the universe.

Behind the figures of the *Baptism* there is a sun-drenched, wind-parched landscape inspired by the rough hilly country around Piero's home town Borgo S Sepolcro (its towers are visible beyond Christ's right hip). As we have already seen, Jan van Eyck incorporated a distant landscape in his *Madonna of Chancellor Rolin* (10,13), and Piero may well have known Flemish paintings which had reached Florence. The landscape of *The Baptism* is not, however, a symbol glimpsed through a window, as it is in van Eyck's painting; it surrounds the figures and, by implication, the spectators too. In Italian art such landscapes made their first appearance in the fifteenth century. Gold backgrounds, which had previously been so popular for devotional images, were suddenly abandoned, for a combination of reasons – economic (shortage of gold) and moral (hostility to conspicuous display), as well as aesthetic. The landscapes which took the place of these backgrounds enabled the figures to appear less hieratically remote from the world and more 'as if actually present'. They seem also to have been appreciated for their own sakes by both painters and their patrons. Thus, in 1485 Domenico Ghirlandaio (1449–94) signed a contract for frescoes he was to paint in S Maria Novella, Florence, agreeing to include 'figures, buildings, castles, cities, mountains, hills, plains, rocks, costumes, animals, birds

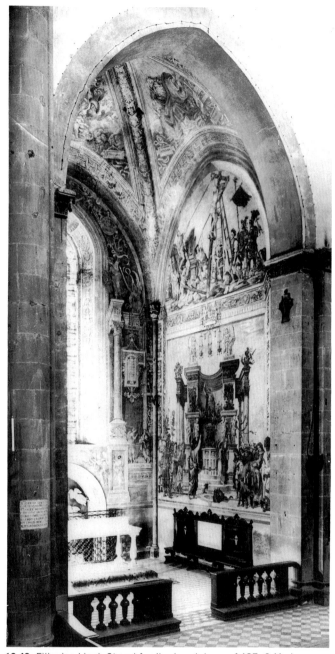

10,42 Filippino Lippi, Strozzi family chapel, begun 1487. S Maria Novella, Florence.

and beasts of every kind'. Similarly, Pinturicchio (Bernardino di Betto, 1454–1513) undertook to paint 'landscapes and skies in the empty part' – or, more precisely, the ground behind the figures – of the pictures he was providing for a church in Perugia.

So there are no 'empty parts' in the paintings of Ghirlandaio and Pinturicchio: their backgrounds teem with activity, as in the Sassetti Chapel, where Ghirlandaio used both townscapes and landscapes (**10,41**). The altarpiece itself is indebted to Flemish art in technique (oil painting) and also in other ways – two figures derive from Hugo van der Goes, for instance (see p. 435). But the landscape in which the Nativity takes place is Italianate and

---

FILIPPINO LIPPI AND FILIPPO STROZZI:

FINANCIAL AND OTHER PROBLEMS OVER THE STROZZI CHAPEL

The commissioning and execution of Filippino Lippi's paintings in S Maria Novella, Florence (10,42), are very fully documented and the problems that beset them, by no means untypical of such enterprises, are recorded in detail. The patron was Filippo Strozzi (1428–91), head of a Florentine bank, who spent large sums on the decoration of churches. 'God having conceded temporal goods to me, I want to show gratitude to Him', he wrote. He shared with other Florentines of his class a burning desire for lasting fame on earth which he hoped to attain by commissioning notable works of art. In 1486 he acquired the right to decorate a chapel in S Maria Novella where he planned to be buried. He began by ordering rich vestments and an altar-frontal embroidered with the Strozzi coat of arms. In the following year he engaged 'Filippo di Filippo', usually known as Filippino Lippi, to fresco its vault and walls. A contract was signed on 21 April 1487.

Let it be known to all that the painter Filippo di Filippo is engaged by Filippo di Matteo degli Strozzi to paint his chapel in S Maria Novella next to the high altar. In the vault there shall be four figures, either Doctors of the Church, Evangelists or others according to the choice of the said Strozzi, and they shall be painted with blue and with gold as richly as possible. The rest of the vault shall be of fine ultramarine blue worth at least 4 large gold florins an ounce, and the ribs of the vault, capitals of the pilasters and cornices shall be adorned with as much gold as is necessary. On each side wall there shall be two narrative scenes of subjects to be determined by the said Filippo Strozzi, and the window wall and the pilasters and the arch inside and out shall be adorned as the said Filippo Strozzi requires, and the dado similarly as Filippo Strozzi orders, and in every place where it is needed gold, pure gold and every other fine and perfect color shall be used. And the said Filippo di Filippo promises the said Strozzi to work in fresco according to the practice of good masters, and with all possible diligence, and all by his own hand, especially the figures. And it is agreed that the said Filippo di Filippo shall

have for the work, that is to say the painting, colors including blue pigment, scaffolding, lime [for plaster] and all else so that the said Strozzi will be required to meet no other expenses, that is to say 300 minted gold florins payable as to 35 at the beginning for wooden scaffolding, lime and other necessities, up to 100 florins when he wants to go to Venice, and the rest by installments according to the progress of the work . . . which he promises to complete by 1 March 1490.

The subjects of the paintings were presumably agreed verbally: four patriarchs, Adam, Noah, Abraham and Jacob in the vault, with scenes from the lives of St Philip and St John the Evangelist on the walls. The visit to Venice for which Filippino was to be paid one third of the total sum was, no doubt, to obtain the fine blue pigment (ultramarine made from lapis lazuli) that could best be bought there. Recent scientific analysis has revealed that he did in fact use ultramarine, not any of the cheaper substitutes.

The painting of the chapel did not, however, proceed according to contract. Nothing had been done by the summer of 1488 when Filippino went to Rome, where he had a far more important and remunerative commission from a cardinal (for the fresco in the Caraffa Chapel, S Maria sopra Minerva, Rome). He began work on the Strozzi Chapel during a brief return visit to Florence in 1489; but little had been done by 1491 when Filippo Strozzi died, leaving directions in his will that up to 1,000 florins was to be spent on completing the chapel with his own tomb, a stained glass window and other furnishings as well as the frescoes. Filippino resumed work in 1494 but soon halted, claiming that the payment due to him was not enough to cover the cost of materials. By applying to a tribunal for arbitration he obtained an extra 100 florins from Strozzi's heirs and the frescoes were finished in 1501. Half a century later Giorgio Vasari (see p. 473) was to write that they were paintings 'which it would be impossible for any invention, design, industry or artifice to improve.'

(Transcription courtesy of E. Borsook)

---

the triumphal arch through which the Magi pass, the Corinthian pilasters supporting the roof of the stable and a sarcophagus behind the Christ child are all emphatically Classical. The setting of the frescoed scenes from the life of St Francis is specifically localized in Florence itself. Pope Honorius confirming the rule of the Franciscan Order, an event which took place in Rome in 1223, is set by Ghirlandaio in Florence, in front of the Loggia dei Lanzi, with Lorenzo de' Medici, his sons and their tutor, the

humanist poet Poliziano, ascending the stairs to witness the event. In the register below, St Francis appears in the sky to resuscitate a dead child in the piazza of S Trinità.

Ghirlandaio retained the 'strip cartoon' system traditional for fresco cycles – not until slightly later was it generally outmoded by large scenes on each wall, as in the cycle by Filippino Lippi (1457–1504) in S Maria Novella in Florence (10,42). Each scene in the Sassetti Chapel records a single incident without 'continuous narrative'. Past events are set in the present, probably to suggest their continuing relevance, and this gives them a sense of immediacy which we still feel today and which must have been much more strongly felt by the painter's contemporaries. But Ghirlandaio or whoever was responsible for the iconographical program may have wished to go further and suggest how the Christian doctrine of eternity embraced both present and past, not excluding the Classical past. Four sibyls look down from the ceiling and in the side walls there are niches adorned with reliefs of centaurs, cupids and bacchantes, enclosing black marble sarcophagi carved with bulls' skulls. These images from the pagan cult of the dead adorn the tombs of the donors, who kneel so piously on either side of the altarpiece.

SECULAR PAINTING

Throughout the fifteenth century, in Italy as in northern Europe, the figurative arts remained predominantly religious. Portraits were painted, modelled and carved, and no longer restricted to members of ruling houses, but they were still rare in comparison with, for instance, images of the Madonna and Child. Mythological scenes were hardly less rare and, as we shall see, were generally given a moral, if not an explicitly religious, significance. Surviving

records written in Tuscany before 1550 name 500 or more religious paintings and sculptures and fewer than 40 secular ones; and although these writers mention only the more prominent artists and works of art (generally ignoring small devotional images and furniture paintings), the proportion is probably correct. There was almost certainly an increase in secular painting in the late fifteenth century, just as in Florence there was an increase in the number and size of large private houses built both in the city and as summer retreats in the surrounding hills.

Yet, as economic historians remind us, the fifteenth century was not a period of economic expansion so much as one of slow and incomplete recovery after a major depression in the mid-fourteenth century. It has, therefore, been suggested that merchants and bankers, who found trade stagnant and agriculture unremunerative, sometimes turned to investment in culture which, thanks to the humanists, had acquired prestige value. The hypothesis is as hard to prove as to disprove. The tendency towards simplicity and restraint in Florentine art and especially architecture may perhaps have been partly economic in origin. In terms of materials and man-hours, a building in the Renaissance style was certainly a less expensive undertaking than a Gothic one with its myriad decorations, and an altarpiece painted simply in tempera

10,43 Florentine School, a *cassone* or large chest, c. 1460. Overall 6ft 8⁷⁄₁₀ins (2.05m) long. Royal Museum of Fine Arts, Copenhagen.

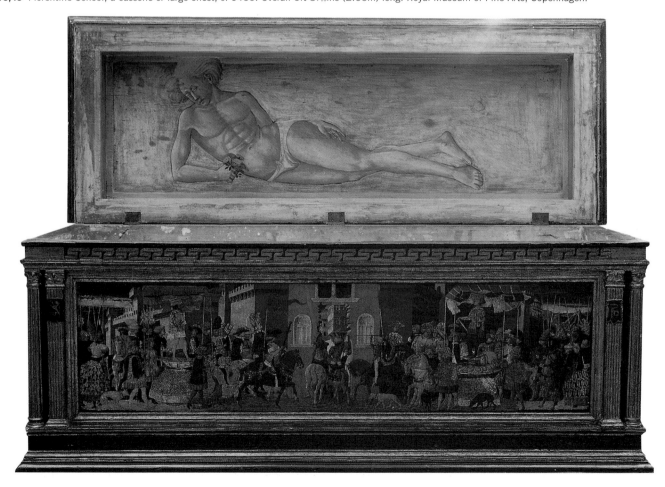

or oils than one with much use of gold and lapis lazuli (the costliest blue pigment) set in an elaborately carved and gilded frame.

The shift in attention from the value of materials to the skill of the artists coincided with, if it did not directly result from, a shortage of gold and silver, which became increasingly acute in the course of the century. Vasari stated that Antonio del Pollaiuolo abandoned a successful career as a goldsmith because he 'foresaw that his art did not promise a lasting fame', and took up painting. This was, of course, written with the benefit of hindsight after many of the finest Florentine works in gold and other precious metals had gone into the melting-pot during a crisis in 1529. But Pollaiuolo was not a unique case. Several other leading Florentine artists began their careers as goldsmiths and then turned to painting, notably Verrocchio, Botticelli and Domenico Ghirlandaio. Ironically, their work as painters has been preserved partly because painting materials had little intrinsic value. If they had continued to work as goldsmiths their works would almost certainly have been melted down and their names forgotten.

Shortage of precious metals may, therefore, have played a part of seldom recognized importance in diverting talent to the art of painting. It certainly gave a fillip to the production of small objects made of humble materials yet designed and decorated with consummate skill – pottery painted as beautifully as enamelled gold vessels (10,54) or little marriage coffers of wood covered with the molded paste called *pastiglia* and worked no less finely than caskets of gold or silver. Household furniture was generally simple – of plain wood covered on special occasions with woven silks or carpets from the eastern Mediterranean – except for the *cassone* or large chest used for storing clothes and linen and often made to hold the bride's trousseau and adorned with the coats of arms of her and her husband's families. *Cassoni* were sometimes very elaborate, reflecting the importance of marriage as a means of forging political and business alliances between leading families. Unfortunately few survive intact, but they reveal a preference for sober Classical ornamentation combined with brightly colored, vivacious figurative scenes on the painted panels.

Many of these painted panels have been preserved as independent pictures after the *cassoni* they decorated were broken up. They usually depict scenes from ancient history or mythology – those with Christian subjects probably adorned the chests which nuns took with them when they entered convents. In style, however, they all maintain until well after the mid-fifteenth century the traditions of International Gothic art, packed with incident, crowded with figures related to one another in intricate surface patterns. Some of the stories come from Homer or Virgil, but the figures are always dressed in the height of contemporary fashion; they are, in fact, indistinguishable from those who enact scenes from the stories of Boccaccio. Greeks and Trojans are clad in shining armour like jousting knights. These paintings have a distinctly courtly air, which reminds one that the Florentines, though city-dwellers, merchants and nominally republicans, still paid lip-service to feudal ideals of chivalry. Some directly allude to marriage, the story of the Romans and the Sabines being among the most popular. The *cassone* illustrated here is one of a pair with paintings on this theme; the panel depicts the reconciliation between the two peoples after Romulus and his companions had carried off Sabine women to be their wives (10,43). Inside the lids of these chests there are paintings of nudes, which would have been seen only by the bride and were probably intended as lucky charms for fair children of the marriage.

BOTTICELLI

Much larger and finer mythological paintings were similarly expected to be charming in the original, magical sense of the word. *La Primavera* (The Spring) by Sandro Botticelli (Alessandro Filipepi, c. 1445–1510) is one of the earliest (10,44). Over 6 feet (2m) high, it is painted on a scale previously reserved for religious pictures. The most notable earlier secular works of art of such a size intended for private houses – or rather the private apartments of palaces – are tapestries on chivalric themes woven in France and Flanders from early in the fifteenth century (10,45). Tapestries were by far the most costly large-scale works of art – much more expensive than paintings – and the *Primavera* may well have been conceived originally as an inexpensive substitute. There is certainly something tapestry-like about its flat composition and especially the flower-strewn ground, recalling the 'thousand-flower' hangings, though the finest of these are slightly later in date. This affinity may partly account for the 'Gothic' quality often noted in Botticelli's exquisitely, almost preciously, graceful and rather weightless figures, so different from those of Masaccio, Piero della Francesca and Uccello. But whereas the figures in a fifteenth-century French or Flemish tapestry belong to the medieval world of chivalry and courtly love, the figures in the *Primavera* come no less obviously from Classical mythology.

Venus stands in the centre, with the blindfolded Cupid hovering over her head. The other figures, reading from left to right, are Mercury, the three Graces, Flora, goddess of flowers and the spring, the earth nymph Chloris, and Zephyr, the west wind. They do not enact any specific scene from ancient mythology and a bewildering number of different interpretations has been put on them. As the messenger of the gods, Mercury had come to be regarded as the patron of those who sought to penetrate the mysteries of the ancient world – the Hermetic philosophers, who were called after his Greek name, Hermes. 'He calls the mind back to heavenly things through the power of reason', wrote Marsilio Ficino, one of the group of Florentine Neoplatonists. And there can be little doubt that the *Primavera* was strongly influenced by ideas current in this group. It seems to have been painted for Lorenzo di Pierfrancesco de' Medici (second cousin of Lorenzo the Magnificent) when he was no more than 14 or 15 years old and Ficino was taking a close interest in his education.

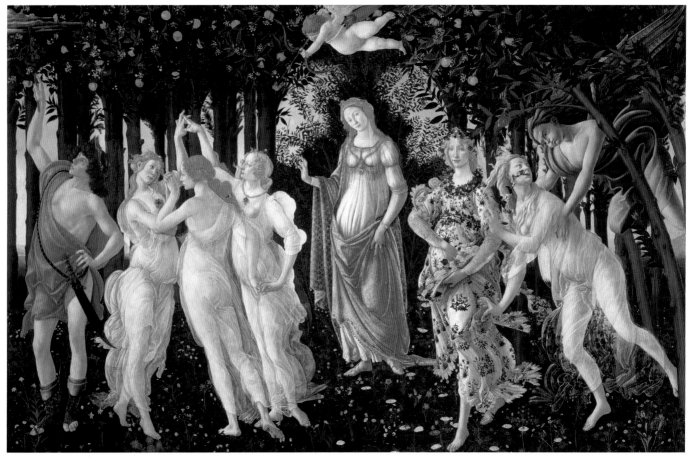

10,44 Sandro Botticelli, *La Primavera*, c. 1478. Panel painting, 6ft 8ins × 10ft 4ins (2.03 × 3.15m). Uffizi, Florence.

In 1478, the probable date of the picture, Ficino wrote the boy a letter in the form of a horoscope, urging him to fix his eyes on Venus, who represented Humanity, 'a nymph of excellent comeliness born of heaven and more than others beloved by God all-highest. Her soul and mind are Love and Charity, her eyes Dignity and Magnanimity, the hands Liberality and Magnificence, the feet Comeliness and Modesty . . . .' This mixture of astrology, Classical mythology and Christian morality typifies Florentine Neoplatonic thought. So, too, does the idea of presenting a didactic lesson in a form that was outwardly attractive yet yielded its inner message only to the initiated, for mysteries were supposed to lose their almost magic power when they were revealed to the profane. It is natural to ask how far Botticelli shared this outlook. The program of the *Primavera* was almost certainly devised for him. But it was Botticelli's individual genius that enabled him to translate the program into a sweetly poignant poetry no less characteristically Florentine – though he seems to have known Alberti's treatise on painting, which recommends that a pictorial narrative should have 'abundance and rarity of object', several figures, some fully clothed, others wholly or partly nude in different poses, frontal or profile 'with hands up and fingers apart' or 'arms relaxed and feet together', each having 'its own action and bending of limb'. He created the visual

equivalent not so much of the obscurantist treatises of Ficino as of the hedonistic songs of his patron Lorenzo the Magnificent, which epitomize all the freshness of the early Renaissance.

Interest in antiquity was complemented by a still deeper preoccupation with astrology. No court of the time was complete without an astrologer to cast horoscopes and decide on propitious moments for taking important decisions. Though condemned by the early Christians, astrology had been revived in Europe by the twelfth century and soon became so influential that it was tolerated by the Church. That the planets and constellations bore the names of pagan deities was unfortunate (attempts to provide Christian alternatives were ineffectual), but they were generally believed to reveal the will of God and in this way astrology, astronomy and Christian theology were reconciled. Above the altar of Brunelleschi's sacristy in S Lorenzo (see p. 424) the cupola is painted with an accurate map of the stars in the sky over Florence on 9 July 1422 – the date of the altar's consecration – and there is a similarly placed map in the Pazzi Chapel (10,1). The signs of the zodiac, in which the pagan gods survived the Middle Ages, recur again and again in the art of the Renaissance, nowhere more prominently than in Palazzo Schifanoia, the summer palace of Borso d'Este, duke of

Ferrara. Here, the walls of the great hall were divided into 12 vertical sections (only seven of which remain intact) frescoed by the chief court painter, Cosimo Tura (1430–95), and a team of artists who were paid by the square yard. The erudite program, derived mainly from an astrological poem of the first century AD, was probably drawn up by one or more of the Classical scholars and astrologers whom Borso d'Este had gathered around him. Each section is devoted to one of the zodiacal months of the year, horizontally divided into three parts.

The *Month of March* (**10,46**), painted by Francesco del Cossa (c. 1436–78), has at the top the presiding deity Minerva seated on a triumphal chariot. As she was the patroness of learning and the crafts, scholars are ranged on one side of her, women engaged in embroidery and weaving on the other. The central band is devoted to the zodiac, with two bizarrely dressed figures representing decans, the spirits who ruled each period of ten days. We come down to earth in the lower register with activities appropriate to the month, courtiers hunting and peasants pruning their vines. In a handsome little Renaissance loggia on the right, Borso d'Este encourages the administration of justice. Each of the other months illustrates one of his virtues and thus the room as a whole celebrates the tiny dukedom of Ferrara as a microcosmic reflection of celestial harmony in which peasants, scholars, women, courtiers and, above all, Borso d'Este have their appointed places. For astrology was regarded not simply as a way of predicting the future, but as a means of discovering the rules of cosmic order.

There were a few humanists who protested at the fatalism of astrology and proclaimed their belief in the

10,45 The *Rose Tapestry*, detail of French or Flemish tapestry, c. 1435–40. Wool, total height 9ft 7ins (2.9m). Metropolitan Museum of Art, New York.

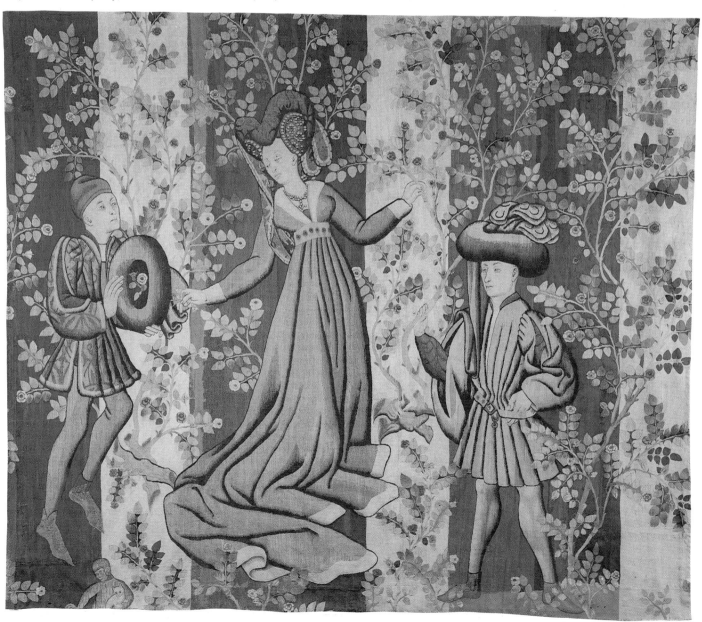

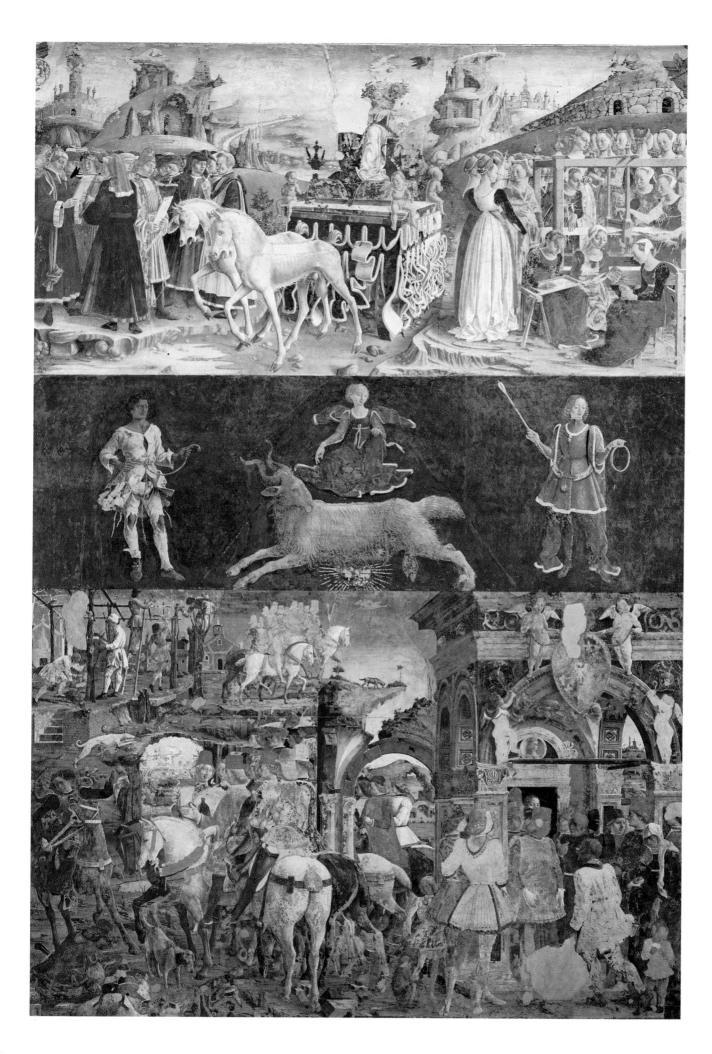

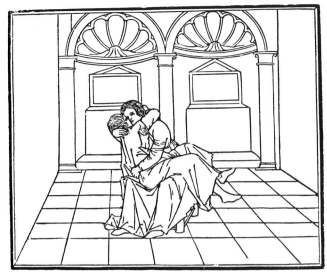

10,47 Woodcut illustration to *Hypnerotomachia Poliphili*, Venice, 1499.

power of man to be his own master, but all succumbed to the lure of the antique mysteries in which eternal truths were supposedly concealed. Notable literary and artistic expression is given to them in a strange rambling allegorical romance, *Hypnerotomachia Poliphili* (Love's Strife in a Dream of Poliphilo), written in about 1460 by a Dominican friar, Francesco Colonna, and published with elegant woodcuts in Venice in 1499 (**10,47**). The combination of a darkly obscurantist text with typography of unprecedented clarity and illustrations in which forms are fully defined by a few confidently drawn lines could hardly be more characteristic of the period.

The art of printing with movable type, first developed in Europe in the mid-fifteenth century (though invented in China 400 years earlier), was initially employed to diffuse religious texts and these were to remain the staple products of printing presses for centuries. An edition of the Bible printed by Johann Gutenberg at Mainz in 1455 was the first major work. Early printed books were conceived as substitutes for manuscripts and many printers left space for illuminators to elaborate capital letters at the beginning of chapters. Humanists (some of whom disapproved of the new invention) and printers seem to have had little influence on one another until the last decade of the century, when Aldus Manutius set up his press in Venice and published the first accurately printed Greek texts and reliable editions of Latin authors, as well as such curiosities as the *Hypnerotomachia*. Not until this moment did printing begin to affect the intellectual life of Europe, which it was eventually to transform.

THE VENETIAN SYNTHESIS

MANTEGNA AND BELLINI

A small painting of St Sebastian by Andrea Mantegna (c. 1431–1506), dating from about 1460, emphasizes many of the characteristic features which had gradually emerged in Italian art of the previous four decades – spatial clarity

10,46 *Opposite* Francesco del Cossa, *Month of March*, 1469–70. Fresco, Palazzo Schifanoia, Ferrara.

by means of perspective, naturalistic landscape background, antique architectural and decorative motifs and an idealized human being, harmoniously proportioned and all but nude (**10,48**). It is signed, below the saint's right elbow, in Greek, as if to underline the painter's insistent Classicism. The story of St Sebastian, an officer in

10,48 Andrea Mantegna, *St Sebastian*, c. 1460. Panel, 26⅘ × 11⅘ins (68 × 30cm). Kunsthistorisches Museum, Vienna.

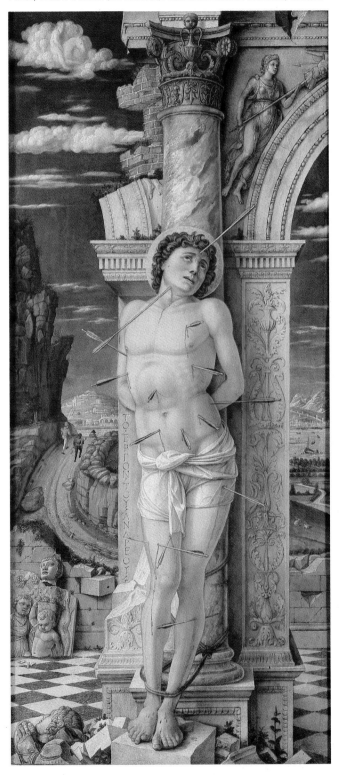

Diocletian's imperial guard, converted to Christianity and condemned to be shot to death with arrows, justified an antique setting.

Mantegna was trained in Padua, where the university was one of the main centres for humanist studies in Italy – or in all Europe – though the local artistic style was still predominantly Gothic. Just after he finished his apprenticeship Donatello arrived in Padua to model the Gattamelata monument and the Classicizing reliefs for the altar of the church of S Antonio (see p. 440). Later, in Venice, Mantegna married the daughter of the painter Jacopo Bellini (c. 1440–70/71), whose drawings of Classical antiquities (Louvre and British Museum) are remarkable for their archeological precision and understanding. At this date, antique sculpture was nowhere more in evidence than in Venice, the Italian city with the closest contacts with Greece, much of which was a Venetian possession from the early thirteenth century until 1460. Four first-century AD bronze horses stood on the façade of S Marco and other ancient Greek or Hellenistic bronze statues seem to have been brought to the city if only to be melted down to make cannons. Similar marble carvings were also to be seen there. On Mantegna all these antiquities must have made a deep impression and he began very early to develop a style of painting more explicitly indebted to Greek and Roman sculpture than that of any other artist of his time.

Vasari was to write that Mantegna 'always maintained that the good antique statues were more perfect and beautiful than anything in Nature. He believed that the masters of antiquity had combined in one figure the perfections which are rarely found together in one individual and had thus produced single figures of surpassing beauty.' Whether or not Mantegna ever made such an uncompromising statement of faith in idealization, these words are relevant to his *St Sebastian*. The young saint's body looks as if it had been carved out of some unusually hard and flawless marble. It is placed against a Corinthian column (with a glancing allusion to Vitruvius's equation between architectural and bodily proportions). Yet in this, as in many other fifteenth-century religious pictures, the pagan world is shown symbolically in ruins. Fragments of statues and reliefs lie on the ground, the building (based on the arch of Septimius Severus in Rome) is fissured and broken. The apparent contradiction is, however, essential to the meaning of the painting – Christianity, personified by the saint, prevails over all human ills and disasters. St Sebastian was a patron of the sick and his intercession was evoked especially in times of plague, of which there were outbreaks (probably bubonic) every 15 years or so in Venice throughout the century. This accounts for the frequency of his appearance in Venetian art.

St Sebastian, paired with Job as the Old Testament type of the pestilence-stricken, is included in the large altarpiece painted by Mantegna's brother-in-law Giovanni Bellini (c. 1430–1516) for the church attached to the hospital of S Giobbe (Job) in Venice (**10,49**). In this painting also there are crisply carved antique ornaments on pilasters and capitals (see Glossary). But the differences

between the two works are striking although Bellini's shallow space is no less real for being restricted by the curved wall of the apse, his forms no less clearly defined for being painted with gentle fluid brush-strokes. The greatest Venetian painter of his time, Giovanni Bellini assimilated the technical and stylistic innovations of early Renaissance art, combining a spring-like freshness typical of the fifteenth century with a new self-confident mastery. Statuesque poses are no longer needed to indicate weight, nor guidelines to indicate perspective recession.

10,49 Giovanni Bellini, *S Giobbe Altarpiece*, c. 1485. Panel, 15ft 4ins × 8ft 4ins (4.67 × 2.54m). Gallerie dell'Accademia, Venice.

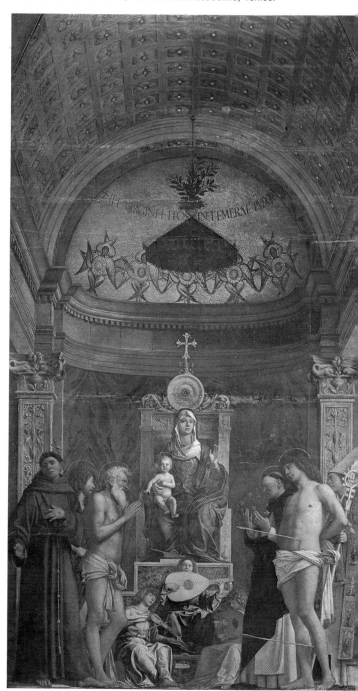

In the *S Giobbe Altarpiece* the barrel vault recalls the architecture of Brunelleschi, but otherwise the setting is distinctly Venetian with inlays of precious marbles, very seldom used in Tuscany, and a half-dome of gold mosaic on which Byzantine seraphim flutter their wings, a reminder of Venetian contacts with Constantinople in the not-so-distant past. The picture is of a type called a *sacra conversazione* (holy conversation), evolved in the fifteenth century by Fra Angelico and others. No longer are the saints separated from one another as in a Gothic polyptych; they stand in an informal group on either side of the Madonna and Child, conversing or communing with each other within a single, unified space. Bringing the saints much closer to the spectator, and representing them much more 'as if actually present' (see p. 448), the *sacra conversazione* beautifully answered the spiritual need for a less remote, less hieratic religious art. On the left of the *S Giobbe Altarpiece* St Francis looks straight out of the picture and with a gentle gesture of his right hand invites the devout to share in a celestial vision where angels play their musical instruments beneath the throne of the Madonna. Each of the saints is an individual, distinguishable by pose and expression as well as traditional attributes. They have a humanity which has little if anything to do with humanism. The most striking feature of the altarpiece and its greatest novelty is, however, its color – not simply that of the Madonna's lapis lazuli robe or the shot silk of the dresses worn by the angelic musicians but the rich color harmonies created by the whole work. Forms are, as it were, built out of colors which merge into one another; and the light which falls on them is no longer a ray of unearthly pallor, but is itself charged with glowing color. It might be said that Bellini introduced 'atmosphere' into painting by opening the hermetically sealed perspective box invented in Florence to admit the glow of real Venetian sunlight, an achievement made possible by oil painting. Bellini had, so to speak, fused the innovations of Flemish and Florentine art. But this was more than a merely technical achievement. He created a new artistic language with a soft Venetian accent, promptly adopted by other painters in the city and articulated with increasing fluency and subtlety in his

10,50 Giovanni Bellini, *Madonna of the Meadow*, c. 1505. Panel, 26½ × 34ins (67 × 86cm). National Gallery, London.

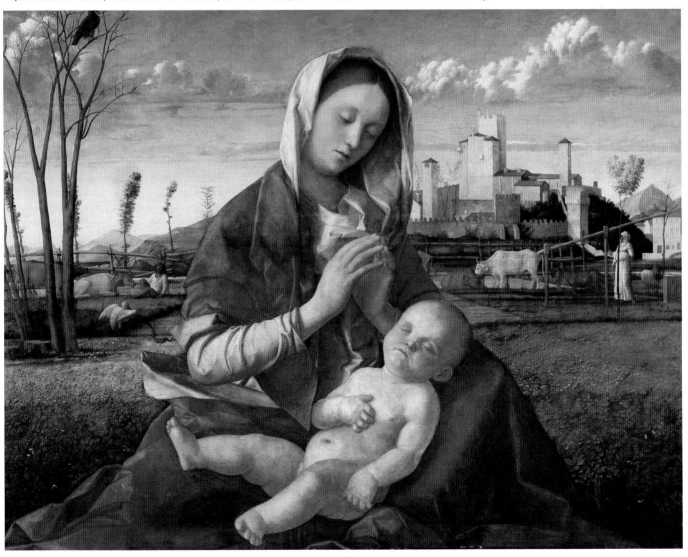

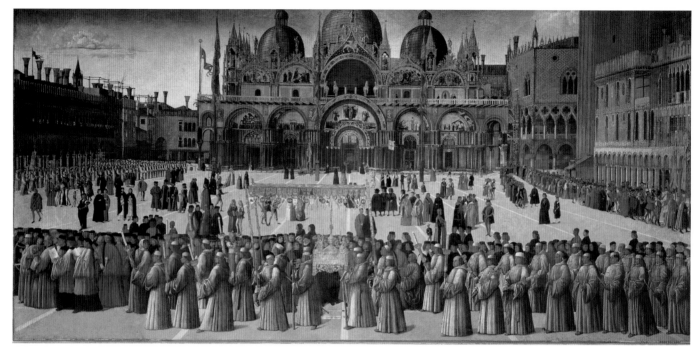

10,51 Gentile Bellini, *Procession in the Piazza S Marco*, 1496. Canvas, 12ft ½in × 24ft 5¼ins (3.67 × 7.45m). Accademia, Venice.

own late works when he was in his seventies. His pictures of the Madonna set in landscapes bathed in the reanimating light of winter sunshine, with a promise of spring in the cool air, are among the most poetical devotional images ever painted, expressing at once the humility and pride of the Virgin mother, and the worshipper's feeling of wonder at the beauty of Creation and the miracle of the Incarnation. In his *Madonna of the Meadow* (**10,50**) the landscape is no mere background but an essential part of the whole image, evoking tranquil meditation and reflecting the mood of the central figures who dominate without detaching themselves from it. Indeed they become part of it. In 1506, when he was nearly 80, he was 'still the supreme master', as Albrecht Dürer called him.

Gentile Bellini (1429–1507), the elder brother of Giovanni, was in his time equally distinguished, but mainly as a painter of historical scenes rather than devotional images. In 1474 he obtained the most important commission given to any artist in Venice, that of replacing the decaying frescoes by Gentile da Fabriano and other masters of the by then outmoded International Gothic style (see p. 417) in the main council chamber of the Doges' Palace. He did this with scenes from Venetian history, painted on canvas; and with them, though they were all destroyed by fire in 1577, he initiated a new and peculiarly Venetian style of narrative painting. Buildings, figures and even the smallest objects were depicted with the empirical realism and meticulous attention to detail of Flemish painters, but without their obsessive symbolism, and set in the rationally structured spaces created by Florentine painters, but without their sometimes over-insistent use of perspective to focus attention on the main subject.

During the next three decades many such paintings in what has been aptly termed the 'eye-witness style' were executed in Venice. They were commissioned for the premises of the lay religious confraternities called *Scuole* (literally 'schools', but this was a uniquely Venetian use of the word) which were at the time the most active patrons of the arts in the city. For the Scuola di San Giovanni Evangelista, for example, Gentile Bellini painted three, including that of a procession in Piazza S Marco (**10,51**), the façade of S Marco glowing with the Byzantine mosaics that were later to be replaced (9,16). An artist of the next generation and the most accomplished practitioner of the style, Vittore Carpaccio (c. 1460–1526) painted for the same Scuola in 1494 *Healing of a Possessed Man*, with a view of the Rialto and the wooden bridge over the Grand Canal (**10,52**). At first sight these paintings might seem to be no more than animated cityscapes. But they had a higher purpose. They all commemorate the miracles worked during the previous hundred years by a relic of Christ's cross which was the Scuola's most cherished possession. Indeed they did more than commemorate them, they 'testified', as might an eye-witness, in support of various written documents concerning the relic's 'almost innumerable miracles'. Gentile Bellini showed the St Mark's Day procession, in which the relic was carried, passing a bareheaded kneeling man who was suddenly inspired to prayer and whose son, far away in Brescia, was cured of a fractured skull at the very same moment. Carpaccio showed in the open loggia on the left of his picture a 'possessed' or insane man healed by the presence of the relic. These were among the miracles that testified to the relic's authenticity as a fragment of the True Cross; and the ascertainable fidelity with which circumstantial details were rendered by Carpaccio served to corroborate the stories about them as matters of fact. There are no supernatural appearances, like that of St

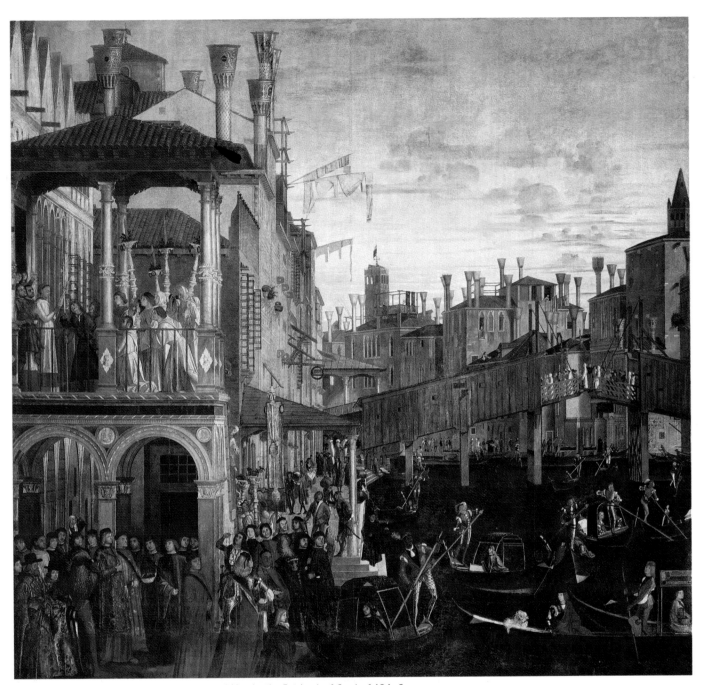

10,52 Vittore Carpaccio, *Healing of a Possessed Man by the Patriarch of Grado*, 1494. Canvas,
11ft 11¾ins × 12ft 9⅛ins (3.65 × 3.89m). Accademia, Venice.

Bellini and Carpaccio

CORPORATE PATRONAGE IN RENAISSANCE VENICE

The Scuola di S Giovanni Evangelista for which Gentile Bellini and Vittore Carpaccio's paintings (10,51; 52) were executed was one of the five main lay religious confraternities in Venice. Called Scuole Grandi, they had been founded in the thirteenth century by groups of laymen who scourged themselves publicly on ceremonial occasions, seeking to atone for the sins of the world by re-enacting the sufferings of Christ. By the end of the fifteenth century there were more than 200 smaller confraternities known as Scuole Piccoli in the city as well. Established for devotion outside the institutional church, most of them admitted women as full members and some developed into mutual-aid associations that provided for the sick, impoverished and aged. Several were more widely engaged in charitable work and a few established hospitals and old people's homes. There were and still are, of course, lay confraternities in Catholic countries, notably the Misericordia, which provides ambulances and first-aid services all over present-day Italy. But the Scuole had distinguishing features and functions as part of the social fabric of Venice.

The membership of the Scuole Grandi was socially mixed. Venice was an oligarchy, and a rigid one. The Scuole were the only places where members of different social strata could meet on equal terms, at least theoretically. Members included 'patricians' descended from old families, who inherited seats in the Great Council and elected from among themselves the Doge, senators and officers of state; 'citizens' descended from families long resident in Venice, often rich but without a vote in government; and lastly the lower class of manual workers, shop-keepers and so on, who made up 85 per cent of the total population. In 1482 the members of the Scuola di S Giovanni Evangelista included, besides 'patricians', such 'citizens' as a ship-owner and dealers in silk and gold, but also a bookseller, a fisherman, a fruit-vendor, a barber and others of the lower class. All members vowed equally to maintain high standards of conduct; notorious offenders were expelled. The state cherished the Scuole as guardians of morality but, at the same time, took steps to prevent them from becoming power bases for politically ambitious patricians or centres of popular discontent, legislating that the governing bodies they elected should be confined to 'citizens', thus excluding both patricians and the lower orders.

Bequests made to the Scuole enabled them eventually to build imposing premises and decorate them lavishly. Narrative paintings were favoured by the governing bodies and those they commissioned from Gentile Bellini and Carpaccio are not only remarkable in themselves but also in being the product of this unusual corporate patronage. For the governing bodies not only selected the artists but chose the subjects to be depicted and appointed a committee to supervise the work. Carpaccio painted complete narrative cycles for three Scuole though only one, that for the Scuola di S Giorgio degli Schiavoni (a confraternity of Dalmatians who manned Venetian ships), still survives in the building for which it was commissioned (**10,53**). What were the motives behind these acts of corporate patronage? They were, first of all, acts of piety like that of giving alms to the poor or lighting a candle before an altar. But were the narratives they commissioned also intended as 'eye-witness' accounts of Venetian life, as visual testimonies to the truth of the miracles and other religious events depicted? Or did they mediate in some way between everyday reality and life as the Venetian 'citizens' of the governing bodies wished and hoped it was? The answer is of interest not only historically but because of what is known about the role of narrative in present-day society. Even when ostensibly mere entertainment – fables, dramas, TV romances or strip cartoons – narrative often functions as a filter to make the ambiguities of everyday life comprehensible and acceptable, to resolve the incongruities of the real world. They give structure and coherence and sometimes even a moral dimension to the untidy and largely inconsequential events of every day. Did Bellini's and Carpaccio's narrative cycles play a similar role?

Enough is known about Venice in the late fifteenth and early sixteenth centuries to exclude the possibility that these narrative cycles were intended to be straightforward reflections of life as it was. They are not to be understood simply as colorful tableaux in the unfolding pageant of ceremonial and popular life in Venice. Although they illustrate to some extent the social structure as well as the physical appearance of the city they are not disinterested neutral records of daily life, not even of ceremonial life. All the conflicts and tensions beneath the surface of Venetian life have been concealed in order to present a happy picture of social harmony and well-being. They celebrate a mercantile ideal of the state as conceived by the well-to-do merchant 'citizens' who commissioned them.

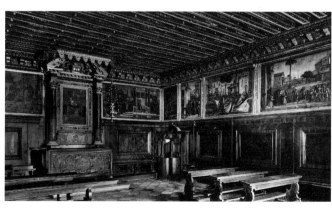

10.53 Oratory of the Scuola di S Giorgio degli Schiavoni, Venice, with paintings by Carpaccio, c. 1502–7. The paintings were originally in a meeting-room on the first floor.

Francis emerging from the sky to resuscitate a dead child in one of Ghirlandaio's frescoes in Florence (10,41). The emphasis is on the everyday world familiar to the pious but hard-headed merchants of Venice at a time when no one, not even humanists, doubted the possibility of miraculous occurrences.

INTERNATIONAL HUMANISM

In the last decades of the fifteenth century, Italian influence gradually began to infiltrate Europe north of the Alps. Matthias Corvinus, king of Hungary (1458–90), not only acquired Renaissance works of art, including marble reliefs by Verrocchio, but employed an Italian architect to rebuild his palaces in the Tuscan manner and Italian sculptors and painters to decorate them with carved marble fountains and frescoes (of which only fragments survive). Such strongly marked Italianate tastes were unusual before the sixteenth century and may have been due partly to his wife, a daughter of the king of Naples, whose arms appear with his own on a spectacular maiolica table service painted with allegories at Faenza or Deruta (**10,54**). But the little Renaissance court at Budapest was altogether exceptional at this date.

The new style was first carried across the continent by illuminated manuscripts of Classical texts, engravings of mythological subjects and printed books, mainly, it seems, along a network of personal contacts between humanists. The reader of a book printed in Italy might find his eye distracted by naked *putti* (see Glossary) frolicking among the crisp fronds of acanthus which sprout from capital letters in many a woodcut initial (**10,55**). These little figures insidiously established a link between learning and the visual language of the Renaissance long before Italian paintings and sculptures had reached northern Europe in any quantity.

10,54 Maiolica plate, Deruta or Faenza, c. 1476. Victoria & Albert Museum, London.

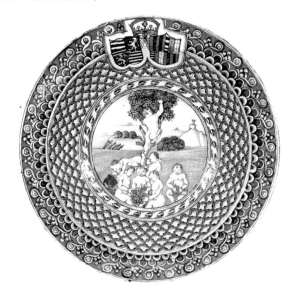

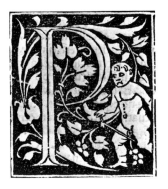

10,55 Initial from a Venetian edition of Virgil of 1495.

DÜRER

It was in the context of international humanism that Albrecht Dürer (1471–1528) created a northern equivalent to the Italian Renaissance style of the fifteenth century. Like many Florentine artists, he began as a goldsmith (in his father's workshop). But he completed his apprenticeship under a Nuremberg painter, who was also a maker of woodcuts, and after journeyman travels in the Rhineland was employed for a while on book illustrations in Basel. In 1494 he went to Venice, then beginning to emerge as the most important centre for humanist book publishing. The reasons for this visit are, however, unknown and he may have gone there primarily to study works of art and to complete his artistic education, just as his lifelong friend Willibald Pirckheimer was then completing his classical education at the University of Padua. Through Pirckheimer, the son of a patrician family of Nuremberg, he made and maintained contact with humanists, who in Germany tended to hold themselves aloof from artists and craftsmen. In these circles, probably, Dürer encountered engravings of mythological scenes by Pollaiuolo and Mantegna, which were quite unlike any northern works of art in that the figures were nude or clad in antique drapery (not modern costume) and thus reintegrated Classical subject-matter with Classical form. He set himself to copy them in pen and ink, soon mastering their style so perfectly that he could work in it independently. It was not, however, with Classical subjects that he established his reputation after returning to Nuremberg in 1495. Apart from portraits, all but one of his paintings are religious. So, too, are most of his many prints, the finest of which have never been surpassed in their concentration of religious thought and feeling – or in technical accomplishment.

The practice of making prints from metal plates, first developed in Germany and Italy in the mid-fifteenth century, was the result of combining two much older techniques – printing from carved woodblocks and engraving silver ornamentally – facilitated by a great improvement in the quality of linen-rag paper. No artist was better fitted by training to bring the process to maturity than Dürer, and his large print of St Eustace is outstanding in point of technique alone (**10,56**). Never before had an engraving suggested such subtle gradations of light and shade, such contrasts of texture and almost of color. The

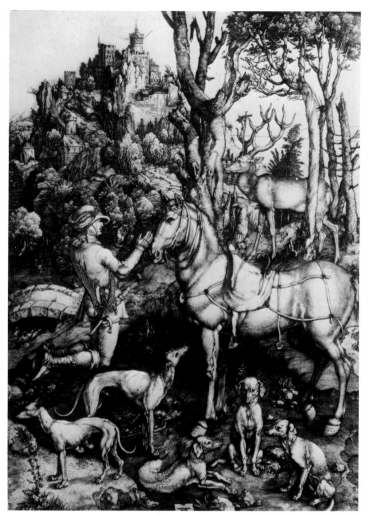

10,56 Albrecht Dürer, *St Eustace*, 1501. Engraving, 14 × 10⅕ins (35.5 × 25.9cm). British Museum, London.

germinates, grows and becomes fruitful of its kind.' Drawings testify to his tireless application; more than 1,700 survive, a far larger number than can be attributed to any earlier artist or any contemporary except, significantly, Leonardo da Vinci (see p. 473). He seems to have had an insatiable urge to draw whatever he observed, including his own face and body.

Few previous artists had portrayed themselves at all, but Dürer painted three half-lengths (two of them life-size) and made several drawings of himself. The first is a fairly large, meticulous silver-point made when he was no more than 13 (Albertina, Vienna). A sheet of sketches dating from his journeyman years includes his own face staring wistfully back from a mirror and beside it his elegantly long-fingered left hand held up to be drawn by the right, as if he wished to compare a reflection in a glass with directly observed reality (**10,57**). Below there is a crumpled cushion and there are more cushions on the back of the sheet, exercises in the technique of rendering an irregular object with hatched lines of varying density. At about the same date he drew his left leg in two positions (British Museum). It was not simply for want of other models that Dürer made these drawings. The self-portrait is marked with his initials – at a time when few

10,57 Albrecht Dürer, *Self-Portrait*, 1493. Drawing, 10⁹/₁₀ × 8ins (27.6 × 20.2cm). Metropolitan Museum of Art, New York (Robert Lehman Collection, 1975).

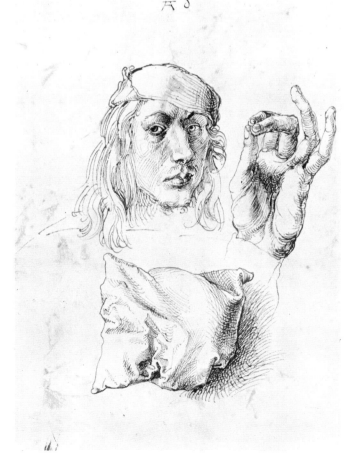

story of St Eustace converted to Christianity, while out hunting, by the vision of a stag with a crucifix between its antlers was a popular one and demanded a landscape setting. And Dürer's landscape reveals the unprecedented sharpness of his eye and cunning of his hand in recording plants and animals – dogs with their alert, knowing look, the horse restively shifting his hind leg, tufts of grass springing from the earth, tree-trunks weather-beaten into strange shapes, even a flight of birds (starlings to judge from its formation) circling the hilltop tower. Dürer delighted in drawing such things, which, in the *St Eustace* print, are invested with special meaning as a revelation of God in the beauty of nature and thus give universal relevance to the saint's miraculous vision. For this is no straightforward transcript of the visible world.

Kunst – a word which meant both knowledge and art in the modern sense of the term – 'is embedded in nature; he who can extract it has it', wrote Dürer. 'No man can ever make a beautiful image out of his private imagination unless he have replenished his mind by much painting from life. That can no longer be called private but has become *Kunst* acquired and gained by study, which

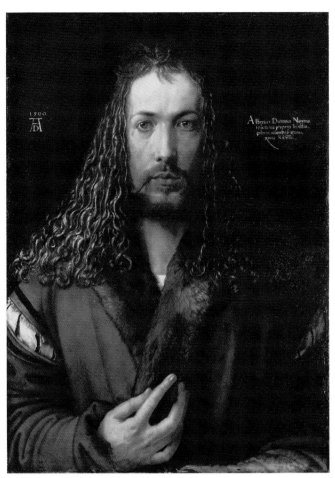

10,58 Albrecht Dürer, *Self-Portrait*, 1500.
Panel, 26⅖ × 19³/₁₀ins (67 × 49cm). Alte Pinakothek, Munich.

artists signed even their most highly finished paintings, let alone sketches – which suggests that he was already highly conscious of himself and of his artistic uniqueness.

Dürer was much preoccupied with his status. Although he had friends in the upper strata of Nuremberg society, notably Willibald Pirckheimer, he ranked among craftsmen along with all other painters and together with carpenters, tailors and so on. Painters were more highly

regarded only in Italy. There, as he wrote to Pirckheimer just before leaving Venice after his second visit in 1505–7, things were very different: 'here I am a gentleman'. A few years earlier he had, indeed, depicted himself very much as a well-dressed, even dandified gentleman in what appears to be the first independent self-portrait ever painted (Prado, Madrid). But another self-portrait is still more extraordinary, for here he took up the hieratic frontal pose normally reserved for kings and for Christ, to whose features he assimilated his own (**10,58**). This can be explained partly as a literal interpretation of the doctrine of the 'Imitation of Christ' and partly by Dürer's conviction that the artist's creative gift came from, and was at least to some extent part of, the creative power of God. In 1512 he was to write: 'This great art of painting has been held in high esteem by the mighty kings many hundred years ago. They made the outstanding artists rich and treated them with distinction because they felt that the great masters had an equality with God, as it is written. For, a good painter is full of figures, and if it were possible for him to live on forever he would always have to pour forth something new from the inner ideas of which Plato writes.'

The reference to Plato recalls the Florentine humanists; but Dürer's attitude was essentially different. He was not concerned with Plato's theory of ideas so much as with the God-given power of the artist to create. Towards the end of his life he wrote: 'Only the powerful artists will be able to understand this strange speech, that I speak the truth: one man may sketch something with his pen on half a sheet of paper in one day, or may cut it into a tiny piece of wood with his little iron, and it turns out to be better and more artistic than another's big work at which its author labours with the utmost diligence for a whole year. And this gift is miraculous. For God often gives the ability to learn and the insight to make something good to one man the like of whom nobody is found in his own days, and nobody has lived before him for a long time, and nobody comes after him very soon.' This remarkable statement of faith in the value of the individual could hardly have been made but for the great revolution in attitudes to the arts initiated by the Italian Renaissance, which had by the end of the fifteenth century achieved so much more than a revival of antique forms.

CHAPTER ELEVEN

THE SIXTEENTH CENTURY IN EUROPE

For the first time artists took their place among the great minds of the age – this is the outstanding feature in the history of sixteenth-century art. The century was dominated by a few artists of commanding personality, all Italians apart from Dürer, who was exceptional in other ways. Their fame and influence were international, spread by printed accounts of their careers and by reproductive engravings. They were courted by popes and emperors and princes, who competed with each other to possess examples of their work. Never before had individual artists won such extensive and exalted acclaim.

The idea that architecture, painting and sculpture were liberal arts, rather than branches of craftsmanship, was due mainly to Alberti (see p. 437). But Alberti had been primarily a writer. To him the knowledge and (strictly non-professional) practice of the visual arts were among the accomplishments of a 'universal man'. Now, with Leonardo, an artist had become a 'universal man'. The shift in emphasis is crucial. Leonardo da Vinci (1452–1519) was a scientist and daring experimental thinker, Michelangelo (1475–1564) a notable poet. It was, nevertheless, as supreme artists that they were extolled, together with Raphael (1483–1520) and Titian (c. 1490–1576), who had no other claims to fame. Their towering achievement overshadowed Western art until well into the nineteenth century.

In general history, however, the main event of the sixteenth century was the great movement for religious reform. By setting up the individual conscience as moral authority, the Protestant Reformation called into question not only the teachings and practices of the Catholic Church, but also the traditions and assumptions underlying European culture, including the visual arts. In spreading new ideas the recent invention of printing was instrumental, for it enabled the writings of the reformers to be disseminated both widely and quickly. What might otherwise have remained a minor dispute among theologians or the heresy of a local sect (like those led by John Wyclif in England and Jan Hus in Bohemia in the late

The visual arts	Historical landmarks
1501–3 Michelangelo, *David* (11,25)	**1503** Julius II elected Pope
c. 1505 Bosch, *Garden of Earthly Delights* (11,3)	**1507** Indulgence to rebuild St Peter's
1508–12 Michelangelo, Sistine Chapel ceiling (11,29; 30)	**1509** Watch invented (Germany)
1509–11 Raphael, Stanza (11,23)	**1515** Francis I king of France
c. 1510–15 Grünewald, *Isenheim Altarpiece* (11,5)	**1516** Ariosto, *Orlando Furioso*
1516–18 Titian, *Assumption* (11,45)	**1517** Martin Luther protests against indulgences
1519-34 Michelangelo, Medici Chapel (11,34)	**1519** Charles V elected Holy Roman Emperor
	1520 Luther excommunicated
	1522 First circumnavigation of the world completed
	1524-6 Peasants' War in Germany
c. 1523 Holbein, *Erasmus* (11,7)	**1527** Sack of Rome by German and Spanish mercenaries
1526 Dürer, *The Four Apostles* (11,10)	**1528** Castiglione, *The Book of the Courtier*
	1532 John Calvin begins work of Reformation in Paris
c. 1532 Correggio, *Danae* (11,56)	**1534** Jesuit order founded. Church of England declares itself independent of Rome
c. 1535 Parmigianino, *Madonna with the Long Neck* (11,58)	**1541** Calvin establishes Church at Geneva
1543 Titian, *Pope Paul III* (11,46)	**1545** Council of Trent begins (ends 1563)
1546–64 Michelangelo, St Peter's (11,41)	**1550** Pierre de Ronsard, *Odes*. Vasari, *Lives of the Painters*
1565 Tintoretto, *Crucifixion* (11,49) Bruegel, *Harvesters* (11,65)	**1558** Elizabeth I queen of England
	1566 Unrest in Spanish Netherlands
1567–9 Palladio, Villa Rotonda begun (11,53)	**1572** St Bartholomew's Day massacre of Protestants in Paris
1573–5 Giovanni Bologna, *Apollo* (11,63)	**1576** Dutch provinces unite against Spain
c. 1597–1604 El Greco, *Resurrection* (11,70)	**1596** Shakespeare, *Midsummer Night's Dream*
	1598 Edict of Nantes grants toleration of Protestants in France

fourteenth and early fifteenth centuries) immediately became an international issue on which every thinking Christian was obliged to take sides. Within a decade of 1517, when Martin Luther (1483–1546) launched his first protest in the small German city of Wittenberg, Western Christendom was irreparably split.

The Protestant Reformation polarized beliefs that originated much earlier. Humanists of the fifteenth century had extolled the importance of the individual. They looked sceptically on the Aristotelianism of medieval theology. They probed the scriptures with the tools of Classical scholarship. And it was the exemplary humanist Desiderius Erasmus (1466–1536) of Rotterdam who was said, already in the sixteenth century, to have 'laid the egg which Luther hatched'. But there were other, complementary tendencies in religious thought like that which had inspired such deeply personal, emotional and undogmatic writings as the *Revelations of Divine Love* by Julian of Norwich and found expression at a less intense level in what was called *Devotio moderna* – the new devotion. This was fostered by the Brethren of the Common Life, groups of pious laymen in the Netherlands and northern Germany who renounced private property to live a communal life without taking monastic vows. Its manual was the *Imitation of Christ* (probably by Thomas à Kempis, d. 1471), a work of anti-worldly and anti-intellectual piety uncomplicated by theological niceties and unencumbered by the popular medieval cults of saints, relics and pilgrimages. It was first printed in 1472; there were more than 20 editions before 1500, and it was repeatedly printed and reprinted in Latin, French, German and English versions in the early sixteenth century. It may have had almost as much influence as the vernacular translations of the Bible that proliferated at the same time. Admired by St Ignatius Loyola (c. 1491–1556), founder of the Society of Jesus, the *Imitation of Christ* testified to a movement for reform within the Roman Church, a movement which gathered strength in the early sixteenth century to become the self-transforming force of the so-called Counter-Reformation.

Luther, who also admired the *Imitation of Christ*, nevertheless followed the opposing tendency. By combining hostility to the ecclesiastical hierarchy and rejection of priestly mediation and outward forms with the widespread yearning for a more direct and personal religion, he evolved a new and distinctive theology of justification by faith – the main doctrinal point on which Protestants parted company from Catholics. It was a theology which placed the burden of deciding what is right and wrong on the individual conscience.

So far as the visual arts are concerned, humanism, the *Devotio moderna* and, later, the Counter-Reformation had a more positive influence than Protestantism. Luther's first protest was against the traffic in indulgences to raise money for rebuilding St Peter's (see p. 490). 'Cannot the Pope build one single basilica for St Peter out of his own purse rather than out of the money of the faithful poor?' he asked. But he was indifferent, rather than hostile, to painting and sculpture and opposed both the veneration and the destruction of religious images. Luther did not promote Iconoclasm. 'I approached the task of destroying images by first tearing them out of my heart', he wrote in 1525; 'for when they are no longer in the heart they can do no harm when seen by the eyes.' Crucifixes and representations of saints were, he ruled, 'praiseworthy and to be respected', but only as 'images for memorial or witness'. There were, however, more extreme Protestants who thought them idolatrous and sinful, notably John Calvin (1509–64), who dominated the Protestant world after the mid-century. Nevertheless, more than one great work of art was inspired by Protestantism during his life-time (11,9; 10).

REFORM AND EARLY SIXTEENTH-CENTURY ART IN THE NORTH

Although the forms, motifs and techniques of Italian Renaissance art spread amazingly quickly, as we have seen (p. 461), they were only gradually accepted in northern Europe. During the first quarter of the sixteenth century the new style coexisted with a still-vigorous Gothic. The tomb of Henry VII and his queen in Westminster Abbey, London, is a case in point (11,1). A conspicuous monument was needed to commemorate the founder of the

11,1 Pietro Torrigiano, Tomb of Henry VII, 1512–18. Gilt bronze figures, about life-size. Westminster Abbey, London.

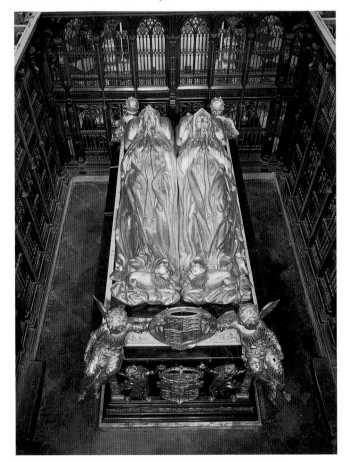

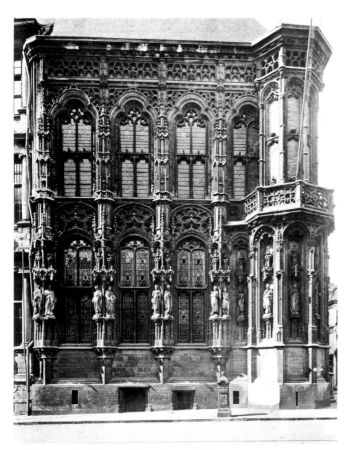

11,2 Town Hall, Ghent, Belgium, begun 1518.

11,3 Hieronymus Bosch, *Garden of Earthly Delights* triptych, left panel *Garden of Eden*, centre panel *The World before the Flood*, right panel *Hell*, c. 1505. Side panels 86 × 36ins (218.5 × 91.5cm), centre panel 86 × 76ins (218.5 × 195cm). Prado, Madrid.

Tudor dynasty, who had re-established royal power in England after 30 years of civil war, and his son Henry VIII looked to Italy for a sculptor. The commission went to the Florentine Pietro Torrigiano (1472–1528), a fellow student with Michelangelo (whose nose he broke in a fight) under Donatello's pupil Bertoldo di Giovanni (see p. 440). The tomb he created is very obviously Italian, with naked *putti* and delicate Classical pilasters surrounding the sarcophagus, angels with alert little Florentine faces seated at its corners, and the effigies of the king and queen sensitively modelled with controlled naturalism.

That the Italian Renaissance style should have been adopted for dynastic monuments in both France and England testifies to its prestige in the north. Already, it seems to have been associated not only with the new humanist learning but also with the new ideal of a monarch who was a patron of scholarship and the arts as well as a military leader and a divinely appointed ruler. The tomb of Henry VII was, nevertheless, surrounded by a bronze screen in the English 'Perpendicular Gothic' style that echoes the flattened Gothic arches of the chapel in which it stands (begun 1503). Even after the tomb was finished, niches in the chapel's walls were filled with statues of saints which adhere so closely to Gothic conventions that they might be mistaken for work of at least a century earlier.

The 'Perpendicular' style is peculiar to England. First developed in the mid-fourteenth century, it persisted until late in the sixteenth (though mainly for secular buildings after the English Reformation in 1532). In fifteenth-century France, Gothic had been elaborated into the 'Flamboyant' style with intricate curvilinear tracery which was not outmoded until the mid-sixteenth century. A more robust but equally rich version of Gothic was evolved in the Low Countries. The Town Hall of

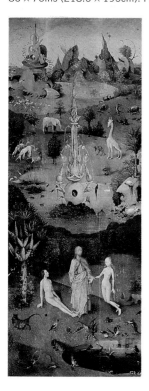

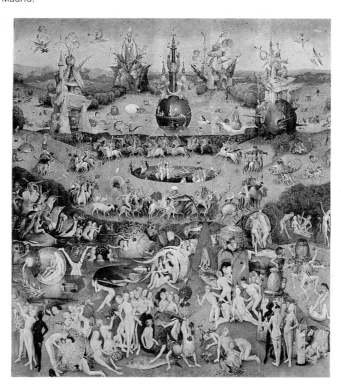

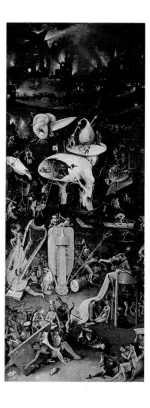

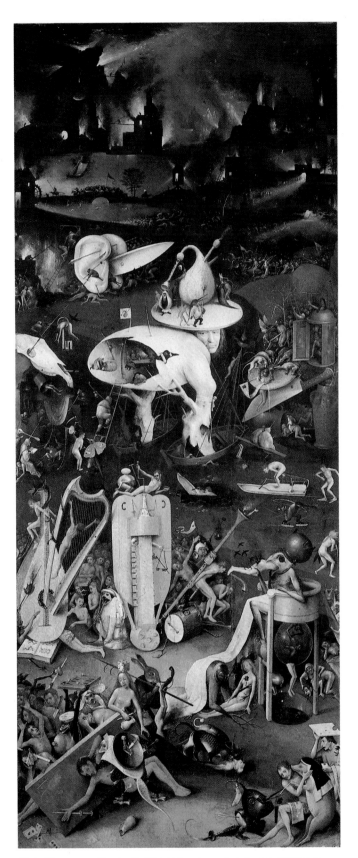

11,4 Hieronymus Bosch, *Hell* (right-hand panel of *Garden of Earthly Delights*), c. 1505. 86 × 36ins (218.5 × 91.5cm). Prado, Madrid.

Ghent is a notable example, one in which the opulence of a great trading centre found expression in an abundance of busy carving (**11,2**). It was begun in 1518, one year after the regent of Flanders, Margaret of Austria, had an addition to her palace at Mechlin (Malines) built in a pure Renaissance style. There cannot be much doubt that in each instance the style was deliberately chosen – the wealthy citizens of Ghent clinging conservatively to the Gothic associated with their civic liberties, the regent adopting the new Classicizing style patronized by the ruling families in the south.

Hieronymus Bosch

In Netherlandish painting the tradition established by Jan van Eyck (see p. 430) lived on into the second decade of the sixteenth century. But the most interesting painter of the time, Hieronymus Bosch (Jeroen van Aken, c. 1450–1516), had more distant artistic origins. Living in the provincial city of s'Hertogenbosch (generally called Den Bosch, hence his name) and apparently working in isolation – though conversant with a wide range of religious, astrological, astronomical and travel literature – he evolved an imagery of disturbing individuality. A large triptych more than 7 feet (215cm) high is perhaps the finest, but also the most perplexing, of his works (**11,3**). It is now called *Garden of Earthly Delights*, although its precise subject-matter and original function remain obscure (for it cannot have been intended as an altarpiece). In the late sixteenth century it was called *Lust* or *Strawberry Painting*. The most convincing interpretation is that the outer panels, when closed, represent the world under the flood, the central panel the world before the flood, flanked by the Garden of Eden on the left, and hell on the right, thus illustrating the origin, indulgence and punishment of sin.

No paintings of the period are more remote from the spirit of the Italian Renaissance than those of Bosch, an almost exact contemporary of Leonardo da Vinci. Bosch stresses the frailty and wickedness, not the beauty and nobility, of humankind. The pleasures of the flesh, which Italian artists celebrated, he condemned as severely as the author of the *Imitation of Christ* – 'Oh how brief, how false, how inordinate and filthy, are all those pleasures!' Musical instruments, which to Giorgione and other Italian artists symbolized a soothing and celestial harmony, were for Bosch the agents of the Devil. In his view of hell they surround the damned, one of whom is crucified on a harp. Perhaps he had in mind the words of Isaiah (5: 11-14):

> *Woe unto them that rise up early in the morning, that they may follow strong drink; that continue until night, till wine inflames them! And the harp, and the viol, the tabret and pipe, and wine are in their feasts; but they regard not the work of the Lord . . . . Therefore hell hath enlarged herself, and opened her mouth without measure: and their glory, and their multitude and their pomp, and he that rejoiceth, shall descend into it.*

Bosch's view of hell is not, however, as was that of medieval artists, a mere aggregate of symbols. His is truly

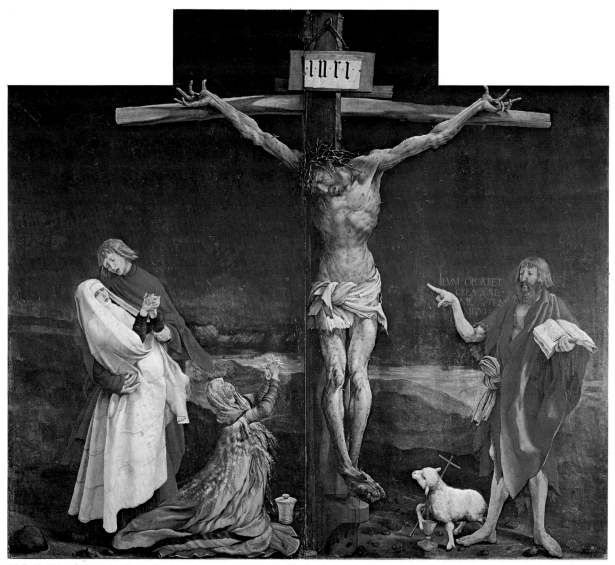

11,5 Matthias Grünewald, *Isenheim Altarpiece*, centre panel, c. 1510–15. Panel, 8ft × 10ft 1in (2.4 × 3m). Musée Unterlinden, Colmar.

a vision. A hallucinatory, unbounded, fluid space, seen from far away and above, is rendered with complete command of the new techniques of pictorial representation (**11,4**). In the chaotic area between the foreground and the burning buildings on the horizon, human figures, demons and various strange and incongruous objects seem to float, all depicted with a delicate precision and sense of form which give them a weird reality. Even the most bizarre are uncomfortably tangible presences. It is this that differentiates them from the demons and monsters abounding in medieval art (9,26). 'He endeavoured to find for his fantastic pictures the most out-of-the-way things, but they were always true to nature', a Spaniard wrote of him in the mid-sixteenth century. Despite the prevalent Classicism of the time, his work was greatly admired and collected, by Philip II of Spain (Titian's patron) among others, and copied in costly tapestry.

GRÜNEWALD

The work of another German painter, Mathis Gothardt Neithardt (d. 1528), enjoyed so little posthumous renown that his very name was for long forgotten. Since the late

seventeenth century he has been known as Grünewald. His major work is the large polyptych he painted for the high altar of the hospital chapel in the monastery of St Anthony of Isenheim (Alsace). The *Crucifixion* (**11,5**) is depicted on the outer side of doors which were opened on Sundays to reveal paintings of the *Annunciation*, *Nativity* and *Resurrection* and, on feast-days, the inner sculptured *corpus* (see p. 469). Of all the tortured Christs in the history of Western art, this makes the most violent impact. His body, torn and bruised by scourging and with a ragged stained cloth around the loins, hangs heavily on the cross, head slumped forwards, eyes closed and mouth open after the last breath of life has escaped. The fingers of the pierced hands strain convulsively upwards and blood flows from the wound in the contorted feet, but physical agony has ceased and the flesh has already begun to turn gangrenous. To suggest the weight of the body, Christ's arms have been disproportionately lengthened. He is also much larger than the four figures on the ground, St John the Baptist, St John the Divine, who supports the fainting Virgin, and St Mary Magdalene kneeling, hands clenched in a paroxysm of grief and prayer. A desolate stony landscape and louring sky close in and complete this harrowing image, painted in quivering brush-strokes, with anguished angularities of line and shrill contrasts of color.

The iconographical program of the altarpiece seems to have been inspired by the mystical writings of St Bridget of Sweden (1303–73), first printed at the end of the fifteenth century. But the *Crucifixion* on its outer doors had a particular purpose and meaning, being permanently visible in the monastic hospital's chapel. There patients prepared themselves spiritually before undergoing medical treatment (mainly for diseases of the blood and skin, including syphilis, which had suddenly struck Europe in the late 1490s). Help for the sick was commonly invoked from the four saints below the cross and also from those on the flanking wings, St Sebastian (see pp. 455–6) and St Anthony, patron of the religious order which ran this and many other hospitals. Grünewald's Crucifixion scene, however, transcends the popular cult of miracle-working saints and reflects profounder beliefs about the meaning of physical suffering. Although sickness was sometimes regarded as punishment for sin, it was also interpreted as an act of grace which could restore the health of the soul. Nothing is 'more profitable to man's salvation than suffering', wrote the author of the *Imitation of Christ*; 'the more the flesh is wasted by affliction, so much the more is the spirit strengthened by inward grace.' Suffering had to be endured for Christ's sake, as the human equivalent of his Passion, and Grünewald's agonized image was intended in this way as a spiritual aid to the sick and infirm.

In form, the *Isenheim Altarpiece* or retable (see Glossary) belongs to a type extremely popular in Germany in the second half of the fifteenth century and first quarter of the sixteenth. It consists of a central element called the *corpus* with sculptured figures, a high superstructure of interlaced Gothic tracery and a base like a predella. Except on feast-days, the *corpus* was concealed behind doors or wings often painted outside and carved in low relief inside. Pride of place was thus given to sculpture rather than painting. The favourite material in south Germany was light, close-grained and easily worked lime-wood, which permitted effects of the greatest delicacy, though it also imposed limitations since only the outer shell of the tree-trunk can be satisfactorily carved. Concave forms and strong verticals determined by the organic structure of the tree tend to predominate. The wood was either coated with gesso and painted naturalistically or, from the late fifteenth century, left plain and varnished.

The makers of these retables were independent artists, in social standing and organization more like panel painters than medieval sculptors and stone-carvers who had been employed as day-labourers in the masons' lodges attached to the great cathedrals and churches. The emergence of these wood-carvers in the second decade of the fifteenth century marks the beginning of large-scale independent sculpture in northern Europe – that is, sculpture independent of architecture. Their carvings are among the outstanding products of the new urban culture of Germany which appeared on the recovery of industry and trade after the devastation of the Black Death (see p. 416). For although their major works were for churches, they were commissioned less frequently by the clergy than by rich merchants, city councils, guilds and lay confraternities. And much of their small-scale work was offered for sale ready-made, e.g. crucifixes and figurines of saints, often bought for private houses. Alongside other skilled craftsmen and tradesmen, they belonged to the middle rank of the society for which they worked and were members of guilds with a voice on the city council. One of the most successful, Tilman Riemenschneider (c. 1460–531), became mayor of Würzburg in 1520–1. The changing social climate that permitted such independence also fostered competitiveness; and this may largely account for the bravura displays of technical skill and the development of strongly marked workshop styles, as means of advertisement no less than self-expression. The long, lean faces and spiralling locks of hair in Riemenschneider's figures, for instance, might be regarded as his hallmarks.

Cross-currents of civic, religious and artistic ideas meet in an imposing retable commissioned by the corporation of Rothenburg-on-the-Tauber, an imperial free city (i.e. one that was self-governing under the emperor). Local craftsmen were entrusted with the framework, but Riemenschneider, working in Würzburg some 30 miles (48km) away, was engaged to carve the figures (**11,6**). Its purpose, to enshrine a relic of Christ's blood which drew

11,6 Tilman Riemenschneider, *Last Supper* from the *Altar of the Holy Blood*, 1499–1505. Limewood, figures up to 3ft 3ins (1m) high. St Jakobskirche, Rothenburg-on-the-Tauber.

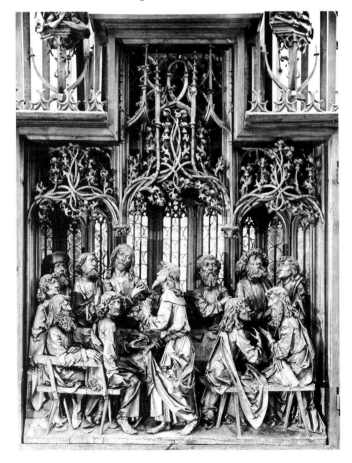

pilgrims to Rothenburg, links it with medieval Catholicism. But in other respects it reflects contemporary attitudes, especially the rising tide of hostility to elaborate religious images as being both temptations to idolatry and vain displays of wealth and pride rather than true piety. Riemenschneider's retable was relatively inexpensive, costing less than a fifth of the sum paid by a rich merchant to Veit Stoss (c. 1450–1533) for the Annunciation group in the church of St Lorenz in Nuremberg (10,3). There is no showy paint or costly gilding on the retable at Rothenburg. The figures in the group of the Last Supper have a sober rustic simplicity. Airs and graces, the elegant Gothic play of curve and counter-curve have been renounced, and with them the complex theological symbolism of medieval art. Riemenschneider returned to the letter of St John's Gospel and gives a straightforward account of the moment when Christ answered the disciples' questioning as to which of them would betray him: 'He it is, to whom I shall give the sop when I have dipped it. And when he had dipped the sop he gave it to Judas Iscariot.' The figures communicate with one another, not with the spectator, and the central position normally reserved for Christ is occupied by Judas, as if to emphasize the illustrative and didactic, rather than devotional, function of the carving.

11,7 Hans Holbein the Younger, *Erasmus of Rotterdam*, c. 1523. Panel, 30 × 20¼ins (76.2 × 51.4cm). Private collection.

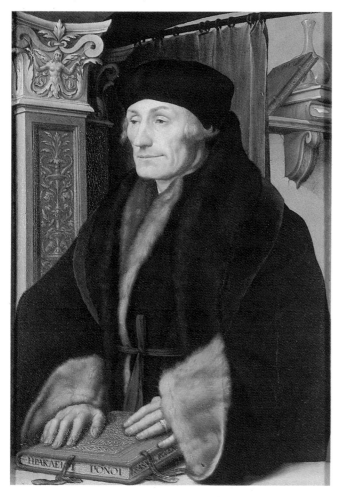

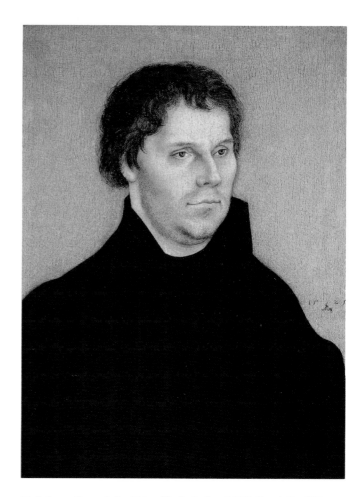

11,8 Lucas Cranach the Elder, *Martin Luther*, 1533. Panel, 8 × 5¾ins (20.5 × 14.5cm). Herzog-Anton-Ulrich-Museum, Brunswick, Germany.

Protestant objections to religious images could hardly have been more effectively forestalled, and this may account for the preservation of the retable after Rothenburg adopted the reformed faith in 1524.

PROTESTANT ART

Riemenschneider supported the peasants against the landed nobility and higher clergy in the Peasants' War of 1524–6, although he was not converted to Protestantism, as was Grünewald, who also sided with the peasants. In the following years both suffered, like other German artists, from a sharp decline in patronage. A print of the 1530s illustrates the plight of sculptors with the lamentable case of one who had been obliged to turn soldier for lack of work. Others were forced to emigrate, including even well-known artists such as Hans Holbein the Younger (1497–1543), who left Basel in 1526 with a letter of introduction from Erasmus saying, 'here the arts are freezing: he goes to England in order to scrape together a little money.' Holbein was welcomed in London and after 1532, when Henry VIII formally ousted the Pope as head of the Church of England, he settled there, eventually becoming court artist.

Born in Augsburg, Holbein spent his youth in Basel, one of the great centres of printing and book production, of humanism and, later, of Protestantism. At first he worked mainly as a religious artist. But he drew illustrations in a copy of Erasmus's sharp attack on the abuses of the Church, *In Praise of Folly* (1509). And after Erasmus settled in Basel in 1521 Holbein painted several portraits of him. One commissioned by Erasmus himself to send to a friend in England is almost emblematical of the great cause for which his name stood in the minds of his admirers (**11,7**). It shows him standing beside a pilaster delicately carved with Classical motifs and resting his sensitive fingers on a book inscribed in Greek 'The Herculean Labours' and in Latin 'of Erasmus of Rotterdam'. The origins of his scholarship are thus made quite explicit, but the purity and truth of his Christian humanism are also alluded to (in the decanter of clear water). It is the image of a new and peculiarly Renaissance type of man, the aristocrat of the intellect.

In Protestant countries there was a demand for portraits of reformers, including Erasmus (although his desire for Christian unity prevented him from abandoning the Catholic Church), and especially of Luther himself, of whom those by Lucas Cranach the Elder (1473–1553) are outstanding (**11,8**). They are the most numerous Protestant works of art produced in the sixteenth century, apart from satirical prints. Attempts were, however, made to express Lutheran ideas in a 'reformed' religious art by Lucas Cranach the Younger (1515–53) and others, above all by Holbein and Dürer. Holbein's *Allegory of the Old and New Testaments* is a doctrinally didactic work, which subtly transforms the significance of traditional Christian imagery (**11,9**). Instead of presenting the Old Testament as a prefiguration of the New, he shows the two in antithesis to underline the differences between old (Roman Catholic) and new (Lutheran) teaching. Moses receiving the Law on Mount Sinai, for instance, is contrasted with the Virgin, towards whom the infant Christ descends bearing a cross. Adam and Eve repenting their sins, the consequence of which is death (a skeleton in a coffin), are contrasted with Christ teaching and, below, trampling on sin and death as he rises from the tomb – with the inscription 'our victory'. In the centre, beneath a tree dead on one side and in leaf on the other, a nude figure representing humankind is seated flanked by Isaiah and St John the Baptist, who direct his attention to the Incarnation, Crucifixion and Resurrection of Christ, which were, for Luther, the essentials of Christianity. In this overt way the Roman Catholic cult (symbolized by Law in various guises on the left side of the painting) is contrasted with Protestant belief in salvation by faith and grace.

Dürer's approach was less militant. In 1519 he underwent a spiritual crisis from which he emerged a fervent admirer of Luther, 'the Christian man who has helped me

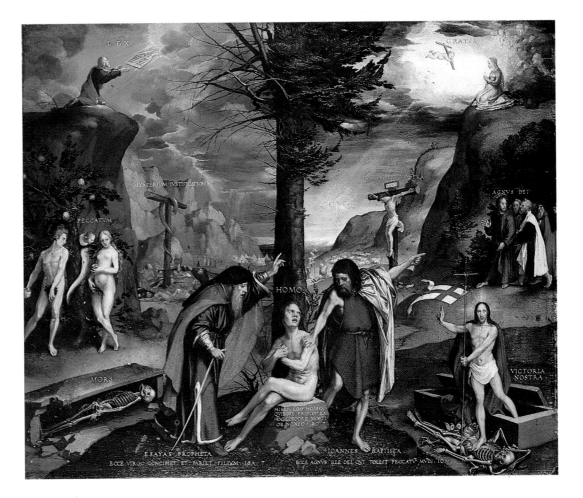

11,9 Hans Holbein the Younger, *Allegory of the Old and New Testaments*, c. 1530. Oil on panel, 19³/₄ × 24ins (50.2 × 61cm). National Gallery of Scotland, Edinburgh.

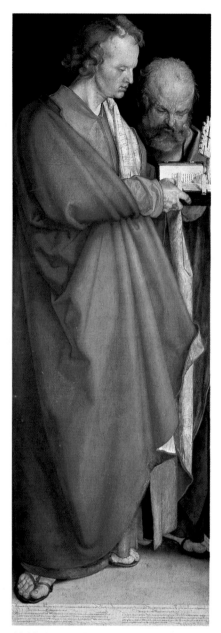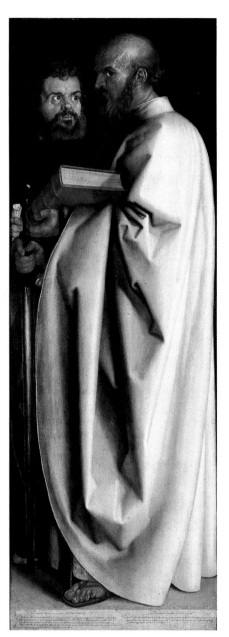

11,10 Albrecht Dürer, *The Four Apostles*, 1526. Panels, each 85 × 30ins (216 × 76.2cm). Alte Pinakothek, Munich.

out of great anxieties' as he called him. The iconoclastic riots and the questioning of the value and function of art that accompanied Luther's preaching and writing deeply affected Dürer and for some years he pondered the uses and abuses of art. In 1526 he presented to the city council of Nuremberg *The Four Apostles*, probably at least partly in gratitude for the peaceful outcome of the religious crisis the city had just gone through when it accepted Lutheranism (**11,10**). The paintings were to be hung in the city hall, not in a church. (They were never, as has sometimes been thought, intended to form part of a triptych.) Four saints or witnesses, three apostles and one evangelist, are depicted. In the left-hand panel St John, Luther's 'favourite evangelist', overshadows St Peter, the founder of the Roman See; in the other panel prominence is given to St Paul, often regarded as the spiritual father of Protes-

tantism, who stands in front of the evangelist St Mark. The painting is unmistakably Protestant.

Dürer is known to have intended the figures to exemplify also the four humours or temperaments – sanguine, phlegmatic, choleric and melancholic – associated with the elements forming the basic substance of all creation. These humours were believed to have been perfectly balanced in Adam and Eve; but since the Fall one predominated over the others in every human body and mind. In so far as the theory of the humours accounts for physical and psychological diversity, it embodied Protestant beliefs about human nature, and thus *The Four Apostles* expresses another aspect of Protestantism. But Dürer went further, illustrating Protestantism at a deeper level. His four figures constitute a divine whole greater than the sum of its parts, like the Lutheran conception of the

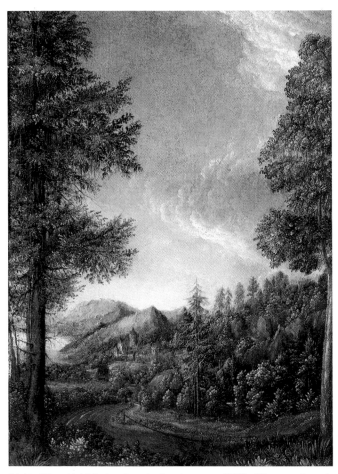

11,11 Albrecht Altdorfer, *Danube Landscape*, c. 1530. Oil on parchment on beechwood, 11⅘ × 8⅗ins (30 × 22cm). Alte Pinakothek, Munich.

Reformed Church, composed of equal individuals without a hierarchy.

Beneath the figures Dürer inscribed lengthy quotations from their writings, in Luther's translation of the New Testament (1522), beginning with a warning to the secular powers against taking 'human misguidance for the Divine word' in these perilous times. He was alluding not only to the Roman Church but also to extreme forms of Protestantism, which had recently come to the surface during the Peasants' War. These he firmly denounced, as did Luther. So the paintings may perhaps also be interpreted as a plea for balance and sanity in a world torn by dissension. Their dignified simplicity and restraint bear the same message. 'When I was young I craved variety and novelty', Dürer told his friend Melanchthon, a Protestant humanist; 'now in my old age, I have come to see . . . that simplicity is the ultimate goal of art.' He eschewed all superfluous detail, rendering draperies in broad swathes of contrasting colors without ornament. There are no haloes. But the figures have a monumental stability and solidity, a serenity and nobility which sanctify them more truly than would any outward sign of holiness.

In his last years Dürer almost totally abandoned secular work, devoting himself mainly to prints of 'apostolic' simplicity illustrating themes so fundamental to Christian

belief that they transcend sectarian differences. (Protestants who were wary of painted images had few objections to prints of sacred subjects.) Other artists with Lutheran sympathies were less rigorous. Albrecht Altdorfer (c. 1480–1538), who was instrumental in bringing a Protestant preacher to the city of Regensburg (of which he was a councillor), painted both sensuous mythological and traditional religious pictures. His drawings, etchings and oil paintings of the rolling hills, rocks, streams and pine trees of the Danube valley may, nevertheless, have had new religious implications (**11,11**). Without any figures or narrative content, they are among the earliest pure landscapes in European art and seem to reflect, as well, ideas then current among Protestant mystics. 'As the air fills everything and is not confined to one place', wrote Sebastian Franck in *Paradoxa* (1533), 'as the light of the sun overfloods the whole earth, is not on earth and none the less makes all things on earth verdant, thus God dwells in everything, and everything dwells in Him.'

THE HIGH RENAISSANCE IN ITALY

The first quarter of the sixteenth century was one of political stress and almost constant warfare in Italy. Florence, still an important artistic centre, passed from republicanism to the autocratic rule of the Medici. Northern Italy was twice invaded by the French, who occupied Milan from 1499 to 1512 and from 1515 to 1525. The Papacy was actively engaged in a struggle to extend its temporal power – Pope Julius II was almost continuously at the head of his troops on military campaigns – and was only checked by the intervention of the Holy Roman Emperor. In 1527 Rome itself was sacked by German and Spanish mercenaries of the army of Charles V. Yet it was during this extremely turbulent period that the art of the High Renaissance came into being, an art of serene and elevated conception, of great but controlled energy and, above all, of Classical balance. It was the creation of a small number of pre-eminent artists – pre-eminent in their own day as in ours – notably Leonardo da Vinci (1452–1519), Michelangelo Buonarroti (1475–1564) and Raphael (Raffaello Sanzio, 1483–1520). Each one was very much an individualist and although sparks of inspiration flashed between them they never formed a group. Supreme technical accomplishment, perfect co-ordination of mind, eye and hand, was attained by all three. Problems which had vexed earlier artists they effortlessly resolved. In their work artistic form is always beautifully adjusted to intellectual content.

LEONARDO DA VINCI

Looking back from the mid-sixteenth century, the Florentine painter, architect and biographer of artists Giorgio Vasari (1511–74) described how the 'revival' of the arts led, under Leonardo, to what Vasari called the 'modern' style, notable for 'boldness of design, the subtlest imitation of all the details of nature, good rule, better order, correct proportions and divine grace, prolific and profound, endowing his figures with motion and breath'. The high position given to Leonardo is the more remarkable in view of the small number of works he completed. His first major painting, *Adoration of the Magi* (Uffizi, Florence), begun in 1481, was left unfinished and so, too, was his large battle scene in the Palazzo Vecchio, Florence (1502–5, invisible since the mid-sixteenth century). His equestrian monument to Francesco Sforza of Milan was never cast and the full-size clay model perished. None of the buildings he designed was erected. Nor did he ever prepare for publication his several thousand pages of illustrated notes on artistic theory, human anatomy, natural history, the flight of birds, the properties of water and numerous mechanical contrivances. 'Great minds often produce more by working less, for with their intellect they search for conceptions and form those perfect ideas which afterwards they merely express with their hands', he wrote. Such ideas presuppose that 'art' is much more than 'craft' and lead directly to the notion of a great artist as 'a genius'.

Leonardo grew up in the Florence of the humanists but took little interest in their Classical erudition and Neoplatonic speculations. He did not learn Latin until he was 40. So he was as independent of Classical as of medieval thought – perhaps the first thinker to be so. Trained as a painter and sculptor, almost certainly in the studio of Andrea del Verrocchio (see p. 443), his interests soon expanded to embrace not only all the arts, but all natural phenomena. His boundless curiosity and appetite for knowledge gradually focused on what Aristotle had called 'entelechy', the condition in which a potentiality becomes an actuality. Hence his preoccupation with the

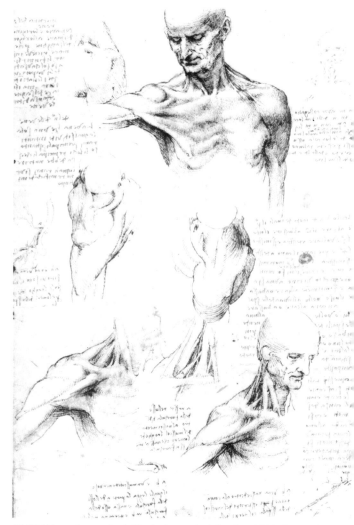

11,12 *Above* Leonardo da Vinci, *Anatomical Studies*, 1510. Pen and ink, 11⅕ × 7ins (28.4 × 19.7cm). Royal Collection, Windsor Castle. Reproduced by gracious permission of Her Majesty The Queen.

11,13 Leonardo da Vinci, *Last Supper*, c. 1495–8. Mural painting, 15ft 1⅛ins × 28ft 10½ins (4.6 × 8.56m). S Maria delle Grazie, Milan.

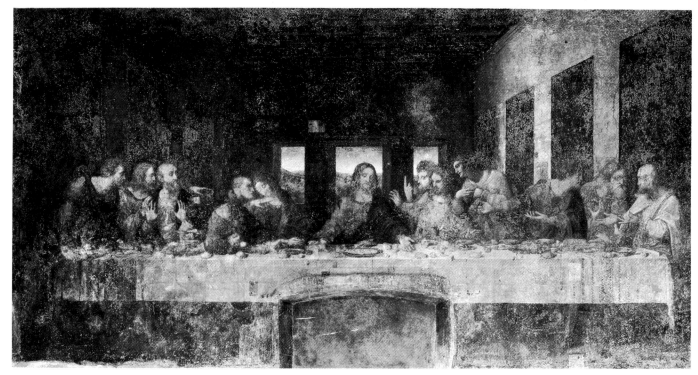

germinal stage in both nature and art, the moment a body is organically complete though still immature, or that in which a painting is fully realized though not yet finished. His passion to understand the structure of the human body led him to dissect corpses and make the first accurate anatomical drawings (**11,12**). Leonardo developed his astonishingly bold empirical approach at a time when scientists still accepted as authorities such ancient Greek and Roman writers as the first- and second-century AD Dioscorides and Galen. 'It seems to me that those sciences are vain and full of error which are not born of experience, mother of all certainty, first-hand experience which in its origins or means or ends has passed through one of the five senses', he wrote. 'And if we doubt the certainty of everything that passes through the senses, how much more ought we to doubt things contrary to these senses such as the existence of God or of the soul or of similar things over which there is always dispute and contention.'

Leonardo's innovatory genius first found full expression in his *Last Supper* (**11,13**). In order, presumably, to avoid the cramping limitations of fresco, which obliges a painter to finish one section of a wall at a time, he experimented with a medium which would allow him to work over the whole composition simultaneously, like an oil painting. Unfortunately the new medium proved not to be durable and there were already signs of decay during his life-time. In general conception his composition follows recent Florentine precedents, with figures set in a pictorial space which extends the real space of the refectory. But the scene is defined more precisely and invested with a wholly new animation. Instead of depicting the disciples in an undifferentiated line, he gathered them in threes, creating a network of formal and emotional connections binding each figure to his neighbours and to Christ in the centre. By selecting the pregnant moment in the Gospel story when the disciples ask Christ which of them would betray him – 'Lord, is it I?' – he was able to depict each one as an individual reacting in a different and psychologically revealing way. He dispensed not only with all the discursive details in which earlier fifteenth-century painters had revelled, but also the emblems and inscriptions previously used to identify the various figures. By facial expression and gesture the disciples identify themselves. They are all larger and – apart from Judas, whose head is in shadow – nobler than life, needing no haloes to indicate their sanctity, although Christ's divine aura is suggested by the natural light from the window framing his head. Leonardo was not a devout Christian, he might almost be called an agnostic, but by translating what had previously been represented as an hieratic ritual into a scene of human tragedy, he paradoxically deepened its religious significance. No more than a few years later, as we have seen, Riemenschneider in Germany represented the succeeding moment in the story of the Last Supper, also as a human drama but one enacted by peasants and lacking both the psychological subtlety and the sense of spiritual elevation conveyed by Leonardo's complex composition.

Careful study of plants and anatomy and the principles of organic growth led Leonardo to construct his paintings according to a similar system, with every part integrated in such a way that there are no apparent beginnings or ends, no sharp transitions. In his *Virgin and Child with St Anne*, for example, he entwined the three figures into a pyramid, within which forms grow out of one another as naturally as a leaf from its stem or a branch from a tree-trunk (**11,14**). This picture also illustrates, much better than the *Last Supper*, the pictorial techniques which were either perfected or, in effect, invented by Leonardo and very soon transformed European painting into a form of art unlike any practised elsewhere in the world: *chiaroscuro* (light and dark modulated to create effects of relief or modelling), *sfumato* (misty, soft blending of colors) and aerial perspective, which indicates distance by grading tones and muting color contrasts. Comparison with such a work of the mid-fifteenth century as Piero della Francesca's *Baptism* (10,40) marks the difference between two ways of seeing and painting. Whereas Piero's landscape background is rendered with telescopic vision and painted like the foreground in local colors (see Glossary), Leonardo's distant mountains melt into a grayish-blue haze. The figures in the *Baptism* have an adamantine solidity; those in the *Virgin and Child with St Anne* have no less weight yet breathe with a yielding softness. Leonardo's picture

11,14 Leonardo da Vinci, *Virgin and Child with St Anne*, 1508–10. Panel, 5ft 6⅛ins × 4ft 3¼ins (1.68 × 1.3m). Louvre, Paris.

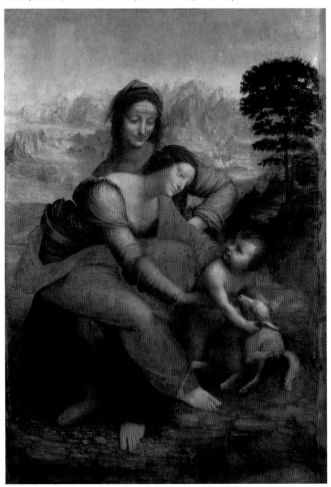

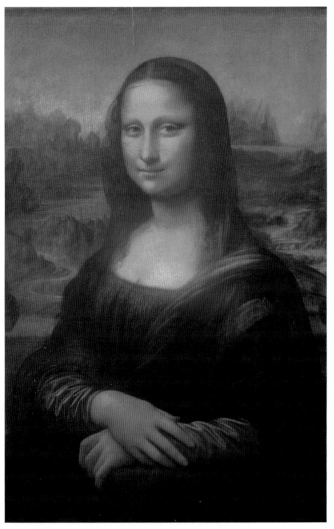

11,15 Leonardo da Vinci, *Mona Lisa*, 1503–6.
Panel, 30¼ × 21 ins (76.8 × 53.3cm). Louvre, Paris.

presents an image of figures in a landscape closer to visual experience, though veiled in a mysterious unworldly atmosphere. Calculated imprecision in rendering the most expressive facial features, the eyes and the corners of the mouths, gives to the faces strangely ambiguous half-smiles, as remote and haunting as that of Leonardo's *Mona Lisa* (**11,15**), the most famous portrait ever painted.

HARMONY, UNITY AND RAPHAEL

Leonardo opened the eyes of artists to great new possibilities in painting, even artists as temperamentally opposed to him as Fra Bartolommeo (1472–1517), 20 years his junior and a man of deeply pious character, who had been inspired by Savonarola to become a Dominican friar. Fra Bartolommeo's finest work is an altarpiece commissioned by Ferry Carondelet, the imperial ambassador to Rome, who is portrayed kneeling on the right, looking at the spectator and pointing to the Virgin and Child borne aloft by angels (**11,16**). Figures are depicted as three-dimensional forms made visible by light, like Leonardo's, but without his hazy atmospheric effects. Their apparently natural poses

are governed by the principle of *contrapposto*, whereby one part of a body is twisted in a direction opposite to another – a right arm counterpoising a left leg, for instance. Two angels in the upper corners are not only posed in this counterbalancing way but also, unlike the mirror-image pairs in earlier art, complement one another, introducing a rhythm of correspondence which runs through the whole composition and binds it together. One gesture echoes another across the panel, holding the gentle, unemphatic movements of the figures in an equilibrium which steadies and concentrates thought, creating a piously reflective mood. A similar holy calm pervades the tranquil landscape stretching far into the distance beyond the door, through which the Virgin and Child appear to have entered.

In painting this altarpiece, Fra Bartolommeo was confronted or confronted himself with the problem of reconciling three-dimensional naturalism with symmetry and poise – the natural with the contrived. The problem taxed the abilities of all High Renaissance artists, as can be seen in Raphael's many ingenious variations on the Madonna and Child theme. In more than one he reached a solution so convincing that it has the apparent simplicity and inevitability of a single axiomatic thought (**11,17**). With figures as natural in pose as in gesture, yet forming a most unnaturally well-balanced design of soft, sweetly melting curves within the curved picture shape, the finest retain, none the less, all the spirituality of an icon. Circularity has complex implications in a devotional image for Christian prayer and meditation – like the cosmic diagrams in a Buddhist *mandala* (see pp. 232, 254). As the writer Baldassare

11,16 Fra Bartolommeo, *Carondelet Altarpiece*, c. 1511. Panel, 8ft 6⅖ins × 7ft 6½ins (2.55 × 2.29m). Besançon Cathedral.

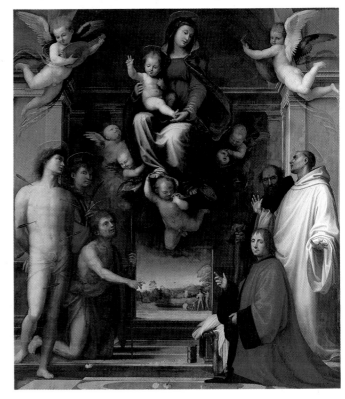

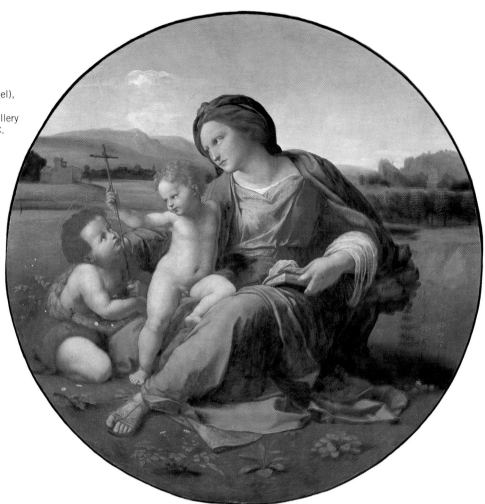

11,17 Raphael, *Alba Madonna*, c. 1510. Canvas (originally panel), 37¾ins (94.5cm) diameter. National Gallery of Art, Washington DC.

Castiglione, who was a friend of Raphael at about this date, put it: 'Beauty is born of God, and is like a circle of which goodness is the centre: and, just as no circle can exist without a centre, so no beauty can exist without goodness.'

The idea of grouping the Virgin and Child with the infant St John the Baptist (an incident never mentioned in the Gospels) was Leonardo's. And it was from Leonardo that Raphael derived his organic system of composition and his subtle use of *chiaroscuro*. Not for him, however, Leonardo's mysterious twilight. Raphael's figures are bathed in the even, limpid sunshine of a mellow summer's day and set in an untroubled landscape with an idyllic distant view of a farmstead and rolling hills. Nor is there any Leonardesque ambiguity in the loving expressions with which they gaze upon one another.

The same ideal of harmonious unity inspired architects as well as painters. Some 50 years later, Palladio wrote that Donato Bramante (1444–1514) was 'the first to bring to light good and beautiful architecture which from the time of the ancients to his day had been forgotten'. In view of the great achievements of Alberti, Brunelleschi and others of their time, this may seem a strange judgement. But Bramante was more radical than any of his predecessors and with the Tempietto (**11,18**), to which Palladio specifically referred, he initiated a new phase in Renaissance architecture. He renounced all superfluous decoration and restored the correct usage of the Classical orders in this little building – a *tholos* surrounded by a

11,18 Donato Bramante, the Tempietto, S Pietro in Montorio, Rome, c. 1504–after 1510.

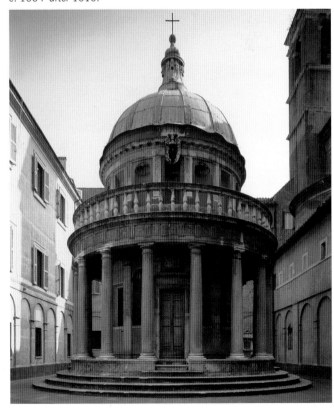

Bramante's Tempietto

ALBERTI, LEONARDO AND THE IDEAL RENAISSANCE CHURCH

The quest for the perfect Christian church obsessed Renaissance architects. How could Christian and humanist ideals be reconciled architecturally? Bramante's Tempietto (11,18) was an attempt to solve the problem. The aim – to achieve a complete Christian–humanist fusion – is manifest not only in such details as the combination of antique Roman Doric columns with, on the entablature, the keys of St Peter and the liturgical instruments of the Mass, but in the whole conception of the building. The traditional circular form of Early Christian *martyria* was developed and transformed by Bramante by applying the Classical vocabulary and symbolism of Renaissance architectural theory. (The Tempietto is a *martyrium* or commemorative chapel marking the spot where St Peter was believed to have been crucified.)

In considering possible shapes for an ideal church, the architect and theorist Alberti (p. 437) had begun with the circle as being that preferred by nature. He cited the globe, the stars, the trees, animals and their nests and many other natural forms, and recommended nine basic geometrical figures, all determined by the circle (squares, hexagons, octagons, etc.). It is notable that the traditional type of Christian church, the basilica, was excluded. A basilica is planned along an axis, longitudinally, and not centrally. Alberti acknowledged the close relationship of the basilica to the temple or church functionally, as they were both seats of justice; but, he emphasized, of human and divine justice respectively. A church should clearly be superior as the seat of divine justice. Only a circular or centrally planned building crowned with

a hemispherical dome like that of the Pantheon symbolizing the cosmos would, he thought, be appropriate.

How should the parts of such august buildings be proportioned? Vitruvius supplied the answer. His famous code of human proportions should be reflected in those of temples and churches. Vitruvius (see p. 193) described how a well-built man fits with extended arms and legs into the most perfect geometrical figures, the circle and square. This simple concept seemed to contain some deep and fundamental truth and it haunted the imagination of architects and artists. Indeed it had been present, intermittently, in many minds since the Middle Ages. The Christian mystic, Hildegard of Bingen (1098–1179), for instance, referred to it and illustrations of it appeared in illuminated manuscripts of her works. But its importance for Renaissance architects was compelling and in about 1485–90 Leonardo made a drawing of it with a translation into Italian of Vitruvius's Latin text appended in his own hand (**11,19**). During these years he and Bramante were working for the Sforza duke of Milan, and Bramante presumably knew this drawing as well as the numerous projects for centrally planned and domed churches that Leonardo made at the same time. Though none foreshadows the Tempietto precisely, Bramante's debt to Leonardo is evident. Their association remained close after they both left Milan in 1500, and when Leonardo visited Rome in 1504 he may well have contributed to the conception of the Tempietto.

The strictly symmetrical concentric effect of Bramante's design came near to realizing Alberti's and Leonardo's ideal Christian church: a free-standing, centrally planned building crowned with a hemispherical dome symbolizing the universe and reflecting celestial harmony in its

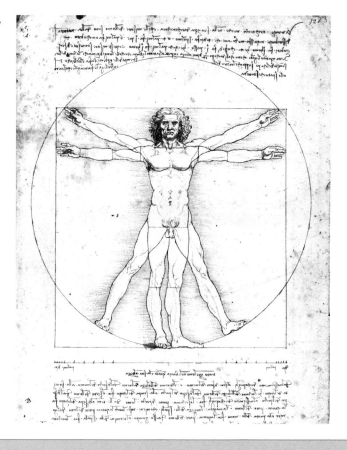

11,19 Leonardo da Vinci, *Human Figure in a Circle and Square, illustrating Vitruvius on Proportion*, 1485–90. Pen and ink, 13½ × 9⅝ins (34.3 × 24.5cm). Accademia, Venice.

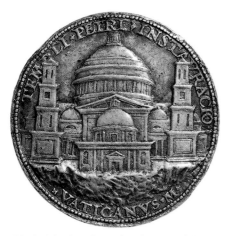

11,20 Cristoforo Foppa Caradosso, medal showing Bramante's design for St Peter's, Rome, 1506. British Museum, London.

proportions and geometry of pure forms. The effect was, however, partly lost by the design not having been fully carried out. The Tempietto was not intended to stand in a square courtyard; it was to have been surrounded by a circular cloister of 16 columns corresponding to those of the colonnade. When approached through the cloister, the lucidity of the whole radial composition would have been vividly apparent. Moreover, by a subtle ocular effect, the Tempietto would have been made to look higher and wider and more monumental and the surrounding area more spacious. As a result, the sense of harmonious unity created by the concentric composition would have been increased, and with it that ele-

11,21 Bramante,
Plan for St Peter's, Rome, 1505–6.

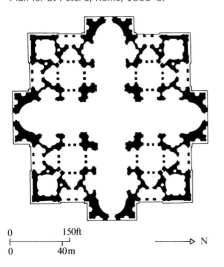

```
0        150ft
|--+--+--+
0        40m
```
→ N

vating and purifying effect required for an ideal Christian church.

In 1506 Pope Julius II embarked on 'renovating the very dilapidated church of St Peter the Apostle in Rome from its foundations up', as he wrote to King Henry VIII of England, and designs for another domed building on a centralized plan were submitted by Bramante and accepted. This time, however, it was to be on a gigantic scale. The design is known from a medal struck when the foundations were laid (**11,20**). Only one drawing in Bramante's hand survives, showing only one half of the Greek cross plan (**11,21**), but his design for the great hemispherical dome on a colonnaded drum was reproduced later in both plan and elevation because it had been such a 'great revelation to architects', as one of them said. Indeed, so overwhelming was Bramante's design that none of his successors at St Peter's, not even Michelangelo, could escape its influ-

ence. Very little was ever built and only the great piers supporting the dome survive in Michelangelo's structure.

Two years after the foundations of Bramante's St Peter's were laid, work began on a pilgrimage church just outside the small hill-town of Todi, north of Rome. The architect named in the contract, Cola da Caprarola (fl. 1499–1519), is otherwise almost unknown. Nowhere, however, was the Christian–humanist ideal of Alberti, Leonardo and Bramante realized in purer form (**11,22**). Crowned with a dome, standing in open ground and offering the same aspect on all sides, without windows at eye-level so that pilgrims and worshippers might not be distracted by the outside world, of a crystalline quality in its geometrical purity in both plan and elevation, S Maria della Consolazione epitomizes the simplicity and clarity of the sober, harmonious aspirations of the High Renaissance.

11,22 Cola da Caprarola, S Maria della Consolazione, Todi, Italy, begun 1508.

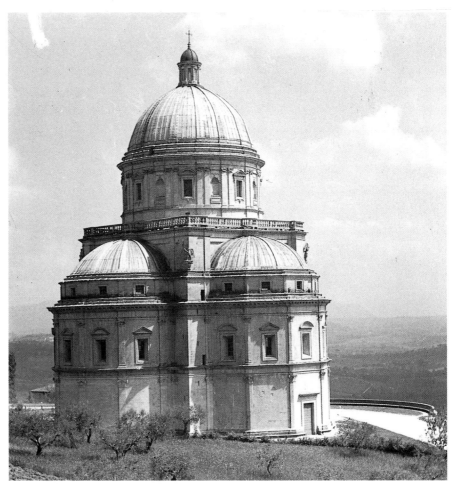

colonnade of equally-spaced Doric columns bearing a flat entablature with metopes and triglyphs (see Glossary), not arches, as had previously been used. It was intended to be set in the centre of a circular peristyle (never built), being conceived not in isolation but as the nucleus of an ordered environment, in which solids and voids, mass and volume, would be held in perfect equipoise.

The Tempietto is a monument rather than a place for congregational worship, for it can hold only a few people. But it embodied the idea of a free-standing, centrally planned church crowned by a hemispherical dome, an idea that had haunted the minds of Italian architects for more than half a century, as a symbol of the concentric cosmos, reflecting celestial harmony in its proportions and geometry of pure forms. Leonardo, a friend of Bramante, experimented with many sketches for churches combining cubes and spheres. And when Bramante was given the task of rebuilding St Peter's in Rome (partly in order to make the presbytery into a memorial to Pope Julius II), he designed the most grandiose centralized church he could conceive standing in the middle of an immense square.

The foundation stone was laid in 1506. St Peter's was not to be built to Bramante's design, but he had, nevertheless, set a new standard of solemn, monumental grandeur.

Bramante was artistic adviser as well as architect to Pope Julius II (1503–13), under whom Rome became, for the first time since antiquity, the centre of European art. Bramante may well have been responsible for engaging Raphael to decorate the Pope's private apartments in the Vatican – generally known simply as *le stanze* (the rooms) – almost immediately after he arrived in Rome from Florence in 1508. Raphael was not yet 26 years old. It was a golden moment, a brief interval of apparent prosperity before the sack of Rome, and Raphael created visions of unequalled grandeur and serenity.

The Stanza della Segnatura (called after the supreme ecclesiastical tribunal which later met there) came first. Originally intended as a library, its paintings allude to the four 'faculties' or branches of humanist learning – theology, philosophy, poetry and jurisprudence – personified in roundels on the ceiling. On one side is the wall devoted to literature, with Classical and modern writers gathered

11,23 Raphael, Stanza della Segnatura with the *School of Athens*, 1509–11. Vatican, Rome.

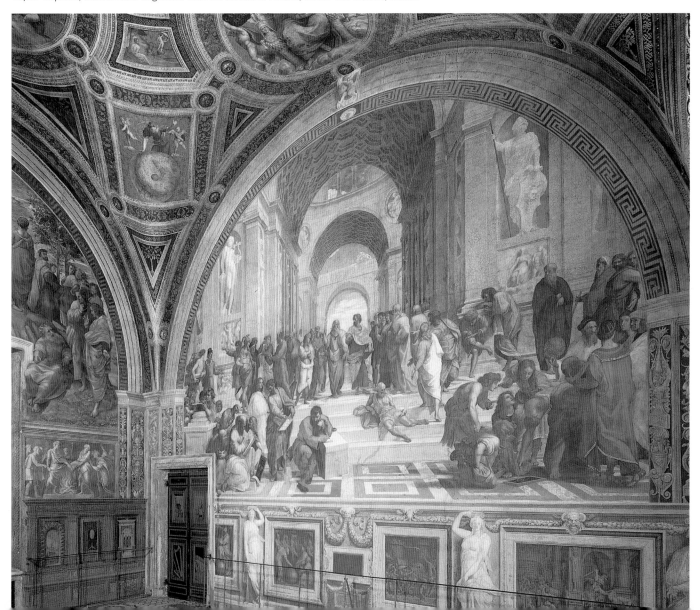

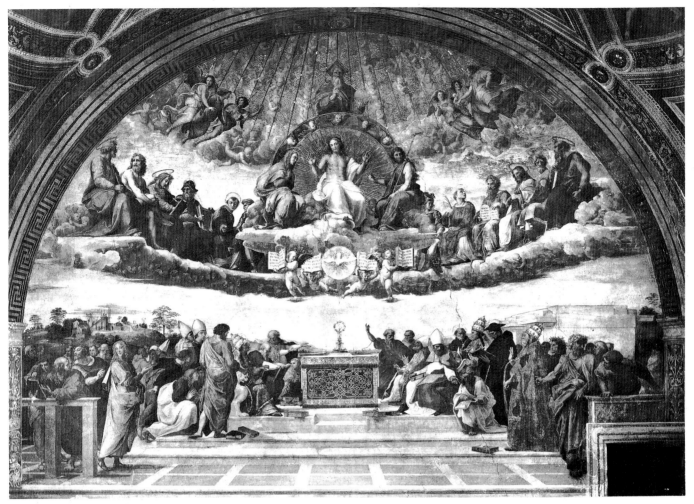

11,24 Raphael, *Disputa* ('Debate on the Holy Sacrament'), 1509–11. Fresco, Stanza della Segnatura, Vatican, Rome.

around Apollo and the Muses on Mount Parnassus. Philosophy is illustrated on the other wall in a fresco of ancient Greek thinkers and scientists, generally if somewhat inaccurately entitled the *School of Athens* (**11,23**), with Plato and Aristotle enshrined in the centre – here, at the very heart of the Papacy. However, this celebration of human reason faces the wall on which Theology is represented by a congregation of saints and Catholic teachers called the *Disputa* or 'Debate on the Holy Sacrament' – the complementary path to truth, reached by faith and revelation (**11,24**). The fourth wall is divided into two parts (below the lunette), with civil law depicted on that adjoining the *School of Athens*, canon law next to the *Disputa*. Thus, a perfect balance is maintained between the different strands in Christian humanist culture.

The general iconographical program seems to have been devised before Raphael took charge in 1509, for a start had already been made on the ceiling. From then onwards he was given a free hand to work out the great compositions, as his numerous preliminary drawings testify. He abandoned the old system of allegorical personifications of abstract ideas (except in the roundels on the ceiling) in favour of scenes in which historical figures enact the subjects. For the *School of Athens* he conjured up an ideal gathering of thinkers actively engaged in philosophical discourse, teaching, learning, talking, pondering, with rapt expressions of mental concentration. In

the centre Plato pointing upwards, perhaps to indicate the source of Platonic Ideas, stands next to Aristotle, whose downward gesture suggests his preoccupation with natural phenomena. Speculative thinkers are grouped on Plato's side; on the other there are 'scientists', including the geographer Ptolemy with Euclid (said to be a portrait of Bramante) demonstrating a geometrical theorem.

The device of placing the two main figures within a framing arch against the sky recalls Leonardo's *Last Supper*. Raphael's composition is, however, more complex than Leonardo's, with 52 figures in as many different poses, yet the same unity within diversity is attained without any deadening sense of symmetry. His insertion of the brooding man identified as Heraclitus in the foreground, just to the left of centre, was a masterly afterthought – as examination of the plaster has shown, for this section of the wall had to be chipped out and replastered to enable Raphael to make the alteration. (Heraclitus is perhaps a portrait of Michelangelo, and Plato of Leonardo.) Contrasts in color, sharp greens, clear blues and a few shot reds and yellows create an animating pattern, which further relieves the formality and exalted solemnity of the general scheme. But the great innovation in the painting is the relationship between the figures and their architectural setting, a grandiose vaulted structure reminiscent of Bramante's unexecuted designs for St Peter's. Whereas in Leonardo's *Last Supper* the figures were set in a predetermined perspective box, here they determine the pictorial space, which is no longer conceived as an extension of the room but as one much larger and wholly independent, yet which neither constricts nor overwhelms. In Raphael's full-scale cartoon for the fresco (Ambrosiana, Milan) there is no indication of the architectural background, which was presumably conceived later and, as it were, built round and for the figures.

Michelangelo

While Raphael was painting the Stanza della Segnatura, Michelangelo was at work on the ceiling of the Sistine Chapel (11,28; 29; 30; 31; 32). Never before or since have two outstanding works of this order been created concurrently in such close proximity. They exemplify, however, two tendencies latent in the High Renaissance but soon to diverge and set off a conflict which has given later European art its stylistic volatility. The two artists were unlike one another in background, as in character.

Raphael, the son of a painter, had begun in the medieval tradition of artist-craftsman, although he rapidly rose socially to end his brief life as a man of conspicuous wealth, the owner of a handsome palace in Rome, with a retinue of domestic servants and a still larger staff of assistants. In his style of life, as in his paintings, he acquired the *sprezzatura* or ease of manner so highly lauded by his friend Baldassare Castiglione in *The Book of the Courtier* (1528) – the quality that 'conceals art and shows that what is said and done is accomplished without difficulty and almost without thinking about it'. Michelangelo was the antithesis of the ideal courtier. Unsociable, mistrustful, moody, untidy, obsessed with his work and almost pathologically proud, he was the archetype of the 'man of genius', a poet as well as a sculptor, painter and architect. At odds with himself and with the world, his introspective imagination revolutionized everything he touched.

He came from an impoverished Florentine family with claims to nobility and always held himself aloof from other artists. 'I was never a painter or sculptor like those

Sources and Documents

Michelangelo's David: Contract and Installation

Michelangelo's *David* (11,25) was commissioned on 16 August 1501 by the board of directors of the cathedral works (called the *Opera del Duomo*) in Florence. The figure had been badly blocked out by another sculptor and abandoned. Michelangelo was to 'make, carry through and complete' it.

He is to do it within the next two years, as from the next 1st September, and at a monthly salary and reward of 6 broad golden florins cash; and whatever he needs for this, the Opera *undertakes to lend and supply, whether it is workmen from the* Opera, *or timber, or anything else he requires. When this work and marble figure have been finished, the Consuls and Operaii who then hold office will judge according to their consciences whether it deserves a higher price.*

Having previously 'removed a certain knob which there was on the figure's breast, with one or two strokes of the chisel', Michelangelo began working 'steadily and strongly' on the *David* early on Monday morning, 13 September. He finished less than two years later. On 25 January 1503 the board of directors called a meeting to discuss the best location for it. Thirty Florentine artists gave their opinion: jewellers, embroiderers, goldsmiths, wood-carvers, sculptors, architects and painters, including Andrea della Robbia, Piero di Cosimo, Giuliano da Sangallo, Perugino, Botticelli and Leonardo. Botticelli and a few others favoured the cathedral as originally intended; but in view of the imperfect condition of the marble a majority, including Leonardo, recommended that it be placed under cover in the Loggia

dei Lanzi. If this recommendation were to be accepted, Giuliano da Sangallo proposed for it a black niche. However, the directors decided to give it a more honorific position in front of the Palazzo Vecchio.

According to Luca Landucci (1450–1519), a dealer in spices and medicinal drugs, whose journal is one of the most informative about art at this time in Florence, the marble was brought out of the workshop near the cathedral on 14 May 1504.

It came out at 24 o'clock, and they broke the wall above the gateway enough to let it pass. That night some stones were thrown at the colossus to harm it. Watch had to be kept at night; and it made way very slowly, bound as it was upright, suspended in the air with enormous beams and a complicated mechanism of ropes. It took four days to reach the Piazza, arriving on the 18th at the hour of 12. More than 40 men were employed to make it go; and there were 14 rollers joined beneath it, which were progressively transferred. Afterwards, they worked until June 1504, to place it on the platform where the Judith *used to stand. The* Judith *was removed and set up upon the ground within the Palace.*

The act of vandalism mentioned by Landucci may have been prompted by local politics, for radical Republicans highly esteemed Donatello's *Judith* which the *David* was to displace. The *David* remained undisturbed outside the Palazzo Vecchio until 1873 when it was removed indoors to the Accademia where it still stands.

(Tr. J. Pope-Hennessy, 1958 [contract]; J. A. Symonds, *Life of Michelangelo*, 1899 [Landucci])

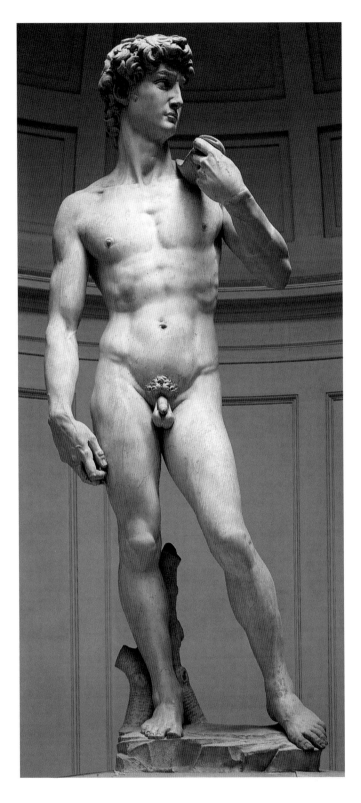

(see p. 451) was to play an important part in sixteenth-century aesthetics.

In Florence in the autumn of 1504 the over-life-size statue of David on which Michelangelo had been working for the previous three years was set up outside the main entrance to the Palazzo Vecchio (now replaced by a copy) (**11,25**). Unlike earlier representations, his *David* is not shown as the victor with his foot on Goliath's severed head, but as the champion of a just cause fearlessly confronting his physically stronger opponent. Placed in front of the seat of government, this provocative adolescent with his muscular torso, straining neck and defiant expression beneath knotted brows was seen by some Florentines as symbolizing their new republic, which had expelled the Medici in 1494. Whether this was uppermost, or present at all, in Michelangelo's mind when working on the figure may be questioned. (Originally the statue was intended for the cathedral exterior.) But as the first nude to be carved on this colossal scale since antiquity, it gave him the opportunity to measure his strength. The effect is audaciously un-Classical. The hands and feet are oversize, muscles and veins are swollen and the gangling limbs are not at rest. But already Michelangelo's conception of the body as the prison of the soul has endowed his heroic figure with an extraordinary sense of pent-up energy – outwardly calm, but inwardly tense and challenging.

The success of the *David* was such that Michelangelo was summoned to Rome to execute for Julius II a free-standing sepulchral monument, on a scale and of a complexity to outdo all others, as part of the new St Peter's designed by Bramante. This was to have been Michelangelo's culminating achievement, combining and unifying architecture and sculpture, and he worked on it intermittently for 40 years, its scale being gradually reduced to that of a wall monument (**11,26**) of which only the over-life-size central figure of Moses is certainly by him. The unfinished slaves intended for it are dispersed (**11,27**). He

11,25 *Left* Michelangelo, *David*, 1501–3.
Marble, about 18ft (5.5m) high. Galleria dell'Accademia, Florence.

11,26 Michelangelo, Tomb of Julius II, c. 1513–45.
S Pietro in Vincoli, Rome.

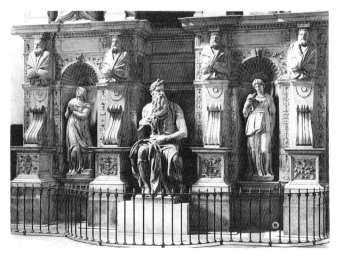

who set up shop', he told his nephew in 1548. Although he served a brief apprenticeship to Domenico Ghirlandaio (see pp. 448–9), his formative years were those he spent in the household of Lorenzo de' Medici (the Magnificent) around 1489 to 1492, studying sculpture under Bertoldo di Giovanni (see p. 440) and living on familiar terms with the young Medici, two of whom were later to become popes, Leo X and Clement VII. Here, too, he encountered the Classical scholar and poet Angelo Poliziano (see p. 449) and the philosopher Marsilio Ficino, whose revival of the Neoplatonic notion of 'Ideas' as metaphysical realities

regarded it as the tragedy of his life. However, in 1508 Julius II persuaded him to paint the ceiling of the Sistine Chapel, of which the upper parts of the walls had been frescoed by leading artists of the late fifteenth century – Botticelli, Domenico Ghirlandaio and Raphael's master Pietro Perugino, among others. The vault measures roughly 133 by 43 feet (40 by 13m), with many curved surfaces, and presented an exceptionally difficult problem as a field for figurative paintings. Michelangelo's solution was one of daring originality. He probably had the advice of theologians for the iconographical program, though he claimed that the Pope had 'let him do what he wanted'. In two sessions, from winter 1508/9 to summer 1510 and February 1511 to October 1512, he painted the upper part of the walls and the whole ceiling in true fresco, almost single-handed.

Michelangelo conceived the ceiling as an imaginary architectural structure rising above the chapel and treated the areas of greatest curvature as continuations of the walls (11,28; 29; 30). Separating off the concave triangles above the windows and at the corners, he painted the spandrels between them as thrones, joined by a cornice that marks the top of the fictive walls, and flanked by pilasters that support 'horizontal' ribs of stone spanning the centre. This imaginary structure provided three distinct zones for figurative paintings, which could thus be given a corresponding hierarchy of content. In the lowest – the lunettes surrounding the upper windows of the real wall and the small vaults above them – he painted the ancestors of Christ. The thrones of the second zone support magnificent figures of prophets alternating with Classical sibyls (11,31), who foretold the coming of Christ. All these are foreshortened from the viewpoint of a spectator on the ground – as if they were within the same space. But the figurative scenes of the uppermost zone, seen through the ribs of stone, present a higher reality and are painted according to their own perspectival laws as independent pictures. They illustrate the first of

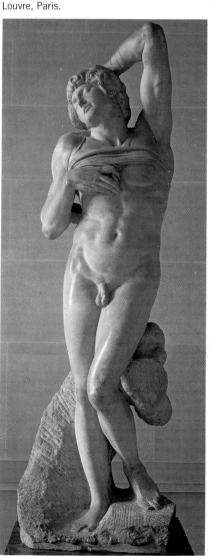

11,27 Michelangelo, *Dying Slave*, c. 1513. Marble, 7ft 6ins (2.29m) high. Louvre, Paris.

11,28 Plan of the Sistine Chapel ceiling, Vatican, Rome.

The frescoes on the ceiling

1	God Separates Light and Darkness
2	God Creates the Sun and the Moon and the Plants on the Earth
3	God Separates the Water and Earth and Blesses His Work
4	Creation of Adam
5	Creation of Eve
6	Fall of Human Race and Expulsion from Paradise
7	Sacrifice of Noah
8	The Flood
9	The Intoxication of Noah

Prophets and Sibyls

10	Zechariah
11	Delphic Sibyl
12	Isaiah
13	Cumaean Sibyl
14	Daniel
15	Libyan Sibyl
16	Jonah
17	Jeremiah
18	Persian Sibyl
19	Ezekiel
20	Eritrean Sibyl
21	Joel

Window niches showing portraits of the first popes

Lunettes and spandrels above the windows with portraits of the ancestors of Christ

22	David Slaying Goliath
23	Judith with the Head of Holofernes
24	The Brazen Serpent
25	The Punishment of Haman

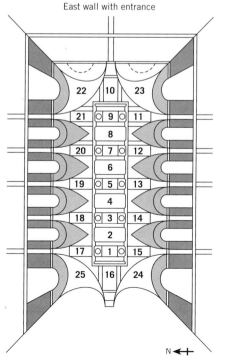

East wall with entrance

North wall with scenes from the life of Christ

South wall with scenes from the life of Moses

N

West wall with *Last Judgement*

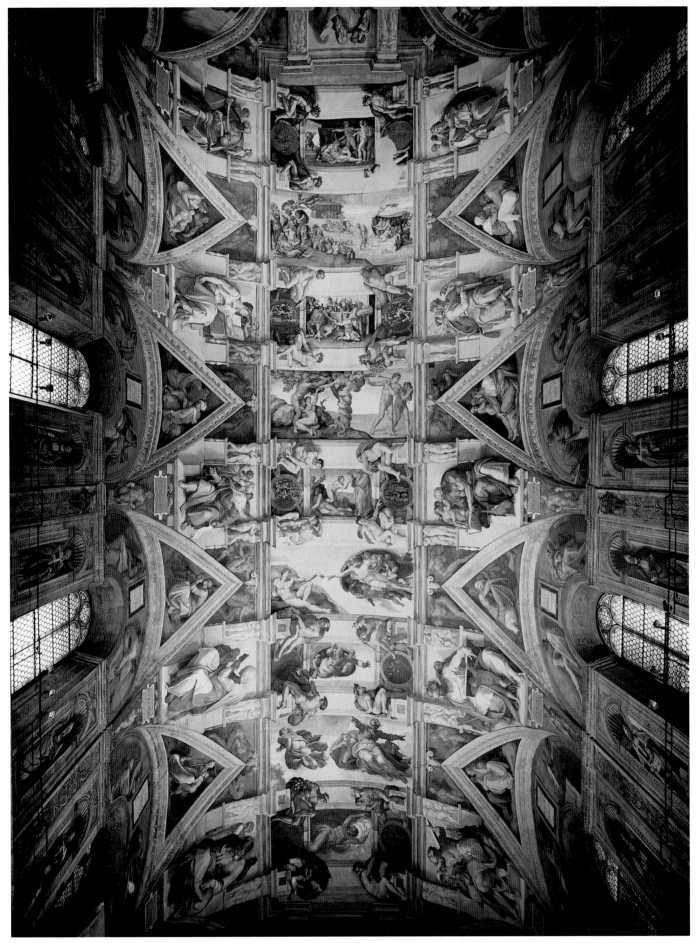

11,29 Michelangelo, ceiling of the Sistine Chapel, Vatican, Rome, 1508–12. Fresco, 45 × 128ft (13.7 × 39m) (after cleaning 1989).

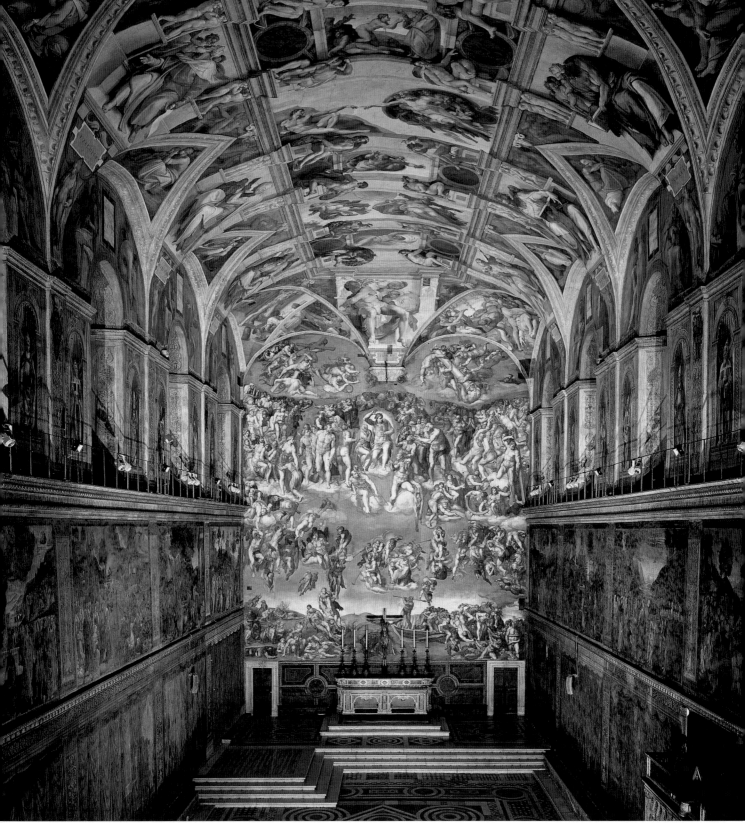

11,30 Michelangelo, Sistine Chapel, showing the ceiling, 1508–12 (after cleaning 1989) and *Last Judgement* fresco on west wall, 1534–41 (after cleaning 19

three periods into which the history of the world was then divided, that before the tablets of the Law were given to Moses and called *ante legem*. (Those *sub lege* and *sub gratia* had already been depicted on the lateral walls.) The relationship between the figures and the fictive architecture in the logical structure of the ceiling has been made more clearly apparent than it had been for centuries by the recent cleaning (completed in 1989) which has also

revealed the vibrance of Michelangelo's palette with its unprecedented shot yellows, acid pinks and sharp greens.

Above the altar Michelangelo recorded the beginning of all things, the androgynous figure of God with cloud-covered face dynamically emerging out of primal chaos, followed by the creation of the sun and moon, and the separation of land from water (**11,32**). In the next scene, Michelangelo's most sublime and justly famous image,

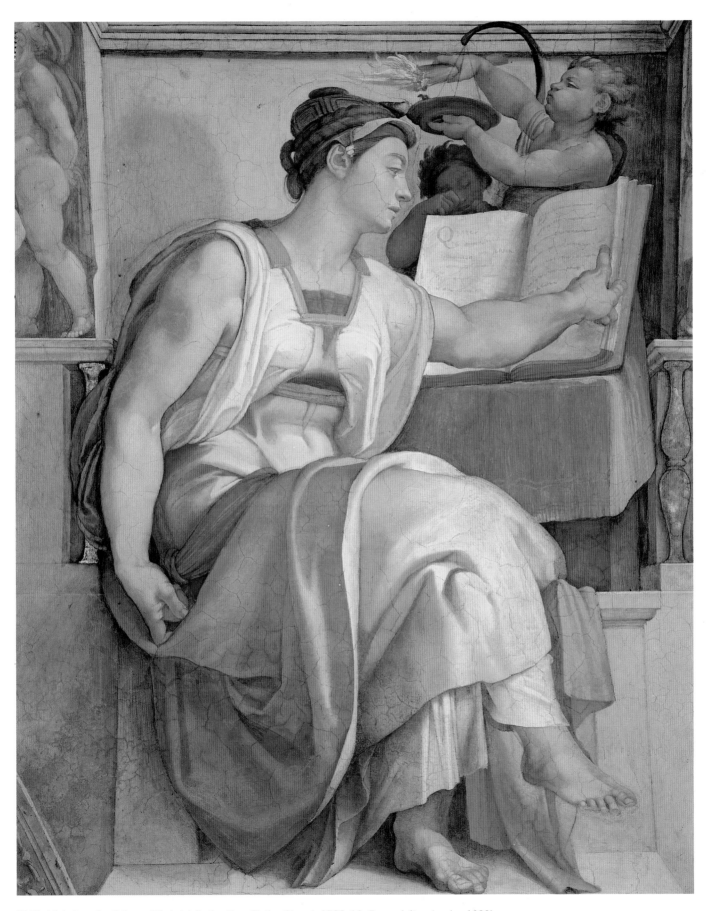

11,31 Michelangelo, *Eritrean Sibyl*, detail of ceiling, Sistine Chapel, 1508–12. Fresco (after cleaning 1989).

11,32 Michelangelo, *God Separates the Water and Earth and Blesses his Work*, detail of ceiling, Sistine Chapel, Vatican, Rome, 1508–12. Fresco (after cleaning 1989).

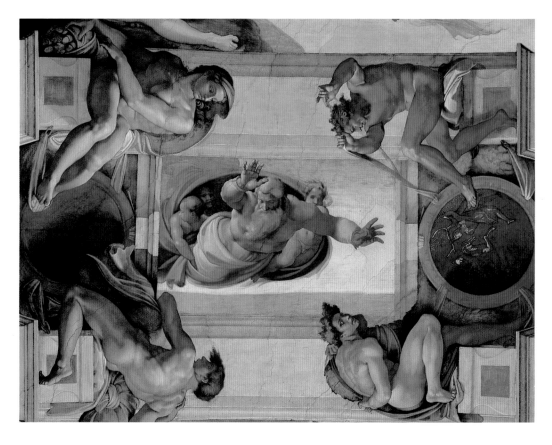

God animates the languid clay of Adam through a tiny gap between their outstretched fingers, imparting the spirit that enables man to move, think and feel. The creation of Eve and a scene which combines the temptation of Adam and Eve with their expulsion from Eden come next. The three final scenes are devoted to Noah, the man chosen by God to continue the human race. Michelangelo began work at this end of the ceiling, proceeding towards the altar with an access of self-confidence, simplifying the compositions and enlarging his designs. (They were intended to be seen from the chancel, where the Pope sat on his throne. To the modern visitor entering the chapel, they read in reverse and upside down.)

Seated on the pilasters (see Glossary) between the thrones of prophets and sibyls are nude adolescents – *ignudi* as they are called – flexing their muscles and showing off their athletic limbs with complete abandon, as if in praise of God's creation. Their pictorial function is to mask the join between the upper zones (they seem to belong to both), and they have been variously interpreted as wingless angels and symbols of the rational soul, though Michelangelo's homosexual leanings must partly account for them. Clearly related to the slaves intended for Julius II's tomb (11,27), they are not, like them, held by the bonds of sin and death. They exult in their carnality. Developing a heightened sensitivity to the human form as he worked along the ceiling, he rendered them in more energetic, almost violent, poses and (another revelation of the recent cleaning) stronger *chiaroscuro* to model their limbs. To Michelangelo the male body made in God's image represented the summit of physical and spiritual

beauty and there can be little doubt that these sensuously painted nudes embodied his deepest longings.

Numerous attempts have been made to expound the meaning and program of the ceiling in interpretations ranging from Neoplatonic to orthodox theological allegory, without, however, accounting for its most striking feature, the complete freedom from convention with which every aspect of the great composition is treated. For Michelangelo's frenzied, whirlwind energy made everything seem superhuman and Olympian, creating a pantheon for the soul's most exalted aspirations, transforming a chapel at the centre of Western Christendom into a monument to his own genius. It is the most extreme instance of the independence that could be won by a great artist.

Raphael was the first artist to respond to the impact of the Sistine Chapel ceiling, and he was perhaps the only one to assimilate it without compromising his own artistic integrity. He must have seen part of it before completing the *School of Athens* with the Michelangelesque figure of Heraclitus. In 1515 he took account of the whole work when designing a set of tapestries to hang beneath it – they cost more than ten times as much as Michelangelo was paid for the ceiling! In Raphael's last great work, the *Transfiguration* (**11,33**), Michelangelo's superhuman, demonic sculptural vision was translated into something much less overpowering but more painterly and dramatic in its rendering of natural and supernatural light, a work in which the combination of grandeur and humanity is unique. The contrast between the serene figures bathed in transcendental light in the upper part and the troubled

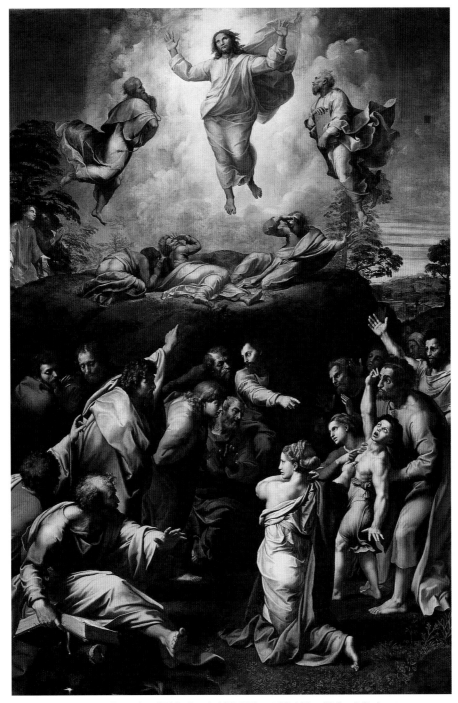

11,33 Raphael, *Transfiguration*, 1517. Panel, 15ft 1½ins × 9ft 1½ins (4.6 × 2.8m). Vatican Museums, Rome.

gesturing of those in the shadows below, who have witnessed the disciples' failure to cure a lunatic boy, enforces the picture's message that only Christ can heal the ills of the world. The words of the boy's father in the Gospel story link the painting with the spiritual crisis of the time: 'Lord, I believe; help thou my unbelief.'

After the Sistine Chapel ceiling Michelangelo returned to Florence, where the Medici had regained power in 1512 and, with the election of a Medici Pope (Leo X, 1513–21), took control of the Papal States. They were now the rulers of central Italy. The new Pope and his cousin (later Clement VII, 1523–34) set about converting the church of S Lorenzo into a dynastic monument by commissioning Michelangelo to design a new façade (never built) and

subsequently a family mausoleum, the Medici Chapel (**11,34**). In plan, in the use of a giant Corinthian order and in the dark-gray and white color-scheme, Michelangelo followed Brunelleschi, whose sacristy matched the new chapel on the other side of the church. But in every other respect his design was revolutionary, especially in the way it broke free from the tyranny of the Classical orders. Windows taper, capitals vanish from pilasters which have recessed panels instead of fluting, tabernacles weigh down heavily on the voids beneath them. Many architectural elements have no structural function at all, the marble cladding simply being carved into simulated architectural forms. In this way Michelangelo evolved a new conception of architecture in which the wall is no

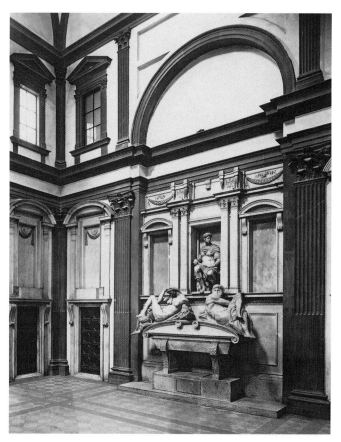

11,34 Michelangelo, Medici Chapel, S Lorenzo, Florence, 1519–34.

longer an inert plane to which ornament may be applied, but a vital many-layered organism. His approach was that of a sculptor removing stone from a block rather than that of a builder raising one structural element on another.

'In hard and craggy stone the mere removal of the surface gives being to a figure, which ever grows the more the stone is hewn away', he wrote in one of his poems. His usual practice was to make a small clay or wax model and then, with few if any assistants, to attack the marble block direct, all but finishing the front before removing the material on either side. For the statues in the Medici Chapel, however, he adopted the process which became normal for European sculptors during the next four centuries – making full-scale models from which assistants could rough out figures for him to finish. Even so, Michelangelo completed only one statue for the Medici Chapel, that of Giuliano de' Medici. This is an idealized image of a young patrician general in Roman military costume, not a likeness. Of the unfinished figures of Day and Night below, Michelangelo wrote a *concetto* or literary conceit of the type beloved by Renaissance writers (including Shakespeare at the end of the century), and its antithetical convolutions are echoed in the elaborate *contrapposto* of all three figures. But they transcend the ingenious artificiality of the *concetto*, just as they seem to burst through the restraining architectural framework, whose angular linearity offsets and heightens their roundness and weight. Iron-muscled Day, with his roughly

worked face staring over a huge, beautifully modelled and smoothly carved shoulder, and heavy-limbed Night, with her tired breasts and creased belly, as if in troubled sleep or exhausted after frantic, impotent struggle, are only equalled by the unfinished slaves for the tomb of Julius II (11,27). Figures of complex three-dimensional form, they are invested with the pathos of the human tragedy, the dualism of body and spirit. Outwardly calm, they seem stirred by some ever-present inward anguish.

Work on the Medici Chapel was interrupted by a political crisis precipitated by Medici ambitions, culminating in 1527, when the unpaid mercenaries of the imperial army – Spaniards and Germans, some of whom were Lutherans – sacked Rome, chasing the Pope out of the Vatican, desecrating churches, burning houses and slaughtering civilians with calculated brutality. It was the worst disaster to have befallen the city for nearly a thousand years. The Florentines took advantage of it to expel the Medici and proclaim a republic, enthusiastically supported by Michelangelo, who was later pardoned by the Pope on condition he resume work on the Medici Chapel. In 1534 he returned to Rome to paint the *Last Judgement* above the altar in the Sistine Chapel (11,30).

The Last Judgement had usually been conceived as reflecting the eternal equity of divine justice. Michelangelo's vision was of a cosmic convulsion. Christ's gesture controls an irreversible and irresistible cyclical motion, raising up the blessed on his right and casting down the damned, towards whom his face is turned with a merciless expression. No attempt was made to give an illusion of depth. The figures are suspended in a single plane, each group being depicted from a different viewpoint, those at the base much smaller than those higher up. This defiance of the normal laws of perspective construction has a deeply disturbing effect and adds to the force of the painting, which powerfully expressed that sublime and awesome quality in Michelangelo's art and personality called by contemporaries his *terribilità*.

Less pronounced is his Neoplatonism, though still present in his conception of divinity as light. He had recently made a drawing of Helios, the sun god, and used the same pose for Christ, beardless, nude and with the muscular physique of a Hellenistic statue, surrounded by an aureole like the sun. Perhaps he was also inspired by the Hellenistic notion of a heliocentric universe, then being given new and scientific validity by Copernicus (1473–1543). While painting the fresco, however, Michelangelo began his passionate friendship with the pious poet Vittoria Colonna, in whose circle he met religious thinkers who held that salvation depended wholly on God's mercy – a belief generically similar to the Protestant doctrine of justification by faith. These were the early years of the Counter-Reformation sponsored by Pope Paul III (1534–49). As a young cardinal he had fathered four illegitimate children; as Pope he became a zealous reformer and tried to steady the Church after the shock of Luther by enquiring into ecclesiastical abuses, sanctioning the Society of Jesus (1540) and convoking the Council of Trent, which, between 1545 and 1563, hardened the lines

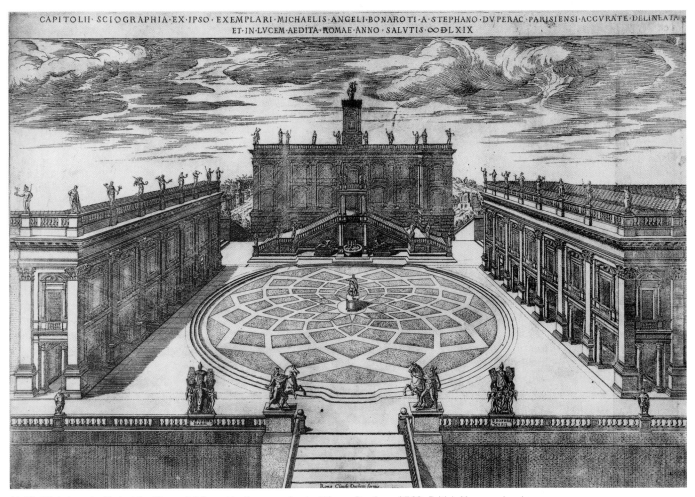

CAPITOLII·SCIOGRAPHIA·EX·IPSO·EXEMPLARI·MICHAELIS·ANGELI·BONAROTI·A·STEPHANO·DVPERAC·PARISIENSI·ACCVRATE·DELINEATA ET·IN·LVCEM·AEDITA·ROMAE·ANNO·SALVTIS·∞DLXIX

11,35 Michelangelo, Project for Piazza del Campidoglio, engraving by Etienne Dupérac, 1569. British Museum, London.

of doctrine, revised the liturgy, initiated the index of prohibited books and laid down rules for religious music and art. Michelangelo's *Last Judgement* reflected something of this new mood, as well as his own increasingly anguished piety – but not enough to satisfy the more literal-minded reformers.

The nude figures gave offence. Nudity in art had come to seem indecent, its antique precedents being pagan and its Neoplatonic justification heretical. The Christian humanism which had inspired the Sistine Chapel ceiling was now seen as the hot-bed of Protestantism. Michelangelo was denounced in 1549 as an 'inventor of filthiness, who cared more for art than for devotion'. After his death, loin-cloths were added to the figures and there were repeated proposals that the whole fresco be erased. Yet no one was more painfully aware of the conflict between art and piety than Michelangelo. 'Now know I well how that fond fantasy / which made my soul the worshipper of earthly art is vain', he wrote in a poem of 1554. He still had ten years to live but, apart from drawings of the Crucifixion and two unfinished groups of the Pietà, carved as a kind of religious exercise, he gave up art. His last years were devoted mainly to architecture.

Shortly after being granted Roman citizenship in 1537 he designed a pedestal for the statue of Marcus Aurelius

(5,62), which had been moved to the Capitoline hill – Campidoglio – at that time no more than a rough hill-top field bounded by two buildings at an oblique angle to one another and the nave wall of S Maria in Aracoeli. He soon worked out a project to transform this unpromising site into one of the most imposing urban spaces in Europe: a trapezoid with the statue set on an oval and very slightly convex pavement of intricate pattern in front of the medieval senators' palace, which was given a new Classical façade and flanked by lower twin buildings, all with the giant order of pilasters that he favoured (**11,35**). Work proceeded slowly and the buildings were not completed (with some modifications) until a century after his death.

In the meantime he was appointed architect of St Peter's in 1546. As we have already seen, Bramante had designed a centrally planned church 40 years before, but funds soon ran out and the sale of indulgences (which provoked Luther's first protest, see p. 465) failed to raise enough to continue it. Although projects for less costly buildings had been prepared, by Raphael among others, little was achieved until Paul III became Pope. Work began in earnest in 1543 under the direction of Antonio da Sangallo (1483/5–1536), a pupil of Bramante. Within a few months of Sangallo's death Michelangelo made a clay model for a bolder, stronger and more tightly organized structure, and in the

Renaissance Urbanism

THE ROME OF SIXTUS V

The Piazza del Campidoglio (11,35) is the most distinguished of several artificially created spaces that by the end of the sixteenth century had made Rome the most imposing example of urban design in Europe – and the most conspicuous demonstration of the power of the Counter-Reformation Papacy. The whole city had been completely transformed, 're-born from its own ashes', as a contemporary remarked. This sweeping reorganization was inspired by a vision of Rome as the capital of Christendom, a great magnet to which pilgrims from all over the world would be drawn to visit the sites associated with the early Christians. When the first Roman churches were built in the fourth and fifth centuries they rose on the city's outskirts where land was available. As a result the great basilicas – S Lorenzo, S Croce, S Giovanni in Laterano, S Maria Maggiore and St Peter's itself – were scattered, usually on peripheral sites. Entering the city from the north, as most pilgrims did, they had to cross a great extent of abandoned land strewn with ancient ruins in order to reach them. To resolve this and bring order out of chaos led to the renewal of the city.

During the Middle Ages when other cities in Italy and in northern Europe had prospered and grown until they burst their boundaries, Rome had contracted and stagnated. The diminishing population clustered in a bend of the river Tiber, the only source of water after the ancient Roman aqueducts had broken down. The situation deteriorated still further in the fourteenth century when the absence of the Pope and his court in Avignon, followed by the Great Schism, left Rome without effective government. Pope Martin V (1417–31), whose election ended the schism, returned to find a largely abandoned city whose population of over a million in imperial Roman times had dwindled to 17,000 living in a slum. He placed this tangle of insanitary streets under a single administration with power, eventually, of expropriation of property and this established the means, while the desolation of the vast area inside the city walls provided the space, for urban development on a uniquely grand scale.

Projects were put forward under Pope Nicholas V (1447–55), probably with the help of Alberti (see p. 437), the first theorist of Renaissance urban design whose conception of the city as a planned human environment, as a work of art, almost anticipated what is now called 'townscape'. But none of their schemes was realized, apart from the removal of the papal residence and seat of government from the Lateran to the Vatican. Several decades later, Bramante (see p. 479) was employed on urban design by Pope Julius II (1503–13) and laid out the via Giulia, the first great street created since ancient Roman times though intended less as a thoroughfare than as a site for new administrative offices and private palaces, all built to a standard height. In the 1530s it was extended by a short street to meet at an acute angle the via Papale – the processional way from St Peter's to the Lateran – and, for purely aesthetic effect, a balancing third street (in fact a cul-de-sac) was added at a similar angle to make a *trivium*, i.e. three streets meeting with geometrically precise convergence at a central point. This was a new element in urban design and was to be repeated on a larger scale and with more dramatic effect at the Piazza del Popolo (11,36) and later elsewhere, notably Versailles (13,52), Catherine the Great's St Petersburg and L'Enfant's Washington DC. Another innovation in urban design followed in 1561 when Pope Pius IV (1559–65), in consultation with Michelangelo, had the wide via Pia (now via XX Settembre) cut through undeveloped land from the Quirinal hill, where a summer palace for the Pope was being built, to the city wall more than a mile away (11,37). Although leading in the direction of a pilgrimage church this was less a pilgrimage route than a vast, elongated piazza flanked by the high garden walls of villas, punctuated by their imposing entrances and terminating in Michelangelo's Porta Pia with its main façade on the inside and not, as was usual, on the outside. Via Pia was, however, no more than a prelude to the sweeping master-plan of Sixtus V and his civil engineer and architect Domenico Fontana (1543–1607) (11,38).

Pope Sixtus V (1585–90), who saw to the completion of the dome of St Peter's, was determined to make Rome the manifest capital of Christendom, a New Jerusalem, with scant respect for pagan remains. His network of streets, wide and smooth enough for carriages, though intended primarily to connect the churches visited by pilgrims, also integrated the whole urban area. To make the plan visible at ground level,

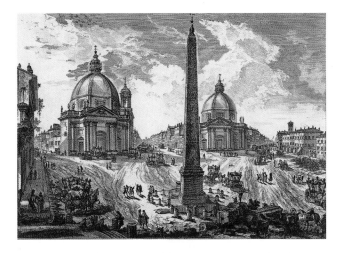

11.36 View of Piazza del Popolo, Rome, c. 1750. Engraving after Piranesi, 17¾ × 21½ins (45 × 55cm). British Museum, London.

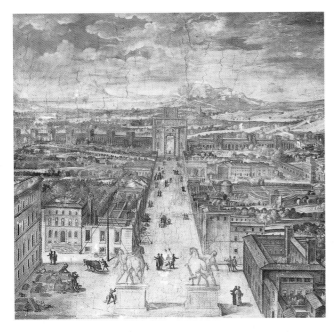

11.37 View of the via Pia, c. 1588. Fresco. Salone dei Papi, Lateran Palace, Rome.

property which became ripe for development. The most notable feature of his and Fontana's city plan was, however, its comprehensiveness, incorporating all the elements of Renaissance urban design in a vast total environment, spatially unified and visually integrated. The regularization of districts, the manipulation of space with streets that open up into piazzas sometimes with panoramic views in several directions, the exploitation of different ground levels, not only answered practical needs but inspired religious aspirations with its scenographic effects. Domenico Fontana, who was in charge of the work, wrote in 1590 that Sixtus had 'stretched the streets from one end of the city to the other and not heeding the hills and valleys they had to cross but flattening here and filling in there, he made them gentle plains and most beautiful sites, and along their routes and in many places there are open views of the lower part of the city in varied and different perspectives. Thus beyond the religious purposes these beauties provide a paradise for the bodily senses.'

the nodal points, formed by the new piazzas created in front of the pilgrimage churches, were marked by huge ancient Egyptian obelisks which Sixtus V raised from the imperial ruins where they had been buried and crowned with iron crosses. (He also had statues of St Peter and St Paul set on the columns of Trajan – 5,65 – and Marcus Aurelius.) At the same time he had a new aqueduct made, the first since antiquity, to bring fresh water to the arid northern area of the city, facilitating urbanization along streets radiating from the central hub of S Maria Maggiore near his own private

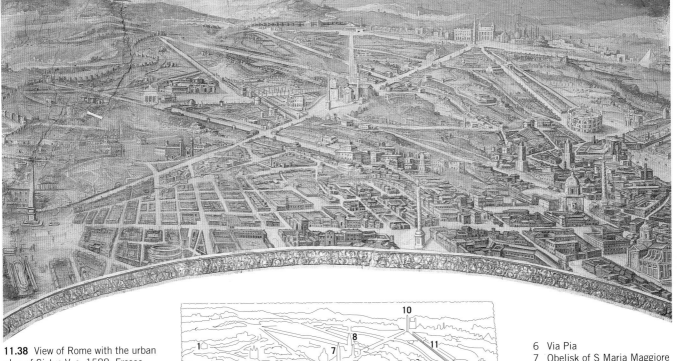

11.38 View of Rome with the urban plan of Sixtus V, c. 1588. Fresco. Salone Sistino, Library, Vatican, Rome.

1 Porta Pia
2 Obelisk in Piazza del Popolo
3 Via del Corso
4 Via Clementia/Paolina Trifaria
5 Via Felice

6 Via Pia
7 Obelisk of S Maria Maggiore
8 S Croce in Gerusalemme
9 Column of Marcus Aurelius
10 Lateran Obelisk
11 Via S Giovanni in Laterano
12 Colosseum
13 Column of Trajan
14 Il Gesù

11,39 Plan of
Michelangelo's
St Peter's.

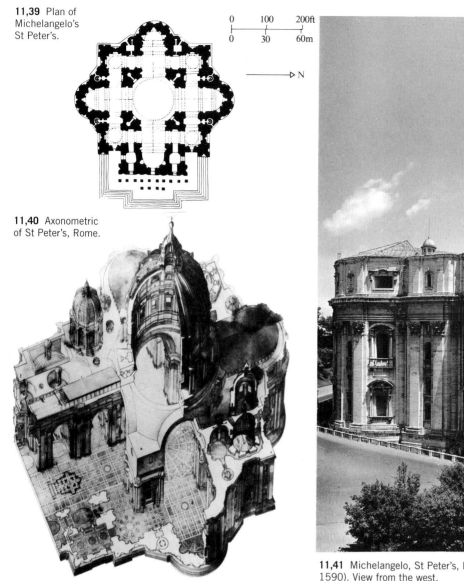

11,40 Axonometric
of St Peter's, Rome.

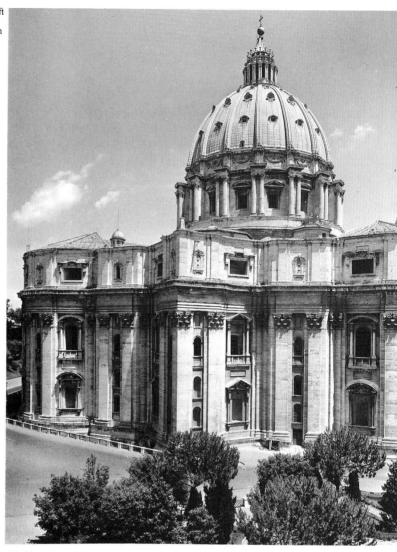

11,41 Michelangelo, St Peter's, Rome, 1546–64 (dome completed by Giacomo della Por
1590). View from the west.

course of the next 18 years the two transepts and the drum of the dome were substantially completed according to his design – or, rather, designs, for he constantly modified his ideas as construction proceeded (**11,39; 40**). Much still remained to be done when he died. The dome was erected between 1588 and 1590 by Giacomo della Porta (c. 1522/33–1602) with considerable modifications, and the centralized plan of the whole building was converted into a Latin cross by Carlo Maderno (1556–1629), who also designed the façade built in 1608–15. Nevertheless, St Peter's owes more to Michelangelo than to any other architect. He created the internal continuum of space flowing round the massive piers that support the dome (13,15). It is his exterior of the transepts, repeated round the apse, and on either side of the nave, that articulates the huge mass of masonry with a supremely dignified rhythm (**11,41**).

On the exterior Michelangelo used giant pilasters of the same Corinthian order as those within but made little attempt to indicate the interior volume of the building, and none to suggest its structural form. Here, as else-where, he made a logical distinction between structure and decoration, the body and its clothes, which enabled him to treat the latter with imaginative freedom. His alternation of wide and narrow bays separated by the pilasters backed by strips, for example, creates deep shadows which lead the eye up to the paired columns around the drum of the dome and its prominent ribs (an element from his design preserved by della Porta). This vertical emphasis recalls the aspiring effect of a Gothic cathedral; but Michelangelo interrupted the insistent upward thrust with the strong horizontal of the cornice and unusually high attic, above and beyond which the dome seems to float – the symbol of heaven being in this way visually detached from the world of mortal endeavour. Like all his works, St Peter's made an immediate impact on younger artists. But later sixteenth-century architects seem to have been attracted more by details which they could imitate (the surrounds of the attic windows, for instance) than by his new and dynamic principles of architectural composition.

THE VENETIAN HIGH RENAISSANCE

Throughout the century Venice remained one of the richest cities in Europe, far richer than any other in Italy. It was a great entrepôt for trade with Asia (as yet little affected by the use of the sea route to India), a flourishing industrial centre for textiles and glass, and the capital of an overseas empire with territories on the mainland of Italy as well. Venice was the only important Italian city to resist political and economic domination by France, Spain or the Papacy, and one of the very few that retained a nominally republican, in fact oligarchic, system of government. Venetian art followed a similarly independent course, partly due to its particular pattern of patronage. The Church did not enjoy in Venice the absolute predominance it did elsewhere in Italy. Both state and private patronage, on the other hand, were considerable, since the governing body of the Serenissima (the 'most serene' republic, as it was called) was intent on making a conspicuous display of power and prosperity as were the luxury-loving families at the top.

GIORGIONE

At the beginning of the century Giovanni Bellini (see p. 456) was, as Dürer wrote in 1506, 'still the best' painter in Venice. But two younger men, Giorgione and Titian, were already becoming known. Giorgione (c. 1476/8–1510) or Giorgio da Castelfranco, a small town on the Venetian mainland, is a very elusive figure, whose only surviving documented work is an all but totally obliterated fresco (Ca'd' Oro, Venice). No more than six easel paintings can reasonably be attributed to him. And yet, there is abundant evidence of his fame. He introduced a new technique, a new style and a new type of picture. He was the first artist to exploit the luminous effects of the new Venetian technique of painting on canvas (rather than panel) with pigments mixed with oil and flexible resins (not the hard resins used in the Low Countries). Great freedom of brushwork with richly opaque and thick, juicy colors was now possible. Unlike the Florentines, Vasari noted, Giorgione made no detailed preparatory drawings on paper or on the canvas itself. He began by roughing out a composition in body-color on the canvas and modified it as he proceeded, defining forms in gradations of tone. Softness of contour, atmospheric subtlety and an evanescent dream-like quality characterize his style – as also, indeed, his subject-matter or, one might almost say, his lack of it. The earliest writer to mention his paintings, the Venetian connoisseur and collector Marcantonio Michiel (d. 1552), might seem sometimes to have been deliberately vague about them – 'a nude in a landscape', for instance. Another is described as 'depicting three philosophers in a landscape, two standing and one sitting looking at the rays of the sun with a sextant'. This survives and shows not only that Michiel's descriptions were accurate, but also that the ambiguous nature of the scene depicted was intentional and reflects Giorgione's very personal conception of the purpose and meaning of art (**11,42**). So eloquently

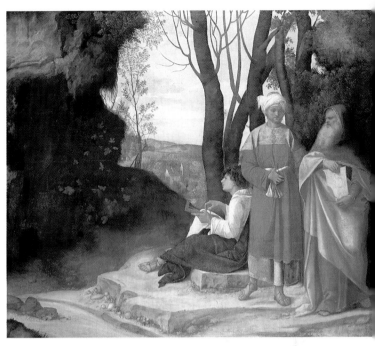

11,42 Giorgione, *Three Philosophers* (finished by Sebastiano del Piombo), c. 1509. Canvas, 3ft 11⅝ins × 4ft 7½ins (1.21 × 1.41m). Kunsthistorisches Museum, Vienna.

could he evoke atmosphere and mood that we do not need to know the precise meaning – the mood is all.

In this instance X-rays reveal that he began by painting the figures in the traditional guise of the Three Magi or 'wise men' – one black, another wearing a crown – not, as was usual, adoring the Christ Child but awaiting the appearance of the star that would announce his nativity. Legend identified the Magi as astronomers or astrologers – 'philosophers' in the terminology of the time. But so effectively did Giorgione remove all traditional attributes of the Magi that they are open to more than one interpretation, for example that they refer to the main tendencies in Venetian thought, the bearded man being associated with Aristotelianism, the man in Oriental costume with Islamic Averroism and the youth with a sextant with the new natural philosophy. Unilluminating though such interpretations are, they invite comparison with Raphael's almost exactly contemporary *School of Athens* (11,23) and emphasize the disparity between the two paintings. It is the mystery and magic, not the rationality, of Renaissance thought that is evoked by Giorgione.

The composition of the *Three Philosophers* is daringly asymmetrical, the figures being balanced by the dark entrance to a cave in the overhanging rock, while the centre opens out on to a warmly glowing landscape beneath the first convincing sunset sky in European art. The figures are in the classical triad of poses – profile, frontal and three-quarters – psychologically detached from one another as from the spectator, yet pictorially inseparable from this lyrically beautiful countryside, as if within a glade and not, as in most earlier paintings, placed in front of a backdrop. The whole painting with its rich colors of falling leaves, dark evergreens and the red of ripe berries is suffused with a hushed, late summer atmosphere of vague apprehension, as the 'philosophers' await whatever revelation is to be vouchsafed to them.

Another Venetian painting of about the same date, entitled *Concert Champêtre*, is entirely secular and, what is more surprising, entirely without any discernible narrative content, mythological or otherwise (**11,43**). A pastoral landscape, with a shepherd and his flock in the distance, recalls the Arcadian setting of Classical and Renaissance bucolic poetry. But one can only speculate as to who the foreground figures are and how and why they have come together – two nude women, one holding a flute, a very fashionably dressed lute-player and a barefoot young rustic with tousled hair. The theme might possibly be harmony, though whether harmony between man and nature, or the sexes, or the classes of society or simply of musical instruments, we are left to guess. Only poets had hitherto captured this air of nostalgic erotic reverie in which everything is, like music, the 'food of love', and the *Concert Champêtre* is best understood as a visual poem. Indeed, Venetians were soon to begin calling such pictures *poesie*. Whether or not it was painted by Giorgione or by Titian, who, according to Vasari, imitated him 'so well that in a short time his works were taken for Giorgione's', this and similar Giorgionesque pictures established a new and immensely influential type, that of the small easel painting intended for the delectation of private collectors – 'cabinet pictures' as they were later to be called. Nothing so sensuous and unintellectual was as yet being produced in Florence or Rome. Only in Venice could be found private patrons rich enough and sophisticated enough to create a demand for such works – patrons like Andrea Odoni, whom Giorgione's pupil Lorenzo Lotto (c. 1480–1556) portrayed in his 'cabinet', swathed in furs and toying with a statuette of Diana of Ephesus by a table strewn with antique gems and coins – an image of cultivated self-indulgence (**11,44**).

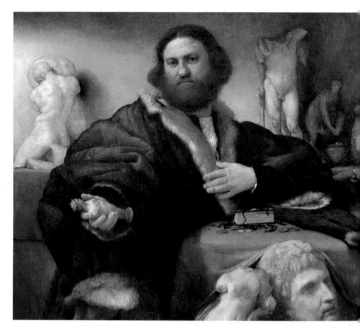

11,44 Lorenzo Lotto, *Andrea Odoni*, 1527. Canvas, 3ft 3⅖ins × 3ft 8⁹⁄₁₀ins (1.01 × 1.14m). Hampton Court Palace, London. Reproduced by gracious permission of Her Majesty The Queen.

TITIAN

Despite lavish private patronage, Venetian artists were dependent on public commissions for fame and fortune. Titian (Tiziano Vecelli, c. 1490–1576) was given his first chance to reveal the full force of his artistic energy when he was asked to paint a vast picture of the Assumption of the Virgin for the high altar of S Maria dei Frari (**11,45**). Hitherto, Venetian altarpieces had been intended to be seen to best advantage from the altar steps; their figures were life-size or less and usually set within simulated architecture conceived as an extension of the church (10,49). Titian's altarpiece, the largest ever painted in Venice, with heroic-scale figures, was designed to catch the eye of anyone entering the west door of the nave, nearly 100 yards away. Its dynamic vertical impulse accords with the Gothic architecture of the church, though the amplitude of the forms, sumptuousness of color and general sense of abundance and health lend its triumphant message a peculiarly Renaissance flavour. All the figures are caught in dramatically expressive movement, the apostles gesticulating on the ground, the Virgin with wind-blown draperies borne up in an aureole of golden light, and the Michelangelesque figure of God the Father with arms extended at a slight slant, as if soaring through the picture plane. Titian's uncompromising departure from Venetian conventions – the picture is said to have dismayed the friars of the church when they first saw it – seems to have been prompted by his knowledge of recent developments in Tuscan art, especially in drawings of the same subject by Fra Bartolommeo. For the Virgin he used a typically Florentine *contrapposto* pose. But the manner of painting is Giorgione's, though much broadened. Contours are brushed in with sweeping strokes and the structure of the composition is created as much by

11,43 Anonymous (Giorgione–Titian?), *Concert Champêtre*, c. 1508. Canvas, about 3ft 7ins × 4ft 6ins (1.09 × 1.37m). Louvre, Paris.

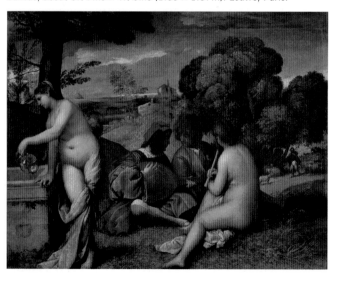

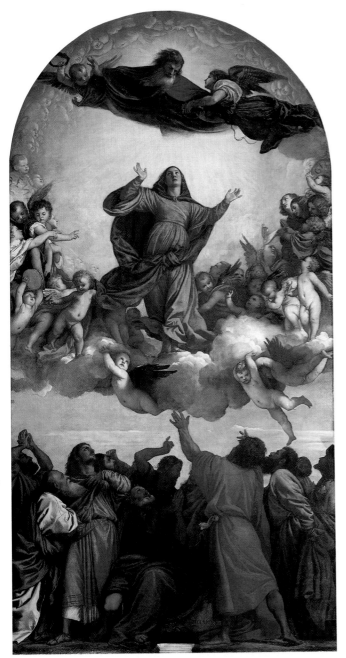

11,45 Titian, *Assumption of the Virgin*, 1516–18. Panel, 22ft 6ins × 11ft 10ins (6.9 × 3.6m). S Maria Gloriosa dei Frari, Venice.

color as by form, with a great triangle of rich red pointing up from the two most prominent apostles to the Virgin's robe and God the Father.

The *Assumption of the Virgin* established Titian's reputation as the leading painter in Venice, with few rivals elsewhere. Indeed, he was perhaps the greatest Renaissance painter of all. He had none of Leonardo's scientific interests or Michelangelo's religious and poetic ones. Nor was he, like Raphael, an architect as well. It was Titian, however, who became in a real sense the founder of modern painting, for he made oil color on canvas the main medium of later Western art. He exploited all its possibilities for the first time, from the animation of the picture surface with vigorous brush-strokes on the rough texture of the canvas to the contrast between rich, creamy highlights thickly laid on and deep, dark hues delicately modulated with glazes.

The *Assumption* was the first of several important altarpieces, but Titian was increasingly occupied with secular commissions, especially after 1532/3, when he painted the Emperor Charles V (Madrid, Prado). Ten years later he was asked to portray Pope Paul III (**11,46**). The relaxed three-quarter length and three-quarter face pose was invented by Raphael, but Titian now developed it in his own more painterly way, absorbing everything into a composition of colors, the heightened flesh-tones of the face contrasting with the surrounding color-scheme of deep values of the same tones. Forms and textures are rendered with amazing skill but only by gradations of tone and variety of touch. Similarly, the compelling impression of authority is conveyed by purely pictorial means. The seated figure with long bony fingers and shrewd lean face directs a steely gaze down towards the spectator.

Paul III tried to lure Titian to Rome. Charles V offered to make him a member of the imperial household, sending him a patent of nobility. But Titian refused. Though far from unworldly, he resisted all their blandishments and clung to his independence. Aided by his close friend, the brilliant, urbane and scandalous writer Pietro Aretino (1492–1556), he made himself the most sought-after painter in Europe. This unique position enabled him to work very largely for whom he wished, at his own pace and on subjects of his own choosing. No earlier artist had achieved such freedom, and the contrast between his

11,46 Titian, *Pope Paul III*, 1543. Canvas, 41$\frac{7}{10}$ × 33$\frac{1}{2}$ins (106 × 85cm). Museo e Gallerie Nazionale di Capodimonte, Naples.

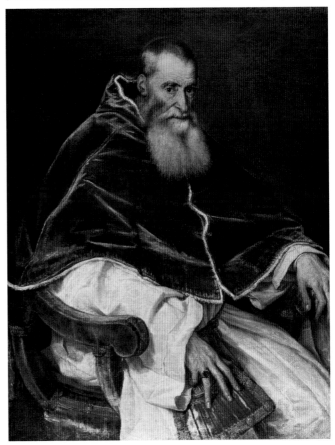

career and that of the constantly thwarted and disappointed Michelangelo is poignant.

A painting of a reclining woman, naked and as large as life, has for long been known as the *Venus of Urbino*, although it lacks all the attributes of a goddess (**11,47**). Titian took the pose from Giorgione's more chaste *Sleeping Venus in a Landscape* (Dresden Gallery), with slight variations to show the figure not only awake but quite frankly inviting her lover (the spectator) with wide-eyed expectation. He also moved her from the fields to the bedroom, where she reclines on ruffled sheets with a pet dog curled up by her feet. In the background there are two attendants, one of whom looks into a chest of the type in which brides kept their trousseau, and it has been suggested that the picture was conceived as an allegory of married love. But Guidobaldo della Rovere, for whom it was painted, called it simply 'the naked woman' and there is no reason to suppose that more, or less, was intended. This image of a woman luxuriating in the warmth and voluptuous softness of her flesh is an uninhibited celebration of the erotic experience raised to the plane of great love-poetry.

Titian's attitude to his subject-matter becomes clearer in the series of *poesie* or erotic mythological scenes he painted for Philip II of Spain. In a letter of 1554 he wrote: 'Because the figure of Danae, which I have already sent to your Majesty, is seen entirely from the front, I have chosen in this other *poesia* to vary the appearance and show the opposite side, so that the room in which they are to hang will seem more agreeable. Shortly I hope to send you the *poesia* of *Perseus and Andromeda*, which will have a viewpoint different from these two.' Evidently, the subjects did not mean a great deal to him, though he had chosen them himself from Ovid's *Metamorphoses*, which he seems to have read in a popular Italian version (not in the original). His aim was neither to illustrate a literary text nor to enrich it with variations, but to create autonomous works of art. His approach to Classical mythology was akin to that of sixteenth-century poets, who also used it simply as a pretext for new and original compositions – Christopher Marlowe's *Hero and Leander*, for example, or Shakespeare's *Venus and Adonis*. In the last picture in the series painted for Philip II Titian derived from the story of Jupiter transforming himself into a bull in order to abduct Europa a wonderful image of the ecstasy, as well as the mystery and fear, involved in the sexual act (**11,48**). Europa's abandoned attitude reveals both her instinctual resistance and her irresistible urge to physical surrender, conveying the terror and the rapture of submission to natural, primal impulses. Her swirling red scarf has the effect of a convulsive cry and her ample flesh seems to quiver with voluptuous anticipation.

By the time he painted the *Rape of Europa* Titian had reached complete mastery of his highly individual handling of paint. The bold rhythm of his heavily loaded brush-strokes could evoke effects of the most sumptuous or the most iridescent color. His early works had been executed with 'a certain finesse and incredible diligence, to be seen from near and far'; Vasari remarked:

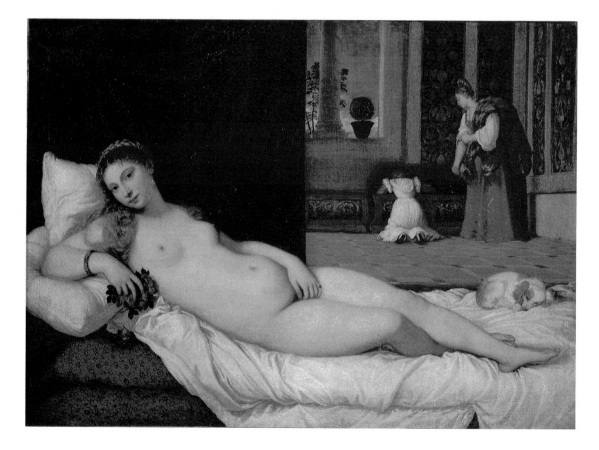

11,47 Titian, *Venus of Urbino*, 1538. Canvas, 3ft 11ins × 5ft 5ins (1.19 × 1.65m). Uffizi, Florence.

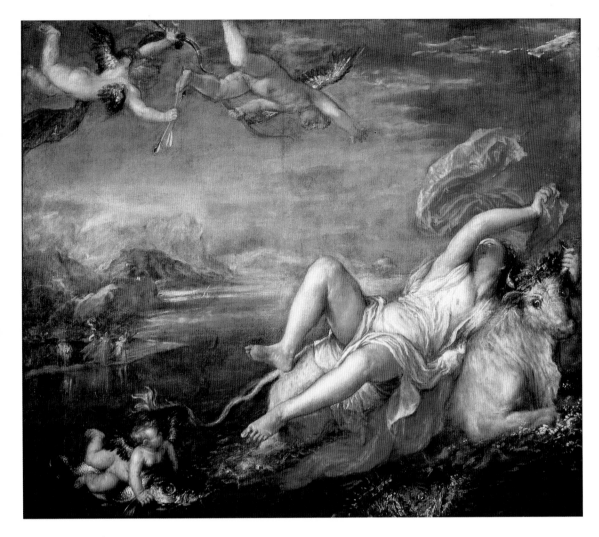

11,48 Titian, *Rape of Europa*, 1559–62. Canvas, 6ft 1in × 6ft 9ins (1.85 × 2.06m). Isabella Stewart Gardner Museum, Boston.

These last pictures are executed with bold strokes and smudges, so that nearby nothing can be seen but from a distance they seem perfect . . . . He went over them many times with his colors and one can appreciate how much labour was involved.

Another contemporary described his unorthodox way of finishing his paintings, 'moderating here and there the finest highlights by rubbing them with his fingers, reducing the contrasts with middle tones and harmonizing one tone with another; at other times, using his finger he would place a dark stroke in a corner to strengthen it, or a smear, almost like a drop of blood, which would enliven some subtle refinement; and so he would proceed.' This method of working was not simply a new technique. It was the outcome of a new attitude to painting. For Titian established the autonomy of the picture as an equivalent – not a mere imitation – of the real world.

TINTORETTO AND VERONESE

From the 1550s Titian worked mainly for Philip II of Spain, leaving his large staff of assistants to turn out pictures, often replicas of earlier works, for less discerning patrons. Although he was by far the most famous Venetian artist, he latterly painted little for the city. Public commissions went to younger painters, notably Tintoretto and Veronese. Tintoretto (Jacopo Robusti, 1518–94) is reputed to have begun in Titian's studio and probably learned his painterly technique there. But his fondness for sharp and often irrational perspective effects, violent foreshortening and gesticulating figures in strenuous muscular movement reveal different susceptibilities, hence perhaps the legend that he aimed to combine the coloring of Titian with the drawing of Michelangelo. Fervently devout, volatile and unworldly, he was the reverse of Titian in character.

Tintoretto grew up in the heady climate of Counter-Reformation piety and his religious pictures have the emotional force of a revelation. An enormous *Crucifixion* he painted for a charitable confraternity engulfs and overwhelms the spectator (**11,49**). The huge panoramic canvas stretches from wall to wall and from wainscoting to ceiling with wide-angle enveloping effect, yet the multitude of tilting, twisting figures, of which those in the foreground are over-life-size, coheres under the visionary lighting into a single dramatic unity. Great plunging diagonals meet and intersect in the body of Christ, isolated above the tumult. There is nothing episodic about this

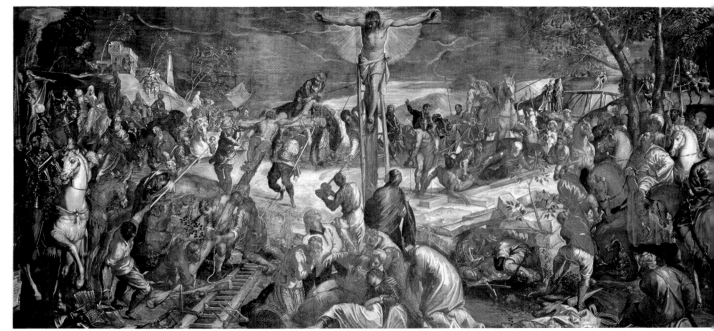

11,49 Tintoretto, *Crucifixion*, 1565. Canvas, 17ft 7ins × 40ft 2ins (5.36 × 12.3m). Scuola di San Rocco, Venice.

intensely dramatic painting; the eye is barely allowed time to take in the superb accomplishment with which individual figures are rendered before being directed to the dominating central cross.

Details, often irrelevant details, are just what catch the attention in a contemporary painting by Veronese (Paolo Caliari, 1528–88) of the Last Supper. When Veronese was called before the Inquisition to explain why he had included dogs, dwarfs, German soldiers and a fool with a parrot, he answered: 'My commission was to make this picture beautiful according to my judgement', adding that 'we painters use the same licence as poets and madmen'. A compromise was reached by calling it *Feast in the House of Levi* (**11,50**). Nothing could be further removed from the noble conception of Leonardo's *Last Supper* (11,13) than this Venetian banquet, though Veronese was a devout Catholic, rather more devout, indeed, than Leonardo. Yet Veronese's is no mere decorative painting. With complete self-assurance he creates an imaginary world of elegance and grandeur, of marble, gold and costly fabrics, in which visual delight in the sumptuous and gorgeous can riot and exult.

11,50 Veronese, *Feast in the House of Levi*, 1573. Canvas, 18ft 3ins × 42ft (5.56 × 12.8m). Gallerie dell'Accademia, Venice.

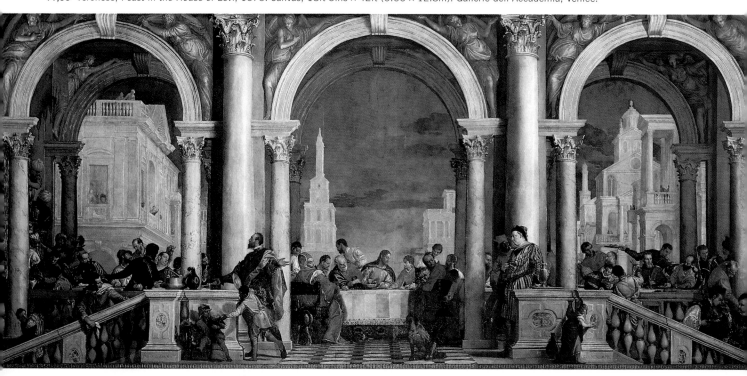

> ## SOURCES AND DOCUMENTS
>
> ## VERONESE'S INTERROGATION BY THE INQUISITION
>
> In 1573 Veronese was examined by the Holy Office on being charged with lack of decorum in his *Last Supper* for the convent of SS Giovanni e Paolo in Venice. The concept of decorum – that a serious subject should be represented wholly in an elevated style – had been taken over from ancient Rome and was highly regarded in the Renaissance. The Holy Office was concerned with Veronese's possibly heretical motives for disregarding it.
>
> **Q**: *In this Supper which you made for SS Giovanni e Paolo what is the significance of the man whose nose is bleeding?*
>
> **A**: *I intended to represent a servant whose nose was bleeding because of some accident.*
>
> **Q**: *What is the significance of those armed men dressed as Germans, each with a halberd in his hand?*
>
> **A**: *This requires that I say 20 words!*
>
> **Q**: *Say them.*
>
> **A**: *We painters take the same licence the poets and the jesters take and I have represented these two halberdiers, one drinking and the other eating nearby on the stairs. They are placed there so that they might be of service because it seemed to me fitting, according to what I have been told, that the master of the house, who was great and rich, should have such servants.*
>
> **Q**: *And that man dressed as a buffoon with a parrot on his wrist, for what purpose did you paint him on that canvas?*
>
> **A**: *For ornament, as is customary.*
>
> **Q**: *Who are at the table of Our Lord?*
>
> **A**: *The Twelve Apostles.*
>
> **Q**: *What is St Peter, the first one, doing?*
>
> **A**: *Carving the lamb in order to pass it to the other end of the table.*
>
> **Q**: *What is the Apostle next to him doing?*
>
> **A**: *He is holding a dish in order to receive what St Peter will give him.*
>
> **Q**: *Tell us what the one next to this one is doing.*
>
> **A**: *He has a toothpick and cleans his teeth.*
>
> **Q**: *Who do you really believe was present at that Supper?*
>
> **A**: *I believe one would find Christ with His Apostles. But if in a picture there is some space to spare I enrich it with figures according to the stories.*
>
> **Q**: *Did anyone commission you to paint Germans, buffoons, and similar things in that picture?*
>
> **A**: *No, milords, but I received the commission to decorate the picture as I saw fit. It is large and, it seemed to me, it could hold many figures.*
>
> **Q**: *Are not the decorations which you painters are accustomed to add to paintings or pictures supposed to be suitable and proper to the subject and the principal figures or are they for pleasure – simply what comes to your imagination without any discretion or judiciousness?*
>
> **A**: *I paint pictures as I see fit and as well as my talent permits.*
>
> **Q**: *Does it seem fitting at the Last Supper of the Lord to paint buffoons, drunkards, Germans, dwarfs and similar vulgarities?*
>
> **A**: *No, milords.*
>
> **Q**: *Do you not know that in Germany and in other places infected with heresy it is customary with various pictures full of scurrilousness and similar inventions to mock, vituperate, and scorn the things of the Holy Catholic Church in order to teach bad doctrines to foolish and ignorant people?*
>
> **A**: *Yes that is wrong; but I return to what I have said, that I am obliged to follow what my superiors have done.*
>
> **Q**: *What have your superiors done? Have they perhaps done similar things?*
>
> **A**: *Michelangelo in Rome in the Pontifical Chapel painted Our Lord, Jesus Christ, His Mother, St John, St Peter, and the Heavenly Host. These are all represented in the nude – even the Virgin Mary – and in different poses with little reverence.*
>
> **Q**: *Do you not know that in painting the Last Judgment in which no garments or similar things are presumed, it was not necessary to paint garments, and that in those figures there is nothing that is not spiritual? There are neither buffoons, dogs, weapons, or similar buffoonery. And does it seem because of this or some other example that you did right to have painted this picture in the way you did and do you want to maintain that it is good and decent?*
>
> **A**: *Illustrious Lords, I do not want to defend it, but I thought I was doing right. I did not consider so many things and I did not intend to confuse anyone, the more so as those figures of buffoons are outside of the place in a picture where Our Lord is represented.*
>
> Veronese was ordered to improve and alter the painting within three months. He did not comply, however, and satisfied the Inquisitors by changing the title to *Feast in the House of Levi* (11,50). This unusually liberal behaviour by the Inquisitors can be explained by the fact that in Venice the Holy Office worked under an agreement that gave the Venetian Republic a part in the trial and a right to withhold the sentence.
>
> (Tr. E. G. Holt, *Literary Sources of Art History*, Princeton 1947. Reprinted by permission of Princeton University Press)

SANSOVINO, PALLADIO
AND THE LAWS OF HARMONY

The loggia in which Veronese's grandees are gathered is reminiscent of the upper floor of the library of S Marco (**11,51**) designed by Sansovino (Jacopo Tatti, 1486-1570), who had left Rome at the time of the sack and settled in Venice. There he was taken up by Titian and Aretino, another refugee from Rome, and together they formed an artistic triumvirate. The library was conceived as part of a grandiose urban scheme for the republic's administrative and ceremonial centre, the vast L-shaped space flowing from the piazza in front of S Marco into the piazzetta outside the Doges' Palace, which the library faces (9,85). One of Sansovino's problems was to marry their façades. He translated the palace's superimposed Gothic arcades, with their squat columns, pointed arches and elaborate tracery, into a true Roman idiom, compensating for the smaller height by adding an exceptionally rich entablature (see Glossary) crowned by a balustrade on which statues and obelisks stand against the sky. Figurative carvings, in the spandrels and on the soffits of the lower arches, take the place of the costly inlays of colored marble previously favoured by Venetians for buildings intended to display conspicuous wealth. The two orders used (and used correctly for the first time in Venice) are Doric and Ionic. Sansovino reserved the 'superior' Composite order for the nearby Loggetta built at the base of the Campanile as a meeting-place for the patricians of Venice – a nice example of the use of the language of Classical architecture to accord with the hierarchic social structure.

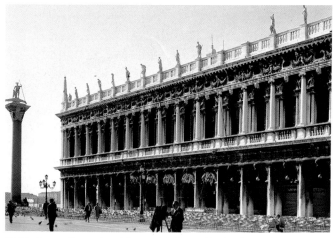

11,51 Jacopo Sansovino, Library of S Marco, Venice, begun 1536.

The library introduced High Renaissance architecture to Venice, and its admirers included Andrea Palladio (1508–80), whose most prominent Venetian building, the church of S Giorgio Maggiore, is on an island just across the water from the Piazzetta (**11,52**). At S Giorgio Maggiore a solution was found to a problem which had vexed Italian architects ever since the beginning of the Renaissance, that of adapting a Classical temple front to a church with a nave and lower side-aisles. Façades had usually been divided into two stories, a wide one across the whole breadth and a narrower upper part corresponding to the nave. But Palladio conceived the façade as two interlocking temple fronts, one based on the height of the nave, the other on that of the aisles. At S Giorgio Maggiore the triangles on either side of the main block are the ends of a pediment, whose base is marked by the string-course between the

11,52 Andrea Palladio, S Giorgio Maggiore, Venice, begun 1565.

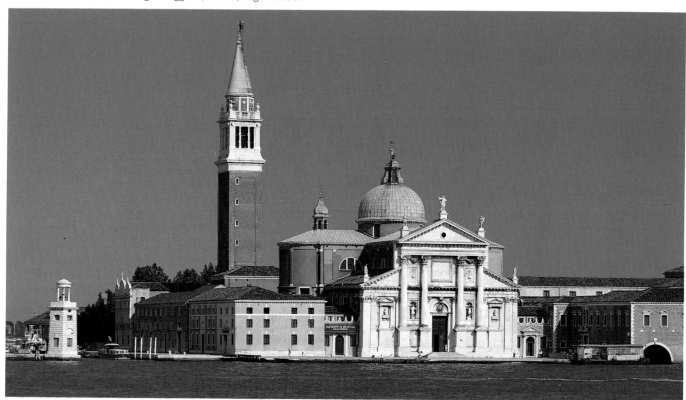

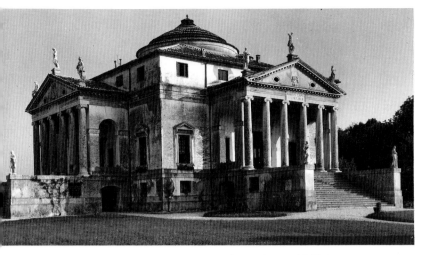

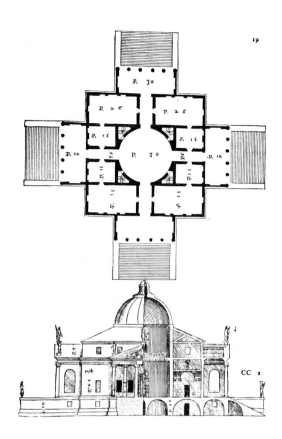

11,53 *Above* Andrea Palladio, Villa Rotonda, Vicenza, begun 1567–9.

11,54 Plan and section of the Villa Rotonda, from *Quattro libri dell'architettura*, 1570.

tall half-columns. Pilasters supporting this structure visually (but not structurally) rise from low bases, whereas the half-columns in the centre are set on high pedestals, giving the façade a strong and un-Classical vertical thrust and at the same time uniting it with the interior, where the same two orders are used in exactly the same way.

Most of the great sixteenth-century Italian architects were also painters or sculptors (Sansovino was primarily a sculptor), and it was said at the time that those who were neither could have 'no eye for what really makes the beauty of architecture'. Palladio was unusual in being a professional architect who practised no other art. Trained in the building craft, he was enrolled in 1524 in the guild of stone-masons and brick-layers of Vicenza, some 40 miles (64km) west of Venice. A local nobleman, Giangiorgio Trissino – humanist, poet and amateur architect – noticing that he was 'a very spirited young man with an inclination to mathematics', undertook, so a contemporary tells us, 'to cultivate his genius by explaining Vitruvius to him and taking him to Rome'. The mathematical theories of the Renaissance, the writings of Vitruvius and the ruins of ancient Rome were to be the interrelated sources of his style. But his designs were saved from theoretical dogmatism and archeological pedantry by his early experience as a working builder.

His practice was mainly domestic – another novelty – ranging from palaces in Vicenza to villas distributed widely over the Venetian mainland. In the mid-sixteenth century, Venetian patricians had begun to turn their attention to farming as a means of maintaining the republic's economic independence from the great grain-producing countries of the north. They improved marshland by drainage, introduced modern methods of cultivation and experimented with new crops, notably maize, then only recently introduced into Europe after it had been found in America. The demand thus created for houses or 'villas' from which estates could be administered was met most successfully by Palladio. He designed buildings of the utmost dignity which could, nevertheless, be constructed by local labour from the simplest and cheapest materials, rough brickwork covered with stucco and needing little if any carved stone. An aristocratic effect was created by the use of

temple fronts to emphasize the main façades, in the mistaken belief that ancient Roman villas had them. La Rotonda outside Vicenza – a suburban retreat rather than a villa in the true sense – has four hexastyle porticoes and is perhaps the most perfect realization of the Renaissance ideal of a free-standing centrally planned building (**11,53**). He designed it to take advantage of a site which he called (in words reminiscent of Pliny the Younger, see p. 195) 'one of the most agreeable and delightful that may be found, on a hillock with gentle approaches and surrounded by other charming hills, all cultivated, that give the effect of a huge theatre'. This sensitivity to landscape, which links Palladio with Giorgione and other Venetian painters, is equally evident in the siting of his other villas, 18 of which survive. They are simpler than the Rotonda, usually with attached farm buildings, and though no two are alike, all are harmoniously proportioned.

To Palladio and his contemporaries, the phrase 'harmoniously proportioned' was no mere figure of speech. The ancient Greeks (traditionally Pythagoras) had discovered that if two chords are twanged, the difference in pitch will be an octave if one is half the length of the other, a fifth if one is two-thirds the length of the other, and a fourth if the relationship is 3:4. It was therefore assumed that a space or solid whose measurements followed the ratio 1:2, 2:3 or 3:4 would be visually harmonious. This belief persisted in the Middle Ages and seems to have been known to some Gothic architects. Indeed, these simple ratios were so often used that they came to condition, almost instinctively, the Western 'sense of proportion' and the Western idea of a well-proportioned building. As Palladio wrote, 'such harmonies usually please very much without anyone knowing why, apart from those who study their causes.' Measurements prominently inscribed on the plans of villas in his

Quattro libri dell'architettura (1570, the first extensive publication by an architect about his own work) suggest that he had in mind also such subtler proportions as those of the major and minor third, 5:6 and 4:5 (**11,54**). They were, however, more easily indicated on the drawing-board than observed on the building-site and, in fact, were rarely followed precisely in construction.

The laws of musical harmony were studied by sixteenth-century theorists and architects not simply to create visually pleasing effects. Harmony had cosmic significance to which Lorenzo, in Shakespeare's *Merchant of Venice*, refers when gazing at the starry sky from the garden of Belmont, a villa near Venice:

> *Look how the floor of Heaven*
> *Is thick inlaid with patines of bright gold;*
> *There's not the smallest orb, which thou beholdest,*
> *But in his motion like an angel sings,*
> *Still quiring to the young-eyed cherubins:*
> *Such harmony is in immortal souls.*

Observance of the laws of harmony was believed to attune all aspects of life on earth to a heavenly ideal. And in Venice particularly the polyphonic consonance of the many voices of the social orders was believed to be essential for the well-being of the most serene republic. Musical metaphors occur frequently in the political theory as well as in the art of the time.

MANNERISM AND MANNERISMS

The term 'Mannerist' – sometimes used in connection with Palladio and more often with Tintoretto – has acquired a bewildering range of meanings. It derives from the Italian word *maniera*, much used in sixteenth-century writings on social behaviour as well as on the arts, to signify not simply a style or manner in the literal sense but also the highly prized quality of stylishness which implied ease of manner, virtuosity, fluency and refinement. This quality was found in the antique statues then most admired and in the works of Leonardo, Raphael and Michelangelo. A distinction was, however, drawn between the stylish and the mannered or affected, i.e. the adoption of another's mannerisms or, paradoxically, the self-conscious display of personal traits. It was in this derogatory sense that the word 'Mannerist' later came to be used for the work of mid- and late sixteenth-century artists, whose paintings in sharp acid colors, with figures writhing in curiously distorted perspective, looked contrived and over-refined to seventeenth-century eyes. The notion of Mannerism as an historical style, following that of the High Renaissance, is much more recent and there are various and contradictory definitions and interpretations of it. It has been construed as either a reaction against or an extension of the ideals of the High Renaissance, as an expression of the spiritual crises of the time or as a sophisticated art created solely for art's sake, a 'stylish style' exemplifying the aesthetic theories of the sixteenth century.

CORREGGIO AND MANNERIST 'LICENCE'

Evolving mutations in Renaissance style can be seen very clearly in the work of two artists, Correggio and Parmigianino, separated by a generation but working at the same time in Parma, some way from the main centres of artistic activity. Correggio (Antonio Allegri, c. 1489–1534) developed from the art of Mantegna and Leonardo, or his north Italian followers, a personal style of the utmost grace and suavity. Michelangelo's Sistine Chapel ceiling, Raphael's *Stanze* and Titian's *Assumption* enlarged his ideas, even though he may have known them only at second-hand from drawings. With his fresco in the cupola of Parma Cathedral he created a work of art no less influential, a new type of ceiling painting which breaks completely through the architecture to open a vision of figures swirling into the heavens and, as it were, whirling the spectator up into the vortex with them (**11,55**). Instead of witnessing the scene as if through a proscenium arch (as in Titian's *Assumption*, 11,45) the spectator is made part of it. Correggio's skill in depicting figures seen from below – *sotto in sù* is the technical term – displaying well-turned limbs as they gyrate in space, set a new standard for illusionism. But his mastery in rendering flesh – no artist has ever painted the blush of a perfect youthful complexion with greater sensitivity – was fully developed only in his oil paintings, whether of saints in graceful adoration or of elegantly amorous Olympians. In one painting Jupiter is about to descend in a shower of gold on Danae, whose virginity her father tried to preserve by incarcerating her in a tower, as the view through the window indicates (**11,56**). The subject had often been cited (by St Augustine among others) as one of dangerously provocative eroticism, but Correggio purged it of gross sensuality. Lubricity is held in check by the tenderness and sweetness of Danae's passively receptive attitude, by the gentleness with which

11,55 Correggio, *Assumption of the Virgin*, detail, 1526–30. Fresco, dome of Parma Cathedral.

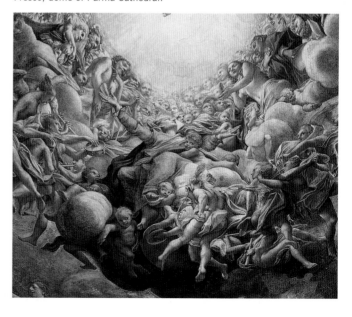

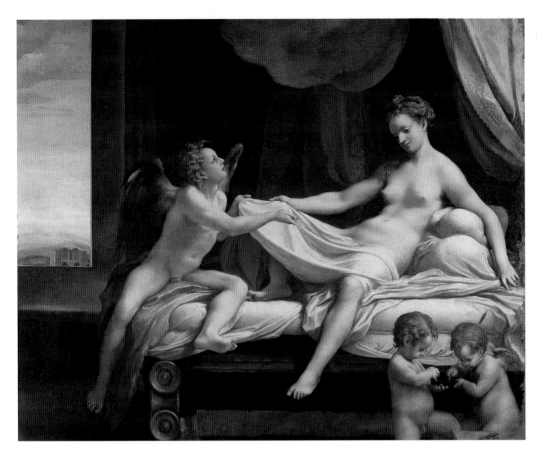

11,56 Correggio, *Danae*, c. 1532. Canvas, 64⅖ × 29ins (163.5 × 74cm). Galleria Borghese, Rome.

Cupid lifts the drapery from her thighs and by the lithe and supple rhythm which the metrical rhyming of their limbs imposes on the composition.

Correggio's paintings perfectly express the early sixteenth-century notion of stylishness, and his idealized images of youthful beauty never pass beyond natural limits. Parmigianino (Francesco Mazzola, 1503–40) went further, pursuing grace and elegance to extremes in his painting known as the *Madonna with the Long Neck* (**11,58**). He was much indebted to Correggio, whose pupil he may have been, and to such late works of Raphael as the *Transfiguration* (11,33) (he spent three years in Rome from 1524 until the sack of the city). But his ideal of feminine beauty seems to have derived less from art and still less from nature than from literary conceits such as that which compared a woman's shoulders, neck and head with a perfectly formed vase (hence that carried by the long-legged angel on the left). Not only the Virgin's neck, but her hands, her right foot and the limbs of the Child are all elongated and refined to an unearthly elegance. Far below and far away in space and time a tiny figure, probably St Jerome, unfolds a scroll in an echoing perspective space and introduces a slightly uncomfortable visionary quality into the otherwise very worldly atmosphere of the painting.

The wilful distortion of the human body in painting was paralleled in architecture by the manipulation of the Classical orders and their enrichments. Michelangelo had given a lead in the Medici Chapel (11,34) and still more boldly in the vestibule to the Laurentian Library attached to the same church, of which Vasari remarked that all architects owed a debt to Michelangelo 'for having broken the chains which made them all work in the same way'. At exactly the same time Giulio Romano (1492/9–1546), formerly a pupil and assistant of Raphael, was indulging in similar 'licence' – a term of approval in the sixteenth century. In 1526 he began at the Palazzo Te then just outside Mantua (**11,57**). As was appropriate for a building in the country, he used the Doric order and covered the walls from ground to entablature with rustication (originally less bulky than restorations have made it). But the spacing of the half-columns is most irregular and midway between each of them a triglyph slips unaccountably down from an otherwise correct frieze. On the side of the courtyard illustrated here windows are frameless, pushed

11,57 Giulio Romano, Palazzo Te, Mantua, 1526–35.

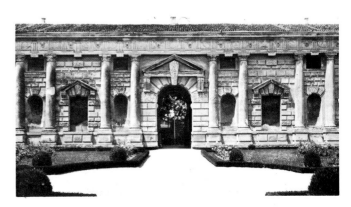

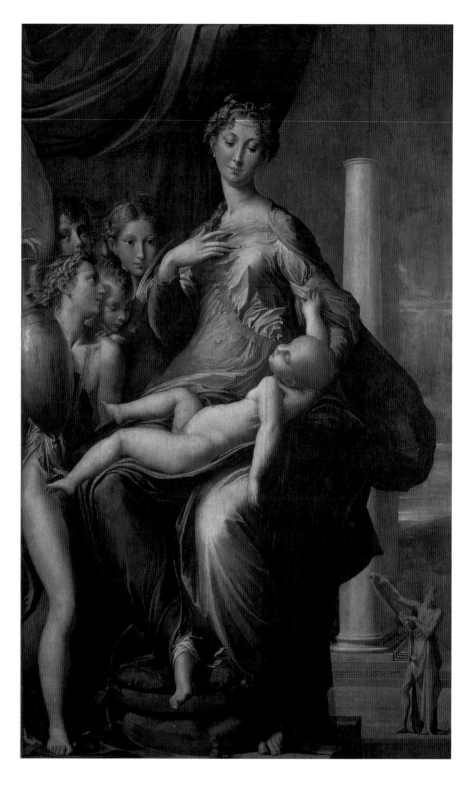

11,58 Parmigianino, *Madonna with the Long Neck*, c. 1535. Panel, about 7ft 1in × 4ft 4ins (2.16 × 1.32m). Uffizi, Florence.

up to the top of the wall and squeezed between the more closely spaced columns; prominence is given to niches below them and blind windows capped by bold pediments in the wider spaces. These contradictions are disturbing, but Giulio Romano's intention seems to have been less to dismay than delight those who knew enough of architectural theory to appreciate his ingenuity. They have an effect akin to that of a rhetorical oxymoron, such as Aretino used in a letter to Giulio Romano: 'always modern in the antique way and antique in the modern way'.

The licence accorded to architects was dependent on their knowledge of the rules they infringed. Treatises cod-

ifying the Classical orders were published by two of the most dashingly stylish architects, Sebastiano Serlio (1475–1554) and Giacomo Barozzi da Vignola (1507–73), an assistant of Michelangelo, whom he succeeded at St Peter's. For his own most important building, however, Vignola renounced all licence in favour of severity and decorum. This was the first and still the main church of the Society of Jesus in Rome (**11,59**). His brief was to accommodate as large a congregation as possible within the limits of an oblong site. 'The Church is to be entirely vaulted over', he was told; 'it is to have a single nave, not a nave with aisles, and there are to be chapels on both

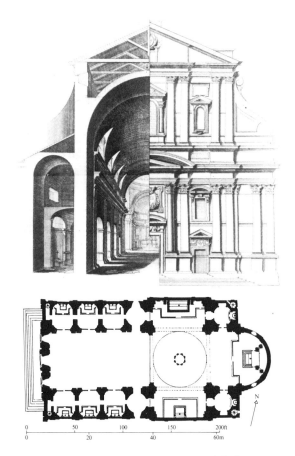

11,59 Vignola, Il Gesù, 1568. Façade by Giacomo della Porta, c. 1575–84 (engraving by Sandrart) and plan.

sides.' By almost completely shutting off the chapels flanking an unusually spacious, 60-foot-wide (18m) nave he successfully combined the centralized scheme of the Renaissance with the longitudinal plan of the Middle Ages. The demands of Counter-Reformation piety were perfectly met by this lucid and simple interior – originally gray and white without any further enrichments – in which there was nothing to distract from the words of the preacher or obstruct the view of the ritual at the high altar. The strong eastward drive of the great tunnel vault and cornice running right through without a break was dramatically emphasized by carefully contrived light effects, notably the contraction and darkening of the last bay before the crossing to make a pause before the flood of light streaming down from the drum of the dome with a wonderful sense of glory and fulfilment. The façade was designed after Vignola's death by Giacomo della Porta (see p. 494), with correctly proportioned Classical elements combined in an entirely un-Classical way.

A sharpening of the distinction between what was deemed appropriate for, respectively, religious and secular art was an immediate consequence of the Counter-Reformation. Michelangelo's *Last Judgement* was censured from a religious viewpoint for the very qualities that most appealed to artists – for what his pupil and biographer Ascanio Condivi called his expression of 'all that the human figure is capable of in the art of painting, not leaving out any pose or action whatsoever'. Such virtuosity was brought to its highest pitch in secular work, often on a small scale and in precious materials, for

example the gold salt-cellar by Benvenuto Cellini (1500–71) (**11,60**). In his autobiography Cellini gave a full account of the genesis, production and meaning of this exquisitely refined *objet de luxe*, which might seem far removed from the exuberant rough and tumble, the fierce passions and jealousies, of the world Cellini lived in and also brilliantly described. The main figures represent Water and Earth 'fashioned like a woman with all the beauty of form, the grace and charm, of which my art was capable', he proudly declared. Their legs are interlaced, giving a sophisticated eroticism to his celebration of the fecundity of nature.

Cellini began this feat of virtuoso artistry in Rome, but completed it in France for Francis I (1515–47), who had made his court at Fontainebleau the most important centre of artistic activity north of the Alps. Italians, beginning with Leonardo, who spent his last years in France, were particularly favoured. French artists followed their lead, realizing Italian ideals in their own slightly different way. Water nymphs from a (dismembered) fountain by Jean Goujon (fl. 1540–62), for example, wear clinging draperies derived from Hellenistic carvings and dance to an Italian tune yet have a curiously bloodless, wraith-like quality quite foreign to the Mediterranean (**11,61**). From France the principle of delicately poised *contrapposto* was transmitted to England and adopted for jewel-like miniature portraits of Elizabethans by Nicholas Hilliard (c. 1547–1619), a student of both Italian artistic theory and of Castiglione's *Book of the Courtier*. To Castiglione's influence was also largely due the acceptance – both socially and artistically – of well-bred, well-educated women artists such as Sofonisba Anguissola (1532/5–1625), the daughter of Cremonese aristocrats. Her miniature portraits brought her international celebrity (**11,62**). She was the first Italian woman to become a famous artist.

11,60 Benvenuto Cellini, salt-cellar of Francis I, 1539–43. Gold with enamel, 10¼ × 13⅛ins (26 × 33.3cm). Kunsthistorisches Museum, Vienna.

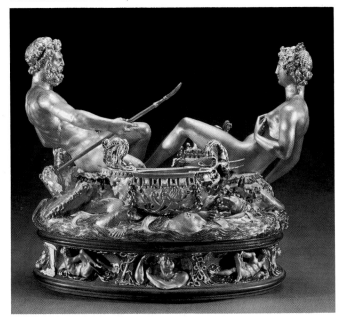

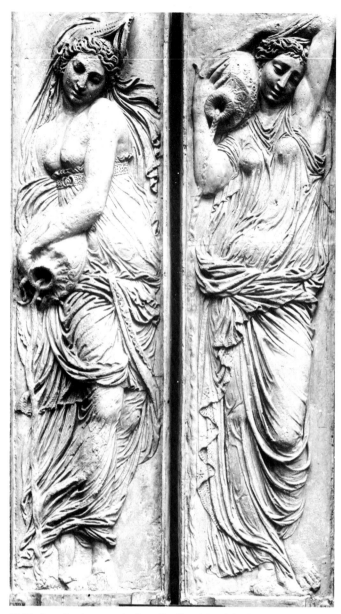

11,61 Jean Goujon, nymphs from the *Fountain of the Innocents*, 1547–9. Stone, 7ft 8½ins (2.35m) high. Louvre, Paris.

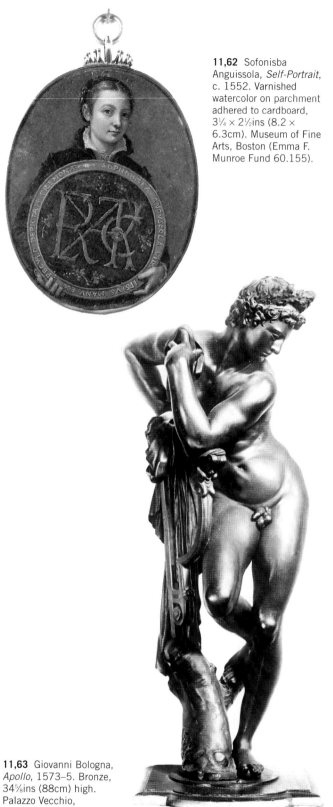

11,62 Sofonisba Anguissola, *Self-Portrait*, c. 1552. Varnished watercolor on parchment adhered to cardboard, 3¼ × 2½ins (8.2 × 6.3cm). Museum of Fine Arts, Boston (Emma F. Munroe Fund 60.155).

11,63 Giovanni Bologna, *Apollo*, 1573–5. Bronze, 34⅝ins (88cm) high. Palazzo Vecchio, Florence.

Contrapposto, which had been understood in the early sixteenth century simply as a means of articulation, was gradually developed to obtain an effect of continuous spiral movement almost as an end in itself. The Roman writer Quintilian's eulogy of the 'distorted and elaborate attitude . . . the novelty and difficulty' of Myron's *Discobolus* (**4,34**) was well known and, although no copy or version of this famous statue had as yet been discovered, sixteenth-century sculptors took to heart Quintilian's recommendation that effects of grace and charm involve 'departure from the straight line and have the merit of variation from the ordinary usage'. Statuettes by Giovanni Bologna (1529–1608) seem almost to have been conceived as essays in smoothly convoluted three-dimensional form, to be appreciated only when they can be seen all round. That of *Apollo* (**11,63**) was modelled to stand in

a niche and Giovanni Bologna compensated for the restriction of viewpoints by the sway of the hips, the curve of the torso and the eurythmic movement of the supple arms and legs to make it appear as if slowly revolving (in fact, there was originally a mechanism to rotate it in its niche). It was commissioned for Francesco de' Medici's *studiolo*, a small room described at the time

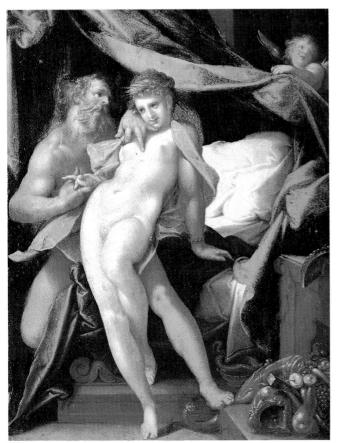

as 'a cabinet of objects that are rare and precious both for their price and their art'. For another such sanctum of visual hedonism, that of the Emperor Rudolf II, a strangely introverted connoisseur of artistic preciosity, Bartholomäus Spranger (1546–1611), painted a series of small pictures in which the provocatively erotic nature of the twisted pose becomes explicit (**11,64**). There are echoes of statues by Michelangelo, of paintings by Correggio and of Giulio Romano's illustrations to pornographic poems by Titian's friend Pietro Aretino in these works, which are Mannerist in every sense of the word and invest sexuality with a stylish perversity.

PIETER BRUEGEL THE ELDER

Many Flemish artists visited Rome and returned to the north, where they practised a showily Italianate style favoured by Church and state. The great exception was Pieter Bruegel the Elder (c. 1525/30–69), who began by painting and drawing for engravers moralizing subjects of a disquieting strangeness looking back to Bosch (see p. 467). Later he became more direct and straightforward, or apparently so, and was often misunderstood as a result. The biographer Karel van Mander (1548–1606) said that there were few of his works which the observer could contemplate 'with a straight face' and he was later nicknamed 'Peasant Bruegel' and 'Bruegel the jester'. But he

11,64 Bartholomäus Spranger, *Vulcan and Maia*, c. 1590. Copper, 9 × 7⅛ins (23 × 18cm). Kunsthistorisches Museum, Vienna.

11,65 Pieter Bruegel the Elder, *Harvesters*, 1565. Panel, 3ft 10½ins × 5ft 3¼ins (1.18 × 1.61m). Metropolitan Museum of Art, New York (Rogers Fund 1919).

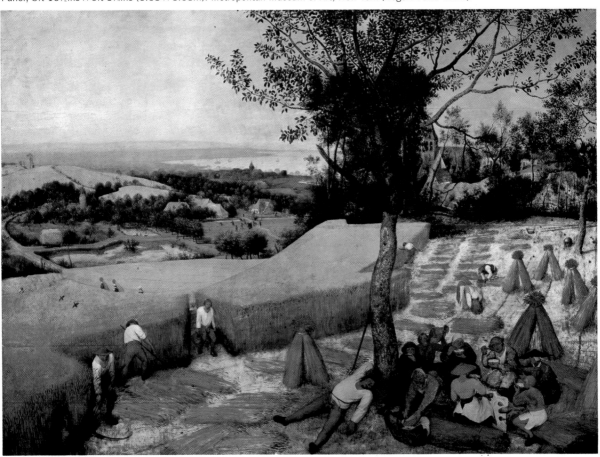

Pieter Bruegel's Months

PATRONAGE IN FLANDERS

Pieter Bruegel's *Harvesters* (**11,65**) was painted as one of a cycle of six pictures each of which illustrated life on the land for two months of the year. *Hunters in the Snow*, for December and January, was another (**11,66**). They were commissioned by an Antwerp financier, Niclaes Jongelinck (b. 1517), a patron of a new type soon to become increasingly common in Europe. He bought works of art as items of interior decoration and as financial assets, combining pleasure with profit. In the fifteenth century rich Flemish burghers had sometimes commissioned paintings for churches, notably the Ghent altarpiece (see pp. 432–3), and small devotional images for their homes. But the main domestic wall decorations were tapestry hangings of all-over leafy designs, called 'verdures', the stock-in-trade of the factories at Arras in Flanders. Figurative tapestries were within the means of very few except the ruling class and higher nobility. Easel paintings of figurative, secular subjects, on the other hand, were far less expensive and could be commercially valuable if by well-known artists; hence their appeal to

a new art-buying public and the increasing production of them.

Niclaes Jongelinck was born into the bourgeoisie of Antwerp, the most prosperous city in the Netherlands under Spanish rule. His paternal grandfather had been a fish-merchant but his father entered the Spanish service and from 1538 was master of the Antwerp mint. He had three brothers, two of whom worked in the mint. The youngest, Jacques, branched out as a maker of medals, rather than coins, and after studying in Italy also as a sculptor of large-scale works in bronze. Niclaes engaged in various financial activities: trade, running a lottery, marine (shipping) insurance and tax-farming or tax-collecting on behalf of the authorities, usually an extremely profitable enterprise. In 1554 he bought a big newly-built house in a recent suburban development just outside the city walls of Antwerp and promptly set about commissioning works of art to decorate it. A local poet wrote a few years later: 'Let Italy send her pupils to visit the house which you, born of good stock from the lesser citizens, possessed of

wealth but an ardent lover of all the arts, also a hater of sordid avarice and its sworn enemy, raised to the stars near proud Antwerp at unusual expense' (tr. I. Buchanan).

The first of the artists he employed was Frans Floris (c. 1518–70), who provided ten large paintings of the *Labours of Hercules* and seven of the *Liberal Arts*, now known from engravings (**11,67**). Floris had been trained in Antwerp and in the early 1540s visited Italy, where he was overwhelmed by Michelangelo, especially by his *Last Judgement* in the Sistine Chapel (11,30). On his return he introduced an Italian Mannerist style of painting to the Netherlands, with such success that he had to employ a large staff of assistants to fulfil the numerous commissions he received. His pictures for Jongelinck, with dignified figures robed in ancient Roman costumes or with violently muscular nude bodies in a variety of athletic poses, could hardly have been more Italianate. The paintings Jongelinck bought in 1565 from Bruegel to decorate a neighbouring room, probably a dining room, were, on the other hand, almost defiantly Flemish in style and subject-matter. Their straightforward, even uncouth, scenes of contemporary low-life were a far cry from the airs and graces of the Classical world of Italy.

In 1566 Jongelinck had to pawn part of his art collection to the city of Antwerp as security for money owed by business associates: 22 paintings by Floris, 16 by Bruegel and one ascribed to Dürer. He seems to have recovered them, however, and shortly afterwards commissioned from his brother Jacques eight bronze life-size nude figures; but even before they were finished he had to pledge them to another Antwerp merchant as security for a loan. He died in 1570 deeply in debt and his works of art were sold.

Floris and Bruegel, who nowadays seem worlds apart in artistic ability as well as style and choice of subject-matter, were equally highly esteemed by their compatriots. Floris, like his Italian contemporaries, was engaged mainly on large church altarpieces,

11,66 Pieter Bruegel the Elder, *Hunters in the Snow*, 1565. Oil and tempera on panel, 3ft 10ins × 5ft 4ins (1.18 × 1.64m). Kunsthistorisches Museum, Vienna.

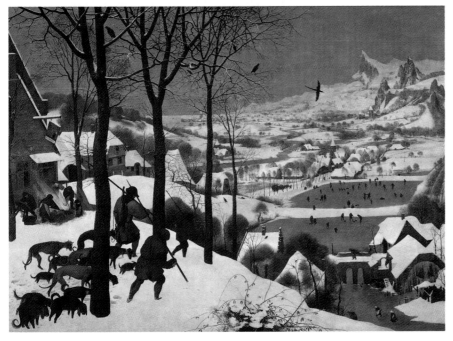

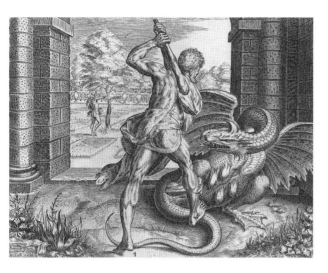

11,67 Frans Floris, *Hercules before the Garden of the Hesperides*, 1555. Engraving by Cornelis Cort after Floris, 8½ × 11¼ins (21.4 × 28.5cm). British Museum, London.

mythological scenes and formal portraits. Bruegel, on the other hand, devoted himself either to drawings for prints of moralizing subjects, which had a very wide diffusion, or easel paintings for private houses, usually of rustic or low-life scenes. The number he painted in no more than 15 years, of which some 60 survive, testifies to the size of the new market he was exploiting. It favoured easel pictures and set a high premium on technical virtuosity and individuality, i.e. on the unique work of art, no matter what the subject-matter was. His patrons and collectors of his work included, besides members of the merchant class, a Spanish cardinal and viceroy, a Habsburg arch-duke and the Holy Roman Emperor Rudolf II, patron of Spranger (11,64) and other stylishly sophisticated Mannerist painters whose effete, delicately serpentine figures make a striking contrast with Bruegel's rough and sturdy peasants.

Bruegel's pictures were admired for their truth to nature. To his friend Ortelius (see p. 512) they seemed not so much works of art as 'works of Nature'. The Flemish art theorist Karel van Mander (1548–1606) praised his 'many comic figures showing the true character of peasants', remarking that in 'a most beautiful picture' of a peasant wedding, the 'faces and limbs, where they are bare, are yellow and sunburnt; their skins are ugly, different from those of town-dwellers'. In this picture, or one like it (11,68), he gave with great skill an impression of veracity not only in the strongly characterized faces and postures of the figures but in the seemingly casual composition cut off abruptly at the sides to suggest an instantaneous record. The most prominent figures are two robust and burly cooks with their backs to the spectator, carrying food on a door wrenched from its hinges to serve as a tray. The bride sits red-cheeked, eyes half-closed and hands clasped, ignored by the rest of the company, some of whom may even be slyly mocking her. Is she already pregnant? An engraving of another painting by Bruegel of the same subject bears the legend: 'But our Bride has already given up dancing. And all for the best too, as she's full and sweet.' At the far right there is a well-dressed sword-bearing gentleman in conversation with a cowled friar, holding themselves aloof from the rowdy merry-making throng, though they may, by their presence, be lending official sanction to the occasion. Bruegel may also have had some general satirical intention. In composition the painting recalls images of the Marriage at Cana but the emphasis on the deadly sin of gluttony is subversive, undermining the sacramental nature of the occasion.

With such paintings Bruegel created a new *genre*. There were, nevertheless, precedents for his scenes of country activities, on a very small scale, on the calendar pages of Books of Hours (see p. 418) illustrating, for instance, the singeing of the hide of a dead pig as shown outside the inn on the left of *Hunters in the Snow*. Having painted miniatures himself, he was surely aware of these calendar pages with their idyllic scenes of rustic harmony, which continued to be made during and after the intermittent and brutally suppressed peasant rebellions in the early sixteenth century. Bruegel's peasants, though much more vigorous – sometimes bursting with life – are also contented whether working or playing outside the towns that depended on the fruits of their labours. Hence, no doubt, the appeal of his pictures to town-dwellers who liked to contemplate, from the comfort of their well-appointed burgher homes, the toil and sweat of rural life in a natural world whose harshness Bruegel did not attempt to mitigate.

11,68 Pieter Bruegel the Elder, *Peasant Wedding*, c. 1565. Oil on panel, 3ft 8⅞ins × 5ft 4ins (1.14 × 1.63m). Kunsthistorisches Museum, Vienna.

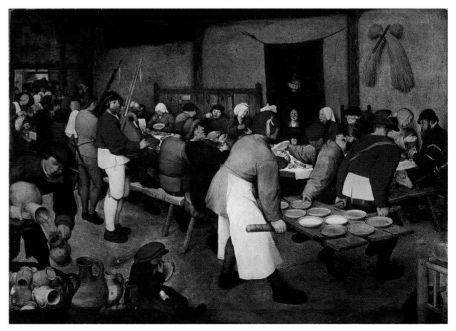

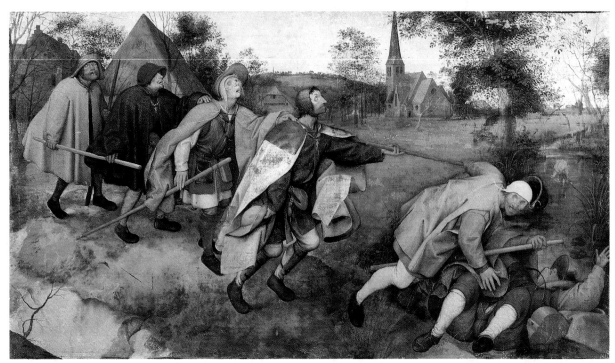

11,69 Pieter Bruegel the Elder, *Blind leading the Blind*, 1568. Tempera on canvas, about 34 × 68ins (86.3 × 172.7cm). Museo Nazionale, Naples.

was by no means a *naïf* painter. He knew Italy as well as any of the Flemish 'Romanists' and his rejection of their modish style was quite deliberate. In Antwerp, where he spent most of his life, he was a valued member of an intellectual circle which included Christophe Plantin, the great scientific publisher, and Abraham Ortelius, then preparing the first modern atlas of the world and later to become official geographer to Philip II of Spain. Bruegel worked for private collectors of educated taste and a large group of his paintings was bought shortly after his death by Rudolf II.

In an obituary tribute, Ortelius extolled Bruegel's fidelity to nature and went on to remark that 'in all his works more is always implied than is depicted'. This is fully borne out by a series of paintings recording the cycle of the seasons, subjects often represented in medieval art (9,87) but treated by Bruegel in an entirely new way and on the large scale normally reserved for religious or mythological scenes. They are essentially paintings of landscape and atmosphere rather than illustrations of 'the labours of the months'. One evokes in rich browns and yellows the burning heat of August in a wide landscape so objectively factual in detail that it is difficult to realize that it is imaginary (11,65). From Italians, especially Venetians, Bruegel had learnt much – notably aerial perspective and the advantage of a high viewpoint – but his figures are far removed from the poetic inhabitants of Arcadia; they are real-life farm labourers, of the earth and earthy. Some are reaping and tying sheaves while others eat and drink; one lies in a stupor. The church half hidden behind the tree reappears in another work, his most disturbing, that of the *Blind leading the Blind* (**11,69**). In this the moral is explicit, whereas in the harvest scene it is implied in the

contrast between the plenitude and generosity of nature and the insignificance of man. The vacuous faces and ungainly limbs of the yokels might suggest that Bruegel saw only their clownish aspects – they recall Shakespeare's rustics. But Bruegel made this lowest class of the social order stand for all humanity. In his paintings men are not, as they are in Italian Renaissance art, the lords of creation. They are almost incidental to his majestic conception of the annual cycle of growth and decay, of death and rebirth. He extols the grandeur of the universe by denying man's central position in it. His peasants are, none the less, individuals and the independent life with which he has endowed them reveals another seam of implied meaning which runs through all his mature work. He was in direct contact with the Dutch moralist Dirk Volckertszoon Coornheert, the leading exponent of an undogmatic tendency in religious thought called Libertinism or Spiritualism, centred on man's personal relationship with God and his duty to overcome sin, to which he is driven by folly. Bruegel probably remained a Catholic, like Coornheert, but he came closer to a Protestant view of the world than any great artist of the century, apart from Dürer and Holbein. Though he did not live to see the worst effects of the Spanish suppression of Protestantism in the Netherlands, he had his wife burn many of his engravings during his last illness. Their inscriptions might be thought 'too biting and too sharp' and he feared that 'most disagreeable consequences might grow out of them'.

El Greco

The Italian mannerisms which Bruegel disregarded were painstakingly learned only to be transformed into a deeply emotional religious art by the last great European painter of the sixteenth century, El Greco (Domenicos Theotoco-poulos, 1541–1614). He was born on Crete, then a Venetian possession, and went as a youth to Venice, where he began by painting icons in the Byzantine style for the Greek community there but soon succumbed to the influence of Titian, Tintoretto and, later, Michelangelo. When he

11,70 El Greco, *Resurrection*, c. 1597–1604. Canvas, 9ft ¼in × 4ft 2ins (2.75 × 1.27m). Prado, Madrid.

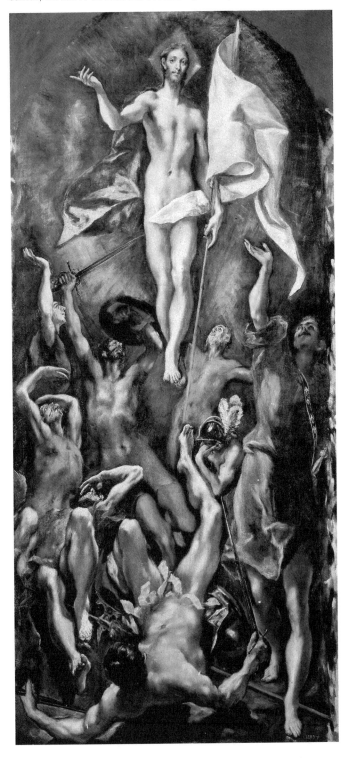

visited Rome between 1570 and 1572 the Counter-Reformation was at its height and all religious art was being scrutinized in strict accordance with the decrees of the Council of Trent to eliminate any imagery which might be misconstrued as profane, pagan or heretical. When Michelangelo's *Last Judgement* (11,30) was attacked and condemned, El Greco is said to have offered to paint something more 'decent and virtuous' as a replacement – a myth, no doubt, but one which indicates the direction of his ambition, to create an art as grandiose as Michel-angelo's yet purged of all sensuality. In 1576/7 El Greco went to Spain, settling in Toledo, where he spent the rest of his life. Spain was then the leading power in Europe with dominions stretching from the Netherlands to Mexico and Peru. In 1571 it had scored a major victory for Christendom with the destruction of the Turkish fleet at the battle of Lepanto. And, of course, the Counter-Refor-mation was nowhere more ardently promoted by both Church and state than in Spain. The most profoundly spiritual of sixteenth-century Catholic mystics were Spanish, notably St Teresa of Avila (1515–82) and St John of the Cross (1542–91), as was also St Ignatius Loyola, the founder of the Society of Jesus.

The aim of El Greco's art was to arouse religious fervour and to elevate the spirit above the everyday world of sen-sory perceptions. But whereas St Teresa, for example, visualized her transcendental experiences in concrete imagery, he translated the physical into incandescent spirituality. In his late painting of the Resurrection lam-bent forms flicker upwards in parabolic curves (**11,70**). The brushwork is ecstatically free, colors are used expres-sively, the white banner in Christ's hand being balanced by shimmering red drapery that has no other function than that of adding vibration to the upper parts of the pic-ture. Figures are elongated to maximum tension, their arms being all but dislocated by emphatic gestures. Violent fore-shortening is used to entirely non-illusionistic effect – for the body of the nude man falling backwards in the centre and for the shins and knees of the sleeping figure beside him. Lighting and spatial relationships are similarly irra-tional. And the traditional iconography of the subject has also been left behind. No tomb is visible. Indeed, the rad-iant figure of Christ suggests the Ascension as well as the Resurrection, and his feet are crossed as if still crucified.

El Greco was a visionary. Though described by a con-temporary in 1611 as 'a great philosopher', he could have said, with St John of the Cross, that he had 'no light or guide other than that burning in the heart'. The books in his library at Toledo included two editions of the works of Dionysius, whose concept of divine light had fired Abbot Suger more than four centuries earlier (see p. 385). And his painting of the Resurrection recalls Dionysius's metaphor for Christ as 'the first radiance' of God the Father. His art seems to have been inspired by the belief that if the human mind could abandon itself to the 'harmony and radiance' of true terrestrial beauty, it would be guided upwards to the divine transcendent cause. He was the last European painter to express such transcendental ideals, and his work brings a great age of Christian art to its close.

Chapter Twelve

The Americas, Africa and Asia

European knowledge of the rest of the world was dramatically and vastly expanded around the year 1500. Vasco da Gama opened up the sea-route round Africa to India in 1497–9 and in 1492–1504 Christopher Columbus's attempts to reach the spice islands of the Far East by sailing westwards led, totally unexpectedly, to the discovery and subsequent exploration of America. Finally, in 1519–22, came the first circumnavigation of the globe. The boundaries of Classical geography were shattered by all this – and there were also some disconcerting implications that could not be ignored. As the Florentine historian Francesco Guicciardini wrote in the 1530s, 'not only has this navigation confounded the affirmations of former writers about terrestrial things, but it has also given some anxiety to the interpreters of Holy Scripture.' A reluctance to take in or an inability to assimilate the new knowledge persisted until late in the sixteenth century, nowhere more obviously than in European reactions to non-European art.

Both Near Eastern and Far Eastern arts had been known in the West since ancient Roman times at least, as we have seen, and if not fully understood were often greatly prized. Motifs from Chinese and Islamic art had long been acclimatized in Europe. But American artifacts, when they first reached Europe, were regarded in quite a different light. Mexican gold, silver and featherwork, sent by Hernán Cortés to the Emperor Charles V, were displayed at Brussels in 1520 and seen by Dürer, who wrote in his diary of these 'wonderful works of art', but neither he nor anyone else seems to have made a visual record of them. Such visual imagery was, perhaps, too strange to be digested. Further examples of Mexican art were imported

The visual arts

c. 100–650 Teotihuacán (12,1)

766 Quiriguá megalith (12,5)
800–1000 Igbo-Ukwu bronze (12,21)
1100–1300 Ife head of queen (12,22)

1200–1400 *Tales of Heiji Insurrection* (12,80)
c. 1300 Li Kan, *Bamboo* (12,64)
1354–91 Alhambra (12,31)

1403–5 Gur-i-Mir, Samarkand (12,34)

c. 1500 Machu Picchu (12,17)
c. 1500–50 Benin bronze head (12,26)
c. 1525–35 Sultan-Muhammad(?), *The Court of Gayumarth* (12,38)

1532 Wen Zhengming, *Seven Juniper Trees* (12,77)
1567–74 Sinan, Selimiye Mosque, Edirne (12,36)

1615–1700 Katsura palace, Kyoto (12,93)
c. 1618 *Imayat Khan Dying* (12,50)
1632–48 Taj Mahal (12,51)

Historical landmarks

c. 200 BC Emergence of Maya civilization in Yucatán
c. AD 100 Foundation of Teotihuacán
c. 800 Foundation of Ife (Nigeria)
1022 Murasaki completes *The Tale of Genji*
c. 1100 Foundation of kingdom of Benin. Islam spreads south of Sahara in West Africa
1191 Zen Buddhism introduced into Japan
c. 1200 Incas found capital city of Cuzco (Peru)
1210 Mongols invade China
1354 Turks cross Dardanelles into Europe
1364 First Ming dynasty emperor ends Mongol rule in China
1370 Aztecs settle at Tenochtitlán (Mexico)
1453 Constantinople falls to Turks
1499 Vasco da Gama reaches India, opens sea-route from Europe to Far East
1502 Safavid dynasty begins rule in Iran, Iraq and Afghanistan
1519–22 Cortés conquers Mexico
1522 First circumnavigation of the world completed
1526 Foundation of Mughal empire in India
1532–4 Pizarro conquers Peru
1571 Turks take Cyprus and Tunis, but their fleet destroyed at Lepanto
1615 Edo (Tokyo) becomes capital of Japan
1620 African slaves imported into N. America
1638 Christianity suppressed in Japan, foreigners expelled
1644 Ming succeeded by Qing dynasty in China
1658 Aurangzeb seizes Mughal throne in India

after the conquest in 1521 – illustrated codices (12,11), masks encrusted with turquoise (12,13) and ingenious pieces of featherwork (12,12). Some were preserved as 'curiosities', but the majority were destroyed – and so, too, was the civilization that had produced them. Still more ruthless was the destruction of work in gold or silver sent to Europe from Peru in 1534. Not a single piece survives.

The ease with which small forces of Spaniards conquered Mexico and Peru fostered the belief, summed up by an Italian shortly before the end of the sixteenth century, that Europe 'was born to rule over Africa, Asia and America'. This preposterous notion is implicit in numerous European paintings and other images of the four parts of the world (14,15). While it prevailed, as it did until well into the nineteenth century, few Europeans were able to see more than a piquant exoticism in works of art from distant, alien traditions. So it is hardly a paradox that the great sixteenth-century expansion in knowledge of the world should have coincided with a resurgence of the Classical tradition in European art.

MESOAMERICA AND PERU

At the time of the Spanish invasion in 1519 Mesoamerica, from the desert just north of modern Mexico City to the tropical rain-forests of Guatemala (an area more extensive than western Europe from Portugal to Germany), was ruled by the Aztecs or Mexica, as they called themselves. They were recent arrivals from further north whose empire had begun to expand less than a century before. But their pervasive artistic style incorporates elements from the earlier arts of the region occupied by groups of people who seem to have been nearly always at war with one another although they had many basic cultural traits

in common. For the Mesoamericans spoke related languages, observed the same 260-day calendar and had similar forms of monarchical government inseparable from their religious ideas and rituals, which included self-inflicted blood-letting, the ball-game and sacrificial offerings of captives. They also shared techniques of building with stone, of carving with stone instruments, of modelling pottery and of painting. But they developed individual artistic styles which overlap chronologically and encroach on one another geographically, with as many similarities and differences as those of Europe.

Before the civilization of the Olmecs on the Gulf Coast disintegrated (see pp. 120–2), another, related to it, emerged in about 600 BC on the west of the central mountain chain. Its ceremonial centre was at Monte Albán (near present-day Oaxaca City), but most of the surviving buildings at this site date from the first millennium AD, when it rose to its maximum importance under the Zapotecs, who spoke a language which survives to the present day. Some 200 miles (320 km) to the north-west, at a place on the Mexican plateau which the Aztecs later called Teotihuacán ('where one becomes a god'), another ceremonial centre was developed from the first century AD into a true city, covering about 8 square miles (2,072 hectares) and with a population of up to a quarter of a million at the height of its prosperity. The residential quarters were laid out on a grid system, but the plan of the whole city was fixed astronomically to provide an earthly reflection of the movement of the heavenly bodies. At its heart an avenue, 130 feet (40m) wide and a mile and a half (2.4km) long, connected massive stepped platforms (12,1) – so-called 'pyramids' but more like ziggurats in form as in function – each of which was originally crowned by a temple approached up a broad flight of stairs. The earliest, and also one of the largest not only here but in all Mexico

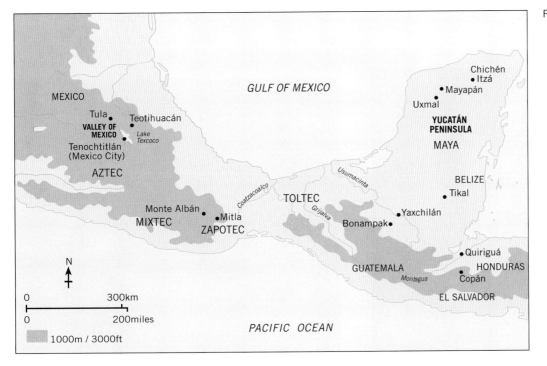

Pre-Columbian Mesoamerica

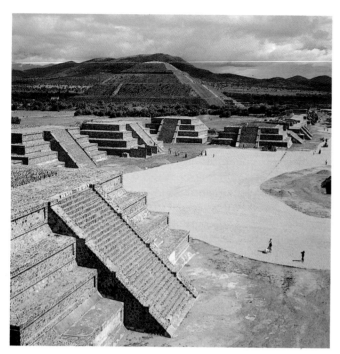

12,1 Teotihuacán, Mexico, 1st to 7th century AD.

(700 feet, 213m, wide and over 200 feet, 61m, high), was sited on axis with the point where the sun set on the day of its zenith passage. It is composed of layers of clay faced with rough stones. A more elaborate system of construction was adopted for the later pyramids – a skeleton framework of piers and slabs of tufa, to stabilize earth and rubble fillings, and finely dressed masonry on the exterior. That at the southern end of the avenue was exceptional in the richness of its relief carvings of plumed serpents and menacing heads composed of circles and squares, perhaps representing the mosaic head-dresses of warriors or the fire serpent identified with warfare (**12,2**). These sculptures

12,2 Pyramid of the Feathered Serpent, detail, Teotihuacán, c. 200–300.

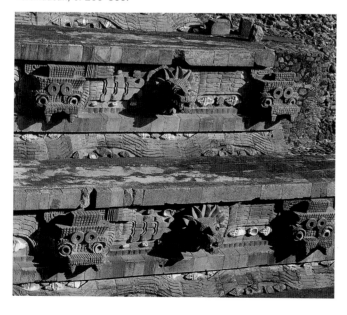

were fortuitously preserved when the platform was enlarged and its surface was covered with painted plaster.

Paintings executed in a fresco technique came to be preferred for the exteriors and interior patios of both religious and secular buildings. And several reveal an accomplishment in the creation of large tightly integrated compositions of small delicately rendered symbolic elements that is unsurpassed in later Mesoamerican art. The sloping inside walls of one structure were painted in shades of red and touches of green and blue, with at least eight almost identical scenes – repetition enforcing the power of the imagery (**12,3**). They represent a ritual of blood-letting, to ensure the fertility of the soil and probably human fertility as well, performed by a celebrant who has pierced his skin with the hard, sharp spine at the tip of the leaf of the maguey plant, a species of agave indigenous to Mexico where it was a source of food and medicine, fibre for textiles, rope and paper, also the intoxicant *pulque* drunk in religious ceremonies. In the centre of each scene a man in profile wearing a huge feathered head-dress, another panache of feathers on his back and a rich garment that indicates his élite status – warrior, priest or both – but completely conceals his shortened torso, stands uttering a prayer or chant indicated by a scroll puffed out from his mouth. On either side the blooded tips of maguey leaves are stuck in the ground. A two-headed serpent with birds in its rectangular coils is depicted in the frieze separated from the main scene by a band of chevrons, apparently associated with the Great Goddess who presided over the life and art of Teotihuacán. By the time these scenes were painted, however, the city was outgrowing the agricultural resources of the surrounding country and a climatic change to semi-desert conditions was being brought about partly by deforestation to provide timber to burn lime for plaster. Teotihuacán was sacked in 650 and no city of equal size was to be built in America for many centuries.

12,3 *Blood-Letting Rite*, from Teotihuacán, c. 600. Pigments on lime plaster, 32¾ × 45¾ins (83.2 × 116.2cm). Cleveland Museum of Art (Purchase from J. H. Wade Fund).

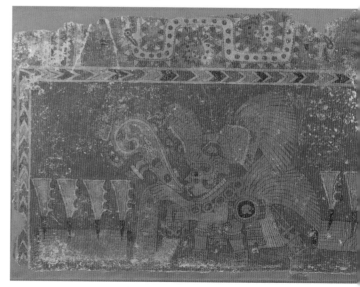

THE MAYA, TOLTECS AND MIXTECS

The civilization of the Maya emerged somewhat earlier than Teotihuacán, was brought to the height of its development at about the same time – the so-called 'Classic' period from the late second century AD – but enjoyed a much longer life in the humid climate of the Yucatán peninsula and present-day Belize and Guatemala. The Maya developed writing in symbols known as glyphs which have been deciphered to provide dates according to their calendar, reckoned from the day 0 which corresponds with 13 August 3114 BC (or would correspond had there been such a calender in Europe), and, although sometimes obscure, to illuminate the religio-social structure of their civilization. A number of independent states were ruled by hereditary monarchs whose power derived from their relationship with the gods. It was believed that the gods had created human beings by a sacrificial act and needed for their sustenance the reciprocal shedding of blood. The two main rituals were those of self-inflicted blood-letting, performed by the rulers as well as their subjects, and of human sacrifice, which occasioned a state of intermittent warfare – not for territorial expansion, but to obtain captives to be offered to the gods.

The cities of the Maya were extensive. Tikal (Guatemala) was one of the largest, covering some 6 square miles (15.5 square km) of hillocks connected by causeways with nine main courts surrounded by the remains of religious buildings. No traces of the dwellings of the population survive. Durable materials seem to have been reserved for the gods (as in much of Asia). And the siting of buildings was governed by astronomical observations relating them to the cosmos, for the Maya were just as much concerned as people in other parts of the world to maintain harmony between the earth and the heavens. In the ritual ball-game, for which courts were built in all temple precincts, the rubber ball flying over the players' heads probably signified the sun – and the sacrifice, which sometimes followed, was no doubt intended to ensure that the sun continued on its daily course.

From the beginning of the 'Classic' period, the Maya built with stone and a remarkably strong burnt-lime cement, from which concrete, used for cores, was subsequently developed. They also refined the technique of corbelled vaulting which had been little used in America. But their temple architecture was predominantly one of exteriors, since all the public rituals were conducted in the open air. At Tikal two unusually steep pyramids topped by temples, rising to a height of some 230 feet (70m), each with an unbroken flight of steps climbing precipitously up its front, faced one another across a spacious square (**12,4**). Here, as elsewhere, the height of each temple was increased by the vertical extension of its rear wall into what is called a 'roof comb', and the whole construction might be described as a high-backed throne set on a dais. At Uxmal in the north, structures with a horizontal accent – usually called palaces, though their original purpose is unknown – were heightened by building up the front wall far above roof level, as a false or flying façade, and

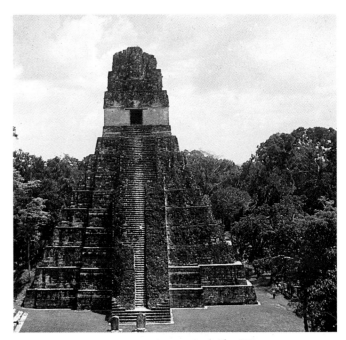

12,4 Stepped pyramid at Tikal, Guatemala, before 800.

sometimes adding a second still higher wall behind it. These flat areas were articulated with stucco relief carvings, some figurative but later geometrical, brightly painted and polished to a glossy surface or enlivened with mosaic.

Large-scale sculpture is mainly in relief rather than in the round. At Quiriguá convolutions of serpents, birds, monsters and human figures were worked over the surface of large boulders called zoomorphs. Megaliths (see Glossary) often of impressive size were carved as *stelae* with images of rulers in full regalia staring out (sometimes from the front and back), surrounded by tropical profusions of hieroglyphs which record their legitimizing ancestry and the precise dates of birth, accession to power, marriage and conquests, and also the day on which the stone was erected – an important ritual event. Stele D at Quiriguá is one of several set up in the reign of king Cauac Sky celebrating his victories over the king of nearby Copán (**12,5**). *Stelae* similar in form but diverse in handling were carved at Copán. For in each of the kingdoms the local styles of sculpture seem to have been developed by artists who sometimes showed marked individuality. A series of reliefs from the façade of a building at Yaxchilán is ascribed to the so-called 'Cookie cutter Master'. One lintel shows, according to the inscription, king Shield Jaguar with the shrunken head of a sacrificial victim in his feathered crown, holding a flaming torch over his principal wife, Lady Xoc, who kneels, pulling a cord knotted with thorns through her perforated tongue to draw blood which drips on to strips of paper that will be burnt and thus transmitted to the gods (**12,6**). The day on which this particular blood-letting rite was performed is also commemorated in the inscription – the equivalent of 28 October 709. Few works of art produced by the Maya reveal as completely their religious and political ideas in an appropriately sacramental style. The stolid impassivity

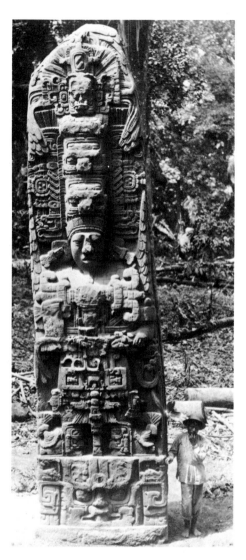

12,5 *Left* Stele D, Quiriguá, Guatemala, 766. Sandstone, 35ft (10.7m) high.

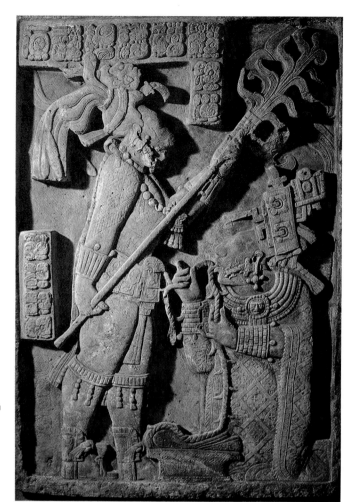

12,6 *Top, right Blood-Letting Rite*, lintel from Yaxchilán, Mexico, c. 725. Limestone, 3ft 8ins (1.11m) high. British Museum, London.

12,7 *Bottom, right Ball-game*, cylindrical vase, c. AD 600–900. Slip on earthenware, 9ins (23cm) high, 6¾ (17.5cm) wide. The Saint Louis Art Museum (Gift of Morton D. May).

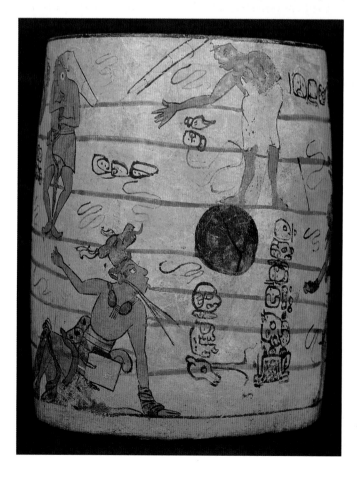

of the figures is set off by the hard-edged clarity and firmly weighted balance of the composition, the mystical meaning of the subject by the realism of the detail (Lady Xoc's patterned robe, the jade ornaments that hang from bands round Shield Jaguar's knees and his jaguar-skin footwear). It is pictorial rather than sculptural; outlines must have been drawn on the surface of the stone, the background cut away and the details incised – with surprising delicacy in view of the fact that only stone tools were available. And it was originally painted in bright colors of which only a few traces remain. Wall-paintings were sometimes more naturalistic and a cycle of about AD 800 at Bonampak (Mexico) includes a battle scene and its aftermath, in which captives wait to be sacrificed with a fatalism that characterizes so much of the figurative art of the Maya.

Paintings on pottery vessels reveal more intimate and often more lively aspects of this civilization. Despite their small size, rarely more than about 12 inches (30cm) high, they are among the most remarkable Mesoamerican works of art. One represents a ball-game that might appear to be a sporting event rather than a solemn ritual, showing players with different facial expressions and in a variety of postures skilfully rendered by contour and flat color (**12,7**).

Recession is indicated by placing the figures on different base-lines. Glyphs, as yet undeciphered, are linked to the men by freely drawn wisps. Many other vessels, dating from the sixth to the eighth century, bear paintings of courtly and ceremonial life, of mythological subjects and of animals, executed in slip (diluted clay), predominantly black, white and shades of red, in a wide range of personal as well as regional styles within the same set of pictorial conventions. The vessels are normally cylindrical and must be rotated in the hand to read the scenes and inscriptions wrapped around them. These paintings are not (as are those on ancient Greek vases) decorative embellishments so much as independent works of art for which pottery served as a convenient support. Nor were they alternatives to more expensive metalwork. And although many were buried with the dead they were not all conceived as grave-goods; some have dregs of cocoa that show they had been used for drinking and repairs indicate they had been so used before burial. Inscriptions naming the notable people for whom they were made suggest that they were symbols of status. And the artists who signed several of the finest examples – their signatures being the only known artists' signatures in pre-conquest America – were scribes who probably painted codices as well (though these have perished), sometimes the sons of ruling families and always members of the educated élite that flourished while the great Mayan monuments were being built.

The structure of Mayan civilization began to crumble in the ninth century. Several cities in the south of their territories were abandoned and the series of dated inscriptions came to an end in 909. (The Maya survived as an ethnic group – their few manuscripts, devoted mainly to the calendar and astronomy, date from between the thirteenth and sixteenth centuries – and there are still some two million living in modern integrated societies as well as traditional communities on the Yucatán peninsula.) People whose features differ from those of the Maya with their sloping foreheads and stepped haircuts appear as rulers in the art of the area. In the far north the ceremonial centre of Chichén Itzá was enlarged under foreign influence though the work was apparently done by Mayan

12,8 The Observatory (*El Caracol*), Chichén Itzá, Yucatán, before 1200.

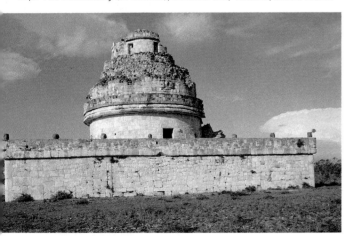

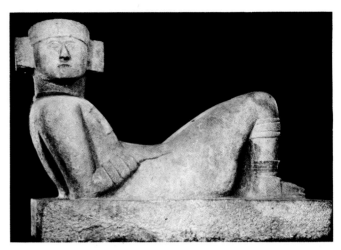

12,9 *Chacmool* from Chichén Itzá, Yucatán, before 1200. Limestone, 3ft 5⁵⁄₁₆ins (1.05m) high. Museo Nacional de Antropologia, Mexico.

artists and artisans. Here the most interesting building, one without precedent in Mesoamerican architecture, is the observatory (**12,8**) enclosing two concentric annular passages with unusually high corbelled vaults and an upper story reached by a winding stair (a *caracol* in Spanish, after which the building is often named). Shafts radiating from the centre of the upper story were directed to transit points of the sun and stars and also to the ball-courts below, thus permitting observation and correlation of heavenly phenomena and earthly ceremonies.

Relief carvings at Chichén Itzá reflect a preoccupation with human sacrifice more obsessive and explicit than in the earlier sculpture of the Maya. On each side of the ball-court – the largest in Mesoamerica – teams are lined up with the leader of one decapitated. There are carvings of warriors marching in procession, files of eagles and jaguars devouring human hearts, and rank upon rank of skulls on poles in front of a platform where the heads of sacrificial victims were probably displayed. But some images have no precedent in the art of the Maya, notably statues of a deity usually called Chacmool (though this is in fact a nineteenth-century name), a reduction of the human figure to severely impersonal geometry, resting on his elbows with knees up and holding in his lap an offering tray but turning his head away from it with apparent indifference, as gods accept the lives of men (**12,9**). Similar statues have been found far away at Tula, Hidalgo, the furthest to the north of all ancient sites in Mesoamerica, and a capital of the Toltecs who, according to later traditions, extended their rule from Mexico into Yucatán.

Tula, Hidalgo, was a densely populated city with a rough grid plan laid out on an arid windy site. Its best-preserved monument is a pyramidal platform originally faced with reliefs of jaguars, eagles holding hearts in their beaks and monstrous creatures (few of which survive). On its summit there was a temple with a presumably wooden roof supported by columns in the form of warriors standing rigidly to attention as if on ceremonial parade, wearing butterfly pectorals and holding spear-throwers in their hands (**12,10**). These columns are all identical with one another, each

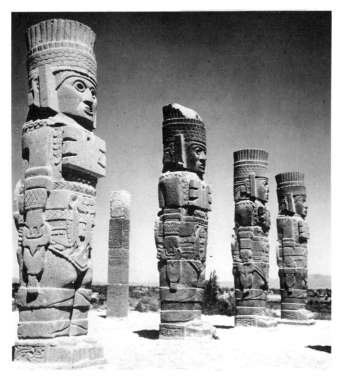

12,10 Atlantean figures on Pyramid of Quetzalcoatl, Tula, Mexico, before 1200. Basalt, 15ft (4.57m) high.

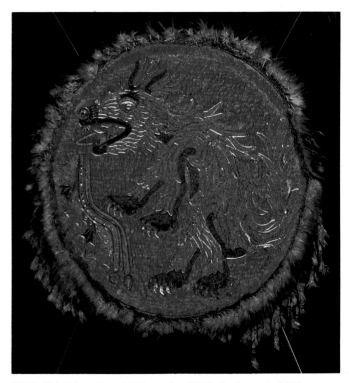

12,12 Shield from Tenochtitlán, before 1519. Featherwork, 27½ins (70cm) diameter. Museum für Völkerkunde, Vienna.

composed of four drums held together by dowels, and they were originally painted in bright colors. Somewhat similar figures appear in reliefs at Chichén Itzá, and whether the art associated with the Toltecs originated in the Valley of Mexico or in Yucatán is an unresolved question. Tula was sacked in the late twelfth century. Chichén Itzá was abandoned slightly later and a new capital of the Yucatán was founded at Mayapán, a walled city, which survived until the mid-fifteenth century though its art and architecture reveal a marked decline in craftsmanship.

There were other civilizations in Mesoamerica, notably that of the Mixtecs who became the dominant power in the mountainous country of the south in the second millennium AD. The finest surviving Mesoamerican manuscripts are Mixtec, painted on sheets of parchment joined to make long strips that could be folded into book-like form – generally, if inaccurately, called codices. They are concerned with rituals, performed in accordance with the all-important astronomical calendar and with the genealogical history of the leading families (**12,11**).

12,11 Page from the *Codex Zouche-Nuttall*, c. 1400–1500. Bodycolor on prepared deerskin, 10ins (25.5cm) high. British Museum, London.

12,13 *God Quetzalcoatl or Tonatiuh*, c. 1500. Turquoise mosaic set in resinous gum over wood, with eyes of pearl shell, 6⅝ ins (16.8cm) high. British Museum, London.

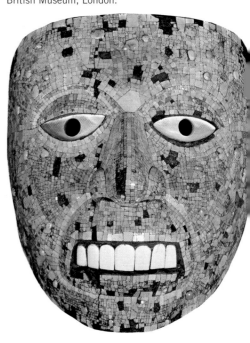

Figures, firmly drawn in black outline filled with brilliant color, are shown frontally or in profile, gesturing with hieratic gravity, and located in space and time by symbols. This is a purely informative art. But elaborate gold jewelry found in Mixtec tombs suggests appreciation of fine craftsmanship. And their craftsmen seem to have been extensively employed by the Aztecs, who conquered much of their territory in the fifteenth century. They are known to have excelled in featherwork, of which a surviving shield with a coyote is perhaps an example (**12,12**). Mixtec craftsmen may also have been responsible for masks coated with turquoise, worn by Aztec priests. Concurrent tendencies towards naturalism and abstract symbolism, present in Mesoamerican art since early times, intersect in these menacing and disconcerting objects (**12,13**).

THE AZTECS

The Aztecs were imperialists able to draw on the artists and craftsmen of their subject peoples, and the art they sponsored combines elements from different traditions. There is a strong reminiscence of Olmec art (see pp. 120–2), for instance, in the figure of a woman giving birth, carved in a greenish stone probably in the Valley of

12,14 *Goddess in Childbirth*, from the Valley of Mexico?, c. 1500. Stone (Wernerite), 8½ins (21.6cm) high. Dumbarton Oaks, Washington DC.

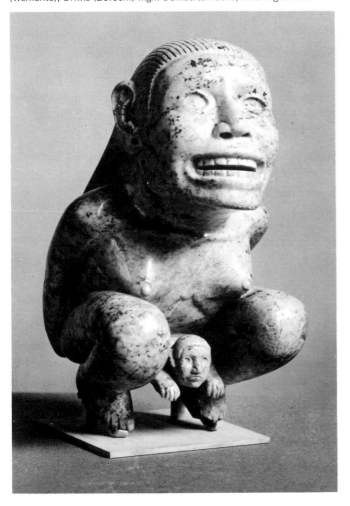

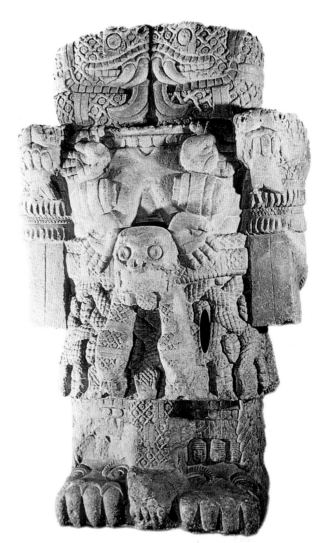

12,15 *Goddess Coatlicue*, late 15th century. Andesite, 8ft 3¼ins (2.52m). Museo Nacional de Antropologia, Mexico.

Mexico about 1500 (**12,14**). The head of a full-grown man (not a baby) emerging from the womb is an indication that the carving had ritual significance. But the straining and grimacing image of a mother in the agony of labour, with the clammy surface of skin in cold sweat, has an expressiveness new to the art of Mesoamerica. A colossal statue of the earth goddess Coatlicue is expressive in a different way, completely dehumanized and yet oppressively real, a terrifying evocation of malignity in nature – with two confronted rattlesnake heads, serpent fangs at her elbows, a skull hanging from a necklace of human hands and hearts above her pendulous breasts and a skirt of entwined snakes. Her feet have feline claws (**12,15**). Most other monsters in the art of the world are docile by comparison.

The last of a succession of northern tribes which infiltrated the Valley of Mexico, the Aztecs settled in about 1370 on the island of Tenochtitlán (where Mexico City now stands) in Lake Texcoco. Here they built the city of spacious palaces and gardens and temple-crowned pyramids which seemed like an enchantment to the first Europeans who saw it. The bloody rites performed in this

SOURCES AND DOCUMENTS

CORTÉS AND DÜRER ON MEXICO AND MONTEZUMA'S TREASURE

Hernán Cortés left Vera Cruz in August 1519 to march on the Mexican capital, Tenochtitlán. His account of the city he conquered is all the more impressive for its cool matter-of-factness. It is, he declares,

as big as Seville or Córdoba. The main streets are very wide and very straight; some of these are on the land, but the rest and all the smaller ones are half on land, half canals where they paddle their canoes . . . . There is also one square twice as big as that of Salamanca with arcades all around, where more than 60,000 people come each day to buy and sell . . . ornaments of gold and silver, lead, brass, copper, tin, stones, shells, bones and feathers.

The cotton market seems to him like the silk market at Granada and, he goes on, they

. . . sell as many colors for painters as may be found in Spain and all of excellent hues.

Among the temples there is one

. . . whose great size and magnificence no human tongue could describe, for it is so large that within the precincts, which are surrounded by a very high wall, a town of some 500 inhabitants could easily be built.

In general, he concludes, with an air of judicious condescension,

I will only say that these people live almost like those in Spain, and in as much harmony and order as there, and considering that they are barbarous and so far from the knowledge of God and cut off from all civilized nations, it is truly remarkable to see what they have achieved in all things.

The gifts that Montezuma sent him shortly after his arrival in Mexico, in the hope of satisfying his greed and deterring him from advancing on the capital, had

had, of course, precisely the opposite effect. Cortés set out immediately for Tenochtitlán and sent Montezuma's treasures to the Queen of Spain and her son Charles V in order to justify his wholly unauthorized activities on the American mainland. A year later Albrecht Dürer saw them displayed in Brussels where Charles halted for a while on his way to be enthroned as Holy Roman Emperor in Aix-la-Chapelle. He wrote in his diary on 27 August 1520:

I saw the things which have been brought to the King from the new golden land . . . a sun all of gold a whole fathom broad, and a moon all of silver of the same size, also two rooms full of the armour of the people there, and all manner of wondrous weapons of theirs, harness and darts, wonderful shields, strange clothing, bedspreads, and all kinds of wonderful objects of various uses, much more beautiful to behold than prodigies. These things were all so precious that they have been valued at 100,000 gold florins. All the days of my life I have seen nothing that has gladdened my heart so much as these things, for I saw amongst them wonderful works of art, and I marvelled at the subtle ingenia of men in foreign lands. Indeed, I cannot express all that I thought there.

Very few, apart from Dürer, had any appreciation of the treasures sent from Mexico though the official historian of the Indies, Peter Martyr, had been amazed by the featherwork. Charles V and his ministers were quite blind to them and soon had the gold and silver melted down and the precious stones extracted. Of all the things seen by Dürer, only one seems to have survived – a codex (now in the National Library of Austria) which had no monetary value and was preserved merely as a curiosity.

(Tr. A. R. Pagden, *Hernán Coréts, Letters from Mexico*, New York 1971 and E. Panofsky, *The Life and Art of Albrecht Dürer*, Princeton 1955)

beautiful setting, however, appalled even those hardened adventurers. Human sacrifice, practised by most other Mesoamericans, had become the central rite of Aztec religion. On dates determined by the astronomical calendar they sacrificed their own people by the thousand – hearts of 20,000 are said to have been torn out on a single occasion – and to obtain more victims they embarked in the mid-fifteenth century on a campaign of imperial expansion, the success of which was largely due to their soldiers' disciplined willingness to confront death. As a result, Cortés was greeted as a liberator by the subject peoples who assisted him in the conquest of Mexico – promptly followed by the suppression of the indigenous religions and the arts they had inspired.

THE INCAS

In Peru the Spaniards found the empire of the Incas, which by one of the most extraordinary and inexplicable coincidences in history had begun to expand at almost exactly the same time as that of the Aztecs. It was still more extensive, occupying, by about 1500, the whole length of the Andes from modern Ecuador to Bolivia, Argentina and southern Chile. Technology was developed here in advance of Mesoamerica, weaving at a very early date (see pp.124–5), metallurgy before the first millennium AD (with the production of a gold and copper alloy, followed c. 700–1000 by bronze) and extensive schemes of agricultural terracing and irrigation. The finest artistic products

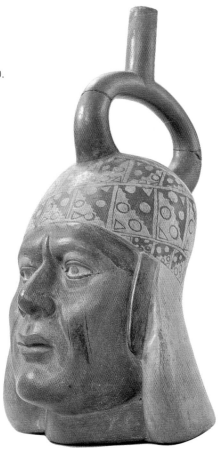

12,16 Portrait vessel, Moche style, AD 200–500. Pottery, 14 × 9½ins (35.6 × 24.1cm). Art Institute of Chicago, Buckingham Fund.

of the people of the Andes were elaborate forms of useful objects, notably textiles and pottery.

For want of written records, the early history of the area can be traced only from artifacts, which reveal a succession of more than local styles. As we have already seen (pp. 122–4), the Chavín style is the earliest of which clear traces remain. Another style originated around the beginning of the first century AD in the valleys of the Moche and Chicama rivers and spread some hundred miles to the south. An aristocratic society living in walled towns built round hillocks seems to have governed a population of farmers working on land irrigated by long aqueducts and canals (still in use today). Its most distinctive artistic products are exceptionally well-made pottery vessels with stirrup-shaped spouts of a type peculiar to South America. Some have globular bodies with vivaciously painted figurative scenes, sometimes overtly erotic. Others are molded or modelled like human heads, whole figures, animals or buildings. The heads are strongly characterized and startlingly realistic (**12,16**). They ponder, frown or sneer in high disdain, some have enigmatic smiles with the hint of a twinkle in the eyes, and one has a broad grin which lights up his whole face. All the vessels were probably made for burial with the dead.

About the seventh century an entirely different style of pottery painting, with abstract designs or severely

12,17 Machu Picchu, Peru, c. 1500.

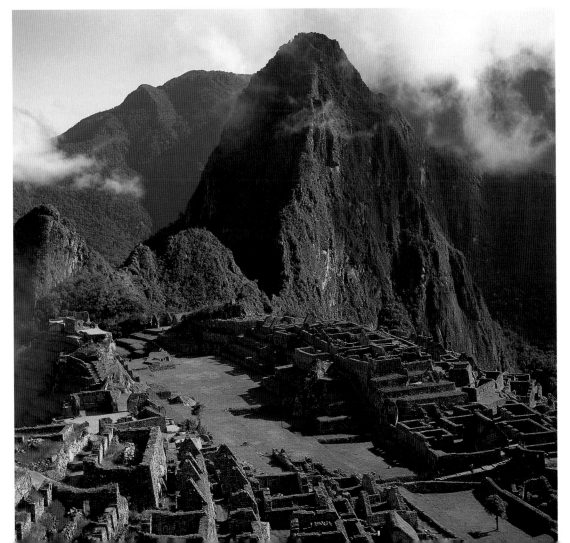

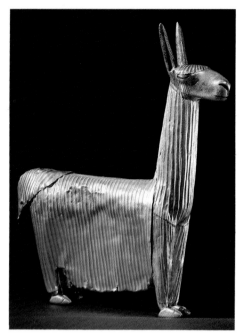

12,18 Alpaca, Cuzco style, c. 1500. Silver, 9⁷⁄₁₆ins (24cm) high. American Museum of Natural History, New York.

stylized natural forms, spread from the south and covered a far wider area, including the Moche valley. It is named after Tiahuanaco, high in the Bolivian Andes, where an ancient ceremonial centre was enlarged with massive stone buildings in the course of the first millennium AD. A deity holding two upright staffs, carved with geometric rectilinearity on a monolithic gateway at Tiahuanaco, is a recurrent motif in pottery painting and textiles, including featherwork. The diffusion of the style seems to have been due to the expansion of a religious cult whose devotees looked askance on the freedom and variety of Moche art (and also on the lively, if less naturalistic, style of pottery painting and textile design centred on the Nazca valley, which likewise died out). There is, however, evidence of the growth of increasingly large political units, one with a populous capital city at Huari, which has given its name to a style allied with that of Tiahuanaco. On the coast further to the north Chanchan (near modern Trujillo), a city founded in about the twelfth century, became in the fourteenth the capital of the Chimú kingdom incorporated in the Inca empire in about 1460.

The Incas, a clan of unknown origin, founded their capital city Cuzco early in the thirteenth century and after some 200 years of local warfare became an imperial power. Their organizing genius was comparable only with that of the Romans. Like that of the Romans, it found expression in large-scale works of civil and military engineering and in an architecture of massive solidity. The great straight 'Royal Road of the Mountains', 30 feet (9m) wide and bordered with walls along its 3,750 miles (6,000km), was the main line in a unifying system of communications which amazed the Spaniards, who had seen nothing like it in Europe. At Cuzco there were huge walls of polygonal masonry ingeniously tenoned and of regular courses of rectangular blocks fixed by grinding the surface of one against those beneath and beside it. Both methods of construction were used and have survived the storms of five centuries at the fortified town of Machu Picchu, built on a saddle of the Andes, with terraced fields on the slopes and a 2,000-foot (610m) drop to the valley below (**12,17**). Types of buildings were simple and standardized throughout the Inca empire, rectangular or circular with windows and doors of uniform trapezoid shape. Architectural decoration was sparse. Geometrical patterns prevail on textiles and on pottery made in a very limited range of utilitarian shapes. Natural forms appear only in small carvings and in gold and silver, made by techniques of embossing and *cire perdue* casting which originated in the northern Andes and were perfected in the Chimú kingdom, whence craftsmen were transported to Cuzco. Llamas, the only beasts of burden, and alpacas, which provided wool for clothing, seem to have been the most popular subjects (**12,18**). There is a rigidity in the art as in the structure of the Inca empire. It was ruled by a despot styled the 'Son of the Sun', administered by an interrelated nobility and populated by an inferior class paying tax by labour service (there was no money and officially no private property) and regimented with totalitarian thoroughness. Indeed, so rigid was the structure that Francisco Pizarro and his 180 Spanish followers, whose arrival coincided with a civil war between two contenders for the thrones, were able to take over the whole system intact by deposing and strangling the last emperor in 1533.

AFRICA

Unlike America, Africa was never cut off from Europe and Asia. Egypt was the most important link, in antiquity closely associated with the civilizations of west Asia and Europe but also ruled for a century by Pharaohs from Nubia (present-day Sudan) before it became a Hellenistic kingdom and thus part of the Roman empire. Christianity spread south to Ethiopia in the fourth century. Egypt was also the bridgehead for the expansion of Islam across northern Africa and down the east coast to maritime cities that had for long been trading with Arabia, Iran, India and beyond – coins of the Tang emperors of China have been dug up on their sites. The Atlantic coast cities of west Africa were linked to the Mediterranean by a network of trade routes with caravan trails across the Sahara. Religion followed commerce and Islam had spread as far as Mali before 1100. Europeans were late comers: not until 1471 did Portuguese mariners sail down the Atlantic coast as far as the equator and not until 1498 round the Cape and up the east coast where they found that towns like Mombasa had 'many fair houses of stone and mortar, very well arranged in streets . . . with doors of wood well carved and excellent joinery'. But Europeans were unable to establish more than coastal footholds until the late nineteenth century. African states, jealous of one another and well able to resist intruding seafarers, generally maintained their independence culturally if not always economically.

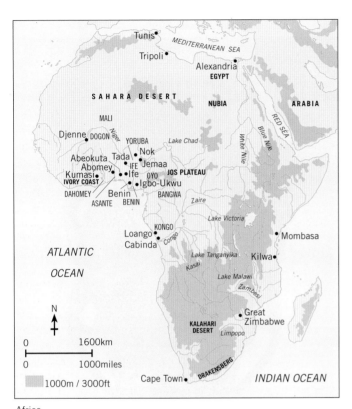

Africa

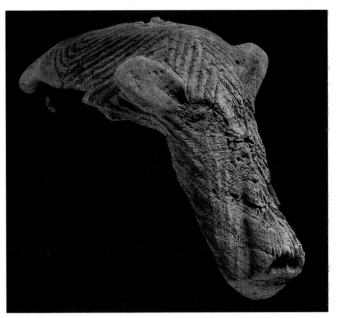

12.19 Zoomorphic head, from Central Africa, c. AD 750.
Wood, 19¾ × 6ins (50.5 × 15.5cm). Royal Museum for Central Africa,
Tervuren, Belgium.

12,20 Cushion cover, from Kongo, Angola, early 17th century. Raffia and
pigment, 9½ × 18½ins (24 × 47cm). Pitt Rivers Museum, Oxford.

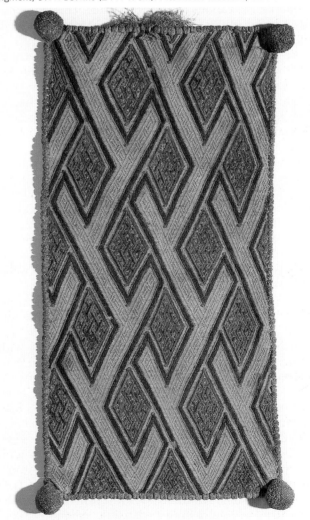

The history of art in Africa south of the Sahara is difficult to trace, partly for the want of written records apart
from travellers' reports of which the earliest of note are
those of the Moroccan scholar Ibn Battuta who visited
south-west Africa in 1331, and Mali in 1352. Surviving
examples of sculpture are of the greatest diversity but the
use of perishable materials condemned much to natural
destruction. The preservation underground far beneath the
water-table in Angola of a carved wooden head of an animal
with a radio carbon date of c. AD 750, was quite fortuitous
(**12,19**). Otherwise the only wood-carvings which can be
dated earlier than the eighteenth century are those brought
to Europe by a German merchant, C. Weickmann, before
1659 (now in Ulm Museum, Germany) and two rather
rough statuettes taken to Italy by way of Portugal in 1695
(now in Museo L. Pigorini, Rome) and thus protected from
the ravages of tropical termites. Similarly a number of early
seventeenth-century raffia palm fibre cloths from the kingdom of Kongo have been by chance preserved in a climate
more favourable than that of equatorial Africa. One, probably a cushion for a royal throne, is no less distinguished
for its sophisticated design than for the technical accomplishment of its weaving with a subtle combination of
smooth areas and pile tufts (**12,20**). Other textiles must
have been woven in earlier times and elsewhere. Works in
enduring materials – stone, terracotta, ivory and metal –
appear to have been produced only in west and southern
Africa, where they probably represent no more than a
minute proportion of the total artistic production. And
even there no objects have been found that date from the
millennium and a half that separates the terracottas of the
'Nok culture' (see p. 125) from the earliest known bronzes.

In Asia and Europe a bronze age was succeeded by an iron age. But in West Africa iron came first and was used before the end of the first millennium BC for making weapons, agricultural implements and perhaps also images which have long since rusted away. Its introduction is celebrated in myths as a great cultural advance and its smelting and forging were until recently accompanied by rituals and guarded by exclusions from worksites, probably of ancient origin. Complete mastery of bronze casting is quite suddenly displayed in examples dating from the ninth or tenth century AD, disinterred at the village of Igbo-Ukwu in eastern Nigeria. A water-pot enclosed in a net of simulated rope is a virtuoso feat of *cire perdue*, and no less elegant in design than accomplished in craftsmanship (**12,21**). Other bronze objects from the same place are encrusted with brightly colored beads or covered with ornamental patterns in shallow relief, and some, of the utmost delicacy, are fashioned like snakes or shells. The alloy of copper, tin and a high proportion of lead is very unusual if not unique, but it is not known where the metals came from, let alone how the tricky skill of casting them was acquired. Robust well-fired pottery vessels with intricate incised and modelled decorations, and many thousands of glass and cornelian beads were found among the bronzes. But nothing is known of the people by and for whom these luxurious objects were made. This extraordinary Igbo-Ukwu art bursts into the archeological record without precedents and vanishes without a sequel.

At Ife, an important religious and political centre in south-western Nigeria, an entirely different and predominantly figurative style of sculpture was created some two centuries later with a self-assurance which could hardly have been attained without a long evolutionary period. The earliest surviving examples were modelled in the twelfth or thirteenth century, some 400 years after the foundation of the city. They include the head of a woman, presumably a queen, which is a paragon of restrained naturalism, a distillation of human features into an image at once serene and intensely lifelike (**12,22**). The elaborate head-dress is rendered in minute detail, but the sculptor departed from such strict verisimilitude in modelling the face with high, thoughtful brow and sensitive mouth. The full lips are emphasized by a slight ridge at their outer edges and the upper eyelids overlap the lower at the corners with just a hint of a living flicker. Several other heads are in the same style, all youthful and to some extent idealized yet differing from one another in a way that suggests that they may have been intended as portraits, with a preference for what the Yoruba of Nigeria call *jijora*, or moderate resemblance to the subject, something between absolute abstraction and absolute likeness. They are modelled in terracotta or cast in copper or an alloy of copper and zinc (technically brass, not bronze) (**12,23**). The holes around the mouth were, it is thought, made to carry a veil of beads. There are also bronze statuettes of kings with stocky bodies clad in elaborate regalia. A still more remarkable cast copper figure, found in the village of Tada on the Niger some 120 miles (192km) north of Ife, may be the work of a sculptor from a related though independent

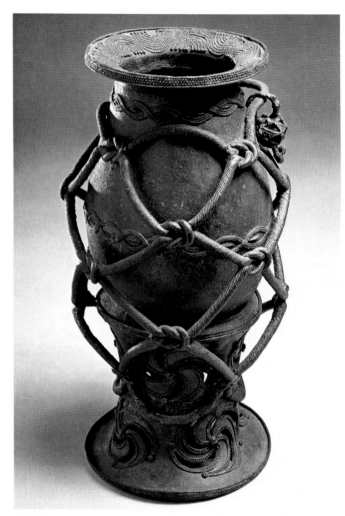

12,21 Roped water-pot on a stand, from Igbo-Ukwu, eastern Nigeria, 9th to 10th century. Leaded bronze, 12¹¹⁄₁₆ins (32.3cm) high. National Museum, Lagos.

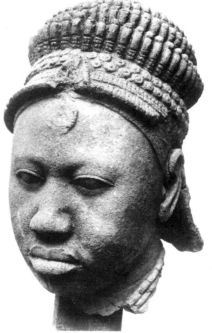

12,22 Head of a queen, 12th to 13th century. Terracotta, 9¹³⁄₁₆ins (25cm) high. Museum of Ife Antiquities, Ife, Nigeria.

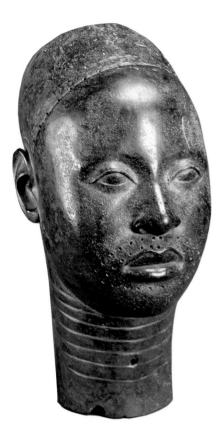

12,23 Head of an ooni (king) of Ife, Yoruba, 12th to 15th century. Zinc brass, 12³⁄₁₆ins (31cm) high. Museum of Ife Antiquities.

school (**12,24**). It is rather over half life-size, natural in bodily proportions and features and in a pose of rhythmic complexity which reveals both complete mastery of sculptural form and technical proficiency in casting. These naturalistic works were, however, produced at the same time as some in which human forms are reduced to barely recognizable abstractions. And further up the Niger at Djenne (Mali), in about the thirteenth century, an entirely different, strenuously expressive, style was created in small figures provocatively thrusting out their chins and pointed beards (**12,25**).

When terracotta and brass heads were first discovered at Ife at the beginning of this century, contact with the Mediterranean was assumed. But they are as close or closer in feeling to contemporary Buddhist art in India and south-east Asia (although there is no evidence of direct contact) as to the art of Europe. In fact, no sculpture of comparable technical accomplishment or spiritual poise and serenity was produced in Europe between the fall of the Roman empire and some centuries after the date of the finest Ife works. Metals may have been imported from beyond the Sahara and the processes of working them learned from Muslim craftsmen, who were the most skilled metalworkers of the time, though never naturalistic. There can, therefore, be little doubt that this west African

12,24 Seated figure from Tada, Middle Niger region, late 13th to 14th century. Copper, 21⅛ins (53.7cm) high. National Museum, Lagos.

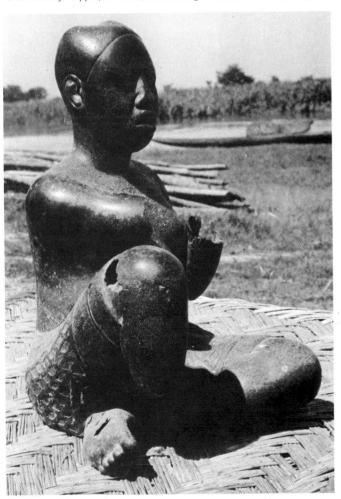

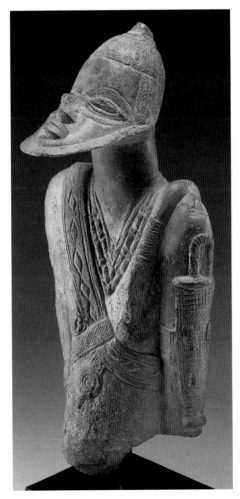

12,25 Bearded male figure from Djenne, Mali, 14th century. Terracotta, 15ins (38.1cm) high. Detroit Institute of Arts (Eleanor Clay Ford Fund for African Art).

art was an indigenous growth conditioned by the need for lifelike images of royalty for funerary rituals and the cult of ancestors from whom kings derived their authority. Significantly, the sculpture produced in the city of Benin after it began to trade with Portugal in the 1480s is more stylized than that of Ife.

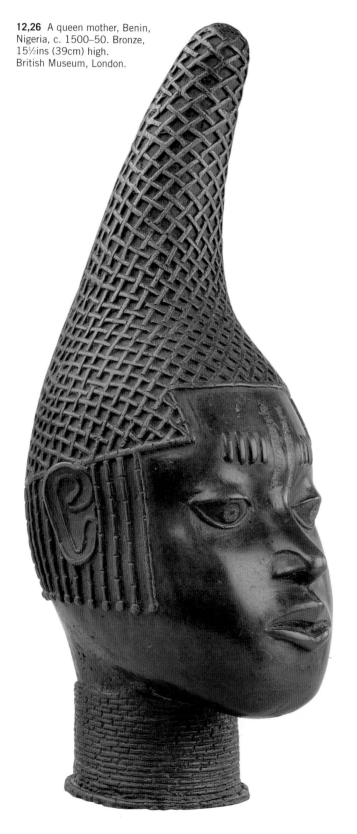

12,26 A queen mother, Benin, Nigeria, c. 1500–50. Bronze, 15½ins (39cm) high. British Museum, London.

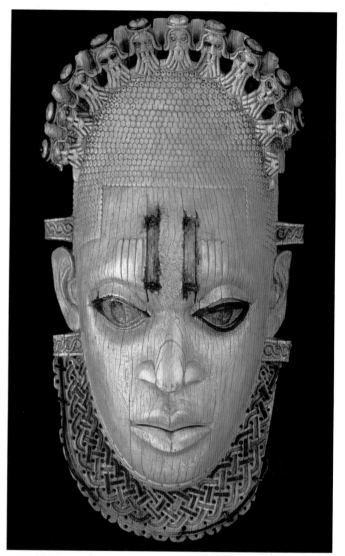

12,27 Pectoral or hip mask, Benin, Nigeria, early 16th century. Ivory, 9¾ins (25cm) high. British Museum, London.

Contradictory local traditions ascribe the founding of the Benin school of sculpture to a master from Ife and to the Portuguese. Affinities with the art of Ife are evident in a noble bronze head of a young queen-mother of which there is more than one version (**12,26**) and in a powerful yet exquisitely carved ivory hip mask believed to have been made for the oba or king of Benin to wear in ceremonies commemorating his mother, who had been alive when the Portuguese arrived (**12,27**). (The long-haired and bearded heads of Portuguese are incorporated in the crown.) The Portuguese traded copper and brass for ivory and slaves and they are represented in a number of relief plaques and statuettes. Originally attached to columns in the oba's palace at Benin, the plaques formed a series illustrating the history and rituals of the realm and are of a rectangular format most unusual in African art. The introduction of this 'framing device' may have been due to European printed book illustrations, which could have reached Benin in the sixteenth century with the Portuguese. Stylistically, however, the plaques have little in

DAPPER ON BENIN

The earliest European account of the royal palace and city of Benin was published in Amsterdam in 1668 by a doctor and compiler of historical–geographical works, Olfert Dapper (d. 1690). Dapper never went to Africa but his account is based on earlier seventeenth-century Dutch reports which seem to have been first-hand. German and English translations appeared in 1670. Dapper included engravings of Benin but they appear to have been made in Europe following the verbal descriptions and not from sketches made on the spot and are therefore of less interest.

According to Dapper, the city walls of Benin were 3 miles (4.8km) long and 10 feet (3m) high, formed by a double palisade of thick tree-trunks bound together with lighter beams and covered with red clay. The gates were of solid wood, 8 or 9 feet (2.4–2.7m) high and 5 feet (1.5m) broad, turning on hinges and giving on to the main streets of the city. There were in all 30 main streets, very straight and broad – 120 feet (36.6m) wide. The houses were laid out in rows and, though seldom of more than one story, they were spacious. Each had its own spring of fresh water. The royal palace, which occupied an area as big as the city itself, interested Dapper's sources as much or more than the city and his account is of great interest, as the palace was destroyed by fire in 1898. According to Dapper:

The king's court is square, and stands at the right hand side when entering the town by the gate of Gotton [Ughoton], and is certainly as large as the town of Haarlem, and entirely surrounded by a special wall, like that which encircles the town. It is divided into many magnificent palaces, houses, and apartments of the courtiers, and comprises beautiful and long square galleries, about as large as the Exchange at Amsterdam, but one larger than another, resting on wooden pillars, from top to bottom covered with cast copper, on which are engraved the pictures of their war exploits and battles, and are kept very clean. Most palaces and the houses of the king are covered with palm leaves instead of square pieces of wood, and every roof is decorated with a small turret ending in a point, on which birds are standing, birds cast in copper with outspread wings, cleverly made after living models.

Dapper goes on to recount that the king

. . . shews himself only once a year to his people, going out of his court on horseback, beautifully attired with all sorts of royal ornaments, and accompanied by three or four hundred noblemen on horseback and on foot, and a great number of musicians before and behind him, playing merry tunes on all sorts of musical instruments . . . . Then the king causes some tame leopards that he keeps for his pleasure to be led about in chains; he also shows many dwarfs and deaf people, whom he likes to keep at court.

(P. Ben-Amos, *The Art of Benin*, London 1980)

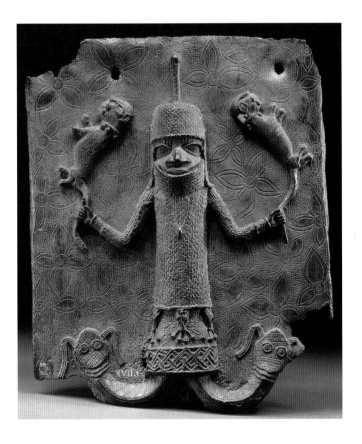

common with European art at the time. Isolated against delicately patterned flat backgrounds, the figures are frontally posed, still in gesture, steady in gaze, scaled according to importance, yet packed with compressed energy. One plaque shows an oba sacrificing or displaying his power over two leopards, which he swings by their tails (**12,28**). His legs terminate in fish, associating him with the sea god Olokun and also, perhaps, alluding to a belief that the king's feet should not come into contact with the soil. The oba traced his ancestry to the son of an ooni (or king) of Ife who was believed to be descended from a god, and this tradition set him apart from his subjects. He held a monopoly of sculpture in brass (chiefs were allowed ancestor figures only in terracotta) and metalworkers were servants of the oba. Benin art was thus predominantly royal and so closely connected with the rituals in the service of divine kingship that it underwent few modifications. Some new types of object were produced in the early eighteenth century, when increased quantities of brass (mainly from trade in slaves) became available. But sculptors went on working according to their own time-honoured traditions, with some loss of

12,28 The oba of Benin in divine aspect, 16th century. Brass, 15½ins (40cm) high. British Museum, London.

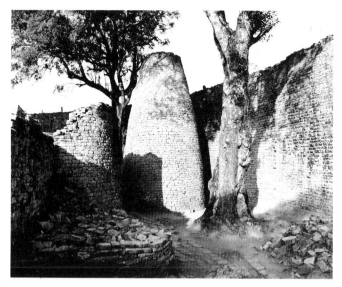

12,29 *Zimbabwe* or Chief's House, c. 1470. Great Zimbabwe, Zimbabwe.

12,30 Plan of Great Zimbabwe.

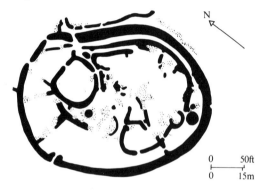

vitality due to artistic inbreeding, until 1897, when a British punitive expedition deposed the oba, sacked his palace and carried off most of its works of art.

The palace of the oba, which sprawled over much of the city of Benin, was constructed of mud-brick and timber with metal facing and consisted of rooms ranged round courts with roofs sloping inwards to carry rainwater into cisterns – rather like a huge ancient Roman villa. Building with stone seems to have been practised only in east Africa. At Great Zimbabwe impressive remains survive (**12,29**), testifying to the size and importance of this once great capital city of a kingdom which stretched from the Zambesi to the Limpopo – covering the main gold-bearing area – and reached its summit of power and wealth in the mid-fifteenth century. They include buildings on elliptical plans and a conical tower within a massive enclosure wall some 30 feet (9m) high and nearly 800 feet (240m) in circumference, faced with neatly cut granite blocks (**12,30**). And there are more than 100 other sites with the ruins of stone buildings. The remains of trading cities on the coast, including that of Kilwa, which the Muslim traveller Ibn Battuta described in 1331 as 'one of the most beautiful and well constructed towns in the world', show how deeply the art as well as the religion of Islam had penetrated this part of Africa.

THE ISLAMIC WORLD

At the beginning of the diary he wrote on the voyage which led to the European invasion of the Americas, Columbus recorded how, a few months before setting sail in August 1492, he saw the Spanish royal banners 'victoriously raised on the towers of the Alhambra'. At the same moment the last Muslim emir of Granada came out of the city gates and kissed the hands of the Catholic sovereigns, Ferdinand and Isabella. Nearly seven centuries of war between Christians and Muslims in Spain had ended. As a result Ferdinand and Isabella took possession of what was perhaps the most luxurious palace in all Europe at that date. Begun as the residence of a Jewish vizier in the mid-eleventh century, when a patchwork of semi-independent Islamic states covered three-quarters of present-day Spain and Portugal, the Alhambra was enlarged into a palace-city after Granada became the capital of an emirate in the late thirteenth century.

Islamic culture flowered under the emirs of Granada, and the Alhambra is the finest monument of the 'Hispano-Moresque' style. It also epitomizes the paradoxical character of Islamic architecture as a whole in its simultaneous appeal to the senses, to the intellect and to the spirit, and especially in its capacity to assimilate elements from other traditions and recast them in forms as distinctively Muslim as the turban and robe of a mullah. The Alhambra belongs to the same tradition of Mediterranean palatial building as the great imperial Roman palaces, of which very much less survives. At the Alhambra a forbiddingly austere and fortified exterior encloses a complex of cool rooms, ingeniously heated baths and sun-drenched courts overlaid with intricately devised and exquisitely wrought decorations to provide settings for a life of cultivated luxury – prominently displaying, however, inscriptions to the glory of Allah with appropriate allusions to the evanescence of all earthly things. There are colonnaded interior courts green with plants and running water as at Domitian's palace in Rome and Hadrian's villa at Tivoli, there are even domed halls of cosmic symbolism like that in Nero's Golden House, but at the Alhambra all these memorably imposing and symmetrically grouped spaces open unexpectedly out of one another, like successive incidents of some rambling story in the *Thousand and One Nights*.

The most elaborate part of the Alhambra, the Court of the Lions, is a Hellenistic peristyle given new life and a wider range of associations by Islamic thought and culture (**12,31**). The slender columns on which the arches are lightly poised are not uniformly spaced, being sometimes single and sometimes coupled in irregular but rhythmical sequence, breaking forward gracefully to form pavilions at either end. Interpenetrating covered and open spaces modulate the light and eliminate harsh contrasts. As it varies in intensity and direction from dawn to dusk, the light subtly changes the structural appearance of the court and the rooms leading off from it, creating almost hallucinatory effects of insubstantiality. Stucco and tiled panels drape walls with abstract patterns of all-over

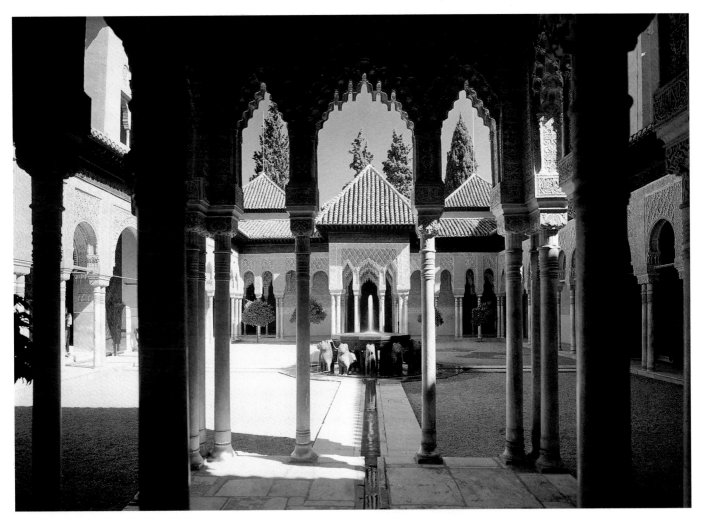

12,31 The Court of the Lions, the Alhambra, Granada, 1354–91.

12,32 *Right* Tile decoration in the Alhambra, Granada, 1354–91.

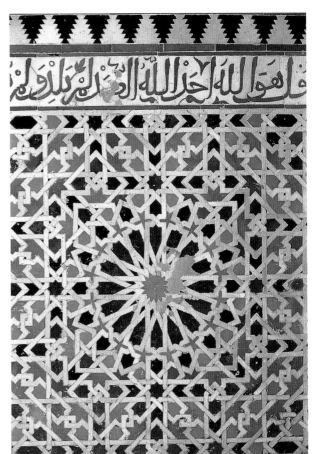

ornamentation, whose predominant geometricity (even of vegetal forms) is profoundly Islamic in its underlying mathematical structure (**12,32**). There is no background, every motif being an active and equal participant in the design. Like the cosmic symbolism of the adjoining domed hall, which is made quite explicit in verse inscriptions, this ornamentation reflects in its myriad divisions and subdivisions certain essential characteristics and values of Islam and has even been interpreted as a visual translation of the cosmic view of Islamic mysticism. No less typically Islamic is its orientation – not outwards but inwards. Light and shade, stone and water, all are interwoven like the delicate motifs on the capitals of columns and on the walls – and like the various levels of meaning which sustain all this fragile sensual beauty. Water sparkles from the central fountain and ripples along four intersecting channels to give a foretaste of paradise, a specifically Islamic holy paradise as described for the faithful in the Koran – 'gardens through which rivers flow, where they shall remain for ever' – as well as a more sensuous paradise of physical well-being, whose possible mystical associations did not exclude occasional orgiastic over-tones. The four water channels also recall the rivers flowing out of Eden, as in the quadripartite gardens or *chahar baghs* of later Iran and India – and as in the complex symbolism surrounding the Fountain of Life in Christian art and thought. In Islamic art, however, symbolism is usually metaphorical rather than allegorical (see p. 181), with consequent ambiguities and sometimes even reversals of meaning. The 12 lions of the fountain, for example, were, according to an eleventh-century poem, originally associated with Solomon, the first great builder of palaces; but when they were re-used in the fourteenth century to form the centrepiece of the court they became 'lions of the Holy War', perhaps with allusion to the taking of Algeciras in 1369, the last triumph for Islam on Spanish soil.

The expulsion of the Muslims from Spain in 1492 was a very minor setback for Islam, which was then in the ascendant on every other sector of its immense frontier, from Africa to Indonesia and across central Asia to the Balkans. But it inspired Ferdinand and Isabella to finance Columbus's epoch-making voyage, the declared aim of which was to contact the 'Great Khan', traditionally believed to be the leading opponent of Islam in Asia. They seem to have been unaware of the changes that had taken place in the previous 300 years. The vast Mongol empire built by Genghis Khan (1167–1227) had been increased

but also divided among his descendants. One grandson, Kubilai, founded the Yuan dynasty of emperors of China, whose rule came to an end after little more than a century in 1368 (see p. 551). Another grandson, Hulagu, who took the dynastic title of ilkhan, became ruler of the western territory from Iran through Mesopotamia to Syria, sacking Baghdad in 1258 (see p. 350). He was a violent anti-Muslim with Christian sympathies, but his great-grandson, who became the fifth ilkhan in 1295, was a Muslim convert. Thus Islam was re-established as the state religion of Iran, which once again became a major centre of Islamic art and culture (see below).

Under the Mongols the decorative arts of China and Iran were brought close together, with influences flowing in both directions, but the religious architecture of Iran maintained or reverted to Seljuk and earlier traditions, despite a hiatus in building activity which lasted almost a century. The *iwan*, which derived ultimately from Sassanian architecture (see p. 343), remained the most characteristic form, a large niche-like structure placed in the centre of one or more interior walls of a court and also used as a portal. At Yazd (some 200 miles, 320km, south-east of Isfahan) an exceptionally tall and fine *iwan*, crowned by minarets reminiscent of Seljuk funerary towers, provides the entrance to the court of the Friday Mosque (**12,33**). This is purely decorative and demonstrative architecture, without any utilitarian purpose, erected with a complicated system of buttressing to support its

12,33 The Friday Mosque, Yazd, Iran, completed by 1330.

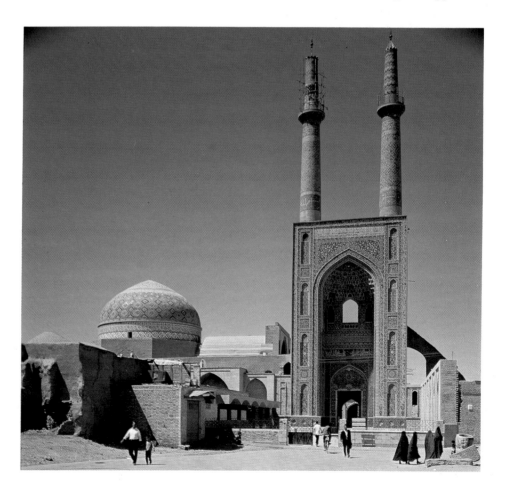

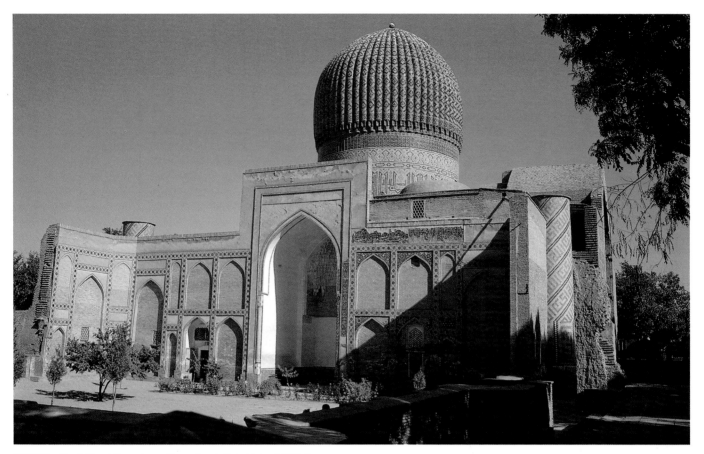

12,34 The Gur-i-Mir of Timur Lang, Samarkand, Uzbekistan 1403–5.

height simply as an embellishment to the earlier mosque. The entire surface is coated with glazed tiles of a type which, from the early fourteenth century, had a dominant role in Iranian architecture, giving to the most substantial constructions a colorful and delicately shimmering fragility (12,41).

The further development of art and architecture in Iran was little affected by changes in dynastic rule. In the early 1380s the area was incorporated in the empire of Timur Lang (1336–1405), a prince of Turko-Mongol descent whose armies swept across Asia, penetrating as far north as Moscow, south into India and west into Anatolia. He is the Tamburlaine of Western literature. But in addition to being a merciless conqueror, he was a notable, if hardly less ruthless, patron of the arts – when a building failed to please he had the architect beheaded! Calling on artists and craftsmen from all the territories he overran, he made his capital city, Samarkand, the wonder of the age. The sophisticated elegance of the mausoleum he had built for his son, and in which he also is buried, might seem to be at odds with his character (**12,34**). The architect was a Persian from Isfahan. Here again colored glazed tiles are used with wonderful effect on the ribbed melon-shaped dome, which gives prominence to the building by rising high above the domed ceiling of the interior chamber. An inscription in Kufic lettering round its drum declares that 'Allah is eternity'.

OTTOMAN ARCHITECTURE

Timur's empire shrank immediately after his death. The petty rulers whom he had held in vassalage regained their independence and the Osmanli or Ottoman Turks resumed their expansion westwards, which Timur had interrupted. A clan from central Asia named after their first notable leader Osman (d. 1324), who had seized control of the Seljuk sultanate in Anatolia (see p. 357), the Ottoman Turks crossed the Dardanelles into Europe in 1354, took Sofia in 1382, drew a noose round Constantinople, which fell to them in 1453, and then moved swiftly on to the conquest of Greece, Serbia and Albania. By 1520 the Ottoman empire had also spread to the south, covering Syria and Egypt, but the drive into Europe continued. Belgrade was taken in 1521, Buda in 1526 and Vienna besieged for the first time in 1529. They even glanced across the Atlantic. In 1513 a Turkish cartographer drew a map of the Americas for his sultan, and in 1580 a Turkish historian of the Spanish colonization of America expressed the hope 'that these valuable lands will be conquered by the family of Islam, and will be inhabited by Muslims and become part of the Ottoman lands'. The peak of power had, in fact, been passed by that date, but Ottoman sultans ruled until 1922 – it was the longest-lived dynasty in the history of Islam.

The first act of Mehmet the Conqueror on taking

Constantinople – or Istanbul, as it was called in colloquial Greek – was to ride to Hagia Sophia (7,41), claim it for Islam, leap on the altar slab and kneel in prayer to Allah. Muslims had always been ready to take over Christian churches. They had also, as we have seen, been adept at bending to their own purposes the architectural styles of the lands they occupied. Even before the Ottomans burst out of Asia their buildings incorporated Byzantine as well as Seljuk elements and had always shown a preference for stone rather than the brick of central Asia. But a new and explicitly Ottoman style, not so much derivative from as challenging the Byzantine achievement, had reached maturity in the late fifteenth century and was crystallized in the sixteenth by Sinan (1489–1588) – Koca Mimar Sinan, 'the great architect Sinan', as he came to be known. Structural logic is its main characteristic, vast spaces vaulted by shallow domes with no dark corners or mysteriously shaded extensions, centralized planning and sober exteriors composed of wide-spreading masses set off by slender minarets like sharp-pointed pencils.

Sinan began his career as a soldier and not until 1538 was he appointed architect to the Sultan Suleyman the Magnificent (1520–66); but the sheer quantity of buildings he designed and saw through to completion in the following 50 years is the most vivid testimony to his genius and bounding energy – and to Ottoman wealth at this period. He is reliably credited with 81 Friday mosques for communal worship, 50 smaller mosques, 55 schools, 34 palaces, 33 public baths and 19 mausoleums, not to mention hospitals, soup kitchens, bridges and other utilitarian structures, notably hydraulic systems, making up a total of 334. The many that survive reveal consistently high standards of design and craftsmanship in execution with perfectly cut masonry, crisp detailing and exquisite glazed tiles made specially in the factories at Iznik and used for cladding interior walls. The contrast with the amount of building achieved by Michelangelo at about the same time, or by any other west European architect before the eighteenth century, is striking. Sinan was also able to realize on the grandest scale the idea of a free-standing centrally planned place of worship which had haunted the imagination of Italian Renaissance architects, most of whose projects remained on paper.

The functional demands for a mosque are, of course, much simpler than those for a Catholic or Orthodox church. All that is strictly necessary is a large hall; and Sinan took the opportunity to create an impressive variety of spaces conditioned only by the availability of building land and the financial resources of his patrons. He regarded as his finest achievement the Selimiye mosque at Edirne (the first Ottoman capital in Europe) built for Suleyman's son and successor Selim II (**12,35; 36**). It had distressed him, he later declared, that nothing had been built to 'rival the dome of Hagia Sophia and it was thought too difficult to build another equally large'. The Selimiye mosque has not only a slightly wider dome

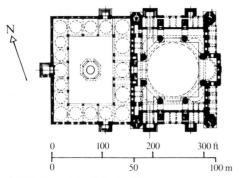

12,35 Plan of the Selimiye Mosque.

12,36 Sinan, the Selimiye Mosque, Edirne, Turkey, 1567–74.

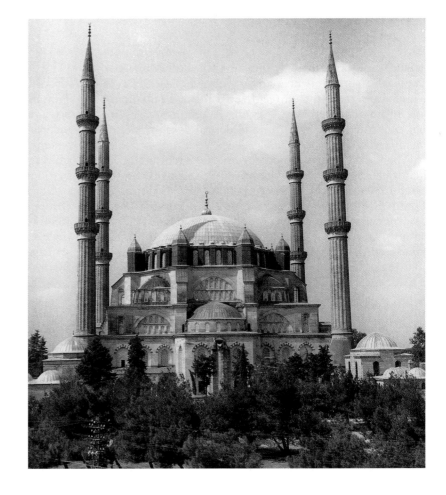

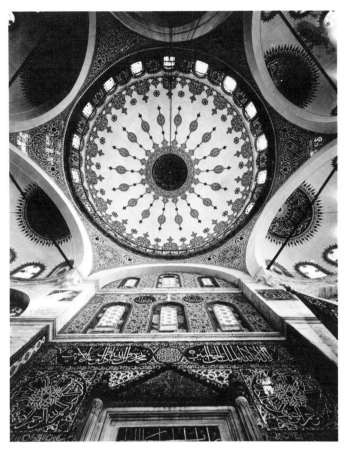

12,37 Sinan, the Sokollu Mehmed Pasha Mosque, Istanbul, 1571.

(more than 100 feet, 30m, in diameter) resting on eight elegant piers of pinkish sandstone but also, as it were, 'corrects' the design of Hagia Sophia with the axiomatic simplicity of its centralized plan – an octagon inscribed in a square – with the clarity and evenness of the lighting, the sparseness of decoration and the monumental regularity of the exterior which perfectly expresses the interior volumes. He created, in fact, one of the world's greatest works of architecture conceived as the molding of space. But he was hardly less successful when working on a smaller scale, as in the Sokollu Mehmed Pasha mosque built for the grand vizier's wife (a daughter of Selim II) on a difficult and limited hillside site in Istanbul (**12,37**). Its plan is a hexagon inscribed in a rectangle with a central dome counterbalanced by four half-domes (creating a spatial effect totally unlike anything in Byzantine architecture). For this more intimate building Sinan devised decorative effects of greater delicacy, with contrasted areas of white marble and panels of glazed tiles, which suffuse a turquoise light through the whole interior.

SAFAVID ART AND ARCHITECTURE

On the eastern frontier of the Ottoman empire the most powerful state was that ruled since 1502 by the Safavid dynasty, covering modern Iran, most of Iraq and much of Afghanistan. The area overlapped the main schism in Islam (see p. 349) for whereas the Ottomans were Sunnite the Safavids, who claimed descent from the Prophet Muhammad's son-in-law and successor, were defenders of a revived and much strengthened Shi'ite faith which they imposed on the state religion, thereby giving Iran the national identity it has retained to the present day. The Safavids also saw themselves as the successors of the rulers of ancient Persia and claimed to be descended from Cyrus the Great. Differences between Ottoman and Safavid arts were, however, due less to political ideals or even religious doctrine than to local traditions and inborn aesthetic preferences, as miniature paintings very clearly demonstrate.

As we have already seen (p. 343), Muslim attitudes to figurative art had from the beginning been very loosely defined. The Koran put a ban only on idols, and traditional teachings about the representation of human beings outside religious contexts were open to more than one interpretation. Figurative scenes were often painted on the walls of palaces and appear in Arabic manuscripts from at least as early as the ninth century. Korans were not illustrated, of course, but were often sumptuously illuminated with abstract ornament. It was from the cross fertilization of this type of work with Chinese Buddhist art, introduced by the Mongols in the thirteenth century, that Iranian miniature painting developed from its immediate origins in Mesopotamia. Already cultivated by the rulers of Shiraz in southern Iran and by Timur Lang's successors, especially at Herat (Afghanistan), it was brought to full bloom under the patronage of the Safavids at their first capital, Tabriz in western Iran.

A miniature of an angel warning Gayumarth, the legendary first shah of Iran, that the idyllic age in which he lives will soon come to an end, is from a manuscript of the Iranian national epic, the *Shahnama* (Book of Kings) by the early eleventh-century poet Abu'l-Qasim Firdawsi (**12,38**). The pose of Gayumarth, the attenuated elegance of the angel, the clouds and the gnarled branches recall Chinese art; but the general effect of jewel-like colors and the fluid rhythm of the composition are essentially Iranian in their synthesis of western (Tabriz) and eastern (Herat) traditions. The painting is attributed to Sultan-Muhammad (fl. c. 1510–45), the greatest painter of the Safavid period and largely responsible for bringing about this synthesis of styles. It is precious in every way, the work probably of several years, with much use of gold and blue lapis lazuli pigment. Such paintings were intended primarily to delight the eye as it follows the curves of the design and lingers in admiration at the vividness of the smallest details, especially the animals. The many miniatures in the volume, commissioned by the first Safavid shah, Isma'il (1502–24), and finished for his bibliophile son Tahmasp (1524–76), were the work of several hands and the pleasure of looking at each one must always have been enhanced by that of comparing it with others. Monotony was avoided by shifts in type of subject, color-scheme, composition and the way in which some scenes are tightly confined within a rectangle, while others burst out, so that the gold-speckled border is read as a back-

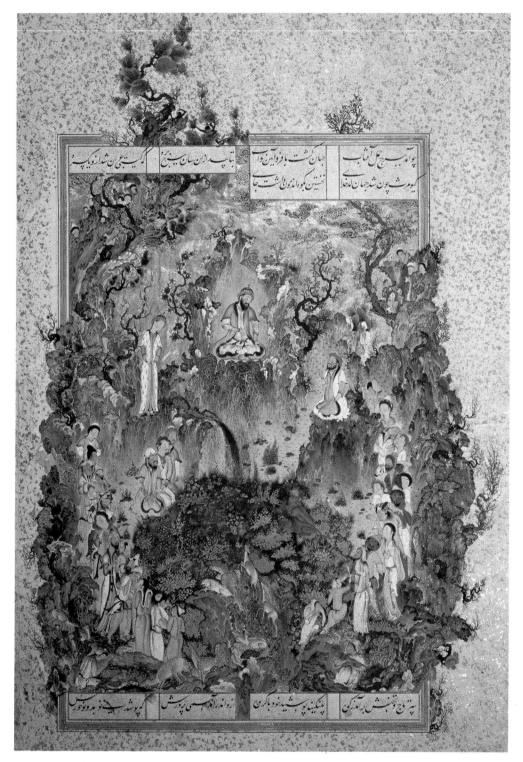

12,38 Anonymous (Sultan-Muhammad?), *The Court of Gayumarth*, from the *Shahnama* (Book of Kings), c. 1525–35. Pigment and gold on paper, 16½ × 11½ins (47 × 31.8cm). Metropolitan Museum of Art, New York.

ground rather than as a frame. Shah Tahmasp employed a retinue of artists who observed the same basic conventions – recession indicated by position on the page rather than diminution of scale, flat color with hatching but no shading – and satisfied the same demands for meticulous craftsmanship, yet were able to command an astonishing range of effects, from the lyrical and visionary to the humorous and delicately erotic.

Miniature painters and calligraphers held important positions at the Safavid courts, close to the shahs who were themselves practitioners of these arts. They also supplied designs for carpets made in the royal workshops. The art of making knotted carpets began with the nomads of central Asia in prehistoric times (see p. 161). Those made in Anatolia, and greatly prized in western Europe during the later Middle Ages and Renaissance, maintained ancient traditions, with foliage and animal forms reduced to geometrical shapes set by the rectangular weave of the ground to which the tufts of woollen pile were knotted. Under the Safavids, however, an entirely different type was developed, technically finer with silk grounds and up to 400 knots of variously colored wool per square inch (6.45cm), and decorated with a profusion of naturalistically rendered flowers and sometimes animals scattered over symmetrical patterns. Two of the finest and largest, said to have been made for the shrine of an ancestor of the Safavid shahs of Ardabil, are signed by 'a servant of the court, Muqsud of Kashan' who was presumably responsible for the design and for overseeing its execution by numerous, mainly female, workers (**12,39**).

Calligraphers in the manuscript studios influenced and sometimes designed the inscriptions painted on ceramic tiles for mosques and other religious buildings. On one of the finest early sixteenth-century *mihrabs*, scrolls and closely integrated floral patterns surround verses of the Koran in the beautiful flowing *thuluth* script (**12,40**). The text across the niche itself is a warning to those who pray negligently or hypocritically, and that running round the arch reads: 'Be constant in prayer, and give alms, and what good ye have sent before your souls, ye shall find it with Allah, surely Allah seeth that which ye do.' Such inscriptions fulfil the same function as figurative imagery in a Christian altarpiece but, incorporated in an apparent eternity of intricately woven motifs, without a focal point and conveying no sense of space or time, they help to concentrate the worshipper's attention beyond the wall which the tiles cover like a shimmering

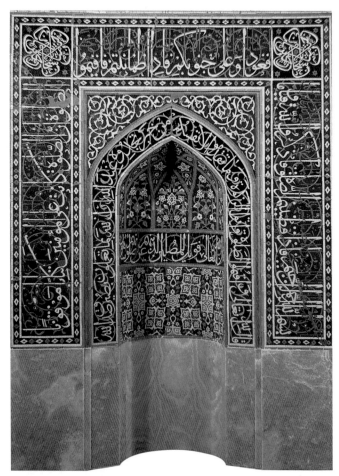

12,40 *Mihrab* from Iran, early 16th century. Tin-glazed earthenware tiles, 6ft 7ins (2m) high. Museum für Islamische Kunst, Berlin.

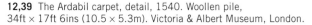

12,39 The Ardabil carpet, detail, 1540. Woollen pile, 34ft × 17ft 6ins (10.5 × 5.3m). Victoria & Albert Museum, London.

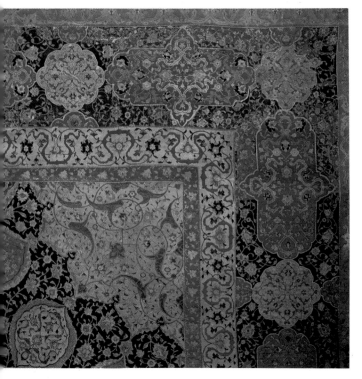

veil. Better than any other medium, painted and glazed ceramic tiles resolve the contradictory purposes of the *mihrab*: to indicate the direction of prayer without becoming an object of devotion. It had simultaneously to proclaim physically and deny spiritually the importance of the *qibla* wall. The only naturalistic motifs are floral and although they have no precise symbolical meanings (like the lily in Christian and the lotus in Buddhist art) they may reflect both the transience of life and mystical Sufi ideas of the immanence of the divine in the natural world.

This *mihrab* is dated to the early Safavid period from which virtually no complete buildings have been preserved. In 1555, Shah Tahmasp moved his capital from Tabriz, perilously near Ottoman territory, to Qasvin where he had a palace built and decorated with paintings on literary themes of which only fragments have survived the earthquakes common in this region. During his long reign Safavid authority was weakened by incursions of the Ottomans who seized two major Shi'ite shrines in Iraq and internally by a power struggle for succession to the throne. After a troubled interregnum, Shah Abbas I (1588–1629) restored order and set about strengthening the state. In the 1590s, he transferred the capital to Isfahan in the centre of the country and had an extensive

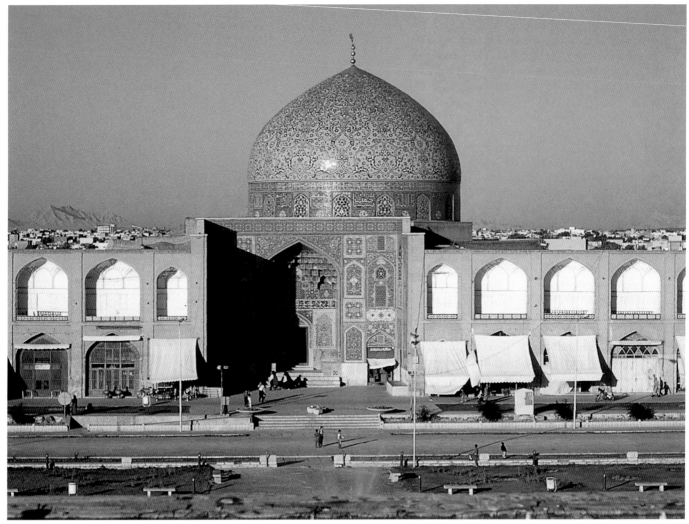

12,41 The Lutfullah Mosque, Isfahan, Iran, begun 1603. View across the new *maidan* from the porch of 'Ali Qapu.

addition to the old city laid out as a spacious complex of mosques, palaces, bazaars, open spaces and tree-lined 'boulevards' – an unprecedented and for long unequalled example of urban design. By an odd coincidence, at almost the same moment, Rome was being transformed on the master-plan of Sixtus V with entirely different motives (see p. 492).

A distinctly Safavid architecture, owing much to the buildings of Timur Lang but lighter in appearance and decorated with a delicate refinement that verges on the precious, was fully developed in Isfahan. The open court-yard entrance to the Lutfullah mosque, begun in 1603, is clad in panels of ceramic tiles which resemble the most exquisite carpets and silk textiles (**12,41**). This small building, which is still more richly decorated inside, prob-ably served as a private oratory for the shah and was later named after Shaykh Lutfullah, an eminent scholar and religious teacher who lived in Isfahan at the invitation of Abbas I. The nearby congregational Shah Mosque (renamed the Imam Mosque after the Islamic Revolution in Iran of 1979), on the other hand, was built 1611–38 to

supplement if not replace the Friday Mosque in the old city – one of the largest in Iran dating from the eighth to the thirteenth century and preserving and combining ele-ments in the styles of different periods, like a European Gothic cathedral. The Shah Mosque is a homogeneous and strictly symmetrical construction on the four-*iwan* plan – built round a square court with an *iwan* in the centre of each of its arcaded sides – developed in central Asia over the previous three centuries but never realized with such serene gravity and balance, such exquisite sensitivity to proportional relationships (**12,42; 43**). All these surfaces, including those of two interior prayer halls for use in winter, are clad in glazed ceramic tiles that dissolve the structure and envelop the worshipper or visitor who feels as if suspended in a haze of reflected color. Both mosques are, of course, oriented towards Mecca but as their façades are on the rectangular *maidan* laid out before they were begun, the great public space for regal ceremonies, mili-tary parades, polo games and commerce, their entrances are skewed, mediating between secular and religious life and art.

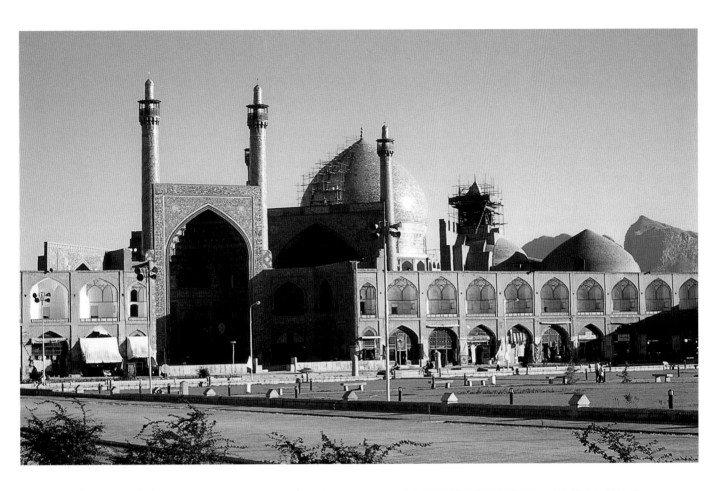

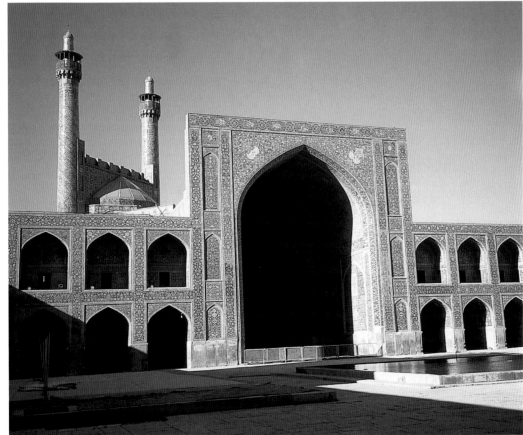

12,42 The Shah Mosque, Isfahan, Iran, 1611-38. View from the new *maidan*.

12,43 The Shah Mosque, Isfahan, Iran, 1611-38.

Isfahan and Samarkand

ISLAMIC URBAN DESIGN

The Shaykh Lutfullah Mosque (12,41) and Shah Mosque (12,42), Isfahan, form part of the large extension to the city laid out for Shah Abbas I from 1598 onwards. This extension constitutes a remarkable innovation in urban design, pioneering new forms and spaces for an improved human environment – salubrious, airy and verdant, with pools and canals and a huge *maidan* or public open space balancing a long shady, tree-lined thoroughfare resembling a mid-nineteenth-century European 'boulevard'. They combine to create an urban complex unparalleled elsewhere in the world at that date and still partly surviving (**12,44**). Yet, innovative though it was in conception, it followed the same process of growth by extension as in earlier Islamic cities rather than by expan-

sion round a stable core as in Europe. When the Muslim armies erupted out of Arabia in the seventh century they took over such ancient cities as Damascus, converting pagan temples and their precincts into mosques and colonnaded streets into covered bazaars. New settlements were limited to garrison towns laid out on a simple grid pattern. Their growth, as at Fustat in Egypt, was by the addition of enclaves outside the original settlement, this process being repeated until eventually a vast area was covered by the urban sprawl of Cairo. Most Islamic cities grew in this way, Isfahan being exceptional only in its sophistication and ameliorative social concerns.

The aim of Shah Abbas I was to create a new political and religious capital combined and integrated with,

as was not unusual in Islam, a new commercial centre. An undeveloped area between the old city and the Ziyamanda river was chosen for it, the great Friday Mosque in the old city being linked to the new Shah Mosque by a new bazaar 1¹/₂ miles (2.4km) long. Shops in a uniform two-story arcade, similar in design to that round the court of the new Shah Mosque and thus visually uniting and harmonizing the secular and religious life of the city, completely surround a huge new oblong twenty-acre (8 hectares) *maidan* – larger than any piazza or square in Europe. Behind them corridors of the bazaar, roofed with a myriad shallow domes, encircle the whole complex. Across the length of the *maidan* the glittering ceramic tile clad *iwan* portal of the Shah Mosque (12,42) faces that, only slightly less richly decorated, of the Royal Mint and entrance to the bazaar. At one third of the length between them the royal palace of Ali Kapu (High Gate), with a lofty slender-columned upper-floor terrace from which ceremonies and parades and games of polo could be watched, rises above the level of the shopping arcades directly opposite the exquisite Shaykh Lutfullah Mosque (12,41). Merchants and artisans were encouraged to move to the new town by the offer of premises at low rents. Nowhere has trade been given a more elegant and welcoming environment.

A major element in the town-plan was the straight avenue 2¹/₂ miles (4km) long, named after the *chahar bagh* or four-fold Islamic garden at its head. With a canal, fountains, trees and flowering shrubs planted along the centre and with ample space for gardens and the houses of the nobility on either side, nothing like it was to be seen elsewhere until the mid-nineteenth century in Europe. It led, moreover, directly to the Ziyamanda river which ventilated it and from it the whole new city. At the junction with the river a bridge, built in 1602, led to a royal park on the opposite bank and also to a suburb where

12,44 Plan of Isfahan, Iran, as developed by Shah Abbas I from 1598 onwards.

1 New *maidan*
2 Bazaar portal
3 The Lutfullah Mosque
4 The Shah Mosque
5 Charar Bagh

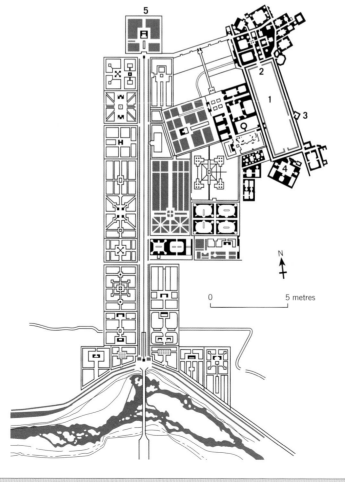

0   5 metres

Armenians from the troubled frontier with the Ottoman empire were settled. Some 50 years later, Shah Abbas II had another bridge built slightly downstream to serve also as a dam, with three lanes separating pedestrian from other traffic and with elegant kiosks projecting out over the rushing waters. Here the public could, and still does, enjoy the cool refreshing air above the dam (**12,45**). Visitors from the smoky overcrowded cities of Europe were impressed. One of them wrote in 1624 that Isfahan was 'so sweet and verdant that you may call it another paradise'.

The only urban project comparable to the Isfahan of Shah Abbas I is at Samarkand, Uzbekistan, where the Registan was begun by Timur Lang's intellectual grandson Ulughbeg in 1417. He built an exceptionally large *madrasa* and *khanqah*, or hospice, for Sufis, the wandering mystics of Islam, facing each other across the Registan or 'place of sand', and in front of a huge caravanserai for merchants on the Silk Route from China to the Mediterranean. However, the Registan was not completed for another two centuries when the *khanqah* was

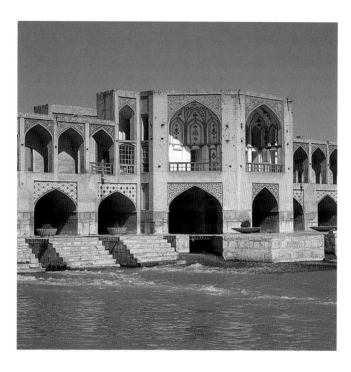

12,45 Shah Abbas II Bridge, Isfahan, Iran, c. 1650.

replaced by a second *madrasa* (in 1616–36) and the caravanserai by a third *madrasa* in the 1650s (**12,46**). Their towering façades, with central *iwans* recalling the solemnity of French Gothic cathedral porticoes and with detached minarets punctu-ating the architectural complex like ancient Roman triumphal columns, embrace with their glittering ceramic tile clad surfaces an architectural space that has been described as 'the noblest public square in the world'.

12,46 The Registan, Samarkand, Uzbekistan, begun 1417 completed 1650s.

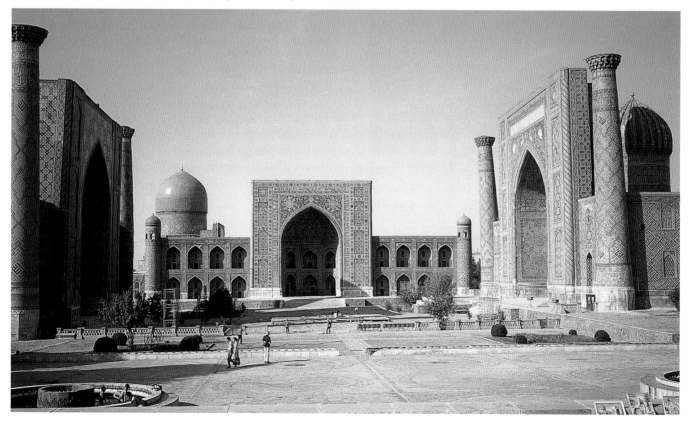

MUGHAL ART AND ARCHITECTURE

From Iran the Safavid art of miniature painting was introduced into India. At the beginning of the sixteenth century the greater part of the sub-continent had for long been ruled by Muslim sultans. In 1526 two military adventurers from Turkestan, Babur (d. 1530) and his son Humayun (1508–56), seized power and founded the Mongol, or Mughal, empire. Humayun was, however, opposed and took refuge for 12 years in Iran at the çourt of Tahmasp, who aided his restoration. During his exile he acquired a taste for Iranian art, especially miniatures, and took into his service two of the best painters employed by the shah, who was beginning to lose interest in illustrated books. Humayun's son Akbar (1542–1605), who consolidated and extended the Mughal empire to Bengal in the east and as far south as the river Godavari, was a still more active patron and assembled court workshops at Agra, Delhi and Fatehpur Sikri with artists from all parts of India, including many Hindus. As a result, Islamic art underwent its most radical transformation.

12,47 Basawan, *Akbar restrains Hawa'i*, c. 1590. Pigment on paper, 13½ × 8½ins (34.5 × 21.7cm). Victoria & Albert Museum, London.

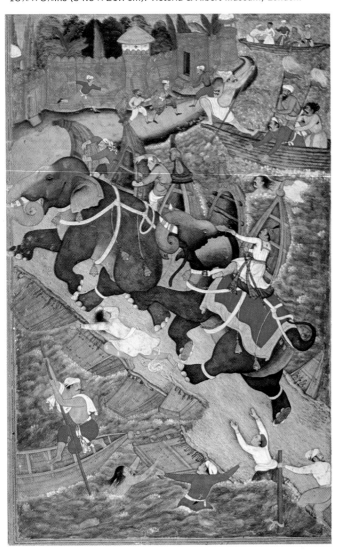

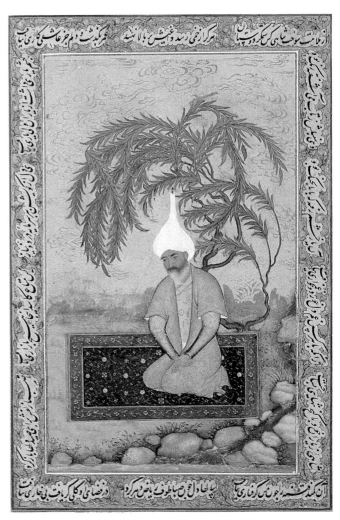

12,48 Sahifa Banu, *Portrait of Shah Tahmasp*, early 17th century. Pigment on paper, 6 × 3¾ins (15 × 9.5cm). Victoria & Albert Museum, London.

Although he was among the wisest of all rulers – perhaps the greatest in a century dominated by emperors, Charles V in western Europe and Suleyman in Turkey – Akbar was almost, if not entirely, illiterate. And this may partly account for his passion for paintings, especially for those with a strong and clearly expressed narrative content – unlike most Iranian miniatures. The history of his long reign was brilliantly illustrated in his own copy of his biography, written about 1586–90 by his minister Abu'l Fazl. One sheet by the Hindu painter Basawan (fl. 1590–1605), who created the classic Mughal narrative style, records a youthful exploit, Akbar's mounting a notoriously intractable elephant and setting it to fight another, which it chased across a pontoon bridge (**12,47**). In technique the painting follows the Iranian practice of drawing in outline and filling with color (draftsman and colorist sometimes being different artists), but the bold contrasts of red, blue, green and yellow owe more to Hindu art, and the suggestion of distance by diminution in scale was probably learned from Europeans, who were welcomed at Akbar's court. Although the subject might seem to be light and anecdotal, it had a symbolic meaning, which

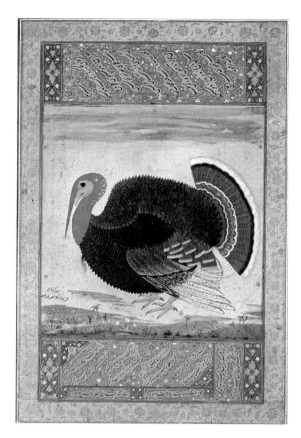

12,49 *Above* al-Mansur, *Turkey Cock*, 1605–27. Pigment on paper, 5¼ × 5⅛ins (13.2 × 13cm). Victoria & Albert Museum, London.

Basawan presented dramatically. Akbar told Abu'l Fazl that he had mounted dangerous elephants in order to put himself at God's mercy and the incident thus illustrates the origin of the vital power that enabled him to triumph over men as well as beasts.

Under Akbar painting was largely an 'official' art, confined almost entirely to the illustration of histories and chronicles and sometimes intended for display at public readings. Many paintings were quite large, for example the 1,400 commissioned in 1567 for the *Hamzanama* (The Tales of Hamza), which were 45 inches (114.3cm) square (only about 100 survive). They generally depict scenes of violence or boisterous energy – battles, sieges, hunts, etc. – and are very different in feeling from Safavid painting. Akbar also commissioned portrait miniatures, but the great master of this famous type of Mughal painting, Abu'l Hasan (b. 1589), worked for Akbar's successor Jahangir (1569–1627), under whom painting became more aristocratic and refined – smaller in scale, lighter in palette and more exquisite – intended for the connoisseur's private delectation. Narrative painting declined and was superseded by album painting, i.e. paintings of animals, birds, flowers, *genre* scenes or portraits, made not as illustrations to a book but as individual works of art to be mounted in an album and enjoyed for their own sakes. One of his albums included, for example, a portrait of Shah Tahmasp by the Mughal princess Sahifa

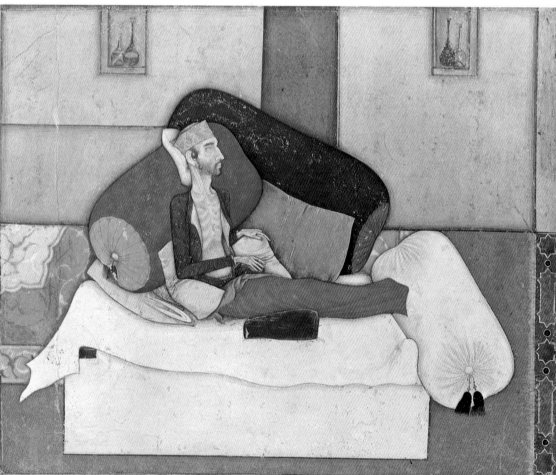

12,50 Anonymous, *Imayat Khan Dying*, c. 1618. Pigment on paper, 5 × 6ins (12.5 × 15.3cm). Curators of the Bodleian Library, Oxford (MS Ouseley Add. 1716, fol. 4v).

Banu, one of several accomplished women artists of this period in India (**12,48**). Boasting of his connoisseurship in his memoirs, Jahangir claimed to be able to attribute not only whole paintings to their author but even the parts of a composite work – 'if anyone has put in the eye and eyebrow of a face, I can perceive whose work the original face is and who has painted the eye and eyebrow'! When the Portuguese at Goa sent him a turkey – a species still rare in the Old World, to which it had been introduced from America a century before – Jahangir commissioned a picture of it from one of his favourite artists, al-Mansur, called 'The Wonder of the Age'. The result is among the most distinguished of all ornithological paintings, capturing the turkey's jauntiness as well as meticulously recording the color and sheen of its plumage with sumptuous effect (**12,49**).

But this detached approach could also lead to other and, to Western eyes, rather disturbing effects, in which the most refined artistic sensibilities are combined with complete and inhuman indifference to the implications of the subject. In 1618, for instance, one of Jahangir's courtiers, reduced to skin and bones as a result of opium addiction, was carried into his presence and, Jahangir wrote, 'as it was a very extraordinary case, I directed painters to take his portrait' (**12,50**). No more coolly objective image of a man confronting death has ever been painted. The beauty of its austerely geometrical structure, its predominantly pallid tone lit only by the carefully placed patches of bright color and the tiny strip of blue and red ornament in the right-hand margin, glows like a fading ember. Every link with the Iranian style of decorative miniature painting has been severed in this extraordinary work.

The early Mughal emperors were no less active as patrons of architecture and the decorative arts than of paintings, most notably Jahangir's successor Shah Jahan (1592–1666). The Taj Mahal at Agra (**12,51**), one of the

12,51 The Taj Mahal, Agra, India, 1632–48.

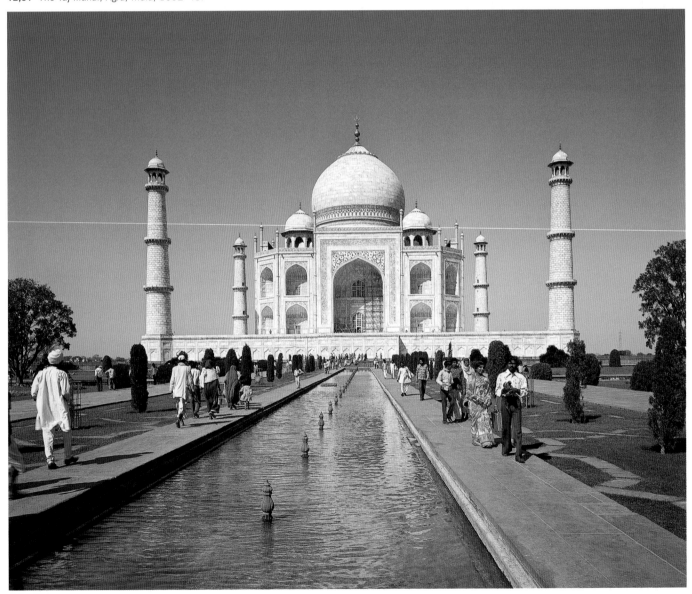

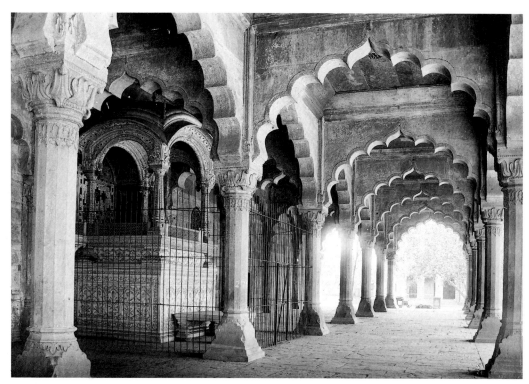

12,52 Audience Hall with royal throne, 1639–48. Red Fort (or Lal-Qila), Delhi.

most famous buildings in the world, grandiose in scale, exquisite in its opalescent color and its refinement of carved and inlaid detail and perfectly balanced in its proportions, was commissioned by Shah Jahan as a mausoleum for his favourite wife Mumtaz Mahal (1593–1631). A tomb for a wife on such a scale was entirely without precedent in Islam and it seems possible that the Taj Mahal was conceived also as an allegory in stone of the day of Resurrection, the Taj itself being a symbolical replica of the throne of God. Certainly the lay-out of four intersecting water channels in the great Persian *chahar bagh* garden, through which the Taj Mahal is approached, symbolized Paradise with its four flowing rivers as described in the Koran.

The architect seems to have been Ustad Ahmad Lahori called 'Wonder of the Age' (d. 1649), a Persian who later designed the audience hall (**12,52**) and other buildings in the Red Fort at Delhi (1639–48). Yet the effect of the huge white marble octagonal structure of the Taj, culminating in its enormous dome with flanking minarets some 140 feet (43m) high, is not wholly Iranian, despite the prominence of Iranian forms such as the *iwan* and the bulbous double-dome like that of Timur Lang's tomb at Samarkand (12,34). The general effect is entirely different from that of any building north of the Hindu Kush. The Taj Mahal is, indeed, the ultimate refinement and culmination of a style developed at Humayun's tomb at Delhi (completed c. 1570), refined at Akbar's new city of Fatehpur Sikri (1568–75) and later still at Akbar's tomb at Sikandra (completed 1613), all of which incorporate and reconcile Hindu and Islamic elements – the latter

including true arches and domes which had been introduced to India by Muslims and remained distinguishing marks of their architecture – as a conscious expression of political and religious policy. For Akbar's success as a ruler was largely due to his winning over the Hindu princes and to his religious tolerance. He even attempted to found a new world-wide religion and had a hall built for discussions between Muslims of all sects, Hindus, Zoroastrians, Jains and Christians.

The architectural activities of the early Mughals were devoted mainly to mausoleums and palaces of rarefied opulence, not to mosques for the mass of the faithful. 'If there is heaven on earth, it is here, it is here, it is here', Shah Jahan had inscribed in his audience hall at Delhi. Yet this essentially courtly art reflects highly developed intellectual interests. The complexities of Indian theology particularly fascinated Shah Jahan's favourite son, the most cultivated member of the family, Dara Shikoh, and it was probably for him that a group of Hindu holy men was depicted (**12,56**) – an amazingly objective record of spiritual experience, quite literally a brown study in color as in subject. This painting also reveals the extent of European artistic influence on Indian art at this date, for the distant view is rendered with aerial perspective and the pose of the *chela* or neophyte in the foreground is taken from an Italian print.

A great change, not only in art, came about after 1658, when Aurangzeb (1618–1707) seized the throne, imprisoned his father Shah Jahan, had his brother Dara Shikoh executed for heresy, and attempted to impose the Sunnite Muslim faith throughout the empire, which he extended

Nur-Jahan and Jahangir

ART AT THE MUGHAL COURT

A decade before the Taj Mahal was begun, white marble inlaid with floral motifs in glowing semi-precious stones had been used for the first time in Mughal architecture on the tomb of a Persian nobleman, the Lord High Treasurer and chief minister of the emperor Jahangir, who gave him the title Itmad-ud-Daula (Pillar of Government) (**12,53**). With its exquisite refinement of detail, this little building on a square plan no more than 70 feet (21.3m) wide is set in the centre of a Persian-style garden with flagged pathways, rectangular ponds and fountains within a walled enclosure. It is entered through tall red sandstone gateways which contrast in both texture and color with the smooth white marble. The predominantly horizontal lines of the building and the spreading cupola over its upper-story pavilion, nicely balanced by only slightly taller minarets, help to create an atmosphere of beatific repose in a paradise of refined sensuality.

It was commissioned in 1622 by Itmad-ud-Daula's daughter. She was born in Persia and in 1611 married Jahangir, who named her Nur-Jahan (Light of the World), complementing his own title which means World Seizer. She is one of the few women who emerge from the anonymity of Mughal harems. A crack shot with a flintlock gun, she went on hunting expeditions with the emperor but was also notable as a patron of the arts and the charitable founder of several orphanages for girls. Jahangir was devoted to her, as his memoirs reveal, and issued gold coins in her name – a distinction for a consort without precedent or sequel in Islam. Having given up alcohol, Jahangir became increasingly addicted to opium which he is said to have eaten with a spoon as if it were cream cheese, and because of this Nur-Jahan came to play a major role in governing the

12,53 Tomb of Itmad-ud-Daula, Agra, 1622–8.

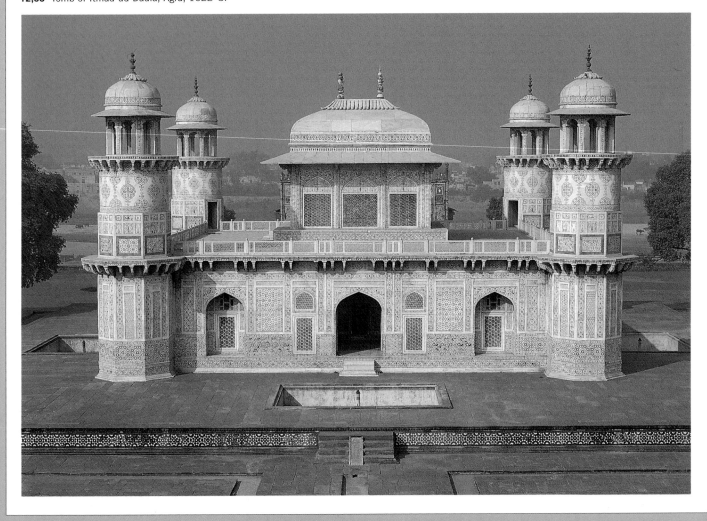

Mughal empire. At the centre of a Persian faction at court she also intrigued against the heir apparent who, when he succeeded as Shah Jahan (Ruler of the World) in 1628, had her banished to Shahdara near Lahore. He had, however, married her niece Mumtaz Mahal for whom he later built the Taj Mahal.

Jahangir was a connoisseur of carpets and other textiles, jewelry and especially hard-stone carvings. But it was during the long reign of his successor that the arts of luxury and also architectural decoration (12,52) were brought to a height of refinement rarely equalled and never surpassed anywhere in the world. A wine-cup made for Shah Jahan in 1656–7 is one of the most beautifully sensual objects ever wrought out of jade, seemingly caressed rather than cut and ground into shape (**12,54**). From the natural lump of soft, rather soapy looking material that limited the form, the artist fashioned a bowl in the semblance of a half gourd out of which an ibex's head, serving as a handle, seems to grow organically. A similar refinement is evident in the design and execution of mats on which prayers were said five times a day. One panel is embroidered on a cotton ground in shades of red, blue and green silk with tiny flowers surrounding a central panel shaped like a *mihrab* (see p. 345) pointing the way to Mecca, with a stylized lily in full bloom (**12,55**). Such floral motifs had been introduced in art from Persia in the reign of Jahangir but were soon given a distinctively Mughal appearance.

Mughal art was quintessentially a court art, inacessible and unknown to the vast mass of the population of subjugated Hindus. The court workshops monopolized the finest materials and employed the most skilful artists to produce luxuries for the emperors and nobility, often as gifts that passed between them. Their sophisticated delicacy is in striking contrast with the brutal reality of the power struggles at the courts they embellished. Their highly civilized and often exquisite refinement derived from Persia; and in this development, Persian-born Nur-Jahan seems to have played a leading role.

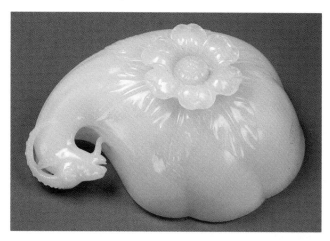

12,54 Wine cup of Shah Jahan, 1656–7. Jade (white nephrite), 7⅜ins (18.7cm) long. Victoria & Albert Museum, London.

12,55 *Below* Embroidered panel, c. 1650–1700. Cotton and silk, 46 × 32ins (117 × 81.3cm). Victoria & Albert Museum, London.

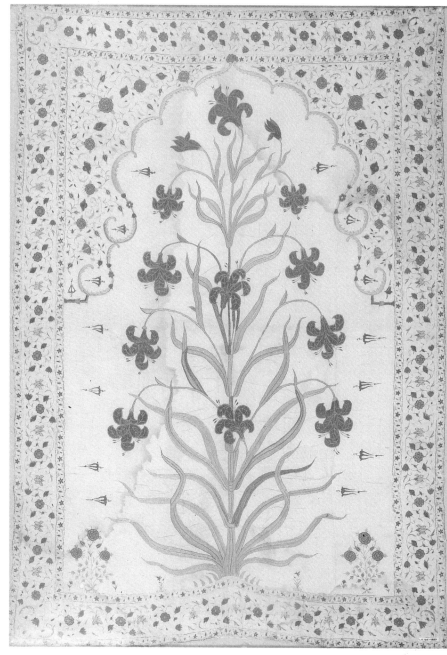

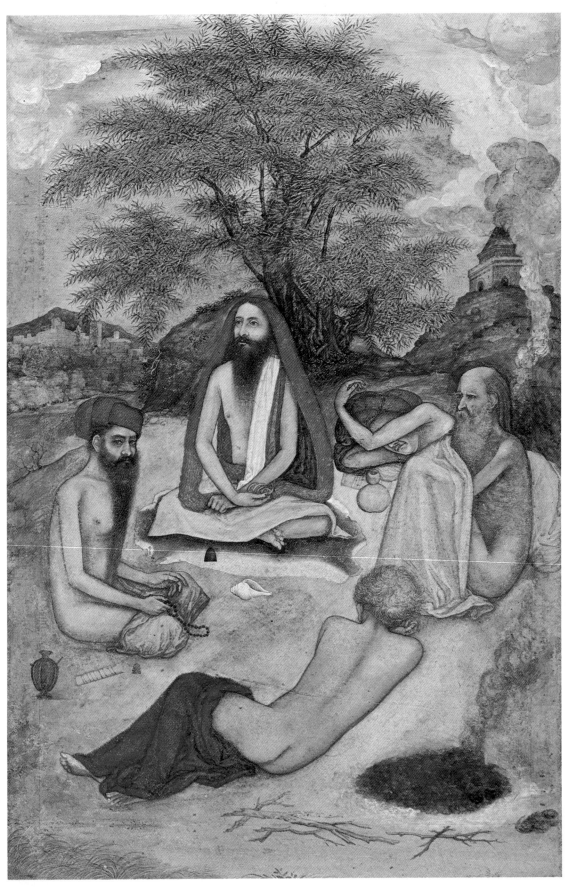

12,56 Anonymous (Govardhan?), *Hindu Holy Men*, c. 1625.
Pigment on paper, 9⅜ × 6ins (23.8 × 15.2cm). Private collection.

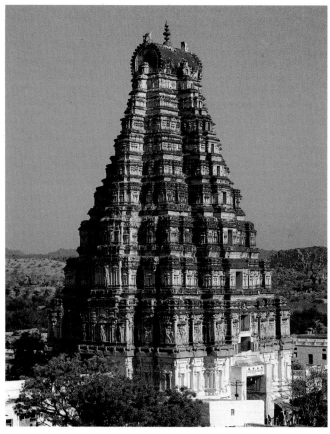

almost to the tip of the peninsula. Under his rule the art of miniature painting was virtually suppressed; he devoted himself to copying out the Koran and building mosques on the sites of Hindu temples which he had demolished. The result of his long reign was, however, divisive and after his death in 1707 India reverted to its pre-Mughal state of internal warfare, which, of course, opened the way to European colonization.

In the far south, never completely assimilated by the invaders who had poured into India from central Asia over the millennia, the tradition of Hindu art lived on, strengthened by an influx of refugees. Here in the early sixteenth century the 10-square-mile (2,590 hectares) city of Vijayanagar had been built with huge temples richly adorned with sculpture (**12,57**), 'so well executed that they appear as if made in Italy', a Portuguese traveller reported in about 1520! But in 1565 it fell to Muslims of the Deccan sultanate, who spent a whole year destroying it with gunpowder and crowbars, though much remained in the depopulated city. The influence of Islamic architecture is apparent in such palatial buildings as the pavilion known as the Lotus Mahal with elegant cusped arches on the ground floor (**12,58**). But the religious buildings were emphatically Hindu, almost defiantly anti-Islamic in

12,57 *Above Gopura* of the Pampapati temple, Vijayanagar, India, 16th century (renovated in the 17th century).

12,58 *Below* Lotus Mahal, Vijayanagar, 16th century.

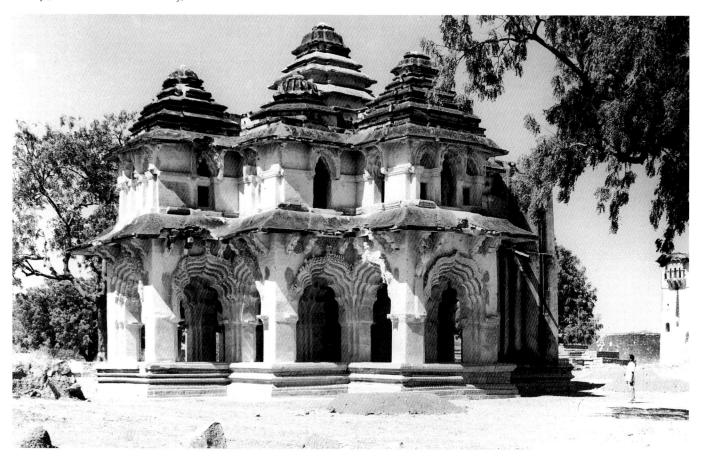

their abundance of figurative sculpture celebrating belief in the plurality of deities. In the empire of Vijayanagar the concept of the temple was widened from that of a single shrine to a complex of dispersed buildings within concentric enclosures entered through tall *gopuras* (gateway towers), increasing in size from the inner to the outer walls, dwarfing the main shrine (usually an ancient one) but making their presence felt from far away. The buildings include subsidiary shrines for the consorts of gods and for their vehicles (Shiva's bull, Vishnu's eagle), colonnades round water tanks for ritual ablutions, *mandapas* (halls) for sacred drama and dance, education and civic meetings. These temples were more fully integrated than before into the life of a town while making the religion of the state more powerfully, visibly manifest. They have an extraordinary abundance of sculpture. Outer columns of *mandapas* were carved with whole cohorts of warriors on life-size horses rearing up over men and tigers (**12,59**). *Gopuras* were entirely covered with stacked friezes on which the deities of the whole Hindu pantheon were modelled in stucco and brilliantly colored (12,57). And the process of enlarging and enriching temples continued for more than a century after the fall of Vijayanagar, most notably in the great temple city of Madurai. These structures make the most violent contrast with the smooth planes and clearly defined masses of such Islamic buildings as the Taj Mahal. The sensuality and carnality of their mountains of writhing forms continue the ancient Indian conception of architecture as sculpture, as a living, organic mass.

SOURCES AND DOCUMENTS

DOMINGO PAES ON VIJAYANAGAR

Domingo Paes, a Portuguese merchant and traveller from Goa, saw the great Hindu city of Vijayanagar at the height of its grandeur and magnificence. His account, written soon after 1520–2, is unusually vivid and graphic.

In this city you will find men belonging to every nation and people, because of the great trade which it has, and the many precious stones there, principally diamonds.

He could not describe the size and extent of it

. . . because it cannot all be seen from any one spot, but I climbed a hill whence I could see a great part of it; I could not see it all because it lies between several ranges of hills. What I saw from thence seemed to me as large as Rome, and very beautiful to the sight; there are many groves of trees within it, in the gardens of the houses, and many conduits of water which flow into the midst of it, and in places there are lakes; and the king has close to his palace a palm-grove and other rich-bearing fruit-trees.

Few of the buildings he described can now be recognized, but of them the Lotus Mahal (12,58) is the most notable. Paes called it 'a little house'.

As soon as you are inside, on the left hand, are two chambers one above the other, which are in this manner: the lower one is below the level of the ground, with two little steps which are covered with copper so gilded, and from there to the top is all lined with gold (I do not say 'gilded,' but 'lined' inside), and outside it is dome-shaped. It has a four-sided porch made of cane-work over which is a work of rubies and diamonds and all other kinds of precious stones, and pearls, and above the porch are two pendants of gold; all the precious stone-work is in heart-shapes, and, interweaved between one and another is a twist of thick seed-pearl work; on the dome are pendants of the same. In this chamber was a bed which had feet similar to the porch, the cross-bars covered with gold, and there was on it a mattress of black satin; it had all round it a railing of pearls a span wide; on it were two cushions and no other covering. Of the chamber above it I shall not say if it held anything because I did not see it, but only the one below on the right side. In this house there is a room with pillars of carved stone; this room is all of ivory, as well the chamber as the walls, from top to bottom, and the pillars of the cross-timbers at the top had roses and flowers of lotuses all of ivory, and all well executed, so that there could not be better, – it is so rich and beautiful that you would hardly find anywhere another such. On this same side is designed in painting all the ways of life of the men who have been here even down to the Portuguese, from which the king's wives can understand the manner in which each one lives in his own country, even to the blind and the beggars. In this house are two chairs covered with gold, and a cot of silver with its curtains.

Less than 50 years later, in 1567, an Italian traveller, Cesare Federici, visited Vijayanagar. He related that after the sack, when the Muslims had returned north, an attempt was made to repopulate the city. He wrote:

It had not been altogether destroyed, yet the houses stand still, but emptie, and there is dwelling in them nothing, as is reported, but Tygres and other wild beasts.

(Tr. R. Sewell, *A Forgotten Empire*, London 1924 [Paes];
S. Purchas, *Purchas His Pilgrimes*, London 1625 [Federici])

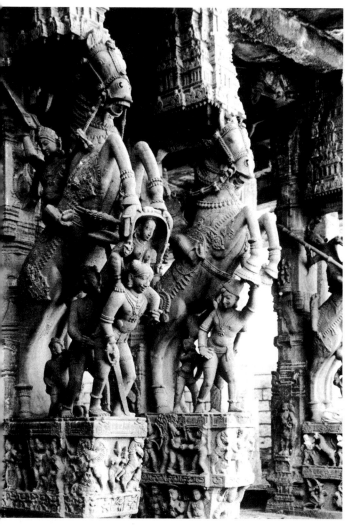

12,59 Sheshagiriraya *mandapa*, Ranganatha temple, Srirangam, India, 16th century.

CHINA

THE YUAN DYNASTY

The Mongol conquest of China, begun by Genghis Khan in 1210 and completed by his grandson Kubilai, who made himself the first emperor of the Yuan dynasty in 1279, brought the greater part of Asia under the rule of a single family. As a result, China briefly became more easily accessible to Europeans. Marco Polo, who travelled extensively in Asia from 1271 to 1295, and served as an official to Kubilai, and Friar Odoric of Pordenone, who went as a missionary to Beijing in 1324, both recorded their experiences; and they were by no means the only European visitors to China. In 1340 an Italian merchants' manual declared the route from the Black Sea to Beijing to be perfectly safe 'whether by night or by day'. In these circumstances greater quantities of silks and other artifacts crossed the continent and Asian motifs were more frequently imitated by European artists and craftsmen than ever before. In a painting by Simone Martini, for instance, St Louis of Toulouse wears a mitre embroidered with dragons of Chinese ancestry, and the dais of his throne is set on a Turkish carpet (9,82). Chinese influence on the arts of Iran was more profound, as we have seen (12,38), and Iranian motifs also passed in the opposite direction to be incorporated in porcelain and metalwork made in China. The Mongols seem, indeed, to have promoted a kind of international Asian style in the decorative arts. But the major Chinese art form, landscape painting, remained largely unknown to the rest of the world (apart from Japan).

Although Marco Polo had nothing but praise for the splendour of Kubilai's court and the efficiency of his administration, the Chinese felt very differently, crushed beneath a burden of taxes which landowners could pay only by pressing on the peasants until they were reduced to serfdom. The country was devastated and a population estimated at 100,000,000 in the early Song period had dwindled under the Mongols to 45,000,000, of whom 7,500,000 were officially reported to be starving. In 1325 there was a popular uprising against Chinese landlords and the Yuan régime, in 1348 rebellion broke out in the east and in 1368 the Mongols withdrew. The first emperor of the native Ming dynasty was installed on the Dragon Throne the same year.

Economically disastrous and relatively short though the Yuan period was, it determined much in the future course of Chinese art. The Mongols were interested especially in the decorative arts; they introduced the manufacture of carpets, commissioned fine metalwork, promoted greater richness of form and color in ceramics and, in general, imposed their 'barbaric' tastes which left their mark even after being tamed by the Chinese. So far as painting is concerned, the most notable direct effect of their rule was on religious art. The population of their vast empire included Muslims, Christians, Daoists and Buddhists of various sects as well as the Shamanists with whom they were most closely associated. Nor was there any religious persecution under the rule of the Mongols. Although they fought savagely against Islamic states in west Asia they put no hindrance on the many Muslims in China as their mosques testify (notably those in Beijing and Xi'an, though these were later rebuilt and are hardly distinguishable, externally, from Chinese temples, with pagoda-shaped minarets). The interests of the Khans in magic, however, led them to promote especially the Tantric Buddhism of Tibet and esoteric Daoism with its alchemy and promise of immortality.

The Yonglegong, a Daoist temple in Shanxi province not far from the Yellow River, dates almost entirely from the Yuan period. Replacing a burned down predecessor, the present buildings were begun in 1247 when the area was already occupied by the Mongols. They are in the simple, dignified style developed in this region under the Liao dynasty (see pp. 283–4), on an axial plan as in all Chinese temples and palaces, with a southern gate leading to a sequence of halls with plenty of space for gardens between them (12,60). (The original arrangement was maintained when the whole complex was moved to its present site in 1959–63 to avoid submergence following the building of a dam.) All the buildings have mural

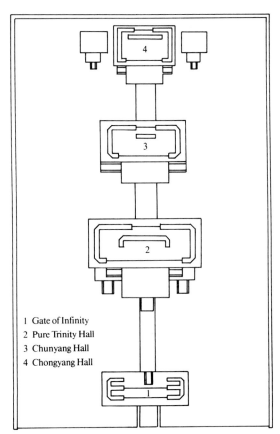

12,60 Plan of Yonglegong, Ruicheng, Shanxi, China.

1 Gate of Infinity
2 Pure Trinity Hall
3 Chunyang Hall
4 Chongyang Hall

élite. Professional painters, who ranked socially with entertainers and prostitutes, were thought to be simply artisans by Chinese connoisseurs and writers on art – who were, of course, almost invariably scholar-painters themselves. These *literati* are often termed amateurs in English but this is misleading, for though they did not practise their art to earn a livelihood their lives were devoted almost exclusively to it – to painting, calligraphy and poetry – and occasionally they might even sell a scroll. The distinction between the professionals and *literati* was educational, and also social, as only the children of the upper classes had access to the classics. In the Yuan period they withdrew more than ever into scholarly seclusion, holding themselves aloof from the world – very few were now important government officials, as some had been in former times – becoming increasingly contemplative and introspective, looking back with reverence to the early art of China, the product of more glorious epochs of national history. Their paintings present convincing images of the natural world – always a prime aim for earlier Chinese artists – but are more concerned with the artist's inner vision. 'A painting is nothing but an idea', wrote Huang Gongwang (1269–1354); 'what matters most when making a painting is the spirit of rightness' – and rightness implied adherence to tradition, both moral and artistic.

A painting of a sheep and goat by Zhao Mengfu (1254–1322) illustrates the Yuan scholar-painters' dependence on the past, in this case early Song realism, their

12,61 Ma Junxiang, *Daoist Deities*, completed 1325. Pure Trinity Hall, Yonglegong, Ruicheng, Shanxi. Wall-painting.

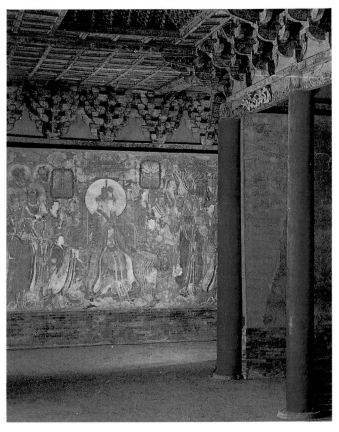

paintings inside them and those in the largest, the Pure Trinity Hall completed in 1325, form a most impressive sequence covering the walls from the dado to the (mainly ornamental) bracketing of the ceiling – some 14 feet (4.25m) high. Here the Daoist deities are shown surrounded by the full court of heaven, celestial generals, 'Jade Maidens' and other attendants, magnificently attired in flowing bejewelled and embroidered robes (**12,61**). The painter, Ma Junxiang, came from Luoyang, the former Song dynasty capital, and worked in a style developed there from Tang period origins. But although he was a masterly painter of figures – comparable in his expressive range and elegant accomplishment of line to Italian painters of a century or more later, such as Francesco del Cossa (10,46) – Ma Junxiang's name is known only because he signed his work in the Yonglegong. Like most other professional artists who worked publicly on a large scale, usually on temple walls, he was ignored by Chinese historians. They did not rank such professionals as 'artists', that is, with those who worked privately, on paper or silk, and did not seek to sell their paintings.

It was in the Yuan period that this rift, which was to mark the whole subsequent history of Chinese painting, opened between professionals, like Ma Junxiang, and the others, the scholars or *literati* as they are usually called, who cultivated painting, mainly in black and white, as an intensely personal and private form of art in accordance with the philosophical and religious ideals of an intellectual

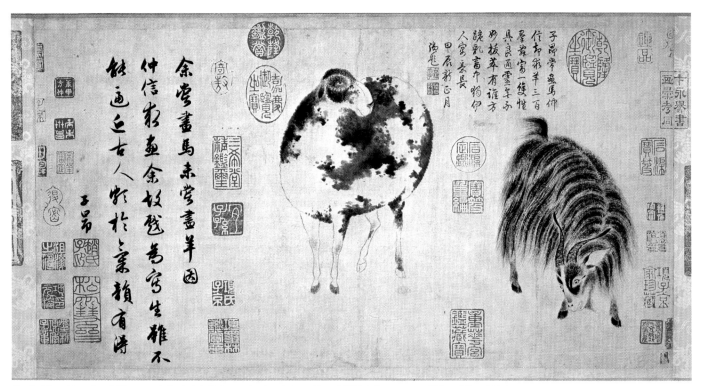

12,62 Zhao Mengfu, *A Sheep and Goat*, detail from a horizontal scroll, c. 1300. Ink on paper, 9⅞ins (25cm) high. Freer Gallery of Art, Smithsonian Institution, Washington DC.

sometimes almost defiant 'amateur' stance and their profound concern for art's inner meaning (**12,62**). In his inscription Zhao Mengfu stated that he had not previously painted these animals and did so now 'for amusement' to please a friend. A goat's characteristic movements are, in fact, brilliantly caught and the texture of its hair deftly suggested by a subtle mixture of wash and dry brush-strokes with very little use of outline. But to Zhao Mengfu such naturalistic effects were no more than a means of capturing the rhythm of life or vital spirit, which can be sensed in natural forms. It could also be sensed in the work of old masters, but could not be injected into a painting simply by copying. Nevertheless, 'the spirit of antiquity' sometimes led, as in his case, to deliberate archaism. He was one of the leaders of a return to the styles of painting practised under the Tang and early Song. He was also one of the few members of the aristocracy of birth as well as intellect – an eleventh-gen-eration descendant of the founder of the Song dynasty with the rank of duke – who accepted office under Kubilai and was given a high position in the civil service – and his 'collaboration' was never entirely forgiven by other scholar-painters who wrote the history of Chinese art.

Both the life and the work of Ni Zan (1301–74), on the other hand, were regarded as exemplary. He came from a rich merchant family, devoted himself exclusively to intellectual pursuits and, impoverished by taxation, in 1352 disburdened himself of his remaining possessions to live on a small houseboat drifting around the beautiful rivers and lakes of south-eastern Jiangsu. Rejecting the delicacy and lyricism of late Song painting (see p. 283), he created an art of austere detachment and understatement without any atmospheric effects or displays of virtuosity. His medium was black ink used with the utmost economy on absorbent paper, which was preferred at this period to glossy silk as a ground. Human figures very rarely appear in his landscapes, which are nearly always of the same imaginary scene, a group of sparsely leaved trees and a scholar's empty pavilion at the edge of a stretch of water with low hills rising from the further shore (**12,63**). 'Their air of supreme refinement and purity is so cold that it overawes men', wrote a late seventeenth-century Chinese painter who likened them to 'waves on the sandy beach, or streams between stones which roll and flow and issue by their own force'. His paintings have the moral qualities extolled by the Chinese, being firm without an undue display of strength, graceful without affectation, informal without being casual – very gentlemanly in their restraint and unpretentiousness and in the stern self-dis-cipline and intense application which underlie them.

Some subjects had strong symbolic overtones for the scholar-painters. The resilient evergreen bamboo, for example, was likened to the perfectly educated gentleman who bends to circumstances, adapts himself to society yet preserves his integrity; and it is hardly a coincidence that the plant was more frequently painted than ever before under the oppressive Yuan dynasty, when these moral qualities were especially called for. Bamboo painting became a distinct *genre*. Its stems and pointed leaves nat-urally had a particular fascination for artists who were also calligraphers, and its constantly changing appearance according to the season, time of day and humidity in the

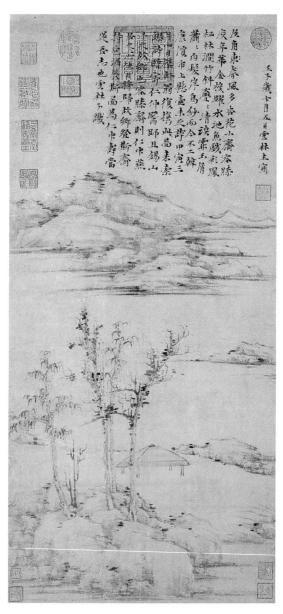

12,63 Ni Zan, *Rongxi Studio*, 1372, inscribed 1374. Ink on paper, 5ft 7ins (1.73m) high. National Palace Museum, Taipei (Taibei), Taiwan.

atmosphere presented a challenge to those who sought, in painting or in words, to grasp the vital spirit of nature. Li Kan (fl. 1260–1310) devoted his life to the plant, travelling as far as Assam to study different species, seeking out earlier bamboo paintings and writing a *Comprehensive Record of Bamboo*. He did not, however, advocate painting it direct from nature. The artist must, he wrote, accumulate his observations until he 'possesses' the bamboo completely in his mind and can depict what he holds in his mind's eye. Only in this way could its vital rhythm pass through the artist on to the paper and thence to the spectator. One of his few surviving scrolls shows two clumps of different species and a single stem painted with equal regard for botanical accuracy, for the naturalistic representation of growing leaves and gently swaying stems surrounded by warm air, and for the intricate organization of brush-strokes in a most carefully thought-out composition, which seems nevertheless to have been splashed on to the paper with spontaneous creative abandon (**12,64**). By being cut at top and bottom, the image is brought up close to the picture plane and the spectator enters, as it were, into intimate relationship with it.

A short handscroll, *Ten Thousand Bamboo Poles in Cloudy Mist*, dated 1308, is by Guan Daosheng (1262–1319), one of the most famous of Chinese female painters and the earliest of those whose work has survived (**12,65**). It is a scene of perfect calm untroubled by the lightest breeze to rustle leaves or disperse the mist that hangs between the beautifully observed bamboos in the foreground and those beyond. Several of her paintings are of bamboos not isolated, as was usual, but growing in clumps by the side of a river, a type of composition of her own devising that was admired and imitated. Indeed the esteem in which her work was held is indicative of the attitude of Chinese collectors and writers generally, gender being of no account to them when considering an artist's ability, especially one, like Guan Daosheng, who was well born, highly educated, in every sense a scholar-painter and married to the still more aristocratic painter Zhao Mengfu. But it was only among the *literati* that

12,64 Li Kan, *Bamboo*, detail from a horizontal scroll, c. 1300. Ink on paper, 14¾ins (37.5cm) high. Nelson-Atkins Museum of Art, Kansas City (Purchase: Nelson Trust).

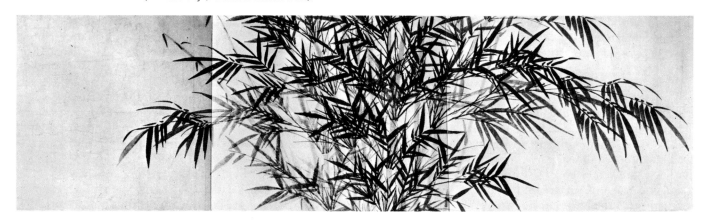

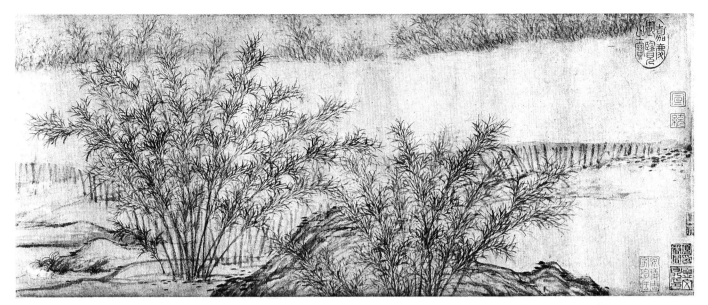

12,65 Guan Daosheng, *Ten Thousand Bamboo Poles in Cloudy Mist*, handscroll, 1308. Ink on paper, 6ins (15cm) high. National Palace Museum, Taipei (Taibei), Taiwan.

women artists were so accepted. And the distinction between scholar-painters and professional painters hardened during the Yuan period, due perhaps to the gradual exclusion of most of the former intellectual élite from government. Nor did the situation improve under the Ming dynasty.

THE MING DYNASTY

Although the Mongols provoked only a negative response from painters, they had a strong and lasting influence on the decorative arts by introducing new techniques. The blue-and-white color-scheme so intimately associated with Chinese porcelain – especially in the West – was evolved under their rule by a marriage of Chinese and Iranian processes and materials. China provided the porcelain, which had been invented much earlier (p. 278), Iran the cobalt-oxide medium used for decorating Near Eastern earthenware. This was the most easily controllable medium for underglaze decorations and was at first used in China for motifs of an Iranian cast on porcelain vessels fashioned like the metalwork of the Mongols. During the Ming period the color-scheme persisted, but all traces of foreign influence were expunged from the designs and Ming blue-and-white porcelain is as purely Chinese in decoration as in form (**12,66**). Similarly, *cloisonné* enamelling introduced under the Mongols came to be used to enrich bronze vessels of shapes which hark back to the Shang period with brightly colored Tang style ornament.

The first Ming emperor, Hongwu (1368–99), was a man of the people and won the throne by force of arms against a hated foreign oppressor. A return to ancient national traditions was thus the order of the day. The civil service was restored with an even less flexible organization than before. Classical Chinese scholarship was revived and in

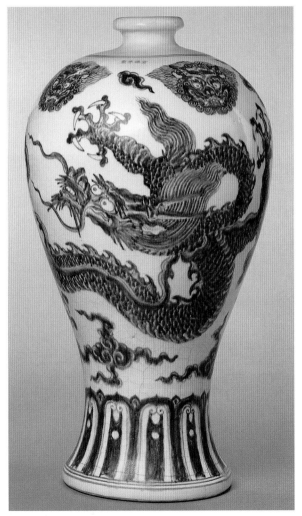

12,66 Meiping Vase, 1426-35. Ming dynasty (Xuande era). Porcelain, 21¾ins (55.2cm) high. Nelson-Atkins Museum of Art, Kansas City (Purchase: Nelson Trust).

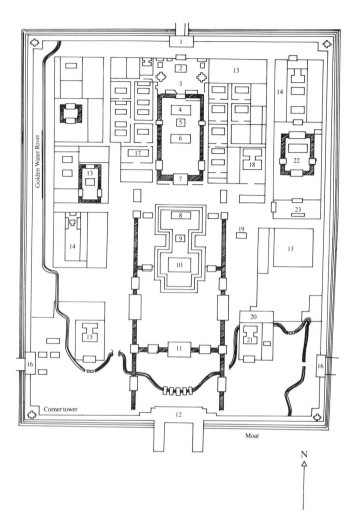

1403 the third Ming emperor, Yongle, initiated the compilation of all knowledge in an 11,095-volume encyclopedia. Respect for tradition was, however, tempered by a growing taste for ostentation. When Yongle moved his capital from Nanjing to Beijing in 1417, he had his palace laid out according to Zhou dynasty ritual, which prescribed that the 'Son of Heaven' should rule from three courts. Raised on the site of Kubilai's palace and using some of the old foundations, it was also designed to outshine the splendour of buildings that Marco Polo had thought 'so vast, so rich and so beautiful that no man on earth could design anything superior'. A 15-mile (24km) wall surrounded the axially planned courts dominated by the three great halls of state, which were later rebuilt and refurbished but always in the same sacrosanct manner, with wooden columns and beams and wide-spreading roofs of shimmering glazed yellow tiles – a color reserved for imperial buildings (**12,67**).

12,67 *Left* Plan of the Imperial Palace, Beijing.

1 Gate of Divine Pride	12 Meridian Gate
2 Pavilion of Imperial Peace	13 Kitchens
3 Imperial garden	14 Gardens
4 Palace of Earthly Tranquillity	15 Former Imperial Printing House
5 Hall of Union	16 Flower Gate
6 Palace of Heavenly Purity	17 Palace of the Culture of the Mind
7 Gate of Heavenly Purity	18 Hall of the Worship of the Ancestors
8 Hall of the Preservation of Harmony	19 Pavilion of Arrows
	20 Imperial Library
9 Hall of Perfect Harmony	21 Palace of Culture
10 Hall of Surpreme Harmony	22 Palace of Peace and Longevity
11 Gate of Surpreme Harmony	23 Nine Dragon Screen

12,68 *Below* The first courtyard of the Imperial Palace, Beijing, with the outer gate on the left, 1420, later restored.

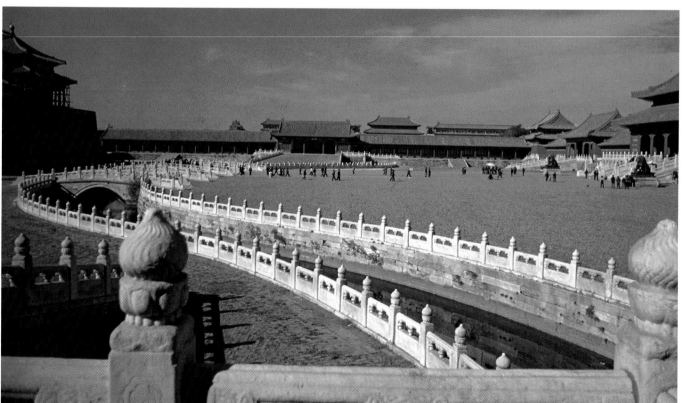

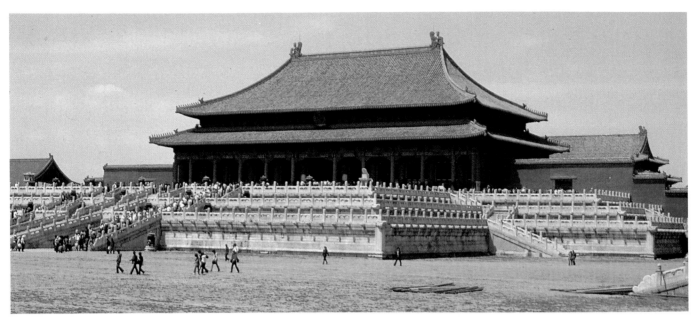

12,69 Hall of the Preservation of Harmony, Imperial Palace, Beijing, 15th century, later restored.

The outer gate (built in 1420, restored in 1647 and 1801) gives access to the first courtyard, crossed by the bow-shaped 'Golden Water River' (**12,68**). A still larger courtyard is reached through the 'Gate of Supreme Harmony' beyond. As Zhou ritual appointed the hour of dawn for the emperor's audiences, it was here that those who were to be received knelt and kowtowed in the gray twilight when the buildings must have looked their most dauntingly impressive. The three main halls are elevated above it on a triple tiered white marble platform. The 'Hall of Supreme Harmony', the only one that can be seen from the level of the courtyard, is about 200 feet (61m) wide and 100 feet (30.5m) deep, with the imperial throne on a high dais against its back wall. It was built in 1669 following an earlier design. The other two buildings on the platform date from the Ming period: the square 'Hall of Central Harmony', where the emperor performed such ancient rituals as that of inspecting seed before the spring

12,70 Street in the Imperial Palace, Beijing.

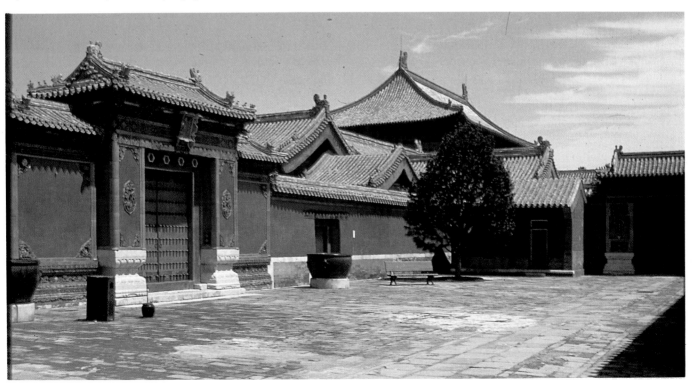

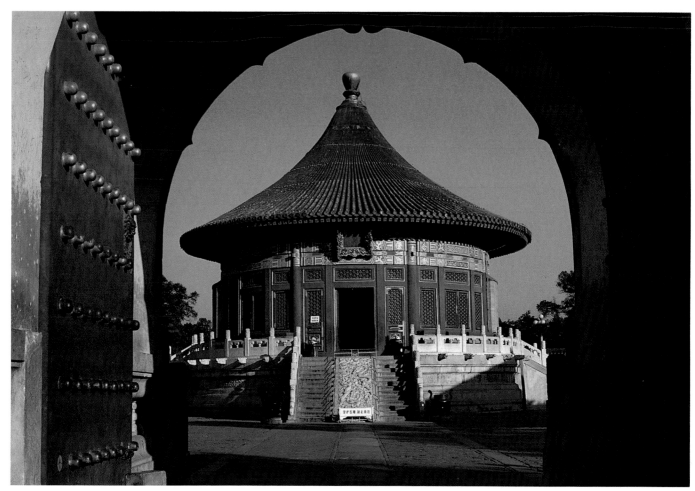

12,71 Imperial Heavenly Vault, Temple of Heaven, Beijing, 1530, restored 1752 and later.

sowing, and the 'Hall of the Preservation of Harmony', where the final part of the highest civil service examination was held (**12,69**). A third courtyard separates the platform from the rest of the Forbidden City which was accessible only to its permanent residents, with the emperor's private palace in the centre, that of the empress behind, and on either side houses for widows and secondary wives in courtyards leading off long, straight streets (**12,70**). Here the rigidity of the plan and the uniformity of the buildings, differing from one another only in size, were relieved, however, by small gardens and a profusion of plants in porcelain pots.

The Imperial Palace was the heart of an empire which, in Chinese eyes, spread over the entire world – foreign ambassadors were received there only as tribute bearers from vassals until well into the nineteenth century. The main buildings lie on the south–north axis of the celestial meridian which determined the whole lay-out. Thus the emperor, who ruled by the mandate of heaven, looked from his throne in the 'Hall of Supreme Harmony' south and down on the world of people as from the pole star. And the rituals he performed were intended to ensure harmony on earth in tune with the harmony of the cosmos. Although cosmic symbolism had been a feature of palatial architecture from a very early date and in many different

parts of the world, notably in Meso- and South America (see pp. 515–6), nowhere was it more strictly observed than in China or on a grander scale. The vast 4-square-mile (10.45 square km) precinct known as the Temple of Heaven, laid out in the Ming period, proceeds from an open-air temple on a mound, where the emperor sacrificed to and communicated with the heavens, to the Imperial Heavenly Vault (**12,71**) and, more than 650 yards (600m) to the north, the much larger triple-roofed 'Hall of Annual Prayers' (rebuilt after 1889; see pp. 697–8), each one built on a circular plan of celestial significance. Cosmology even guided the planning of private residences, which always had their main buildings facing south. The Imperial Palace was, furthermore, a kind of model of the administrative structure of the aptly named Celestial Empire, divided and sub-divided into units of identical form.

Vast underground palaces excavated as tombs for the Ming emperors some 30 miles (48km) to the north of Beijing have similarly symmetrical plans and were hardly less sumptuous. Their several rooms were faced with stone and vaulted, unlike the temples at ground level above them which are of normal Chinese timber construction with yellow glazed roof-tiles similar to the halls of the Imperial Palace. They are approached along a 'spirit road' flanked by large statues of men and monsters and of life-size camels and elephants carved with a bold realism recalling Tang dynasty sculpture (**12,72**). But a memorial pillar by one of the gates with a delicately cut relief of a dragon materializing out of a tight pattern of clouds is, perhaps, more typical of Ming taste (**12,73**).

Conservatism, naturalism and opulence characterize the style of painting favoured at the Ming court. *Winter Scenery* by Lü Ji (1477–1521), with snow, water, rocks, gnarled trees, a brightly feathered cock pheasant, two small birds, flowers of prunus and bright-red camellias, derives from the bird and flower paintings of early Song artists, who would, however, have contented themselves with two of its elements and half its color (**12,74**). The rushing torrent binds the composition together and gives the whole work a vigour conspicuously lacking in later renderings of similar subjects, which were exported in quantity to Europe and gave a misleading impression of Chinese art. Such a painting was intended to grace the wall of a princely palace, not to be scrutinized in the seclusion of a scholar's sanctum. It is a highly professional performance by one of the most gifted members of the imperial academy, who were, as already mentioned, despised as little better than craftsmen by the gentlemen amateurs.

12,74 Lü Ji, *Winter Scenery*, hanging scroll, c. 1500. Ming dynasty. Ink and color on silk, 5ft 9ins (1.75m) high. National Museum, Tokyo.

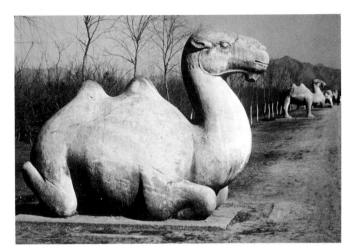

12,72 Camel, 15th to 16th century. Ming dynasty. Stone, about 8ft 2ins (2.5m) high. Approach to the Ming tombs near Beijing.

12,73 Memorial pillar, 16th century. Ming dynasty. Marble. Ceremonial gateway before the Ming tombs near Beijing.

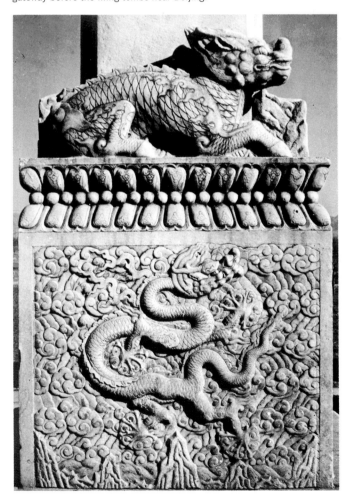

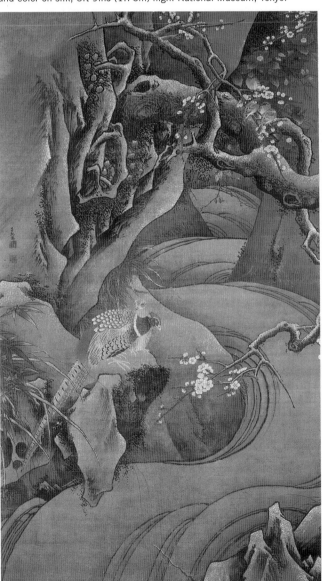

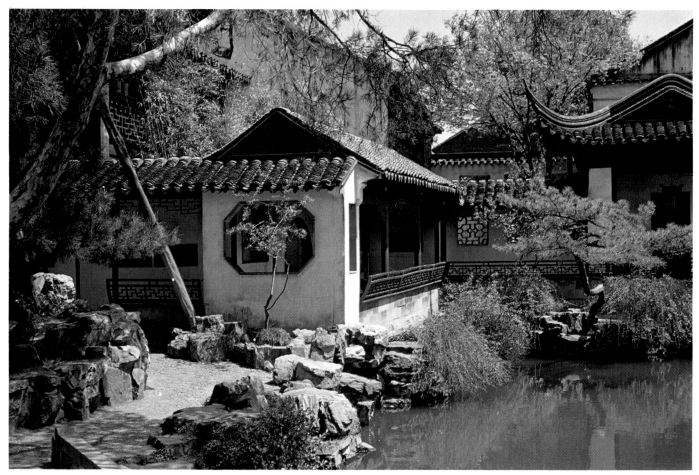

12,75 The Wangshiyuan garden, Suzhou, China. 16th century. Ming dynasty.

The first Ming emperor was hostile to the scholar-painters and they in turn were repelled by the court and court intrigues of his successors. The more exquisite and financially independent settled far away from the capital in the sunnier climate of Hangzhou and Suzhou, where they cultivated their talents and, quite literally, their gardens – designed as three-dimensional landscape paintings with trees and curiously shaped rocks framed by the columns and trellis-work of the covered walks (**12,75**). Devoted exclusively to scholarship and the liberal arts of painting, calligraphy (see Glossary) and poetry, they were amateurs only in the sense that they did not sell their work. A small album leaf on which Shen Zhou (1427–1509) depicted himself standing aloof from the world on a mountain (**12,76**) conveys their aims and attitudes as neatly as the wistful poem at which he gazes:

> *White clouds like a belt encircle the mountain's waist.*
> *A stone ledge flying in space and the far, thin road.*
> *I lean on my bramble staff and gazing into space*
> *Make the note of my flute an answer to the*
> *surrounding torrent.*

> (Tr. R. Edwards)

In the Ming period the artist's poem was conceived more frequently than before as an integral part of the work of art both visually and intellectually, and as much attention

was paid to its calligraphy as to the painting itself. Shen Zhou was a close student and able imitator of the old masters, who now included Ni Zan and other admired amateurs of the Yuan period, and he developed various styles, which he employed according to the mood of his subject. For the *Poet on a Mountain Top* he used his broad

12,76 Shen Zhou, *Poet on a Mountain Top*, album leaf, late 15th century. Ming dynasty. Ink on paper, 15¼ins (38.7cm) high. Nelson-Atkins Museum of Art, Kansas City (Purchase: Nelson Trust).

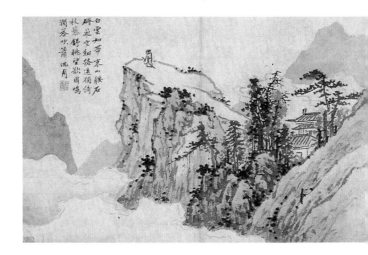

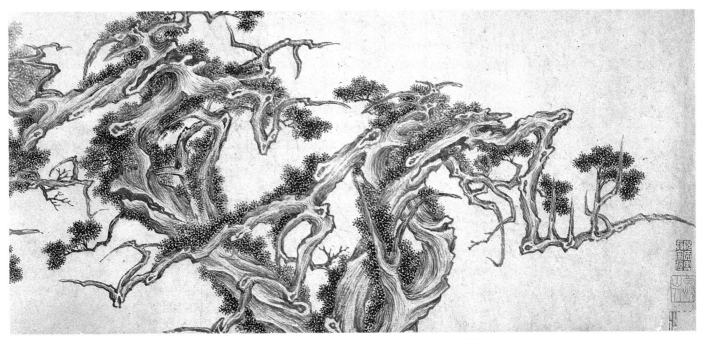

12,77 Wen Zhengming, *Seven Juniper Trees*, detail of handscroll, 1532. Ming dynasty. Ink on paper, 11⅛ins (28.3cm) high. Honolulu Academy of Arts, Hawaii.

manner, with thick brush-strokes, dots of various sizes to represent vegetation and mark the main accents, united by graded ink washes. In his later years he attracted the friendship of Wen Zhengming (1407–1559), who took up painting seriously only after he had failed the civil service examination 28 times and held for a short while a minor post as an historian at the academy in Beijing. Despite his late start, Wen Zhengming developed a highly personal style especially in paintings of juniper trees, symbols of vitality in old age, and much more besides (**12,77**). The scroll, from which a detail is illustrated here, has an inscription referring to the trees as 'flawless idols, spirits infinite' that 'hallow the Palace of the Stars, attendants subservient to Heaven's majesty'. But it demonstrates also an intense feeling for and grasp of pure form new to Chinese painting.

'Painting is no equal to mountains and water for the wonder of scenery, but mountains and water are no equal to painting for the sheer marvels of brush and ink', wrote Dong Qichang (1555–1636), summarizing a belief that had become prevalent among the scholar-painters and tended to remove art ever further from the direct representation of nature. Conventional elements of landscape painting were pulled apart and reorganized in a monumental format, from which he rigorously excluded everything, including atmospheric effects, that might appeal to sentiment (**12,78**). Paramount importance was given to the brush-strokes dragging the ink thinly over the surface so that the paper shows through, concentrating densely in only a few areas. The effect is daunting in its austerity. Of the major painters of the Ming period he alone was a true *wenren* or scholar-official, and he rose to be president of the all-important Board of Ceremonies. As an examiner he was so severe that he provoked a student uprising and his treatment of his peasants was so autocratic that they revolted and burnt his house. Authoritarian also in his

12,78 Dong Qichang, *Autumn Mountains*, detail of handscroll, early 17th century. Ming dynasty. Ink on paper, 15⅛ins (38.4cm) high. Cleveland Museum of Art.

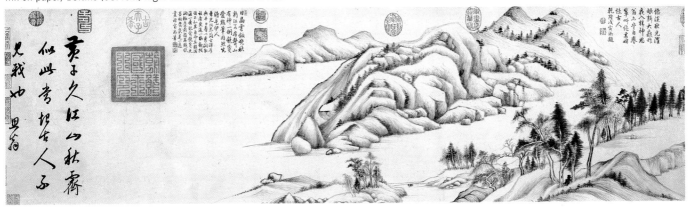

attitude to art, he wrote influential treatises enumerating the few painters of the Song, Yuan and Ming periods who should be imitated – all of them scholars and constituting the core of what came to be called the Southern School. But the emphasis he placed on the spiritual qualities in works of art led him to make a proviso ignored by many later Chinese painters: 'Those who study the old masters and do not introduce some changes are as if closed in by a fence. If one imitates the models too closely, one is often still further removed from them.' In this way he justified his own bold originality – and also the still more radical individuality manifested by a few Chinese painters in the later seventeenth and eighteenth centuries (see Chapter 16).

JAPAN – KAMAKURA TO EDO

Attempts by the Mongols to invade Japan in 1274 and 1281 were thwarted and the national style created more than a century earlier (see p. 291) continued to flourish in isolation throughout the Kamakura period (1185–1333). A tendency towards naturalism, more conspicuous in secular work than in religious images – which derived iconographically from the Buddhist art of China – is felt especially in portraiture, the art in which the Japanese had earlier shown pre-eminence (6,127) and which now developed in both painting and sculpture, perhaps in connection with the cult of ancestors. A statue of a military lord, Uesugi Shigefusa, for instance, is preserved in a temple built by his

---

SOURCES AND DOCUMENTS

DONG QICHANG ON PAINTING: THE STUDY OF NATURE AND OLD MASTERS

Dong Qichang's voluminous writings (undated, but published soon after his death in 1636) were devoted mainly to establishing a canon of masters of landscape painting, all literary men of the Song and Yuan periods, who provided models to be followed.

Someone has said that each one must form his own school, but that is not right, he declared, citing the different artists who had excelled in depicting, respectively, willow trees, pine trees and old trees.

These are traditional and cannot be altered, and even if they were modified, they will not be very far removed from the original sources . . . . Thus, if one combines in the drawing of trees the most beautiful points of the old masters and does not waste one's force on stones, the trees will become quite naturally beautiful and moist. Those who nowadays wish to follow the old masters prepare a volume of copies after their trees to serve as a bag of supplies.

Copying should, nevertheless, be combined with direct observation:

One should observe every morning the changing effects of the clouds, break off the practising after painted mountains and go out for a stroll among the real mountains. When one sees strange trees, one should grasp them from the four sides. The trees have a left side, which does not enter in the picture, and a right side which does enter; and it is the same way with the front and back. One should observe them thoroughly and transmit the spirit naturally, and for this purpose the form is necessary. The form, the heart and the hand must correspond mutually, and one must forget all about the imagination (what the spirit offers). Then there will, indeed, be trees in the picture, which have

life also on the silk; they will be luxuriant without being crowded, vigorous and elegant without blocking the view, all fitting together like members of one family.

He also gave advice about other elements in a landscape:

The painted figures must be looking about and speaking. The flowers and fruits must move in the wind and be sprinkled with dew; the birds should flutter and the animals run. The spirit must be taken from the real things. Mountains and waters, woods and springs must be pure, quiet, solitary and vast. Houses and cottages must have depth and be receding (into the picture). Bridges and ferries must be represented with people who are coming and going.

Such details were no doubt dependent on the study of nature but the principles of composition had been established by the old masters:

When the old masters composed large pictures, they made only three or four sweeping divisions and accomplished thus the whole composition. It contained many fine parts, but these were subject to the general effect which was the main point.

He remarked in another passage which has a general relevance:

Whenever one paints a landscape one must pay attention to proper dividing and combining; the spacing (distribution of the parts) is the main principle. There is the spacing of the whole composition and the spacing of the parts of the picture. If one understands this, one has grasped more than half of the principles of painting.

(Tr. O. Sirén, *The Chinese on the Art of Painting*, Peking 1936)

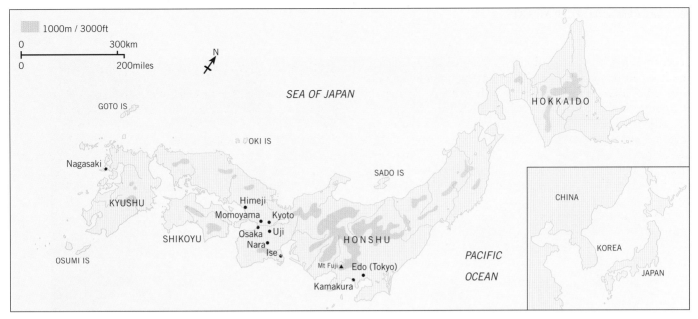

Japan

descendants (**12,79**). Formal, frontally posed with only the slightest deviation from symmetry in the position of the hands, his body completely engulfed in the billowing drapery of court dress, which indicates his status in Japanese feudal society, it is, nevertheless, the portrait of an individual, a speaking likeness of a member of the ruling class – even though it was, in fact, carved a century after the subject's death. There are several other portrait sculptures of the same period, similar in pose and costume, holding the same ceremonial slats, but each one with marked individuality of features and expression. The realism of such works reflects a taste for the down-to-earth, a

12,79 Anonymous, *Uesugi Shigefusa*, 14th century, Kamakura period. Painted wood, 27½ins (70cm) high. Meigetsuin, Kamakura, Kanagawa prefecture, Japan.

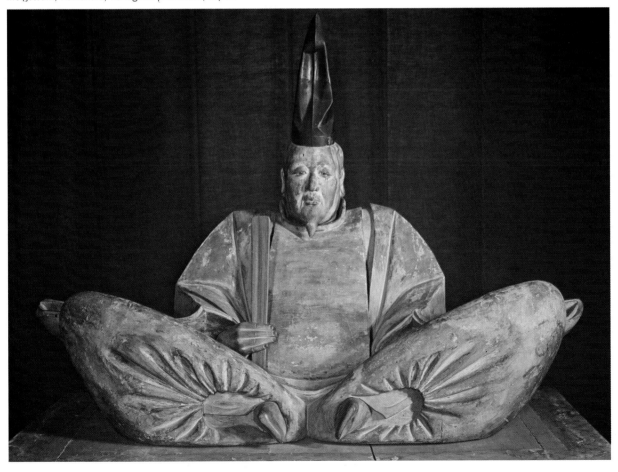

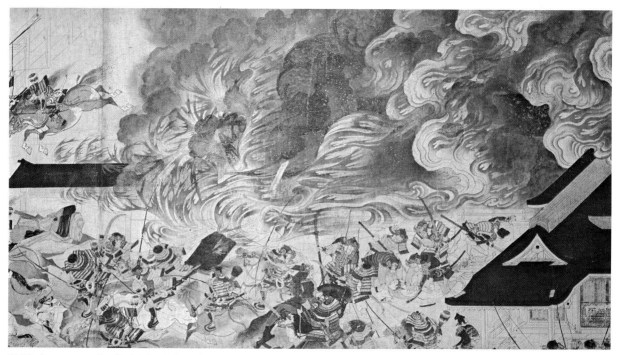

12,80 Anonymous, *Scroll with Depictions of the Night Attack on the Sanjo Palace*, detail, from the *Illustrated Scrolls of the Events of the Heiji Era*, second half of 13th century. Kamakura period. Ink and colors on paper, 16¼ins (41.3cm) high. Museum of Fine Arts, Boston (Fenollosa-Weld Collection).

taste prevalent among the aristocracy at the time and perhaps more often expressed in painting, where it was combined with the Japanese flair for bold, decorative design.

The art of narrative painting on scrolls, originally introduced to Japan from China with Buddhism, was secularized in about the eleventh century, when works of fiction were illustrated, notably Lady Murasaki's famous *Tale of Genji*. Such paintings are called *Yamato-e*, 'Japanese paintings', to distinguish them from those in the Chinese manner. The scrolls, rarely as much as 15 inches (38cm) high but up to 30 feet (9.1m) long to include numerous scenes, differ from the panoramic landscapes of Chinese painting both in format (narrower and much longer) and in style and subject-matter. As a Chinese writer of the time remarked, Japanese painters 'portray the natural objects, landscapes and intimate scenes of their own country. Their pigments are laid on very thick, and they make much use of gold and jade colors'. Dismayed by its complete lack of philosophical content, he was able to commend this type of painting only 'for the way it shows the people and customs of a foreign land in an unfamiliar quarter, a country which is rude and out of the way, uncivilized, lacking ceremonies and propriety'.

Recent events were recorded on several *Yamato-e* scrolls of the thirteenth century, such as the war between rival branches of the imperial family which broke out in Kyoto in 1159 and ended with the establishment of the dictatorship at Kamakura. A succession of scenes is presented in bright, sharply contrasting colors, all painted from a bird's eye viewpoint with architecture slanting diagonally across the paper and sometimes open to show interiors – a characteristic of *Yamato-e*. Emphasis is on

telling circumstantial details, especially of military costume, and on swift energetic action which leads the eye excitedly forward from one turbulent episode to the next (**12,80**). Bullocks draw carriages with whirling wheels, horses gallop, running soldiers rattle sabres and brandish long bows in a mêlée, which is, none the less, composed with decorative aplomb and great narrative skill to suggest constant movement from right to left. Glorifying the thrill of battle and expressing a love of martial pageantry, which members of the Japanese upper class shared with contemporary chivalry in Europe, these scrolls are a very far cry from the reveries of Chinese scholar-painters of about the same time (6,106). Before the end of the Kamakura period, however, the influence of Chinese painting was reasserted.

Japanese attitudes to China resemble in many ways those of Europeans to ancient Greece and Rome. Chinese literature, both secular and religious, had the prestige accorded to Latin in Europe, and Chinese art had a similar kind of classical status, although it was, of course, the product of a living contemporary culture. (The Japanese responded to changes in Chinese art rather as Europeans from the fifteenth century onwards continued to discover new aspects of antiquity.) Some Japanese artists contented themselves with direct copying. But many produced interpretations which differ almost as much from Chinese paintings as from *Yamato-e*. Two distinct styles were in fact practised concurrently, with some interchange between them, rather as Japanese forms of Buddhism coexisted with Shinto beliefs and practice. And the influence of Chinese art is strongest in paintings inspired by Chan Buddhism (see pp. 279–80).

THE INFLUENCE OF ZEN BUDDHISM

The Chan sect had little influence in Japan until the early Kamakura period when it quite suddenly began to attract a large following under the leadership of two Japanese monks who had travelled in China. Although reputedly of Indian origin, Chan had been developed since the sixth century as a distinctively Chinese form of Buddhism, strongly influenced by Daoist ideas of nature. Its first monasteries in Japan were built in direct imitation of Chinese prototypes and some were headed by Chinese abbots. It had, nevertheless, so many features peculiarly acceptable to the Japanese at this time that it was soon naturalized as Zen (the Japanese pronunciation of Chan) and became an integral part of their civilization, as it has remained ever since. Its complete assimilation may have been partly due to affinities with indigenous Shinto, similarly a religion without ethics, dogmas, scriptures or devotional icons. And in the early thirteenth century Zen had a special relevance for the new social class that was beginning to dominate the country under the Shoguns.

Undogmatic and unsystematic, anti-logical, intuitive, non-theological to the point of being almost irreligious, Zen made a direct appeal to the *daimyo* and *samurai* (barons and knights in European terms) who despised the effete ceremonial life of the imperial court and seem to have had little time for the arcane rituals and esoteric doctrines of Mahayanist Buddhism. It provided a strenuous practical discipline to fortify the individual's struggle for self-knowledge and against self-ness. Frugal simplicity of life and indifference to both sensual pleasure and physical pain were extolled. Book learning, rational argument and philosophy were dismissed as valueless. Zen masters taught by baffling the disciple's mind with paradoxes of inconsequential discourse – the *koans* or problems – until it broke through to direct vision of 'things as they are', the ultimate reality. Warfare could be seen as a life-and-death struggle, uninhibited by fear, not only with the enemy but also with the self – for to the Zen Buddhist the self is the greatest enemy.

Zen is perhaps best understood as a lifelong process of education of mind and body. The larger monasteries were, indeed, teaching establishments not only for aspiring monks but also for the sons of *samurai*. Among their buildings, axially planned in the Chinese manner and expressing the severe disciplinary aspect of the sect, pride of place was given not to a temple or image house but to a lecture-hall where the focal point was not a statue of the Buddha but a simple throne on a raised dais where the abbot sat and taught. Virtually the only Zen sculptures are portraits of distinguished teachers, often the founders of monasteries, and they could hardly be more obviously Japanese – there is a special Japanese name, *chinso*, for this type of statue. That of Muji Ichien (1226–1312), probably carved immediately after his death (most Japanese portraits were posthumous), is an amazing feat of realistic characterization, 'warts and all' – there is one on his left eyelid (**12,81**). He is relaxed in pose, dressed in the simple robe of his order and holds in his hand a whisk to brush

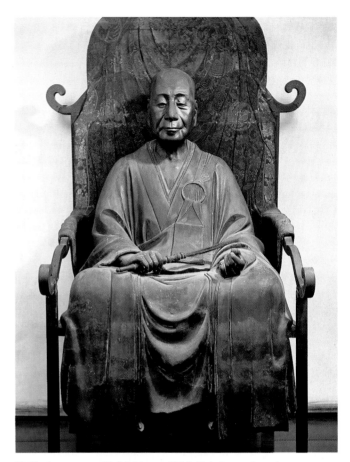

12,81 Anonymous, *Muji Ichien*, c. 1312. Polychromed wood, 3¼ins (79.4cm) high. Chomoji, Aichi prefecture.

aside idle thoughts. It is a down-to-earth likeness of an aged master who had come to terms with the human condition and left as his final message to his disciples a brief poem: 'A seagull floats over the sea / Seven and eighty years / The wind rests, the waves are still / Calm as in the days of yore.'

By the fifteenth century Zen monasteries had become the main cultural centres in Japan. At this time, and for the last time, relations with China were close. The monks read and wrote nature poetry in Chinese. They also admired and practised ink painting in the Chinese manner as a means of breaking through the barriers of the physical world to ultimate reality. A Zen tenet states that 'many colors blind the vision'. These communities still preserve some of the finest early Chinese Chan paintings, including the *Six Persimmons* by Muqi and the imaginary portrait of Li Bai by Liang Kai, two of the originators of the style and more highly regarded in Japan than in their own country (6,102; 103). The greatest Japanese master of ink painting, Sesshu (1420–1506), was trained in Zen monasteries and became a *gaso* or priest-painter – the existence of such a denomination indicates the importance given to painting by Zen Buddhists. Sesshu travelled in China in 1467–9, studying both art and the natural landscape, which was to be a permanent source of inspiration for him. There is nothing imitative about his work, however, as his *Winter Landscape* shows (**12,82**). Instead of the

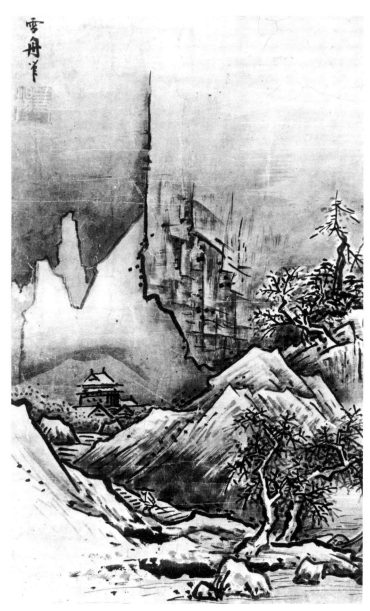

12,82 Sesshu, *Winter Landscape*, c. 1495. Muromachi period.
Ink and faint color on paper, 17¾ × 10⅝ins (45 × 27cm).
National Museum, Tokyo.

delicate brushwork and soft atmospheric effects of Chinese painting, his landscapes are firmly structured in bold, jagged linear designs. Conventional elements of Chinese landscape, gnarled trees, rocks, distant crags, jutting cliffs, a temple and a diminutive human figure climbing up to it, are rendered as if suddenly revealed in the cold, flattening illumination of a flash of lightning – a sudden vision corresponding to the mental spasm of transcendental Zen experience.

Ink painting was also practised by artists less closely associated with Zen, notably Kano Masanobu (1434–1530), the founder of six generations of painters – one of the several dynasties which play a leading role in the history of Japanese art. His serene vision of the Chinese philosopher Chou Mao-shu admiring lotuses from a boat

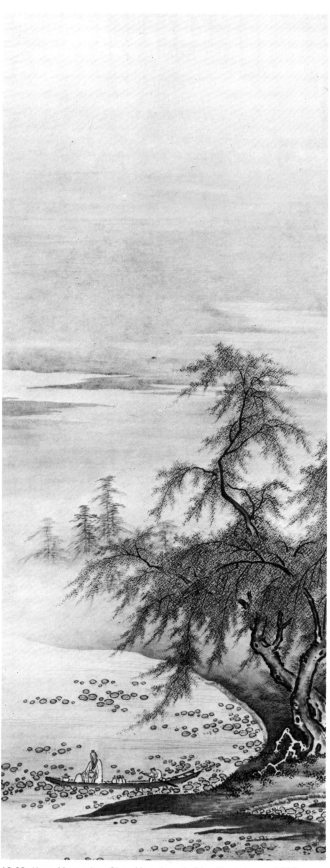

12,83 Kano Masanobu, *Chou Mao-shu admiring the Lotus*, c. 1500. Muromachi period. Ink and faint color on paper, 35⅜ × 12⅝ins (89.9 × 32cm). National Museum, Tokyo.

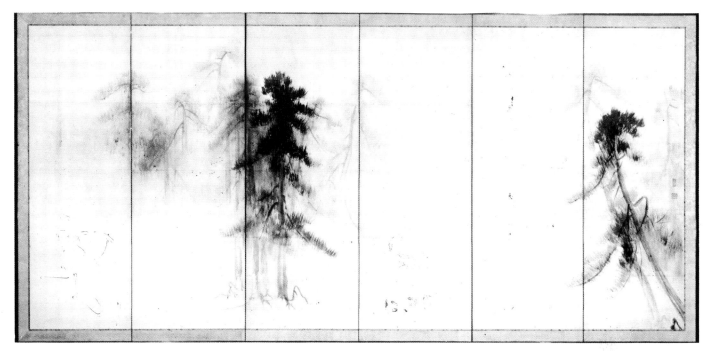

12,84 Hasegawa Tohaku, *Pine Trees*, 1539–1610. Momoyama period. Ink on paper, 5ft 1in (1.55m) high. National Museum, Tokyo.

in a lake is an exemplary illustration of the Zen love of nature and of virtue, but it is painted with as much attention to subtle decorative effect as to literary or moral content (**12,83**). It is a hanging scroll of the format which became popular from the fifteenth century onwards with the introduction of the *toko-no-ma* or picture alcove, still a common feature of the Japanese interior. Screens were also painted in ink monochrome. A pair by Hasegawa Tohaku (1539–1610) of pine trees exploits the splashed ink technique used by Zen masters, including Sesshu, in a composition which takes to its limit Japanese daring and economy in asymmetrical design (**12,84**).

Such exquisite and delicate effects were, however, rather unusual on screens, which were more often boldly painted with the brilliant colors of the *Yamato-e* palette and a great deal of gold. Painted screens and sliding panels were used to enliven the otherwise austere, bare and completely unfurnished rooms of the period, such as still survive in the castles built for the *daimyos* or feudal lords. After the Muromachi period (1334–1573) of almost constant civil war, castles were built to combine elegance with strength and were sometimes sited with hardly less regard for the views they afforded of the surrounding landscape than for defence. At Himeji, massive stone fortifications are surmounted by a five-story structure of wood coated in white plaster, with a complex arrangement of gables and eaves tilted up at the corners which gives it an almost weightless appearance (**12,85**). The high base was made necessary by the introduction of fire-arms from Europe in the mid-sixteenth century, and the departure from the single story normal for secular buildings in Japan may also be due to Western influence although the earthquake-resistant structural technique is peculiarly Japanese, similar to that of pagodas, with massive tree-

trunks passing through the seven stories and locking together the horizontals in a unitary framework.

In the architecture of the *Mahayana* Buddhist sects, on the other hand, the main change after the thirteenth century was towards the greater enrichment of traditional forms. Many temples destroyed in the civil wars were reconstructed, e.g. the huge imposing Daibutsuden or 'Great Buddha Hall' of the Todaiji at Nara, rebuilt for a second time in 1708 on a slightly reduced plan but with the addition of a curved 'pediment' above a window in the centre of the façade (6,118). The rebuilding of the main halls of the large Zen monasteries was more rigidly conservative, retaining the style and axial planning of their Chinese prototypes. But their living quarters and also the smaller Zen establishments, of which there are many in the hills around Kyoto, were conspicuously plain externally (though often with finely painted sliding screens inside), similar to simple private houses, informally planned with rooms looking on to gardens which are sometimes composed only of rocks placed with careful irregularity in raked gravel.

Zen retained its hold on Japanese life in the more peaceful climate of the Edo period (1615–1867, called after the capital, which was renamed Tokyo in 1868) during which contacts with China were limited. A new decorative element appeared in paintings of Zen subjects. A hanging scroll of the monk Choka meditating up a tree by Tawayara Sotatsu (d. 1643) is doubly revealing (**12,87**). Strongly characterized and sometimes grotesquely caricatured images of patriarchs and masters of the sect were commonplaces of Zen art which had their origin in China. Sotatsu's source was, in fact, a much earlier Chinese woodblock print which showed the whole tree and clearly delineated the monk. But he transformed the figure with

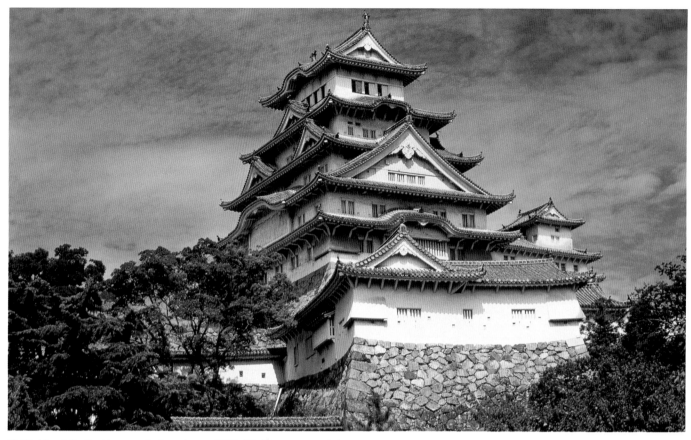

12,85 Himeji Castle, Hyogo prefecture, Japan, 1601–13. Momoyama period.

a softer touch and more delicately irreverent wit, barely indicating the trunk of the tree and leaving the rest altogether to the imagination. Fluid graceful brushwork is combined with a keen appreciation of the decorative possibilities of daring asymmetry. Sotatsu was a professional artist, not a monk. A screen he painted with poppies on a gold ground that glints through their petals reveals, nevertheless, how a work of art with a mainly decorative purpose could be interfused and animated with a Zen feeling for nature (**12,86**).

12,86 Tawayara Sotatsu, *Poppies,* detail, pre-1643. Edo period. Ink, colors and gold on paper, 4ft 11ins (1.5m) high. Museum of Fine Arts, Boston (Gift of Mrs W. Scott Fitz).

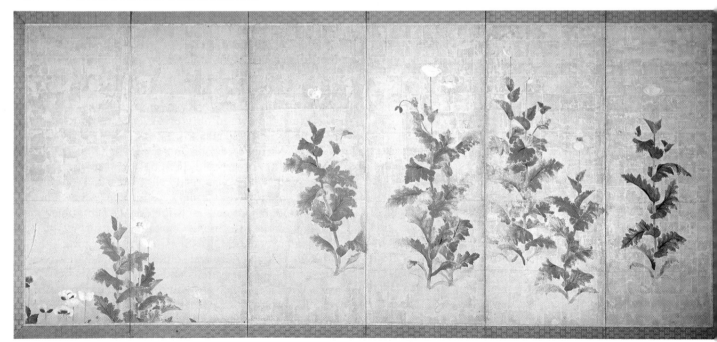

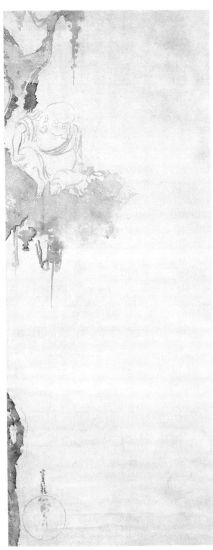

12,87 Tawayara Sotatsu, *Zen Priest Choka*, pre-1643. Edo period. Ink on paper, 37¾ × 15¼ins (96 × 38.8cm). Cleveland Museum of Art (Norman O. Stone and Ella A. Stone Memorial Fund).

12,88 Tea-ceremony rooms, Daitokuji monastery, Kyoto, Japan, c. 1573–1615. Monoyama period.

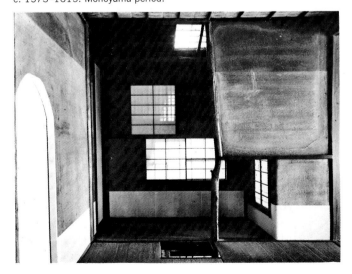

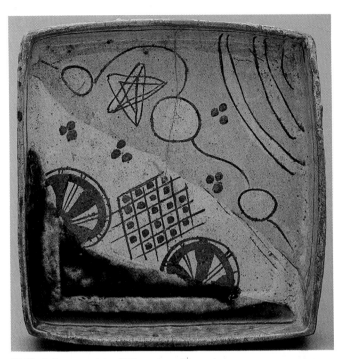

12,89 Oribe ware plate, 17th century. Edo period. Stoneware with green and transparent glaze, submerged wheel decoration in brown slip, 8ins (20.3cm) diameter. Seattle Art Museum (Eugene Fuller Memorial Collection).

Among the laity Zen ideals were most prominently expressed in the unceremonious ritual of the tea-ceremony or *Cha-no-yu*, with its formal informality, its sophisticated cultivation of the unsophisticated, its artificial naturalness. Tea drinking, introduced from China with Buddhism, was a feature of social life in Zen monasteries. By the late sixteenth century rooms set apart for it had acquired a style, or rather a contrived non-style, being constructed of roughly worked natural materials, stripped tree-trunks, bamboos and reeds, rectangular in plan but with irregularly, one might think haphazardly, placed windows (**12,88**). To capture this spirit in the city, small thatched tea-houses (*chachitsu*), surrounded by appropriately natural and apparently untended gardens with lichened stones, moss and fallen leaves, were erected in the grounds of palaces and upper-class houses. Here, under the guidance of a tea-master, who was both arbiter of taste and censor of behaviour, a select company would meet in an atmosphere of quiet harmony to drink tea and to admire and discuss poetry, paintings and arrangements of flowers. The vessels used were of coarse pottery, at first peasant wares imported from China but later pieces made expressly for the purpose in Japan, erratic in shape, uneven in surface and with decorations of seemingly artless spontaneity (**12,89**). They were, and still are, admired for the correspondence of form, texture and weight according to an aesthetic which defies logical analysis. Appreciation of accidental effects, irregularity and asymmetry, which sharply distinguishes Japanese from Chinese attitudes to the arts, is nowhere more clearly reflected than in these little cups and bowls.

Namban Screens

THE JAPANESE ENCOUNTER WITH EUROPEANS

The arrival of Europeans in Japan in the mid-sixteenth century was vividly recorded by Japanese painters on screens of traditional form but in a totally different style from that developed by the Zen masters (12,84). In the bright, clear colors of the national *Yamato-e* palette (see p. 564), with a great deal of gold leaf, they depict all-over narrative scenes of great galleons and swarms of lively figures of merchants and mariners, including a few Africans (**12,91**). All are rendered with the closest attention to their characteristic gestures as well as details of costume and physiognomy. However, it is not only in their cool, down-to-earth descriptive manner that they differ from the work of Zen and other artists of the time. They record a cultural phenomenon that did not occur elsewhere in Asia: that peculiarly Japanese fascination with novelty and curiosity about alien cultures.

The first Europeans to land in Japan were Portuguese – some sailors shipwrecked in 1541 followed by a trading expedition two years later. As they arrived from the south they were called *Namban*, or southern barbarians, according to Japanese cosmology. At this time the country was embroiled in the wars between the *daimyo*, or feudal barons, that were bringing the Muromachi period to an end (see p. 567). Traders thus found a welcoming market for European fire-arms, previously unknown in Japan. In 1549 the Jesuit Francis Xavier disembarked with three companions and, as a representative of the king of Portugal, was well received at the imperial court at Kyoto, given permission to preach and to found a Christian mission which was to have far greater success than any in China. Jesuits concentrated on converting members of the feudal upper class who seem to have been attracted by the Jesuits' dissociation from China and everything Chinese; though perhaps still more by

the prospect of buying arms from the traders who accompanied the missionaries. Spanish Franciscans who arrived shortly afterwards preached the gospel to the masses. By 1582 there were some 150,000 Christian converts and the number was still growing. It seemed possible that Christianity would soon be established as firmly as Buddhism had been a millennium before (see p. 288).

Missionaries and traders brought with them furniture of types never seen before by the Japanese, who copied their forms but decorated them with inlay work of a kind recently introduced from Korea. A folding stand to hold an open missal on an altar is among the finest, of wood covered in lacquer inlaid with gold leaf and slivers of mother-of-pearl (**12,90**). The Jesuit emblem – the letters IHS, the cross and nails of the Crucifixion – is surrounded by geometrical motifs. There are flowers typical of Japanese decorative art on the base.

The spread of Christianity in Japan was aided by Oda Nobunaga, a general who with the help of Euro-

12,90 Missal stand, late 16th century. Wood decorated with black lacquer, gold and silver lacquer and shell inlay, 14 × 13⅜ × 18⅛ins (35.8 × 34 × 46cm). Tokyo National Museum.

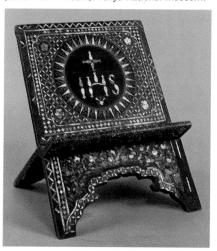

pean guns seized control of Japan in 1576 and supported Christians as a counterweight to the rich and influential Buddhist communities, as well as mediators in trade with the West. He was, however, assassinated in 1582 and his successor, the more ruthlessly powerful Toyotomi Hideyoshi, became increasingly suspicious of the missionaries. They were under the protection of the kings of Portugal and Spain who had already established colonies elsewhere in Asia and the Philippine Islands. In 1587 he issued an edict expelling European priests in the hope of controlling the religious movement without losing the benefit of foreign trade. But Spanish Franciscans continued to proselytize the restive lower classes. In 1597 seven of them and nineteen Japanese converts were crucified at Nagasaki. This was the first of many campaigns of persecution which continued intermittently until only a very few indigenous Christians remained alive. All foreigners had meanwhile been expelled, apart from Protestant Dutch traders who were confined to an island in Nagasaki Bay.

Hideyoshi was, like so many soldiers, a devotee of the Zen tea-ceremony (see p. 569). He was also anxious to unite the country by reviving Confucianism as the official ideology, 'the foundation of our relationships between sovereign and minister, parent and child, husband and wife', now unfortunately being undermined by Christianity, as he wrote in a letter in 1591. By a curious coincidence, in the very same year he commissioned for one of his castles the earliest recorded *Namban byobu* – screens on which Europeans were depicted. He was so much amused, perhaps even impressed, by the 'southern barbarians' that he and his courtiers sometimes dressed up in the hats, cloaks and baggy breeches of Portuguese fashion. Other Japanese

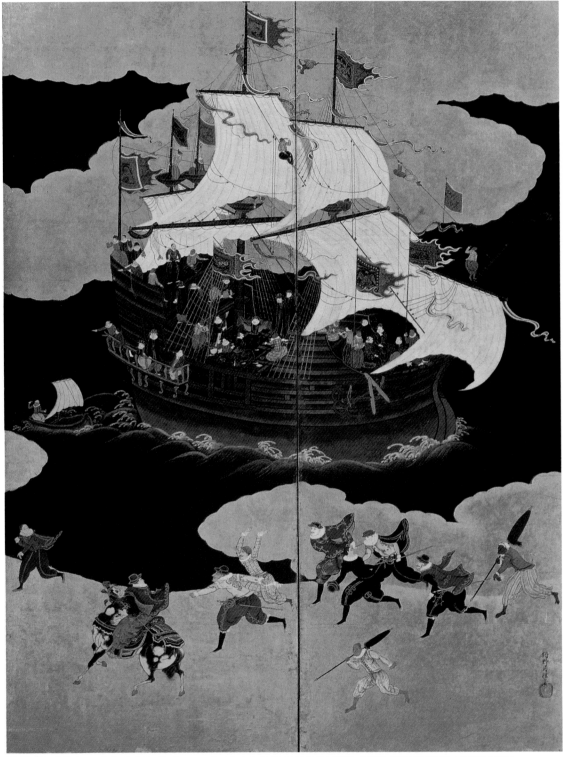

12,91 Kanô Naizen, *Arrival of the Portuguese*, two leaves from a six-leaf screen, 1593. Gold leaf and color on paper, 5ft 1in × 11ft 10⅞ins (1.55 × 3.63m) overall. Kobe Shiritsu Namban Bijutsukan, Kobe, Japan.

similarly succumbed to a taste for Occidentalism, the mirror image of European Orientalism. For these *Namban* screens were essentially and purely decorative, without any of the religio-philosophical overtones of such Zen screens as that by Hasegawa Tohaku. They were often painted from sketches made on the spot at Nagasaki harbour, as was that by Kanô Naizen (1570–1616) who sketched at Nagasaki in 1593 (12,91). The grotesque features, the garishly colored costumes and the uncivilized deportment of the barbarians are uncompromisingly recorded, to the delight of the Japanese, no doubt. They continued to be painted for some decades after the proscription of Christianity in Japan.

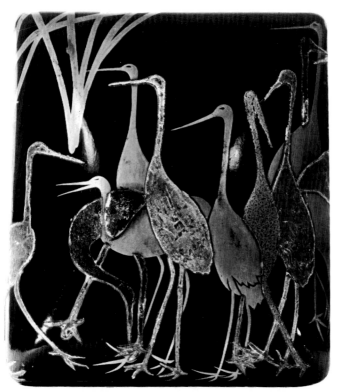

12,92 Writing box, 17th century. Edo period. Black lacquer on wood, gold paint, inlaid lead and pewter, 8½ × 9⅛ins (21.6 × 23.2cm). Seattle Art Museum (Gift of the late Mrs Donald E. Frederick).

The peace brought to Japan by the centralized government of the Edo period encouraged trade and the rise of a prosperous merchant class. In these circumstances secular art flourished as never before. Painted screens for the domestic interior were produced in quantity and some are among the most beautiful examples of purely decorative art ever created. A pair by Ogata Korin (1658–1716), one of the leading painters of his period, combines mastery of both abstract patterning and naturalistic representation (**12,95**). The gracefully swaying stems of the chrysanthemums are set off by the rigid rectilinear panels and the schematic rendering of the stream, and their blossoms grouped in twos and threes and fours create a kind of fugal rhythm. Colors are limited to azurite blue, emerald green, jade green, gold and, for the blossoms, pure white modelled in relief. Such screens were, of course, luxury products, but their opulence is restrained. They are quintessentially Japanese in form, style and subject-matter.

12,93 Katsura palace, Kyoto, Japan, 17th century. Edo period.

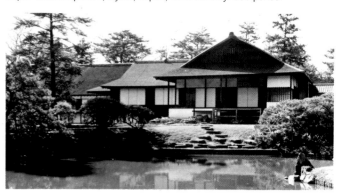

Devotees of the tea-ceremony were, nevertheless, just as appreciative of the most exquisitely finished works of art and craftsmanship, such as lacquer boxes painted in gold and inlaid with metals (**12,92**).

A similar, though less extreme, taste for simplicity and formal informality also governed the design of the finest example of seventeenth-century Japanese architecture, the Katsura palace at Kyoto, built for a prince of the imperial family (**12,93**). It is a single-story building with an asymmetrical, totally unmonumental plan (**12,94**). A succession of rooms opening out of one another vary in size but are all proportioned according to a module derived from the standard 6-by-3-foot (180 by 90cm) straw mat, which unobtrusively unites the separate rooms into a harmonious spatial flow. The exterior is uncompromisingly rectilinear in contrast to the garden setting, where all straight lines are carefully avoided. The module observed in the interior determines the proportions of the windows, which are likewise related asymmetrically to the gables of the roof. From every point of view – there is no main façade in the European or Chinese sense – a most delicate balance is maintained between horizontals and verticals, solids and voids, the linear and the spatial. Decoration is reserved for the interior walls, some of which are sliding panels and can be drawn back to unite rooms. Both inside and out the carving of the woodwork is of the utmost precision, satisfying a demand for meticulous workmanship complemented by that for rusticity in the nearby tea-house.

12,94 Plan of Katsura palace.

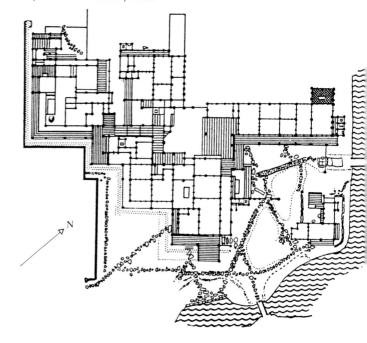

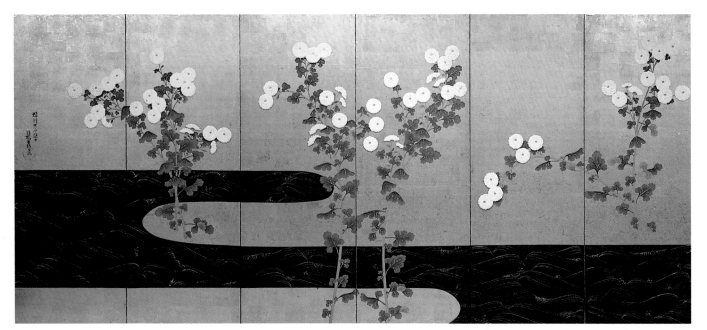

12,95 Ogata Korin, *Chrysanthemums by a Stream*, c. 1700. Edo period. Color and gold on paper, 5ft 7ins (1.7m) high. Cleveland Museum of Art (Gift of Hanna Fund).

The integrity of this style of painting was preserved throughout the Edo period by conservatism and the isolationist policy of the government. Japan cut itself off from the rest of the world in 1638, when Portuguese traders, who had first arrived in 1542, were expelled. Christianity, introduced by St Francis Xavier, was proscribed. Thereafter trade with Europe was carried on through the Dutch, whom the Japanese held at arm's length, allowing them no closer than an island off Nagasaki harbour. Exports, mainly lacquer and porcelain, were specially designed for the foreign market, and thus Europeans had for long a very partial and misleading impression of Japanese art, as they had, for similar reasons, of Chinese art.

CHAPTER THIRTEEN

THE SEVENTEENTH CENTURY IN EUROPE

The rise of the Dutch republic was the most momentous event in the history of seventeenth-century Europe, coinciding with the decline of Spain and the Thirty Years' War (1618–48) which devastated Germany and destroyed the authority of the Holy Roman Empire. Holland, and six other provinces of the Netherlands which rebelled against Spanish rule (1579–1609), became one of the richest of European states and by far the least intolerant. Its prosperity was founded on free enterprise at home and world-wide maritime trade. So, too, was that of England, where the principle of parliamentary government was gradually being accepted. Throughout Europe, but especially in the north, there was a revolt against long-established authority, most notably in scientific thought, where great advances were made in astronomy and mathematics. An experimental and inductive approach to the physical sciences proposed by Francis Bacon (1561–1626) at the beginning of the century was widely accepted by the end. Above all, Western philosophy was freed from two millennia of dependence on Plato and Aristotle by René Descartes (1596–1650), whose *Discourse on Method* (1637) set forth a new theory of knowledge, an extreme form of scepticism that led, by a systematic process of doubt, to the famous conclusion: 'I think therefore I am'. This made mind more certain than matter, and the individual mind the most certain of all, with subjective implications that were far-reaching. Though French and a Catholic, Descartes wrote and published his works in the Dutch republic.

This great explosion of speculative thinking did not have any immediate effect on the visual arts. (For a time art and thought moved 'out-of-phase', although the sudden flowering of Dutch painting followed relatively quickly, see p. 598.) Moreover, it coincided with the recovery of the Papacy from the blow of the Protestant Reformation so that Rome became once again a great artistic centre; while in France autocracy triumphed and was given its most magnificent expression.

The visual arts	Historical Landmarks
1597–1600 Carracci, Farnese ceiling (13,2)	**1600** Giordano Bruno burned for heresy in Rome
c. 1601 Caravaggio, *Conversion of St Paul* (13,1)	**1605** Cervantes, *Don Quixote* Pt I. Bacon, *Advancement of Learning*
1616–17 Rubens, *The Miracles of St Francis Xavier* (13,5)	**1616** Death of Shakespeare. Roman Church condemns Copernicus
	1618 Thirty Years' War begins
c. 1620 Artemisia Gentileschi, *Judith Slaying Holofernes* (13,11)	**1620** Puritans land in New England
	1623 Election of Pope Urban VIII
1624–33 Bernini, *Baldacchino* (13,15)	**1624** Cardinal Richelieu first minister in France
	1625 Charles I king of England
	1632 Galileo Galilei, *Dialogue on Copernicus*; obliged to recant 1633
1633 van Dyck, *Charles I* (13,10)	**1635** Richelieu founds Académie française
c. 1635 Rubens, *Landscape with Rainbow* (13,8)	**1637** Descartes, *Discourse on Method*
1642 Rembrandt, *The Night Watch* (13,32). Borromini, Sapienza begun (13,23)	**1642** Jansenism condemned by Pope. Civil War begins in England
	1643 Louis XIV king of France
1645–52 Bernini, *Ecstasy of St Teresa* (13,17)	**1649** Charles I beheaded: England a Free Commonwealth
1656 Velázquez, *Las Meninas* (13,29)	**1656–7** Blaise Pascal, *Lettres provinciales* against Jesuits
1660–70 Claude Lorraine, *Landscape* (13,27)	**1660** Restoration of Charles II as king of England
1667–70 East front of Louvre (13,51)	**1661** Personal rule of Louis XIV begins in France
c. 1669 Rembrandt, *Return of the Prodigal Son* (13,38). Versailles begun (13,53)	**1667** John Milton, *Paradise Lost*
	1672 Isaac Newton, Law of Gravitation
c. 1670 Vermeer, *The Art of Painting* (13,48)	**1685** Revocation of Edict of Nantes: emigration of French Protestants
1675–1710 Wren, St Paul's (13,49)	
1689 Hobbema, *The Avenue, Middelharnis* (13,41)	**1689** Peter I Czar of Russia

NEW BEGINNINGS IN ROME

In Rome new life was breathed into old forms by two artists from northern Italy, Annibale Carracci (1560–1609) and Caravaggio (Michelangelo Merisi, 1571–1610). Although they were later to be seen as the founders of two irreconcilably divergent tendencies (idealism and naturalism), both were equally admired in their own time, often by the same people. In 1600, indeed, an ecclesiastical lawyer commissioned for his funerary chapel in S Maria del Popolo, Rome, an altarpiece from Annibale Carracci and two paintings for the side walls from Caravaggio.

In one of the latter, the *Conversion of St Paul*, naturalism has completely replaced the symbolism usual in religious painting (**13,1**). There are none of the rhetorical antitheses and stylish 'figures of art' beloved by the Mannerists of the mid-sixteenth century. It has the directness of the spare New Testament account of how Saul the persecutor of the Christians was miraculously converted into an apostle, as if Caravaggio had accepted the robustness and conviction of High Renaissance art but rejected its idealism. St Paul is a coarse-featured young soldier with a first growth of beard, his horse a sturdy piebald held by an old man with wrinkled brow and balding head – one of the peasants whose prominence in later pictures

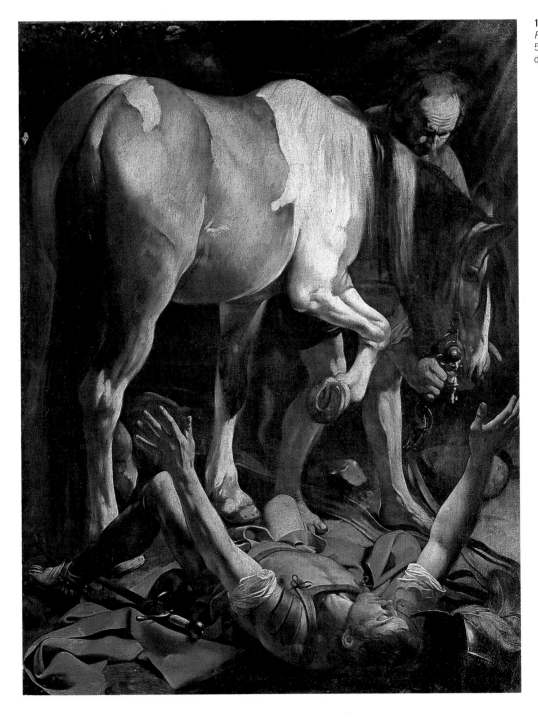

13,1 Caravaggio, *Conversion of St Paul*, c. 1601. Canvas, 7ft 6½ins × 5ft 8⅞ins (2.3 × 1.75m). S Maria del Popolo, Rome.

NATURE, IMITATION AND INVENTION: THE FORMATION OF ACADEMIC THEORY

In treatises that formed the basis of instruction for academies of art from the seventeenth to the nineteenth century, the terms 'Nature', 'Imitation' and 'Invention' were key-words but they had meanings different from those understood today. Nature with a capital N signified the creative power operating in the physical world and also the pure essence of its creations which artists were exorted to 'imitate', especially in their representations of the human figure. Imitation in this sense, clearly, did not mean mere copying but rather the apprehension and rendering of some underlying principle. Likewise, invention did not imply originality: it referred to the selection and presentation of subject matter in 'history pictures', that is to say paintings of significant and morally uplifting human actions derived from the Bible, classical mythology and, usually ancient, history.

The authors of these treatises, from Alberti to Bellori, were classically educated men who looked to the founders of Western philosophy for guidance – to Plato and his concept of 'ideas' and to Aristotle who held that men and women should be represented not as they are but as Nature intended them to be. These philosophers had, in fact, been no more than marginally concerned with the visual arts; but as the Greeks had categorized painting and sculpture, together with poetry and music, as mimetic or imitative arts, it was assumed that their theories were applicable to all. And a bridge between literary and artistic theory was provided by a phrase in the *Ars poetica* of Horace: *ut pictura poesis* ('poems are like paintings') to which Horace added that some give pleasure close up, others from a distance, some at first glance, others when they have been seen ten times. However, Renaissance and later theorists divorced the three words *ut pictura poesis* from their context, reversed their meaning and quoted them repeatedly in support of the concept that paintings should be like poems with morally uplifting subject-matter, intended to instruct as well as to delight.

The foundations of Renaissance art theory were laid by Leon Battista Alberti (see pp. 437–8) in his treatise *De pictura* written in 1435. The aim of painting is, he wrote, to 'represent things seen' but painters should idealize or 'add beauty' to what they see by 'taking from all beautiful bodies each praiseworthy part' – and he cited the legend of Zeuxis employing five models for a single image (see p. 149). He also suggested that painters could be assisted by poets whom they might rival in narrative pictures, the highest form of visual art in his opinion. *De pictura* had a limited circulation and was not published until 1540 (in Latin, 1547 in Italian) at a time when painters were seeking to justify their demands for recognition as practitioners of a liberal art rather than a craft. It was followed by other treatises, similar but usually more pedantic as were the lectures

on artistic theory delivered later in the century at the newly established state-supported academies (see p. 579), such as those given at the Academy of St Luke in Rome by its president, the mannerist painter Frederico Zuccaro (1540/3–1609). However, the version that was to dominate academic teaching was not formulated until the mid-seventeenth century in Rome.

In 1664 Giovanni Pietro Bellori (1613–96), an antiquarian and historian, not an artist but a close friend of Nicolas Poussin (see p. 592) who probably advised him, gave a lecture at the Academy of St Luke entitled: *The Idea of the Painter, Sculptor and Architect*. Here, he expounded a modified version of Platonism, transferring it from a metaphysical to a practical realm and locating the Idea in the mind or imagination of the artist. 'The Idea of the painter constitutes the perfection of natural beauty, and unites the truth with the verisimilitude of what appears to the eye', he declared. He criticized such artists as Caravaggio for copying the defects of common nature; others for not studying common nature at all but working instead 'in a mannerist way' from a 'fantastical idea', and others, the worst of all, for plagiarising the ideas of fellow artists, 'creating works that are not legitimate children but the bastards of Nature.' Artists, he believed, should study both common nature and also its 'corrected beauties' as revealed in 'the most perfect antique sculptures'. Thus, in academies of art, students drew from the nude model in life-classes, supplemented, however, by plaster casts of the most famous antique statues. Bellori's lectures were printed in 1672 as the preface to his *Lives of Modern Painters, Sculptors and Architects*, beginning with Annibale Carracci. To Carracci's frescoed ceiling in Palazzo Farnese (13.2) he devoted some thirty pages as being exemplary, with its mythological 'histories' and their moral significance, of his theories and teaching.

Bellori dedicated his *Lives* to the French minister Jean-Baptiste Colbert (see p. 611), protector of the Royal Academy in Paris, and his theories became the basis of French academic teaching. They were supplemented by those of several Frenchmen who had studied in Rome, notably Bellori's friend Charles-Alphonse Dufresnoy (1611–68) whose *De Arte graphica* was widely translated; Charles Lebrun (see p. 611) a disciple of Poussin and later the dictatorial director of the French Academy; and finally, André Pélibien (1619–95) who compiled the most coherent academic doctrine in which the hierarchy of *genres*, rising from still-life (common nature) to landscape, portraits and, at the top, history painting with morally improving narratives, was established. With this academic theory culminated. Its concepts dominated the visual arts in Europe until the late eighteenth century and were not eclipsed until well into the nineteenth.

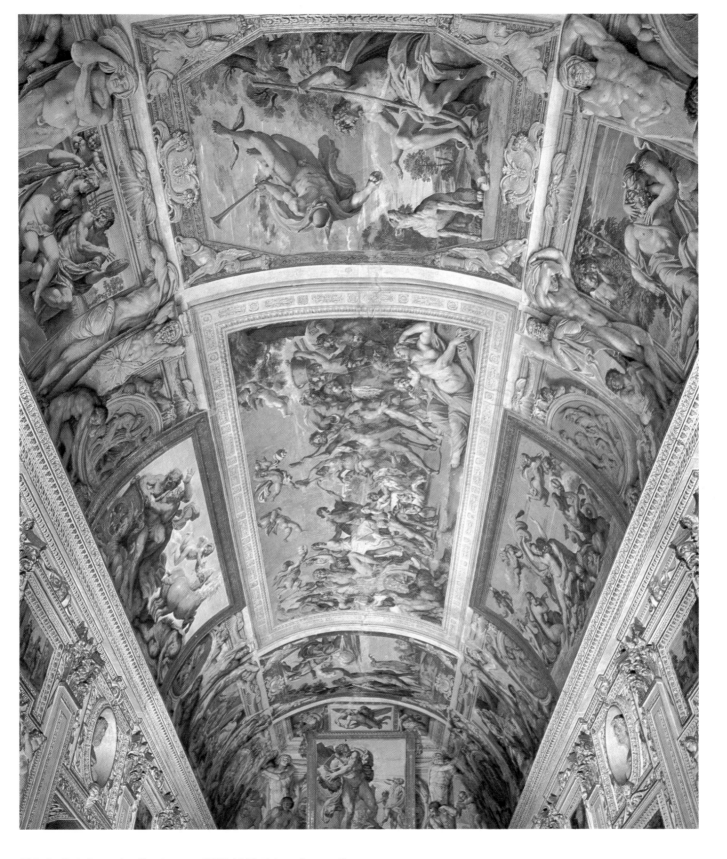

13,2 Annibale Carracci, ceiling frescoes, 1597–1600. Palazzo Farnese, Rome.

by Caravaggio shocked some contemporaries. Rough textures are rendered with illusionistic skill. This is not, however, naturalism for its own sake. The painting effectively illustrates, as the contract specified, 'the mystery' of St Paul's conversion. His arms and hands are spread to embrace the divine light which blinds him and penetrates his heart. Caravaggio was almost certainly aware of the importance placed by St Ignatius Loyola's *Spiritual Exercises* on the senses rather than the intellect as a means of attaining spiritual understanding, and his picture, with its life-size and lifelike figures, is an open invitation to participate in the mystery of conversion. Significantly, it makes its most dramatic effect when seen from a kneeling position at the entrance to the chapel.

Only three years after this painting was completed the Dutch painter and writer Karel van Mander (1548–1606) published a report of the 'remarkable things' Caravaggio was doing in Rome:

> *He holds that all works are nothing but* bagatelles, *child's work, whatever their subject and by whomever painted, unless they be painted after life and that nothing could be good and nothing better than to follow Nature. Whence it is that he will not do a single brush-stroke without close study from life which he copies and paints. Surely this is no wrong way to achieve a good end. For to paint after drawings, even though they be done after life, is nowise as reliable as to face life and to follow Nature with all her different colors.*
>
> (*Het Schilder-Boeck*, Haarlem 1604, tr. W. Friedlaender)

This contradicts practically all the theoretical writings of the sixteenth century, yet van Mander called it 'an example for our young artists to follow' – and follow it they did. Within a decade Caravaggism, as it came to be called, had spread throughout Italy to Spain, France and the Netherlands. There was a proliferation of pictures with unidealized, boldly illuminated figures set against dark, mysterious backgrounds. But van Mander also spread the news of Annibale Carracci's recent work in Palazzo Farnese, Rome (**13,2**).

Annibale Carracci broke with the immediate past no less decisively than Caravaggio. His first biographer, the influential art theorist Giovanni Pietro Bellori (1613–96), claimed that he rescued painting from 'Mannerism' – a term which now took on its pejorative meaning (see p. 504). The Sistine Chapel ceiling (11,29; 30) was one source of inspiration for the Palazzo Farnese ceiling, but Carracci rationalized Michelangelo's scheme, clarifying the distinction between levels of reality. The decorative structure, with simulated stucco reliefs of Atlantes and bronze medallions, is painted illusionistically, skilfully fore-

13,3 David Teniers, *The Picture Gallery of Archduke Leopold Wilhelm of Austria*, c. 1647. Canvas, 3ft 5¾ins × 4ft 2¾ins (1.06 × 1.29m). Prado, Madrid.

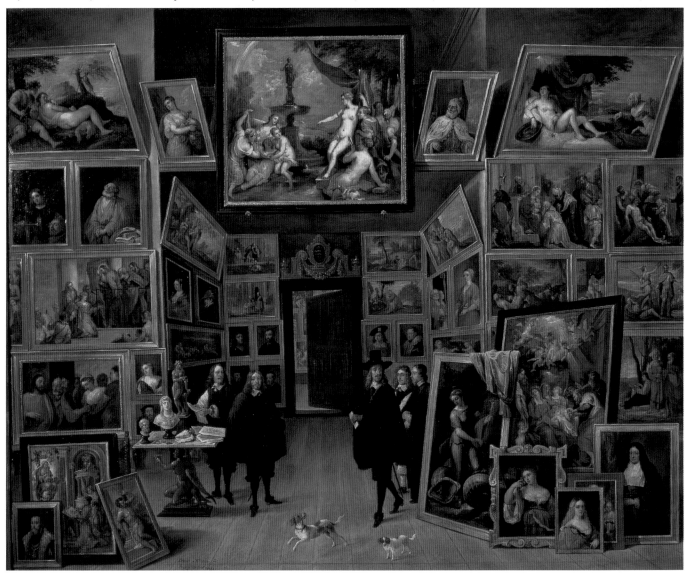

shortened and lit as if from the real source of light below, whereas the narrative scenes, celebrating the divine power of love, are rendered like framed pictures (*quadri riportati*) placed in front of the decorative structure. They are painted in a style inspired by Raphael and antique sculpture, evenly lit, Classically composed with figures parallel to the picture plane.

Annibale Carracci also differed from Caravaggio in his working methods. Some 500 drawings were made in the process of working out his design for the Farnese ceiling. He, his brother Agostino (1557–1602) and their cousin Lodovico Carracci (1555–1619) were all indefatigable draftsmen. They drew everything, compositions for painting, models in the studio, people in the street, and the first caricatures (they invented the word). At mealtimes they sat with bread in one hand and a piece of charcoal in the other. Their aim was fidelity to nature, but to a nature purified of all grosser elements, and in pursuing it they turned for guidance to antique sculpture and the masters of the High Renaissance. Annibale Carracci was no theorist, but his work soon came to be extolled as the exemplar of a rationalized version of sixteenth-century aesthetic theory, substituting for the Neoplatonic metaphysical 'Idea' (see pp. 220–1) an ideal derived purely from art itself. For more than two centuries it was to provide the basis of all academic teaching.

In Bologna in the 1580s the Carracci had organized gatherings of artists called the *Accademia degli Incamminati* (academy of the initiated). It was one of several such informal groups that enabled artists to discuss problems and practise drawing in an atmosphere calmer and more studious than that of a painter's workshop. The term 'academy' was more generally applied at the time to literary associations, membership of which conferred intellectual rank. The first academy of artists was founded in Florence in 1563 and had similar social ambitions, together with the more practical purpose of freeing painters and sculptors from the restrictions of the craft guilds. The two types of academy were combined at the Academy of St Luke in Rome, which, from the early seventeenth century, provided lectures on theory, instruction in design and facilities for life-classes to supplement the training given to an apprentice in a master's workshop. Similar academies sprang up elsewhere in Italy and in northern Europe, most notably in Paris, where art education was to be more highly organized than anywhere else (see p. 611).

Alongside, and perhaps not unconnected with, the rise of academies was the widespread growth of art-collecting in the seventeenth century, both of old masters and contemporary works, which naturally led to art dealing. This diverted attention from large-scale mural painting and other traditional forms towards the more easily transportable and negotiable easel painting, which now began to occupy in European art a place of prime importance. It was, and is, a unique phenomenon, without parallel in other cultures. Vast collections were made by Charles I of England, Philip IV of Spain, the self-exiled Queen Christina of Sweden, Cardinal Mazarin, the ruler of France during Louis XIV's long minority, not to mention minor noblemen and rich bankers. Part of the collection made by Archduke Leopold Wilhelm of Austria, governor of the Spanish Netherlands, is recorded visually – a room stuffed with paintings by Giorgione (the *Three Philosophers* [11,42] is visible on the right), Titian (the top row) and other Venetians (**13,3**). Raphael's *St Margaret* is propped against a large sketch by Rubens for a *Circumcision*. In such surroundings devotional images were separated from portraits, still-life paintings, landscapes and mythological scenes only by their gilt frames and thus tended to lose whatever religious meaning they originally had. They were looked upon quite simply as works of art like all the others: pictures acquired mainly to demonstrate the owner's status, wealth and discriminating taste. A preference for the already rare and very expensive works by High Renaissance masters agreed with academic teaching, but there were also, by the mid-seventeenth century, perceptive collectors sensitive to qualities other than those stressed by theorists – such as freedom of handling and licentiousness of subject-matter – and in the subsequent history of European painting their taste was to be increasingly important.

BAROQUE ART AND ARCHITECTURE

Like many other stylistic labels, 'Baroque' was first used as a term of critical abuse. It has a curious etymology, being derived from two words current in the sixteenth century, the Italian *barocco* referring to tortuous medieval pedantry, and the Portuguese *barrocco*, a deformed pearl. Both signified deviation from a norm, and in this sense mid-eighteenth-century theorists took them up to describe works of art, and especially architecture, which seemed to them impure and irrational. Although no longer pejorative, the term is still used to isolate a single strand from the tightly woven fabric of seventeenth-century art, that strand of predominantly religious emotionalism, dynamic energy and exuberant decorative richness which was generated in Rome and spread all over Europe and beyond, including the European colonies in America and India. The distinction between this so-called 'Baroque' and other seventeenth-century styles, such as those of the 'Naturalists' and 'Classicists', is not easy to define. Despite superficial differences, there are similarities which run deep, and the art of the seventeenth century is best understood as a whole, as a nexus of various stylistic impulses. Essentially, it was the creation of strong-minded individualists, among whom were some of the greatest of all European artists. Apart from Peter Paul Rubens (1577–1640), they were all born within a few years of each other: Nicolas Poussin (1594–1665), Gianlorenzo Bernini (1598–1664), Anthony van Dyck (1599–1641), Diego de Velázquez (1599–1660), Claude Lorraine (1600–82) and Rembrandt van Rijn (1606–69).

RUBENS AND VAN DYCK

Rubens stands somewhat apart, not only because of his age but also because of his social background, for he was an active and high-ranking diplomat as well as a painter. The son of a prominent lawyer and alderman of Antwerp, Rubens was given a Classical education and then lived for a period in a noble household to acquire aristocratic manners before beginning his training as a painter. In 1598 he qualified as a master in the Antwerp artists' guild and two years later left for Italy, where he lived and travelled in some style while pursuing his artistic career at the little ducal court of Mantua. Back in Antwerp in 1609 he was appointed court painter to the Habsburg regent of the Netherlands and very soon he was the most highly esteemed artist in Europe, occupying a position analogous to that of Titian in the previous century.

No artist ever studied the works of the Italian masters more diligently and closely than Rubens – he copied them in literally hundreds of drawings and painted sketches. Although he copied them in order to learn by exploring the means of pictorial representation, his robust sensuality and fertile imagination stamped his copies, like everything that came out of his studio, with a strongly individual character. A painting of the gods Castor and Pollux carrying off the daughters of Leucippus (**13,4**), for example, may well have been inspired partly by Titian's *Rape of Europa* (11,48), which he had copied in Spain. There are also reminiscences of Veronese in the glossy

silken draperies, and his debt to Flemish painters, especially Pieter Bruegel, is evident in the landscape. All these disparate influences have, however, been completely absorbed and transmuted in the heat of Rubens's imagination. A new and very personal ideal of female beauty, full-breasted, broad-waisted, more womanly than girlish, as natural in amplitude of figure as in innocent freedom from coquetry, is celebrated with full-blooded exuberance. The dimpling and puckered flesh of his female nudes is painted in pearly translucent colors both suggesting the smoothness and warmth of skin and enabling him to depict the blush on a cheek without so much as a hint of cosmetic artifice – a rare achievement in paint.

In the *Rape of the Daughters of Leucippus* the two women are in precisely complementary poses, the one presenting almost a mirror image of the other. Such antitheses were not uncommon in sixteenth-century paintings but Rubens used them without the usual rhetorical emphasis, simply in order to enhance the swirling impression of dynamic movement. Rejecting the stability of a pyramidal composition, he designed the picture as a diamond of intersecting diagonals within which the large swinging movement, the twist and counter-twist of intertwined forms, so typical of 'Baroque' art and architecture, gives a sense of expansive ascension, a suggestion of rapture rather than rape. There is no violence; the central figure seems to float upwards, merely supported on the brawny arms of the two gods. Despite the theme, the effect is curiously unerotic – rather as Rubens's religious pictures are unmystical.

Whether he was painting a mythological or a sacred subject, Rubens concentrated on the vitality and corporeality of the figures, seeking in this way to bring the supernatural world within the grasp of human experience. Many of his religious paintings were for Jesuit churches, including a whole cycle for one in Antwerp, where, a contemporary wrote, 'the magnificence of the interior of the edifice turns the thoughts to the abode of heaven'. The original austerity of their mother-church in Rome (11,59) was abandoned by the Jesuits in Antwerp, on a contested frontier of Catholicism, where they spared no pains to uplift the minds of beholders by dazzling their eyes. Two huge canvases depicting the first Jesuit saints, Ignatius Loyola and Francis Xavier, were placed alternately above the high altar. That of St Francis Xavier (1506–52), who had preached the gospel in India, Ceylon, south-east Asia and Japan, records the miracles he performed and celebrates the world-wide mission of the Society of Jesus (**13,5**). It is very much a Eurocentric vision of the world. Only the recumbent Hindu with shaved head on the left is Asian. The pagan temple from which the idol topples down has Corinthian columns, and the saint himself stands in the attitude of a Roman emperor addressing his troops – a motif taken from the Arch of Constantine. As several drawings reveal, Rubens made studies from life for individual figures but the final work is built up in color and light rather than by line. The episodic nature of the subject enabled him to represent in subtly differentiated facial expressions a wide gamut of human emotions, for

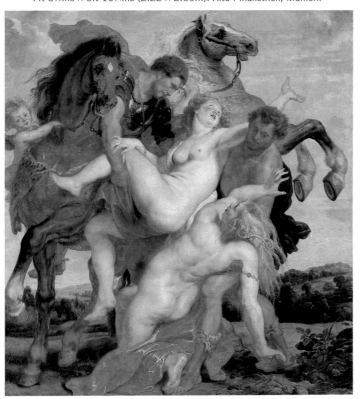

13,4 Rubens, *Rape of the Daughters of Leucippus*, c. 1616–17. Canvas, 7ft 3½ins × 6ft 10¼ins (2.22 × 2.09m). Alte Pinakothek, Munich.

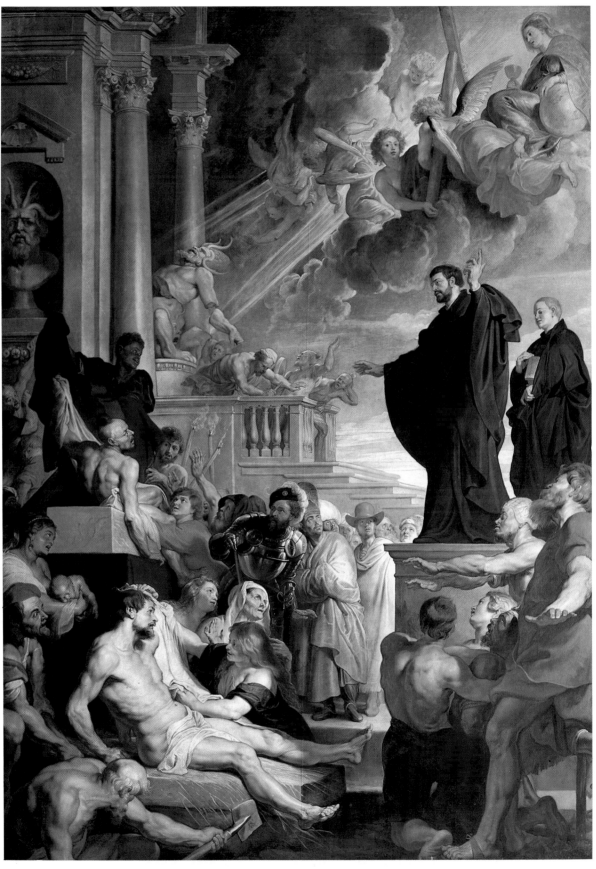

13,5 Rubens, *The Miracles of St Francis Xavier*, 1616–7.
Canvas, 17ft 6⅝ins × 12ft 11½ins (5.35 × 3.95m).
Kunsthistorisches Museum, Vienna.

The Jesuit Missions

EVANGELIZATION AND COLONIZATION

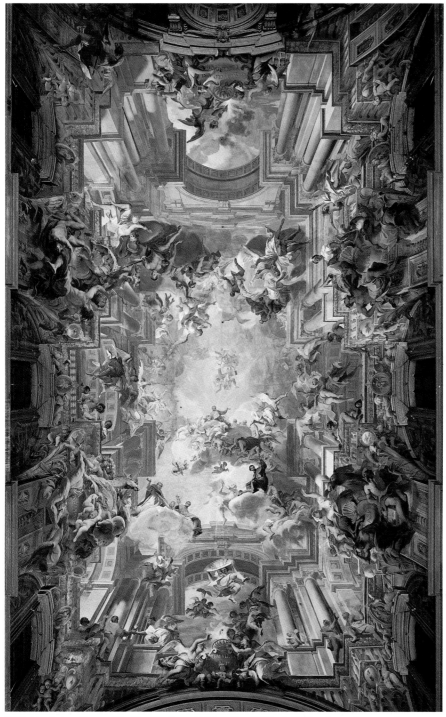

13,6 Fra Andrea Pozzo, *The Glorification of St Ignatius*, 1691–4. Ceiling fresco in nave of Sant'Ignazio, Rome.

The altarpiece of *The Miracles of St Francis Xavier* painted by Rubens in 1616–17 is one of many glorifications of Jesuit missionaries (13,5). In 1691–4 Andrea Pozzo (1642–1709), a lay brother in the Society of Jesus, 'wishing to represent the great zeal of St Ignatius in propagating the Catholic faith throughout the world' (as his first biographer recorded), covered the ceiling of the church dedicated to him in Rome with a vast allegorical fresco (**13,6**). This celebrates the contribution of the Jesuits to the triumph of Catholicism. A ray of light passes from Christ to St Ignatius whence it is refracted by way of St Francis Xavier and other missionaries to personifications of the four continents seated above tumbling figures of the heathen and heretical enemies of the Catholic Church. All the figures are depicted as if seen from below; the walls of the church are projected upwards with an almost vertiginous effect and the roof of the church is notionally lifted off to reveal a vision of heaven. The geometrical precision of the perspective in this celestial–terrestrial vision seemingly corroborates the truth of the painting's message although there is, in fact, only one place, marked with a metal plaque in the floor, from which it can be seen as a wholly convincing optical illusion. And only from a Catholic and Eurocentric viewpoint could the message it conveys be fully accepted.

For the personifications of the continents, Pozzo resorted to iconographic models devised in the late sixteenth century. They are shown as women: Asia riding a camel, Africa black-skinned on a crocodile, America bare-breasted, wielding an arrow and wearing a feather head-dress, and, most significantly, Europe with one hand holding a sceptre, the other resting on an orb, and a royal crown on her blond hair. The figures thus illustrate the preposterous but widely accepted notion, summarized in 1591 by an Italian associate of the Jesuits, that Europe, though the smallest of the continents, 'was born to rule over Africa, Asia and America'. Hence the vogue in seventeenth- and eighteenth-century Europe for allegories of the continents in paintings (14,15), tapestries, prints, sculptures (13,19), and even in ceramics, silver and furniture. They appear in both religious and secular art, for the processes of evangelization and colonization went hand in hand. Indeed, Christianity took root only where European colonies were firmly established – in the Americas, the Philippines and a few other islands; in Africa and Asia only in very limited coastal areas that were initially no more than trading stations. Missionaries, nevertheless, wrote optimistic accounts of their activities in the interior of India and China, incidentally including detailed and commercially very useful information about the natural resources and products. The customs and religious beliefs of the inhabitants they usually thought outlandish.

13,7 Albert Eckhout, *Tapuya War Dance*, c. 1641–3. Canvas, 9ft 7¾ins × 6ft (2.94 × 1.83m). National Museum of Denmark, Copenhagen.

Europeans felt a need to impose order on the diversity of peoples revealed to them by the discoveries of the fifteenth century when the sea route round Africa to India and the Far East was opened and the American continent explored. In 1590 a Spanish Jesuit in Peru, José Acosta, divided the population outside Christendom into four hierarchically arranged categories: first those who were literate like the Chinese and Japanese; then those like the Mexicans and Peruvians who lived in stable settlements with organized government and religion; below them the 'savages' subdivided between those with the rudiments of organized life and the rest who, in José Acosta's view, were like wild beasts. His aim was to demonstrate that each class called for a different approach from missionaries, who were urged to study the beliefs of the people they sought to convert. This basic system of classification, which implied a process of social evolution from 'savagery' to civilization, was also adopted by the European powers for their colonial administrations and was to survive little altered until the late nineteenth century.

Between 1638 and 1643 the Dutch governor general of Brazil, Count Johann Mauritz of Nassau-Siegen, employed a team of scientists and artists to record every feature of the colony, landscape, flora, fauna and inhabitants. The latter were portrayed by Albert Eckhout (c. 1607–65) who, in one of several paintings of Brazil, shows men of a Tapuya tribe performing a war dance, stark naked and brandishing their weapons as they gyrate while two women hum an accompaniment (**13,7**). Drawings reveal that he based the picture on studies of individual figures drawn from the life in order to present an ethnographically accurate illustration. The result is an extraordinarily vivid image of a way of life that missionaries and colonizers were anxious to suppress as a hindrance to the Christianization and commercial exploitation of the territory, a process that has, alas, continued to the present day. Eckhout's painting would have been regarded by Europeans simply as a visual document. In works of art, until the late eighteenth century they preferred fanciful figures of docile Americans, Africans and Asians, sometimes busy producing goods to be enjoyed in civilized luxury in Europe, as in Giovanni Battista Tiepolo's frescoed ceiling of 1752–3 in the Prince-Bishop's palace at Würzburg (14,15).

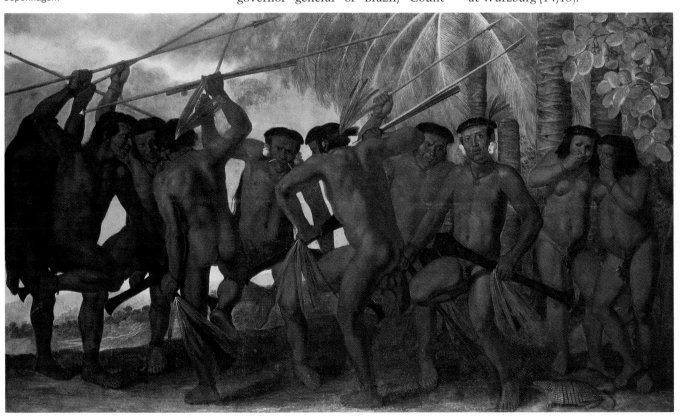

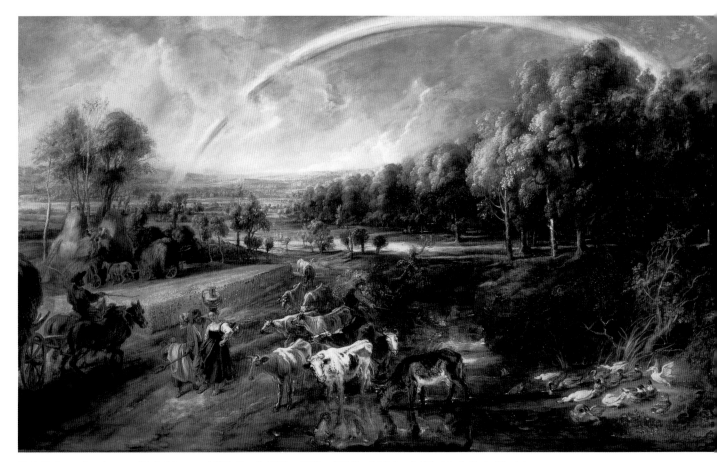

13,8 Rubens, *Landscape with Rainbow*, c. 1635. Panel, 37¼ × 48½ins (94.6 × 123.2cm). Alte Pinakothek, Munich.

he shared to the full his contemporaries' interest in what were called the 'passions of the soul' and is said to have composed a treatise on the subject 'with appropriate illustrations after the best masters, especially Raphael'. In this respect, indeed, he may have sought to rival Raphael's *Transfiguration* (11,33) in *The Miracles of St Francis Xavier*. His principal achievement was, however, to unify this 17-foot-high (5.2m) composition with a sweeping spiral which curls round the saint and his attendant in their black habits, silhouetted against the sky. The eye is led, and the mind follows, a line from the blind men groping their way forward in the lower right corner, to a man who has been raised from the dead, past the sick Hindu and along the beams of light striking the temple to the visionary personification of Faith in the heavens.

'I am by natural instinct better fitted to execute very large works than little curiosities', Rubens wrote in a letter of 1621. 'I have never lacked courage to undertake any design, however vast in size or diversified in subject' – as his 21 12-foot-high (3.7m) canvases illustrating the life of Marie de Médici, queen of France, confirm. (Painted between 1621 and 1625, they are now in the Louvre, Paris.) Yet his small, intimate works are unsurpassed in their combination of delicacy and robustness. The head of his bright-eyed smiling first wife, Isabella Brant, is one of the most arresting (13,9).

The *Portrait of Isabella Brant* also exemplifies Rubens's essentially painterly vision, even in a chalk drawing. His prodigious ability to define form fully in a small rapid sketch had, however, a dubious side-effect; it enabled him to turn over to his staff of assistants much of the work commissioned from him. Often he would add no more than the final touches to a painting (though he honestly adjusted his prices according to the extent of his own participation). The rate of production was such that his studio has been likened to a factory. This is rather misleading, for it was a studio directed by a genius, who, moreover, never let it slip from his control.

He made a fortune and in 1635 bought a country estate, the Château de Steen, a few miles south of Antwerp. But he did not retire. The surrounding country inspired a series of paintings which suddenly revealed, in his late fifties, a new aspect of his art. For although he had often sketched views from nature, only now did he depict the scenery of Flanders for its own sake and on a large scale (13,8). Pride in land-ownership may have prompted these works, which he evidently painted for himself. But they seem to be still more deeply personal – celebrations, as it were, of the goodness and plenitude of creation on the part of a middle-aged man who had recently married a second wife, 27 years his junior, and was fathering a new family of children. Very vividly do they convey, in the generous all-embracing

'Baroque' rhythm of their great arcs and spirals, a sense of perpetual growth and change as the earth revolves in its diurnal course, and a sense, too, of an ageing man's longing to catch and hold the fleeting moment, all of which gives them a deeply moving human dimension. Rainbows appear, storm-clouds roll away and through them sunlight, which always seems brighter after rain, strikes on patches of meadow land and glistens on wet leaves, while the work-aday life of the farm goes on undisturbed – buxom milk-maids lead the cattle home to the byre, men build stacks of new-mown hay, geese paddle in the flowing stream.

Of Rubens's many assistants and followers, Anthony van Dyck (1599–1641) was the most notable. He painted both religious and mythological subjects, but it was as a portrait painter that he excelled and in 1632 he was appointed court painter to Charles I (1625–49) in England. In deference to Charles I's obsession with the idea of kingship van Dyck portrayed him some 20 times in a variety of richly symbolic roles – as the knight of St George and commander of armies, as the perfect Renaissance gentleman cultivated in mind and body, self-assured and unaffected in manner, as faithful husband and fond father both of his children and of the nation. Charles I, in fact of diminutive stature and rather plain features, was

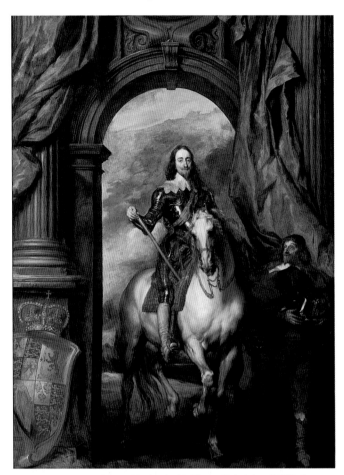

13,10 Anthony van Dyck, *Charles I with M. de St Antoine*, 1633. Canvas, 12ft 1in × 8ft 10¼ins (3.68 × 2.7m). Buckingham Palace, London. Reproduced by gracious permission of Her Majesty The Queen.

13,9 Rubens, *Portrait of Isabella Brant*, c. 1622. Black, red and white chalk with light washes on light-brown paper, the eyes strengthened with pen and black ink, 15 × 11⅝ins (38.1 × 29.5cm). British Museum, London.

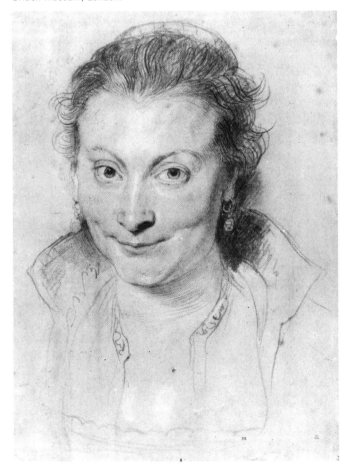

wonderfully transfigured in these portraits. In one he appears in imperial guise mounted like Marcus Aurelius, but on a nobler horse and riding through a triumphal arch (**13,10**). A low viewpoint silhouetting the king against the sky within a grandiose architectural framework – a device used to exalt saints in altarpieces – was here employed in the service of divinely appointed monarchy. It must have looked still more imposing in its original position, at the end of a long gallery hung with pictures of ancient Roman emperors by Giulio Romano and Titian, some of the finest works in the great art collection Charles I amassed. The propagandist value of paintings by both old and modern masters was nowhere more fully exploited.

The Easel Painting in Italy

But despite the fame of Rubens and van Dyck, the works of art most eagerly sought by collectors were Italian. At the beginning of his reign Charles I had invited to England two painters of the Bolognese school. They refused to undertake the journey and he was obliged to make do with Orazio Gentileschi (1563–1639), joined for a short time by his daughter Artemisia (1593–1652), the first prominent woman artist in Italy since Sofonisba Anguissola (11,62).

She was a follower of Caravaggio, but such works as her gory picture of *Judith Slaying Holofernes* exploit *chiaroscuro* and an unidealized vision of common humanity to such violent effect that his canvases seem quite restrained in comparison (**13,11**). Slowly and deliberately carving off the head of Holofernes, Judith holds her body back from the spurting blood. The subject had often been represented, sometimes as an allegory of tyrannicide. But this picture seems to have been intended simply as a vivid reconstruction of the story told in the apocryphal Book of Judith and as a virtuoso feat of dramatic naturalism for inclusion in a collection of works of art – it was bought by the grand duke of Tuscany on the advice of Galileo. A late seventeenth-century Florentine described it as arousing 'not a little terror' and the conjunction of a woman painter with a homicidal heroine may have added a sense of alarm. Artemisia specialized in scenes in which women play a dominant role. But although she had good reason to distrust men – she was seduced by her teacher of perspective and when her father brought him into court *she* was tortured with the thumb-screw to ascertain the truth of her evidence – her choice of subjects was probably determined as much by the expectations of her patrons as by her personal feelings. A rather cool, businesslike character is revealed in her letters.

Artemisia Gentileschi worked for most of her career in Naples, where naturalism flourished under the patronage of Spanish rulers and the stimulus of such Spanish painters as Jusepe de Ribera (1591–1652), who lived there from 1616 onwards. In Rome, on the other hand, despite the great popularity of small pictures of peasants and beggars – usually by Flemish artists settled in the city – idealization was demanded in large religious and mythological works. Hence the success of Guido Reni (1575–1642), a Bolognese painter long resident in Rome who adopted Caravaggio's dramatic *chiaroscuro* to spotlight the nobility of his figures. He was an almost exact contemporary of Rubens and his first master was a Mannerist painter from Antwerp, but he soon moved into the circle of the Carracci. Even in such a mature work as *Atalanta and Hippomenes* the ballet-dancer poses of the figures, the delicately contrived pattern of their limbs and the fluttering ribbons of drapery, with no possible functional purpose, recall the stylishness of the sixteenth century (**13,12**). These youthful bodies are, however, more substantial as well as more naturally proportioned, and the sensuous painting of their flesh declares a debt to Correggio. The picture is, furthermore, composed like an antique low relief – or like one of the *quadri riportati* on the ceiling of Palazzo Farnese – with movement parallel to the picture plane. Guido Reni took the subject from Ovid's story, overlooking its feminist implications to create, like Artemisia Gentileschi, what is essentially a collector's piece.

Another artist from the region of Bologna, known by his nickname Il Guercino, the man with a squint (Giovanni Francesco Barbieri, 1591–1666), began by working in a rich painterly manner, but later adopted a lighter palette and less dramatic lighting in order, so he told a friend, 'to satisfy as well as he could most of the people,

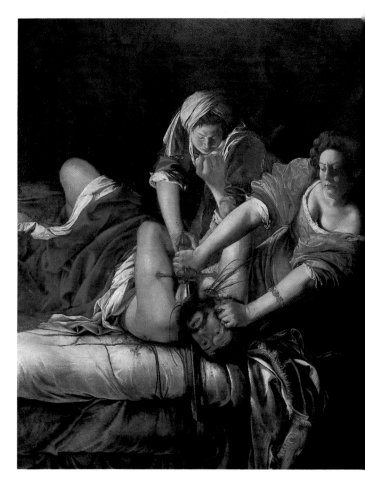

13,11 Artemisia Gentileschi, *Judith Slaying Holofernes*, c. 1620. Canvas, 6ft 6⅓ins × 5ft 4ins (1.99 × 1.63m). Uffizi, Florence.

especially those who commissioned paintings and had the money to pay for them'. Some regretted the change, however, and in 1660 a Sicilian collector asked him to paint a canvas in his 'early powerful manner' as a pendant to a Rembrandt. That Rembrandt should have been held up as a model by a Sicilian patron at this date is noteworthy, as is the admiration for his etchings that Guercino declared

13,12 Guido Reni, *Atalanta and Hippomenes*, c. 1625. Canvas, 6ft 9ins × 9ft 9ins (2.06 × 2.97m). Prado, Madrid.

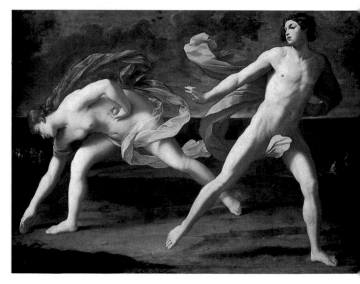

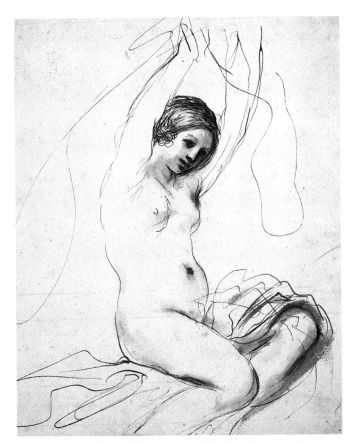

13,13 Guercino, *Woman Undressing*, c. 1620. Pen, ink and wash on paper, 10 × 8⅛ins (25.6 × 20.7cm). British Museum, London.

in his reply. Guercino's own graphic work was almost as extensive as Rembrandt's and was likewise done mainly for his own pleasure or as working drawings, such as that illustrated here (**13,13**) – a masterly study from life, entirely natural in attitude, the full form of the model's body being caught with a few swift strokes of the quill-pen and a very sparing application of wash. These drawings were not conceived as finished works of art, but as notes of visual ideas for his own use or the instruction of pupils and he was always reluctant to sell them.

BERNINI

Paradoxically, Guercino's stylistic regression towards a restrained Classicism in painting coincides with the rise to pre-eminence of the artist from whose work the idea of Baroque exuberance is mainly derived, Gianlorenzo Bernini (1589–1680). Like Michelangelo a century before, Bernini regarded himself primarily as a sculptor, though he was no less gifted as an architect and was also a painter and poet. And he was similarly indebted to the patronage of artistically enlightened popes. He was the first artist with the self-confidence to confront Michelangelo's achievement without flinching. But in character they were antithetical. Bernini was extrovert, sociable, witty in conversation, aristocratic in manner and way of life, a good family man, conformist in his no less profound piety, little interested in philosophical speculation and untroubled by doubts. He was an astonishingly fast worker with a demonic drive to complete whatever he undertook, a systematic and extremely efficient organizer of large teams of assistants.

For half a century he dominated the artistic scene in Rome and no single man contributed more to the city's present appearance. 'You are made for Rome and Rome is made for you', Pope Urban VIII is said to have told him.

Bernini was the son of a sculptor and first made his name with mythological groups and portrait busts. The latter he continued to carve throughout his career and none of his other works better displays his astonishing technical virtuosity, his ability to chisel and rasp white marble into the semblance of flesh, hair and drapery, even to give a suggestion of color. The portrait of Francesco I d'Este, duke of Modena, is a triumph of art over that most artificial of all European conventions – the bust (**13,14**). It succeeds in evoking the presence of a whole figure by means only of the head and armless shoulders. The lifelike impression is due not only to the illusionism of the carving but, still more, to balanced asymmetry in a composition of opposed diagonals. The face is to the left and the centre folds of the cloak to the right of the main axis, while the direction of the gaze is countered by that of the drapery, which descends from one shoulder to swirl up into a buoyant billow over the other. Bernini, who never saw the duke, complained of the difficulty of working from a painted portrait, but this may have helped him to attain that concentration on problems of form rather than of description which makes the bust memorable. In the process he created one of the most vivid images of regal hauteur, setting a new standard for royal portrait sculpture, which he was unable to surpass, even in his bust of Louis XIV at Versailles.

Bernini received his first papal commission when only 26 years old. The newly elected Pope Urban VIII (1623–44) entrusted him with the task of creating a *baldacchino* or canopy for the main altar of St Peter's, above the tomb believed to contain the remains of St Peter and St Paul. This gigantic 95-foot-high (29m) structure, of bronze

13,14 Bernini, *Francesco I d'Este*, 1651. Marble, 3ft 3⅜ins (1m) high with base. Galleria e Museo Estense, Modena.

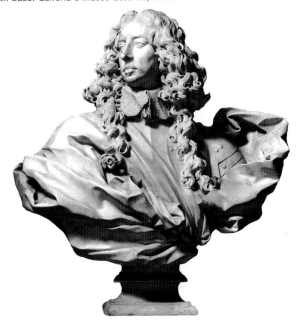

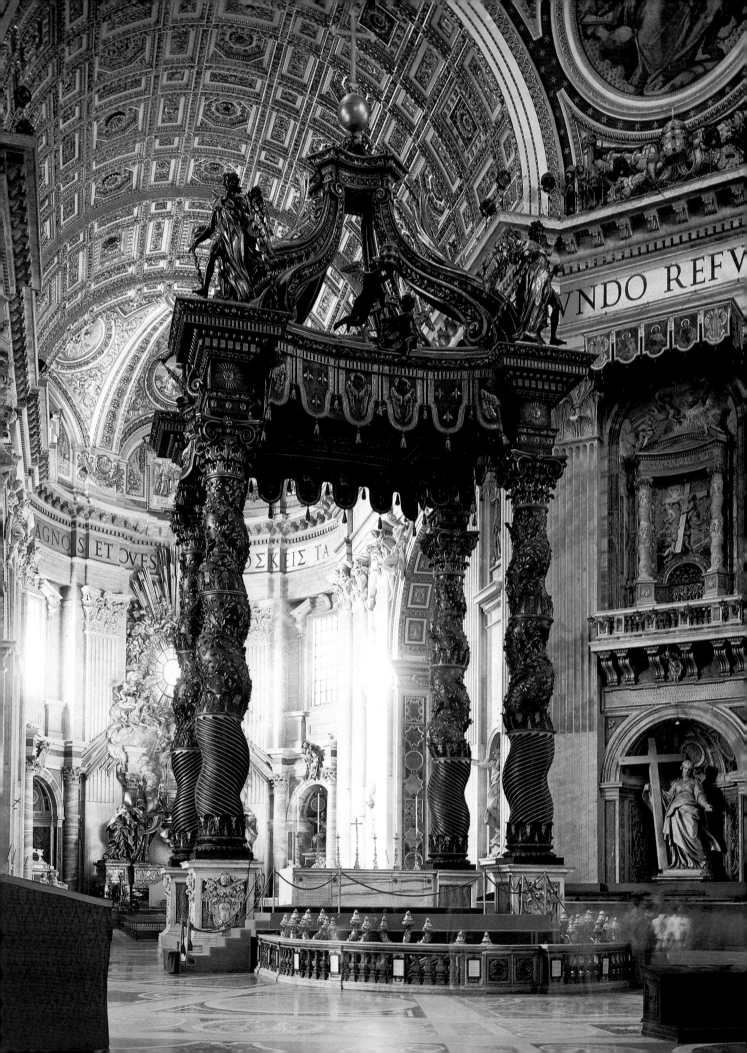

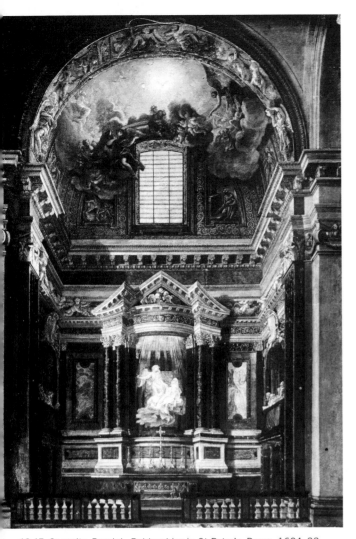

in golden yellow skies with purple clouds – an unprecedented use of color. The lower niches were filled with colossal statues of the two men and two women associated with the relics, each expressing a different 'passion of the soul', the men gazing ecstatically towards the heavens, the women towards the sacrifice at the altar. In this way the whole crossing, with the *baldacchino* marking the centre, became a total work of art in which all the elements are conceptually and visually woven into a seamless fabric of associations – a grandiose conception celebrating the continuity of the Church and its triumph over the Reformation. The theme was brought to its climax outside when Bernini added, 1656–67, two great colonnades enclosing an oval piazza. These reach out and around it like, Bernini said, the motherly arms of the Church, 'which embrace Catholics to reinforce their beliefs, heretics to re-unite them with the Church and unbelievers to enlighten them with the true faith'.

Bernini's aim at St Peter's was to proclaim the unity of the Catholic Church by combining all available artistic means, unifying architecture, sculpture and painting into what was called at the time *un bel composto* – a beautiful whole. On a less colossal scale he achieved the same unified effect in a chapel commissioned by Cardinal Federico Cornaro as his own burial-place and as a memorial to his family, dedicated to St Teresa of Ávila (**13,16**). It is dazzlingly rich and sumptuous from inlaid floor to frescoed vault,

13,17 Bernini, *Ecstasy of St Teresa*, detail of Cornaro Chapel altar. Marble, 11ft 6ins (3.5m) high. S Maria della Vittoria, Rome.

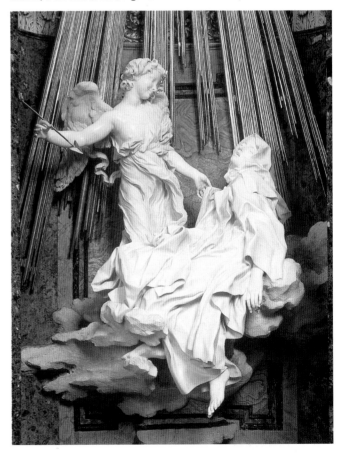

13,15 *Opposite* Bernini, *Baldacchino* in St Peter's, Rome, 1624–33. Gilded bronze, 95ft (29m) high.

13,16 *Above* Bernini, Cornaro Chapel, S Maria della Vittoria, Rome, 1645–52. Anonymous 18th-century painting. Staatliches Museum, Schwerin.

embellished with gilding, rose majestically to reaffirm the centrality of the crossing not only for the church but also for all Christendom (**13,15**). The elements of the design were traditional but combined in a new way, which offended some contemporaries. Its twisted columns are greatly enlarged versions of those believed to have come from Solomon's temple in Jerusalem (incorporated in Constantine's basilica and later re-used by Bernini, see below); the tasselled valance simulates the fabric of a canopy carried on staves, usually for a priest bearing the sacrament in a procession, and the superstructure recalls a type of ciborium often suspended over an altar. Symbolically, therefore, its message was plain to all believers and the triumphant visual flourish of its huge twisting columns, buoyant scrolls and dynamic sculpture epitomizes the grandeur, flamboyance and emotionalism of the Counter-Reformation.

Bernini's new conception of the crossing of St Peter's did not stop there, however. Michelangelo's great piers were transformed to allude to four famous relics enshrined within them. In the upper niches Bernini re-used the twisted columns from Constantine's basilica to flank reliefs of the relics borne by white marble angels set

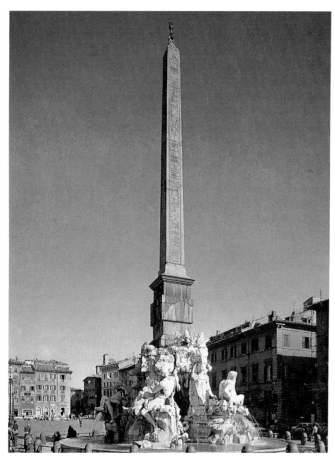

13,18 Bernini, Fountain of the Four Rivers, 1648–51. Travertine and marble. Piazza Navona, Rome.

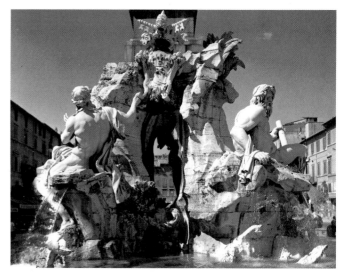

13,19 Bernini, detail of the Fountain of the Four Rivers.

the complex architectural elements built up of various colored marbles (predominantly yellow and green) with flashes of gilt bronze and the shallow space lit with such ingenuity that it has often been likened, rather misleadingly, to a theatre. The central feature is a white marble group of the saint's ecstasy, illuminated from above by a hidden window and carved with supreme illusionistic mastery (**13,17**) – as are also the half-figures of the Cornaro family behind their marble-draped praying desks (not theatre boxes) on the side walls. Such realism was entirely appropriate to St Teresa's visions of the angel:

> *In his hands I saw a long golden spear and at the end of the iron tip I seemed to see a point of fire. With this he seemed to pierce my heart several times so that it penetrated my entrails. When he drew it out, I thought he was drawing them out with it and he left me completely afire with love of God. The pain was so sharp that it made me utter several moans; and so excessive was the sweetness caused me by this intense pain that one can never wish to lose it, nor will one's soul be content with anything less than God. It is not bodily pain, but spiritual, though the body has a share in it – indeed, a great share.*

(St Teresa, *Vida*, tr. E. A. Peers)

The pious Bernini, who worshipped each day at the Gesù and cherished the *Imitation of Christ* (see p. 465), responded instinctively to the sensual imagery of St Teresa's mystical writings and did not minimize the body's 'great share' in the spiritual experience. His angel,

reminiscent of a cupid by Correggio (11,56), and his St Teresa, head thrown back, mouth open and eyes closed in an attitude of physical abandon, have obvious erotic overtones and aroused adverse comment from contemporaries. But Bernini goes beyond a direct representation of her experience – so direct that her convulsive condition might almost be diagnosed by a twentieth-century psychologist – to hint at the phenomenon of her levitation after receiving communion and also her miraculous transformation into a beautiful young woman at the moment of her death, so that the group becomes a richly allusive image of that state, midway between heaven and earth, when spirit and matter meet.

The rest of the chapel sets the saint's individual salvation in a universal context. The institution of the Eucharist is shown in relief on the altar frontal, the dead rise from their graves on the inlaid floor, the Cornaro family meditate on and participate in the divine mysteries. High overhead, angels carry a scroll with the message of salvation in words spoken by Christ to St Teresa in a vision but addressed to every believer: 'If I had not created heaven already, I would create it for you alone.'

While work was proceeding on the chapel Bernini was engaged on another major undertaking, the fountain in Piazza Navona, which has a cognate theme – even though, at first sight, it may seem an extravaganza (**13,18; 19**). It was designed as the base for an antique obelisk (see Glossary), interpreted as a symbol of divine light and eternity, crowned by the dove of the Holy Spirit, the personal emblem of Pope Innocent X (1644–55), who commissioned it. Four gigantic figures seated in contrasting poses personify the great rivers (the life-giving waters) of the four continents, each with a characteristic animal – the American river Plate has an armadillo. But they are also associated with the four rivers flowing out of Paradise and the central rock with the hill of Calvary. Thus the idea of salvation through the Church is interwoven with that of Catholic triumph over the four parts of the world in a complex *concetto* of the kind beloved by the seventeenth-century intelligentsia. Others were less enthusiastic, however, and verses posted nearby declared: 'We want bread more than obelisks and fountains – bread, bread, bread.'

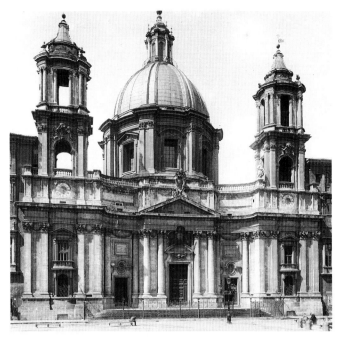

13,20 Francesco Borromini, S Agnese in Piazza Navona, Rome, 1653–5, completed 1666 by other hands.

BORROMINI

The great church façade towering behind the fountain was designed mainly by Francesco Borromini (1599–1667), with concave centre and a dome not, as was usual, set back but seeming to rise up from it (**13,20**). Borromini was a stone-carver by training and in 1619 came to Rome, where he was employed as a decorative sculptor and draftsman. Later he worked under Bernini, on the *baldacchino* at St Peter's among other projects, but temperamental incompatibility kept them apart. Borromini was morose, quarrelsome, frustrated and neurotic – eventually

13,21 Borromini, interior of dome,
S Ivo della Sapienza, Rome, begun 1642.

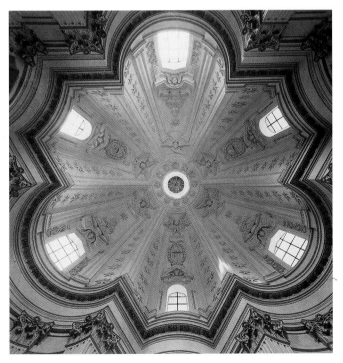

he committed suicide. The liberties he took with the rules laid down by Vitruvius prompted Bernini to remark that he had been 'sent to destroy architecture'. But he had, in fact, greater knowledge of ancient Roman architecture than Bernini and he was more deeply concerned with structural problems – and far more daring in solving them, often with thrilling spatial effects. His work makes a stronger intellectual than emotional appeal. He was an

13,22 Schematic plan of S Ivo della Sapienza.

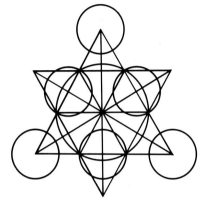

13,23 S Ivo della Sapienza. Section, from a 17th-century engraving.

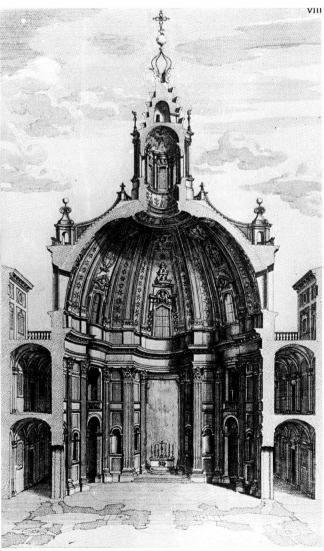

inspired geometrician and it is tempting to suggest that the new Galilean conception of the regular irregularity of the planetary orbits – though condemned by the Roman Church – emboldened him to reject the simple cubes, cylinders and spheres of earlier cosmic significance, on which so many architectural designs had been based.

His independent career began late, in 1634, and he succeeded in completing relatively few buildings, of which S Ivo della Sapienza is one of the finest (**13,21; 22; 23**). His ingenious plan of intersecting equilateral triangles and circles creates a very unusual hexagonal central space. Built as the chapel of the Archiginnasio (later the university) of Rome, the main purpose of the new building was to provide suitable space for the preaching of sermons to the students. Borromini was thus freed from the restrictions of the usual Counter-Reformation church plan and devised a single large enclosing shell of complex homogeneity. The dome is unprecedented in conception, being formed simply by the continuation of the walls upwards and inwards until they meet in the circle of light beneath the lantern. There are no intervening elements. Complete spatial unity is attained without any loss of variety or movement. Symbolism also played a part, however, in this remarkable design. It is said that the plan was based on a schematic drawing of a bee with folded wings from the Barberini family coat of arms of Pope Urban VIII, who was reigning when Borromini began work. The six-pointed 'star of David' made by the intersection of two triangles is a symbol of wisdom especially appropriate for a university chapel and as such it appears in the stucco decorations of the dome. The whole was, in fact, conceived as a symbol of wisdom (*sapienza*) associated with the descent of the Holy Ghost, which gave the apostles knowledge of tongues at Pentecost, and a gilded dove hovers in the centre of the lantern. A curious feature of the exterior, a spiral ziggurat-like crown (see Glossary) for the lantern, may allude to the confusion of tongues, which was interpreted as the Old Testament parallel to the Pentecostal gift of tongues.

For interiors Borromini used none of the rich materials in which Bernini delighted. That of S Ivo is entirely of stucco originally painted white or in shades of off-white. Many of the larger Roman churches were, however, decorated at this time with frescoed vaults opening into visions of heaven. In S Maria in Vallicella (known as the Chiesa Nuova), for which Rubens had painted the high altarpiece in 1608, the dome was frescoed with the Holy Trinity in Glory and the conch of the apse with the Assumption of the Virgin (**13,24**). The influence of Correggio's cupola at Parma is obvious (11,55); it had demonstrated how such an exhilarating sense of levitation could be conveyed. But the compositions are more forcefully articulated in great swirling scrolls, and what was more important at the time, the subjects are much more clearly legible. They are by Pietro da Cortona (Pietro Berrettini, 1596-1669), the leading Italian painter of his generation and also a notable architect, though overshadowed by the more inventive Borromini and the more grandiose Bernini.

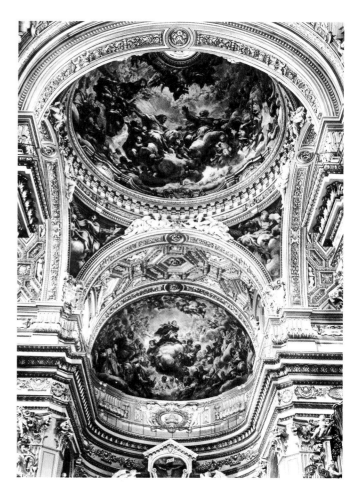

13,24 Pietro da Cortona, *The Trinity in Glory* (dome), 1647–51; *Assumption of the Virgin* (apse), 1655–60. Frescoes. S Maria in Vallicella, Rome.

POUSSIN AND CLAUDE

The most distinguished painters working in Rome in the mid-seventeenth century were not Italian but French: Nicolas Poussin (1594–1665) and Claude Lorraine (1600–82), both of whom spent the greater part of their lives in the city. Poussin arrived in 1624. He was well educated, with a command of Latin literature that won the admiration of Roman men of letters, but as an artist he was slow in developing. For a while he worked in the studio of Domenichino (Domenico Zampieri, 1581–1641), a Bolognese who had assisted Annibale Carracci on the gallery in Palazzo Farnese. By 1628 Poussin had so far mastered their style that he was given the important commission for a large altarpiece in St Peter's. But his work did not please and he never painted again for a church or other public building in Rome. Instead he concentrated on relatively small pictures for the cabinets of collectors, especially those whose intellectual interests he shared. Turning away from contemporary Roman art, Poussin looked for inspiration first to the Venetians, as can be seen in a picture of about 1630 in which the robust, athletic figures, rich colors, golden light and succulent, free handling of paint all recall Titian, several of whose finest works were then in Rome (**13,25**). Titian's sensuous vitality has, nevertheless, been completely transmuted in this evocation of the autumnal, elegiac mood of bucolic poetry. Shepherds are depicted fingering the words on a sarcophagus, *Et in Arcadia Ego* – I, that is to say death, am present

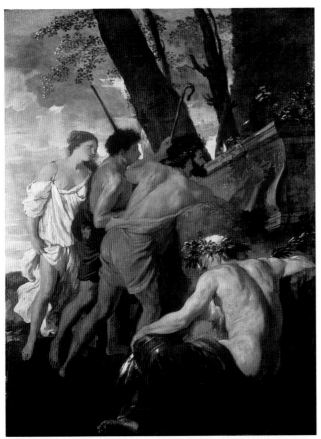

also in Arcadia. No Classical source for the inscription is known and Poussin probably invented it. The Classical concision and restraint of these lapidary words point up similar qualities in the painting and perfectly express his melancholy at the transience of pleasure.

By the time he painted *The Holy Family on the Steps* (**13,26**) Poussin's art had almost reached its final stage of stoical severity. This grave painting unites Raphaelesque and Michelangelesque forms with the idea of the Virgin as the 'stairway to heaven' in a single image of still perfection. There are no merely decorative details: every element has both a symbolic meaning and a pictorial function in the deceptively simple balance of the composition. The exquisitely painted basket of apples, for instance, alludes to the forbidden fruit and the fall of man redeemed by Christ. Poussin wrote of one of his pictures that it should be framed so that 'in considering all its parts, the eye shall remain concentrated and not dispersed

13,25 *Left* Nicolas Poussin, *The Arcadian Shepherds*, c. 1630. Canvas, 39¾ × 32¼ins (101 × 82cm). Devonshire Collection, Chatsworth, Derbyshire, England.

13,26 *Below* Nicolas Poussin, *The Holy Family on the Steps*, 1648. Canvas, 28½ × 44ins (72.4 × 111.7cm). Cleveland Museum of Art (Purchase, Leonard C. Hanna Jr. Bequest).

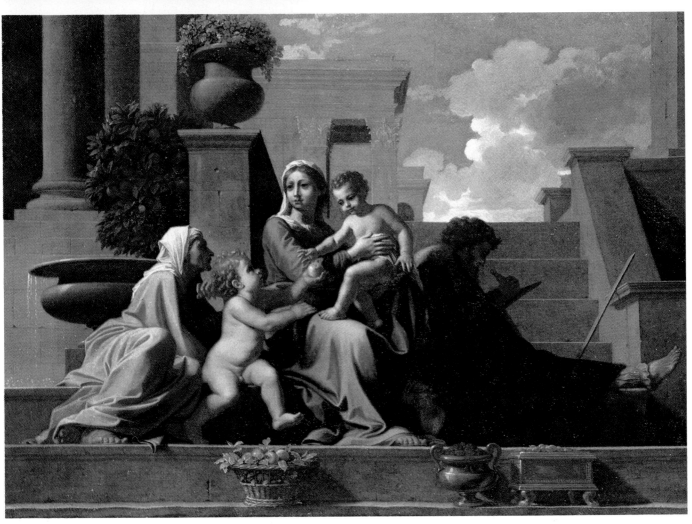

beyond the limits of the picture.' His paintings demand and reward such attention, like poems that must be learned by heart before they are fully understood. Poussin was, as Bernini remarked, pointing to his forehead, 'a painter who works up here'.

The name of Claude Gellée, known as Claude Lorraine, is often coupled with that of Poussin and the two artists certainly knew one another, though they were as different in character and in art as were the two great French dramatists of the same period, Corneille and Racine. Claude had no Classical education; he was trained as a pastry-cook in his native Lorraine and went in his early teens to Rome, where he learned to paint as an assistant to a decorative artist. He remained there for the rest of his life, apart from a few years in the 1620s. He appears to have read Latin poetry only in translation, yet his pictures fixed the image of its landscape indelibly on the European mind. The 'Classical landscape' was virtually his creation, and the idea of landscape as one of the higher

art forms in the West was largely due to him. Until the mid-seventeenth century it had not even been recognized as an independent *genre* (except in the Netherlands). Claude's landscapes were bought by kings, notably Philip IV of Spain, and the aristocracy of Europe – patrons of a different type and class from the intellectuals, lawyers and officials who admired Poussin's more intellectually demanding work. Claude's success was such that by 1635 his works were being so extensively forged that he began to keep records of the originals, drawing their compositions and noting their purchasers in a volume called the *Liber Veritatis* (now in the British Museum).

Claude's landscapes (**13,27**) have acquired a timeless appearance, a kind of inevitability that makes it difficult to appreciate their novelty. They represent the pastoral world of a Classical Golden Age, a recurring theme in European literature and art, but Claude's immediate inspiration came from the countryside around Rome itself – the *campagna* – which, surprisingly, had not pre-

13,27 Claude Lorraine, *Landscape with the Father of Psyche sacrificing to Apollo*, 1660–70. Canvas, 5ft 9ins × 7ft 3¾ins (1.75 × 2.23m). National Trust (Fairhaven Collection), Anglesey Abbey, Cambridgeshire, England.

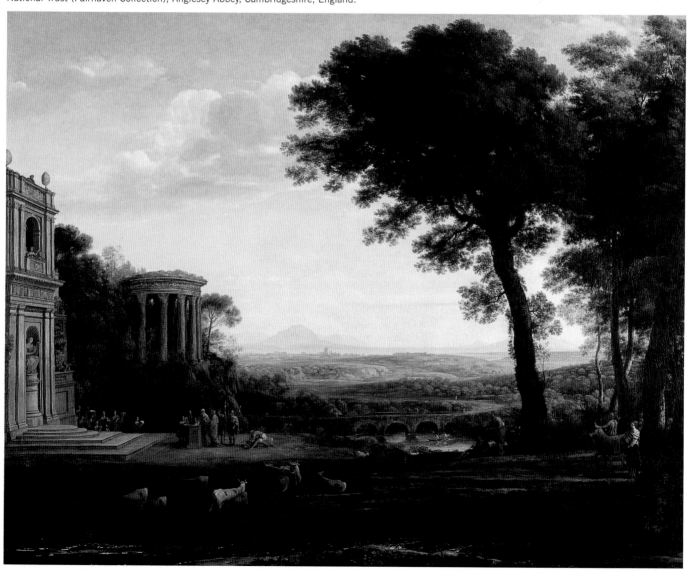

viously attracted painters apart from those in search of ancient ruins. He spent days on end with his sketchbooks in these miles and miles of solitary, gently undulating pastures, observing and registering their undramatic, almost monotonous features under varying effects of natural light. Ancient myth acquired a new reality in his pictures which are at once idealized and closely observed – wide views of subtle diversity, with an open foreground, prominently placed trees just off-centre or to one side and here and there unobtrusive but skilfully placed features, such as a bridge or a copse, to lead the eye along a slowly winding path through the gentlest gradations of tone to the bright horizon. His principal innovation was in the treatment of light emanating from the horizon towards the spectator – reflected by water, absorbed by stone, penetrating the outer branches of the great oaks which throw shadows into the foreground, and unifying the whole composition. He generally avoided the blaze of noonday with its dramatic contrasts of sunshine and shade, preferring the more evenly diffused glow of morning and early evening. Nothing more closely links him with his contemporaries than this preoccupation with light, connecting him with artists as diverse in every other way as Caravaggio, Bernini, Rembrandt, Vermeer and Velázquez.

VELÁZQUEZ

Diego de Velázquez (1599–1660) was among the many artists who visited Rome in the mid-seventeenth century – he was there in 1630 and again in 1650–1 – drawn, like most of the others, by the ruins of antiquity rather than by contemporary Roman art and architecture. He began in a style of solid, almost sculpturesque realism influenced, if only indirectly, by Caravaggio, whose work was then beginning to reach Spain. Spaniards responded instinctively to such straightforward realism. Miguel de Cervantes (1547–1616) in the prologue to *Don Quixote* (1605) significantly used a pictorial metaphor for the 'plain and simple' style of writing he strove for, and Velázquez's almost exact contemporary, Francisco de Zurbarán (1598–1664), began in the same way. Zurbarán's pictures of praying monks – painted mainly for monasteries in South America as well as Spain – combine to a unique degree down-to-earth actuality with the rapt intensity of Counter-Reformation mysticism (**13,28**). The subsequent development of the art of Velázquez was, however, quite different.

In 1623 Velázquez entered the service of the young king Philip IV (1621–65), who took a strong personal liking to him and almost monopolized his production for the rest of his life. The royal collection opened Velázquez's eyes to the splendour of Venetian art, especially Titian, whose great series of *poesie* adorned the palace in Madrid. They confirmed Velázquez in his natural predilection for the painterly – and his indifference to Raphael and the more linear tradition. Eventually he was to go beyond even Titian's subtle handling with broken and fluid brushstrokes, sometimes with such thinly applied paint that the texture of the canvas shows through.

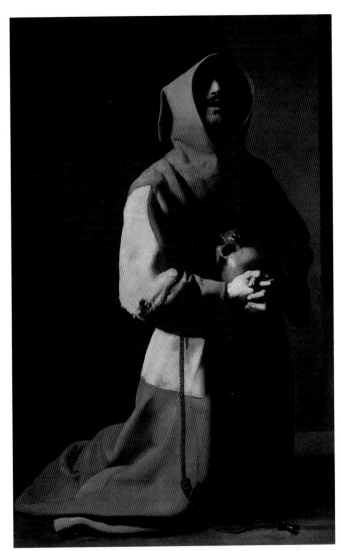

13,28 Francisco de Zurbarán, *St Francis in Meditation*, c. 1639. Canvas, 60 × 39ins (152 × 99cm). National Gallery, London.

The picture originally called 'The Family of Philip IV', better known as *Las Meninas* (The Maids of Honour), is Velázquez's supreme achievement, a highly self-conscious, calculated demonstration of what painting could achieve and perhaps the most searching comment ever made on the possibilities of the easel painting (**13,29**). Already before the end of the seventeenth century an Italian artist called it 'the theology of painting' and it is indeed essentially a painting about painting. The central figure is the five-year-old Infanta Margarita, daughter of Philip IV and his second wife, who are reflected in the looking-glass on the far wall. She is attended by two maids of honour, from whom the picture takes its modern title. Two court dwarfs stand behind the large sleepy dog, a lady-in-waiting and a male official are engaged in conversation and a member of the queen's staff can be seen through the doorway at the end of the room. Velázquez himself, palette and brushes in hand, stands by a gigantic canvas. All the figures are members of the royal household including the painter, who had risen to the high rank

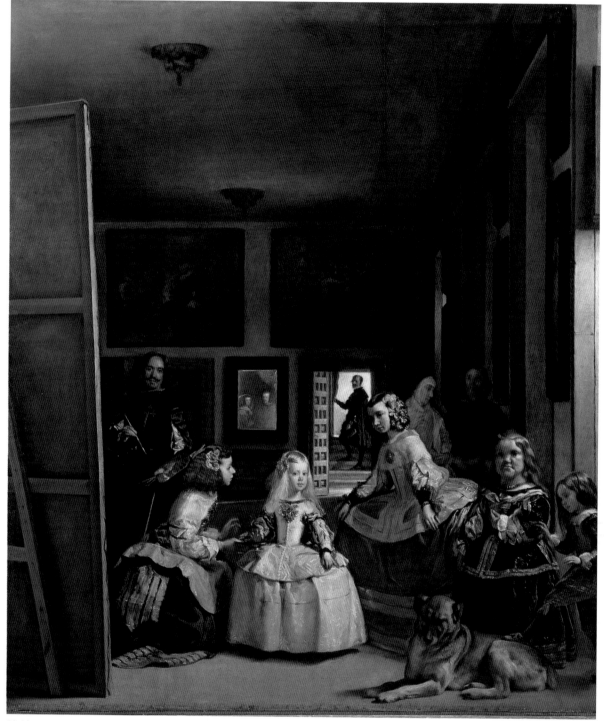

13,29 Velázquez, *Las Meninas*, 1656. Canvas, 10ft 7ins × 9ft ½in (3.23 × 2.76m). Prado, Madrid.

of chamberlain. There were no precedents for such a picture, recording an apparently casual incident of no significance in the life of the court and painted on a scale hitherto reserved for full-length formal portraits and historical subjects. But behind what appears to be no more than a moment captured in the mirror of art there are several layers of meaning.

Las Meninas is, first of all, a demonstration of the painter's unique power to represent life as it takes place before our eyes and thus to arrest time, to stop the clock for ever at a certain moment. The apparently quite haphazard disposition of the figures and the artist's neutral,

uninvolved attitude towards them are such that the effect of the painting has often been likened to that of a snapshot. In fact, of course, so convincing an illusion of reality can be created only by great and concealed artifice. Similarly, the completely dispassionate way in which the grotesque ugliness of the female dwarf is recorded makes us believe in the exquisite beauty of the infanta and her attendants. The naturalism of these figures is further set off by the contrast with the dim reflections in the looking-glass and the dimmer pictures on the wall above it. And the presence in the painting of the painter himself recalls the ingenious play with levels of reality in those passages

SOURCES AND DOCUMENTS

PACHECO ON ART IN THE SERVICE OF RELIGION

The painter Francisco Pacheco (1564–1654) was the most important Spanish writer on art in the seventeenth century. Through his uncle, a canon of the cathedral of Seville, he knew an erudite circle of poets, humanist scholars and theologians and numbered among his friends El Greco and his son-in-law Velázquez. An inspector of art for the Inquisition of Seville, he faithfully followed the teachings of the Council of Trent (1563) and his *The Art of Painting, Its Antiquity and Greatness* (Seville 1649) is notable for the inquisitorial spirit with which he expounded his conception of the role of painting in the service of Catholicism.

The principal aim of a painter as a Christian artist should be, he wrote, 'to achieve a state of grace through the study and practice of this profession'. Thus, he went on,

. . . we can say that painting, which before had imitation as its sole aim: now, as an act of virtue, takes on new and rich trappings; and, in addition, it elevates itself to a supreme end – the contemplation of eternal glory. And as it keeps men from vice so it leads them to the true devotion of God our Lord.

It would be hard to overstate the good that holy images do: they perfect our understanding, move our will, refresh our memory of divine things. They heighten our spirits . . . and show to our eyes and hearts the heroic and magnanimous acts of patience, of justice, chastity, meekness, charity and contempt for worldly things in such a way that they instantly cause us to seek virtue and to shun vice, and thus put us on the roads that lead to blessedness.

Besides what has been said, there is another very important aspect of Christian painting, which concerns the goal of the Catholic painter, who, in the guise of a preacher, endeavors to persuade the people and to bring them, by means of his painting, to embrace religion.

This goal of persuading people will be achieved differently according to circumstances, just as in the case of the orator who, having as his basic desire to convince his audience, will nevertheless argue now for war, now for peace, now to punish or forgive or reward, and so on. Thus the painter may have several ends in mind, depending on the diversity of things he is called upon to depict. But I say that the principal goal of Christian images will always be to persuade men to be pious and to lead them to God . . . even though other specific goals may also be involved, such as leading men to penitence, to suffering with pleasure, charity, contempt of the world, or to other virtues, which are all ways of uniting men with God, which is indeed the highest end that the painting of sacred images can aspire to . . . .

If it seems that I have departed from my intention in order to deal with the question of holy images, I will insist that if they are not the sole aim of painting, they are, nevertheless, the most illustrious and majestic part of it, the part which gives it greatest glory and splendor, because they are employed [to show] the holy stories and divine mysteries that teach the faith, the works of Christ and His Most Holy Mother, the lives and deaths of the holy martyrs, confessors and virgins, and all else that pertains to this. And because it imposes strict obligations of truth, naturalness, and decorum, wherein so few achieve success even though they be great painters, it is the most difficult part of this noble art.

(Tr. J. Brown)

in *Don Quixote* where the Don and Sancho Panza refer to the book in which they appear and to its author. Yet there is no trace at all of the contrived, of the slick optical trickery of *trompe l'oeil* painting, in this greatest of all visual illusions. Velázquez's handling of paint was exceptionally free, and as one approaches *Las Meninas* there is a point at which the figures suddenly dissolve into smears and blobs of pigment. The long-handled brushes he used enabled him to stand back from the canvas and judge the total effect – an enclosed space naturally illuminated from the windows on the right wall, the door and, most important of all, the area in front of the picture plane, that is to say that part of the room in which the king and queen notionally stand. These three sources of light eliminate harsh and stagey shadows. Moreover, the rectangular pictorial space provides a framework within which the figures seem to have come together accidentally, without being 'composed' at all. They are unified by their rela-

tionship not to one another but to the spectator standing in the position apparently occupied by the king and queen, whose reflections appear in the looking-glass. In this way the spectator becomes part of the whole, being drawn into the picture just as the worshipper is involved in such a very different work of art of the same years as Bernini's chapel in S Maria della Vittoria in Rome (13,16).

A secondary theme of *Las Meninas* is that of painting as a liberal art and, by extension, that of the status of the artist. The latter was very much on Velázquez's mind when painting the picture, for he was just then seeking admission to one of the orders of military knighthood which would have raised him to noble rank. Their ancient statutes, however, excluded all 'manual' workers as well as those of Moorish and Jewish ancestry and thus the question as to whether painting was a liberal or merely a mechanical art was crucial. The question had been hotly disputed in Spain for some time. Liberal status carried substantial practical advantages, such as exemption from taxes and military service. There were many, including the famous dramatist Lope de Vega (1562–1635), who supported the painters' claim and *Las Meninas* can be interpreted as the artist's contribution to the debate. The two paintings on the far wall of the room, for instance, are copies after works by the ennobled Rubens illustrating divine participation in the arts. Moreover, Velázquez portrayed himself as a court official wearing his badge of office, the keys, in his belt. In fact, he was admitted two years later to the proudest of all the Spanish noble orders, that of S Iago (St James), whose cross was later, at the king's behest, painted on his breast.

DUTCH PAINTING

The importance of the Dutch republic in the intellectual life of seventeenth-century Europe can hardly be exaggerated. It was the one country where there was freedom of speculation, the one country where Descartes from France and Spinoza, the heretical Jew from Portugal, could write and publish their revolutionary philosophical works. Although the revolt in the Spanish Netherlands had begun with the resistance of trading cities to Philip II's policy of centralizing the government of his empire, which threatened to deprive them of their ancient privileges, it soon became a struggle for religious as well as civic liberty. For the Spanish ideal of 'one king, one law, one faith' had led to the remorseless persecution of Protestants, thousands of whom took refuge in the seven United Provinces (usually, if inaccurately, called Holland after the richest of them), which, as already mentioned, formally renounced allegiance to Philip II in 1581 and were given tacit recognition of independence in 1609. Although attempts were made to impose Calvinism as the established faith, other Protestant sects were tolerated, asylum was given to Jews who had fled from persecution in Spain and Portugal, an official ban on Catholics was liberally interpreted and free-thinking was unchecked.

The Dutch republic was unique in other respects, a federation surrounded by unitary states, far more democratic than other nominal republics (Venice, for instance), defensive rather than aggressive in foreign policy, with an economy based not on agriculture but on commerce. Aristocracy went out with the Spaniards; the powers of the princes of Orange, who held the title of stadtholder (governor) for most of the century, were severely restricted. Bankers, merchants, shippers and manufacturers constituted the upper class and under their patronage secular painting flourished as never before and as nowhere else. 'As for the art of painting and the affection of the people to pictures, I think that none go beyond them', wrote an English visitor to Amsterdam in 1640:

> . . . *all in general striving to adorn their houses, especially the outer or street rooms, with costly pieces – butchers and bakers not much inferior in their shops, which are fairly set forth, yea many times blacksmiths, cobblers, etc. will have some picture or other in their forge and in their stalls. Such is the general notion, inclination and delight that these country natives have to paintings.*

> (*The Travels of Peter Munday in Europe and Asia: 1608–1667*, spelling modernized)

It was, of course, exclusively easel paintings that were being bought. And by their development of all the various *genres* – landscapes, seascapes, portraits, low-life scenes, still life, etc. – the Dutch brought easel painting to its highest pitch. It could almost be claimed that European art found its most distinctive form in Dutch seventeenth-century painting. There was little or no demand for altarpieces or other large-scale devotional paintings, or for grandiose architecture or sculpture.

HALS

Frans Hals (c. 1581/5–1666), generally regarded as the founder of the Dutch school of painting, specialized in portraits – usually of fellow citizens of Haarlem, singly or in groups – and in portrait-like pictures of figures from contemporary life. In the latter, which were primarily studies of expression and character, he was unrestricted by his sitters and free to work out his individual manner of painting. The picture known as *The Merry Drinker* (**13,30**) was probably conceived as an allegory of the sense of taste or of drinking, perhaps also with political overtones (a medal of Prince Maurice of Orange associates the drinker with the anti-burgher faction, which came near to converting the young republic into a monarchy). But whatever implications may have been intended, they are completely swallowed up by the immediacy of this image of forceful physical reality. With bibulously flushed face, eyes twinkling, mouth slightly open as if about to speak, one hand impetuously raised, the other clutching a glass of wine, the man seems surprised by the spectator's appearance before him. The impression of instantaneous life is created by the apparent spontaneity of the brushwork, flicks of dark paint for beard and mustaches, smears of white for reflections on the glass and the sweaty forehead, dark slashing strokes for the creases in the sleeve and a jagged outline suggesting sudden movement. Much of the animating sparkle comes from the highlights added as final touches, 'putting in his handwriting', Hals is reported to have said – and the phrase is significant. In the competitive Dutch art world a premium was set on individuality and also on novelty, with the result that painters' reputations swiftly rose and declined. Hals, whose broadly painted works caught so brilliantly the boisterous optimism of the first decades of the Dutch republic, fell out of favour in the 1640s, when smoother styles, influenced by van Dyck, were introduced to portray newly enriched citizens with their recently acquired aristocratic manners. Often in debt, probably for want of work, Hals continued to receive commissions for portraits but, almost in defiance of current trends, continued to handle his brush as freely as ever and adopted an increasingly sombre palette. His arresting group portrait

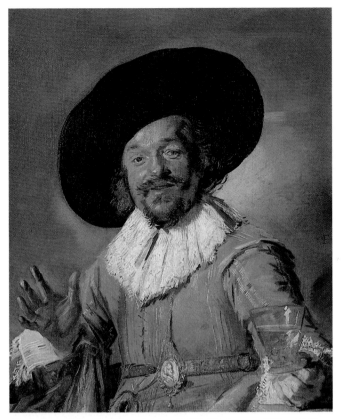

13,30 Frans Hals, *The Merry Drinker*, 1628–30. Canvas, 31⅞ × 26⅛ins (81 × 66.5cm). Rijksmuseum, Amsterdam.

of the female governors of the poor-house for old men in Haarlem of about 1664 is painted in puritanical whites, grays and deep, glowing blacks (**13,31**). The strong characterization of the five heads, differing from one another in expression as much as in feature, carries total conviction. A maid-servant standing on the right and the youngest of the women on the left look towards the three simply but obviously well-dressed governors in the centre who stare out of the canvas with shrewd, world-weary candour as if assessing whether a candidate they are interviewing for admission is truly deserving. Yet they too bear with patience the poignancy of lonely old age. As Hals was then over 80 and had been at times almost destitute – though he had recently been given a small pension by the city of Haarlem – it is tempting to see this picture as his long pondered and deeply felt comment on their and his own human predicament in a small, provincial Dutch town. It has even given rise to the myth that he was, himself, an inmate of the poor-house. However, he seems in fact to have been adequately paid for this picture and a companion portrait group of the male governors – adequately, that is to say, for commissions given by a poor-house. Many other Dutch artists similarly suffered the vicissitudes of fortune, most notoriously Rembrandt, who differed from Hals in almost every other respect.

13,31 Frans Hals, *Regentesses of the Old Men's Home*, c. 1664. Canvas, 5ft 7⅛ins × 8ft 2⅓ins (1.71 × 2.5m). Frans Hals Museum, Haarlem.

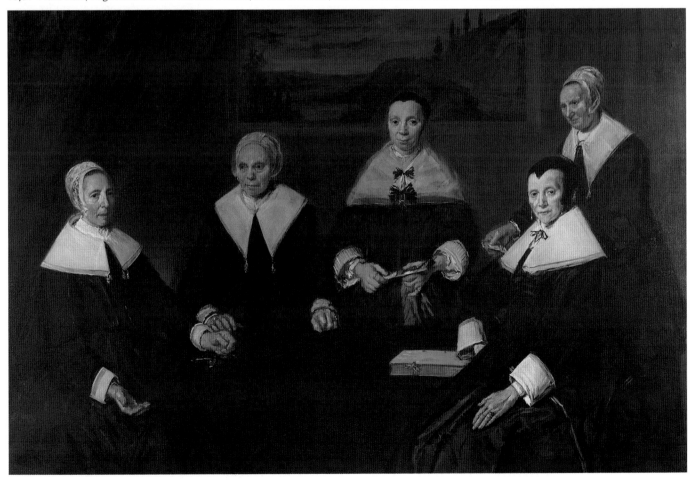

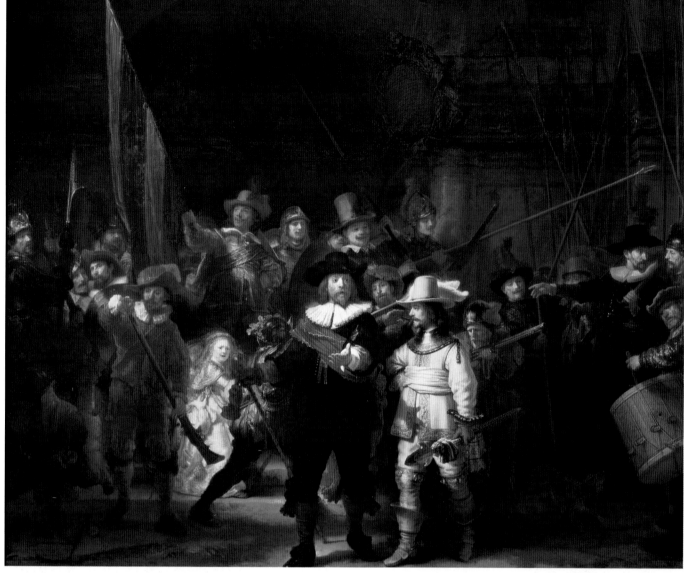

13,32 Rembrandt, *The Night Watch* (*The Company of Captain Frans Banning Cocq*), 1642. Canvas, 12ft 2ins × 14ft 7ins (3.7 × 4.45m). Rijksmuseum, Amsterdam.

REMBRANDT

Rembrandt Harmensz van Rijn (1609–69) began with small, very smoothly painted Biblical scenes, in which spiralling compositions learned from Rubens were painted with the strong *chiaroscuro* of the Dutch followers of Caravaggio. Throughout his life Rembrandt was to be unusually responsive to the work of other artists, notably Italians of the Renaissance and even, very exceptionally at this date, non-European artists – he owned and copied Mughal miniatures. But every influence was completely assimilated in his work, which reflects an uninterrupted course of development throughout his life, both artistic and spiritual. After 1631/2, when he moved from his native Leiden to more prosperous Amsterdam, the main commercial centre of the Dutch republic, he was soon recognized as the leading painter of the day, especially for portraits. The work traditionally called *The Night Watch* (**13,32**) – though it is neither a night scene nor does it depict soldiers mounting a watch – was commissioned as a group portrait

of a militia company and finished in 1642. By then Dutch militia companies had become little more than male drinking and dining clubs. Frans Hals portrayed those of Haarlem seated around banqueting tables. But Rembrandt devised a more dramatic solution to the problem of integrating numerous portraits into a pictorial composition by showing the company issuing from its headquarters for a ceremonial parade, perhaps that on the occasion of Marie de Médici's official reception in Amsterdam in 1638. This enabled him to present an insignificant incident as a grand historical spectacle on a huge scale – the figures are life-size and the canvas was originally larger (it was cut down on all sides when it was removed to the Town Hall in 1715, with a serious loss on the left destroying the symmetry of the background architecture).

The whole vast canvas throbs with bustling activity: a drum beats, a dog barks, banners and pikes are raised, excited children run between the militiamen. Rembrandt pulled out every stop to create a resonantly thrilling atmosphere with rich contrasts of light and shade, brilliant and drab color, a great variety of poses, gestures and facial expressions in opposed movements across and out of the picture plane, in a complex spatial design which leads the eye on a zigzag backwards and forwards. The composition is focused on the captain dressed in black with an orange-red sash and his lieutenant in lemon-yellow, colors which shimmer in other parts of the canvas. Frans Banning Cocq,

the captain, was a wealthy merchant and the other militia-men, each of whom paid a subscription for the picture scaled according to the prominence he was given in it, probably came from the upper ranks of Amsterdam society. Militia companies kept alive memories of the heroic days of struggle against authoritarian Spain and some of the older men in the picture may well have been veterans. But it was, above all, the triumph of the Dutch republic with its loose (if by no means egalitarian) social structure and exaltation of private enterprise that was being celebrated. Rembrandt spared no pains to create as convincing an illusion of actuality as possible in this image of self-possessed and somewhat self-satisfied burghers walking out of the picture to meet us on their own terms.

The Night Watch was always regarded as Rembrandt's outstanding achievement. Subsequently, his reputation and prosperity declined for reasons quite unconnected with it. As a result of being less in demand as a portrait painter, he later came to depend for sitters on members of his own circle – and himself. No earlier artist had ever portrayed himself so frequently. He began in the 1620s and went on throughout his life, leaving some hundred or more self-portraits in paintings and etchings which con-stitute a unique pictorial autobiography, though this is unlikely to have been his intention. Most were probably made as studies of character and expression and may well have been bought as such by collectors unaware of whom they represented. He takes on a variety of roles, as rebel-lious youth, bourgeois citizen, armed knight, eccentric in flamboyant Oriental costume, jovial reveller, saint and sage. His rough and powerful features, broad face and bulbous nose, appear in several pictures of himself as a painter. In one, dating from the last sad years after his bankruptcy in 1656, he is white-haired, deeply thought-ful, as if rising indomitably above a sea of troubles (**13,33**). It is so completely dispassionate, so sublimely impartial, that Rembrandt might almost seem to have shared with one of Descartes's followers, Arnold Geulincx (1624–69),

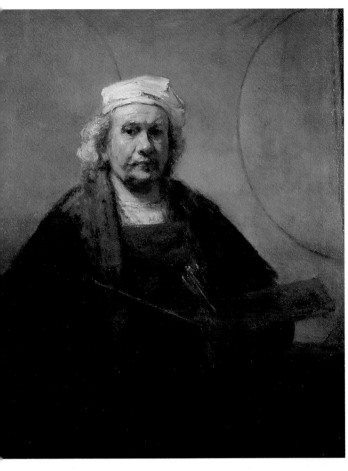

13,33 Rembrandt, *Self-Portrait*, c. 1660. Canvas, 45 × 38ins (114.3 × 96.5cm). The Iveagh Bequest, Kenwood, London.

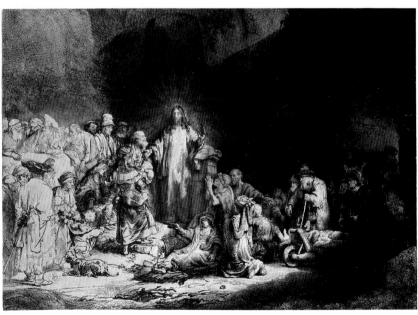

13,34 Rembrandt, *Christ Healing the Sick* (the 'hundred-guilder print'), c. 1648–50. Etching, 11 × 15½ins (28 × 39.3cm). British Museum, London.

Rembrandt's 'Hundred-guilder Print'

The Development of Graphic Processes

Among the various graphic processes used in Europe from the fifteenth century onwards (see p. 461), those of etching and drypoint engraving were exceptional. As developed by Rembrandt, among others, they enable an artist to etch or engrave a design on a copper plate in successive stages. At each stage the design can be checked and modified, if need be radically. The advantage of this for the artist is very great. It not only facilitates corrections and revisions but permits the artist to continue evolving a composition almost indefinitely while working on the copper plate. No other media allow this to quite the same degree, and this aspect of the process is as important as, if not more important than, that of its reproductive possibilities. The development of mechanical reproduction, which was to have so great an effect and influence on all the visual arts, came very much later.

For an etching, the plate is first coated with a thin layer of wax through which the artist draws with a steel needle. It is then dipped into an acid bath for several minutes so that the acid can eat into (etch) the lines made by the needle. When the wax has been removed they will hold ink and the design can then be printed in reverse on a sheet of paper pressed on to the surface. Trial or proof prints can be made at every stage; similarly the process of drawing through the wax may be repeated, and some parts of the plate may be varnished so that unvarnished lines are more deeply etched. Alternatively, the artist may work directly on the plate without waxing it by scratching it in drypoint – that is, with a sharply pointed, sometimes diamond tipped tool – or by engraving it with a burin which makes deeper V-shaped incisions.

Different types and quality of line are made by these instruments. An etching needle, with which an artist can work as freely and as lightly or heavily as when drawing with a pen or pencil on paper, makes lines of even thickness. The drypoint instrument needs more hand-pressure and raises a burr of metal which holds ink and gives the line a soft, velvety richness. The engraver's burin is more difficult to handle and leaves a sharper, harder line. In the course of printing the various types of line are gradually weakened, but in varying degrees. Whereas several hundred prints of uniform quality can be made from an engraved plate, no more than 50 of excellent quality and perhaps some 200 of good quality can be made from an etched plate. Very many fewer can be made from a drypoint plate: usually no more than ten impressions. Later the burr begins to wear away. Worn or damaged plates were often reworked and each time this was done

a new edition (called a state) was issued. When executed by the original artist such reworking was usually confined to strengthening weak lines and making minor adjustments, generally only to details. Rembrandt's most popular prints were issued in as many as eight states, the last of which are often disfigured by clumsy work carried out by engravers who had obtained the plates after Rembrandt's death.

Rembrandt made use of all these processes. He began with pure etching in about 1625 but was soon to finish his plates with drypoint. In *Christ Healing the Sick* (13,34), the figures on the left are etched but in the course of intermittent work on the plate over several years he made increasing use of drypoint and the

13,35 Rembrandt van Rijn, *The Three Crosses*, State II, c. 1653. Drypoint and etching on vellum, 15⅛ × 17¾ins (38.4 × 45cm). The Metropolitan Museum of Art, New York (Gift of Felix M. Warburg and his family).

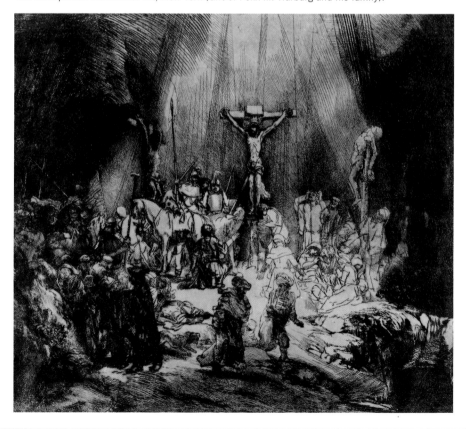

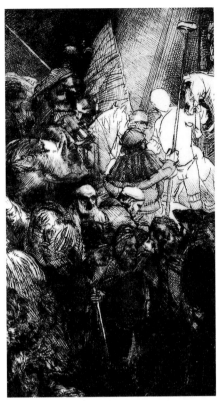

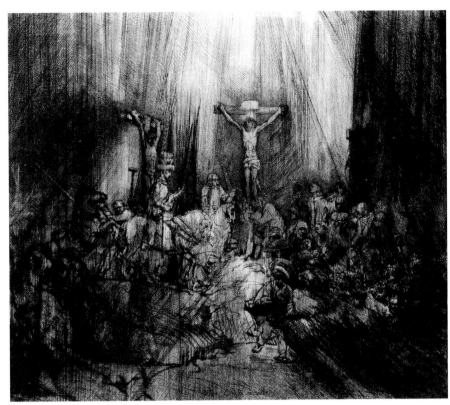

13.36 Rembrandt van Rijn, *The Three Crosses*, detail of State III, 1653. British Museum, London.

13,37 Rembrandt van Rijn, *The Three Crosses*, State IV, c. 1660. Drypoint and etching on paper, 15⅛ × 17¾ins (38.4 × 45cm). British Museum, London.

engraver's burin to enrich the shadows and create an effect of light, as if emanating from Christ. The resulting effect is painterly rather than draftsmanly. There are differences between not only the various states of this print but also, due to the gradual wearing-down of the drypoint burrs, the impressions of a single state. This accounts for the high price said to have been paid for a particularly fine example, the 'hundred guilders' by which it is known.

From about 1640–60 Rembrandt seems to have given more time to drawing and print-making than to painting. Some prints of these years were in drypoint with some use of the burin but no etched lines. He issued that of *The Three Crosses* in several states; the second was printed, unusually, on vellum rather than paper (**13,35**). Each time he made minor alterations to repair damage, readjust the balance of light and shade, eliminate some details and emphasize others (**13,36**). The fourth state of about 1660 is the product of a radical reworking. The scene is darkened, strong shafts of light from heaven are replaced by a mysterious flicker, fore-ground figures and many distracting details have been eliminated in order to attain an effect of almost archaic simplicity – the thief crucified on Christ's left has been completely obscured while a man on horseback has been inserted in front of the one on Christ's right (**13,37**). Figures previously shown communicating with one another are now isolated and either look towards Christ or gaze out of the composition. Attention is focused on Christ's death and what had started as a slightly diffuse illustration of the Gospel narrative has been transformed into a deeply pondered image of timeless significance.

The English writer John Evelyn referred in 1662 to the 'incomparable Reinbrand [sic] whose etchings and engravings are of a particular merit'. During his life-time and for more than a century afterwards, Rembrandt's international fame was based less on his paintings than on his prints. They were diffused all over Europe. Unlike the large, highly finished engravings (often reproductions of paintings) that were intended to be framed and hung, most of Rembrandt's prints were small, some quite tiny, and were usually kept in a portfolio. Demanding and rewarding microscopic examination, they appealed to a growing public of collectors who set a high premium on the individuality of the artist's touch and rarity – that of, for instance, trial proofs and early states, of which some impressions were unique. Such collectors were often artists, like Rembrandt himself, who built up a notable collection of prints and drawings. Drawings were similarly valued and collected for the insight they gave into the act of creation, their spontaneity often being lost in the finished paintings for which they were studies. Many of Rembrandt's prints have the same immediacy. Even in such a finished work as that of *Christ Healing the Sick* some of the figures are outlined without modelling; and one head was left as a blank oval in the first three states of *The Three Crosses* (13,35; 36). It may be significant that the public for prints included and was perhaps dominated by members of the newly emerging 'professional' classes who were beginning to play a notable role in artistic patronage at this date.

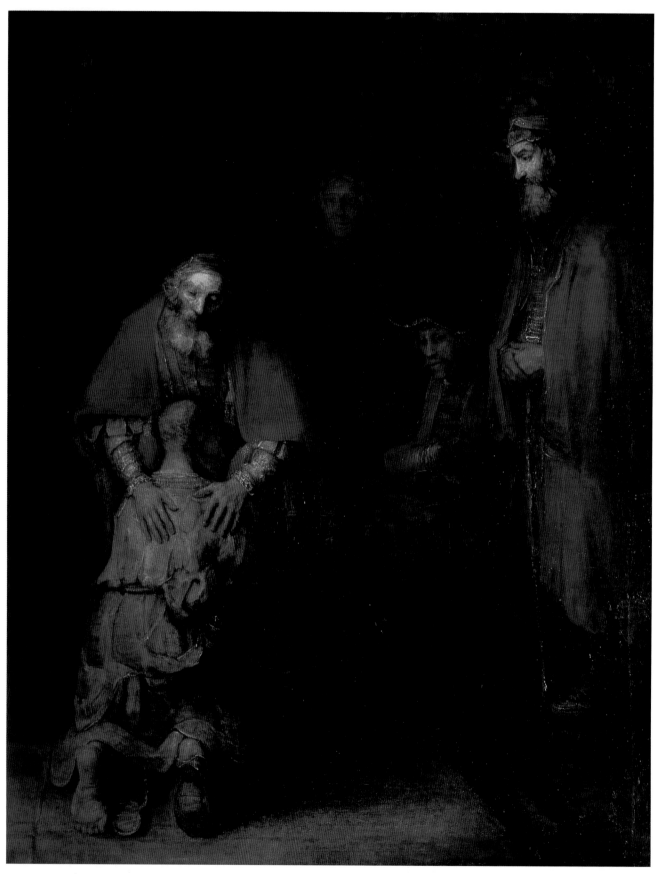

13,38 Rembrandt, *Return of the Prodigal Son*, c. 1669.
Canvas, 8ft 8½ins × 6ft 10ins (2.65 × 2.08m).
State Hermitage, St Petersburg.

then teaching at Leiden, the belief that the soul is neither stimulated by nor moves the body but simply observes it. Yet this burly, dishevelled figure conveys in its simple frontality and static pose an impression of inwardness and meditation. A great but unassuming dignity and natural nobility are inherent in its simple forms, emphasized by the two great arcs on the wall behind.

Despite his supreme gifts as a painter of portraits, Rembrandt seems to have thought of himself as, above all, a religious painter – not of devotional images, however, but interpretations of sacred subjects. He was a Calvinist by upbringing but associated in Amsterdam with members of the undogmatic, pacifist Mennonite sect, which accepted no authority apart from the Bible and strove to follow the teaching of the Sermon on the Mount. Their ideals permeate his *Christ Healing the Sick* (**13,34**), known as the 'hundred-guilder print' from the price allegedly paid for a fine impression in Rembrandt's life-time. Although he made full use of Baroque compositional devices to lead the eye on an undulating three-dimensional course, it is far removed in spirit from a Baroque altarpiece or such Counter-Reformation displays of religious fervour as Rubens's *Miracles of St Francis Xavier* (**13,5**). Both are complex figure compositions, but the miracle Rembrandt represents is one of spiritual not physical healing. No artist has ever depicted the poor and derelict, the outcasts of society, with greater sympathy than Rembrandt and here they fill the entire right-hand half of the print; the well-dressed and healthy are on the other side. All are equally and deeply pensive, communicating with something within themselves that leads beyond themselves. Sombreness, mystery and a dark, flickering spirituality pervade the whole scene.

The 250 or more etchings which spread Rembrandt's fame across Europe were public works of art, even though they are small in size and often appear to be unfinished – he is said to have declared a work to be completed 'when the master has achieved his intention by it'. On the other hand, the large religious pictures of his later years are intensely private, as personal in their interpretations of scripture as in expression and technique. In that of the *Return of the Prodigal Son* his power of creating a palpable physical presence with broad, thick brushwork is undiminished (**13,38**). The weary body of the kneeling son is sensed beneath the tattered garments, and the slight pressure of his father's aged hands on his shoulders is felt as well as seen. Resonant, sombre colors have an interior warmth which glows like embers in the scarlet and gold of the father's garments. But Rembrandt concentrates attention on the relationship between the main figures, flooded in mysterious, supernatural light, which catches also the face and folded hands of the unbendingly virtuous elder brother. No display of emotion, no gestures, no movements even, disturb an atmosphere of absolute calm. The essential meaning of the parable is embodied in this remarkably simple but deeply felt and pondered image of humble repentance and tender fatherly forgiveness, of homecoming as a metaphor for death and man's innermost contact with the divine.

LANDSCAPE

Very soon after the founding of the Dutch republic, that epoch-making event in seventeenth-century Europe (see p. 574), an altogether new way of seeing as well as depicting the undramatic, flat, watery and almost featureless local scene became evident in numerous pictures. The painters responsible for this sudden development owed something to Flemish art of the fifteenth and sixteenth centuries, especially the mastery of aerial perspective, but their landscapes are never settings for Biblical or mythological stories nor are they images of rural labour like Pieter Bruegel's *Months* (11,65; 66). They are without narrative content. They differ in other ways, too, from landscapes painted elsewhere in Europe in the seventeenth century. Rarely do they express pride in private possession, like Rubens's views of his own estate (13,8); still less do they attempt to recall a Classical past like paintings by Claude Lorraine (13,27).

A remarkably large number of seventeenth-century Dutch landscape paintings survive: some 1,200 by Jan van Goyen (1596–1656), for example, which would alone testify to their popularity. Rarely commissioned by individual patrons, they were usually painted 'on speculation' for a wide public, sold on the open market and bought, as inventories reveal, largely by town-dwelling merchants, members of the professional classes, tradesmen and the better-off artisans, rather than by the aristocracy who preferred Italianate views. Although they may have been regarded partly if not mainly as decorations for the home, they also had some otherworldly and patriotic significance. The Bible and nature were commonly believed to be the twin sources of divine understanding. 'God's goodness appears on every sand-dune's top', wrote the pious Calvinist Constantijn Huygens (1596–1687), an exact contemporary of van Goyen. The recurrence in paintings of the towers of medieval churches that had, of course, been converted to Protestant use, was a reminder of the Protestant origin and providential protection of the republic. Explicit symbolism, however, remained rare. And although many of these paintings were exquisitely refined in touch, perfectly balanced in tone and composition, the vast majority sold for very modest sums and were distinctly rough-and-ready feet-on-the-ground images of local scenery, apparently naturalistic and insistently, recognizably Dutch. They are symbolic in that they form part of an iconography of nationhood, part of a shared set of ideas and memories and feelings that bind a people together.

Above all, they are manifestly of contemporary scenes. The buildings, river craft, modern means of land transport, the dress worn by the figures incorporated in them all declare this. At first sight they might seem to be direct transcripts from nature; but although they are very often of identifiable tracts of land and could even, sometimes, seem to have affinities with map-making, they are in fact seldom topographically accurate. The aim was verisimilitude – what the Dutch painter and art theorist Samuel van Hoogstraten in 1678 called *keurlijke natuurlijkheid*, selective likeness to nature. Artists felt free to modify, adjust and rearrange what lay before their eyes.

Jan van Goyen was perhaps the most gifted as well as the most prolific of the artists who specialized in this type of landscape painting in the first half of the century. One of his largest and finest is a view of Rhenen, a town southeast of Utrecht on the northern bank of the Rhine and the frontier of the seven provinces that made a compact to resist Spanish tyranny in 1579 (**13,39**). This marked the beginning of the struggle for Dutch independence. Rhenen had a strong attraction for painters and was depicted at least 26 times by van Goyen as well as by several others. It is an inhabited landscape, indeed a work-a-day landscape, with shipping on the river, three men in a punt on a backwater in the foreground, foot-travellers on the right, a coach drawn by four horses and a man on horseback ambling forwards. All these elements and also the medieval walls of the town are, however, absorbed into a vision of peace and harmony painted in tans, browns and grayish greens, gradually lightening in tone

from the dark foreground strip to the low horizon that suggests an infinite expanse of land and water beneath the gently billowing clouds of the luminous sky. As in so many Dutch landscapes two-thirds of the canvas is given to sky, and here the neatly placed church tower marks the same proportional relationship horizontally.

An artist of the next generation, Jacob van Ruisdael (1628/9–82), adopted a less restricted palette and sometimes a dramatic manner, as in his painting of the windmill at Wijk bij Duurstede on the river Lek, a branch of the Rhine (**13,40**). He greatly exaggerated the size of the mill, a utilitarian modern building that dominates the small town (the massive fifteenth-century archbishop's castle is just visible to the left of the mill) and he eliminated both the town wall and an entrance called the Vrouwen Poort (Women's Gate) which he replaced with the figures of three women. Nevertheless he took care to show in the church tower on the far right a clock-face set up in about 1668, and he gave prominence to the palings that had to be constantly renewed to reinforce the river

13,39 Jan van Goyen, *View of Rhenen*, 1646. Canvas, 3ft 4ins × 4ft 5½ins (1.02 × 1.36m). The Corcoran Gallery of Art, Washington DC, William A. Clark Collection, 26.95.

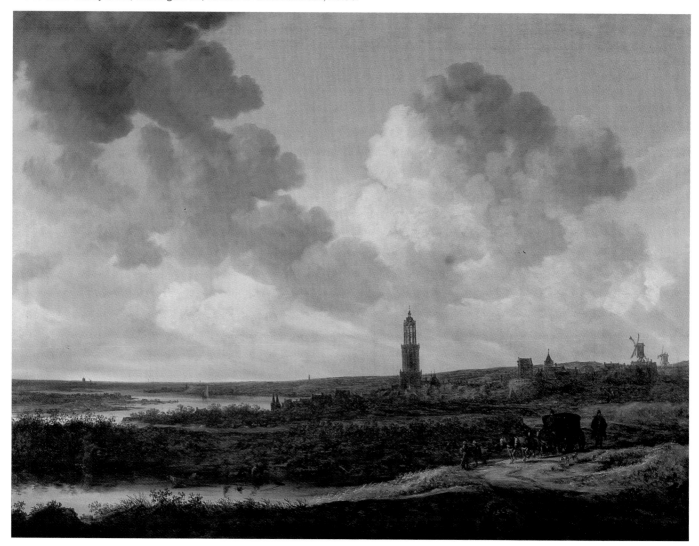

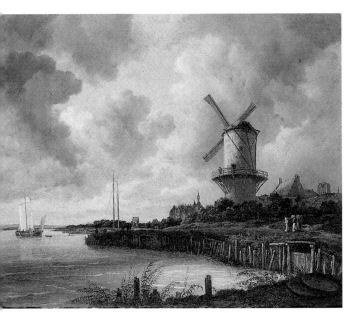

13,40 Jacob van Ruisdael, *Windmill at Wijk*, c. 1665.
Canvas, 32⅔ × 39¾ins (83 × 101cm). Rijksmuseum, Amsterdam.

career working in the austere manner of Jan van Goyen, he soon adopted a light tonality, colorful palette and smooth technique akin to that of the several Dutch artists who visited Italy, bathed their canvases in the warm air of the Mediterranean and were much patronized by the upper classes after their return. He was born in the flourishing port and trading city of Dordrecht, worked mainly for its patrician families, married a rich widow in 1658 and gave up painting soon afterwards. His canvases radiate an atmosphere of well-being. One of his several views of Dordrecht is lit by the glow of the setting sun reddening clouds and reflected in the still water (**13,42**). The fishing fleet is in port and the Dutch flag flutters on a tall-masted ocean-going vessel, a reminder of the prosperity of the Netherlands from trade and a rapidly growing overseas empire.

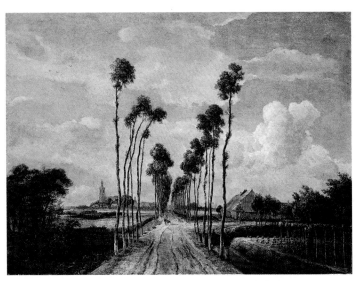

13,41 Meindert Hobbema, *The Avenue, Middelharnis*, 1689. Canvas, 3ft 4¾ins × 4ft 7½ins (1.04 × 1.41m). National Gallery, London.

bank and protect the land from floods. Windmills fascinated him, as his other paintings and many drawings of them reveal, and they were of course a characteristic feature of the Dutch countryside. However, they had also been given a bewildering range of symbolic meanings by Dutch writers. Their sails had been associated with Christ's cross, the grain they ground with the Eucharist, and so on. And they had also been illustrated as emblems of fortune, folly, virtue, etc. How far Ruisdael intended the mill at Wijk to convey any of these meanings it is impossible to say. He may simply have wished to suggest how it harnessed one force of nature just as the palings on the river bank protected the land from another. However, he gave this modern mill the heroic presence accorded to Ancient Roman buildings in Classical landscapes.

In *The Avenue, Middelharnis* of 1689 by Meindert Hobbema (1638–1709), who had studied under Jacob van Ruisdael, the combination of contemporaneity and timeless symbolism is more explicit (**13,41**). The avenue of pollarded alder trees is known to have been planted in 1665 and a beacon just visible beyond the barn was put up in 1682. Nowadays, after three centuries, the picture may seem to be just an unforgettable image of a tract of country which could in itself have had little interest and no pictorial possibilities, an instance of extreme simplicity, almost banality, being raised by small but subtle adjustments to the sublime. The device of placing the avenue of lanky trees dead centre so that it draws the eye along the muddy road, into the picture and up to the calmly luminous sky, cannot, however, have been without some spiritual intent, and indeed it would, to a Protestant mind, inevitably recall the straight and narrow path of virtue that leads to heaven.

The style of painting developed by Aelbert Cuyp (1620–91) was quite different. Although he began his

13,42 Aelbert Cuyp, *The Maas at Dordrecht*, 1650–90. Canvas, 38½ × 54ins (97.8 × 136.8cm). The Iveagh Bequest, Kenwood, London.

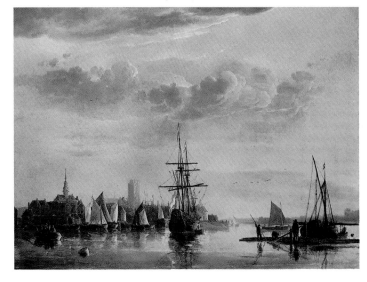

STILL LIFE AND GENRE

Rembrandt's art was exceptional in its range as well as its profundity. Nearly all other Dutch artists of the time specialized, some very narrowly. A painter of still life, for instance, would often restrict himself to a single class of objects. Willem Kalf (1619–93), one of the most gifted, depicted group after group of almost identical luxury objects such as silver flagons, Turkish rugs and Chinese porcelain bowls with oranges and lemons (expensive fruits in northern Europe at this date). His sense of composition was no less sure than his illusionistic skill, enabling him to create sumptuous, restful harmonies of shapes, colors, textures, reflections and transparencies (**13,43**). Even when contemporary scientific interests – notably botany and zoology – were engaged, sheer visual delight in the variety and abundance of nature usually remained uppermost in artists' minds, as is very evident in the flowerpieces of Rachel Ruysch (1664–1750), the first woman to achieve an international reputation as a major artist (**13,44**). The immediate predecessors of these different types of still life incorporated such symbols of mortality as a skull or a burnt-out candle as a *memento mori*, the reminder of death which is also an invitation to enjoy the pleasures of life. But the tradition of depicting household objects went back to the fifteenth century.

In the favours of the Dutch art-buying public, scenes of ordinary everyday indoor life vied with landscape and still life. Such *genre* pictures (as they came to be called in the

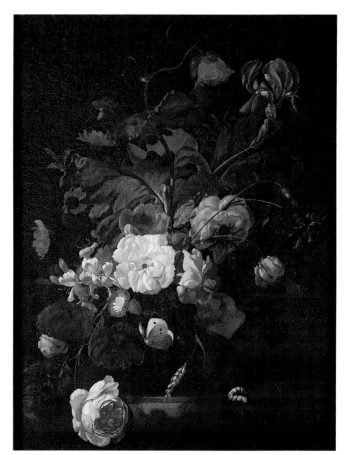

13,44 Rachel Ruysch, *Flowers in a Vase*, 1698. Canvas, 23 × 17½ins (58.5 × 44.5cm). Städelsches Institut, Frankfurt am Main.

13,45 Gerard ter Borch, *The Gallant Officer*, c. 1662–3. Canvas, 26⅔ × 21⅝ins (67 × 55cm). Louvre, Paris.

13,43 Willem Kalf, *Still Life*, c. 1650–90. Canvas, 28⅛ × 24⅜ins (71.5 × 62cm). Rijksmuseum, Amsterdam.

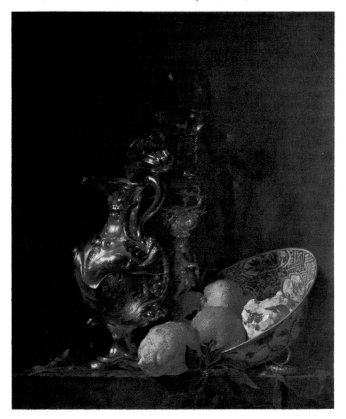

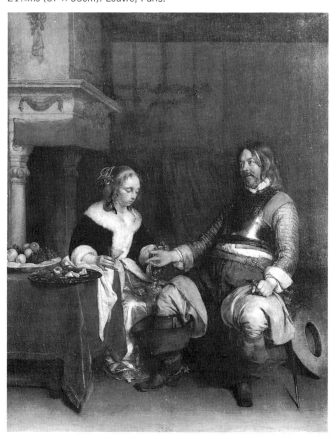

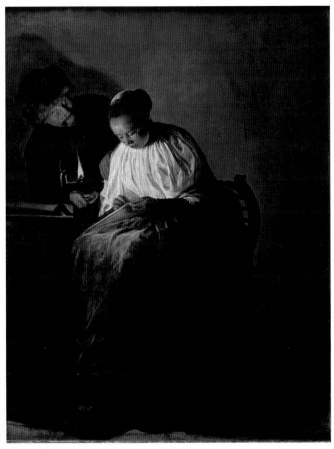

13,46 Judith Leyster, *The Proposition*, 1631. Panel, 11¹¹⁄₁₆ × 9½ins (30.9 × 24.2cm). The Mauritshuis, The Hague.

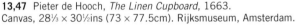

13,47 Pieter de Hooch, *The Linen Cupboard*, 1663. Canvas, 28⅓ × 30½ins (73 × 77.5cm). Rijksmuseum, Amsterdam.

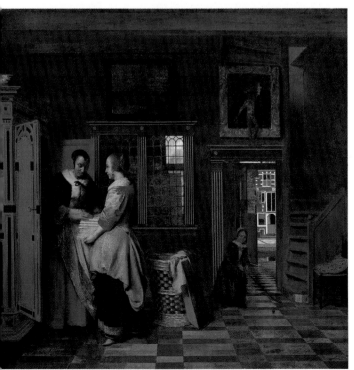

late eighteenth century), small in size, sharply detailed and representing a familiar world, were perfectly adapted for the living-rooms of middle-class houses and accurately mirrored the outlook of their owners. They have often been seen, in fact, as prime examples of an art called into being by its patrons, in this instance hard-headed merchants who distrusted the imagination and idealization. The realism of these paintings was not, however, an end in itself, for most if not all of them originally carried a moral message, sometimes expressed ambiguously as in *memento mori* still-life pictures. Many allude to sexual transgression, but so dispassionately that they offer the spectator a choice of luxuriating in its licence or ruminating on its iniquity, raising the problem of Christian free-will, which had not been allayed by the Calvinist doctrine of predestination. *The Gallant Officer*, a seduction scene by Gerard ter Borch (1617–81) is a good example (**13,45**), and it emphasizes how unusual, indeed unique, was such a painting as that by Judith Leyster (1609–60) in which a woman ignores her 'suitor' and his unwelcome attentions, refusing his proffered palm full of coins (**13,46**). *The Linen Cupboard* by Pieter de Hooch (1629–after 1688), on the other hand, provides a glimpse of a perfectly ordered household with well-polished floors, a maid handing laundered linen to her mistress and a child quietly playing (**13,47**). Above the door there is a statuette of Mercury, god of commerce, holding a money-bag. It is a rare image of domesticity invested with poetry by restrained warmth of color, delicate gradations of light, and the spatial complexity of a view through another room and a door to the sunlit house on the far side of a canal.

VERMEER

Jan Vermeer (1632–75) also specialized in moralizing *genre* pictures. He painted very little – no more than 35 surviving pictures can be attributed to him – and apparently supported his large family as an innkeeper and art dealer. But he stands out from his contemporaries on account of his extreme, almost tremulous sensitivity in the rendering of light and his unusual, predominantly blue and yellow color-schemes. The extraordinary luminosity of his paintings was achieved by a virtually new technique based partly on optical experiments but mainly on observation and an intuitive awareness of the subtleties of interpenetrating reflected colors. His method of capturing the sparkle of light in minute pearl-like dots beyond the contours of objects is unique. And the evenness of focus in his pictures makes them seem so limpid and objective that they have the effect of panels of clear glass – windows on to interiors in which all conflicts have been resolved. They have often been mistaken for straightforward renderings of daily life, and one was believed to represent the artist himself at work in his studio until it was discovered that his widow entitled it *De Schilderconst* (*The Art of Painting*). The painter is dressed in sixteenth-century Burgundian costume and the model is posed with the attributes of Clio, the Muse of

England. Dutch influence dominated the decorative arts and domestic architecture (brick with stone dressings). A more Italianate style had, however, been introduced early in the century for royal buildings by Inigo Jones (1573–1652) and it was to this tradition that the greatest English architect, Christopher Wren (1632–1723), turned when designing St Paul's Cathedral and 51 parish churches in London to replace those destroyed in the great fire of 1666.

By training, Wren was a mathematician and astronomer – professor of astronomy at Oxford, 1661–73 – with an eminently practical and experimental mind. For the cathedral, the first to be built for the Church of England, he was required 'to frame a Design handsome and noble, and suitable to all the ends of it, and to the Reputation of the City and the Nation' (**13,49; 50**). He approached the task in the empirical spirit of his fellow scientists in the Royal Society, who included Isaac Newton, gradually working out the design like a series of experiments as the building went up. Although the foundations were laid in 1675 and the chancel completed in 1697, he did not settle on the definitive form of the dome and west towers until after 1700. In the course of the work he studied engravings of Bramante's design for St Peter's in Rome and the Tempietto (11,18), also more recent Italian and French buildings. But his imagination or inventiveness, still more apparent in the ingenious variety of his parish church

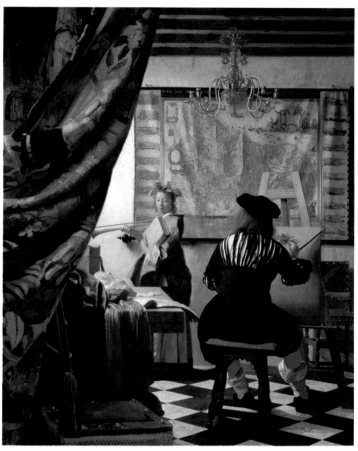

13,48 Jan Vermeer, *The Art of Painting*, c. 1670. Canvas, 3ft 11¼ins × 3ft 3⅜ins (1.2 × 1m). Kunsthistorisches Museum, Vienna.

History (**13,48**). The rich curtain recalls the swathes of drapery used in official portraits (13,10). On the wall there is a recently printed Dutch map of the Netherlands, such as were hung in many houses of the period and appear in other paintings by Vermeer. But the presumably allegorical meaning of *The Art of Painting* remains unknown. Was Vermeer perhaps making a claim for painting as a liberal art, as Velázquez did in *Las Meninas* (13,29)? (Dutch as well as Spanish artists were then seeking recognition for their status and trying to dissociate themselves from the craft guilds.) If so, the claim went unheeded. Soon afterwards French influence became dominant throughout the Netherlands. Vermeer's name was omitted from the academically inspired histories of Dutch art and his work was almost entirely forgotten until rediscovered in the mid-nineteenth century.

ENGLAND AND FRANCE

There were close cultural links between the Dutch republic and England, despite differing political alliances which twice led to war. English books were translated into Dutch but in the visual arts influence was mainly, if not entirely, in the opposite direction. The English bought Dutch pictures and several Dutch artists, following Rubens and van Dyck, worked and sometimes settled in

13,49 Christopher Wren, St Paul's Cathedral, London, 1675–1710.

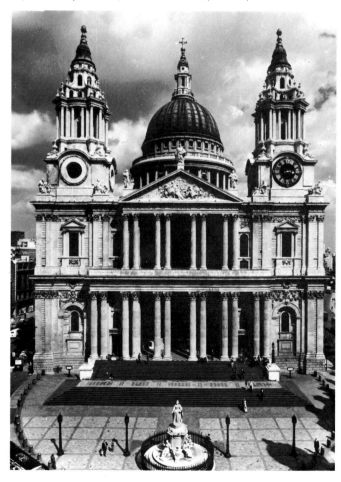

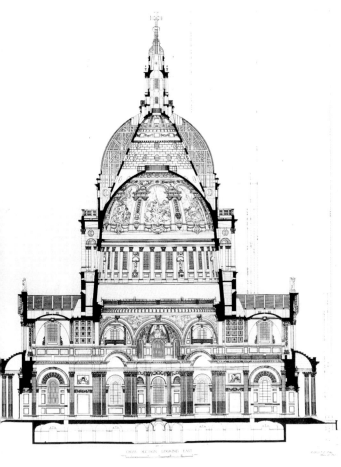

13,50 Cross-section of St Paul's Cathedral.

designs, was essentially practical, and St Paul's has none of the transcendent spirituality felt in even the most intellectual of Italian Baroque churches (13,23). Imposing but not overpowering, it strikes a middle path between Classical puritanism and Baroque exuberance. St Paul's and the city churches were, however, the products of exceptional circumstances. In England, as in the Dutch republic, the arts owed little to Church or state patronage in the late seventeenth century.

Different artistic aims and ideals were pursued in France in the second half of the century. Here the visual arts were enrolled, ordered and paraded in the service of autocracy. No artistic style is more directly expressive of the political ambitions and achievements of a monarch than that named after Louis XIV (1643–1715), nor more clearly marked by the peculiar circumstances of its conception. Before Louis XIV began his long personal rule in 1661, the main obstacles to the centralized organization of an absolutist state had already been removed. Under him the ancient feudal nobility were reduced to purely courtly functions, allowing recently ennobled families (the *noblesse de la robe*, as they were called) to become powerful and, eventually, to hold the principal ministries of state. It was among this section of the upper class that the greatest French painter of the time, Nicolas Poussin, found buyers for his late and most severely stoical works;

and it was for one of the richest of them, the finance minister Nicolas Fouquet, that the architect Louis Le Vau (1612–70) designed a luxurious château at Vaux-le-Vicomte, which prefigured Versailles. All the visual arts, including garden design, were exploited at Vaux-le-Vicomte in a style of Classical authority, logical clarity and imposing splendour well adapted to glorifying absolutism. Louis XIV was greatly impressed, so much so that he had Fouquet arrested for embezzlement and took over his architect, artists and craftsmen.

The organization of the arts in the service of the monarchy was one of the great administrative achievements of Jean-Baptiste Colbert (1619–83), a man of humble origin who became Louis XIV's adviser on political, economic, religious and artistic matters. He gathered the best tapestry weavers, furniture makers and other craftsmen into a single factory, the Gobelins, to produce furnishings for the royal palaces under the direction of Charles Lebrun (1619–90), a painter much influenced by Poussin. Colbert also reformed the Parisian Academy of painters, converting it almost into a part of the civil service and developing it as a teaching institution to provide the most thorough system of artistic training ever devised. Its inherent tendency to codify and regularize – as well as its authoritarian tone – is exemplified in Lebrun's lectures on how to represent the passions 'correctly', as well as by the practice of sending promising students to Rome to study and copy the most famous works of antique sculpture and Renaissance painting.

In a memorandum to the king, Colbert wrote: 'Your Majesty knows that apart from striking actions in warfare, nothing is so well able to show the greatness and spirit of princes than buildings; and all posterity will judge them by the measure of those superb habitations which they have built during their lives.' The first task confronting the king was the completion of the Louvre, the royal palace in Paris. In 1665 Bernini was summoned

13,51 Claude Perrault, Louis Le Vau and Charles Lebrun, east front of the Louvre, Paris, 1667–70.

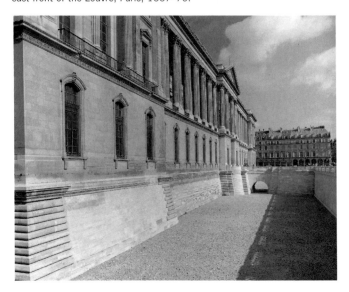

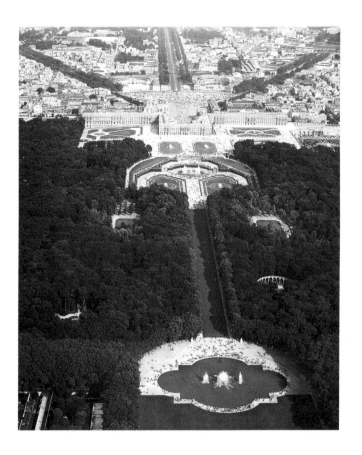

to advise. But his designs were rejected. The king selected one of two alternative designs presented by a committee consisting of Lebrun, Louis Le Vau and Claude Perrault (1613–88), a scientist and student of Classical architecture. With its correct Roman detailing, its clarity in the definition of masses and its dry, crisp elegance in articulation, the new east front is more strictly Classical than any earlier building in France (13,51). There was, however, no precedent for the coupled columns or the segment-headed windows which contribute so notably to its 'modernity'.

While the east front of the Louvre was being built Louis XIV decided to make his main residence outside Paris at Versailles. A relatively small château built by his father was enlarged first by Le Vau and then by Jules Hardouin-Mansart (1646–1708) into the largest and most grandiose palace of the world, set in a vast park laid out by André Le Nôtre (1613–1700) to extend its symmetry over the whole surrounding landscape (13,52). In addition to providing a complete environment for the unending ritual of court life, the palace of Versailles was a manifestation of Louis XIV's determination to shine as the greatest ruler

13,52 *Left* Louis Le Vau and Jules Hardouin-Mansart, Palace of Versailles, 1669–85. Aerial view.

13,53 Garden façade of the Palace of Versailles.

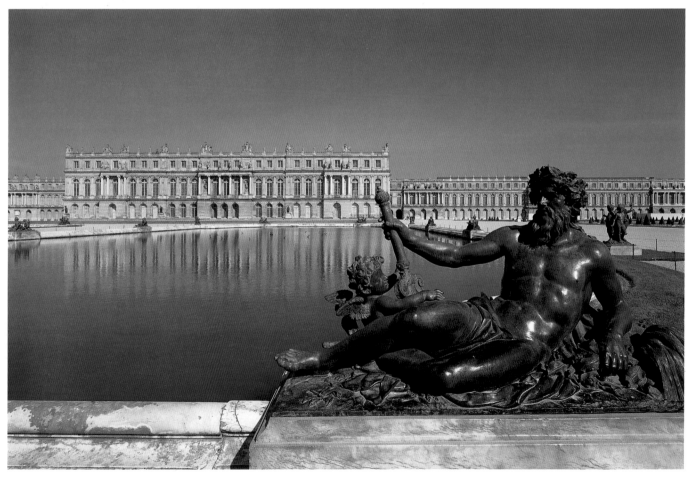

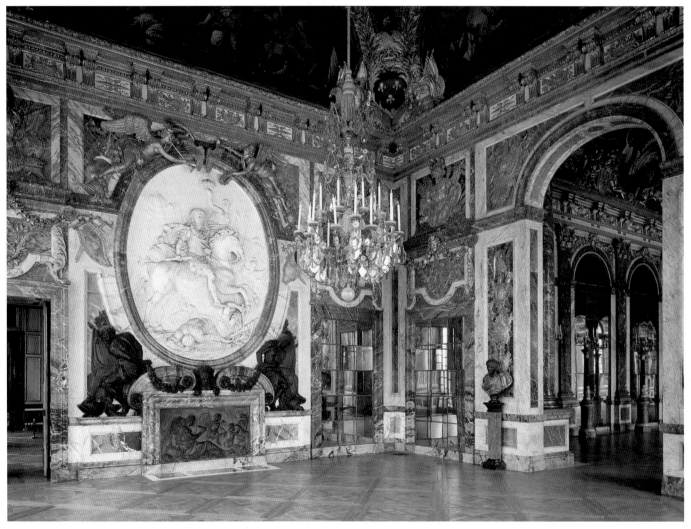

13,54 Antoine Coysevox, *Louis XIV on Horseback*, 1683–5. Stucco relief, over-life-size. Salon de la Guerre, Palace of Versailles.

in Europe. The work of several generations of designers, artists and craftsmen over nearly half a century, carried out piecemeal and not according to a single predetermined plan, the whole complex of buildings and gardens is, nevertheless, unusually consistent in conception (**13,53**). The king's personal approval was necessary for even minor decorative details – most of which alluded either directly or symbolically to himself.

A great series of state rooms was created after 1678, when the wars against Spain, the Dutch republic and the Holy Roman Empire came to an end with notable territorial advantages to France. On the ceiling of the Galerie des Glaces – the very long central gallery named after the tall mirrors lining the wall opposite large windows looking out on to a completely artificial man-made landscape as far as the eye can see – Lebrun translated the history of the wars into the pictorial language of Classical mythology with the king figuring in the guise of Apollo. In the Salon de la Guerre, which leads into it, a huge stucco relief of

the king, larger than life on horseback, by Antoine Coysevox (1640–1720), is set among panels of colored marbles and gilt bronze reliefs beneath a painted ceiling, again by Lebrun (**13,54**).

As Louis XIV intended, Versailles caught the attention of all Europe. It became the ideal for every royal household and even the sultan of Morocco competed with it at Meknes. Christopher Wren almost certainly had it in mind when enlarging Hampton Court Palace near London for Louis XIV's main antagonist, William of Orange, stadtholder of the Dutch republic and from 1688 king of England. In France, however, there was a reaction against its formality and towards the end of the century voices were raised against the dominant Classicism of the Academy. Admirers of Rubens contested the supremacy of Poussin and, for the first time, the taste of middle-class patrons who collected Dutch and Flemish *genre* paintings began to play a part in determining the course of French art.

CHAPTER FOURTEEN

ENLIGHTENMENT AND LIBERTY

Almost everything that distinguishes the modern Western world from earlier centuries – industrialized production, bureaucratized government, the new conceptions that science introduced into philosophy, the whole climate of thought and opinion – overlapped during the eighteenth century with the old political and social order, the *ancien régime*. It was the last period in which it was widely believed that 'kings are by God appointed', the first in which it could be claimed as 'self-evident' that (in the words of the American Declaration of Independence, 1776) 'all men are created equal, that they are endowed by their Creator with certain unalienable Rights, that among these are Life, Liberty and the Pursuit of Happiness'. The incompatibility of these claims with traditional systems of monarchic or oligarchic government was not shown up until the last decade of the century, when the French Revolution gave a new and explosive meaning to ideas of 'liberty, equality and fraternity'. Yet, the revolution with which the century ended was by no means inevitable or even foreseen. Enlightened despots of the *ancien régime* – notably Frederick the Great of Prussia (1740–86) and Joseph II of Austria (1780–90), even to some extent Louis XVI of France (1774–93) – strove, together with their efficient administrators, to promote material progress and enforce justice, toleration and humanitarianism, often overriding the ancient privileges of the nobility, the clergy and the city corporations.

Until the end of the century Christianity retained its hold, unquestioned by the mass of the population in Protestant as well as in Catholic countries. This is clearly reflected in the arts. Despite the development of operatic and chamber music, much of the most memorable music was religious in the period beginning with Johann Sebastian Bach (1685–1750) and Georg Friedrich Handel (1685–

The visual arts	Historical landmarks
1711–22 Pöppelmann, Zwinger (14,11)	**1714** George I king of England
	1715 Louis XIV dies: regency until 1723
c. 1717–18 Watteau, *The Dance* (14,2)	**1719** Defoe, *Robinson Crusoe*
	1720 National bankruptcy in France
1730 Restout, *The Death of St Scholastica* (14,1)	**1735** Linnaeus, *System of Nature*
1739 Chardin, *The Governess* (14,6)	**1738** First spinning machine patented in England
1743 Hogarth, *Marriage à la Mode II* (14,19)	**1740** Frederick II (the Great) of Prussia
1745–54 Zimmermann, the Wieskirche (14,13)	**1751–72** Diderot and d'Alembert, *Encyclopédie*
1752–3 Tiepolo, Würzburg ceiling (14,15)	**1754** First iron-rolling mill (England)
	1759 English take Quebec, opening way to annexation of Canada (1763)
1760–9 Adam, Syon House (14,22)	**1762** Rousseau, *Social Contract*
	1764 Winckelmann, *History of Art*
c. 1770 West, *Death of General Wolfe* (14,25)	**1771** First spinning mill (England)
1771–2 Fragonard, *The Meeting* (14,7)	**1773** Jesuits suppressed. Boston Tea Party
	1774 Louis XVI king of France
	1776 American Declaration of Independence. Gibbon, *Decline and Fall* Vol. I
1784–5 David, *The Oath of the Horatii* (14,29)	**1783** Peace of Versailles: USA recognized by European powers
1785–96 Houdon, *George Washington* (14,27)	**1787** Mozart, *Don Giovanni*
1787–93 Canova, *Cupid and Psyche* (14,28)	**1789** Fall of Bastille; Declaration of Rights of Man
1789 Houdon, *Thomas Jefferson* (14,26)	**1791** Paine, *Rights of Man*
	1792 Wollstonecraft, *Rights of Women*. First steam-powered loom (England)
1793 David, *The Dead Marat* (14,30)	**1793** Louis XVI executed
	1799 Bonaparte First Consul

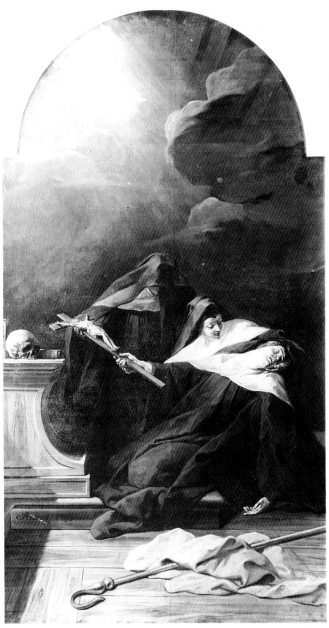

14,1 Jean Restout, *The Death of St Scholastica*, 1730. Canvas, 11ft 1¼ins × 6ft 2¾ins (3.38 × 1.9m). Musée des Beaux-Arts, Tours.

(**14,1**). But in every other way it is exceptional, both in the intensity of religious feeling conveyed and in the refinement and exquisite, almost tremulous, restraint of the artistic handling. Yet even in this deeply felt and moving image a religious experience tends to become a drama of 'sensibility', that most eighteenth-century of emotional states. There is hardly a suggestion of any miraculous or heavenly mitigation of the loneliness of death. But if secular works continued to account for only a part of the total production of French, German, Italian and Spanish painters and sculptors, it is the part that stands out in the perspective of history. Similarly, the thinkers of the Enlightenment who questioned Christian teaching were a tiny minority and very few of them rejected religion altogether. But the brilliance of their writing – and the force of their (often wishful) thinking – was such that the whole century is sometimes called 'the age of reason'.

The Enlightenment radiated out of the philosophical and scientific thought of the seventeenth century, especially that of Descartes (see p. 598), of John Locke (1632–1704), who propounded a philosophy based on empirical observation and common sense, and of Isaac Newton (1642–1727), who provided a rational explanation of the laws determining the structure and working of the universe. Despite many and profound differences, the leaders of the eighteenth-century Enlightenment shared a faith in the power of the human mind to solve every problem. They believed in human perfectibility and in the possibility of human omniscience. And in this optimistic belief all physical phenomena were studied and categorized and all aspects of human behaviour were scrutinized from a strictly rational viewpoint – political systems, social customs, religious practices. Everything that seemed to them worth knowing was ordered and encapsulated in the great French encyclopedia, which began to appear in 1751. It aimed to survey knowledge according to rational philosophical principles. *'Dare to know!* Have the courage to use your understanding; this is the motto of the Enlightenment', the German philosopher Immanuel Kant declared in 1784, although in his case it eventually led him to lay bare the inadequacies and fallacies of rationalism (see p. 643).

FRENCH ROCOCO ART

The delicate, sensual and often capricious art of the first half of the eighteenth century, especially in France, seems at first sight to be at odds with the rational thought of the Enlightenment. Indeed, most contemporary theorists criticized it from this point of view. Later, in the revolutionary era, it was dubbed Rococo – a frivolous confection of shells and shell-like forms – and dismissed as an attempt to satisfy the whims of a dissipated upper class. But if it lacked a closely reasoned theory, it was not without a rationale. Demands for freedom from academic restrictions and 'rules', for an appearance of spontaneity and for novelty were its motivating forces. Its genius lay in nuances, subtle juxtapositions of forms, gentle gradations and minglings of colors, the elusive dancing

1759) and ending with Wolfgang Amadeus Mozart (1756–91) and Joseph Haydn (1732–1809). In Catholic Europe there was no decline in the building and decoration of churches, monasteries and religious foundations, nor in the production of paintings and sculptures for them. Much of it, however, was uninspired and imitative of earlier models, especially in France, and the few notable exceptions usually reflect religious tendencies of the time no less exceptional among Catholics, such as the movement towards greater simplicity of external forms and increased concentration on personal devotion and piety. A painting by Jean Restout (1692–1768) of the death of St Scholastica, the founder of the Benedictine order of nuns, is in this sense typical in that the order had recently been a centre of controversy and conflict with the Vatican

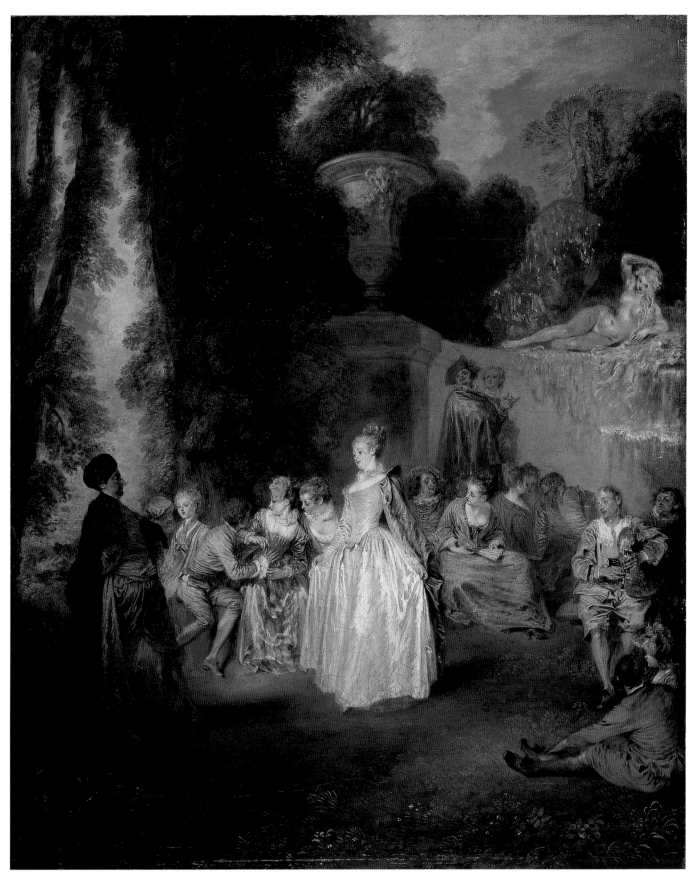

14,2 Antoine Watteau, *The Dance* (*Les fêtes vénitiennes*), c. 1717–18.
Oil on canvas, 21½ × 17¾ins (54.6 × 45cm). National Gallery of Scotland, Edinburgh.

rhythms of only slightly differentiated motifs. Classically inspired rules of pictorial compositions were light-heartedly infringed, the Vitruvian orders of architecture were abused or ignored. There was widespread recognition that – in the words of Alexander Pope's *Essay on Criticism* (1711) – 'some beauties yet no Precepts can declare', and that there:

> *Are nameless graces which no methods teach*
> *And which a master-hand alone can reach.*

Such qualities could be judged only by 'taste', which Voltaire (François Marie Arouet, 1694–1778), the leading spirit of the Enlightenment in France, defined as 'a quick discernment, a sudden perception, which, like the sensations of the palate, anticipates reflection; like the palate it relishes what is good with an exquisite and voluptuous sensibility, and rejects the contrary with loathing and disgust.' Without knowledge of the Classical rules, however, the man of taste could not savour the piquancy of deviations from them. Taste was an attribute of the educated class only.

The Rococo first developed in France, where Classicism had been made the guiding principle of a rigorous system of artistic instruction (see p. 611). In 1699 Louis XIV called for paintings more light-hearted and 'youthful' than those previously commissioned for Versailles, where work was still in progress. He also transferred his favours from artists who supported the official doctrine of the Academy to those who dissented from it. The quarrel between these two parties hinged on the relative importance of drawing and color, epitomized by Poussin and Rubens, from whom they took their names. *Poussinistes*, led by Charles Lebrun (director of the Academy), declared that drawing, which appealed to the intellect, was superior to color, which appealed only to the eye. *Rubénistes* argued that color was necessary for a truthful imitation of nature, which they held to be the prime aim of art. That color made an impression on the senses rather than on the intellect was for them an advantage. Philosophical support could be found in John Locke's influential *Essay Concerning Human Understanding* (1690), which claimed that all ideas derived ultimately from experience and that none was innate. The implications for aesthetics were soon realized, and in 1719 a leading French theorist, Jean-Baptiste Dubos (1670–1742), remarked that what was apprehended through the mind seemed pale and insipid in comparison with what was apprehended through the senses. Pictures affect people more deeply than poetry because they 'act upon us directly through the organ of sight; and the painter does not employ artificial signs to convey his effect . . . the pleasure we derive from art is a physical pleasure.'

WATTEAU, DE TROY AND THE ROCOCO INTERIOR

The greatest of early eighteenth-century painters, Antoine Watteau (1684–1721), came from outside the circle of artists employed by the court and was not of a theoretical turn of mind. He was born at Valenciennes, which had been part of the Spanish Netherlands until six years before, and his training was that of an artist-craftsman. His admiration for Rubens and the great sixteenth-century Venetian colorists seems to have been instinctive. He painted a fairly wide range of subjects: religious pictures, portraits, military scenes and mythological pieces. But his individual genius found scope especially in *fêtes galantes* – fanciful visions of well-dressed men and women enjoying themselves in the open air. In them his contemporaries could catch a reflection of their own ideals of civilized life (14,2). Pictures of this type were indebted to the early sixteenth-century Venetians, especially to the Giorgionesque *Concert* (11,43), which was then in the royal collection at Versailles, though they are almost insistently up-to-date in other ways. *The Dance* (later named *Les fêtes vénitiennes*) is set in a park of a type which had only recently been laid out, with much less constraint than hitherto in the treatment of plants and much more freedom in the design of stonework and statuary, striking a new balance, one might almost say creating a fusion, between the works of man and of nature. This balance between the artificial and the natural is equally apparent in the poses of Watteau's figures and, indeed, in the composition as a whole with its deceptive air of informality.

It may be questioned whether the picture is quite so simple and straightforward a celebration of the pleasures of this world as it seems. The man in fancy-dress Oriental costume on the left may be a portrait of the artist Nicolas Vleughels, the dancing young woman in the centre is perhaps an actress of the day and the bagpipe player on the right is probably Watteau himself, dressed in peasant costume. Fantasy and reality and the interplay between them are the painting's theme. There was a deep strain of irony in Watteau's character – 'he was born caustic', a contemporary remarked – and this gives his work its 'edge' and a sometimes haunting poignancy, a combination of sadness and sensuality. Few artists have more faithfully recorded the sheen of silk with such keen awareness that it is no more than a superficial evanescent effect of texture and light. The exquisite world he created in his *fêtes galantes* is largely a fantasy, but none the less poetically 'true'. That he had struck a penetrating chord is indicated by their vast progeny, not only in painting, but also in porcelain, lacquer, textiles, enamel, silver, even gold snuff-boxes. And his influence was still more pervasive than these might suggest: prints after his paintings and drawings proliferated all over Europe and inspired artists as diverse as Boucher, Gainsborough and Goya.

Another aspect of the early eighteenth-century French ideal of civilized life is recorded in *A Reading from Molière* (14,3) by Jean-François de Troy (1679–1752). It probably illustrates a scene from a novel or a play, but the characterization of each individual is so sharp and the details of decoration in the room are depicted with such precision that it has often been thought to be a portrait group. The figures are dressed in the height of fashion of the late 1720s (two of the ladies wear silks of a pattern

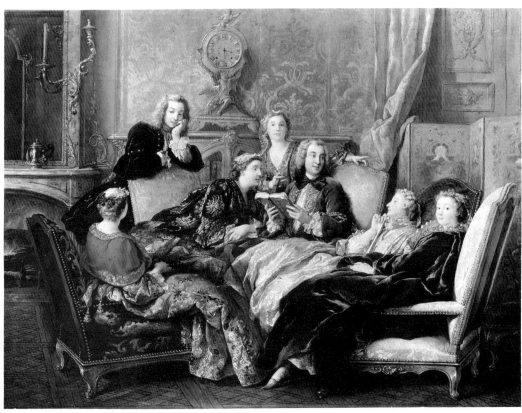

14,3 Jean-François de Troy, *A Reading from Molière*, c. 1728. Oil on canvas, 28½ × 35¾ins (72.4 × 90.8cm). Collection Marquess of Cholmondeley.

14,4 Gabriel-Germain Boffrand, the Princess's Salon, Hôtel de Soubise, Paris, 1737–40.

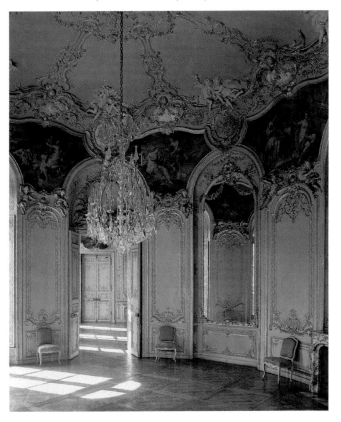

woven at Lyons in 1728), but they are perfectly at ease in their finery. Five of them are absorbed in one another, two others stare out of the canvas as if to include the spectator in their cultivated circle. The varying, glancing directions of their gaze, as much as the contrasting colors and textures, break down what might otherwise have been too formal and self-consciously composed a group. For the accent is on informality and modish contemporaneity. The only link with the past is the volume of Molière, the great comic moralist who had satirized with supreme verve the pomposities, absurdities and pretences of society in the early years of the reign of Louis XIV.

The room in which the reading takes place is flooded with light, with looking-glasses playing a part in its diffusion (that over the chimneypiece reflecting one on the opposite wall). Every detail of decoration is of calculated, informal elegance: the tendril curves of the ormolu candle-sconces and similar motifs on the walls, the clock with figures signifying the triumph of love over time, the screen painted with decorations after Watteau, the carving on the lower rail of the chairs with their delicately turned cabriole feet. But the room is designed as much for comfort as for elegance: a screen stands in front of the door, which would have been a commanding as well as a draughty feature in a formal room, the chairs are lower and more thickly upholstered than hitherto, inviting their occupants to recline indolently.

Most French buildings of this period have been altered (if only by refurnishing) and none provides as vivid an impression of their original atmosphere of sophisticated and cultivated ease as de Troy's painting. The finest surviving French interior is probably the Princess's Salon in the Hôtel de Soubise, Paris (14,4). It is on the upper floor of a pavilion (with a very reticent, almost plain, exterior typical of domestic architecture in France at the time) designed by Gabriel-Germain Boffrand (1667–1754) and completed in 1739–40. Even now this room seems to have been conjured up rather than constructed, so insubstantial are the walls, so effervescent the decorations, which hover above. The effect is due partly to the oval plan (very popular in France in these years), which creates a looser effect than the rectangle or circle, and partly to the manipulation of light, which floods into the room only just above floor level from tall arched windows reflected in corresponding looking-glasses. Boffrand provided the general design but the success of the decorative scheme is due to the team of artists and craftsmen who executed the various parts, interlocking with one another to create a total work of art. The carved and painted woodwork of the walls, the delicate stucco decorations on the ceiling, and white reliefs of cupids above the 'openings' (door, windows and looking-glasses) have no less importance than the inset paintings of the fable of Cupid and Psyche by Charles-Joseph Natoire (1700–77), a leading Parisian artist of the day but one who was prepared to adapt his compositions to the unusually shaped cartouches determined by the window arches and the undulating curves of the cornice. It is a fairly large room for a private house, even by the standards of the previous century, but so airy and light as to seem intimate in scale. For the Rococo not only introduced a taste for small rooms – such as boudoirs – but answered a demand for rooms adapted to their human purposes and to a human scale. Tall pilasters (see Glossary) and all other decorative elements which might dwarf the occupants were excluded.

BOUCHER, CHARDIN AND FRAGONARD

The Salon in the Hôtel de Soubise is one of the best examples of what was called in France at the time the *genre pittoresque* – a style which subordinated architectonic to 'pictorial' motifs. Its repertory of ornament was of shells, flowers, wayward tendrils, sprouting leaves and patterns of scrolls. Lightness, elegance, gaiety and, of course, novelty were the aims of the designers who created this decorative style, Nicolas Pineau (1684–1754) and Juste-Aurèle Meissonier (c. 1693–1750). But there is more to their curvilinear forms than a taste for whimsicality. Their organic character lends them a sensuality, a carnality almost, which becomes quite explicit in such a painting as *Hercules and Omphale* by François Boucher (1703–70), in which the gilded sofa with a cupid emerging out of its curved leg is so appropriate a piece of furniture for a scene of sensual rapture and abandon (14,5). The picture is somewhat exceptional for Boucher, who usually left more to the imagination. But all his work, even his religious painting, exults in the same voluptuous sensibility.

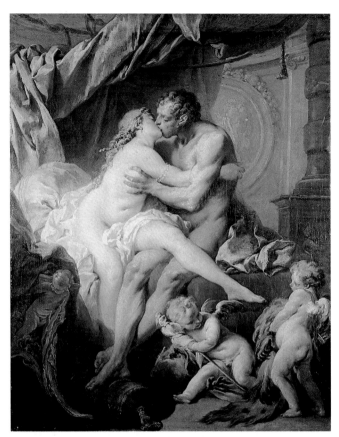

14,5 François Boucher, *Hercules and Omphale*, c. 1730. Oil on canvas, 35½ × 29⅛ins (90.2 × 74cm). Pushkin Museum, Moscow.

It seems a far cry from the paintings of Boucher to those of his contemporary Jean-Siméon Chardin (1699–1779). Boucher's scenes are often set in, and were probably intended for, the boudoir, his palette is light with an abundance of pearly flesh tints and a hint of cosmetics, his handling has an easy juicy fluency beneath a sparkling and highly finished surface. An air of perfumed and powdered artifice is pervasive. Chardin painted downstairs, often below stairs; his colors are subdued with the grays and browns of rough worsted to offset plain white linen; his paintings seem to have been built up slowly, methodically with thick blocks of pigment. Everything is simple and wholesome – not, as in Boucher, fancy and succulent. Yet both artists, if for totally different reasons, appealed to much the same patrons; both were, for instance, represented in the collections of Louis XV and his mistress Mme de Pompadour, the king of Sweden, the king of Prussia and Catherine the Great of Russia, not to mention numerous wealthy amateurs of art. *The Governess* (14,6) was bought by a rich Parisian banker, who later sold it to the prince of Lichtenstein.

Chardin's paintings may have been appreciated by the rich simply because they provided a piquant contrast to their pampered lives. In many there are moral overtones of a reassuringly upper-class kind – the governess, with her work-basket beside her, reproves her young charge, whose idleness is indicated by the battledore, shuttlecock and cards on the floor. The picture is, indeed, in the

SOURCES AND DOCUMENTS

DIDEROT ON BOUCHER, GREUZE AND CHARDIN

The French novelist, essayist and editor of the great French *Encyclopedia*, Denis Diderot (1713–84), regularly reviewed the Paris Salons in the 1760s. He avoided theory and wrote as if standing before the work of art, allowing his impressions time to sink in. A rather stern, secular morality informed his judgements, however, and led him to put a high value on the instructive and elevating. Some prominent artists he dismissed as frivolous. Of Boucher, for instance, he wrote:

What a waste of talent and time! This man is the ruin of our young painting students. As soon as they are able to hold brush and palette, they begin to sweat over garlanded putti, to paint rosy and dimpled behinds, and to indulge in all sorts of extravagances . . . .

In contrast, his response to the sober, moralizing paintings of Greuze was keenly sympathetic; he wrote of two paintings by him in 1765:

I consider these sketches are masterpieces of composition . . . there is nothing labored or artificial about them, but the interest is simple and striking, yet appeals to all. But nowadays there is so little real feeling for art that perhaps these sketches will never be painted as pictures, and if they were, Boucher would sooner sell 50 of his commonplace indecent puppets than Greuze these two sublime compositions.

Eventually Diderot came to rank Chardin even above Greuze, writing of him:

Here is the real painter; here is the true colorist. This magic is beyond comprehension. There are thick layers of paint, laid one on top of the other, which inter-

penetrate from the bottom to the top layer. In other places, it is as if a vapor had been breathed on the canvas; in others still, as if a light foam had been thrown on it . . . . Come close, and everything becomes confused, flattens out and vanishes; move back, and everything takes shape once again and recomposes itself.

Some years later, between 1776 and 1781, Diderot summed up his thoughts on art in a collection of aphoristic fragments from which the following have been selected:

Every work of sculpture or painting must be the expression of a great principle, a lesson for the spectator – otherwise it remains mute.

A question which is not as ridiculous as it may seem: is it possible to have pure taste, when one's heart is corrupt?

Everything common is simple, but everything simple is not common. Simplicity is one of the chief characteristics of beauty; it is essential to the sublime.

I am no Capuchin, but I confess that I should gladly sacrifice the pleasure of seeing attractive nudities, if I could hasten the moment when painting and sculpture, having become more decent and moral, will compete with the other arts in inspiring virtue and purifying manners. It seems to me that I have seen enough tits and behinds. These seductive things interfere with the soul's emotions by troubling the senses.

The moment an artist thinks of money, he loses his feeling for beauty.

(Tr. L. Eitner, *Neoclassicism and Romanticism*, vol. 1, Englewood Cliffs 1970)

moralizing tradition of Dutch seventeenth-century *genre* scenes, which were very popular with collectors (despite academic disapproval) throughout the eighteenth century. Chardin is often called the painter of the *bourgeoisie*, but the moral code he illustrated was extolled (if often infringed) by the upper as well as by the middle class. The low-life figures in his pictures are usually servants in what appear to be well-to-do households. But Chardin also appealed for his pictorial mastery, his almost miraculous power to evoke the substantial reality of objects. 'He is the one who understands the harmony of colors and reflections', wrote Denis Diderot, the most sensitive art critic of the century, in 1763. 'O Chardin! it is not red, white and black you mix on your palette: it is the very substance of objects, it is the air and the light you take with the tip of your brush and fix on the canvas.'

The robust sensitivity of Chardin and the tender sensuality of Boucher had some influence on Jean-Honoré Fragonard (1732–1806), who was apprenticed to the

former for six months and to the latter for slightly longer before being absorbed into the official system of art education, in Paris and Rome. His first major painting, of 1765, was bought for the Crown and he was accepted for membership of the Academy, though he never became an Academician and rarely showed his work at the biennial Salons – the only important art exhibitions in eighteenth-century France. There were enough private collectors in Paris who appreciated his genius as draftsman and painter for him to opt out of the official art world. His series of large pictures of *The Progress of Love* was commissioned by Louis XV's mistress Mme du Barry for a pavilion at Louveciennes.

The four scenes of *The Progress of Love* are set in a park with statues and stone balustrades amongst a luxuriant growth of flowers and free-growing trees. In the first, a girl as exquisite as porcelain is surprised by a youth climbing over a wall (14,7). There is an ejaculatory force in the composition, echoing the subject-matter, with lines shooting upwards and outwards, and the girl in a pure white dress in the centre of it all. Everything has been set in motion by the precipitate arrival of the youth; flowers and leaves seem to tremble with excitement, even the statue is animated, preventing Cupid from snatching an arrow from her. And the whole canvas is painted with amorous energy in vibrating flecks of bright pigment.

With Fragonard the Rococo took on palpitating new life; and that was probably why Mme du Barry found *The Progress of Love* unsuitable for her new pavilion. She returned the paintings to Fragonard and commissioned Joseph-Marie Vien (1716–1809) – an older and indifferent artist, but one more closely in touch with current developments in the arts – to paint a series of panels on the same theme, but with solemn Classical temples in the background, figures in antique not contemporary costume and greater emphasis on sentiment than on impulsive 'natural' urges. By this date the critical opposition to the Rococo, voiced periodically throughout the century, had grown too loud for anyone as fashion-conscious as Mme du Barry to ignore it. Even so *mondaine* an artist as Marie Louise Elisabeth Vigée-Lebrun (1755–1842) adopted at about this time a restrained, plain style, though still expressive of the cult of sensibility (**14,8**).

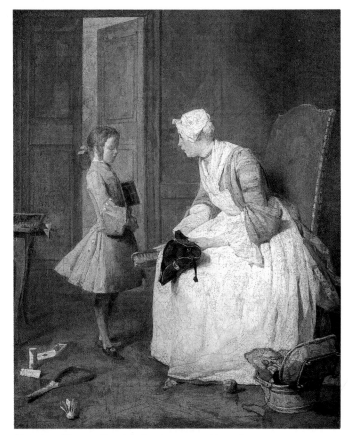

14,6 Jean-Siméon Chardin, *The Governess*, 1739. Oil on canvas, 18⅓ × 14¾ins (46.7 × 37.5cm). National Gallery of Canada, Ottawa.

14,7 Jean-Honoré Fragonard, *The Meeting*, from *The Progress of Love*, 1771–2. Oil on canvas, 10ft 5ins × 8ft (3.18 × 2.44m). Frick Collection, New York.

14,8 Marie Louise Elisabeth Vigée-Lebrun, *The Artist and her Daughter*, c. 1785. Canvas 51⅛ × 37½ins (130 × 94cm). Louvre, Paris.

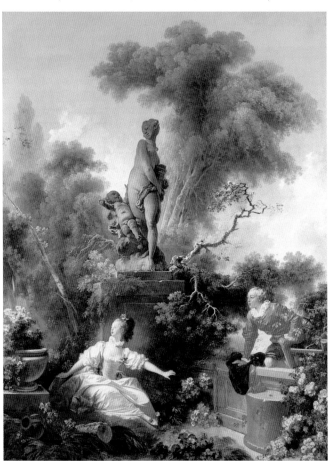

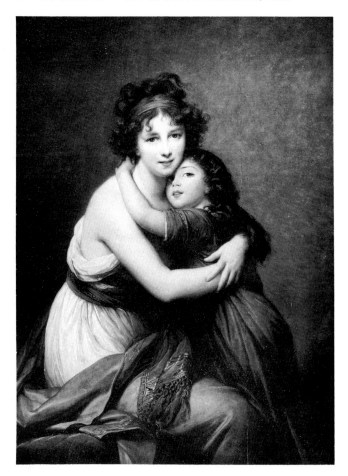

Fragonard and Greuze

SEX OBJECTS AND VIRTUOUS MOTHERS

The lightly veiled eroticism of Fragonard's *The Meeting* (14,7), which proved too much for Madame du Barry, had been given much more explicit expression five years earlier in *The Swing* (**14,9**). A woman on a swing was an established motif in French Rococo art, especially in paintings of *fêtes galantes*, those poetic celebrations of the aristocratic life of leisure. Children were occasionally shown enjoying the pastime, very infrequently men. Women and girls monopolized it and the swing soon acquired further connotations. It seemed to epitomize the pleasure-loving, licentious spirit of the *ancien régime* and in particular the fickleness and inconstancy ascribed to women, especially in high society, their teasing changes of mind if not of heart in the perpetual to-and-fro game of light-hearted, feet-off-the-ground flirtation.

The origin of Fragonard's *The Swing* is by chance known. The writer Charles Collé recorded having met the painter Gabriel-François Doyen on 2 October 1767, who said to him: 'Would you believe it!' A gentleman of the court had sent for him shortly after a religious painting of his had been exhibited in Paris and when Doyen presented himself he found him at his 'pleasure house' with his mistress. 'He started by flattering me with courtesies', Doyen related, 'and finished by avowing that he was dying with a desire to have me make a picture, the idea of which he was going to outline. "I should like", he continued, "to have you paint Madame (pointing to his mistress) on a swing that a bishop would set going. You will place me in such a way that I would be able to see the legs of the lovely girl, and better still, if you want to enliven your picture a little

more . . ." I confess, M. Doyen said to me, that this proposition, which I wouldn't have expected, considering the character of the picture that led to it, perplexed me and left me speechless for a moment. I collected myself, however, enough to say to him almost at once: "Ah Monsieur, it is necessary to add to the essential idea of your picture by making Madame's shoes fly into the air and having some cupids catch them."' Doyen did not accept the commission, however, and passed it on to Fragonard. The identity of the patron is unknown, though he was at one time thought to have been the Baron de Saint-Julien, the Receiver General of the French Clergy, which would have explained the request to include a bishop pushing the swing. This idea as well as that of having himself and his mistress portrayed was evidently dropped by the patron, whoever he may have been. The picture was depersonalized and, due to Fragonard's extremely sensuous imagination, became a universal image of joyous, carefree sexuality.

The theme is that of love and the rising tide of passion, as intimated by the sculptural group in the lower centre of the picture. (Dolphins driven by cupids drawing the water-chariot of Venus symbolize the impatient surge of love.) Beneath the girl on the swing, lying in a great bush, a tangle of flowers and foliage, is the young lover, gasping with anticipation. The bush is, evidently, a private place as it is enclosed by little fences. But the youth has found his way to it. Thrilling to the sight now offered him, the youth reaches out with hat in hand. (A hat in eighteenth-century erotic imagery covered not only the head but also another part of the male body when inadvertently exposed.) The feminine counterpart to the hat was the shoe and in *The Swing* the girl's shoe flies off her pretty foot to be lost in the undergrowth. This idea had been suggested originally by Doyen, as he recounted to Collé, and in

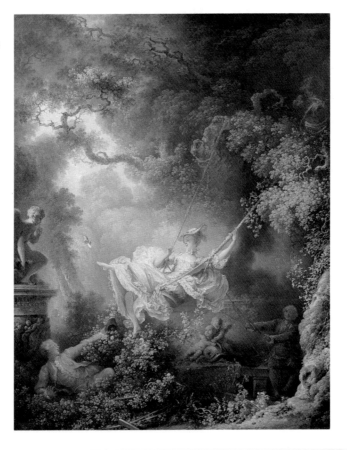

14,9 Jean-Honoré Fragonard, *The Swing*, 1767. Canvas, 31⅞ins × 25¼ins (81 × 64.2cm). Wallace Collection, London.

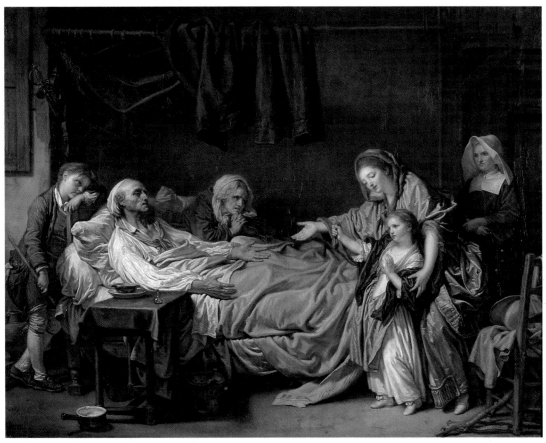

14,10 Jean-Baptiste Greuze, *The Benefactress*, 1775. Canvas, 3ft 8ins × 4ft 9½ins (1.14 × 1.47m). Musée des Beaux Arts de Lyon.

French paintings of the period a naked foot and lost shoe often accompany the more familiar broken pitcher as a symbol of lost virginity.

However, all these erotic symbols would lie inert on the canvas had not Fragonard charged the whole painting with the amorous ebullience and joy of an impetuous surrender to love. In a shimmer of leaves and rose petals, lit up by a sparkling beam of sunshine, the girl, in a frothy dress of cream and juicy pink, rides the swing with happy, thoughtless abandon. Her legs are parted, her skirts open; the youth in the rose-bush, hat off, arm erect, lunges towards her. Suddenly, as she reaches the peak of her ride, her shoe flies off.

Conjugal love was also celebrated by Fragonard and by other painters of the time with the same, or almost the same, vibrant sensuality. The joys of family life were extolled, usually from the point of view of the husband, and motherhood was associated above all with sexual gratification. But later, as the social and moral climate changed, other aspects of the

female sex were emphasized, notably that of the Virtuous Mother or woman as the consoler and dispenser of charity. These moralizing works were created for a new and different public. Whereas Fragonard and other hedonistic Rococo painters had worked for private patrons and often, as in the case of *The Swing*, strictly for private consumption, the painters who extolled such themes as that of the Virtuous Mother had a larger and more general public in mind. By the second half of the eighteenth century visitors to the biennial Salons had become quite numerous and were not drawn from any particular class of society. The effect of their patronage soon began to be felt and its influence was greatly augmented by their purchase of prints after the paintings they admired, thus creating a new and wider public for art.

The Benefactress (**14,10**) by Jean-Baptiste Greuze (1725–1805) is typical of this new *genre*. A well-dressed woman is visiting an elderly sick man, apparently in hospital and attended by a nun who stands in the

background. Visiting the sick was one of the Seven Acts of Mercy derived from the Gospel according to St Matthew and the woman has brought her daughter with her to teach her Christian virtue. Though not exhibited in the Salon, since Greuze had quarrelled with the Academy, the painting quickly became known and its absence was publicly regretted. It was thought an eloquent and edifying work, sublime in sentiment as in feeling. Diderot, who never tired of repeating how Greuze 'spoke to vital moral issues', would have greatly admired it as exemplifying 'that poetry that touches our feelings, instructs us, improves us and invites us to virtuous action'. Even six years later it was singled out for its exceptional tenderness in the depiction of moral subjects – and, it might be added, one in which a woman is given the central role as the noble exemplar of Christian virtue. It was a far cry from the world of thoughtless escapades with women as sex objects so beloved by Fragonard less than a decade earlier.

THE ROCOCO IN GERMANY AND ITALY

In France the Rococo emerged in opposition to the teaching program of the Academy, which, nevertheless, continued to exert a restraining influence and forcefully reasserted its authority in the 1750s. German Rococo, on the other hand, although sometimes directly indebted to France, developed from an exuberantly Italianate Baroque. Borromini (see p. 591) and the north Italian architect Guarino Guarini (1624–83), who were always regarded with suspicion by the French, inspired the spatial complexity, intricacy of form and elaboration of surface textures which German architects exploited to the point where architectonic verticals and horizontals all but dissolve. The distinction between Baroque and Rococo in Germany, as in Italy, is one of degree, which can be measured only subjectively. (The presence or absence of the Classical orders is no more than a convenient rule-of-thumb aid to categorization.)

The Zwinger in Dresden (14,11) is of such light-hearted ebullience that it mocks stylistic classification. Incredible as it may seem, the architect Matthaeus Daniel Pöppelmann (1662–1736) claimed that he designed it according to the Vitruvian rules; he called it a 'Roman theatre'! Classical prototypes can, of course, be found for all the decorative elements which he distended and contracted, combined and dismantled and reassembled, without any inhibiting deference to the Roman sense of decorum. In conception, however, this extraordinary building goes back to ephemeral 'festival' architecture. Elaborate, open-air festivals had played an important part in European court life ever since the Renaissance, combining entertainment with instruction – about the magnificence, wisdom and power of princes. The Zwinger (the word means simply 'outer courtyard') replaced a wooden amphitheatre to provide a permanent setting for parades, carousels and other pageants.

14,11 Matthaeus Daniel Pöppelmann, pavilion in the Zwinger, Dresden, 1711–22.

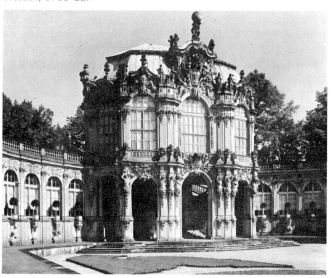

The patron was Augustus the Strong (1694-1733) and the statue of Hercules crowning the 'grand stand' of the Zwinger symbolized both his strength and the burden he had assumed as king of Poland and elector of Saxony. Aspiring to build a palace to outshine all others, he dispatched Pöppelmann on a study tour of Austria and Italy to pick up ideas, but the Zwinger was the only part to be erected. After his return Pöppelmann made a succession of designs which show him gradually moving away from the boldness and massiveness favoured in the late seventeenth century, towards ever greater intricacy and richness, perhaps at the behest of Augustus, whose taste in art was for the exquisite and opulent. (He founded the Meissen factory in 1710, the first to produce true porcelain in Europe.) The Zwinger owes much of its enchanting effect to the unusually happy collaboration between architect and sculptor, Balthasar Permoser (1651–1732), under whose guiding hand the wall surfaces were animated with flowers and masks, leering satyrs and muscular term-figures. Together they produced a unique integration of architecture and sculpture. All that is lacking is color, originally provided by the costumes of the performers in the festivities for which the Zwinger was created.

The Zwinger is exterior architecture (the rooms in the pavilions were something of an anticlimax even before they were burnt out in 1945), though of a very unusual kind. For the vast courtyard was conceived as if it were an interior, an enclosed space which can be fully appreciated only by walking through it or looking down into it from the upper windows of the pavilions. Early eighteenth-century architects were generally more concerned with the manipulation of space than with form. This is equally apparent in French town-houses and south German churches, which seldom give an external hint of the splendours within.

The Wieskirche (or 'church of the meadow'), in open country near Füssen and Oberammergau in southern Bavaria, has an undistinguished exterior. Inside is a miracle of light and color and swirling all-encompassing decorative motifs, giving the visitor coming through the door an extraordinary feeling of welcome and joy (14,12; 13). This was, of course, the intended effect, for it is a pilgrimage church. The architect, Dominikus Zimmermann (1685–1766), was by training a craftsman – a worker in stucco – who retained throughout his life a peasant vitality and unquestioning piety. But he had a highly sophisticated understanding of architectural space and a feeling of the utmost refinement for ornament. In the Wieskirche the rather broad oval of the nave flows into an oblong chancel, drawing the visitor towards the altar not only by the curvature of the walls and the disposition of the columns but also by the intensification of color and the richness of the decoration – from the predominantly white nave, with motifs picked out in gold, pinks and blues, to the glowing pink chancel, with details in shining white. Structure dissolves, leaving the decorative motifs as if suspended in space; even the large and elaborate pulpit seems to hover in mid-air.

Such church interiors – and there are many in central Europe – gave the visitor and especially the peasant pilgrim

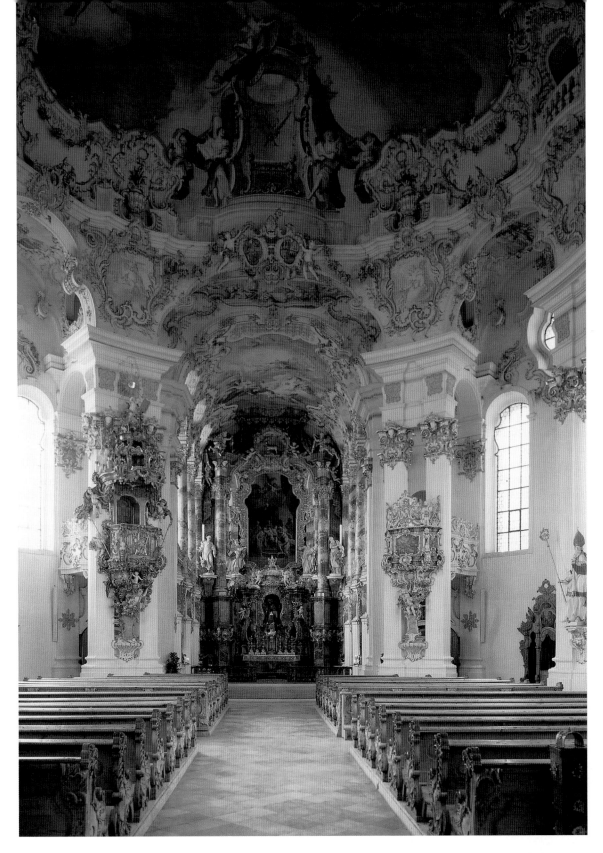

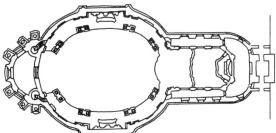

14,12 *Above* Dominikus Zimmermann, the Wieskirche, Bavaria, 1745–54.

14,13 *Left* Plan of the Wieskirche.

a vision of heaven. This was their main purpose. At Ottobeuren the prior of the abbey asked Johann Michael Fischer (1692–1766) to design a church that would be 'new, splendid and worthy of the King of Heaven and Earth'. Yet their ostentatious decorations, even their colors, have religious significance as well. The Wieskirche, for instance, is dedicated to Christ Scourged and the red columns in the chancel symbolize his blood. It is without the slightest sense of impropriety that simple piety is combined here with a taste for the modish and fantastical. No hint of secularization is implied, rather the reverse – the sanctification of the secular.

Among the sculptors who worked for the churches in Bavaria, Ignaz Günther (1725–75) was outstanding. His statues are of wood, often painted in naturalistic colors, but the rusticity of the medium is offset by the almost unnatural grace of his tall, light-footed figures, which perfectly blend sophistication with guileless innocence. The two are contrasted and combined in the group of a very chubby, earthy peasant-boy Tobias clutching the hand of a delicately poised and rather superior angel from the court of heaven (**14,14**). Günther had studied late sixteenth-century statues in Munich, and the influence of Italian Mannerism, especially the serpentine figure (see p. 508), is very evident in his, as in many other Rococo, sculptures. But he was also heir to the German tradition of naturalistic wood-carving, which reached back to the Middle Ages, when the idea of saints and angels dressed in the height of fashion had seemed no more untoward or irreligious than it did to him. Although he was appointed sculptor to the elector of Bavaria in 1754, the unmistakably Germanic and religious character of his work set him apart from other artists employed at the court.

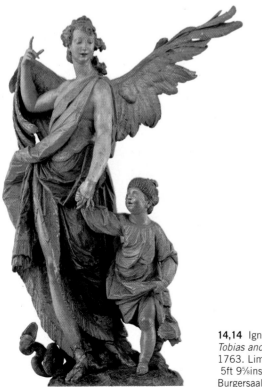

14,14 Ignaz Günther, *Tobias and the Angel*, 1763. Limewood, 5ft 9⅝ins (1.77m) high. Burgersaal-Kirche, Munich.

TIEPOLO, GUARDI AND CANALETTO

In the mid-eighteenth century the courts of the many German principalities looked to France for leadership in fashion; in some even the language spoken was French. The *genre pittoresque*, diffused by engraved designs, influenced architectural decorations and the furnishings made to accompany them. The Bavarian court architect François Cuvilliés (1695–1768) had been trained in Paris and introduced into Germany a kind of hyper-Rococo version of French interior design, notably at the Amalienburg and in the Residenz at Munich. But in painting (as in operatic music) Italy still retained its prestige. Thus, when the prince-bishop of Würzburg wished to add the crowning touch of magnificence to his vast palace, he called in the greatest (and most expensive) fresco painter of the time, the Venetian Giovanni Battista Tiepolo (1696–1770).

At Würzburg Tiepolo painted the ceiling of the Kaisersaal – the main state room, suitable for the entertainment of the Holy Roman Emperor – and the ceiling above the staircase that leads up to it. The staircase is itself an imposingly dramatic creation by Johann Balthasar Neumann (1687–1753), the most gifted and prolific German architect of his time, a master of elegant and ingenious spatial compositions of great intellectual and visual complexity. Here Tiepolo was required to record the fame of the prince-bishop Carl Philip von Greiffenklau, trumpeted to the corners of the earth and beyond to the gods on Olympus – an unpromising program, which he made, nevertheless, the vehicle for what is perhaps his finest work, sparkling with Venetian light and color (**14,15**). Unlike most previous ceiling paintings, it was intended to be seen from a succession of viewpoints. The eye of a visitor climbing the first flight of the staircase from the rather cavernous ground floor is caught immediately by a nude woman with feathers in her hair symbolizing America – the New World, source of prodigious natural riches. A turn to right or left on the half-landing brings into view bizarrely dressed figures and exotic animals representative of Asia and Africa. Ascending either of the twin flights leading to the main floor the visitor is finally confronted with Europe and the portrait of the prince-bishop suspended in a sky teeming with gods and goddesses and cupids and figures of fame. The whole ceiling, a vast area of nearly 6,000 square feet (557 square m), is painted with astonishing illusionistic bravura and a complete command of the fresco painter's resources. It is also enlivened by flashes of Tiepolo's visual wit. The architect, Neumann, for instance, in the uniform of an artillery officer with a svelte dog beside him, is portrayed reclining on the *trompe-l'oeil* cornice which connects the frescoed surface of the ceiling with the relief decorations on the walls. Painting, architecture and sculpture (stucco figures and huge shells in the corners) interpenetrate to create a total environment masking the frontier between reality and fiction.

The ceiling presents a view of the world cherished by Enlightenment thinkers who were fascinated by distant countries – their flora and fauna, their peculiar artifacts,

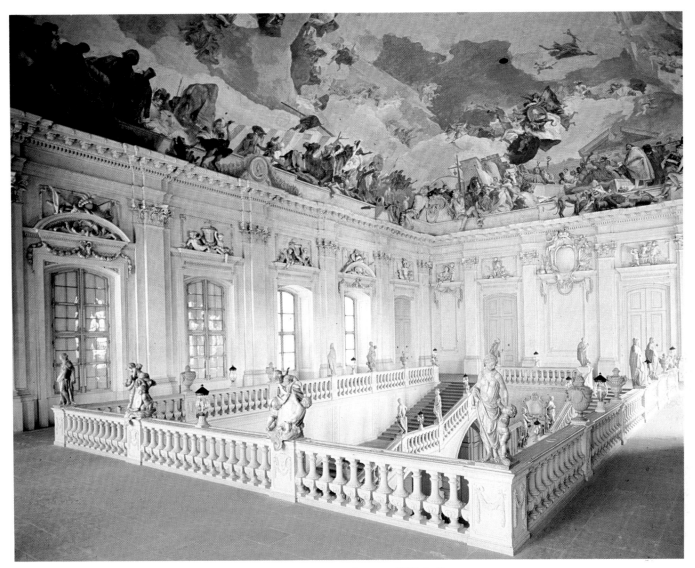

14,15 Giovanni Battista Tiepolo, staircase ceiling of the Residenz, Würzburg, Germany, 1752–3. Fresco.

and the customs and religious beliefs of their strangely beautiful people – but unquestioning in their faith in European superiority. On Tiepolo's ceiling Africa, America and Asia produce the goods to be enjoyed by Europe in civilized comfort. There are enticing bundles and casks on the shore of Asia, where merchants examine ropes of pearls held out by a turbaned Oriental. Europeans, on the other hand, are able to devote themselves to the arts of music, architecture, sculpture and painting. But Tiepolo's view of the world was not only Eurocentric – it was Venetocentric. The ceiling is a tribute to his own Venetian school and especially the art of Paolo Veronese (pp. 500–1). The livery of the page-boys, who appear in several parts of the ceiling, is sixteenth-century Venetian and the throned female figure symbolizing Europe (to the left of the musicians) is almost directly copied from one of Veronese's allegories of the city of Venice.

Local patriotism is apparent in much of the art of eighteenth-century Italy. Italians had already begun to live on their artistic past. The Bolognese clung tenaciously to

their early seventeenth-century masters. Rome was dominated by the Classicism of the High Renaissance. Venetians looked back to the richness and color of Titian, the elegance of Veronese and the dramatic lighting effects of Tintoretto (see pp. 499–500). Francesco Guardi (1712–93) is perhaps best understood as the last exponent of a tradition initiated by Tintoretto. He began as a figurative painter working with his brother Gianantonio (1699–1760). But his fame rests mainly on the views of Venice, which beautifully capture the sparkle of sunshine on domes and towers and the eerie mystery of its dark canals and passages (**14,16**). Very few are dated nor is much known of the public for which he painted them. He certainly did not have the success with rich foreign visitors to Venice enjoyed by Canaletto (1697–1768), whose cool clear views of the city (**14,17**) were much to the taste of the English, who were his chief patrons and some of whom had themselves portrayed while in Venice by Rosalba Carriera (1675–1757), the most distinguished portrait painter of her day in Venice or, indeed, in Italy (**14,18**). Under the

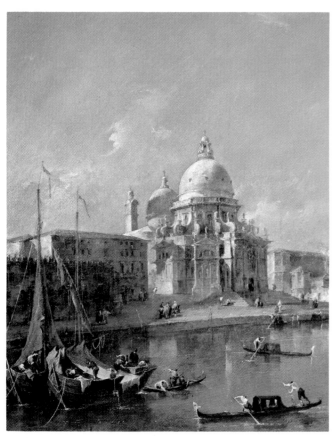

14,16 Francesco Guardi, *Santa Maria della Salute*, Venice, c. 1765. Oil on canvas, 19 × 15⅛ins (48.3 × 38.4cm). National Gallery of Scotland, Edinburgh.

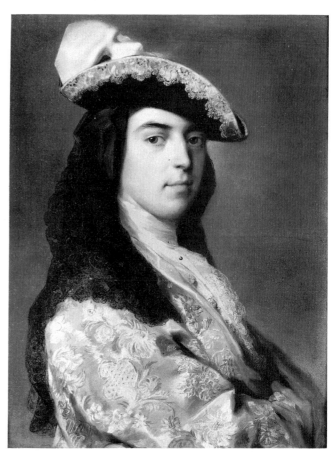

14,18 Rosalba Carriera, *Charles Sackville, 2nd Duke of Dorset*, c. 1740. Pastel on paper, 25 × 19ins (63.5 × 48.3cm). Lord Sackville Collection, Knole, Kent, England.

14,17 Giovanni Antonio Canal called Canaletto, *Venice: The Bacino di S Marco on Ascension Day*, 1732–5. Canvas, 30¼ × 46ins (76.8 × 116.8cm). Windsor Castle. Reproduced by gracious permission of Her Majesty The Queen.

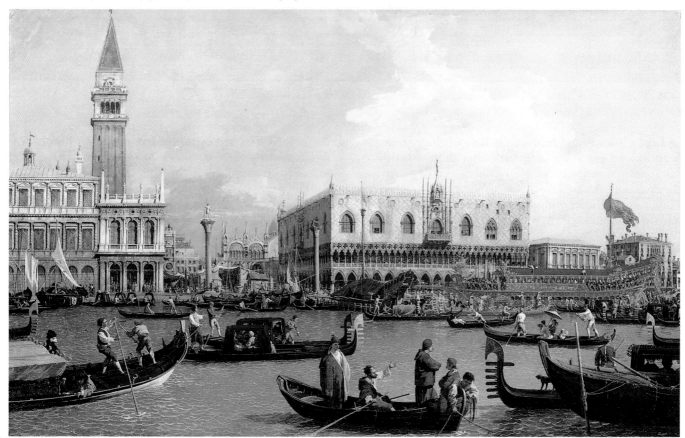

lightning brilliance of Guardi's flicks and dabs of color, buildings, gondolas, sailing ships, men and women in flurrying cloaks, all seem to dissolve into aerial fantasies. That the government of Venice was also on the point of dissolution may be no more than a coincidence; only four years after Guardi's death the city fell to the French republican army of Napoleon.

English Sense and Sensibility

The Italian Baroque, which inspired German architects, was viewed askance in Great Britain from the early eighteenth century. 'How affected and licentious are the works of Bernini', wrote the Scottish architect Colen Campbell (1676–1729). 'How wildly Extravagant are the designs of Borromini, who has endeavoured to debauch Mankind with his odd and chimerical Beauties' (*Vitruvius Britannicus*, 1715). This combination of rational and moral disapproval isolated Great Britain from the rest of Europe in artistic matters. Campbell was the spokesman for a group of architects, including the earl of Burlington (1694–1753) and other wealthy amateurs, who advocated a return to Classical principles by way of Andrea Palladio (see p. 502). Burlington indeed built for himself at Chiswick near London one of the several English versions of Palladio's La Rotonda. Houses in the Neo-Palladian style, created in England and taken up in the American colonies, make an effect of robust self-assurance, unaffected good manners and very solid prosperity. They also had political and social implications. Their Classicism

was Roman and seemed to embody the republican virtues extolled by Cicero and for many years thrashed into every English schoolboy, but never more highly valued than after the development of constitutional monarchy which, under George I (1714–27), gave political power to a land-owning oligarchy. A Neo-Palladian house declared its owner's respect for propriety and decorum and with its dressed stonework, columns and pediment, marked his social standing far more obviously than the seventeenth-century brick-built gentleman's house.

Hogarth and Gainsborough

This social aspect of the style is well brought out in paintings by William Hogarth (1697–1764). In the second scene of his *Marriage à la Mode* series an ill-matched couple (young viscount and city merchant's daughter) are shown in a typical Neo-Palladian room with columns and Classical ornament (**14,19**). Italianate pictures on the walls indicate upper-class taste. But there are also some telling 'frivolities', Chinese porcelain figures on either side of a Roman bust on the chimneypiece and a preposterous Rococo clock on the right. To Hogarth such objects symbolized heartlessness or affectation – deviance from nature in life and art. Yet his attitude to the Rococo was equivocal. He was closely associated with the decorative designers who cultivated an English version of the *genre pittoresque*, for furniture, metalwork and the title-pages of books. The wonderfully free brush-strokes of his paintings suggest the influence of contemporary French artists.

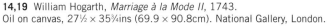

14,19 William Hogarth, *Marriage à la Mode II*, 1743. Oil on canvas, 27½ × 35¾ins (69.9 × 90.8cm). National Gallery, London.

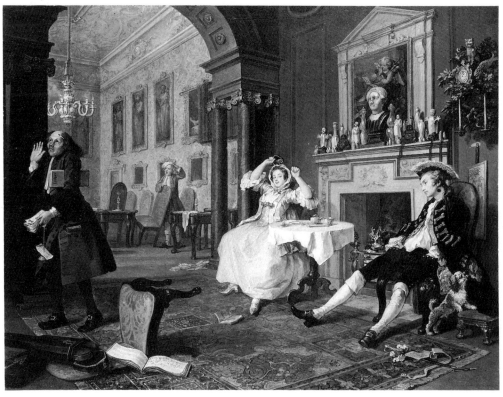

And he chose French engravers active in England for the prints which made him and his paintings famous.

Hogarth was most sharply set off from his contemporaries on the continent by moral attitudes which were secular rather than Protestant, derived from common sense as much as from bourgeois values. This was the morality preached by the two leading journalists and writers of the time, Joseph Addison and Richard Steele. Hogarth's satire on the fashionable marriage of convenience, which leads to unhappiness and immorality, may well have been inspired by an essay Addison wrote for the *Spectator* in 1712, celebrating the ideal of marriage based on love – in comfortable financial circumstances, of course. The theme was taken up by countless English novelists and playwrights. Love was presented as a 'natural' passion, but one which should be restrained within a reasonable framework of social conventions. Addison in his essays and Alexander Pope in his poetry extolled the related ideas of nature and liberty – words which then had meanings different from those they were to acquire at the end of the century and retain to the present day. The natural was then understood simply as the opposite of the artificial, the affected, the aberrant. Nature signified not the wild and lawless, but the divinely ordered universe, as revealed by Newton, in which everything had its appointed place. Liberty could be regarded as 'natural' only within this structure, which provided the model for the social system.

These ideas, or rather these assumptions, lie behind one of the most eloquent English pictures of the mid-century, the portrait of the Suffolk squire Robert Andrews and his wife Mary – a well-matched couple from the same stratum of county society – painted shortly after their wedding in 1748 by the young Thomas Gainsborough (1727–88) (**14,20**). This wonderfully fresh little painting is eminently natural, especially the very precisely rendered background, clearly the record of an actual place. Despite their fine clothes, there is more than a touch of rustic provincial awkwardness in Mr and Mrs Andrews, who make as striking a contrast with the figures in French outdoor scenes as does the Suffolk landscape with the balustraded, be-statued gardens of France depicted by Watteau and Fragonard (14,2; 7). The landscape in which the pair are shown, presumably at their request, is their own estate. They are placed at the point where their park with its clumps of trees merges into their well-cultivated farm-land with its neat hedges and gates, stooks of recently cut grain in the foreground and sheep grazing a distant meadow.

LANDSCAPE AND CLASSICISM

The landscape park, perhaps the most important British contribution to the visual arts of the eighteenth century, could be regarded as a symbol of liberty, in contrast with the rigidly formal gardens of Versailles, in which the

14,20 Thomas Gainsborough, *Mr and Mrs Andrews*, c. 1749. Oil on canvas, 27½ × 47ins (69.8 × 119.4cm). National Gallery, London.

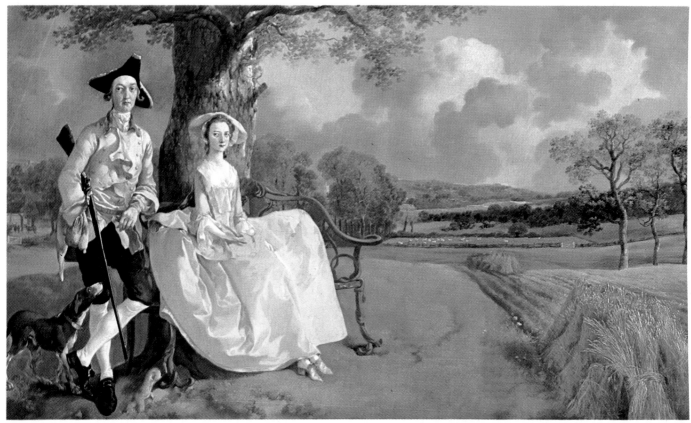

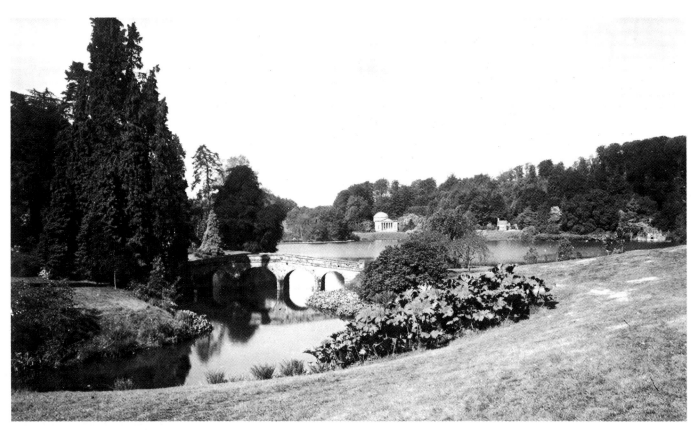

14,21 The Park at Stourhead, Wiltshire, laid out 1743.

domination of nature could be equated with autocracy. A park often had a monument to British liberty – in the form of a ruin recalling the Barons' Wars and *Magna Carta* or a temple of British worthies – liberty as defined by Locke and enjoyed by the propertied class. The ditch or 'ha-ha', which separated a gentleman's park from the surrounding world of unimproved nature, was a most discreet, indeed almost invisible barrier, although one no less firmly set and effective than that dividing the owners from other ranks of society. An ideal of self-assured informality, unostentatious wealth, untyrannical power and unpedantic learning is reflected in these parks and landscape gardens. Like the Neo-Palladian country-house, they were the product of a Classically based culture, created by and for the well-bred and well-read. Sometimes it was directly associated with ancient Rome. At Stourhead in Wiltshire Henry Hoare (the son of a banking family which had made a vast fortune after the revolution of 1688) transformed his estate into a Virgilian landscape of running brooks, lakes, groves of mixed trees, Classical temples and a sibyl's grotto (**14,21**). The effect is reminiscent of paintings by Claude (13,27). As in other English parks, there is a note of nostalgia for youthful days on the Grand Tour to Italy, which completed a Classical education. But the main purpose of the makers of these landscape gardens was more serious: to penetrate and, as it were, to liberate an ideal lying beneath the common face of nature.

The Classical past permeated British culture throughout the eighteenth century. Deviations into Gothic and Chinese architectural styles merely afforded amusing contrasts to emphasize the supremacy of the Classical norm. But attitudes began to change in the mid-century. When the architect Robert Adam (1728–92) went to Italy on his Grand Tour in 1754 he quickly realized that the Neo-Palladian houses he had previously built in Scotland bore scant resemblance to the monuments of ancient Rome. Like the Italian engraver and architect Giovanni Battista Piranesi (1720–78), he responded to the richness, variety and magnificence of imperial Roman architecture. These were the qualities he strove to recapture in the houses he began to design soon after setting up his practice in London in 1758. The ancient Roman baths (p. 217) inspired him to make imaginative use of contrasted shapes and sizes of rooms and to plan an interior as a series of dilating and contracting spaces. At Syon House near London, where he remodelled the shell of an early seventeenth-century building, a severe entrance hall, accented horizontally, opens into a seemingly lofty square room of imperial Roman splendour with great gilt trophies of arms on the walls and tall green marble columns topped by gilded statues (**14,22**). The following two rooms are oblong but with contrasted decor, a dining-room with copies of famous antique statues in niches, and a drawing-room where the unit and scale of the decorations are decreased to create a more intimate, relaxed effect.

century Bolognese masters. His desire was to emulate the 'grand style', but he was shrewd enough to see that the market for 'history pictures' (mythological as well as religious) was very limited in England, where the old masters were much collected but living painters were patronized mainly as portraitists. He therefore devoted himself to elevating the art of portraiture. Male sitters were posed by him in the attitudes of antique statues; ladies were treated almost like figures in mythological compositions. Lady Sarah Bunbury (one of the most famous beauties of the day, whom George III had wanted to marry) he depicted as a priestess sacrificing to the Graces (**14,23**). This grand style was reserved, however, for his socially grander sitters; men of letters, such as Dr Johnson, were portrayed in more natural poses and in the clothes they normally wore. Although he became the most fashionable English portrait painter of his time, Reynolds despised fashion, exhorting young artists to rise above it. In 1771 he

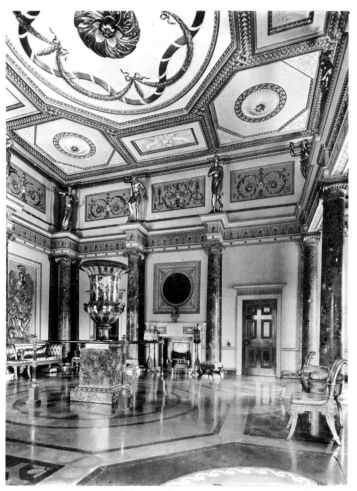

14,22 Robert Adam, Anteroom, Syon House, Middlesex, 1760–9.

14,23 Sir Joshua Reynolds, *Lady Sarah Bunbury Sacrificing to the Graces*, 1765. Oil on canvas, 7ft 10ins × 5ft (2.42 × 1.52m). Art Institute of Chicago (W. W. Kimball Collection).

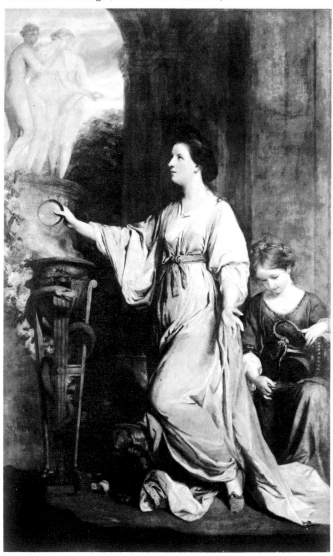

Not only the wall surfaces but also the furniture, the carpets, even the door-knobs and key-hole guards were designed in Adam's office. In his interiors the architect rules supreme; craftsmen became merely the mechanics executing designs as precisely as possible. The style he created therefore lent itself well to industrial production. Pottery designed in his manner and made in the Staffordshire factory of Josiah Wedgwood (1730–95), for instance, was the work of simple artisans following predetermined patterns. The craftsman's individual touch was no longer needed. One of the results was a widening of the gap between artists and craftsmen, especially in England, where industrialization was more advanced than elsewhere. For this and other reasons artists demanded recognition of their superior status and this was partly achieved by the foundation of the Royal Academy in 1768.

The first president of the Royal Academy, Sir Joshua Reynolds (1723–92), knighted the year after its foundation, was obsessed by status, personally, professionally and nationally. The son of a clergyman-schoolmaster, he came from a social stratum above most English artists of his day and, as a youth, declared his ambition to be more than an 'ordinary painter'. Like Robert Adam he made the Grand Tour to Rome, where he saturated himself in the work of Raphael, Michelangelo and the seventeenth-

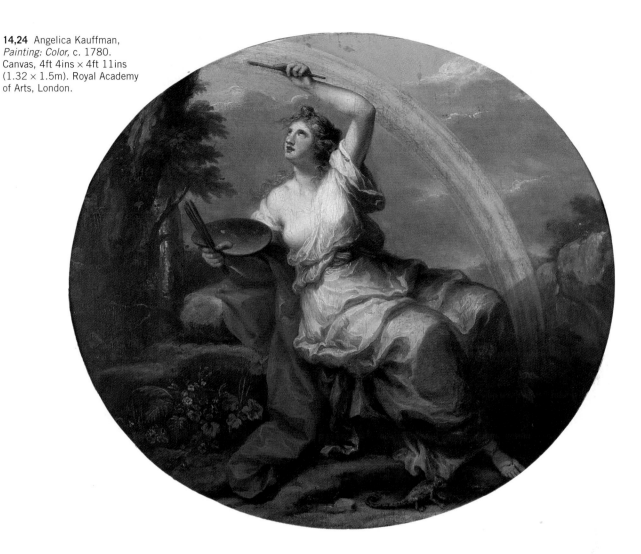

14,24 Angelica Kauffman, *Painting: Color*, c. 1780. Canvas, 4ft 4ins × 4ft 11ins (1.32 × 1.5m). Royal Academy of Arts, London.

declared in one of the *Discourses* he delivered year after year at the Royal Academy: 'If a portrait painter is desirous to raise and improve his subject, he has no other means than by approaching it to a general idea.' He should change 'the dress from a temporary fashion to one more permanent, which has annexed to it no ideas of meanness from its being familiar to us.'

Angelica Kauffman (1741–1807), a close friend of Reynolds, was boldly determined to paint historical subjects as well as portraits. She was cosmopolitan, born in Switzerland, trained in Italy, settled in London in 1766, married first a Swedish adventurer (a bigamist who soon absconded) and second a Venetian painter, spent her final years in Rome and worked for an international clientele. In London she was one of the two women to be founder members of the Royal Academy (otherwise an exclusively male preserve until the 1920s). It is a mark of the esteem in which she was held that in 1779 she was commissioned to paint four large oval canvases for the ceiling of the Academy's lecture room, where generations of students were to be taught. They represent the essential elements of painting: color (**14,24**), design, composition and genius or invention. Kauffman knew such theoretical writers as Winckelmann (see pp. 636–7), of whom she painted a

portrait, but her ovals for the lecture room were not at all pedantic. The allegorical personifications, though influenced by traditional iconography, express her own ideas and interpretations and, furthermore, they are all self-portraits. *Color*, in a loose dress with one breast bare, lifts her brush either to paint a rainbow across the sky or to match its colors on her palette.

The central panel in the lecture room ceiling, *The Graces Unveiling Nature*, was by the American painter Benjamin West (1738–1820), who had known Kauffman in Italy before they both settled in London. He too was intent on painting historical subjects, usually from ancient history with the figures correctly attired in antique costume. But Reynolds is said to have been shocked when he heard that West was painting a scene from modern history with the figures in contemporary dress. It represented the death of General James Wolfe as victor over the French at the battle of Quebec, a turning-point in the war that made Canada a British colony (**14,25**). There were accepted traditions for the depiction of such a scene. It could be treated as an allegory with personifications of victory, war and so on; or as an heroic scene with the figures in Classical costume; or as straight reportage. Although the latter was denigrated by theorists,

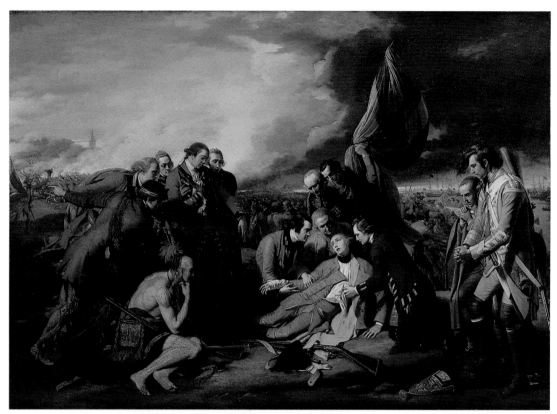

14,25 Benjamin West, *Death of General Wolfe*, c. 1770. Oil on canvas, 4ft 11½ins × 7ft (1.53 × 2.15m). National Gallery of Canada, Ottawa (Transfer from the Canadian War Memorials, 1921. Gift of the 2nd Duke of Westminster, Eaton Hall, Cheshire 1918).

West combined it with the others: the costumes suggest reportage, the poses Classicism, while the figures are at the same time symbols and flesh-and-blood individuals who might have been present when Wolfe died. The pensive Indian in the foreground, for instance, is both a personification of America and a 'portrait' of one of the British Mohawk auxiliaries. The picture was conceived in the grand style with echoes of the old masters – Wolfe is in the attitude of Christ in a *Deposition* by van Dyck. Only the costumes would have to be changed to convert it all into a scene from Biblical, Classical or medieval history.

But contemporary costume was important for another reason. The sense of reality it gave reinforced the truth of a painting's moral message. West drew from the particular incident a general significance: the calm courage with which the hero faces death. And his picture also reflects the current shift in emphasis from the concept of divine judgement and eternal life to that of judgement by posterity and immortality on earth. Wolfe, it is suggested by West, will live in the memory of those around him; and through them the story of his heroic death will be transmitted to future ages. The painting is a secular apotheosis, a rationalization of a Renaissance or Baroque altarpiece, with the angel carrying a crown of martyrdom replaced by a soldier who cries: 'they run, I protest, they run', and the martyr by a hero (a Protestant, of course, for the war in Canada was against a Catholic power). It also made an appeal to 'sensibility', that proneness to emotion, more

particularly the emotion of sympathy, which led to the cult of the tender heart and 'generous tear', complementing hard-headed rationalism among the cultivated in the eighteenth century. The 'man of sensibility' was much admired.

The prodigious popularity enjoyed by prints of West's *Death of Wolfe* (the engraver is said to have earned £15,000) was, however, largely due to a turn of political events. Only five years after the picture was exhibited in London the Declaration of Independence was signed in Philadelphia and North America suddenly became the promised land of the Enlightenment. Both the Declaration and the constitution of the United States were based on the rational principles of natural law – the 'self-evident' rights to which we have already alluded (see p. 614). And when Americans wished to give artistic expression to these political ideals they turned to the most famous works of Classical antiquity, not because they were fashionable in Europe, but because they embodied – or seemed to embody – aesthetic principles no less eternally and universally valid. Thus, Thomas Jefferson (1743–1826) selected the Maison Carrée at Nîmes (5,37) – 'without contradiction . . . the most perfect and precious remain of antiquity in existence', he called it – as the model for the state capitol of Virginia, designed by him in collaboration with the French architect Charles-Louis Clérisseau (1721–1820), formerly drawing-master to Robert Adam.

Neo-Classicism, or the 'True Style'

The founders of the United States were often seen, and sometimes represented, as figures from the ancient world. Benjamin Franklin was portrayed wearing a toga like a Roman senator. But Jefferson wears modern dress in his bust (14,26) as does George Washington in the statue carved on Jefferson's recommendation for the state capitol of Virginia (14,27). The author of these works was Jean-Antoine Houdon (1741–1828), the leading French portrait sculptor of his day. Houdon combined unusual directness, almost an innocence, of vision with great dexterity of hand. In one bust after another he brings us jowl to jowl, eye to illusionistically sculptured eye with a large number of his most eminent contemporaries – Voltaire, Diderot, Rousseau and other luminaries, as well as the leaders of the American Revolution. Repetitions of these portraits were produced in Houdon's studio in various sizes and media as images for the cult of great men of modern times that was promoted by thinkers of the Enlightenment. Whether the sitters are shown wearing their own hair or wigs, whether bare-necked with stylized antique drapery around their shoulders or with cravats and contemporary clothes, these busts have an air of being perfectly natural. And in this way they answered the call to renounce Rococo affectation and 'return to nature' that was reiterated with increasing vehemence in the second half of the eighteenth century.

Reaction against the Rococo set in almost simultaneously in France, Germany and England in the 1750s,

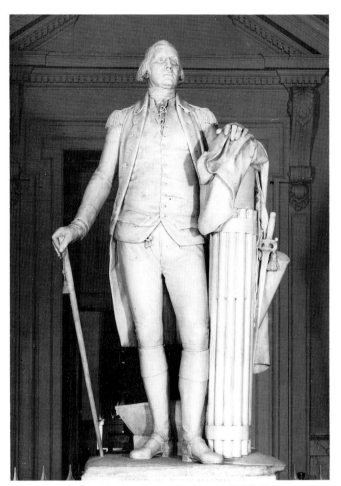

14,27 Jean-Antoine Houdon, *George Washington*, 1785–96. Marble, 6ft 2ins (1.88m) high. State Capitol, Richmond, Virginia.

14,26 Jean-Antoine Houdon, *Thomas Jefferson*, 1789. Marble, 21½ins (54.6cm) high. Library of Congress, Washington DC.

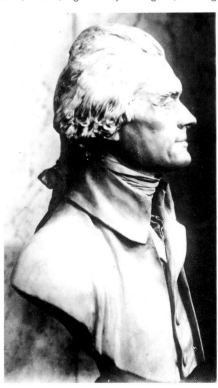

though from diverse and complex intellectual motives. Thinkers of the Enlightenment played an important part with their demand for logic, clarity, simplicity and moral rectitude. Jean-Jacques Rousseau (1712–78), the fiercest critic of the evils of contemporary social life and the most impassioned advocate of the cultivation of natural sentiments, called in 1750 for a didactic art – for statues and paintings of 'the men who have defended their country or those still greater who have enriched it by their genius'. In words that bring to mind paintings by Boucher (14,5), he condemned 'images of every perversion of heart and mind, drawn ingeniously from ancient mythology'. Simultaneously a less high-minded, more general nostalgia for the glory of the 'great century' of Louis XIV led to condemnation of the style which had flourished in its aftermath. There was also a demand for a 'new' art, the retrieval or creation of what was called at the time the 'true style' and, much later, Neo-Classicism. In England this demand reflected national self-consciousness and the ambition of artists, such as Reynolds, to found a national school on a par with those of sixteenth-century Italy. In Germany it was colored by bourgeois hostility to the Francophile culture of the princely courts.

The term 'Neo-Classical', coined in the mid-nineteenth century, gives a misleading impression, implying a

---

SOURCES AND DOCUMENTS

WASHINGTON AND JEFFERSON: ANTIQUE VERSUS MODERN DRESS

On 24 June 1784 the Assembly of the State of Virginia voted to commission a statue of George Washington and asked Thomas Jefferson, who was about to succeed Benjamin Franklin in Paris as American Minister to France, to find the best sculptor in Europe. Houdon was reputed to be the best, Jefferson reported, and he lost no time in speaking to him about the commission. It was agreed that the statue should be life-size but Houdon did not think it could be done, as was proposed, from a full-length portrait to be painted for the purpose by Charles Willson Peale. However, Jefferson told Washington,

. . . he is so enthusiastically fond of being the executant of this work that he offers to go to America for the purpose of forming your bust from the life, leaving all his business here in the meantime. He thinks that being there three weeks with you would suffice to make his model in plaster with which he will return here and the work would employ him three years. Mr Houdon is at present engaged in making a statue of the king of France.

By July 1785 the terms of the contract had been settled: 25,000 livres (1,100 pounds sterling) for the statue and pedestal plus expenses and 10,000 livres life insurance in case Houdon should die on the voyage. Jefferson again remarked that, in order to go to America and take Washington's 'true figure by actual inspection and measurement', Houdon would leave several royal portraits unfinished and withdraw, not without some difficulty, from a commission from the empress of Russia. Since Washington would have Houdon as his guest at Mount Vernon for a week or more Jefferson went on to add that

. . . as a man, he is disinterested, generous, candid and panting after glory, in every circumstance meriting your good opinion. He brings with him a subordinate workman or two, who of course will associate with their class only.

Houdon and three assistants arrived in Philadelphia on 14 September but as their luggage had been mislaid they did not reach Mount Vernon until 2 October at night, 'after we were in bed (about eleven o'clock)', wrote Washington. He noted in his diary for 7 October that he had 'sat today as I had done yesterday, for Mr Houdon to form my bust', but apart from a lengthy note on the process of preparing plaster of Paris he did not remark further on the sculptor's visit. Houdon made

a terracotta model of a bust of Washington (still at Mount Vernon, signed and dated: HOUDON F. 1785) and from this he must have made a plaster mold and at least one plaster cast. By January 1786 he was back in Paris.

One question remained to be answered. In what dress – antique or modern – should Washington be shown? Jefferson took the matter up and in August Washington replied that,

. . . not having sufficient knowledge of the art of sculpture to oppose my judgement to the taste of connoisseurs, I do not desire to dictate in the matter. On the contrary, I shall be perfectly satisfied with whatever may be judged decent and proper. I should even have scarcely ventured to suggest, that perhaps a servile adherence to the garb of antiquity might not be altogether so expedient, as some little deviation in favour of the modern costume, if I had not learnt from Colonel Humphreys, that this was a circumstance hinted in conversation by Mr West to Mr Houdon. This taste, which has been introduced in painting by West, I understand is received with applause, and prevails extensively.

Modern dress, introduced by Benjamin West in his *Death of General Wolfe* (14,25), had attracted a great deal of attention though its appropriateness for sculpture was still controversial. To what extent Washington was aware of the importance and implications of contemporary costume is unknown. But he may well have wished to distance himself from portraits of rulers in Europe which were usually in antique or antique-seeming costume. Both Jefferson and Houdon still favoured antique dress. Houdon visualized Washington as a modern Cincinnatus, protector of agriculture, now retired to his own acres but still leading his people in peace as he had in war. Jefferson was firmly convinced of the appropriateness of antique dress for such works and wrote some years later that he was sure

. . . every person of taste in Europe would be for the Roman, the effect of which is undoubtedly of a different order. Our boots and regimentals have a very puny effect.

Nevertheless, despite his seeming diffidence, Washington had made his preference for modern dress quite clear and modern dress it was to be.

(H. H. Arnason, *The Sculptures of Houdon*, New York 1975)

---

style devoted essentially to the revival of antique forms. Ancient Roman buildings and antique statues had, in fact, been admired, imitated and sometimes directly copied throughout the first half of the eighteenth century. Their pre-eminence had never been seriously doubted. But they were revealed in a new light by Johann Joachim Winckel-

mann (1717–68), who effected a complete reappraisal of the art of antiquity (as understood since the Renaissance) and suggested the means for the regeneration of that of his own time. His first book, *Thoughts on the Imitation of Greek Works of Art* (Dresden 1755, translated into English 1765), broke away from the dry antiquarianism of earlier Classical scholarship. Writing from the point of view of an aesthete, a 'man of sensibility' and a man of the Enlightenment, he understood and discussed Greek statues as living works of art of eternal relevance (albeit without realizing how many of them were not originals). To him they embodied the essence of the Greek spirit, its liberty and love of the good, the beautiful and the true. 'The only way to become great and, if possible, inimitable', he wrote, 'is by imitation of the ancients' – not by the straightforward copying of antiquities, of course, but by emulating their essential aesthetic and moral qualities, which he defined in a famous phrase as 'noble simplicity and calm grandeur'. Winckelmann's fusion of the ideas of the Enlightenment with the art of antiquity set such familiar works as the *Apollo Belvedere* (5,5) in a new perspective, together with the recent discoveries at Herculaneum from 1738 and Pompeii from 1748 (see p. 186). But Winckelmann went further than that. He gave a sense of aspiring purpose to the reaction against the Rococo. And his shift in emphasis from form to spiritual essence contributed to the creation of a new theory of the arts which was expressive rather than mimetic (or imaginative in Aristotle's sense), with still more far-reaching consequences.

CANOVA AND DAVID

Winckelmann's influence was pervasive but it was most strongly felt in Rome, where he lived from 1755 to 1768 and where most of the statues he extolled were to be seen. Here it was that the sculptor Antonio Canova (1757–1822) and the painter Jacques-Louis David (1748–1825) underwent a kind of artistic revelation and conversion. Canova began his career in the Venice of Guardi, carving figures which have the graceful lightness and sensuous charm of those in Tiepolo's frescoes. Before he was 20 he had astonished Venetian connoisseurs with his technical virtuosity. But in 1779 he visited Rome, where he settled permanently next year, fell in with an international (predominantly British) set of artists, archeologists and theorists, and began to evolve a new sculptural style of revolutionary severity and uncompromising idealistic purity. His austere monument to Pope Clement XIV (SS Apostoli, Rome), completed in 1787, won him international renown and also numerous commissions. He was hailed as the continuer of the ancient Greek tradition, the modern Phidias.

The free-standing statues and groups Canova went on to carve in a gentler, less impersonal style were even more widely acclaimed. Their subjects were drawn from Classical mythology, sometimes challenging comparison with the most highly admired antiquities. But they are always suffused with the sensibility of his own time. His *Cupid and Psyche* is as far removed in feeling from Greek or Roman sculptures as from those of the earlier eighteenth century (**14,28**). Representing the moment, in the version of the fable by Apuleius, when Cupid revives the dying Psyche, it is a complex image of love and death, of eroticism purged of sensuality, of idealism made tangible and

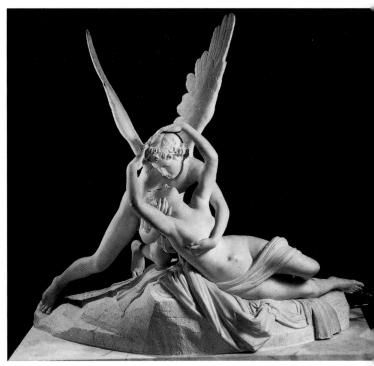

14,28 Antonio Canova, *Cupid and Psyche*, 1787–93. Marble, 5ft 1in (1.55m) high. Louvre, Paris.

accessible by human passion. Nor is it less complex when viewed solely as a three-dimensional composition of interlocking forms in contrapuntal harmony, revolving through a series of mellifluous and apparently effortless transitions. The figures, wholly absorbed in one another without so much as a glance towards the spectator, form a self-contained entity and demand to be seen as such. The group has to be shown in a central position. In addition to 'reviving' the art of sculpture (in the eyes of his contemporaries), Canova liberated it from the architectural settings to which most works, apart from portraits, had been bound since the early seventeenth century. It is also a sign of the times that some of his new statues were intended for museums – the first great works of art to be created specifically for this purpose. Museums were now regarded for the first time as institutions for public education.

Jacques-Louis David, like Canova, began in a distinctly mid-eighteenth-century manner. He was a product of the French system of artistic education shortly after it had been made more rigorous, a student at the Academy in Paris and then from 1775 to 1780 at the French Academy in Rome. He went back to Rome in 1784 to paint his first major work, *The Oath of the Horatii* (**14,29**). It was commissioned for the Crown as one of a number of pictures with the didactic purpose of improving public morality through the visual arts. The subject was probably proposed and certainly approved by Louis XVI's minister for the arts. But David himself was responsible for selecting, one might say inventing, the particular scene or incident, which is not described in ancient or later literature. The three Horatii brothers are

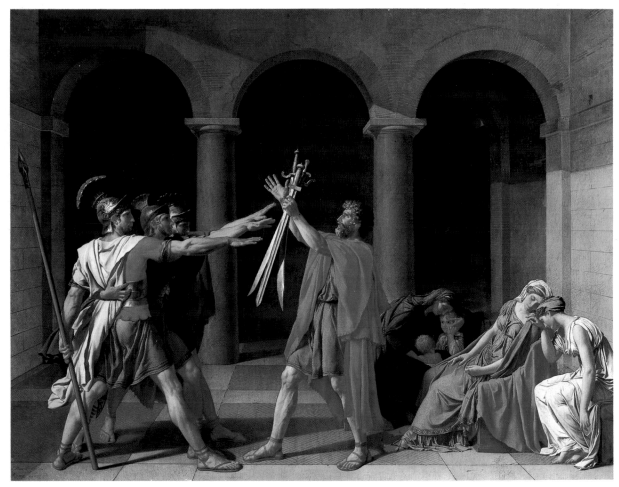

14,29 Jacques-Louis David, *The Oath of the Horatii*, 1784–5. Oil on canvas, about 14 × 11ft (4.27 × 3.35m). Louvre, Paris.

shown selflessly resolving to sacrifice their lives for their country, a premonitory overture stating the great themes of a story from the early history of ancient Rome told by Livy and dramatized by the seventeenth-century French tragedian Pierre Corneille. (To settle a political dispute the three Roman Horatii fought three brothers from the neighbouring city of Alba; the only survivor was one of the Horatii who, on returning victorious to Rome, killed his sister for lamenting the death of one of the Alban brothers, her betrothed lover.)

The nobility of ancient Roman stoicism and patriotism is the message, which David conveyed with an appropriately stoic directness and economy of visual means. Style is fused with subject-matter in this evocation of an heroic world of simple, uncomplicated passions and blunt, uncompromising truths. Masculine courage and resolve is contrasted with feminine tenderness and acquiescence; the taut muscles of the brothers, vibrant with an almost electric energy, are balanced, across the noble aspiring stance of their father, by the softly pliant draperies and meltingly compassionate gestures of their mother and sisters. Compositional lucidity is reinforced by the limpid early morning clarity of the lighting and the pristine purity of color, as well as the rudimentary simplicity of the shallow box-like space with its primitive

Doric columns and semicircular arches. David followed up this work with another on the same vast scale (more than 10 feet, 3m, high) and still more severe in subject – the ancient Roman consul Brutus seated in his house while lictors carry in the bodies of his two sons, who have been executed at his command for treasonable conspiracy (Louvre, Paris). It was also painted for the Crown and exhibited at the Salon in 1789, a few weeks after the Bastille had been stormed. Both pictures are revolutionary in an artistic sense; but whether they were so politically, as was later only too easily assumed, is uncertain.

The events of 1789 – the demolition of the Bastille, which demonstrated that the king had lost control of Paris, the formation of a national assembly and its declaration of the Rights of Man, the nationalization of Church property, the abolition of feudal rights, riots throughout the land – forced on every Frenchman a political choice of the utmost gravity. David threw in his lot with the revolutionary extremists of the Jacobin club. He was elected to the Convention in 1792 and voted for the death of the king, he became a member of the police committee of 'General Security', which was mainly responsible for administrating the Terror, and when more moderate views began to prevail in 1794 he was imprisoned. During the Jacobin years he devoted his art to the new republic, finding the style he had forged for pictures of ancient virtue to be the perfect vehicle for commemorating the 'martyrs' of the Revolution in paintings hung in the Convention – the journalist Jean-Paul Marat murdered in his bath by Charlotte Corday, the young Joseph Barra shot by royalist troops, and Lepeletier de Saint-Fargeau, a fellow member of the Convention, killed by a royalist during the trial of Louis XVI. *The Dead Marat* is the most deeply moving of David's works and perhaps the greatest 'political' picture ever painted (**14,30**). The absolute minimum of detail necessary to recreate the historical moment is used. For the painting's significance is universal, a stark image of the finality of death in which the unrelenting horizontality of the composition is broken only by the downward accent of the right arm, which seems to deny any hope of redemption above. The upper part of the canvas is a limitless, empty void. It is a revolutionary icon, a secular Pietà, intended to immortalize Marat in the memory of his fellow men, as ruthless in its logic and unyielding in its austerity as the political ideals of the Jacobins – a fitting memorial to the writer who had extolled 'the despotism of Liberty'.

14,30 Jacques-Louis David, *The Dead Marat*, 1793. Oil on canvas, about 5ft 3ins × 4ft 1in (1.6 × 1.25m). Musées Royaux des Beaux-Arts de Belgique, Brussels.

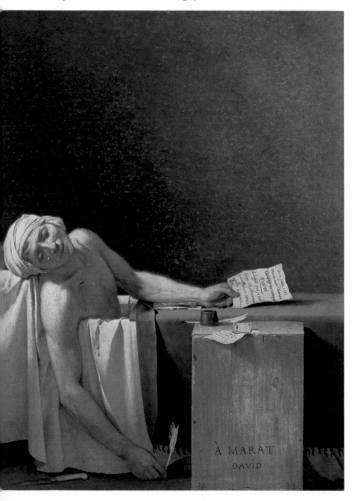

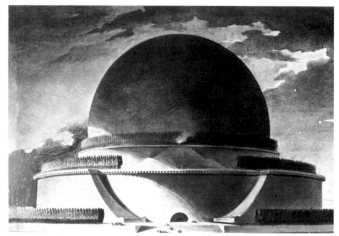

14,31 Etienne-Louis Boullée, *Design for Monument to Isaac Newton*, 1784. Ink and wash on paper, 5^{7}/₁₆ × 25⅝ins (39.2 × 65cm). Bibliothèque Nationale, Paris.

Architectural parallels to David's radical style of the 1790s, but without the political significance he gave it, may be found in the designs of Etienne-Louis Boullée (1728–99) and Claude-Nicolas Ledoux (1736–1806). In the work of both the mid-century reaction against the Rococo was given a positive direction, a return to the antique leading to the creation of a new architecture of astonishing boldness and simplicity. They participated in a general movement to reject the Baroque system of architectural composition, that process of fusing and interlocking of parts so that one flows almost imperceptibly into those adjacent to it, together with the mesh of decoration which made such an organic unification possible. Stark contrasts between the various masses of a building or group of buildings were emphasized with interior volumes clearly expressed on the exterior. A marked preference was shown for unbroken contours, clear-cut lines, right-angles, openings of simple shape punched in the walls with no surrounds to soften the impact. Emphasis shifted from free-flowing space to static mass and what the English poet Mark Akenside (1721–70) called 'the pure forms / Of Triangle or Circle, Cube or Cone'.

Such an architecture of pure geometry could be taken to its logical conclusion on paper, as in Boullée's project for a monument to that great hero of the Enlightenment, Isaac Newton (**14,31**). The exterior was intended to suggest a planet, the interior the night sky with stars lit by holes bored through the shell. Like the Pantheon in Rome, it is composed of a cylinder and sphere; but Boullée went back beyond antiquity to the primal Platonic essences. The monument has no antique elements apart from the sarcophagus. The architect 'ought not to make himself the slave of the ancients', Boullée wrote; he should become the 'slave of nature' – but of nature as understood by Newton and subsequent thinkers, an orderly structure, not the impenetrable mystery which was soon to fire the imagination and trouble the souls of the Romantics.

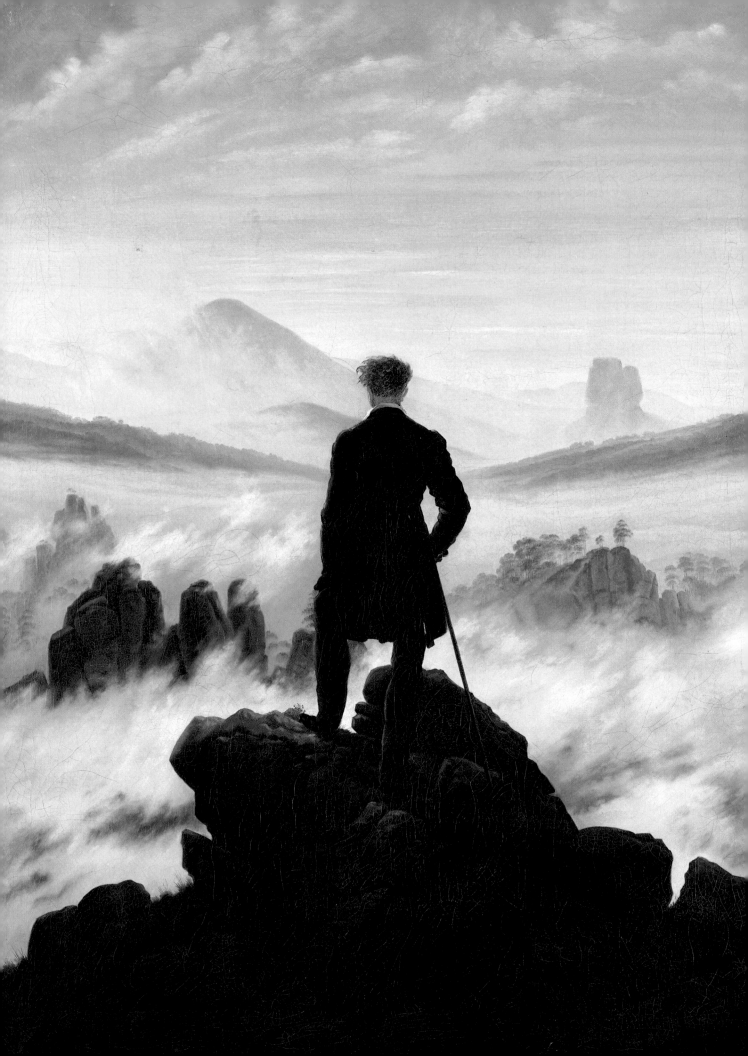

PART FOUR

THE MAKING OF THE MODERN WORLD

Opposite Caspar David Friedrich, *The Wanderer above the Mists*, detail, c. 1817–18. Oil on canvas, 29½ × 37¼ins (74.8 × 94.8cm). Kunsthalle, Hamburg.

CHAPTER FIFTEEN

ROMANTICISM TO REALISM

In the last decade of the eighteenth century and the first of the nineteenth, attitudes to the arts, as to life in general, underwent a profound change which has influenced Western thought to the present day. Out of the turbulence of the revolutionary epoch there emerged ideas which soon became basic assumptions for artists, architects, writers, musicians and the public for whom they worked – ideas about the artist's individual creativity, the uniqueness of his work and his relationship to the rest of society, about artistic sincerity and integrity, about the relative importance of expression and representation and, above all, about the power of the artist to transcend logical processes of thought and break through to states of mind beyond or below conscious control. An art based on the optimism of the Enlightenment and of its faith in reason and human perfectibility could not long survive the

French Revolution. The insufficiency of reason, the power of fanaticism and the role of chance in human affairs, the bewildering internal contradictions which make such rational concepts as those of liberty and equality irreconcilable, had all been made painfully apparent by the course the Revolution took. Initial, eminently reasonable reforms installing a constitutional monarchy had led to republicanism and thence, uncontrollably, to the Terror and the 'despotism of Liberty', followed by the autocracy of Napoleon's imperial rule.

These political events coincided with almost equally revolutionary changes in philosophy. Science now seemed to make the universe more, rather than less, mysterious. Isaac Newton's mechanistic conception of creation – an orderly system set in motion by 'a divine clock-maker' – gave way to one that was dynamic and organic. The

The visual arts	Historical landmarks
1800 Benoist, *Portrait of a Black Woman* (15,6)	**1798** Wordsworth and Coleridge, *Lyrical Ballads*
	1802 Peace of Amiens
	1804 Napoleon crowned Emperor by Pope. Beethoven, *Eroica Symphony*
1814 Goya, *The Third of May 1808* (15,8)	**1812** Napoleon enters and retreats from Moscow
1814–15 Constable, *Stour Valley and Dedham Vale* (15,21)	**1814** First effective steam locomotive
c. 1817–18 Friedrich, *The Wanderer* (15,19)	**1815** Waterloo
	1818 Byron, *Don Juan*
1819 Géricault, *The Raft of the 'Medusa'* (15,12)	**1826** Fenimore Cooper, *Last of the Mohicans*
1824–5 Constable, *The Leaping Horse* (15,22)	**1830** July Revolution. Louis Philippe king of the French
1830 Delacroix, *Liberty* (15,17)	**1831** Faraday discovers electromagnetism
1834 Corot, *Volterra* (15,28)	**1834** British abolition of slavery
1839–52 Barry and Pugin, Houses of Parliament (15,34)	**1837** Victoria queen of England
	1839 Invention of photography
1840 Turner, *The Slave Ship* (15,24)	**1840** Proudhon – 'Property is theft'
1841–52 Upjohn, Trinity Church (15,35)	**1845** Wagner, *Tannhäuser*
1845 Bingham, *Fur Traders* (15,48)	**1848** Revolutions in France etc. Fourth Republic. Marx and Engels, *Communist Manifesto*
1849–50 Courbet, *A Burial at Ornans* (15,38)	**1849** Ruskin, *Seven Lamps of Architecture*
1852–62 Millet, *The Man with a Hoe* (15,39)	**1852** H. Beecher Stowe, *Uncle Tom's Cabin*
1859–63 Ingres, *Turkish Bath* (15,14)	**1857** Flaubert, *Mme Bovary*. Baudelaire, *Fleurs du mal*
1863 Manet, *Luncheon on the Grass* (15,40). O'Sullivan, *Gettysburg* (15,57)	**1859** Darwin, *Origin of Species*
1867 Manet, *The Execution of Emperor Maximilian* (15,41)	**1861** American Civil War begins. Women gain vote in Australia
1875 Eakins, *The Gross Clinic* (15,54)	**1865** Lincoln assassinated
1878 Muybridge, *Galloping Horse* (15,58)	**1870** France declares war on Prussia. Napoleon III capitulates

classification of natural species by Linnaeus (Carl von Linn, 1707–78) and others led to the dawning realization that they had not been created in definitive form but were the products of a long evolutionary process. Speculative theories of evolution were put forward in France by Jean-Baptiste Lamarck (1744–1829) and in England by Erasmus Darwin (1731–1802), grandfather of Charles Darwin (see p. 671). At the same time philosophy was given a new direction by Immanuel Kant (1724–1804), who shifted its focus away from problems amenable to empirical investigation and rational deduction from self-evident axioms to an analysis of the most general concepts and categories. He brought to an end the heroic attempt to make philosophy a branch of natural science, breaking completely with traditions of both rationalism and empiricism. The distinctions he made between types of statement, according to the evidence they require and the interconnection between the concepts they presuppose, provided a new basis for the discussion of religious beliefs, morals and also aesthetics, which, for the first time in Western thought, moved from the periphery to the centre of philosophical systems. Goethe, in an essay of 1799 on Winckelmann (see p. 636), remarked that no educated man could with impunity reject or oppose the philosophical movement initiated by Kant – a tribute from the greatest creative writer to the greatest thinker of the time. The movement led, nevertheless, to a Romantic philosophy which Goethe lived to deplore.

Unlike previous revolutions, the French Revolution had ecumenical claims: its armies set out to revolutionize the world and its ideas spread beyond Europe to South America, the Near East and India. It began a period of constant political and social unrest. In France it had effected the transfer of power from the old aristocracy to the bourgeoisie. Subsequent French governments, irrespective of their ostensible political color and the upheavals which brought them to power, all depended for survival on their ability to protect bourgeois society from the twin dangers of Jacobin republicanism and a return to the privileges and restrictions of the *ancien régime* – the Directory (1794–9); the rule of Napoleon as first consul from 1799 and as emperor from 1804; the restored Bourbon monarchy (1815–30); the constitutional monarchy of Louis-Philippe (1830–48); the Second Republic (1848–51) and the Second Empire of Napoleon III (1851–70), followed by the Third Republic.

Outside France, reaction triumphed after 1815, though there were revolutions in many different places in 1830 and 1848 simultaneous with those in Paris, all led by members of the middle classes who demanded participation in government. In countries under foreign rule (Belgium until 1830, parts of northern Italy until 1866) they were also fired by ideals of nationalism. Everywhere there was conflict between forces of continuity (monarchy, landed aristocracy and Church) and forces of change. A rapid rise in the population, the spread of industrial production and the enrichment of its entrepreneurs, a drift from the country to the cities and the consequent emergence of an urban proletariat occasioned the growth of new social structures which could not be regulated by the old systems of government based on the notion of a static order and immutable values.

The Industrial Revolution began in England in the 1780s with the mass production in mechanized factories of goods for mass consumption. Here industry was unhampered by the guild restrictions, trade unhindered by the local customs barriers, which had survived on the Continent. Expansion was made possible by the exploitation of overseas markets, especially in the still growing colonial empire (the annexation of India amply compensating for the loss of the United States). Classes enriched by industry were placated by parliamentary reforms. But the cost in human suffering at a lower social level was appalling. 'From this foul drain the greatest stream of human industry flows out to fertilize the whole world', the French political analyst Alexis de Tocqueville wrote of Manchester in 1835. 'From this filthy sewer pure gold flows. Here humanity attains its most complete development and its most brutish, here civilization works its miracles and civilized man is turned almost into a savage.'

Just over a decade later conditions in Manchester convinced Karl Marx (1818–83) that the system of industrial production provided the key to the problem of historical change. Assisted by his friend Friedrich Engels (1820–95) – the representative in Manchester of a German cotton firm – he wrote *The Communist Manifesto* (London, 1848) which called for 'the forcible overthrow of all existing social conditions'. Although it had little immediate effect, this pamphlet acquired within two decades the status of a holy text and came to be accepted by about half of the human race. It differs from previous political declarations in that its prime concern is not with the rights of man or systems of government but with theoretical certainties. The dialectical process of history would, Marx believed, inevitably lead to the triumph of the proletariat.

Artists were as much affected as everyone else by the political and social conflicts of the early nineteenth century. And since these upheavals lend themselves to interpretation as conflicts between progressives and reactionaries, a similar structure has been superimposed upon the history of art during this period. However, the parallel is not exact. Painters and sculptors and architects who were artistically innovatory did not always hold advanced political views. Even the most politically engaged artists were usually more concerned with 'artistic freedom' than with political liberty. They worked mainly for a middle class to which they themselves, or most of them, belonged – the 'bourgeoisie' against which Marx directed his invective. And this public demanded an escapist art: evocations of distant times, distant lands, happy country folk and the beauties of nature. Similarly, urban designers and architects, employed by the expanding middle-class, supplied buildings that gave illusions of grandeur with classicizing or medievalizing façades and correspondingly evocative interiors. Only the vast, many-storied factories built by industrialists in England, Blake's 'dark Satanic mills', were baldly utilitarian and made few, if any, concessions to aesthetic tastes. Their advanced techniques of

Factories and Public Parks

OWEN, NASH AND OLMSTED

By the early nineteenth century, especially in Britain, the industrial revolution had led to the proliferation of factories around which workers lived in a heavily polluted environment. The first attempt to provide an alternative was small-scale but none the less remarkable. In 1800 Robert Owen (1771–1858) became part owner of a cotton mill at New Lanark in the beautiful Clyde valley of southern Scotland and astonished his contemporaries by beginning to build a settlement for his employees with a school, infirmary, community centre and co-operative shop, not simply barrack-like dormitories as was usual at isolated factories. He also paid regular wages, provided security for the sick and aged, limited the hours of work to ten and one-half a day and employed no children under the age of ten. These departures from current practice, modest though they may nowadays seem, won international fame for New Lanark. As a model for factory management it attracted many visitors, including the Czar of Russia, whose comments on Owen's utopian socialist schemes, first set out in *A New View of Society* (London 1813) are, however, unrecorded.

Owen went further in his *Report to the Committee of the Association for the Relief of the Manufacturing and Labouring Poor* (London 1817), recommending the establishment in the countryside of self-supporting 'villages of co-operation' for 800 to 1,200 inhabitants engaged in manufacturing and agriculture (**15,1**). Unable to realize this project in Britain he turned to the wide open spaces of the USA, acquired a small German Protestant settlement in Indiana in 1825, named it New Harmony and employed an architect to make an elaborate model for its buildings which were to exploit the most up-to-date techniques of construction, ventilation and lighting. But no work on the site was ever done, Owen lost four-fifths of his fortune, returned to England and spent the rest of his life promoting Trade Unionism, the Co-operative Movement and Spiritualism. Contemporaneously, the French social theorist Charles Fourier (1772–1837) was developing his *phalanstère* project, a large building to be owned jointly by some 1,600 inhabitants with a communal dining-hall, library, workshops and private apartments opening on to interior streets, the exterior recalling that of the Palace of Versailles. Similar communes, smaller in size and with simpler buildings, were established in France and the USA. But the utopian projects of Owen and Fourier had greater influence when shorn of their Socialist ideology. From the 1830s paternalist factory owners, recognizing that the physical and moral welfare of their employees was no less important than the oiling and maintenance of machinery, built so-called 'company towns'. Each one usually had a church or chapel for worship according to the owner's denomination, a school, a library, a single shop and a public park for quiet recreation, but no tavern where alcohol could be sold. Not surprisingly many workers preferred the rough and tumble of some nearby town.

Such utopian projects and 'company towns' in fact evaded the problems created by the continual growth of industrial cities. It had been recognized already in the seventeenth century that greenery could help to purify polluted air, hence the introduction of squares planted with trees and shrubberies which became a conspicuous feature of property development in London and which were to be included in the planning of Philadelphia and other colonial cities in America. London also had the benefit of vast royal parks, often called 'the lungs of the city', and most European capitals also had royal parks partly open to the public. However, it was not until 1789 that the first park intended specifically for the public was created, the *Englischer Garten* at Munich on land donated to the city by the Elector (ruler) of Bavaria. As the name indicates, it was laid out like an English landscape park (see pp. 630–1) to provide the general public with pleasures previously available only to the owners of large estates. This type

15,1 Robert Owen, design for a 'Village of Cooperation' from his *Report to the Committee for the Relief of the Manufacturing Poor*, London, 1817.

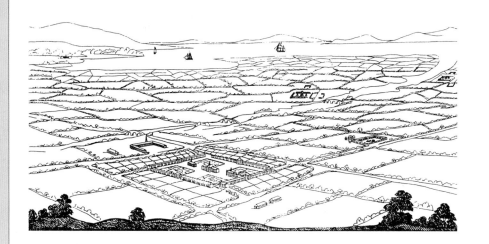

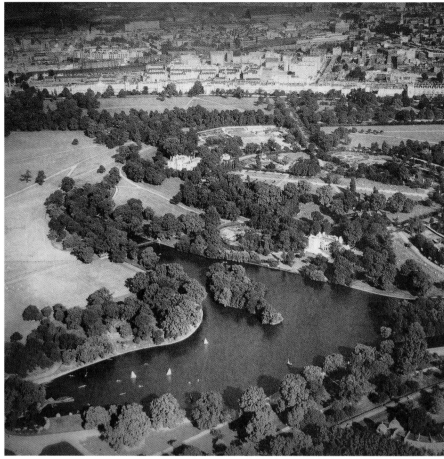

15,2 John Nash, Regent's Park, London, 1811–30. Aerial view looking east.

new ship-building town of Birkenhead near Liverpool, was visited in 1850 by the American Frederick Law Olmsted (1822–1903) who noted that it was 'enjoyed equally by all classes' whereas in 'democratic America there was nothing to be thought comparable with this People's Garden' (15,3). Olmsted was at that time a journalist, but in 1858 he won, in collaboration with the architect Calvert Vaux (1824–95), the commission to lay out New York's Central Park on an 843-acre (341.2-hectare) site at what was then the north end of Manhattan's rectangular grid of streets. The area, far larger than Birkenhead's 60 acres (24 hectares), permitted the creation of a more varied landscape of seemingly wild woodlands, lakes, hills and plains with an innovatory separation of footpaths from carriageways by means of bridges and tunnels (15,5). It was intended, Olmsted wrote, 'in a directly remedial way to enable men to better resist the harmful influences of ordinary town life and to recover what they lose from them'. Whether or not this was in fact to be realized, it remains one of the most remarkable artistic achievements of the century, despite later alterations and encroachments. Many other public parks were created in America and Europe while most of the projects for improving lower-class housing remained on paper.

of park with irregular lakes, gentle hillocks and paths meandering among clumps of trees, was also to be adopted in England for middle-class residential developments and suburbs. One of the first was Regent's Park, London, designed in 1812 by the architect and town-planner John Nash (1752–1835), surrounded by terraces of houses disguised by façades to give each block the appearance of a great palace and so placed that their windows had views similar to those seen from upper-class country-houses (15,2).

A landscape park was, however, thought to be more than just visually pleasing; it partook of that spiritually regenerative influence which nature was believed to exert. In the USA, the first intended for the public was Mount Auburn outside Boston, designed in 1831 primarily as a cemetery. The creation of parks for working-class areas began in Germany and England in the 1840s, a decade of poverty and political turbulence in the industrial centres. Three were laid out in notoriously insalubrious Manchester. Another, in the

15,3 Joseph Paxton, Birkenhead Park, Liverpool, 1843–4.

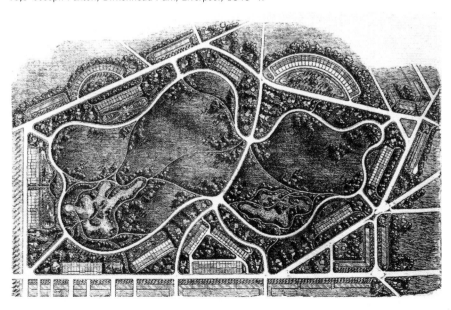

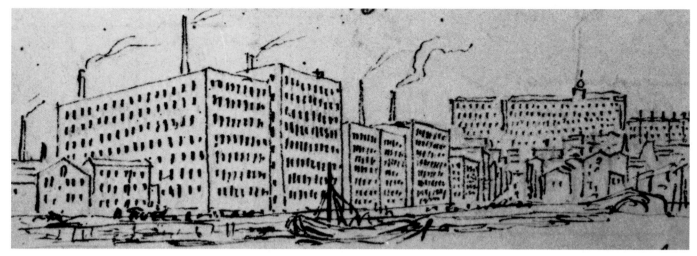

15,4 Karl Friedrich Schinkel, *Union Street, Ancoats, Manchester, England, with the McConnel and Murray Mills fronting the Canal*, 1826. Pen and ink. Staatliche Museen Preussischer Kulturbesitz, Berlin.

construction with iron, to reduce the risk of fire, impressed visitors including the great Prussian architect Karl Friedrich Schinkel (see p. 668) who sketched a group in Manchester in 1826 (**15,4**). Here, he wrote, 400 new cotton mills had been erected in the post-war boom, 'several as big as the royal palace in Berlin, thousands of smoking obelisks from steam-engines around them' and already 'as blackened with smoke as if they had been in use for a hundred years'. Already, however, overproduction had led to a trade recession with thousands of the unemployed gathering in the streets and he was 'very much in doubt as to what might come of this frightful state of affairs'. Successful factory owners, he noted had country-houses and parks in pleaasant valleys not far but far enough away, while accommodation for the workforce was left to speculators whose rows of cheap red-brick 'back-to-back' houses sprawling out from industrial towns soon became slums.

The 'Condition of the Working Class in England' (the title of Engels's first book published in 1844), which had already been described with horror by the novelist Charles Dickens (1812–70), raised problems that preoccupied many, those who feared revolution as well as political revolutionaries. How might the living conditions of the proletariat be ameliorated? By building new industrial settlements in the clean air of the open country? Or by purifying the polluted atmosphere of cities and by inserting patches of country as public parks for outdoor recreation in the urban fabric? The latter was to be widely adopted, becoming throughout the West a distinctive feature of nineteenth-century urban design, with New York's Central Park, begun in 1863, as the most extensive example (**15,5**). All the proposed remedies were founded on a belief in the physically healing and morally regenerative power of nature, a belief which had inspired so many Romantic poets and artists from Wordsworth to the landscape painters in Europe and America.

ROMANTICISM

Romanticism was the response to the situation at the beginning of the century, or rather an infinite number of individual responses to a constantly changing situation. There was no single Romantic attitude nor can the variety of Romantic ideas be encapsulated in a simple formula. The word 'Romantic' was adopted, as writers of the time remarked, simply for lack of another to define what had previously eluded definition. The term 'Romance' had originally been used in the Middle Ages to distinguish songs in the French vernacular from those in Latin and traces of this sense survived. But the eighteenth-century reappraisal of medieval literature and art played no more than a part in what was to amount to a complete revaluation of all the arts of all countries and times, including Classical antiquity. For the Romantics judged works of art, literature and music not by predetermined rules, but according to the sensibility of the individual. They were reluctant to accept any guide apart from their own inner light.

Whereas Neo-Classical artists had striven after a style of impersonal clarity for the expression of universally relevant and eternally valid truths, the Romantics sought to express only their own feelings, beliefs, hopes and fears in all their myriad forms. John Constable (see p. 659) said that painting was for him 'but another word for feeling', Caspar David Friedrich (see p. 657) that the artist's only law was his own feelings. The poet Charles Baudelaire (1821–27), who was also the greatest and most discerning writer about the visual arts of his time, later remarked that 'Romanticism is precisely situated neither in choice of subject nor in exact truth, but in a way of feeling.' All this is evident in, for instance, the new importance given

15,5 *Opposite* Frederick Law Olmsted and Calvert Vaux, Central Park, New York, planned 1858, begun 1863.

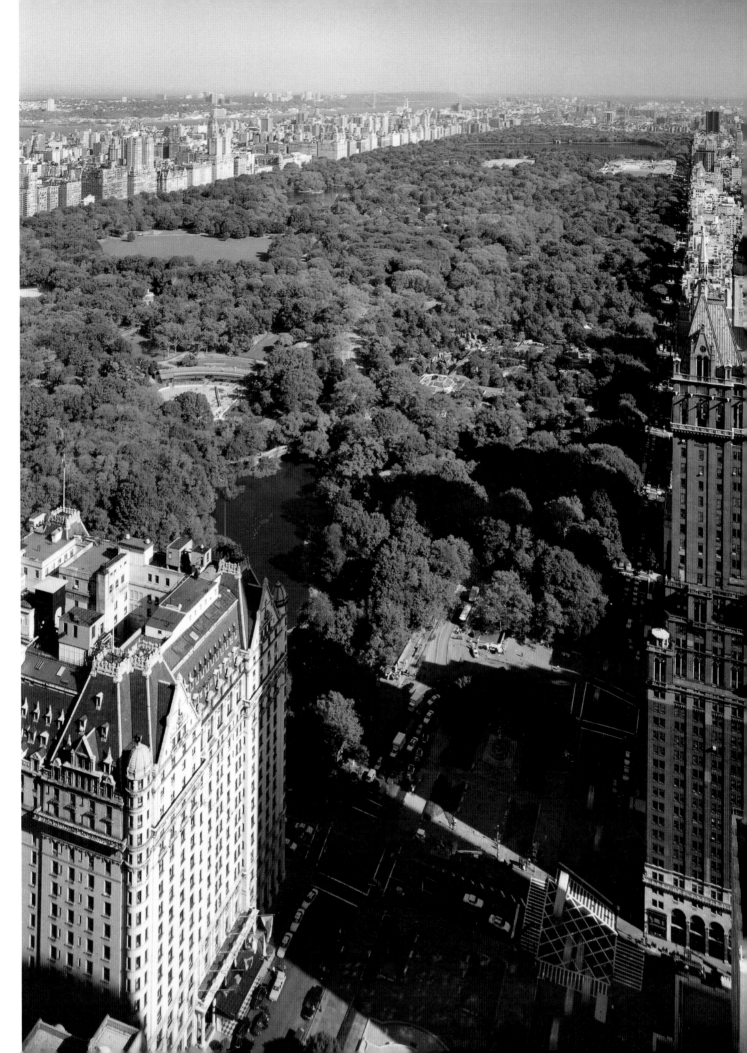

to the sketch – as the least premeditated form of art – and thus to the free handling of materials which reveal in the most direct manner possible the individuality of the artist's 'touch'. However an equally intimate, even idiosyncratic, view of the world could also be conveyed in meticulously detailed, impersonally precise drawings, and tightly handled paintings which expressed the artist's hypersensitive response to the exquisiteness of natural form – e.g. by the German 'Nazarene' artists. In such complexities and apparent contradictions the essence of Romanticism eludes definition.

Romantic attitudes precluded the development of a single style. Romanticism was neither simply a reaction against nor a development from earlier styles. Rather, a number of individual styles radiated out from the still centre of Neo-Classicism. The relationship of Neo-Classicism and Romanticism is therefore quite different from that between Baroque and Rococo, or from that between Gothic and Renaissance. Neo-Classicism was not rejected but fragmented. Ideas latent in Neo-Classical theory (especially in the writings of Winckelmann, see pp. 636–7) were developed independently. As a former pupil of Jacques-Louis David later remarked, the new movement in French painting was a revolution but not an insurrection. David himself, after the fall of Robespierre and his own imprisonment, had relaxed the austerity of his Jacobin pictures and went on to portray the great individualistic genius of the day, Napoleon.

THE HEIRS OF DAVID

Among David's pupils at the beginning of the Revolution there were a few young women, notably Marie Guillemine Leroulx de la Ville, better known under her married name as Mme Benoist (1768–1826). It was 'easy to see from the purity of drawing that she was a pupil of David', a critic remarked when her arresting portrait of a black woman was shown at the Salon in 1800 (15,6). With this exquisitely painted image of great visual sensitivity, the soft black skin set off by the crisp white freshly laundered and ironed drapery and head-dress, Marie Benoist made a radical break with the eighteenth-century tradition of representing non-European people as picturesquely exotic 'types'. It is very obviously the portrait of an individual, and a highly finished portrait rather than an *étude* or study from the life such as were done mainly as demonstrations of an artist's technical ability. On the other hand, it differs from contemporary portraits of white women. They were sometimes shown in daring *décolleté* (with a very low neck-line), but only occasionally with such prominent exposure of the breasts. This painting might therefore seem to have pandered to male voyeurism even though it was painted by a woman and without having been commissioned. At this time female nudity was associated either with a divinity (as in statues of Venus) or with personification (as in Kauffman's self-portrait as *Color*, 14,24, or Delacroix's *Liberty Leading the People*, 15,17) or with scientific ethnographic illustrations of people in a state of nature. Marie Benoist's painting does

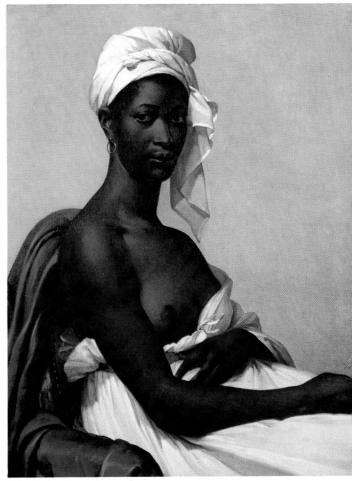

15,6 Marie Guillemine Benoist, *Portrait of a Black Woman*, 1800. Oil on canvas, 32½ × 25ins (81 × 65cm). Louvre, Paris.

not fall into any of these categories; yet the bare breast of her black woman would seem to have some, perhaps ambiguous, significance. Since it was almost certainly painted on the artist's own initiative and remained in her possession until 1818 when it was bought by the French state for, eventually, the Louvre, it is tempting to see in it some personal commitment. Might not Marie Benoist have been involved not just with this black woman, whom she painted with such warmth of human feeling, but with the general issue of liberty as brought to public attention by the abolition of slavery and the emancipation of women? Influenced by numerous prints of black men and women wearing caps of liberty and often barebreasted, published after the decree of 1794 abolishing slavery throughout French territory, Marie Benoist may have linked this enlightened act with the emancipation of women, which was being much discussed at the time, although it remained little more than a fond hope for the future. She was one of a number of women artists who had begun to achieve prominence in eighteenth-century France despite the restrictions put in their way, for they were not admitted to the official art schools, let alone the life-class. These restrictions were maintained during most of the nineteenth century and women contributed much less to the visual arts than to the literature of Romanticism, even though there was a notable increase in the number of professional women painters. Exclusion from the life-class inhibited them from depicting figure subjects, which continued to be regarded as the highest form of art. (Marie Benoist's first works had been moral subjects such as *Innocence between Virtue and Vice* – with vice personified as a handsome young man, not, as was usual, as a woman. But her career was cut short at the Restoration when her royalist husband became one of the king's ministers and it was thought unbecoming for her to work as a professional painter. So she gave it up.)

David's favourite and most successful pupil was Antoine-Jean Gros (1771–1835), who reflected the aspirations of the empire as vividly as his master had expressed those of the republic. On one vast canvas after another he celebrated the glory of Napoleon and the benefits of his régime. He began with an incident in the Egyptian campaign of 1799 – General Bonaparte visiting his plague-stricken troops in Jaffa (**15,7**). It is an essay in the grand style, combining reportage to evoke verisimilitude (rather than to reconstruct the historical moment) with allegory

to stress the picture's significance. The various symptoms and effects of the plague are illustrated – bubonic sores, emaciation, feverish thirst and vomiting – and one of Bonaparte's aides holds a handkerchief to shield his nose from the stench. But the immaculate general is invulnerable, almost immortal, touching a sick man with the gesture of a divinely appointed healer-king, if not that of Christ.

The very carefully thought-out program of *Napoleon in the Plague House at Jaffa* links it with the morally improving pictures painted for the crown in the late eighteenth century. But propaganda takes the place of enlightened didacticism in this glorification of an individual, whom the spectator is invited not to emulate but to venerate. Neo-Classical simplicity, clarity, purity of line and color have given way to richness, complexity and bravura handling of paint. Gros had learned as much from Rubens as from David. There is, however, a dichotomy between the sharp-edged precision with which Bonaparte and his attendants are rendered and the more broadly painted other figures. And although this was obviously intended to focus attention on the central group, it was soon to have exactly the opposite effect – both pictorially, as the freer

15,7 Antoine-Jean Gros, *Napoleon in the Plague House at Jaffa*, 1804. Oil on canvas, 17ft 5ins × 23ft 7ins (5.32 × 7.20m). Louvre, Paris.

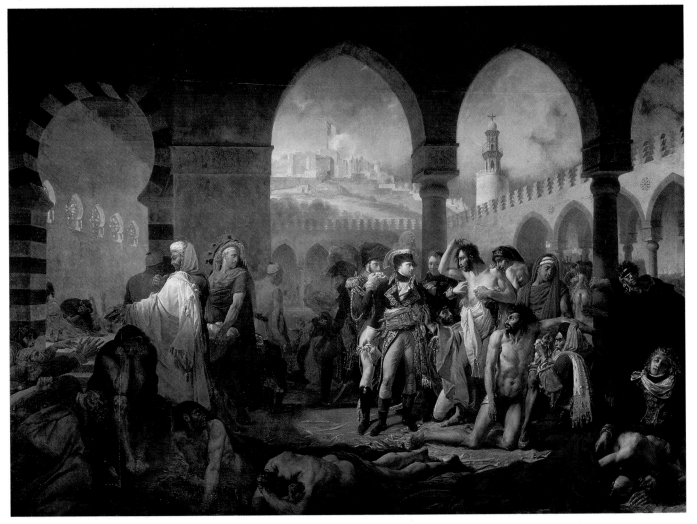

style of painting initiated by Gros became more wide-spread, and emotionally, as attention shifted from the personality of Napoleon Bonaparte to the heroic suffer-ings of his troops (often to be depicted on the retreat from Moscow).

GOYA

By stressing the realistic at the expense of the idealistic or classic elements in David's work, Gros created a new type of modern history picture. He became the most influen-tial painter of his generation, partly through prints which disseminated his major compositions. Francisco de Goya (1746–1828), a far greater artist, may initially have con-ceived his two paintings *The Second of May 1808* (Prado, Madrid) and *The Third of May 1808* (**15,8**) as replies to Gros. In both composition and subject-matter *The Third of May 1808* seems to be a direct riposte to the faintly absurd *Capitulation of Madrid* (Versailles) by Gros and perhaps also a disenchanted comment on the stoic heroism of David's *Oath of the Horatii* (14,29). Goya's French soldiers echo the stance of the Horatii, but they

shoot a group of defenceless civilians rounded up in Madrid after the previous day's uprising against the French army of occupation. But the emphasis is placed on, and the spectator's sympathy directed to, the victims, especially the man in a white shirt who stands with out-stretched arms before the faceless firing-squad.

Goya, an almost exact contemporary of Jacques-Louis David, established himself in the 1780s as the leading painter in Spain, specializing in religious pictures and por-traits, and much employed by the royal court. He also knew well one or two of the few Spaniards who welcomed the Enlightenment and shared their hatred of injustice, religious fanaticism, superstition and cruelty. It was in this spirit that he made his first great series of etchings, *Los Caprichos* (The Caprices), published in 1799, the year he was appointed first painter to the king (**15,9**). Inscrip-tions set out the morally improving message of these didactic prints; but their perturbing view of a disjointed world inhabited by ignoble, barely human creatures of bestial appetites and impulses indicates how far Goya had already begun to move away from his early optimistic faith in the power of reason and the possibility of human

15,8 Francisco de Goya, *The Third of May 1808*, 1814. Oil on canvas, 8ft 6ins × 11ft 4ins (2.6 × 3.45m). Prado, Madrid.

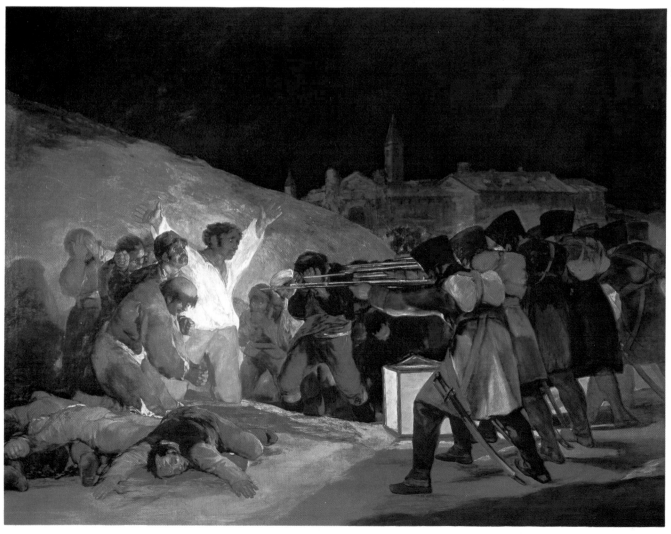

amelioration. Doubts gave way to disbelief and despair in the still more terrifying prints of his *Los Desastres de la Guerra* (The Disasters of War), prompted by the atrocities of the French troops in their attempt to suppress the popular uprising against Napoleonic rule in Spain – the conflict in which the word 'guerrilla' acquired its modern meaning (**15,10**). They are images of inhuman cruelty that go far beyond moral protest to denude the victims, as well as the victors, of all trace of nobility in body and mind, disclosing not simply the impotence of reason but the uncontrollable forces of unreason and madness lurking in the human brain. Later, in 1820–3, he covered the interior walls of his house outside Madrid with the so-called Black Paintings, which defy rational analysis and were perhaps a means of releasing and exorcizing the phantoms which possessed him and haunted his imagination (**15,11**). These broodingly private works were rarely seen before they were moved to the Prado in Madrid in 1881. Nor were *Los Desastres* published until 35 years after Goya's death.

The Third of May 1808, on the other hand, was intended for public exhibition. Goya painted it just after the restoration of the Spanish Bourbon monarchy in 1814, to commemorate the beginning of the Spanish war of liberation, and evidently intended to suggest that the men

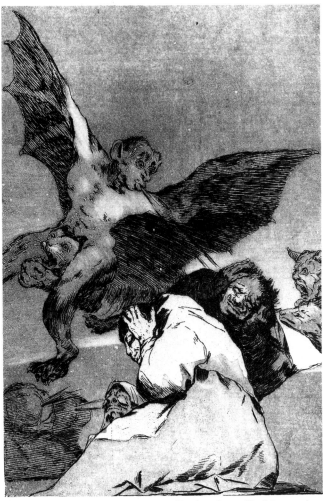

15,9 Francisco de Goya, *Blowers (Soplones)*, no. 48 of *Los Caprichos*, 1799. Etching and aquatint, 8⅓ × 6ins (21.5 × 15cm). Victoria & Albert Museum, London.

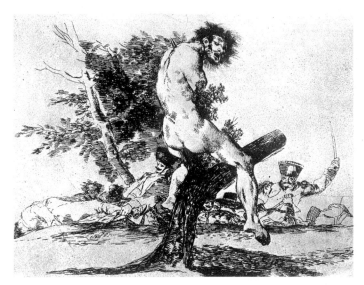

15,10 *Above* Francisco de Goya, *That is Worse (Esto es peor)*, no. 37 (32) of *Los Desastres de la Guerra*, 1812–15. Etching, 6¼ × 4¼ins (15.7 × 10.7cm).

15,11 *Right* Francisco de Goya, *Saturn Devouring one of his Children*, 1820–3. Wall-painting in oil detached on canvas, 57⅞ × 32⅝ins (146 × 83cm). Prado, Madrid.

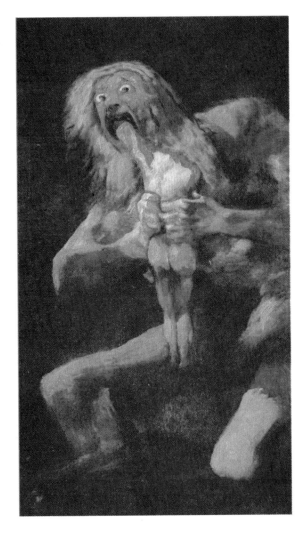

who were shot in 1808 had not died in vain. But it has a wider and deeper meaning as a secular martyrdom, one without any ray of hope that the manifest evils of this world will be righted in the next. The only source of illumination is the soldiers' gigantic lantern, perhaps a symbol of the remorseless logic of the Enlightenment, in which Spanish intellectuals, including Goya, had earlier placed their hopes of salvation. Everything seems to have failed, the Enlightenment as much as the Church represented by the towers in the background and the tonsured monk among the condemned. Only the individual artist and his vision remain to give meaning to a chaotic world – and Goya's vision was already too embittered and violent by 1814 to permit any relief or distraction from the horror of the subject by delicacy of brushwork or harmony of colors such as had 'neutralized' savage subjects in earlier art.

GERICAULT

The shift in emphasis from heroism to suffering, from victors to victims, is also apparent in the work of the French painter Théodore Géricault (1791–1824). His first exhibited work, of 1812, was a painting of a cavalry officer thrilling to the music of battle, the boom of cannon and the white of grape-shot – his next, of 1814, was of a wounded cuirassier retiring from the field (both in the Louvre). He was a painter of a socially new type: middle-class with a private income large enough to enable him to work without commissions. (Such financial independence helped to establish the notion of artistic independence.) When he set out to make his reputation at the Paris Salon of 1819 he took a subject very much of his own choosing and painted it on a vast scale: the survivors from the wreck of a French government frigate, *La Méduse*, in the Atlantic in 1816 (**15,12**). When the ship foundered, the captain and the senior officers took the only seaworhty lifeboats and cast 150 passengers and crew adrift on a makeshift raft on which only 15 survived a horrifying ordeal of 13 days.

The men on the raft were not heroes in any accepted sense of the word. Neither courageous endurance nor stoic self-control was displayed by any of them: they behaved as men all too frequently do in moments of crisis, those who survived did so simply from a crude animal urge to live. They suffered atrociously but in no good or noble cause; they were victims of incompetence, not of human or divine malevolence. But Géricault raised their plight to a level of universal significance. His picture questions conventional attitudes to the perennial prob-

15,12 Théodore Géricault, *The Raft of the 'Medusa'*, 1819. Oil on canvas, 16ft × 23ft 6ins (4.91 × 7.16m). Louvre, Paris.

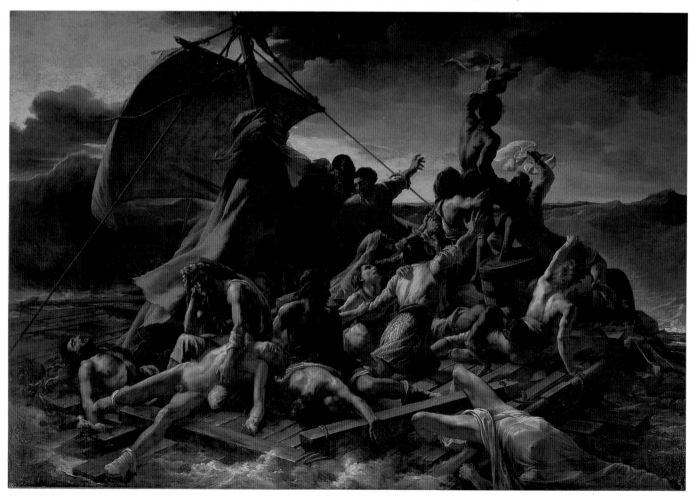

lems of heroism, hope, despair and suffering, providing only a disturbingly equivocal answer. When the picture was first exhibited, comments in the press were strongly colored by the scandal of *La Méduse* (the captain was a returned royalist émigré). By elevating a topical 'low-life' subject to such a colossal and heroic scale, Géricault might seem to have been attacking by implication not only the long-established hierarchy of *genres* but also the recent Bourbon restoration. Later it came to be regarded as a political allegory of a more profound type. 'France herself, our whole society is on that raft', the historian Jules Michelet wrote in 1847, when the clouds of revolution were again gathering over the country.

Despite its provocative subject, *The Raft of the 'Medusa'* was well received by the artistic establishment. Géricault was awarded a gold medal and given a commission for a large religious painting, which he passed on to the young Delacroix (see pp. 654–5). His pyramidal composition was of an academically approved type. Individual figures were depicted with the healthy physique of Greek athletes and not at all realistically – not, as they appeared when rescued, bearded, emaciated, covered with sores and wounds. In the Salon of 1819 it was Jean-Auguste-Dominique Ingres (1780–1867) who was censured for daring innovations in his paintings of an odalisque and of a scene from Ariosto's epic of chivalry.

INGRES

The *Odalisque* of 1819 was the first of the many nudes in Near Eastern settings which Ingres painted in the course of his long career, including the *Odalisque with a Slave* (**15,13**) and the *Turkish Bath* (**15,14**), on which he proudly inscribed his age – 82. The poses and background 'props' vary from one to another; but all reveal the same fleshy, erotic sensuality expressed with the utmost refinement of line, often in bright, rather acid colors. It is, in fact, the unexpectedness of the contrast between the warm voluptuousness of the subject-matter and the cool, sharp precision of the painting, between the languorous atmosphere and the carefully worked smooth surface, which gives these pictures their unnerving hold on our imagination. The composition of the *Odalisque with a Slave* is as tightly integrated as the pattern on a Persian carpet, with one element echoing another, the coil of the hookah's tube and the ripple of the odalisque's arms, the slant of her torso and of the lute, the two left feet one above the other. Colors are sharply juxtaposed and repeated with different effects of contrast over the canvas, a bright scarlet recurring in such a way as to suggest the twanging notes of the lute. The blond complexion of the odalisque is set off by the swarthy slave girl and the black eunuch, the soft smoothness of her boneless body by the caressing silks and satins on which she wallows with sensuous abandon, her nakedness enhanced by the thin drapery around her legs and thighs, her pearl necklace and jewelled bracelets.

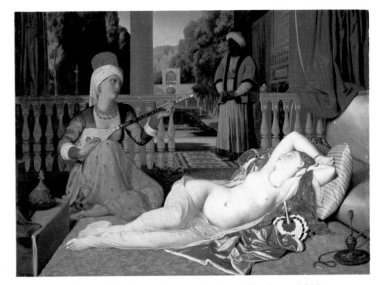

15,13 Jean-Auguste-Dominique Ingres, *Odalisque with a Slave*, 1842. Oil on canvas, 28 × 39⅜ins (71 × 100cm). Walters Art Gallery, Baltimore.

Ingres seems almost to have believed that a woman's place was in the harem. The fashionable ladies in his portraits are often loaded with golden chains, decked out to accentuate the opulence of well-rounded shoulders and plump arms, frequently posed against mirrors as if to suggest that such expensive and delectable objects should be seen, as well as fondled, in the round. Mme Moitessier,

15,14 Jean-Auguste-Dominique Ingres, *Turkish Bath*, 1859–63. Canvas, 3ft 6½ins (1.08m) diameter. Louvre, Paris.

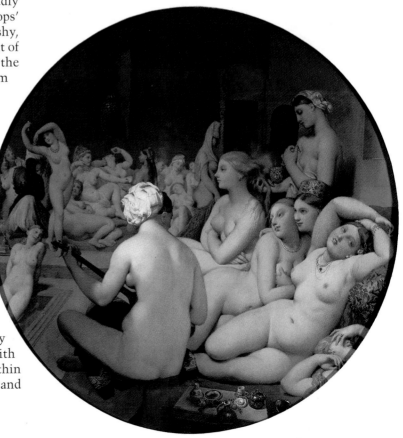

dressed in black lace and tulle with roses in her hair, standing in front of a damask, silk or paper wall-covering the color of Parma violets, exudes a hot-house luxuriance (15,15). She slightly looks down on the spectator, with a devouring expression of sexual superiority. After his early years in Rome, where he was obliged to earn his living from portraiture – mainly by exploiting his supreme gift as a draftsman in drawings of northern visitors to the city – Ingres would depict only those sitters with whom he felt some rapport. The Junoesque Mme Moitessier appealed to him for what he called her 'terrible beauty' and he gave her the air of an inscrutable goddess, her arms placed almost – but significantly not quite – in the pudic gesture of an antique Venus (see p. 152). Paradoxically, she acquires a timeless quality from the fashionable decor, which might seem to have been included gratuitously but which, in fact, plays an important part in the composition. The appearance and personality of the sitter, like the real-life original of a character in some great novel, provided Ingres

15,15 Jean-Auguste-Dominique Ingres, *Madame Moitessier*, 1851. Oil on canvas, 4ft 9¾ins × 3ft 3½ins (1.47 × 1m). National Gallery of Art, Washington DC (Samuel H. Kress Collection, 1946).

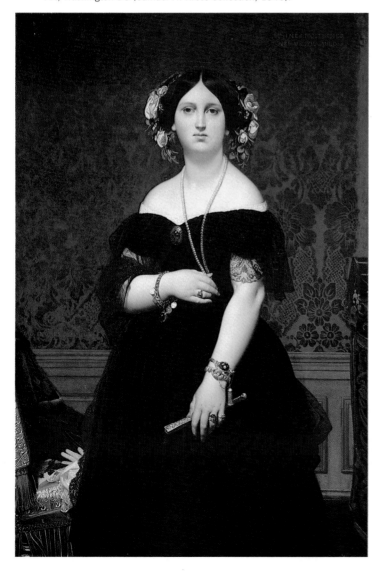

with no more than a point of departure for a complex work of art. Mme Moitessier becomes part of a pattern of curving lines. The composition is much subtler than it may seem at first sight – the bold vertical axis running down from the parting of the hair provides a central line against which Ingres plays off gentle asymmetries – and so is the predominantly black, pink and violet color-scheme, made vibrant by a tiny patch of turquoise in the chair.

DELACROIX

A pupil of David in the late 1790s, albeit an unruly one, Ingres became by the mid-nineteenth century the self-appointed guardian of the Classical tradition – the devotee of Raphael, the champion of 'line' and the great opponent of the colorist Eugène Delacroix (1798–1863). A caricaturist pictured them in single combat, one wielding a pencil, the other a paintbrush. Delacroix, born after the Revolution, was almost a generation younger than Ingres. As a student he was swept off his feet by Géricault, with whom he struck up a friendship, posing for one of the figures in *The Raft of the 'Medusa'* (the dead youth lying on his face in the centre foreground). His ambition was to paint large history pictures in the grand manner, in the tradition of Michelangelo and Rubens. And he succeeded so well that his first exhibited work (*The Bark of Dante*, 1822, now in the Louvre) was bought for the crown – he was always to be favoured by the state, receiving more and also more important official commissions than Ingres. But he developed an increasingly personal style of dynamic energy and richness of color, applied in great sweeps and splashes, which reached a climax in his *Death of Sardanapalus* (**15,16**). Even his admirers quailed before this vast canvas.

Depicting the story of the king of Nineveh, who, when besieged, ordered the massacre of his entire retinue before he too was immolated in his palace, the *Death of Sardanapalus* was inspired by (though not taken directly from) a tragedy by Byron, the most famous poet of the day. An intoxicating atmosphere of violence and sexual licence hangs over this voluptuous picture. It pulsates with color and flashes with light which glances off gold and pearls and precious stones. The sinewy virility of the black slave killing a horse, and the beautiful passionate bodies of the women in attitudes of frenzied exhaustion, or of pain which is almost rapture, give an orgiastic appearance to the scene of carnage. Although the subject is antique, and details in the painting are taken from antique art, nothing could be further removed from the Neo-Classical ideal of 'noble simplicity and calm grandeur'. It is also a far cry from the torpid world of the harem pictured with such cool and calculating eroticism by Ingres. The *Death of Sardanapalus* is composed in bold masses, which roll like clouds of smoke from a furnace across the canvas. Spatial relationships are ambiguous, conventional rules of perspective are disregarded, anatomy is wilfully distorted, an illusion of solidity is created by daring color relationships, flecks of blue and gray on flesh tones, not by firm contours and carefully graded

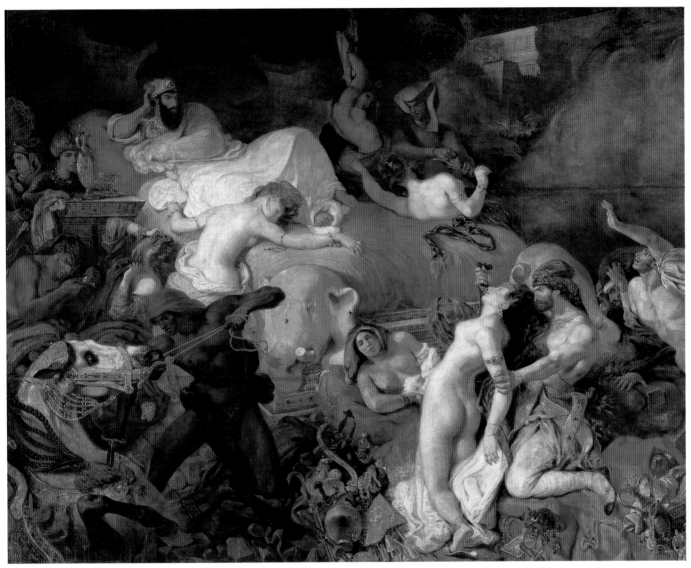

15,16 Eugène Delacroix, *Death of Sardanapalus*, 1828. Oil on canvas, 12ft 10ins × 16ft 3ins (3.92 × 4.96m). Louvre, Paris.

modelling. The picture is a kind of manifesto of artistic autonomy and of the Romantic belief in the painter as creator and destroyer, of both art and life.

The picture was shown in 1828 in the last Salon held under the Restoration, at a moment when Romanticism in the arts was being equated with liberalism in politics. Delacroix's next major work *The 28th July: Liberty Leading the People* (**15,17**) commemorated the revolution of July 1830 and was shown in the first Salon of the new régime under Louis-Philippe. For this evocation of fighting on the barricades – perhaps the most famous visual image of revolution ever created – he returned to the combination of grand style and reportage, allegory and real life. It is more idealized than the many other representations of the July days, but also more vivid and much more disturbing – as contemporaries seem to have appreciated. Bought by the state, it was judged too inflammatory to be exhibited for long and was withdrawn until immediately after the 1848 revolution, though not made permanently accessible to the public until 1861. Accom-

panied by an urchin brandishing pistols, a high-hatted bourgeois and a proletarian with a sabre, Liberty herself, with bayoneted rifle in one hand, tricolor in the other, advances inexorably towards the spectator, from whom she turns her head to rally her followers. Her attitude and the life-size corpses underfoot – one recalling a figure in *The Raft of the 'Medusa'* (**15,12**) – suggest that Delacroix was aware of her two-faced nature, of the distinction between negative liberty, or freedom from oppression, and positive liberty, or freedom to impose an ideal way of life. Indeed, the picture brings to mind a remark made by the French novelist and liberal politician Benjamin Constant (1767–1830): 'Human beings are sacrificed to abstractions; a holocaust of individuals is offered up to the "people".'

For committed and unequivocally political images one must turn to the caricaturists of the day, who worked for the increasing number of newspapers. A new reproductive technique, lithography (invented in 1798), was widely used – a process of print-making, from drawings on stone

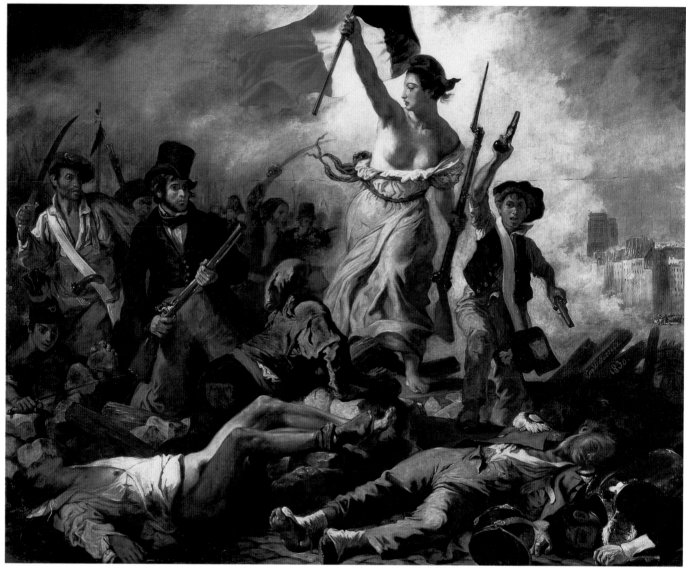

15,17 Eugène Delacroix, *The 28th July: Liberty Leading the People*, 1830. Oil on canvas, 8ft 6ins × 10ft 7ins (2.59 × 3.25m). Louvre, Paris.

in greasy chalk, which calls for no intermediary engraver and preserves the artist's individual touch. Typically Romantic effects of spontaneous fluency could be obtained. In one caricature lithograph after another the painter and sculptor Honoré Daumier (1808–79) satirized the absurdities and pomposities of the newly rich bourgeois, especially judges and lawyers and reactionary politicians, sometimes recording the horrific results of their actions. Daumier was deeply committed to liberalism and yet, when he drew *Freedom of the Press: Don't Meddle with It* (**15,18**), he was perhaps almost as much concerned with artistic as with political freedom. Press censorship had been one of the immediate causes of the revolution of 1830 in France and in this print of 1834 the printer who has knocked out the last Bourbon king stands ready to take on Louis-Philippe. The muscular working man, fists clenched, sleeves rolled up and open shirt revealing a hairy chest, is certainly no pallid abstraction. He is an individual prepared to defend the integrity and

15,18 Honoré Daumier, *Freedom of the Press: Don't Meddle with It*, 1834. Lithograph, 12 × 17ins (30.7 × 43.1cm).

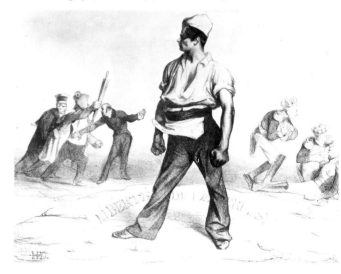

HEINE ON DELACROIX'S
LIBERTY LEADING THE PEOPLE

The German poet Heinrich Heine (1797–1856) left Germany for Paris in 1831, largely for political reasons. He reviewed the Paris Salon that year where Delacroix's *Liberty Leading the People* was outstanding, in Heine's opinion, because there prevailed in it 'a great thought'. It represented, he wrote:

a group of the people during the Revolution of July, from the centre of which – almost like an allegorical figure – there rises boldly a young woman with a red Phrygian cap on her head, a gun in one hand, and in the other a tri-colour flag. She strides over corpses calling men to fight – naked to the hips, a beautiful impetuous body, the face a bold profile, an air of insolent suffering in the features – altogether a strange blending of Phryne, fishwife, and goddess of liberty. It is not distinctly shown that the artist meant to set forth the latter; it rather represents the savage power of the people which casts off an intolerable burden . . . . And there we have it! A great thought has ennobled and sainted these poor common people, this rabble, and again awakened the slumbering dignity of their souls.

There is no picture in the Salon in which the colour is so sunk in as in the July Revolution of Delacroix. But just this absence of varnish and sheen, with the powder-smoke and dust which covers the figures as with a grey cobweb, and the sun-dried hue which seems to be thirsting for a drop of water, all give to the picture a truth, a reality, an originality in which we find the real physiognomy of the days of July.

Among the spectators were many who had been actors or lookers-on in the Revolution, and these could not sufficiently praise the picture. 'Matin!' exclaimed a grocer, 'these gamins fought like giants'.

(Tr. C. G. Leland, *The Works of Heinrich Heine, The Salon*, London 1893)

independence of his craft, 'true, formidable and sincere' – as Daumier himself was to be described by Victor Hugo (1802–85), the leader of the French Romantic movement in literature.

The value of sincerity in art and literature is now so generally assumed that it is often forgotten how recently it was recognized. Its appreciation as a desirable artistic quality is essentially Romantic. (None of Tiepolo's contemporaries would have bothered to ask whether he was 'sincere' in extolling the prince-bishop of Würzburg!) The value of sincerity was implicit in the Romantic conception of the work of art as being, above all, an expression of

the artist's feelings and convictions, especially those which seemed to lie beyond the bounds of logical discourse. In 1824 the young Delacroix wrote in his journal: 'I find precisely in Mme de Staël the development of my ideas about painting. This art, like music, *is higher than thought*; and both are superior to literature – in their vagueness.' He was referring to Germaine de Staël, the French writer whose book on Germany (*De l'Allemagne*, 1813) was the main channel through which the ideas of German philosophers and poets reached both France and England.

ROMANTICISM AND PHILOSOPHY
FRIEDRICH

German Romanticism was very much a home-grown product, strongly colored by the ideas of nationalism developed by the philosopher Johann Gottfried Herder (1744–1803) and by the new concept of *Deutschheit* or Germanness, which crystallized during the War of Liberation against Napoleonic France in 1813–15. Painters were much more closely associated with poets and philosophers in Germany than in France, especially with those who, in the wake of Immanuel Kant, began to question accepted Enlightenment views about human reason, religion, nature and the meaning and purpose of the arts. Caspar David Friedrich (1774–1840) was attacked by a critic of the old guard partly because his paintings were supposed to reflect the transcendental ideas of the new school of philosophy. The relationship was not simple or direct; nor was it supposed to be so. Critics did not imagine that Friedrich's paintings were based on programs drawn up for him by philosophers (as had been the case with Botticelli and the *Primavera*; see pp. 451–2). Friedrich sought to express in paint thoughts and emotions which could not be put into words. What he said of a fellow artist's works applies perfectly to his own: 'Just as the pious man prays without speaking a word and the Almighty hearkens unto him, so the artist with true feelings *paints* and the sensitive man understands and recognizes it.'

Friedrich came from a pious north German Protestant background which conditioned his attitude to art as well as to religion. His refusal to make the art student's traditional pilgrimage to Rome may well have been prompted by anti-Catholic sentiments. He was opposed to the notion of authority in any form, whether of the Academy or the Church. His firm faith in the inner light and his insistence on the 'private judgement' of the individual as the only valid guide to the interpretation of the 'Bible of nature' are at once artistic and religious in a quintessentially Protestant way. Hence the tone of intimacy and mystery, the strange and moving power of his landscapes, which seem to be the product of strenuous solitary self-examination. Crystal-clear precision of detail and an even, flat surface emphasize this withdrawn quality. But their simultaneously sharp focus and vague, dissolving air of unreality, their literalness combined with the heightened

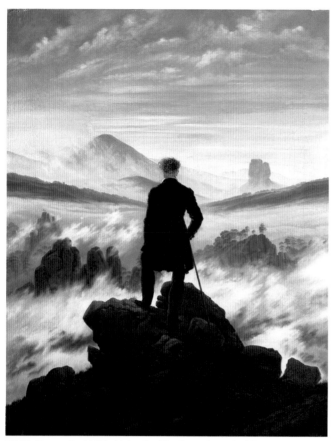

15,19 Caspar David Friedrich, *The Wanderer above the Mists*, c. 1817–18. Oil on canvas, 29½ × 37¼ins (74.8 × 94.8cm). Kunsthalle, Hamburg.

'mood' of poetry make us almost painfully aware of an element of uncertainty that lies at the heart of Friedrich's work and his grappling with the problems of art and reality – with the agonizing doubts of the man of faith confronted with a natural world in which divine order could no longer be seen. His figures usually stand apart, as if in some way extraneous to the landscape – like the man in *The Wanderer above the Mists* (**15,19**) – neither of its world nor of ours, standing on the edge of reality. Motionless, isolated, they seem to be both within and yet somehow outside nature, at once at home in it and estranged – symbols of ambiguity and alienation. Great visual subtlety, a unique manner of seeing and representing, gives his paintings an extraordinary power. The viewpoint is rarely that of a naturalistic painter with his feet on the ground; we are, as it were, suspended in mid-air when we look at his pictures. *The Wanderer above the Mists* is depicted from a point in space on a level with the wanderer's head.

BLAKE

The art of the great English mystic, poet and painter William Blake (1757–1827), like that of Friedrich, confronts a world in which the certainties of both Christianity and the Enlightenment had been clouded over. Blake accepted much of Enlightened thought, subscribing

to its demand for tolerance and social justice, welcoming the revolutions in America and France. But like other Romantics, he found that Enlightenment thinkers had failed to answer some vital questions and left a void at the centre of their system. His attitude to Neo-Classical artistic theory was similar: he accepted its demands for high seriousness, universality and purity, but rejected its submission of the imagination to reason. The God-given faculty of imagination should control the fallible human understanding, he believed, and not vice versa. When Reynolds (see pp. 632–3) wrote in his *Discourses* that 'in the midst of the highest flights of fancy or imagination, reason ought to preside from first to last', Blake commented: 'If this is True, it is a devilish Foolish Thing to be an Artist.'

Blake's art and writings (which cannot be fully understood independently of one another) reflect his burning need to resolve the agonizing conflicts in his own mind – to reconcile imagination with understanding, the ideal of man with the experience of men, and, above all, his intuitions of the divine with accepted ideas of god, whether as the jealous God of the Old Testament or as the rationalists' 'prime mover' of a mechanistic universe – whom he called Mr Nobodaddy. In some of his finest prints, executed in series with a dialectical inner logic, an irreconcilability is, however, acknowledged and accepted. That of Newton, for example, a nude of flawless Classical beauty, immersed in the waters of materialism, turned in on himself as he studies geometrical ratios, is accompanied by a print of Nebuchadnezzar, the man who abandoned reason – one of Blake's most terrifyingly memorable images (**15,20**). Reason may be insufficient, as the Newton print suggests, but Nebuchadnezzar's bestial sensuality is no better.

The figures in both these prints were derived from earlier artists whom Blake admired, Newton from Michelangelo and Nebuchadnezzar from Dürer. Both are drawn with the firm outlines advocated by Neo-Classical theo-

15,20 William Blake, *Nebuchadnezzar*, 1795. Color print finished in watercolor, 17¼ × 24¼ins (44 × 61.5cm). Tate Gallery, London.

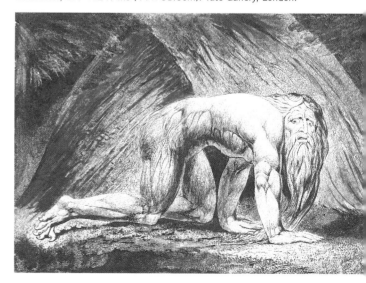

rists and filled in with watercolor (they are engravings from which very few prints were pulled, each being colored by hand). But the prototypes have been given a new and intensely personal significance in Blake's wholly individual mythology, and the method of representation suggests that their philosophical meaning was more important to Blake than their tangibility. 'The Nature of my Work is Visionary and Imaginative', he wrote in 1810:

> *This world of Imagination is the world of Eternity; it is the divine bosom into which we shall all go after the death of the Vegetated body. The World of Imagination is Infinite & Eternal, whereas the world of Generation, or Vegetation, is Finite & Temporal. There Exist in that Eternal World the Permanent Realities of Every Thing which we see reflected in this Vegetable Glass of Nature.*
>
> ('A vision of the Last Judgement', in *The Complete Writings of William Blake*, ed. G. Keynes, 1957)

This idea can be traced back by way of the Protestant mystics (see pp. 470–3) to the Neoplatonists (see p. 220). But Blake's religious and artistic thought was too deeply personal to be systematized or categorized.

ROMANTIC LANDSCAPE PAINTING
CONSTABLE

The 'vegetable glass of nature' was just what appealed most to John Constable (1776–1837), who declared his ambition to be, above all, a 'natural painter'. One of his most beautiful paintings of his native Vale of Dedham shows men at work on a dunghill (**15,21**). No painter ever represented the English countryside with greater fidelity, the sparkle of dew on grass, the glint of sunshine on sappy leaves, the noble form of great elms, the enthralling intricacies of the hedgerow, and as a result his paintings are very much more than straightforward topographical records. He sought to recapture in them a childhood vision of the harmony of nature in all its innocent purity and to re-examine it in the light of mature reflection – to use it as a touchstone against which all experience, of nature and art and his sense of being part of creation, might be tested. In this his affinity with William Wordsworth (1770-1850), whom he knew and whose profoundly reflective autobiographical poetry he loved, is very evident.

Constable, the son of a fairly prosperous farmer and mill-owner, was brought up in the flat lands of East Anglia. His native landscape was not wild. It had been

15,21 John Constable, *Stour Valley and Dedham Church*, 1814-15. Oil on canvas, 21⅞ × 30⅝ins (55.5 × 77.8cm). Museum of Fine Arts, Boston (Warren Collection).

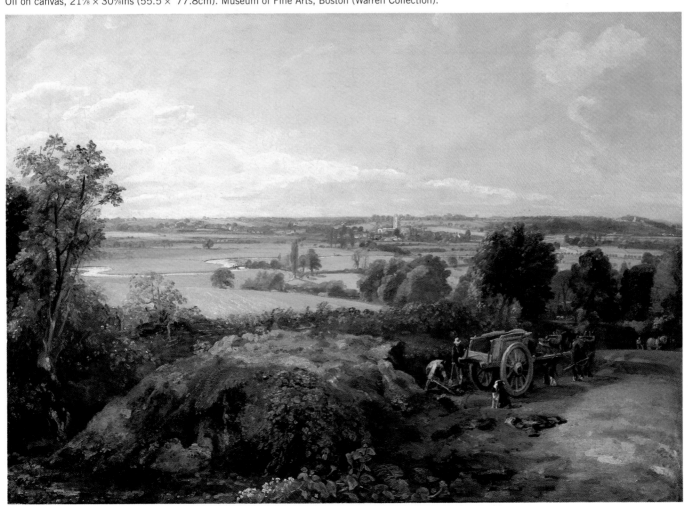

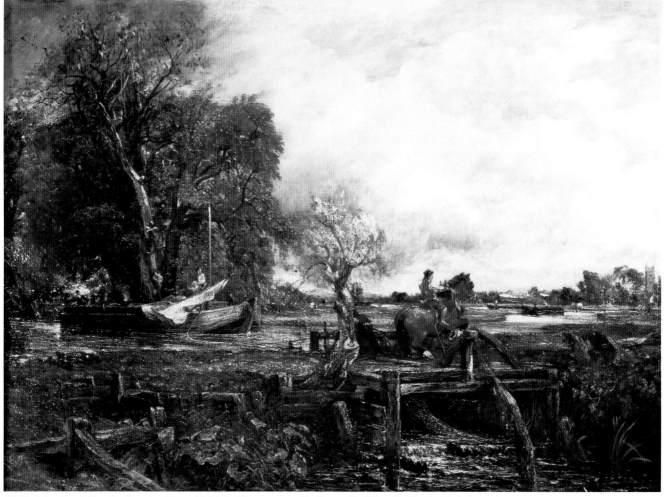

15,22 John Constable, *The Leaping Horse*, 1824–5. Oil on canvas, 4ft 8ins × 6ft 1⅝ins (1.42 × 1.87m). Royal Academy of Arts, London.

formed by the labour of his relations and their neighbours over many generations. He preferred painting man-made canals and dams, he said, to the mountain brooks and waterfalls that inspired Romantic poets. 'The sound of water escaping from mill-dams, etc., willows, old rotten planks, slimy posts and brickwork, I love such things', Constable wrote in 1821. 'As long as I do paint, I shall never cease to paint such places.' In nearly all his pictures the land is worked. The dung which fertilized the fields, no less than the rain that watered them, the mills in which the grain was ground, the boats in which it was transported by canal to the city, all played their parts in the divine harmony of the physical world as he understood it. The tower of Dedham parish church recurs constantly in his Suffolk landscapes, a reminder rather than a symbol of the presence of God. In the picture illustrated here, he placed it immediately above the dunghill.

Constable's vision of the English landscape culminates in a series of seven large pictures – 'six-foot canvases' he called them – of scenes near his childhood home, a landscape so unspectacular that it had not previously been thought worth recording at all, let alone on this grand scale. Each of them represents the harmony of the elements, epitomized by the reflection of sky in water. The pulse-beat of the universe can be felt in the movement of the clouds, the ripples on the stream and the shimmer of leaves on the great trees as a summer breeze passes over them, as well as in the bustle of human figures and animals. Each picture is centred on some workaday occurrence, sometimes of a slightly unexpected kind – a lumbering cart-horse rearing to leap a barrier, for instance – which links it with a particular moment of vision. In this way they form pictorial equivalents to the 'spots of time' of Wordsworth's *The Prelude* – those vividly remembered moments of childhood that 'retain a renovating virtue' and through which in later life 'our minds are nourished and invisibly repaired'. Constable prepared these pictures with great care, proceeding from drawings to full-size sketches. To modern eyes, the sketches strike first and deepest, by their apparent spontaneity and truth to nature, the bravura of handling, with heavily loaded brush-strokes and pigments dashed on and worked with a palette knife, the bold massing of forms, the sparkling highlights and rich shadows. The quietly contemplative finished pictures seem deliberate, perhaps over-elaborated. But Constable would not have agreed. He wrote of a sketch as something which 'will not serve more than one state of mind & will not serve to drink at again & again'. His six-foot sketches were attempts to recapture the original moment of vision, the finished pictures his mature reflections (**15,22**). The relationship is akin to that between a diary and an autobiography.

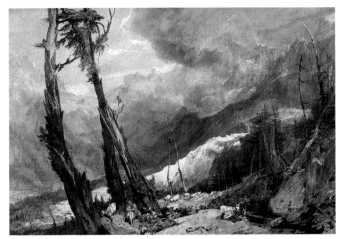

15,23 Joseph Mallord William Turner, *Glacier and Source of the Aveyron, Chamonix*, 1802–3. Watercolor on paper, 27 × 40ins (68.5 × 101.5cm). Yale Center for British Art, New Haven, Connecticut (Paul Mellon Collection).

TURNER

The mature landscapes by Constable's contemporary Joseph Mallord William Turner (1775-1851) are no less obsessively personal, though in a very different and often ambiguous manner that was often misunderstood by contemporaries. His painting of *The Slave Ship* (**15,24**) was ridiculed in the press as 'a passionate extravagance of marigold sky and pomegranate coloured sea'. Only his most perceptive admirer, John Ruskin (1819–1900), recognized it as 'the noblest sea that Turner has ever painted, dedicated to the most sublime of subjects and impressions'.

Of another seascape the artist himself remarked: 'I did not paint it to be understood'. In some ways Turner was more of a 'natural observer' than Constable, less reflective, more impulsive, more concerned with visual appearances and especially with fleeting effects of light. He was also more concerned with the practice of painting as an end in itself. Mists which transform and unite disparate objects visually, and skies in shot reds and yellows with the deep radiance of the rising or setting sun, are natural paradigms of the art of painting, and eventually Turner seems almost to have identified the pigments which he applied to paper or canvas with the atmospheric coloring which hangs between the artist and the object depicted. For he conceived painting neither as the composition of clearly defined solid forms nor as the imitation of nature, but simply as the manipulation of opaque and translucent pigments on a flat surface. He sought to recreate rather than represent effects of light – in his own words 'admiring Nature by the power and practicability of his Art, and judging his Art by the perceptions drawn from Nature'.

He began (like Constable and Friedrich) with topographically accurate views in watercolor, a medium of great antiquity and much used in the Orient but only occasionally in Europe, notably by Dürer, before the second half of the eighteenth century, when it was extensively taken up for small-scale landscapes, especially in England. Prodigiously gifted, he very soon attracted official recognition and was elected associate of the Royal

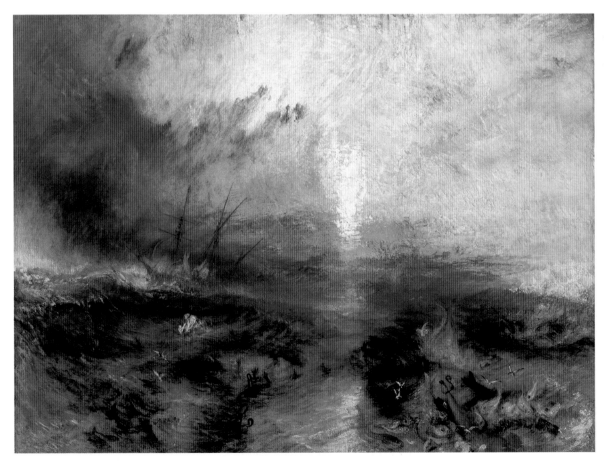

15,24 Joseph Mallord William Turner, *The Slave Ship*, 1840. Oil on canvas, 35¾ × 48¼ins (90.8 × 122.6cm). Museum of Fine Arts, Boston (Henry Lillie Pierce Fund).

Turner's Slave Ship

IMAGES OF SLAVERY

Turner's *Slave Ship* (15,24) retains its power to shock partly, perhaps, because the effect is delayed. This glorious sunset at sea is not immediately seen as the setting for an atrocity. When the significance of the painting is recognized it becomes one of the most disturbing of all visual images of the Atlantic slave-trade. Turner's great admirer, John Ruskin, acquired it and kept it for a while but, despite his appreciation of its great painterly qualities, sold it because the subject – 'the throwing overboard of the dead and dying, who are seen struggling in the water surrounded by sharks and gulls – had, he used to say, become too painful to live with'. The Atlantic slave-trade, a crime against humanity, had been initiated as soon as Europeans began to colonize the Americas and was still increasing in the mid-eighteenth century when Christians (mainly Quakers in America and England), inspired by a new idea of benevolence as a moral imperative, and free-thinkers with new notions of freedom as a natural right, began to campaign for its abolition. Partly as a result of their endeavour it was abandoned by Denmark in 1792 (with effect from 1803) and subsequently by Britain, the USA, France and finally Brazil in 1831 though it continued there illicitly on a very large scale for another two decades. Legislation against the trade tended to be decreed only by governments that recognized it as a hindrance to their other commercial interests. It was only the trade in slaves, not slavery itself, with which they were concerned. Slavery itself was regarded strictly as a domestic issue for each country concerned. It remained legal in Britain and its colonies until 1834, in France and its colonies until 1848, in the USA until 1865, in the Spanish colonies until 1873 and in Brazil until 1888. In each instance slavery was abolished as a result of a combination of humanitarian demands with economic and political pressure. The motives of the abolitionists were often mixed and the visual images they inspired were as often equivocal.

Artists were, however, enrolled to advance the abolitionist cause, the two most influential images being those commissioned by the British Society for Effecting the Abolition of the Slave Trade: its emblem of 1787 with a chained black slave begging to be freed (0,13) and a diagram of a slave ship illustrating the inhuman way in which Africans were stowed when crossing the Atlantic. Artists focused attention on the slave-trade rather than on slavery, as freedom was a politically sensitive issue, especially after the French Revolution. In France, Théodore Géricault projected but never painted a large picture on the theme of the slave-trade to which there may be an allusion in *The Raft of the 'Medusa'* (15,12), his depiction of survivors from a ship wrecked on its passage from the French colony of Senegal, adrift on the Atlantic with an African at the summit of the pyramid of misery.

A lithograph after a drawing by Johann Moritz Rugendas (1802–58) exhibited in the Paris Salon of 1827 gives a nauseating glimpse of the hold of a slave ship bound for Brazil with Africans in attitudes ranging from despair to sullen resignation. They are crowded together in the fetid atmosphere while a corpse is carried out by white sailors (**15,25**). This was the first image of the slave-trade shown in these official exhibitions but it attracted little attention. In the Salon of 1835 Auguste-François Biard (1798–1882) exhibited a large painting (now lost) of slaves being sold after arrival on an American coast. Such a painting would have had little appeal for private collectors and Biard may well have hoped that it would be bought for the national museum of contemporary French art; but it was not, probably because the subject was too contentious while slavery was still legal in the French colonies. The British, on the other hand, were preening themselves on having abolished slavery and Biard sent to London an equally large painting of slaves being assembled on the African coast for transport to America (**15,26**).

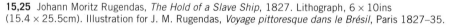

15,25 Johann Moritz Rugendas, *The Hold of a Slave Ship*, 1827. Lithograph, 6 × 10ins (15.4 × 25.5cm). Illustration for J. M. Rugendas, *Voyage pittoresque dans le Brésil*, Paris 1827–35.

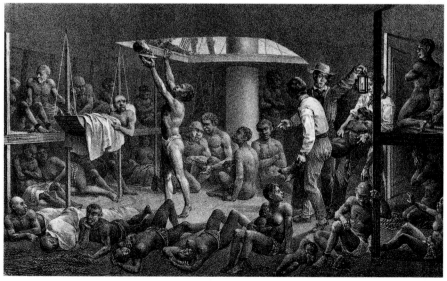

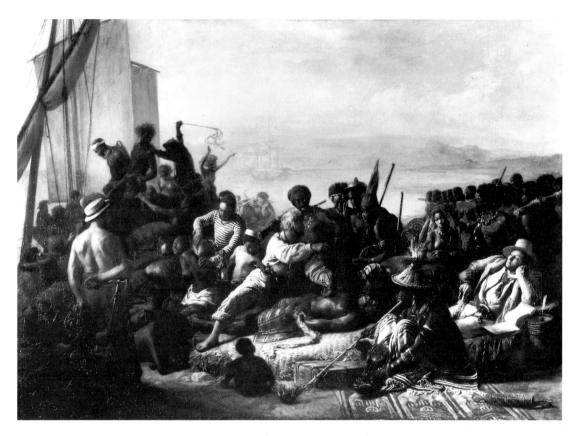

15,26 François Biard, *The Slave Trade*, 1840. Canvas, 5ft 4⅛ins × 7ft 6⅛ins (1.63 × 2.29m). Wilberforce House, Hull City Museums and Art Galleries, UK.

It was shown in the Royal Academy's summer exhibition in 1840 which opened a month before the first international convention of the British and Foreign Anti-Slavery Society was due to meet. That Turner showed *The Slave Ship* in the same exhibition is no mere coincidence; he must have been well aware of preparations for the convention.

Biard's painting was well received by British critics who emphasized that not only the slaves but the men selling them were Africans. They praised it for 'representing with fearful accuracy the atrocious deeds of the miscreants who traffic in this abominable trade'. However, such admirable abolitionist sentiments could be combined with racist attitudes. One critic remarked that 'helpless animal suffering is displayed in the wretched groups driven to market, with little more intelligence in their misery than the flock of sheep driven to the shambles', noting 'the wretched and brutalized chief, feathered and tricked out in finery, bartering his war captives, or, perhaps, even his own kindred, for luxury and gold, the enjoyments and uses of which only touch his dull sense

faintly'. To the British public at this date slavery was a distant phenomenon arousing self-righteous indignation. It could be safely condemned, however, as it was also a barrier to the commercial exploitation of Africa.

In the USA slavery was a constantly smouldering problem. African Americans were not infrequently depicted but their status as free men or women or slaves was rarely made clear. In 1841 the Artist Fund Society of Philadelphia refused to exhibit the portrait by Nathaniel Jocelyn (1796–1881) of Cinque, a West African who had led a mutiny on a Spanish slave ship (**15,27**). Imprisoned in the USA, he was tried for piracy and acquitted. The secretary wrote that it was 'contrary to usage to display works of the character, believing that under the excitement of the times, it might prove injurious both to the proprietors and the institution'. The portrait had been commissioned by a leading abolitionist, Robert Purvis, who was himself classified as 'a black' because his mother was the freeborn daughter of a slave, although his father was white. And he remarked that it had been excluded from the exhibition because the sitter was a

hero and 'a black man has no right to be a hero'. This image of proud defiance makes a striking contrast with most European paintings of enslaved Africans; they arouse pity rather than admiration.

15,27 Nathaniel Jocelyn, *Cinque*, c.1840. Canvas, 30¼ × 25½ins (76.8 × 64.8cm). New Haven Colony Historical Society, New Haven (Gift of Charles B. Purvis, 1898; 1971.205).

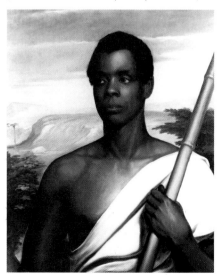

Academy in 1799 and a full member in 1802 (Constable had to wait for associateship until 1819 and did not become an Academician for another ten years). His early style is seen at its best in such large watercolors as *Glacier and Source of the Aveyron, Chamonix*, painted immediately after his first Continental tour in 1802 (**15,23**). It is a 'Romantic landscape' in the eighteenth-century meaning of the phrase. There is not so much as a hint of the transcendental overtones which were to hang over the paintings of Friedrich (15,19), nor of the Wordsworthian 'joy of elevated thoughts' emanated by Constable's. The viewpoint has been carefully selected so that the scene can be portrayed accurately within the well-established conventions for sublime prospects. Only in its slightly broader technique does it differ from mountain views by John Robert Cozens (1752–97), which Turner had studied. Turner's oil paintings of the same period, with pigment dashed on to the canvas and much use of the palette knife and heavy scumbling (see Glossary), depart more radically from accepted academic manners and shocked conservative critics. The Swiss painter known as John Henry Fuseli (1741–1825), professor of painting at the Royal Academy in London, formulated an axiom that 'the less the traces appear of the means by which a work has been produced, the more it resembles the operations of nature'. The nature Turner perceived could rarely be smoothly rendered by an art which conceals art. His technique responded with increasingly violent color and handling to his ever more pessimistic preoccupation with the clash of elemental forces in natural cataclysms. The conventional components of landscape diminish in importance. Everything becomes transmuted into light and water, as in *The Slave Ship* (15,24), where the frail-masted vessel is no more than a spectral presence overshadowed by angry storm clouds and floundering in primal chaos. The full title given to this astonishing picture when exhibited at the Royal Academy, London, in 1840 was *Slavers Throwing Overboard the Dead and Dying – Typhon Coming On*, alluding to a malpractice that emphasized the inhumanity of the Atlantic slave-trade. Much publicity had been given to the atrocity committed by the captain of a British ship, the *Zong*, who had a large number of sick slaves thrown overboard in order to claim insurance payable for cargo lost at sea. (The legal category 'cargo lost at sea' normally referred to animals and inanimate cargo washed overboard.) The most sharply defined element in the composition (lower right corner) is a single dark-skinned leg with a shackle on its ankle surrounded by predatory birds and fish as it sinks into the waves. This is not, however, the record of a particular historical incident so much as a deeply pessimistic cosmic vision in which humanity struggles vainly against elemental forces. A fragment from Turner's poem *The Fallacies of Hope*, printed in the catalogue, ends with the lines: 'Hope, Hope, fallacious Hope!/Where is thy market now?' In many of his other late paintings (which he did not exhibit) there are no signs of humanity at all, just seas and skies of glowing color charged with the mysterious energy of a creative force.

COROT AND THE *Etude*

In France the transformation of the art of landscape painting in the Romantic period was more gradual than in Germany and England, but perhaps more far-reaching. If less affected by the transcendental ideas of Romantic poets and thinkers, it was no less deeply influenced by the new demands for spontaneity, emotional authenticity and artistic freedom. Jean-Jacques Rousseau (see p. 635) had already, in the late eighteenth century, extolled the beauty and morally improving power of uncorrupted nature. Still more influential was the cult of the individual sensibility he promoted. But French landscape painting did not, as might be supposed, develop in conflict with academic theory and practice. Indeed, landscape was given an academic respectability it had previously lacked by the institution in 1817 of a scholarship at the French Academy in Rome for a painter of 'historic landscapes' – that is to say idealized Italianate views based on the precedents of Claude and Poussin (see pp. 592–5). Close study of nature was, nevertheless, required. Drawing and painting in the open countryside became the equivalent of the figurative painter's studies in the life-class. Precise records of trees and rocks, of the effects of light and atmosphere, made out of doors for their own sake (not as preparatory sketches) were seen as prerequisites for the creation of imaginative compositions painted in the studio. They were called studies or *études*. The practice was by no means confined to France. Constable worked in much the same way and Turner referred to 'pictures of bits' and 'pictures made up of bits'. The impact one of Constable's 'six-foot canvases' made when shown in Paris in 1824 was due to his having preserved the freshness of an *étude* in a large exhibition piece.

Jean-Baptiste-Camille Corot (1796–1875), the greatest French landscape painter of his time, was trained under a 'historical landscape' painter, though he soon 'took up the study of nature all on my own'. Like Gericault and other Romantic artists, he had sufficient independent means for his modest needs, and this enabled him to devote more time to *études* than most artists could and rather less to exhibition pieces (though he regularly contributed landscapes with Biblical or mythological subjects to the Paris Salon). Many small views of the Italian and French landscape, freely painted with a loaded brush, display Corot's unique sensitivity to the varying quality of light and atmosphere and to the subtlest gradations of tone. Tone, rather than line and color, indicates form, suggests distance and unites the various components of a landscape into an artistic whole. His aim, he said, was 'to reproduce as conscientiously as possible what I see before me'. But he also remarked that 'in striving conscientiously to imitate, I do not lose for a moment the emotion that possessed me', for 'if we have been truly touched, the sincerity of our emotion will be transmitted to others'. So entirely convincing is the naturalism of these *études*, so free are they from artificial framing and other devices, that his compositions seem to have been determined simply by choice of viewpoint – like that of a photographer. In

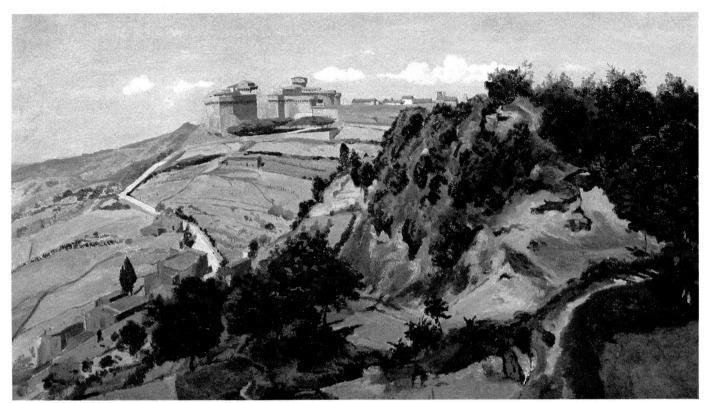

15,28 Jean-Baptiste-Camille Corot, *Volterra*, 1834. Oil on canvas, 18½ × 32¼ins (47 × 82cm). Louvre, Paris.

one of Corot's views of Volterra, for instance, a hillock covered with nondescript scrub is given greater prominence and no less pictorial importance than the distant citadel, which is the main object of interest (**15,28**). It dates from just four years before 1839 when Louis-Jacques-Mandé Daguerre (1787–1851) in France and William Henry Fox Talbot (1800–77) in England publicly announced their independent inventions of photography.

PHOTOGRAPHY

The inventors of photography seem to have been motivated by an urge akin to that of contemporary landscape painters in their *études*: to capture single spots of space and time as records of visual appearances rather than evocations of the ideal that was supposed to underlie the common face of nature. In this way both were strongly influenced by Romantic notions. Fox Talbot recalled how the stimulus for his invention came to him. On his honeymoon in 1833 he tried to sketch the landscape around Lake Como – a famous Italian beauty-spot – with the aid of a device that enabled an artist to see in a prism his subject and the paper on which he was working. Handicapped by lack of training as a draftsman, he gave up, but recalled how he had seen in a *camera obscura* 'the inimitable beauty of the pictures of nature's painting which the glass lens of the Camera throws upon the paper in its focus – fairy pictures, creations of a moment and destined as rapidly to fade away'. And he thought 'how charming it would be if it were possible to cause these natural images

to imprint themselves durably and remain fixed upon the paper'.

Although the desire was aesthetic, somewhat similar to that which had recently led to the development of lithography as a means of directly reproducing an artist's handling of chalk (see pp. 655–6), the means were scientific, optical and chemical, and already separately available. The *camera obscura* to which Fox Talbot referred was a sixteenth-century invention derived from much earlier observations – that images of objects are projected on to the side of a dark chamber by light passing through a very small aperture. And this device, developed as a box with a lens, mirror and ground-glass screen, had been used occasionally by artists for a very long time, including probably Vermeer and certainly Canaletto, though rarely as more than a preliminary aid for depicting townscapes. It had also been discovered, early in the eighteenth century, that some chemicals darkened on exposure to light; but not until about 1800 was their possible use for recording images explored, first of all with only partial success by Thomas Wedgwood (1771-1805), son of the Staffordshire pottery manufacturer with an interest in the reproduction of ornament. In France Nicéphore Niépce (1765-1833), who was concerned mainly with lithography and other reproductive techniques, succeeded between 1816 and 1827 in fixing the images in a *camera obscura* on metal and glass plates. The results were not very brilliant, but the potentiality of the process was immediately recognized by Daguerre to whom its secret was imparted. An artist by training, Daguerre was familiar with the *camera*

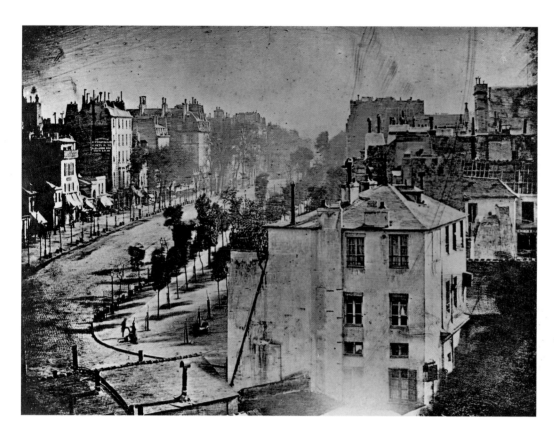

15,29 Louis-Jacques-Mandé Daguerre, *Boulevard du Temple, Paris*, c. 1838. Daguerreotype. Bayerisches Nationalmuseum, Munich.

15,30 *Below* Anonymous, *Frederick Douglass*, 1847. Daguerreotype. National Portrait Gallery, Smithsonian Institution, Washington DC (William Rubel Collection).

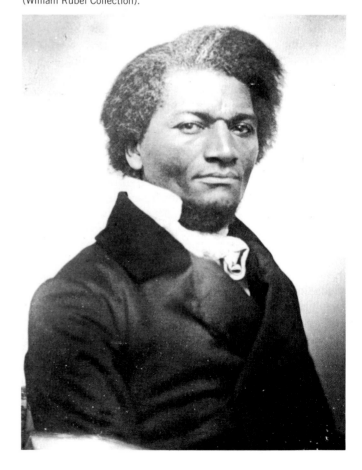

obscura, which he had used as an aid in painting vast illusionistic *dioramas* (dramatically lit panoramas) that enjoyed great popular success in Paris. He developed the process and by 1837 was able to record a Parisian street scene on a copper plate coated with silver, one of the first daguerreotypes – a name he was to patent two years later (**15,29**). Meanwhile, Fox Talbot had been experimenting quite independently in England and before 1839 fulfilled his ambition to fix naturally projected images by an entirely different two-stage process, for his camera recorded a negative image on translucent paper which had to be fixed, placed over another sheet of sensitized paper and again exposed to light to make a positive print.

Daguerre's process, which was soon technically improved, was widely adopted for some two decades in Europe and especially America where it answered a rapidly growing demand for portraits. The first of the American daguerreotype studios was opened in 1840 and by 1853 there were 86 in New York City alone. More than 400,000 daguerreotype portraits were taken in the state of Massachusetts in 12 months in 1854–5. Quite suddenly portraiture had been made available to an incomparably larger section of the population than ever before – to anyone who could afford $2 and, eventually, no more than 12 cents, a minute fraction of the sum demanded by any painter. Novelty may partly have accounted for the success of the daguerreotype but there can be little doubt that the desire to be portrayed with absolute fidelity by a process that was one of the marvels of modern science reflected the outlook of an increasingly materialist culture.

The vast majority of sitters were members of the

middle classes. But some were famous people including, for instance, the ex-slave Frederick Douglass, whose daguerreotype portrait taken at the time of his election as president of the New England Anti-Slavery Society suggests the strength of mind that was to make him the leader of African Americans – far better, indeed, than do any of the painted portraits of him in which his features were softened (**15,30**). As Nathaniel Hawthorne remarked in 1851, 'heaven's broad and simple sunshine' could bring out in daguerreotypes 'the secret character with a truth no painter would venture upon'. That they were so revealing was not always seen as an advantage, however. Painted portraits, usually the result of some collusion, conscious or unconscious, between sitter and artist, lost none of their appeal for those who could afford them. And they also provided models of composition for cameramen. That the figures in daguerreotypes are stiffly posed with expressions of fixed solemnity may have been due not only to the need to keep stock still during exposure (initially for several minutes in bright light) but also to a desire for dignified images that could be handed down to posterity. They were covered with glass to protect their surfaces and many were framed like painted portrait miniatures.

Daguerreotypes tended to be regarded as alternatives to paintings. They included not only portraits but also views of buildings and panoramas of whole cities – the inventor's own point of departure. And each one was a unique object. Fox Talbot's process, on the other hand, permitted a number of prints to be made from a single negative – rather as lithographs were pulled from the stone. When he published *The Pencil of Nature* (in six instalments, 1844–6) he was at pains to point out that each one of the 24 illustrations in every copy was a print made from a negative by the agency of light alone without the aid of an artist's hand. It revealed the possibilities of his invention as a new means of artistic expression. His choice of subjects was, however, strongly conditioned by conservative ideas of what was suitable to be represented – or picturesque in the simplest meaning of the word. And one, *The Open Door*, very clearly reveals that the 'artist's hand' had in fact been at work, propping up a broom and hanging a lantern on the wall while waiting for the sun to illuminate the scene as he wished (**15,31**). It is as carefully composed as any still-life painting and not without allegorical overtones in its reference to the light of nature contrasted with the lantern. In his comment on this photograph he wrote: 'We have sufficient authority in the Dutch school of art for taking as subject for representation scenes of daily and familiar occurrence. A painter's eye will often be arrested where ordinary people see nothing remarkable. A casual gleam of sunshine, or a shadow thrown across his path, a time-withered oak, or a moss-covered stone may awaken a train of thoughts and feelings, and picturesque imaginings.' He significantly called his negatives calotypes – beautiful images: a conjunction of Classical Greek words.

Fox Talbot's process was soon taken up by those who were prepared to pay him a fee, most notably Robert Adamson (1821–48) who worked in collaboration with a Scottish painter Octavius Hill (1802–70) for four years, taking a vast number of photographs in and around Edinburgh. Their partnership began when Hill was commissioned to paint a group portrait of the convention that

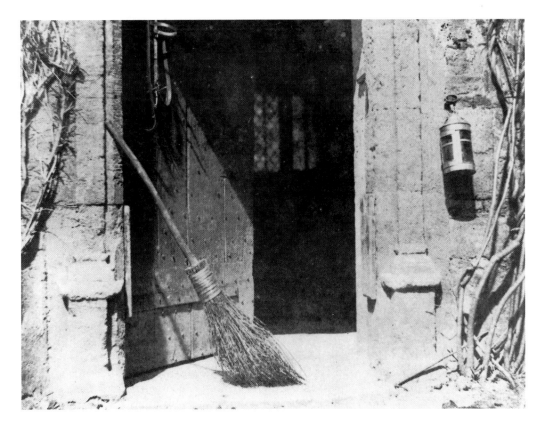

15,31 William Henry Fox Talbot, *The Open Door*, 1843. Salted paper print from a calotype negative. Fox Talbot Collection, Science Museum, London.

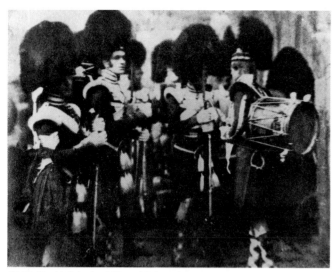

15,32 David Octavius Hill and Robert Adamson, *Highland Guard*, c. 1844–5. Salted paper print from a calotype negative. Royal Photographic Society, Bath.

founded the Free Church of Scotland in 1843, and to save himself the task of drawing the heads of 457 men and women (as was usual for such a work) decided to work from photographs of them instead. They also photographed numerous scenes from daily life, sometimes all too obviously posed but occasionally spontaneous, as in that of the Highland Guard (**15,32**). Individual prints were exhibited and, like etchings and engravings, sold by art dealers. Due to the rough surface and uneven texture of the paper, prints from a calotype were much less precisely defined than daguerreotypes, 'and this is the very life of it', Hill remarked; they 'look like the imperfect works of man – and not the much diminished perfect work of God'. Other photographers made much use of the process for evocative landscape. And although it was superseded in the 1850s by the introduction of glass negatives which permitted greater sharpness of definition, somewhat hazy effects were often sought and preferred by photographers who conceived their prints as, primarily, works of art rather than visual documents.

The idea that photography was – or might become – a new medium for artistic expression did not go unchallenged. In 1859 Charles Baudelaire, the poet and great art critic who pleaded for an art of 'modern life', launched an attack. From the moment of its invention, he wrote, 'our squalid society rushed, Narcissus to a man, to gaze at its trivial image on a scrap of metal'. He particularly objected, and with ample justification, to photographs of people dressed and posed as in paintings of historical subjects. 'If photography is allowed to supplement art in some of its functions, it will soon have supplanted or corrupted it altogether', he protested. 'If it be allowed to encroach upon the domain of the impalpable and the imaginary, upon anything whose value depends solely upon the addition of something of a man's soul, then it will be so much the worse for us!' Photography had answered one of the demands of the Romantics – that for direct records of visual appearance, and as such they were

regarded by Fox Talbot as products as well as representations of nature – but its apparent automatism suggested that it could not express the unique sensibility of an artist, what Corot had called 'the emotion that possessed me'. For the possibility of any felt or seen imprint of the artist's 'touch' in handling, for instance, was very limited, as were other means for personal expression.

From the beginning, the relationship between photography and painting was complex. As we have seen, subjects and viewpoints selected by the early photographers were determined, whether consciously or not, by generally admired types of painting. Influences in the other direction are more difficult to trace. Delacroix, among others, made drawings from photographs of nude figures who had, however, usually been posed in the attitudes of models in academic life-classes – themselves often derived from antique Classical statues! More significantly, photography also provided records more accurate than ever before of earlier works of art and especially of architecture – products of and at the same time contributions to that interest in history which dominated so much of nineteenth-century thought.

IN WHICH STYLE SHOULD WE BUILD?

Romantic ideas put a heavy burden on architects, who were far more dependent than painters on the demands of patrons and much more constrained by stylistic conventions and technical possibilities. But the need for a 'new architecture' to embody the ideals of the nineteenth century was keenly felt and repeatedly expressed from the 1820s onwards, following the precipitate decline of the 'Empire Style' promoted by Napoleon. *In which style should we build?* was the title of a book published in 1828 by the German critic Heinrich Hübsch. 'Every epoch has left its own style of architecture', wrote the leading Prussian architect Karl Friedrich Schinkel (1781–1841). 'Why should we not try whether a style of our own might also be found?'

Schinkel was trained under the brilliant but short-lived Friedrich Gilly (1772–1800), whose designs have a geometrical purity and rational severity akin to those of Boullée (14,31). Subsequently Schinkel adopted and adapted a number of historical styles – Greek, Roman, Romanesque, Gothic, Italian Renaissance – and sometimes made precocious use of cast iron for decoration as well as construction. But his buildings always have an individual feeling for mass, for the delicate balance of proportions and for sharp, clean detailing which gives a precision-tooled rather than hand-carved effect, though without any sense of the mechanical. His theatre in Berlin (badly damaged in 1945) consists of rectangular forms compactly interlocked in such a way that it presents a visually exciting composition from whatever point of view it is seen – not just four façades to be confronted head-on (**15,33**). An Ionic portico marks the entrance with an appropriately dramatic gesture, but other antique elements are reduced to simple geometry. Ornament is minimized throughout. In later buildings Schinkel reduced

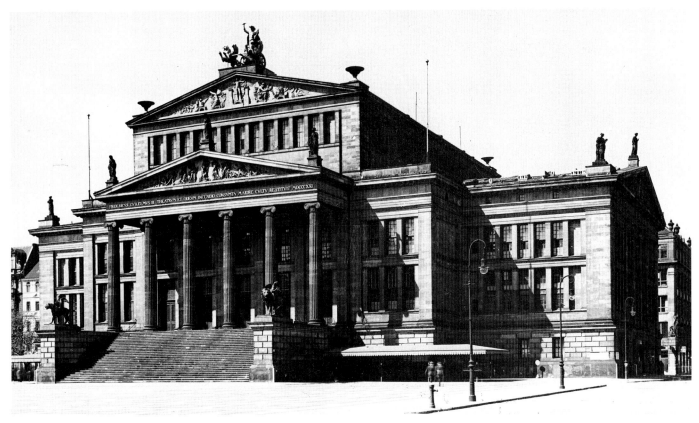

15,33 Karl Friedrich Schinkel, Theatre in Gendarmenmarkt, Berlin, 1818–21.

his means almost to proportional relationships alone. 'The scope of architecture is to render beautiful what is usable, useful, purposeful', he wrote; adding elsewhere, however, that 'mere need cannot give us beauty'. Qualities which he called 'the historic and the poetic' were necessary in architecture.

Schinkel was unusual in his concern with architectonic, rather than stylistic, problems. Most of his contemporaries tended to equate architecture with the use of period styles, which were imitated, or rather relived, with ever greater fidelity as information about them became more detailed and more widely diffused. Once Neo-Classical faith in the 'true' style underlying all others had faltered, an ever widening choice opened before architects and their patrons. Eclecticism was, however, discountenanced; a building was expected to conform in all its parts to a single style. Before the beginning of the nineteenth century Classical architecture had been divided into Greek and Roman. Now medieval architecture, which had been termed 'Gothic' in eighteenth-century England, was divided and subdivided into chronological and local styles, each with its own rules and historical associations.

In England, Gothic had survived longer and was revived earlier than elsewhere in Europe, survival overlapping revival in the early eighteenth century. Nevertheless, the decision taken in 1836 to rebuild the recently burnt-out Houses of Parliament in London in a medieval rather than a Classical style was the flashpoint for violent controversy. Classicists stressed the rationality of Greek

and Roman architecture. But Gothic had for some time been regarded as a national style, evolved at the time of the Barons' Wars which had led to the granting of *Magna Carta* – the supposed foundation stone of British liberties. Something of a compromise was reached in the building eventually erected (**15,34**), to the general design of Charles Barry (1795–1860) with profuse Gothic ornament inside and out by Augustus Welby Northmore Pugin (1812–52). For, although the silhouette, with the massive Victoria Tower providing a robust vertical accent at one corner and the more delicate clock-tower (Big Ben) piercing the skyline at the other, is eminently picturesque (as many painters were to discover), the plan is quite logical in its clarity, ornaments are regular and repetitive, and each section of the building is strictly symmetrical. Pugin himself is said to have complained that the river front was 'all Greek' – a Classical structure in medieval costume.

In 1836, the year of the first design for the Houses of Parliament, John Constable condemned the Gothic Revival as a 'vain endeavour to reanimate deceased art, in which the utmost that can be accomplished will be to reproduce a body without a soul'. This was a highly Romantic idea. In the eighteenth century no one had questioned the principle of imitation in architecture, nor had buildings been expected to have souls. But Pugin turned the anti-revivalist argument to his advantage. For him, Gothic art had never died; it had merely fallen into disuse after the Renaissance and Reformation. Gothic, he proclaimed, was not a style, but a principle as eternally

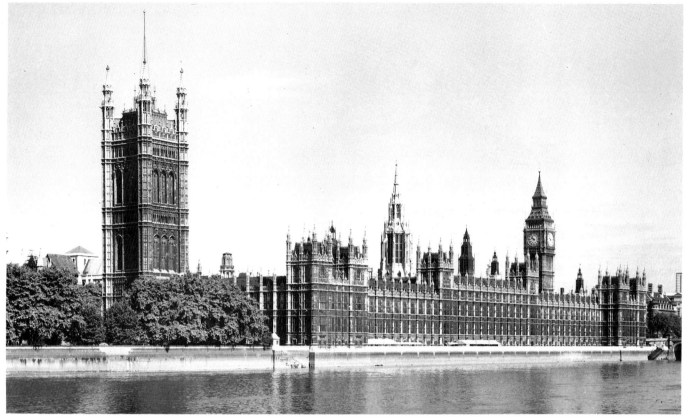

15,34 Sir Charles Barry and Augustus Welby Northmore Pugin, Houses of Parliament, London, 1839–52.

PUGIN ON THE PRINCIPLES OF CHRISTIAN ARCHITECTURE

Barry's designs for the Houses of Parliament (15,34) were accepted the same year, 1836, as Pugin published the first of his polemical books on Gothic architecture: *Contrasts; or, A Parallel between the Noble Edifices of the fourteenth and fifteenth centuries and similar Buildings of the Present Day; shewing the Present Decay of Taste*. It was, he wrote, inspired by 'no other feelings but that of advancing the cause of truth over that of error'. Pugin's conversion to Gothic had come simultaneously with his conversion to Roman Catholicism and he lamented equally the 'fallen condition' of humanity in architecture as in religion and stressed the need for 'sincerity' in both. If Gothic was to be truly revived, its principles must be understood and followed. Merely to copy its forms and ornamentation, as in the eighteenth century, was futile if not immoral. Medieval methods of building must be revived and the nature of building materials respected so that architecture might once again truthfully express its structure and function. In this way Pugin freed honestly constructed Neo-Gothic buildings from the stigma of being shams; and by shifting the emphasis from styles to principles of construction he provided the basis for later functional theories (see p. 827) whose results would have horrified him.

The 'true principles of Pointed or Christian Architecture' could be reduced to two great rules, he wrote:

1st, that there should be no features about a building which are not necessary for convenience, construction, or propriety; 2nd, that all ornament should consist of enrichment of the essential construction of the building. The neglect of these two rules is the cause of all the bad architecture of the present time . . . .

In pure architecture the smallest detail should have a meaning or serve a purpose; and even the construction itself should vary with the material employed, and the designs should be adapted to the material in which they are executed.

Strange as it may appear at first sight, it is in pointed architecture alone that these great principles have been carried out; and I shall be able to illustrate them from the vast cathedral to the simplest erection. Moreover, the architects of the middle ages were the first who turned the natural properties of the various materials to their full account, and made their mechanism a vehicle for their art.

(A. Welby Pugin, *The True Principles of Pointed or Christian Architecture*, London 1841)

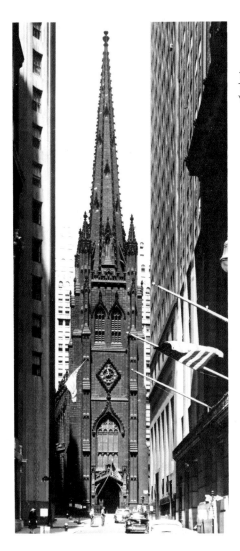

15,35 Richard Upjohn, Trinity Church, New York City, 1841–52.

valid as the teaching of the Roman Church, to which he had been converted. He propounded two 'great rules': 'first, that there should be no features about a building which are not necessary for convenience, construction or propriety; second, that all ornament should consist of enrichment of the essential structure of the building.' These principles were fulfilled in Gothic architecture and only in Gothic architecture, he declared. Greek temples were marble copies of prototypes in wood, and therefore shams. Gothic was the perfect expression of construction in stone or brick and, therefore, true. In this way, by a nimble shift in emphasis from styles to principles, from the integrity and the imaginative faculty of the architect to the nature and potentialities of his media, Pugin freed the Gothic Revival building from the stigma of being a deception. His ideas were to be given far wider circulation by the militant anti-Papist John Ruskin (1819–1900), a writer of genius and social reformer as well as an art critic.

Pugin's principles were widely accepted by architects throughout the English-speaking world (also to some extent in France and Germany). But Gothic was usually adopted for its historical associations as much as for its structural rectitude. Thus, Richard Upjohn (1802–78) – born in England but trained in America – admitted a 'deceptive' plaster vault to his otherwise correctly stone-built Trinity Church, New York (**15,35**). It is in the English early fourteenth-century style particularly dear to

High Church Anglicans and to Episcopalians, partly as the 'classic' phase of Gothic in England (richer than Early English, purer than Flamboyant and Perpendicular) and partly, it seems, because it had been evolved before John Wyclif's propositions for reform had been condemned in 1382. Upjohn built Gothic churches only for Episcopalians. For Congregationalists he adopted a round-arched Early Christian or Romanesque style.

HISTORICISM AND REALISM

History dominated not only architecture, but nearly every aspect of Western thought throughout the nineteenth century, very largely taking the place occupied by reason in the eighteenth. (The German term *Historismus* or Historicism was coined to describe this tendency.) Political, social and economic as well as artistic problems were referred to historical precedents and principles. Both Hegel and Marx founded their philosophies on historical studies. Where eighteenth-century naturalists had classified species, those of the nineteenth sought to trace their evolution – notably Charles Darwin (1809–82) in *The Origin of Species* (1859). 'When we regard every production of nature as one which has had a history', he wrote, 'how far more interesting, I speak from experience, will the study of natural history become!' In literature historical novels such as those by Walter Scott in Great Britain, James Fenimore Cooper in the United States, Victor Hugo in France and Alessandro Manzoni in Italy attained unprecedented popularity. The majority of operas had historical settings, Giuseppe Verdi's *Il Trovatore* (1853), *Don Carlos* (1867) and *Aida* (1871) being among the most famous. The exhibition halls of Europe and America were crammed with statues of figures from medieval and later history, and with pictures of historical events over an ever widening time-range – from the very dawn of human life with the ape-men of popular science to the French Revolution and its heroes, and victims.

Late eighteenth-century painters had used medieval as well as antique historical subjects as moral exemplars. Historical anecdotes with few didactic overtones were more to the taste of the nineteenth century, telling and touching glimpses of how people had lived and loved and died in former days: the past recorded for its own colorful sake. Although such subjects were painted by Ingres and Delacroix, the artists who scored the greatest popular success were those who held to a middle course, avoiding all extremes. They were called the painters of the *juste milieu* (happy medium), a phrase popularized in a political sense by Louis-Philippe, who announced in 1831 his wish to avoid both an excess of popular power and the abuse of royal power. The *genre* demanded detail – local color in a literary as well as in an artistic sense – and detail rendered with illusionistic veracity: the button-hole of a cloak, the pommel of a dagger. Artists were obliged to engage in historical research to guard themselves against anachronisms. *The Execution of Lady Jane Grey* by Paul Delaroche (1797–1856), the acknowledged leader of the *juste milieu* in France, was one of the most famous of

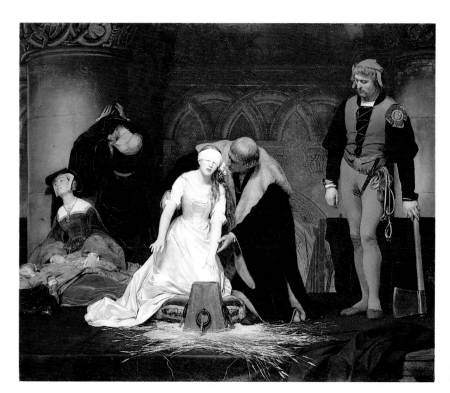

15,36 Paul Delaroche, *The Execution of Lady Jane Grey*, 1833. Oil on canvas, 8ft ¾in × 9ft 9ins (2.46 × 2.97m). National Gallery, London.

15,37 *Opposite* William Holman Hunt, *Our English Coasts*, 1852. Oil on canvas, 17 × 23ins (43.2 × 58.2cm). Tate Gallery, London.

these historical pictures, clearly composed and painted with consummate technical ability (**15,36**). The lighting is dramatic, concentrated on the heroine in her shimmering white silk dress, with an effect comparable to that of the final scene of a play or opera, a tragedy vividly enacted by substantial flesh-and-blood figures. The subject is eminently pathetic – the death on the scaffold of the hapless Lady Jane Grey, unwillingly elevated to the English throne (in 1553) in opposition to Mary Tudor – and would have been quite familiar to a French middle-class public alert to any possible parallels between English history and their own. Choice of subject was, indeed, all-important for such paintings, to catch popular attention when first exhibited and later to secure a wide and very profitable diffusion of prints after them.

Pictures of this type were produced in every European country and also in the United States of America. Sometimes they had overt political overtones, especially in Italy, where subjects alluding to the *Risorgimento* or struggle for national unification and independence were as popular for paintings as for operas – the battle of Legnano, for instance, at which the German emperor was defeated by the Milanese in 1176. Despite, or perhaps because of, their appeal to the general public, they were, however, scorned by the more serious painters and writers. If they reflected Romantic notions of history, they seldom answered Romantic demands for artistic authenticity, for originality of vision and individuality of touch, and for the expression of the painter's own feelings and intimate convictions. It was against their superficial Romanticism – which helped to give the whole Romantic movement a bad name – that a number of young artists in France, England and Germany rebelled in the mid-century.

THE PRE-RAPHAELITES

In England a group of artists – William Holman Hunt (1827–1910), John Everett Millais (1829–96), Dante Gabriel Rossetti (1828–82) and four others – founded the Pre-Raphaelite Brotherhood in 1848. The name is somewhat misleading, for they did not advocate a return to the art of the period before Raphael (as a group of German painters known as 'Nazarenes' had done nearly half a century earlier), nor did they know very much about it. Their declared aim was a 'return to Nature' and a renunciation of academic practices which they traced back by way of Joshua Reynolds ('Sir Sploshua', as they called him) and the seventeenth-century Bolognese school to the first imitators of Raphael. The name was chosen, Holman Hunt said, 'to keep in our minds our determination ever to do battle against the frivolous art of the day'. He was soon drawn to religious subjects, though of a highly allusive type (**15,37**). *Our English Coasts* is a comment on the defencelessness of the English Church against attacks from the Papacy (Pope Pius IX had just proclaimed the re-establishment of the Roman Catholic hierarchy in England). But it is also, and more notably, a wonderfully faithful, naturalistic view of the Sussex coastal landscape, diligent in its attention to details of natural forms clearly lit by bright cold seaside sunlight. The picture was, in fact, painted in the open air, a practice occasionally adopted by Constable but rare, except for *études* like those of Corot (15,28), before the mid-century. Informality of composition and a curious evenness of focus give it a kind of 'snapshot' immediacy. The original title was soon forgotten and it came to be regarded as a pure landscape without any ulterior meaning.

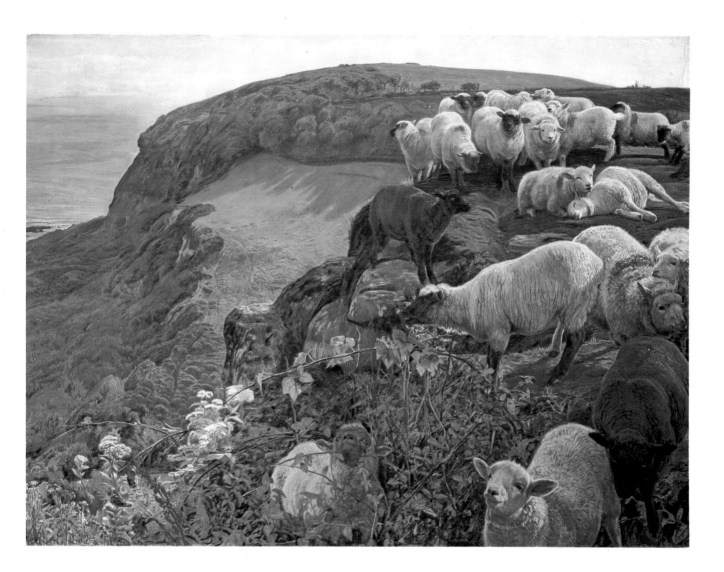

COURBET

A much greater painter in France, Gustave Courbet (1819–77), reacted against the 'frivolous art of the day' in a very different manner. He began with portraits, including more than one of himself in medieval costume, but soon discarded what he called the 'trappings of Romanticism'. After the exhibition of his first major work, *A Burial at Ornans* (**15,38**), in 1850–1, he was called a Realist, just as, he wrote, the title of Romantic was imposed on 'the men of 1830'. The remark occurs in Courbet's preface to the catalogue of the one-man show he set up in 1855 to display pictures which had been excluded from the international exhibition in Paris. This revealing document, which constitutes a manifesto of Realism, continues:

> I have studied, outside system and without prejudice, the art of the ancients and the art of the moderns. I no more wanted to imitate the one than to copy the other; nor, furthermore, was it my intention to attain the trivial goal of art for art's sake. No! I simply wanted to draw forth from a complete acquaintance with tradition the reasoned and independent consciousness of my own individuality. To know in order to be able to create, that was my idea. To be in a position to translate the customs, the ideas, the appearance of my epoch, according to my own estimation; to

> be not only a painter, but a man as well; in short, to create a living art – this was my goal.

Courbet had not cast off all Romantic ideas along with the trappings of Romanticism. But his paintings show better than his writings how his forceful personality and the circumstances of his life led him to create an art far removed from that of Delacroix, not to mention Delaroche. He was the son of a fairly well-to-do farmer at Ornans, near the Swiss border, and went in 1839 to Paris, where he taught himself to paint by studying in the Louvre and in the *ateliers libres* (open studios), which for a small fee provided a model but had no formal curriculum. His circle of friends included Baudelaire and Pierre-Joseph Proudhon (1809–65), originator of the phrase 'property is theft', whose Socialist views he shared.

Painting of Human Figures, Historical Record of a Burial at Ornans, as Courbet himself entitled it, is a painting on the same grand scale as Gros's *Plague House at Jaffa* (15,7), Gericault's *Raft of the 'Medusa'* (15,12), Delacroix's *Sardanapalus* (15,16) and *Liberty Leading the People* (15,17). But the grand style which survives in those great canvases – *grandes machines*, as they came to be called – is lacking, although there is a distant and perhaps significant echo of the 'bourgeois' group portraits of Dutch seventeenth-century art. There are no heroic gestures. There is no firm centre to the vast composition.

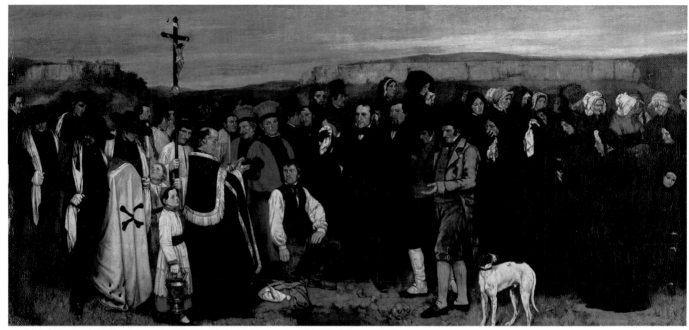

15,38 Gustave Courbet, *A Burial at Ornans*, 1849–50. Oil on canvas, 10ft 3ins × 21ft 9ins (3.14 × 6.63m). Louvre, Paris.

Concepts

ART FOR ART'S SAKE: AESTHETICISM VERSUS REALISM

The concept of 'art for art's sake', of the autonomy of a work of art, without any moral, social, political or any other didactic purpose, was at the centre of much nineteenth-century thought though as often attacked as commended. Its origin can be traced back to Immanuel Kant (see p. 643) who, in *The Critique of Judgement* of 1790, broke with traditional aesthetics by analyzing the previously unified notions of the good, the true and the beautiful as discrete categories. Appreciation of beauty is, he argued, subjective and disinterested – unaffected by an object's purpose. In simplified form, his philosophy was diffused by Germaine de Staël in her book on Germany of 1813 (see p. 657); and the catch phrase 'l'art pour l'art' was coined in 1818 by the French philosopher Victor Cousin (1792–1867). The concept appealed strongly to Romantics in revolt against academic rules.

Among the latter, the French poet Théophile Gautier (1811–72) published in 1835 a novel *Mademoiselle de Maupin* with a preface which came to be regarded as the manifesto of 'art for art's sake'. In it he exposed the hypocrisy of prudish moral censors and went on to repudiate the belief that the value of works of art depends on their utility. 'What is the good of music? what is the good of painting?', he asked. 'There is nothing truly beautiful that can be used for anything; everything that is useful is ugly, for it is the expression of some need. . . . The most useful room in a house is the latrine.' With greater subtlety, Charles Baudelaire (see p. 676) emphasized the autonomous integrity of works of art. Painting, he wrote, is 'an evocation, a magical operation' which makes its effect by color and line, with its own principle of life to be found only in the soul of the artist.

The doctrine of 'art for art's sake' could, however, be evoked simply as a justification for hedonistic aestheticism, as in the writings of Whistler (see p. 719) in England or of Edmond Goncourt (1822–96) in France, among others. Goncourt, an enthusiast of eighteenth-century painting and Japanese prints, remarked that 'Art sets out from the useless: it aims towards that which is agreeable for the few. It is the egotistic adornment of aristocracies.' Such a definition was, of course, anathema to social reformers and proponents of Realism in the arts. Pierre-Joseph Proudhon (1809–65), the foremost French socialist and author of the phrase 'property is theft', wrote in an interpretation of the Realism of his friend Courbet:

> '. . . it is not true that the only aim of art is pleasure, for pleasure is not an end; it is not true that it has no other aim but itself, for everything sticks together, everything is conjoined, everything has an aim in humanity and nature. . . . Art has the objective of leading us to the knowledge of ourselves. . . . It was not given to us to feed ourselves with myths, to intoxicate ourselves with illusions . . . but rather to deliver ourselves from these harmful illusions by denouncing them.*

Nevertheless, aestheticism was prevalent in Europe and America by the end of the century when Georgi Plenkhanov (1857–1918), founder of the first Russian Marxist association, wrote that 'art for art's sake' develops when artists feel 'a hopeless contradiction between their aims and the aims of the society to which they belong.'

The group of figures looking in different directions, each absorbed in his or her sad thoughts, seems hardly to have been composed at all; yet it is very subtly organized, with breaks which give the frieze-like arrangement a slow dirge-like rhythm, and a masterly use of a limited range of colors, so that the blue stockings of the man by the dog and the red costumes of the men who have carried the coffin lend the russet and black-and-white scheme a sombre autumnal resonance.

The subject is insistently commonplace – just a burial at Ornans, no matter whose. Death is a leveller in more than one sense, uniting round the grave members of the various strata of rural society, the priest, the mayor, farmers and farm-labourers, with their wives and children. Courbet set the scene in the new cemetery at Ornans, opened the year before he began the picture. And he painted the figures, including among them his father and sisters, as large as life and just as plain, with such frankness that his Parisian critics supposed that he had intended to ridicule the priest with his slightly inane expression, the red-nosed coffin-bearers, the gaunt-faced women. Courbet's aim was simply to record the most solemn act in the life of any community as it really takes place and his calm and straightforward honesty of purpose is felt throughout the great painting and gives it its continuing power. The scene is dominated by the crucifix. As a Socialist, Courbet would hardly have questioned its importance, for life in the French countryside was still dominated by the Church. Socialism and Christianity were never so closely allied as they were at this moment in France, on the eve of Napoleon III's seizure of power. But later, in 1873, after his political and anti-clerical ideas

had hardened and he was an exile in Switzerland as a result of his involvement in the Paris Commune in 1871, Courbet said that *A Burial at Ornans* was 'worth nothing'. By this time he had come to share Marx's view that 'Christian Socialism is but the holy water with which the priest consecrates the heart-burnings of the aristocrat'.

MILLET

The main figures in Courbet's picture were members of the rural bourgeoisie, to which his own family belonged. His near-contemporary Jean-François Millet (1814–75) specialized in depicting the rural proletariat, the people who had no possessions. But he, too, was misunderstood. As the painter Camille Pissarro (1830–1903), a convinced Anarchist, later remarked:

> Because of his painting The Man with a Hoe, *the Socialists thought Millet was on their side, assuming that an artist who had undergone so much suffering, this peasant of genius who had expressed the sadness of peasant life, would necessarily have to be in agreement with their ideas. Not at all . . . . He was just a bit too Biblical. Another one of those blind men, leaders or followers, who, unconscious of the march of modern ideas, defend the idea without knowing it, despite themselves!*
>
> (Letter to his son, 2 May 1887, tr. T. J. Clark)

Millet's obstinate refusal to accept the Socialist interpretations put on his work was part of the myth he created about himself as the uneducated peasant who had worked on the land until he was 21. In fact, he was the son of a far

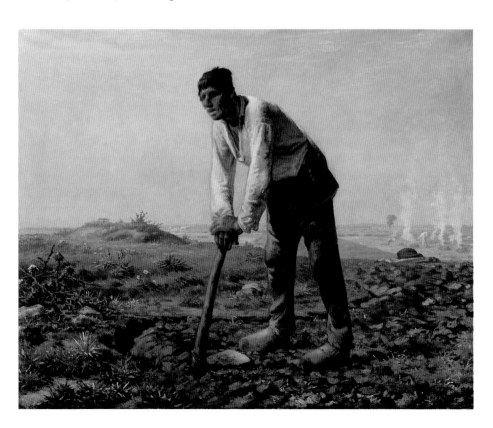

15,39 Jean-François Millet, *The Man with the Hoe*, 1852–62. Oil on canvas, 32 × 39½ins (81 × 100cm). J. Paul Getty Museum, Malibu, California.

from indigent farmer who sent him (aged 18) to study art at Cherbourg. In 1837 he went to Paris, where he became a favourite pupil of Delaroche (see pp. 671–2), but was embittered by failure to win a scholarship to the French Academy in Rome. From 1849 he lived at Barbizon, a village on the fringe of the forest of Fontainebleau (south of Paris), where a group of naturalist landscape painters led by Théodore Rousseau (1812–67) – the so-called Barbizon School – had settled.

But if Millet the 'peasant painter' is largely a myth he was not politically disingenuous. The peasants he depicted belonged to the class which still accounted for more than half the French population yet had benefited least from the growing mid-century prosperity. In Marx's view of society they were no more than dim background figures, destined to form the rank and file of 'industrial armies for agriculture'. But *The Man with the Hoe* (**15,39**), brutalized by toil, stopping for a moment in his task of hacking the stubborn soil, personifies a more fatalistic and pessimistic view in an image of eternal human labour and poverty. It recalls a description of a peasant by the sixteenth-century essayist Michel de Montaigne, one of Millet's favourite authors. But the image goes back further, to the Book of Genesis and God's judgement on Adam: 'Cursed is the ground for thy sake; in sorrow shalt thou eat of it all the days of thy life; thorns also and thistles shall it bring forth to thee, and thou shalt eat the herb of the field. In the sweat of thy face shalt thou eat bread, till thou return unto the ground . . .'. Millet's view of life was deeply fatalistic, redeemed only by his power to express it with an epigrammatic terseness and force of composition, a tautness of line combined with great delicacy and refinement in handling of paint. Yet the tillers and sowers and gleaners he depicted with an uncompromising realism that seemed shocking to many contemporaries soon came to be veiled in a nostalgia which gave the innumerable reproductions of them an irresistible sentimental appeal to city-dwellers. For the rural world was on the eve of a momentous change as a result of the mechanization of agriculture (already well under way by this date in the United States).

SOURCES AND DOCUMENTS

BAUDELAIRE: 'WHAT IS THE GOOD OF CRITICISM?'

The French poet Charles Baudelaire (1821–67) was the most discerning of ninteenth-century art critics. His first signed publication was a review of the 1845 Salon and he went on reviewing exhibitions throughout his life, never taking the position of a detached observer. He wrote as an artist, a poet, personally involved in and directly confronting the problems of the painters and sculptors whose work he discussed. For Baudelaire the source of art lay solely in individual artists' image-making faculties, in their imagination, and in the force of their ideas. From them came all its vitality and its capacity to respond to 'Modern Life'. He called for an art that would, above all, take account of the transformation of ninteenth-century society and he ended his 1845 Salon review with a passionate appeal for a painter who would interpret the age to itself: a painter with an imaginative grasp of its paradoxical spasms of 'heroism' amid its moral and spiritual desolation.

There is no lack of subjects, nor of colors, to make epics. The painter, the true painter for whom we are looking, will be he who can snatch its epic quality from the life of today and can make us see and understand, with brush or with pencil, how great and poetic we are in our cravats and patent-leather boots. Next year let us hope that the true seekers may grant us the extraordinary delight of celebrating the advent of the new!

He renewed his appeal the following year, ending his Salon review by remarking:

I observe that the majority of artists who have attacked modern life have contented themselves with public and official subjects – . . . with an ill grace . . .

and he went on to urge them to open their eyes to

. . . the thousands of floating existences – criminals and kept women – which drift about in the underworld of a great city . . . we have only to open our eyes to recognize our heroism.

And again:

The life of our city is rich in poetic and marvellous subjects. We are enveloped and steeped as though in an atmosphere of the marvellous; but we do not notice it.

There was, however, a more general problem.

What is the good of criticism? What is the good? – A vast and terrible question mark which seizes the critic by the throat from the very first step in the first chapter that he sits down to write. . . . I sincerely believe that the best criticism is that which is both amusing and poetic: not a cold, mathematical criticism which, on the pretext of explaining everything, has neither love nor hate, and voluntarily strips itself of every shred of temperament . . . . To be just, that is to say, to justify its existence, criticism should be partial, passionate and political, that is to say, written from an exclusive point of view, but a point of view that opens up the widest horizons.

(J. Mayne, *The Mirror of Art*, London 1955. The first extract is from the Salon of 1845; the rest are from the Salon of 1846, first published as a booklet, Paris 1846)

MANET

The realities of contemporary life were given a different and more straightforward interpretation by Edouard Manet (1832–83), who outlived Courbet and Millet by less than a decade but seems to belong to another, later period, being often hailed as the 'first modern painter'. He claimed no more than the simple merit of having 'merely tried to be himself and not someone else'. As he wrote in the catalogue of the one-man show he organized when excluded from the International Exhibition in Paris in 1867: 'The artist does not say today, "Come and see faultless work", but "Come and see sincere work." This sincerity gives the work its character of protest, albeit the painter merely thought of rendering his impressions.' Rebelliousness and conformism are found side by side in Manet. He was both a convinced Socialist and a respectable bourgeois (from an upper-middle-class family). Few artists have leaned more heavily and obviously on masters of the past – Raphael, Giorgione, Titian, Velázquez, Hals, Watteau, Chardin, Goya – yet made a clearer break with traditional ways of painting. His *Luncheon on the Grass* (*Déjeuner sur l'Herbe*, **15,40**) is both a modernized version of and a comment upon such *fêtes champêtres* as that attributed to Giorgione or Titian (11,43), together with allusions to a sixteenth-century print after a mythological composition by Raphael. He wanted both to be accepted by the Salon, and to shock its organizers and visitors, as he did even more flagrantly with *Olympia* (17,9) which was immediately recognized as depicting a prostitute (see p. 714). Hankering after official recognition, he aspired to paint a monumental public work in the great French tradition. But the nearest he came to realizing this ambition was with *The Execution of the Emperor Maximilian* (**15,41**), which was debarred from public exhibition until 1879 because of its subject.

The death of the Archduke Maximilian of Austria in 1867 was the last event in the tragic story of Napoleon III's ill-starred attempt to create a client state in the New World. Maximilian had been made emperor of Mexico with the support of French troops, and when they were withdrawn he was captured and shot by Mexican nationalists. In Manet's picture, however, the firing-squad is dressed not in Mexican but in French uniforms, and in this way Maximilian is made to appear an innocent victim of the imperial régime, which Manet hated (the point was taken by the censors, who banned the publication of his lithograph of the composition). The device also made it easier for Manet to adhere strictly to his 'realist' aims. Photographs (which were much used as visual 'aids' by Courbet and other artists at this date) provided him with a record of the event. But he employed as models soldiers from a nearby barracks so that he need trust only his own eyes to depict their stance and the blue serge and pipe-clay of their uniforms. And his eyes told him that most previous artists had falsified visual appearances. Just as Delacroix found that shadows are not simply darkened local colors, so Manet perceived that the half-tones of academic painters were merely a pictorial convention. He strove to eliminate them from his work. His constant study of the old masters, and also of Japanese prints (see

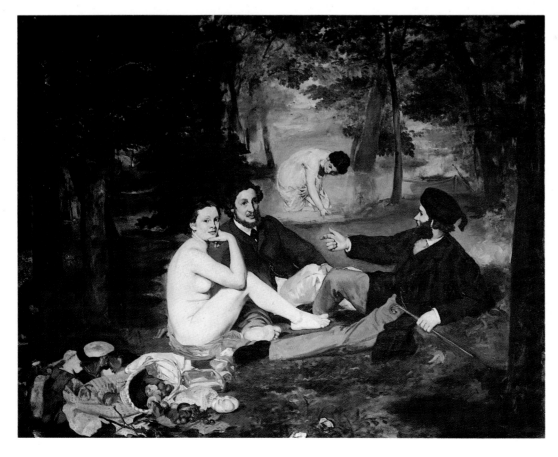

15,40 Edouard Manet, *Luncheon on the Grass (Déjeuner sur l'Herbe)*, 1863. Canvas, 7ft × 8ft 10ins (2.14 × 2.79m). Musée d'Orsay, Paris.

pp. 718–21), and his practice of incorporating elements from them in his paintings were methods of testing his vision against theirs.

When Manet painted *The Execution of Maximilian* he clearly had in mind Goya's *The Third of May 1808* (15,8), which he knew from a print, but the two pictures are essentially dissimilar. Manet's picture lacks the drama and pathos of Goya's. It is dispassionate; contemporaries thought it unfeeling. There is no indication of where his sympathies lay, with the nationalists or with their victims, no pictorial suggestion of anything above or beyond the ostensible subject. The matter-of-fact attitude and expression of the captain of the squad, cocking his rifle on the right, sets the tone of the scene, which the painter seems to observe with the same disinterested, almost casual, curiosity as the figures looking over the wall (a kind of mirror-image of the picture's viewers). It is an example of the way in which Manet redefined the Romantic notion of sincerity to signify not so much emotional integrity as artistic honesty – direct painting from the motif without studio tricks and subterfuges. He made another attempt to work on the grand scale in 1879 by

offering to paint murals of socially significant scenes (markets, railways and docks) for the council chamber of the Hôtel de Ville in Paris. But his proposal was turned down and thereafter he worked on medium- or small-sized pictures for private collectors (see pp. 711–6).

The motto of the Realists, *il faut être de son temps* – one must be of one's own time – was in origin a Romantic idea, the counterpart of the new sense of history or historicism. Justifying a rejection of superficially Romantic themes, it encouraged artists and writers to select unpicturesque, unconventional and sometimes sordid subject-matter. But this did not necessarily involve any break with the past in the manner of painting as sharp as that made by Courbet and Manet, nor did it inevitably imply a rebellious attitude towards the social system. The picture of an iron rolling-mill by Adolph von Menzel (1815–1905) is a case in point (**15,43**). Menzel's sympathy with the spirit of the 1848 revolution is commemorated in his unfinished painting of the funeral of those killed in the March uprising in Berlin (Kunsthalle, Hamburg). But most of his work is divided between freshly painted studies from life, either landscapes or domestic interiors, such as that by

15,41 Edouard Manet, *The Execution of the Emperor Maximilian*, 1867. Oil on canvas, 8ft 3ins × 10ft (2.52 × 3.05m). Kunsthalle, Mannheim.

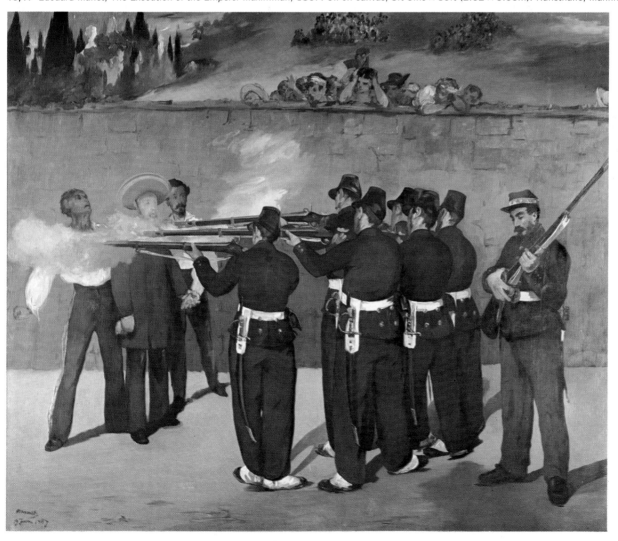

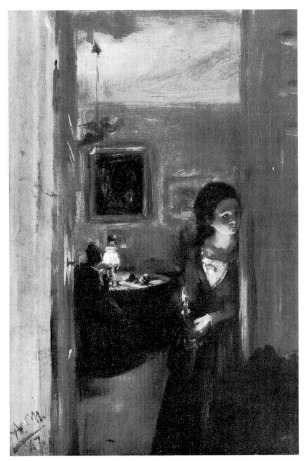

lamplight of his sister at their family home (**15,42**), and large historical pictures, often scenes from the life of Frederick the Great, almost pedantic in their dependence on research and fully approved by the Prussian state and the Berlin Academy (where he became a professor in 1856). Despite the industrial subject, the *Iron Rolling-Mill* is painted with the same studied accuracy of detail, the same virtuoso command of oil paint and the same ability in organizing large figurative compositions to give an impression of spontaneity. It is a highly dramatic and at the same time realistic celebration of what Menzel called the 'Cyclopean world of modern engineering', a description of, rather than a comment on, man's relationship with the machine.

In Russia a realist movement was launched with the publication in St Petersburg in 1855 of an essay by Nikolai Chernyshevskii (1828–89) entitled *The Aesthetic Relation of Art to Reality*, demanding that the arts concern themselves with current social and moral problems. This involved style as well as content for, he wrote, 'a work of art must contain as little of the abstract as possible; everything must be expressed concretely in living scenes and individual images'. An outspoken critic of the autocratic Czarist régime, he was sentenced to hard labour in Siberia but managed to write a novel, *What Is To Be Done?*, which circulated clandestinely and inspired a generation

15,42 *Above* Adolph von Menzel, *Living-Room with the Artist's Sister*, 1847. Oil on paper, 18 × 12½ins (46.1 × 31.6cm). Neue Pinakothek, Munich.

15,43 *Below* Adolph von Menzel, *Iron Rolling-Mill*, 1875. Oil on canvas, 5ft 2¼ins × 8ft 4ins (1.58 × 2.54m). Staatliche Museen, Berlin.

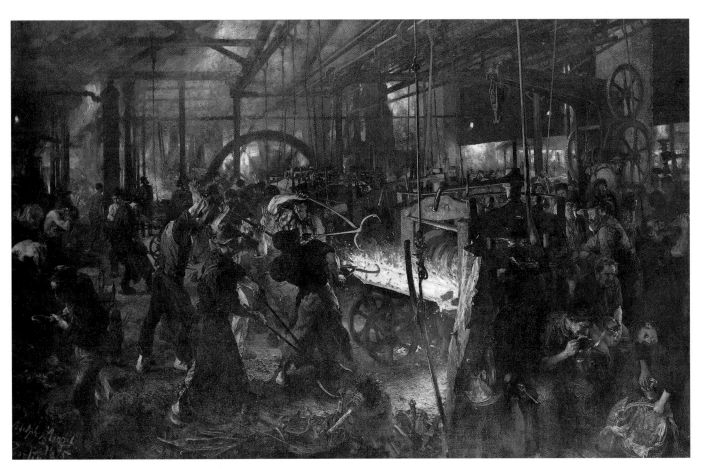

of artists during the following decades of revolutionary terrorism and government repression. Its admirers included the painter Il'ia Efimovich Repin (1844–1930) and other artists who formed an association to exhibit their works in provincial towns, with aims akin to those of the Populists who went to the country to propagate revolutionary ideas at the base of the social structure.

Repin turned his attention to revolutionary subjects at the time of the mass arrests of Populists in the 1870s, painting works with such titles as *The Arrest of a Propagandist*, *Revolutionary Meeting* and *Revolutionary Woman Awaiting Execution* which were, however, too explicitly political to be exhibited. So they failed to carry their message beyond his studio. Although not an active revolutionary, he recognized that 'all the slavery, the merciless punishment, the arbitrariness of power call forth such horrible opposition and such horrifying events' as the assassination of the Czar Alexander II in 1881. In a letter to a friend in 1883 he remarked: 'With all my meagre strength I strive to embody my ideas in truth. The life around me upsets me too much; it gives me no rest, but demands the canvas. Reality is too shocking to allow one to embroider its patterns peacefully, like a well-bred young lady.' At the time he was beginning work on his large painting *They Did Not Expect Him*, which he showed in a travelling exhibition in 1884 (**15,44**).

Among politically motivated realist pictures this work is unusual in the calculated obliqueness of its approach. It shows an obviously middle-class interior rendered in great detail, quite neutrally, including a maidservant wearing an apron. The man with haggard features whose return is unexpected is one of the Populists imprisoned or exiled to Siberia but amnestied by Alexander III, whose police concentrated on rounding up more potentially violent

15,44 Il'ia E. Repin, *They Did Not Expect Him*, 1884. Canvas, 5ft 3⅛ins × 5ft 6ins (1.61 × 1.68m). Tretyakov Gallery, Moscow.

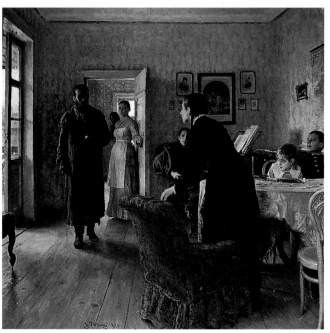

revolutionaries. On the wall there is a portrait of a Populist writer who had collaborated with Chernyshevskii. But there is also a photograph of Alexander II lying in state which suggests that the exile's family had remained loyal to the Czar while he had followed Bakunin's demand to 'stifle all tender feelings of family life, of friendship, love and gratitude . . . by a single cold passion for the revolutionary cause'. Repin focused on the moral problem confronted by revolutionaries whose activities could endanger their families as well as themselves. Although he had been in sympathy with the Populists he was by this date politically a moderate, a friend of the great advocate of passive resistance, the thinker, social reformer and novelist Lev Nikolayevich Tolstoy. Repin was to become the president of the St Petersburg Academy and in 1917 left revolutionary Russia for Finland, where he spent his last years. His works were, nevertheless, to be extolled by the Communist régime as models for Social-Realist painters.

THE USA

In the United States, artists equated being of their own time with being of their own country. Subjects from the Bible, Classical mythology and ancient history were little favoured. Portraits, *genre* scenes, still lifes and especially landscapes were preferred. Thomas Cole (1801–48) declared that artists who depicted American scenery had 'privileges superior to any others. All nature here is new to art.' There were no stretches of country like the Roman Campagna which had been painted over and over again for centuries. He had been born in England and not until after emigrating to the United States, at the age of 17, did he begin to work as an artist, painting views of the Hudson River Valley which immediately found buyers in New York. In 1839 he was one of the founders of the Apollo Association in New York, later called the American Art Union, which exhibited, bought and sold contemporary American works of art. Selling paintings by lottery and supplying prints of them to all who bought tickets, the organization extended the possibility of collecting to a large section of the population across the whole continent. Its managers imposed on themselves the task of building up 'a national school of art'. Inspiration derived from antique statues and European old masters 'defies the spirit of the age', they declared. 'Modern artists have no hope but modern art.'

Cole and a number of other artists in New York were called by an early critic 'The Hudson River School' and the label stuck although they did not limit themselves to painting the scenery of the valley. They sketched in the open air, preferring uncultivated nature 'fraught with lessons of high and holy meaning, only surpassed by the light of Revelation', as the theorist among them, Asher B. Durand (1796–1886), wrote in his *Letters on Landscape Painting* (New York 1855). In their finished pictures, nevertheless, they adopted the formal conventions of European painters, the dark foreground strip and strong *repoussoirs* (see Glossary) and usually included a few small human figures to indicate scale. A younger painter,

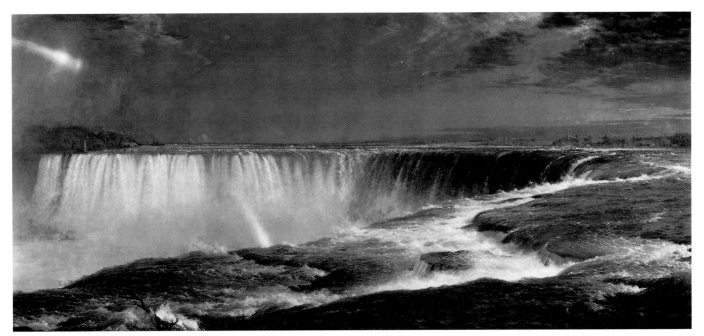

15,45 Frederic Edwin Church, *Niagara*, 1857. Oil on canvas, 3ft 6½ins × 7ft 6½ins (1.08 × 2.3m). Collection, Corcoran Gallery of Art, Washington DC (Museum purchase, 1876).

Frederic Edwin Church (1826–1900), abandoned such devices in his vast panoramic view of Niagara Falls (**15,45**), which was exhibited alone in a commercial gallery in New York in 1857 and hailed as 'perhaps the finest picture yet done by an American; at least that which is fullest of feeling'. One of the wonders of the world, the Falls on the frontier with Canada had come to be regarded as a kind of American emblem, attracting numerous artists and still more tourists. There is, however, no sign of this in Church's picture; the spectator is made to feel alone, a solitary, standing perilously on the edge of the roaring tide, overwhelmed by the spectacle of the water's volume and impetuous, irresistible force. Despite the grandiose size and theme it is painted with great delicacy of coloring, violets and pinks setting off the whiteness of the falling water. The rainbow in the mist of foam is a natural phenomenon but gives the picture another dimension, suggesting the religious awe experienced by many visitors to the place. Charles Dickens had written: 'I felt how near to my Creator I was standing.' Church devoted most of his painting to the Horseshoe Falls on the Canadian side; but the rainbow, perhaps significantly, arches over the United States on the left of the canvas.

America presented artists with natural wonders exceeding in grandeur of scale anything to be seen in Europe. Albert Bierstadt (1830–1902) began in 1859 to explore the as yet little known and seldom depicted mountains, chasms and canyons of the Far West which he sketched and photographed, gathering material to be assembled on huge canvases. Although reared in Massachusetts from the age of two, he had been born in Germany, returned there for his artistic education at the Düsseldorf Academy where there were several American

students, and subsequently crossed and re-crossed the Atlantic. The controlled composition and meticulous handling of detail in his stupendous 10-foot-wide (3m) *Among the Sierra Nevada Mountains in California* reveal his German training, while the more fluidly painted clouds suggest the influence of Turner, whose work he admired (**15,46**). This is not an exact topographical record but a composite impression of sunshine breaking through clouds after a storm in the mountains, with a calm lake, waterfowl and deer, 'a perfect type of what our scenery ought to be, if it is not so in reality', a writer in the *Boston Post* remarked. He painted this astonishing picture far from California, while on a visit to Rome, and exhibited it in Berlin, London and Paris, presumably as a means of establishing an international reputation to impress American collectors with the prestige of Europe. It was bought by Alvin Adams of Watertown, Massachusetts, an American express mail magnate. Bierstadt sold equally large Far West landscapes to other entrepreneurs actively engaged in opening up the region, notably to one of the financiers of the Central Pacific Railroad.

Such carefully selected and idealized prospects of vast areas of land with still unexploited natural resources had an obvious appeal for Americans who shared the belief, first summarized at the time by John O'Sullivan (1813–95), in 'our manifest destiny to overspread the continent allotted by Providence for the free development of our yearly multiplying millions'. They also captured what the historian Francis Parkman (1823–93) called the 'stern and solemn poetry that breathed' from the primeval American wilderness. Ever since the seventeenth century Americans had defined themselves in relation to the wilderness that was steadily being eroded in the nineteenth century to the regret of an increasing number of people, including

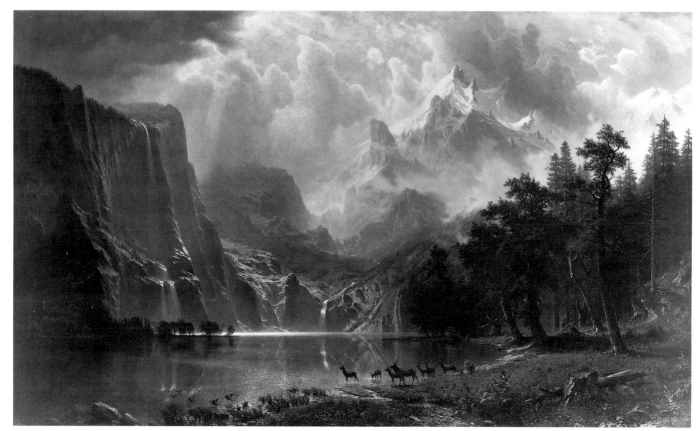

15,46 Albert Bierstadt, *Among the Sierra Nevada Mountains in California*, 1868. Oil on canvas, 5ft 11ins × 10ft (1.83 × 3.05m). National Museum of American Art, Smithsonian Institution, Washington DC.

most notably Henry David Thoreau (1817–62). In 1864, despite the Civil War, Congress passed an act to protect the spectacular Yosemite Valley in the Californian Sierra Nevada, and in 1872 some 2,000,000 acres (800,000 hectares) of north-west Wyoming were designated the Yellowstone National Park. These were the first instances anywhere in the world of large-scale wilderness preservation – a cultural phenomenon of, eventually, global impact – but one that could have been initiated and realized only in a country with a booming industrial economy. Its most active promoters included Frederick Law Olmsted, the leading landscape architect of the time and designer of New York's Central Park and other public parks created so that the urban masses might enjoy the physical and moral benefits of nature (see p. 646).

The unspectacular flat farmland in the eastern seaboard was just as much part of the American scene as the wilderness in the Far West but it attracted few painters apart from Martin Johnson Heade (1819–1904). Although he travelled extensively in the 1860s in the United States, South America, the West Indies and Europe, he returned repeatedly to the East Coast, to Massachusetts, Rhode Island and New Jersey, painting more than 100 views of their salt marshes. These landscapes nearly always include haystacks deployed over a seemingly infinite space of meadows with winding streams or ponds left by the retreating tides, only occasionally with a few cows, human figures or the sail of a small boat to

break the uninsistent horizontality (**15,47**). They are essentially depictions of light from skies that are clear or cloudy, rarely thundery, refracted through the damp atmosphere at various times of day, from dawn to dusk, accurately recorded but by no means simply as meteorological studies. Evoking a mood of serene meditation, they seem to have been inspired by feelings akin to those described in 1836 by Ralph Waldo Emerson (1803–82): 'Standing on the bare ground – my head bathed in the blithe air and uplifted into infinite space – all mean egoism vanishes. I become a transparent eyeball; I am

15,47 Martin Johnson Heade, *Sunset over the Marshes*, c. 1863. Oil on canvas, 10¼ × 18¼ins (26 × 46.4cm). Museum of Fine Arts, Boston (M. and M. Karolik Collection).

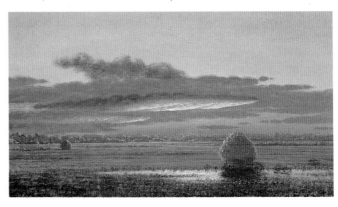

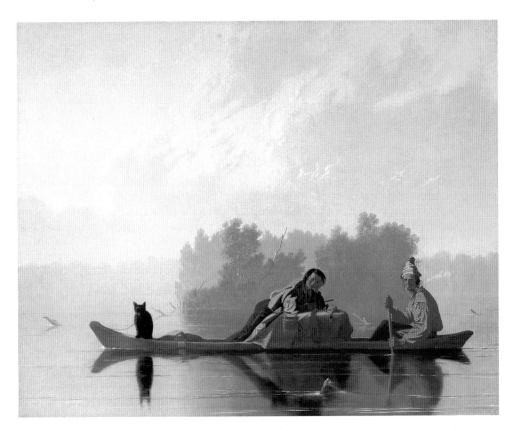

15,48 George Caleb Bingham, *Fur Traders descending the Missouri*, 1845. Canvas, 29 × 36½ins (73.7 × 92.7cm). Metropolitan Museum of Art, New York (Morris K. Jesup Fund, 1933).

nothing; I see all; the currents of the Universal Being circulate through me; I am part and parcel of God.' This transcendental attitude to nature, prevalent in the mid-century, was probably shared by Church (a close friend of Heade) and Bierstadt. Heade's paintings of the salt marshes are, however, uncontaminated by ulterior ideas and although he found purchasers for them, he achieved only a modest reputation. Long before his death he was forgotten and not rediscovered until the 1940s.

The term 'luminist' was coined in the 1950s to classify the works of Heade and a few of his contemporaries. It could, nevertheless, be applied equally well to the magical *Fur Traders descending the Missouri* of 1845 by George Caleb Bingham (1811–79) (**15,48**). Rarely has the effect of early morning light dissipating a mist been as beautifully evoked. The contrast between the trees materializing out of haze and the sharply focused figures in brightly colored clothes, reflected in the slowly moving water, gives the picture a dream-like quality. This sets it apart from the majority of outdoor *genre* scenes, which enjoyed a popularity second only to landscapes in the United States at this time. The demand was for pictures that preserved the myth of simple, happy, rustic life, rendered with close attention to circumstantial detail and without any hint of social tension. Bingham's picture was bought by the American Art Union for a miserable $75 and sold at its annual lottery in 1845 after his original but slightly disturbing title *French Trader and His Half Breed Son* had been changed to that by which it is still known. In the following year the same association bought from Bingham for $290 a painting of men making merry on a Missouri

flatboat, in better accord with the tastes of its members. It later distributed almost 10,000 engravings of it across the continent.

The demand for pictures of outdoor life continued after the Civil War, which provoked the most anxious heart-searchings on the problem of national identity, more sharply reflected in writing than in the visual arts. Winslow Homer (1836–1910) was one of the painters who devoted themselves mainly to this type of work although he diverged from his predecessors both in choice of subject and style. The first painter of international standing to be born and trained and to work almost exclusively in the United States, he began his career as an illustrator for various periodicals. During the Civil War he was sent to the front to make drawings for *Harper's Weekly* and there found himself alongside photographers recording the same events. Photography suggested new ways in which three-dimensional reality might be projected on to a flat surface, but the highly individual style he began to evolve after the war owed as much to painters of the previous two or three decades. In 1867 he visited France and shortly after his return painted his view of *Long Branch, New Jersey* (**15,51**), a popular resort with fashionably dressed figures – the kind of scene often depicted by such French artists as Eugène Boudin (see p. 709). In its asymmetry, its silhouetted forms and its light, bright color-scheme (white, pale blues, fresh greens and sandy yellows) it is also quite close to contemporary work by Manet. But this may be no more than a coincidence. The way in which the composition is cut (especially in the lower left-hand corner) could have been learned either from Japanese

Caleb Bingham's Fur Traders

ART AND THE FRONTIER

Caleb Bingham's *Fur Traders descending the Missouri*, or, as he originally titled it, *French Trader and His Half Breed Son* (15,48), was exhibited at the American Art Union in New York in 1845 with another canvas complementary in composition and subject as well as size, entitled *Indian Figure – The Concealed Enemy* (**15,49**). Conceived as pendants, the two pictures evoke life in the state of Missouri when it was still on the western frontier of the United States. The 'French trader' is a representative of the so-called *voyageurs* or trappers who had often married Native American women; the 'Indian' has the hairstyle and body paint of an Osage. Both were out-of-date by the 1840s, however, for by then large companies with steamships (not canoes) had taken over the fur trade

and the Osage nation, after being assigned land in Kansas under the Indian Removal Act of 1830, had been expelled from Missouri by a military campaign in 1837. But Bingham's paintings of a West that had already vanished were calculated to appeal to the public in the eastern states at a time when the Leatherstocking novels, that great epic of the northwest frontier by James Fennimore Cooper (1789–1851), were being widely enjoyed. They also answered the Art Union's patriotic demand for pictures that 'distinguished this country from all others'.

In New York Bingham was called 'the Missouri Artist' but in his native Missouri he was equally well-known as a politician. The son of a successful farmer at Franklin, he was a self-taught painter. In 1838 he visited

Philadelphia, bought casts of antique sculpture, drawings and prints which he copied and soon achieved some local success with portraits and outdoor *genre* scenes. At the same time he began to take an active part in local politics, joining the Whig party (later to be renamed Republican). In the run-up to the presidential election of 1841 he was among the speakers at Whig rallies, for one of which he painted a large banner (now destroyed). The Whig candidate William Henry Harrison was elected and Bingham moved to Washington in the hope of Whig patronage. In this he was disappointed and after three years returned to Missouri in time to take part in the next presidential campaign, supporting the candidacy of Henry Clay. For this he painted three banners, one of which (now known only from contemporary descriptions) showed on the front Clay with a farmer and also a railroad, merchant shipping and factories. On the back there was a prairie in its uncultivated state with buffalo racing across it. Another banner proposed by Bingham but refused by the party committee would have shown the frontiersman hero of Missouri, Daniel Boone, 'engaged in one of his death struggles with an Indian'. His pictures of the *Fur Traders* and the *Concealed Enemy* date from the same year and similarly contributed to the mythology of the American frontier.

Clay had been the only senator who protested against the treatment meted out to Native Americans by the Indian Removal Act, though he seems to have objected mainly to the way in which it was enforced, and to the Democrats' policy of further territorial expansion. The aim of his 'American System' was to encourage agriculture, commerce and industry in the lands already occupied. The Democratic President Andrew Jackson expressed, nevertheless, a

15,49 George Caleb Bingham, *Indian Figure – The Concealed Enemy*, 1845. Canvas, 29¼ × 36½ins (74.3 × 92.7cm). Stark Museum of Art, Orange, Texas.

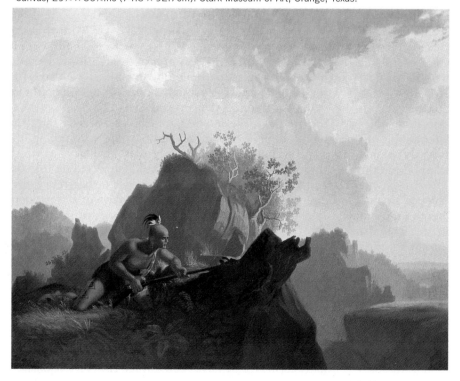

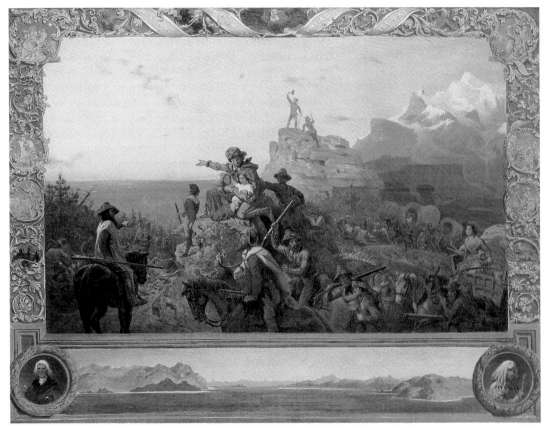

15,50 Emanuel Gottlieb Leutze, *Westward the Course of Empire Takes its Way (Westward Ho!)*, 1861. Canvas, 33¼ × 43⅜ins (84.5 × 110.2cm). National Museum of American Art, Smithsonian Institution, Washington DC (Bequest of Sara Carr Upton).

majority view when he remarked in 1837: 'The states which had so long been retarded in improvement by the Indian tribes residing in the midst of them are at length freed from the evil, and this unhappy race – the original dwellers in our land – are now placed in a situation where we may well hope that they will share the blessings of civilization.' Native Americans had been regarded as enemies of civilization ever since the beginning of European occupation and their alliance with the British during the Revolution did not help them. Bingham's *Concealed Enemy* was only one of innumerable hostile images.

Paintings and sculptures of the exploration and settlement of North America, commissioned from the 1820s onwards for the Capitol in Washington, promoted the ideology of national expansion then current: that the white Christian settlement and the consequent displacement of the Indian were a providential consummation of God's civilizing plan. Native Americans were not excluded altogether, as were African Americans, but they usually figured as obstacles to progress. In a triumphalist painting by Emanuel Leutze they are marginalized (**15,50**), just as the surviving tribes had been by federal policy relocating them to the arid edges of the western frontier. They appear in Leutze's decorative frame, enmeshed in scrolls on either side of the symbolic eagle, above a celebration of expansion to the West. Emanuel Gottlieb Leutze (1816–68) was born in Germany, taken as a child to Philadelphia but in 1841 went to Düsseldorf where he spent the next 18 years, sometimes sharing his studio with other painters from the United States, notably Bierstadt (see p. 681). He made his reputation there with large pictures of American and other historical subjects, notably *George Washington crossing the Delaware* (Metropolitan Museum, New York) of 1851. After returning to the United States he obtained the commission for the painting in the Capitol even though the Civil War was then at its height. He promptly went to sketch the Rocky Mountains and soon completed the model illustrated here. The title *Westward the Course of Empire Takes its Way* was taken from a poem written in Bermuda in 1728–30 by the Irish philosopher and Anglican clergyman (later bishop) George Berkeley (1684–1783) suggesting the historical inevitability of the 'rise of empire and the arts' to the west of Europe. Leutze illustrates the pregnant moment when the emigrants sight the promised land from the mountains (a view through the Golden Gate of San Francisco Bay is in the predella). But the dominant pyramid in the composition would indicate, rather, the stability of an empire already won. When painting the 20- by 30-foot (6 × 9m) mural in the Capitol, Leutze made some significant departures from the model, adding to the crowd of figures in the foreground one – only one – African American, the first allowed to appear anywhere in the Capitol. Hitherto references to the African presence in the United States had always been excluded. Lincoln's Emancipation Proclamation, issued in September 1862 while Leutze was at work on the mural, presented a Unionist view of the state of the nation.

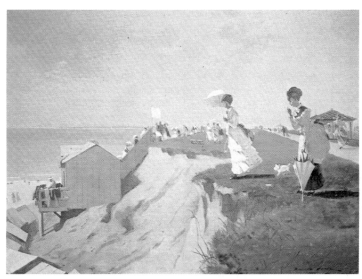

15,51 Winslow Homer, *Long Branch, New Jersey*, 1869.
Oil on canvas, 16 × 21¾ins (40.6 × 55.2cm). Museum of Fine Arts,
Boston (Hayden Collection).

observing eye. Sometimes they recall passages from the fiction of Henry James (1843–1916), who admired Homer, though in rather simple terms. 'He is a genuine painter, that is, to see and reproduce what he sees, is his only care', James wrote of him in 1875. 'He not only has no imagination, but he contrives to elevate this rather blighting negative into a blooming and honourable positive.'

Homer did, in fact, concern himself more deeply than any other artist of his generation with what was certainly the most serious issue of the post-bellum period: the plight of African Americans freed from slavery but not integrated into democratic society. *Dressing for the Carnival* of 1877, painted in bright, vibrant pigments, might at first sight appear to record nothing more than a picturesque, sun-drenched southern scene, with light striking forms of great solidity (**15,52**). Closer inspection reveals sorrow in sunshine. The man in the centre is being dressed in a clown's costume by two women whose expressions are anything but festive. Even the children seem unnaturally subdued. That two of them hold miniature American flags suggests that the man is getting ready to take part in the Centennial Fourth of July celebrations, and Homer may well have witnessed some such scene on that very day in Virginia. In one southern town, however, African Americans wearing militia uniforms who had taken part in a Centennial parade had been harassed, and several were killed a few days later. Before Homer finished the picture the situation had taken a turn for the worse. The contested election in the fall of 1876 led to a compromise whereby the southern Democrats accepted a Republican president on the tacit understanding that Federal troops would be withdrawn from the South and no further effort be made to implement the Fifteenth Amendment enfranchising all people irrespective of their

prints (see pp. 718–21) or from photographs. The picture has a distinctly American air, an insistence on the plain, solid and wholesome reality of everyday things – the beach-hut with its uncompromisingly geometrical blank wall – and also a sense of open spaciousness in which figures are all individually distinct, sometimes almost estranged from one another. The similarity of stance of the two women in the foreground only emphasizes the absence of connections between them. They even look in different directions. As in other paintings by Homer, there are undercurrents of psychological tension, and the sharpness of focus suggests also the detachment of the artist as an

15,52 Winslow Homer, *Dressing for the Carnival*, 1877. Canvas, 20 × 30ins (50.8 × 76.2cm). Metropolitan Museum of Art, New York (Amelia B. Lazarus Fund, 1922).

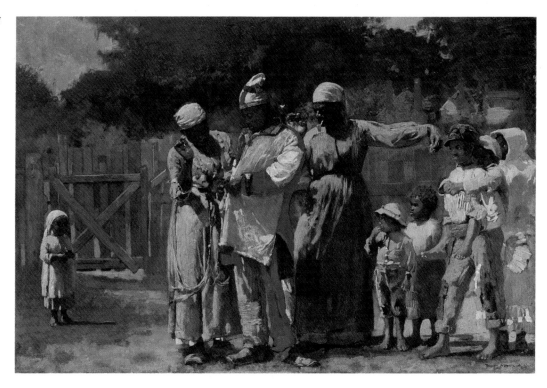

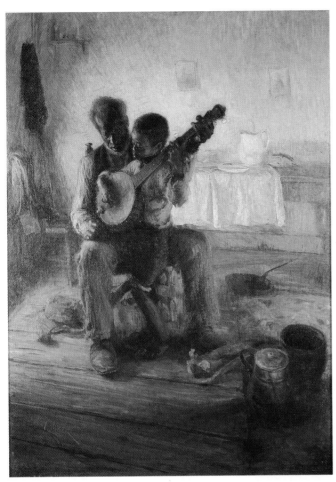

15,53 Henry Ossawa Tanner, *The First Lesson*, c. 1893. Oil on canvas, 48 × 35ins (121.9 × 88.9cm). Hampton University Museum, Hampton, Virginia.

'race, color or previous condition of servitude'. The hopeful period of Reconstruction had ended and segregation was to be ever more strongly enforced. So the closed gate and the clown's costume in *Dressing for the Carnival* may have some symbolic significance.

During the following decades African Americans were more frequently included in *genre* scenes than ever before, nearly always as whites wished to see them in life, on the other side of the color bar. They went on being shown according to the formulae that had been devised to suggest that slaves were contented: either grinning or dancing, if not in attitudes of servile deference. Such images perpetuated the myth of a stable social structure. Other victims of the economic system were similarly depicted, without so much as a hint that all might not be well. Artists were not expected to record the misery of the poor in the land of freedom. 'Whatever the surrounding evil, for the artist the sun is always at the zenith. His business is to put whatever part of nature he paints in the best possible light', Moncure F. Conway (1832–1907), the Virginian writer who had been an outspoken opponent of slavery, remarked in 1871. 'The reformer's zeal, much less his discontent, admirable elsewhere, is inconsistent with the repose of spirit which wins beauty to the side of the artist.'

This was not, however, completely to preclude images that diverged from the stereotypes. African Americans were sometimes portrayed as human individuals, notably by Henry Ossawa Tanner (1859–1937). The son of a theologian who became a bishop of the African Methodist Episcopal Church in Philadelphia, Tanner was partly of African descent, pale skinned but classified as a 'black' in the United States. As such he was persecuted by a gang of white youths when he studied at the Pennsylvania Academy of Arts. He began by painting straightforward landscapes, seascapes and outdoor *genre* scenes and in 1891 went to study in Paris where he was to live for most of the rest of his life. In 1893 he returned on a visit to Philadelphia and, as he wrote at the time, 'painted mostly Negro subjects . . . because of a desire to represent the serious and pathetic side of life among them'. One of these, which he titled *The First Lesson* (**15,53**), shows an elderly man teaching a small boy to play the banjo, a subject which would usually and conventionally have been treated in a comic manner, like an episode in a minstrel show. He probably chose it for that very reason, in order to subvert the stereotype. The two figures are shown wholly absorbed in what they are doing, unaware of any spectator. This image of a human relationship is, in fact, as serious and touching as one between a white grandfather and his grandson, with the implication that African Americans should be regarded in the same way.

At the Philadelphia Academy, Tanner had been taught and befriended by Thomas Eakins (1844–1916), the most distinguished artist working in the United States apart from Homer, from whom he differed in nearly every way. Homer's paintings are small in size (he was also an accomplished watercolorist). Eakins worked on a grander scale and his first major painting, *The Gross Clinic* (**15,54**), has life-size figures in the foreground. As a youth in Philadelphia he had attended anatomy classes at a medical college as well as drawing at the academy. Then he went to Paris and studied under Jean Léon Gérôme (1824–1904), a pupil of Delaroche and a highly finished painter of historical subjects (mainly antique). But it was Rembrandt, Velázquez and Ribera who inspired him to create a nineteenth-century American equivalent to their 'realism'. He may even have intended to rival Rembrandt's *Anatomy Lesson of Dr Tulp* (Mauritshuis, The Hague) with *The Gross Clinic*, which shows a celebrated American surgeon, Dr Samuel Gross, directing an operation on a man's thigh in front of a class of students. Eakins depicted not the investigatory dissection of a corpse (as Rembrandt had done), but remedial surgery on an anaesthetized patient – one of the triumphs of modern science. Skilful control of light, which falls on Dr Gross's forehead and hand and the patient's naked limb, makes it also a highly dramatic composition, showing how far Eakins's debt to Rembrandt went beyond choice of subject-matter. For this is no casual record of a daily event in the life of a busy surgeon. The concentrated expression of concern on Dr Gross's face, the dramatic lighting and the imposing composition give the picture the solemnity of a meditation on the mysteries of science.

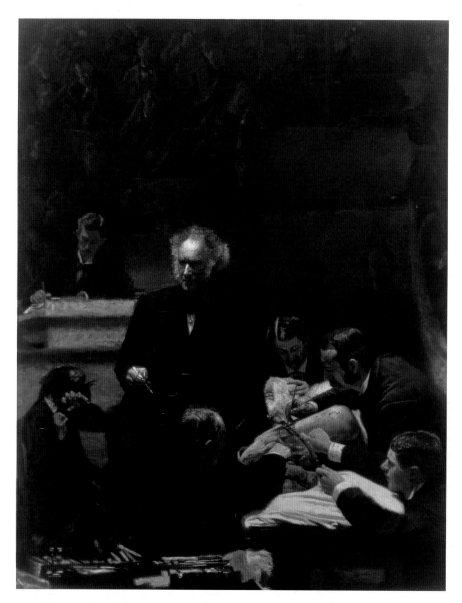

15,54 Thomas Eakins, *The Gross Clinic*, 1875. Oil on canvas, 8ft × 6ft 6ins (2.44 × 1.98m). Jefferson Medical College, Philadelphia.

PHOTOGRAPHY COMES OF AGE

A small black-and-white reproduction of *The Gross Clinic* might at first sight be mistaken for a photograph, though one of a later period. Photographs had been taken of similar scenes in operating theatres; but with figures formally ranked, stiffly posed and patiently holding solemn expressions, they give a far less convincing impression of reality than the painting, due partly to the need for long exposures and strong even lighting. Yet the criticism most insistently levelled at the works of Courbet and other Realists was that they resembled daguerreotypes. This was absurdly wide of the mark but carried the implication that photography was no more than a scientific process for visual record. Whether it could be considered an art was the subject of acrimonious discussion and was the main point at issue in a lawsuit fought in the courts of Paris in 1861–2 which ended with the judge's ruling that photographs could be – the conditional tense is significant – products of thought and spirit, of taste and intelligence, bearing the imprint of a personality and thus works of art. They were, nevertheless, excluded from the Salons after 1850 (when a few had been

hung among lithographs), being shown from 1859 in separate officially sponsored annual exhibitions at the Palais de l'Industrie. They were also barred from the exhibitions of the Royal Academy in London, though one colored by hand was unknowingly accepted in 1861. And this general exclusion was to continue into the twentieth century.

By the 1850s the technical limitations of photography had been much reduced and at the same time more clearly recognized as defining its character and unique possibilities. Photographic images are purely tonal, composed of shades of gray or brown until the development of color photography (based on a limited range of hues) and familiarity with them began subtly to affect perception and ways of seeing – of seeing both nature and works of art. Artists who petitioned against the French legal decision of 1862 that photographs 'could be' works of art were led by Ingres and others who worked in a linear, rather than a tonal, painterly style – significantly, Delacroix refused to lend his name to the petition. The camera can record only degrees of light – as the poet Alphonse de Lamartine put it, photography 'is more than an art, it is a solar phenomenon, where the artist collaborates with the sun'. This was clearly recognized by Gaspard-Félix Tournachon

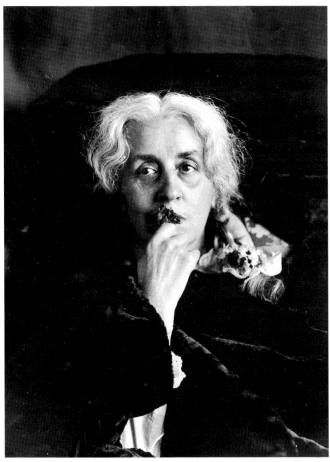

15,55 Nadar (Gaspard-Félix Tournachon), *The Photographer's Wife*, 1853. Gelatin silver print from a collodion negative. Menil Foundation, Houston.

knowledge of how to use it became ever more easily accessible, an increasing number of amateurs took up photography and in portraying family and friends often succeeded in penetrating character far better than the majority of professionals. Julia Margaret Cameron (1815–79) is the most famous, not only because she had the good fortune to number among her sitters such distinguished friends as the poet Tennyson, the Victorian 'sage' Carlyle and the astronomer Herschel. Her photographs are the most vivid images of these great men in rugged old age, surpassing in this any of the painted or sculpted portraits of them. Those of the very young are equally remarkable, capturing brief moments of perfect physical beauty and, sometimes, the ungainliness and, for their elders, the rather unnerving knowingness of childhood. She entitled one, perhaps jokingly, *Paul and Virginia* with reference to Bernardin de Saint Pierre's late eighteenth-century story of juvenile innocence, but made no attempt to conceal the fact that the subject was two children of her own time – one 'showing off', the other shy – posed before the camera (**15,56**).

Although photographs could be works of art, the great majority were and still are valued also, sometimes exclusively, as instantaneous records of moments of truth – just because they are photographs. They are not simply representations but direct reflections of the real world providing incontrovertible evidence of how things appeared. Hence the importance of portraits, views of buildings and

15,56 Julia Margaret Cameron, *Paul and Virginia*, c. 1867. Albumen print. Royal Photographic Society, Bath.

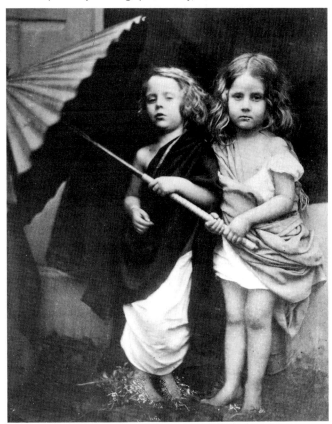

known as Nadar (1820–1910). 'The feeling for light' is essential for a photographer, he wrote in 1856. 'It is how light lies on the face that an artist must capture.' No one more adventurously explored what a camera could record; he went up in a balloon and down into the catacombs to photograph Paris from above and below. But his most memorable images are of writers, artists and musicians who were among his friends and, perhaps best of all, his wife in whom the pensive expression and steady gaze, combined with a suggestion of suppressed tension in the nervously clutched hand, coalesce in a penetrating portrait (**15,55**). Nadar had begun his career as a caricaturist, emphasizing physical features that reveal character, and he put this experience to brilliant, if entirely different, use in photographic portraiture.

'Photography is a marvellous discovery, a science that has attracted the greatest intellects, an art that excites the most astute minds – and one that can be practised by an imbecile. Photographic theory can be taught in an hour, the basic technique in a day', Nadar remarked. What could not be taught was how to 'grasp the personality of the sitter. To produce an intimate likeness rather than a banal portrait, the result of mere chance, you must put yourself at once into communion with the sitter, size up his thoughts and his very character.' As equipment and

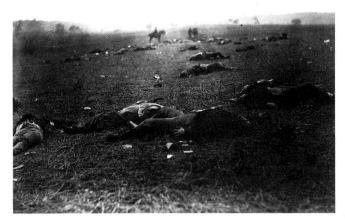

15,57 Timothy H. O'Sullivan, *A Harvest of Death, Battlefield of Gettysburg*, Pennsylvania, July 1863. Albumen print. Rare Books and Manuscript Division, New York Public Library, Astor, Lenox and Tilden Foundations.

eral hundred others. Working for a public convinced of the righteousness of its cause, they had no inhibitions about recording the disasters of war for which the blame was put on the enemy. Earlier paintings of warfare had celebrated heroism and victory. But Timothy H. O'Sullivan (1840–82), the most brilliant of Brady's men, photographed dead soldiers of the Union lying with their boots stolen and pockets rifled on the field of Gettysburg (**15,57**). Although intended primarily, no doubt, as reportage this is no mere casual image of the aftermath of battle. The viewpoint must have been very carefully selected to give a horizontal emphasis, suggesting more dead men stretching out on either side of the image field, balanced by a central axis which leads the eye from the sharply focused figure in the foreground past the horseman and two other survivors to the misty distance.

At this period photographers were still prevented from recording swift action by the need for exposures of several seconds. The development of more sensitive plates and the invention of a mechanical shutter, open for less than one thousandth of a second, enabled Eadweard Muybridge (1830–1904) to catch the movements of animals and humans. He was an Englishman – his original name was Edward Muggeridge but he preferred what he believed to be its Anglo-Saxon form – who worked mainly in the United States where he began by photographing landscapes. In 1878 he succeeded in taking 12 shots of a galloping horse with cameras ranged beside a race-track (**15,58**). The result was astonishing for it showed that the so-called 'flying gallop' in which horses had been depicted since ancient Egyptian times, with all four legs extended off the ground, was the result of an optical illusion. Thomas Eakins, who was one of the first to be impressed

glimpses of historical events which have documentary interest as distinct from their artistic qualities. The camera cannot lie; but it was soon appreciated that it need not tell the whole truth. In 1855 Roger Fenton (1819–69) was sent by the British government to the theatre of war in the Crimea to take photographs that would disprove reports of the disastrously blundering military leadership. During the American Civil War (1861–5) photographers were in the front line, mainly with the forces of the Union. Mathew Brady (1823–96), who had run a successful portrait studio, organized a corps of about 20 cameramen to record every aspect of the conflict, and there were sev-

15,58 Eadweard Muybridge, *Galloping Horse*, 1878. Albumen print. George Eastman House, Rochester, New York.

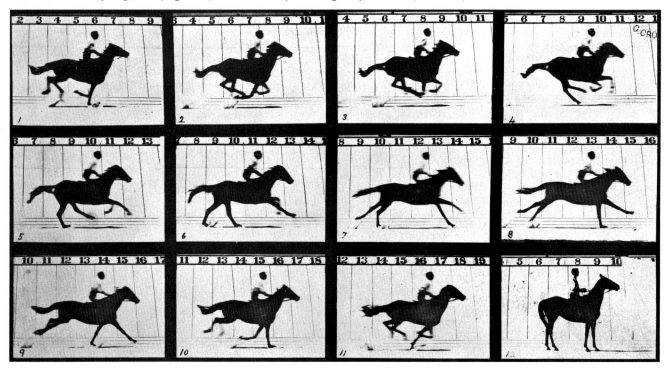

by the work of Muybridge, collaborated with him for a time and evolved his own system for photographing his studio models in fleeting movement, though he was also among the first to appreciate the limited use of such photographic records as aids in painting. In general, naturalistic painters took immediate account of Muybridge's photographs. They were available printed directly from the negatives, published on 781 sheets sold separately or bound into 11 volumes entitled *Animal Locomotion, an Electro-Photographic investigation of successive phases of animal movements* (1887). Thereafter, nudes in a greater variety of poses than those that could be held by a model in a life-class began to appear in academic paintings. Horses in the 'flying gallop' vanished from battle scenes. But the main effect of this work and others that followed was in helping to define the relations between art and the visual, phenomenal world. For the photograph reveals details that are not normally noticed (as Fox Talbot had remarked) and also, in the abrupt suspension of time, it catches moments that are unregistered by the human eye – the spokes of a rotating wheel, for instance, which appear to the human eye to be blurred. 'The artist is truthful and photography lies', Rodin remarked (see pp. 727–9). And photographers with artistic ambitions continued to prefer soft-focus prints of motionless subjects.

Documentary photographers, on the other hand, seized on the most recent technology. Jacob A. Riis (1849–1914) in 1888, with a relatively small camera and flash-light powder (invented the previous year), explored and recorded the slums of New York (**15,59**). His declared aim was to show 'as no mere description could, the misery and vice he had noticed . . . and suggest the direction in which good might be done'. In his book *How the Other Half Lives* (1890) some of his shots were reproduced by the recently developed half-tone process which made cheap widespread diffusion of photographic images possible, though it tended to smudge detail and soften their impact. He also made lantern slides for lectures which he is said to have enlivened with 'humorous and adventuresome anecdotes'. It is hard to imagine Courbet, Millet or Eakins doing such a thing! Riis's photographs, in fact, enabled members of the middle class to go slumming without discomfort, to intrude on the life of the poor without undermining current beliefs that misery as well

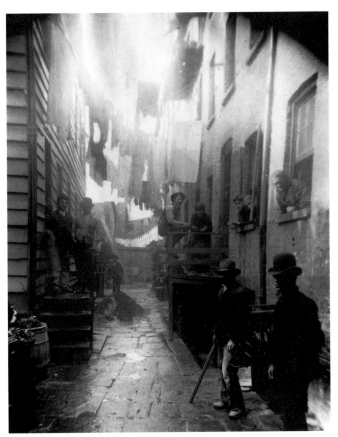

15,59 Jacob A. Riis, *Bandits' Roost, New York*, 1888. Gelatin silver print from the original negative. The Museum of the City of New York, New York.

as vice was caused by moral weakness. Whether consciously or not, his choice of viewpoints, and also his selection of the photographs he thought worth preserving, were usually conditioned by traditional artistic principles of composition which had the effect of distancing if not neutralizing sordid subject-matter. The same may be said of the many early photographs of daily life in India, China and other faraway places. They helped to confirm the belief of Westerners in their own moral as well as economic and technological superiority. For such scenes paintings and drawings were gradually superseded by photographs – all the more insidious in their supposedly innocent objectivity.

CHAPTER SIXTEEN

EASTERN TRADITIONS

'The Great Exhibition of the Works of Industry of All Nations' held in London in 1851 was a glorification of material progress. According to the Prince Consort, who presided over the organizing committee, it presented 'a living picture of the point of development at which the whole of mankind has arrived' and marked 'the new starting point from which all nations will be able to direct their further exertions'. More than 100,000 exhibits were brought together from all parts of the world, specimens of raw materials, hand-tools and handicrafts, machines and their products both utilitarian and decorative, to form a celebration of Europe's still continuing colonial expansion together with the Industrial Revolution. The unprecedented display was housed in the Crystal Palace, itself a marvel of the new technology, being constructed almost entirely of cast iron and glass (17,35). It was little admired by architects at the time and there were a few high-minded critics who also condemned the vulgarity and overwrought ingenuity of many of the examples of Western decorative art on show, reserving their praise for works of hand-craftsmanship which harked back to pre-industrial traditions. But no dissident voice seems to have been raised against the exhibition's resounding declaration of faith in the triumph of man over nature and of

Europeans over the rest of the world, both of which were blandly assumed to be providential. The commemorative catalogue's account of the Indian exhibits – 'the works of people whom many conceive as placed beyond the pale of civilization' – conceded that some techniques had originated in Asia, while adding that they had, of course, 'matured' in Europe! Subsequent international exhibitions in Paris and Vienna gave greater space to non-European countries but made similar claims for European superiority in the arts as well as in technology – claims which went unquestioned at the time.

By 1851 a very large part of the inhabitable world was ruled by Europeans or by men of European descent, and throughout this vast area European artistic ideals gradually infiltrated. In India, for instance, the art of miniature painting had a brief but very beautiful reflowering at the courts of Hindu rulers in Rajputana and the Punjab and among the British nabobs and their retainers from the mid-eighteenth century to the 1820s, but slowly faded with the extension of British control (16,1). Not only did British officials demand work in European styles, but the semi-independent princes who were the only other patrons followed their example. Western art also penetrated the politically autonomous states of Asia. The

The visual arts	Historical landmarks
c. 1650-1700 Yun Shouping, *Lotus Flower* (16,2). Gong Xian, *Landscape* (16,3)	**1682** Manchus complete conquest of China
	1685 Chinese ports opened to foreign trade
	1690 English founded trading station at Calcutta
1732 Hua Yan, *Conversation in Autumn* (16,5)	**1736** Qianlong emperor of China
c. 1740 Emperor Qianlong's throne (16,7)	**1763** *Dream of the Red Chamber* left unfinished on death of author
c. 1790 *Dr George Wombwell* (16,1) Utamaro, *The Hour of the Boar* (16,10)	**1764** British East India Company takes Bengal
	1794 Qajar dynasty in Persia founded
1794 Sharaku, *The Actor Segawa Tomisaburo* (16,11)	**1824** British take Rangoon
c. 1800 Kiyonaga, *Interior of a Bath-House* (16,9)	**1839** British take Hong Kong
1817 Hokusai, *Manga* (16,12)	**1843** With annexation of Sind British control Indian subcontinent
1823–9 Hokusai, *The Great Wave* (16,13)	**1850–66** Taiping rebellion against Manchus in China
1857 Hiroshige, *Maple Leaves* (16,14)	**1854** Commodore Perry forces Japan to open ports to foreigners
	1857 Indian 'Mutiny'
	1858 China admits foreign ambassadors
	1859 French occupy Saigon
	1863 French take Cochin-China, impose protectorate on Cambodia
	1869 Meiji period, Tokyo capital of Japan
1889 Hall of Annual Prayers, Temple of Heaven (16,8)	**1877** Queen Victoria proclaimed empress of India

among its masters), probably originating in Buddhist art. His album-leaf of a lotus is a superbly accomplished essay in what the Chinese call 'boneless' painting – color washes with no outlines (16,2). The forms and textures of the waxy leaves and fragile translucent petals are recorded with the greatest fidelity in a composition so delicately balanced as to seem entirely natural, the movement of reeds swirling round the flower being steadied and closed on the left by two columns of free, strong calligraphy. This is not, however, a straightforward botanical illustration. The symbolism with which Buddhists endowed the lotus has been subsumed in a more general feeling for the creative force or *dao* inherent in all nature. The painting is a product of the concentrated meditation which Yun Shouping admonished artists to cultivate before putting brush to paper. 'You must exclude all human presence', he wrote, 'then the creative dynamism is imparted to your hand and the original inspiration spreads in abundant measure.' He preserved, in fact, the ideals of the scholar-painters, although he was obliged to sell his work – an indignity to which they had rarely been reduced – in order to support himself and his father, a former Ming official. His album-leaves won him recognition as the last of the great flower painters and they were extensively copied in later years, sometimes, it seems, at second if not third hand, with a conspicuous slowing down of 'creative dynamism'.

Opposition to the new régime was not necessarily accompanied by a nostalgic return to the art of earlier times. Gong Xian (1617/18–89), who seems to have gone underground during the first years of Manchu rule, was perhaps the most notable of the individualist landscape painters. Dissociating himself from acknowledged schools, he remarked, 'there has been nobody before me and there will be nobody after me'. His was a distinctly bleak personal view of the world and he invested traditional subject-matter with a sadness sometimes close to despair. There are no human figures in his hand-scroll of a ghostly landscape with a tomb-like temple and forbidding cliffs,

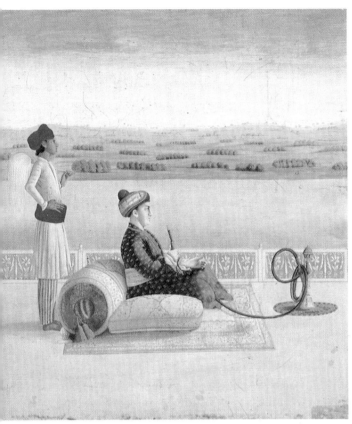

16,1 Anonymous, *Dr George Wombwell, Lucknow*, c. 1790. Gouache on paper, 21½ × 10ins (32.3 × 25.5cm). Fondation Custodia, Collection Frits Lugt, Paris.

Ottoman sultans of Turkey, for instance, built palaces and even mosques which owed as much to French as to Islamic architecture. Shahs of the Qajar dynasty, who ruled Iran from 1794 onwards, encouraged the imitation of European models, including portraiture in oils. Examples of Chinese decorative art shown at the Great Exhibition incorporated Italian Renaissance motifs; but these were very uncharacteristic and were made exclusively 'for export'. Indigenous traditions were, however, maintained in China itself, Thailand and Japan.

QING-DYNASTY CHINA

The alien Qing or Manchu dynasty, from Manchuria north of the Great Wall, displaced the last of the Ming emperors in 1644 and in 1682 completed the conquest of China, which they ruled until 1911. As Manchuria had for some time been a cultural province of China, the advent of the Qing made a much less violent impact on life and art than that of the Yuan four centuries earlier. They brought with them no new artistic style. Before the beginning of this period, however, Chinese painting had already become quite eclectic with a wide range of styles, both conservative and original.

Yun Shouping (1633-90) worked in a tradition of flower painting which went back many centuries and had been popular at the Song court (where an emperor had been

16,2 Yun Shouping, *Lotus Flower*, late 17th century. Qing dynasty. Watercolor on paper. Osaka Museum, Osaka, Japan.

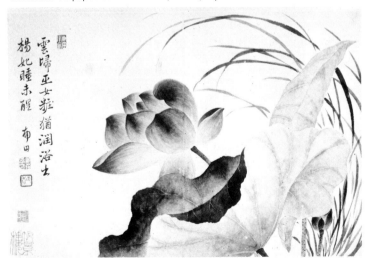

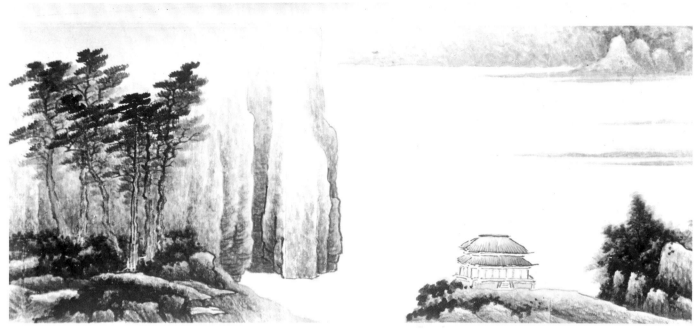

16,3 Gong Xian, *Landscape*, detail, late 17th century. Qing dynasty. Ink on paper, 10½ins (26.7cm) high. Nelson-Atkins Museum of Art, Kansas City (Purchase: Nelson Trust).

which rise sheer out of glazed, almost unnaturally still waters (**16,3**). The technique he developed was also unorthodox, with much use of heavy masses of black ink broken by occasional glints of light, uniform short brush-strokes and a profusion of small dots which give an effect of haziness. In an inscription on one of his works he summed up an attitude to art which had been developing during the previous century. In antiquity there were pictures but no paintings, he wrote.

A picture represents objects, portrays persons, describes events. In a painting this is not necessarily so.

(Tr. M. Loehr)

Of course, painting was never thought of as being other than representational, but the emphasis changed. Subject-matter was of less importance than handling, and subject-matter was in any case rather limited – 'clouded mountains, mist-enveloped trees, steep rocks, cool springs, plank bridges and rustic dwellings', according to Gong Xian; he added: 'there may be figures or there may be none'. Similar distinctions were to be made independently in Europe in the nineteenth century (see pp. 707–9), though their implications were not fully realized until the twentieth.

This attitude led the most gifted painters of the Qing period to an almost obsessive concern with technique. *Conversation in Autumn* by Hua Yan (1682–c. 1762) is a virtuoso performance with color-washed mountains in the 'boneless' manner, contrasts of wet and dry ink, quick flicks of the brush, and slow, steady, well-loaded strokes (**16,5**). Yet it very vividly conveys both the love of mountain scenery and the ideal of disinterested intellectual companionship which had been recurrent themes in Chinese literature and art for more than a millennium. Hua Yan was regarded as an eccentric, even though he did

not go to such extremes as Gao Qipei (c. 1672–1734), who painted with the tips of his fingers and with his long nails split into quill-like pens. The inscription claims *Conversation in Autumn* to have been 'inspired by the ideas of Yuan masters', but it is a very free interpretation rather than a direct imitation. In a similar spirit a few seventeenth-century painters, including Gong Xian, occasionally drew inspiration from European prints brought to China by Jesuit missionaries. But Chinese and Western attitudes to art were incompatible, as was recognized even by Wu Li (1632–1719), a Chinese painter converted to Christianity and ordained priest. 'Our painting does not aim at likeness, nor does it depend on fixed pattern; and we call it spiritual and untrammelled', he wrote; that of Europeans 'is all concerned with shadow and light, front and back, formal likeness and fixed patterns over which they work laboriously . . . and their brushwork is not like ours'. Quite simply, as one of the emperor Kangxi's court painters, who admired European craftsmanship, put it: 'Foreign painting cannot be called art'. Most eighteenth-century Chinese painters were content to imitate the old masters in scrolls and album-leaves which are often pleasing and almost invariably competent as a result of intensive training, but very rarely have any sense of the profound religious and philosophical ideas which lay behind the finest paintings of the past. They seem often to have resorted to such books as *The Painting Manual of the Mustard Seed Garden* (1679–1701) with woodcut illustrations showing how to depict trees, rocks, waterfalls and so on in the approved styles of the Song, Yuan and Ming periods. There were, nevertheless, artists of great ability among the orthodox painters who remained faithful to the teachings of Dong Qichang (see pp. 561–2), for example the painter Wang Hui (1632–1717). His copies after old masters are deceptive in their apparently total

Wang Hui and Others: Portrait of An Qi
PAINTERS AND PATRONS UNDER THE QING DYNASTY

A scroll depicting the *Portrait of An Qi* is marked very clearly by attitudes to the arts prevalent in early eighteenth-century China (**16,4**). The inscription states that in 1715 Tu Luo painted the portrait, Yangjin the landscape and 'the 84-year-old Wang Hui added the bamboo and the rock'. Tu Luo, otherwise unknown, was probably a professional who specialized in portraiture and, as such, was excluded from histories of art written by the *literati*, who focused attention on landscape. One of the few theorists who discussed portraits (Wang Yi during the Yuan period) wrote that the portrait painter should proceed as if painting a

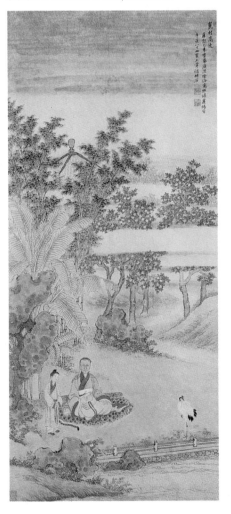

16,4 Tu Luo, Yangjin and Wang Hui, *Portrait of An Qi*, 1715. Ink and color on paper, 47¾ × 21⅝ins (121.8 × 53.5cm). Cleveland Museum of Arts, Cleveland.

landscape, memorizing the 'five mountains' or projections of the subject's face during a 'lively conversation' – not, during a formal sitting – and work from memory. In the late Ming period (early seventeenth century) a few of the *literati* painted portraits of their friends in this way. Otherwise portraits were hardly regarded as works of art at all. The vast number painted in the eighteenth century, including those of emperors and their concubines, were the work of the despised professionals who rarely presumed to sign their names. Tu Luo gave some individual character to the features of An Qi, perhaps influenced by European art, especially the work of the Jesuit Giuseppe Castiglione (1688–1766), who had settled in China and was much patronized by the emperor Kangxi. From a Chinese viewpoint, however, this scroll's artistic merit lay in its landscape setting painted by the elderly Wang Hui (1632–1717) and his assistant Yangjin (1644–after 1726).

Wang Hui strove to maintain the life-style and artistic standards of the *literati* although he was obliged to live by his brush. He was one of the 'Four Wangs', painters from Jiangsu province who shared the same family name (though only two were relations) and were generally regarded as the most distinguished traditionalists of the early Qing period. His aim was, he wrote, to synthesize the styles of the past, 'the brushwork of the Yuan, the construction of mountains of the Song, and the spirit resonance of the Tang'. He was, in fact, employed mainly on copies and pastiches in these different styles. In 1692, however, he was summoned to Beijing to direct an imperial commission for 12 hand-scrolls with a total length of some 650 feet (200m) illustrating 'the Kangxi emperor's tour of the south' and depicting in bright colors thousands, perhaps almost a million, tiny figures passing over mountains, along rivers and through towns (now in the Palace Museum, Beijing). None of the true *literati* would have undertaken a task so far removed from their ideal of

painting. For them painting was a form of meditation on nature. However, when 'the Kangxi emperor's tour of the south' was finished, Wang Hui was named 'the pure and shining' painter of landscape and offered a permanent position at court by the emperor. But he chose to remain as he was and resumed painting his previous type of work, with an enhanced reputation that may have impressed such patrons as An Qi.

An Qi was the son of a Korean who had settled in Tianjin (on the coast not far from Beijing), found employment in government service and made a fortune in the semi-underground salt-market. He was one of the many beneficiaries of the growing prosperity of China during the peaceful reign of Kangxi. Like the Manchu emperors themselves, he immersed himself in Chinese culture and became a discriminating connoisseur, assembling and cataloguing a notable collection of calligraphy and paintings which included one of the few surviving scrolls that may date from as early as the sixth century as well as many from later periods, most of which were to pass eventually to the insatiably acquisitive emperor Qianlong and are now in the National Palace Museum, Taipei. An Qi had himself portrayed by Tu Luo as a scholar, like those depicted in the early seventeenth century. Holding a scroll and with a bundle of others beside him, he is seated on a tiger-skin rug and attended by a diminutive boy servant. The garden is of the artificially natural kind created by the *literati* for their own delight and private pleasure, with the ancient rocks they so much admired. It also has symbolic overtones. The crane in the foreground was a bird associated with the Daoist immortals. The bamboo painted with such tender feeling by Wang Hui was a symbol of the perfectly educated gentleman (see p. 553). There are auspicious autumnal chrysanthemums in flower. And a tree loaded with golden fruit disingenuously alludes to ancient riches.

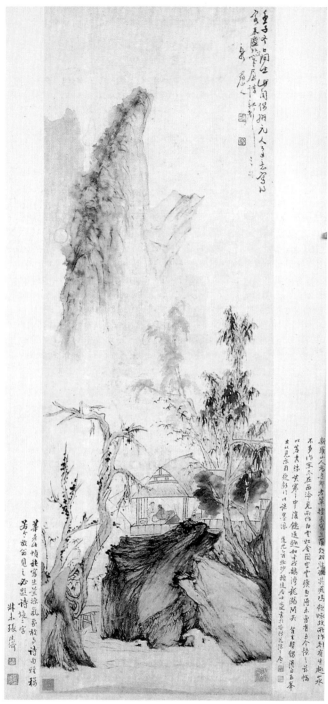

16,5 Hua Yan, *Conversation in Autumn*, hanging scroll, 1732. Ink and color on paper, 45⅜ × 15⅝ins (115.3 × 39.7cm). Cleveland Museum of Art, Cleveland, Ohio (John L. Severance Fund).

and unquestioning fidelity. They also have qualities admirable in themselves which distinguish his original work, such as his contribution to the collaborative portrait of An Qi (16,4). The precision of brush-strokes and control of nuances so evident in them were qualities more highly valued than originality by members of the imperial court and the newly emerging class of patrons which included rich merchants.

ARCHITECTURE AND THE DECORATIVE ARTS

Despite, or perhaps because of, their foreign origins, the first Qing emperors enforced the strictest observance of ancient Chinese traditions in the complicated rituals of the court, the elaborate system of administration, in education, literature and the visual arts. At the imperial palace – the Forbidden City within the city of Beijing – the great audience hall, called the Hall of Supreme Harmony, built in 1627 but damaged by the peasant rebellion which preceded the Manchu seizure of power, was promptly restored in 1645. In the complete reconstructions of 1669–99 and 1765 and in subsequent refurbishings there appear to have been no significant deviations from the original form and decoration, including the double roof with yellow glazed tiles which shone like gold, red lacquer and gilt woodwork, all of which followed much more ancient prototypes. There was no more potent symbol of the continuing authority of the Son of Heaven.

Other buildings in the Forbidden City were restored if not entirely reconstructed. Painted decorations, delicately chiselled white marble balustrades, elaborately carved wooden ceilings, richly colored pottery finials on roofs and plaques set in walls date mainly from the eighteenth and nineteenth centuries (16,6). The whole vast complex was given its present appearance under the Qing. And the same can be said of the majority of temples throughout China. Whether built entirely or only partly in this period, however, they are in the style developed under the Ming. (Relatively few buildings from earlier than the fifteenth century survive.)

16,6 Gateway with ceramic decoration, Imperial palace, Beijing. 19th century.

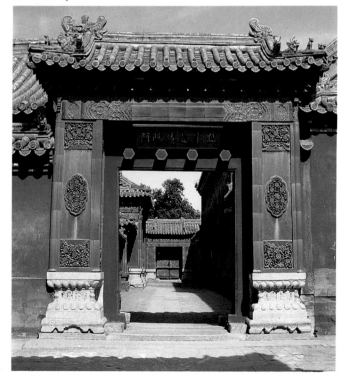

Tradition governed the plans, forms and decoration of upper-class residences in Beijing and other cities, which were always composed of several courtyards surrounded by one-story buildings to house the various branches of an extended family. The way of life, the prevailing etiquette, the pleasures and pains of such households – the master, his wife and concubines, children and numerous servants some of whom were virtually slaves – is memorably evoked in one of the greatest works of Chinese literature, Cao Xueqin's long novel *The Story of the Stone* (alternatively called *The Dream of the Red Chamber*) first published in 1792. Few such buildings have survived the revolutions of the twentieth century (the most notable – though untypical – is the home of the Kong family, descended from Confucius, at Qufu in Shandong province) but numerous examples of the furniture, tablewares and decorative objects made for them have been preserved.

The decorative arts were lavishly patronized by the Qing emperors. Kangxi (1662–1722) rejuvenated the Ming imperial porcelain factories and established in the palace precincts workshops for lacquer, glass, enamel and jade. Their products set standards of excellence which other craftsmen strove to emulate in household objects for an increasingly large public of government officials and merchants, who prospered under Manchu rule. Chinese preoccupation with technical refinement, which could have so deadening an effect on painting, was more stimulating when directed towards the decorative arts. In perfection of craftsmanship the finest examples of eighteenth-century Chinese porcelain have never been surpassed, even though they may lack the subtleties of surface texture which distinguish Tang and Song wares. (The differences are most clearly apparent in the imitations of earlier wares which began to proliferate under the Qing emperors.) Nor have jade and lacquer ever been carved with more delicate precision.

A lacquer throne (**16,7**) demonstrates the skill of the imperial craftsmen in this extremely exacting process (see p. 118). It was made for the emperor Qianlong (1737–96) with the decorative elaboration that became increasingly prevalent during his long reign. Motifs include the imperial dragon in sinuous pursuit of a fiery pearl signifying the sun, but quite without the menacing vigour of Ming dragons. Symbols are, in fact, so closely interwoven that they are almost lost in a blaze of opulence. Their devaluation was perhaps partly a result of contact with the West, for by this date many Chinese craftsmen were working largely for the European market, crowding fanciful decorations on porcelain, lacquer and enamels to satisfy a European craving for exoticism. Qianlong himself acquired a taste for European art, albeit one no better informed than the taste of contemporary European monarchs for Chinese art. While they were raising fragile *Chinoiserie* pavilions at Potsdam and elsewhere, he had a summer palace built in the European Rococo style (almost totally destroyed in 1860). He also employed a Jesuit missionary, Giuseppe Castiglione, who lived in China from 1716 onwards, to paint for him in a hybrid

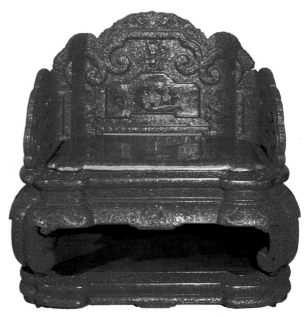

16,7 Throne of the Emperor Qianlong, c. 1740. Red lacquer, 3ft 11ins (1.19m) high. Victoria & Albert Museum, London.

Sino-Italian manner with linear perspective and shading. Yet he seems never to have doubted the supremacy of Chinese culture, and he assembled the largest of all collections of works by earlier Chinese artists as well as by contemporaries who imitated them.

As the Western powers forced their way into China from 1842 onwards, obtaining trading concessions by warfare, settling in the 'treaty ports' including Shanghai, and building in their own national styles, Chinese artists and their patrons became ever more inflexible in maintaining their own traditions. In 1860 the British and French, taking advantage of a civil war, sent in a military expedition which penetrated as far as Beijing. The numerous buildings of the Summer Palace, scattered round a lake to the north-east of the city, were sacked and burned down. But in 1888 the whole vast area was laid out anew with temples and pavilions linked by long covered colonnades in the traditional style as 'The Garden where Peace is Cultivated', for the notorious dowager empress Cixi (1835–1908), an enthusiastic if undiscriminating patron of the arts and herself a painter (like her near contemporary Queen Victoria in this although in no other respect). She was censured at the time for diverting to this work funds already earmarked for the navy. But no criticism was aroused by the complete reconstruction of the Hall of Annual Prayers of the Temple of Heaven in Beijing which was struck by lightning and burnt down in 1889; it was deemed essential for the good of the empire. In form and size it was an exact replica of its predecessor, set on a triple-tiered white marble terrace and built entirely of wood, rising to a height of 123 feet (43m), with a triple cone-shaped roof of dark blue glazed tiles topped by a gilded ball (**16,8**). The circular plan, unusual in Chinese architecture, is directly related to the idea of the heavens. Inside there are concentric circles of 12 columns to

16,8 Hall of Annual Prayers, Temple of Heaven, Beijing. Begun 1889.

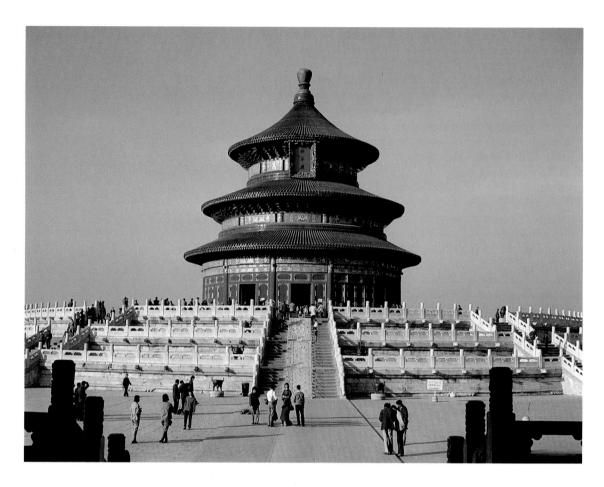

represent the months of the year and the hours of the day, surrounding four taller columns for the seasons. The carved and especially the painted decorations were, however, executed in a somewhat slapdash manner.

The Hall of Annual Prayers was approached only by the emperor and his entourage but its deep blue roofs could be seen from far away as a potent symbol of imperial rule 'by the mandate of heaven'. It is the most prominent of the widely spread out complex of buildings in the Temple of Heaven, *Tiantan*, constructed in the early Ming period and (like the Imperial Palace) much restored in the mid-eighteenth century. The reigning emperor went there at the beginning of the first month of the calendar, to offer sacrifices and pray for good harvests, and also at the winter solstice to 'speak with the heavens', telling them of the events of the previous year. It was thus rather more than a mere symbol. On the first Chinese National Day, after the revolution which deposed the last Qing emperor, a minister of the new government went there to offer sacrifices to the Supreme Lord on behalf of the republic. And the president Yuan Shikai, who was attempting to establish himself as emperor, made a ceremonial visit at the winter solstice of 1914.

During the troubled half-century that followed the revolution of 1911, attempts were made to bring Chinese art into conformity with the West. Academies were founded and students were obliged to draw from casts and, to the horror of conservatives, from nude models. Ju Pon (Xu Beihong, 1895–1953) is the best known of those

who sought a compromise between their own tradition and the realism of late nineteenth-century Western art. There were, however, a number of artists who looked neither to European nor to Chinese traditionalists but followed the lead of their own 'individualists' of the early Qing period in confronting the challenge of Western culture in the twentieth century without relapsing into a synthetic Sino-Western style – such artists as Huang Binhong (1864–1955) and Fu Baoshi (1904–65). Later the influence of certain European twentieth-century artists, notably Paul Klee (1879–1940), whose sensibilities were akin to the Chinese in their delicacy and extreme refinement, were absorbed into new forms of Chinese painting by Zao Wou-ki (Zhao Wuji, b. 1921) and others.

JAPAN IN THE EDO PERIOD

A late eighteenth-century Japanese print of the type known as *Ukiyo-e* (see below) is a very far cry from any Chinese work of art (**16,9**). Indeed, it would not have been thought a work of art at all in China – nor were such prints so regarded by upper-class Japanese. They were essentially a popular art. Subject-matter is all-important and often of an extremely plebeian and unelevating nature. Forms are indicated by firm, curving or rigidly straight lines and there can have been no sense of spontaneity in handling, no subtle variations of brushwork, even in the drawings from which such prints were made.

The scene depicted is one of common everyday life: a group of women in a communal bath-house with a squatting man, whose head and knees are glimpsed through openings into an adjoining room – perhaps the voyeur artist himself. Extremes of realism and stylization, of awkwardness and elegance, are combined in the naked and dressed figures. Throughout the emphasis is on recording a casual moment. Figures are informally grouped and posed, the upper body of the woman in the background is cut off by the wall on which there are prints of birds flying over the sea, suggesting another level of artistic reality. However, the effect of unsophisticated artlessness is contrived with a consummate skill, which astonished European artists when they first saw *Ukiyo-e* in the second half of the nineteenth century. Edgar Degas (see pp. 716–8) hung the specimen illustrated here over his bed.

Japan was effectively isolated from the rest of the world from the 1630s, when Christianity was suppressed and Portuguese traders were expelled. So eighteenth- and nineteenth-century Japanese art is exclusively the product of Japan's peculiar political, social and economic structure. Throughout the Edo period (1615–1867) the role of the emperors in their palace at Kyoto was no more than ceremonial. Power had shifted into the hands of the shoguns (dictators) of the Tokugawa family, who ruled from Edo (later renamed Tokyo). Although they paid lip-service to Neo-Confucian ideals of wise government, the dominant class below them was not one of scholars but of *daimyos* and their *samurai* (feudal lords and knights). There were four distinct social strata, with the military at the top, then farmers, followed by artisans with merchants below. Officially, all occupations were determined by heredity, the art of painting thus being limited to the sons or adopted sons of painters (though exceptions were made and some members of the military families voluntarily relinquished their privileges to become artists). But laws which stopped upward social mobility permitted development within the classes so long as they did not threaten the authority of the military caste. During the long period of peace following two centuries of civil war, the *samurai* were, in fact, impoverished. Merchants, on

16,9 Torii Kiyonaga, *Interior of a Bath-House*, c. 1800. Ink and color on paper, 15 × 20ins (38.7 × 51cm). Museum of Fine Arts, Boston (William Sturgis Bigelow Collection, by exchange).

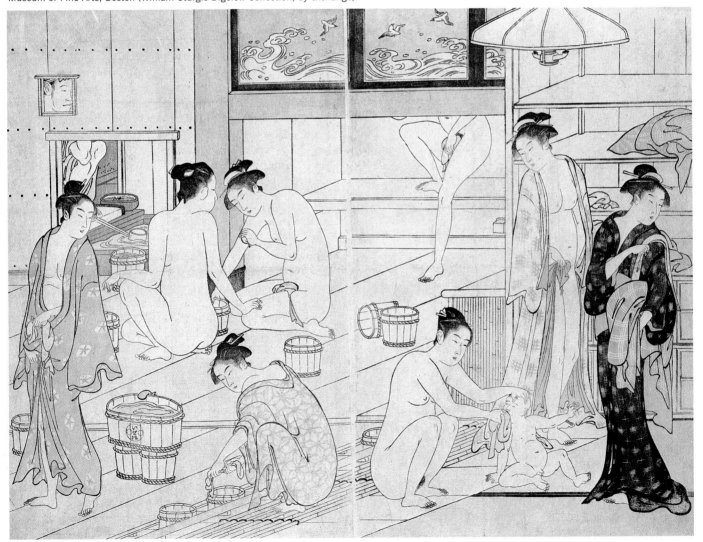

the other hand, prospered and increasingly commanded the services of artists and craftsmen. They quite consciously maintained the high standards reached in the seventeenth century in screen painting and lacquer and went on indulging the traditional and peculiarly Japanese taste for complementary extremes – exquisite porcelain (made in Japan since 1616) of elegant form and refined decoration being produced side by side with rough tea-ceremony pottery wares of ostensibly artless simplicity. Chinese influence was rarely felt except in landscape painting, patronized exclusively by the intelligentsia and sometimes practised by them as well in emulation of the scholar-gentlemen painters of earlier times in China.

The principal innovation was the *Ukiyo-e* print created for and mainly by the lower ranks of society, especially the urban lower class in Edo (Tokyo) itself, which grew into a huge bustling prosperous city under the rule of the shoguns. *Ukiyo-e* expressed the tastes and interests of a sub-culture with an artistic mastery unequalled anywhere else in the world at any time. No other art form comparably secular, plebeian (sometimes explicitly anti-aristocratic) and strictly topical has ever attained the

16,10 Kitagawa Utamaro, *The Hour of the Boar*, c. 1790. Polychrome woodblock print, 9½ × 15ins (24.5 × 38cm). British Museum, London.

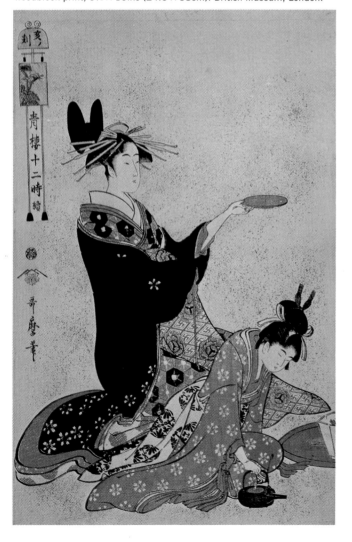

distinction of the *Ukiyo-e* popular print. The word 'Ukiyo-e' was originally applied to a 'painting of the floating world', that is to say the changing or fashionable scene. But the print-makers of the late eighteenth and early nineteenth centuries gave it a wider meaning, equivalent to 'modern'. The most gifted of them were able to invest the grossest and most trivial subject-matter with a strangely haunting beauty as well as to inject a new proletarian vigour into traditional themes.

The origins of *Ukiyo-e* can be traced back to two diverse sources, to popular religious prints and to *Yamato-e* or 'Japanese-style paintings' of scenes from daily, though usually courtly, life (see p. 564). The technique of wood-block printing had been introduced from China with Buddhism in the eighth century and was later developed for the illustration of printed Buddhist texts and, from the early seventeenth century, of love poems and romances. Printed books were at first regarded as substitutes for the expensive hand-written and painted scrolls which they imitated – sometimes printed sheets were joined to form scrolls. But picture books for the masses were also produced, most notably by Hishikawa Moronobu (c. 1625–95), generally regarded as the founder of *Ukiyo-e*. Although he had been trained in the most conservative traditions, he turned to representing popular subjects, especially of the Yoshiwara or brothel district of Edo. In the 1670s he also began to design single-leaf prints, which evidently enjoyed enough popularity for his lead to be followed. Subjects ranged from the flowers and birds that had for so long delighted the Japanese to portraits of beautiful women, usually the flaunting 'queens' of Yoshiwara, to scenes of furious fornication. Most of them are small and were probably intended to be kept in albums, but the larger ones could be mounted on hanging scrolls. They were printed in black on white paper, and color had to be added by hand. But in the second half of the eighteenth century the technique of polychrome printing was very rapidly developed, and further widened the appeal of *Ukiyo-e*. The first multicolored prints were fairly expensive and their buyers probably the richer merchants, rather than artisans. The process of making them was cooperative and differed from that used in Europe. An artist's drawing was pasted on to a panel of pear or cherry wood and all but the fine lines was cut away to make a block from which to print sheets. These sheets were used for the cutting of other blocks, sometimes as many as 15, one for each color, brushed on to it in a water-soluble pigment. Impressions were taken not with a press but by placing the paper on the block and rubbing the back with a circular tool, skilful manipulation of which could produce subtle variations of tone.

In the fully developed *Ukiyo-e*, women have pride of place, young, elegant in deportment, dressed in the height of urban fashion from the tips of tiny feet to jet black hair beset with combs and bodkins. They figure singly, clutching exquisitely patterned kimonos to their slender forms with an air of mild surprise, and in groups, in the bath-house (16,9), idling away an afternoon on a river-boat, watching the moon rise or catching fireflies on a warm

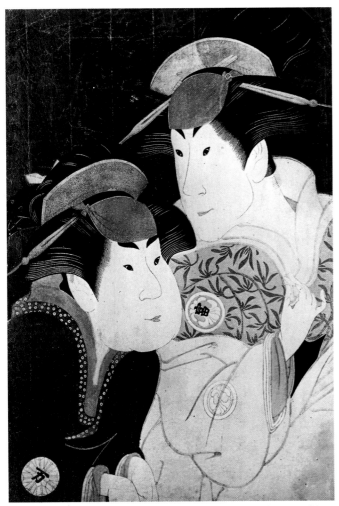

16,11 Saito Sharaku, *The Actor Segawa Tomisaburo as Yadorigi*, 1794. Polychrome woodblock print, 14¼ × 9¼ins (36.2 × 23.5cm). Art Institute of Chicago (Clarence Buckingham Collection).

summer's night. They are invariably creatures of sensual pleasure, often recognizable as the highly sophisticated prostitutes for whom Edo became famous. One is shown daintily handing to her unseen client a saucer of warm sake which her apprentice assistant has prepared (**16,10**). It is entitled *The Hour of the Boar* (9 to 11 pm) and comes from a set depicting 'Twelve Hours of the Green Houses' (i.e. brothels) by Kitigawa Utamaro (1753–1806), one of the first and greatest masters of the *genre*. The Kabuki theatre, a form of entertainment more popular and thrilling than the formal and intricately symbolical *No* dramas favoured by the aristocracy, provided numerous subjects for print-makers. Saito Sharaku (fl. 1794–5) specialized during his very brief career in portraits of actors, notably the star female impersonators (**16,11**). Realism merges into carica-ture in these prints and it is hard to tell whether the exag-geratedly arch expression on Segawa Tomisaburo's face is a record or a criticism of his performance. Sharaku was himself a *No* actor in the service of a *daimyo*. His work reveals, none the less, the full decorative possibilities of the medium, with bold patterns of color set off by the metallic sheen of a mica background, a substitute for the gold which the lower classes were not allowed.

HOKUSAI AND HIROSHIGE

The greatest *Ukiyo-e* master of the early nineteenth cen-tury, Katsushika Hokusai (1760–1849), was a pupil of a theatrical print-maker, like Sharaku, but set no limits to his own subject-matter. As prolific as he was gifted, he made some 30,000 drawings, most of which were repro-duced as book illustrations. An unparalleled record of the life of his time, especially street life in and around Edo, is presented in the 15 volumes of his *Manga*, which he began to publish in 1814. No human activity seems to have escaped his sharp observant eye and expressive brush. His line is sinewy, his style virile, his view of humanity humorously objective. He made no attempt to disguise the physical gracelessness of, for instance, acro-bats caught unaware of their observer (**16,12**). Late in life he signed himself 'the old man mad about painting'. His most important contribution to the art of the polychrome print was, however, in landscapes quite unlike any previ-ously depicted in Japan or China: very strongly colored views which are instantly recognizable yet are neither realistic nor idealized. Mount Fuji's snow-covered cone recurs in them, glimpsed in the most famous from the

16,12 Katsushika Hokusai, page from *Manga*, vol. 8, 1817. Woodcut, 9 × 5¾ins (22.8 × 14.6cm). British Museum, London.

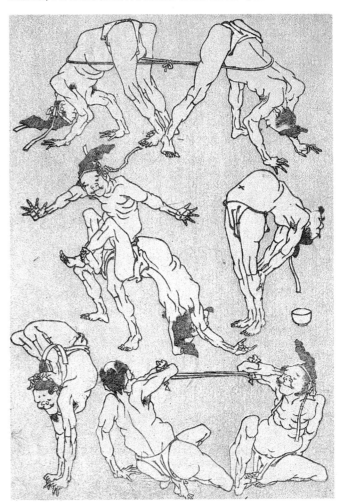

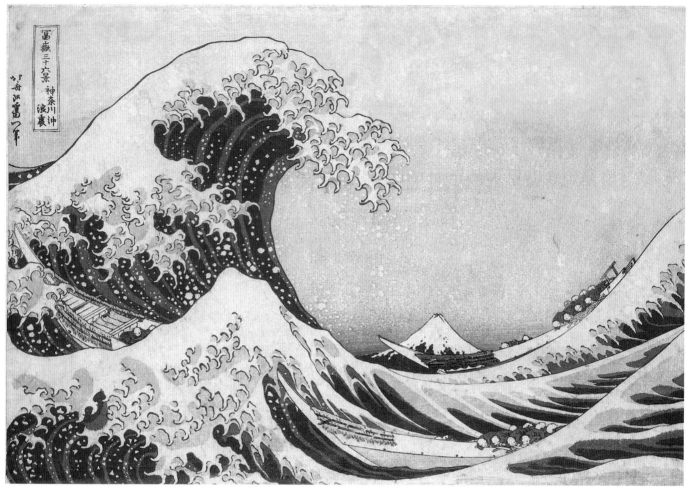

16,13 Katsushika Hokusai, *The Great Wave off Kanazawa*, 1823–9. Polychrome woodblock print, 10 × 14ins (25.5 × 37.5cm). Victoria & Albert Museum, London.

trough of a great wave breaking into spray like dragon-claws over fragile boats (**16,13**). His prints reveal the intense response to natural forms and the genius for decorative pattern-making which have always characterized Japanese art when least dependent on China. The same can be said of the landscape prints by his younger contemporary Ando Hiroshige (1797–1858), which came to epitomize Japan for the Japanese as well as for Westerners. They are more realistic and less stylized than Hokusai's, yet often more poetic in feeling. In many he adopted the novel device of depicting distant views through a 'framing' foreground of plants, irises in one, maple leaves in another (**16,14**).

Four years after Hokusai died the isolation of Japan was broken and his prints were almost immediately imported into Europe, where they had an electric effect on painters attempting to find a way out of the conventions of Western art (see pp. 718–21). In 1854 the American naval commodore Matthew Calbraith Perry forced the Japanese to open their ports to foreign traders. Radical internal changes quickly followed. In 1868 the last of the shoguns was obliged to resign under pressure from a group of *samurai* who seized power in the name of the 15-year-old Meiji who had recently succeeded as the 122nd

emperor. To make a distinct break with the immediate past both the court and the new administration were established at Edo, renamed Tokyo (literally Eastern Capital). The art of the following Meiji period (1868–1912) was conditioned by two apparently contradictory tendencies towards extremes of westernization and aggressive nationalism. Western technology was rapidly assimilated and the process of transforming a mainly agrarian feudal country into an industrialized nation began. Simultaneously, on the other hand, worship of the emperor as a living god was revived and an attempt was made to constitute Shinto as the one national religion with the suppression of Buddhist sects, many of their temples and works of art being destroyed as a result. Competition with the West led to the introduction of oil painting (although mainly for traditional Japanese subjects, notably landscapes) and the mass-production both for export and the home market of porcelain overburdened with Japanese decorative motifs of a wholly untraditional garishness. But calligraphy was unaffected; and painting on scrolls and screens for Japanese houses was little influenced by Western art. In country regions pottery, lacquer and textiles continued to be made as before and, so far from being 'westernized', soon began to inspire European and

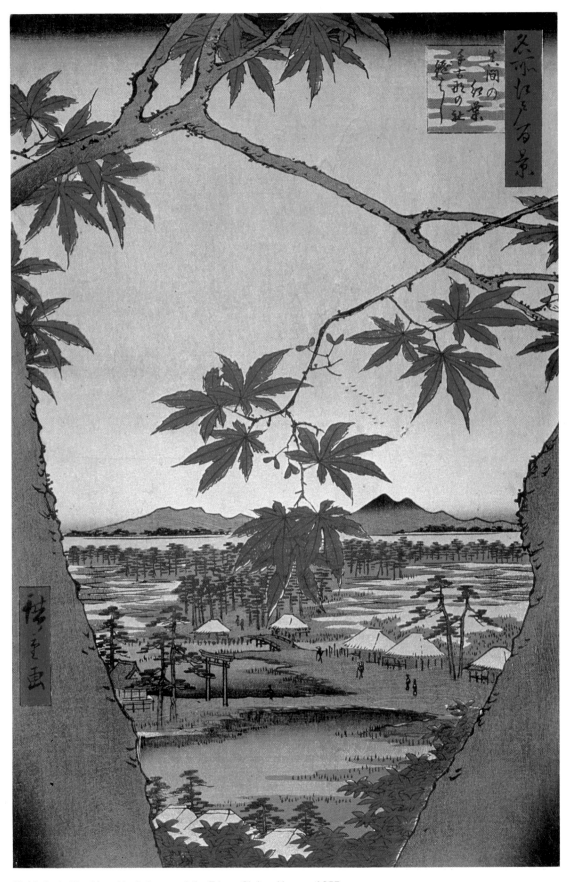

16,14 Ando Hiroshige, *Maple Leaves at the Tekona Shrine, Mamma*, 1857.
Polychrome woodblock print, 13¾ × 9⅜ins (35 × 24cm).
British Museum, London.

SOURCES AND DOCUMENTS

HOKUSAI AND FRANK LLOYD WRIGHT ON THE JAPANESE PRINT

Hokusai was 75 years old when he published the first volume of *One Hundred Views of Mount Fuji* in 1834. This work was in a sense a prayer for the gift of immortality that was believed to lie hidden within the heart of the volcano, and to express his hope he announced a change of name – his fifth – to 'Manji, Old Man mad about Painting'. He was in fact to live another 15 years, not dying until 1849. His signature was followed by his well-known declaration:

From the age of six I had a penchant for copying the form of things, and from about 50, my pictures were frequently published; but until the age of 70, nothing that I drew was worthy of notice. At 73 years, I was somewhat able to fathom the growth of plants and trees, and the structure of birds, animals, insects, and fish. Thus when I reach 80 years, I hope to have made increasing progress, and at 90 to see further into the underlying principles of things, so that at 100 years I will have achieved a divine state in my art, and at 110, every dot and every stroke will be as though alive. Those of you who live long enough, bear witness that these words of mine prove not false.

Some 70 years later, by which time Japanese prints were already well-known in the West and had become very influential (see p. 718), the American architect Frank Lloyd Wright gave a lecture in Chicago at a Japanese exhibition including works by Hokusai. He said:

The unpretentious colored wood-cut of Japan, a thing of significant graven lines on delicate paper which has kissed the color from carved and variously tinted wooden blocks, is helpful in the practice of fine arts, and may be construed with profit in other life-concerns as great.

It is a lesson especially valuable to the West because, in order to comprehend it at all, we must take a viewpoint unfamiliar to us as a people, and in particular to our artists – the purely aesthetic viewpoint . . . . Go deep enough into your experience to find that beauty is in itself the finest kind of morality – ethical, purely – the essential fact, I mean, of all morals and manners . . . .

Now speaking in a language all the clearer because not native to us, beggared as we are by material riches, the humble artist of old Japan has become greatly significant as interpreter of the one thing that can make the concerns, the forms, of his everyday life – whether laws, customs, manners, costumes, utensils or ceremonials – harmonious with the life principle of his race – and so living native forms, humanly significant, humanly joy giving – an art, a religion, as in ever varied moods, in evanescent loveliness he has made Fujiyama – that image of man in the vast – the God of Nippon.

(H. Smith, Introduction to *Hokusai, One Hundred Views of Mount Fuji*, London 1988; F. L. Wright, *The Japanese Print. An Interpretation*, New York 1912)

American designers and craftsmen. It was this apparently uneasy dualism – political nationalism and cultural pluralism – which was to underlie the remarkable development of Japanese art and especially architecture in the later twentieth century (see pp. 860–1).

Westernization was imposed on Japan only by the Japanese themselves – as Chinese civilization had been in the sixth century. By the end of the nineteenth century, however, most of southern and south-eastern Asia was under the direct control of European colonialists who promoted archeology but took scant interest in living indigenous arts. Thailand – or Siam as it was then called – was almost unique in retaining its independence. The kingdom of Sukhothai, which had emerged on the edge of the former Khmer empire in the early thirteenth century (see p. 262), was absorbed into that of Ayutthaya, which in the fifteenth century spread over most of the area of modern Thailand and beyond into Burma and Cambodia (Angkor was taken in 1431). But the states of south-east Asia were intermittently at war with one another and in 1767 the city of Ayutthaya was sacked by the Burmese; a new capital – the present-day Bangkok – was founded further to the south, with no pains spared to make it more impressive than its predecessor.

Under a succession of powerful kings, Thailand prospered. After the mid-century the administration was modernized and such archaic practices as slavery were abolished. Western technology was introduced for building and the old custom of reserving permanent materials for religious structures was broken, although houses continued to be built mainly of wood and religious (*Theravada* Buddhist) architecture and sculpture remained traditional, the basic form of monastic halls evolved at Ayutthaya being followed to the present day. Earlier styles were sometimes revived by sculptors who imitated the Buddha statues of the Sukhothai period (**16,15**), and there are similar historicist elements in architecture. In the precinct of Wat Phra Keo, the temple of the Royal Palace

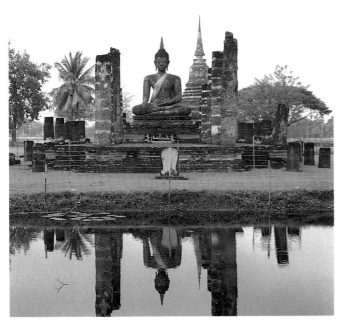

16,15 Statue of the Buddha, 19th century.
Laterite and plaster. Sukhothai, Thailand.

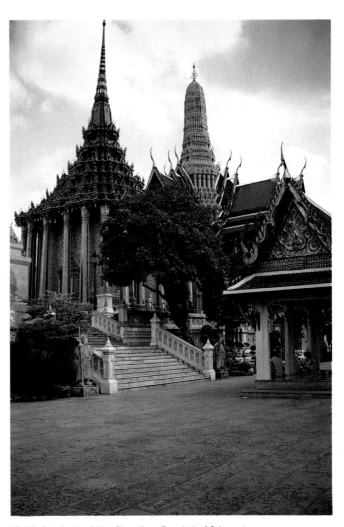

16,16 Precincts of Wat Phra Keo, Bangkok. 19th century.

in Bangkok, the library for sacred books with its elegantly pointed roof and the main structure of the 'pantheon' (enclosing statues of Thai kings), with roofs terminated at their gable ends by arching snake-head finials, are in elaborated versions of the Ayutthaya style, but the latter is crowned by a tall stone spire which harks back to the temples of the Khmer (**16,16**). These buildings have a self-confident vitality akin to that of the more exuberant historicist architecture of nineteenth-century Europe. The flamboyance of their lavish gilding, mosaics of colored glass shimmering in the tropical sunlight, and panels of porcelain may seem to Western eyes almost jazzy. But similarly colorful decorations originally covered many earlier buildings in south-east Asia and elsewhere that are now reduced to brown and ochre ruins.

CHAPTER SEVENTEEN

IMPRESSIONISM TO POST-IMPRESSIONISM

Only three years after the great Universal Exhibition of 1867 in Paris, which had celebrated the still expanding French colonial empire and established Paris in Western eyes as the artistic capital of the world, France suffered the most humiliating defeat in her long history. The Franco-Prussian War ended in surrender, followed by political collapse and revolution. The first German emperor was crowned at Versailles in 1871, while in Paris the Commune was repressed with a ferocity far exceeding anything witnessed in 1830 or 1848. Yet these traumatic events left remarkably little trace. A bourgeois empire was succeeded by a bourgeois republic. 'Plus ça change plus c'est la même chose' was a quip of the time. 1871 was not a turning point, hardly even a date in French intellectual or artistic history. Apart from the now ageing Courbet, who was imprisoned and heavily fined for his part in the Commune, most artists were unengaged if not indifferent. Monet and Sisley, for example, avoided the troubles at home by going to London for some months. Their friend, the critic Théodore Duret, went off on a world tour.

As if to celebrate bourgeois stability the most typically Second Empire monument in Paris – the Opéra, designed in 1861 by Charles Garnier (1825–98) – opened some years after the Second Empire had been succeeded by the Third Republic (17,1). The flamboyant opulence and ostentation, the meaningless eclecticism of this Neo-Renaissance Neo-Baroque extravaganza, with its lavish sculptural decorations, luxurious display of costly materials and ample, buxomly curved furnishings, epitomize the tone of both régimes and periods and the showy pomposity of officially sponsored art. Among the life-size sculptural groups on the façade was one of a frenetic bacchanalian dance by Jean-Baptiste Carpeaux (1827–75) – a virtuoso display of naturalistic, painterly sculpture. Carpeaux's verve and lightness of handling combine with a vigorously sensual

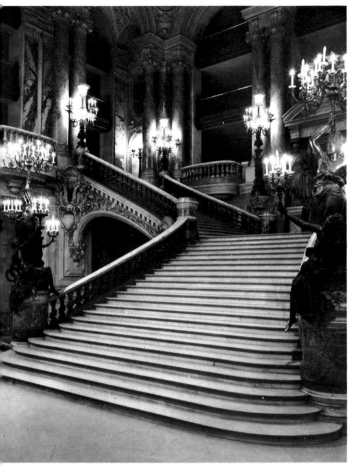

17,1 Charles Garnier, Opéra grand staircase, Paris, 1861–74.

feeling for human form in this joyously rhythmical, freely swinging and whirling composition of solids and voids (**17,2**). It was, however, the one feature of the building to be severely criticized – for indecency. The rendering of naked flesh was too lifelike for the prudish and attempts were made to deface it.

IMPRESSIONISM

Attacks on artists by an outraged public were a regular feature of mid-nineteenth-century life, not only in France. But it was in Paris that the situation became acute with the opening in 1863 of a Salon des Refusés for works rejected by the official Salon, and later with the holding of independent exhibitions, notably by the Impressionists. These marked the first stage in an attempt to evade the tyranny of the official art-world, which controlled, through the Salons, the only road to professional acceptance and success for an artist in France. Hostility to these initiatives was of an intensity that is now difficult to comprehend. Even at the time, Manet was never able to understand why such paintings as his *Luncheon on the Grass* (15,40) had been refused by the Salon, still less why it and others aroused such a storm of abuse. Of course, the general public, accustomed to the smooth brushwork and careful finish of Salon painting, had some difficulty in

'reading' Impressionist paintings with their rough handling and broken color patches spotted all over the surface, as if they were casual sketches. The few critics who noticed the early Impressionist exhibitions pointed this out, though not all of them were unfavourable. 'By Michalon', one critic wrote,

> *'What on earth is that?'*
> *'You see . . . a hoarfrost on deeply ploughed furrows.'*
> *'Those furrows? That frost? But they are palette-scrapings placed uniformly on a dirty canvas. It has neither head nor tail, top nor bottom, front nor back.'*
> *'Perhaps . . . but the impression is there.'*
> *'Well, it's a funny impression!'*

(L. Leroy in *Charivari*, 25 April 1874)

The Impressionists never completely won over the official art-world, but they were recognized by the cultivated

17,2 Jean-Baptiste Carpeaux, *The Dance*, 1867–9. Plaster, about 15ft × 8ft 6ins (4.6 × 2.6m). Musée de l'Opéra, Paris.

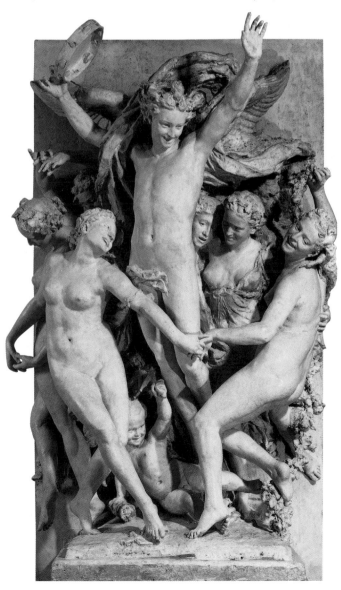

intelligentsia. Eventually Monet was so successful that he could employ six gardeners at his country-house at Giverny. Yet even as late as 1900 the Academician Jean-Léon Gérôme (1824–1904) is said to have stopped the French president from entering the Impressionist room at the Universal Exhibition with the words: 'Arrêtez, monsieur le Président, c'est ici le déshonneur de la France'! Such anecdotes fuelled a Romantic myth about the artist's 'alienation' from society.

Few, if any, of the Impressionists ever thought of themselves in these terms. So far from being rebels, some of them were, like Manet, of good, solid bourgeois origins and enjoyed to the full the advantages of their position. Their paintings embody precisely those values which true rebels would have scorned. They convey a typically middle-class vision of happiness – unintentionally, of course, for the Impressionists claimed to be quite uninvolved emotionally with their subject-matter. Theirs is a sunny, friendly, convivial world in which everyone enjoys robust good health and relaxes out of doors during a perpetual midsummer weekend. Carefree and extrovert, with more than enough to eat and drink, they while away the hours with music and laughter and casual flirtation (17,7).

This can already be seen in the huge, life-size painting of a picnic which Claude Monet (1840–1926) hoped would make his name at the 1866 Salon but which he never finished (17,3). Like many other young Parisians, Monet and his friends passed summer weekends picnicking at Fontainebleau and with this painting he tried to answer Baudelaire's demand for an art of 'modern life' by recording an everyday theme in a strictly objective, dispassionate spirit of on-the-spot observation. In its dual concern for contemporaneity of subject and optical truth, Monet's painting sums up the aims of young avant-garde artists in mid-nineteenth-century Paris. But it was not until 1869, when Monet and Pierre-Auguste Renoir (1841–1919) spent the summer together at Bougival on the Seine, that Impressionism may be said to have been born. So closely did they work together that some of their paintings can scarcely be distinguished one from another, notably those of the restaurant and swimming place 'La Grenouillère' (17,4). No paintings had ever before shown such innocent, unquestioning joy in the visible world.

Impressionism had no aesthetic theory nor any definable program – both Monet and Renoir detested theorizing – but it may be thought of, in broad terms, as the final stage of Realism (see pp. 673–80). It reflects the positivist,

17,3 Claude Monet, sketch for *The Picnic*, 1865–6. Canvas, 4ft 3¼ins × 5ft 11¼ins (1.3 × 1.81m). Pushkin Museum, Moscow.

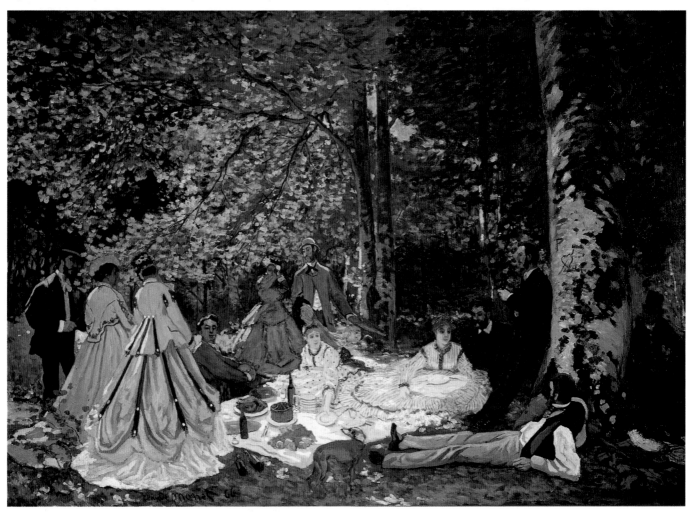

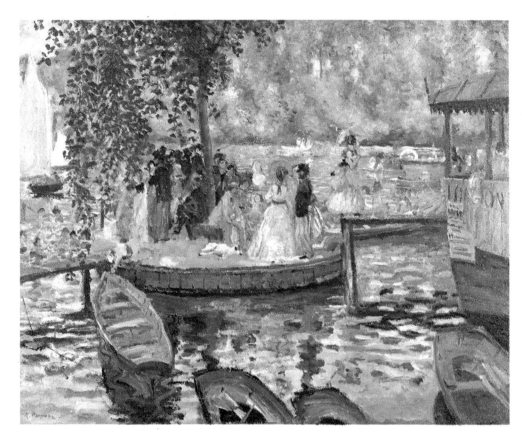

scientific attitudes of the mid-century, when the study of optics and the physiological principles of visual perception were being intensively pursued by Hermann L. F. von Helmholtz (1821–94), the color theorist Michel Eugène Chevreul (1786–1889) and others (see below). Positivism, as a philosophical system, was largely the creation of Auguste Comte (1798–1857), who taught that non-scientifically verifiable explanations of natural phenomena, including human life, are inadmissible – that our sense perceptions are the only acceptable basis of knowledge. The influence of these ideas was already apparent in the Realists' rejection of the past (and future) as a source of subject-matter. They believed that artists should deal only with the world around them. They should invent nothing. Their concern should be solely with the truth and actuality of contemporary experience. For the Impressionists this meant that artists should restrict themselves to what lay within their range of vision at the place and time they were painting. They sought to give a totally objective transcription of the everyday world, to escape from the studio and academy into the streets and open air and capture their immediate, momentary impressions with the greatest possible fidelity. For them the present became the instant of consciousness in which one is aware of existence. Had not Baudelaire said that 'modernity is the transitory, the fleeting, the contingent'? Yet a degree of artifice inevitably entered into their work, even some of the most apparently spontaneous of Monet's 'impressions' being dependent on devices learnt from Japanese prints.

The archetypal Impressionist painting is a landscape or other out-of-doors subject, comparatively small in scale and painted largely or entirely on the spot and not in the studio, with a high-toned palette of clear, bright colors applied with varied, broken brushwork to a canvas primed with white (not the traditional brown). They tried to catch the prismatic character of natural light by using spectrum colors evenly and in small touches so that they blend optically when seen from the right distance. The composition, apparently as casual as a snapshot, is constructed entirely with color (optical colors in place of local colors) and relies as little as possible or not at all on tonal contrasts. All these elements had been anticipated separately by earlier painters to a greater or lesser degree but their combination was new. Many had even been taught at the academies, though only for sketches or *études* (see p. 664). Monet's friend and teacher Eugène Boudin (1824–98) specifically recommended this, and Baudelaire, writing in 1859, singled out Boudin's *études* for praise while recognizing the gulf that separated them from 'finished' pictures. Now, however, it was not just the sketch but the finished picture which was painted in the open air, so that the truth of the first immediate impression of the scene would not be lost. Other artists had occasionally painted complete, finished canvases out of doors from at least as early as the 1820s, notably Corot, the Barbizon School painters and Charles-François Daubigny (1817–78), the Dutch artist Johan Barthold Jongkind (1819–91) and, in England, Constable and later Ford Madox Brown (1821–93) and Holman Hunt (15,37), who pursued a Ruskinian conception of truth to nature (see p. 672). But the Impressionists went much further.

MONET

Impression – Sunrise (**17,5**) the painting which gave the movement its name when it was exhibited in 1874 – is a good example of how Monet constructed a whole composition in terms of color alone (blues and greens setting off yellows and orange instead of contrasting dark and light tones) and of his exploitation of a high viewpoint to eliminate the foreground and, usually, the horizon as well. Outlines have also been eliminated. In fact, nothing is clear-cut and solid. For Monet experienced nature as distant things veiled in atmosphere, as vibrations or sensations of light and color rather than as shapes and forms. All 'content' or subject-matter, in the traditional sense, has gone, too. Light and atmosphere are the subject – the visual effects of mist, smoke and murky reflections in the dirty water of a harbour. This is simply the record of a fleeting moment, a glimpse of the sun as it rises through the rapidly dissolving mists of dawn. A few minutes, a few seconds later the sun will have climbed higher and changed color, the small boat will have moved, everything will look different.

Monet tried to recreate in pigment an equivalent for his optical sensations or (as the scientists who were just then exploring the problems of visual perception would have said) the neurological reactions of the retina to stimuli received from light rays reflected by the phenomenal world. Monet told a young American artist in 1889, '"When you go out to paint, try to forget what object you have before you – a tree, a house, a field, or whatever. Merely think, here is a little square of blue, here an oblong of pink, here a streak of yellow, and paint it just as it looks to you, the exact color and shape, until it gives you your own naive impression of the scene before you." He said he wished he had been born blind and then had suddenly gained his sight so that he could have begun to paint in this way without knowing what the objects were that he had before him. He held that the first real look at the *motif* was likely to be the truest and most unprejudiced one.' For this reason his pictures are usually without any sense of deep space. To the innocent eye, it was thought, the world would look flat. As his contemporary, Hermann von Helmholtz, the founder of a physiological theory of perception, pointed out: 'The instant we take an unusual position and look at the landscape with the head under one arm, let us say, or between the legs, it all appears to be like a flat picture.' In fact, according to the scientific theory of the time, we do not see the third dimension. All we see is a medley of color patches. Monet's conviction that it is our knowledge of what we see which falsifies our

17,5 Claude Monet, *Impression – Sunrise*, 1872. Canvas, 19½ × 25½ins (49.5 × 64.8cm). Musée Marmottan, Paris.

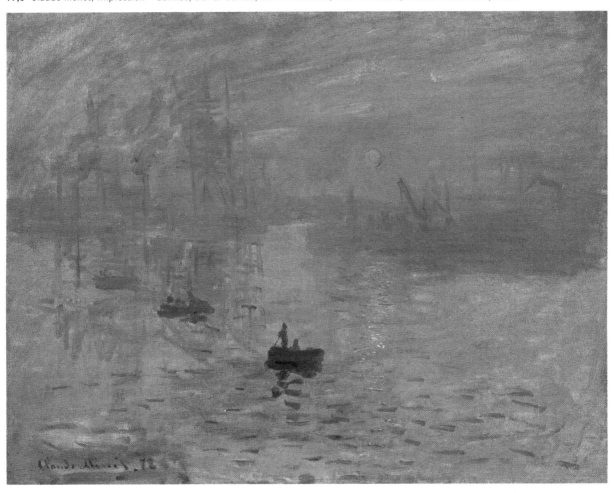

LAFORGUE ON IMPRESSIONISM

The French poet Jules Laforgue (1860–87) knew most of the Impressionist painters. Their aims were close to his own in poetry and he worked surrounded by pictures by Monet, Sisley, Renoir and others. His interests were wide and included science and, through Charles Henry who was later to be the influential friend of Seurat and the Neo-Impressionists, experimental psychology as well. An essay he wrote in 1883 for an exhibition in Berlin of Pissarro, Degas, Renoir and others is one of the earliest and most penetrating analyses of the Impressionist movement and its implications. He wrote:

Object and subject are . . . irretrievably in motion, inapprehensible and unapprehending. In the flashes of identity between subject and object lies the nature of genius.

Laforgue's essay is the first coherent expression of the modern view of art, continuing in the path of Baudelaire, who had written in 1860 that 'Modernity is the transitory, the fleeting, the contingent . . . .'

The Academic Eye and the Impressionist Eye: Polyphony of Color. *In a landscape flooded with light, in which beings are outlined as if in colored grisaille, where the academic painter sees nothing but a broad expanse of whiteness, the Impressionist sees light as bathing everything not with a dead whiteness but rather with a thousand vibrant struggling colors of rich prismatic decomposition. Where the one sees only the external outline of objects, the other sees the real living lines built not in geometric forms but in a thousand irregular strokes, which, at a distance, establish life. Where one sees things placed in their regular respective planes according to a skeleton reducible to pure theoretic design, the other sees perspective established by a thousand trivial touches of tone and brush, by the varieties of atmospheric states induced by moving planes . . . .*

Explanation of Apparent Impressionist Exaggerations. *The ordinary eye of the public and of the non-artistic critic, trained to see reality in the harmonies fixed and established for it by its host of mediocre painters – this eye, as eye, cannot stand up to the keen eye of the artist. The latter, being more sensitive to luminous variation, naturally records on canvas the relationship between rare, unexpected, and unknown subtleties of luminous variation. The blind, of course, will cry out against willful eccentricity. But even if one were to make allowance for an eye bewildered and exasperated by the haste of these impressionistic notes taken in the heat of sensory intoxication, the language of the palette with respect to reality would still be a conventional tongue susceptible to new seasoning. And is not this new seasoning more artistic, more alive, and hence more fecund for the future than the same old sad academic recipes?*

Program for Future Painters. *Some of the liveliest, most daring painters one has ever known, and also the most sincere, living as they do in the midst of mockery and indifference – that is, almost in poverty, with attention only from a small section of the press – are today demanding that the State have nothing to do with art, that the School of Rome (the Villa Medici) be sold, that the Institute be closed, that there be no more medals or rewards, and that artists be allowed to live in that anarchy which is life, which means everyone left to his own resources, and not hampered or destroyed by academic training which feeds on the past. No more official beauty; the public, unaided, will learn to see for itself and will be attracted naturally to those painters whom they find modern and vital. No more official salons and medals than there are for writers. Like writers working in solitude and seeking to have their productions displayed in their publishers' windows, painters will work in their own way and seek to have their paintings hung in galleries. Galleries will be their salons.*

(Tr. W. J. Smith by permission of *Art News*, where published May 1956; originally published by Gurlitt Gallery, Berlin, October 1883 and later as *L'Impressionisme* in *Mélanges posthumes*, J. Laforgue, *Oeuvres complètes*, Paris 1902–3)

vision eventually led him to pursue what he called 'instantaneity' by painting series of views of the same subject – whether a haystack or a cathedral didn't matter to him – at different times of day, in varying conditions of light and atmosphere, and later to explore ever more fleeting and evanescent effects of light, on and through water especially. Cézanne is reported to have said: 'Monet is only an eye but, my God, what an eye!' Monet was, indeed, gifted with a uniquely sensitive instrument for recording the subtlest gradations of tone, the most exquisite sensations of color. He expressed the quality of light in terms of paint on canvas more brilliantly than any artist before or since. But he was not unaware of the ambiguities and contradictions inherent in Impressionism (see p. 721) – nor was his vision quite so innocent as he claimed.

MORISOT, RENOIR AND MANET

Alfred Sisley (1839–99), the purest if also the simplest Impressionist of them all, remained true to the movement's

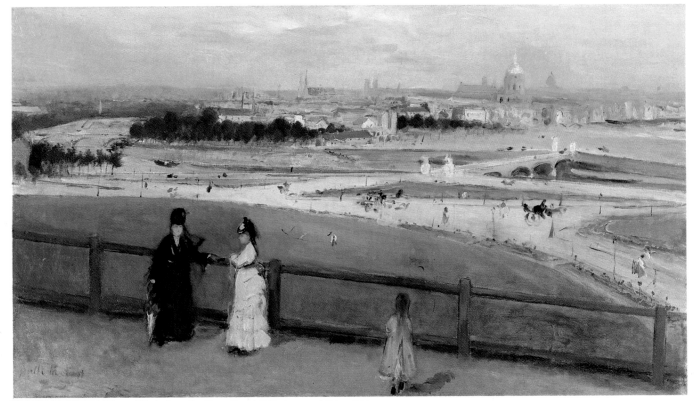

17,6 Berthe Morisot, *View of Paris from the Trocadéro*, 1872. Canvas, 18¹/₁₆ × 32ins (45.9 × 81.4cm).
Collection of the Santa Barbara Museum of Art (Gift of Mrs Hugh N. Kirkland).

original impulse, though its inspiration flagged in his later work. Berthe Morisot (1841–95), who had begun as a follower of Corot, evolved an individual style of great freshness and spontaneity strikingly evident in the casual composition and fluid brushwork of *View of Paris from the Trocadéro* (**17,6**). This painting has obvious affinities with a view of the Paris World's Fair in 1867 (Oslo, National Galeriet) by Manet, a close friend whose brother she was to marry. In a way typical of the development of Impressionism, the two artists influenced one another, she preceding him in painting out of doors. Her *View of Paris from the Trocadéro* is, however, very much a personal view rather than a cityscape. She painted it from the end of the street in which she was living in the western suburb of Paris called Passy, on high ground between the Trocadéro Gardens and the Bois de Boulogne. The two well-dressed ladies and the child in the foreground were probably neighbours if not relatives. Passy had been semi-rural when the Morisots settled there in the 1850s and although more built-up by the 1870s was still regarded as suburban, favoured by well-to-do bourgeois for its quietness and clean air as a healthy place for children. On weekdays, while men conducted their business affairs in the city, it became a social space occupied by women and children. This seems to be the true subject of Morisot's painting rather than the distant view of Paris to which, in fact, the two ladies – separated from it by the railings, the garden and the river – pay no attention at all. Paris was the city of men, of the poor and the very rich (the spires of

Sainte Clotilde, the church of the aristocratic Faubourg Saint-Germain, are just visible on the skyline). Passy belonged to women – bourgeois women – who were said to 'descend' to Paris only rarely.

From 1874 Morisot exhibited regularly with the Impressionists but in the 1880s began to give greater attention to solidity of form, while continuing to paint subjects of immediate personal significance. Renoir also began to feel he had exhausted the possibilities of Impressionism, 'wrung it dry', as he said. Although he had initially taken the lead with his 'rainbow palette', Renoir had always been more traditional than Monet in his concern with the human figure, and his *Boating Party* of 1881 is still fully Impressionist (**17,7**). Its diaphanous brushwork beautifully catches the trembling leaves and shimmering water and quivering vibrations of air inundated with blazing summer light filtered through canvas awnings on to clean white linen and cut glass and soft human flesh. But by 1882, after a trip to Italy, Renoir had serious doubts about Impressionism's lack of form and composition, and lack of content, and he sought renewal notably with the female nude in developing more traditional forms and methods.

Manet's *Bar at the Folies-Bergère* was finished the same year (**17,8**). He never exhibited with the Impressionists, but from the early 1870s onwards he associated himself with them and their illusionistic innovations, experimenting with the spectrum palette while retaining the firm structure of his earlier, more broadly handled,

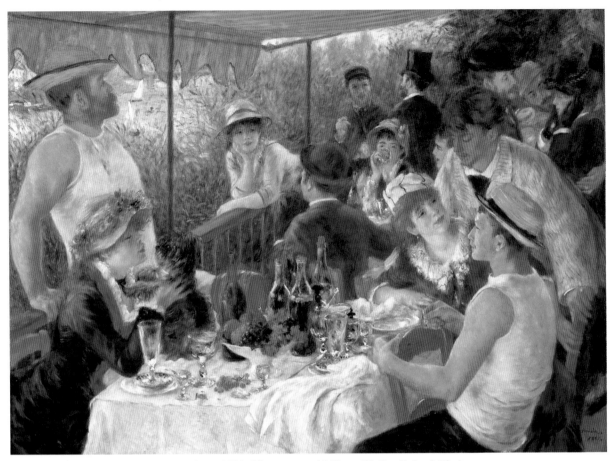

17,7 Pierre-Auguste Renoir, *The Boating Party*, 1881. Oil on canvas, 4ft 3ins × 5ft 6ins (1.3 × 1.73m). Phillips Collection, Washington DC.

17,8 Edouard Manet, *A Bar at the Folies-Bergère*, 1881–2. Oil on canvas, 37½ × 51ins (95.2 × 129.5cm). Courtauld Institute Galleries, University of London.

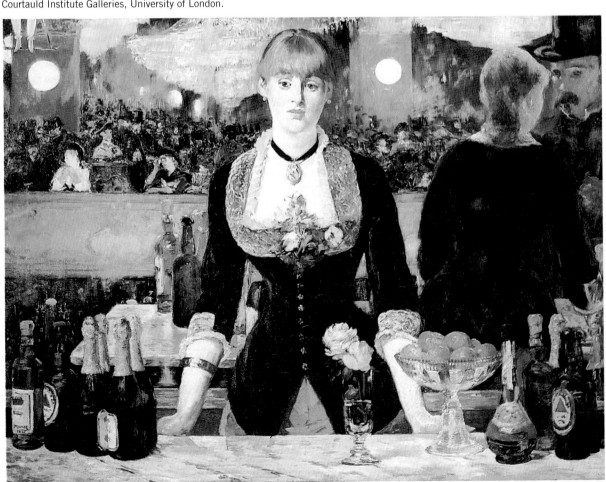

Degas and Manet

CITY LIGHTS AND THE EXPLOITATION OF WOMEN

When Degas exhibited his *Women on the Terrace* (17,15) at the Third Impressionist Exhibition in Paris in 1877 it was the subject that attracted attention, not the Impressionist handling and novel 'mixed media' technique, nor the extremely refined artistic and innovative formal qualities that we now value. To contemporary Parisian eyes the women were obviously prostitutes. 'Monsieur Degas seems to have issued a challenge to the Philistines', wrote one critic. 'You must have seen these rouged, shop-soiled creatures, oozing with vice, cynically recounting their business of the day: you know them and will come across them again in the boulevard.' Twelve years previously an even greater scandal had been caused by Manet's *Olympia* (17,9), for this too was unmistakably the portrait of a prostitute – in every way more brazen, and painted life-size. A young woman, completely nude except, tit-illatingly, for her slipper, a bracelet and a choker round her neck, reclines on a dishevelled bed, with a black woman bringing her a bunch of fresh flowers and, in the lower right corner, a black cat with tail erect.

Manet's *Olympia* was shown at the Salon of 1865, the most important artistic event of the year for the Parisian public. The name 'Olympia' was itself enough to make them raise their eyebrows, as the better-class brothels were full of Floras, Aspasias, Lucretias, etc. The public whose gaze met Olympia's level stare, and the unblinking eyes of the cat, was astounded. 'Never has a painting excited so much laughter, mockery or catcalls', one critic remarked. Daumier drew a bourgeois family gaping at it in bewilderment (17,10). Less able artists caricatured it. At least 30 critics derided it in the press, complaining loudly of the seemingly brash and slap-dash way it was painted as well as of the embarrassingly provocative and explicitly 'modern' subject. Emile Zola, a personal friend of Manet and soon to become famous as a novelist of the seamier side of contemporary city life, answered them by concentrating on the picture's painterly qualities. 'You wanted a nude, and you chose Olympia, the first that came along', he wrote as if addressing the artist. 'You wanted luminous bright patches and you put in a bouquet of flowers. You wanted black patches and you placed a Negress and a cat in the corner. What does it all mean? You hardly know and neither do I.' This was, of course, disingenuous. Zola must have recognized in the alley-cat, at least, a symbol of sexual promiscuity. It was true, however, that in this painting Manet was developing a new manner in pictorial representation, experimenting with tone, making strong contrasts between

17,9 Edouard Manet, *Olympia*, 1862–3.
Canvas, 4ft 3ins × 6ft 3ins (1.3 × 1.9m). Musée d'Orsay, Paris.

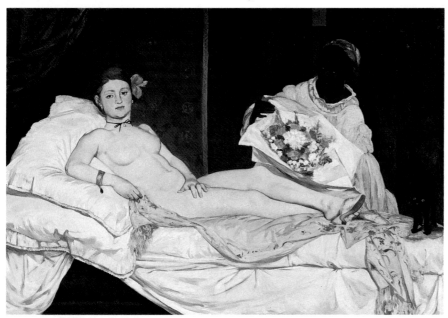

17,10 Honoré Daumier,
Before the Painting of M. Manet, 1865.
Lithograph. Bibliothèque Nationale, Paris.

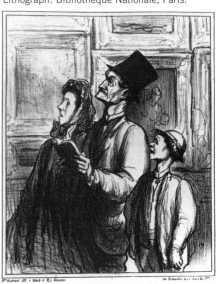

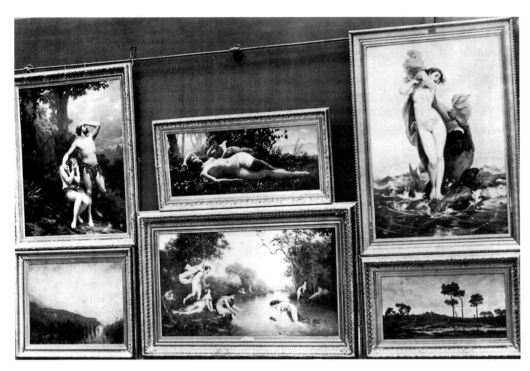

related shades at either end of the scale and eliminating the softening intermediate range. That is one of the reasons why it made such an impact on young artists, who recognized it as marking a breakthrough. After Manet's death they were to prevent its exportation to America by subscribing to buy it for the Louvre.

It is easy enough to see why *Olympia* offended the general public if it is compared with other female nudes exhibited in the same Salon and bought by the French state for museums (**17,11**). In handling it could hardly be more unlike these daintily colored and smoothly painted canvases. Olympia's slender adolescent body is also in striking contrast to their voluptuous figures, which exemplify the accepted form of bourgeois femininity and sexuality. Full-bosomed, narrow-waisted, wide-hipped women populated one Salon after another and made a strong erotic appeal to men of the Second Empire whose wives were tightly corseted to give their bodies the same ample contours even when fully dressed. Women in pornographic photographs of the time are similarly fleshy and buxom. In paintings they were politely distanced in time and space, transformed into goddesses rising from the foam of southern seas or reposing in Arcadian glades. They dis-

play their bodies freely, though invariably without pubic hair, as undemanding objects of desire waiting for male embraces. They are passive bearers of meaning, not makers of meaning, for the determining male gaze which projects its voyeuristic fantasies on to them.

Manet was not simply reacting against the *kitsch* style of such paintings; he believed he was furthering the great tradition of European painting and was dismayed by the hostility and incomprehension with which his work was received. Titian's so-called *Venus of Urbino* (11,47), of which he had painted a copy when a student, was almost certainly a prime source of inspiration, as were the odalisques by Ingres (15,13), whom he greatly admired, though his attitude to both painters was not without irony. That Titian's *Venus* was then thought to have been a courtesan is no coincidence. But Olympia differs from these precedents. Her raised head and the eyes of the cat confront the spectator as if he has just entered the room. She holds his look, plays to it as if 'signifying' male desire. The spectator's eye is drawn to her left hand, not softly furled like that of Titian's Venus in an overtly provocative gesture, but emphatically clamped down as if to veil the absence of a penis and arousing in the critics

an anxiety that they could allay only by ridicule.

Prostitution was accepted in nineteenth-century France as a necessary evil, officially controlled by law. If registered with the police, prostitutes were licensed to work as *filles publiques* in brothels or *filles en carte* soliciting in the streets, both subject to medical examinations. According to Zola, Olympia aged 16 was painted by Manet in 'her youthful tarnished nakedness . . . a *fille* of our own time, whom we have often met in the streets'. The model, Victorine Meurent (1844–1927), was then 16 years old, as Zola said, but she is not known to have been a *fille en carte*. She frequently sat for Manet, who painted her at least nine times (notably in *Luncheon on the Grass*, (15,40), and she later became a painter. In *Olympia* Manet gave her the luxurious setting of a courtesan, above the system of police surveillance, one whose favours were reserved for the upper bourgeoisie – hence their embarrassment. In fact most prostitutes probably evaded surveillance and a writer complained in 1870 that 'they are everywhere, in the café concerts, the theatres, the balls. They are on all the promenades, in front of most of the cafés', as in *Women on the Terrace* by Degas. They were an inescapable part of modern city life.

flat manner. Manet often worked at Argenteuil in 1874, painting idyllic, hedonistic riverside scenes together with Monet and Renoir. But his *Bar at the Folies-Bergère*, painted shortly before he died, is an achievement of a different kind. Urban night-life and the anonymous vitality of the streets and cafés, bars and cabarets appealed to the Impressionists as to Naturalist writers like Zola and Maupassant and the recognition of their visual interest for a painter was one of Impressionism's greatest discoveries. The combination of the artificial and the natural, of illusion and reality, in this nocturnal world provided preeminently 'modern' images of contemporary life. Manet's painting is one of the most subtle and evocative of them. It is largely a reflection of a reflection, the entire background being a mirror. We look into a reflection of the cabaret behind us. The picture has virtually no depth at all; indeed by cutting off the bar along the bottom edge of the canvas Manet indicates that it extends outwards rather than inwards. This complex conception is, however, slightly ambiguous (why are we not reflected in the mirror? and who is the top-hatted man talking to the barmaid?) – but Manet also caught, in the barmaid's empty stare, something of the loneliness and disillusion of city life, of that sense of isolation and alienation so typical of the modern sensibility.

DEGAS

The painter most deeply involved in the representation of urban life was Edgar-Hilaire Degas (1834–1917). Although he exhibited with the Impressionists, his relationship to them is problematical, for landscapes were not a major interest and he painted in the studio, seldom if ever on the spot. Moreover he was consistently concerned with drawing and with the art of the past. But his sense of actuality was as authentic as that of any of the Impressionists and in some ways he was more radical than they were. He preferred the tawdry and seedy night-life of gas-lit streets and cafés to the fresh and jolly open-air world painted by Monet and Renoir. 'For you natural life is necessary; for me, artificial life', he remarked to an Impressionist friend one evening at the Cirque Fernando while an acrobat, Miss La La – the subject of one of his finest paintings – was literally hanging by her teeth high above them.

Degas had 'fallen in love with modern life', wrote Edmond de Goncourt apropos of the paintings of laundresses and ballet-dancers he saw stacked against Degas's studio walls in 1874. Illusion and reality – the tinselly disguise and the naked truth – are artfully contrasted in these deceptively informal compositions (**17,12**). All the gossamer prettiness and glitter seen 'out front' vanish

17,12 Edgar Degas, *Ballet Rehearsal*, 1874. Canvas, 23 × 33ins (58 × 84cm). Burrell Collection, Glasgow Museums & Art Galleries.

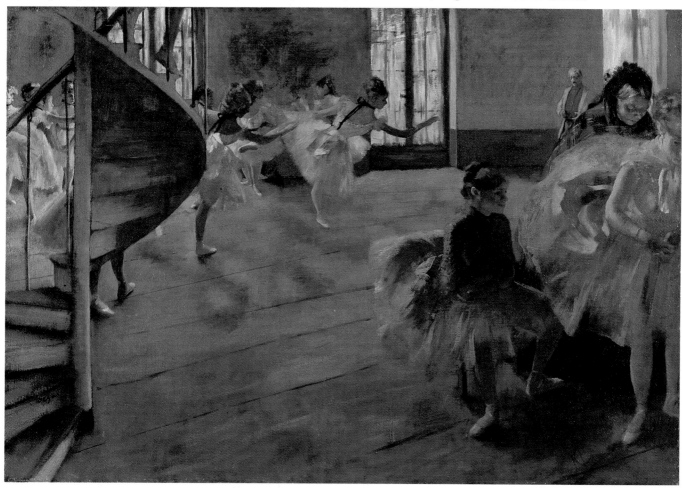

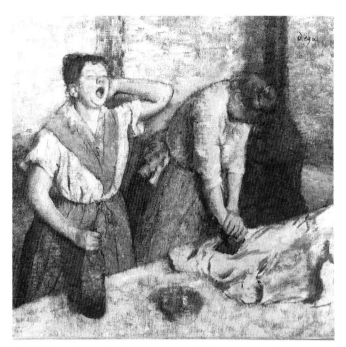

17,13 Edgar Degas, *Two Laundresses*, c. 1884.
Canvas, 29⅞ × 32¼ins (76 × 81.5cm). Louvre, Paris.

backstage. There the dancers go through backbreaking work-outs at the bar or squat, breathless with fatigue, their features sagging, muscles bulging, as their bodies relax gracelessly, with legs sprawling wide apart, totally devoid of erotic or any other charm. Even more cynical in observation are the paintings of laundresses and washer-women, yawning and scratching their backs (**17,13**).

It is largely these paintings and his later pastels of women bathing and drying themselves after their morning tub that gave rise to the idea of Degas the miso-gynist. But his detachment was artistic rather than emo-tional. 'The nude', he told the Irish writer George Moore, 'has always been represented in poses which presuppose an audience, but these women of mine are honest, simple folk, unconcerned by any other interest than those involved in their physical condition. Here is another, she is washing her feet. It is as if you looked through a key-hole.' Certainly, it is this so-called keyhole aesthetic that gives his work such biting reality, most of all in his sculp-ture. Although Degas exhibited only one sculpture during his life-time – the *Little Dancer of Fourteen* (1881) – he was deeply and continually involved with sculptural problems and was certainly as great an artist in plastic as in pictorial media. Renoir always insisted that Degas was the greatest sculptor of the nineteenth century. Such fig-ures as that of the dancer looking at the sole of her right foot are conceived so completely and fully in three dimen-sions that they cannot be appreciated from one viewpoint only (**17,14**). They must be seen from various positions as the spectator moves round them, as with the most sophis-ticated and accomplished sculptures of the past, such as Giovanni Bologna's *Apollo* (11,63).

Degas goes beyond Giovanni Bologna, however, not only by concealing his virtuosity more completely, but

also by his interpretation of sculptural form itself. This has been described as 'sculpture from within'. For his con-ception of the human form surpasses mere nakedness. For him the human body was an infinitely complex and malle-able organism, never still, endlessly changing. So the materiality of his figures sometimes seems almost provi-sional, as if their bodies had not yet quite taken on their final form. Created in privacy and never cast until after Degas died, these astonishing sculptures lack the revolu-tionary use of real materials (muslin, satin, human hair) which made one critic claim that the *Little Dancer of Fourteen* had 'overthrown the tradition of sculpture' at one stroke. But they are perhaps even more radically modern. And they rival the most exquisite of his pastels and mixed-media paintings in sensitivity of handling.

By the late 1870s Degas had given up oil painting for pastel or a mixture of oil paint and pastel and sometimes other media as well – gouache, ink and watercolor – even combining them with monotypes or other print media as in *Women on the Terrace* (**17,15**). This work is small in scale only, for it sums up many aspects of his art, not least his extraordinary ability to disguise the artificiality of a picture's construction by making it all appear an effect of chance. 'A painting', he said, 'is an artificial work existing outside nature and it requires as much cunning as the per-petration of a crime.' The women sitting at a café seem to have been caught as in a snapshot by someone strolling along the boulevard or passing by in a bus or tram. In fact, the composition is ingeniously contrived, with carefully judged cut-offs and croppings of figures to give an effect of discontinuity. Some of these devices Degas had learnt from Japanese prints. Though by no means the first in

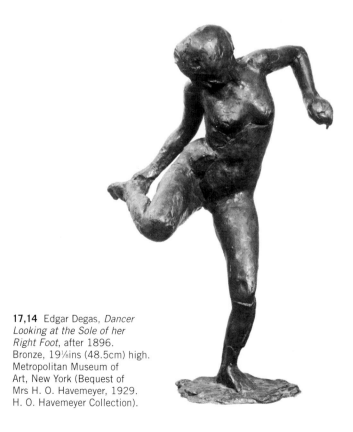

17,14 Edgar Degas, *Dancer Looking at the Sole of her Right Foot*, after 1896. Bronze, 19⅛ins (48.5cm) high. Metropolitan Museum of Art, New York (Bequest of Mrs H. O. Havemeyer, 1929. H. O. Havemeyer Collection).

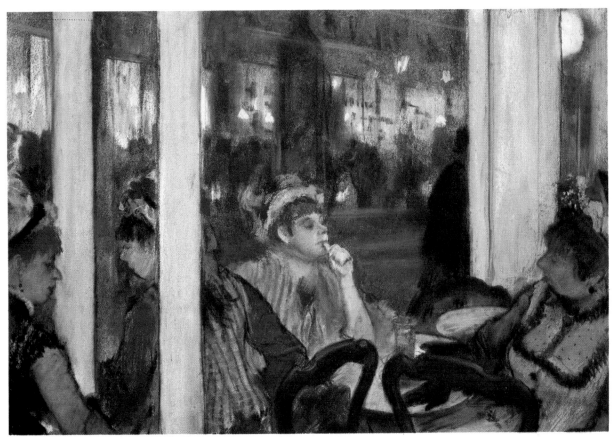

17,15 Edgar Degas, *Women on the Terrace*, c. 1877. Pastel over monotype on paper, 15¾ × 23½ins (40 × 60cm). Louvre, Paris.

Europe to admire and collect Japanese art, he was deeply interested in it from the 1870s onwards and a Kiyonaga bath-house scene always hung over his bed (16,9). But so completely and with such understanding and tact did he assimilate Japanese influence into his own art that its presence is almost unrecognizable.

JAPONISME

Japanese prints dramatically affected the whole course of Western art in the latter half of the nineteenth century. They provided a catalyst which helped painters to throw off the spell of the Classical tradition, free themselves from the authority of the old masters and seek new conceptions in art, new ways of seeing. 'Looking at them', wrote Edmond de Goncourt in 1863, 'I think of Greek art, boredom in perfection, an art that will never free itself from the curse of being academic.' Japanese prints were usually popular, if not vulgar, in subject-matter, unorthodox in their viewpoint and as fresh and brilliant in color as they were vivacious in form. It was from them, Degas confessed, that he had learnt what drawing really meant – that it was 'a way of seeing form'. Without them Monet and the Impressionists would not have been able to realize so quickly and so completely their new vision of the world. 'Well, it may seem strange to say it', wrote Théodore Duret, author of the first serious discussion of Impressionism (1878), 'but it is none the less true that before the arrival among us of Japanese books, there was no one in France who dared to seat himself on the banks

of a river and put side by side on his canvas a roof frankly red, a white-washed wall, a green poplar, a yellow road, and blue water.' Almost certainly Japanese prints were more influential than photography (see pp. 665–8), as we have already suggested in connection with Degas (himself a keen photographer). Indeed, the influence may well have moved as much or more in the opposite direction, from Japanese prints and naturalistic painters to photographers. *The Snow Garden from Marsh Leaves* by Peter Henry Emerson (1856–1936), for instance, very strongly suggests the inspiration of Japanese art – though of screens (12,84) more than of prints – in its choice both of subject and of viewpoint, with the plants in the foreground separated from the distant trees and buildings by a blank snowy space (**17,16**). Emerson was an advocate of soft-focus who applied to photography the theories of Helmholtz (see p. 709), arguing that the camera should record sharply only what the eye perceives at a given moment. His attitude to evenly diffused focus, recording every detail of a scene with equal precision, was akin to that of the Impressionists to local color. He mentioned in 1891 having had discussions on the relationship between art and nature with a 'great painter', almost certainly Whistler (see below), who may well have directed his attention to the art of Japan which was just then so subtly modifying Western ways of seeing and representing the natural world. *The Snow Garden* was taken after these discussions.

Nineteenth-century *Japonisme* was completely different from earlier Orientalisms – seventeenth- and eighteenth-century *Chinoiserie*, for instance. That had been essentially an art of fantasy and exoticism, of sophisticated caprice and elegant mockery. No attempt was made to understand Chinese art or the principles on which it was based. Not until the mid-nineteenth century did Western artists approach any non-Western art in a sufficiently receptive and humble frame of mind to learn from it. And so potent was the impact when they did that every major late nineteenth-century painter (with the possible exception of Cézanne) was to be influenced by it, often fundamentally. Indeed, the history of modern art in the West is to a much greater extent than is commonly realized that of the liberating and vitalizing effect of successive waves of discovery by Western artists of alien cultures, first Japanese and then African, Polynesian and indigenous American.

Japanese woodblock prints became widely accessible after 1854, when Japan was reopened to foreigners by the United States – it had been closed since 1638, though the Dutch were allowed a trading station at Nagasaki – and the first artists to show Japanese influence in their work were American, John La Farge (1835–1910) and James Abbott McNeill Whistler (1834–1903). Whistler lived in London from 1859 onwards and became the most radical of the aesthetes, an apostle of 'art for art's sake' (see p. 674). At first his *Japonisme* amounted to little more than the use of Japanese motifs, but by the early 1860s he had begun to immerse himself in Oriental art and was trying to absorb it creatively into his own. Complete assimilation was achieved a few years later in such works as *Nocturne in Blue and Silver, Cremorne Lights* (**17,17**), in which all explicitly Oriental borrowings have been eliminated. An empty expanse of smooth water with a very high skyline almost becomes an undefined space, with here and there delicate hints of objects floating freely in it. Though naturalistically conceived, the exquisite adjustment of lines and intervals approaches some abstract 'arrangement' of colors so that the painting is, in effect, a translation into Western terms of Japanese art.

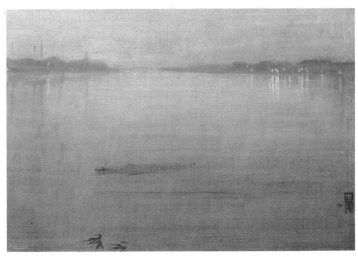

17,17 James Abbott McNeill Whistler, *Nocturne in Blue and Silver, Cremorne Lights*, 1872. Oil on canvas, 19¾ × 29¼ins (40 × 74cm). Tate Gallery, London.

17,16 Peter Henry Emerson, *The Snow Garden from Marsh Leaves*, c. 1895. Photogravure print from a negative. Metropolitan Museum of Art, New York (Gift of Robert Hershkowitz in memory of Samuel J. Wagstaff, Jr., 1988, 1069.1).

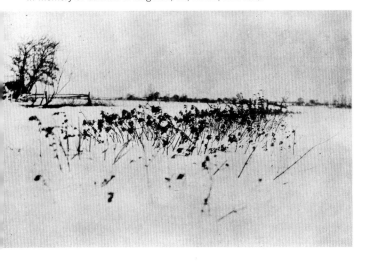

Whistler's *Nocturne in Blue and Silver* was painted the same year as Monet's *Impression – Sunrise* (17,5) and comparison between them reveals how much both were indebted to Japan. Impressionism might seem to be the antithesis of Japanese art, and Monet, as Impressionism's purest exponent, the painter least open to Oriental influence. Yet he was closely caught up in it from the day he first bought a Japanese print when a 17-year-old student to his last great paintings of water-lilies in his Japanese garden (19,4). The freshness and brightness of color, the unorthodoxy of design and subject-matter all appealed to him. More important, Japanese art indicated a way to solve the problem which increasingly obsessed him, that of how to combine and reconcile pictorial three-dimensional illusionism with the flat painted surface as a field for invention. This became a central concern for all late nineteenth-century painters and it was in connection with it that Japanese influence is most strongly felt, especially in the work of artists like Lautrec, who confronted the problem directly and in its simplest terms, or in the remarkable and technically innovative color prints of Mary Cassatt (1844–1926), the most significant American artist of her generation, who exhibited with the Impressionists in Paris from 1879 onwards (**17,18**).

Henri-Marie-Raymond de Toulouse-Lautrec (1864–1901) revolutionized the art of poster-making by flattening illusionistic space in the Japanese manner and uniting the pattern of the pictorial elements with that of the lettering. The development of lithography into a polychrome medium converted posters, which had earlier been confined mainly to typographic announcements, into a new form of public art, which Lautrec brought to sudden maturity. In his *Jane Avril au Jardin de Paris* (**17,19**) the lack of modelling, the economy of line and the integration of blank paper into the composition all derive from Japan, as does the truncation of the boldly foreshortened cello and its use as a framing device. The pictorial elements merge with the frame and the lettering into a

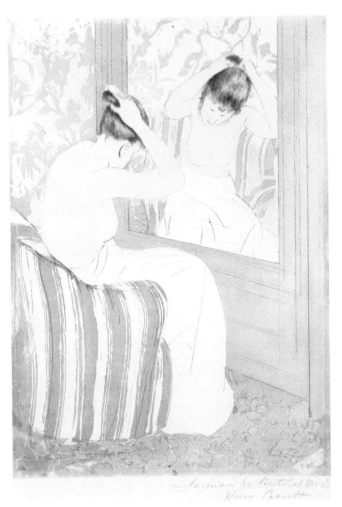

17,18 Mary Cassatt, *The Coiffure*, 1891.
Color print with dry point, soft-ground and
aquatint, 14⅜ × 10½ins (36.5 × 26.7cm).
The Cleveland Museum of Art
(Bequest of Charles T. Brooks).

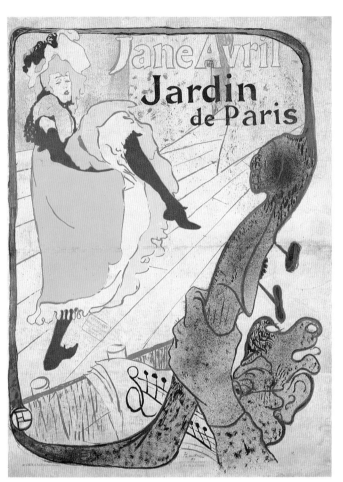

17,19 Henri de Toulouse-Lautrec, *Jane Avril au Jardin de Paris*, 1893.
Lithograph, 50⅕ × 37ins (129 × 94cm). Musée de la Publicité, Paris.

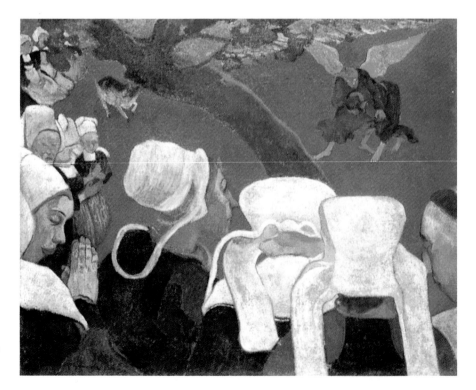

17,20 Paul Gauguin, *The Vision after the Sermon*,
1888. Canvas, 28¾ × 36¼ins (73 × 92cm).
National Gallery of Scotland, Edinburgh.

flat pattern so that the dancer's vivacious, gawky body makes a Hokusai-like calligraphic flourish on the same frontal plane as the uptilted perspective of the stage and footlights.

Japanese influence is hardly less strong in the work of Symbolist painters, especially Paul Gauguin (see pp. 724–7), who enthusiastically collected Japanese prints, decorated his primitive studio in the South Seas with them and combined their influence with that of other non-European cultures in his own work. In his first completely Symbolist painting, *The Vision after the Sermon* (**17,20**), the 'vision' of Jacob wrestling with the angel is derived from a drawing of a similar hand to hand combat in Hokusai's *Manga*. But Japanese influence goes deeper. It is felt in the whole conception of the picture, in the flattened forms with dark contours, the absence of shadows, the unmodulated areas of pure, sometimes unnaturalistic colors, as in the dominant red ground. With van Gogh (see p. 724) the debt to Japan also went far beyond the occasional use of Japanese motifs, remarkable though van Gogh's copies after Hiroshige and his other directly Japanese-inspired paintings are. Van Gogh's involvement with Japanese art during the last four years of his life was perhaps more extensive and more complex than that of any other artist of the period.

NEO-IMPRESSIONISM

The crisis within Impressionism, to which we have already alluded (see p. 712), became a conscious reaction by the mid-1880s, when young artists sought to move away from and beyond it. Impressionism's dependence on nature and on the objective recording of visual appearances, its concentration on the fleeting and casual at the expense of the enduring and monumental, seemed to them to be self-imposed limitations which had led to formlessness, sketchiness and the lack of any sense of elevation or deeper meaning. The latter especially – the triviality of content – was deplored, although earlier it had been thought one of Impressionism's virtues. To Renoir what had seemed most significant about Impressionism was that it had 'freed painting from the importance of the subject (under Louis XV I would have been obliged to paint nothing but specified subjects). I am at liberty to paint flowers and call them simply flowers, without their needing to tell a story.' Now artists wanted art to have, once again, some avowed and significant purport, to be more 'meaningful'.

Of course, their reaction oversimplified the issues; Impressionism was deeply ambivalent, hence the difficulty the Impressionists had in defining their aims. Their concept of the 'impression' was both objective and subjective, going some way beyond a straightforward

17,21 Georges Seurat, *Bathers, Asnières*, 1883–4. Canvas, 6ft 7⅛ins × 9ft 10⅛ins (2.1 × 3m). National Gallery, London.

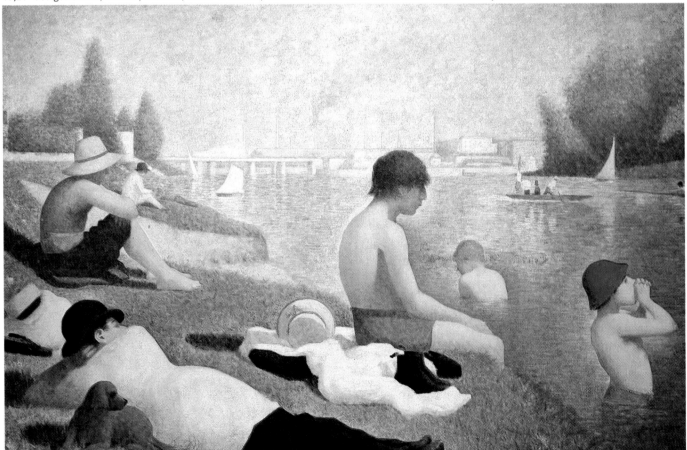

'accurate view of nature' to include the individual and unique 'sensation' of a particular artist. Monet, for example, would talk about 'my very own impression' and said he always worked better in solitude according to 'just the impression of what I felt, I, all alone'. Similarly, Pissarro referred to his own 'sensation' as being 'the only thing that counts'.

SEURAT, DIVISIONISM AND SOCIALISM

One solution to the crisis was indicated by Georges Seurat (1859–91) in the *Bathers, Asnières* (**17,21**). This huge and monumental rendering of a weekend riverside scene near Paris is a combination of opposites, of Impressionist contemporaneity and naturalism with academic gravity and formality. It is as joyous a celebration of sunlight as anything by Monet or Renoir, but the transitoriness and sketchiness of their renderings of similar, typically Impressionist, subjects (**17,4**) have been replaced with a sense of timeless universality – as in some mythological scene by Pierre Puvis de Chavannes (1824–98), an academic painter whose subtlety and refinement were admired by artists despite his rather pallid idealizing imagery. Comparison of the *Bathers* with Puvis's *Pastoral* (**17,22**), exhibited at the Salon the previous year, shows that Seurat's relation to this academic master went deeper than might be supposed. But Seurat was a great deal more than just a 'modernizing Puvis'. Based on numerous small impressionistic sketches done quickly on the spot, the *Bathers* was composed in the studio and painted slowly and methodically in a new technique invented by Seurat to impose logic and discipline on Impressionist discov-

eries. He called it 'chromo-luminarism', but it is better known as 'Divisionism' (or 'Pointillism'). The *Bathers* is painted evenly all over with short brush-strokes uniformly separated and not directional – in later works these became dots like the tesserae in mosaics – each a pure color juxtaposed (or 'divided') instead of being mixed on the palette, so as to fuse optically in the eye of the spectator when seen at the right distance. Increased luminosity would, it was hoped, result, especially when the juxtaposed colors were complementary (red-green, yellow-violet, orange-blue, etc.). Divisionism was a systematization of Impressionist practice (from the color and other theories of Michel Eugène Chevreul, Ogden N. Rood and Charles Henry especially), but its laborious, painstaking application contrasts with the spontaneity and freshness of Impressionist brushwork. Similarly, the sharp hard-edged outlines of Seurat's figures and their arrangement along parallel diagonals, combined with the predominant horizontality implied by the left–right direction in which all but one of the figures gaze, create a firm structural effect very different from the evanescent atmospheric imprecision of Impressionist painting.

Seurat's scenes of modern urban life also differ from those of the Impressionists in being less bourgeois and more working-class. His political stance is uncertain, but several of his followers, notably Paul Signac (1863–1935), who became the spokesman for the Divisionists or Neo-Impressionists as they were called from 1886 onwards, were active supporters of the Socialist-Anarchist movement in France. Signac was quite explicit about the social and political inspiration of their art. While abjuring any crudely propagandist intentions, the Neo-Impressionists,

17,22 Pierre Puvis de Chavannes, *Pastoral*, 1882. Canvas, 10⅛ × 15⅝ins (25.7 × 39.7cm). Yale University Art Gallery (Mary Gertrude Abbey Fund).

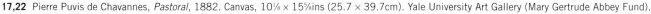

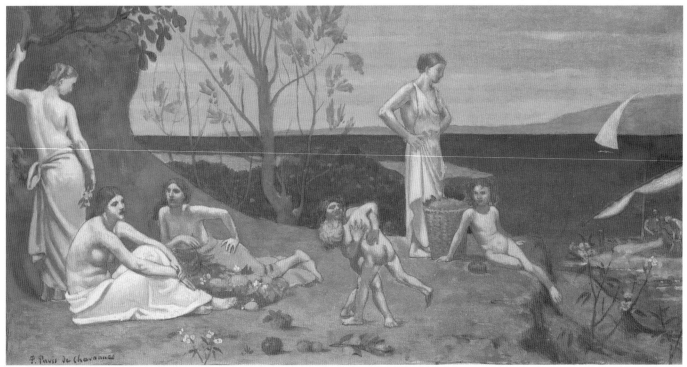

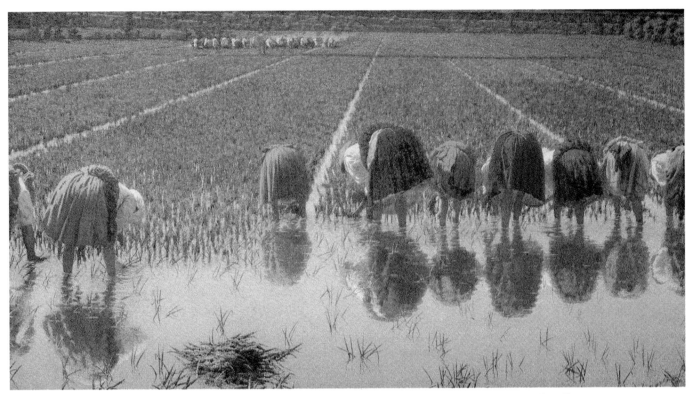

17,23 Angelo Morbelli, *For Eighty Cents*, 1895. Canvas, 48¾ × 27½ins (124 × 70cm). Civico Museo Antonio Borgogna, Vercelli.

he wrote, bore witness with paintings of proletarian subjects to 'the great social struggle that is now taking place between the workers and capital'. It would be an error, he went on, 'to require a precise socialist tendency in works of art'. But 'pure aesthetes, revolutionaries by temperament', who painted 'what they see, as they feel it' do very often 'give a hard blow of the pick-axe to the old social structure . . .' ('Impressionistes et Révolutionnaires' in *La Révolte*, June 1891, tr. L. Nochlin).

Neo-Impressionist paintings by Signac, Pissarro, Henri-Edmond Cross and other members of the group now seem more lyrical and carefree than politically provocative. But socialism played a very positive role in the work of the Italian *Divisionisti*, who developed independently of the French. In such paintings as *For Eighty Cents* (**17,23**) by Angelo Morbelli (1853–1919), a social message is very forcefully conveyed without any attempt at pathos and without any loss in subtlety of color, handling or composition. It depicts peasants weeding rice fields near Casale Monferrato in Piedmont and was recognized immediately as a powerful indictment of the appalling conditions in which women were condemned to work – 'in the asphyxiating heat' and 'stench of the waters of the rice fields under the blaze of the June sun'. Yet this social protest is combined with exquisite visual effects of transparency and luminosity rendered with a very personal Divisionist technique, in which the predominant greens are opposed not by their complementary (red) but by their contrast in terms of light rays (purple). The intricately woven brush-strokes of Morbelli's specially devised three-pointed brush run in parallel threes.

During the last few years of his tragically short life, Seurat began to explore the expressive possibilities of line and color in a systematic, scientific manner and, had he lived, his ideas would probably have resulted in a kind of scientific 'synthetism' parallel to the more intuitive synthetism of Gauguin and the Symbolist painters of the Pont-Aven school. For Symbolism, in varying forms, was to be the main subjective current of anti-Impressionism during the last two decades of the century.

SYMBOLISM

Many young artists, seeking ways of escape from objective naturalism, turned to imagination and fantasy, to the intimate private world of the self, which Baudelaire had made into a cult, as well as to Baudelaire's theory of 'correspondences' and expressive equivalences. The idea that color might have a directly expressive rather than a merely descriptive function was traced back to Delacroix and the Romantic painters; similar potentialities were now found in line and form though without going so far as to suggest that emotion and subjective experience might be communicated by non-representational pictorial means.

The movement was heralded for poets by the Symbolist Manifesto (1886) of Jean Moréas, who rejected the naturalism of Zola and other writers in favour of a totally new school, whose aim was 'to clothe the *Idea* in sensual, perceptible form'. A further declaration by the Symbolist poet Gustave Kahn was more explicit.

We are tired of the everyday, the near-at-hand and the contemporaneous; we wish to be able to place the development of the symbol in any period, even in dreams (dreams being indistinguishable from life) . . . . The essential aim of our art is to objectify the subjective [the externalization of the Idea], *in place of subjectifying the objective* [nature seen through the eyes of a temperament]. *Thus we carry the analysis of the Self to the extreme.*

(G. Kahn in *L'Evénement*, 1886)

The relationship of the poet and artist to his subject was reversed; instead of seeking their motifs in the tangible, external world, they now looked inwards so that feelings and ideas became the starting-point of works of art. Rejection of Impressionism and Neo-Impressionism followed, quite consciously and explicitly in the case of the painter Emile Bernard (1868–1941). Until 1886 Bernard had been painting in a Neo-Impressionist manner. That autumn he visited Signac's studio to 'obtain the latest word on the chromatic researches of the theoreticians of optics'. Experiencing a sudden revulsion, he abandoned Neo-Impressionism in order, as he later wrote, 'to allow ideas to dominate the technique of painting'. He destroyed all his Neo-Impressionist work and left Paris for Brittany, a backward area where village life was still untainted by urban civilization. There, at Pont-Aven mainly, he experimented with rustic, archaic subjects and anti-naturalistic techniques until he reached a simplified style of bold outline and flat color (called 'Cloisonnism'), which, he claimed, became the catalyst for his friend Gauguin's *Vision after the Sermon* (17,20), the first major example of Synthetism or pictorial Symbolism.

GAUGUIN AND VAN GOGH

Paul Gauguin (1848–1903) had given up a profitable career as a stockbroker in 1883 in order to paint and had twice exhibited with the Impressionists before settling in Brittany in 1886. By that date he had already formulated – in letters and no doubt also in conversation – the essence of his new style, but it was Bernard's pictorial innovations that finally released him from the last vestiges of Impressionism and enabled him to realize paintings in which dream and memory predominate. 'Art is an abstraction', he wrote from Pont-Aven in 1888, 'extract it from nature, dreaming before it, and think more of the creation which will result than of nature.' Gauguin had probably seen Breton village festivals, including one with wrestling matches, red banners and bonfires, before painting the *Vision after the Sermon*, but this painting is essentially of something not seen. It is the record of something imagined and interpreted in visual metaphors. At first glance, too, it might seem to present both an outward and an inner experience – the priest and the peasants and their recollection of the sermon they have just heard (on Jacob wrestling with the angel) – but the 'vision' is a double one, the religious vision of the Breton women and the artist's

imaginary vision of them and of the power of the faith that moves them.

Gauguin's Symbolist, expressive aims were shared by the Dutch painter Vincent Willem van Gogh (1853-90), for whom art was a means of personal, spiritual redemption. Van Gogh's is a unique case. He did not become an artist until 1881 and for him it was truly a 'calling'. He threw himself into it with all the fervour of a religious convert. 'To try to understand the real significance of what great artists, the serious masters, tell us in their masterpieces, that leads to God', he wrote in 1880. Between then and 1890, when he committed suicide after intermittent periods of insanity and several months as a voluntary inmate of an asylum, he painted over 800 pictures – not to mention drawings and his voluminous correspondence with his brother Theo and others, one of the most tormented and relentless accounts of the search for self in literary history and one of the fullest expositions ever given by an artist of his ideas about the meaning and purpose of art. During the last 70 days of his life he painted 70 canvases. Of all these hundreds of fully realized, if hastily executed, pictures he succeeded in selling only one, though the effect on him of this neglect and of the poverty and obscurity in which he lived should not be overstressed. His reaction, shortly before his suicide, to the one favourable mention his work received in the press during his life-time was remarkably level-headed.

Van Gogh had studied theology to become a pastor in a depressed coal-mining area of Belgium. In becoming an artist he satisfied his craving for spiritual fulfilment in work which, he believed, could and should be socially useful. 'I am good for something, my life has a purpose after all', he told his brother Theo in 1880. 'How can I be useful, of what service can I be? There is something inside of me, what can it be?' Each of his paintings became a cry of anguish as he struggled to release his violent, frustrated passions. 'I have a terrible lucidity at moments', he wrote in 1888. 'I am not conscious of myself any more, and the picture comes to me as in a dream.' Writhing, flame-like forms and agitated brushwork transmit with almost hallucinatory power the convulsions of his tormented sensibility and, in such baleful works as *The Night Café* (**17,24**), the state of almost permanent anxiety and sense of instability which threatened to engulf him. It is painted in disharmonies of red, green and yellow, he wrote, 'to express the terrible passions of humanity . . . the idea that the café is a place where one can ruin oneself, go mad or commit a crime. So I have tried to express, as it were, the powers of darkness in a low public house, by soft Louis XV greens and malachite, contrasting with yellow-green and harsh blue-greens, and all this in an atmosphere like the devil's furnace, of pale sulphur. And all with an appearance of Japanese gaiety.'

The concept of art as a new religion, as a way of life to which the artist is called and to which he gives himself up utterly, was an article of faith for Gauguin as much as for van Gogh. Both were inspired by a similar quest to recover the sincerity and purity of simple, unspoilt people, uncorrupted by civilization and modern urban life. Such myths

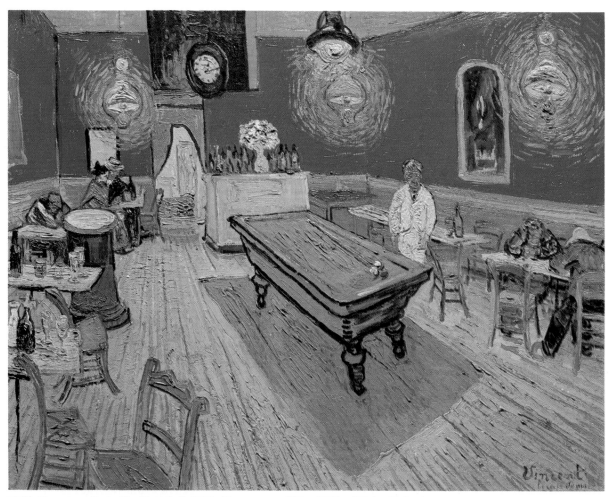

17,24 Vincent van Gogh, *The Night Café*, 1888. Oil on canvas, 28½ × 36¼ins (72.4 × 92.1cm).
Yale University Art Gallery (Bequest of Stephen C. Clark, 1903).

of the primitive have haunted the Western imagination ever since Classical times, going back far beyond Romantic ideas of the 'noble savage' to that of an earthly paradise where men lived in a state of nature. But no artist before Gauguin had ever tried to put it into practice and go native himself. Gauguin turned his back on Europe and sailed for the South Seas in 1891, settling in a native village in Tahiti.

Innocence and knowledge, the savage and the civilized, became central themes for Gauguin after he left Europe, though he found that he was no more able to shed Western civilization in Tahiti than he had been in Pont-Aven. In fact, his paintings became less, rather than more, 'primitive' in the South Seas. Though more exotic in subject and color, the essential elements of his style remained unchanged. And since he had taken with him a stock of photographs and reproductions – of ancient Egyptian reliefs, the Parthenon frieze, a Rembrandt drawing, Borobudur reliefs, and so on – and drew on them as freely as he had previously on Japanese prints and rustic Breton sculptures, his South Seas paintings are often more obviously eclectic. His synthetic method of constructing a picture became quite self-conscious after the shock and stimulus of his new surroundings wore off, as he revealed in his

description of the genesis of the *The Spectre Watches Over Her* (**17,25**). It began by his being 'captured by a form, a movement' of a young Tahitian, of whom he made a carefully rendered drawing with 'no other preoccupation than to execute a nude'. He then felt impelled to 'imbue it with the native feeling, character and tradition' and introduced the bright *pareo* and yellow bark-cloth which would 'arouse something unexpected in the spectator'. To suggest a background of 'terror', he added some purple. In this way, 'the musical part of the picture' was all set out. The 'idea' of the picture, however, which had come to him as he worked on it and which is already felt in his use of the word 'terror', had not yet been made visual. To do that he had to reconsider the whole work once again. 'I see only fear. What kind of fear?' he asked himself.

Certainly not the fear of Susanna surprised by the Elders. That does not exist in Oceania. The Tupapau *(Spirit of the Dead) is clearly indicated. For the natives it is a constant dread. Once I have found my* Tupapau *I attach myself completely to it, and make it the motif of my picture. The nude takes second place.*

What can a spirit be for a Maori? . . . she thinks

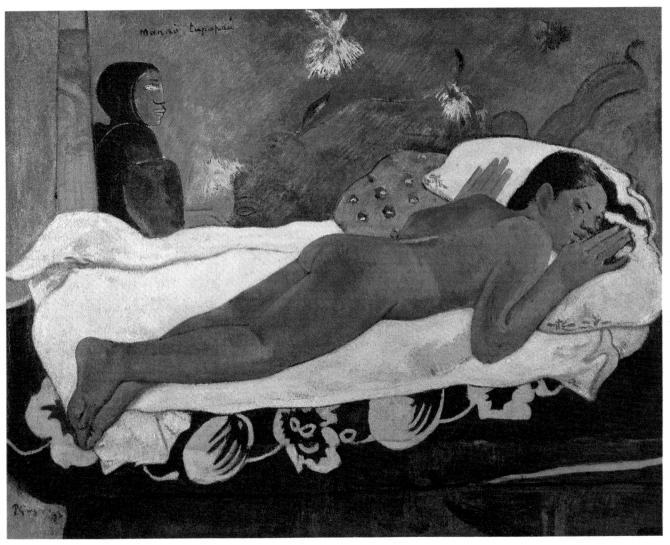

17,25 Paul Gauguin, *The Spectre Watches Over Her (Mana'o tupapa'u)*, 1892. Canvas, 28¾ × 36¼ins (73 × 92cm).
Albright-Knox Art Gallery, Buffalo, New York (A. Conger Goodyear Collection).

17,26 Paul Gauguin, *Where do we come from? What are we? Where are we going?*, 1897.
Oil on canvas, 4ft 6¾ins × 12ft 3½ins (1.39 × 3.74m). Museum of Fine Arts, Boston (Tompkins Collection).

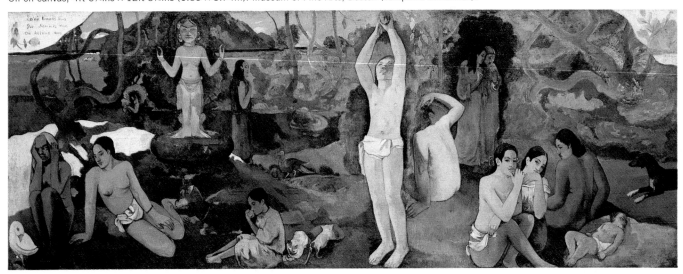

necessarily of some she has seen. My spirit can only be an ordinary little woman. The title has two meanings, either she thinks of the spirit: or, the spirit thinks of her.

(From Gauguin's manuscript
'Cahier pour Aline', tr. R. Goldwater)

The Spectre Watches Over Her illustrates Gauguin's Synthetist-Symbolist creative process and also, very significantly, his extraordinary understanding of Polynesian culture and religion, informed by the most unusual (for a European) intimacy of his engagement with indigenous Tahitian and Marquesan society. Their complex sexuality is expressed and felt with personal empathy, notably in the androgynous nude figure, though it recalls, perhaps rather too overtly, well-known Classical sculptures of hermaphrodites. But his achievement was, none the less, great. His anti-naturalism and emphasis on poetic and rhythmical effects, on purity of line and creative autonomy of color, his appeal to the imagination, to dreams, to the unconscious and to the primitive, all these were to be enormously influential. 'I wanted to establish the right to dare everything', he said. 'The public owes me nothing, since my pictorial *oeuvre* is but relatively good; but the painters who today profit from this liberty owe me something.'

ALLEGORIES OF MODERN LIFE:

MUNCH AND RODIN

Gauguin's largest work, *Where do we come from? What are we? Where are we going?* (**17,26**), painted as a kind of personal testament before he attempted suicide in 1897, is less daring than many of his earlier paintings but more typically Symbolist in its subject-matter, an allegory of human life from infancy to old age. Allegories also preoccupied several other artists of the period, notably Edvard Munch (1863–1944) and Auguste Rodin (1840–1917). Munch left Norway in 1889 to study in Paris, where he felt the impact of Impressionism, and of Seurat, van Gogh and Gauguin. But he belonged essentially to a dark Northern world of brooding introspection and neurotic obsessions, the deeply pessimistic, fatalistic world of Ibsen's and Strindberg's plays, and his paintings and lithographs are similarly expressive of states of mind – often unbalanced and bordering on the pathological – in sequences having a continuous, cumulative effect. The theme of his *Frieze of Life*, which occupied him over many years, is suffering through love. A cycle of intensely subjective images re-enacts the emotional states of attraction, union, disenchantment, jealousy and despair. Though never completed, it forms the most powerful statement left by any artist of *fin-de-siècle* disillusion and culminates in Munch's most famous painting, *The Scream* (**17,27**). 'I stood there, trembling with fear', he wrote. 'And I felt a loud, unending scream piercing nature.' The despair and terror experienced by the foreground figure are made visible in the landscape and sky, which writhe with agonized streaks of arbitrary color –

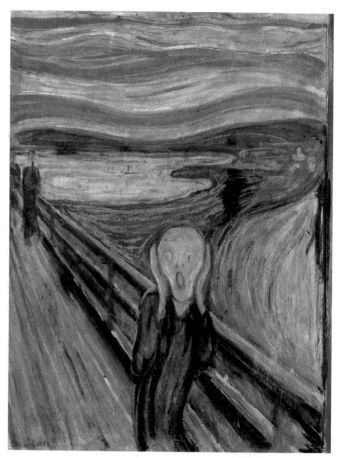

17,27 Edvard Munch, *The Scream*, 1893. Oil, pastel and casein on cardboard, 35¾ × 29ins (91 × 73.5cm). National Gallery, Oslo.

red, yellow and green – as if the scream was expanding in waves of neurotic, unreasoning fear.

Rodin objected to being called a Symbolist and distrusted his visionary powers. He always worked from nature like an Impressionist painter and, in fact, one of his early works was so realistic that he was accused of having made it up from casts taken from a living model. Yet his sculptures are much more than just naturalistic feats of descriptive modelling; they portray states of mind and feeling. His one-time secretary, the Austrian poet Rainer Maria Rilke, said that Rodin's was an art 'to help a time whose misfortune was that all its conflicts lay in the invisible'. In his most ambitious work, *The Gates of Hell* (**17,28**), which occupied him for 20 years and was never finished, the pessimism and anxiety and psychic distress of the *fin-de-siècle* period take on material form and become visible with the same immediacy as in Munch's and van Gogh's paintings. Indeed, some figures in the Gates of Hell closely parallel Munch's, notably the kneeling youths with arms upstretched and heads thrown back, emitting, as Rodin said, 'cries lost in the heavens' (**17,29**). If less obsessive, less pathologically expressive, they are quite as powerful images of despair as Munch's *The Scream*, and the spectator's delayed awareness that they are casts from the same model only adds to the unnerving effect. Moreover, in its whole conception as a

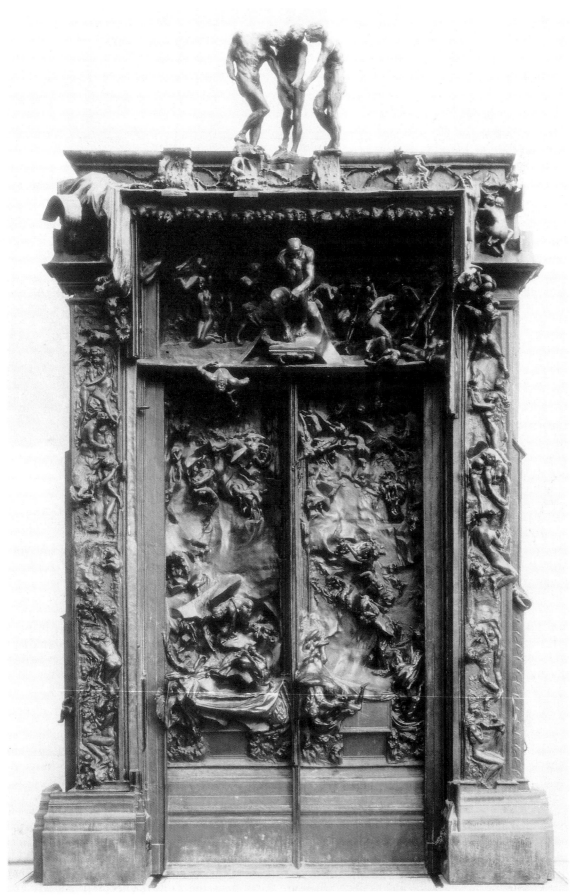

17,28 Auguste Rodin, *The Gates of Hell*, 1880–1917. Bronze, 18ft (5.49m) high. Musée Rodin, Paris.

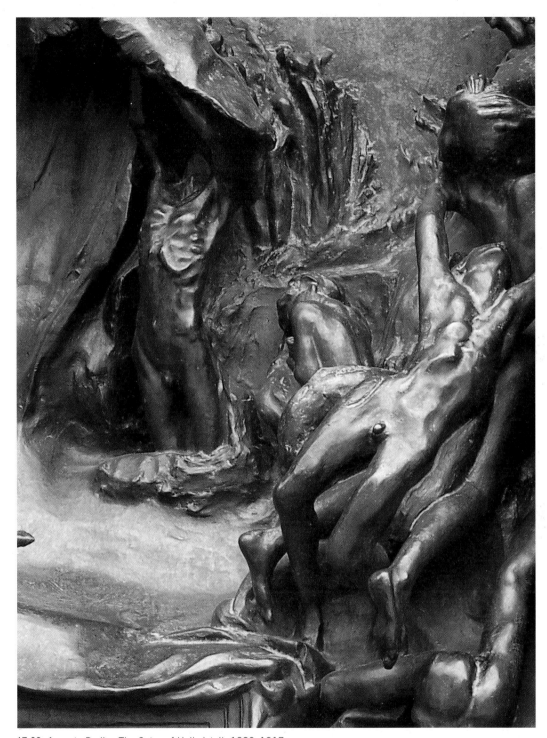

17,29 Auguste Rodin, *The Gates of Hell*, detail, 1880–1917.

modern Inferno of perpetual flux, this huge monumental portal with its amorphous indeterminate composition, inconsistencies of scale and dizzying shifts of direction, is a disturbing symbol of psychic instability. Rodin may not have been as great or as innovatory a sculptor as Degas: he was the last great exponent of an old tradition, rather than the first of a new. But the imaginary world he created is comparable in power with the tormented visions of van Gogh.

ART NOUVEAU AND THE NEW ARCHITECTURE

Munch's *The Scream* is exactly contemporary with the Tassel House in Brussels (**17,30**) by Victor Horta (1861–1947), and three years later, in 1896, Munch's first exhibition in Paris was held in a recently opened gallery called 'Art Nouveau', which gave the new style its name and had been designed by another Belgian architect,

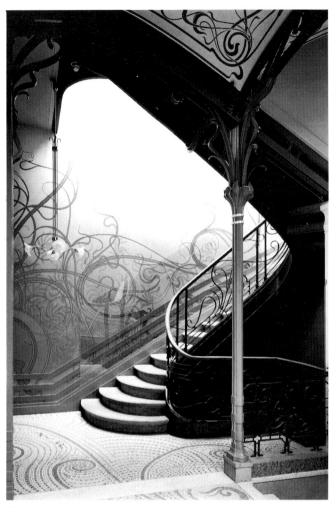

17,30 Victor Horta, Tassel House, Brussels, Belgium, 1892–3.

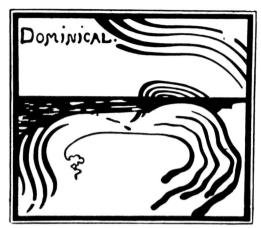

17,31 Henry van de Velde, *Dominical*, 1892.
Lithograph, 12¾ × 10¼ins (32.5 × 26cm).

17,32 Henry van de Velde, *Tropon*, 1898.
Lithograph, 11½ × 8½ins (29 × 21.5cm).

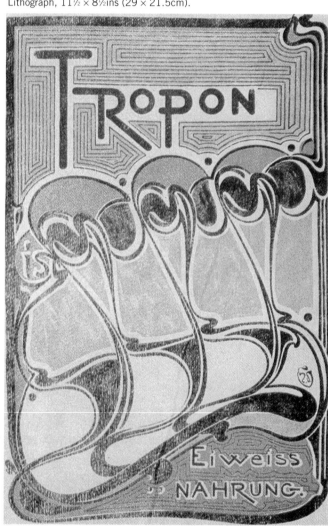

Henry van de Velde (1863–1957). These coincidences are
not irrelevant. For the slithery, undulating, plant-like
curvilinear patterns of the Tassel House interior, so characteristic of Art Nouveau, have affinities with the
swelling and writhing lines of *The Scream* and other
works by Symbolist painters, including Gauguin and
van Gogh.

The connection between Symbolism and Art Nouveau
is, however, formal only. Whereas the tortured lines of *The
Scream* have great suggestive and expressive force, the
linear patterns of the Tassel House are smooth and relaxed
and purely decorative. The same superficial similarities
and radical differences can be seen very clearly in two
small, but masterly, designs by van de Velde (**17,31; 32**). In
one, the woodcut title-page for a volume of poems,
Dominical, by Max Elskamp, the design is expressive as in
Symbolist painting. Suggestions of both space and mood
are vividly conveyed without either modelling or foreshortening. The poster for Tropon tinned foods, on the
other hand, though equally linear, lacks any suggestion of
depth nor are there any emotional overtones or hints of
further meaning, or indeed of any meaning at all. The design
is flat and ornamental. Its extreme economy of means and
non-representational character relate it, rather, to early

attempts at industrial design being made in Germany at
about the same date by Peter Behrens (see p. 782).

Despite the odour of decadence which hangs about a
great deal of Art Nouveau, the movement was, in fact, a
positive one, the last of several earnest endeavours to

achieve a truly contemporary and 'modern', i.e. non-period-imitation, style. Historicism (see p. 671) and the revival of historical styles had repeatedly provoked, as a reaction, a demand for a 'style of the nineteenth century'. But buildings like the Crystal Palace (17,35) which exploited new industrial materials and methods and attempted to answer the call to be 'of one's own time', taken over from the Romantics by the mid-century Realists, were seldom accepted as 'architecture' by their contemporaries. Art Nouveau was the first conscious and successful attempt to halt the succession of historical revivals (Greek, Roman, Gothic, Byzantine, Early Christian, Romanesque, Italian Renaissance, French Renaissance, Jacobean, Elizabethan, and so on) and replace them with something which had no links, or at any rate no obvious links, with the past. Connections with Rococo ornament and Celtic ornament can be traced, as well as debts to the Pre-Raphaelite painters and to the English designer, poet and theorist William Morris (1834–96) and the Arts and Crafts Movement. But an essentially 'new' style was certainly achieved by the more extreme Art Nouveau designers, notably the Spanish architect Antoni Gaudí (1852–1926), some of whose buildings in Barcelona combine entirely free, asymmetrical, jagged planes with fiercely extravagant and arbitrary forms so that there are no straight walls, no right-angles and everything undulates in an unprecedentedly organic interplay of exterior and interior (**17,33; 34**).

The rapid diffusion of Art Nouveau all over Europe was due largely to another late nineteenth-century phenomenon – the lavishly illustrated art magazine made possible by new reproduction processes following the invention of photography. Art magazines now had international circulations and they, together with the international exhibitions which were also a feature of the 1890s, could make an artist's work known very quickly and widely. Thus the Scottish Art Nouveau architect Charles Rennie Mackintosh (1868–1928) was better appreciated and more influential in Vienna than in Glasgow.

SULLIVAN AND THE SKYSCRAPER

Art Nouveau soon reached the United States, where, however, an indigenous type of proto-Art Nouveau ornament had already been created by the architect Louis Henry Sullivan (1856–1924), though this was not to be of great significance. Sullivan's importance lies elsewhere, in an architecture far more radically contemporary than anything conceived by Art Nouveau architects in Europe. Already in 1892 Sullivan had written that 'it would be greatly for our aesthetic good if we should refrain entirely from the use of ornament for a period of years in order that our thought might concentrate acutely upon the production of buildings well formed and comely in the nude'.

Sullivan worked in Chicago, not hitherto a centre of architectural achievement. But a devastating fire in 1871 was followed by a building boom and this induced a sudden and extraordinary outburst of architectural invention, which Sullivan brought to maturity by giving the sky-

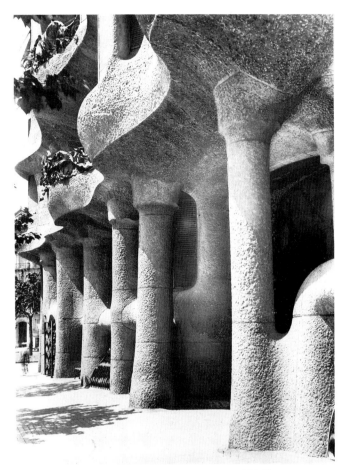

17,33 Antoni Gaudí, Casa Milá, Barcelona, Spain, 1905–7.

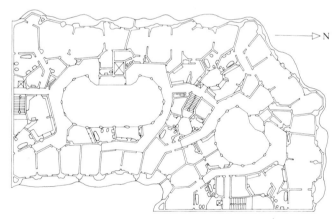

17,34 Plan of Casa Milá.

scraper its classic form. Office buildings in New York had reached 10 or 12 stories by the 1870s and to go beyond this was impossible with traditional materials. Further development depended on the introduction of metal framing, which took place in Chicago in 1883 when William Le Baron Jenney (1832–1907) built the Home Insurance Building (demolished). Skeleton construction free from load-bearing walls soon followed with Holabird & Roche's Tacoma Building in Chicago of 1886–9, though the new principle of construction was not expressed externally.

The Crystal Palace and the Statue of Liberty

METAL AND NEW BUILDING METHODS

Metal as a building material was to be crucial for the development of the skyscraper in Chicago in the 1880s, as we have seen (see p. 731), and it was to be hardly less determining an influence on later nineteenth-century architecture in both the USA and Europe. It had been in partial use for some time, however, first for bridges, of which that at Coalbrookdale, England (1775–6), was notable, and then for iron-framed buildings beginning with Benyon, Bage and Marshall's mill at Shrewsbury, England, in 1796. Metal also facilitated the mass-production of building parts, which quickly followed, so that by the 1840s there were 'cast iron districts' in several American cities – especially New York, where the cast-iron façades introduced by James Bogardus (1800–74) also played a role in the development of prefabrication. This was one of the most important innovations brought about by the Industrial Revolution. By the mid-century completely prefabricated houses of iron were being shipped from England all over the world; one was erected on the Calaba river in central Africa in 1843–4, not to mention the 'portable' houses of the Australian pioneers and the Californian Forty-Niners, or the prefabricated metal churches of colonial missionaries. But the epoch-making event in the history both of metal and prefabrication in building was the construction in 1851 of the Crystal Palace in London (**17,35**) by Joseph Paxton (1803–65), a gardener and designer of greenhouses. It was intended as a temporary structure to house the Great Exhibition of the Works of Industry of All Nations held in London in 1851, a celebration of the wonders of the Industrial Revolution and the new technologies introduced by science.

The Crystal Palace, 1,848 feet (563m) long and 408 feet (124m) high, was constructed almost entirely of cast iron and glass. The great novelty, little appreciated at the time, was its prefabrication. All the component parts had been mass-produced in factories and then assembled on the site, greatly reducing the need for skilled labour as well as saving time. It was the Industrial Revolution's answer to a construction deadline of nine months. No single prefabricated part was allowed to weigh more than a ton (1016kg), and the length of the largest

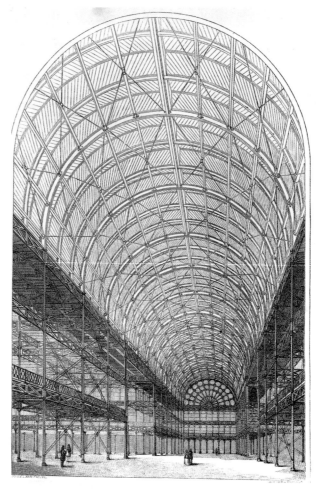

manufacturable pane of glass (4ft 1in, 124.5cm) provided the module for the whole building. Nothing could have been more remote from all earlier principles of design than this purely utilitarian module and, being a temporary and strictly utilitarian structure, it was disassembled when the exhibition closed and rebuilt on another site in the London suburbs. The Crystal Palace was seldom admired by architects of the time. Indeed most of them refused to regard it as 'architecture' at all. Ornamentation having been dispensed with, the

17,35 Joseph Paxton, the Crystal Palace, London 1851. Engraving by R. P. Cuff after W. B. Brounger. Drawings collection, Royal Institute of British Architects, London.

building was without the stylistic and historical references to earlier architecture with which professional architects then felt obliged to clothe their buildings (see pp. 668–9). Even when fully aware of the great innovative possibilities for design and construction offered by new materials and technology, architects were reluctant to abandon the past with its traditional forms and styles. This resulted in visual juxtapositions and contradictions such as that of St Pancras Railway Station and Hotel in London of 1866–76. There a remarkable and ingeniously designed train shed, with a span of 75 feet (22.9m) and for many years the widest in the world, was hidden from public view immediately on its completion. An elaborate and colorful Neo-Gothic hotel of bright red Nottingham bricks with red and gray granite and beige stone was erected in front of it. Similarly, though much less stridently, the American bridge builder John A. Roebling (1806–69) in his Brooklyn Bridge (**17,36**), with a span more than half again as long as any earlier bridge, sustained by galvanized cast-steel cables that were spun in place, combined this feat of pioneering technology with huge, dramatically imposing masonry piers pierced with Gothic arches. Such juxtapositions reveal the disturbing schizophrenia of a period

17,36 John A. Roebling, Brooklyn Bridge, New York, 1869–83.

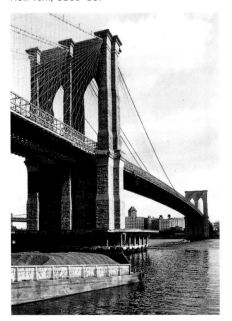

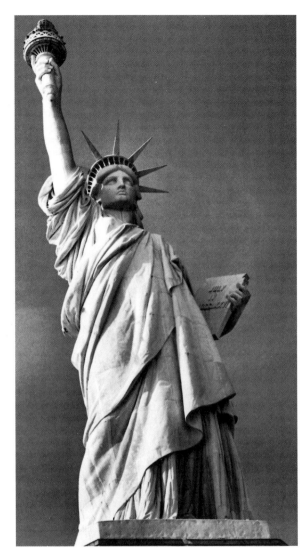

17,37 Frédéric Auguste Bartholdi, *The Statue of Liberty* (originally entitled *Liberty Enlightening the World*), New York Harbour, 1870–86. Hammered copper over wrought-iron pylon designed by Gustave Eiffel, 150ft (46m) high from base to top of torch.

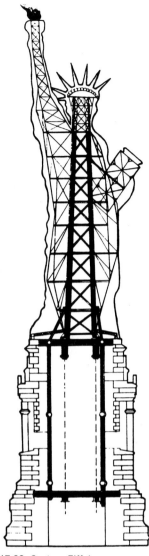

17,38 Gustave Eiffel. Diagram of the construction of *The Statue of Liberty*.

obsessed with the past and its artistic styles and at the same time unable to resist the glamour (and practical advantages) of the new technologies that science and the Industrial Revolution were making available.

The same underlying conflict can be felt, though not seen, in reverse in the Statue of Liberty in New York Harbour. Here the billowing, hammered-copper drapery of a colossal antique Roman Augusta figure symbolizing Liberty Enlightening the World is sustained by an elaborately calculated wrought-iron pylon designed by the French engineer Gustave Eiffel (1832–1923). The complex armature he created consists of a pylon 97 feet

(29.5m) high, with horizontal struts, angle girders, and double diagonal bracing that laces the entire pylon into a powerful, rigid, trussed unit (**17,37; 38**). On its upper two levels is hung the more complex trussed asymmetrical girder that swings out and rises a total of 65 feet (19.8m – 40ft 7ins or 12.4m above the top of the pylon) to form the core of the torch arm. The extraordinary resilience of the pylon and arm structure can be strongly felt by anyone rash enough to stand on the torch on a gusty day, where one senses the 150-foot-high (46m) armature responding like a giant, powerfully elastic spring to the buffeting of the wind.

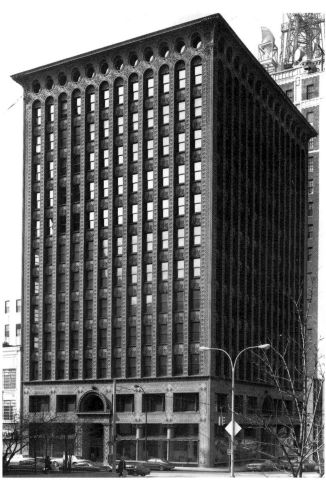

17,39 Louis H. Sullivan, Guaranty Building, Buffalo, New York, 1894–5.

It was Sullivan who made the classic statement of it with the Guaranty (Prudential) Building in Buffalo (**17,39**). In this monumental building the underlying grid of the structural steel frame dominates and controls the whole design so that complete independence from all period styles is reached. The façades become simple but rhythmically beautiful patterns of windows and sills between elegantly slender vertical members, the whole being read as a protective skin stretched between the corner piers, attics and mezzanine floors. The latter, together with the ground story, are conceived as forming a huge pedestal with the main piers isolated by slightly setting back the shop windows. These great piers seem to lift the building right off the ground, allowing space to flow under and into it. Moreover, the building's purpose as well as its hollow-cage structure is expressed in a way that illustrates and interprets Sullivan's famous words, 'form follows function', without any of the doctrinaire rigidity of later functionalists who made his remark their slogan.

DOMESTIC ARCHITECTURE

Skyscapers were American, but another architectural phenomenon had meanwhile occurred on both sides of the Atlantic almost simultaneously – the medium-sized middle-class architect-designed detached house. No aspect of nineteenth-century art and architecture is so quintessentially bourgeois. Up to this date the history of domestic architecture had been little concerned with that of any but the upper classes. If architects designed domestic buildings on a small scale they did so only as picturesque 'retreats' or follies or as adjuncts (vicarages, etc.) to some noble mansion on a large estate. Now middle-class clients began commissioning architects independently to serve their own particular needs. In England a 'picturesque' tradition for the small detached house had begun with John Nash (1752–1835), and the famous Red House at Bexley Heath which Philip Webb (1831–1915) built for William Morris in 1859–60 was still in this tradition, simple and comfortable but with an individual plan to suit the client's special requirements. In the United States a comparable development took place in New England and culminated with the Shingle-style houses of Henry Hobson Richardson (1838–86), which are remarkable for their open internal planning and free compositions (**17,40**), qualities which made Richardson's Neo-Romanesque but no less idiosyncratic public buildings influential in Europe. In England towards the end of the century, Charles Francis Annesley Voysey (1857–1941) brought this informal rustic trend in domestic architecture to its unassuming, but masterly, conclusion with such houses as Norney in Surrey (**17,41**). Voysey's houses were never grand or imposing, never representative in any sense, but were most sensitively planned in intimate relation to nature, with perhaps an old tree preserved near the front door and surrounded by ample and rambling gar-

17,40 Henry H. Richardson, Stoughton House, Cambridge, Massachusetts, 1882–3.

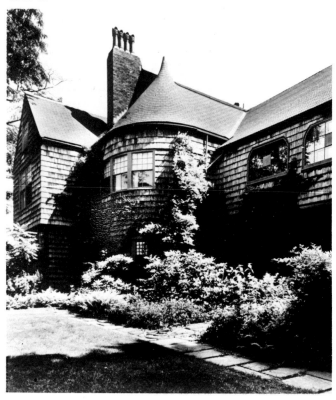

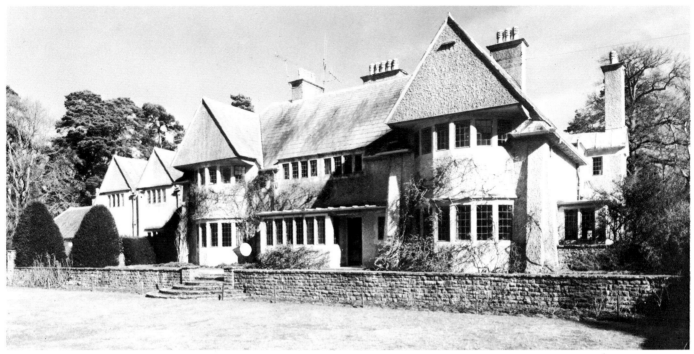

17,41 Charles F. A. Voysey, Norney, near Shackleford, Surrey, England, 1897.

dens. They spread with ease and have low, comfortable, cosy rooms. All is reasonable and friendly and wholesome – the perfect expression of the middle-class city-worker's dream of a lost rural bliss.

CEZANNE

The same post-Industrial Revolution nostalgia for country life inspired much nineteenth-century art, Impressionism above all, and it profoundly informed that of the greatest late nineteenth-century artist, Paul Cézanne (1839–1906). Cézanne, however, was to go far beyond Monet's and Renoir's celebrations of the sunlit natural world. No painter understood so well the limitations and inner contradictions of Impressionism. 'One must reflect', he is recorded as saying. 'The eye is not enough, reflection is needed.' His paintings are the result of prolonged meditation in front of nature, not of the instantaneous recording of its fleeting effects. He wanted to make 'something solid and enduring' out of Impressionism, which seemed to him to lack simplicity, grandeur and, especially, that sense of underlying structural unity that can transform into a whole even the most fragmentary view.

'Art is a harmony parallel to nature', he wrote in an often quoted phrase. The problem was how to adapt the discoveries of Impressionism to this end; how to remain faithful to the truth of visual sensations without sacrificing all sense of order; how to regain form and solidity without losing the brilliance of Impressionist color; indeed, how to regain it by color alone and, in addition, reconcile the flat surface of the canvas with an illusion of depth. For Cézanne had to a unique degree the faculty of

seeing both depth and pattern at the same time and he felt that a picture should exist as a flat design before it creates a three-dimensional illusion. To young artists around the turn of the century, when his work was first becoming known, the magnitude and loneliness of his quest seemed heroic.

Cézanne had exhibited with the Impressionists in 1873 and 1877 but left Paris after a few years and returned to his home town, Aix-en-Provence, where his father was a prosperous banker. There he dedicated himself to his art in isolation and solitude. Of independent means, he had no need to find buyers for his paintings and was almost completely forgotten and unknown until 1895, when his first one-man show was held in Paris at the instigation of Camille Pissarro, with whom Cézanne had worked many years earlier. Thereafter his work gradually won recognition, though widespread knowledge of it – even among avant-garde artists and collectors – came only with the memorial exhibition of 56 paintings at the 1907 Salon.

From the first, Cézanne was attracted by still life. He could set it up in the studio and keep it almost indefinitely for contemplation, apples and other long-lasting fruits being favourites, though they sometimes had to be replaced by wax replicas before he finished painting them. Completely absorbed in what lay before his eyes, he would go on organizing and reorganizing his visual responses until he saw his subject 'correctly'. 'If only I could realize' was a phrase repeatedly on his lips and the term 'realize' was evidently of central importance to his conception of his goal. By it he seems to have meant the process of transforming nature into something amenable to the closed and artificial world of the painted canvas. And to his mind this could only be done by making

CEZANNE TO EMILE BERNARD

Cézanne's letters are sometimes awkward in expression and even ungrammatical but they give an invaluable insight into his aims as an artist. The difficulty he had in expressing himself in words recalls his struggle to 'realize' in painting and they convey, not without pathos, the single-minded sincerity with which he met his daily self-imposed challenge. The painter and critic Emile Bernard (1868–1941) had been a prominent member of Gauguin's Symbolist circle at Pont-Aven in the eighties and nineties when he first saw Cézanne's paintings. He wrote a brief biography of him in 1891. But they did not meet until 1904 when Bernard went to Aix. Their subsequent correspondence is the most important source for Cézanne's thoughts about art and the nearest he ever came to composing a coherent body of theoretical writing. On 15 April 1904 he wrote to Bernard his now famous words, which should not, of course, be understood literally as a prescription to reduce everything to simple geometry.

. . . *treat nature by the cylinder, the sphere, the cone, everything in proper perspective so that each side of an object or a plane is directed towards a central point. Lines parallel to the horizon give breadth – that is, a section of nature or, if you prefer, of the spectacle that the Pater Omnipotens Aeterna Deus spreads out before our eyes. Lines perpendicular to this horizon give depth. But nature for us men is more depth than surface, whence the need of introducing into our light vibrations, represented by reds and yellows, a sufficient amount of blue to give the impression of air.*

A month later he told Bernard that he was:

. . . *progressing very slowly, for nature reveals herself to me in very complex forms; and the progress needed is incessant. One must see one's model correctly and experience it in the right way.*

And in late July 1904 he reaffirmed his belief that to 'achieve progress nature alone counts, and the eye is trained through contact with her'. This he emphasized again a year later:

The Louvre is the book in which to learn to read. We must not, however, be satisfied with retaining the beautiful formulas of our illustrious predecessors. Let us go forth to study beautiful nature, let us try to free our minds from them, let us strive to express ourselves according to our personal temperaments.

Late the following year Cézanne wrote in one of his last letters to Bernard a couple of brief paragraphs that might almost be an artistic testament. He thanked Bernard for giving him the opportunity to describe

. . . *the obstinacy with which I pursue the realization of that part of nature, which, coming into our line of vision, gives the picture. Now the theme to develop is that – wherever our temperament or power in the presence of nature may be – we must render the image of what we see, forgetting everything that existed before us. Which, I believe, must permit the artist to give his entire personality whether great or small.*

Now being old, nearly 70 years, the sensations of color which give light, are the reason for the abstractions which prevent me from either covering my canvas or continuing the delimitation of the objects when their points of contact are fine and delicate; from which it results that my image or picture is incomplete. On the other hand the planes are placed one on top of the other from whence neo-impressionism emerged, which outlines the contours with a black stroke, a failing that must be fought at all costs. Well, nature when consulted gives us the means of attaining this end . . . .

Shortly before he died, in a letter to his son Paul, he referred again to the danger for an artist of frequenting museums and relying on the 'schemata' provided by the great artists of the past. Bernard, for example,

. . . *simply turns his back in practice on what he expounds in his writings; his drawings are merely old-fashioned rubbish which result from his dreams of art, based not on the emotion of nature but on what he has been able to see in the museums, and more still on a philosophic mind which comes from the too great knowledge he has of the masters he admires.*

(J. Rewald ed., *Paul Cézanne's Letters*, tr. M. Kay, London 1941)

visible that unifying harmony which unveils itself little by little to the artist in answer to some profound demand of the spirit.

It was the agonizing difficulty he had in 'realizing' combined with the constant struggle to integrate his natural sense of flat pattern with his consciousness of solid form that led to what were sometimes thought to be awkwardnesses and clumsy distortions in his work. In one of his best known still-life paintings, for instance, the horizontal surfaces seem to tilt upwards and there are other features which make the perspective appear incorrect (**17,42**). Yet an extraordinary sense of monumental gravity and grandeur, of everything having found its duly appointed place as in some sonorous Bach chorale, is

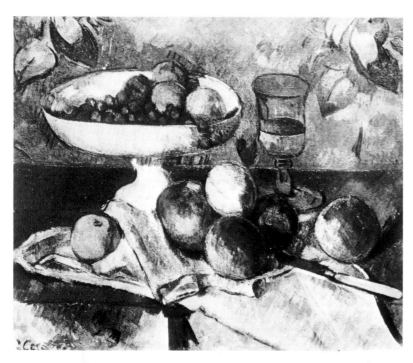

17,42 Paul Cézanne, *Fruit Bowl, Glass and Apples*,
1879–82. Canvas, 18 × 21½ins (45.7 × 54.6cm).
Private collection, Paris.

17,43 *Below* Paul Cézanne, *Mont Sainte-Victoire*, 1885–7.
Canvas, 25¾ × 32⅛ins (64.5 × 81.6cm). Metropolitan
Museum of Art, New York (Bequest of Mrs H. O. Havemeyer,
1929. H. O. Havemeyer Collection).

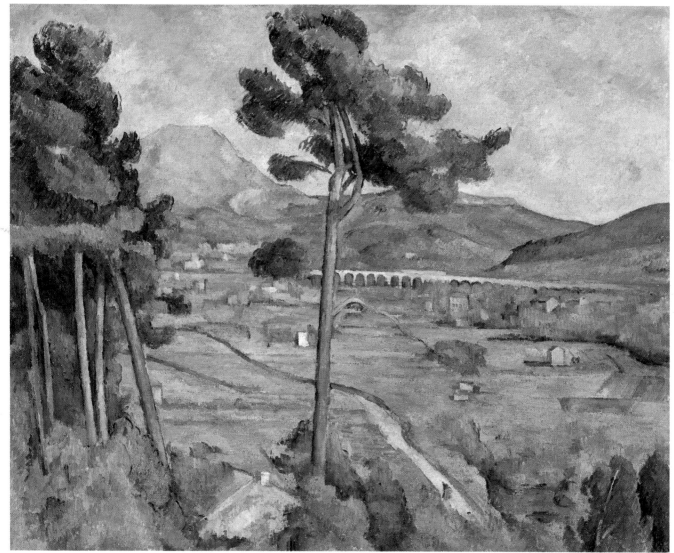

evoked by this quite modest depiction of a commonplace subject. The design is very closely-knit, every part of the canvas being equally worked. Moreover, apart from the bowl and glass, everything has been reduced to its essential form, either spherical or rectangular, which enforces a great sense of weight and mass. The same heavily rounded curves echo each other across the canvas, creating rhythms of such momentum and pull that all the objects depicted take on the same elementary shapes – like rocks and stones ground smooth into cognate forms by the endless motion of the tides. Thus, the ellipses of the bowl and glass become rounded oblongs and the bowl's stem is set very slightly off-centre to accord with the general design. Evenly worked with thick, regular brush-strokes slanting from right to left as they descend without regard to the contours of the objects, the whole surface of the painting is united into a rich consistency, like enamel or lacquer, and saturated with color.

Cézanne's voluptuous sense of color and passion for solid construction produced unprecedented effects of mass and volume in still-life painting. With the more evasive subject of landscape the problem of rendering depth in space by color became crucial. Linear perspective and tonal modelling would detract from the truth of his optical impressions and were therefore to be avoided. 'Color must reveal every interval in depth', he said, through the recession of cool colors, the advance of warm colors and variations in intensity. The challenge this presented released all the boldness and largeness of his vision. It was partly in response to it that he began, after about 1882, to paint more thinly with a restricted palette of pale greens, earth colors and a wide range of blues, with which limited means the scenery of his native Provence – scenery which had hardly ever been painted before – was endowed with all the nobility of a Classical landscape. The seeming simplicity and straightforwardness of his views of Mont Sainte-Victoire conceal most complex and refined constructions (**17,43**). Parallel lines, echoing forms, balancing contrasts unite into a surface pattern elements that also represent things in depth so that complete integration of his dual vision is attained. We look out across the valley, past an evergreen pine, towards Mont Sainte-Victoire. He was to paint this great rocky outcrop near Aix again and again, in all seasons and at all times of day, until, towards the end of his life, its odd, almost unreal contours came to symbolize the exaltation he experienced before, as he put it, 'the depth and breadth of nature or, if you prefer, the spectacle that the Pater Omnipotens Aeterna Deus spreads out before our eyes'. The spirituality inherent in Cézanne's work is felt most deeply in his last majestic, but sombre, paintings of this strange mountain – remote, unchanging, divine in its inti-

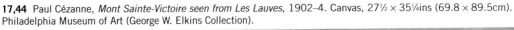

17,44 Paul Cézanne, *Mont Sainte-Victoire seen from Les Lauves*, 1902–4. Canvas, 27½ × 35¼ins (69.8 × 89.5cm). Philadelphia Museum of Art (George W. Elkins Collection).

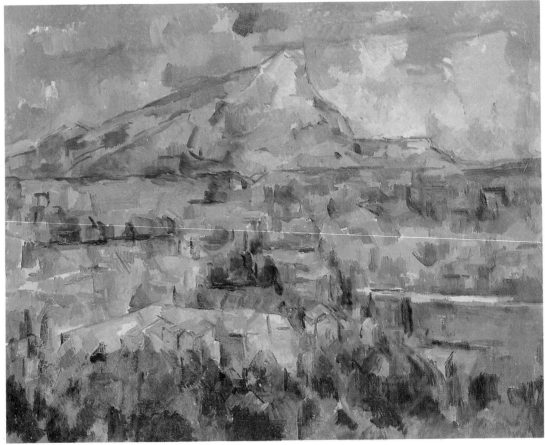

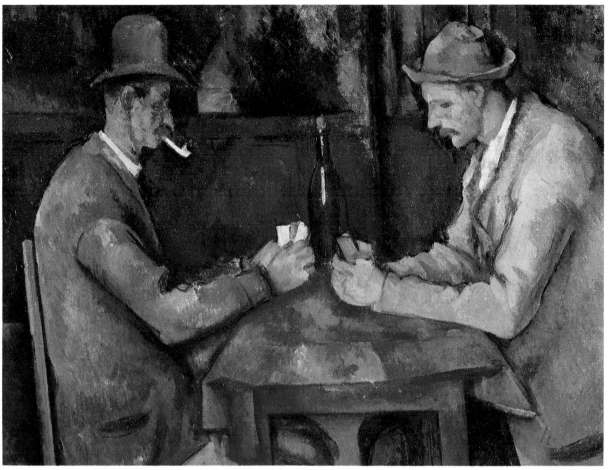

17,45 Paul Cézanne, *Cardplayers*, c. 1890–5. Canvas, 18¾ × 22½ins (47.5 × 57cm). Louvre, Paris.

mations of eternity – silhouetted against a serene or lowering sky (**17,44**).

The absence of figures or of any 'human interest' in Cézanne's landscapes and still-life paintings should not be understood as implying in any way an impersonal attitude or that he was concerned mainly with formal artistic problems. His portraits, especially of his own household, are among the finest of all his works. Those of his gardener Vallier and of an old woman with a rosary – said to have been an aged nun who had escaped from a convent, and was found wandering and taken in as a servant by Cézanne – have all the monumental gravity of his landscapes, as well as a deeply-felt and pondered humanity. Though anonymous, his groups of card players in a local café are equally intimate and filled with human warmth.

One of the last depicts two of his peasant neighbours facing each other in silent concentration across a rickety café table (**17,45**). It sums up his achievement in a totally unconventional image of bold frontality and horizontality broken right down the middle by a vertical line which would have been anathema to an academician. The extreme refinement of its resonant harmonies of purples, deep blues, black, reddish brown and yellow tan combine with its restraint and directness and unpretentious simplicity to convey all the moral dignity of Cézanne's single-minded pursuit of an ideal. With such great works he gave an answer – not the only answer but a wonderfully coherent one – to the basic questions Impressionism had raised about art and nature, perception and reality, and about the nature of reality itself.

CHAPTER EIGHTEEN

INDIGENOUS ARTS OF AFRICA, THE AMERICAS, AUSTRALIA AND OCEANIA

The term 'primitive art' was coined at the beginning of the present century to categorize objects which had not previously been regarded in the West as 'works of art' at all, that is to say objects from areas on the margin of or beyond the cultural influence of Europe, the Near East, India, China and Japan. In a pioneer study of *Primitive Culture* (1871) Edward Tylor, the first professor of anthropology at Oxford, mentioned the arts only in so far as they illuminated his problem of 'determining the relation of the mental condition of savages to that of civilized man'. Ethnographical museums founded in the nineteenth century – Copenhagen 1841, Berlin 1856, Leiden 1864, Cambridge, Mass. 1866, Dresden 1875, Paris 1878 among others – all adopted the same attitude. Their aim was to illustrate the ground base from which Western civilization had supposedly ascended and they can now be seen as monuments to that cult of progress enshrined in Charles Darwin's *The Origin of Species* (1859), subtitled *The Preservation of Favoured Races in the Struggle for Life*.

Objects formerly preserved as odd and isolated examples of human ingenuity in cabinets of 'natural and artificial curiosities' – *Wunderkammern*, as they were called in Renaissance Germany (see pp. 514–5) – were set together with prehistoric artifacts in the context of the evolution of material culture. Their alien strangeness was neutralized to some extent by incorporation into that cult of history or 'historicism' which became one of the dominant preoccupations of Western thought in the nineteenth century. The majority of exhibits in ethnographical museums were weapons and other utensils brought back by explorers, traders and missionaries from Africa, America and, after the mid-eighteenth century, the islands of the South Pacific. More specialized collections were built up by the colonial powers. Colonial exhibitions were also held (Amsterdam 1883, London 1887, Tervuren, outside Brussels, 1897), their aim being quite clearly indicated in the entrance to the museum at Tervuren by contemporary European sculptures personifying

The visual arts	Historical landmarks
pre-1779 Kukailimoku (18,3)	**1776–9** Cook's third voyage, NW coast of America and Hawaii
pre-1821 A'a from Rurutu (18,4)	**1804–5** Lewis and Clark cross N. America
pre-1823 Staff-god from Rarotonga (18,5)	**1807** British abolition of slave-trade
pre-1835 Maori canoe prow (18,6)	**1830** French begin conquest of Algeria
c. 1840 Tlingit bear screen (18,25)	**1840** British take New Zealand
c. 1842 Ancestor figure (18,7)	**1846** Melville, Typee: *a Peep at Polynesian Life*
c. 1850 Tlingit mask (18,24)	**1851** British occupy Lagos (Nigeria)
	1859 Oregon completes US expansion across N. America
	1864 British annex southern Ghana
	1873–4 First British war against Asante: capital sacked
	1874 British annex Fiji Islands
	1878 British-Zulu massacres. Treaty of Berlin partitions Africa among European powers
	1879 Rebellion against European colonists in Lesotho
c. 1880 Tlingit 'totem-pole' (18,18)	**1880** France annexes Tahiti
	1885 Belgian Congo acquired by king of the Belgians. Germany annexes Tanganyika, Zanzibar and northern New Guinea
c. 1890 Wobé mask (18,43)	**1891** Gauguin settles in Tahiti
Kota reliquary figure (18,41)	**1893** Guinea and Ivory Coast become French colonies
	1897 Benin sacked by British
	1898 United States annexes Hawaii and Philippines
c. 1900 Bangwa king and mother of twins (18,39)	**1902** Conrad, *Heart of Darkness*
	1904 Nationalist risings in German W. Africa suppressed
c. 1910 Asmat memorial poles (18,11)	**1919** German colonies in Africa pass to Britain and France

Belgium bringing peace, prosperity and Christianity to the Congo!

Although the ideas and assumptions on which these museums were based have fallen into disrepute, together with the colonialism they celebrated, the word 'primitive' is still applied to the objects exhibited in them (although nowadays 'tribal' is sometimes preferred). The term 'primitive' has positive as well as negative overtones with reference to urban man's regression from the primal state of nature – a recurrent theme in Western art and literature (pastoral poetry being among its finest expressions), and one of special relevance in the heavily urbanized and industrialized West of the late nineteenth century, as we have seen (p. 725). The heterogeneous carvings, paintings and compositions in various materials which the term has been stretched to cover have little in common except their divergence from Western conceptions, especially of naturalism, and the fact that they evolved – like nearly all major artistic forms at all times and places – in intimate association with religion and magic. They are expressions of humanity's common and unending endeavour to live in harmony with, or to control, natural and supernatural forces; very seldom are they merely decorative in intention. They were, however, products of widely dissimilar social groups which integrated the arts into complex structures of laws, customs, morals, knowledge and beliefs. And, unlike the illustrative art of the proselytizing world-wide religions, 'primitive art' tends towards the deliberately arcane. The precise significance of a cult object, the mask worn in a ritual, the carving on the support of a house, or the painting on a shield, was limited to the initiated, sometimes to no more than a single sector of the community, and it has become ever less accessible as the structures of these societies have been transformed, if not completely disrupted, by contact with the West.

OCEANIA

The vast stretch of the Pacific known as Oceania is conventionally divided into three geographical and cultural areas: Polynesia, a triangle with sides some 4,000 miles (6,400km) long from New Zealand to Hawaii in the north and Rapanui – or Easter Island as it is more widely known – in the east; Melanesia, comprising New Guinea and a group of islands stretching to the western limits of Polynesia; and Micronesia, a scattering of small islands north

Oceania

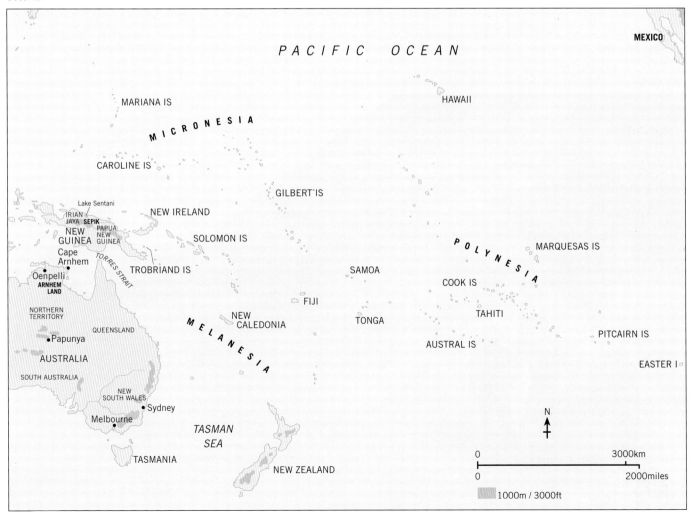

of Melanesia. The original populations immigrated from Asia. After about 26,000 BC a succession of groups settled in Melanesia, which has remained multilingual. Polynesia was the last part of the world to be populated – Fiji by 1300 BC, Tonga by 1200 BC and Samoa by 1000 BC. Not until shortly before the beginning of the Christian era did people occupy the westerly Fiji islands and then spread to Hawaii and Easter Island in about AD 300–600, and to New Zealand in about AD 750–1000. They were horticulturalists, fishermen and expert canoe-builders with an hereditary hierarchy and spoke a single Austronesian language. The dialects subsequently developed in the various subgroups of islands thus had the same origin, and the arts similarly branched from a single root-stock.

POLYNESIA

After the initial settlement Polynesia remained isolated from the rest of the world until the mid-eighteenth century. Although Fiji had been visited by A. J. Tasman in 1643 and Easter Island by another Dutch sailor, Jacob Roggeveen, in 1722, it was only in the 1760s that Europeans reached Tahiti in the centre of the Polynesian triangle – an English naval captain, Samuel Wallis, in 1767, the French scientist and explorer Louis de Bougainville next year and James Cook on his three voyages of discovery (1768–79). To these explorers, especially the observant Cook with his trained naturalists and artists, we owe most of our knowledge of Polynesian culture. For contact with the outside world was fatal for the Polynesians, who soon succumbed to diseases carried from Europe, especially syphilis. Their way of life was changed by the introduction of metal tools and fire-arms; their traditional beliefs and rituals were undermined by Christian missionaries.

Easter Island's great monolithic heads and half-length figures, up to 60 feet (18.3m) high, are the most imposing Polynesian sculptures (18,1). More than 600 survive, carved over a long period from about AD 900 to 1500, perhaps as late c. 1700, when the majority were thrown down, probably in a tribal war, and others were left unfinished in the volcanic crater where they were quarried. Bodies are summarily rendered and the heads are no more than giant masks, all with the same forceful features, prominent noses, pursed lips, long ears, massive brows and deep sunken eye-sockets. Some, wearing cylindrical crowns of red rock, were set with their backs to the sea on stone platforms beneath which the dead were buried near the shore. Others are thought to have marked three long avenues across the interior. By the time of Cook's visit the islanders seemed to have lost interest in them; but Cook recognized their connection with the cult of ancestors of a ruling caste. They are now known to have been symbols of the power which, throughout Polynesia, ruling chiefs were believed to inherit from the gods and retain after death when they were themselves deified. In this way they are comparable with other images of divine kingship – the faces inscrutably staring out from the towers of

18,1 Monolithic images, AD c. 900–1500, on the slopes of Ranoraraku, Easter Island.

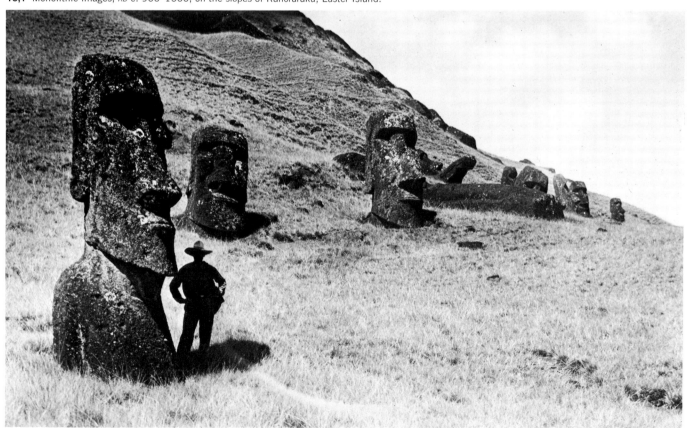

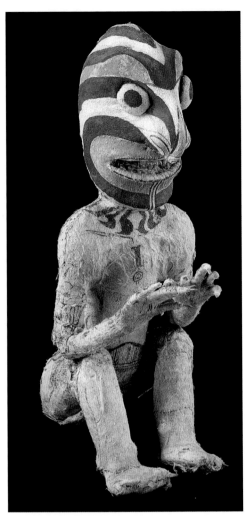

18,2 Seated figure, from Easter Island, pre-1899. Painted wood and bark-cloth, 15ins (38cm) high. Peabody Museum of Ethnology and Archeology, Harvard University, Cambridge, Mass.

Angkor Thom (6,67) (contemporary with some Easter Island statues), for instance, or the much earlier ancient Egyptian royal statues and the Great Sphinx (2,30) – and are likewise the expressions of an hereditary politico-religious structure. Their peculiar jutting, block-like form is probably due mainly to the nature of the only material available for large-scale work, a grainy, easily worked tufa. But only stone, shell and bone implements were available.

Elsewhere in Polynesia stone sculptures were carved, though not on so gigantic a scale nor in such quantity. Greater use was made of wood, which was scarce on Easter Island and could be used only for small figures (18,2) and the plaques inscribed with symbols of arcane significance. In the Hawaiian Islands some images of gods were composed of basketry covered with red, yellow and black feathers, dogs' teeth in their mouths and pearly shells for eyes (18,3). Priests carried them in religious ceremonies and also in battles, which were almost a ritual, attended by chiefs wearing similarly made helmets and capes of the finest featherwork – a prerogative of the gods and the ruling clans descended from them. The example illustrated here was one of several collected by Cook in

1779 when he was hailed as a god by the Hawaiians (although they later killed him). They are the earliest examples known (now widely dispersed in museums). Basketry and featherwork quickly perish in the tropics, and so also does wood.

Few wood-carvings date from much before the arrival of Europeans, and the vast majority of those produced in the following decades were destroyed as Christianity spread across Polynesia in the nineteenth century. Only a few were saved, mainly by missionaries who sent them to Europe for exhibition as trophies of their victory over heathenism. One of the most remarkable was collected in 1821 by an English missionary who recorded its significance (18,4). A'a, the deified ancestor of the ruling clan on the island of Rurutu (in the Austral group south of Tahiti),

18,3 The war-god Kukailimoku, from Hawaii, pre-1779. Feathers over wickerwork, pearl shells and dog teeth, 3ft 4¾ins (1.04m) high. British Museum, London.

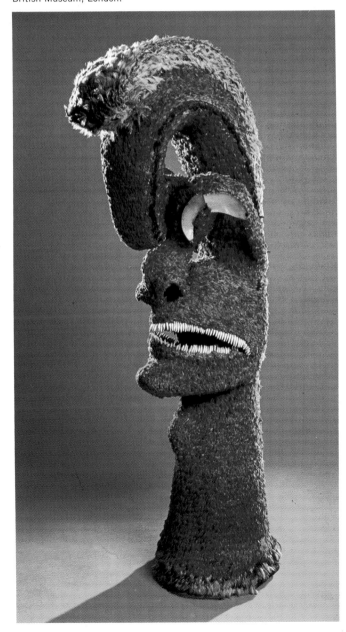

is shown with his progeny, tiny figures in relief, which take the place of his physical features, and a number of statuettes enclosed in a cavity in the back. The phallic shape of the figure emphasizes its procreative symbolism. Other cult figures called staff-gods, from Rarotonga (in the Cook Islands west of Tahiti), similarly combine images of gods with their descendants (**18,5**). They ranged in length between 28 inches (71cm) and 18 feet (5.5m) and were carried and displayed horizontally. At one end there is a highly schematized blade-shaped head and arms of the progenitive god with a succession of little figures rising from his body, alternately full-face and in profile – those in profile with penis erect. The staff itself terminated in a phallus. But this elaborately carved sexual imagery had less importance for the Rarotongans than the feathers and pieces of shell representing the soul of the god and enclosed in yards of bark-cloth wound round the centre of the staff. Missionaries called them idols, though the Polynesians regarded cult images as no more than temporary 'receptacles' into which the spirit of a god might be induced by rituals. (Idolatry, the worship of man-made objects rather than of the spirits they represent, is, in fact, a very rare phenomenon in any part of the world.) Simpler figures, alway naked, usually male, sometimes intended to stand on the prows of canoes, were carved elsewhere in Polynesia in a remarkably wide variety of local styles. All of them expressed similar beliefs in religion and magic.

The Maori, whose forebears were probably canoe parties from central Polynesia driven to the shores of New Zealand by storms, created an art conditioned by a colder climate, different natural resources and a social structure based on kinship rather than on class hierarchy. They excelled in relief carving, often on a large scale, for canoes (**18,6**) and for the lintels, barge-boards and posts of assembly houses, communal storehouses and stockades protecting villages. The indigenous *totara* and *kauri* pine, light, tough, durable and much softer than the types of wood found in tropical Polynesia, permitted effects of greater elaboration and curvilinear vitality. Whole surfaces were intricately worked with spirals (a favourite motif), scrolls and chevrons. A large relief of an ancestor, club in hand, tongue protruding from open mouth, joints of limbs rendered as spirals which suggest the capability of movement, is characteristic (**18,7**). It is one of a series attached to supports in an assembly house, the physical embodiment of a tribe, where its members were surrounded and protected by the benevolent spirits of ancestors – menacing only to outsiders.

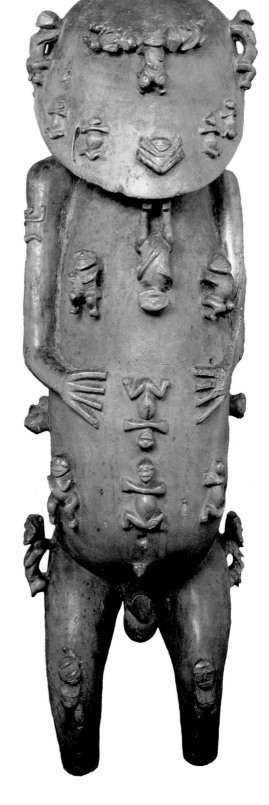

18,4 *Right* The god A'a, from Rurutu, Austral Islands, pre-1821. Ironwood, 3ft 8ins (1.12m) high. British Museum, London.

18,5 Staff-god, from Rarotonga, Cook Islands, pre-1823. Wood, 28½ins (72.5cm) long. University Museum of Archeology and Anthropology, Cambridge, England.

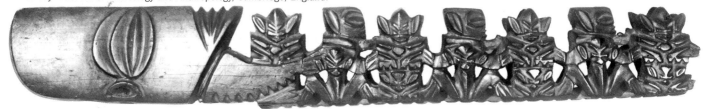

CAPTAIN COOK AND THE ARTS OF THE PACIFIC

On the three voyages of discovery between 1768 and 1779 made by Captain James Cook (1728–79) neither he himself nor any of the draftsmen he took with him were greatly impressed by the arts and crafts they found. They were interested in them as curiosities, their descriptions frequently using the term 'curious', which at the time meant strange, odd or peculiar though also, sometimes, finely worked, i.e. of good craftsmanship. The draftsman Sydney Parkinson (d. 1771), for instance, described New Zealand paddles as 'curiously stained' and the Maoris themselves as 'curiously tattooed'. Occasionally he went further, saying some woodwork was 'very ingeniously wrought' and a flaxen garment 'ornamented with a beautiful wrought border'. Cook himself admired Tahitian canoes, of which he wrote that

. . . they have high curved sterns, the head also curves a little and both are ornamented with the image of a Man carved in wood, very little inferior of the like kind done by common ship carvers in England.

In Cook's opinion the carving on New Zealand canoes was 'neither ill designed nor executed' (18,6), and Parkinson went even further:

The men have a particular taste for carving their boats, paddles, boards to put on their houses, tops of walking sticks, and even their boat valens are carved in a variety of flourishes, turnings and windings, that are unbroken; but their favourite figures seems to be a volute, or spiral, which they vary many ways, single, double, and triple, and with as much truth as if done from mathematical draughts: yet the only instruments we have seen are a chizzel, and an axe made of stone. Their fancy, indeed, is very wild and extravagant, and I have seen no imitation of nature in any of their performances, unless the head, and the heart shaped tongue hanging out of the mouth of it, may be called natural.

A more favourable view was taken on Cook's second voyage. Maori cloaks, for instance, had such 'elegant borders' that they 'might have passed for the work of a much more polished nation'. However, the explorers were perplexed by the sculpture on Easter Island (18,1). Of one figure Cook's German draftsman, Georg Foster (1754–94), remarked that the

. . . eyes, nose, and mouth were scarcely marked on a lumpish ill-shaped head; and the ears, which were excessively long . . . were better executed than any other part, though a European artist would have been ashamed of them.

On Cook's last voyage he explored, in the spring of 1778, the Alaskan and north-west coast of America where he was greatly intrigued by Nootkan wood bird masks, of which he wrote in his journal:

The men on some occasions wore Masks of which they have many and of various sorts such as the human face, the head of birds and other Animals, the most of them both well designed and executed. Whether these masks are worn as an Ornament in their public entertainments, or as some thought, to guard the face against the arrows of the enemy, or as decoys in hunting, I shall not pretend to say; probably on all these occasions. The only times however we saw them was by some of the chiefs when they made us a ceremonious visit and in some of their Songs.

(R. Joppien and B. Smith, *The Art of Captain Cook's Voyages*, New Haven and London 1985)

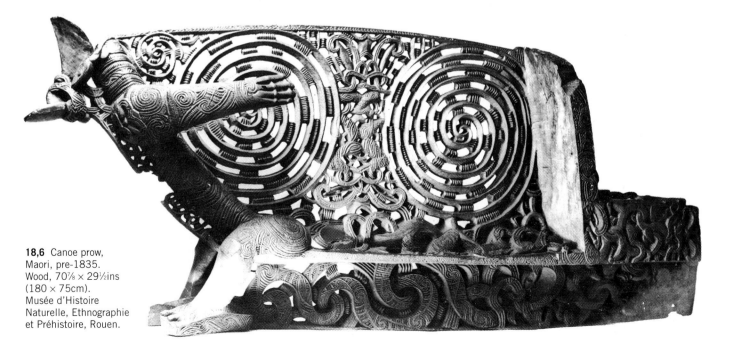

18,6 Canoe prow, Maori, pre-1835. Wood, 70⅞ × 29½ins (180 × 75cm). Musée d'Histoire Naturelle, Ethnographie et Préhistoire, Rouen.

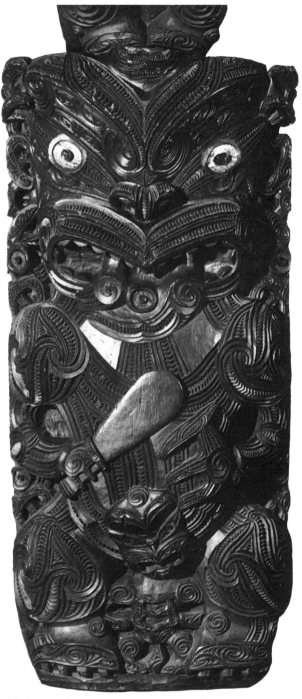

course, used for a very widespread and ancient practice in many cultures, see p. 161.) Body painting, from which tattooing developed, is probably the oldest of the arts of mankind and the one which most obviously distinguished human beings from other creatures. Lasting no more than a single life-time, it is also the least permanent and yet, paradoxically, so strongly regulated by tradition passed from one generation to another that it may well have kept alive motifs which appear in other, more enduring media widely separated in time and space. Tattooing in the most intricate designs, clearly of remote origin, was and still is practised all over the area between China, Indonesia and the South Pacific (**18,8**).

The decoration of the living human body is closely associated with that of the shield made to protect it. Shields are perhaps the most telling instances of the various ways in which art had been used to give additional meaning or magic power to a utilitarian object. Reliefs and paintings applied to them seem to have been seldom merely ornamental, even if they indicated no more than the bearer's membership of a group or his status within it. The precise significance of such designs is, nevertheless, often elusive. The painting on a shield from the Trobriand

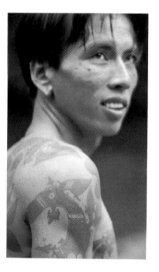

18,8 *Left* Tattoo patterns used by the Iban of Sarawak.

18,7 Ancestor figure, c. 1842. Wood, 55 × 25⅛ins (139.5 × 64cm). National Museum of New Zealand.

The face is strikingly reminiscent of bronze ritual vessels made in Shang dynasty China about two millennia before New Zealand was populated. Other Maori carvings are still closer to the *taotie* masks in their combination of two profiles with a frontal view (2,63).

No direct connection can be established, but perhaps the tattooing with which the Maori, like other Polynesians, covered their bodies may provide a clue. (The word tattoo is, like the word taboo, of Polynesian origin, introduced into European languages by Cook but now, of

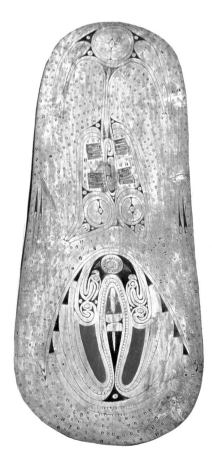

18,9 *Right* Shield from the Trobriand Islands, late 19th century. Painted wood and cane, about 33ins (84cm) high. University Museum of Archeology and Anthropology, Cambridge, England.

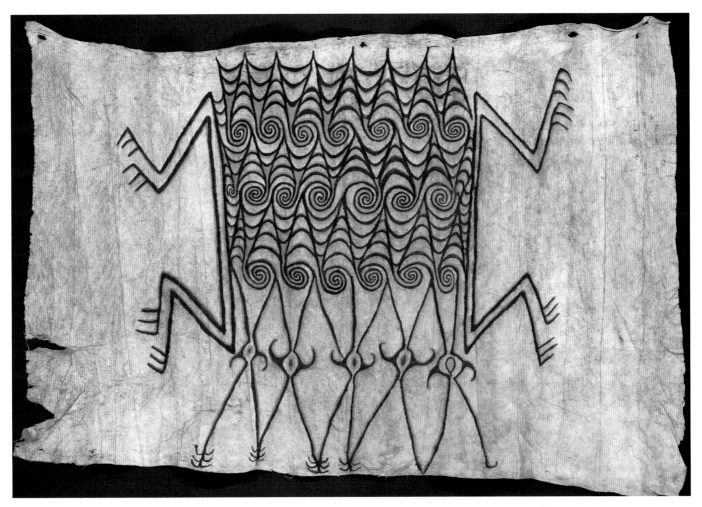

18,10 Mourning garment, collected in 1926 from Saboiboi, Lake Sentani, Irian Jaya.
Black and red pigments on bark-cloth, 3ft 8ins × 5ft 9ins (1.12 × 1.75m). Museum für Völkerkunde, Basel.

Islands off New Guinea has been variously interpreted by well-informed anthropologists as the representation of a witch – a Melanesian Medusa intended to petrify an enemy with fear – or a copulating couple (**18,9**). There are several other shields from the same area, similarly painted with symmetrical curvilinear forms, derived apparently from parts of the human body, which suggest not only an arcane symbolism but also aesthetic preferences peculiar to Trobriand Islanders.

An enthralling composition of scrolls flanked by angular motifs is painted on a sheet of bark-cloth from the Lake Sentani area on the north coast of Irian Jaya (western New Guinea) (**18,10**). This type of material, though fabricated also in Africa and South America, is a distinctive product of Oceania and often called *tapa* (the corruption of an Hawaiian word). Many travellers, including Herman Melville in his semi-fictional *Typee* (1846), described how strips of the fibrous inner bark of the mulberry and other trees were soaked, scraped and laboriously hammered into supple paper-thin sheets, almost exclusively by women – their most notable contribution to the arts and crafts of Oceania. The islands echoed with the clear, ringing, musical sound of the hammer-blows as the women

worked to satisfy the perennial need for cloth. Much was sun-bleached to a dazzling whiteness, otherwise dyed red or yellow, or enlivened with paintings in a range of styles conditioned by local traditions and also historical events. It was used for clothing the living and shrouding the dead, for covering masks and figures of wood or wicker, and increasingly from the mid-nineteenth century it was sold to foreigners, sometimes having been made specifically for them. More notable are the pieces, up to three yards (2.74m) wide and several hundred long, which continued to be made for rituals of exchanging gifts, a notable feature of life in the islands, then rolled and stored in élite houses as status symbols. Because of the perishable material, the paintings may have had only a temporary, one might say topical, significance that is now irrecoverable even when they have by chance been preserved – as in the case of the sheet illustrated here, though the angular elements resemble the motif of the praying mantis that recurs in the art of head-hunting groups (18,10). Such cloths were worn as mourning garments and hung above graves in the Sentani area. (Although now superseded by imported textiles for practical purposes, bark-cloth is still made by women in some islands for ceremonial use but mainly for sale.)

MELANESIA AND MICRONESIA

In Melanesia a still wider range of artistic styles was evolved than in the scattered islands of Polynesia. They can be broadly grouped, just as the 800 or so languages spoken in New Guinea have been categorized in linguistic groups called phyla – though, strangely, these do not correspond with the artistic styles. Their diversity reflects the corporate individuality of the many small tribes which were until very recently in a state of almost constant warfare. The Asmat on the marshy coastal plain of south-western New Guinea, for instance, developed their own kind of memorial for victims of head-hunting raids: tall poles, up to 37 feet (11.3m) high and carved from single tree-trunks with human figures balanced precariously on top of one another (**18,11**). As head-hunting had a ritualistic sexual significance, these poles were also believed to promote fertility and the elaborately worked

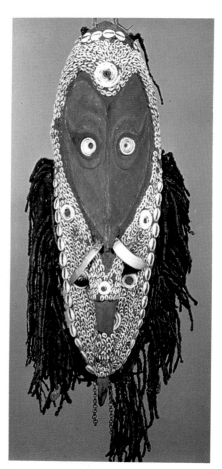

18,12 Mask from Kanganaman, Middle Sepik, Papua New Guinea, collected 1950–3. Wood with overmodelling, cowrie inlays and boar tusks, 23¼ins (59cm) high. Tropical Museum, Amsterdam.

18,11 Asmat memorial poles, from Irian Jaya, early 20th century. Wood, paint and sago-palm leaves, 17–18ft (5.2–5.5m) high. Metropolitan Museum of Art, New York (Michael C. Rockefeller Memorial Collection of Primitive Art, Gift of Nelson A. Rockefeller and Mrs Mary C. Rockefeller, 1965).

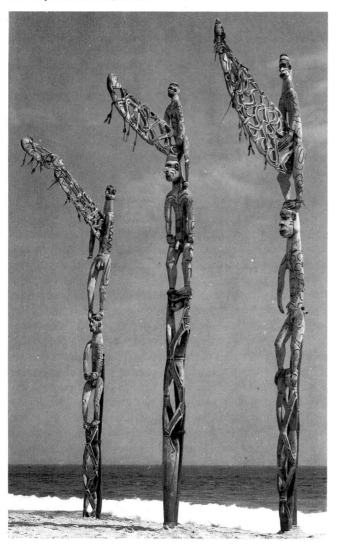

projecting member is phallic. Poles with the same function and significance were carved by the neighbouring Mimika but in a different style, more solid and much less elegant and dynamic. In the valley of the Sepik river in northern New Guinea a rich variety of styles of carving was and still is practised. Masks intended to be worn or carried in rituals or hung on the wall of a hut are the most striking products, brilliantly colored and often embellished with shells, boar-tusks, feathers and locks of human hair (**18,12**). A long-nosed face recurs in many and they all incorporate symbolic elements (the chin extended into a phallus), displaying amazing ingenuity in the assembling of materials to create images of supernatural vitality. Large wooden hooks made to be hung from roof-beams to carry baskets for food, clothing and precious objects are often intricate works of sculpture incorporating human figures or long-nosed heads similar to those of masks (**18,13**).

In the island of New Ireland, north-east of New Guinea, artistic attention centred on the *malanggan*, a term that covers ceremonies commemorating the dead as well as the statues, masks, carved and painted boards, and string instruments used in them. Many of these objects were made for a single, particular ceremony and thrown away afterwards. Ancestor figures, on the other hand, were preserved for a time in huts built specially for them (**18,14**). They are of an impersonal, collective character, not, apparently, representations of individuals. Usually symmetrical in structure, they are carved with great intricacy from

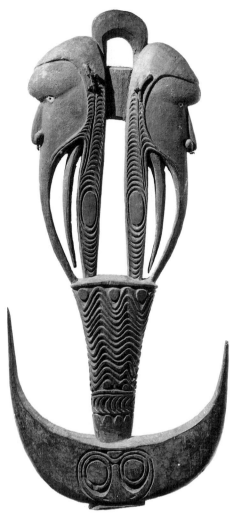

18,13 Double-ended suspension hook, from Middle Sepik, Papua New Guinea, early 20th century. Carved and painted wood, 29⅛ins (74cm) high. Musée de l'Homme, Paris.

single blocks of wood, painted in bright colors, sometimes inlaid with shells and usually provided with plant fibres for hair. Although they are recognizably human in inspiration, the extensive use of open-work in the carving and the complex painted patterns on the surface reduce their solidity, giving them an insubstantial, perhaps intentionally 'spiritual' rather than corporeal appearance. Diverse styles of carving were practised in different parts of the island, although it is no more than 200 miles (320km) long and very narrow. These sculptures from New Ireland have, none the less, a generic similarity which sets them apart from other types or styles of Melanesian art.

There were few hereditary chieftainships in Melanesia, so there is little or no dynastic art. Power within a tribe was acquired by individual prowess (in head-hunting or other ways) and this goes far to explain the lack of interest in objects intended to endure for more than a short while. Few surviving examples of Melanesian art can be dated earlier than the mid-nineteenth century. And although traditional ways of tribal life survive in New Guinea and masks continue to be made much as before, even if with metal tools, the rituals·for which they are made have, with the pacification of the island, lost much of their power. In the Sepik region the building of a ceremonial house is nowadays marked by the killing of pigs, instead of men, and their skulls are now hung from its roof. Paradoxically, however, the population has declined since head-hunting was virtually suppressed. In 1932 the great anthropologist Bronislaw Malinowski, who devoted his life to the study of Melanesia, remarked: 'Ethnology is in a sadly ludicrous, not to say tragic, position, that at the very moment when it begins to put its workshop in order . . . the material of its study melts away with hopeless rapidity.'

18,14 *Below Malanggan* masks and figures, New Ireland. Bamboo, palm and croton leaves and painted wood. Museum für Völkerkunde, Basel.

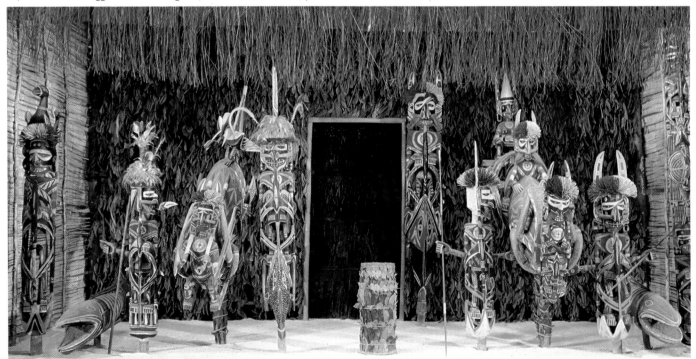

AUSTRALIA

Human settlement began early, perhaps as much as 70,000 years ago when Australia was easily accessible by land from Asia. As a consequence of a great rise in the sea-level about 14,000 years ago, however, the continent was isolated from the rest of the world (apart from Papua New Guinea by way of islands in the Torres Strait) until the arrival of British settlers little more than 200 years ago. The vast landmass was peopled by small widely dispersed groups with uncentralized social structures who subsisted by hunting and gathering. Although they spoke different languages, they had similar religious beliefs and rituals focused on the natural environment with social and moral codes established by mythical ancestors who moved across the land creating all things. For this complex of ideas, which provides the main subject-matter of their art, survivors of the original population, categorized as 'Aborigines', have adopted a pidgin-English word, 'Dreamings', derived from a mistranslation and given a meaning quite distinct from European notions of dreams. 'Dreamings' are not visions experienced in sleep. Nor are they confined to events in the story of human genesis. They are ever present in natural species, sacred places, whole stretches of land and the paths traversed by the creator ancestors. In the course of the nineteenth century, as the British appropriated all the more fertile areas of the continent, the original nomadic way of life gradually disappeared until it barely survived outside the central desert and the tropical north. There the indigenous arts are still practised with great vitality in diverse regional and individual styles.

Some paintings on rock surfaces are, perhaps, the earliest discovered anywhere in the world. They can be dated from about 40,000 BC, though the majority are much later – some even from the 1960s. They range from 'negative' imprints made by spraying pigments round outstretched hands to representations of human and mythological beings, animals and plants rendered either schematically or naturalistically. Unlike Prehistoric paintings in Europe,

18,15 Nguleingulei, *Anteater*, c. 1950.
Paint on wood bark, 18⅞ × 11⅕ins (48 × 30cm).
Anthropology Research Museum, University of Western Australia, Perth.

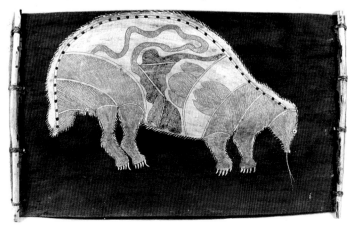

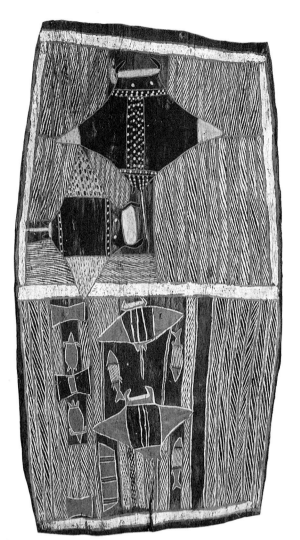

18,16 Bunnugga, *Sea Piece*, c. 1950. Paint on wood, 16½ × 33ins (42 × 84cm). Anthropology Research Museum, University of Western Australia, Perth.

they remained visible at sacred sites over the millennia and testify to an extraordinary continuity of artistic activity which is also evident in paintings on impermanent surfaces including the earth and the human body. Paintings on perishable bark stripped from eucalyptus trees are all relatively recent and, indeed, are still made by the inhabitants of Arnhem Land from whom most of our information about the meaning of this art has been obtained. They express a view of the world in which there are no clear distinctions between the secular and the sacred, natural and supernatural, past and present, or even the visible and the invisible. Some, uniquely Australian, show both the exterior and interior of animals as in X-rays. Fish were depicted in this way, probably in the first millennium BC, on a cliff overhang in what is now the Kakadu National park (Northern Territory). An anteater painted in about 1950 by Nguleingulei who lived at Gunbalanaya in northern Arnhem Land is naturalistic in outline, catching the carefully observed movement of the creature's snout and protruding tongue, and at the same time conceptual in the rendering of its formalized entrails (**18,15**). Other paintings of the same time and area resemble maps or charts like that by the Gumatj-speaking artist Bunnuga, representing the sea with thorn-backs, king-fish, two turtles and a canoe among the reefs of Cape Arnhem (**18,16**).

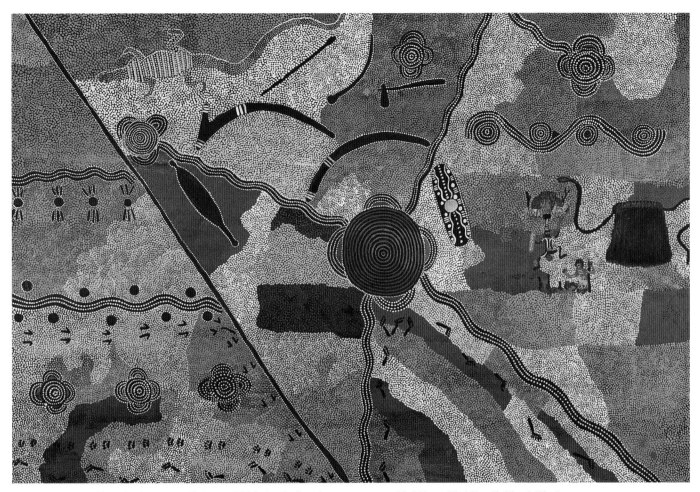

18,17 Tim Leurah Tjapaltjarri, *Wallaby Tjukurrpa*, 1982. Synthetic polymer on canvas, 3ft 11ins × 5ft 10ins (1.21 × 1.79m). National Gallery of Victoria, Melbourne, Australia.

Paintings were and still are a means of preserving the ethos of a group. All members of a community learned to draw or paint as part of their initiation into its mysteries, many of which have never been divulged to outsiders. And the act of painting could be a ritual in itself, most obviously in painting combined with assemblage on sand, as practised in the central desert. The elders who are guardians of faith and morals as well as the secrets of a group are thus the most important artists. Traditions govern style of representation as well as subject-matter, leaving scope, nevertheless, for individual expression and consequently for change as well as continuity, most obviously evident in the work of the last decades. Synthetic pigments have been very successfully adopted, in place of the red and yellow ochres, white kaolin and black charcoal that were the only ones previously available, and applied to composition board, canvas or paper as well as bark. But artists still work in the traditional way, moving around the support placed on the ground and thus evolving compositions quite different from those painted on an upright. And traditional subjects continue to be depicted.

Wallaby Tjukurrpa (or Dreaming) by Tim Leurah Tjapaltjarri (c. 1939–84) who lived at Papunya in the centre of the continent is a kind of landscape both spiritual and geographical (**18,17**). The central roundel, representing a soakage and sacred site asssociated with the rock wallaby, is surrounded by half-circles of ceremonial participants rendered by dots, and several similar configurations denote camp-sites. To the left there is a shield decorated for a ceremony and further to the left a group of men depicted naturalistically. The upper right corner is filled by a large lizard whose tracks are shown together with those of the wallaby in the lower right. Hunters are represented by their footprints and weapons – boomerangs, hafted stone axe, club and spear. The background is composed of delicately applied dots of smoky gray, olive green, yellow, violet, red ochre and umber to create an opalescent shimmer as of the artist's own environment seen through a slight heat-haze. This is one of many paintings executed, increasingly from the 1960s, by professional artists, women as well as men, for sale to outsiders. They have helped to strengthen cultural traditions that had been under attack ever since the arrival of British settlers and, more recently, by an official policy of assimilation as well as the urbanization of many Aborigines. And their dispersal has drawn international attention to the values of Aboriginal culture and the plight of people dispossessed of the land on which it is based.

THE AMERICAN NORTH-WEST

The 1,000-mile (1,600km) stretch of the north-west coast of America – the north-east of the Pacific – from southern Alaska to the state of Washington, provided an ideal environment for the growth of stable communities. Despite the northerly latitude, the climate is temperate. Natural resources were originally so rich that the inhabitants could subsist by fishing, hunting and gathering, without the need to domesticate stock or cultivate the land. Forests yielded abundance of wood for buildings, for boats and also for sculpture, sometimes on a large scale. Beyond them the rocky mountains were an impenetrable barrier against marauders. The history of the area is obscure until the 1770s, when exploration by Europeans began – James Cook was among the first and collected the earliest surviving examples of its art. It appears to have been settled in the mid-first millennium AD by tribes of diverse origins speaking languages which are still mutually unintelligible: from the north, the Tlingit, the Haida mainly on Queen Charlotte Island, the Tsimshian and the Bella-Coola on the coast and, at the southern end, the Kwakiutl and Nookta (also known as Nuuchanuta) on Vancouver Island. The culture to which they contributed has, nevertheless, an underlying homogeneity and a visual character as distinct from that of the Polynesians as from that of the nomads of the North American plains and forests.

The peoples of the American north-west engaged in trade as well as warfare with one another, and this may partly account for the diffusion of cultural traits and artistic motifs throughout the area. They were also linked by belief in shamanism, that most ancient form of magic which they shared with the hunting tribes of Siberia and had probably inherited from common forebears in the remote past. Despite very different myths of creation and ideas of supreme deities, all acknowledged the power of shamans to make contact with the spirits of the forests and the waters, to heal the sick and predict the future. Much of their art was concerned with the shaman's equipment of masks and other ritual objects. But the rest is secular and springs from a preoccupation with the hereditary basis of their complex social structures.

The Tlingit and other 'nations' or language groups were aggregates of autonomous village communities composed of one or more families, each with its own chief, who inherited his position through matrilineal descent. They had no centralized political or religious organization, but cohesion was given by extensive networks of kinship established through marriage, both men and women being obliged to marry outside the larger divisions of clans and moieties (or halves) into which they were born and into which the social group was divided by matrilineal or patrilineal descent. Thus families built up riches by marriage without any one family acquiring a dominant position. Although politically on a par with one another, their chiefs competed in displays of riches, especially in the potlatch, a feast accompanied by exchanges of gifts and the dramatic performance of myths connected with the history of the family.

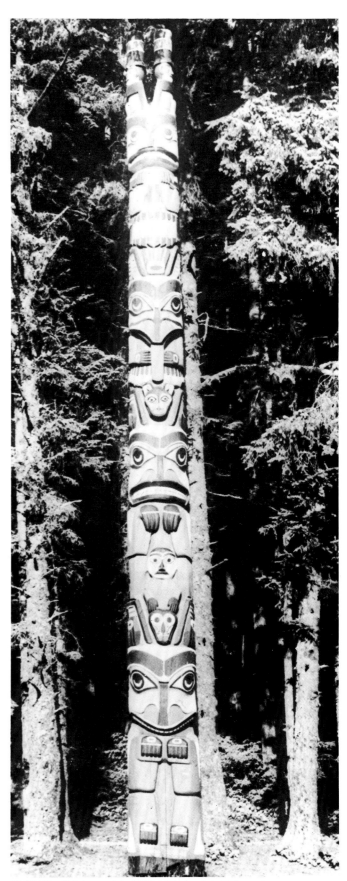

18,18 Tlingit 'totem-pole' at Sitka, Alaska, late 19th century. Carved and painted wood.

The so-called 'totem-poles' (**18,18**), the most distinctive artistic product of the north-west, were similarly conspicuous declarations of prestige and the genealogy by which it had been attained, equivalents to the coats of arms of the European nobility. These magnificent sculptures that probably originated as funerary monuments were first described by travellers in the late eighteenth century though none survives from before the mid-nineteenth. Each one was carved from a single trunk of cedar and the increasing availability of metal tools both permitted and encouraged more complex compositions and greater height – up to 90 feet (27.4m). Their superimposed figures – eagles, beavers, whales and so on – were crests which a chief inherited from his lineage, his clan and his moiety. They were not objects of worship, nor were the animals carved on them, strictly speaking, totems with which a group of people had a supernatural relationship although they might represent guardian spirits. Poles were designed according to a governing principle of bilateral symmetry, with their various elements interlocked so that they seem to grow organically out of one another, creating a unity of symbolism, form and surface. In the Haida village of Skidegate, posts sometimes enshrining the ashes of a cremated chief, and marked with a record of the number of potlaches he had given, were erected outside each of the houses inhabited by an extended family, and there were similar though shorter posts indoors. Sculptors among the Haida worked, and still work today, also on a small scale, carving masks of wood and minute figures of argillite (a stone similar to slate), one of which illustrates the myth of the bear-mother, a woman writhing in agony as a creature – partly human and partly bear-cub – sucks at her breast (**18,19**).

Masks are the most varied of the carvings from the north-west, where they were an essential part of communal life. In style they range from an almost abstract symbolism to combinations of human and animal features and to a lifelike naturalism sometimes bordering on caricature, taken to its extreme in Tlingit war helmets (**18,20**). Some differences must have been due to those between the cultures in which they were created; but

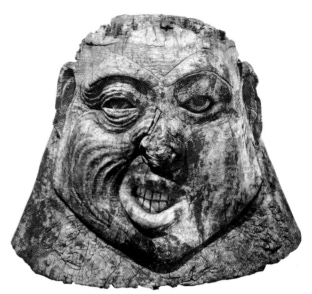

18,20 Tlingit war helmet, from south-east Alaska, early 19th century. Wood, 12ins (30.5cm) high. American Museum of Natural History, New York.

their place of origin cannot always be ascertained as they seem to have passed from one contiguous nation to another in the course of trade or warfare. Although carvers worked according to established conventions, no two masks are exactly the same and those with basic similarities reveal varying degrees of skill. On a Tsimshian mask of a male face, for instance, the remarkably sensitive modelling around the eyes and mouth which, together with the asymmetrical painting of the tattoos on cheeks and forehead, gives an unusually vivid impression of mental anguish, could only have been achieved by a carver of exceptional ability (**18,21**).

18,21 Tsimshian mask, c. 1875. Wood, paint, applied hair and fur, 12¾ × 9 × 7ins (30.5 × 24.8 × 17.8cm). Private collection.

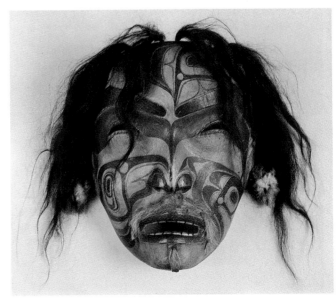

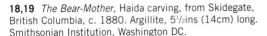

18,19 *The Bear-Mother*, Haida carving, from Skidegate, British Columbia, c. 1880. Argillite, 5¹/₂ins (14cm) long. Smithsonian Institution, Washington DC.

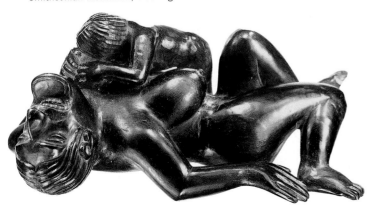

A Shaman's Mask

ART AND MAGIC

The word 'shaman' was originally used by the Tungus, nomads of eastern Siberia, to designate a man whose association with the world of spirits enabled him to control the weather, predict the future and, especially, heal the sick or mentally deranged. It was subsequently applied elsewhere to men, rarely women, believed to have similar occult gifts. The term 'shamanism' derived from it is, however, something of a misnomer in so far as it implies a consistent body of religious beliefs evolved at some very early period and diffused across the world. In some places shamans had the role of priests. But the creation myths and cosmologies of the cultures in which they functioned, including those of autonomous groups of the American north-west, were of great diversity; and sometimes they had positions alongside those of the leaders of organized religions, notably Buddhism and Daoism. The spirits with whom they associated were usually in an intermediate zone between mortals and the creator gods, a zone occupied by innumerable spirits.

A man became a shaman, or claimed to have become one, as a result of a traumatic experience, sometimes also by inheritance from a relative (a maternal uncle in matrilineal societies), usually followed by a period of apprenticeship to acknowledged shamans. The story of an Inuit (or Eskimo) shaman is characteristic. While running from a summer camping place to his village he saw a shaman who had died in the previous year descending from the moon in a boat. This shaman was then transformed into a grotesque figure with one large eye dancing towards the Inuit, who ran away but found he had been possessed by it and some months later was himself accepted by his fellow villagers as a shaman. Among the Tlingit a man who had inherited the possibility of becoming a shaman retired to the mountains, where he lived on nothing but roots and leaves until he met and obtained the help of a spirit, usually the soul of a sea-mammal or land animal, that of the land otter being the most powerful. His status as shaman was confirmed when he had effected a cure which depended on his faith in his own magic power combined with that of the sick person and the expectations of the group within which the relationship between the two was located. A shaman might also detect witches, foretell the movement of animals that were killed for food, accompany and advise war parties, and preside over rites of passage, birth, initiation and death.

Although shamans had great importance among the nomads of central and north-eastern Asia their equipment of costumes, drums and so on was impermanent. Only among the settled communities of the American north-west did they leave traces in durable artifacts, notably the carved wood masks which express and record so much of their ethos. These are also among the world's most arresting works of sculpture, incidentally so because they were not intended to make any such appeal but simply to identify the shaman with his spirit helper, though this would be best effected by one that was skilfully carved and painted. He had a number of them to be worn on different occasions. Some have lifelike human faces (18,21), others incorporate animal forms (18,24). Many are mainly animal, notably the Tsimshian mask of a sea spirit with the snout of a whale and five human heads emerging from its back (**18,22**). Such masks were made either by the shaman himself or by carvers working under his direction to represent the spirits with whom he had communed. Despite this personal origin they seem usually to have been passed on from one generation to the next. The mask transformed its wearer and without it the shaman was like any other member of his community.

18,22 Tsimshian sculptor, Shaman's mask of a sea spirit, c. 1850–75. Carved and painted wood, 21½ins (54.6cm) long. Royal Ontario Museum, Toronto.

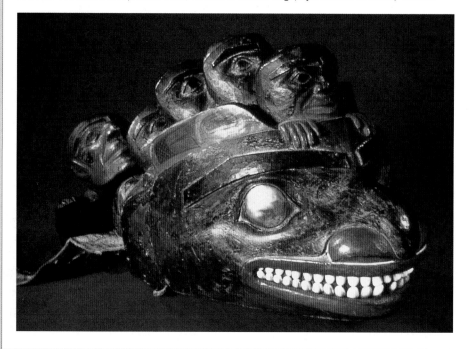

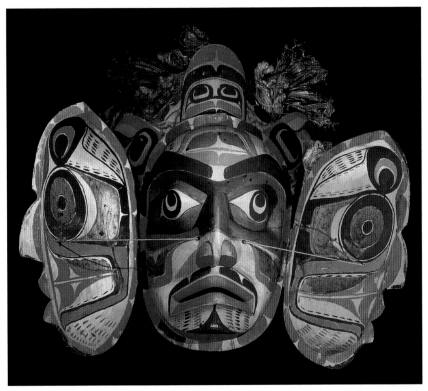

18,23 Kwakiutl Transformation Mask, late 19th century. Carved and painted wood with plant fibres, 19³/₄ (50cm) high. Field Museum of Natural History, Chicago.

18,24 *Right* Tlingit mask, mid-19th century. Carved and painted wood with shell, 9¼ins (23.5cm) high. Musée de l'Homme, Paris.

ceremonies. Many Tlingit masks were made for shamans and incorporate the animals that were believed to be their spirit helpers (**18,24**). Conjuring up forces of nature from the ocean, the forests or the sky, they mediated like the shamans themselves between life on earth and the inscrutable powers around and above.

Whatever their purpose, masks were carved with a feeling for bold sculptural form. Paintings, on the other hand, are emphatically flat and non-naturalistic. They are mainly of animals rendered by devices which mysteriously recur in the arts on both sides of the Pacific. Sometimes the animals are, as it were, split open and their features rearranged so that all can be shown on a flat surface. This device was used by the ancient Chinese and also by the Maori in New Zealand (**18,7**). Physical features were also incorporated inside one another, as in the Animal style of the ancient Scythians (**4,53; 56**). Faces stare out from the ears, eyes, nostrils, paws and limb-joints in a

The major differences between these masks were determined by their purpose. Some were representations of chiefs and their ancestors and were made to be displayed at commemorative potlaches and treasured as heirlooms. Although they appear to record the styles of facial tattooing customary in different groups, it is difficult to say how far they were intended to be portraits, in the European sense of the word, rather than generalized images, even though Haida artists in the mid-nineteenth century carved what appear to be faithful likenesses of visitors of European origin. Many masks, sometimes quite large, were carved to be worn in dance-dramas which re-enacted and kept alive the cohesive myths of a culture. These performances were usually given indoors during the long winter nights, and when the masks were seen by the flickering light of torches they must have had an awe-inspiring supernatural presence. Transformation masks of the Kwakiutl are the most elaborate, made in two layers so that a narrator or actor could, by pulling strings, open the outer one to reveal that inside and transform its character from, for instance, a sea-monster or a bear into a human being. The example illustrated here shows a mask of the setting sun half open to reveal a grimacing human face (**18,23**). Some of them represented spirits and so were akin to the masks worn by shamans in their various functions, foretelling the future, controlling the weather, healing the sick or conducting initiation

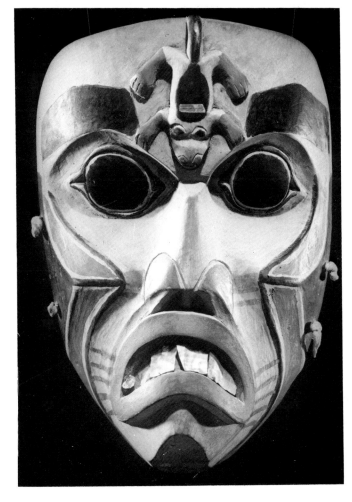

painting of a brown bear (**18,25**). The large scale (15 feet, 4.6m, high), the broad sweep of the general design and the simple color-scheme combine to give imposing monumentality to an image conjured up from a world which parallels that of reality. The brown bear was a Tlingit clan crest and this painting was executed in about 1840 on the interior wall of a chief's house in Wrangell, Alaska, but is said to have been copied from an earlier prototype.

THE PLAINS AND THE ARID LANDS OF NORTH AMERICA

A buffalo skin dating from shortly before 1830, when it was acquired by a European explorer, is a notable example of the art of the Sioux, who lived on the great central plains of North America (**18,26**). To the eyes of an outsider it is a wonderfully well-controlled abstract composition with its few elements of red and black so placed on the blank ground that it suggests, perhaps fancifully, the spaciousness of the open windswept country. Several other robes have similar 'box and border' motifs. They were painted by women to be worn in the puberty rites of girls and there can be no doubt that the designs had a symbolic significance, probably related to earth and the idea of an earth mother, known only to initiates and consequently lost to us. Anthropologists have found that other symbols in North American art were diversely interpreted by men and women and also by members of neighbouring tribes. Examples later in date tend to have more colors and were sometimes hung with glass beads obtained from European-American traders.

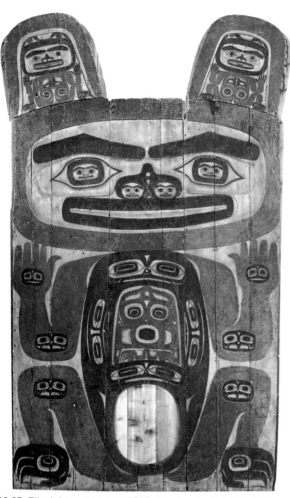

18,25 Tlingit bear screen, c. 1840. Wood and paint, 15 × 9ft (4.57 × 2.74m). Denver Art Museum, Denver, Colorado.

18,26 Painted hide, from the Dakotas. Sioux. 4ft 5⅛ins × 6ft ⅞in (1.35 × 1.85m). Linden Museum, Stuttgart.

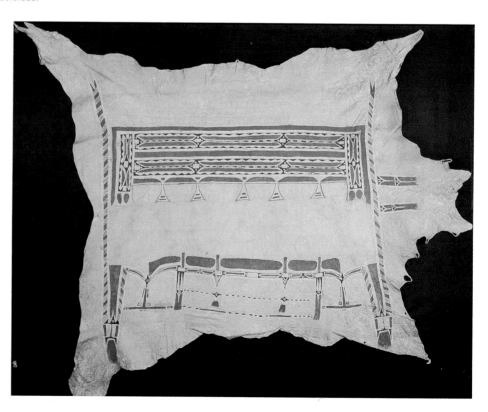

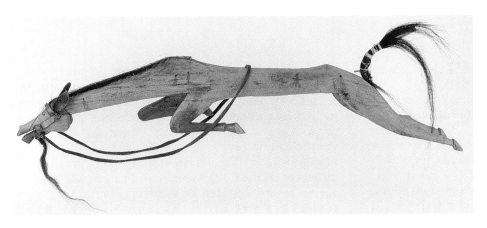

18,27 Horse effigy, from the Dakotas. Sioux. Wood, leather, horsehair, paint. South Dakota State Historical Society, Pierre, South Dakota.

In the mid-nineteenth century the Sioux constituted a very large group of tribes living in the Dakotas, Minnesota and Nebraska. They spoke dialects of the same language (Siouan) and shared a cosmology that involved belief in a Great Spirit and the power of shamans (who were sometimes also tribal chiefs). Their social structures were hierarchical, dominated by polygamous men. Women performed domestic tasks and were more closely involved in the arts than men, who were often absent from the settlements, occupied in hunting and warfare. These people of the Plains seem to have led more peaceful, semi-agricultural lives before the arrival on their frontiers of Europeans, who brought with them not only lethal diseases but also horses and fire-arms. Horses, introduced from the Spanish colonies but not numerous until the late eighteenth century, brought about a complete change in the way of life, greatly facilitating the hunting of buffalo, and providing increased mobility which encouraged territorial expansion with the result that tribes living far apart became engaged in war with one another. This was soon reflected in the arts. Much attention was given to horse trappings. Horses were painted on buffalo skin robes to record the exploits of the men who wore them. The carving of a galloping horse that conveys the exhilarating fleetness of almost air-borne movement felt by a rider is, however, unique in the art of North America (18,27). As the capture of horses was one of the aims of warfare, this figure was probably intended to be displayed in a victory dance. It was collected by a missionary, Mary C. Collins, who lived among the Sioux. She made friends with Sitting Bull, the great shaman and chief and one of the leaders of a movement for the purification and revitalization of indigenous culture associated with the Ghost Dance religion. This was to lead, tragically, to the decimation of his people and the confinement of survivors on reservations.

Native American artifacts differ from one another as much as the physical environments and cultural structures of the societies in which they were produced. Many were of impermanent materials and the history of their development can rarely be traced back beyond the time when they were first acquired by outsiders. In the southwest, however, baskets made as early as the eighth millennium BC have been preserved by the arid climate. Pottery was also made there, as nowhere else in North America. Basketry was very widely practised, mainly by women, in a rich variety of techniques determined by the availability of materials. Like the majority of pottery vessels throughout the world, baskets were intended primarily for use as containers though sometimes also to please the eye. Not until the late nineteenth century, at the time of a general reassessment of handicrafts, did European-Americans begin to recognize that baskets could have artistic merits comparable with those of ceramics. This led to their production specifically for collectors and not as utilitarian objects.

Women of the Washoe tribe, hunters and gatherers living around Lake Tahoe on the border of Nevada and California, who had previously made rather rough baskets for domestic use, were engaged to work for this new market of collectors. The most celebrated, Dat So La Lee (meaning wide hips), who preferred to be known by her Anglo name Louisa Keyser (c. 1850–1925), was employed by the owners of a clothing and curio emporium in Carson City, Nevada, who from 1895 gave her food, lodging and medical care in return for her entire production. In these circumstances she developed her own artistic gifts to devise a new technique as well as an individual style of ornament. The *degikup*, or offering basket, which took her nearly a year in 1917–18 to weave from willow, redbud and bracken fern in an unconventional form of her own devising (18,28), is one of the most aesthetically pleasing examples of basketry, as well as an unusually successful product of acculturation, that process of culture change brought about by the interaction of two societies with different traditions.

18,28 Dat So La Lee, basket, 1918. Willow, bracken fern, redbud bark. Clark Field Collection, Philbrook Art Center, Tulsa, Oklahoma.

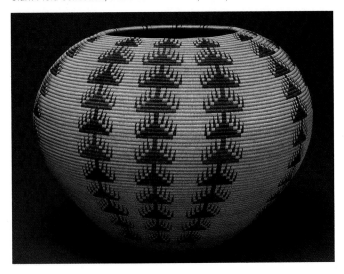

AFRICA

The art of Africa south of the Sahara permits no generalizations that are not equally applicable to the art of
humankind as a whole. It had a diversity of functions,
media and styles as great as that of the other continents.
Nor did it evolve in complete isolation; Africans were
trading overseas with Asia and Europe long before Europeans penetrated the interior. On the west coast objects
were made for export (mainly from ivory) at least as early
as the sixteenth century. As in other parts of the world,
arts were practised mainly in religious contexts, which
included cults of ancestors and kingship, for related
didactic purposes to perpetuate ancient traditions as well
as to satisfy a need for symbols of wealth and power. Religious beliefs were localized. There was no unifying religion with a clearly defined iconography. Even in areas
where Islam had been the official creed since the twelfth
century and in those where there had been a Christian
majority since the mid-nineteenth century, animistic and
pantheistic cults survived. African art is, furthermore, the
product of many ethnic groups with their own languages
and ways of life. It was created within diverse social organizations ranging from small communities of hunters and
gatherers, nomads and farmers to the centrally organized
kingdoms of Benin, Dahomey, Kongo and Asante.

All the usual materials for artistic production were
employed: stone, metals, clay, wood, ivory, fibres, skins,
many different pigments, as well as the horns and teeth of
wild animals, feathers, shells and dried grasses. Figurative
paintings appear, mainly in the south, over a very long
time-span, from small charcoal and ochre images of animals on fragments of shale, dated c. 25,000 BC, to more
than 15,000 rock paintings, executed until late in the
nineteenth century by diverse hunting and gathering
groups loosely classified as the San (formerly called
Bushmen). That they have some similarities with the
coeval rock paintings of Australia (see p. 750) can be no
more than a coincidence but an interesting one. For, like
the rock engravings of north-east Africa (1.14) but unlike
the prehistoric cave paintings of Europe, they were permanently accessible and could thus help to preserve traditions of pictorial representation. The interior of a rock
shelter in the southern Drakensberg (South Africa) was
covered probably in the late eighteenth century, for
example, with images of humans including shamans and
of animals, notably the eland (a species of large antelope)
that had multiple symbolic associations (18,29). It was
believed that shamans could heal the sick, attract beasts
that were a main source of food, call down rain and, in
trance, enter the spirit world to travel extracorporeally in
animal form. In the fragment illustrated here they are
shown in various postures, one lying down in a trance
with his feet transformed into cloven hoofs.

Paintings on movable surfaces, apart from shields and
bark-cloth garments, were uncommon until recent times.
The major two-dimensional art was textile and non-
figurative, practised with as much technical skill as
sensitivity to color and flat patterning. As we have
already seen, weaving had been developed into a non-
figurative art by the early seventeenth century (12,20). In
the kingdom of Asante (modern Ghana), which rose to
power and wealth in the eighteenth century, some of the
finest of all textiles, generally called *kente*, were woven in
cotton and, from the early nineteenth century, also silk
obtained by unravelling imported European and Chinese
pieces to make fabrics of an entirely different appearance
(18,30). Long strips woven on horizontal looms were
stitched edge to edge for large panels that could be
worn like togas. Great ingenuity was applied to the

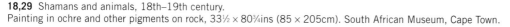

18,29 Shamans and animals, 18th–19th century.
Painting in ochre and other pigments on rock, 33½ × 80¾ins (85 × 205cm). South African Museum, Cape Town.

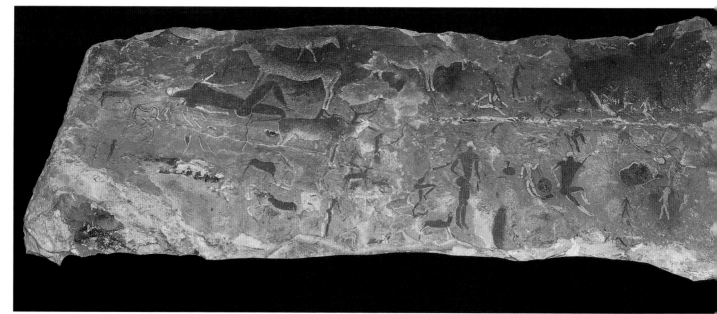

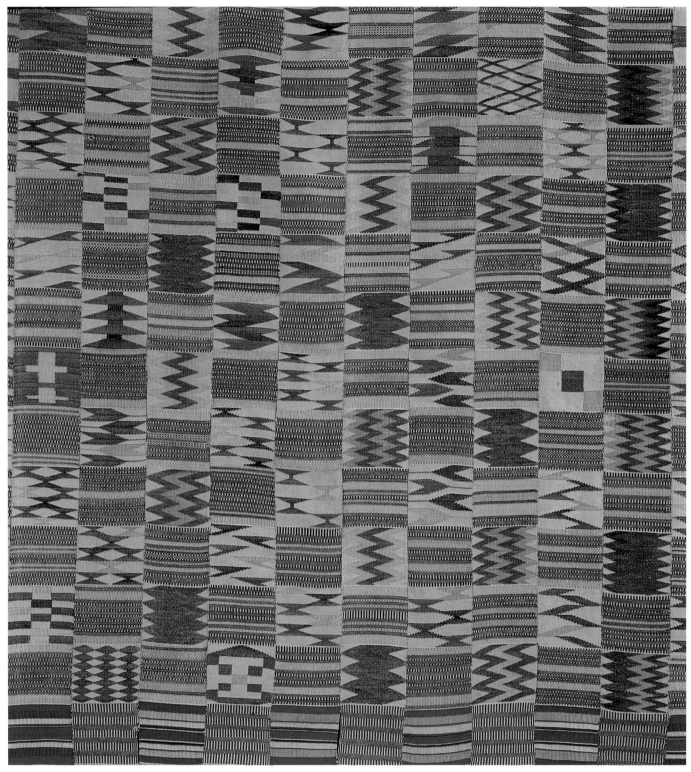

18,30 *Kente* cloth, 19th or 20th century. Cotton and silk detail from a panel 5ft 10½ins × 5ft 11ins (1.79 × 1.8m). Fowler Museum of Cultural History, University of California, Los Angeles.

manipulation of colored warp and weft threads to create patterns of rectangles filled with diverse (sometimes symbolic) motifs determined by the weave, so that every piece was a unique work of art and given a title – 'skill is exhausted' for the one illustrated here. Silks known as *adwinasa* were reserved for the king, who had first choice, and for local chiefs. Cotton fabrics with somewhat similar patterns were made for common use and are still hand-woven in Ghana though now with synthetic as well as natural fibres.

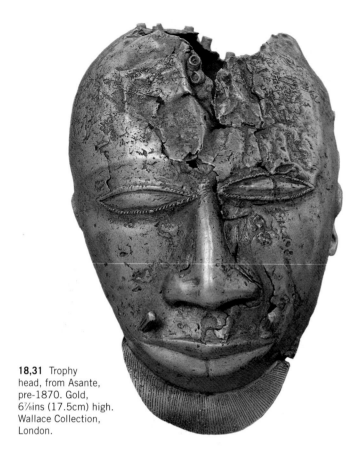

18,31 Trophy head, from Asante, pre-1870. Gold, 6⅞ins (17.5cm) high. Wallace Collection, London.

The major contribution of Africa to the arts of the world has been in sculpture – sculpture including, of course, assemblages and all artifacts in three dimensions ranging from figures for shrines, items of royal regalia and masks to stools and other furnishings that were more than merely utilitarian. Figurative sculptures were created at least as early as c. 400 BC (see p. 125). The art of casting in metal was perfected by the ninth century AD (see p. 526). At the court of the obas of Benin, brass figures, heads and reliefs were cast from the fifteenth century until the city was sacked by the British in 1897 and its treasures dramatically revealed to the world (see pp. 528–30). A naturalistic art of small-scale metal sculpture flourished from the seventeenth century in the area dominated by the kings of Asante. An impressive gold head was one of several made to commemorate enemy leaders slain in battles to subdue neighbouring peoples (**18,31**). The eyes are closed and a gag was originally suspended over the mouth from the two projecting pegs. It was part of the royal treasure in the capital city of Kumasi sacked by the British in 1874. Asante and its dependent territories were notable also for the development of a secular and popular art unusual in Africa: little weights for measuring gold dust cast in brass in the form of lively human figures and animals, sometimes illustrating proverbs, made from the seventeenth to the early twentieth century.

Between the kingdoms of Asante and Benin (modern south-west Nigeria, Benin and Togo), the land of the Yoruba – one of the largest African ethnic groups – was united in the sixteenth century to form the Oyo kingdom.

By the early nineteenth century, however, this area had been fragmented into small states with a religious centre at Ife. Their rulers seem to have vied with one another in the decoration of palaces with carved wood verandah posts and doors in a style which may have been developed from the art of Ife, though very little survives from the intervening millennium. If there was such continuity there were also changes due to political circumstances and the achievements of individual artists, as is clearly evident in works of the late nineteenth and early twentieth centuries. A pair of doors from the palace of the ogoga or king of Ikere (Nigeria) records a novel subject, the visit in about 1895 of a British colonial administrator, who is shown carried in a litter on the right-hand panel (**18,32**). The sculptor was Olowe of Ise (d. 1938), who carved similar doors for other Yoruba rulers and seems to have originated a technique of carving figures in high relief with projecting heads cut free from the background. In the same period, however, different styles were adopted by other Yoruba sculptors whose names are recorded. They all specialized in secular works which permitted greater individuality of handling than cult images associated with the spirit world and the traditions of a group into which adolescents were initiated. The latter were valued for their efficacy in serving the cult, not for any aesthetic appeal they might have. Indeed, the individual sculptor was thought so subordinate to the object he created that he was, as it were, absorbed into it, sometimes to such an extent that his name was kept secret until the work had fallen out of use.

The majority of African sculptures connected with popular religious beliefs and magic practices were of iron, which soon rusts away in the tropics, or of wood, which usually perishes in less than a century. Some, like body paintings, were executed for a single occasion. We thus have no more than scanty and incomplete knowledge of the history of the arts in which Africans sought to express their relationship with fellow beings, the natural environment, the mysterious forces of good and evil, life and death. There is evidence to show that some symbolic motifs were unchanged over long periods, as in the arts of Europe and Asia. A wooden divining tray acquired by a German collector in the early seventeenth century (Ulm Museum) is almost identical with others carved some 300 years later. But artistic and other cultural traditions were subject to change. African art of the nineteenth and early twentieth centuries is best understood as the product of a long process of development, conditioned by extensive folk migrations, by the rise and fall of states, by the introduction of materials and techniques from outside, and, no less, by the work of individual artists.

Continuity and change are evident in uniquely African power figures of the type that used to be called fetishes (a term now obsolete in this context on account of the entirely different meaning given to it in psychological studies). They were products of collaboration between sculptors, patrons who wished to control natural or supernatural forces and diviners who provided substances to which magical properties were ascribed by ancient tradi-

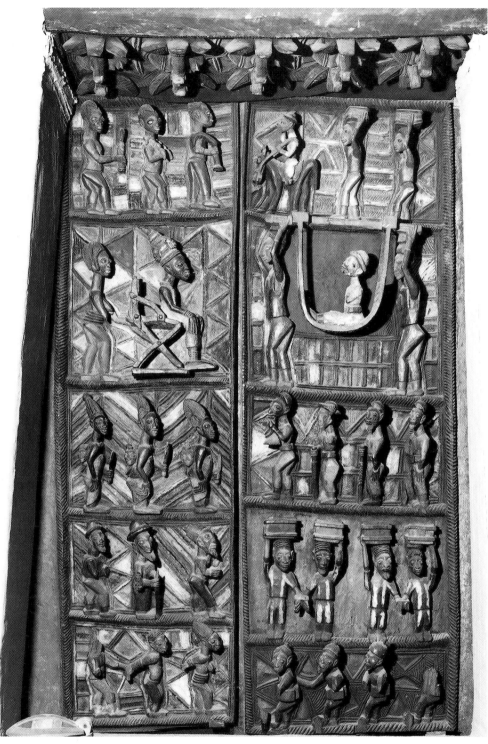

18,32 Olowe of Ise, entry doors for the palace of the ogoga of Ikere, c. 1916.
Painted wood, 6ft 11⅞ins (2.13m) high. British Museum, London.

tions. Very often, however, the figures incorporated pieces of mirror glass taken to Africa no earlier than the sixteenth century, usually much later. It was believed that evil spirits of malevolent human beings would be repelled by reflections of themselves, or else that the mirror would, so to speak, absorb the image of the looker who would then be destroyed by the magic substances embedded in the power figure. Mirror glass gave a more perfect reflection than pieces of polished stone or shell which had probably been used before it became available. Power figures were not revered and treasured like images in shrines (or the analagous reliquaries of Buddhist and Christian cults); they were discarded once their purpose had been achieved or they were found to be ineffective.

Palace Doors from Ikere

AFRICAN IMAGES OF EUROPEANS

The status of the ogoga of Ikere was conspicuously demonstrated by the elaboration and fine craftsmanship of the doors and verandah posts carved for his palace by Olowe (see p. 760), probably the most highly regarded Yoruba sculptor of the early twentieth century (18,32). The time and skill expended were an indication of the riches and power of the ruler who had commissioned them. The figurative scenes carved on them had, of course, a more precise significance. On the left leaf the ogoga himself is shown wearing his beaded crown and seated on a throne. His principal wife from whom, according to Yoruba tradition, he derived his sovereignty, stands behind him. Below them are three other wives, each with a baby cradled on her back. On the next register, three men with beards, not usually worn by the Yoruba, are foreigners, and the one with a fez on his head is clearly a Muslim, perhaps a trader. The outsiders most frequently seen in Yoruba towns were Muslims from the north. On the other leaf of the door, facing the ogoga, a European carried in a litter and identified as a British Travelling Commissioner named Captain Ambrose is shown as a visitor or ambassador rather than as a colonial overlord, and he cuts a somewhat pathetic figure. Above, a man on horseback rides in front of two porters, and below four men, two of whom wear European hats, seem to be part of his entourage. Two pairs of men chained at the wrists and carrying burdens on their heads – evidently captives or slaves – fill another panel on this leaf of the door, though whether or not they should be associated with Captain Ambrose is uncertain. In the very rich program of sculptural decorations carved for the palace at Ikere he is no more than incidental. He was, however, represented riding a horse on a door carved by Olowe for another palace (now in the Nigerian Museum, Lagos).

These images of a British captain had a significance similar to those of Europeans in the court art of Benin, where the Portuguese had been granted trading concessions in the late fifteenth century. Portuguese soldiers who had served the oba or king of Benin in campaigns against the neighbouring states were shown with their muskets and cross-bows in brass statuettes and plaques incorporated in the decoration of the royal palace. Bearded faces of Portuguese form the crown of an ivory mask probably carved to be worn on the hip of the oba in commemorative rites for his mother, who had witnessed the first arrival of Europeans (12,27). Such images indicated the power of the ruling family.

By the late nineteenth century relations between Africans and Europeans in this part of the continent had undergone a complete change. Although Europeans had secured no more than footholds here and there on the coast from which to conduct the Atlantic slave-trade, they initiated a spiral of destruction in which African rulers became involved in wars with one another to obtain captives to sell to the slave-traders. In exchange they were given fire-arms which they used in further wars. The abolition of the slave-trade by the European powers in the early nineteenth century helped to bring peace to a ravaged country while, at the same time, opening it up to other forms of exploitation. In 1851, for instance, the British signed an anti-slave-trade treaty with the king of Lagos, an island just off the West African coast, which was constituted a British colony a decade later. From there trading companies could penetrate into the interior and in the course of the next half century the whole of modern Nigeria became a British protectorate in which local rulers were nominally independent but ceded some rights in return for protection from neighbouring states, especially the colonies of other European powers. Captain Ambrose appears to have been the first British colonial official to visit Ikere and other small Yoruba states in the interior. By the time Olowe carved his image on the door, however, Nigeria had been formally designated a colony in which local rulers retained little of their former power. The doors were sent to London to be shown in the British Empire Exhibition of 1924 and were acquired for the British Museum from the ogoga, who commissioned Olowe to carve another pair.

A nearly life-size wooden statue of a European soldier was carved in about 1900 by a sculptor of the Baule group of people living in the French Ivory Coast colony (18,33). His heart-

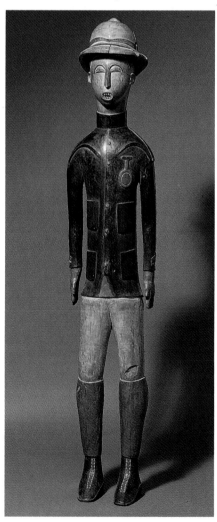

18,33 Anonymous Baule sculptor, *French Colonial Officer*, c. 1900. Carved and painted wood, 4ft 10⅝ins (1.49m) high. Staatliches Museum für Völkerkunde, Munich.

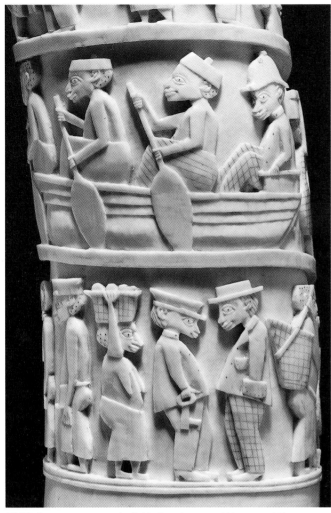

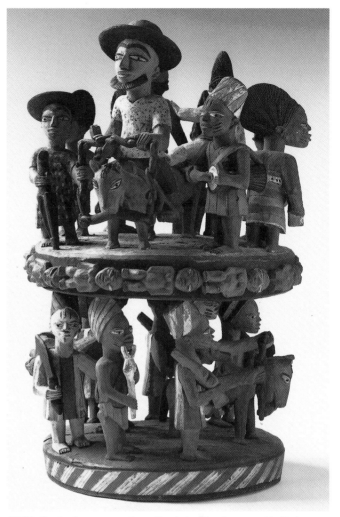

18,34 Anonymous carver in Cabinda or Loango, *Africans and Europeans*, c. 1850–1900. Detail of carved ivory tusk, total length 27ins (68.5cm). Staatliches Museum für Völkerkunde, Munich.

18,35 Yoruba figure group, from Abeokuta, Nigeria, second half of 19th century. Painted wood, 32⅜ins (82.3cm) high. Hamburgisches Museum für Völkerkunde, Hamburg.

shaped face resembles those on masks carved in the same region. But the sculptor took pains to record details of costume, tropical helmet, tight-fitting uniform, jacket with a medal on the chest, and boots. The bodily proportions and stiff military pose, standing to attention, are quite unlike those of the Baule or any other African images that were so avidly collected in early twentieth-century Europe and admired by such artists as Picasso. Whether that of the European soldier was commissioned by a European or an African, it reveals the sculptor's flexibility and his ability to adapt his style for a novel task. The same may be said of figures of Europeans carved for export on ivory tusks from the mid-nineteenth century in the region of the Zaire estuary (now the Democratic Republic of Congo). On one, several Europeans, including two men in conversation – probably a merchant and a store-keeper holding a huge key – and another seated in a canoe, have a somewhat comic look but are rendered with the same attention to characteristic costumes and facial expressions as the many Africans surrounding them (**18,34**). It may be noted, however, that this tusk is topped by the figure of a monkey.

Europeans often seemed uncanny to Africans, who sometimes believed that they became possessed by them, as by evil spirits. They were always aliens and might be ridiculed, especially in plays for exclusively African audiences. The original meaning of a carved wood group crowned by the figure of a moon-faced missionary, riding a horse and surrounded by a band of African musicians, is nevertheless obscure (**18,35**). It was probably carved by Ojerinde who in 1854 established a notable sculpture workshop at Abeokuta (Nigeria), some 50 miles (80km) north of Lagos. One of the Africans on the lower tier has his body covered with white clay and lines painted on his face for a local religious rite. Naked corpses carved around the platform dividing the two tiers are probably sacrificial victims. But does the group allude to the suppression of human sacrifice by missionaries and colonial officials? Or does it absorb Christianity into traditional African beliefs and practices? Such large sculptures were carried on the heads of young men in popular dance festivals that were at the same time fertility rites and entertainments. (Their size and weight were intended to test the ability of dancers to sway and jump while wearing them.) The group with the missionary was certainly intended for an African public whose ambivalent attitude to Europeans it clearly reflects.

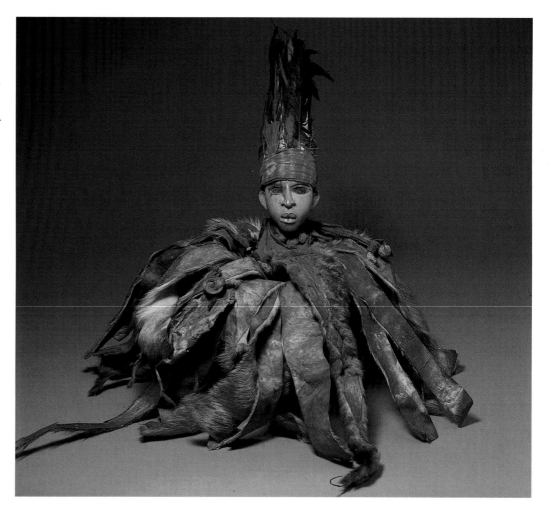

Yet some are superb works of sculpture, none more striking than that from Mayombe (Zaire) (**18,36**). The head of a young man, pale in skin color like many inhabitants of this region, is carved with sensitive naturalism and set among swathes of leather and skins and feathers, royal insignia that suggest the power of the substances embedded behind the mirror-glass eyes. Other power figures, called *nkondi* in the Kikongo language, bristle with iron nails driven into them to activate their magic, to cure or to kill, but also as a kind of solemn oath confirming a contract between merchants, for example, or declaring a truce in warfare (**18,37**). These nails are of European make (wooden pegs may have been used earlier) and it has been suggested that the idea of investing them with supernatural potency was inspired by crucifixes – in the sixteenth and seventeenth centuries Christianity was the state religion of the kingdom of Kongo (on either side of the Zaire river) where these figures have been found.

Iron had, however, a much older symbolic significance derived from its use in agriculture, hunting and warfare some centuries before the birth of Christ (see p. 125). In traditional African societies smelters and forgers of iron belonged to a distinct hereditary caste and in some there was a close association between metallurgy and kingship, connected also with notions of nature, fertility and political control. But ancient rituals tended to inhibit large-scale production. Increasing quantities of pig-iron were imported and it was, indeed, partly to obtain it that Africans became embroiled in the vicious spiral of the

Atlantic slave-trade, selling captives for metal that could be forged into weapons to obtain more captives. Among the Yoruba, users of iron implements worship the god Ogun, who introduced the metal to their ancestors, and wear iron amulets (formerly including miniature slave manacles). The neighbouring Fon ethnic group in Dahomey (now the Republic of Benin) worshipped the god of iron and war under the name of Gu. And here, in about 1860, King Glele (1858–89) commissioned a life-size statue representing – though not portraying – himself and his father as a warrior in the guise of Gu, with a large sword in each hand and a crown of miniature weapons and tools on his head – one of the most compelling of all African images (**18,38**). Although King Glele also commissioned a brass statue showing Gu naked (Fondation Dapper, Paris), divinities were seldom represented as directly as this in African art which focused on the spirit conceived as 'resident' in matter rather than on the spirit's physical manifestation. It is this fundamental difference in conception and approach that divides African sculpture from Western and most Asian sculpture. However, the angularity and asymmetrical pose of the Gu figure are unusual. It is, in fact, unique: the work of a sculptor-smith said to have been Akate Akpele Kendo who was taken prisoner of war in King Glele's first military victory and then set up in a smith's compound just outside the royal palace in Abomey. With rods and sheets of scrap metal, hammered and twisted and bent, he created an image in which the symbolism of the material

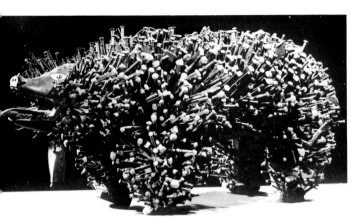

18,37 Magic animal, from Loango, Republic of the Congo, late 19th or early 20th century. Wood with iron nails and blades, 35ins (88cm) long. Musée de l'Homme, Paris.

18,38 Akate Akpele Kendo, *Warrior*, c. 1860. Iron, 5ft 5ins (1.65m) high. Museé de l'Homme, Paris.

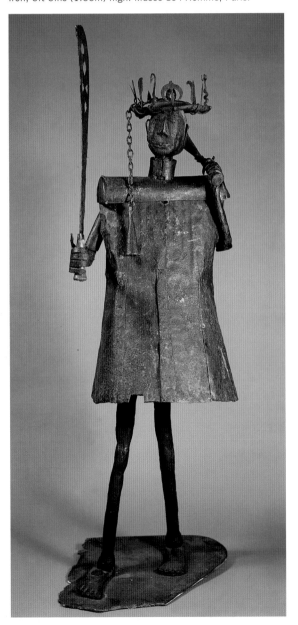

itself and the form so forcefully given to it have equal importance. The power to bring victory in war was ascribed to it and it was predominantly housed in a military shrine surrounded by large-scale weapons in the palace when not being carried to a battlefield to threaten and menace Glele's enemies. It was hailed there as *Agoije* and was thought to yell 'Watch out' as it advanced.

The creation of wood sculptures was in many parts of Africa accompanied by rituals, from the felling of a tree and propitiation of its spirit to some kind of sacrifice on the work's completion. The predominantly curving, organic forms of sculpture in wood seem, furthermore, to express the dynamistic belief widespread in Africa: belief in the energy immanent in all nature which integrates and reconciles the cults of spirits, ancestors, kings and the impersonal magic of power figures. Organic forms are ordered and controlled by simplification and symmetry even in representations of figures in motion, as in the half life-size statues from the Bangwa kingdom in the Cameroon grasslands – the work of a single sculptor, though whether they were intended to complement one

18,39 A king and a mother of twins, from the kingdom of Bangwa, Cameroon, late 19th or early 20th century. Wood, 34½ and 34¼ins (87.6 and 87cm) high. Private collection.

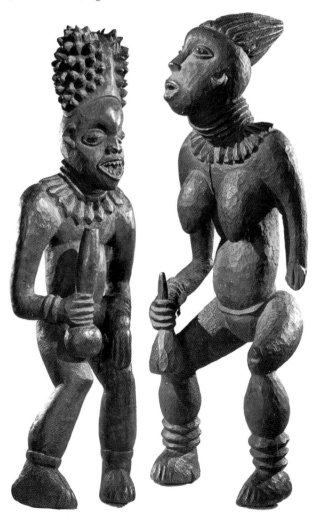

ders as well as the static frontal pose. That the social structure of Yombe clans was matrilineal – descent being traced through the maternal not paternal line – is no coincidence. Emphasis is on motherhood and there is a striking divergence between this carving and the fertility symbols of other cultures that overtly suggest the erotic appeal of the female body for men. The statuette is one of several that seem to be the work of a single sculptor. But some maternity figures from the same region are remarkably diverse in treatment, and the two groups have been ascribed to unnamed sculptors as different from one another as any two Europeans who depicted or carved images of the Madonna – similarly though coincidentally a regal figure. There is no better indication of the role played by individual artists in Africa – as much as anywhere else in the world.

Reliquary guardian figures created by the Kota in Gabon could hardly be more different in their flatness, spare geometrical symbolism and apparent negation of individuality as well as naturalism (18,41). They were carved in wood covered with sheets and bands of copper to be placed over wickerwork baskets containing the skulls and bones of chiefs, notable warriors, founders of villages and other distinguished ancestors. Not intended to represent the people whose relics they guarded, they are perhaps the most effective of all images of quite literally disembodied spirits with eyes staring out of elliptical faces

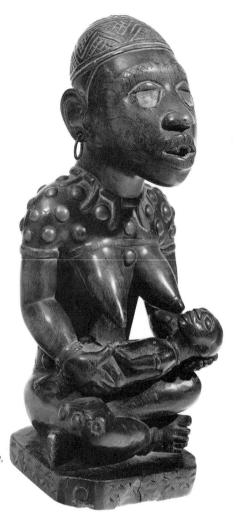

18,40 *Maternity Figure*, from Zaire, pre-1913. Yombe. Wood, 10ins (25cm) high. Rietberg Museum, Zürich.

another is uncertain (18,39). One represents a king with an elaborate head-dress necklace of leopard claws and in one hand a phallic shaped container for palm-wine – symbols of royal power. The other, with a cowrie necklace and bracelet carries a rattle which identify her as a mother of twins and thus a woman who has been accorded an important position in a Cameroon palace and takes a leading role in fertility rituals. The youthful appearance that both share with nearly all African figurative carvings reflects a preoccupation with the cycle of life – with growth and flowering – rather than with any concomitant aesthetic qualities. Although they do not come from the Yoruba region, they also have qualities valued by the Yoruba in sculpture, qualities that can only be called aesthetic: modified naturalism, 'visibility' or clear articulation of parts, and shining surfaces which afford a play of flickering light and shade. The woman especially has the flexibility of body and the coolness or detachment of expression particularly admired in dance.

Similar qualities are apparent in the statuette of a woman with a baby in her lap from an entirely different culture, that of the Yombe living in Zaire (18,40). It is a personification of maternity, a symbol of fertility raised to the highest level of royalty by the jewelry on the shoul-

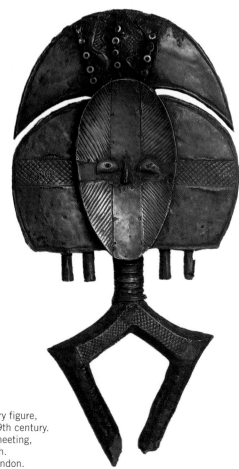

18,41 Kota reliquary figure, from Gabon, late 19th century. Wood and copper sheeting, 26¾ins (68cm) high. British Museum, London.

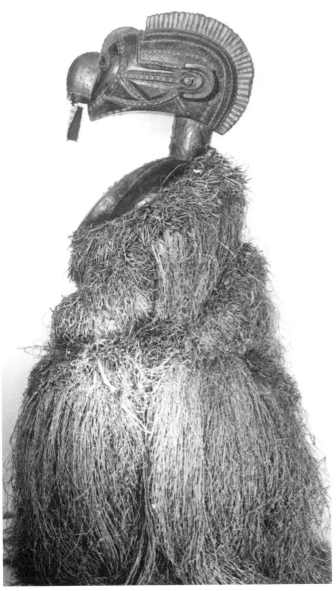

18,42 The goddess Nimba, from Guinea, late 19th century. Carved wood with copper nails and natural fibres, 7ft 2⅜ins (2.2m) high. Musée de l'Homme, Paris.

They were worn in rites with various purposes, to propitiate the dead, to gain security and survival, to promote human fertility and to increase food supply in a world where uncertainty was always a menacing presence, and to ensure the continuity and stability of a social group, initiating the young into its traditions and preserving its myths by dramatic presentation. Some masks were worn on the top of the head so that they could be seen only by

18,43 Ceremonial mask, from Wobé or Grebo, Ivory Coast, late 19th century. Painted wood, feathers and fibres, 11ins (28cm) high. Musée de l'Homme, Paris.

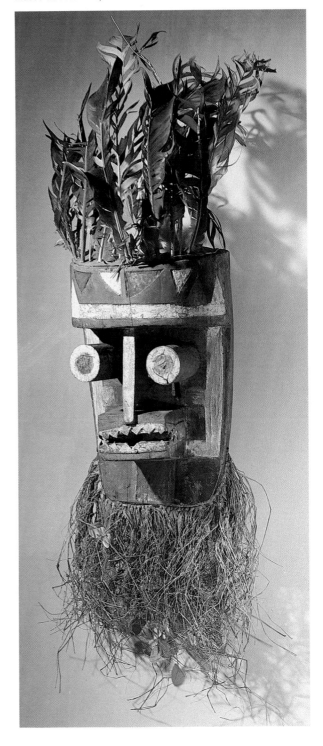

crowned by elements in the form of the crescent moon and with wing-like elements on either side, supported on angled struts probably to be understood as arms. The basic form permitted, nevertheless, much variation in the treatment of the surface – engraved or modelled in very low relief – the use of copper wire and sometimes sheets of brass as well as copper providing a contrast in colors.

But sculptured images, many of which were rarely seen and some never displayed once they had been completed, did not have the prominence in African cultures that they had in those of Europe. In Europe, literacy has tended to destroy the instinctive orchestration of the senses and to focus attention on the static image as on a statement in black and white. In Africa, as in north-west America and Melanesia (though curiously not Polynesia), much artistic activity was devoted to masks made to be seen in movement as part of a ceremonial often accompanied by music.

the spirits of the air, but generally they were visible to all participants and set off by elaborate costumes concealing the wearers who were completely transformed into animated images. Among the Baga of Guinea, heavy carved wood busts of Nimba, goddess of maternity, were at the time of the rice harvest carried on the shoulders of dancers who could see out through holes in the breasts but who were hidden by rustling skirts of fibres (**18,42**).

A mask from the Sassandra river area of the Ivory Coast was made for the Poro society, a male organization that directed diverse public functions, initiatory, civic, religious, administrative, judicial and social (**18,43**). It is roughly composed of unnaturalistic and non-representational forms which are given the appearance of a terrifying human head by their arrangement – a flat oblong panel with a semi-circular block for a brow, cylinders for eyes, a vertical strip for a nose. It is of a type valued only when it was being worn. Among the Dogon

18,44 Dogon Dancers wearing Sirige and Female Warrior masks. Photograph taken in 1972 or 1975. Metropolitan Museum of Art, New York (The Photograph Study Collection. Gift of Lester Wundermann, 1996).

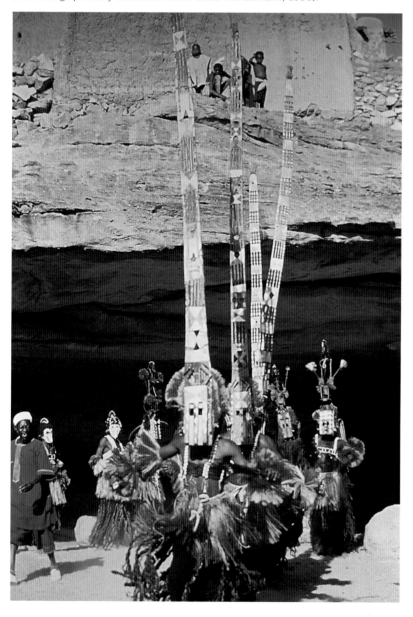

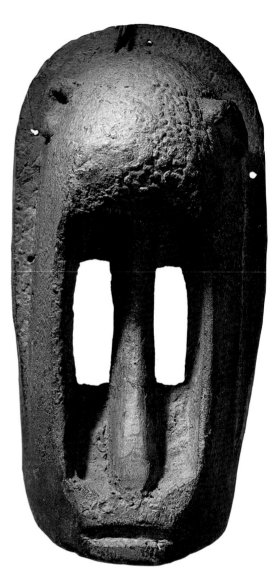

18,45 Dogon 'Black Monkey' mask, from Mali, late 19th century. Carved wood, 14½ins (37cm) high. Musée de l'Homme, Paris.

in Mali many masks were fragile and discarded after use. A photograph taken in 1972 or 1975 shows four Dogon dancers transformed into a powerful spirit called Sirige, by masks with immensely tall superstructures, followed by two other dancers with masks of a female warrior spirit celebrating the courage of women. Women fought alongside men (**18,44**). Such masks had the power to capture and control life-forces when activated in ritual dances in which the skill of their makers and the adroitness of their wearers were of equal importance. Yet many are powerful works of sculpture: notably the sombrely impressive 'Black Monkey' mask carved to be worn in dances which terminated a period of mourning (**18,45**).

Some masks were, nevertheless, preserved in treasuries and brought out for use in such important ceremonies as initiation rites and royal installations. Elaborate examples embellished with copper, cowrie shells and beads were made in the small but rich kingdom of Kuba, in the Kanai river region of the central Congo (Zaire), a stable state with an oral tradition of a succession of rulers dating back to the seventeenth century (corroborated by references to Halley's comet). One of a set of three masks, worn to enact a myth of the origin of royal power, personifies Mbwoom, a Pygmy, who fights with his elder brother, the king, for the affections of their sister – though Mbwoom is identified also with commoners in the realm and the sister with women in general (**18,46**). This is, in fact, a specimen of court art, marked by refinement of craftsmanship as well as costliness of embellishment. But in some uncentralized small-scale social groups where

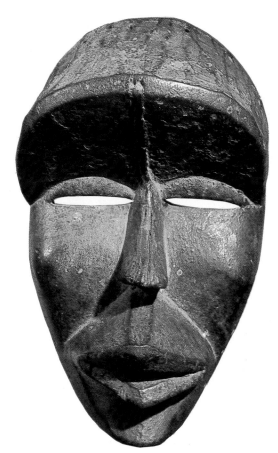

18,47 Dan ceremonial mask, from Ivory Coast or Liberia, late 19th century. Wood, 9⅝ins (24.5cm) high. Musée de l'Homme, Paris.

18,46 Kuba Mbwoom helmet mask, from Zaire, late 19th century. Wood, brass, cowrie shells, beads and seeds, 13ins (33cm) high. Musée Royale de l'Afrique Centrale, Tervuren, Belgium.

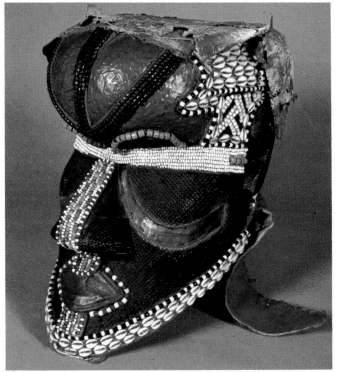

masks were assembled for specific occasions others were carved in hard wood to be handed down from one generation to another. Those carved by the Dan on the Ivory Coast (Côte d'Ivoire) to embody an ideal of feminine beauty correspond with aesthetic preferences verbally expressed by the sculptors as symmetry about a vertical axis with balance, rhythm and harmony between their various masses, surfaces and lines (**18,47**). These three-dimensional qualities, which have appealed so much to European and American artists since the early twentieth century, survive even when such a carving is shown in isolation. But the arts of Africa, like those of Oceania, Australia and the American north-west, lose their all-important fourth dimension when uprooted and taken out of their ritual contexts – just as people living in urbanized and industralized societies tend to lose their sixth sense.

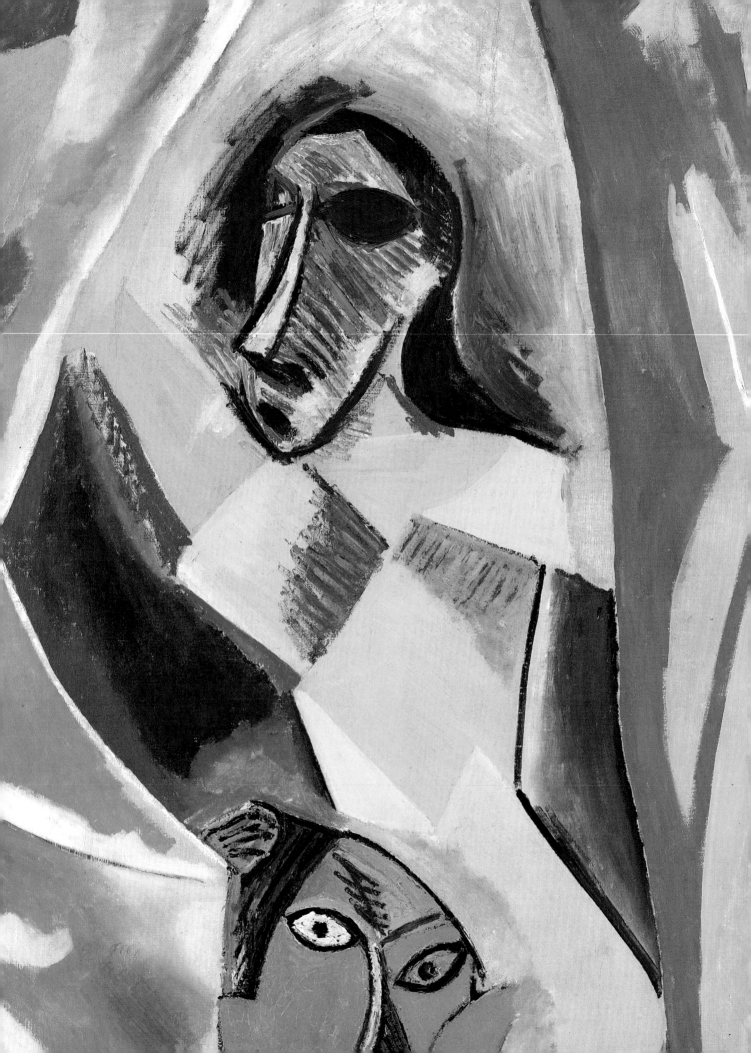

PART FIVE
TWENTIETH-CENTURY ART

Opposite Pablo Picasso, Detail of *Les Demoiselles d'Avignon*, Paris, begun May, reworked July 1907.
Oil on canvas, 8ft × 7ft 8ins (2.44 × 2.34m). The Museum of Modern Art, New York
(Acquired through the Lillie P. Bliss Bequest).

CHAPTER NINETEEN

ART FROM 1900 TO 1919

By the beginning of the twentieth century the revolt against all forms of naturalism was in full swing and the decade before the First World War was to be one of the most daring and adventurous in the whole history of Western art. Fundamentally new ideas and methods were put forward – in painting, sculpture and architecture, in literature and music and in philosophy and science as well – and the radical innovations of these years underlie all later developments, even today. Two opposing tendencies which had been increasingly felt towards the end of the nineteenth century, the subjectivism of the Symbolists and the objectivism and transcendent 'otherness' sought by Cézanne, were intensified and explored ever more self-consciously. Each was to be taken to its ultimate extreme, bringing to an end artistic traditions going back to Giotto and the early fourteenth century. Already by about 1912 the limits had been reached in one direction with the first completely abstract work of art. Artists then found themselves confronted by an insoluble

dilemma as they oscillated frantically between the cult of pure form and the cult of inner truth – though the dilemma was more apparent than real.

The search for new ways of looking at the world, combined with an urge to break down all accepted conventions and preconceptions, is characteristic generally of the period around the turn of the century. Quite close parallels between innovations in the arts and in philosophy and thought – notably in Henri Bergson (1859–1941) and Benedetto Croce (1866–1952) – can be found. But the theories which were to have the profoundest effect on Europeans and others generally were those of the Viennese psychologist Sigmund Freud (1856–1939), whose *Interpretation of Dreams* was published in 1900. Freud's revolutionary theories about the role of the subconscious, especially of the sexual urge, transformed early twentieth-century attitudes and values. His emphasis on the importance of understanding the instinctual side of human nature, his assertion that the emotions and sensations,

---

The visual arts

1904	Wright, Larkin Building (19,44)
1906	Matisse, *The Joy of Life* (19,3)
	Derain, *The Pool of London* (19,9)
	Modersohn-Becker, *Mother and Child* (19,13)
1907	Rousseau, *The Snake-Charmer* (19,1)
	Picasso, *Les Demoiselles d'Avignon* (19,2)
	Monet, *Water Lilies* (19,4)
1907–9	Wright, Robie House (19,43)
1908	Matisse, *Harmony in Red* (19,10)
	Braque, *Houses and Trees* (19,21)
1908–9	Picasso, *Three Women* (19,23)
1909	Behrens, AEG factory (19,16)
1910	Picasso, *Female Nude* (19,24)
1911	Braque, *The Portuguese* (19,25)
1911–14	Gropius and Meyer, Fagus Works (19,46)
1912	Delaunay, *Simultaneous Contrasts* (19,30)
1912–13	Picasso, *Guitar* (19,27)
	Goncharova, *Cats* (19,38)
1913	Kandinsky, *Improvisation No. 30* (19,18)
	Braque, *Le Courrier* (19,26)
	Balla, *Abstract Speed* (19,32)
	Mondrian, *Composition VII* (19,41)
	Stella, *Battle of Lights, Coney Island* (19,35)
1914	Marc, *Fighting Forms* (19,20)
	Duchamp-Villon, *The Horse* (19,36)
1915	Picasso, *Harlequin* (19,29)
	Brancusi, *The Prodigal Son* (19,37)

Historical landmarks

1900	Freud, *Interpretation of Dreams*. Planck evolves quantum theory
1901	Queen Victoria dies
1902	Boer War ends. Debussy, *Pelléas et Mélisande*
1903	First powered flight (USA)
1904	Russo-Japanese war
1905	Abortive revolution in Russia. Einstein, Special Theory of Relativity. Five cent cinema opens in Pittsburgh
1907	Bergson, *Creative Evolution*
1909	Model T Ford. Diaghilev ballet in Paris. Stein, *Three Lives*
1910	Plastics developed
1911	Agadir crisis. Kandinsky, *Concerning the Spiritual in Art*. Strauss, *Der Rosenkavalier*
1913	Proust, *Swann's Way*. Stravinsky, *Rite of Spring*
1914	First World War begins
1915	Dardanelles. Second battle of Ypres
1916	First battle of the Somme

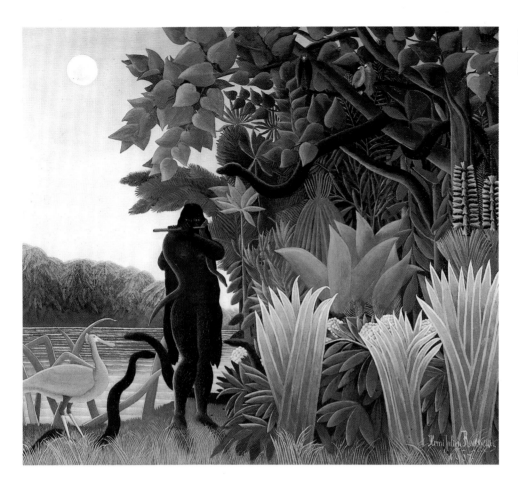

19,1 Henri Rousseau, *The Snake-Charmer*, 1907. Canvas, 5ft 6½ins × 6ft 2⅜ins (1.69 × 1.9m). Musée d'Orsay, Paris.

especially the unconscious urges, are more important than rational thought as a key to human behaviour, were to have profound effects, in art no less than in other fields.

This climate of ideas naturally favoured primitivism – that so-called 'myth of the primitive' to which we have already alluded in connection with Gauguin (see pp. 724–5), the belief that a superior spontaneity, energy and sincerity reside in the ethos of indigenous peoples. As a result, artists now became aware for the first time of the sculpture and painting of Africa and Oceania as 'art', all the more stimulating for being so completely at odds with Western traditions. It could still be seen only in ethnographical and anthropological museums, not in art galleries. But in their search for directness and immediacy of instinctual response, artists increasingly turned away from civilized 'fine art' in favour of the supposedly primitive, especially 'Negro' sculpture (African was not distinguished from Oceanic); and they went on to embrace naive and folk art, even the art of children. In 1911 the writer André Gide declared, in a phrase already in circulation, that 'the time for gentleness and dilettantism is past. What are needed now are barbarians.' By 1915 African sculpture was being claimed as among the greatest ever created. As Braque, an artist little influenced by it overtly, confessed: 'Negro masks also opened a new horizon for me. They permitted me to make contact with instinctive things, direct manifestations that ran counter to a false traditionalism which I abhorred.'

NEW WAYS OF LOOKING

As if by coincidence, the first decade of the century witnessed the culmination of *le Douanier* Rousseau's unique career. Henri Rousseau (1844–1910), a retired customs collector, hence his nickname, was the only naive artist of undoubted genius who has ever lived. And it is significant that his genius was recognized only by the few other artists and writers of genius of the day, notably by Picasso, who owned several of his paintings and gave a now famous banquet in his honour in 1908. Rousseau had started to paint in middle age without training of any kind, though he went to public art exhibitions and was aware of recent developments. But his technical and conceptual naivety endowed him with the innocent eye of a savage without his ever leaving Paris. His imagination teemed with exotic images of mysterious and menacing tropical jungles – true landscapes of the unconscious (**19,1**). The poet Guillaume Apollinaire (1880–1918) wrote that while painting such scenes Rousseau felt their imaginative reality so intensely that he had to throw open the window to escape from his self-induced spells. Though depicted with obsessive exactness and particularity, every detail is subordinated by his extraordinary natural gift for design to the hypnotic drum-beat rhythm of the interweaving verticals and diagonals of his compositions. Violence and terror are completely exteriorized in them.

19,2 Pablo Picasso, *Les Demoiselles d'Avignon*, Paris, begun May, reworked July 1907. Oil on canvas, 8ft × 7ft 8ins (2.44 × 2.34m). The Museum of Modern Art, New York (Acquired through the Lillie P. Bliss Bequest).

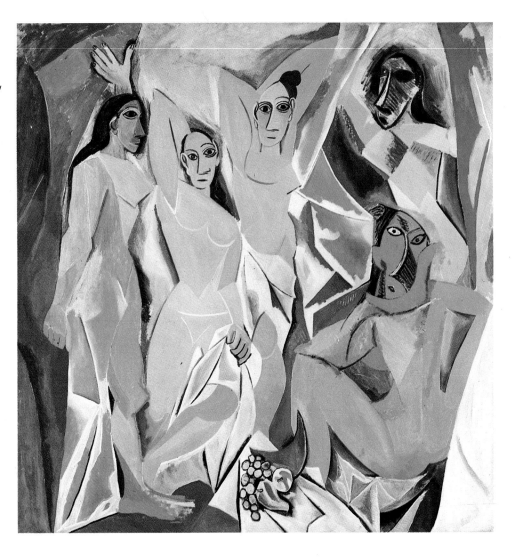

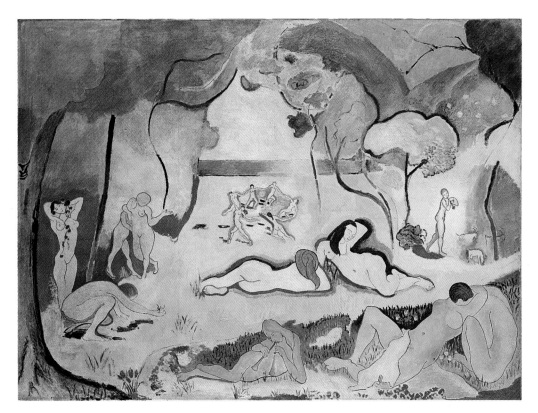

19,3 Henri Matisse, *The Joy of Life*, 1906. Canvas, 5ft 8¾ins × 7ft 10ins (1.75 × 2.39m). Barnes Foundation, Merion, Pennsylvannia.

Jostling the enormous canvases by Rousseau in Picasso's studio were numerous African masks and Oceanic sculptures. Picasso was not the first artist in Paris to discover African sculpture, but it was for him, as he later acknowledged, a creative revelation and source of liberating energy. It impelled him on a headlong course, the immediate effect of which can be seen in *Les Demoiselles d'Avignon* (**19,2**). The two right-hand figures were repainted after he had felt the emotive power of African sculpture (though he claimed not to have seen the ethnographic collection at the Trocadéro until later). This monumental composition marks a decisive turning-point, for with it Picasso made a revolutionary break with traditional, Western, illusionistic art. Instead of treating the picture as a window opening on to the visible world beyond, he conceived it simply as a painting, as a complex of invented forms, flat or nearly so. 'It was my first exorcism-painting', he said many years later, though not just 'because of the forms'.

In painting *Les Demoiselles* Picasso quite deliberately set out to produce a major work – he had the huge canvas specially lined – probably in response to two challenges: Matisse's *The Joy of Life* (**19,3**), which had caused a stir at the 1906 Salon, and Cézanne's late monumental figure compositions, which were just then becoming known and seemed to represent a last noble attempt to recreate the Classical tradition. 'Around 1906 Cézanne's influence gradually flooded everything', Picasso is reported as saying in 1930. *Les Demoiselles d'Avignon* (named after a red-light district in Barcelona, Picasso's home town), began as a brothel scene with allegorical overtones suggested by a sailor seated among the naked women and a student holding a skull. Picasso eliminated these figures at an early stage, and with them any symbolical, iconographical or anecdotal significance he may have originally intended the painting to carry. Its eroticism, however, became ever more aggressive and savage the more radically he absorbed primitive images and forms into it – a ravening eroticism at the very opposite pole of sensuality to that of the Salon painters or to that of Ingres, whose *Turkish Bath* (15,14) may well have been an initial source for one or more of *Les Demoiselles*.

Picasso had turned to various sources for inspiration, notably to Cézanne and Iberian (pre-Roman Spanish) sculpture (4,61), before African art opened his eyes to new ways of regarding the visual world. African art struck him as *plus raisonnable*, he explained – that is, more conceptually structured than the art of the West, more dependent on 'knowing' than on 'seeing'. So, abandoning the single viewpoint and normal proportions, reducing anatomy largely to geometrical lozenges and triangles, he completely re-ordered the human image. It is this total departure from long-accepted Western conventions that makes *Les Demoiselles* so revolutionary a work of art. Its creation involved a major intellectual 'breakthrough', opening up new approaches not only to the treatment of space and form (see pp. 786–90) but also to the evocation of previously unexpressed emotions and states of mind and the rejection of all the comfortable, contrived coherences of representational art. He may even have gone so far as to reject stylistic unity. Was the painting abandoned unfinished, as is usually assumed? It seems quite likely that the stylistic rupture on the right-hand side was left intentionally unresolved.

Monet is seldom mentioned in this context, although it was during these years that he began his last great series of paintings. Impressionism culminated with these – his *Nymphéas (Water Lilies)* – and if the new concept of painting embodied in *Les Demoiselles* had a single origin it could be identified as a reaction against Impressionism's illusionistic aesthetic and air of civilized refinement. Certainly, nothing could be further from the rough handling and harsh and jagged forms of *Les Demoiselles*, its shrieking lack of harmony, its flat, unmodulated color areas and violent centripetal composition, than the delicate brushwork, exquisitely subtle color harmonies and expansive centreless compositions of the *Water Lilies* Monet was painting at the very same moment (**19,4**).

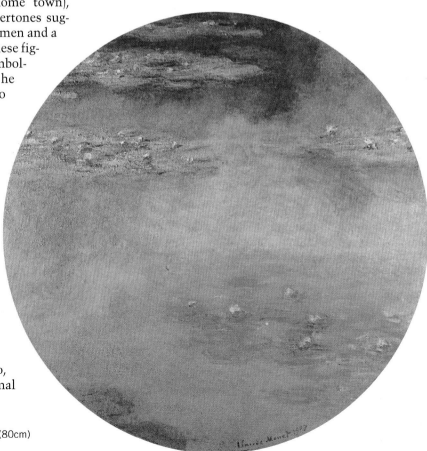

19,4 Claude Monet, *Water Lilies*, 1907. Canvas, 31½ins (80cm) diameter. Musée d'Art et d'Industrie, Saint-Etienne.

Picasso's Demoiselles

ANARCHISM, COLONIALISM AND ART AS EXORCISM

Picasso's *Demoiselles d'Avignon* (19,2) did more than open up new approaches to form and space in painting. It had further meanings both for the artist and for his friends in Paris, who were the only people to see it for many years. Various influences had been absorbed into the painting during its long period of gestation – diverse influences such as Iberian sculpture, late Cézanne figure painting and even El Greco, whose *Vision of St John the Divine* (Metropolitan Museum of Art, New York) provided a source, in reverse, for the three left-hand demoiselles. But African art was the final and determining catalyst. It impelled Picasso on a breakneck course when he 'discovered' it after he had begun the painting. African sculpture's overwhelming appeal was twofold. It held out a key towards solving Picasso's dual problem: how to radicalize structure and form without losing important issues of content and allusions to real-life concerns.

African art could be seen in Paris from at least as early as the 1890s not only in the Ethnographical Museum but in junk-shops where 'fetishes' from the French colonies were often on sale. Picasso and his painter friends Vlaminck, Derain and others, who were soon to 'discover' African art, must have been quite familiar with it for some years though without, apparently, being more than mildly interested until current events in France brought the whole subject of Africa up, and in a very pointed way. A French colonial scandal hit the headlines in 1904–5. Arbitrary executions and murders by two French colonial officials, Gaud and Toqué, were made known and widely publicized, notably in the illustrated weekly *L'Assiette au beurre*, to which Picasso's painter friends Juan Gris and Frank Kupka – both to become prominent Cubist painters later – frequently contributed. A special

issue on *The Torture of Blacks* came out in March 1905. The most shocking instances were those of the so-called 'hunts' and the 14 July festivities in the French Congo. One of the 'hunts' was illustrated, the white hunters in their Safari suits and topee hats rising from their camp-stools to take aim as a covey of naked Africans was driven past them by, presumably, French army 'beaters'. In the same issue Bastille Day, of all days – the day when the beginning of the French Revolution is celebrated all over France – was illustrated with a lithograph of the festivities at Brazzaville, the capital of the French Congo (**19,5**). French colonial officials are here shown applauding and jeering at the spectacle of an African being dynamited to make a human firecracker.

The Gaud-Toqué scandal was eventually hushed up but there were

fierce debates in the Chamber of Deputies and a widespread sense of public outrage. Anti-colonial societies were promoted and remained active until 1910 or later. At one of their meetings Pierre Quillard, whom Picasso knew, made a remarkable speech in which he never condescended or pitied the Africans but asked his 'brothers of another skin and another color to please forgive us for the crimes we have committed against them'. Quillard, like several of Picasso's friends, was a declared anarchist and although Picasso does not seem ever to have committed himself, at any rate politically, he was as open to the appeal of anarchism as they were. For it was the anarchist cultivation of independence of mind, freedom of action and experience for its own sake that attracted artists and intellectuals. The great interest

19,5 Bernard Naudin, *'La Fête du 14 Juillet à Brazzaville'*, cartoon from *L'Assiette au beurre*, 11 March 1905.

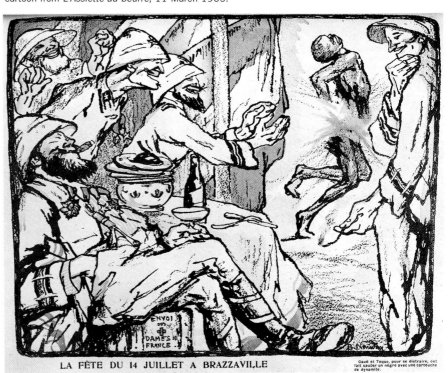

LA FÊTE DU 14 JUILLET A BRAZZAVILLE

Gaud et Toqué, pour se distraire, ont fait sauter un nègre avec une cartouche de dynamite.

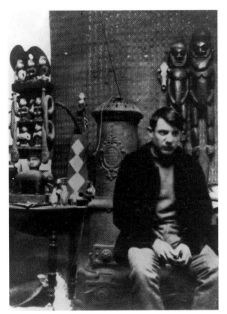

19,6 Gelett Burgess, *Picasso in his Bateau-Lavoir studio*, 1908. Photograph. Musée Picasso, Paris.

Picasso was never very forthcoming about African art and what it had meant to him. But in 1937 he gave to the writer André Malraux an unusually candid account of his first visit to the Ethnographical Museum some 30 years previously. Every detail was imprinted on his memory as if it had happened the previous day. 'I was all alone. I wanted to get away. But I didn't leave. I stayed, I understood that it was very important,' he told Malraux. 'The masks weren't just like any other pieces of sculpture. Not at all. They were magic things . . . .

They were against everything – against unknown, threatening spirits. I always looked at fetishes. I understood; I too am against everything . . . . Spirits, the unconscious (people still weren't talking about that very much), emotion – they're all the same thing. I understood why I was a painter. All alone in that awful museum, with masks, dolls made by the redskins, dusty mannikins. *Les Demoiselles d'Avignon* must have come to me that very day, but not at all because of the forms; because it was my first exorcism-painting – yes absolutely!'

19,7 Pablo Picasso, *Mother and Child*, 1907. Canvas, 31⅞ × 23⅝ins (81 × 60cm). Musée Picasso, Paris.

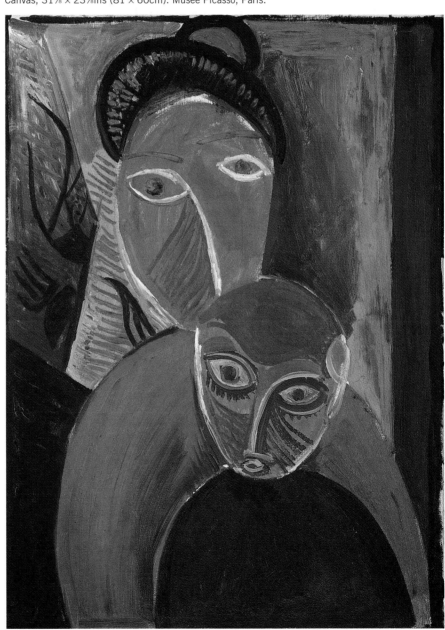

suddenly taken by Picasso and his anarchist friends in the 'dark continent' and African art was motivated in this way: it was a radical avantgarde gesture, a provocative and not simply an appreciative, still less an aesthetic, response.

Picasso's intimate involvement is illustrated by a photograph of him in 1908 in his Paris studio taken by an American writer, Gelett Burgess, who published it in 1910 in an article entitled 'The Wild Men of Paris'. For this Picasso posed himself surrounded by his African and Oceanic sculptures (**19,6**). The previous year he had painted a wilder and even more provocative work than *Les Demoiselles*, a small painting he entitled *Mother and Child* quite clearly based on a traditional Madonna and Child composition, complete with halo and the blue robe of heaven that the Madonna traditionally wears (**19,7**). The transformation of such an easily and immediately recognizable white man's holy icon through what would have been thought in 1907 a crude and brutalizing African manner of painting, evoking associations of tribal magic, superstition, irrationality, darkness and horror, was an unmistakably anarchic gesture. It exploited a familiar anarchic strategy of inversion to equalize and level the 'savage' with the 'civilized'.

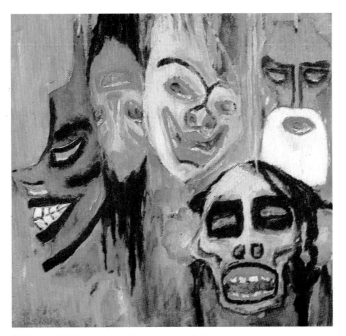

19,8 Emil Nolde, *Masks*, 1911. Canvas, 28¾ × 30½ins (73 × 77.5cm). Nelson-Atkins Museum of Art, Kansas City (Gift of the friends of art).

Monet's aim was still the presentation of an immediate experience of nature, but his water-lily garden at Giverny held for him intimations of infinity and his contemplative visions of it give the illusion of a glimpse into an endless whole. His almost spaceless views downwards, on to and through the surface of the pool, become shimmering, impalpable curtains of color. The natural world disappears into near-abstract patterns of vibrating light and atmosphere. The implications of such paintings were, in fact, quite as radical as those of Picasso's, albeit Monet's approach had been along an alternative route.

If Picasso was a pioneer in the appreciation of African art for its formal qualities, other artists, who had discovered such art as early or even earlier, responded more emotionally. The Fauve painters (see below), to whom Picasso probably owed his introduction to African sculpture, were less overtly influenced by it, but by 1904 in Germany artists were recognizing as 'art' much of the contents of their ethnographic museums and German artists were to be perhaps more deeply influenced by it than were any others. For them it meant essentially a sensual awakening. What fascinated them was its power and directness and immediacy. As the painter Emil Nolde said, it was 'its absolute primitiveness, its intense, often grotesque expression of strength and life in the very simplest form' that impressed them. In his series of *Masks* (**19,8**) Nolde began the process by which these qualities were to be absorbed and interiorized by German artists. A few years later the Expressionist painters of *Der Blaue Reiter* group in Munich (see below) were exploring an even wider range of the arts. In their 'almanac' of 1912 they illustrated examples from New Caledonia, the Malay Peninsula, Easter Island, the Cameroons, Brazil and Mexico as well as Russian and Bavarian folk art and

children's drawings and paintings. Renaissance art was omitted altogether except for one El Greco. As the painter Franz Marc, co-author of the almanac with Kandinsky, wrote earlier that same year: 'We must be bold and turn our backs upon almost everything that until now good Europeans like ourselves thought precious and indispensable.' By that time Kandinsky had already made the second great twentieth-century artistic breakthrough – comparable with that of Picasso – when he painted the first of his abstract *Improvisations*. In them his debt to African art was as great as Picasso's had been in *Les Demoiselles*, but in his case it was instinctive. Of his sympathy and 'spiritual relationship' with what he regarded as primitive art and artists Kandinsky said that 'like ourselves, these artists sought to express in their work only internal truths, renouncing in consequence all considerations of external forms'.

THE FAUVES AND EXPRESSIONISM

Paris was still the cultural capital of Western civilization, and it was there that an exhibition, which has since come to be regarded as the first 'event' in twentieth-century art, took place in 1905. At the Salon d'Automne that year a group of young painters headed by Henri Matisse (1869–1954) exhibited a roomful of works of such strident colors, rough handling and distorted anti-naturalistic drawing that they were dubbed *Les Fauves* (Wild Beasts). The art historian Elie Faure referred to them as young 'primitives' in his introduction to the catalogue and their spiritual affinity with naive art was emphasized by hanging in the same room with their paintings one of the *Douanier* Rousseau's more disturbing jungle visions, *Hungry Lion*.

Matisse was the oldest of the group and the only major artist among them. Of the others, André Derain (1880–1954) and Maurice Vlaminck (1876–1958) were the most gifted. Derain's views of London of 1905 and 1906 summarize the Fauve achievement in their exploitation of violent and quite arbitrary color, what Derain called

19,9 André Derain, *The Pool of London*, 1906. Canvas, 25⅞ × 39ins (65.7 × 99cm). Tate Gallery, London.

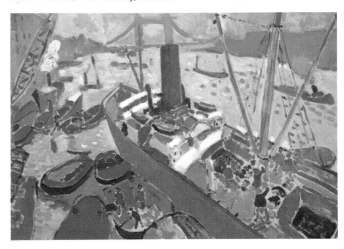

'deliberate disharmonies' (**19,9**). The clashing yellows, purples, blues, greens and reds are expressive of his emotional reaction to the subject, asserting with the utmost intensity his own personal vision. All naturalistic effects have been abandoned. By freeing color from its traditional descriptive role in representation, the Fauves led the way to its use as an expressive end in itself.

MATISSE

The key Fauve painting is Matisse's *The Joy of Life* (19,3), in which color is used even more subjectively than by Derain, while the forms are so drastically simplified that they become a pure linear pattern unifying the picture surface into a single spatial plane, not without some lingering reminiscences of Art Nouveau.

The Joy of Life has an ostensible subject and one which might even seem to look back to the Classical pastoral tradition of Arcadia. Such references were avoided in future. In *Harmony in Red* (**19,10**) Matisse summed up

and completed the Fauve revolution with a vibrant composition of line and flat areas of color, a brilliant essay in pure, childlike creative play with the simplest possible pictorial means – a few contrasting warm and cool colors and some curving and some straight lines. Perspective and modelling have gone completely; space is reduced to a minimum; light has become simply a function of flat color, not a reflection from a lighted surface. Above all, a child's simplicity and innocence bordering on the gauche are combined with an almost barbaric sense of decoration. Color floods the room and turns into something elemental, enveloping the spectator so that we begin to share in the exhilaration of the artist's self-identification with his medium.

'What I am after, above all, is expression', wrote Matisse in his *Notes of a Painter* in 1908. 'The whole arrangement of my picture is expressive. The place occupied by figures or objects, the empty spaces around them, the proportions, everything plays a part.' *Notes of a Painter* was widely read and immediately translated into

19,10 Henri Matisse, *Harmony in Red*, 1908. Canvas, 5ft 11ins × 7ft 2½ins (1.8 × 2.2m). State Hermitage, St Petersburg.

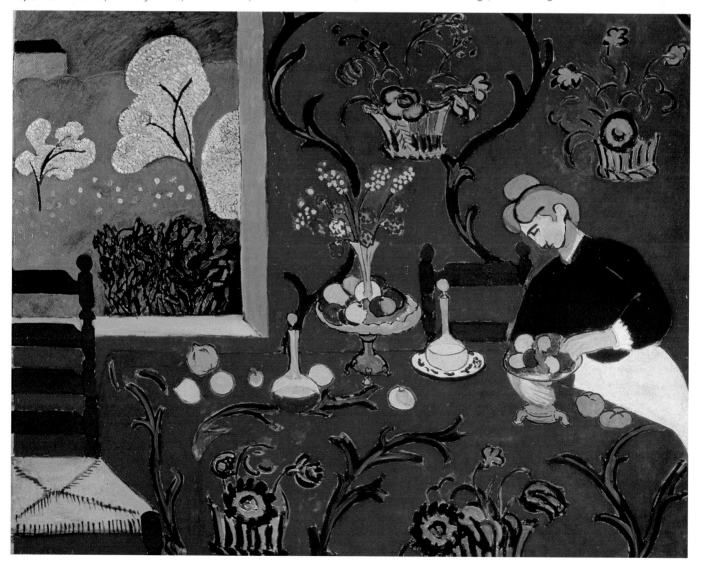

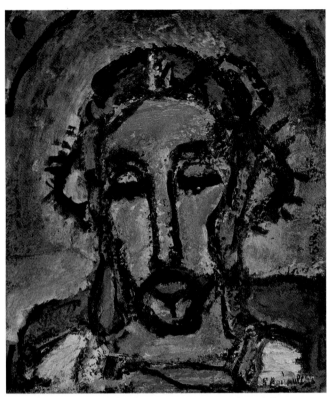

19,11 Georges Rouault, *Ecce Homo*, 1952. Panel, 31½ × 29ins (80 × 74cm). Vatican Museums, Rome.

German and Russian, but although Matisse set out the method he proposed for an art intended to express emotional responses with apparent spontaneity and vividness, he avoided saying anything that might be taken for a program. Perhaps his most revealing comment was that his 'choice of colors does not rest on any scientific theory; it is based on observation, on feeling, on the very nature of each experience', and that his goal was 'to reach that state of condensation of sensations which constitutes a picture'. He also described how slowly and how laboriously his paintings were achieved. Their apparently impetuous spontaneity is quite misleading. They were, in fact, created by a long, progressive process of continual small adjustments until the relationships of color to color, shape to shape and color to shape reached what he felt to be exactly the 'right' balance. The process was self-observant and introverted. His art grew out of art. As he painted he watched his reactions to every brush-stroke, and his reactions to his reactions, and went on painting and repainting until the process gathered its own momentum and the picture emerged of itself, as if out of his subconscious. When painting, he wrote, he was 'conscious only of the forces I am using and I am driven on by an idea that I grasp only as it grows with the picture.'

The Fauves never became a movement, never developed a consistent artistic theory, and by 1908 their loose association began to dissolve. It had been very short-lived. Some members had broken away even earlier, notably Georges Rouault (1871–1958) who was to become the finest religious painter of the twentieth century (**19,11**).

He had, in fact, very little in common with the Fauves apart from the deliberate cultivation of coarse pictorial means for ardent emotional ends, in his case glowing colors separated by thick dark outlines recalling fragments of early medieval stained glass windows. (He began as a stained glass painter and restorer.) His pictures are personal confessions of spiritual anguish and of faith in a revitalized Catholicism, his position being analogous to that of polemical French Catholic writers of his day, such as Léon Bloy, Charles Peguy and Jacques Maritain, who became his friends and admirers. Like Bloy, he found the truths of religious experience and, like van Gogh, the inspiration for his most 'sacramental' images among the poor and destitute and other outcasts and rejects of industrial society. The typical Fauve painting is, of course, quite devoid of social comment. Rouault was an Expressionist in the wider European sense and was perhaps closer to German painters such as Emil Nolde than to any of his French contemporaries.

THE GERMAN EXPRESSIONISTS

Emil Nolde (1867–1956) was a lonely figure in whose work deeply religious and intensely human feelings are conveyed. He regarded himself as a kind of mystic evangelist. Though a good deal older than most German Expressionists, he matured late and his full artistic powers were not revealed until after 1900. By then, largely under the influence of the philosopher Friedrich Wilhelm Nietzsche (1844–1900), a whole generation of writers and artists in central Europe was awaiting a violent change, their work exuding a heavy, oppressive atmosphere of unease, guilt and foreboding. The novels and stories of Franz Kafka (1883–1924) are the supreme example. In the visual arts this mood of apprehension and dread had found expression around the turn of the century in the work of

19,12 Käthe Kollwitz, *Outbreak*, 1903 (no. 5 in *Peasants War* series). Etching, aquatint and engraving, 19½ × 22¼ins (49.4 × 56.6cm). British Museum, London.

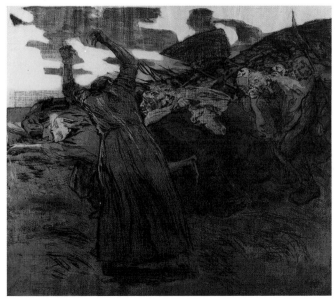

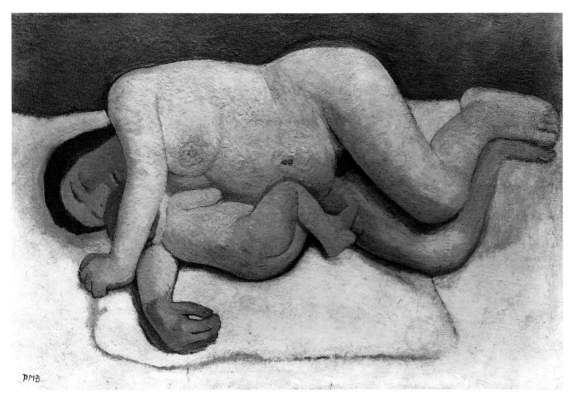

19,13 Paula Modersohn-Becker, *Mother and Child*, 1906. Canvas, 31½ × 49ins (82 × 124.7cm). Private collection, Bremen.

Käthe Kollwitz (1867–1945), who might be called a pioneer Expressionist had she not always been fiercely independent and outside any group. She considered herself to be a realist. In 1903 she issued a series of seven prints depicting events in the Peasants' War of the early sixteenth century, which had left much of Germany devastated (see p. 470). The uprising was eventually repressed with barbaric violence by the landlords and employers. In one print in Kollwitz's series, *Outbreak* (**19,12**), the legendary figure of Black Anna stands with arms upraised, urging on an angry mob of rebellious workers armed with picks and staves and other farm implements.

However, German Expressionist painting, as developed in the immediate pre-First World War years, was concerned increasingly with the psychological situation of contemporary man, and Expressionist painting originated in a revolt in favour of a new spontaneity and intensity of inner vision. Artists felt impelled to confess their moods of anxiety, frustration and resentment towards the modern world. Even more subjective than the Fauves, they sought *Durchgeistigung* or the charging of everything with spiritual significance, with soul, their fervent nationalism and self-consciously anti-French bias making such painters as Grünewald (11,5) seem especially valid. For them primitive art was primarily an emotional and spiritual experience and Nolde, for instance, was able to absorb the impact of African and Oceanic art into his own, deeply personal Christian images, which acquired almost ecstatic force from their brutal simplifications and raw colors. When a critic told him to soften his work he replied, 'It is exactly the opposite that I am striving for, strength and inwardness.'

The first organized group of German Expressionists, *Die Brücke* (The Bridge), was formed in Dresden in 1905, but its goals had been foreshadowed in the work of Munch (see p. 727), who was living in Berlin during these years, and in that of Paula Modersohn-Becker (1876–1907), whose sensual, earthy and very unladylike maternities (**19,13**) are among the most deeply feminine works of art ever created. But she died young, before her genius could flower in the glow of Expressionism. In the *Brücke* manifesto the leading painter in the group, Ernst Ludwig Kirchner (1880–1938), wrote that, 'He who renders his inner convictions as he knows he must, and does so with spontaneity and sincerity, is one of us.' However, the group did not move far beyond its origin in avant-garde protest against academic naturalism, even in Kirchner's Berlin street scenes with their dandies and prostitutes (**19,14**), compelling images though they are of the modern city as the devourer of human souls and fermenter of anxiety. The group's most striking achievement was in graphic art. Rejecting all the delicate atmospheric subtleties achieved with such enormous technical skill and ingenuity by the Impressionists and Post-Impressionists in lithography and various complicated mixtures of graphic media, the *Brücke* artists exploited the simplest and crudest methods of woodblock and lino-cut with brutal but often very powerful effect (**19,15**). In them their primitivism found a perfect vehicle for distilling the ferment of introspective emotions.

The term 'Expressionist' was first used in 1911 by Wilhelm Worringer (1881–1965, author of *Form in Gothic* and *Abstraction and Empathy*, see pp. 783–4) in connection with van Gogh and Matisse. Soon it was being quite

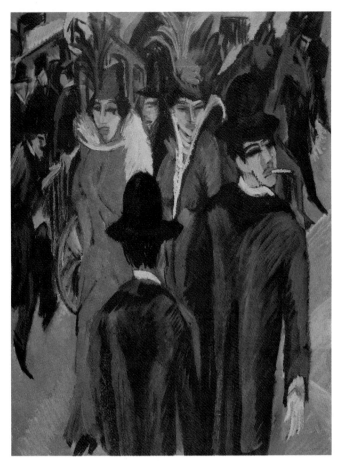

19,14 Ernst Ludwig Kirchner, *Berlin Street Scene*, 1913. Canvas, 6ft 6¾ins × 4ft 11ins (2 × 1.5m). Brücke Museum, Berlin.

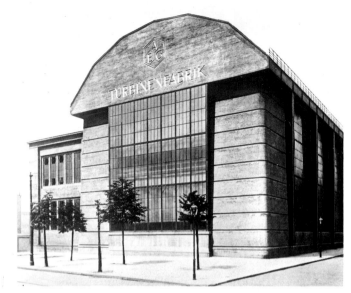

19,16 Peter Behrens, AEG turbine factory, Berlin, 1909.

widely applied to artists and even to architects, though Expressionist architecture is not easy to define. However, in Germany and northern Europe, where Expressionists could find roots in their native (Gothic) traditions, organic Art Nouveau forms coalesced with the anti-Classical simplifying trend in industrial building in ways which enabled architects to mold buildings 'expressively' and mark every form with their creative will. They went some way towards that 'total transposition of a personal idea into a work' which Kirchner had demanded of artists, and in this sense such architects as Hans Poelzig (1869–1936) and Erich Mendelsohn (1887–1953) may be called Expressionist. The most obviously Expressionist buildings are the former's Grosse Schauspielhaus in Berlin (1918–19, destroyed) and the latter's Einstein Observatory at

19,15 Karl Schmitt-Rottluff, *Die Brücke* membership card, 1911. Woodcut on orange card, 6¾ × 5ins (17 × 12.7cm). Brücke Museum, Berlin.

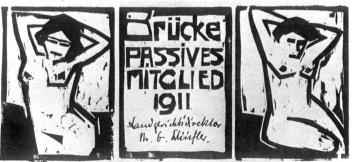

Potsdam (1919). The Schauspielhaus especially, with its fantastic cavernous stalactite-ceilinged interior round a central circular stage, was a truly innovatory conception inaugurating a new departure in theatre design. But other pre-war buildings in Germany were also and perhaps more essentially, though less obviously, Expressionist. The famous AEG turbine factory in Berlin of 1909 by Peter Behrens (1868–1940), for example, is not functional in any simple utilitarian sense but rather monumentally expressive of the energy it houses, both in its form (like a giant piece of machinery) and in its application of the latest technologies (glass and steel) (**19,16**). Similarly expressive is the great Centennial Hall of 1911 at Wrocław (formerly Breslau) by Max Berg (1870–1947). And it was among architects, it should be noted, that the alliance in these years of a leftist political utopianism with the artistic avant-gardes was most pronounced. Their ideology of individual creativity and the autonomy of the imagination led naturally to forms of anarchism.

Whereas the Fauves and the artists allied to the *Brücke* group had all been in varying degrees representational, those of the slightly later *Der Blaue Reiter* (The Blue Rider) group in Munich between 1911 and 1916 took the crucial step beyond the world of visual appearances and created some of the first completely abstract or non-objective works of art. The question of who painted the first abstract picture may be endlessly debated. Certainly Kandinsky, the leading *Blaue Reiter* painter, was not the only artist who began, around 1910–12, to eliminate all references to objective reality in his work. There were others in France, Italy, Russia, Holland and elsewhere (see pp. 834–5). But Kandinsky was different in that he did so in order to strengthen the imaginative and emotional and spiritual content of his paintings. There is nothing of the coldly theoretical and geometric about his first abstract pictures. On the contrary, they are warmly spontaneous and organic. Discerning critics and others were immediately persuaded by them. 'I cannot any longer doubt the possibility of emotional expression by such abstract visual signs', wrote Roger Fry in 1913 after seeing one of

Kandinsky's *Improvisations* in London. 'They are pure visual music.'

As Fry realized, the origins of abstract art go back to Romantic theories that in their essential nature all the arts – music, poetry, painting, sculpture and architecture – are one and that the ultimate artistic experience would be synaesthetic (a synthesis of perception and response on many levels) – a Wagnerian *Gesamtkunstwerk* or total art work. Stimulated by their awareness of the directly affective character of music, which communicates without the aid of description or narrative or any appeal to anything outside itself, the Romantics were already conscious of the expressive power of shapes and colors, of brush-strokes and textures, of size and scale, and of the possibility that the visual arts might become as autonomous as music. In this way the trend towards abstraction began. During the later nineteenth century, artists successively approached and withdrew from the threshold of non-representational art, though the Symbolists and others such as Whistler in his *Nocturnes* (17,17) came close to crossing it with their use of colors and forms to evoke sensations.

KANDINSKY

The Russian painter Vassily Kandinsky (1866–1944) lived in Munich from 1896 until war broke out in 1914, with lengthy visits to Italy and Paris. A highly educated and widely cultivated man, he had given up a university professorship in law in order to become an artist. In his early work he adopted the flat patterns, broad color areas and rhythmic lines of German Art Nouveau, as had his companion Gabriele Münter (1877–1962), with whom he settled at Murnau, south of Munich, in 1909. Münter's *Boating* (**19,17**) of the following year synthesizes the expressiveness of Fauve color with the simplified forms bounded by strong, dark contour lines borrowed from Bavarian glass painting, to which she had introduced Kandinsky, as well as to other peasant and folk arts. Kandinsky stands while Münter rows the boat and we see him as if through her eyes. It was at Murnau that they were to take together the decisive step towards abstraction. Kandinsky's lyrical and resonantly Slav sense of color – he said he had always experienced music in terms of color and color primarily as an emotional effect – gradually lost its descriptive function and became detached from form. Yet he approached abstraction cautiously. He himself dated his full understanding of its possibilities to an evening in 1910 when he accidentally failed to recognize one of his own canvases which was stacked the wrong way up and saw a picture 'of extraordinary beauty, glowing with inner radiance'. This revelation of the inherent expressive properties of color and form convinced him that the representation of nature was quite superfluous for his art. It also accorded with the predominantly anti-materialist, mystical bent of his mind, for he was deeply interested in the occult and the theosophical theories of Rudolf Steiner (1861–1925), who believed that art and artistic experiences were the best stimulant for

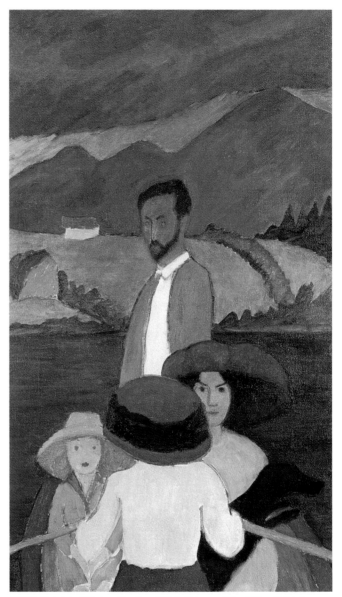

19,17 Gabriele Münter, *Boating*, 1910. Canvas, 49 × 29ins (124.5 × 73.7cm). Collection, Milwaukee Art Museum (Gift of Mrs Harry Lynde Bradley).

an understanding of the spiritual. Steiner was living in Munich during these pre-war years and Kandinsky probably knew him and certainly attended his lectures. He may even have been influenced by theosophical drawings of 'thought forms'. In other ways, too, his 'revelation' of abstract art was in keeping with much of the advanced thought of the day, for example that of the French philosopher Bergson, who insisted on the importance of the intuitive in the apprehension of truth, or that of the pioneer *Gestalt* psychologists who asserted that shape, size, color, spatial orientation, etc. regularly produce certain perceptual effects, from whence it follows that there are 'meanings' intrinsic within forms and colors by which they convey themselves directly, irrespective of the context. The publication in Munich in 1908 of Worringer's *Abstraction and Empathy*, in which abstract tendencies in art are attributed to man's need to withdraw from the

SOURCES AND DOCUMENTS

KANDINSKY ON COLOR

Color played a key role in Kandinsky's theories about the essential expressive or 'spiritual' value of art and its autonomy, that is, its independence from naturalistic appearances. He developed his theories into a program for abstract painting in his *Concerning the Spiritual in Art* (1912), from which the following extracts are taken:

Letting one's eyes wander over a palette laid out with colors has two main results:

1. There occurs a purely physical effect, . . . The spectator experiences a feeling of satisfaction, of pleasure, like a gourmet who has a tasty morsel in his mouth. Or the eye is titillated, as is one's palate by a highly spiced dish. It can also be calmed or cooled again, as one's finger can when it touches ice. These are all physical sensations and as such can only be of short duration. They are also superficial . . . .
2. The second main consequence of the contemplation of color, i.e., the psychological effect of color. The psychological power of color becomes apparent, calling forth a vibration from the soul . . . .

Sight must be related not only to taste, but also to all the other senses. Which is indeed the case. Many colors have an uneven, prickly appearance, while others feel smooth, like velvet, so that one wants to stroke them (dark ultramarine, chrome-oxide green, madder). Even the distinction between cold and warm tones depends upon this sensation. There are also colors that appear soft (madder), others that always strike one as hard (cobalt green, green-blue oxide), so that one might mistake them for already dry when freshly squeezed from the tube.

The expression 'the scent of colors' is common usage.

Finally, our hearing of colors is so precise that it would perhaps be impossible to find anyone who would try to represent his impression of bright yellow by means of the bottom register of the piano, or describe dark madder as being like a soprano voice . . . .

Anyone who has heard of color therapy knows that colored light can have a particular effect upon the entire body . . . . red light has an enlivening and stimulating effect upon the heart, while blue, on the other hand, can lead to temporary paralysis . . . .

In general, therefore, color is a means of exerting a direct influence upon the soul. Color is the keyboard. The eye is the hammer. The soul is the piano with its many strings.

The artist is the hand that purposefully sets the soul vibrating by means of this or that key.

(Vassily Kandinsky, *Über der Geistige in der Kunst*, Munich 1912, tr. K. C. Lindsay and P. Vergo, *Kandinsky; Complete Writings on Art*, London 1982)

materialistic world and find a 'resting-place in the flight of phenomena' was also more than a coincidence.

In 1910 Kandinsky finished writing his own book *Concerning the Spiritual in Art*, though it was not published until 1912. In it he formulated his concept of non-representational art as one originating in some 'inner necessity' of the artist to find a 'spiritual' art form free from all references to the external world. In themselves abstract formal qualities were of as little importance to Kandinsky as representational qualities: they became meaningful only in so far as they expressed the artist's innermost feelings and antimaterialistic values and thus created a true spiritual reality. He was keenly aware of the danger that abstract art might be misunderstood and would be seen as mere decoration – indeed, of the danger that an art of pure colors and forms might degenerate into meaningless decorative patterns – 'something like a necktie or a carpet', as he wrote.

So in his early abstract paintings of 1911 to 1913 he retained hints and suggestions of recognizable subject-matter, hidden or disguised images, in order to lead the spectator into his spiritual world and apocalyptic visions, as in *Improvisation No. 30* (**19,18**). Kandinsky's 40-odd *Improvisations* were, he said, 'largely unconscious, spontaneous expressions of inner character, non-material in nature'. In No. 30, however, two cannons are quite clearly recognizable in the right-hand bottom corner and indeed the painting acquired the sub-title *Cannons*. When questioned about this in 1914 Kandinsky replied: 'The designation *Cannons*, selected by me *for my own use*, is not to

19,18 Vassily Kandinsky, *Improvisation No. 30*, 1913. Canvas, 3ft 7¼ins × 3ft 7¼ins (1.1 × 1.1m). Art Institute of Chicago (Arthur Jerome Eddy Memorial Collection).

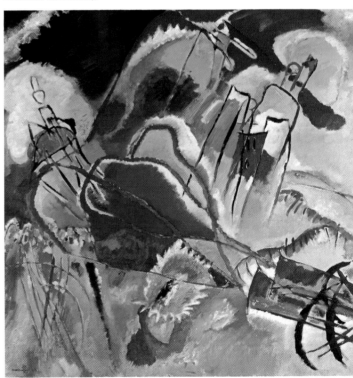

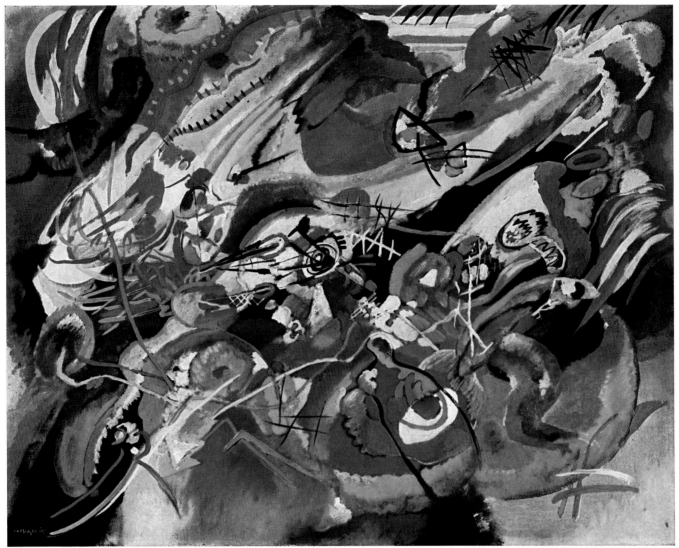

19,19 Vassily Kandinsky, *Study for Composition VII* (no. 2), 1913. Canvas, 30⅓ × 34¾ins (78 × 99.5cm). Städtische Galerie im Lenbachhaus, Munich.

be understood as indicating the contents of the picture. These contents are indeed what the spectator *lives*, or *feels* while under the effect of the *form and color* combinations of the picture . . . which I have painted rather subconsciously in a state of strong inner tension. So intensely did I feel the necessity of some of the forms that I remember having given loud-voiced directions to myself, as for instance, "But the corners must be heavy!"'

Kandinsky seems to be implying that the cannons had taken shape while he painted without his consciously intending them and that the spectator should similarly allow his subconscious free play when looking at the picture. How far he actually went in such paintings towards the automatic creative processes of later twentieth-century artists is uncertain. His more fully evolved *Compositions* of these same years were certainly consciously planned and carefully worked out in preliminary drawings and sketches; and it was with his *Compositions* that he finally succeeded in suppressing representational elements altogether. He described them in 1912 as 'expressions of a slowly formed inner feeling, tested and worked over repeatedly, and almost pedantically . . . . Reason, consciousness, purpose play an overwhelming part. But of

calculation nothing appears: only feeling.' A work such as *Composition VII* (**19,19**) constitutes a true landmark in the history of painting, for the forms, the colored shapes, have no equivalents in the world of appearances at all. Moreover, there is no perspective and thus no spatial relationships as we normally apprehend them: the colored shapes float and gyrate in a continuously expanding and contracting space unknown to our conscious selves but akin to that of dreams.

MARC

Franz Marc (1880–1916) was the only other important member of the *Blaue Reiter* group, though it was not until shortly before he was killed in the First World War that he approached Kandinsky's degree of symbolic abstraction. His work is dominated by passionate feelings for animals, which he thought more beautiful than human beings and through which he believed humans could experience closer affinities with nature. It was a need to find symbolic forms to convey his emotions on 'submerging himself in the soul of the animals' that impelled his search for a non-representational art echoing

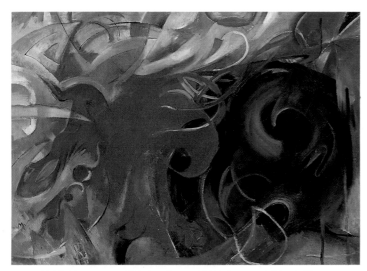

19,20 Franz Marc, *Fighting Forms*, 1914. Canvas, 35¾ × 51¾ins (91 × 129cm). Bayerische Staatsgemäldesammlungen, Munich.

what he called the 'absolute rhythms of nature'. By 1911, the year in which he and Kandinsky formed *Der Blaue Reiter* group in Munich, Marc had already abandoned local color in such paintings as his famous *Red Horses and Blue Horses*. The following year he saw examples of Futurist and Orphic paintings in Paris (see pp. 793–7). Inspired by their dynamic innovations, he embarked on his last works, notably *Animal Destinies* (1913, Kunstmuseum, Basel) and the almost completely non-representational *Fighting Forms* (**19,20**), painted early in 1914 but left unfinished when war broke out and he was called up. Two whirling embryonic forms, one expanding red, the other contracting dark blue, seem to be on the point of impact, symbolizing the universal psychic energy animating both human and non-human creation.

CUBISM

The word Cubism is a misnomer and hinders rather than helps the understanding of a subject which has always resisted precise definition. Neither Picasso nor Braque would ever say what they meant or intended in inventing Cubism – no doubt for much the same reason that T. S. Eliot always refused to explain *The Waste Land*. It has no meaning beyond or outside itself. As the poet Archibald MacLeish wrote: 'A poem should not mean but be.' However, 'Cubism' became the label of a movement in 1911 when a group of artists (not including Picasso and Braque, from whom they all derived) exhibited together in Paris and were written about as Cubists. The following year exhibitions were held all over Europe – again without Picasso and Braque – and a book entitled *Du Cubisme* was published by two of the painters, Albert Gleizes (1881–1953) and Jean Metzinger (1883–1956). In 1913 the Armory Show in New York made Cubism known in America.

If Picasso and Braque held themselves aloof from the movement they had initiated, they were probably better

aware than any of their contemporaries of its implications; for it raised the question of figuration as against abstraction as a conscious and serious issue. On this matter Picasso's views are known. 'There is no such thing as abstract art', he is reported to have said. 'You must always start with something.' So whatever later abstract artists were to derive from Cubism – and it became the immediate source of a stream of abstract movements such as Orphism, *De Stijl*, Constructivism, etc. (see pp. 793–9) – it was certainly never intended by its creators to be non-representational.

PICASSO AND BRAQUE:
ANALYTICAL AND SYNTHETIC CUBISM

Pablo Picasso (1881–1973) was an infant prodigy. Already in 1900 when he first came to Paris from Barcelona, he had mastered every trick in the academic painter's repertoire and several of his Blue and Rose Period paintings of 1903 to 1906 are remarkable for their wistful poetry and extreme delicacy and refinement of color and handling. The contrast between his paintings of these years, such as the *Family of Saltimbanques* (**19,22**) and *Les Demoiselles d'Avignon* (19,2), painted only two years later, is quite startling. In subject the two paintings are alike. Both depict social outcasts – street musicians and itinerant circus performers in the former, prostitutes in the latter – yet they seem worlds apart. A gulf, and not just an artistic

19,21 Georges Braque, *Houses and Trees*, 1908. Canvas, 28¾ × 23⅜ins (73 × 59.5cm). Kunstmuseum, Berne (Hermann and Margrit Rupf Foundation).

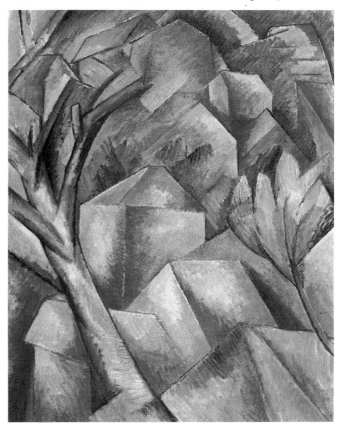

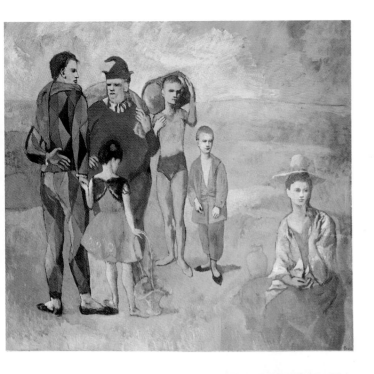

gulf, seems to separate them. *Les Demoiselles d'Avignon* was a complete and deliberate *volte-face*. Its crudity and apparent clumsiness were intentional. Moreover, it posed the pictorial problems with which Cubism was to wrestle and illustrates very clearly the influences of its two main sources: first of all Cézanne, whose late works (17,44) foreshadowed Cubism even more profoundly than his famous injunction to treat nature in terms of the sphere, the cylinder and the cone would suggest; and secondly, African sculpture, in which Picasso recognized the key to his problem of creating an art simultaneously representational and anti-naturalistic. This is, perhaps, as near a simple definition as is possible of so slippery a concept as Cubism, and it is significant that Picasso's debt to African art should be most obvious in the most Cubist features of the painting, for example the squatting figure on the right in which he abandoned perspective and the single view-point in order to combine several views in a single image. Cubism is partially prefigured in other ways as well:

19,22 *Above* Pablo Picasso, *Family of Saltimbanques*, 1905. Oil on canvas, 6ft 11¾ins × 7ft 6⅜ins (2.13 × 2.3m). National Gallery of Art, Washington DC (Chester Dale Collection).

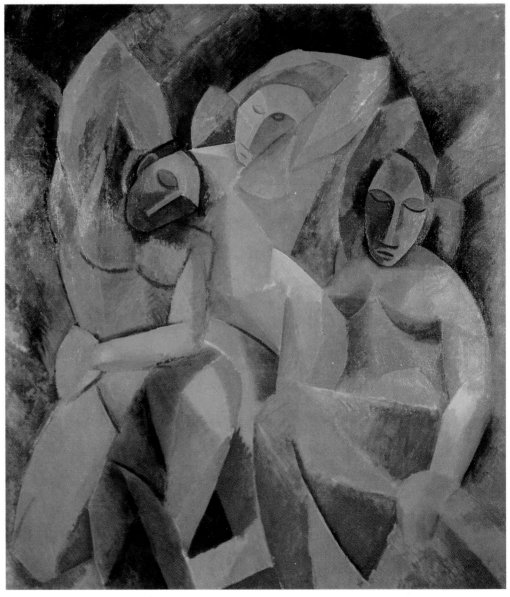

19,23 Pablo Picasso, *Three Women*, 1908–9. Canvas, 6ft 6¾ins × 5ft 10½ins (2 × 1.79m). State Hermitage, St Petersburg.

notably in the way figures are broken up into flat surfaces meeting at sharp angles (later called 'faceting'); in the way light is used arbitrarily and anti-perspectivally, different forms being lit from different directions as required by the general design; in the way space has been almost completely eliminated, as if the figures were being projected forwards out of the picture by the stiff but pliable metallic material behind, which seems to buckle out between them while taking on a correspondingly angular, faceted form from the pressure of their bodies against it so that the foreground merges into the background; and above all in the way the whole picture is conceived as an independent construction – what the Cubists were later to call a *tableau-objet* or picture-object.

Very soon after painting *Les Demoiselles* Picasso met Georges Braque (1882–1963), who was at first as shocked as everyone else by its wilful ugliness. But shortly afterwards his own painting began moving, more coolly and soberly, in a parallel manner to Picasso's and from 1908 until 1914, when Braque was called up for military service, they worked together. Cubism was invented jointly by them. Theirs was a uniquely close and intimate collaboration, closer and more prolonged than that of Monet and Renoir in the early years of Impressionism. They were, Braque once said, 'like mountaineers roped together'. Indeed, at one point (in 1911) their works can hardly be distinguished and they themselves were uncertain later who had painted which pictures.

At first Braque seems to have taken the lead, but by late 1908 both he and Picasso were on the threshold of Cubism with such works as *Houses and Trees* (**19,21**) and *Three Women* (**19,23**). Cézanne was now the predominant influence, most obviously in the geometrical simplifications of the Braque, where natural forms have been broken up into a semi-abstract all-over design of tilting, overlapping planes compressed into so shallow a space that they seem to move outwards towards the spectator instead of inwards towards a vanishing point. But the Picasso is hardly less indebted to Cézanne. It was originally conceived in his 'African' manner, with brashly contrasted colors articulated with vigorously brushed striations, as in the right-hand figures of *Les Demoiselles*. He then completely repainted it in a more controlled and consistent way with a very narrow range of close-valued colors (mainly terracottas and muted greens) so that the whole picture has a faceted surface without intervals or gaps, the figures and the ground forming a single, rock-like mass. It is less spatial, more volumetric and sculptural than the Braque. The huge figures are palpably bulky, while the picture itself remains flat, like a stone relief – and static, as if filled with a primordial stillness.

From 1910 onwards Picasso's paintings gradually became less sculptural, their fragmented contours and transparent planes hovering in indeterminate yet somehow shallow, luminous space, so that his and Braque's work during these years of so-called Analytical Cubism – 1910 to 1912 – might be described as a painterly dissolution of their 1908/9 manner. The term Analytical Cubism, introduced some years later by the Spanish

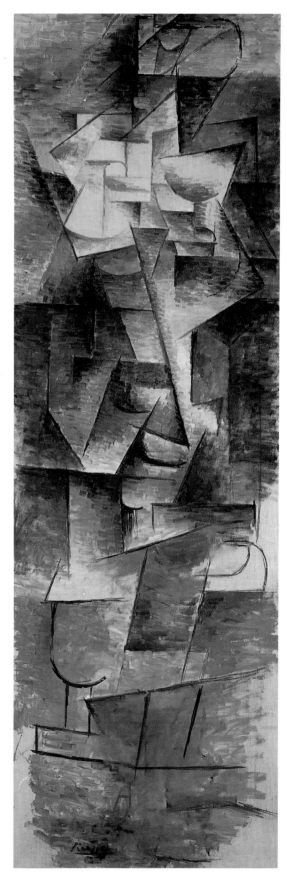

19,24 Pablo Picasso, *Female Nude*, 1910. Canvas, 73¾ × 24ins (187 × 61cm). National Gallery of Art, Washington DC (Ailsa Mellon Bruce Fund, 1972).

SOURCES AND DOCUMENTS

BRAQUE AND PICASSO ON CUBISM

Braque's aphorisms on art, said to have been originally jottings on the margins of drawings, were first collected and published in 1917. They emphasize the autonomy of Cubism, its 'constitution of a pictorial fact' and its status as a form of representation. The following is a selection from the 20 published in 1917.

1. In art progress consists not in extension but in the knowledge of its limits.
2. The limits of the means employed determine the style, engender the new form and impel to creation.
3. The charm and the force of children's paintings often stem from the limited means employed. Conversely the art of decadence is a product of extension.
4. New means, new subjects.
5. The subject is not the object; it is the new unity, the lyricism which stems entirely from the means employed.
6. The painter thinks in forms and colors.
7. The aim is not to reconstitute an anecdotal fact but to constitute a pictorial fact.
8. Painting is a mode of representation.
9. One must not imitate what one wishes to create.
10. One does not imitate the appearance; the appearance is the result.
11. To be pure imitation, painting must make an abstraction from appearances.
12. The senses deform, the mind forms. Work to perfect the mind. There is no certainty except in what the mind conceives.
13. Nobility comes from contained emotion.
14. Emotion must not be rendered by an emotional trembling. It is not something that is added, or that is imitated. It is the germ, the work is the flowering.
15. I love the rule which corrects emotion.

(First published by P. Reverdy in *Nord-Sud*, December 1917; tr. from E. Fry, *Cubism*, New York and London 1966)

Picasso's only recorded discussion of Cubism was with an American critic, Marius de Zayas, in 1923. As the following extracts reveal, he was sceptical of attempts to intellectualize Cubism. For him it was an art like any other, to be judged by results and not intentions. His remarks were first published, in a translation which he approved, in New York in 1923.

In my opinion to search means nothing in painting. To find, is the thing . . . . We all know that Art is not truth. Art is a lie that makes us realize truth; at least the truth that is given us to understand. The artist must know the manner whereby to convince others of the truthfulness of his lies . . . . They speak of Naturalism in opposition to modern painting. I would like to know if anyone has ever seen a natural work of art. Nature and art, being two different things, cannot be the same thing. Through art we express our conception of what nature is not . . . .

Cubism is no different from any other school of painting. The same principles and the same elements are common to all . . . . Many think that Cubism is an art of transition, an experiment which is to bring ulterior results. Those who think that way have not understood it. Cubism is not either a seed or a foetus, but an art dealing primarily with forms and when a form is realized it is there to live its own life.

Mathematics, trigonometry, chemistry, psychoanalysis, music, and whatnot, have been related to Cubism to give it an easier interpretation. All this has been pure literature, not to say nonsense, which brought bad results, blinding people with theories.

Cubism has kept itself within the limits and limitations of painting, never pretending to go beyond it. Drawing, design, and color are understood and practiced in Cubism in the spirit and manner that they are understood and practiced in all other schools. Our subjects might be different, as we have introduced into painting objects and forms that were formerly ignored. We have kept our eyes open to our surroundings, and also our brains.

(Originally published as 'Picasso Speaks' in *The Arts*, May 1923)

Cubist painter Juan Gris (1887–1927), is another misnomer in so far as it implies any rational process of dissection. But forms were increasingly fragmented and Picasso and Braque both tended not to work from any visual model, not even a still life set up in the studio, and this inevitably led towards abstraction and a more intellectual kind of painting in which the depicted objects were to disintegrate to a point only just short of total unrecognizability. How far and how quickly they were to move away from anything like verisimilitude can be seen in Picasso's *Female Nude* and Braque's *The Portuguese* of 1910 and 1911 respectively (**19,24; 25**).

In the *Female Nude* the effect is hardly sculptural at all any longer, for it is quite massless, a configuration of floating, overlapping and eliding planes open to space and suggesting a flimsy tower built of pieces of cardboard leaning against or propped on top of each other. The tilting of these planes, combined with the lines, which sometimes form their edges and sometimes do not, creates a delicately poised spiral of ambiguities. In *The Portuguese*

19,25 Georges Braque, *The Portuguese*, 1911. Canvas, 45⅞ × 32ins (117 × 81.5cm). Kunstmuseum, Basel.

the traditional relationship between figure and ground has given way to a unified pictorial configuration in which the shapes seem to float close to the picture plane in a sharply contracted space. In both paintings the near monochrome color (predominantly ochres and silvery grays), the dry, matt surface and the extreme degree of fragmentation are all characteristic of Analytical Cubism. So, too, is the way the ostensible subjects hover like after-images behind the geometrical structures. Braque left only just enough clues for his to be recognized; Picasso went further. His subject may not, in fact, have been a female nude but a mother and child, and this uncertainty emphasizes how unimportant subject-matter was for the Cubists – seldom more than a pretext, in fact, and always extremely limited and studio-centred.

It was this introversion, this concentration on pictorial structure and language at the expense of subject-matter which led to the Cubists' assertion of the essentially autonomous nature of the work of art – all of which, combined with their fastidious restraint and good taste in handling, might suggest some latent 'art for art's sake' and Symbolistic affinities. Much of Picasso's earlier work had been strongly Symbolist in tone. And it is in Symbolist writings that comparable conjunctions to those of Cubist paintings can be found, mysterious verbal structures which afford only the most partial glimpses of external reality.

That the artists themselves realized how dangerously near they had come to total abstraction is shown by their beginning to include small but easily recognizable details, such as the stencilled lettering in *The Portuguese*, in their later Analytical Cubist pictures. And it was probably this, too, which led to the next and perhaps the most important step of all in Cubism as a source for later developments in twentieth-century art – the invention of *collage* (paste-up). In a still life of May 1912 Picasso incorporated a ready-made facsimile, a piece of commercial oilcloth printed with imitation chair-seat caning, to indicate the chair on which the still life rested. In a sense this was the logical outcome of Cubism. Certainly, the Cubist aesthetic could go only one step further, which Picasso duly took when he began incorporating actual objects or parts of them into his pictures. In doing this he went beyond the play with natural and artistic reality in his first *collage* with chair-seat caning, for he now introduced 'real' elements in such a way that they could be understood in either sense or in both senses simultaneously.

A further refinement of *collage* was invented by Braque when he limited the pasted-on elements to pieces of paper. *Papiers collés*, as they are called, are necessarily and absolutely flat and with them illusionistic space was finally eliminated altogether, though spatial relationships might still be indicated by overlapping. The virtue of *papiers collés*, however, lay in the method's ambivalence. The strips of pasted paper could be arranged according to an aesthetically independent (or abstract) scheme, while still signifying the color and form of the objects drawn over them. The breathtaking skill with which this duality could be manipulated by Braque is beautifully displayed

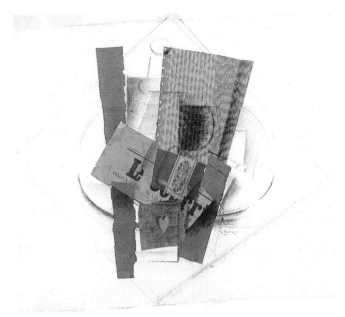

19,26 Georges Braque, *Le Courrier*, 1913. Pasted paper and charcoal, 20 × 22½ins (51 × 57cm). Philadelphia Museum of Art (A. E. Gallatin Collection).

in *Le Courrier* (**19,26**). The carafe, wine-glass, cigarette packet, newspaper and playing-card, which provide the subject, seem to hover over the square table-top like disembodied presences. They can be sensed rather than seen through the gossamer web of an abstract 'arrangement' of pasted-on planes of color.

Whereas Braque used *collage* logically and soberly as an instrument on which to draw out tender and sonorous chords of visual harmony, Picasso delighted in the opportunities it gave him to display his audacity in paradox and visual wit, turning one substance into another as if by visual alchemy – newspapers into violins and so on – and extracting new meanings out of old forms by combining them in unexpected ways or in unusual contexts. It also enabled him to attain the ultimate Cubist ideal of the *tableau-objet* – a constructed object independent of, but recreating, the external world. 'The purpose of the *papier collé*', he later said, 'was to give the idea that different textures can enter into a composition to become the reality in the painting that competes with the reality in nature. We tried to get rid of *trompe l'oeil* to find a *trompe l'esprit* . . . . If a piece of newspaper can become a bottle, that gives us something to think about in connection with both newspapers and bottles, too. This displaced object has entered a universe for which it was not made and where it retains, in a measure, its strangeness. And this strangeness was what we wanted to make people think about because we were quite aware that our world was becoming very strange and not exactly reassuring.'

The words printed on the newspaper cuttings, cigarette packets, bottle labels, etc. used in *collages* may have had some urban associative value for the artists but seldom if ever any other verbal significance, and it is misleading to read any into them. Indeed, the importance of *collages* lies in the fact that, divorced from their artistic context, the

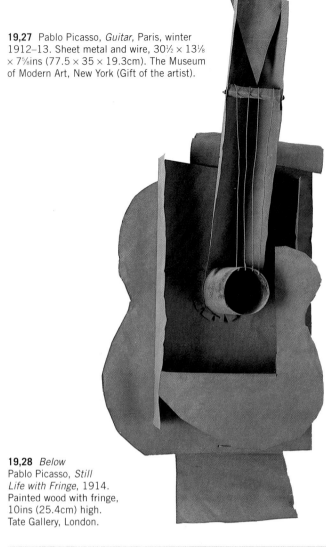

19,27 Pablo Picasso, *Guitar*, Paris, winter 1912–13. Sheet metal and wire, 30½ × 13⅛ × 7⅜ins (77.5 × 35 × 19.3cm). The Museum of Modern Art, New York (Gift of the artist).

19,28 *Below*
Pablo Picasso, *Still Life with Fringe*, 1914. Painted wood with fringe, 10ins (25.4cm) high. Tate Gallery, London.

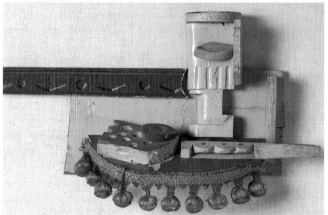

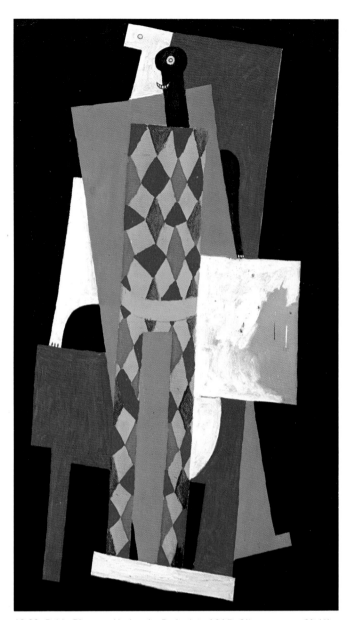

19,29 Pablo Picasso, *Harlequin*, Paris, late 1915. Oil on canvas, 6ft ¼in × 3ft 5⅜ins (1.84 × 1.05m). The Museum of Modern Art, New York (Acquired through the Lillie P. Bliss Bequest).

individual elements used to create their imagery are quite meaningless and of no intellectual or aesthetic value – a supreme demonstration, in fact, of the artist making something beautiful and meaningful out of nothing.

The first Cubist sculpture also dates from 1912 and, Picasso claimed, slightly preceded *collage*. Braque had for some time been making cardboard models of objects as aids in working out his Cubist paintings and Picasso followed him. But it was Picasso who saw in them the possibility of Cubist sculpture. He remade one in sheet metal

and wire and thereby effected a sculptural revolution (**19,27**). It is impossible to exaggerate the radical nature of Picasso's impact on sculpture: it was more radical even than on painting. With the *Guitar* he changed, at one stroke, the whole nature of sculpture. Until now all Western sculpture had been carved in stone or wood or modelled in clay and cast in bronze or other metal. Picasso's sculptures were made of wood, tin, cardboard, paper, string and other materials, sometimes of a distinctly ready-made character, and they were constructed or put together by the same process of assemblage as were his *collages* – though his debt to African sculpture, particularly to a Wobé mask he owned, is obvious (18,43). Sculpture was liberated by him from its traditional materials and techniques and subject-matter and was given a new intellectual dimension – as was appreciated at the time, notably by Boccioni and Tatlin (see pp. 795, 821–2). And since Picasso's constructed objects themselves represent objects they attained in a high degree that autonomy which the Cubists sought. The *Guitar* also manages to retain some of the ambiguities and contradictions of Cubist paintings, being flat yet not quite flat, half spatial and half solid, decorative yet austere and harsh. Later his constructions were more light-hearted or seemingly so. The *Still Life with Fringe* (**19,28**) hangs a snack on the wall with wooden salami, slices of bread, knife and a half-full wine-glass (the latter rendered as a rather crude three-dimensional planar model of an Analytical Cubist painting of a glass). A dark wood-grained strip of dado with carved motifs painted in *trompe l'oeil* and, below, a piece of real golden-thread fringe complete this apparently rough and simple, but in fact most sophisticated, compound image. Cubist sculpture of a few years later by Jacques Lipchitz (1891–1973), Henri Laurens (1855–1954) and Alexander Archipenko (1887–1964) is tame by comparison. Most sculptors, such as Aristide Maillol (1861–1944), went on using the traditional techniques and materials and subject-matter, limited almost exclusively to nude (female) figures.

The last, or Synthetic, phase of Cubism developed alongside *collage* and became in a sense the mirror image of Analytical Cubism, for the artists now worked back from abstraction to representation, not the other way round. As in *collage*, the object is depicted with forms not originally derived from it. Flat and colored shapes are arranged decoratively on the canvas, creating a substructure through which the object is made visible by subsequent adjustment and added signs. The pictorial surface remains an arrangement of flattened forms bearing no relation to the shape of the figure or object portrayed and looking almost as if they have been cut and pasted on to the canvas. Yet the subject is clearly recognizable. At the time Picasso thought his Synthetic Cubist *Harlequin* (**19,29**) the 'best thing I have done', and it epitomizes the style in its daring simplicity, its bright, almost dazzlingly decorative color and its unconcealed disunities. By this date Picasso was again working on his own, for Braque, who was invalided out of the French army in 1917, never resumed his collaboration with Picasso after they had parted on his being called up in 1914.

ORPHIC CUBISM

Although Cubism had been the invention and creation of Picasso and Braque alone, there were already by 1914 a number of deviant or subsidiary Cubisms, of which the first to emerge as a new and identifiable movement was Orphism or Orphic Cubism. This was heralded in 1912 by Apollinaire, a close friend of Picasso, as a form of 'pure painting' in which the subject would no longer count at all. The painters involved were Robert Delaunay (1885–1941), Sonia Delaunay-Terk (1885–1979), Fernand Léger (1881–1955), Marcel Duchamp (1884–1968) and Francis Picabia (1879–1953). The Delaunays were interested mainly in color, at that date banished by Picasso and Braque from their work, but they nevertheless adopted a Cubist planar structure for their Orphic works (**19,30**). They are compositions of prismatic colors dispersed evenly across the

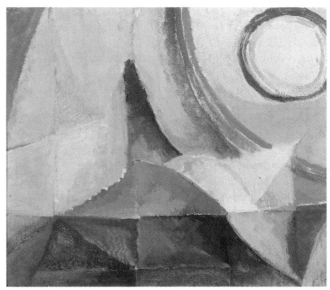

19,30 Sonia Delaunay, *Simultaneous Contrasts*, 1912. Canvas, 21⅝ × 17⁹⁄₁₆ins (55 × 45.5cm). Musée National d'Art Moderne, Paris.

19,31 Fernand Léger, *Contrast of Forms*, 1913. Canvas, 51⅜ × 38⅜ins (130.5 × 97.5cm). Philadelphia Museum of Art (Louise and Walter Arensberg Collection).

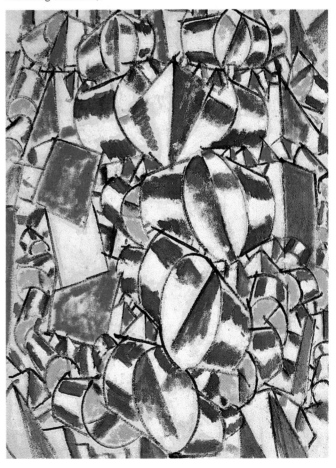

canvas in simultaneous contrast and change. Their subject and that of Robert Delaunay's *Circular Forms* series of 1913 is light and its source, the solar disc, also the source of life itself – for life springs like color from a prism, Delaunay believed. Sonia Delaunay's paintings were more lyrical and to her the whole movement probably owed its main impulse. Her conception of color is quite remote from that of Kandinsky, for whom it was a vehicle of indefinable emotions. But the vibrancy of Delaunay's color conveys a dynamism consonant with the dynamism of life if not quite fulfilling the claims made for Orphism by Apollinaire: 'Works of the Orphic artist must simultaneously give a pure aesthetic pleasure, a structure which is self-evident, and a sublime meaning, that is, a subject. This is pure art.'

Léger's relationship to Cubism was more personal and closer than Delaunay's and he created what might be described as a genuine alternative. Already in 1910 he had begun to emphasize in his work the hard, gleaming geometric forms of his subjects, reducing figures to tubular structures in increasingly mechanized compositions. Like the Delaunays, he believed that painting should be concerned with contrasts, but contrasts not only of color, but of line and form. Instead of the dynamism of light, his paintings are about the dynamism and discord and tensions of modern urban life. Gradually he eliminated nearly all representational elements until his compositions reached, around 1913/14, what he called 'Contrasts of Forms', tubular forms and flat areas being rhythmically set off against each other so as to achieve the maximum contrast and plastic vigour (**19,31**). The result came close to abstraction, but Léger's concern with formal values was always combined with a passion for contemporary life and technology, for everything up-to-date and dynamic, so that he became, after his release from military service in 1917, the artist *par excellence* of the Machine Age.

FUTURISM

Unlike other modern movements, Futurism was not concerned solely with the arts. It was less a style than an ideology. Launched in Milan in 1908 by the Italian poet Emilio Filippo Tommaso Marinetti (1876–1944), it had almost immediate international impact with the publication of the Futurist Manifesto in Paris the following year, and a series of further manifestos and public appearances spread the Futurist idea throughout Europe, from Italy to Czarist Russia and even to the United States. Futurism became better and more widely known than Cubism – a phenomenon quite out of proportion to the value of all but very few of its achievements.

Exhilarated by the noise and speed and mechanical energy of the modern city, Marinetti wanted to obliterate the past, especially the cult and culture of the Italian past – 'Burn the museums! Drain the canals of Venice!' – and replace it with a new society, a new poetry and a new art based on new dynamic sensations. 'We declare', he wrote in the Manifesto, 'that the splendour of the world has been increased by a new beauty: the beauty of speed . . . . A screaming automobile that seems to run like a machine-gun is more beautiful than the Victory of Samothrace.' Of the artists who rallied to Marinetti's call, the most articulate as well as the most gifted, both as

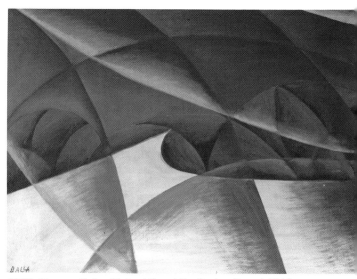

19,32 Giacomo Balla, *Abstract Speed the Car has Passed*, 1913. Canvas, 19¾ × 25¾ins (50 × 65.3cm). Tate Gallery, London.

painter and sculptor, was Umberto Boccioni (1882–1916). He was mainly responsible for the manifestos of Futurist painting in 1910, in which it was proclaimed 'that universal dynamism must be rendered as dynamic sensations; that movement and light destroy the substance of objects'. Later, after he and the other Futurist painters had been to Paris and seen Cubist painting, he formulated their aim as being 'to represent not the optical or analytical impression but the psychical and total experience'. As this suggests, they were as close to the Expressionists as to the Cubists. But they borrowed freely from the Cubist vocabulary of broken forms and, in fact, could not have realized their 'dynamic' visions without them. Their fundamental divergence from Cubism is, however, evident not only in their emphasis on intuition and action but also in their rejection of centralized, static compositions in favour of what they called 'simultaneity'. Their pictures were conceived as small sections only of continuous wholes. The action which is the subject of the painting passes through it and has no centre, as in Balla's *Abstract Speed the Car has Passed* (**19,32**), a typical Futurist work. Giacomo Balla (1871–1958) painted the famous *Dog on a Leash* based on multiple-exposure photographic studies of movement (see p. 690), but in his other works the dynamism is less superficial and in his studies called *Iridescent Interpretations*, begun in 1912, he created some of the earliest non-objective paintings.

Boccioni's paintings were more naturalistic and his triptych entitled *States of Mind* (1911–12) has considerable poetic power. In his *The City Rises* (**19,33**) he succeeded in giving memorable expression to an aspect of contemporary life with which the Futurists identified, that of urban life. Unfortunately their urbanistic ambitions were unrealized because of the war in which the outstanding Futurist architect Antonio Sant'Elia (1888–1916) was killed, too early to have had a chance to do any actual building. But his projects and drawings create a remarkable vision of the industrial and commercial metropolis of the future, with

19,33 Umberto Boccioni, *The City Rises*, 1910. Oil on canvas, 6ft 6½ins × 9ft 10½ins (1.99 × 3.01m). The Museum of Modern Art, New York (Mrs Simon Guggenheim Fund).

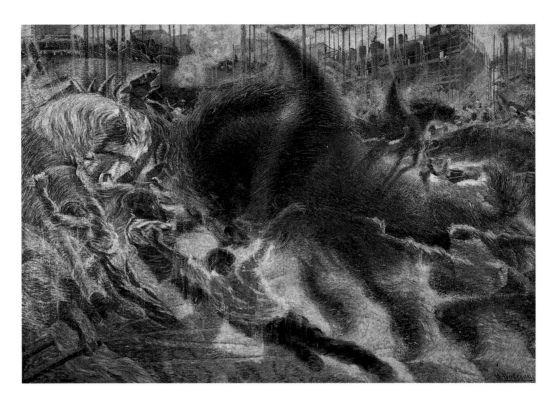

19,34 Umberto Boccioni, *Unique Forms of Continuity in Space*, 1913. Bronze (cast 1931), 43⅞ × 34⅞ × 15¾ins (111.2 × 88.5 × 40cm). The Museum of Modern Art, New York (Acquired through the Lillie P. Bliss Bequest).

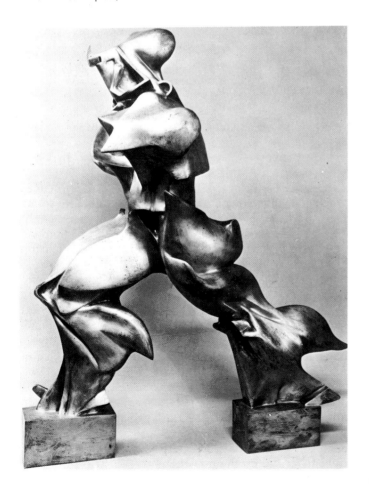

stepped-back skyscrapers, traffic lanes at different levels and factories with boldly curving fronts. It was to this Futurist utopia that Boccioni's sculptures belonged and it was as a sculptor that he excelled. In *Unique Forms of Continuity in Space* (**19,34**) he succeeded in giving full expression to the movement's aims in memorable form. The figure does not so much symbolize movement as realize it through a sequence of surfaces which seem to be constantly dissolving and reforming. He here achieved what he had been seeking, 'not pure form, but *pure plastic rhythm*; not the construction of the body, but the construction of the *action* of the body'.

Boccioni went even further in his *Technical Manifesto of Futurist Sculpture* of 1912, which parallels, if it does not anticipate, the breakthrough made that year by Picasso with his first constructed sculptures (19,27). Boccioni proclaimed the 'absolute and complete abolition of the finite line and closed-form sculpture. Let us tear the body open and let us enclose the environment in it.' And he went on to suggest that 'transparent planes of glass, of sheet metal, wires, electric lighting outside and inside, could indicate the planes, the directions, the tones and half-tones of a new reality'. Other untraditional materials are later proposed – cardboard, iron, cement, horse-hair, leather, cloth, mirrors, even built-in motors to give sculpture actual movement. The only surviving example of Boccioni's constructions is, however, rather less revolutionary than his Manifesto. He was killed in the First World War and in 1916 Futurism came to an end. An attempt to revive it after the war foundered in its alliance with Fascism.

Futurism was a short-lived, meteoric episode, but it had more lasting effects and a much wider influence than is sometimes thought. In America its exuberance and

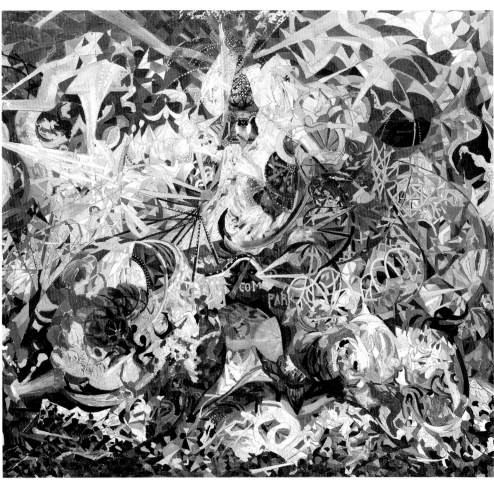

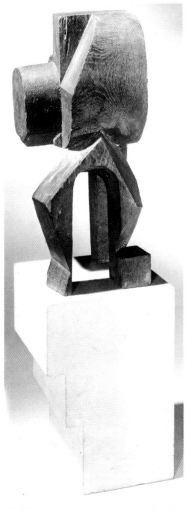

19,35 Joseph Stella, *Battle of Lights, Coney Island,* 1913. Canvas, 6ft 4ins × 7ft ¼in (1.93 × 2.14m). Yale University Art Gallery (Gift of the Société Anonyme).

19,37 Constantin Brancusi, *The Prodigal Son*, 1915. Oak on stone base, 17½ins (44.5cm) high, base 12½ins (31.3cm) high. Philadelphia Museum of Art (Louise and Walter Arensberg Collection).

19,36 Raymond Duchamp-Villon, *The Horse*, 1914. Bronze (cast c. 1930–1), 40 × 39½ × 22⅜ins (101.6 × 100.1 × 56.7cm). The Museum of Modern Art, New York (Van Gogh Purchase Fund).

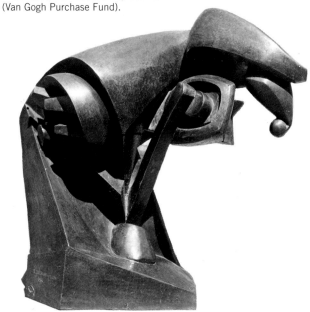

optimism were reflected in such works as Joseph Stella's *Battle of Lights, Coney Island* (**19,35**) of 1913. Nearly all contemporary European movements in the arts were touched by it, including Cubism in its last, synthetic phase, which may not have been uninfluenced by Futurism's anarchic vitality. The brilliant young Duchamp brothers in Paris certainly were. The extraordinary dynamism of *The Horse* (**19,36**) by Raymond Duchamp-Villon (1876–1918), brother of Marcel Duchamp (see p. 803), clearly owes something to Boccioni and Futurist painting. This remarkable work, in which vital animal energies are given mechanistic forms symbolizing the locomotive apparatus or machinery of a horse, is outstanding in its relentless, though not quite complete, abstraction. The tendons and muscles are just recognizable, coiled in upon themselves in an image compact of potential energy – of mechanical horse-power.

The Romanian sculptor Constantin Brancusi (1876–1957), who settled in Paris in 1904, may also have been stimulated by the Futurists, although he never became involved with them in any way. At least one of his early sculptures seems to have been partly prompted by their dynamism and machine aesthetic (**19,37**). The 'primitive' and folkloric origins of Brancusi's art – tribal African sculpture and the peasant artifacts of his native Romania – were, of course, completely at odds with Futurist aspirations and tend to conceal his affinities with them. Brancusi's unique sense of form, of form cut rather than modelled or carved or constructed in space, and his almost rapturous feeling for surface textures and the inherent qualities of his medium, all found expression in wood sculptures such as *The Prodigal Son*. Wood's tensile strength and its amenability to different types of handling (chopping and sawing, as well as carving) are exploited in this small work and give it an organic, hand-made quality of a kind the Futurists abhorred. However, Brancusi's later and most famous sculpture, *Bird in Space* (20,45), embodies glistening, precision-tooled, high-speed effects more eloquently than any Futuristic work of the pre-First World War period.

ABSTRACT OR NON-OBJECTIVE ART

One of the implications of Cubism – an implication that Picasso and Braque always resisted – was that, since the shapes within a painting could be conceived and seen as existing independently of whatever they stood for in the world of appearances, art could therefore be – perhaps should be – abstract, an absolutely self-sufficient entity of value entirely in and for itself. Such ideas were not new. They go back to Romantic theories of the early nineteenth century, as has been mentioned in connection with Kandinsky, who was embarking on his exploration of the non-objective in about 1910–12. The abstract art to which Cubism gave the creative impulse was, however, ideologically different from Kandinsky's. The Cubists had broken down their subjects into abstract or semi-abstract shapes which were predominantly geometrical. This seemed to confirm the belief that the underlying laws of art correspond to those of geometry and mathematics, although they played only an incidental role in Orphic Cubism (19,30), which became completely abstract as we have seen. But there were to be others who aspired to embody universal laws in their art and believed that this could be achieved only with abstract forms originating in the artist's mind. Despite the rarefied, intellectual nature of this approach, it led to abstract art being conceived as a kind of model for an ideal harmony between human beings and their environment. It thus acquired a sense of social destiny linking it with contemporary political and social theory.

SUPREMATISM AND THE FOUNDING OF DE STIJL

Avant-garde art could be seen in pre-war Czarist Russia almost as well and as easily as in Paris, for exhibitions of contemporary Western art were regularly held in Moscow and St Petersburg from 1910 onwards. In fact, the chief patrons of both Picasso and Matisse were at that time wealthy Moscow merchants whose collections were open to the public. Russian artists were thus aware of all the latest trends and in 1912/13 the first Russian abstract movement emerged, led by Mikhail Larionov (1881–1964)

and Natalia Goncharova (1881–1962), whose painting *Cats* (**19,38**) is a prime example. The movement was called Rayonism by Larionov because his abstract paintings resembled rays of light, as did Goncharova's, which were often appropriately entitled – *Electricity* or *Dynamo Machine* or such like. But the movement's importance was mainly as a focus of artistic theory and inspiration for their contemporaries, above all for Kasimir Malevich (1878–1935) and a younger generation who were to form the Constructivist movement during and after the Revolution (see pp. 821–3), notably Liubov Serbeevna Popova (1889–1924) among the painters (**19,39**).

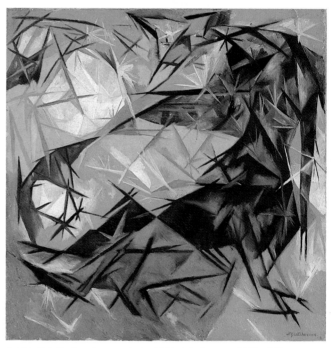

19,38 Natalia Goncharova, *Cats*, 1912–13. Canvas, 33¼ × 33ins (84.4 × 83.8cm). Solomon R. Guggenheim Museum, New York.

19,39 Liubov Serbeevna Popova, *Painterly Architectonic*, 1917. Oil on canvas, 31½ × 38⅝ins (80 × 98cm). The Museum of Modern Art, New York (Philip Johnson Fund).

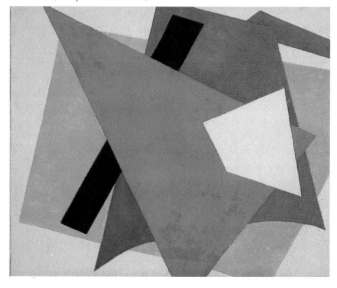

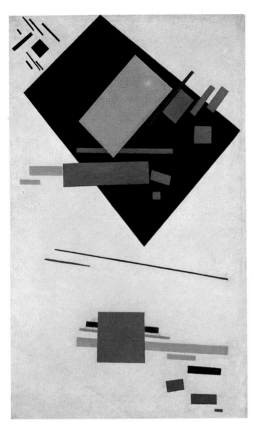

19,40 Kasimir Malevich, *Suprematist Composition, Black Trapezium and Red Square*, after 1915. Canvas, 24⅜ × 39¾ins (62 × 101.5cm). Stedelijk Museum, Amsterdam.

In 1912 Malevich was painting in a style he called Cubo-Futurist, which indicates his sources accurately enough. In 1913, however, he had gone far beyond them towards an absolutely pure and geometric form of total abstraction. This he called Suprematism and the first Suprematist picture, a black square on a white square, he claimed to have painted in 1913, though the movement was not publicly proclaimed until the following year. Malevich had much in common with Kandinsky and his theosophical speculations, though he was a devout Christian of a deeply mystical cast of mind. By Suprematism he meant 'the supremacy of feeling in creative art' and this, he believed, could be best expressed by the simplest, most elemental visual forms, such as the square, which convey the supremacy of mind over matter, over the chaos of nature. In his *Black Square on a White Ground*, he wrote, 'all reference to ordinary objective life has been left behind and nothing is real except feeling . . . the feeling of non-objectivity'. In his most famous painting, *White on White* of about 1918, the square has shed this vestigial materiality and merges with infinity. Abstraction can go no further, at any rate in theory.

However, Malevich also developed a progression of shapes, the square being followed by the circle, the triangle, two equal squares side by side, squares unequal in size but balanced by color, and so on. It was the more dynamic and complex compositions he was able to create with these elements, such as *Black Trapezium and Red*

Square (**19,40**), that influenced Alexander Rodchenko, El Lissitzky, Vladimir Tatlin and others who turned his pure and lofty conceptions to practical use in the post-Revolutionary period (see pp. 821–3). Despite his belief in art as a spiritual and strictly non-utilitarian activity, Malevich welcomed the Revolution and stayed on in Russia. But in 1922 he announced the end of Suprematism.

The most cerebral and at the same time most idealistic of the abstract movements was the Dutch group *De Stijl* (The Style), founded in Amsterdam in 1917 by the painters Piet Mondrian (1872–1944) and Theo van Doesburg (1883–1931) and the architect Jacobus Johannes Pieter Oud (1890–1963). They felt, Mondrian said later, that Cubism had not accepted 'the logical consequences of its own discoveries; it was not developing abstraction towards its ultimate goal'. Mondrian, who had passed from Impressionism through Symbolism, settled in Paris in 1911 and lived there until war broke out in 1914. He knew the Cubists and their work very well, but from the first pursued an individual and solitary path towards a more spiritual form of art. Though obviously indebted to Cubist painting for their subtle ochre and gray color harmonies and the firmly centralized compositions fading out towards the edges, Mondrian's pre-war paintings were already so abstract that it was sometimes impossible to detect their subjects. These were often, unlike the studio subject-matter of the Cubists, organic structural forms such as trees, and it is perhaps for this reason that his work is so dynamic, so close-textured and vibrant (**19,41**). 'It took me a long time', he wrote, 'to discover that particularities of form and natural color evoke subjective states of feeling which obscure pure reality. The appearance of natural form changes, but reality remains. To

19,41 Piet Mondrian, *Composition VII*, 1913. Canvas, 3ft 5⅛ins × 3ft 8¾ins (1.05 × 1.14m). Solomon R. Guggenheim Museum, New York.

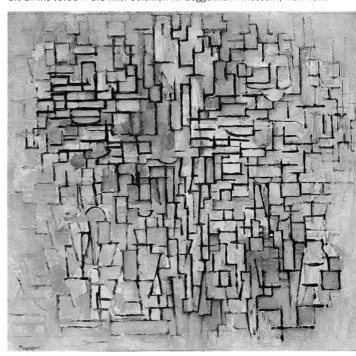

create pure reality plastically, it is necessary to reduce natural forms to constant elements of form, and natural color to primary color. The aim is not to create other particular forms and colors, with all their limitations, but to work toward abolishing them in the interest of a larger unity.'

High-minded ideals of absolute purity, harmony and sobriety inspired all the *De Stijl* artists – and also provided a model for the perfectly balanced organism they believed it possible for man to become both as an individual and in society as a whole. The markedly ethical overtones of all this reflect their sternly Calvinist background, which also accounts for their sense of dedication and mission. Van Doesburg is reported to have said that 'the square is to us as the cross was to the early Christians'. However, the great achievements of *De Stijl* – the buildings of Rietveld and the mature work of Mondrian – belong to the years after 1918 and are discussed in the next chapter.

ARCHITECTURE

FRANK LLOYD WRIGHT

The course of architecture in the first two decades of this century paralleled in many ways that of the other arts, except in one respect. The United States moved for the first time to a central position with the buildings of Frank Lloyd Wright (1869–1959), the greatest American architect to date. Wright began in the office of Louis Sullivan (see pp. 731, 734), whom he revered and with whose Guaranty Building in Buffalo (17,39) steel-skeleton skyscraper construction achieved its classic statement. Sullivan had allowed the underlying grid of the structural steel frame to dominate and control his whole design so that complete independence of all period styles was at last reached, the façades being reduced to a simple, totally unornamented but rhythmically beautiful pattern of mullions and sills. This represented quite as radical a break with the past as that made a few years later in Europe by young artists and architects, and it was comparable in its direction. Indeed, Sullivan anticipated much of the most advanced architectural thought in Europe around the turn of the century. It is not without significance that the Austrian architect Adolf Loos (1870–1933), whose famous *Ornament and Crime* of 1908 was to become the gospel of functionalism and the modern movement in architecture, was studying in Chicago in the 1890s, where he doubtless became familiar with Sullivan's slogan 'Form follows Function'.

Frank Lloyd Wright came from this same background but his genius carried him far beyond it. He had an instinctual, an almost animal, sense of architecture as shelter and of its relation to nature, of the possible affinities between man-made and natural structures, so that his buildings grow out of their environments in a way and to a degree not to be found in the work of any other architect anywhere. He aimed at what he called 'organic architecture', by which he meant 'an architecture that develops from within outwards in harmony with the conditions of

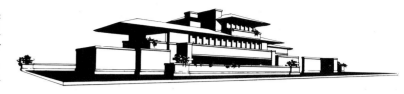
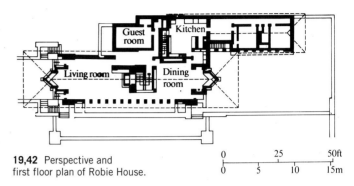

19,42 Perspective and first floor plan of Robie House.

19,43 Frank Lloyd Wright, Robie House, Chicago, Illinois, 1907–9.

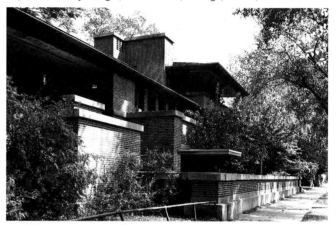

its being'. This can be felt already in his early 'prairie houses', which reflect in their ground-hugging design the long, low-lying far horizons of the great plains of the Middle West, where the slightest vertical projection is instantly visible. His prairie houses culminated in the extended horizontality and free-flowing interior-exterior spaces of the Robie House, Chicago (19,42; 43). The precise detailing and good workmanship – it is built of fine Roman brick – tend to conceal the extreme radicality of this remarkable building. Symmetry has gone completely, as has the controlling conception of the façade, the main entrance being tucked away far off-centre. Instead, the interior spaces, which are not at all articulated but unified and interpenetrating, are allowed to determine the form. Walls have become mere screens and the whole design is dominated by the long lines of the parapeted balconies and cantilevered roofs projecting far out without vertical supports (hip roofs but so low that they look like slab roofs). These and other clean-cut rectangular features elaborate the composition plastically in a way that is very suggestive of Cubism. Even more so is Wright's handling of space – sometimes closed, sometimes open – and the way he plays with voids and solids as design equivalents.

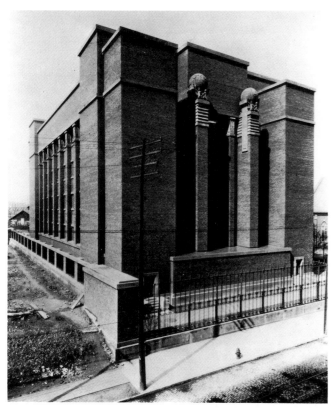

19,44 Frank Lloyd Wright, Larkin Building, Buffalo, New York, 1904 (demolished 1950), rear façade before removal of sculptural decoration.

19,45 Frank Lloyd Wright, Larkin Building, Buffalo, New York, 1904, interior of administration building.

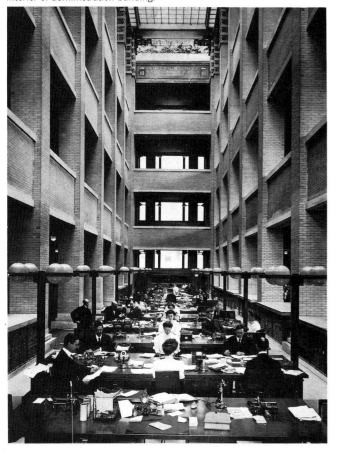

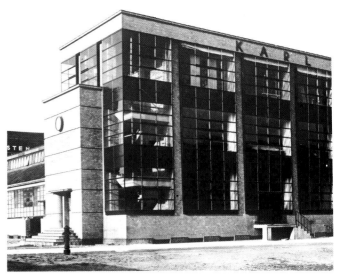

19,46 Walter Gropius and Adolf Meyer, Fagus Shoe Factory, Alfeld, Germany, 1911–14.

Wright did not aim simply to design a house. His 'organic architecture' was also conceived as a polemic in favour of cultural integration. 'An organic entity, this modern building', he wrote in 1910, 'as contrasted with the former insensate aggregation of parts. Surely we have here the higher ideal of unity as a more intimate working out of the expression of one's life in one's environment. One thing instead of many things; a great thing instead of a collection of small ones . . . . In organic architecture, then, it is quite impossible to consider the building as one thing, its furnishings another and its setting and environment still another.' He had already gone some way towards realizing this ideal integration in his Larkin Building at Buffalo, NY (**19,44; 45**), now demolished, in which all the furniture and office equipment and fittings were designed by him. The furniture was of steel.

Wright's fame was international by 1910, partly as a result of a magnificent folio publication of his work issued in Berlin that year. His influence, however, was less great. Germany was by then approaching the pre-eminent position it was to hold in Europe for the next few decades in architecture and architectural theory. In the Fagus Shoe Factory at Alfeld near Hanover (**19,46**) Walter Gropius (1883–1969) and Adolf Meyer (1881–1929) anticipated to an amazing extent the International Style of the post-war years – glass curtain-walling, flat roof without cornice, an unrelieved cubic block with the corners left free of any support, ornament limited to the simplest horizontal banding. The total effect is one of transparent volume, not solid mass. Yet it remains bound, by its modular grid, to the past and to a traditional feeling for symmetry.

CHAPTER TWENTY

BETWEEN THE TWO WORLD WARS

The First World War made a deeper mark on Western culture than did the Napoleonic Wars a century earlier. It brought to an end a long period of almost uninterrupted material progress and prosperity in Europe, cutting short a great outburst of creative genius in the late nineteenth and early twentieth centuries. Western civilization has never fully recovered from it. Fine paintings and works of art went on being produced in the 1920s and 1930s, notably by Picasso, Braque and Matisse, but they were much less adventurous and innovative than before. The rigour and force of the great Cubist and Fauve paintings are quite lacking in Braque's and Matisse's post-war work, exquisite though it often is. Both painters increasingly indulged their extraordinary gifts in displays of extreme 'good taste' and refinement in color, texture, handling and all those purely painterly qualities valued and highly cultivated in Paris. The relaxed tension is reflected in their subject-matter: oysters and lemons and sunny Riviera landscapes, languorous nudes and beach scenes,

exotic fruits and flowers and all the undemanding and soothing delights of bourgeois comfort which had so miraculously survived the war. Picasso, too, had lost the relentless single-mindedness of his Cubist years and succumbed to the multiple opportunities his pictorial intelligence had opened up, sometimes painting in two or three different styles at the same time (**20,1; 2; 3**). Throughout the inter-war period Paris remained the capital of Western art – as of *haute couture* and fashion design – though it had begun to lose its influential position in most other cultural and scientific fields.

DADA AND SURREALISM

Dada and Surrealism, the two related movements which dominated the inter-war years, had already been prefigured before 1914, but, as Lenin wrote from his Swiss exile in 1917, war is 'a great accelerator of events'. Its impact was felt as quickly in the arts as in social, political and

The visual arts	Historical landmarks
1917 Duchamp, *Fountain* (20,5)	**1917** USA enters war. Bolshevist revolution in Russia
1919–20 Tatlin, Monument to Third International (20,30)	**1918** Second battle of the Somme, Armistice
1921–2 Matisse, *The Moorish Screen* (20,8)	**1919** Versailles Peace Conference. Communist Third International. First splitting of atom (UK)
1922 Le Corbusier, Contemporary City Plan (20,47)	**1920** First public radio broadcasts (USA and UK)
1923 Picasso, *Seated Harlequin* (20,3) Duchamp, *Large Glass* (20,5)	**1921** Schoenberg, *Suite for Piano* Op. 25
1924 Rietveld, Schröder House (20,35)	**1922** Mussolini, March on Rome. Eliot, *Waste Land*. Joyce, *Ulysses*
1924–5 Lissitzky, *Proun 99* (20,31)	**1923** USSR established. General Motors established
1927–32 Lutyens, Memorial (20,38)	**1924** Death of Lenin
1928 Brancusi, *Bird* (20,45)	**1925** Hitler, *Mein Kampf*. Kafka, *The Trial*. Pound, *XVI Cantos*
1928–30 Le Corbusier, Villa Savoye (20,42) van Alen, Chrysler Building (20,48)	**1926** Baird invents television. Berg, *Wozzeck*. Scott Fitzgerald, *The Great Gatsby*
1929 Braque, *Guéridon* (20,7) Ernst, *Les femmes 100 têtes* (20,16)	**1927** Proust, *Time Regained* (posthumous). *The Jazz Singer* (first commercial sound film)
1930 Mondrian, *Fox Trot A* (20,37)	**1928** Yeats, *The Tower*
1930–1 Picasso, *Head of a Woman* (20,22)	**1929** Wall Street Crash
1931 Dali, *The Persistence of Memory* (20,17) Mies, Living-room (20,44)	**1932** Roosevelt president of USA. Auden, *The Orators*
1933 Heartfield, *A Pan-German* (20,27)	**1933** Hitler German Chancellor. 'New Deal' in USA
1934 Magritte, *Le viol* (20,19)	**1935** Italy invades Abyssinia
1934–5 Lloyd Wright, Broadacre City project (20,41)	**1936** Spanish Civil War begins. First regular TV broadcasts (UK)
1936 Oppenheim, *Object* (20,18)	**1937** Whittle invents jet engine. Nazi exhibition 'Degenerate Art'
1937 Picasso, *Guernica* (20,49)	**1938** Germany annexes Austria. Munich crisis
1938 Miró, *Head of a Woman* (20,21)	**1939** Germany invades Poland: Second World War begins

economic life, for example, in Dada, which was launched from a cabaret in Zürich almost next door to Lenin's lodgings. Not that Lenin had anything to do with Dada. So far as is known, he was quite unaware of it. The cafés and cabarets of Zürich teemed with revolutionary exiles, not all of them political revolutionaries. Writers such as James Joyce, musicians such as Igor Stravinsky, as well as artists and intellectuals of every kind, congregated in wartime Switzerland. They went there – or to the United States, which remained neutral until 1917 – to avoid the war and protest against the society which had unleashed it. It was early in 1916, when the German and Allied armies were stalemated in the trenches at Verdun on the Western Front, that Dada emerged.

A state of mind rather than a literary or artistic movement, according to its spokesman the Romanian poet Tristan Tzara (1886–1963), Dada was anarchic, nihilistic and disruptive. Dadaists mocked all established values, all traditional notions of good taste in art and literature, the culture symbols of a society based, they believed, on greed and materialism and now in its death agony. The name Dada – a nonsense, baby-talk word – means nothing, so was well suited to Dada's wholly negative nature. Dada even denied the value of art, hence its cult of non-art, and ended by negating itself. 'The true Dadaist is against Dada.'

The Zürich Dadaists were mainly writers and poets, as were also the only notable artists among them, Sophie Taeuber-Arp (1889–1943) and Jean (Hans) Arp (1887–1966),

20,1 Pablo Picasso, *The Pipes of Pan*, 1923. Canvas, 6ft 8¾ins × 5ft 8¾ins (2.05 × 1.75m). Musée Picasso, Paris.

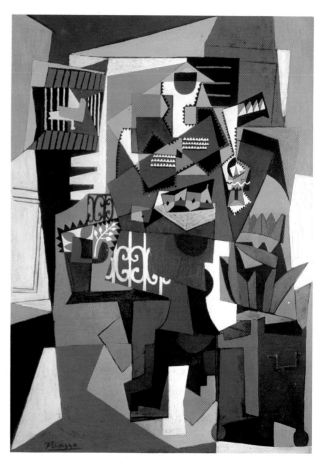

20,2 Pablo Picasso, *The Bird-Cage*, 1923. Canvas, 6ft 7⅛ins × 4ft 7¼ins (2.01 × 1.4m). Collection Mr and Mrs Victor W. Ganz, New York.

20,3 Pablo Picasso, *Seated Harlequin (Portrait of the Painter Jacinto Salvado)*, 1923. Tempera on canvas, 51½ × 38¼ins (130.5 × 97cm). Kunstmuseum, Basel.

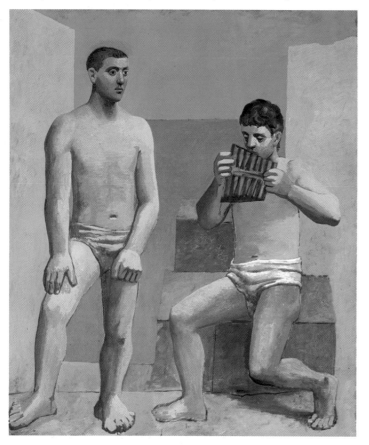

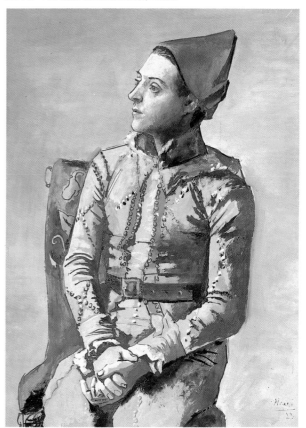

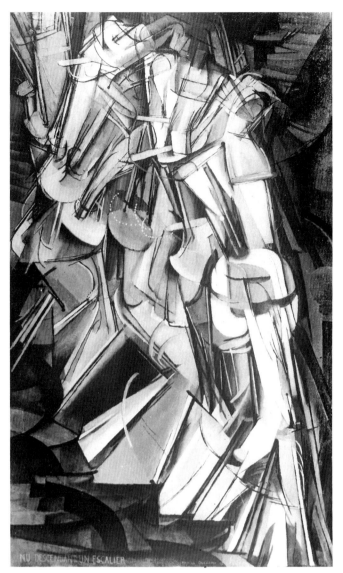

20,4 Marcel Duchamp, *Nude Descending a Staircase, No. 2*, 1912. Canvas, 58 × 35ins (147 × 89cm). Philadelphia Museum of Art (Louise and Walter Arensberg Collection).

whose experiments with automatism and the laws of chance led to some remarkable and quite fortuitously beautiful *papiers collés*. They tore up colored papers and let the pieces fall haphazardly, fixing them (sometimes after slight adjustments) in the abstract patterns they had formed. Much more radically non-art, however, were Duchamp's ready-mades, first exhibited in 1915 in New York, where he spent most of the war years.

DUCHAMP

Marcel Duchamp (1887–1968), the younger brother of the sculptor Duchamp-Villon (see p. 796), was perhaps the most stimulating intellectual to be concerned with the visual arts in the twentieth century – ironic, witty and penetrating. He was also a born anarchist. Like his brother, he began (after some exploratory years in various current styles) with a dynamic Futurist version of Cubism, of which his painting *Nude Descending a Staircase, No. 2* (**20,4**) is the best known example. It caused a scandal at the famous Armory Show of modern art in New York in

1913. Duchamp's ready-mades are everyday manufactured objects converted into works of art simply by the artist's act of choosing them. Duchamp did nothing to them except present them for contemplation as 'art'. They represent in many ways the most iconoclastic gesture that any artist has ever made – a gesture of total rejection and revolt against accepted artistic canons. For by reducing the creative act simply to one of choice 'ready-mades' discredit the 'work of art' and the taste, skill, craftsmanship – not to mention any higher artistic values – that it traditionally embodies. Duchamp insisted again and again that his 'choice of these ready-mades was never dictated by an aesthetic delectation. The choice was based on a reaction of visual *indifference*, with at the same time a total absence of good or bad taste, in fact a complete anaesthesia.' However, he may be thought to have protested too much about this. His ready-mades do have, willy-nilly, a certain visual attraction and distinction.

The earliest was a bicycle-wheel mounted on a kitchen stool (1913); the most outrageous was the *Fountain* (**20,5**), an industrial porcelain fitting for a public urinal, set sideways and signed 'R. Mutt'. When it was rejected by the New York Independents in 1917 it was defended (anonymously but probably by Duchamp himself) as follows: 'Whether Mr Mutt with his own hands made the fountain or not has no importance, he CHOSE it. He took an ordinary article of life, placed it so that its useful significance disappeared under the new title and point of view – created a new thought for that object.' In other words, the significance of ready-mades as 'art' lies not in any aesthetic qualities that may or may not be discovered in them, but in the aesthetic questions they force one to contemplate.

Together with a wealthy Cuban painter, Francis Picabia (1879–1953), Duchamp formed a New York wartime Dada group – Dada in spirit if not in name. Picabia's satirically simplified drawings of actual or invented mechanical forms conveying private symbolic meanings – in deliberate contrast to Futuristic machine aesthetics – paralleled the most extreme and baffling of Duchamp's works, *The Bride Stripped Bare by her Bachelors, Even*, often

20,5 Marcel Duchamp, *Fountain*, 1917. Ready-made, 24ins (61cm) high.

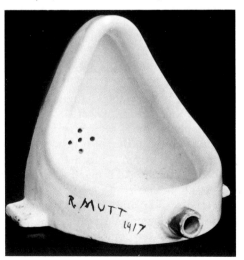

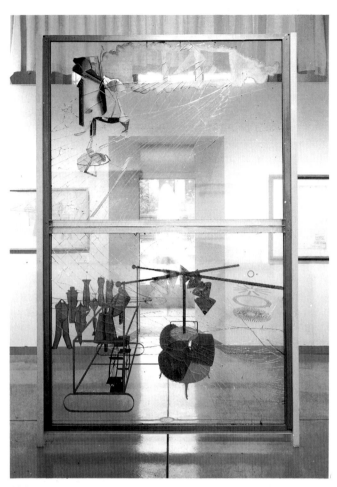

20,6 Marcel Duchamp, *The Bride Stripped Bare by her Bachelors, Even*, 1915–23. Oil and lead foil between glass, 9ft 1¼ins × 5ft 9⅛ins (2.78 × 1.76m). Philadelphia Museum of Art (Bequest of Katherine S. Dreier).

known as the *Large Glass* (**20,6**). Duchamp had been evolving this extraordinary configuration in his mind since 1912 and worked intermittently on the actual construction, in oil paint, lead wire and foil, dust and varnish between two sheets of glass, in New York between 1915 and 1923, when he abandoned it unfinished. In 1927 it was shattered on returning from an exhibition in Brooklyn. The glass cracked in complementary directions due to its being transported in two halves, one on top of the other, and this entirely fortuitous effect 'completed' his work, Duchamp declared.

The *Large Glass* is an insoluble enigma and was intended to be so. It is an illusion of an illusion, all the more disorienting because the changing 'real world' on the other side of the glass forms part of it, as well as the viewer, who is occasionally caught in its reflectivity. It can be deciphered only in the most general terms. In the upper half the bride, a fusion of mechanical and biological functions that Duchamp had evolved separately in an oil painting of 1912, is shown undressing while she both attracts and repulses her suitors, whose orgasmic frustrations are indicated diagrammatically in the bottom half. Is it simply a joke? – a complicated and meaningless visual puzzle? When questioned about it Duchamp once

said that 'there is no solution because there is no problem'. Whatever its meaning may be – and it has inspired the most varied and abstruse interpretations ranging from Hindu mysticism to medieval alchemy – it has been enormously influential. For painters and artists of every kind it has become a talisman. They have recognized in it the most fully committed and radical opposition to a purely visual conception of art. It asserts the value of the work of art as a 'sign', as a 'machine for producing meanings' and for compelling the active contemplation and creative participation of the viewer. Duchamp was quite explicit about this. It was not his intention, he said, to make 'a painting for *the eyes*'. He wanted to put painting once again at the service of the mind. If his work was dubbed 'literary' and 'intellectual' that wouldn't bother him, he said. The term 'literature' has a very vague meaning. 'And in fact until the last hundred years all painting had been literary or religious: it had all been at the service of the mind.' This quality was only lost during the nineteenth century – culminating in Impressionism and Cubism. Dada had been for him, he went on, an extreme protest against such purely visual attitudes to painting.

Duchamp always kept on the margin of politics but the Dada movement had obvious political implications, especially during the immediate post-war years in Berlin. The German painter Max Ernst (1891–1976), for instance, held a notorious exhibition in Cologne in 1920, entered through a public lavatory. Visitors to a Surrealist exhibition were met by a young girl in communion dress reciting obscene poems and were then handed an axe with which to destroy the exhibits. By such provocative gestures against the pomposities of respectable bourgeois society, by mocking everything that was taken seriously, especially everything that was revered as 'art' and 'culture', Dadaists might seem to have been preparing the way for a new social, intellectual and artistic order. Few of them had any such positive intentions, of course. But their successors, the Surrealists, did have. The Surrealists had close links with political revolution and, for a time, with the Communist Party. They were even welcomed by the Soviets. Lenin's commissar for education and the arts, Lunacharsky, is reported as saying: 'The Surrealists have rightly understood that the task of all revolutionary intellectuals in a capitalist régime is to denounce bourgeois values. This effort deserves to be encouraged.' However, the alliance did not last long. After four years those Surrealists who had joined the party left it.

Bourgeois values, it should be remembered, were being celebrated during these same years by two of the acknowledged masters of modern art, Braque and Matisse, as well as by such accomplished painters as Pierre Bonnard (1867–1947). Braque's *Le Guéridon* (**20,7**), Matisse's *The Moorish Screen* (**20,8**) and Bonnard's *Nude in the Bath* (**20,9**) express, or at any rate imply, an ideal of physical and psychological well-being – of well-heeled comfort and ease – that represents everything Dadaists and Surrealists most disliked. They had to admit, reluctantly, the sheer beauty of Matisse's work, but they deplored his influence

further than they did in the rendering of color as it actually exists in Nature. But art and Nature are two different things . . . . And progress came upon us faster than anyone expected . . . before we had realized our intentions completely.'

With the passage of time, however, Bonnard's paintings, especially his great bathroom scenes of the late 1920s and 1930s, have come to be recognized as the consummation of a peculiarly French ideal of modest but civilized living – informal, unpretentious, relaxed and with a natural 'good taste' that banishes any hint of vulgarity, particularly that of the newly rich. They are loosely painted with apparently spontaneous impressionistic brush-strokes, as if they had been quickly sketched one glowing late summer morning and then perhaps just touched up here and there the following day. So the vision remains always not quite fully realized, slightly insubstantial, almost as if about to vanish into the shimmering colors of which it is composed. These remarkable paintings are difficult to accommodate in a view of twentieth-century art that presupposes a logical sequence of movements. Clement Greenberg posed the question in an article of 1948. 'The problem for criticism is to explain why the cubist generation and its immediate successors have, contrary to artists' precedents, fallen off in middle and old age, and why belated impressionists like Bonnard and Vuillard could maintain a higher consistency of performance during the last 15 years . . . . And why, finally, Matisse,

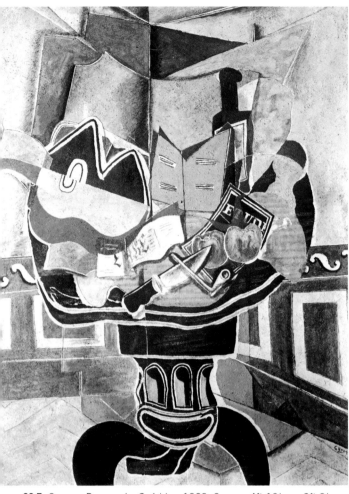

20,7 Georges Braque, *Le Guéridon*, 1929. Canvas, 4ft 10ins × 3ft 9ins (1.47 × 1.14m). Phillips Collection, Washington DC.

and everything he stood for. With consummate and apparently effortless skill Matisse had finally achieved that 'art of balance, of purity and serenity devoid of troubling or depressing subject-matter' of which he had long dreamed – an art which would appease and soothe 'like a good armchair' and embody all those qualities of good taste and well-bred refinement and restraint so prized by the bourgeoisie. In his youth Bonnard had belonged to the Symbolist vanguard with his friend the painter Jean Edouard Vuillard (1868–1940) and others. They exhibited under the name of 'Nabis' (meaning 'prophets') and they did indeed foreshadow later developments, notably with the strong, flat areas of color in paintings by Paul Sérusier (1864–1927). By the 1920s, however, they were painting charming '*intimiste*' pictures, visions of a cosy bourgeois world of provincial domesticity – in Bonnard's case safely sheltered in the Mediterranean sunshine near Cannes. Though refined and eminently civilized they were too insistently private and self-indulgent and pleasure-loving to be taken very seriously in the post-war climate. Picasso thought them old-hat, 'a potpourri of indecision'. Bonnard himself said that he and his friends had been 'left hanging in the air' by the First World War. They had wanted to take 'the same direction as the impressionists but to go

20,8 Henri Matisse, *The Moorish Screen*, 1921–2. Canvas, 36¼ × 29¼ins (92 × 74.3cm). Philadelphia Museum of Art (Bequest of Lisa Norris Elkins).

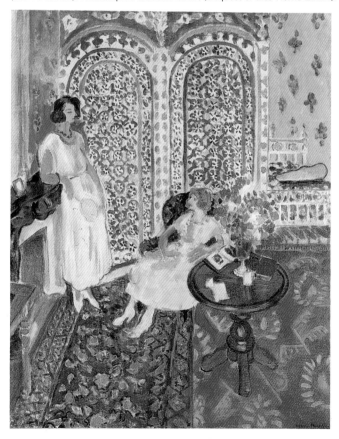

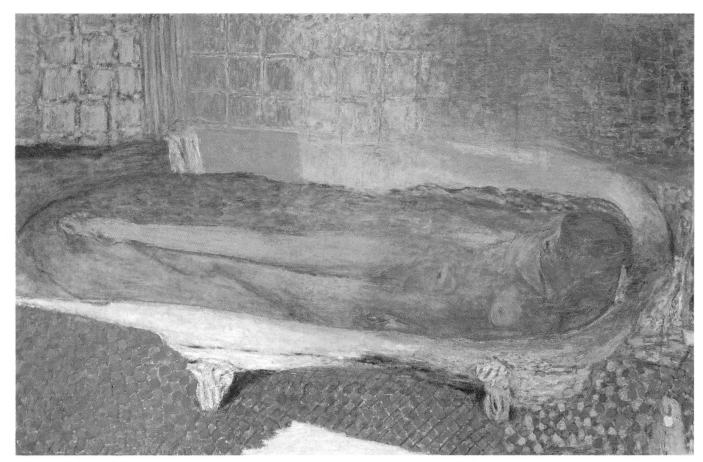

20,9 Pierre Bonnard, *Nude in the Bath*, 1935. Oil on canvas, 36⅝ × 57⅞ins (93 × 147cm). Musée d'Art Moderne de la Ville de Paris.

with his magnificent but transitional style, which does not compare with cubism for historical importance, is able to rest so securely in his position as the greatest master of the twentieth century.' Greenberg could only explain the phenomenon as being one of the results of what he called the 'debacle' of the 'age of experiment', by which he meant, in the visual arts, Cubism. For Greenberg, the 'cubist mission and its hope, coincident with that of Marxism and the whole matured tradition of Enlightenment, of humanizing the world' was central. Whatever feats the late Fauvism and late Impressionism of Matisse and Bonnard had been capable of, Cubism remained supreme, the 'epoch-making feat of twentieth-century art, a style that has changed and determined the complexion of Western art as radically as Renaissance naturalism once did'. Even Picasso succumbed for a time – though patently without conviction – to the post-war call to order promoted by the supremely versatile poet, playwright, film-maker and artist Jean Cocteau (1889–1963), with whom he had already collaborated in designing sets and costumes for Diaghilev's Russian Ballet. Suave and immensely adroit but insipid Ingresque portraits now alternated with gigantic, inflated Pompeiian evocations of the Classical Mediterranean world and a highly decorative and brilliantly colored form of flat-patterned Cubism. No other major artist had ever before painted in several utterly different styles

simultaneously (20,1; 2; 3). Such heterogeneous displays go beyond mere stylistic versatility. But it was only some years later that an all-consuming sensuality and physical passion once again fired Picasso's powers of metamorphosis to create works comparable in impact with those of the pre-war years (20,22).

AMERICA AND THE PRECISIONIST VIEW

Almost as difficult as Bonnard to accommodate in any sequential account of the period between the two World Wars are the American painters Edward Hopper (1882–1967) and Charles Sheeler (1883–1965). In relation to the dominant movements of the time – Abstraction, Realism and Surrealism – they would naturally fall into the second, but neither would have accepted such a classification. Nor did they allow themselves to be associated with any contemporary realist groups in the USA, whether that of the American Scene painters or that of the Regionalist painters of the New Deal era, notably Thomas Hart Benton (1889–1975), Grant Wood (1891–1942) and John Steuart Curry (1897–1946). Indeed Hopper indignantly rejected the imputation. 'The thing that makes me so mad is the American Scene business', he told an interviewer in 1964. 'I never tried to do the American scene as Benton and others did. I think the American Scene painters caricatured America. I always wanted to do myself.' Whereas they had embraced an almost jingoistic form of American artistic isolationism and retreated into the Midwestern agricultural heartland in search of authentic, conservative American values, Hopper depicted the urban scene almost, but of course not quite, in the same spirit as had German Expressionists such as Kirchner before the war (19,14). It had both attracted and repelled the Expressionists, feeding their neuroses and deepening their sense of loneliness. For Hopper, too, the industrial metropolis was the great theme – the city as condenser of modern life with its sensations of alienation and disinheritance – though with quiet despair and even resignation, without the Expressionists' premonitions of hysteria.

If far from ever being avant-garde, Hopper's paintings were formed by his years in Paris and his close study of French nineteenth-century art, especially that of Manet. But the unnerving consistency of his vision came from the New World, from his unrelentingly close observation of his local down-town neighbourhood when he returned to New York. Hopper lived through the Depression that began after the Wall Street Crash of 1929 and his work was never free afterwards from its echoes. His deserted city streets of fly-blown shopfronts, well-lit but unattended suburban filling-stations, lonely coffee drinkers sitting in empty diners (20,10), a solitary man gazing forlornly out of the window of an elevated train – they are all lent great pathos and also a sense of moral dignity by the honesty and restraint with which Hopper depicts them. It was as if he had wanted to testify to his solidarity with them in their mutual concern about 'the predicament of being American'.

Charles Sheeler was no less city-loving than Hopper and imbued with the same Protestant ethic. He began as a commercial photographer specializing in architectural subjects, with a special interest in early American vernacular building. But later he turned to contemporary scenes, pioneering the use of sharp-focus effects, especially after 1920 when he collaborated on a film *Manhatta*, named after Walt Whitman's poem *Mannahatta*, in which skyscrapers and other city buildings are seen from

20,10 Edward Hopper, *Automat*, 1927. Oil on canvas, 28⅛ × 36ins (71.4 × 91.5cm). Des Moines Art Center Permanent Collection 1958.2.

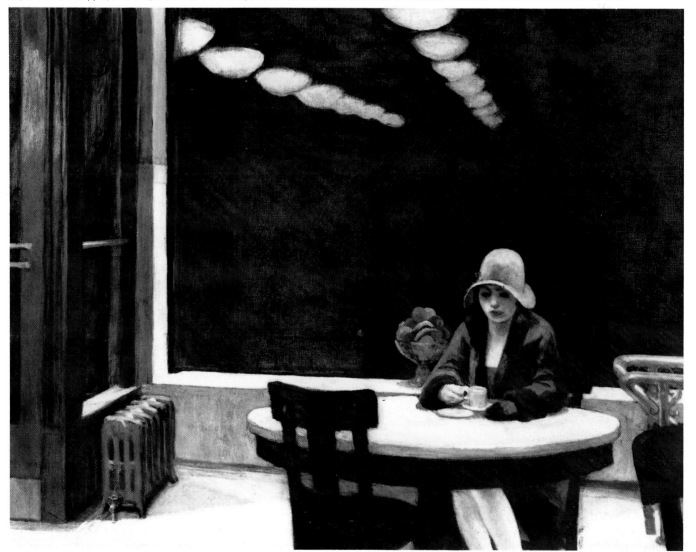

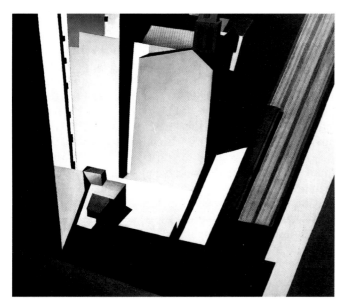

20,11　Charles Sheeler, *Church Street E1*, 1920. Oil on canvas,
16 × 19ins (40.6 × 48.5cm). Cleveland Museum of Art
(Mr and Mrs William H. Marlatt Fund, 77.43).

extreme angles, diagonally from above or below. He used
the same perspectives in paintings such as *Church Street
E1* (**20,11**); the combination of title and subject is exemplary and the strong contours and daring perspectives of
the camera's view are combined with the planar surfaces
he had admired in Cubism. They inaugurated a new style,
soon to be called Precisionism, in which strict geometry
and a love of technology were combined to mirror modern
America. In 1927–8 Sheeler was commissioned by the
Ford Motor Company to record their River Rouge Plant in
Michigan and this confirmed him in his admiration for
mechanization and the technological approach. Sheeler's
vision of America is strangely uneasy: it is that of a
cleansed and dehydrated paradise. His so-called landscapes are depopulated, although everything in them is
man-made – the roads, the railways, the gasometers,
power-plants, water-towers, the cranes and machinery
and, of course, the imposing factories.

DIEGO RIVERA AND THE MEXICAN MURALISTS

In the cultural relations between North and South
America in the first half of the twentieth century the
Mexican painter Diego Rivera (1866–1957) played a key
role. No artist is more relevant to the debate over 'indigenous' or 'national' as against 'international' styles in art,
a debate that was to be taken up fiercely at the time by
both Communists and Fascists in Europe as well as in
North and South America. After more than ten years in
Europe between 1908 and 1921, mainly in Paris where he
knew Picasso and frequented Cubist painters without
ever wholly accepting Cubist aesthetics, Rivera was persuaded to return to Mexico and join the national movement. The new Mexican government had brought the
ten-year civil war to an end and had launched a program

to create a popular public art accessible to the masses.
Before leaving Europe Rivera made a lengthy visit to Italy,
where he studied intensively the great cycles of Renaissance fresco painting by Giotto, Masaccio, Piero della
Francesca, Mantegna and Michelangelo. He began to see
himself as the artist destined to play a crucial role by
uniting the indigenous arts of the Pre-Columbian with
those of the new post-colonial Mexico. He joined the
Communist party at the same time. Soon he was
accepted, alongside Orozco and Siqueiros (see pp. 810–1),
as the leader of the new Mexican art and with his strange
combinations of mechanical shapes with the faces and
bodies of Mexican peasants, transformed by reference to
Pre-Columbian sculptures and Italian Renaissance frescoes, Rivera created some of the most effective and
powerful paintings in the service of politics in the twentieth century. 'For the first time in the history of art', he
claimed, 'Mexican mural painting made the masses the
hero of monumental art.'

Among his first and in many ways his most successful
works, because they are the most direct and easily comprehensible, were the gigantic murals he painted between
1923 and 1928 round one of the patios of the Ministry of
Public Education in Mexico City – no less than 117 fresco
panels covering 17,220 square feet (1,600m²) of wall. They
established his reputation. Soon he was being sought by
North American patrons ambitious to launch a similar
public art in the United States, though they had nothing
in common with Rivera politically. Indeed the best
known of the millionaire American capitalists figure
prominently among the villains in his Mexico City
murals. In one panel John D. Rockefeller, J. P. Morgan and
Henry Ford with their bejewelled and fashionably dressed
wives are seated sipping champagne while a golden ticker-
tape of the stock exchange unwinds before them, with the
Statue of Liberty converted into a table-lamp. His slightly
later, more nationalistic and less politically combative
series of murals, recounting the *History of Cuernavaca
and Morelos* in the Cortes Palace, Cuernavaca, was commissioned by one of them, Dwight D. Morrow, the American ambassador. Quite soon after this Rivera accepted
commissions from the San Francisco Stock Exchange, the
Detroit Institute of Arts and the Rockefeller Center in
New York, though the last was cancelled because Rivera
refused to omit Lenin.

Why did Rivera accept these commissions from the
hated capitalists? He had just returned from a slightly
stormy year in the Soviet Union as a guest of the Communist government. Meanwhile the grim years of the
Depression had begun in the USA. Perhaps he hoped to
spread the light of social and political awareness, if not
the Communist gospel itself. 'Mural painting must help
in man's struggle to become a human being', he wrote,
'and for that purpose it must live wherever it can; no place
is too bad for it, so long as it is permitted to fulfill its primary functions of nutrition and enlightenment.' It was in
this optimistic spirit that he carried out a commission
from the San Francisco Art Association although it was
stipulated that he was not to paint anything 'of a political

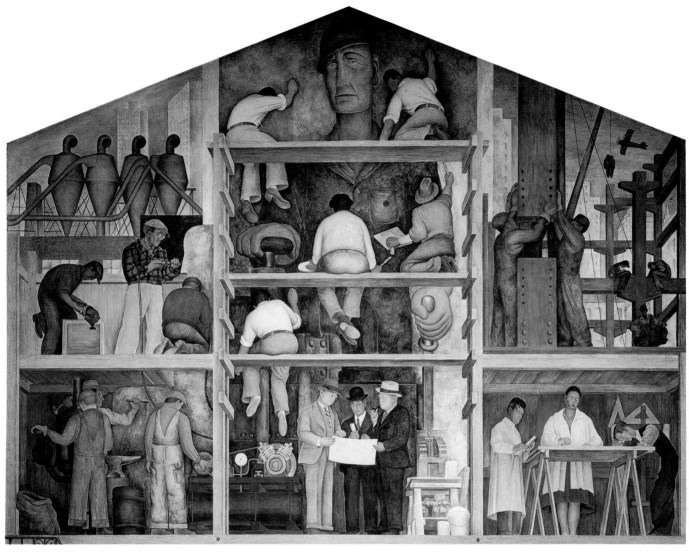

20,12 Diego Rivera, *The Making of a Fresco, showing the Building of a City*, 1931. Fresco, 21ft 8ins × 30ft 4ins (6.6 × 9.25m). San Francisco Art Institute, San Francisco, California.

nature'. The strength of his public art is seen at its most serene in this mature work (**20,12**). Though strictly secular and materialist it has a solemn, quietly confident, almost a sacramental gravity and monumentality. His Cubist apprenticeship and his admiration of Italian Renaissance fresco painting had left him with a love of mathematical construction and what he called 'secret' geometry which found fulfilment here; the device of a builder's scaffolding spread across the composition is skilfully used to frame the five scenes. Rivera himself is in the centre, seen from behind, with his assistants; below, the factory managers stand at the feet of a giant worker towering above them in his overalls, with the benign, imperturbable presence of some great Buddha figure. Other workers, including designers, are shown to the right and left. It calmly celebrates an aspect of the American Dream that Rivera had allowed himself to glimpse before the confrontation with John D. Rockefeller brought his American honeymoon to an end.

BRETON, DE CHIRICO AND ERNST

Surrealism was as anti-bourgeois and as consciously disruptive generally as Dada, but it lacked Dada's anarchic spontaneity. It had a theory and a program and eventually became almost doctrinaire. However, most Dadaists rallied to it when the poet André Breton (1896–1966), who became the leader and theorist of the movement, issued the first Surrealist Manifesto in Paris in 1924. This was concerned almost exclusively with poetry and imaginative literature (hardly at all with the visual arts), but it made an eloquent appeal for the total emancipation of writers and artists from all restraints. The aim was to explore the world of psychic experience revealed by Freud and by psychoanalytic research and to transmute 'those two seemingly contradictory states, dream and reality, into a sort of absolute reality, of surreality . . .'.

Breton had had some experience as a military psychiatrist during the war and had later visited Freud in Vienna. Surrealism's ideological origins clearly lie in Freud's

Orozco, Rivera and Siqueiros

ART AND POLITICS

Though politics have influenced the visual arts throughout history in many and different ways, most notably under the Ancient Roman Empire and during the revolutionary and counter-revolutionary years of the nineteenth century, they have seldom played so prominent a role as they did during the 1920s and 1930s. Relations between Communism and the arts were close, though they followed a zigzag course both in Russia and in western Europe (see pp. 821–3); Fascism and Nazism were also actively concerned with art as propaganda; and the period closed with one of Picasso's major works which is also his only explicitly political painting (20,49). However, it was in Mexico that the relationship between politics and art during these years was most fruitful, partly because the Mexican artists themselves formulated much of the theoretical base on which their program for a new public art was erected, and partly because it was combined with the quest to rediscover their national identity. By the time Rivera painted his *The Making*

of a Fresco, showing the Building of a City (20,12) the revolutionary fervour of his early years had relaxed, but it continued to inform all his work and it is in this context that his paintings and also those of his some-time companions José Clemente Orozco (1883–1949) and David Alfaro Siqueiros (1894–1974) should be seen.

Mexico had thrown off Spanish colonial rule in 1821 and there followed a turbulent century marked by the loss in 1848 of New Mexico, Texas, California, Nevada, Utah, Arizona and parts of Colorado and Wyoming to the USA. Twenty years later Napoleon III made his disastrous attempt to take over the country and install the arch-duke Maximilian as emperor (15,41 and see p. 678). By 1910, when the Mexican Revolution began, 90 per cent of the peasants had been dispossessed of their land and were forced to live under an iniquitous system of debt peonage to their oppressive landlords, not all of whom were Mexicans. A decade of civil war ended in 1920 with the election of Alvaro Obregón as president and the installation of a

revolutionary nationalist, rather than a full-scale communist or socialist, régime. It immediately and actively promoted an ambitious cultural program for which Siqueiros (whose most remarkable works were painted much later) drew up a formal 'Declaration of Social, Political and Aesthetic Principles' in 1922, from which the following extract is taken.

The noble work of our race, down to its most insignificant spiritual and physical expressions, is native (and essentially Indian) in origin. With their admirable and extraordinary talent to create beauty, peculiar to themselves, the art of the Mexican people is the most wholesome spiritual expression in the world and this tradition is our greatest treasure. Great because it belongs collectively to the people and this is why our fundamental aesthetic goal must be to socialize artistic expression and wipe out bourgeois individualism.
We repudiate so-called easel painting and every kind of art favoured by ultra-intellectual circles, because

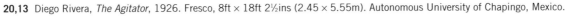

20,13 Diego Rivera, *The Agitator*, 1926. Fresco, 8ft × 18ft 2½ins (2.45 × 5.55m). Autonomous University of Chapingo, Mexico.

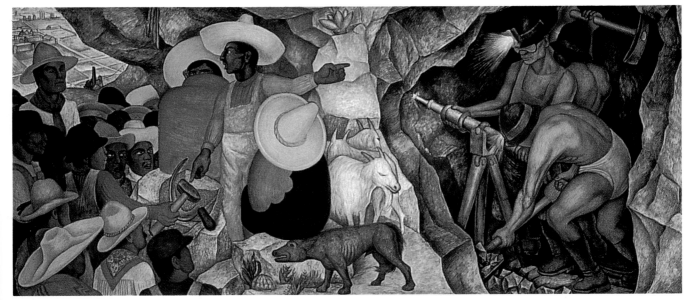

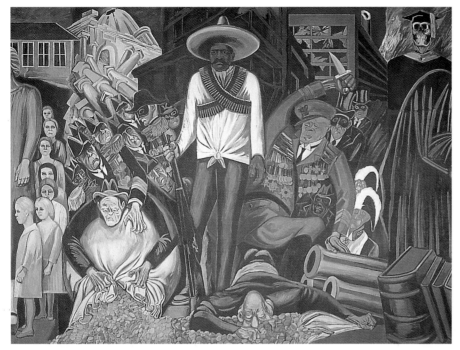

20,14 José Clemente Orozco, *American Civilization – Latin America*, detail of post-Cortesian section, 1932. Fresco, about 9ft 10ins × 9ft 10ins (3 × 3m). Commissioned by the Trustees of the Dartmouth College, Hanover, New Hampshire.

it is aristocratic, and we praise monumental art in all its forms, because
it is public property.

We proclaim *that at this time of
social change from a decrepit order to
a new one, the creators of beauty
must use their best efforts to produce
ideological works of art for the
people; art must no longer be the
expression of individual satisfaction
which it is today, but should aim
to become a fighting, educative art
for all.*

(D. A. Siqueiros, *Art and Revolution*,
London 1975, tr. S. Calles)

Before Rivera had completed his
first great cycle of murals for the
Ministry of Public Education (see
p. 808) he painted another and only
slightly less ambitious series for the
National Agricultural School at
Chapingo just outside Mexico City.
Agrarian and land reform issues had
been central to the Mexican Revolution ever since 1910 and in devoting
this entire cycle to them Rivera was
able to realize more completely than
in any other work his two great
didactic themes, that of the social and
political revolution and that of
Mexico's national identity. Mexican

Indians and peasants had begun to
figure increasingly in his murals as
personifications of Mexico and at
Chapingo they naturally took a central role together with the land itself,
to which the whole cycle was conceived as a hymn based on Emiliano
Zapata's words, 'here it is taught to
exploit the land not the man'. There
are panels devoted to *The Partition of
the Land* and to *Good* and *Bad Government*, the latter recalling, if only
in name, the frescoes by Lorenzetti in
Siena (9,83). In the former chapel of
the Agrarian School buildings two
carefully balanced series depict in
complementary manner the revolutionary transfer of the ownership of
the land and the biological and geological evolution of the earth, thus
conveying Rivera's vision of the one
as a counterpart of the other. The whole
theme is summarized in two panels
on either side of the chapel entrance,
one depicting *The Agitator* (**20,13**),
the other *The Blood of the Revolutionary Martyrs Fertilizing the Earth.*

In contrast to Rivera's work in the
USA, that of Orozco became more
rather than less outspoken, notably in
the murals he painted for the Baker
Library of Dartmouth College in

Hanover, Massachusetts, in 1932.
Orozco was in no way inhibited by
the fact that Dartmouth College had
become a prestigious East Coast bas-
tion of white Anglo-Saxon privilege
despite having been founded specifically to provide education for North
American Indians. Indeed the College's equivocal past set the theme:
that of a continent characterized by
the dualities of its conflicting Indian
and European historical experiences.
Orozco's conception of the American
'idea' centred on the myth of Quetzalcoatl and was represented on the
two main walls of the library with
murals of America's Pre-Columbian
civilization confronting post-Cortés
America. The final panels in the
series show, firstly, a chilly world of
puritan conformity with white
school-children standing obediently
around their straight-laced woman
teacher. In contrast, Hispanic or Latin
America is represented by a tragic
but also potentially heroic world
in which the rebel Emiliano Zapata
stands as the only upright figure
among corrupt politicians and generals (**20,14**). Orozco said apropos this
powerful image that the 'best representation of Hispanic-American idealism, not as an abstract idea but as an
accomplished fact, would be, I think,
the figure of a rebel. After the destruction of the armed revolution (whether
against a foreign aggressor or local
exploiter or dictator) there remains
a triumphant ideal with the chance
of realization. If there is any need
for expressing in just one sentence
the highest ideal of the Hispanic-
American here, it would be as
follows: "Justice whatever the cost".'
Zapata is being stabbed in the back
by a North American general in
Orozco's mural and, significantly,
the general is accompanied by some
of Zapata's own countrymen as well as
by foreign businessmen. In the final
panel Orozco delivered his deeply
pessimistic judgement on modern
America. Echoing Quetzalcoatl's condemnation of his people's worship of
false gods, he castigated his contemporaries' false knowledge and their
worship of money and power and the
violence of their blind nationalism.
As a final gesture of despair he
painted in the background a junk
heap, the detritus of an industrial and
consumer society.

SOURCES AND DOCUMENTS

LOUIS ARAGON, MAX ERNST AND OTHERS ISSUE A SURREALIST DECLARATION

Surrealism began as a literary movement but almost immediately took on a wider revolutionary-politico-cultural role. Following Breton's first Surrealist Manifesto (1924), the Surrealists issued a Declaration in 1925; its signatories were headed by the Communist poet Louis Aragon (1897–1982) and included, among others, the painter Max Ernst.

With regard to a false interpretation of our enterprise, stupidly circulated among the public,

We declare as follows to the entire braying literary, dramatic, philosophical, exegetical and even theological body of contemporary criticism:

1. *We have nothing to do with literature;*
   But we are quite capable, when necessary, of making use of it like anyone else.
2. Surrealism *is not a new means of expression, or an easier one, nor even a metaphysic of poetry.*
   It is a means of total liberation of the mind and of all that resembles it.
3. *We are determined to make a Revolution.*
4. *We have joined the word* surrealism *to the word* revolution *solely to show the disinterested, detached, and even entirely desperate character of this revolution*
5. *We make no claim to change the* mores *of mankind, but we intend to show the fragility of thought, and on what shifting foundations, what caverns, we have built our trembling houses.*
6. *We hurl this formal warning to Society: Beware of your deviations and* faux-pas, *we shall not miss a single one.*
7. *At each turn of its thought, Society will find us waiting.*
8. *We are specialists in Revolt.*
   There is no means of action which we are not capable, when necessary, of employing.
9. *We say in particular to the Western world:* surrealism *exists. And what is this new ism that is fastened on us? Surrealism is not a poetic form. It is a cry of the mind turning back on itself, and it is determined to break apart its fetters, even if it must be by material hammers!*

(Déclaration du Bureau de Recherches Surréalistes, tr. R. Howard from M. Nadeau, *The History of Surrealism*, New York 1965)

theories, and Freud's methods became the model for writers' and artists' explorations of the unconscious, at first with automatic writing, which released the mind from conscious control so that images from the subconscious could float

to the surface. Although Breton later thought his early definition of Surrealism had been too narrow it is worth recalling his main points: 'pure psychic automatism, by which we propose to express verbally, in writing, or by any other means, the real process of thought . . . . Surrealism is based on the belief in the superior reality of certain forms of association neglected heretofore, in the omnipotence of the dream, in the disinterested play of thought.'

Breton named Freud as one of the three great precursors of Surrealism – one of three men who had, he said, revolutionized modern life from its roots. The other two were Trotsky and, curiously but rather typically, an obscure author known as the Comte de Lautramont (but really Isidore Ducasse), who had written a collection of evil and sadistic prose poems entitled *Les Chants de Maldoror* (1868), from which the Surrealists took their motto – 'As beautiful as the chance meeting on a dissecting table of a sewing-machine and an umbrella.' Various other precursors were mentioned, all of them writers. Painters and sculptors were notable for their absence. However, it was to be mainly through the visual arts that Surrealism reached a wide public and Breton later acknowledged its debt to several artists, notably de Chirico, whom he called 'the supreme Surrealist painter'.

Giorgio de Chirico (1888–1978) was a perplexing figure. Between 1911 and 1919 he created some of the most powerful and disturbing images in modern art – ominous evocations of desolate Italian piazzas in which the key to some impending catastrophe seems to be for ever locked

20,15 Giorgio de Chirico, *Mystery and Melancholy of a Street*, 1914. Canvas, 34¼ × 28⅛ins (87 × 71.4cm). Private collection.

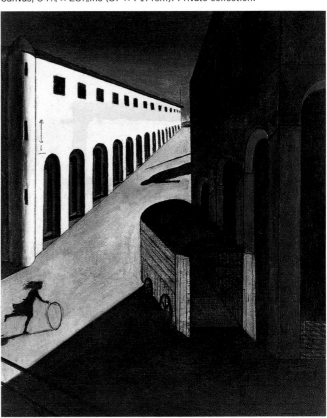

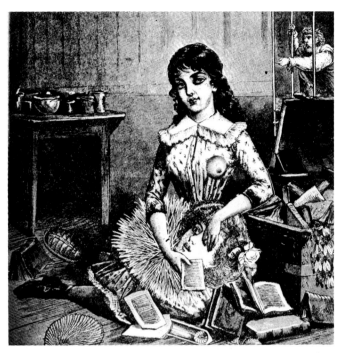

20,16 Max Ernst, plate from *Les femmes 100 têtes*, 1929.

(**20,15**). They are all the more disturbing for being so apparently naive and bland. De Chirico was by no means naive. Yet he abandoned the world of dreams and nightmares in 1919 for a succession of increasingly contrived and academic styles which greatly embarrassed the Surrealists. He was equally embarrassed by their adulation and when they denounced his later work he retaliated by denying the authorship of his early and best paintings, and by executing inferior copies to confuse them! In this, if in nothing else, he revealed himself to be a true Surrealist after all.

The first Surrealist exhibition was held in Paris in 1925, the same year as another, much larger, exhibition in which Le Corbusier and exponents of both the International Modern and Art Deco styles were present (see p. 832). The Surrealist exhibition included the former Dadaists Hans Arp and Max Ernst as well as Joan Miró and several others, the only notable absentees being René Magritte and Salvador Dali, who joined the movement later. Ernst was the first and most successful practitioner of what might be called artistic Freudianism. The Freudian idea of the inner dictation of messages from the subconscious in dreams or psychic, dream-like states and of the possibility, therefore, of attaining complete liberation of the unconscious mind in art so that the writer and artist would simply stand by as spectators at the birth of their works (as Ernst himself was to put it), led Surrealist poets to automatic or unconscious writing. Ernst now invented a visual equivalent which he called *frottage* (rubbing). By taking rubbings with black lead from worn floorboards and other surfaces, as children do with paper and pencil on coins, Ernst created some mysteriously beautiful and suggestive images. 'I was surprised', he wrote, 'by the sudden intensification of my visionary capacities and by the hallucinatory succession of contradictory images superimposed, one upon the other.' In theory his method avoided conscious control and thus bypassed all questions of taste or skill, but in practice, of course, the surfaces to be rubbed had to be selected and the rubbings were usually cut and arranged, so that *frottage* is not wholly comparable to automatic writing.

The alternative route to Surrealism, according to Breton, is the recording or '*trompe l'oeil* fixing' of dreams and this was taken by Ernst in his *collage* novels. These brilliantly exploit that principle of chance juxtaposition which disorientates and disrupts our sense of reality – as epitomized in Lautramont's metaphor quoted above. By means of such unexpected combinations and confrontations a new sense of reality or surreality is created. Ernst's first *collage* novel *Les femmes 100 têtes* of 1929 – untranslatable since '100' means either 'a hundred' or 'without' when spoken in French – contains 149 *collage* images or 'ready-made realities'. These were put together by Ernst from various sources, mainly from nineteenth-century wood-engraved book illustrations, cut out and recomposed by free association. The narrative thus created is convincingly dream-like and frequently borders on the nightmare (**20,16**). Only very rarely did Ernst achieve the same dead-pan, enigmatic and compelling quality in his paintings.

DALI, MAGRITTE AND MIRÓ

The Spanish painter Salvador Dali (1904–89) also tried to capture the hallucinatory clarity of dreams in his so-called 'hand-painted dream photographs', of which *The Persistence of Memory* is perhaps the most unnerving (**20,17**). Time stands still within the dreamer's mind, as in Freud's timeless unconscious, so that in Dali's arid, airless landscape the metal watches go limp and stop for ever. They even melt and decompose, attracting iridescent insects as they take on organic shapes such as that of the watch drooping like some rotting fruit on the bare branch of a dead tree. Dali outlined his creative method in his book *La Femme Visible* (1930). It went a stage beyond that of the most radical Surrealists so far, and for their passive automatism he substituted what he called a 'paranoiac and active advance of the mind'. He proposed a state of mind that would be permanently disoriented. The only difference between himself and a madman, he said, was that he wasn't mad! 'I believe that the moment is near when by a procedure of active paranoiac thought it will be possible to systematize confusion and contribute to the total discrediting of the world of reality.' The paranoia which he claimed to be responsible for his visual images – especially his double images – has little or nothing to do with medical paranoia, but some of them are genuinely disquieting and quickly became famous. However, Dali's cynical self-promotion eventually led to his excommunication by Breton.

Freudian symbolism – phallic noses, fetishistic hair – is very obvious in Dali's work and pervades Surrealist imagery generally, as in one of the movement's most famous works, *Object*, known as *Luncheon in Fur* (**20,18**), by Meret Oppenheim (1913–85). Her combination of hair

20,17 Salvador Dali, *The Persistence of Memory*, 1931. Oil on canvas, 9½ × 13ins (24.1 × 33cm). The Museum of Modern Art, New York (Given anonymously).

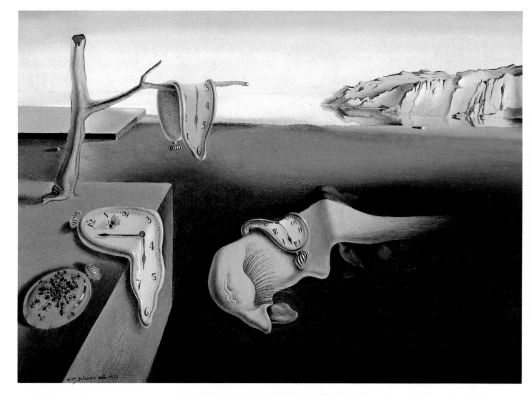

20,18 *Below* Meret Oppenheim, *Object*, 1936. Fur-covered cup, saucer and spoon: cup 4⅜ins (10.9cm) diameter; saucer 9⅜ins (23.7cm) diameter; spoon 8ins (20.2cm) long; overall 2⅞ins (7.3cm) high. The Museum of Modern Art, New York (Purchase).

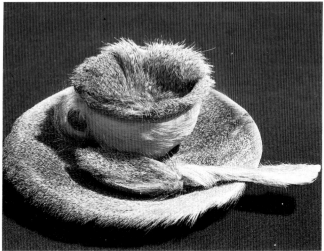

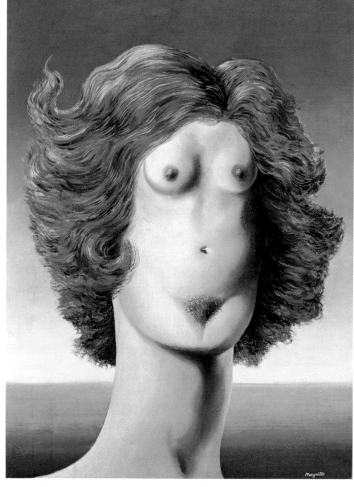

on porcelain, the furry with the slippery, the hirsute with the polite and smooth, fuse subliminally in an unforgettably Freudian way. The Belgian painter René Magritte (1898–1967) also used such imagery. But whereas Dali's paintings were disturbing, Magritte's are truly disruptive – all the more so for being executed with an intentionally banal technique used by Magritte when he worked as a designer of posters, advertisements and wallpapers. They challenge our assumptions about art and reality and, furthermore, they are totally without any meaning in so far as they resist explication as distinct from interpretation. Their titles are striking but the connection of their titles with the visual image almost always turns out to be ambiguous, or non-existent. *Le viol* (**20,19**) is typical. The superimposition on a head of a female torso with pubic

20,19 René Magritte, *Le viol*, 1934. Oil on canvas, 28¾ × 21¼ins (73 × 54cm). Menil Collection, Houston.

mouth, above a swollen and suggestively phallic neck, would be, without the title, no more than an image in bad taste. By adding *Le viol* – a word whose suggestiveness is lost when translated as 'The Rape' – Magritte intimates some 'meaning', which in fact doesn't exist. But it has the effect of a slow fuse. *Le viol* was recognized by the Surrealists as a powerful statement of their aims and Breton used a drawing for it as the cover of his *What is Surrealism?* in 1934. Breton appreciated Magritte as an artist 'who detected what could result from relating concrete words of great resonance . . . with forms which deny or at least do not rationally correspond to them'.

The Mexican painter Frida Kahlo (1907–54) was, like Meret Oppenheim, dubbed one of Surrealism's 'discoveries'. No modern artistic movement gave women such prominence, albeit problematic and ambivalent, or elevated the image of woman to as significant a role in the creative life of the male artist, as did Surrealism. 'The problem of woman', Breton wrote in 1929, 'is the most marvellous and disturbing problem in the world.' The 'problem' was, however, defined in exclusively, and usually anxiety-ridden, explicitly Freudian, male terms. When Breton convened the famous Surrealist meeting to discuss sexuality, no female was present. Women were viewed solely as a projection of male desire and needs, as inaccessible muse, innocent child, castrating temptress or object of sadistic gratification. This made their participation in the movement somewhat problematic though a number were to be active in it. Kahlo met Breton when he went to Mexico in 1938 partly to meet Trotsky, who was then living as a guest of Diego Rivera (see p. 808), Kahlo's husband. The famous anti-Stalinist manifesto of that year, *Towards a Free Revolutionary Art*, appeared under the joint signatures of Breton and Rivera but was in fact largely written by Trotsky. A self-portrait by Kahlo hung in Trotsky's study and was admired by Breton, who welcomed her into the Surrealist movement. However, she always remained defiantly outside it. She was, as she stated so clearly, painting her own reality. And she not only asserted her independence of vision, but also recognized the inherent misogyny in Surrealist fantasies and that there could not be an authentic place in the movement for a woman artist with an identity independent of male projections (fantasies).

Her work consists almost entirely of self-portraits in which she explored the reality of her own body and her consciousness of it, of the dualities of sexual and cultural identity. Though publicly celebrated as an exotic beauty enjoying with Rivera a rich and tempestuous life, she saw herself in sober terms. Chronic ill-health and suffering marked her and she was in almost constant pain as a result of a streetcar accident in her late teens which left her partially disabled for life. Her marriage to Rivera ended by subordinating her both as an artist and as a human being, and her divorce took place while one of her most piercingly honest self-portraits, *The Two Fridas* (**20,20**), was being painted. The two Fridas are the one Rivera loved and the one whom he no longer loved, this duality being coupled with that of her traditional Mexican

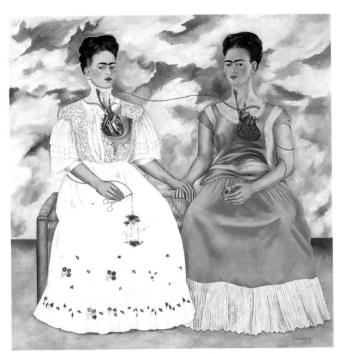

20,20 Frida Kahlo, *The Two Fridas*, 1939. Oil on canvas, 5ft 9ins × 5ft 9ins (1.75 × 1.75m). Museum of Modern Art, Mexico City.

persona and that of the modern woman. They hold hands but the artery joining them has been ruptured. The Frida scorned tries to stay the flow of blood with a pair of forceps and they go on sitting, side by side, one dressed in a high-necked elegantly stitched traditional Mexican bridal dress, the other in a contemporary sleeveless and low-necked garment, bearing witness in their own persons to women's fate. In *The Second Sex*, Simone de Beauvoir had held up the image of the mirror as the key to the feminine condition. Women concern themselves with their own images, she asserted, men with the enlarged self-images provided by their reflection in a woman. Kahlo epitomizes the former, the Surrealists the latter.

It was a Spaniard, however, the Catalan painter Joan Miró (1893–1983), whom Breton thought (correctly) would turn out to be 'the most Surrealist of [us] all'. Miró had undergone several conversions before being drawn to Surrealism – to Fauvism, to Cubism in 1919 after he met Picasso, and to Dada a few years later. Surrealism offered a new direction for his art and helped him to free himself from previous influences. He evolved what Breton called a 'pure psychic automatism', allowing his subconscious full play in the creation of semi-abstract forms. 'I begin painting', he said, 'and as I paint the picture begins to assert itself, or suggest itself, under my brush. The form becomes a sign for a woman or a bird as I work.' Many of his early Surrealist paintings have a wonderful child-like innocence of fantasy and gaiety of free invention. But with the outbreak of the Spanish Civil War and the looming probability of another world war his vision darkened. His forms became increasingly sinister and amoeba-like – or 'biomorphic' as they were called – floating in an

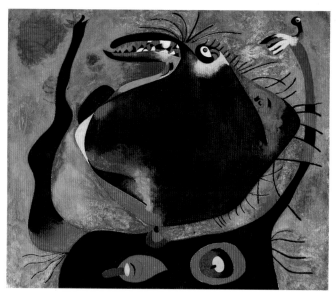

20,21 Joan Miró, *Head of a Woman*, 1938. Canvas, 18⅛ × 21⅝ins (46 × 55cm). Minneapolis Institute of Arts.

immaterial space like medical specimens in a jar of spirits. Such works as his *Head of a Woman* (**20,21**) gave savage expression to the sense of impending horror widely felt in Europe at the time and were equalled in intensity only by Picasso's *Guernica* (20,49). When war broke out in 1939 most of the Surrealists, including Breton, took refuge in New York. They went on working, holding exhibitions and other public manifestations, attracting into their orbit such artists as the Armenian-born Arshile Gorky (see p. 836), and helped to sow the seeds of post-war American movements, notably Abstract Expressionism.

WELDED METAL:
A REVOLUTION IN SCULPTURE

The Dada and Surrealist discovery that self-sufficient works of art could be created by combining useless pieces of scrap metal and other junk in unexpected ways was one of their most fruitful insights. Picasso's *Head of a Bull*, made from the saddle and handle-bars of a bicycle, is the best-known example. Such works involved more than just the use of discarded materials but it was their introduction into artists' studios of industrial metals, especially iron, that opened the way to the second and final stage of the remarkable revolution in twentieth-century sculpture that Picasso had initiated in 1912. His so-called Cubist sculptures were made with pieces of wood, tin, cardboard, string and other discarded materials, put together by a process of assembly similar to that used for his *collages* (see pp. 791–3). Now he took the next and crucial step away from 'closed' or solid form to 'open' or constructed form, that is to say towards sculpture which, instead of being carved from a block or built up or molded or assembled as were Cubist sculptures, is freely constructed around an empty core of space. Forged metal or welded

metal bars and plates were needed for this and Picasso sought the collaboration of a skilled metalworker, Julio González (1876–1942). He had known González since their youth in Barcelona. They had both left Spain in the late 1890s and settled in Paris, where González worked mainly as a decorative artist, making metal boxes, brooches, necklaces and such like. Not until 1927 did he branch out into sculpture, probably at the instigation of Picasso. However, without González the development of modern sculpture might have been very different.

González came from a family of metalworkers in Barcelona, where iron was used for decorative purposes all over the city, notably on buildings in the lively Catalan version of Art Nouveau (17,33). One of the admirers of the González family metalwork wrote that in their sooty workshop, 'under the singing chorus of constant hammering on the anvil, I think I see springing from the fire . . . an art without aesthetic rules or absurd restrictions, an art free as smoke, born from fire, and wrought in fire'. It was from Julio González's workshop in Paris that Picasso and he together made the leap into open-form sculpture, first with Picasso's wire figures, for which he made drawings in 1927–8, and then in constructed metal pieces by both González and Picasso. Though González assisted Picasso in the forge he worked independently as well. Picasso was to be, if anything, less daring and radical than González in exploiting the spatial and other possibilities of the new medium they had invented. Even some of his visually most startling welded metal sculptures did not break

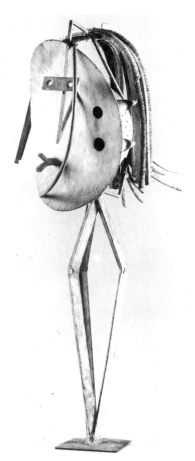

20,22 Pablo Picasso, *Head of a Woman*, 1930–1. Painted iron, sheet metal, springs and found objects (colanders), 3ft 3¾ins (1m) high. Musée Picasso, Paris.

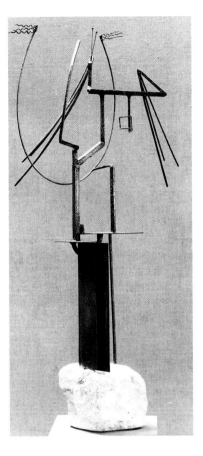

20,23 Julio González, *Woman Combing her Hair II*, 1934. Iron, 47⅝ × 23⅝ × 11⅖ins (121 × 60 × 29cm). Moderna Museet, Stockholm.

away completely from his pre-First World War work but combined assembly with welding. The everyday objects he incorporated in them were not completely reworked. In the *Head of a Woman* (**20,22**), for example, the vegetable colanders, wire springs and other found objects remain easily recognizable. In a González sculpture, on the other hand, such as his *Woman Combing her Hair II* (**20,23**), not only are the parts reworked so that they have lost their original, functional meaning but, more important, the sculpture is not conceived as a solid form but as a collection of elements composed in and around space. The elements appear as if in a constant state of flux as the spectator moves round them.

The concept of open-form metal sculpture, so fully realized by González, was to be carried a stage further by the Americans Alexander Calder (1898–1976) and David Smith (1906–65). Calder was trained as a mechanical engineer but abandoned this career and in 1926 went to Paris where he worked as a sculptor, combining his knowledge of metals and engineering with Constructivist and Surrealist theories he picked up there. Surprisingly quickly he developed a vocabulary of flat biomorphic shapes, based on Miró's paintings, which he suspended in space either from the ceiling or from a tripod. Bases were eliminated and kinetic sculpture with moving parts soon followed. Attempts had previously been made to add mobility to sculpture but they had all relied on clockwork or other motors and this gave them a mechanical air. Calder evolved lightweight, delicately balanced sculptures which were set in motion by the currents of air around them. Duchamp was among the first to appreciate them and gave them their name, mobiles. Calder's later free-standing sculptures of metal that did not move were to be called stabiles.

Most of Calder's mobiles and stabiles are abstract but some have affinities with the animate world, as is indicated by the titles he gave them, such as *Lobster Trap and Fish Tail* (**20,24**). This piece vividly suggests the graceful movement of swimming fish as it slowly gyrates in currents of air. A light-hearted sense of fantasy is also evident in such works by Calder. They recall Klee's sophisticated delight in the whimsical as expressed in paintings such as his *Twittering Machine*.

The descendant of blacksmiths, David Smith was familiar from his youth with iron, steel and other metals and with working with them. He also acquired some knowledge of factory tools and equipment at the Studebaker factory in Indiana. Later he began painting in New York, but only in about 1930 did he turn decisively to metal sculpture after having seen reproductions of work by González and Picasso. By 1932–3, when Calder exhibited his first mobiles in Paris, Smith had established a studio in the Terminal Iron Works in Brooklyn. His painterly beginnings were to mark his early sculptures but he already had the boldness to defy traditional forms and attitudes by inventing what were later to be called 'space frames' as a means of creating in sculpture a pictorial plane for a frontal yet three-dimensional composition. His early welded iron and steel sculptures resemble airborne drawings in space. However, the finest of them date from after the Second World War, during which he worked as a welder at the American Locomotive company plant at Schenectady, New York (21,10).

20,24 Alexander Calder, *Lobster Trap and Fish Tail*, 1939. Hanging mobile, painted steel wire and sheet aluminium, about 8ft 6ins high × 9ft 6ins diameter (2.6 × 2.9m). The Museum of Modern Art, New York (Commissioned by the Advisory Committee for the stairwell of the Museum).

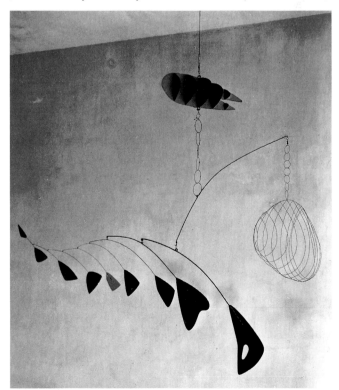

PHOTOGRAPHY AND MODERN MOVEMENTS

During the inter-war period the relationship between photographic and other visual images became more complex than before. As we have seen (pp. 665–8), some nineteenth-century painters had taken photographs and many had used them as aids, while photographers had been strongly influenced by paintings in their choice of subject-matter, angles of vision and indeed in their whole conception of the photographic image. But despite the reiterated claim that photographs could be works of art, they were still generally regarded as belonging to a distinct and inferior category, lacking the unique hand-made quality and artistic prestige of a painting, drawing or even an etching which was usually one of a strictly limited number of 'pulls' or prints. They were also, as a result of the mass-production of easily manipulated cameras and the automatic processing of prints, taken by literally millions of men and women, mostly amateurs, few of whom were aware of, and still fewer in sympathy with, the changes that had transformed art since the mid-nineteenth century. Moreover, while self-consciously 'artistic' photographers clung to traditional ideas of composition in softly focused images, the main technical developments in the medium, facilitating greater sharpness of definition and instantaneity of vision, were equally out of phase with those in the other arts.

20,25 Alfred Stieglitz, *Equivalents*, c. 1927. Gelatin silver print. Philadelphia Museum of Art (The Alfred Stieglitz Collection).

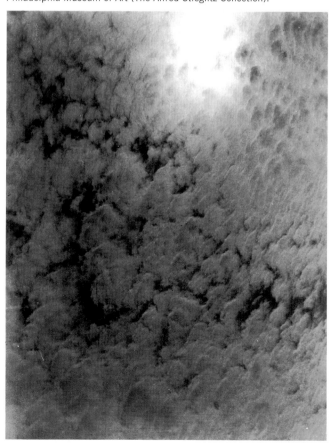

In the early twentieth century a few painters, notably Giacomo Balla in Italy and Marcel Duchamp in France (see pp. 794, 803), drew inspiration from photographs of figures in movement of the type initiated by Muybridge and Eakins. But not until the war years did photographers begin to join up with the ranks of the pictorial avant-garde. In 1917 the American Alvin Langdon Coburn (1882–1966), who had previously photographed such 'unartistic' subjects as smoking factory chimneys, invented a device based on the kaleidoscope to make a series of entirely non-representational images called by his friend, the poet Ezra Pound, Vortographs (from Vorticism, the short-lived British child of Cubism). The key figure in the United States, however, was Alfred Stieglitz (1864–1946) who, after technological training in Germany, settled in New York where he began to photograph the modern city-scape bringing out, as a contemporary remarked in 1899, 'the sentiment and tender beauty in subjects previously thought devoid of charm'. In 1902 he founded a society in New York called the Photographic Secession to associate it with groups of artists who seceded from academically sponsored exhibitions in Austria and Germany. And from 1905, in collaboration with Edward Steichen (1879–1973), an American photographer who lived for a time in Paris, he directed a small gallery at 291 Fifth Avenue, New York, where in addition to photographs there were paintings by Picasso and Matisse and African sculptures, exhibited there for the first time in America. This brought him into contact with the New York Dada group (see pp. 801–4) – it was due to his photograph that Duchamp's *Fountain* (20,5) became notorious. He also promoted the work of the more adventurous young American painters including Arthur G. Dove and Georgia O'Keeffe, to whom he was married in 1924 (see p. 835). No one did more to introduce the most recent European artistic ideas to America, and to establish photography as a means for their expression. At first sight, however, his own photographs – delicately sensitive portraits, nudes, landscapes – seem to make no clear break with the past. Only those of clouds, which he entitled *Equivalents*, have obvious affinities with contemporary paintings of the kind he admired (**20,25**). 'I wanted to photograph clouds to put down my philosophy of life – to show that my photographs were not due to subject-matter.' Studies of clouds had often been painted since the early nineteenth century but Stieglitz's attitude to them was entirely different for in their insubstantial, shifting and dissolving forms he caught combinations of light and shade which he felt to be equivalent to his emotions.

Stieglitz declared: 'I was born in Hoboken. I am an American. Photography is my passion. The search for truth my obsession.' He was exclusively a photographer and he notably expanded, without breaking, the normal bounds of the medium. The same could be said of Edward Weston (1886–1958) whose sharply focused photographs of plants, strangely shaped fruits, the section of an artichoke or segment of the human body, often have the heightened presence and rigour of non-representational images. But the approach of younger artists closely

Berlin – for a type of *collage* called photomontage. As we have seen, Picasso and Braque had been making *collages* since 1913 (pp. 791–3), works of extreme refinement and sophisticated visual wit. But in post-First World War Berlin, Hannah Höch (1889–1979), John Heartfield (1891–1968) and others exploited it for broader and more audacious purposes, in mockery of the popular bourgeois pastimes of gluing together cut-outs for decorative or sentimental effect. Like all Dada creations, the first photomontages – made of fragments of photographs, pieces of newsprint and so on, assembled in apparent disorder – were subversive of all respectable middle-class values and of fine art (the German word montage means 'assembly', as in mechanized industrial production). They expressed the chaos of capitalist society during the war and its immediate aftermath. But despite the use of photographic prints incongruously juxtaposed – to attack both Expressionism and illusionism at the same time – photomontages were unique objects and, as such, works of art sometimes with a strong aesthetic appeal that was probably unintended. They were the point of departure for some of the most effective of all political images, notably those by Heartfield when he found himself confronting enemies far more dangerous than Expressionist painters and the complacent bourgeoisie. Heartfield was the son of a Socialist writer, changed his name from Helmut Herzfeld as a mark of protest during the war, and afterwards helped to found the German Communist party (the Nazis in 1933 forced him to emigrate, first to Prague, then to London, but true to his principles he was to return and settle in East Germany in 1950, like his friend the dramatist Bertold Brecht). His numerous anti-Nazi photomontages – 'One Man's War Against Hitler', he entitled an exhibition of them in London in 1939 – were intended for reproduction in periodicals and on posters. The majority were composed of photographs of leading Nazis cut out and juxtaposed with other images – Julius Streicher and the mangled corpse of a murdered man, for instance – with inscriptions to underline their message (20,27). A few have a more general significance, notably the poster *As in the Middle Ages so in the Third Reich*, combining a photograph of a male nude impaled on a swastika beneath a straight photograph of a Gothic carving which Heartfield misinterpreted (it symbolized humanity on the wheel of divine judgement and not judicial torture). Such works make a stronger point than hand-drawn caricatures, simply because they are composed of photographs, direct images of reality carrying conviction even when the joins between one image and another are apparent. It is hardly surprising that photomontage was soon taken up for Nazi propaganda and commercial advertising – to falsify reality.

Praising Heartfield, the German writer Walter Benjamin remarked in 1934 that apart from his work and that of a very few others photography had become 'more and more subtle, more and more modern, and the result is that it is now incapable of photographing a tenement or a rubbish heap without transfiguring it . . . It has succeeded in turning abject poverty itself, by handling

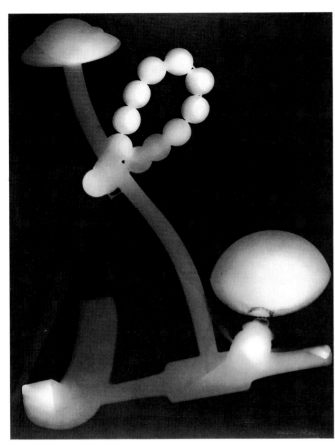

20,26 Man Ray, *Photogram*, 1923. Gelatin silver print, 11½ × 9⅛ins (29.1 × 23.3cm). The Museum of Modern Art, New York (Gift of James Thrall Soby).

involved in Dada was entirely different. Emanuel Rudnitsky, who called himself Man Ray (1890–1976), was trained as a painter and was taken up in New York by Picabia and Duchamp – he photographed the dust gathering on Duchamp's *Large Glass*. They introduced him to the Dada circle in Paris when he settled there in 1921. On a sudden impulse one day in his dark-room, he placed some objects on a piece of sensitized paper, turned the light on for a moment and developed the print, which the poet Tristan Tzara declared to be pure Dada. Man Ray went on to make more of these camera-less photographs or Photograms, selecting ordinary but disparate, opaque and translucent objects to be placed over the paper and create images of strange ambiguity, concrete and abstract at the same time (**20,26**). Each one was unique but 12 were published in a volume entitled *Les champs délicieuses* (*Delectable Fields*, Paris, 1922) with a characteristically abstruse introduction by Tzara who remarked that Man Ray 'presents to space an image that goes beyond it; and the air, with its clenched hands, and its advantage of surmounting all, captures it and keeps it in its breast'. Camera-less images made by others soon afterwards are however less close to the ideals of the Dadaists than to those of the Surrealists among whom Man Ray soon became a leading figure.

Photography was put to other uses by a Dada group in

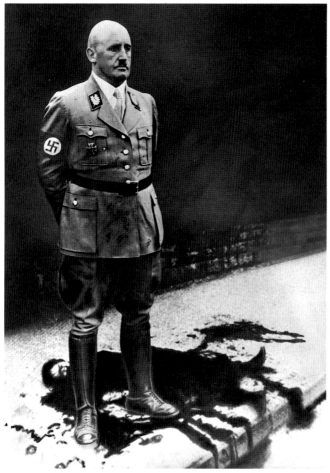

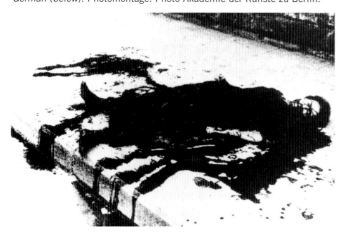

20,27 John Heartfield, *A Pan-German*, 2 November 1933 (*above*) and Stuttgart police photograph of a 'peace-time murder victim' used in *A Pan-German* (*below*). Photomontage. Photo Akademie der Künste zu Berlin.

power to shock has survived, undiminished by the passage of time. 'After looking at these pictures', the poet and critic Lincoln Kirstein wrote in 1938, 'with all their clear, hideous and beautiful detail, their open insanity and pitiful grandeur, compare the vision of a continent as it is, not as it might have been or as it was, with any other coherent vision that we have had since World War I. What poet has said as much? What painter has shown as much?' *Migrant Mother, Nipomo, California* of 1936 very soon became the most famous of these photographs (**20,28**). It was taken by Lange who had begun as a formal portrait photographer but, shocked by the effects of the Depression, turned to making documentary records of the homeless and unemployed, and joined Stryker's team. 'Whatever I photograph I do not molest or tamper with or arrange', she wrote. 'Whatever I photograph, I try to show as having its position in the past or in the present.' But the group of the migrant mother staring into the face of adversity with her three children could not have been more effectively composed by a sculptor. And although intended to do no more than expose the contemporary situation in California, it seems to express the misery of the displaced in all times, including our own. Another photographer, Margaret Bourke-White (1904–71), toured the southern states with the novelist Erskine Caldwell, making an independent survey of the social scene published in an inexpensive and

20,28 Dorothea Lange, *Migrant Mother, Nipomo, California*, 1936. Gelatin silver print. Library of Congress, Washington DC.

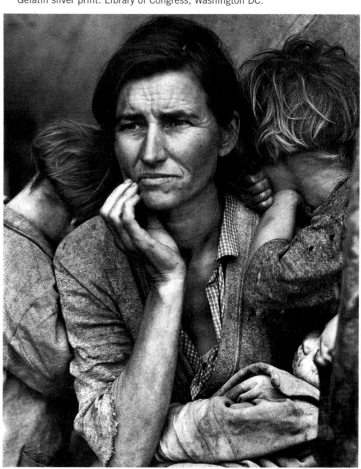

it in a modish, technically perfect way, into an object of enjoyment.' This brings to mind many, though not all, of the photographs of rural poverty in the United States taken during the Depression years for the official Farm Security Administration, both to document the plight of evicted share-croppers and to justify government spending on their resettlement. They were the work of a team that included some outstanding photographers, notably Walker Evans (1903–75) and Dorothea Lange (1895–1965), under the direction of Roy E. Stryker (1893–1976). Their

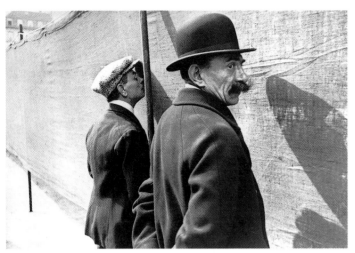

20,29 Henri Cartier-Bresson, *Brussels*, 1932. Gelatin silver print.

widely diffused book *You Have Seen Their Faces* (1937) with the aim of shaking the complacency of city-dwellers who treasured a myth of rustic well-being.

By this date instantaneous photographs – snapshots – were being taken throughout the world. But no one was more adept at stealing from the passing urban scene images that reveal the vagaries of human behaviour than the Frenchman Henri Cartier-Bresson (b. 1908), who roamed the streets with a camera as his third eye to catch a psychological fourth dimension. His *Brussels* is one of the most memorable of all photographs (**20,29**). He gives the impression of being no more than an impartial observer, so carefully does he preserve the neutrality of the camera's eye, but his selection of subjects (and of the photographs he chose for reproduction from the vast number he took) was determined by a finely developed intellect. As a youth, he had been much impressed by the Surrealists, the poetry of the Symbolists, the psychology of Freud and the sociology of Marx. From 1936 he worked for a Communist newspaper in Paris. In most of his photographs, however, apart from those recording the Spanish Civil War, his political sympathies are rarely made explicit. Those of the bourgeoisie are more gently humorous than censorious, though none the less subversive. His friend and fellow Communist, the writer Louis Aragon who had earlier made great use of disturbing images in his Surrealist poetry, remarked in 1936 with Cartier-Bresson in mind: 'Photography has abandoned the studio and lost its static, academic character – its fixity. It has mixed into life; it has gone everywhere taking life by surprise; and once again it has become more denunciatory than painting . . . . The strange part of this rediscovery is that, suddenly, when timid painting has long since renounced daring compositional arrangements, photography produced at random, in the streets or anywhere, the earliest audacities of painters.' Photography and the other visual arts, after their brief moment of intimate association in the 1920s, each helping to define the role of the other, had, finally, gone their own way. Man Ray, who practised both, said that he photographed what he could not paint and painted what he could not photograph.

CONSTRUCTIVISM, *DE STIJL* AND THE INTERNATIONAL STYLE

ART AND REVOLUTION

As we have already seen, Malevich and other artists in Russia welcomed the Revolution in 1917, and during the confused and turbulent years that followed a number of them, among whom were some of the most original and radical artists and architects of the time, enjoyed a brief honeymoon of official recognition. The avant-garde seemed to have come into its own at last. Lunacharsky, a writer and playwright long resident in Paris, and the first commissar for education and the arts, gave them full support and encouragement, as did also Trotsky. Lenin was indifferent.

Among the painters Malevich, Marc Chagall (1889–1985) and Kandinsky (see p. 783) were prominent. But the leaders of the most progressive new movement, Constructivism, were the architects, sculptors and designers Vladimir Tatlin (1885–1953) and El (Eleazer Markevich) Lissitzky (1890–1941). Tatlin had seen Picasso's assemblages in Paris in 1913 and after his return to Russia he went on to make similar constructions out of various everyday material, but without any representational elements so that they were completely abstract – among

20,30 Vladimir Tatlin, Project for the Monument to the Third International, 1919–20.

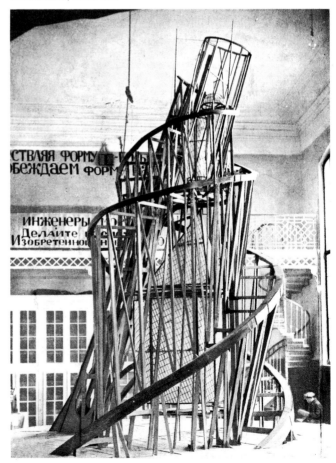

the first of their kind anywhere. They later took on architectural significance in his decor for the Moscow Café Pittoresque of 1917. In 1919 he began his Monument to the Third International, a gigantic double skew spiral of openwork girders with revolving halls suspended at different levels, the whole construction to be a third of a mile (530m) high (**20,30**). Though it was never realized, Tatlin's design became a symbol of revolutionary modernism and of the Constructivist spirit of utilitarian simplicity and respect for the logic of materials. Constructivist ideology was largely anti-aesthetic, reflecting Marx's contention that the mode of production of material life determines social, political and intellectual processes. Its aims were primarily social, utilitarian and materialist. The artist's mission was to express the aspirations of the revolutionary proletariat and enhance the physical and intellectual conditions of society as a whole – hence the Constructivists' eager acceptance of machine production, architectural engineering, manufactured materials, photographic and other modern means of mass communication. Much of their best and most influential work, apart from architecture, was to be in typography and publicity and exhibition design.

20,31 El Lissitzky, *Proun 99*, 1924–5. Canvas, 50¾ × 39ins (129 × 99cm). Yale University Art Gallery (Gift of the Société Anonyme).

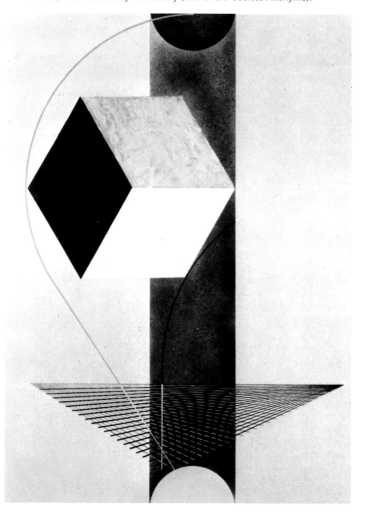

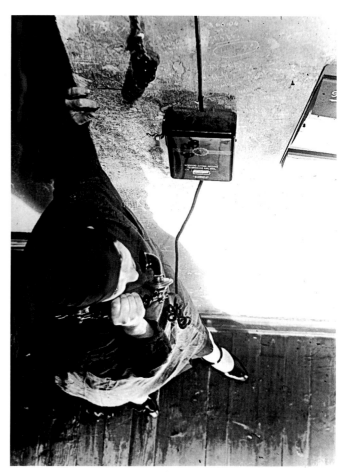

20,32 Alexander Rodchenko, *At the Telephone*, 1928. Gelatin silver print, 15½ × 11⅞ins (39.3 × 29.1cm). The Museum of Modern Art, New York (Mr and Mrs John Spencer Fund).

Lissitzky's best-known Constructivist work, his Lenin Tribune project of 1920, failed, like Tatlin's, to get off the drawing-board. But his paintings, which he called Prouns – an invented word meaning 'For the New Art' – are strongly architectural in character and fully express his vision. He described a Proun as 'a station for changing from architecture to painting', and they often seem to hover halfway between an isometric projection and an abstract composition (**20,31**). The one illustrated here is typical in its cool precision, like that of an engineer's drawing, of the Constructivist machine aesthetic. A cube is suspended in space above a grid of perspective lines and in front of a slightly off-centre bar of color anchored top and bottom by semicircles. The subtle play with intervals and weight and balance is essentially architectural.

However, the Constructivist utopia was short-lived. After the introduction of Lenin's New Economic Policy in 1921 the movement's usefulness began to be seriously questioned and several of its members hastened to leave Russia. In 1921 Lissitzky went to Germany, where he remained intermittently for the next nine years. It was largely through him that Constructivist ideas reached the West. In Russia their legacy remained mainly on paper, the Moscow workers' clubs by Constantin Melnikov (1890–1974) and Ilia Golossov (1883–1945) being the outstanding Constructivist buildings to survive, especially the latter's club, Zoniev, Moscow, of 1926–7. Alexander Mikhailovich Rodchenko (1891–1956), a close associate of Lissitzky and Tatlin, stayed on in Russia. He was an artist with a wide range of talents who began as a painter, became a master of photomontages – some of which are among the most forceful visual expressions of the ideals of the Revolution – and a very notable graphic and industrial designer. No one was more deeply convinced of the role of art as a catalyst for social change, but his work soon came to be thought too intellectually élitist. From 1925 he was active mainly as a photographer and although some of his images of construction workers served for propaganda, his adoption of unusual viewpoints with the camera tilted sharply up or down was similarly criticized (20,32). In 1942 he returned to painting and evolved an abstract-expressionist style directly opposed to the artistic policy of the régime and anticipating, very strikingly, the work of Jackson Pollock in the United States (see pp. 835–8).Rodchenko, however, was an exception. The suppression of artistic groupings in 1932 signalled a radical change in Soviet artistic policy and finally eliminated all modernist tendencies in favour of various revival styles in architecture and of Socialist Realism in the figurative arts – attempts to bridge the gap between avant-garde and working-class culture, between the artist and the masses, which foundered in a banal official style lacking both the creative originality of élitist work and the genuine vitality of popular art.

THE BAUHAUS

In post-war Germany, too, there were many who believed that the artist could help to bring about new social conditions through the creation of new visual environments. The Bauhaus at Weimar became the centre of such aspirations not only in Germany, but in Europe generally. It had been launched in 1919 by Gropius (see p. 800), who combined the two originally separate Schools of Art and Crafts and of Fine Art into one institution, for which he coined the name Bauhaus (House of Building). This alluded to his conviction that, as with the medieval cathedral, a building ought to be the meeting place of all teaching in the visual arts. His aim was unification in art and design. 'The ultimate goal of the Bauhaus is the collective work of art', he wrote, 'in which no barriers exist between the structural and decorative arts.' Artists and architects would work together towards the great goal of 'the building of the future'. In the early years of the Bauhaus he was influenced, through the Viennese *Sezession* group and *Werkstätte*, by the ideas of William Morris and the English Arts and Crafts movement (see p. 731) combined with Expressionist fervour and utopianism. However, this changed in about 1922 through contact with *De Stijl* (see p. 798), which Lissitzky had joined on leaving Russia temporarily in 1921. Ever more austere and purposeful, the Bauhaus now moved in a similar direction towards stark cubic simplicity and functionalism, notably in industrial design. Whereas early Bauhaus

WALTER GROPIUS ON THE BAUHAUS

The enormous influence of the Bauhaus was largely due to its early promotion of fully integrated modern design principles with a view to mass production and industrialization. This eminently rational, technological program was combined with the utopian spirit prevalent in the immediate post-First World War years. In the following extract Gropius summarizes the goal of the Bauhaus teaching curriculum.

The culminating point of the Bauhaus teaching is a demand for a new and powerful working correlation of all the processes of creation. The gifted student must regain a feeling for the interwoven strands of practical and formal work. The joy of building, in the broadest meaning of that word, must replace the paper work of design. Architecture unites in a collective task all creative workers, from the simple artisan to the supreme artist.

For this reason, the basis of collective education must be sufficiently broad to permit the development of every kind of talent. Since a universally applicable method for the discovery of talent does not exist, the individual in the course of his development must find for himself the field of activity best suited to him within the circle of the community. The majority become interested in production; the few extraordinarily gifted ones will suffer no limits to their activity. After they have completed the course of practical and formal instruction, they undertake independent research and experiment.

Modern painting, breaking through old conventions, has released countless suggestions which are still waiting to be used by the practical world. But when, in the future, artists who sense new creative values have had practical training in the industrial world, they will themselves possess the means for realizing those values immediately. They will compel industry to serve their idea and industry will seek out and utilize their comprehensive training.

(W. Gropius, *Idee und Aufbau des Staatlichen Bauhaus Weimar*, Munich 1923; tr. from H. Bayer, W. and I. Gropius, eds., *Bauhaus 1919–1928*, New York 1938)

designs had been in reality crafts products adjusted to give the appearance of industrial production, Gropius was now converted to machine aesthetics, acknowledging that machine work could produce qualities of its own. He also realized that the differences between industry and handicraft are due less to the nature of the tools employed than

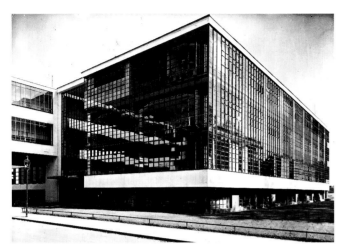

20,33 Walter Gropius, workshop wing of the Bauhaus, Dessau, Germany, 1925–6.

Community in Wisconsin where Frank Lloyd Wright, whose early buildings had influenced Gropius quite notably, encouraged his students to become individualists. The Bauhaus aimed to produce prototypes for the mass production of things in daily use, an aim that was best realized in furniture, the chromium-plated tubular steel chair designed by Marcel Breuer in 1925 being the most characteristic example. It is still in production some 90 years later.

In 1925 the Bauhaus moved to Dessau, where Gropius designed for it a new building in which the school's functional and corporate ideals were admirably exemplified (**20,33**). A complex of workshops, studios, classrooms, showrooms, library, offices and living quarters, it was unified externally by a clean, precise and unornamented yet welcoming asymmetrical arrangement of intersecting rectilinear blocks. Vast expanses of glazed walls were made possible by a supporting skeleton of steel beams and reinforced concrete columns, exterior walling being reduced in the workshop wing to two narrow white strips at top and bottom. It became the paradigmatic International Style building for the next half century and survived the Second World War intact. However, it was closed as a school by the Nazis in 1933; Gropius had already resigned in 1928 to be succeeded by Mies van der Rohe. The staff dispersed, carrying the Bauhaus ideals with them, notably to the USA where Gropius taught at

to the subdivision of labour in one case and individual control by a single craftsman in the other. His emphasis on the need for co-operative work on problems of industrial design and on the designer's creative responsibility to society reflected his left-wing political sympathies. They produced an atmosphere at the Bauhaus which was very different from that prevailing a few years later at Taliesin

20,34 Paul Klee, *Sunset*, 1930. Oil on canvas, 18⅕ × 27⅝ins (46.2 × 70.2cm). Art Institute of Chicago (Gift of Mary and Leigh B. Block).

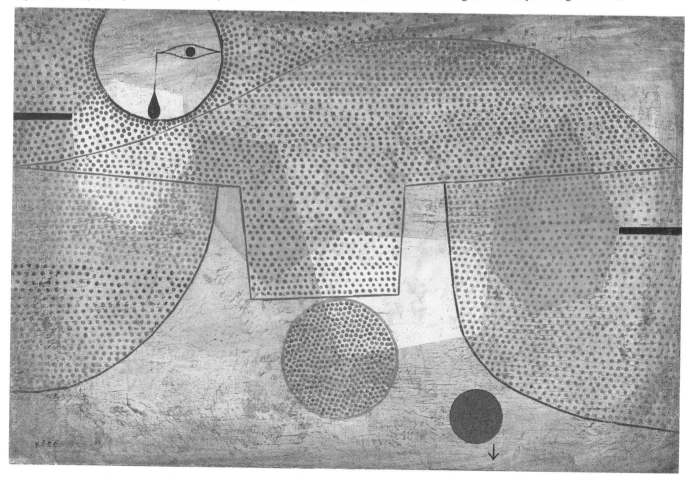

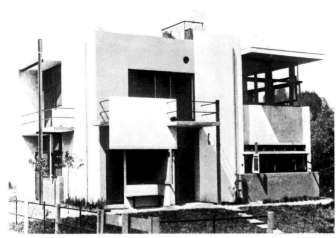

20,35 Gerrit Rietveld, Schröder House, Utrecht, The Netherlands, 1924.

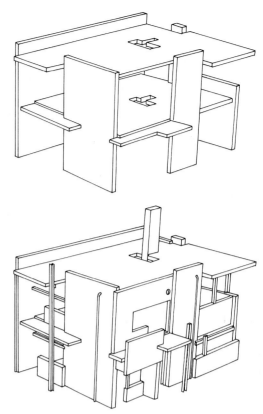

20,36 Elements of construction, Schröder House.

Harvard and Mies van der Rohe at Chicago, where the former Bauhaus teacher László Moholy-Nagy (1895–1946) founded the Chicago Institute of Design in 1937 (now the Illinois Institute of Technology). At the same time the 'White City' at Tel Aviv (Israel) was developed by refugee architects from Germany in the Bauhaus style of which it is a unique example on an urban scale.

The distinguished artists who had joined the Bauhaus included both Kandinsky and the Swiss painter Paul Klee (1870–1940) while several others, such as Mondrian, went as visitors. Klee usually worked on a small scale yet his paintings were far from unambitious. The title he gave his Bauhaus lectures on the principles of design, *Pictorial Thinking*, indicates the intellectual nature of the visual arts as he understood them. His thought was grounded in German Romantic philosophy and later writings on psychology, notably by Freud and Jung, as subsequently taken up by the Surrealists. He sought the essentials of form and elemental symbols, approaching the latter through the irrational stimulus of free-association (for example his 'doodling', which could be understood as a form of psychic automatism). The art of children and of what were then called 'primitives', to which he had been introduced by the German Expressionists, was important for him in his effort to rid himself of traditional European pictorial sources. (He had been a member of the *Blaue Reiter* group in Munich before the First World War.) In such works as *Sunset* (**20,34**), his imagination and fantasy found release in linear abstractions which incorporate both elemental natural forms and pictographic signs, whose potential he developed.

De Stijl's theorist, the painter Theo van Doesburg lectured to Bauhaus students at Weimar in 1922, and *De Stijl*'s leading architect Gerrit Thomas Rietveld (1888–1964) completed in the early 1920s his paradigmatic work, the Schröder House in Utrecht (**20,35; 36**). This small semi-detached suburban villa foreshadowed all the features that were to distinguish the style advocated at the Bauhaus and later throughout Europe and America, where it was to be called the International Style

– asymmetrical composition, unrelieved cubic shapes of clean-cut precision, slab roofs often cantilevered out at the corners, large windows in continuous horizontal strips, a complete absence of moldings and other ornamentation and a predilection for white rendering. Solidity gave way to transparent volume. Skeletal construction, free from load-bearing walls and oppressive monumental openings, enabled architects to realize that feeling of openness and apparent weightlessness which is the International Style's most attractive characteristic.

MONDRIAN

The Schröder House might almost seem to be a realization in three dimensions of a painting by Mondrian. Piet Mondrian (see p. 798) became the greatest painter of the inter-war years – that is to say he was the greatest to reach maturity during these years. And it is no coincidence that the greatest sculptor of the time, Constantin Brancusi (see pp. 796–7), should have been nominated to succeed him when he resigned from *De Stijl* in 1924. Mondrian resigned, needless to say, on a question of principle. He carried the high-minded Calvinist purity of the movement to such lengths that even van Doesburg could not follow him. Mondrian would not allow the use of diagonals! This may seem absurd. But Mondrian's asceticism and single-mindedness were inseparable from the intensity of his vision and of his utopian outlook. The universal harmony his art celebrated would one day, he believed, control all forms and activities of life.

20,37 Piet Mondrian, *Fox Trot A*,
1930. Canvas, 3ft 7¾ins (1.1m) diagonal.
Yale University Art Gallery (Gift of the Société Anonyme).

His task he conceived as being primarily that of discovering 'pure means' whereby the universal harmony, the ultimate reality behind appearances, could be made clear. Cubism, he said, had stopped short of complete fulfilment. It had failed to realize the implications of its discoveries and thus had not gone on towards abstraction. Mondrian totally renounced the world of physical appearances. Identifying a picture firmly with the foreground plane and limiting himself to lines and rectangles and to the primary colors and black and white, he strove to create 'an art of pure relations'. By this he meant not something static but dynamic, not a symmetry and balance but a life-giving tension. And the effect is sometimes almost lyrically intense. In one of his most stark and challenging paintings, *Fox Trot A* (**20,37**), this is achieved with only three straight black lines on white – an economy of means unsurpassed even by the Chinese. Of course, the simplicity is quite deceptive. The longer we look at this apparently elementary diamond-shaped configuration, the more complex and ambiguous it becomes.

Mondrian's economy of means included denying himself the aid of modelling and perspective, yet one is made immediately and very acutely aware of depth and space in this painting. Depth – even if only a hair's breadth – is implied by the overlapping of lines and forms on the flat plane of the canvas. The edges of the upturned square or 'diamond' seem to have cropped the rectangular forms created by the lines, which thus appear to recede below the surface, passing under the edges and continuing into space – or rather they would appear to do so were it not that the edges are slightly raised. (The framing-strip is set back twice, thus emphasizing the surface and the graphic power of the exposed edges, round which the black lines continue down the sides to the first framing-strip.) The ambiguity this creates is not the only one, however. The crossing of the vertical and horizontal lines near the right-hand bottom edge implies a similar crossing beyond the edge on the left, and the grid pattern thus formed could be indefinitely prolonged in all directions so that what we see is part of a larger whole, perhaps an infinity – were it not, once again, for an ambiguity. For no clear indication is given at the top, corresponding to that at the bottom, as to the formation of the lines beyond the top edges. Yet these ambiguities only sharpen our awareness of the spatial harmonies implied in this great painting.

Of course, the painting need not be read in this way at all. It can be looked at simply as a limited plane surface with flat marks on it making an asymmetrical design complete in itself, a design of four triangles of unequal size and a large five-sided polygon. The three lines are of unequal thickness, however, and this introduces another ambiguity. Is the central area to be read as a space, or as a solid set slightly at an angle?

These ambiguities combine with the uncertain sense of balance or symmetry (although a hidden geometric stability is suggested by, for example, the right vertical exactly bisecting the right diagonal edges) and, above all, with the lack of centrality to set up a most subtle tension distributed across the whole picture surface. There is no fading away at the edges, as in traditional pictures, even in Cubist pictures. The edges are as important as any other area. But although there is no focus, nothing is inert. Everything is irregular. No two spaces are the same size or shape. Even the tonal values of the white areas are not quite even, for the pigment is most delicately brushed, reminding one of the vividly sensuous response to the art of painting displayed by Mondrian in his early work, before he renounced all such physical delights (19,41). Austere it may be, but *Fox Trot A* is filled with a sense of liberation, of emancipation even. It has that frankness and openness which is so strongly felt in the work of progressive architects and designers during these years.

LE CORBUSIER AND MIES VAN DER ROHE

It is this straightforward, no-nonsense quality that marks the buildings of the two leading architects of the time, the Swiss painter-architect Charles-Edouard Jeanneret (1887–1965), known by his pseudonym Le Corbusier, and the German architect-designer Ludwig Mies van der Rohe (1886–1969), who became director of the Bauhaus in 1930. It even had a tonic effect on some well-established architects such as Auguste Perret (1874–1954) in France and, in England, Edwin Lutyens (1869–1944), whose reputation had been based on moderate-sized suburban and country houses around 1900, houses of great originality in their sense of massing and house-and-garden integration. But his First World War memorials strike a deeper note (**20,38**). And they reflect in their simplicity and gravity an

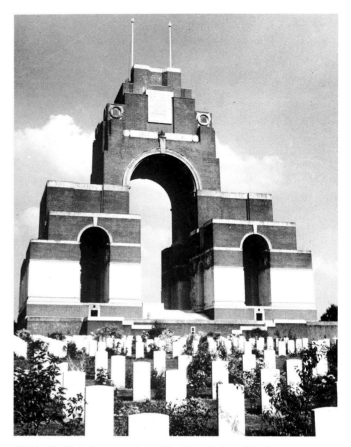

20,38 Sir Edwin Lutyens, Memorial to the Missing of the Somme, Thiepval, France, 1927–32.

awareness of those reductionist trends in contemporary architecture which were quite alien to his immediately previous and later work (e.g. the Viceroy's House, New Delhi, of 1921–31, whose architectural rhetoric now rings as hollow as that of the declining empire it celebrated).

Le Corbusier's famous definition of a house as 'a machine for living in' has often been misunderstood and misused in order to denigrate him. He did not mean that a house ought to be an artless, soulless mechanical capsule fit only for robots to inhabit. For him, as for the Russian Constructivists and the Bauhaus architects, the machine was something wholly beneficial. He thought that a house ought to be conceived, designed and produced in a rational manner (as were motors, cars and aeroplanes) and that traditional, irrationally planned and designed houses simply frustrated the promise of the new age and the good life for all that the machine could bring. Many other gifted young architects and designers were inspired by the same generous ideals. Our aim, said Gropius of the teachers and students at the Bauhaus, is a 'clear organic architecture, whose inner logic will be radiant and naked, unencumbered by lying façades and trickeries; we want an architecture adapted to our world of machines, radios and fast motor cars, an architecture whose function is clearly recognizable in the relation of its forms.'

Cities of the Future

LE CORBUSIER AND FRANK LLOYD WRIGHT

Le Corbusier's Contemporary City for 3 Million Inhabitants (20,47), the population of Paris at the time, and his book on town planning, *Urbanisme* of 1925, put forward radically updated and rigorously logical solutions to problems that had become ever more pressing since the industrial revolution. He listed the imperatives:

1. We must de-congest the centres of our cities.
2. We must augment their density.
3. We must increase the means for getting about.
4. We must increase parks and open spaces.

Measures already taken, including the construction of wide streets to ease circulation, like those imposed on Paris under the Second Empire by Baron Georges Haussmann (1809–91), the insertion of great public parks (see p. 644) and the creation of garden suburbs for the middle classes, were to his mind no more than palliatives. He demanded new cities designed for contemporary life and shaping future developments; but he was by no means the first to do so.

Several forward-looking urban projects had been devised in the previous half-century. The most immediately influential was that by Ebenezer Howard (1850–1928), who published in London in 1898 *Tomorrow: A Peaceful Path to Real Reform*, reprinted four years later with the significant new title *Garden Cities of Tomorrow*. Inspired by the social criticism of John Ruskin and William Morris, Howard, who was not an architect, spent five years in the USA, where he came under the spell of the Transcendentalist philosophy of Ralph Waldo Emerson and Henry Thoreau (see pp. 682–3), and he returned to London convinced that the social system could be transformed without revolutionary violence by imaginative town-planning, by providing for

an alternative way of life in new cities. This gave him the idea of his lifetime: that of the Garden City conceived as an independent city, not a suburb, situated in the green countryside and provided with countrified housing as well as industry and all cultural amenities. It would be communally owned and economically self-sufficient but larger and more complex than the communes projected earlier by Robert Owen and Charles Fourier (see p. 644). Set within a wide green belt of farmland, the municipal buildings would be sited centrally in a park surrounded by glass-roofed shopping arcades and then rings of streets for houses with a peripheral zone for factories to be powered by electricity (20,39). Population was ideally to be 32,000, not more than 58,000, and for overflow he recommended smaller satellite towns, each in its own green belt and interconnected by railroad and canal. Howard's great idea was

20,39 Ebenezer Howard, Garden City Ward and Centre, 1898.

1 Garden	10 Grand Avenue
2 Museum and gallery	11 Boulevard Columbus
3 Hospital	12 Boulevard Newton
4 Library	13 Railway station
5 Theatre	14 Allotments
6 Concert hall	15 Dairy farms
7 Town hall	16 Large farms
8 Central park	17 First Avenue
9 School	18 Fifth Avenue
	19 Railway line

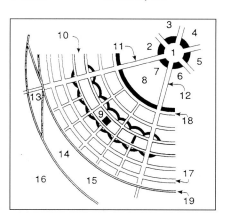

realized in the first garden city, Letchworth, 40 miles (64.4km) north of London, begun by Raymond Unwin (1863–1940) in 1903 though it did not progress as smoothly as had been anticipated and concessions had to be made to allow private ownership. Other developments of the same type followed in Britain, Germany and the USA, all marked by nostalgia for pre-industrial village life, with houses in cosily traditional styles, on winding tree-lined streets planned without much regard for the increasing number of automobiles, except as a danger for pedestrians.

Already before the First World War other, more radical, solutions had been proposed, notably those for a Città Nuova in 1914 by the Italian Futurist architect Antonio Sant'Elia (see p. 794) and those for a Cité Industrielle in 1904–17 by Tony Garnier (1869–1948). It was not until 1925, however, that Le Corbusier wrote that 'modern urban planning comes to birth with a new architecture' and 'an immense, overwhelming brutal step in evolution has destroyed links with the past'. For the congested centres of old cities he had only one solution: complete reconstruction on a geometrical plan with multi-level highways. 'Winding streets are for donkeys', he declared; 'straight roads are for men' – that is, for automobiles. Although he tacitly accepted some of Howard's ideas, notably those of the 'green belt' and of 'zoning' to separate areas for different functions, his contemporary city was not to incorporate public parks but to be itself one vast expanse of green in which high-rise buildings could be deployed. It was to have at its centre a railroad station roofed as a landing-ground for air-taxis shuttling to an airport outside the city of which the centre was to be surrounded by skyscrapers 600 feet (185m) high. He illustrated his ideas with a plan for urban renewal in Paris involving the

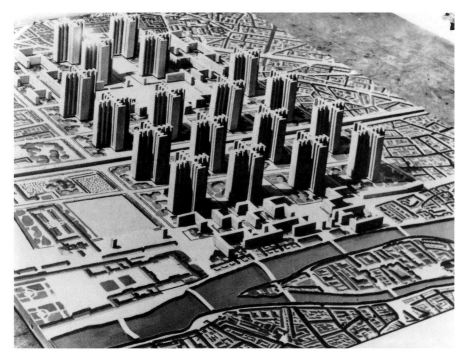

20,40 Le Corbusier, *Plan Voisin* for Paris, 1925.

schools'. Like Ebenezer Howard, to whom he owed an undeclared debt, he aimed at reforming society by creating a new environment. He wanted to enable Americans to free themselves from the tyranny of centralized urban capitalism as well as from centralized urban planning and thereby regain the rural virtues of individual freedom and self-reliance on a Jeffersonian model. His utopian Broadacre vision was never realized but his ideas survived and acquired new relevance after the Second World War with the spread of decentralized suburban development. In the USA such residential projects as Levittown at Hicksville, NY (1947–51), which successfully fused American individualism with collective planning for house-seeking demobbed GI's, vividly recalled Wright's Usonian visions with each of its 16,000 or more open-plan Cape Cod houses on its own site with car-port next to the front door.

20,41 Frank Lloyd Wright, model of the Broadacre City project, 1931–5.

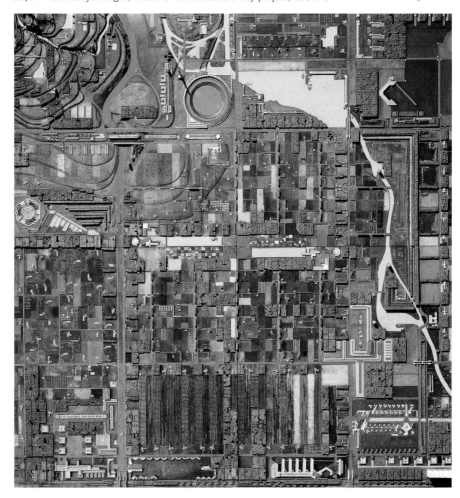

demolition of several hundred acres of old buildings on the right bank of the Seine to make a green area from which 18 glass-fronted skyscrapers would rise (**20,40**). None of these visionary schemes was to be realized, though his ideas were given international authority by the International Congresses of Modern Architecture (CIAM) in 1933 as the 'Athens Charter'.

Contemporaneously, Frank Lloyd Wright (see p. 799) was working out his very different, decentralized and rural Broadacre City project of 1931–5. Centralized planning had, Wright believed, been rendered unnecessary and obsolete by the automobile and telephone. Four miles (10.36km) square, Broadacre was to consist mainly of small-holdings of at least 1 acre (0.4 hectare) and a single-family house built of prefabricated parts according to the wishes and needs of the occupants, these 'Usonian' (United Statesian) houses embodying the same social-reformist ethos (**20,41**). Like Le Corbusier, Wright thought of himself as a prophet, but of a curious kind in which the progressive and conservative were uniquely blended. In his writings, the emphasis is always on the individual unit, on the 'little farms, little factories, little

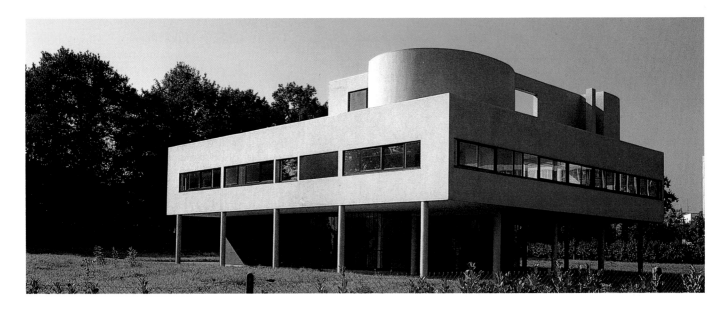

20,42 Le Corbusier, Villa Savoye, Poissy, France, 1928–30.

20,43 Section of the Villa Savoye.

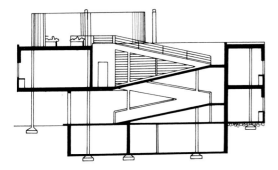

This vision came near to realization in Le Corbusier's Villa Savoye of 1928–30 just outside Paris (**20,42; 43**) and in Mies van der Rohe's Berlin project the following year for a single-family suburban house, complete with furniture (**20,44**). Mies van der Rohe was essentially an architect of steel and glass, Le Corbusier of ferro-concrete, but both exploited to the full the possibilities offered by skeleton construction for a spatially free and open architecture. The Villa Savoye is a cube on stilts or pillars of reinforced concrete called *pilotis*. This was a favourite device of Le Corbusier, and by allowing space to flow under and through the building, it very strongly enhanced that look of volume as opposed to mass which we have already noted in Rietveld (20,35). Le Corbusier went some way further than Rietveld, for the cubic volume of Villa Savoye is hollowed out on three sides, mainly on the south-east and south-west so that sunlight can flood right into the centre of the building. And since load-bearing walls had been eliminated the interior could be left quite free. One wall facing the interior terrace is glazed its whole length from top to bottom. Being open on every side, moreover, it has no façade, no front and no back. That the building should be impossible to comprehend from any single viewpoint only confirms how completely Le Corbusier had achieved his objective of total interpenetration of outer and interior space.

The same principles underlie Mies van der Rohe's 1931 Berlin project, in which the walls are very obviously just screens to be moved or walked around as is convenient (20,44). Here, however, the machine aesthetic finds expression also in the furniture, which has the elegance of a finely adjusted precision tool – the famous 1929 Barcelona chair in the foreground and tubular steel cantilever chairs of 1926 in the background all breaking decisively with the Arts and Crafts tradition in favour of design for standardized mass production. Mies van der Rohe's tubular steel chairs were not the first of their kind. The Dutch architect Mart Stam (1899–1986) had introduced the cantilever principle in 1924 and the Hungarian-born architect Marcel Breuer (1902–81) evolved the first chromium-plated steel chairs at the Bauhaus in 1925. But Mies van der Rohe's chairs, with their immaculate finish, poise and elegance, are the classic statement of this revolutionary design concept. They are deceptive, however, for despite their appearance of having been designed for mass production they, in fact, require careful hand-finishing in order to produce the desired 'machine-made' look.

20,44 Ludwig Mies van der Rohe, Living-room, single-family house project for Berlin, 1931.

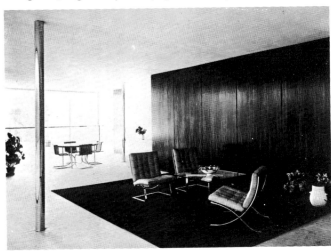

BRANCUSI AND MOORE

A similar ambivalence can be felt in the sculpture of Constantin Brancusi (see pp. 796–7) during these years, though he approached the ideal of absolute form from an entirely different point of view to that of the Bauhaus. By this date Brancusi's point of view had become ever more subjective and spiritual, almost mystic. And, unlike most sculptors before and since, he executed all his works himself by hand. He believed in old-fashioned hand-craftsmanship. Direct carving, he said, was the 'true road to sculpture'. Yet not only did he frequently have his marble works cast in bronze – thus denying the autonomy of the medium – but the extremely subtle and refined surfaces, on which he worked for days and weeks in solitude like a secular monk, carefully conceal all trace of his hand so that they look as if they have been machine-tooled.

There are many versions of most Brancusi sculptures, for he was constantly refining on the original idea. He made some 15 versions of *Bird in Space* from 1923 onwards, of which the one illustrated here is the tenth (**20,45**). Although it neither resembles a flying bird nor suggests the aerodynamics of bird flight, there are analogies which powerfully suggest a continuous rising motion and the poetry of flight. The shining immaculate surface of the highly polished bronze and the streamlined form convey a euphoria of speed and of effortless elevation and ascent. A sense of release from gravity and from everything earthly and confining is imparted so that all our aspirational yearnings seem to be voluptuously fulfilled as in a dream of flight.

The British sculptor Henry Moore (1898–1986) was, like Brancusi, exceptionally sensitive to the tactile and other inherent qualities of the materials he used, and he used a large variety. Whether alabaster or African wonderstone, clay or concrete, marble or lead, pynkado wood or *lignum vitae*, the materials often seem to have suggested not only the form but the subject of his sculptures. This can be sensed even in his most abstract pieces, such as his *Two Forms* of 1934 (**20,46**). Embodying ideas of vulnerability and protection, these smoothly and tenderly enfolding forms become an elemental image of the mother and child relationship. One form might, it is sensed, be extended to clasp and enclose the other or, alternatively, the compact form might be tightly, almost invisibly, fitted into the other. A more than simply formal internal–external relationship is expressed in this two-piece sculpture.

In such works Moore went as far as he was ever to go in the direction of open-form sculpture as pioneered by González and Picasso only slightly earlier (see p. 816). Yet he sought to break away from traditional European sculpture, rejecting Classical Graeco-Renaissance forms in favour of the vital force and formal vigour he found in

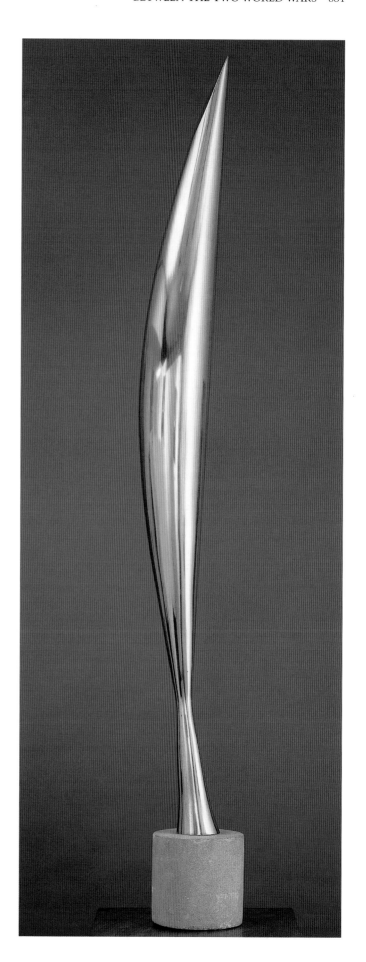

20,45 Constantin Brancusi, *Bird in Space*, 1928. Bronze (unique cast), 54 × 8½ × 6½ins (137.2 × 21.6 × 16.5cm). The Museum of Modern Art, New York (Given anonymously).

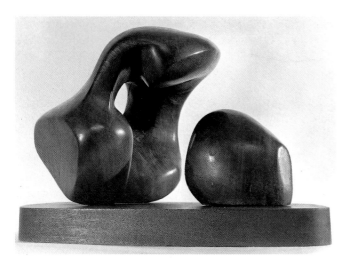

20,46 Henry Moore, *Two Forms*, 1934. Pynkado wood, 11 × 21½ × 12⅛ins (27.9 × 54.6 × 30.8cm) including oak base (irregular). The Museum of Modern Art, New York (Sir Michael Sadler Fund).

ancient Mexican and Sumerian and other non-European sculpture. 'For me', he wrote in 1934, 'a work must first have a vitality of its own. I do not mean a reflection of the vitality of life, of movement, physical action, frisking, dancing figures, and so on, but that a work can have in it pent-up energy, an intense life of its own, independent of the object it may represent. When the work has this powerful vitality we do not connect the word Beauty with it. Beauty, in the later Greek or Renaissance sense, is not the aim of my sculpture.' The universality of his approach was remarkable. As he later observed, the 'same shapes and form-relationships are able to express similar ideas at widely different places and periods of history, so that the same form-vision may be seen in a Negro and a Viking carving, in a Cycladic stone figure and a Nukuoro wooden statuette'. However, a deeply conservative strain remained embedded in his sensibility and this, together with a tendency simply to rely on size to lend his work monumentality, resulted eventually in a decline in the visual impact of his post-Second World War work, well-suited though it often was for public sculpture.

ART DECO

Streamlining became one of the hallmarks of an unfunctional modernism taken up by architects and designers of the late twenties and thirties and only recently has it become possible, with the passage of time, to recognize this – Art Deco, as it is now called – as having been an authentic style of the period parallel with the International Style. The vigour and vitality of popular culture, which the International Style had sacrificed to purism, found exuberant release in Art Deco. It is significant that the 1925 Paris exhibition of decorative art, after which the style is named, included Le Corbusier's Pavillon de l'Esprit Nouveau, in which some of his most brilliant and forward-looking concepts were displayed, but this attracted very little attention and was relegated to the periphery by the exhibition organizers. In architecture Art Deco found its most notable expression in New York, where the Chrysler Building (**20,48**) and Radio City Music Hall with its jazz-age furniture and fittings by Donald Deskey epitomize the style. It was, in fact, only in New York – at Rockefeller Center, of which Radio City Music Hall forms part – that one of the great new urban planning conceptions of the twenties came anywhere near realization on the grandiose scale envisaged by Le Corbusier and others. Le Corbusier published a number of total plans for

20,47 Le Corbusier, plan for a Contemporary City for 3 Million Inhabitants, 1922.

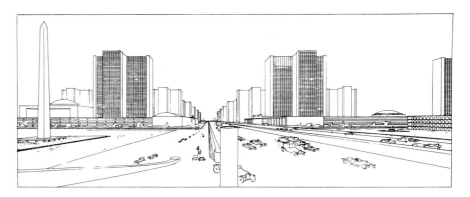

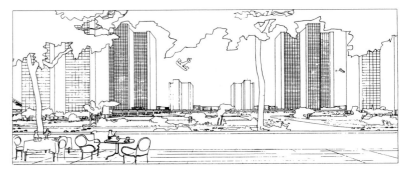

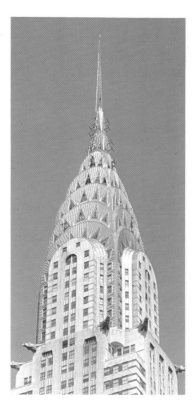

20,48 William van Alen, the Chrysler Building, New York, 1928–30. Spire of stainless steel.

Manhattan. The buildings are disposed and co-ordinated as a unit. Of course, the park setting, which was all-important to Le Corbusier, is sadly lacking as well as a good deal else of his utopian scheme for a modern city. But it introduced for the first time into a living city centre a unified planning concept on the large scale he had imagined.

While the Rockefeller Center was going up in New York the lights were already beginning to grow dim once more in Europe. By the end of 1936 the Spanish Civil War had broken out and in April of the following year the first in a new catalogue of atrocities took place when the small, unprotected Basque village of Guernica was destroyed by Nazi bombers in the service of Spanish Fascists. Picasso's most famous painting commemorates this inhuman act of criminal brutality (**20,49**). It is by far his largest and is in many ways his most ambitious work, for his aim was to press into ideological service all the sophisticated pictorial techniques of modern art. Such an enterprise might seem impossible. But his rage and indignation at the merciless slaughter of defenceless refugees and unarmed civilians so fuelled his visual imagination that images which he had created in earlier paintings for their privately expressive or purely formal qualities were now transformed into symbols which could be understood by everyone. The dying horse which had been the tragic protagonist in many of his bull-fight paintings here takes on universal significance, as does the implacable bull which he had recently drawn as the Minotaur for a Surrealist periodical to embody all the irrational forces in man and nature. But the agonized heads of mothers and the cruel malformations of wounded limbs and hands welled up spontaneously from his subconscious under the impact of this terrible and premonitory event.

cities with a centre of glass curtain-wall skyscrapers symmetrically arranged in a park setting, with lower buildings and complex traffic circulation systems in between – his Contemporary City for 3 Million Inhabitants of 1922 is the most dazzling (**20,47**). Rockefeller Center is a group of 14 buildings occupying three blocks cut out of the narrow-scale gridiron street system of mid-town

20,49 Pablo Picasso, *Guernica*, 1937. Canvas, 11ft 5½ins × 25ft 5¾ins (3.5 × 7.8m). Museo Nacional Centro de Arte Reina Sofia, Madrid.

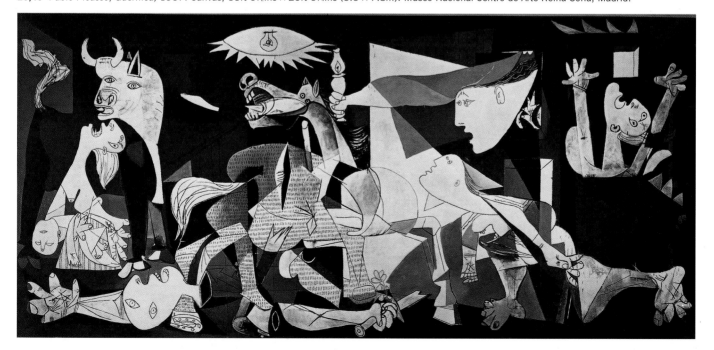

CHAPTER TWENTY-ONE

POST-WAR
TO POST-MODERN

Although the United States had been in the forefront of developments in Western architecture ever since the late nineteenth century and, with Frank Lloyd Wright, had played a leading role in the early twentieth century, it was not until after the Second World War that New York superseded Paris as the focal point of new art in the West. The meeting of the American and Russian armies on the river Elbe in Germany in 1945 symbolized much more than the end of the war in Europe. It marked the end of European imperialism and of European rule overseas and, with the loss of political and economic power, the end of European cultural predominance in the West.

The exodus of intellectuals and artists from Europe to America in the 1930s was symptomatic of this impending decline. They went as refugees from political and racial persecution, mainly from Nazi Germany. The greatest scientist of the twentieth century, Albert Einstein, fled to the United States in 1933 and he was followed by many other intellectuals including musicians such as Béla Bartók, Arnold Schoenberg and Igor Stravinsky, and numerous artists, of whom Hans Hofmann (1880–1966) was the first. Hofmann left Germany for America in 1932 just before the Nazis came to power. A few years later Max Beckmann (1884–1950), George Grosz (1893–1959) and some of the leading Bauhaus figures (including Gropius, Mies van der Rohe, Marcel Breuer, Ludwig Hilbersheimer, László Moholy-Nagy, Josef Albers) escaped to the United States, and a new Bauhaus, later called the Institute of Design, was opened in Chicago. After the fall of France in 1940 a further influx of refugees arrived from Paris, among them several of the most notable painters and sculptors of the time – Léger, Mondrian, Gabo, Max Ernst, Dali, Chagall, Lipchitz and others, most of whom settled in New York.

Thus the two major European movements of the inter-war years were transferred to New York, the rational, formalistic Purist-Abstract trend being represented by

The visual arts	Historical landmarks
1945–50 Mies, Farnsworth House (21,41)	**1945** German surrender. USA drops atomic bomb on Hiroshima
1947 Gorky, *Betrothal II* (21,3)	**1947** Cominform established
1950 Pollock, *Autumn Rhythm* (21,4)	**1949** Communist republic of China. Orwell, *1984*
1953 Matisse, *The Snail* (21,12)	**1950** Korean War begins
1954 Still, *1954* (21,6)	**1952** Beckett, *Waiting for Godot*
1955 Giacometti, *Head of Diego II* (21,13)	**1953** Death of Stalin. Korean armistice. First hydrogen bomb (USA).
1956 Rothko, *Green on Blue* (21,7)	Cage, *Imaginary Landscape No. 4*
Hamilton, *Just what is it* (21,20)	**1957** USSR launches Sputnik I. European Common Market established
1958 Johns, *Three Flags* (21,16)	**1958** Pasternak, *Dr Zhivago*
1959 Rauschenberg, *Monogram* (21,17)	**1959** Resnais, *Hiroshima mon amour*. First transistorized digital computer
1960 Stella, *Tuxedo Park Junction* (21,27)	(USA). Castro takes over Cuba
1962 Oldenburg, *Giant Hamburger* (21,21)	**1961** First man in space (USSR). Berlin Wall erected. Vietnam War begins
Bacon, *Three Studies for a Crucifixion* (21,24)	**1962** Second Vatican Council: Catholic liturgy vernacularized.
1963 Frankenthaler, *Canal* (21,14)	Satellite TV transmission starts
1964 Warhol, *Disaster 22* (21,23)	**1963** Kennedy assassinated
Twombly, *Untitled 1964* (21,39)	**1964** Dylan, *The times they are a'changing*.
1965 Lichtenstein, *Big Painting No. 6* (21,19)	The Beatles, *I Want to Hold Your Hand*
Venturi, Chestnut Hill House (21,45)	**1965** US offensive in Vietnam
1966 Hesse, *Hang Up* (21,30)	**1968** Martin Luther King assassinated
1969 Christo, *Wrapped Coast* (21,31)	**1969** First man on the moon (USA)
1970 Smithson, *Spiral Jetty* (21,32)	**1970** Germaine Greer, *The Female Eunuch*
	1973 Recession begins in USA. Vietnam War ends
1974–6 Isozaki, Kaijima House (21,50)	**1974** Watergate: Nixon resigns. Solzenitsyn, *The Gulag Archipelago*
1976 Guston, *The Painter* (21,36)	**1976** Death of Mao Zedong
1978–9 Moore, Piazza d'Italia (21,46)	**1978** First 'test tube' baby born
	1979 US hostages seized in Iran

Mondrian, Léger and the Bauhaus designers, the anti-rational, emotional, expressive trend by the Surrealists Ernst, Dali and André Breton (as well as by Marcel Duchamp, who had been a semi-permanent resident in New York ever since 1915). In Paris these two movements had usually been thought antithetical if not mutually exclusive. But American artists, quite oblivious of this, were open and receptive to both. There had been, in fact, a small but strong and steady current in America towards abstraction ever since the first decade of the century, for emotional and expressive rather than formal ends. The artists who explored this vein were usually loners – America has always been rich in gifted mavericks – and it is only now that they can be seen as having in some ways foreshadowed post-Second World War painting in New York. Of these forerunners Arthur Garfield Dove (1880–1946) was the first; indeed, his 1910 'extractions' from nature, as he called them, are among the earliest abstract paintings anywhere (see p. 818). That he was aware of the Romantic origins of his art is revealed by his remarking that his ambition was to take nature in its most elemental aspects, wind and water and sand, and simplify everything to 'color and force lines and substances, just as music has done with sound' – a highly Romantic analogy illustrated by such paintings as *Fog Horns* (**21,1**). Though less consistently abstract, Georgia O'Keeffe (1887–1986) created a vocabulary of personal forms which often hover ambiguously between representation and abstraction as they are transmuted into symbols. Filmy, quivering and sometimes extremely sensuous and voluptuous, they seem to take on a life of their own (**21,2**). But remarkable though Dove, O'Keeffe and one or two other isolated American artists were – and O'Keeffe became for a time a modern culture heroine, like the dancer Isadora Duncan and the writer Gertrude Stein, for the new liberated woman – it was the Surrealists from Paris in wartime New York who, with automatism and other techniques for releasing the unconscious, were to point the way ahead into the world confronting young American artists in 1945.

21,1 Arthur G. Dove, *Fog Horns*, 1929. Canvas, 18⅛ × 26⅛ins (46 × 66.4cm). Colorado Springs Fine Arts Center (Gift of Olive B. James).

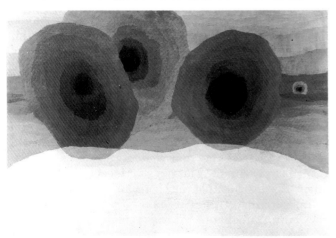

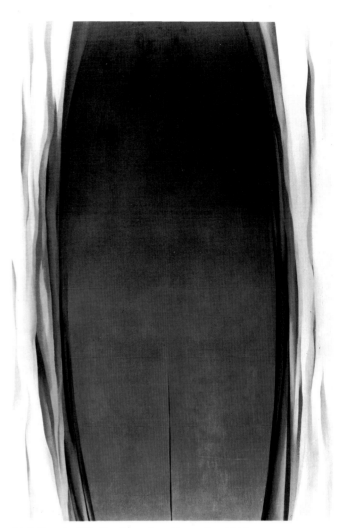

21,2 Georgia O'Keeffe, *Green-Gray Abstraction*, 1931. Canvas, 36 × 24ins (91.5 × 61cm). Private collection.

ABSTRACT EXPRESSIONISM

The New York painters who came to notice in the late 1940s and 1950s did not form a movement, though they all knew each other and were close contemporaries in age. Jackson Pollock (1912–56) was one of the youngest, with Franz Kline (1910–62), Ad Reinhardt (1913–67) and Robert Motherwell (b. 1915). The others, a few years older, were all born within three years of each other – Adolph Gottlieb (b. 1903), Mark Rothko (1903–70), Willem de Kooning (1904–97), Clyfford Still (1904–80) and Barnett Newman (1905–70). Their work has no uniform stylistic traits. Some of them painted with apparently uncontrolled and quite haphazard spontaneity, others with the most austere self-restraint. Superficially they might seem to have very little in common with each other. They had no program. They issued no manifestos. But they all brought to their work a feverish energy and extremism as typically American as their taste for the colossal – and they all felt themselves to be in the same human predicament, all equally subject to the same complex fate of being Americans in the aftermath of the Second World War. The painter Barnett Newman wrote in 1945: 'The war, as the Surrealists predicted, has robbed us of our hidden terror, as terror can only exist if the forces of tragedy are unknown. We now know the terror to expect. Hiroshima showed it to us. We are no longer in the face of a mystery. After all, wasn't it an American boy who did it?'

But what they all thought and felt in common found expression in highly personal works of art. It was the critics who gave them a label – Abstract Expressionists or Action Painters. They never used and probably never thought of themselves in these terms. Their aims were unformulated, except by critics, one of whom, Harold Rosenberg, became their unofficial spokesman. 'At a certain moment', he wrote in 1952:

> . . . the canvas began to appear to one American painter after another as an arena in which to act – rather than as a space in which to reproduce, re-design, analyze or 'express' an object, actual or imagined. What was to go on the canvas was not a picture but an event.
>
> The painter no longer approached his easel with an image in his mind; he went up to it with material in his hand to do something to that other piece of material in front of him. The image would be the result of that encounter.

Abstract Expressionism or Action Painting differed from other phases of modern art because, as Harold Rosenberg put it, it had a different 'motive for extinguishing the object.'

> The new American painting is not 'pure' art, since the extrusion of the object was not for the sake of the aesthetic. The apples weren't brushed off the table in order to make room for perfect relations of space and color. They had to go so that nothing would get in the way of the act of painting. In this gesturing with materials the aesthetic, too, has been subordinated. Form, color, composition, drawing, are auxiliaries, any one of which – or practically all, as has been attempted logically, with unpainted canvas – can be dispensed with. What matters always is the revelation contained in the act.
>
> ('The American Action Painters', 1952, repr. in The Tradition of the New, 1959)

It was the business of putting paint on canvas that alone counted for the Action Painters and led them to abstraction. They did not represent their emotions or sensations but enacted them before the canvas.

A crucial figure in the evolution of Abstract Expressionism was the painter Hans Hofmann. He had an intimate, first-hand experience of Cubism, Fauvism and Expressionism, having lived between 1904 and 1914 in Paris, where he knew Picasso and Matisse among others, and later in Munich where he had in his keeping during the First World War most of Kandinsky's early, transitional paintings, transitional between Expressionism and abstraction. In New York Hofmann's art-school became the centre from which a synthesis of Cubism and Fauvism, a new unity of color and form reflecting his belief in the duality of the world of art and the world of appearances, was propagated.

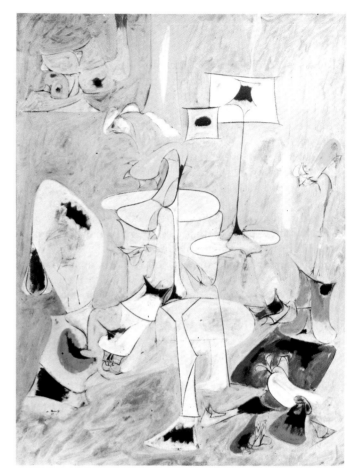

21,3 Arshile Gorky, *The Betrothal II*, 1947. Canvas, 50¾ × 38ins (129 × 96.5cm). Whitney Museum of American Art, New York.

He himself was a strong personality and he achieved in his own work an unusual combination of painterliness and abstraction, especially in the early 1940s when he experimented with 'drip' techniques and mixed media – oil paint, India ink, casein, aluminium paint, etc. For him painting meant creating form with color and his definition of composition – a 'push-pull' of formal and color tensions across the surface of the canvas – became celebrated. His teaching was very influential. But it was the Armenian painter Arshile Gorky (1905–48), whose family had emigrated to America in 1920, who became the effective catalyst between European and the new American painting.

Whether Gorky is best understood as the last Surrealist or the first Abstract Expressionist may be endlessly debated. He spent many years working patiently through a series of obsessive master-pupil relationships, culminating with Kandinsky and Miró, before, in the last years of his short life, he suddenly came into full command of his extraordinary gifts. He succeeded in reconciling the previously irreconcilable, the abstract painterliness propagated by Hofmann with Surrealist imagery as well as with something of the literariness of André Breton, who admired and encouraged him. In Gorky's last attenuated, tortured paintings the embryonic forms seem about to melt and fuse with the gauzy, mysteriously colored flux in which they float, so that they hang for ever in suspense in an indeterminate world of being and not-being (**21,3**). They are private myths. 'I do not paint in front of nature', Gorky said, 'but from within nature.'

POLLOCK AND DE KOONING

The role of leading Abstract Expressionist painter, which Gorky would probably have taken had he lived, was filled by an even more disturbed and melancholy artist, Jackson Pollock, an archetypal American loner – raw, violent and consumed by neuroses and frustrations. He was born in Cody, Wyoming – the home of Buffalo Bill – spent his childhood in Arizona and grew up in southern California; his familiarity with south-west Indian art, especially sand painting, was to remain with him always and re-emerged as a seminal influence in his great Abstract Expressionist paintings. However, nothing in his early life prepares one for his paintings of the early 1950s – his admiration for the intense, subjective landscapes of Albert Pinkham Ryder (1847–1917), his apprenticeship to the mural painter Thomas Hart Benton (1889–1975), his acceptance and later rejection of Social Realism, especially that of the Mexicans David Alfaro Siqueiros (1898–1974) and José Clemente Orozco (1883–1949), his veneration for Picasso and especially for *Guernica* (20,49), his familiarity with Surrealist automatism and Jungian analysis – all these may have contributed to, but they do little to explain or account for, the totally unprecedented nature of such paintings as *Autumn Rhythm* (**21,4**).

Pollock's finest work belongs to a relatively brief period, 1947 to 1951. He was not a naturally gifted painter and wrestled in rage and fury at his inability to master traditional techniques. Suddenly it seems to have come to him, as if in a revelation, that he could find fulfilment by exteriorizing this struggle, by making the act of painting its own subject. Abandoning easel and palette – even brushes – he began to drip, to pour and spatter and fling

the paint on to canvas laid out like a piece of sailcloth on the floor. In this way the marks on the canvas were liberated from any possible representational significance; they simply recorded his engagement with the medium, forming a graph, as it were, of his emotions as he struggled with the viscosity of paint. 'My painting does not come from the easel', he wrote in 1947.

I hardly ever stretch my canvas before painting. I prefer to tack the unstretched canvas to the hard wall or the floor. I need the resistance of a hard surface. On the floor I am more at ease. I feel nearer, more part of the painting, since this way I can walk around it, work from the four sides and literally be in *the painting. This is akin to the method of the Indian sand painters of the West . . . . When I am in my painting, I'm not aware of what I'm doing. It is only after a sort of 'get acquainted' period that I see what I have been about. I have no fears about making changes, destroying the image, etc. because the painting has a life of its own. I try to let it come through.*

('My Painting', *in Possibilities*, I, 1947/8)

Indian sand paintings were executed rhythmically by trickling sand of different colors to form ephemeral symbolic images, as part of a religious rite, and a similar state of transport accompanied the creation of Pollock's paintings. He would gyrate freely round the canvas or into it, spilling and pouring and flinging the colors from cans of Duco and other aluminium and enamel paints as he spun round whirling his arms in great arcs and hemicycles in a kind of dervish dance. His whole body was involved, not just his hands and arms. (He was filmed while painting.) But despite the frenzy, his movements were not completely

21,4 Jackson Pollock, *Autumn Rhythm*, 1950.
Canvas, 8ft 9ins × 17ft 3ins (2.67 × 5.26m). Metropolitan Museum of Art, New York (George A. Hearn Fund 1957).

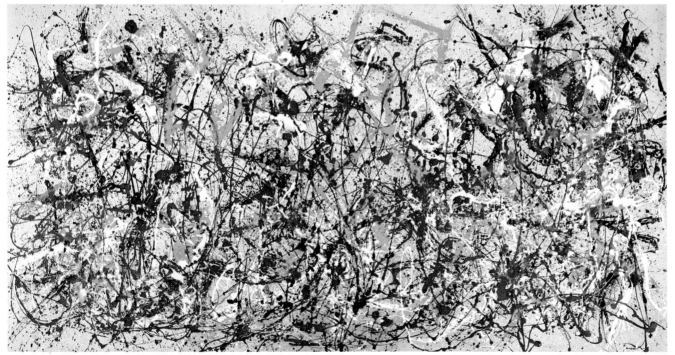

uncontrolled, as he later admitted. 'When I am painting I have a general notion as to what I am about. I can control the flow of paint. There is no accident, just as there is no beginning and no end.'

This indeterminateness and sense of limitlessness is one of the most striking characteristics of Pollock's work. He used extremely large canvases – 'portable murals' they were sometimes called – so large that the spectator has the sensation of being enveloped and engulfed by them as the eye moves from one swirling vortex of color to the next. The nets and skeins of paint he dribbled and poured, one over the other from edge to edge across the huge expanse of the picture field, form an endlessly rhythmical palimpsest of repetitive patterns, interpenetrating and partaking of each other like some great Islamic composition of *thuluth* lettering (12,40), and with a similar exquisiteness of surface expanding into infinity beyond the painting itself. The spectator's vision oscillates between the near and the far, between the microscopic and the telescopic, as if witnessing some galactic or atomic explosion. Whether this sublime effect of pure creative force was consciously intended is uncertain. Pollock said his over-all method was simply 'the natural growth out of a need'.

Pollock remained an isolated figure. He joined no group or societies of artists and had no pupils or followers. Willem de Kooning was the closest to him artistically if not temperamentally, and they now tend to be seen together as the leaders of the Action Painting wing of Abstract Expressionism. De Kooning had emigrated from Holland to the United States in 1926, became a friend of Gorky, with whom he shared a studio for a time, and by the late 1940s was already recognized as one of the major Abstract Expressionists. He was the only one to remain to some extent representational, even making the human figure a principal theme. But his abstract work is perhaps more intense (**21,5**). Aggressive and harsh, often rather raw in color with juicy, fleshy pinks and lurid yellows and tart greens, the texture thick and heavy as if it had been relentlessly worked and reworked over again and again, his pictures have none of the delicacy and neurotic volatility of Pollock's. Moreover, they are never completely abstract. The shapes are always vaguely suggestive, pressing against each other with charged brush-strokes in dense and crowded compositions which almost burst out of the picture field.

The other notable exponent of this type of gestural painting was Franz Kline (1910–62). He began in the late 1930s by painting city scenes in New York, and his later, almost wholly abstract black-and-white oil paintings were also inspired by the dynamism and violence of urban America. In them, he insisted, he was 'painting experiences': he was not creating formal abstractions, any more than he was painting 'bridge constructions or skyscrapers'. However, his work is often very evocative of just such urban configurations.

21,5 Willem de Kooning, *Excavation*, 1950. Canvas, 6ft 8⅛ins × 8ft 4⅛ins (2.04 × 2.54m). Art Institute of Chicago.

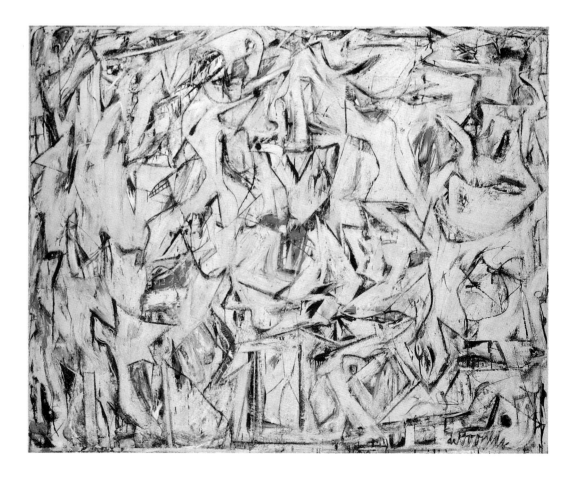

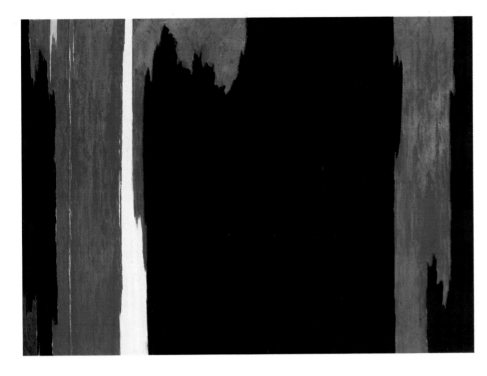

21,6 Clyfford Still, *1954*, 1954.
Canvas, 9ft 5½ins × 13ft (2.88 × 4.96m).
Albright-Knox Art Gallery, Buffalo, New York
(Gift of Seymour H. Knox).

STILL, ROTHKO AND NEWMAN

Abstract Expressionist painting divides into two groups: that of the gestural or 'Action' painters, whose work is discussed above, and that of the color-field painters, of whom Clyfford Still, Mark Rothko and Barnett Newman were the outstanding exponents. Still was in some ways a comparable figure to Pollock and mediates between the two groups. Born in North Dakota and brought up in the Far West and in Canada, he was another loner and solitary, even in New York, where he lived during the 1940s and 1950s. He wrote then of the 'journey that one must make, walking straight and alone . . . . Until one has crossed the darkened and wasted valleys and come at last into clear air and could stand on a high and limitless plain.' The religious, almost Messianic tone is characteristic.

In 1943 he joined Rothko and Adolph Gottlieb in writing a now-famous letter to the *New York Times* in which the Abstract Expressionist point of view was first adumbrated. 'To us art is an adventure into an unknown world which can be explored only by those willing to take risks', they wrote. 'We favour the simple expression of the complex thought. We are for the large shape because it has the impact of the unequivocal. We wish to reassert the picture plane. We are for flat forms because they destroy illusion and reveal truth . . . we profess spiritual kinship with primitive and archaic art.'

Still was a pioneer, like Pollock, of the very large-size canvas – the 'portable mural'. He also, more consciously perhaps than the others, initiated that reorientation away from European and especially French culture and traditions which was shared to some extent by Rothko, Newman and others. (Still described the Armory Show, which introduced 'modern' art to the United States in 1913, as having 'dumped upon us the combined and sterile conclusions of western European decadence'.) By 1946 his vision had found its natural form of expression and his work was to remain remarkably consistent from then onwards (**21,6**). Large asymmetrically placed, jagged planes or planar formations – for the paint is so thickly laid on in great slabs of color that the surface can be, and often is, worked over like a relief – extend right across the canvas without overlaying or standing out against each other. There is a feeling of density but very little, if any at all, of space. The shapes are usually suggestive of tawny hides or tattered bill-boards or of the fissured rock-face or shale in deep gorges and canyons, the colossal elemental detritus of some geological 'fault'. The paint surface is strangely dry and scaly, and this, combined with Still's rawly assertive palette of earth browns and maroons, acid yellows and chalky whites, lends his enormous abstract compositions a primitive power akin to the incommensurable landscapes of the American West.

Mark Rothko was born in Russia and emigrated to the United States with his family in 1913. As melancholy and misanthropic as Pollock and Still, he painted in an increasingly sombre way and in 1970 he committed suicide. But he was perhaps the greatest of the three artists. Certainly he was more fully aware than were they of the spiritual dimensions attainable in abstract art and his mature works are deeply religious. They are objects for contemplation. They demand silence and the spectator's complete absorption in them.

'I am not interested in relationships of color or form or anything else', Rothko is reported as saying in 1957:

I am interested only in expressing the basic human emotions – tragedy, ecstasy, doom and so on – and the fact that lots of people break down and cry when confronted with my pictures shows that I communicate with those basic human emotions. The people who weep before my pictures are having the same religious experience I had when I painted them. And if you, as you say, are moved only by their color relationships, then you miss the point.

(S. Rodman, *Conversations with Artists*, New York, 1957)

Although Rothko did not make so aggressive a rejection of the easel painting as did Pollock and Still, his work is equally enveloping in scale. Soft, hovering, cloudy forms with frayed edges fill almost the entire surface of his pictures. But whereas with Pollock it is the texture of the paint that becomes expressive, with Rothko the texture of the canvas is allowed to remain as if it had been dyed rather than painted. He soaked his paints into the canvas and the two or three banks of colors which form the composition are scumbled over the other very thinly painted areas, creating an effect of luminous grandeur unique to Rothko. In contrast with the austere simplicity of the forms the color is very opulent and subtle; the forms glow and throb as the spectator stands before them on the brink, as it were, of an enormous luminous void (**21,7**).

Like Rothko, whose ambitions ultimately went beyond the subjectivity of Abstract Expressionism, Barnett Newman sought a new form of art which could carry some general human significance. Though his paintings may appear to be no more than arrangements of color and space, his many statements reveal the importance Newman gave to subject-matter. For him art was a quest to attain the unknowable and the sublime. 'I believe that here, in America', he wrote:

> . . . some of us, free from the weight of European culture, are finding the answer, by completely denying that art has any concern with the problem of beauty and where to find it . . . . We are reasserting man's natural desire for the exalted, for a concern with our relationship to the absolute emotions . . . . We are freeing ourselves of the impediments of memory, association, nostalgia, legend, myth, or what have you, that have been the devices of Western European painting. Instead of making cathedrals out of Christ, man, or 'life', we are making it out of ourselves, out of our own feelings.

('The Sublime is Now' in *Tiger's Eye*, no. 6, 1948)

21,7 Mark Rothko, *Green on Blue*, 1956.
Canvas, 7ft 5¾ins × 5ft 3¼ins (2.28 × 1.61m).
University of Arizona Museum of Art (Gift of Edward J. Gallagher Jr.).

21,8 Barnett Newman, *Vir Heroicus Sublimis*, 1950–1.
Oil on canvas, 7ft 11⅜ins × 17ft 9¼ins (2.42 × 5.42m).
The Museum of Modern Art, New York (Gift of Mr and Mrs Ben Heller).

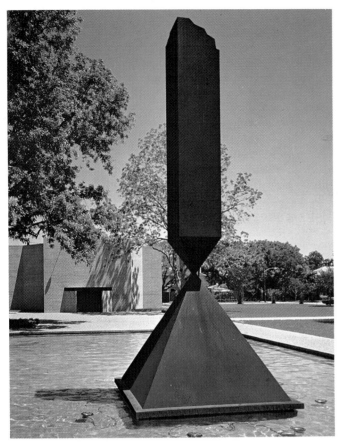

21,9 Barnett Newman, *Broken Obelisk*, 1963–7. Steel, 25ft 1in (7.65m) high. Institute of Religion and Human Development, Houston, Texas.

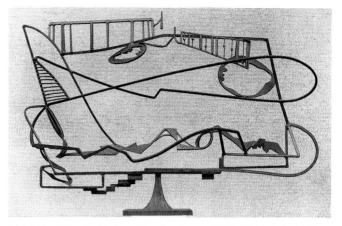

21,10 David Smith, *Hudson River Landscape*, 1951. Welded steel, 75 × 49½ × 16¾ins (190.5 × 125.7 × 42.5cm). Whitney Museum of American Art, New York.

21,11 David Smith, *Cubi XVIII and Cubi XVII*, 1963–4. Stainless steel, 9ft 8ins and 9ft (2.95 and 2.74m) high. Museum of Fine Arts, Boston, and Dallas Museum of Fine Arts.

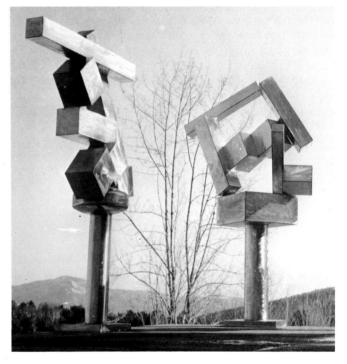

By the 1950s he was painting the kind of picture he was writing about – *Vir Heroicus Sublimis* (**21,8**), for example, a huge canvas covered with an even flat field of red divided by four narrow, sharp-edged stripes or 'zips', as he called them, running from top to bottom and varying slightly in color and width. Such paintings went further even than Mondrian in reducing pictorial language to its basic elements, though whether they can bear the weight of meaning their titles sometimes suggest may be doubted. In 1966 Newman entitled a series of 14 such canvases *The Stations of the Cross* (1958–66). Rothko, too, was working on a great (his last) series of paintings at this time for a chapel designed and built specially for them at Houston, Texas, approached past a memorable sculpture by Newman. In this Newman's exalted and tragic conception of art found a form more readily accessible than in painting – a great burnished pyramid of steel (symbol of timeless stability) bearing at the point of perfect intersection and balance the tip of an upturned and broken obelisk (symbol of man's flawed but perennial aspirations) (**21,9**).

Abstract configurations carrying implications akin to meaning and with references to human hopes and anxieties were created by the sculptor David Smith (see p. 817), who shared many of the interests of the Abstract Expressionists without being publicly associated with them. He was trained as a painter in New York, turned to sculpture in the early 1930s and always maintained that there was no essential difference between the two media. His sculptures tended to be conceived frontally and were built up in a pictorial manner that defied gravity. His early

open-form metal constructions were indebted to Picasso and González to whom, he said, he owed his 'technical liberation'. But his post-war work owed as much or more to his own experiences as a welder on an automobile assembly line at the Studebaker factory and later in a locomotive factory during the war. His sculptures in the late 1940s and 1950s were open and linear, sometimes radiating from a centre like metal calligraphy but also creating pictorial, three-dimensional scenes like 'drawings in air' enclosed within 'space frames', as they were called. At first some residual Surrealist influence may be felt, for example in their linearity, which recalls psychic automatism, and in the subliminal violence of their imagery. Later the curvilinear rhythms and all-over compositions of such pieces as *Hudson River Landscape* (**21,10**) recall contemporary paintings by Pollock, and in them Smith achieved a comparable freedom and lyrical sense. However, he felt even more strongly a strange affinity with crude metal and large, heavy machinery. He was in no way alienated from the machine age and in his last years, before his early death in an automobile accident, began several series of large, rugged pieces in stainless steel which initiated a new era in American sculpture. Despite the massive scale of his *Cubi* pieces (**21,11**), for example, they are never heavy but have a dynamic quality and taut sense of balance which contradicts their density. Their surfaces were always carefully re-worked so that they take the colors, without reflections, of the open landscape settings in which he visualized them. Delicacy and strength, the natural and the manufactured, are combined with an almost Hemingwayesque sensitivity.

EUROPEAN SURVIVORS

Abstract Expressionism with its great achievements, despite its sometimes overweening transcendentalist claims, was a uniquely American phenomenon. Nothing comparable emerged in Europe in the immediate aftermath of the war. During these same years of the late 1940s and early 1950s, however, Matisse, by then in his eighties and partly bed-ridden, created some of the most lyrically ebullient and joyous of all his works. In 1947 he had finished a book, *Jazz*, with pages of hand-written text and illustrations made with cut and colored papers. This was to be the technique that sparked off the last phase of his long artistic evolution, the most serene and perhaps the most fully resolved of all – 'a flowering after 50 years of effort', he called it. Papers were colored in gouache (see Glossary) and prepared by him, then cut and arranged. 'Cutting into color reminds me of the direct action of the sculptor carving stone', he said, and the method had for him more than just physical advantages. In it he conceived an extraordinary variety and richness of composition in color, from designs for stained glass windows and wall decorations to book-jackets. In the year before he died, his art reached its consummation in such large-scale cut-outs as *A Memory of Oceania* and *The Snail* (**21,12**), which sums up his lifelong quest to regain that innocence he had first discovered around the turn of the century in so-called primitive art. 'Seeing is of itself a creative operation, one that demands effort', he wrote in 1953.

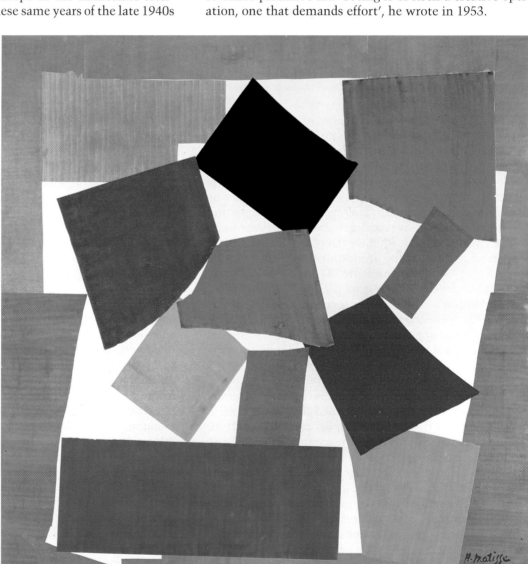

21,12 Henri Matisse, *The Snail*, 1953. Painted, cut and pasted paper, 9ft 4¾ins × 9ft 5ins (2.86 × 2.87m). Tate Gallery, London.

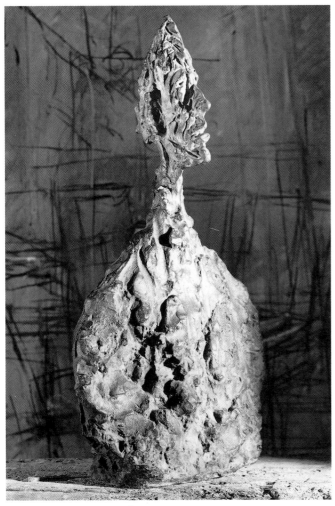

21,13 Alberto Giacometti, *Head of Diego II*, 1955. Bronze, 22¼ × 12⅕ × 5⅞ins (56.5 × 31 × 15cm). Private collection.

Everything we see in our ordinary life undergoes to a greater or lesser degree the deformation given by acquired habits, and this is perhaps especially so in an age like ours, when cinema, advertising and magazines push at us a daily flood of images which, all ready-made, are to our vision what prejudice is to our intelligence. The necessary effort of detaching oneself from all that calls for a kind of courage, and this courage is indispensable to the artist who must see all things as if he were seeing them for the first time. All his life he must see as he did when he was a child.

(*Le Courrier de l'UNESCO*, vol. VI, no. 10, 1953)

The Swiss sculptor Alberto Giacometti (1901–66) had made remarkable Surrealist sculptures in the 1930s in Paris, particularly metal constructions and 'erotic-kinetic objects'. They were related, indirectly and rather distantly, to the open-form sculptures of Picasso, González and Calder of the same years. On his return to Paris from Switzerland after the war, Giacometti changed direction completely and in about 1947 began making small, frontally seen bronze figures which he subsequently went on to develop into the series of elongated stem-like skeletal figures in bronze for which he is best known. In them optical distance becomes an inherent quality of the subject, as with hazy figures seen from afar, and they have been interpreted as symbols of man's spiritual alienation in tune, perhaps uniquely so, with the ideological climate of the immediate post-war years as anticipated by and crystallized in the philosophy of Existentialism. The Existentialist philosopher Jean-Paul Sartre himself wrote discerningly about Giacometti's sculpture at this time. But later, in the 1950s, Giacometti underwent another artistic crisis and evolved a final, visionary, indeed almost mystical, conception of his art. He now thought of it as a kind of magical reduplication of the reality that lies behind appearances, aiming to evoke that mysterious sense of metaphysical 'being', the impact of a 'real presence' in the religious sense of the term (as when the bread and wine are consecrated in a Catholic Mass). In 1954 Sartre wrote that one day Giacometti would come nearer than any previous artist 'to achieving the impossible when his portraits would affect us with all the force of a corporeal presence'. The sometimes painted bronze heads he made during the last years of his life, usually of intimates and often of his brother, to whom he was very close, almost realized this. It was not his aim to create likenesses but a reality in real space corresponding to the essence of a personality (**21,13**). As a perceptive critic wrote at the time, 'They are the most rudimentary representations of corporeality one can imagine, almost a negation of the organic existence of their subjects, but for all that the more deeply probing, knowing and silent, like the faces of old men . . . . They are the nuclei of personalities, and they dominate the surrounding space with their silence.'

POST-PAINTERLY ABSTRACTION

By the early 1960s Abstract Expressionism had reached its apogee and the artistic climate in both the United States and western Europe was rapidly changing. Post-war austerity and constraint were being succeeded by consumer-society affluence and prosperity and the short-lived optimism of the Kennedy years. Analyzing the situation, the critic Clement Greenberg ruminated on the various possibilities the future held for artists. After the 'turgidities of Abstract Expressionism', he wrote, what was needed was a more disciplined, formalist art, one that recognized and concentrated on essentials and, he went on, 'the irreducibility of pictorial art consists in but two constitutive conventions or norms, flatness and the delimitation of flatness'. Already by 1952 an original technique of staining unsized canvas by pouring pigment on to it had been pioneered by Helen Frankenthaler (b. 1928) and her breakthrough from Abstract Expressionism inspired a new movement – Color Field Painting or Post-Painterly Abstraction (**21,14**). The artists whose work attained the desired coolness, restraint and elegance were Morris Louis (1912–62), Kenneth Noland (b. 1924) and Jules Olitski (b. 1922). Their paintings were highly esteemed throughout the 1960s, as were also the geometrical abstractions of Op

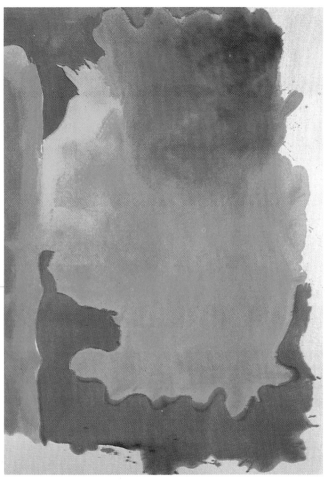

21,14 Helen Frankenthaler, *Canal*, 1963. Acrylic on canvas, 6ft 9ins × 4ft 9½ins (2.06 × 1.46m). Solomon R. Guggenheim Museum, New York.

21,15 Bridget Riley, *Crest*, 1964. Emulsion on board, 5ft 5½ins × 5ft 5½ins (1.66 × 1.66m). Private collection.

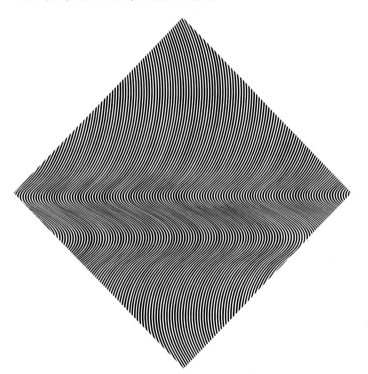

Art and its exploitation of optical devices for, at its best, more than just illusionistic tricks. Bridget Riley (b. 1931), in particular, went on to create some of the most poetically insidious metaphors for the uncertainties and spiritual unease of the 1960s (**21,15**).

JASPER JOHNS AND ROBERT RAUSCHENBERG

In the mid-1950s, just when Abstract Expressionism was celebrating its triumphs and was being conscripted to advertise all over the world the power and beneficence of American liberalism, the exponents of Non-Objective art in New York were confronted with blatantly representational images of Jasper Johns (b. 1930) and Robert Rauschenberg (b. 1925). They were called Neo-Dada at the time, though the connection was slight. But both painters incorporated in their works, sometimes in the most literal way, representational imagery and even recognizable objects, often of the most commonplace kind. *Three Flags* (**21,16**) is painted in encaustic, an old master technique of great antiquity which gives an elaborate and sensitively worked and unmistakably 'fine art' surface to a very edgy subject for the sophisticated public, to whom it was primarily addressed. Was Johns mocking the flag? or art?

According to the artist such subjects attracted him precisely because they were conventional and depersonalized, familiar and available to all, 'things the mind already knows', he said. 'They gave me room to work on other levels.' He also said he was interested in them because they 'suggest the world rather than suggest the personality', thus contradicting the basic assumptions of Abstract Expressionism with its heroicizing of the individual artist's power of self-expression. Johns went on to paint further series of similarly banal subjects entitled *Targets*, identifying in them the image with the field as he had done so strikingly in the flag paintings. They have been interpreted as a sustained meditation on meaning in art,

21,16 Jasper Johns, *Three Flags*, 1958. Encaustic on canvas, 30⅞ × 45½ins (78.4 × 115cm). Whitney Museum of American Art, New York (50th Anniversary Gift of the Gilman Foundation, Inc., the Lauder Foundation, A. Alfred Taubman).

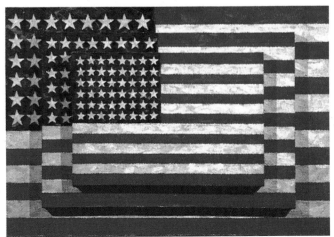

MODERNISM AND FORMALISM

The terms Modernism and Modern Art – as in the name of the New York museum founded in 1939 – have come to signify the innovatory arts of the late nineteenth century and the first three quarters of the twentieth. The concept of Modernism was most clearly embodied in the International Modern architecture of Gropius and Le Corbusier in the 1920s. This went far beyond the demands made ever since the 1820s (see p. 668) for a distinctive style of its own time, to a complete negation of the concept of style itself. Their buildings were purged of ornament and all nostalgic references to the past, emphasized function, exploited new technology and, in urban developments, proposed solutions appropriate to the social condition of the twentieth century. The past and all past styles were rejected also by avant-garde painters and sculptors with results ranging from Expressionism, Cubism, Futurism and abstract or non-objective art to Surrealism and Abstract Expressionism. For them, as for Baudelaire in the mid-nineteenth century (see p. 676), the experience of modernity was the defining challenge.

The need felt by artists to be 'of their own time' led to an approach that stressed innovation above all, an impulse to seek new solutions to pictorial and sculptural problems. Engagement with contemporary themes and with the norms of contemporary culture was felt to be essential for a 'modern' artist as was acknowledgment of the fundamental changes marking the history of the West in the last 150 to 200 years – changes including political developments both in practice and theory (especially Marxism), industrialization and scientific advances of all kinds. This had culminated in the Realism and Naturalism of the late nineteenth century with such painters as Manet and the Impressionists who were concerned with everyday themes in an objective, dispassionate spirit. Some of their paintings could,

however, be understood – if not misconstrued – in another way as abstract surfaces devoid of content; and the possibilities inherent in this duality led artists eventually to Formalism and the exploration of pure form in an art that is completely autonomous, concerned only with itself.

Formalism, as understood by mid-twentieth century artists, was defined by the New York critic Clement Greenberg (1909–94) who saw the art object as being essentially self-contained and self-sufficient, with its own rules, its own order, its own materials; independent of its maker, of its audience, and of the world in general. He saw the artist's calling as one of self-purification and art as a phenomenon characterized mainly, if not exclusively, by surface and pattern. In 1961 he wrote that the unique and proper nature of an art lay in what was unique to the nature of the medium:

> . . . *Realist, illusionist art had dissembled the medium, using art to conceal art. Modernism used art to call attention to art. The limitations that constitute the medium of painting – the flat surface, the shape of the support, the properties of pigment – were treated by the Old Masters as negative factors that could be acknowledged only implicitly or indirectly. Modernist painting has come to regard these same limitations as positive factors that are to be acknowledged openly.*

Greenberg's narrow and rigid attitude found its justification in Post-Painterly Abstraction (see p. 843), a movement he ardently promoted and supported. Eventually he aroused hostility, first of all from Conceptual artists; and his extreme version of Modernism can now be seen as belonging essentially to the Cold War Years and in some respects limited by its reflection of that ideological and political climate.

its construction and its elusiveness, and on the problems of perception – of seeing what we know and knowing what we see. Like Duchamp ready-mades, the *Three Flags* raises as many questions as it answers. But while demonstrating that art can make anything abstract, even a subject as highly charged as Old Glory, it remains supremely and ironically elusive and paradoxical. And Johns' work was to become ever more so with such complex and labyrinthine paintings as *Periscope (Hart Crane)* of 1963, which seems to echo from the deep a passage in Crane's poem 'Cape Hatterass' and has itself been likened to a submerged labyrinth.

Exactly contemporary with the first *Flag* painted by Johns in 1955 was Rauschenberg's *Bed*. He had smeared paint, as might an 'Action Painter', on the clean white cotton sheets, pillow case and cosy looking patchwork quilt of his own bed and then stood it upright on a gallery

wall. It was as challenging a gesture as the American flag paintings by Johns, and like them depended on Duchamp who had removed his *Fountain*'s 'function' by placing it upright and painting a signature and date on it. From *Bed* Rauschenberg went on to make his first 'combine' paintings, that is, paintings in which real objects, including photographs, are affixed to or combined with the painted surface. Part of his purpose in using three-dimensional objects as elements was to break away from the illusionary space that the Abstract Expressionists retained. He wanted, he said, 'to act in the gap between' art and life. In this he was at one with the composer John Cage whom he knew and was influenced by. Like Cage he sought to 'unfocus' the spectator by images of simultaneous and multivalent suggestibility. In one of the most daring and, because of its overt sexuality, most provocative of his combines, entitled *Monogram* (**21,17**), he reversed the process of *Bed* by

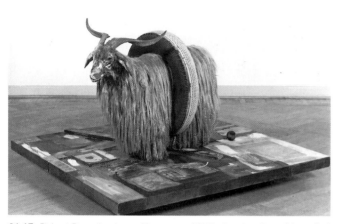

21,17 Robert Rauschenberg, *Monogram*, 1959. Construction with stuffed ram, automobile tyre, *collage* and acrylic, 4 × 6 × 6ft (1.22 × 1.83 × 1.83m). Moderna Museet, Stockholm.

21,18 Robert Rauschenberg, *Retroactive I*, 1964. Oil and silk-screen on canvas, 7 × 5ft (2.13 × 1.52m). Wadsworth Atheneum, Hartford, Connecticut (Gift of Susan Morse Hilles).

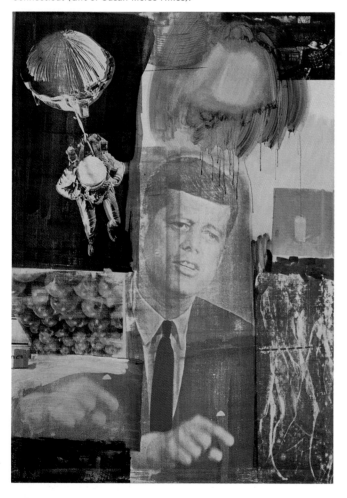

removing the painting from the wall and putting it on the floor with an Angora goat stuffed through a tight and much used automobile tyre standing in the middle. The painting itself, in which *collage* elements of wood and

metal are united together with broad gestural brush-strokes of paint, lies unequivocally flat. With its visual puns, *Monogram* has both hidden and not-so-hidden meanings.

One of the artists most affected by the impact of the home TV set in the sixties was Rauschenberg. The daily and nightly parade of interchangeable images which become almost Surrealist in their arbitrary juxtapositions, turning everything into a disposable spectacle, renewed his interest in creating two-dimensional works. He had begun already to adapt a *frottage* technique for transferring magazine or newspaper pictures by a process of silk-screen stencilling tried out by Andy Warhol, and he developed it for works uniting the most disparate themes and subjects, as in *Retroactive I* (**21,18**). These were inked and screened directly on to canvas in gridlike patterns he had taken over from Dada. He then added here and there swirls or drips of paint. However, these seemingly more traditional works, because of their format, belied Rauschenberg's multifarious visual interests. He participated with Cage in what may have been one of the first 'happenings', anticipating Beuys (see p. 864), and began experimenting with engineers and scientists in the possible future uses of advanced technology in the arts.

POP ART

The main reaction provoked by Abstract Expressionism was, however, to be much more brash than anything by Johns or Rauschenberg. *Big Painting No. 6* by Roy Lichtenstein (1923–97) represents this reaction – Pop Art – at its most blatant (**21,19**). The Abstract Expressionist brush-stroke is treated by Lichtenstein impersonally, even ironically, to make a visual comment on the excessive subjectivity of their cult of the gestural manipulation of paint as a means of unfettered, spontaneous self-expression. He renders it as if he were painting a still life of some graphic material for a paint manufacturer's display stand on a background of Benday pattern (closely spaced dots used for shading in comics and commercial art). 'We think the last generation, the Abstract Expressionists, were trying to reach into their subconscious, and more deeply than ever before, by doing away with subject matter', he wrote in 1966.

> *When we consider what is called Pop Art – although I don't think it is a very good idea to group everybody together and think we are all doing the same thing – we assume these artists are trying to get outside the work. Personally, I feel that in my own work I wanted to look programmed or impersonal but I don't really believe I am being impersonal when I do it . . . . But the impersonal look is what I wanted to have.*
>
> (*Artforum*, 1966)

Pop Art – defined as 'making impersonality a style' by using the imagery of commercial art and other mass media sources – emerged simultaneously but quite independently in Britain and the United States. The *collage, Just what is it makes today's homes so different, so appealing?* by the English painter Richard Hamilton (b. 1922) may

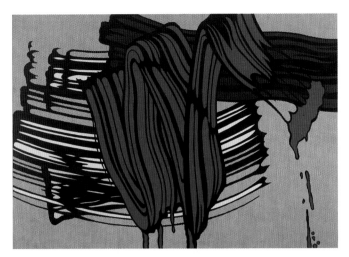

21,19 Roy Lichtenstein, *Big Painting No. 6*, 1965. Acrylic on canvas, 7ft 8ins × 10ft 9ins (2.34 × 3.28m). Kunstsammlung Nordrhein-Westfalen, Düsseldorf.

21,20 Richard Hamilton, *Just what is it makes today's homes so different, so appealing?*, 1956. Collage, 10¼ × 9¼ins (26 × 23.5cm). Kunsthalle, Tübingen.

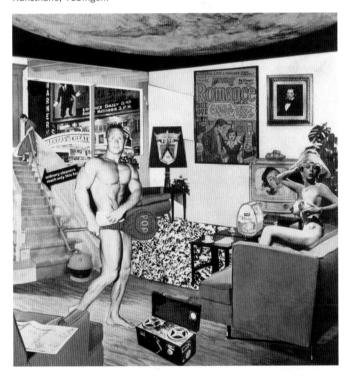

be considered the first truly Pop work of art (**21,20**). It incorporates or alludes to male and female pin-ups, TV, pulp romance, consumer durables, packaging, the movies, automobile heraldry – even the word Pop on the muscle-man's racket. When first exhibited in London, it was misconstrued as an attack on art or on the consumer society. On the contrary, Hamilton explained, he was aiming at a new art which would be 'popular, transient, expendable, low cost, mass produced, young, witty, sexy, gimmicky, glamorous and big business'. It was not intended as 'a sardonic comment on our society', he said. 'I should like to think of my purpose as a search for what is epic in everyday subjects and everyday attitudes.'

But whereas mass media imagery had an exotic glamour for Europeans, it was simply banal and common-

place to American artists. American Pop Art therefore had from the beginning an ambivalence and complexity lacking in its European counterparts. Awkward and provocative questions were posed, for example, by the *Giant Hamburger* (**21,21**) of Claes Oldenburg (b. 1929). Made of painted sailcloth, grossly inflated in scale (it measures some 7 feet, 2m, across) and stuffed with foam so that it is disturbingly soft, like a feather bed, the *Giant Hamburger* denies all traditional notions of sculpture in which surface generates volumes and it widened the boundaries of art by making the spectator aware of something as art that doesn't look like a work of art at all. Oldenburg felt passionately the need to bring art back into ordinary life after the hushed solemnities and high seriousness of Abstract Expressionism. He sold his works in simulated stores with other miscellaneous goods as if they were intended for the supermarket, not an art gallery. 'I am for an art that embroils itself with the everyday crap and still comes out on top', he said.

If Lichtenstein and Oldenburg represent Pop Art at its most brash, Andy Warhol (1928–87) represented its most extreme and subversive form. Warhol was a successful commercial artist on Madison Avenue, working for *Glamour* and other magazines, before he became a painter and later a film-maker, sculptor, writer, director of a pop group and the creator of a Pop lifestyle. He stood all theories of mass culture on their heads, notably Walter Benjamin's Marxist predictions of the suffocation of art in the glut of commercial images. Warhol said he liked mechanical repetition and wanted to be a machine himself. 'I think it would be terrific if everybody was alike.' He made a cult of being boring and banal and superficial – 'just look at the surface of my paintings and films and me, and there I am. There's nothing behind it.' His paintings were done for him by assistants – with a silk-screen technique he was the first to use for painting – and even his subjects were pre-selected, for they were the most popular

21,21 Claes Oldenburg, *Giant Hamburger*, 1962. Painted sailcloth stuffed with foam, 4ft 4ins × 7ft (1.32 × 2.13m). Art Gallery of Ontario, Toronto (Purchase, 1967).

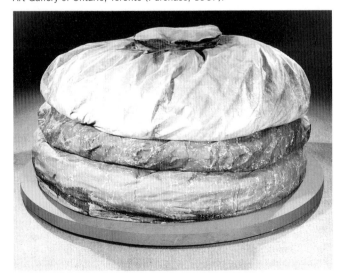

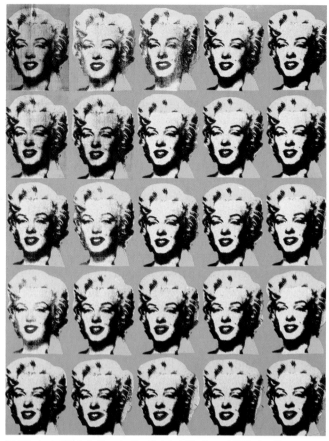

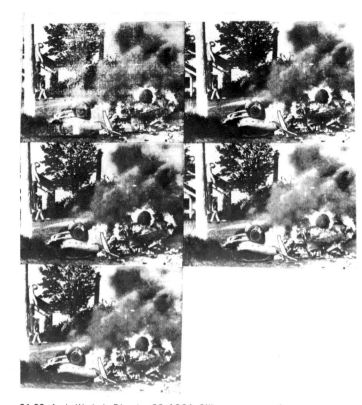

21,23 Andy Warhol, *Disaster 22*, 1964. Silk-screen enamel on canvas, 8ft 10ins × 6ft 10ins (2.69 × 2.08m).

21,22 Andy Warhol, *Twenty-five Colored Marilyns*, 1962. Acrylic on canvas, 6ft 9ins × 4ft 9ins (2.06 × 1.45m). Collection of the Modern Art Museum of Fort Worth (Benjamin J. Tillar Memorial Trust, acquired from the collection of Vernon Nikkel, Clovis, New Mexico, 1983).

(Campbell's soup, Marilyn Monroe [**21,22**]). This extreme form of non-choice also governed his compositions or non-compositions, which reduce everything to nullity by repetition and trivialization. However, a degree of motivation clearly entered into the most powerful, his various *Disaster* series, in which the real horror lies in the refinement of taste with which the mindless repetition and banality of the conception are treated as much as in the grisly subject itself (**21,23**).

Though a generation older, the Anglo-Irish painter Francis Bacon (1909–91) was the only European artist creating works of comparable power in the 1960s and since he too relied largely on existing images (press photographs, films, etc.) his paintings have some, albeit distant, connections with current artistic developments in America. For Bacon art was a 'method of opening up areas

21,24 Francis Bacon, *Three Studies for a Crucifixion*, 1962.
Oil with sand on canvas, each panel 6ft 6ins × 4ft 9ins (1.98 × 1.45m). Solomon R. Guggenheim Museum, New York.

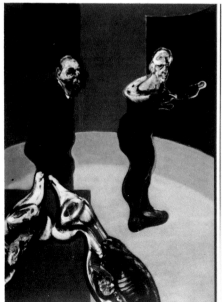
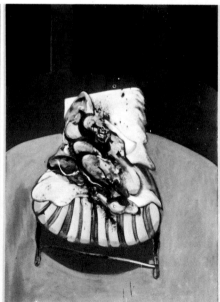
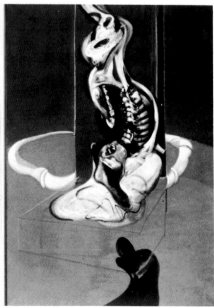

of feeling rather than merely an illustration of an object'. The Crucifixion becomes an ambiguous horror enacted in a shoddy, claustrophobic hotel bedroom, with bodies like partially dismembered carcases grappling in some unnamable sexual embrace (**21,24**). There are beautiful, even exquisite passages of paint in this 'triptych' and it is the incongruity, or rather the total dissociation, of theme and handling which, as with Warhol, conveys that sense of obsessional guilt which is the painting's real subject. In the United States, however, Bacon's work seemed merely decadent, irrelevantly European.

PHOTOGRAPHIC IMAGERY

The importance photography was to attain in the 1980s and the later twentieth century in the work of such artists as Gilbert and George (22,25), Cindy Sherman (22,19; 20), Anselm Kiefer (22,14), and Gerhard Richter (22,15; 16) had already been foreshadowed in the 1960s by Andy Warhol (21,23) and other Pop artists, notably Richard Hamilton in his *Just what is it makes today's homes so different, so appealing?* (21,20). Indeed it might be claimed in retrospect that the whole ethos of that traumatic decade, and its tensions and stresses for Americans especially, was more memorably expressed by photographers than by any other artists. Such compelling images as *Boy with a straw hat ...* , *1967* by Diane Arbus (**21,25**) seem now to encapsulate the predicament of that baffled generation – the trusting, bland incomprehension with which Middle America, in its innocence and simplicity of heart, confronted the inflamed passions of the times. Diane Arbus

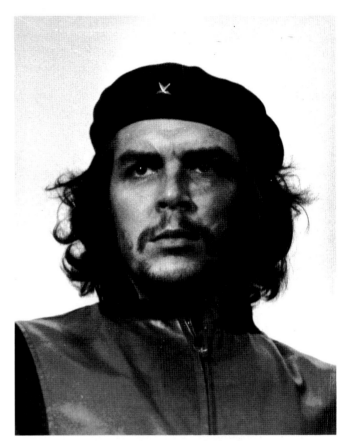

21,26 Alberto Korda, *Che Guevara*, 1960. Photograph.

(1923–71) had begun, like Andy Warhol, in the world of fashion magazines but broke away, she said, to seek with her camera 'things which nobody would see unless I photographed them'. She felt that the camera could, if carefully and imaginatively used, have the power to reveal inner mysteries and psychological truths – hence her attention to identical twins and misfits of all kinds, whom she portrayed with extraordinary insight.

It is significant that the best-known visual image of the time, indeed the most famous of all modern revolutionary images, should have been a photograph and not a painting, print, sculpture or other 'work of art' in the traditional sense (**21,26**). The famous portrait of Che Guevara by Alberto Korda (b. 1928) was taken in March 1960 at a party rally in Cuba after the explosion of a sabotage bomb. Korda selected it from the many he took that day as the best likeness. But it is more than a good likeness or any ordinary press-photograph. Seen from below, the still youthful Che (then 32 years old) with his ruffled hair, a Communist badge in his beret, an upward 'inspired' look in his glowing eyes, makes an impression very different from that of other contemporary politicians with their rhetorical gestures and forced smiles. It was eventually reproduced in every form and format imaginable and used not only in the press and on posters and other propaganda material but also, much simplified, on T-shirts. Few other photographs ever taken have won such universal recognition as a potent icon. It is an extremely forceful projection

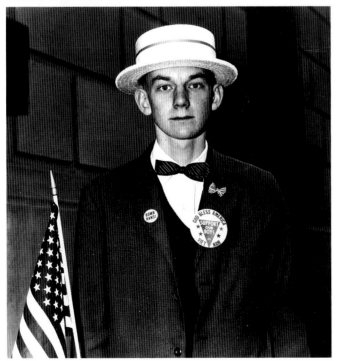

21,25 Diane Arbus, *Boy with a straw hat ...* , *1967*. Gelatin silver print. Fogg Art Museum, Harvard University Art Museums, Cambridge, Mass. (National Endowment for the Arts Grant. © Estate of Diane Arbus 1971).

of a peculiarly mid-twentieth-century hero. And it contributed not a little to Che Guevara's fame as an important political figure outside Latin America and perhaps also there as well. For a largely inarticulate off-beat generation, it came to symbolize many of their aspirations, especially in the student uprisings of 1968, the year after Che was killed as a guerrilla fighting against the rightwing government of Bolivia.

MINIMAL AND CONCEPTUAL ART

The most self-consciously American of all post-war artistic movements was Minimalism, which aimed at complete purity and integrity, the reduction of art to that which is intrinsic to its medium and the elimination of all that is not. By reducing the artist's means to an apparent minimum, it was hoped that an absolutely unitary activity would result – as well as a unitary experience for

21,27 Frank Stella, *Tuxedo Park Junction*, 1960. Enamel paint on canvas, 10ft 2ins × 6ft 1⅝ins (3.1 × 1.87m). Stedelijk van Abbemuseum, Eindhoven, Netherlands.

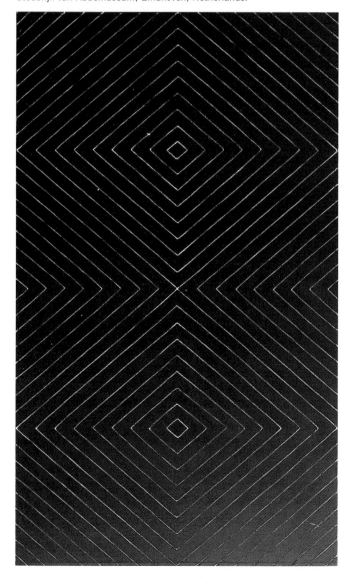

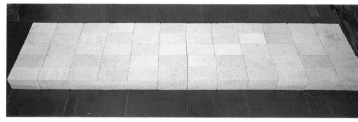

21,28 Carl André, *Equivalents*, 1966. 120 firebricks, 5 × 106½ × 22½ins (12.5 × 274 × 57cm). Saatchi Collection, London.

the spectator. 'All I want anyone to get out of my paintings . . . is the fact that you can see the whole *idea* without any confusion', the painter Frank Stella (b. 1936) remarked. 'What you see is what you see.' Though Stella did not 'invent' Minimalism, his 'Black Paintings' of 1959–60 – large canvases covered with 2½-inch (6.4-cm) wide black stripes arranged in predetermined, symmetrical patterns – were notable in reducing the role of the artist to a minimum as regards the execution of the artwork (**21,27**). The even application of paint to raw canvas, sometimes simply tracing the edge of the canvas in parallel lines to the centre, eliminated individual gesture and self-expression, the two qualities valued above all by the Abstract Expressionists. Not only expression but also illusion and even the allusion of symbols and metaphors were abandoned and art became an intellectual game in which the form of the artwork and the identity of its maker were irrelevant. They were statements of impersonality and opened up the narrow path that Minimalists were to follow during the next decade. In sculpture they were to go even further than in painting towards total impersonality, confining themselves to describing their conceptions in words or drawings and delegating the execution of them to others. The mechanical precision and bare surfaces of work by Donald Judd (1928–94), Robert Morris (b. 1931) and Carl André (b. 1932) exemplify the self-sufficiency and literalness they aimed at, often depending on the repetition of quite characterless manufactured units such as builders' bricks or metal plating, as in André's *Equivalents* (**21,28**). This recalls Stella's 'Black Paintings' in its systematic accumulation of identical units. But André's work is far from being as simple as it looks, embodying more than a single theory or intellectual attitude and foreshadowing later developments in Conceptual Art. André described his sculptures in terms of the transformation from 'form' and 'structure' to 'place'. They were often created for a specific setting and tend to control how the spectator uses and perceives the space. In order to avoid any human associations and to give equal value, in terms of gravity, to each component, they are conceived horizontally, usually laid out on the floor. In this way the art work is linked to the environment. It can be seen from any point of view and, as it can be walked over, includes a temporal element as well. Yet the reductive essence of such works harks back to Malevich (19,40), to the non-art of Duchamp as well as, more specifically, to the teaching of the former Bauhaus designer Josef Albers (1888–1976) and his *Homage to the Square* paintings of the late 1950s. The Minimalists, however, were perhaps more keenly aware than their precursors of some of the implications of their extreme position. As Robert Morris

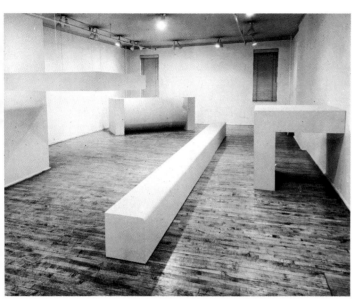

21,29 Robert Morris, Exhibition at the Green Gallery, New York, 1964.

observed: 'A single, pure sensation cannot be transmissible because one perceives simultaneously more than one as parts of any given situation: if color, then also dimension; if flatness, then texture, etc.' And he doubtless had his own recent work in mind (**21,29**) when he went on to remark:

> *Simplicity of shape does not necessarily equate with simplicity of experience. Unitary forms do not reduce relationships. They order them. If the predominant, hieratic nature of the unitary form functions as a constant, all those particularizing relations of scale, proportion, etc. are not thereby cancelled. Rather they are bound more cohesively and indivisibly together. The magnification of this single most important sculptural value, shape, together with greater unification and integration of every other essential sculptural value makes on the one hand, the multipart, inflected formats of past sculpture extraneous, and on the other, establishes both a new limit and a new freedom for sculpture.*
>
> (*Artforum*, February 1966)

The rigorously intellectual nature of Minimalism, together with the artists' self-absorption and their ironic detachment from 'content' as well as from artistic or craft traditions, including the personal handling of the media on which so much of the appreciation of earlier non-representational art had been based, all combined to severely limit its appeal. By the late 1960s, however, some of the Minimalists had begun to break away from the movement's excessively reductive forms and reintroduced a sense of visible process. Eva Hesse (1936–70) was one of these Post-Minimalists, as they were called. Her informal sculptural arrangements were hung from the ceiling or leant against a wall or spilt out over the floor, and they were of unconventional and often pliable and impermanent materials including latex, rubber, fibreglass, rope and cloth. She said she wanted her pieces to be 'non art, non connotive, non anthropomorphic, non geometric, no nothing, everything, but of another kind, vision, sort'. An

early work, *Hang Up* (**21,30**), parodied in an almost Dada anarchic spirit one of the basic, fundamental tenets of Western art, the picture frame. She played with its two-dimensional and three-dimensional attributes and its role as an arena for the artist's self-expression. Her frame is bound up with cloth bandages but is quite empty and the protruding metal rod could not serve to hang it up on a wall except back-to-front and sideways.

This evolution towards the elimination of the hand-made work of art was finally achieved in the late 1960s with Conceptual Art and the 'dematerialization of the art object'. The central theory of Conceptual Art is that the work of art is essentially an idea which may, or may not, generate a visible form. It had been anticipated in the 1950s by Robert Rauschenberg's friend the American composer John Cage, whose 1954 piece entitled *4'33"* consisted of 4 minutes and 33 seconds without music – just silence broken by whatever sounds happened to occur during the indicated period of time. Four years later an exhibition in Paris by the painter Yves Klein (1928–62) consisted of a completely bare art gallery painted white inside and blue outside. It was entitled *La Vide* and asserted the artist's power to take possession of an experience without converting it into a physical work of art.

21,30 Eva Hesse, *Hang Up*, 1966. Acrylic on cloth over wood and steel, 6ft × 7ft × 6ft 6ins (1.83 × 2.13 × 1.98m). Art Institute of Chicago (Gift of Arthur Keating and Mr and Mrs Edward Morris by exchange).

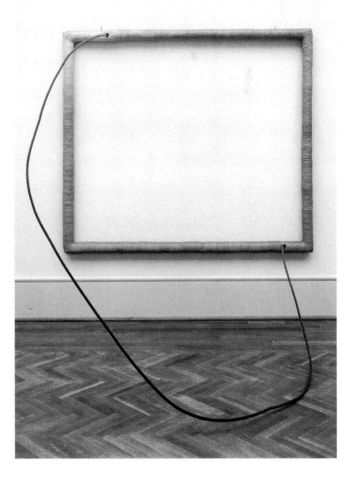

EARTH AND LAND ART

The so-called 'transient works' by the Bulgarian-American artist Christo (Christo Javacheff, b. 1935) exist first of all in the artist's mind. In fact several have never been realized, and those that have been were usually dismantled later. But they survive as 'concepts', together with detailed and elaborate plans: sketches, inventories, instructions, schedules and, for those that were executed, photographs. His early works included projects in which objects were stacked (that for a great *mastaba* formed by stacking 2,000,000 oil barrels at Abu Dhabi begun in 1979,

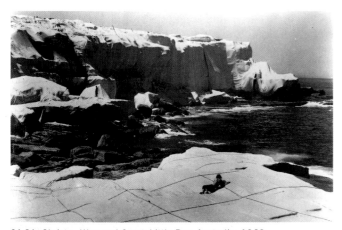

21,31 Christo, *Wrapped Coast*, Little Bay, Australia, 1969. Surface area of project 1,000,000 ft² (93,000m²).

for instance) or the wrapping of objects or buildings in fabric and then binding them with ropes, notably that of some 1,000,000 square feet (93,000m²) of the Australian coastline (**21,31**). In 1976 he created *Running Fence*, 24½ miles (39.4km) of white woven synthetic fabric crossing the hills of Sonoma and Marin Counties, California, to the Pacific, and in 1983 he surrounded 11 small islands in Biscayne Bay off Miami with 6,500,000 square feet (603,850m²) of pink woven polypropylene fabric, turning them into huge flamingo pink water-lilies when seen, ideally, from the air. In the USA, where the landscape had since the nineteenth century been one of the most powerful national metaphors as an artistic subject (see p. 680), it now became itself a medium of artistic expression and eventually led to complete transformations of the natural physical world. Nothing comparable had been seen before anywhere in the world, apart from the gigantic earthworks in Peru of the first millennium BC and those in North America of a slightly later date (3,49; 50). The mud and rock coil in Great Salt Lake, Utah, by the former Minimalist sculptor Robert Smithson (1928–73), was the most notable (**21,32**). Like other earthworks it was generated by the artist's deeply American response to the landscape. 'As I looked at the site', Smithson wrote, 'it reverberated out to the horizons only to suggest an immobile cyclone . . . . The shore of the lake became the edge of the sun, a boiling curve, an explosion rising into fiery prominence.' It was also linked to the minuscule and near-at-hand, for the salt crystals that grew on the jetty were formed in the shape of a spiral. 'The Spiral

21,32 Robert Smithson, *Spiral Jetty*, Great Salt Lake, Utah, 1970. About 1,500ft (457m) long, 15ft (4.6m) wide.

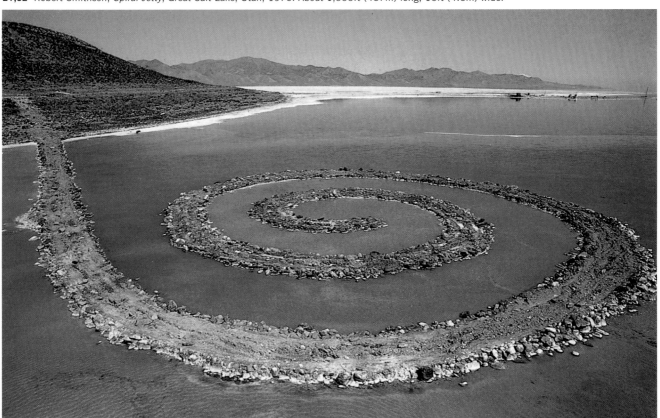

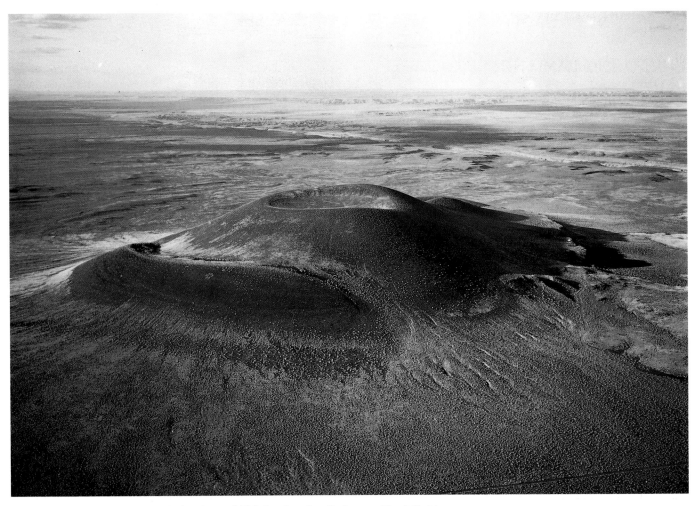

21,33 James Turrell, *Roden Crater Project*, begun 1974. San Francisco Peaks, near Flagstaff, Arizona.

Jetty could be considered one layer within the spiralling crystal lattice, magnified trillions of times', Smithson said. 'So it is that one ceases to consider art in terms of an object.'

Two years earlier, in 1968, Walter De Maria (b. 1935) had created his first landscape work, *Mile Long Drawing*, in the Mojave Desert in California and a few years later, in 1974–7, the astonishing *Lightning Field* in New Mexico. The former consists of two parallel lines traced across the burnt-dry, caked and crackled flat earth surface of the desert; the latter is a grid of 400 stainless steel poles spaced 200 feet (61m) apart and stretching about a mile (1.6km) on an east–west axis and a third of a mile (0.5km) on a north–south one. The poles are planted in such a way that their tips are aligned. Lightning occurs frequently at this high altitude, striking De Maria's work in a spectacular way, though he has stated that the lighting effects are more important than the lightning. The piece almost disappears in the brilliant sunshine of midday and only becomes fully visible in the raking light of dawn or dusk. It is an ingenious perceptual and conceptual conundrum on a gigantic scale.

The ultimate earthwork was to be realized with the appropriation of the earth itself as an art form – one attuned to the cycles of the cosmos. For the *Roden Crater Project* (**21,33**) an entire dormant volcano in northern Arizona has been taken over by James Turrell (b. 1943). In 1973 Nancy Holt (b. 1938) had created a cosmic viewing site in the Great Basin Desert, Utah, by aligning four concrete drainage or sewerage tubes in an X-shape to mark the extreme points of the sun's position on the horizon during the summer and winter. The tubes are perforated with holes that locate specific stars and serve, like Stonehenge, to link the seasonal cycle of earth and sun to the movements of the heavens. In a similar fashion but on a much greater scale and with increased complexity the *Roden Crater* will disclose views into infinity. The site recalls Stonehenge, if only in its circularity and astronomical accuracy, which it combines with the geometry of its geological conic form and its allied dimension of geological time. Turrell, trained in perceptual psychology and an enthusiastic spare-time pilot, was already well-known for his 'Projection Pieces' in which space was defined by using ambient light, neon or xenon light, projected through constructed rooms or 'sensing spaces' which had the huge and awesome feeling of elevation of three-dimensional Rothko paintings. The spaces Turrell is creating inside the tawny-red dormant volcano cone will function as observatories for celestial lighting events, culminating in a phenomenon known as celestial vaulting. From the bottom of the crater the spectator will look up through the recontoured elliptical rim of the volcano to see the sky like an arching roof, composed of light but seemingly solid, as if through the *oculus* of a giant Pantheon.

PHOTO-REALISM AND NEW IMAGE PAINTING

The extreme purism and formalism of Minimalist art did not fail to arouse reactions, of which Photo-Realism (Super-Realism or Sharp Focus Realism) was the most obvious, though it is often misunderstood. So far from being a revival of academic realism this style is as objective and object-oriented as Minimalism itself. Naturalistic imagery and illusionistic space are presented in the form of flat snapshots or color slides rendered with *trompe l'oeil* virtuosity. Richard Estes (b. 1936) is the best-known exponent (**21,34**) though Chuck Close (b. 1940) was more startling when his work first appeared in the late 1960s. His gigantic, deadpan, close-up frontal heads are as static and iconic as any Minimalist work.

The Photo-Realists had no connection with the New Image or New Figurative painters who emerged in the late 1960s in the USA. Nor did a Super-Realist return to traditional forms of representation occur elsewhere. Representation had never been abandoned in Europe, where figurative painters such as Balthus (Balthazar Klossowski de Rola, b. 1908) and David Hockney (b. 1937) were both prominent and highly esteemed. Hockney had at first been classified as a Pop artist, which he denied, but found fulfilment in the USA, where he settled on discovering in California a scene as liberating and as stimulating visually and sensually as had Matisse when he went to Morocco some 50 years earlier (**21,35**). In the USA, however, the return to figurative painting in the 1960s was understood immediately as a gesture of rejection and as a challenge, all the more so because it was launched by a well-known Abstract Expressionist. Philip Guston (1913–80) had been a student friend of Jackson Pollock, with whom he was expelled from a Los Angeles art school in 1930. He subsequently took an active part in the whole course of mid-twentieth-century art in America, working first as a muralist for the WPA/FAP (Works Progress Administration Federal Arts Project), for whom he and others invented a 'New Deal Style'. This was influenced both by the Mexicans, notably Rivera, and by the

21,34 Richard Estes, *The Solomon R. Guggenheim Museum*, 1979. Canvas, 31⅛ × 55⅛ins (79 × 140cm). Solomon R. Guggenheim Museum, New York.

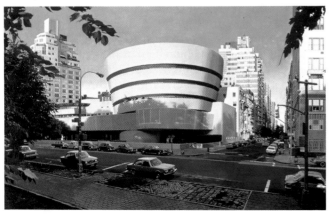

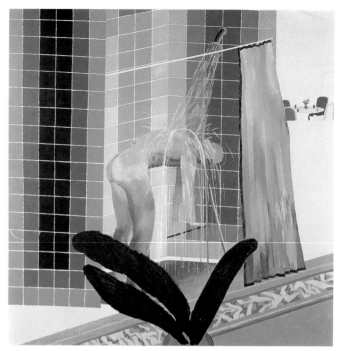

21,35 David Hockney, *Man Taking Shower in Beverly Hills*, 1964. Acrylic on canvas, 5ft 5½ins × 5ft 5½ins (1.67 × 1.67m). Harry N. Abrams Family Collection, New York.

American Regionalists, especially by Pollock's teacher Thomas Hart Benton (1889–1975). After the war Guston turned to abstraction with softly colored, tremulously though often quite thickly painted canvases which were to establish him as the 'lyric poet' of Abstract Expressionism. His sudden about-face when he revived figuration in 1967–8 was all the more striking in that his painting became simultaneously almost grotesque in its deliberately brash and gross handling (**21,36**). The subject-matter included Klu Klux Klansmen, huge heads and clumsy still lifes of indeterminate but somehow menacing import. With their ironic strangeness and cartoon-like linear configurations, Guston's late works heralded New Image painting which, however, was seldom to meet the challenge he had so forcefully issued.

In the 1950s Leon Golub (b. 1922) was one of the Chicago 'monster school' painters obsessed with the theme of human corruptibility. His gigantic paintings of life-size tormented human beings give an impression of fleshless figures consisting only of muscles and tendons because of his peculiar technique of scraping and roughening the unstretched canvases on which he preferred to work. They went deliberately against the current and in New York were thought peripheral. Only after the nightly TV news reports from Vietnam ceased did Golub's raw yet also disturbingly cool depictions become acceptable. He had painted two series of life-size narrative scenes entitled *Napalm* and *Vietnam* in the 1970s. They were intended, as are all his paintings, to shock; and the more effectively because they were 'art' on a big scale and could be seen only in art galleries and not on the banal TV screen. His consistency in confronting contemporary issues is impressive and he went on painting atrocities after the Vietnam War ended with huge life-size or over-life-size narrative series entitled *Mercenaries*, *Interrogation* and *White Squads*.

21,36 Philip Guston, *The Painter*, 1976.
Oil on canvas, 6ft 2ins × 9ft 8ins (1.88 ×
2.95m). Collection of Richard E. Lang,
Jane M. Davis, Medina, Virginia.

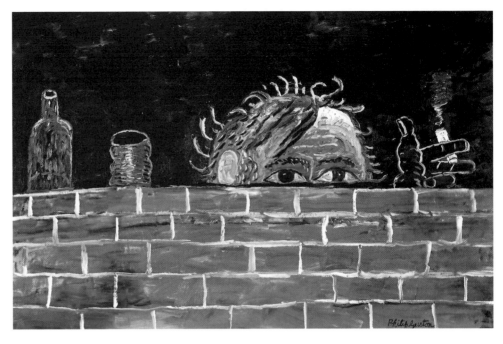

'Most of these paintings have to do with Latin America, some with South Africa', Golub said in 1987, 'but by extension they apply to New York or Chicago or London. They can get away with it better in Latin America today, in El Salvador, than they might be able to do in London or New York, but these incidents still occur in major cities through police force or inadvertence, so-called inadvertence . . . . So, terrorism at one level, or sadism at another level, depending on how you view it. We see ourselves in noble terms and we see the others as monsters. They may see us as monsters and see themselves in noble terms.' The spectator is made to assist at these gruesome events. Our complicity is assumed. In *Mercenaries V* (**21,37**) our eyes are on a level with the victims' behinds and we seem to have caught the leering, half-witted mercenary in the act. Action has been suspended, though only provisionally. The canvas, scraped with a meat-cleaver so that pigment remains only in the interstices of the weave and in the fibres themselves, looks as if it has been rubbed raw. The surface is painfully delicate and tender. Golub's handling of paint is as sensitive as his themes are harsh and crude.

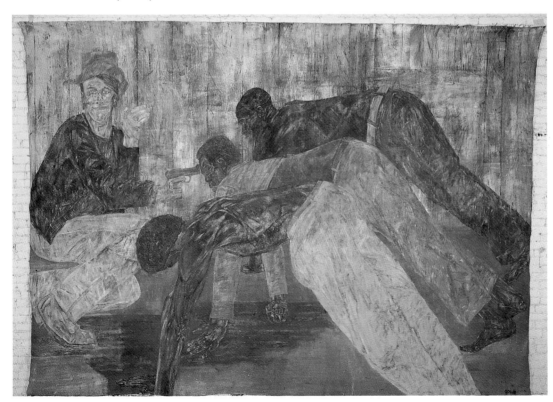

21,37 Leon Golub,
Mercenaries V, 1984. Acrylic
on linen, 10ft × 14ft 4ins
(3.05 × 4.37m). Saatchi
Collection, London.

BODY ART AND PROCESS ART

The premise of all Post-Minimal and Conceptual Art is that the artist's product is of less significance than the idea and process which brought it into being and of which it is only the record – hence Conceptual art's close

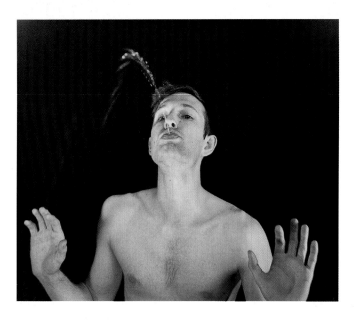

involvement with photography. Indeed it is difficult to believe that Robert Smithson's earthworks, Christo's wrappings or such works of body art as the *Self Portrait as a Fountain* by Bruce Nauman (b. 1941) would ever have been conceived if they could not have been photographed (**21,38**). More important, however, especially for Conceptual art's influence on later developments in photography, was its understanding of it simply as a language, as a carrier of ideas and cultural messages, and not as an artistic category. Pop artists such as Warhol also recognized this, of course (21,23). The photograph was not thought of by them as an 'art object' to be appreciated for its formal, expressive or other aesthetic qualities, notably those that had come to be valued as essentially 'photogenic'. Accepted ideas about the art of photography were undermined, together with the supremacy of the silver gelatin print and the cult of precision. For Conceptual artists photography was simply a tool, for visual exploration or for pure imagination, and since it was outside the prevailing value-system of the art-world it was much to be preferred to other image-making media.

Conceptual artists such as Vito Acconci (b. 1940) and Edward Ruscha (b. 1937) made notable photographic works, usually in series such as Acconci's *Twelve Pictures* of 1969 and Ruscha's *Thirty-four Parking Lots in Los Angeles* of 1967, but the most fruitful for later

21,38 *Above* Bruce Nauman, *Self Portrait as a Fountain*, 1966, from the series *Photograph Suite*. Chromogenic-development print. Sheet and image 20 × 23⅝ins (51 × 60.5cm). Collection of Whitney Museum of American Art, New York (Purchase 70.50.9).

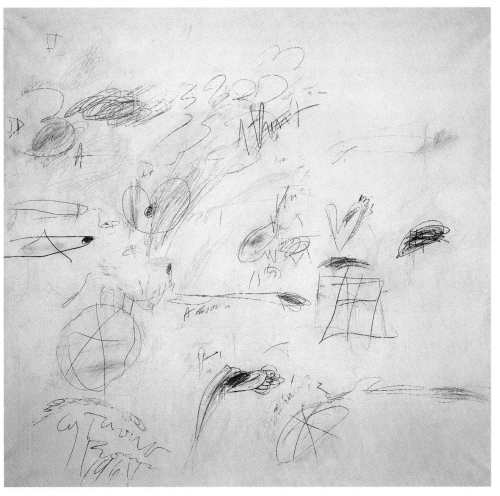

21,39 Cy Twombly, *Untitled 1964*, part of a triptych now dispersed, 1964. House paint, crayon, pencil on canvas, 6ft 6¾ins × 6ft 10½ins (2 × 2.06m). Saatchi Collection, London.

developments have been the works of John Baldessari (b. 1931) in the USA and, in Germany, of Bernhard and Hilla Becher (see p. 867), whose influence reached its height in the 1980s. Keenly aware of the effect of movies, television, advertising, photojournalism, etc. in our media-saturated environment, Baldessari's work is a prolonged and increasingly ambivalent commentary on its imagery, full of hidden messages and paradoxical meanings, both intentional and unintentional.

As the Swiss painter Paul Klee (see p. 825) had stressed, 'the work of art is above all a process of creation: it is never experienced as a mere product'. Canvases by the American Cy Twombly (b. 1929) often give the impression of pictures in the making with false starts partly erased, beginnings undeveloped. Jotted lines, words and numbers in lightly handled pencillings, touches of crayon, smudges of paint – equivalents both mental and pictorial to the sweepings of a floor – are scattered or just allowed to drift across the surface. These memory traces, both collective and personal, are widely dispersed and the emptiness in which they float recalls the use of space in Chinese and Japanese scrolls – space for reverie and musing. The combination of images and lettering also recalls Oriental art, although the former are rarely precise and the latter, though clear, is deliberately not calligraphic, as in *Untitled 1964* (sometimes called *A Roma*) (**21,39**). There is also a suggestion of Zen enlightenment or awakening resulting from irrational questions and answers, especially in the contrast between the appearance of graffiti scrawled on a public lavatory wall and the intellectual allusiveness of the names written on the canvas or used in a title – Virgil, Goethe, Tatlin. As these names, and also such resonant titles as *Orpheus*, *Leda and the Swan*, *Ode to Psyche* are alone enough to reveal, Twombly is steeped more deeply in Mediterranean culture than other modern American artists. (He has lived in Rome since 1957.) His paintings and drawings remain obviously, one might say obstinately, 'works of art' to be framed and hung on a wall.

In the 1960s, however, the concept of art as a process coincided with a deepening revulsion among artists against the art market and the whole system into which they were inevitably drawn. By insisting that art is not to be identified with a special kind of object (an exhibitable, reproducible kind of object which could become a commercial commodity) or with a special location (art gallery or museum) they hoped to find a way of eluding the system – especially the system's elaborate structures for endowing their work with an exclusiveness, rarity value and luxury character they did not want it to have.

MODERNISM AND POST-MODERNISM

It was during the seventies that the purist trends from Post-Painterly Abstraction to Minimalism came to be seen as the last stage of Modernism. And they seemed increasingly to lay the whole modern movement open to the charge of artistic narcissism, especially in the United States, where Minimalism was at its most extreme.

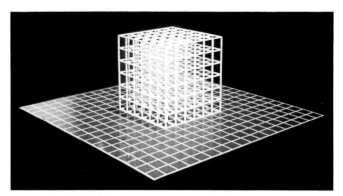

21,40 Sol LeWitt, *Untitled Cube (6)*, 1968. Painted steel, 15¼ × 15¼ × 15¼ins (39 × 39 × 39cm). Whitney Museum of American Art, New York (Gift of the Howard and Jean Lipman Foundation, Inc.).

Certainly they were self-referential to an unusual degree. Sculpture looked more and more like architecture, the Minimal grid becoming a characteristic form, almost an emblem, as, for example, in *Untitled Cube (6)* by Sol LeWitt (b. 1928) (**21,40**). 'Presently', wrote a young American painter, John Perrault, in 1979, 'we need more than silent cubes, blank canvases and gleaming white walls. We are sick to death of cold plazas and monotonous curtain wall skyscrapers.' Protest at this type of urban development had become increasingly vociferous, albeit from the viewpoint of residents rather than architects, since 1961 when Jane Jacobs (b. 1916) published her *Death and Life of Great American Cities*, a passionate appeal for a return to traditional urban life with its social and occupational diversity, streets as places of human interaction and a mixture of old and new buildings. Architecture, much more clearly and consistently than painting and sculpture, had displayed the modern movement's high-minded austerity and self-abnegation and it now invited relaxation with hedonistic 'impurities'. And it was in architecture that the current situation was first polarized as Modernism and Post-Modernism.

Although purely European in origin, the International Style had come to be seen as characteristically American. Gropius and other leading members of the Bauhaus staff emigrated to America in the late 1930s and it was there, in the immediate post-Second World War years, that the style found its greatest exponent in Mies van der Rohe (pp. 827, 830). Very few of his designs had been executed in Europe. In those optimistic post-war years, however, no statement of pure, ideal form was too Platonic for realization in America and the clean, healthy and, above all, rational beauty of Mies van der Rohe's designs seemed to symbolize the new technology and its utopianism. Such 'ideal' solutions to design problems as the Farnsworth House (**21,41**) and the Lake Shore Drive apartments (**21,42**) combine cubic simplicity with elegant precision of detail and immaculate finish in compositions of supreme poise and balance. A progeny of curtain-walled metal and glass skyscrapers proliferated, especially in the United States, beginning with the Lever House, New York (1951–2), by Gordon Bunshaft (1909–90) of the firm Skidmore, Owings and Merrill. However, there were those

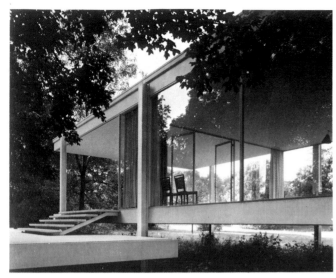

21,41 Mies van der Rohe, Farnsworth House, Fox River, Illinois, 1945–50.

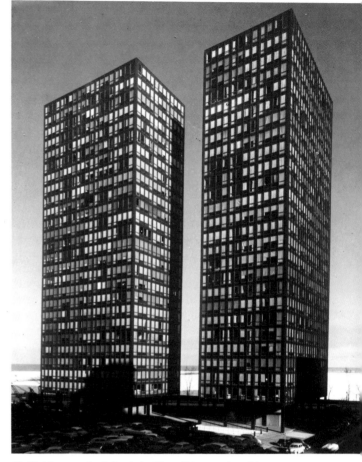

21,42 Mies van der Rohe, Lake Shore Drive apartment houses, Chicago, Illinois, 1950–2.

who judged even Mies van der Rohe's masterly designs to have been sublime failures. (Dr Farnsworth found her house far too expensive to live in and tried, unsuccessfully, to sue the architect.) The critic Lewis Mumford probably spoke for many when he wrote that:

> *Mies van der Rohe used the facilities offered by steel and glass to create some elegant monuments of nothingness. They had the dry style of machine forms without the contents. His own chaste taste gave these hollow glass shells a crystalline purity of form; but they existed alone in the Platonic world of his imagination and had no relation to site, climate, insulation, function, or internal activity; indeed, they completely turned their backs upon these realities just as the rigidly arranged chairs of his living rooms openly disregarded the necessary intimacies and informalities of conversation.*

> (*The Case against Modern Architecture*, 1964)

Hostility to the purism and impersonality of the International Style was felt soon after 1945 in prominent works by Frank Lloyd Wright (see pp. 799–800) and Le Corbusier (see pp. 827–30). Of course, Wright had always gone his own way and never subscribed to any movement or 'style', but his circular ramp design for the Guggenheim Museum in New York of 1943–59 (intended originally for a drive-in planetarium) was taken as a deliberate affront by functionalists and, indeed, it did assert the value of idiosyncrasy, especially in an urban context (21,34). Le Corbusier

21,43 Le Corbusier, Notre Dame du Haut, near Ronchamp, France, 1950–4, from the south-east.

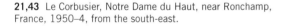

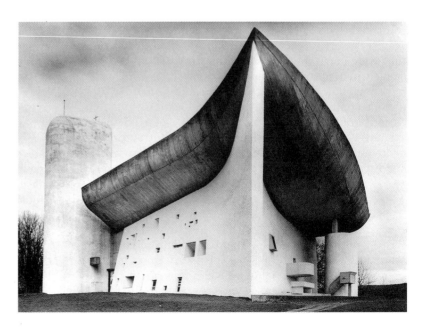

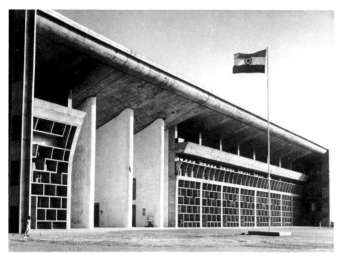

21,44 Le Corbusier, High Court Building, Chandigarh, India, 1956.

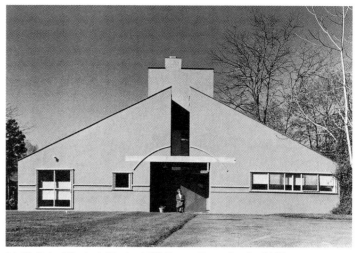

21,45 Robert Venturi, Chestnut Hill House, Pennsylvania, 1965.

had abandoned Purism in his paintings some years before the Second World War – he was both painter and architect – but it was not until about 1950 that Expressionism made itself felt in his architecture with amoeboid curves, biomorphic forms and irregular plans. The pilgrimage chapel on a hilltop near Ronchamp in central France (**21,43**) flouts all the geometrical, rational principles of his earlier work. Though he disclaimed any specific religious inspiration, this small building is richly suggestive of meaning and goes beyond architectural symbolism to intimate a new architectural language of metaphor. In the High Court Building he designed a few years later as part of his new government centre at Chandigarh in India, the conflict between plasticity and geometricality, which makes the Ronchamp chapel so dynamic, was resolved with powerful monumentality on a heroic scale (**21,44**).

These works sparked off a number of equally sculptural, almost irrational, aggressively rough and chunky, so-called

Brutalist buildings by young architects all over the world in the late 1950s and early 1960s – Paul Rudolph (1918–97) in America, James Stirling (1926–92) in Britain, Kenzo Tange (b. 1913) and several others in Japan. But it was only in the 1970s, following the publication of *Complexity and Contradiction in Architecture* and *Learning from Las Vegas* by the architects Robert Venturi (b. 1925) and Denise Scott Browne (b. 1931) that a more radical and fully articulate reaction to the still flourishing International Style emerged. Called Post-Modernism, it was the creation of architects trained in the austere discipline of the International Style, which they sought to transform by extending its élitist language 'into the vernacular, towards tradition and the commercial slang of the street' (Charles Jencks, *The Language of Post-Modern Architecture*, 1978).

The utopian, collectivist, revolutionary, technological and functional ideology which was supposed to have sustained Modernism in architecture – and gave it a single

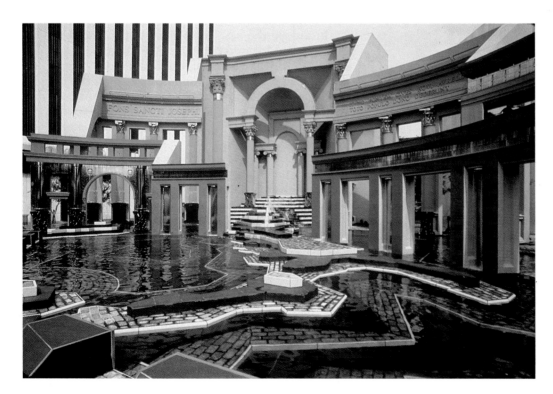

21,46 Charles Moore, Piazza d'Italia, New Orleans, 1978–9.

rationally determined goal – was rejected in favour of something deliberately less idealistic and earnest but, it was hoped, more democratic. The eclecticism to which this led ranged from Pop imagery to a piquant historicism, notably in Venturi's own buildings. The house he designed for his mother (**21,45**) revives traditional principles and characteristic forms of pre-Modern architecture – symmetry, for instance, and the gable like a Mannerist broken pediment – but they are set in opposition to the Modernism of flat planes and standard detailing, so that the contradiction gives the building meaning. Later manifestations have been less sophisticated and more stagey, not always unintentionally. In 1964, Charles Willard Moore (1925–93) praised Disneyland as one of America's outstanding public spaces and an embodiment of the American Dream which inspired his own work. The Piazza d'Italia he designed for the Italian-American community in New Orleans (**21,46**) is rich in color, some of which is provided by neon lighting, with columns, a temple front and a fountain spilling into a map of Italy. A more monumental example is the Public Service Building by Michael Graves (b. 1934) in Portland, Oregon (**21,47**). Here International Modernism, exemplified by huge areas of plate glass, is treated as one of several 'historical' styles, together with skyscraper imagery, Art Deco and Art Nouveau trimmings (fluttering fibreglass garlands), the purist

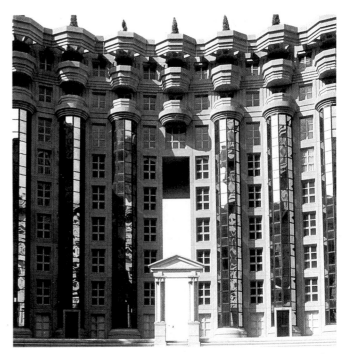

21,48 Ricardo Bofill, the Palace of Abraxas, Marne-la-Vallée, near Paris, 1978–83.

21,47 Michael Graves, Portland Public Service Building, Portland, Oregon, 1979–82.

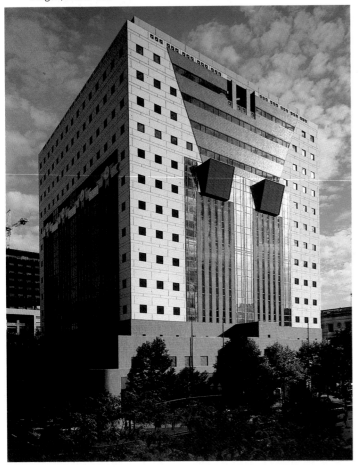

'revolutionary' architecture of late eighteenth-century France and such transformed Classical elements as huge pilasters and a gigantic red keystone. 'Discipline, the backbone of architecture as a civic art, is ridiculed', a practitioner of International Modernism complained – in words which vividly recall the objections raised by traditionalists half a century earlier to the work of Le Corbusier! But Graves's aim has been to create in a city of impersonal concrete and steel-and-glass boxes a building that exploits the metaphorical riches of the language of architecture with multiple layers of form, space and symbolism. It is a building that speaks not only to a professional élite, but also to the man in the street.

In Europe the best-known 'revisionist' architects are the Spaniard Ricardo Bofill (b. 1939) and the Italian Aldo Rossi (1931–97), whose ostensibly autonomous architecture is manifestly derived from the past. Bofill's extensive and grandiose housing project 'Les Arcades du Lac', near Versailles, openly challenges comparison with the Château de Versailles itself. Commenting on it, Bofill remarked that it takes 'without copying, different themes from the past, but in an eclectic manner, seizing certain moments in history and juxtaposing them, thereby prefiguring a new epoch'. Such Neo-Historicist aspirations are apparent in his equally grand Palace of Abraxas, a public housing development in the Parisian suburbs (**21,48**). The forms of Aldo Rossi's buildings are often taken from Boullée (see p. 639), but are raised to what he calls 'an exalted rationalism, emotional and metaphorical', and have mostly, like Boullée's, remained on paper. The generous hopes for a richer, more allusive and vivacious architecture that inspire Post-Modernism have perhaps been best attained in Japan, where the combination of popular 'content' and sophisticated 'form' had once before been realized in art. Architects such as Arata Isozaki (b. 1931), Kisho Kurokawa (b. 1934) and Minoru Takeyama (b. 1934)

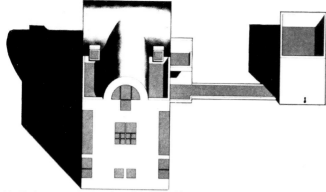

21,49 Axonometric drawing of Kaijima House.

21,50 Arata Isozaki, Kaijima House, Kichijoji, Musashino City, Tokyo, 1974–6.

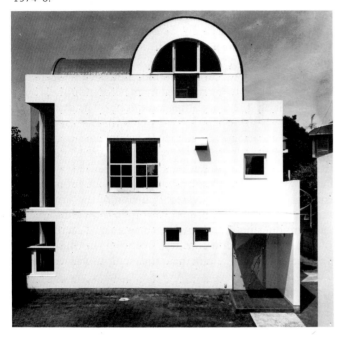

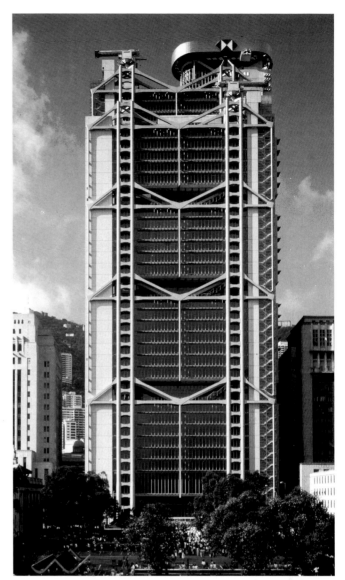

21,51 Norman Foster, the Hongkong and Shanghai Bank, Hong Kong, completed 1986.

have some of the same elegance (without gentility) and proletarian taste (without vulgarity) as the great masters of the *Ukiyo-e* prints (16,14). Isozaki's highly personal use of even the simplest forms, especially cylinders and cubes, achieves an effect of internationalism quite distinct from that of the International Modern style in its allusions to the architectural heritage of the world (**21,49; 50**). That he should acknowledge debts to Palladio, Sinan and Boullée, as well as his own Japanese cultural background, is a sign of our own pluralist times.

The architectural and design movement known as High Tech – a concept or approach to architecture rather than a style – is, in a sense, opposed to Post-Modernism. Its careful avoidance of all references to vernacular building and popular, proletarian taste, so much cultivated by Post-Modernism, marks its distinctive stance in this respect. Based on modern technology and emulating the no-nonsense simplicity and lightweight precision engineering of, for instance, supersonic aircraft construction, High Tech has no ambition to go beyond this aesthetically – or so its exponents declare though, of course, its great achievements depend on their finely-tuned sense of proportion and balance and other aesthetic qualities.

High Tech is unique among internationally significant movements of this century in being exclusively English in origin (tracing its ancestry back to Paxton and the Crystal Palace [17,35]) and predominantly so in its subsequent development, though several of its most notable works have been built outside the UK – in France, Hong Kong and the USA – by English architects. Lloyd's of London (1986) by Richard Rogers (b. 1933) and the Hongkong and Shanghai Bank Headquarters in Hong Kong, also completed in 1986, by Norman Foster (b. 1935) are High Tech's finest achievements to date. Indeed the Hongkong Bank Headquarters epitomizes the movement – elegant, sophisticated and totally of our own time, without any concessions to taste, good or bad (**21,51**). High Tech can be seen as the culmination of several Modernist trends and as sparking off, as a result, various reactionary responses such as the traditional 'fake Georgian' development at Richmond Riverside, London, of 1984–9 by Quinlan Terry (b. 1937), and the less genteel but equally 'fake New England' development in New York Harbour of the same years, known as Port Liberté, by François Spoerry (b. 1912).

CHAPTER TWENTY-TWO

TOWARDS THE
THIRD MILLENNIUM

The decade of the 1980s, like that of the 1780s, was overshadowed by the political events which marked its end. The bicentenary of the French Revolution – the first stage in a long process that was eventually to lead to Communism – was celebrated in 1989 just a few months after the fall of the Communist régimes in eastern Europe. Political and social structures there crumbled. Soon afterwards the Communist Party lost control of the Soviet Union, which then broke up into independent states. The Cold War had ended. But no new era of peace, let alone prosperity, began. Some Communist parties remained in power, notably in China where, in July 1989, a several-day-long public demonstration in Tiananmen Square, Beijing, was suppressed by the army in front of the TV cameras of the world. Less stable régimes in Central and South America, in Africa and India, became even more so, with local and civil wars proliferating. A threatening sense of insecurity, deepened by the uncontrollable spread of AIDS as a possibly global pandemic, combined with increasing awareness of the disastrous consequences of overpopulation, ecological destruction, depletion of resources and atmospheric pollution, created widespread apprehension and unease.

Against this sombre background, the awesome spectacle of a mass culture being diffused by mass communications, together with the consumer products of multinational industries, confronted the world, both East and West. Attempts to resist, mainly in Islamic countries, were rarely effective, yet this ever-spreading homogeneity was accompanied by and perhaps partly aroused a contradictory phenomenon in the arts – that of probing and explorative diversity. A vast expansion of the 'imaginary museum' of art and architecture known from photographs and reproduction, combined with increased facilities for travel after the mid-century, resulted in more open attitudes generally. Paintings and sculptures created in

The visual arts	Historical landmarks
1979 Chicago, *The Dinner Party* (22,18)	
1980 Gilbert and George, *Black Church Face* (22,25)	**1980** Reagan elected President of USA. First report by Center for Disease Control of AIDS
1981 Serra, *Tilted Arc* (22,4)	
1981–8 Kabakov, *The Man who Flew into Space from his Apartment* (22,33)	
1982 Kruger, *Untitled (You Invest in the Divinity of the Masterpiece)* (22,22)	**1982** Falklands War between UK and Argentina. Israel invades Lebanon. Satellite TV introduced
1983 Sherman, *Untitled No. 120* (22,20)	**1984** Indira Gandhi assassinated
1984 Baselitz, *Mocking (Die Verspottung)* (22,13)	**1985** Gorbachov gains power in USSR. Compact discs revolutionize music industry
1985 Beuys, *Plight* (22,2) Rodriguez and Abramson, *Orisha/Santos* (22,28) Polke, *Watchtower III* (22,17)	**1986** Chernobyl accident in USSR. Fax machines revolutionize international communication
1986 Koons, *Rabbit* (22,9)	**1987** Gorbachov's *glasnost* and *perestroika*
1987 Toya, *Woods* (22,29)	**1988** Bush elected President of USA. Salman Rushdie, *Satanic Verses*. Toni Morrison, *Beloved*
1987–9 Gehry, Vitra Design Museum (22,5)	
1988 Richter, *18 October 1977* (22,15)	**1989** Fall of Communist governments in eastern Europe. Tiananmen demonstration suppressed in Beijing
1989 Gober, *Cat Litter* (22,24) Yongping, *Reptiles* (22,32)	**1990** German reunification. Nelson Mandela released from prison
1989–90 Holzer, Installation 'Jenny Holzer' (22,21)	**1991** Gorbachov falls. Gulf War. War in Yugoslavia
1990 Kiefer, *Jason and the Argonauts* (22,14)	**1992** Dissolution of USSR. Clinton elected president of USA
1991 Hammons, *House of the Future* (22,27)	**1993** NAFTA treaty signed by USA. Internet system links 5 million users
1991 Hirst, *The Physical Impossibility of Death in the Mind of Someone Living* (22,26)	**1994** First non-racial elections in South Africa
1992 Hill, *Tall Ships* (22,34)	**1994–6** Russian army defeated in breakaway republic of Chechnya
	1997 Deng Xiaoping dies. Hong Kong handed back to China. Kabila overthrows government of Mobutu

different cultures and for different purposes, and by no means always as 'works of art', were displayed in travelling exhibitions and illustrated in books, periodicals and the daily press, where they were also frequently appropriated for commercial advertising. Developments and innovations in contemporary art could be and were made known instantaneously all over the world; international and even intercontinental exhibitions were held in the East as in the West. As never before, artists became aware of abundance and variety in the arts of the whole world from prehistory to the present day, provoking anxious and often introspective enquiry into the meaning and purpose of art and, in particular, into its status and criteria of value. The assumption that it consists of paintings and sculptures of a certain 'quality' or 'style' has been questioned; the latter terms especially have been discredited along with connoisseurship, aesthetic values and the conception of art as something that happens as a result of the artist's genius. Such questions could hardly arise when art was predominantly sacred, as it still is in much of Asia and Africa. (One of the largest statues of the Buddha in the world was erected and dedicated in Hong Kong in 1994.) In the West, art has lost not only its religious meaning but also that of current secular ideologies. As a result, much of the most significant work of the late twentieth century turned its back on the political and other forces of a society that has enshrined art in hierarchical structures deeply uncongenial to its makers.

Distinctions formerly drawn between the 'fine' arts, 'primitive' art, vernacular or 'folk' art, also between painting, sculpture and the crafts, have been blurred and then eliminated. The idea of 'progress' in art and related concepts of a 'mainstream', an 'avant-garde' and of forward-looking 'movements' have all been questioned together with the desirability of permanence, not to mention 'quality' and 'taste'. The prestige of the unique art object and of the artist's individual creativity has been challenged. (No single figure today has or could have the dominant position of Picasso who, indeed, posed these very questions long before he died in 1973.)

Art made against this background of revaluation in the light of late twentieth-century thought and theory has been called Post-Modern, a slippery term that gained currency in the 1970s first of all for architecture (see pp. 857–9) and then for painting and sculpture that could no longer be covered by the word 'modern' as used in the title of New York's Museum of Modern Art, founded in 1929 to exhibit work that was modern at that date but is now termed Modernist. Much of the art of the 1980s and early 1990s has in fact been directed against accepted aesthetic and other values as promoted up to now by museums of modern art and the art trade, without being anti-modern in the sense that Renaissance art was anti-Gothic or Neo-Classical art anti-Rococo. There has been continuity as well as change. But Post-Modernism has been articulated in opposition to Modernism and the terms it favoured: purity as an end and decorum as an effect; historicism as a setting and the museum as the context; the artist as original and the art work as unique. The importance of the media as such to Modernism, with its emphasis on purity, was challenged; Post-Modern art seeks space between, across or outside them, in new or neglected media such as video or photography, and in a diversity of forms, often being dispersed, textural or ephemeral. Thus not only the role of the artist and the values that authenticated art have all been questioned but, essentially, the whole cultural field has been opened up and transformed. As the critic and theorist Craig Owens pointed out: 'Appropriation, site specificity, impermanence, accumulation, discursivity, hybridization – these diverse strategies characterize much of the art of the present and distinguish it from its modernist predecessors.' Appropriation – direct copying undertaken to contest the notion of originality as a title to fame – was taken to its furthermost limit by Sherrie Levine (b. 1947), who began in 1980 to exhibit her photographs of photographs by famous male photographers. A site specific work is one made for a particular location, often in the open air, where it is expected to disintegrate. Impermanence is a feature also of most indoor installations set up for a single occasion. They differ from one-person exhibitions of works of art well placed in a room (like the sculptures of Robert Morris, see 21,29) in that they create whole environments which often include junk and found natural objects, even living creatures, including the artist. Their walls may be covered in texts. Alternatively they may consist of multiple computer-controlled video screens, the most vital of recent developments. In their reference to current social and other problems, installations differ most strikingly from Modernist works of art (except Duchamp's) conceived as self-contained and self-sufficient entities.

Modernism had been a liberating force for writers and musicians as well as artists; but the premium it set on their originality and the autonomy of their works tended to separate the arts from life. Post-Modernism, on the other hand, both in its theory and its general outlook, extends not only to the arts but also to other fields, notably to sociology, philosophy, post-Freudian psychology and the theory of language. It has itself been very strongly influenced by 'deconstruction' theory, that is to say, by the analysis of the processes by which meaning is constructed in words which condition attitudes to such issues as those of gender and ethnic diversity (many notable art works of the 1980s and 1990s are composed simply of words). And whereas Modernism was exclusively Western, Post-Modernism is a global phenomenon and thus closely associated with pluralism and multiculturalism. The pluralist idea that different cultures are incommensurable and cannot be judged by a single set of criteria goes back to the eighteenth century; but it was usually applied only to non-Western cultures on an assumption of Western superiority. Not until recently has pluralism been adopted as a critique of the Eurocentrism of Modernist art. Multiculturalism (a term coined in the early 1980s) is an assertion that people of different ethnic origins can coexist in a single place, look across frontiers of race, gender and age without prejudice or illusion and learn to think against the background of a hybridized society. Adopted as a social policy in the USA and Australia, it has sometimes been administered by members of the governing class as a defence strategy and means of control. It has also been exploited for the expansion of the art market. Even so, it has demonstrated that the art produced in the USA is by no means dominated by, let alone confined to, that of European Americans. Post-Modernist questioning of Western artistic assumptions has been destructive only in helping to break down barriers to mutual understanding between people and attacking not so much Modernist art as the social and political institutions and practices with which it had been associated. It released energies for the making of arts that were politically challenging, aesthetically contradictory, emancipatory and interdisciplinary – that responded to the exigencies of life in all parts of the world in the late twentieth century.

QUESTIONING MODERNISM

The most provocative questioner of all received ideas about art was the German sculptor Joseph Beuys (1921–86), the creator of intensely personal but widely relevant, transient yet haunting images. His words, not least as a teacher, and his charismatic personality as well as his works inspired a generation of artists all over the world. After serving in the *Luftwaffe* during the war, he studied at the eminently traditional Düsseldorf Academy, where he was appointed professor of monumental sculpture in 1961. A decade later he was fired, mainly as a result of his political activity as the founder of the German Student Party in 1967 and the Organization for Direct Democracy in 1970. His sculptures were assembled from junk and such unconventional materials as animal fat, felt and beeswax, which had special significance for him. When shot down over the Crimea in 1943 he had been rescued by nomads who covered his body with fat and felt and seem also to have introduced him to their belief in shamans. 'My objects are to be seen as stimulants for the transformation of the idea of sculpture or of art in general', he said in an interview in 1978. 'They should provoke thought about what sculpture *can* be and how the concept of sculpture can be extended to the invisible materials used by everyone.' His aim was to create what he called 'Social Sculpture', based on how people mold and shape the world in which they live. As a teacher, his guiding principle was that 'one can no longer start from the old academic concept of educating great artists – that was always a happy coincidence. What one can start from is the idea that art and experience gained from art form an element that flows back into life.'

His 1965 performance or 'happening', or what he preferred to call 'action', entitled *How to Explain Pictures to a Dead Hare*, was an examination in complex tableau form of the problems of thought and communication with reference also to ritual, magic and myth, including his own semi-mythical life (**22,1**). In an empty picture gallery in Düsseldorf, with his head covered in a mixture of gold leaf and honey, which he regarded as spiritual (a holy substance), wearing shoes one of which had a sole of lead, the other of felt, he muttered inaudibly for three hours to a dead hare cradled in his arms. He took the hare to the pictures on the walls and, he recorded, 'I explained to him everything that was to be seen. I let him touch the pictures with his paws and meanwhile talked to him about them . . . . I explained them to him because I really do not like explaining them to people. Of course there is a shadow of truth in this. A hare comprehends more than many human beings with their stubborn rationalism.' Beuys was, above all, a teacher whose message was concerned more with life than with art in the sense of the term then generally accepted.

In some of his performances or 'actions' he used the lecturer's conventional equipment. Dressed in a costume that became part of his persona – felt hat, hunting jacket and boots – with constantly changing expressions on his handsome face, he moved in a kind of shamanistic dance, talking and drawing on blackboards. During an exhibition lasting several weeks in London in 1974 he drew each day on one of 100 blackboards which, scattered over a platform with three standing on easels, finally constituted a work of sculpture itself that he entitled *Directional*

22,1 Joseph Beuys, *How to Explain Pictures to a Dead Hare*, 1965. Performed at Galerie Schmela, Düsseldorf.

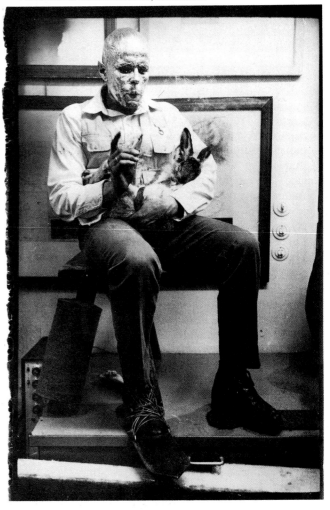

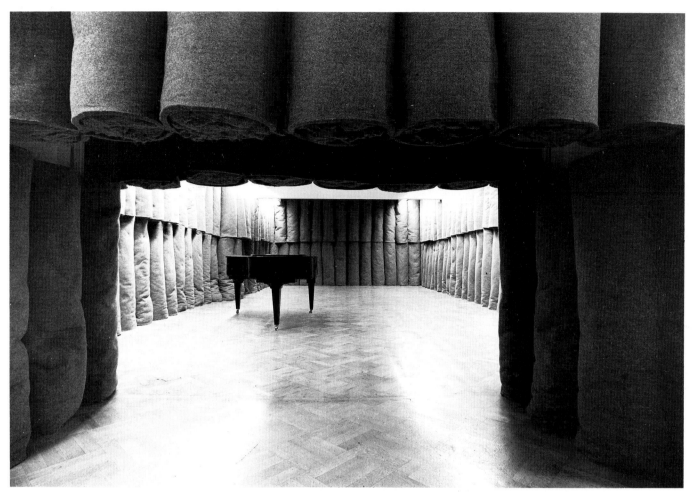

22,2 Joseph Beuys, *Plight*, 1985. Installation with felt, grand piano, blackboard and clinical thermometer. Centre Georges Pompidou, Paris. Courtesy, Anthony d'Offay Gallery, London.

Forces. As channels of communication blackboards have the force of social power normally exerted to conserve the structure that Beuys wished to undermine. A blackboard is included also in his last and perhaps greatest work, *Plight,* an installation of compelling power, set up in London in late 1985 a few months before his death, which succeeded in encapsulating his vision of late twentieth-century fate (**22,2**). Two rooms completely insulated by a dual row of felt rolls – with only a grand piano, on which lay an unused blackboard and a clinical thermometer, to occupy the silent, claustrophobic, prison-like/womb-like space – created a deeply resonant metaphor not just for the artist's condition, but for the human condition imprisoned within current political, cultural and social systems.

The work of Beuys, his 'actions', installations and other assemblages of unconventional materials, was in no single respect unprecedented. With its strong social commitment it exemplifies, nevertheless, tendencies that began to gather strength in the 1970s and diverged in a variety of ways from the central principles of Modernist art as previously understood. A still wider range of media – including drawings, sculpture, neon light, performance art, still photography, video and laser beam holograms (see Glossary) – has been used by the American artist Bruce

Nauman (b. 1941) to express a complex of philosophical, ethical, political, social and sexual concerns and positions. His detachment and distance from the Modernist art world is evident simply by listing them. Painting is conspicuous by its absence. Born in Indiana, he began his career in California (later moving to New Mexico) and did not even visit New York, the capital of Modernist art, until 1968. He went for the opening of an exhibition of his own work which immediately attracted international attention. His early *Self Portrait as a Fountain* of 1966 (21,38) alludes playfully to Duchamp (20,5), whose influence is pervasive in both Modernist and Post-Modernist art. Nauman has, however, been less preoccupied with the definition of 'art' than of self, and in many of his later works even incorporates wax casts of parts of his body. In another early work the very Beuysian sentence 'the true artist helps the world by revealing mystic truths' is written in a spiral of neon. He has made much use of words that flash in neon contradictory commands, 'live and die/die and live/live and live', or comments, 'Human Nature/knows/doesn't know/care . . .' in numerous combinations and permutations. Torture was the theme of a sculpture he entitled *South American Circle* in 1981, and he has similarly referred to the politics of gender in *Punch & Judy (Kick in*

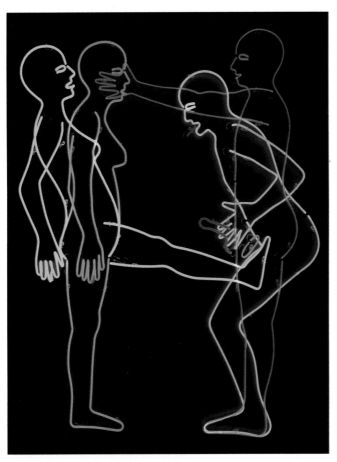

22,3 Bruce Nauman, *Punch & Judy (Kick in the Groin/Slap in the Face)*, 1985. Neon and glass tubing mounted on white aluminium, 77 × 61 × 14ins (195.6 × 154.9 × 35.6cm). Courtesy, Leo Castelli Gallery, New York.

the Groin/Slap in the Face) – outlines of life-size figures in alternating blue and red neon (**22,3**).

The shift in emphasis from form to meaning in the work of Beuys, Nauman and others was opposed not only by the older artists, critics and museum curators. 'There's a real trend now to demean abstract art as not being socially relevant', the American sculptor Richard Serra (b. 1939) complained in 1976. 'I've never felt, and don't feel now, that art needs any justification outside of itself.' Born in San Francisco of Russian and Spanish immigrants, he worked his way through college and became fascinated with metals used in the steel mills. Eventually he began using vulcanized rubber and neon tubing for abstract formations and then, using molten lead thrown into the corners of rooms, he evolved a sculptural equivalent to Pollock's action painting (see p. 837). Subsequently he preferred pure geometrical forms of increasing size, especially steel plates propped against or piled on top of one another, precariously resisting the laws of gravity and giving a new meaning to the term Minimalist that was applied to him. In 1979 he was commissioned to make a work of sculpture for Federal Plaza, New York, by the city's General Services Administration. The result was the *Tilted Arc*, a curved wall of Cor-ten steel 120 feet (36.6m) long, 12 feet (3.66m) high and 2½ inches (6.4cm)

thick, tilting inwards by 12 inches (30.5cm) (**22,4**). Serra had promised that 'after the piece is created, the space will be understood as a function of the sculpture', a reversal of the commonly accepted idea of outdoor sculpture as an embellishment of its surroundings. He had already executed a number of 'site specific' abstract sculptures for urban spaces and believed that in conceiving them 'one has to consider traffic flow, but not necessarily worry about the indigenous community, and get caught up in the politics of the site'. They had often aroused local hostility but not as violent as that directed at the *Tilted Arc*. In the ensuing controversy the work was opposed as a hazard to police surveillance of the square and defended as an anti-authoritarian political gesture. It was supported by the Modernist establishment of museum curators and dealers but decried by many art critics, who saw it as the authoritarian imposition of a single, and to their minds outmoded as well as socially irrelevant, form of art on the general public. Finally, the General Services Administration, which had commissioned and spent $175,000 on it, yielded to public protest in 1989 and ordered the *Tilted Arc*'s removal. However, the conflict between Modernism and Post-Modernism continued.

The work of Richard Serra is nothing if not imposing and most of his site specific pieces have been successful. Although usually categorized as Minimalist, they are so

22,4 Richard Serra, *Tilted Arc*, 1981. Cor-ten steel, 12ft × 120ft × 2½ins (3.66m × 33.6m × 6.4cm). Federal Plaza, New York (Removed by General Services Administration, Washington DC, 1989). Courtesy, The Pace Gallery, photo Kim Steele.

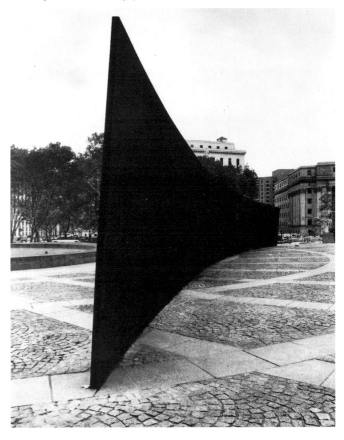

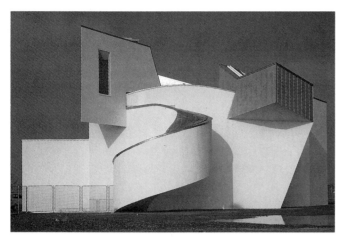

22,5 Frank Gehry and Associates, Vitra Design Museum, near Basel, Switzerland, 1987–9.

historically inspired detailing of Post-Modernism or the elegant rationalism of High Tech than this extraordinary building with its apparent confusion of curved and slanting, sharply angular forms. Gehry intended it to be clad in sheet steel and 'look like an old oil can'. The Swiss patron insisted on a smooth plastered finish with a limited use of sheet steel, but even so the museum challenges the validity of all and any architectural rules. And Gehry was able to develop his ideas on a larger scale in the Guggenheim Museum, Bilbao, Spain, completed in 1997 (see p. 11).

It is no more than a coincidence that a series of photographs of *Gas Cleaning Plants (details)* (**22,6**) by the German photographers Bernhard and Hilla Becher (b. 1931 and 1934) dates from the same years as the Vitra Museum and the controversy over Serra's *Tilted Arc*. The Bechers had begun to make and exhibit their standardized photographs of warehouses, cooling towers and other features of the dirty industrial environment some years earlier and they had first been brought to international attention by an article in *Artforum* of 1972 by the Conceptualist/Minimalist artist Carl André, who recognized their affinities with his own enigmatic works (21,28). The seeming literal-mindedness, the apparent dumbness of their repetitive grid-format typologies, make their images compelling, sometimes almost mesmerizing – and also suggestive of their possibly equivocal nature.

The English sculptor Tony Cragg (b. 1949), who settled in Germany in 1977, alluded in his work to the industrialized and natural worlds, to both organic and inorganic matter. Trained as a scientist, he calls himself an 'extreme materialist' and defines his art as a 'visual material language'. He began by assembling pieces of broken plastic which he arranged on a floor in the color sequence of the spectrum in *New Stones – Newton's Tones* of 1978. His works in three dimensions include forms based on hand-tools, rather old-fashioned laboratory equipment and, in *Raleigh* of 1986–7, a bollard and foghorns resting on a

only in the simplicity of their forms, like the gigantic iron cubes made for a temporary exhibition in the Tate Gallery, London, in 1993. Their surfaces are rough and the play of light gives them a powerful vitality which brings their formal purity down to earth. They have been described as examples of 'dirty realism', a term coined in 1983 for writings published at about that date and dealing with everyday life in a world cluttered with the oppressive debris of modern consumerism. The same term has been been applied to buildings designed by a friend of Serra, the Canadian-born architect Frank Gehry (b. 1929), working in Los Angeles. In 1970 he began to make use of such harsh industrial materials as corrugated iron, sheets in steel, zinc and copper, chain-link fencing and large exposed girders. The Vitra Design Museum erected in an industrialized wasteland outside Basel in Switzerland is typical (**22,5**). Nothing could be further removed from the ascetic geometry of the International Style, the

22,6 Bernhard and Hilla Becher, *Gas Cleaning Plants (details)*, 1988.
Gelatin silver prints, mounted, each 20 × 16ins (50.8 × 40.6cm), total 20½ × 50¾ins (52.1 × 128.9cm). Sonnabend Gallery, New York.

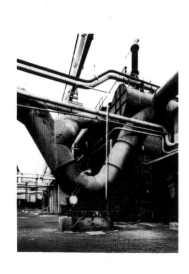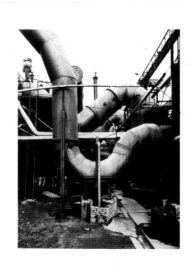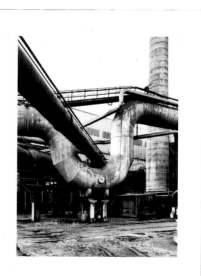

chunk of granite, all enlarged to monumental proportions (**22,7**). Executed in traditional materials, stone and cast metal, they also have traditional qualities of free-standing sculpture in the relationship of surface textures to their bold forms, which are fully revealed only when seen from a succession of viewpoints. Their relationship with the objects on which they are based is, nevertheless, equally significant, and it is this that so strikingly distinguishes them from any abstract work of sculpture conceived as a thing in itself.

The work of the American Jeff Koons (b. 1955) is far more radical and provocative. He has described himself as a 'person who is trying to lead art into the twenty-first century'. No other artist has, in fact, more brazenly and engagingly but also humorously, with a deadpan look of

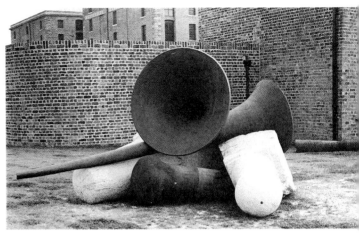

22,7 Tony Cragg, *Raleigh*, 1986–7. Cast iron and granite, 5ft 8⅞ins × 6ft 6¾ins (1.75 × 2 × 3.5m). Collection of the artist.

22,8 Jeff Koons, *New Hoover Convertibles, New Shelton Wet/Drys 5-Gallon Doubledecker*, 1980–7. Five vacuum cleaners, Plexiglas, fluorescent lights, 99 × 54 × 28ins (251.5 × 137.2 × 71.1cm).

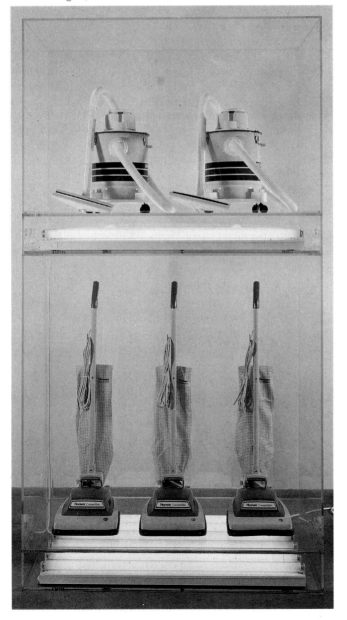

innocence, challenged the notions of art that have been current in the West for three millennia. His widely publicized works have made it more difficult than ever to evade speculation about the relationship of art to craft and mechanical production, the artist's role as maker, conceiver or appropriator, and the distinctions commonly drawn between the high art enshrined in museums and commercial art, decoration, kitsch and pornography. Such issues had of course been raised before, by Duchamp and Picabia (see pp. 803–6), by the creators of Pop Art (see p. 846), especially Warhol, and in different terms by Beuys, but always in a climate of twentieth-century aesthetic agnosticism. Koons seems to assume that they have been resolved and it is this bland assumption that such distinctions have no relevance which makes his work so disturbing.

After art-school education in Baltimore and Chicago, employment by The Museum of Modern Art in New York (selling museum memberships) and a few years as a financially successful commodities broker on Wall Street, Koons began his sudden rise to celebrity in 1979. His first works of art were plastic flowers and toys mounted on pedestals. A series called 'The New', initiated in 1980 with an exhibition at the New Museum of Contemporary Art in New York, consisted of brand new vacuum cleaners in sealed, fluorescently lit, Plexiglas cases (**22,8**). The idea of transforming utilitarian objects into art simply by selection had been started by Duchamp. Koons's cases of vacuum cleaners, however, differ from Duchamp's readymades as much in intention as appearance. The appliances have a specific meaning in that they were made for cleaning and, although unused and never to be used, embalmed in their hermetically sealed case, they will forever remain clean. Koons has declared that he was 'interested in a psychological state tied to newness and immortality, the gestalt came directly from viewing an inanimate object – a vacuum cleaner – that was in a position to be immortal'. The careful disposition of the objects behind the perfectly transparent walls of their rectangular case recalls the spare constructions of Sol LeWitt

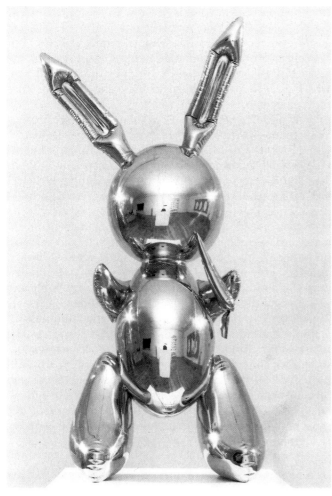

22,9 Jeff Koons, *Rabbit*, 1986. Stainless steel, 41 × 19 × 12ins (104.1 × 48.3 × 30.5cm). Anthony d'Offay Gallery, London.

'Cicciolina', he has concentrated on recording their ecstatic love making, with no holds barred, in large photographs and sculptures for which he claims a religious significance which makes them seem still more outrageous to the general public and the artistic establishment. Koons is nevertheless much closer to popular culture of the late twentieth century than the creators of Pop Art had been in the 1960s. Whereas they distanced themselves from the images they appropriated, he works with the techniques and within the structure of mass culture while coolly exposing its hidden strategies.

NEO-EXPRESSIONISM

By the early 1980s, as the controversy over the *Tilted Arc* shows, Abstraction was widely felt to have become a new orthodoxy, a specifically Modernist orthodoxy, austere and rigorously puritanical, imposed on the public by an élite of critics and museum curators. Non-representational work of the greatest refinement and quiet strength continued to be produced by such painters as Robert Ryman (b. 1930), Brice Marden (b. 1938) and Agnes Martin (b. 1912), that by the last being perhaps the most notable (**22,10**). But Abstraction and especially Minimalism aroused as fierce a reaction as had any academically approved style of the past. The usual pattern of conflict between generations sharpened and, as it were, went into reverse. Minimalist understatement, elegance and good taste, its astringency as well as its restraint – its 'anorexic aestheticism'– was confronted by a youthful, subversive but vehemently backward-looking tendency on both sides of the Atlantic. Illusionism and expressiveness were reclaimed for the creation of new figurative imagery

22,10 Agnes Martin, *The Gate 1985*, 1985. Acrylic and pencil on canvas, 6 × 6ft (1.83 × 1.83m). Courtesy, The Pace Gallery.

(21,40) even though Koons claims, 'I have always placed order in my work not out of respect for Minimalism, but to give the viewer a sense of economic security.'

Basketballs floating or suspended in glass aquarium tanks could still more easily, if deceptively, appeal to taste formed by Minimalism. In his show of 1985 entitled *Equilibrium* they were, however, exhibited together with rubber aqualungs cast in heavy bronze – for sinking rather than floating. *Rabbit* of 1986, the stainless steel cast of a child's inflatable rubber toy, similarly reverses the function of the object from which it is derived (**22,9**). What had been warm and cuddly has been transformed into something cold and resistant. And it takes on a distorted hands-off reflection of the viewer who approaches it. It invites comparisons with Brancusi's abstract metal sculptures but only to make them irrelevant. Later works exhibited under the title *Banality* are still more truculently defiant of both conventional 'good taste' and of Modernist reactions against it: sentimental porcelain figurines, wooden statuettes and posies of flowers of the kind sold in tourist souvenir shops, carved to his specifications by German craftsmen who sign them. Since 1991, when he married the Italian soft porn movie actress Illona Staller known as

together with a return to a more painterly handling of pigments. Instead of the cool and immaculate, delicately ascetic, almost antiseptic, Minimalist surface, several artists reverted to one that was quite extravagantly gestural, messy and tough looking, especially in the USA and Germany. They have been called Neo-Expressionists or practitioners of Gestural Figuration, a term that associates them with, while distinguishing them from, the gestural painting of the Abstract Expressionists.

In Italy a similar development took place at the same time. *Midnight Sun II* of 1982 by the Neapolitan painter Francesco Clemente (b. 1952) reclaims not simply figuration but symbolism, fantasy and overt eroticism (**22,11**). In his youth Clemente was much influenced by the teaching of Beuys and the paintings of Cy Twombly (see p. 857). 'What I hope to have learned from Twombly is a certain elegance and sense of editing', he has remarked. By 1980, however, Clemente had become associated with a number of other Italian figurative painters grouped as the Trans-avant-garde to suggest that they had crossed – one might say side-stepped – the path of what was then regarded as the avant-garde. He has worked, often on a grand scale, in all the traditional media – oils, gouache, pastel, mosaic, and even encaustic and fresco. Few artists have benefited more from improved facilities for travel: he now has home bases in three continents, in Rome, New York and Madras. He has also drawn inspiration from diverse sources: from Classical mythology, Christianity, Buddhism and Hinduism. In *Midnight Sun II*, eyes

floating on a field have sails like those of ships on ancient Greek vases. The two main figures are in the pose of ecstatic lovers carved on Hindu temples (6,46). But looking out from behind them there is the face of the artist himself, with almond eyes and close-cropped hair, who figures in many of his paintings, like a shaman summoning up spirits from the past.

The leading American exponent of Neo-Expressionism or Maximalism, as it is sometimes called to emphasize its anti-Minimalist impulse, is Julian Schnabel (b. 1951). His enormous *Pre History: Glory, Honor, Privilege and Poverty*, painted in oil on pony skin with antlers attached to it here and there, typifies Maximalism in its crude energy and overweening ambition as well as its total lack of inhibitions (**22,12**). At first Schnabel concentrated, or seemed to concentrate, on size and surface, building up his outsize pictures with plaster, broken crockery and urban debris as if to violate Minimalist purity and integrity of surface as brutally as possible and make weightily palpable the often enormous, overscale images. An impression of brashness and bluntness of statement is conveyed. But it is perhaps misleading. The images lour through the richly worked density of pigments without disclosing their meaning fully, if at all. Moreover, surface and image never quite combine and unite. An uneasiness lurks behind the apparent openness, an uneasiness that marks to a greater or lesser degree most of the work of the other Neo-Expressionists, notably in Germany.

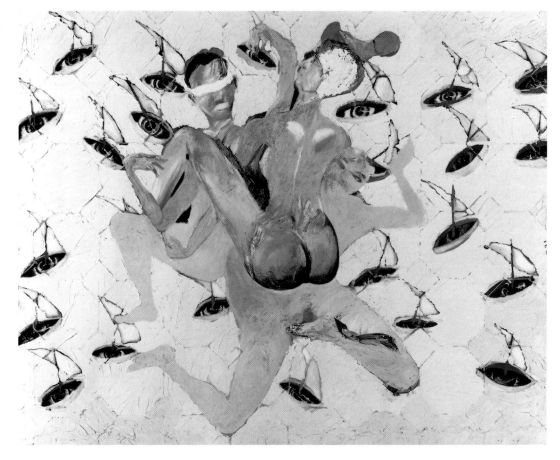

22,11 Francesco Clemente, *Midnight Sun II*, 1982. Oil on canvas, 6ft 7ins × 8ft 2½ins (2 × 2.5m). Tate Gallery, London.

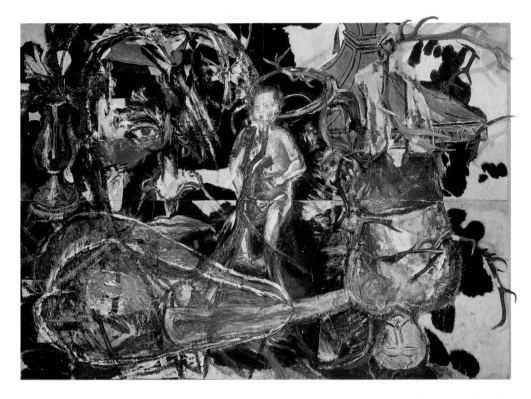

22,12 Julian Schnabel, *Pre History: Glory, Honor, Privilege and Poverty*, 1981. Oil and antlers on pony skin, 10ft 8ins × 14ft 9ins (3.24 × 4.5m). Saatchi Collection, London.

22,13 *Below* Georg Baselitz, *Mocking (Die Verspottung)*, 1984. Oil on canvas, 8ft 2½ins × 6ft 7ins (2.5 × 2m). Waddington Gallery, London.

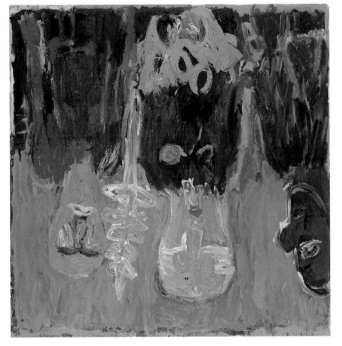

Among the *Neue Wilden* or New Savages, as they are called in Germany with overt reference to the early twentieth-century Expressionists, the most prominent is Georg Baselitz (b. 1938). Indeed the whole post-Minimal figurative and painterly movement might be said to culminate in Baselitz's assertive and single-minded art. He has always claimed that his work is essentially abstract, or rather is focused on aesthetic, pictorial problems, and has no connection with that of the Expressionists (embarrassingly resurrected at this time as exponents of German national genius, with strong political implications). But his imagery often evokes the same extreme emotional and psychological states as are found in van Gogh, Munch and Nolde, from whom his paintings also contain explicit quotations. From 1969 onwards Baselitz turned his world upside down, inverting the images in his paintings with scary consistency – ostensibly to neutralize their meaning and subjective effect. But in his work of the eighties this intention is belied by their evident seriousness and evocative power. When, as in *Supper at Dresden* of 1983 or *Mocking (Die Verspottung)* (**22,13**), with its allusion to the Mocking of Christ, or the large *Resurrection* of 1984, the image is of a kind that is deeply embedded in the viewer's visual consciousness, its inversion seems, in some mysterious way, only to increase its disturbing power. Certainly these paintings cannot be approached simply as abstractions, no matter how luscious and delectable the sheer handling of paint. They must also be understood metaphorically.

In the work of another German artist, Anselm Kiefer (b. 1945), intellectual content is predominant, even if the significance of his signifiers is sometimes deliberately arcane. His sombre, brooding, thickly worked and overlaid paintings revive taboo images: Wagnerian myths and

heroes and also, very provocatively, more recent, guilt-ridden legends and memories from the Nazi past. He has been called a 'history painter' and describes himself as 'bringing to light things that are over, that are forgotten', exposing what many would prefer to forget and leave buried. His paintings often start from photographs which not infrequently remain on the canvas overlaid with brush-strokes or scrawled with words in paint or charcoal – haunting works even when seriousness relapses into a portentous solemnity. His photographic albums, bound

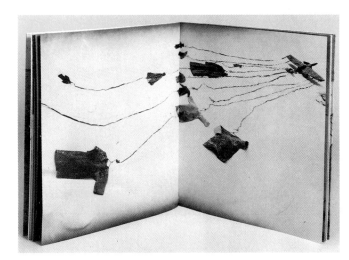

22,14 Anselm Kiefer, *Jason and the Argonauts*, 1990.
Photograph of installation.

by himself, recording sequences in the landscape or special installations in the studio, are more convincing. Saturated with the past, indeed sometimes looking as if they themselves had been buried under rubble and sediment, the detritus of an unwanted history, they powerfully convey a melancholy, elegiac mood, notably in *Jason and the Argonauts* of 1990 in which lead airplanes drag behind them charred and mangled night-shirts – childhood dreams mingling with adult nightmares (**22,14**).

If Kiefer's debt to German Romanticism and Expressionism is self-evident, Gerhard Richter's antipathy to both is no less obvious. Born in Eastern Germany in 1932, Richter moved to the Federal Republic in the West in 1960 and studied at the Academy in Düsseldorf. His two most remarkable groups of paintings, of 1988–9, combine

large non-representational diptychs suggestive of sombre forest landscapes with a series of apparently quite straightforward and conventional representational images derived from police photographs of the last days of the Baader-Meinhof or RAF (Red Army Faction), the most notorious terrorist group in post-war Germany. Their urban guerrilla warfare culminated in the kidnapping and murder of Hans Martin Schleyer, president of the German Federation of Industries, the most important representative of the power of capitalism. Eventually the leaders were caught and three of them, Andreas Baader, Gudrun Ensslin and Carl Raspe, died on the same night in their separate cells in the high-security Stammheim prison built specially to house them. According to the official version of events that night, which leaves many questions unanswered, they committed suicide. (There has never been a full enquiry into their deaths.) The title of Richter's cycle, *18 October 1977* (**22,15**), refers to the date of their common funeral.

Richter's cool, laconic, low-key approach to this deeply disturbing subject is conveyed by his carefully distanced and controlled technique as well as by the detachment inherent in working from photographs. The smooth, immaculate surfaces of the 15 paintings might seem to spurn any close involvement but their reticence and discretion, their 'ineloquence', draw the spectator slowly but all the more compulsively into the emotional and other complexities of the subject. 'I come from East Germany and am not a Marxist', Richter is reported as saying, 'so of course at the time I had no sympathy for the ideas or ideology of these people.' In fact he rejects not only their ideology but all ideologies. 'I consider every type of belief, from astrology to every higher religion and all greater ideologies, superfluous and life-threatening'; the Baader-Meinhof were important to him for symbolizing the

22,15 Gerhard Richter, *18 October 1977*, 'Shot Down (1)', 1988. Oil on canvas, 3ft 3ins × 4ft 6½ins (1 × 1.4m). Museum of Modern Art, Frankfurt am Main.

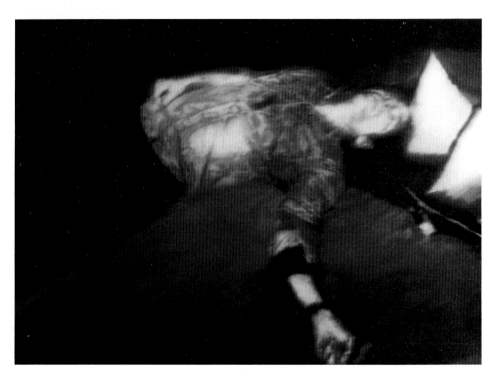

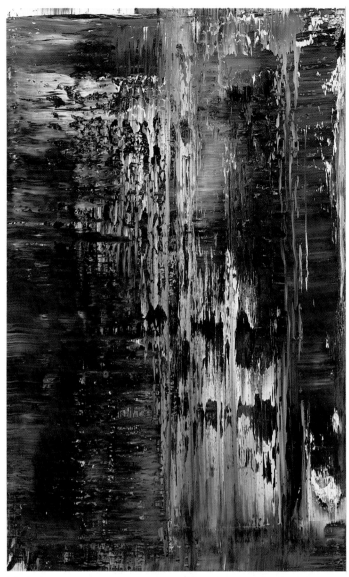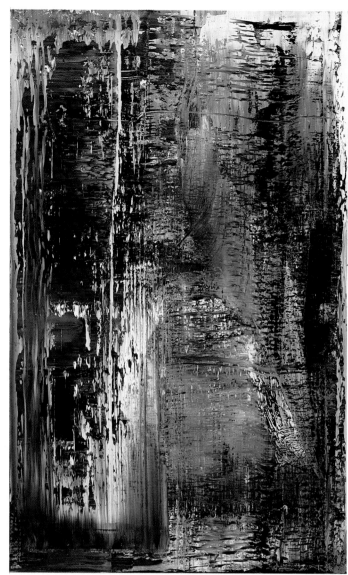

22,16 Gerhard Richter, *December*, 1989. Diptych, 10ft 6ins × 6ft 6¾ins (3.2 × 2m) each.

failure of all the idealisms and utopias of youth, especially the illusion that it is possible to change the world.

The slowly cumulative effect of the fifteen *18 October 1977* paintings, their sense of distance from the subject, their restrained and melancholy tonality, their dirge-like repetitions, all combine to create an oppressive, self-contained season of gloom which awes the viewer into silence. Their pathos lies in the absence of any declamatory gesture. They are to be understood as the equivalent of funeral music, filled with compassion for youth and its lost hopes and illusions.

Significantly, however, these sombre, deeply pessimistic paintings were followed by a group of three diptychs – *January, December* (**22,16**) and *November* – in which the artist's personal emotional involvement, previously so firmly repressed, found relief at last in 'abstraction'. Richter had for some years worked simultaneously in two divergent, apparently contradictory styles – representational and abstract – and often juxtaposed

them intentionally when his paintings were exhibited. In fact this duality or rather diversity of styles is the most remarkable aspect of his work. But the ambivalent yet compulsive relationship between the two 'modes' had never been so fully expressed as in these two groups of paintings of 1988–9. Richter has said that 'art has to do with life' and he must have agreed with Beuys, whom he knew when studying at Düsseldorf, that what is important is that art and the experience gained from art should 'flow back into life'.

While at the Düsseldorf Academy Richter made friends with a younger artist, Sigmar Polke (b. 1941), who had escaped from Communist East Germany at the age of 12. Together in the 1960s they founded what they called Capitalist Realism, though both soon abandoned it to work in different directions. Aware of American Pop Art, Polke began by using similar imagery derived from advertisements for consumer goods but in an entirely different spirit, depicting them as the objects of desire they still were in a Germany that was only beginning to recover from the deprivations of the immediate post-war period. He went on to parody Modernist styles with an engaging irony; a Color Field painting in gray and black lacquer on a rectangular canvas was inscribed as if by a typewriter: *Higher Powers command; paint the upper right corner black*. Restlessly experimental, he made use of printed furnishing or dress fabrics, even blankets as well as canvas for supports on which he painted in an astonishing variety of unconventional materials, some of which have alchemical significance. Some of the colors he used changed completely according to the light on them and he chose a few with chemical properties that ensure change according to temperature and humidity. Several of his works defy reproduction or, rather, can be reproduced only as they appear at a single moment. His experiments with media formed part of his search for new means of expression; his subject-matter is more important. *Watchtower III* of 1985, painted on canvas with silver, silver nitrate, iodine, Cobalt II, chloride and artificial resin, is one of a number of hallucinatory visions of the same subject (rendered with different materials) (**22,17**). The hut on its high scaffolding has multiple significance as a look-out for hunters (a feature of the landscape in many parts of Germany) or for soldiers guarding the frontier or the iron curtain between East and West Germany, or for the guards of

22,17 Sigmar Polke, *Watchtower III*, 1985. Silver, silver nitrate, iodine, Cobalt II, chloride and artificial resin on canvas, 9ft 10⅛ins × 7ft 4⁹⁄₁₆ins (3 × 2.25m). Staatsgalerie, Stuttgart.

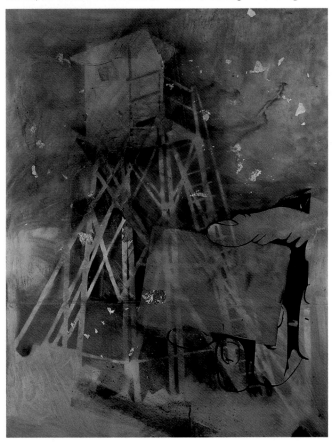

concentration camps. It looms up as a ghostly presence suggesting that the viewer of the painting is under surveillance, seen as well as seeing.

In 1988 Polke made a series of paintings in preparation for the bicentenary of the French Revolution that was to be celebrated as a mixed blessing in the following year. Using more conventional materials than usual, he concentrated on subject-matter, deriving his imagery from prints published in the early 1790s. In *Liberty, Equality, Fraternity* three severed heads are held aloft on pikes in front of a church spire. The contrast between the title and the image seems to be not merely ironical so much as a reminder of the violence with which the humanist ideals of the Enlightenment had been achieved in the Revolution, stated quite simply as a matter of fact. The other eight canvases in the series similarly record the bloodshed that was played down, if not forgotten, in the majority of bicentennial celebrations. They seem to be a response not only to the events of 1789 but to the conflicting views of liberty held in East and West Germany in 1988 and even more, perhaps, to Polke's own conception of a painting as a place of aesthetic and extra-aesthetic conflict.

ART AS IDENTITY

In 1979 Judy Chicago (b. Judy Cohen 1939), a painter of abstract floral vaginal images, exhibited *The Dinner Party*, the most elaborately emblematic feminist work of art ever made (**22,18**). She had begun some five years earlier with the idea of a dinner table set for 13 (the number of men at the Last Supper and of women in its traditional antitype, the witches' coven), with plates painted and place mats embroidered by more than 100 women under Chicago's direction. Each plate and place mat alluded to a woman who had distinguished herself in the history of Western civilization. The number was soon tripled and three tables were made, forming an equilateral triangle, a symbol of the feminine that dates back to prehistory but which had now also come to indicate the equalized world that feminists demanded. Each table referred to a chronological period: from pre-patriarchal prehistory to the end of the ancient Roman period, from the beginning of the Christian era to the Reformation, and from the seventeenth to the twentieth century. Providing an alternative to the Christian periodization (before the law, under the law and under Grace), the tables begin at the time when women had social and political control and show, as Chicago had written, 'the eventual domination of women by men, tracing the institutionalizing of that oppression and women's response to it'. The tables, set for 39 guests who include the Egyptian queen Hatshepsut (see p. 96), Georgia O'Keeffe (see p. 835) and Virginia Woolf, among other artists and writers, were placed on a floor of triangular porcelain tiles painted in gold lustre with the names of a further 999 distinguished women to suggest that those at the table 'had risen from a foundation provided by other women's accomplishments'. Butterflies, symbolizing liberation and the yearning to be free, are painted on the dinner plates. To quote Chicago herself, 'The butterfly

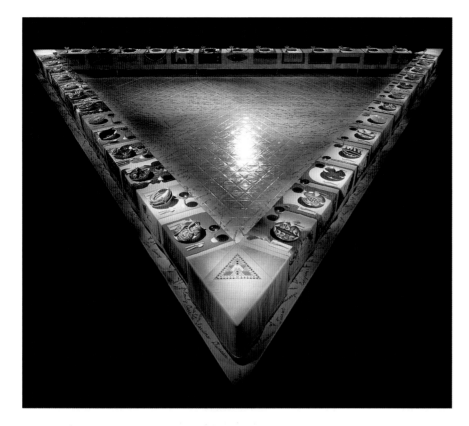

22,18 Judy Chicago, *The Dinner Party*, 1979. Multi-media, 48 × 48 × 48ft (14.63 × 14.63 × 14.63m) installed.

22,19 *Below left* Cindy Sherman, *Untitled Film Still*, 1980. Photograph.

22,20 *Below* Cindy Sherman, *Untitled No. 120*, 1983. Photograph. Courtesy of the artist and Metro Pictures.

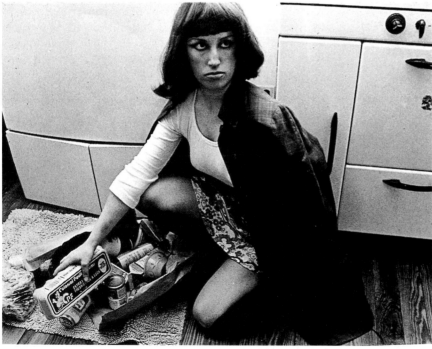

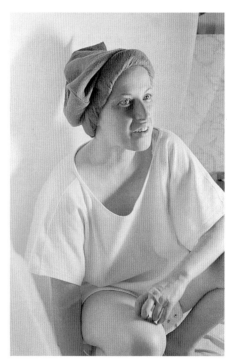

form undergoes various states of metamorphosis as the piece unfolds. Sometimes she is pinned down; sometimes she is trying to move from larva to adult state; sometimes she is nearly unrecognizable as a butterfly; and sometimes she is almost transformed into an unconstrained being . . . .' She went on to remark that the women in *The Dinner Party* 'tried to make themselves heard, fought to retain their influence, attempted to do what they wanted. They wanted to exercise the rights to which they were entitled by virtue of their birth, their talent, their genius, and their desire; but they were prohibited from doing so – were

ridiculed, ignored, and maligned by historians for attempting to do so – because they were women.'

Other feminist works of art have been less symbolic and polemical. Photography has been extensively used to create fictional narratives or to invent a theatre of the self or other works with which to identify imaginatively. Women have played a key part in these developments, especially Cindy Sherman (b. 1954) with her self-portrait photographic icons in which a fragmentary conception of the self is insidiously and sometimes very disturbingly expressed. Beginning with her 1980 series of *Untitled*

Film Stills, based on the eight-by-ten black-and-white glossy publicity print (**22,19**), but soon adopting color for much larger works (**22,20**), Sherman has manufactured a series of masks of herself based on current myths, stereotypes and media images of women, deconstructing, as it were, each female character she assumes. For her the photograph is the modern equivalent of the mask: it offers the opportunity to show all of ourselves – except one. Masquerading her various 'selves' through mocking photographic scenarios, she makes us aware that these are not just images of women but signs of difference, markers or templates of masculinity. If women are such ironic players of the 'feminine', she suggests, it is because, in their effort to elude masculine concepts of femininity, their true selves remain elsewhere. We can never reach the figure within the sign.

An entirely different strategy was developed by Jenny Holzer (b. 1950) to address wider issues than feminism from, nevertheless, a woman's viewpoint. She uses language as a medium and billboards, posters, T-shirts, tractor hats, cast bronze plaques, inscribed stones and most notably the flashing signs of light-emitting diodes (LED) as vehicles for conveying her message. 'I wanted to get context in there, something different than the content of abstract art', she said of such early works as her *Truisms*, one-line statements in capital letters of which EVERYONE'S WORK IS EQUALLY IMPORTANT, HUMANISM IS OBSOLETE and MEN ARE NOT MONOGAMOUS BY NATURE are typical. They were publicly displayed all over the city of New York and not a few were duly edited, scrawled over or erased by passersby. Out of reach, her electronic sign above Times Square in 1985–6 read PROTECT ME FROM WHAT I WANT. From 1983 she created installations. In that of 1989–90 in the Guggenheim Museum in New York, 330 of her bewilderingly banal and/or inflammatory texts – 'mock clichés', she calls them – went spiralling around the inside of Frank Lloyd Wright's building in moving yellow, green and red colored lights while others were carved on the tops of 17 granite benches (**22,21**). The juxtaposition of the quick-moving, flashing, ephemeral action of up-to-the-minute technology and the static, long-lasting, hand-engraved lettering on stone with its intimations of antiquity and mortality was, of course, an essential component of the disorienting vortex of meanings she created. 'The individual statements may be simple', she remarked of her several sequences, 'but the entire series is not, and the way single sentences play off each other is not.'

Barbara Kruger (b. 1945) also uses words as weapons aimed directly at the spectator. But her posters, photographs and installations usually include appropriated images as well. After beginning her career as a graphic designer, working on the fashion magazine *Mademoiselle* in New York, she spent four years teaching in Los Angeles and became increasingly preoccupied with the political and social issues on which her art has been focused. Although influenced, like many of her contemporaries, by the literary, social and psychological theoretical writings of Roland Barthes, Michel Foucault, Jacques Lacan and Jean Baudrillard, her individual viewpoint is expressed with a panache more typical of a world they would not wish to be associated with – that of public relations. Its manipulative practices are skillfully turned against themselves in her attacks on political and commercial

22,21 Jenny Holzer, *Installation 'Jenny Holzer'*, 1989–90. Solomon R. Guggenheim Museum, New York. Extended helical tricolor LED signboard and 17 Indian red granite benches.

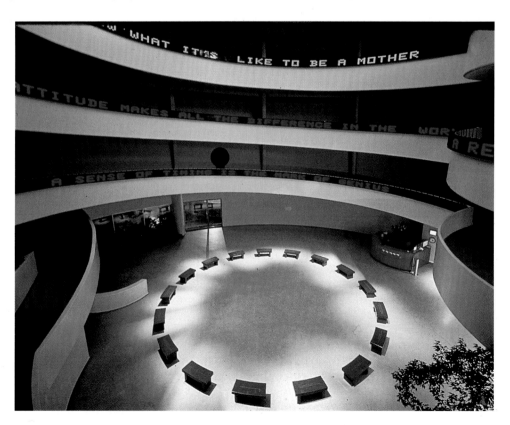

manipulation. Her phrases are as terse as the most effective slogans used in commercial advertising and the visual images combined with them just as eye-catching and memorable. A hand holds a red card with white lettering, 'I shop therefore I am' – an adaptation of Descartes's famous dictum (see p. 574) – on a photographic silk-screen print to define consumption as the mark of identity, replacing thought in a world dominated by consumerism. 'We don't need another hero' is printed across a poster, displayed in Europe as well as the USA, showing a girl pointing to the flexed muscles of a small boy who might in another context be promoting some medicine to increase virility. 'Do I have to give up me to be loved by you?' floats on an anatomical color photograph of a living human heart. Invariably Kruger has used ungendered pronouns – I, you, we – assuming the gender of the writer and reader while also recognizing that the place of the viewer in language is unsettled and unaligned. Many of her works refer directly to the arts. Beside a photograph of the profile of a marble bust of a woman, the words 'Your gaze hits the side of my face' are a reminder that in most works of Western art women have been depicted for the delectation of men, and also that the gaze has the power to arrest, to petrify, its object. 'You Invest in the Divinity of the Masterpiece' is inscribed on a detail of the hands in Michelangelo's *Creation of Adam* (11,29) in a work that is a critique of the commodification of art and at the same time of the notion of artistic creativity as masculine (**22,22**). The most famous image of patriarchy in Western art is deconstructed.

In this and many other ways women artists have reacted against an iconography reflecting and perpetuating gender distinctions within the structure of patriarchal culture. Miriam Schapiro (b. 1923), who had begun by working in the dominant language of formalist abstraction, turned in the 1970s to combine painting with *collages* of textiles which she called *Femmages*, a word invented to include assemblage, *découpage*, photomontage, 'as they were practiced by women using traditional women's techniques to achieve their art – sewing, piercing, hooking, cutting, appliquéing, cooking and the like – activities also engaged in by men but assigned in history to women'. The strategy of subverting a stereotype by changing its context has been adopted by African American women in protest against racism and sexism at the same time. In the 1980s Faith Ringgold (b. 1930), a painter, took up quilting, a traditional craft practised exclusively by women throughout North America. Each of a series of large panels entitled *Bitter Nest* combines multicolored triangles of fabric (like those composing a normal quilt) with paintings in acrylic illustrating the story of a black woman doctor told in neat handwriting on columns running down each side (**22,23**). Her other story quilts refer to slavery, the murder of children in Atlanta, street life in New York and to the writers and musicians of the Harlem Renaissance of the 1920s. Quilting appears originally to have been introduced into America from Africa by slaves, and Ringgold, proud of her ancestry on the other side of the Atlantic, has made use of imported African textiles in these works.

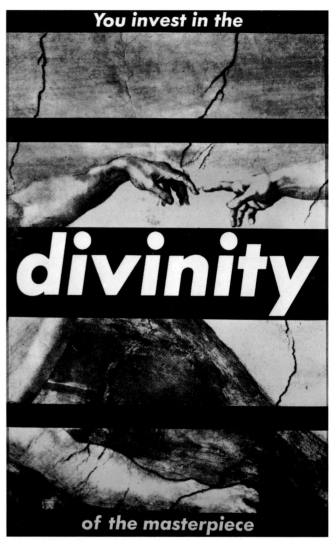

22,22 Barbara Kruger, *Untitled (You Invest in the Divinity of the Masterpiece)*, 1982. Unique photostat, 5ft 11¾ins × 3ft 9⅝ins (1.82 × 1.16m), with frame, 6ft ⅞in × 3ft 10¾ins (1.86 × 1.19m). The Museum of Modern Art, New York (Acquired through an anonymous fund).

The politics of gender, race and class have been addressed in a different way, and from the viewpoint of a homosexual man, by Robert Gober (b. 1954). He does not so much call for liberation as expose a social structure dominated by heterosexual men. Nor is his work in any way a celebration of homoerotic desire; rather the reverse. The male body is shown only in part in his installations, truncated, lying down fully dressed with candles stuck in it, or vulnerably naked and pierced with drain holes, suggesting perhaps life draining away from an AIDS victim. His pious Roman Catholic background may account for his attitude to his sexual orientation and also for his extensive use of symbols: votive candles, kitchen sinks in which guilt may be washed away. The polished metal drain filter-head he includes in many of his works, almost as a signature, has a cross at its centre. Other everyday domestic objects are transformed by him into complex symbols in installations which recall Surrealist paintings but are rather more disturbing: they engulf the visitor in an environment of equivocal symbolism.

22,23 Faith Ringgold, *Bitter Nest Part II: Harlem Renaissance Party*, 1988. Acrylic on canvas, printed, tie-dyed and pieced fabrics, 7ft 10ins × 6ft 10ins (2.39 × 2.08m). Faith Ringgold, Inc.

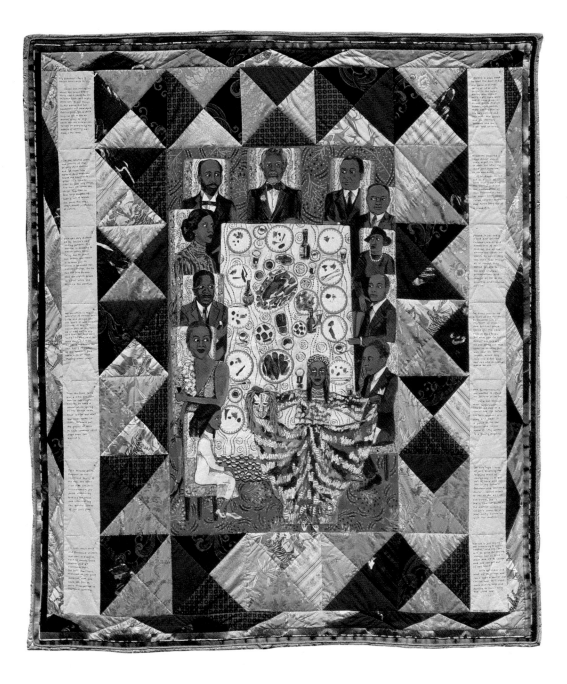

A room first set up in the Paula Cooper Gallery, New York, in 1989 has as its centrepiece a white satin bridal dress of the kind which, according to male orthodoxy, every young woman aspires to wear (**22,24**). It is beautifully made, stitched by Gober himself, who insisted on doing what is normally regarded as women's work. There is, however, no body inside; the dress is hollow, a sham. Its whiteness is a very ancient symbol of virginal purity, but its train drags in the dirt. Propped against the walls of the room there are bags (in fact modelled in plaster and painted by Gober) boldly labelled *Cat Litter*, material to absorb bad smells which, in the context created by Gober, refer to married life. The bags of cat litter were, Gober has said, 'to a large degree a metaphor for the couple's intimacy – that when you make a commitment to an intimate relationship that involves taking care of the

other person's body in sickness and health . . . . I was juxtaposing a low symbol with a high symbol and a deflated symbol with an inflated one.' The delicately colored yellow and blue wallpaper, which may seem at first sight to have been made for some cosy middle-class parlour, has repeated motifs of a white man sleeping and a lynched black man hanging from a tree. Is the one having guilty nightmares about the other? Or is he ignoring his plight? Or are they both victims of the same social system? 'You can't quite pin it down', Gober remarked of the meaning of this combination of images which 'yields so many different responses about what is happening . . . . And then something's literally missing in the story, if you look at it as a story – and you kind of have to. You have to supply that; what was the crime, what really happened, what's the relationship between these two men?'

In England Gilbert and George (Gilbert Proesch, b. 1943, and George Passmore, b. 1942) are the most notable of the artists who have broken away from abstract aestheticism to engage in self-identification. They were known first as performance artists for their 'Singing Sculptures' in which they used themselves as art material, as had Conceptual artists like Yves Klein and Vito Acconci, albeit in their own distinctive way, nattily dressed in formal three-piece suits and singing a popular song of the 1930s. In the late 1970s they embarked on photopieces which addressed contemporary social, racial and sexual issues directly and even provocatively – and were somewhat marginalized by the establishment for that reason. Their work cuts too near the bone. In the most impressive of these extraordinary, often mammoth size tableaux, such as *Death after Life* of 1984, which is over 45 feet (13.7m) long – a size that precludes satisfactory reproduction – they created a psychedelic dreamworld of industrial pollution, in a spiritual rather than a physical sense, prominently figuring themselves as if living through the troubles of modern life for our edification, like preacher painters in the past who had visions and then illustrated them. More complex and, perhaps, more truly 'innocent', they have a deeply Romantic low-church Protestant approach in these visual sermons, which in their earnestness recall Victorian stained glass windows expounding texts from Ruskin and William Morris.

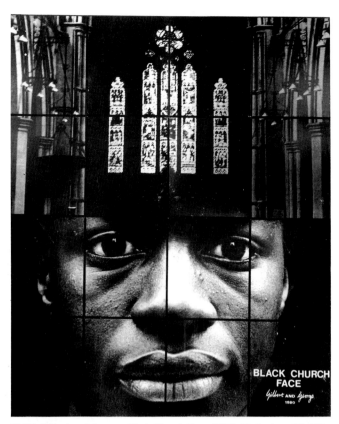

22,25 Gilbert and George, *Black Church Face*, 1980. Photopiece, 7ft 11ins × 6ft 7ins (2.42 × 2.01m). Michael Sonnabend Collection, New York.

22,24 Robert Gober, *Cat Litter*, 1989. Installation, Paula Cooper Gallery, New York.

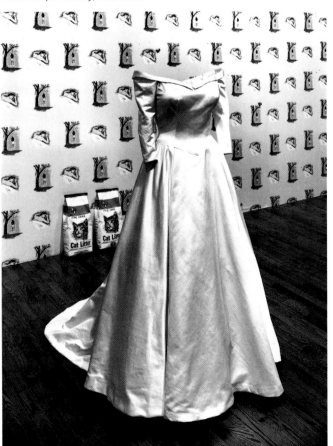

If sometimes stiff and awkward, works by Gilbert and George are imposing and moving in a way that is not easy to explain. In *Black Church Face*, for instance, the images of a black youth full-face and, above, that of the interior of some disused suburban London Neo-Gothic church coalesce in a subliminal way, with many layers of possible meanings (**22,25**). Is the open, trusting gaze about to be wiped off the face of the black youth by a sanctimonious Church? Or is it simply about to be crushed by the white man's empty legacy of a decaying civilization? Or is the white man's burden now about to be inherited and re-animated by good black blood? In the USA it could have other and no less relevant meanings. Or is it, after all, intended non-racially, just as the political and sexual photopieces by Gilbert and George may be intended non-politically and non-sexually in order to achieve aesthetic autonomy in this way? 'To be with Art is all we ask' has become their greeting card motto (with still further possibilities for ambiguity).

Much of the young British art ('yBa' so-called) of the 1990s is similarly ambiguous and similarly obsessed by the sex-and-violence and other criminal or semi-criminal symptoms of decaying big-city centres, likewise by an urge to address 'real life' social issues. Rachel Whiteread (b . 1963), for example, made concrete casts of the interior walls of a three-story Victorian row-house scheduled for demolition so that they would remain when the original brickwork, doors and windows were removed, leaving a record or rather a memorial, not so much of the building

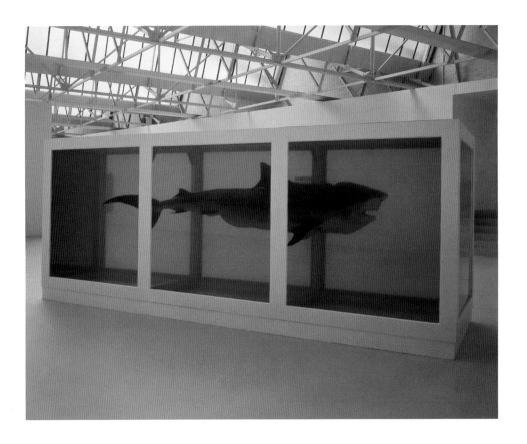

22,26 Damien Hirst, *The Physical Impossibility of Death in the Mind of Someone Living*, 1991. Tiger shark, glass, steel, 5% formaldehyde solution, 7 × 17 × 7ft (2.75 × 8 × 2.75m). Saatchi Collection, London.

as of the lives that had been confined within it. It provoked thought not merely about artistic form and content but about urban destruction and renewal and the plight of the deprived. Perhaps significantly, it was to be demolished partly in response to opposition in a working-class area. Whiteread has also made casts in colored translucent resin of the spaces under chairs, converting voids into solids that have a transitory appearance and evoke ideas of presence and absence, life and death. The work of Damien Hirst (b. 1965) is more violently disturbing. In 1990, he exhibited *A Thousand Years*, a large glass case divided into two compartments in one of which flies are born, feed off a putrefying cow's head, mate and pass into the other chamber where they are killed by a blue-light 'insect-o-cutor' of the type used in butcher's shops. His titles, so far from being merely descriptive, form part of each work, giving it a further dimension. *The Physical Impossibility of Death in the Mind of Someone Living*, for example, gives to a 14-foot (4.26m) tiger shark floating in a formaldehyde solution like a specimen in a natural history museum a new meaning outside and beyond science. The viewer is made to wonder at its immaculate streamlined form and terrifying open jaws (**22,26**). *Some Comfort Gained from the Acceptance of the Inherent Lies in Everything* is Hirst's ambiguous 1996 title for the sections of a cow's body preserved in 12 glass cases between which viewers walk, enthralled or repelled by the congealed complexity of its exposed organism. For such works the context – and the presence of an exhibition-going public – is crucial. However, there is a gap between a work that acknowledges the role of context and one that asserts that art is totally context dependent, i.e. by where and how it is installed.

POST-MODERN MULTICULTURALISM

During the second half of the twentieth century an increasing number of African American, Native American, Latino American and Asian American artists not only resisted acculturation but found new ways of expressing themselves without either severing links with their own traditions or ignoring global developments in Modernism and Post-Modernism. David Hammons (b. 1943) is among the most notable. He was born at Springfield, Illinois, and trained mainly as a commercial artist in Los Angeles but soon began making assemblages that contrasted the Stars and Stripes with emblems of racial and cultural stereotypes. In 1974 he moved to Manhattan, abandoned making saleable artifacts and turned to installations incorporating African American hair and such urban detritus as chicken bones, paper bags and empty bottles. These were shown at the non-profit 'Just Above Midtown' gallery where such works were acceptable to a public that responded to Joseph Beuys. Beuys visited New York in 1974. Whether or not Hammons was directly influenced by him, it was in the same year that he took his art from the gallery to the streets where, he said, 'the audience is much more human and their opinion is from the heart'. On vacant lots and other sites in Brooklyn, Lower Manhattan and Harlem, he set up assemblages that combined African cult objects with local junk to create an ongoing experience of life in the USA. Addressing his work to his fellow African Americans, he often alluded to basketball, the 'poverty game' that is cheap to play, demands skill and has been a route to success for many young black men. In Harlem in 1983 he set up a telephone pole topped with a basketball hoop, entitling it *Higher Goals*.

When invited to take part in the 1991 exhibition of temporary installations at Charleston, South Carolina, to be entitled 'Places with a Past', he discovered that although the city had an important place in the history of African Americans – who made up 56 percent of the population – few were to be involved in the show. For a site in their residential area he thought up a ramshackle house in the style of Southern black dwellings as his contribution to the exhibition. In the course of construction it evolved functionally into a permanent learning centre where young people of the neighbourhood could develop a sense of pride in their culture; it was called *House of the Future* (**22,27**). Architectural elements were assembled from the district: a doorcase, window frames, weatherboarding, columns, railing and three types of roof covering. A can of pineapple juice, alluding to the carved pineapples that grace the entrance gates of many upper-class houses in Charleston, was hung in the gable. The upper floor became a studio for a young painter, Larry Jackson. A quotation from the African American Ishmael Reed was painted on the back of the house: 'The Afro American has become heir to the myths that it is better to be poor than rich, lower class than middle or upper, easy going rather than industrious, extravagant rather than thrifty, and athletic rather than academic.' On the opposite side of the house, Hammons laid out a small garden in which he planted a tall flag-pole to fly his version of the Stars and Stripes in the red, black and green colors of Black Nationalists. And he replaced advertisements for cigarettes with a large photograph of local children gazing hopefully up to the studio. No recent work of art conveys its message with greater earnestness and directness.

An installation set up in the Museum of Contemporary Hispanic Art, New York, in 1985 by Jorge Rodriguez (b. 1944), a Puerto Rican, and Charles Abramson (1945–87), an African American, is far more complex in its imagery but no less compelling. It was entitled *Orisha/ Santos: An Artistic Interpretation of the Seven African Powers* (**22,28**). Abramson was a *santero*, or priest of the Santeria religion, a synthesis of Roman Catholic and African cults which was originated by slaves in Brazil and the Caribbean and now has some 100,000,000 adherents in Latin America and 5,000,000 in the USA. The *Orisha/ Santos* installation assembled objects of the kind placed on altars in the homes of believers together with curling steel sheet sculptures made for the occasion by Rodriguez. The seven African powers of the title are Elegua, Ogun, Obatala, Orunia, Ochun, Yemaya and Shango – gods of the crossroads, war, peace, divination, erotic love, maternal love and fire – represented according to the iconography of Catholic saints. Yemaya, goddess of maternal love, thus appears in the guise of the Madonna and Child. By such means slaves had disguised the African deities to whom they prayed while appearing to conform to the Christian faith to which they had been involuntarily converted. Nowadays in the USA, Santeria remains a religious cult

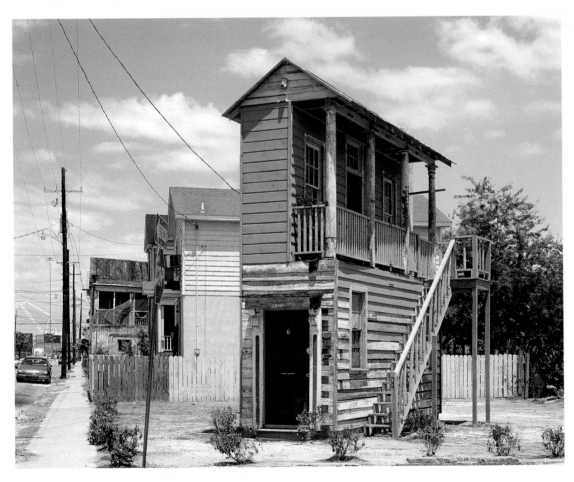

22,27 David Hammons, *House of the Future*, Charleston, South Carolina, 1991.

but is also a means by which Latino immigrants preserve their identity, enabling them to retain links with the places of their own or their parents' birth and their remote ancestry on the other side of the Atlantic. *Orisha/Santos* is a public testimony to the continuing vitality of Puerto Rican culture and its ability to absorb influences from European American art, both iconographically and conceptually. Juan Sanchez (b. 1954), born in New York but a supporter of Puerto Rican *independistas*, has deconstructed neo-colonialism in his mixed media Ricanstructures; Native American artists, on the other hand, such as Jaune Quick-to-See Smith (b. 1940), have equally effectively taken over techniques from European art, which had so often appropriated their images. There were, of course, precedents for this creative synthesizing from different points of departure.

In an international, intercontinental context of global media and global markets in which the industrial products of the West and Japan are prominent and ubiquitous, cultural frontiers are being eroded and forms of global art seem imminent. Reactions by individual artists to these

developments have been diverse, nowhere more so than in heavily industrialized, economically boyant Japan. National costumes are still worn there, mainly by women, on formal occasions in cities of towering skyscrapers, while Western-dressed businessmen with international connections take part in the Zen-inspired tea-ceremony. Japanese designers of consumer goods and their packaging are recognized as among the most sophisticated in the world while, at the same time, practitioners of the traditional arts of pottery, weaving, lacquer and doll-making are equally honored in Japan, where they are officially called 'Holders of Important Intangible Cultural Properties' though more usually known as 'Living National Treasures'.

There had been no word for 'visual art' in Japanese until the late nineteenth century, when translators of Western languages devised one: *bijutsu*. This means literally 'technique of beauty'. Subsequently, a distinction was drawn between national and foreign techniques and styles. Students in Japanese art schools still have to choose between a course in *nihonga* – traditional ink-and-

22,28 Jorge Rodriguez and Charles Abramson, *Orisha/Santos: An Artistic Interpretation of the Seven African Powers*, 1985. Installation at the Museum of Contemporary Hispanic Art, New York.

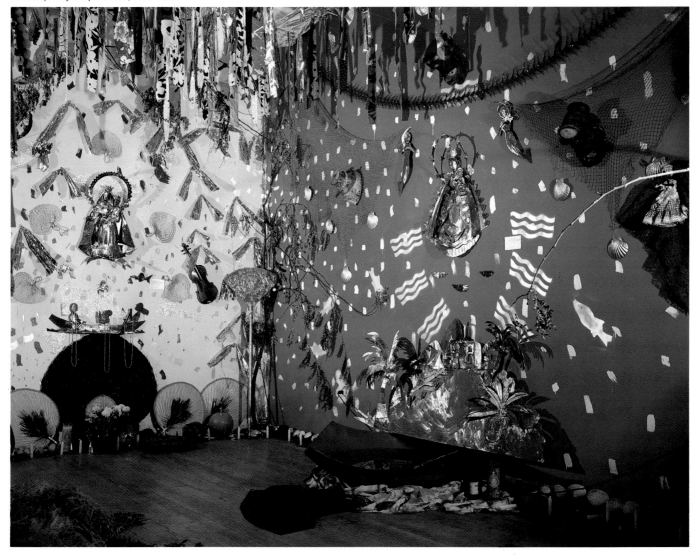

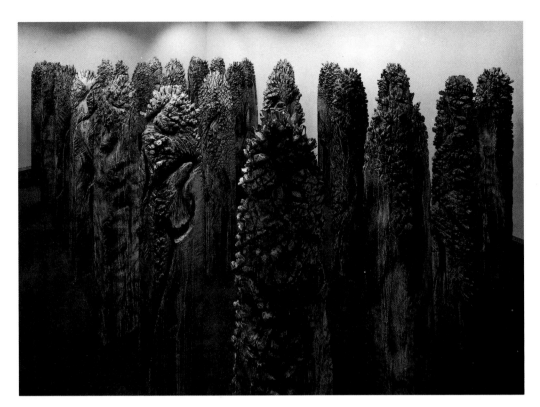

22,29 Shigeo Toya, *Woods*, 1987. Acrylic and wood, 83⅞ins × 11¾ins (213 × 29.8cm). Ludwig Forum für Internationale Kunst, Aachen.

wash painting – or in *yoga* – drawing from plaster casts of Classical Greek and Roman sculpture and the life model. For each of these types of art there are mutually incompatible support structures, galleries and markets. However, several artists who recently opted out of the system, refusing either to follow styles little altered since the late eighteenth century or to be submerged by contemporary currents from the West, have succeeded in re-inventing Japanese art.

Woods by Shigeo Toya (b. 1947), a group of 28 wooden pillars each nearly 7 feet (2.1m) high, ranked in a regularly spaced cohort, owes little if anything to Western art (**22,29**) except, of course, for the recognition of sculpture's non-naturalistic possibilities. Even in the West the idea of assembling such an installation was relatively recent. Crudely worked, cut with a chain-saw and unpolished, these boldly textured forms share that feeling for organic materials which had been a distinguishing feature of Japanese art for centuries, associated with Buddhist and Shinto attitudes to nature. They bring to mind the rough pottery vessels made for the tea-ceremony (see p. 569), the rocks in a raked sand garden of a Zen monastery, the woodwork of a Shinto shrine. Knots of the tree-trunk among the carved excrescences of the surface reveal the structure of the wood, emphasized also by the application of dark acrylic paint and wood ash to heal incisions. Apparently rising through the floor on which they stand, they create a feeling of reverence and terror experienced in a dark forest in which primal forces of growth and decay, creation and destruction, life and death, are subliminally present. From each one a deeply scarred, haggard human face looks out, above the eye-level of spectators and as if, also, above the concerns of humanity. Toya says that he

was inspired by a storm-tossed forest in which the trees seemed to writhe and moan like living beings. He has associated *Woods* also with the chimney stacks of crematoria where the last rites are performed for the majority of Japanese.

Yasumasa Morimura (b. 1951) has responded to the cult and commodification of Western art in Japan by appropriating and subverting its images. He challenges both Western and Japanese notions of good taste and, indeed, of art itself. Like most of his compatriots his knowledge of European painting was limited to reproductions of late nineteenth-century French pictures supplemented by a few originals bought by Japanese collectors for world record prices and with world-wide publicity. Selecting revered icons of early modern art by Manet and others, he reconstructed their settings in plaster and photographed himself made-up and dressed or undressed in the poses of their figures. (Recently he has worked from transparencies of the paintings and using computer technology inserted his image in digitized files to produce prints.) In his version of Manet's *Olympia* (see pp. 714–5), which he entitled *Portrait (Twin)*, he took the place of both Olympia and the black servant (**22,30**). The result has several layers or interwoven threads of significance. Most obviously it is a witty travesty of a picture known for its painterly qualities but made over-familiar from flat reproductions which obliterate all trace of the expressive brushwork. Prostitution, the true subject of the original work, is associated by Morimura with the commodification of art; and he goes on to cross gender and ethnic frontiers as well. Transvestitism is, of course, institutionalized in Japan in the Kabuki theatre where the female parts are taken by male actors who are, however, always

22,30 Yasumasa Morimura, *Portrait (Twin)*, 1988. Photograph, 6ft 10⅝ins × 9ft 10⅛ins (2.1 × 3m). Collection of the artist (Courtesy, Luhring Augustine, New York).

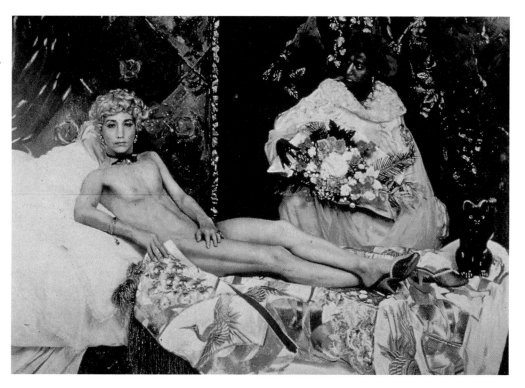

voluminously clothed. There is a taboo on nude figures in Japanese 'fine art' although they figure in popular *Ukiyo-e* prints, some of which are explicitly pornographic and banned from public exhibition. Morimura's ethnic crossover may also allude to the nowadays common Japanese practice of having portrait photographs doctored to Westernize the eyes, as well as to the more costly plastic surgery for the same purpose. *Portrait (Twin)* is, however, more than a light-hearted satire on contemporary Japanese fashions in life and art. It undermines the stability of *genres*, genders and genes as understood in the West as well as Japan.

New forms of artistic expression have been developed recently in China from a background not unlike that of Japan, different though the two countries are in their political, social and economic histories. After the fall of the Qing dynasty in 1912, oil painting and the training methods of European academies were introduced in China as part of an official policy of modernization, equated with Westernization. Many artists went on working in ink and wash, continuing a tradition that has survived, with individual modifications only, to the present day. An art that had been practised in the past exclusively by and for an élite was, however, regarded by Mao Zedong as anti-revolutionary. In 1942 he had called for a style of painting that would be 'closely linked with the masses; give expression to their thoughts and feelings and serve as their loyal spokesman'. His preference was for oil paintings and prints in a style he called Socialist Idealism (rather than Socialist Realism as in Russia), dedicated to the heroization of the Party and especially himself.

Under the Communist régime established in 1949, artists who refused to comply were marginalized. During the Cultural Revolution of 1966–76 they were persecuted, but immediately afterwards allowed to work undisturbed. Practitioners of traditional techniques still found favour with the Party leaders, who focused their hostile attention on the activities of younger artists 'corrupted' by foreign influences. Until 1980 very little was known in China about recent Western art except that it was a product of bourgeois capitalism. Gradually, however, illustrated books and periodicals began to circulate and works by European artists were shown in exhibitions; those by the socially committed Käthe Kollwitz (19,12) and by Picasso, a member of the Communist Party, attracted most attention. Robert Rauschenberg's travelling exhibition of his own works dedicated to world peace, Overseas Cultural Interchange, went on view in Beijing in 1985 and in the course of the next five years Chinese artists became aware of ideas and the means of expressing them developed in the West over the best part of a century. Expressionism, Dada, abstract art, Surrealism, Action Painting, Minimalism, Pop Art and Land Art all provided points of departure for experiment, as well as much facile imitation. There were explosions of artistic energy that had been repressed by hallowed traditions as well as by the official policy of Mao's government. Illustrated periodicals informed artists of what was taking place in Chinese cities far distant from one another. After three years of preparation a large exhibition, 'China/ Avant-garde', representing all current non-academic artistic trends, was mounted in the Chinese National Gallery, Beijing, in February 1989. It included installations and photographs of performance art as well as drawings in pen and ink and oil paintings. A rope extending through the building was provided by artists in the southern coastal town of Xiamen and bore labels inscribed 'Xiamen Dada'. The exhibition opened to the sound of gunshot as two artists fired at their own works and, as a result of further happenings, it was twice closed by the police during its two-week run. Three months later artists took an active part in the massive political demonstration in Tiananmen Square which was suppressed by the army on 4 June. A clampdown on all forms of art tending towards Westernization or expressing 'bourgeois liberalism' immediately followed but was relaxed in 1992.

Fang Lijun (b. 1963) was one of the youngest artists represented in the 'China/Avant-garde' exhibition in 1989, the year he graduated from the Beijing Academy's faculty of graphic reproduction. After beginning with small figurative paintings in grisaille he developed a strikingly individual style. His pictures of bald men rendered in a light-toned palette of white, blues and pink are disturbing and memorable, brutal and delicate at the same time (**22,31**). These men, uniformly dressed, have uniform smiles of threatening inanity on their scrubbed pink faces. 'To paint the human body I use unmixed paint, sold by the manufacturers under the name "flesh color"', he said. 'If it appears absurd to the eye, it proves just how absurd we are in many of the ideas we regard as natural; paint manufacturers only produce "flesh color" world-wide in this way because the vast majority believes that flesh looks like that.' His art is ostensibly one of political 'no comment' but it mocks the attempt to regiment the multiethnic population of the People's Republic. Fang Lijun and others of his age group, are called by their elders a lost generation; and he replies: 'This is nonsense put about by others who want us to think, live and function so well that we satisfy their egotistic needs like their battery

22,31 Fang Lijun, *Group Two No. 3*, 1992.
Oil on canvas, 6ft 6¾ins × 6ft 6¾ins (2 × 2m). Collection of the artist.

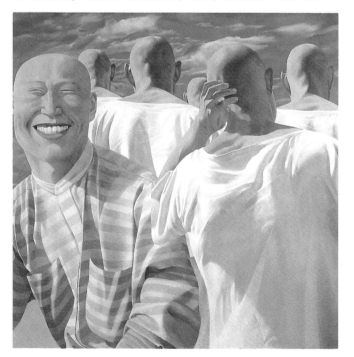

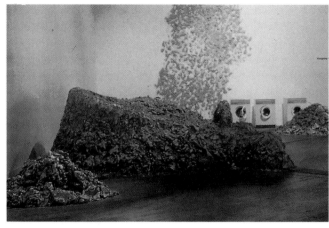

22,32 Huang Yongping, *Reptiles*, 1989. Washing machines and papier mâché, 46 × 23 × 13ft (14 × 7 × 4m). Installation, at 'Les Magiciens de la terre', 1989. Centre Georges Pompidou. Grande halle de la villette, Paris.

hens. But we will not do it. We neither obey the rules of life imposed by them nor collect a salary as public servants as they do. But we do not starve, we have more money than they do, are more relaxed and happy, have more women and have time to have fun and travel. That is why we are called the lost generation. But deep in their hearts the people think that we are a generation that should be shot.'

Huang Yongping (b. 1954) was one of the founders of the Xiamen Dada group represented in the 'China/Avant-garde' exhibition of 1989 but emigrated to Paris in the same year. The originators of Dada had attacked the bourgeois materialism of Europe (see p. 802), but Huang Yongping adopted their strategies in an entirely different socio-political climate to express ideas inspired by Ludwig Wittgenstein's philosophy of language, the Deconstructionists and other works by Michel Foucault and Jacques Derrida (translated into Chinese in the 1980s), and still more by the irrationalism of Taoism and Chan or Zen Buddhism. In 1987 he put the pages of a history of Chinese art and the translation of a history of modern art in the West into a washing machine and exhibited the mangled remains as a cleansed amalgam of Eastern and Western culture. Expanding on this theme, he created *Reptiles* (**22,32**), an installation for the 'Magiciens de la terre' exhibition in Paris in 1989, lining up washing machines against the wall and placing in front of them heaps of pulped Chinese and French Communist newspapers in the form of a giant turtle, an emblem of immortality often carved as a gravestone in China. 'What history has left is a large mass of writings and texts', he wrote in the same year. 'We are in the middle of a large rubbish heap, underneath we find culture – philosophy, religion and art. It can be manipulated and sorted out at will. If you do not raise this from the garbage (our history, our thinking and our culture) you will be oppressed by different theories, values and readings.' The global relevance of his Deconstructive art is confirmed by the installations he has exhibited in Belgium, England, Germany, Italy, Japan and the USA.

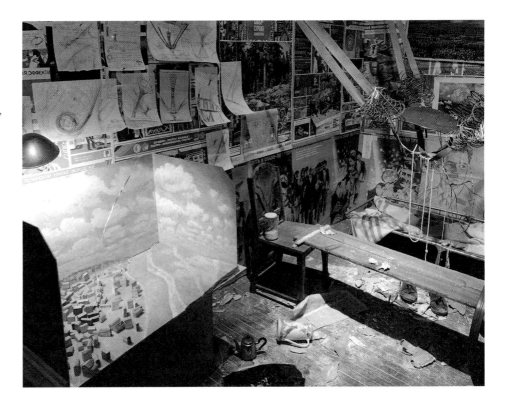

22,33 Ilya Kabakov, *The Man who Flew into Space from his Apartment*, 1981–8. Installation. From *Ten Characters*, Ronald Feldman Fine Arts, 1988. Photo: James Dee, Courtesy, Ronald Feldman Fine Arts, New York.

Installations have since the early 1980s become the most effective vehicles not so much for artistic expression as for the release of artists' demands, hopes, frustrations and fears. Ilya Kabakov (b. 1933) is among those who have created environments of deeply personal yet widely relevant significance. He was born and grew up under Stalin's rule in the Soviet Union, where he led an artistic double life. While employed as a book illustrator acceptable to the régime, he found an outlet for his dissidence in drawing and paintings executed with the skills he had acquired as a Socialist Realist graphic artist. In the course of a decade and a half he compiled some 70 'albums' (in fact boxes) in which he mounted on cards of uniform size his interrelated illustrations of contemporary daily life, records of extraordinary events and evocations of the inner turmoil and manias of people striving to 're-order the universe', together with such written texts as philosophical and religious commentaries summarizing conflicting moral standards, quotations from Russian literary classics and also reports made by Soviet citizens about one another.

Since leaving Russia for the West in 1988, he has re-used many of these sheets in installations such as *The Man who Flew into Space from his Apartment* (**22,33**). Though he makes little, if any, distinction between image and text, his installations are not simply assemblages of them. In an interview in 1992 he remarked: 'I am primarily occupied with the relationship between the object and space, the place of the object in space, and that space does not entirely absorb the object, so that the relationships between them turn out to be problematic. My installations are dedicated to an elucidation of these relationships – the formal problems coincide here with purely personal ones.' He speaks of packaging the emotional content of his work in 'sufficiently rigid, constructive form that I call "total installation"'. It is 'important in the formal sense that I use in my installations things that were supplanted during the era of minimalism: a plot, literature, live speech, human content. These things have been forgotten, they have "rested" well for a time and therefore they can be constructively used again. Thus, content and purely formal problems here are closely intertwined.' (From 'A Conversation with Ilya Kabakov and Boris Goys' in *Parkett* 34, 1992, pp. 35–9).

The Man who Flew into Space from his Apartment is a shattered room in a Russian tenement, littered with the careful drawings of machines invented by its occupant, a crazy reincarnation of Leonardo da Vinci, who has catapulted himself through the ceiling. Kabakov began to make the drawings and invent the story in the early 1980s before he had been allowed to travel outside the Soviet Union to what then seemed to him and to many Russians the paradise in the West. The installation exhibited in Paris in 1989 is not, however, simply a record of disillusion with the Communist utopia, still less of the frustrations of life under a system that was disintegrating. It gained rather than lost as a result of subsequent political events. For its subject is the unresolved conflict between the desire for a rational (even if utopian) social order and the yearning for an unrestricted (even if self-destructive) personal freedom. This has been a recurrent theme in Russian literature from Tolstoy and Dostoyevsky to the present day and, like the great nineteenth-century novels set in Russia, has world-wide relevance. Kabakov has told his story of the man who flew into space in words, as he has other similar narratives of escape. In his installations, however, the realism, irony and fantasy of the stories are unfolded visually without any apparent intervention by the author, which allows the images to reverberate against one another.

VIDEO ART

In a world in which television has become the principal conditioner of opinion, belief and prejudice – and also, in close circuit for monitoring, a potentially ever-present eye – artists have discovered in video installations a new and unprecedented art form. We watch and are watched on TV screens that supposedly cannot lie. Andy Warhol shot some video films in the early 1960s. Nam June Paik (b. 1932), Korean-born but active mainly in the USA, began in 1963 to exploit the medium for sequences of non-representational images. His *TV Clock*, for instance, consisted of 24 monitor screens each showing a Zen-inspired colored band at a slightly different angle. Like Warhol and also the artists who organized and filmed happenings in China and elsewhere, Paik treated the video camera as an extension of the artist's eye, and the screen as the equivalent of a painting. It was not until much later that the great and completely innovatory artistic potential of video was recognized, enabling video installation artists to exploit fully its power as metaphor and to create a new kind of metaphoric 'narrative'. Later still this was to be taken a step further. Only in the late 1980s was it realized that video mimics not the eye but the mind, the process not of sight but of thought. With this remarkable discovery, video installation artists such as Bill Viola (b. 1951) and Gary Hill (b. 1951) have made it a medium that can capture the stream of consciousness. Their recognition of the difference between purely retinal stimulations and the flow of images called up by thought, or by literature or music, has enabled them to explore the myriad possibilities of the new medium. These go far beyond the purely visual and both artists have abandoned abstraction, with which they began, in favour of the human figure and natural phenomena, with which they induce in the viewer various and deepening states of contemplation. Viola, directly inspired by both Christian mysticism and Tantric Buddhism, has confronted the mysteries of birth and death in his *Nantes Triptych* of 1992. Three separate video panels, each over 15 feet (4.6m) high, show his wife giving birth, his mother dying and, on a black-and-white screen between these two color panels, the artist swaying and drifting underwater.

Initially Gary Hill's video installations were inspired by Abstract Expressionist painting but soon the human figure and the human voice were incorporated, notably in his *Primarily Speaking* of 1983. But in 1992 he abandoned the spoken word in *Suspension of Disbelief*, some 30 monitors stripped of casings and placed side by side along a steel beam showing images of the bodies of a woman and a man flowing along the screens as the camera passes over them at different speeds, sometimes so fast that the eye cannot focus clearly on any image, though the general impression lasts in the mind's eye. The anatomies of the two bodies overlap, fade, sometimes blend but are never harmonized in a single coherent space.

Tall Ships, also of 1992, is similarly but almost eerily without sound (**22,34**). The title recalls Longfellow's lines about 'ships that pass in the night and speak each other in passing . . . . Only a look and a voice, then darkness again and a silence.' Black-and-white images of passers-by, such as might be encountered in any street in the USA, are dimly projected on the walls of a dark corridor. They are small and distant but when a spectator stops in front of one of them an electronic switch sets it in motion. Each figure advances out of the darkness to assume life-size; some try to make contact, a little girl runs forward, a man with a reproachful look on his face approaches and then turns away. All this happens as if behind an impenetrable wall of glass. There is a suggestion of the shades of the living in the ancient mythological underworld. Yet the viewer has the sensation of being looked at still more than of looking, of being placed in the position of the 'other', a reminder that one human being can never truly make contact with another; there is always some final barrier. Gary Hill reaches out to touch the impenetrable solitude at the heart of consciousness, turning up the light to show the darkness.

22,34 Gary Hill, *Tall Ships*, 1992 (composite image). Video installation.

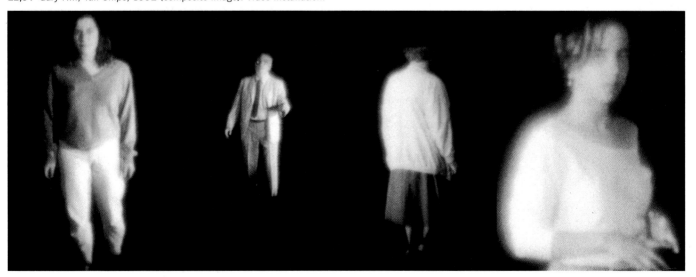

GLOSSARY

ARCADE of PIERS or COLUMNS or in rare cases by a screen wall.

Aisles

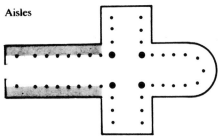

A

ABACUS The flat slab on top of a CAPITAL, bearing an ARCHITRAVE, ARCH or LINTEL.

ABSTRACT ART The term has two main applications: 1. Art that is non-representational, purely autonomous and makes no reference to an exterior world, e.g. Suprematism, Abstract Expressionism; 2. Art that 'abstracts' its images from the visible world, e.g. Cubism.

ACADEMY A place of study or society to advance the arts or sciences, named after the place Akademia in Athens where Plato taught. (Akademia was named after a legendary Attic hero, Akademos.) The first academy of art, founded in Florence by Giorgio Vasari in 1563, was an association of artists who hoped thereby to promote their status from that of artisans to that of practitioners of a 'liberal art'. The French royal academy founded in 1648 and the many later academies (e.g. the British Royal Academy, founded in 1768) were also institutions for teaching with facilities for studying the art of the past and the nude model in a LIFE-CLASS.

ACANTHUS Mediterranean plant with thick, prickly leaves, the supposed source of much foliage ornament as on Corinthian CAPITALS (4,45).

ACROPOLIS The citadel of a Greek city, built at its highest point and containing the chief temples and public buildings, as at Athens.

ACROTERIA Small PLINTHS for statues or ornaments placed at the apex and ends of a PEDIMENT; also, more loosely, both the plinths and what stands on them.

ACRYLIC PAINT A synthetic MEDIUM developed c. 1960, quick-drying and retaining brightness. It permits effects of transparency and IMPASTO but is generally used for work in flat color (21,19).

ADOBE Mud-brick, sun-dried but not fired.

AEDICULE A shrine, formed by two COLUMNS supporting an ENTABLATURE and PEDIMENT, enclosing a statue in a classical temple; the term is also used for the similar framing of a door, window or niche with two columns, half-columns or PILASTERS supporting a GABLE, LINTEL, etc.

AERIAL PERSPECTIVE, *see* PERSPECTIVE.

AGORA The open space in a Greek or Roman town used as a market-place or general meeting place, surrounded by PORTICOES as in a FORUM.

AISLE Part of a church or hall parallel to the main span and divided from it by an

ALABASTER A fine grained stone of which there are two distinct types. One, a carbonate of lime, was used for carving in ancient Egypt and Mesopotamia (2,2). The other, a sulphate of lime, was much used for small-scale carvings in Europe from the Middle Ages onwards.

ALBUMEN PRINT A photographic PRINT on paper coated with egg-white (albumen) and sensitized with a solution of silver nitrate, in general use 1850–c.1920.

ALTARPIECE A devotional painting or sculpture placed on, above or behind an altar, peculiar to Catholic Europe where it was introduced in the early thirteenth century when priests began to celebrate Mass with their backs to the congregation. Many depict multiple scenes and are on several panels (see POLYPTYCH, TRIPTYCH), hinged so that they can be concealed or revealed as required. *See also* PREDELLA, REREDOS.

AMBO A stand raised on two or more steps, for the reading of the Epistle and the Gospel, a prominent feature in early medieval Italian churches. Sometimes two were built, one for the Epistle and one for the Gospel, on the south and north sides respectively. After the eleventh century the ambo was replaced by the PULPIT.

AMBULATORY An AISLE surrounding the CHOIR or CHANCEL of a (usually medieval) Catholic church (9,35).

Ambulatory

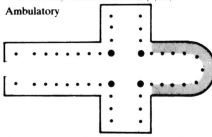

AMPHITHEATRE An elliptical or circular space surrounded by rising tiers of seats, as used by the Romans for gladiatorial contests (5,42).

AMPHORA A tall two-handled vessel with an egg-shaped body, spreading neck and, usually, a wide foot. Used by the ancient Greeks and Romans for oil, wine, etc.

ANASTASIS Byzantine painting of Christ's Harrowing of Hell (9,70).

ANG In Chinese roof construction a long transverse BRACKET arm with the function of a lever. An *angdou* is placed directly under a roof sloping downwards to the eaves.

ANICONIC A religious image without any devotional function.

ANNULAR Ring-shaped, as in an annular BARREL VAULT or annular passage.

ANTEFIX An ornamental block used in Classical architecture to conceal the ends of the roof tiles, later used decoratively.

Antefix

APADANA The COLUMNED (HYPOSTYLE) audience-hall of Persian kings, e.g. at Persepolis, *see* p. 114.

APOCALYPSE The last book of the New Testament, devoted to revelations of the future; hence, a prophetic disclosure or revelation.

APPROPRIATION The copying of images for purposes different from those for which they were originally intended, e.g. the reproduction of a famous work of art in a commercial advertisement. From the early 1980s appropriation has also been adopted as a means of challenging the premium put on artistic originality.

APSARAS Heavenly maiden of the Buddhist paradises; in Hindu art, a member of Indra's seraglio (6,65).

APSE VAULTED semicircular termination of a building, usually a church (7,11; 7,33; 9,20).

APSIDAL, *see* APSE.

AQUATINT A PRINT from a metal plate coated with a porous resin on which the design has been 'stopped out', i.e. painted with a RESIST varnish to prevent it being bitten by acid. The process is repeated to the required degree of complexity, including sometimes the addition of ETCHED lines.

AQUEDUCT An artificial channel for carrying water, usually an elevated masonry or brick structure supported on ARCHES, invented by the ancient Romans (5,41).

ARABESQUE Intricate surface decoration of plant forms, spirals, knots, etc. without human figures (*see also* GROTESQUE).

ARCADE A range of ARCHES on PIERS or COLUMNS, either free-standing or blind, i.e. attached to a wall.

ARCH The spanning of an opening by means other than that of a LINTEL. The most primitive form was made by CORBELLING. True arches are curved and so constructed that the downward THRUST of the weight of their own material and/or of that above is converted into outward thrusts resisted by the flanking material. There are various types and forms of arch of which the Basket, Horseshoe, Lancet, OGEE, Stilted and Tudor are notable.

ARCHAIC Antiquated or old-fashioned; but when used in connection with Greek art the term refers to that of a specific period c. 600–500 BC, *see* pp. 127–35.

ARCHITECTONIC Pertaining to architecture or expressing the spatial and other qualities peculiar to architecture.

ARCHITRAVE The lowest part of an ENTABLATURE, *see* ORDERS.

ARCHIVOLT The continuous molding on the face of an ARCH, also the underside of an arch.

ARCUATED A building dependent structurally on ARCHES as distinct from one constructed on the post-and-lintel or TRABEATED principle.

ARMATURE Framework on which sculpture in clay is supported.

A SECCO, *see* FRESCO.

ASHLAR Hewn rectangular blocks of stone laid in regular courses.

ASSEMBLAGE An art-work composed of three-dimensional objects, either natural or manufactured, usually junk.

ASYMMETRY Without SYMMETRY.

ATLANTES Full-length or half-length male statues used instead of COLUMNS, especially by German Baroque architects; also called *telamones*. *See also* CARYATID.

ATRIUM Inner courtyard of an Etruscan and ancient Roman house (5,34), also the forecourt of an Early Christian church, *see* p. 302.

ATTIC In Classical architecture the story above the main ENTABLATURE; or more loosely, the upper story of a building if less high than the others; or the space within a sloping roof.

AUREOLE Light encircling the head or body of a sacred personage, see also GLORY, MANDORLA, NIMBUS.

AVANT GARDE Literally, the vanguard; more loosely, those in advance or ahead of their time – or thought to be so.

AXIAL COMPOSITION One with a central AXIS and bilateral SYMMETRY.

AXIAL PLAN Planned longitudinally or along an AXIS. *See also* CENTRALLY PLANNED.

AXIS An imaginary straight line about which the earth or any other body rotates; or, in art and architecture, an imaginary straight line passing centrally through a figure or composition, a FAÇADE or GROUND-PLAN, so as to give an impression of balance.

B

BALDACCHINO Canopy over a throne, altar, etc. (13,15).

BALUSTRADE A series of balusters (short posts or PILLARS) supporting a rail.

BAPTISTERY A building for Christian baptismal rites containing the FONT; often separate from the church.

BARREL VAULT, *see* VAULT.

BASALT A very hard, durable, dark colored (usually black) stone used for sculpture in ancient Egypt and the Near East, *see* p. 56.

BASILICA An ancient Roman COLONNADED hall for public use, later adopted as a building type for Early Christian churches. The Christian basilica had acquired its essential characteristics by the fourth century: oblong PLAN, longitudinal AXIS, timber roof either open or concealed by a flat ceiling, and a termination either rectangular or APSIDAL. It is usually divided into a NAVE and two or more AISLES, the former higher and wider than the latter, lit by

CLERESTORY windows and with or without a GALLERY. *See* p. 303.

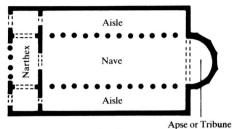

Basilica

BAS-RELIEF, *see* RELIEF.

BATTER The inclined face of a wall.

BAY Vertical division of the exterior or interior of a building marked by FENESTRATION, an ORDER, BUTTRESSES, units of VAULTING, etc.

BAZAAR Persian word for market (*suq* in Arabic), usually an irregular conglomeration of alleys, roofed or covered with awnings, lined with shops and entered through gates that can be closed at night. In the early nineteenth century the word bazaar or bazar was adopted in the West for markets for charity, later for shops selling miscellaneous goods.

BENDAY A process of shading by means of small uniform dots, invented by the New York printer Benjamin Day (1838–1916) for cheap photographic reproductions; also imitated by Pop artists, notably Lichtenstein.

BLIND ARCADE, *see* ARCADE.

BODHISATTVA One capable of attaining Buddhahood but who renounces *Nirvana* and chooses selflessly to remain on earth to help others.

BOLLARD A thick post of wood, metal or stone for securing ropes and hawsers, usually on a ship or wharf but also elsewhere; also, by analogy, similarly shaped posts used in series to limit vehicular access to an area, sometimes with intervening chains.

BOOK OF HOURS A private prayer-book containing the devotions for the seven canonical hours of the Roman Catholic Church (matins, vespers, etc.), liturgies for local saints and sometimes a calendar. Intended for lay use, they were often elaborately illuminated.

BOSS A projection, usually ornamental, covering the intersection of RIBS in a VAULT or ceiling.

BRACKET A small supporting piece of stone or other material to carry a projecting weight; often a scroll or VOLUTE in form.

BRASS An alloy of copper, zinc and often other metals which usually takes on a yellow color when polished. Until the nineteenth century the words brass and BRONZE were interchangeable, and to the present day works in brass (e.g. Benin sculptures, *see* pp. 528–9) are sometimes erroneously described as bronzes.

BREVIARY A prayer-book containing the daily prayers, psalms and hymns generally intended for use by the clergy.

BROKEN GROUND Short thick strokes of OIL PAINT applied over a GROUND to represent shimmering effects of light.

BROKEN PEDIMENT, *see* PEDIMENT.

BRONZE An alloy, mainly of COPPER (95% to 99%) and tin, sometimes with small quantities of lead and/or other metals, that can be formed by CASTING. It was first produced by the second millennium BC (Bronze Age) in Mesopotamia and China and, although gradually superseded by IRON for most of its initial purposes (tools, weapons, etc.), it remained the metal most often used for sculpture until the twentieth century. The term bronze is often applied loosely to sculpture in BRASS and COPPER.

BUDDHIST RAILING A barrier of stone carved to resemble a wooden fence, with horizontal slats woven through the verticals, made to surround a STUPA (as at Sanchi, *see* pp. 227–8), but also carved in RELIEF as a symbol.

BURIN A tool with a sharp metal point used for ENGRAVING, mainly on metal, and especially in PRINT-making.

BURR A rough ridge of copper on either side of the line made by a needle in DRYPOINT PRINT-making; also the uniformly rough surface of a plate prepared for MEZZOTINT.

BUTTRESS A projecting support built against a wall to give additional strength, usually to counteract the lateral THRUST of an ARCH, VAULT, etc. A *flying buttress* is in form an arch or half-arch transmitting the thrust of a vault or roof from the upper part of a wall to an outer support, *see* p. 392.

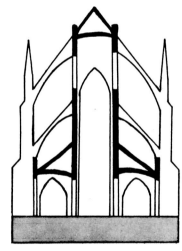

Flying buttresses

C

CABINET PICTURE A small picture intended to be examined closely and at leisure, like a precious object or curiosity. The term derives from the seventeenth–eighteenth-century 'cabinet of curiosities' in which precious objects were kept and displayed.

CALLIGRAPHY Fine (literally 'beautiful') handwriting (8,1).

CALOTYPE The name patented in 1841 by W. H. Fox Talbot for his photographic process by which an image projected on a sheet of sensitized paper is chemically fixed as a negative and may be placed over another sheet of sensitized paper and exposed to light to make a positive PRINT. This was the first negative–positive process, the basis for others by which it was superseded.

CAMEO A gem, hardstone or shell having two layers of color, the upper of which can be carved in RELIEF and the lower used as a GROUND (5,57).

CAMERA OBSCURA The forerunner of the photographic camera: a dark chamber in which images of objects outside are projected on to a wall by light admitted through a pin-point aperture or lens. Developed in the seventeenth century as a portable box with a mirror to receive the image which would be seen through a ground-glass screen on top, it was occasionally used by artists as an aid for drawing. The invention of photography followed the discovery of light-sensitive chemical substances that could fix such images.

CAMPANILE Italian for bell-tower, usually one built separate from but near a church.

CANTILEVER A projecting beam, canopy, etc., supported by a downward force behind a fulcrum. It is usually anchored at one end by the weight of the structure above. Being without external bracing, it appears to be self-supporting.

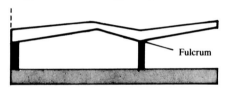

Cantilever

CANVAS A coarse unbleached cloth woven from hemp or flax, much used in the West as a support for OIL PAINTING since the fifteenth century. For this purpose it must be stretched over a wooden armature (called a stretcher) and PRIMED with neutral colored paint to provide an integrated surface.

CAPITAL The upper member of a COLUMN. See ORDERS.

CARDBOARD A stiff type of thick, compressed paper sometimes used in the West, from the early nineteenth century, as the support for OIL PAINTINGS, usually small (17,27).

CARTOON A full-size drawing for a painting. (In modern usage, a satirical or comic drawing, especially one in a newspaper.)

CARTOUCHE An ornamental panel, like a SCROLL or sheet of paper with curling edges.

CARYATID A full- or half-length female statue used as a support instead of a COLUMN, see 4,20; if carrying a basket it is called a canephora. The term is also used loosely for male statues serving the same function, see ATLANTES. See also HERM, TERM.

CASEIN Milk protein mixed with PIGMENTS for painting.

CASEMATE A VAULTED room built within the thickness of a rampart or other fortification.

CASTING A sculptural process often used for the reproduction of a sculpture,

MEDAL, etc., the term *cast* being used primarily in this sense. In casting a liquid MEDIUM (e.g. molten BRONZE, plaster) is poured into a mold. There are various methods, *see* CIRE PERDUE.

CELLA The body of a Classical temple as distinct from its PORTICO and COLONNADES; by extension, the chamber for a cult image in any temple.

CENTERING Wooden framework used in construction of ARCHES and VAULTS, removed (or 'struck') when the mortar has set.

CENTRALLY PLANNED A building which radiates from a central point, as distinct from one on an AXIAL PLAN.

CERAMIC A nineteenth-century term covering PORCELAIN, FAIENCE and all types of pottery.

CHAITYA A Sanskrit word for a sacred mound, especially a Buddhist STUPA. A *chaitya*-hall is a building or, more usually, an artificial cave, with an APSE enclosing a stupa (6,8; 9). A *chaitya*-arch is an English term for a recurrent motif in Hindu architecture resembling in miniature the arches (derived from the cross-section of a VAULTED wooden building) which crown the entrances to *chaitya*-halls.

CHALICE Wine cup used at Mass; called a Communion Cup in reformed churches.

CHALK Calcium carbonate, a white substance used for drawing, ground to powder and mixed with PIGMENTS for PASTELS, also a component of GESSO.

CHAMPLEVÉ, *see* ENAMEL.

CHANCEL That part of the east end of a church in which the main altar is placed, reserved for the clergy and choir and often separated by a screen (Lat. *cancellus*, hence the term) from the rest of the church. The term is now often used for the whole continuation of the NAVE east of the CROSSING.

Chancel

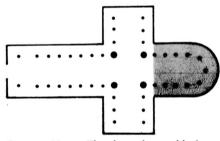

CHAPTER HOUSE The place of assembly for the discussion of business in a MONASTERY.

CHARCOAL Charred wood used for drawing, probably from very ancient times though the first recorded reference is in ancient Rome.

CHASHITSU A small Japanese building, or room, for the tea ceremony (12,88).

CHASING The tooling of a metal surface to add decoration (as on silver) or remove blemishes from a CAST (e.g. BRONZE) object.

CHATTRA An honorific Indian umbrella canopy, also one simulated in stone as on the mast of a Buddhist STUPA (6,6), in Hindu temple architecture or Indian palace architecture.

CHEVET French term for the east end of a church, comprising the CHOIR, AMBULATORY, APSE and radiating chapels if there are any (9,36).

CHIAROSCURO In painting, the manipulation of light and shade to give the effect of MODELLING.

CHIGI Japanese name for the scissors-like FINIALS on the roof of a Shinto temple.

CHLORITE or CHLORITE SCHIST A hard dark green stone used for sculpture in ancient Egypt (2,40).

CHOIR That part of a church where divine service is sung, usually part of the CHANCEL. A partition of wood or stone separating the choir and chancel from the NAVE and TRANSEPTS is called a *choir screen*. Often elaborately carved, it corresponds to the ICONOSTASIS in a Greek Orthodox church.

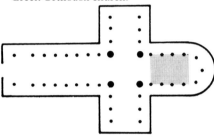

Choir

CHROMOGENIC COLOR PRINT A photographic PRINT made by a process using dyes incorporated in SILVER GELATIN emulsion, invented in the USA in the 1930s and first perfected by Kodak.

CIBORIUM A type of BALDACCHINO, a canopy supported on COLUMNS over the altar of a church.

CIRE PERDUE Lost wax – a process of making a CAST from a model in wax by enclosing it in clay, melting the wax out and filling the resulting mold with molten metal (usually BRONZE) or plaster.

CLERESTORY The upper stage of the NAVE walls of a BASILICA or church, rising above the AISLE roofs and pierced with windows (9,45).

CLOISONNÉ, *see* ENAMEL.

CLOISTER An enclosed space, usually an open court surrounded by covered passages, in a Christian MONASTERY.

CLUSTER PIER Synonym for COMPOUND PIER.

CODEX A manuscript bound as a book, hinged with facing pages, as distinct from a SCROLL, which it superseded in the fourth century AD.

COFFERING Decoration of a ceiling, a VAULT or an arch SOFFIT, consisting of sunken square or polygonal panels, as in the Pantheon in Rome (5,49).

COLLAGE A composition made by gluing pieces of paper, cloth etc. on a CANVAS or other GROUND (19,26).

COLLODION NEGATIVE A glass plate coated with a light-sensitive emulsion of collodion (gun cotton dissolved in alcohol) and other chemicals, inserted in a camera and exposed while still wet, to make a photographic negative. This type of negative was much used from 1850 until the 1870s.

COLLOTYPE A process allied to LITHOGRAPHY, for printing photographs by transferring images from negatives to plates coated with gelatin, which hardens on exposure to light and absorbs ink, invented in 1855 and soon improved.

COLONNADE A row of COLUMNS carrying an ENTABLATURE or ARCHES.

COLOR The sensation produced on the eye by light rays. The seven main rays that make up the visible spectrum are subdivided into three primary colors or *hues* – red, yellow and blue – each of which has a complementary color composed of the other two. Color *values* are determined by the amount of light different hues reflect (yellow has a high, blue a low value), irrespective of the *saturation* or purity of the hue. *See also* LOCAL COLOR.

COLOSSAL ORDER A Classical ORDER of giant COLUMNS rising from the ground through more than one story (11,41).

COLOSSUS A statue very much more than life-size.

COLUMN A free-standing upright member of circular section normally intended as a support though sometimes constructed independently as a monument (5,65; 6,1). In Classical architecture it consists of a shaft, CAPITAL and, except in Greek Doric, a base, *see* ORDERS. The twisted column that appears in Baroque architecture was supposed to derive from prototypes in Solomon's temple and is called a *solomonic column*.

COMPOUND PIER A PIER with several ENGAGED (sometimes detached) shafts or demi-shafts against its faces, much used in Romanesque and Gothic architecture (9,23; 9,35).

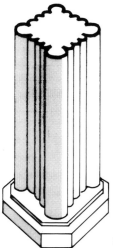

Compound pier

COMPUTER GRAPHICS Two-dimensional art-works created by computer.

CONCRETE An ancient Roman invention. Unlike modern concrete, which can be mixed and poured, ancient Roman concrete had to be laid in courses, though a slow-drying mortar was discovered in the time of Augustus. It became a determining factor in the development of Roman architecture, *see* pp. 199–201, but was forgotten and unused for over a thousand years afterwards. Revived in late eighteenth-century France, it was much developed from the mid-nineteenth century

onwards and its use (especially as FERROCONCRETE) has radically influenced the form of much modern architecture.

CONTÉ CRAYON A non-greasy stick of powdered GRAPHITE and clay with red ochre, soot or blackstone, used for drawing.

CONTOUR An outline defining a form.

CONTRAPPOSTO A pose in which one part of the body is twisted in an opposite direction to another, *see* p. 476).

COPPER A pure metal that can be formed by hammering or CASTING. For sculpture it was sometimes used on its own but more often as an alloy in BRASS and BRONZE.

CORBELLING Masonry courses each built above the one below as a BRACKET or to form a rough ARCH, VAULT or dome, *see* p. 48 (2,55).

CORINTHIAN ORDER, *see* ORDERS.

CORNICE In Classical architecture the top, projecting section of an ENTABLATURE, also any projecting ornamental MOLDING along the top of a wall, ARCH etc.

CORPUS Latin for body, a word used in several senses, e.g. for an artist's body of works or *oeuvre*, for the central part of a POLYPTYCH, *see* p. 469.

CRAMP or CLAMP In stone construction, a metal bar or pin used to bind together blocks of the same course. *See also* DOWELL.

CRAYON Powdered PIGMENT mixed with wax or paraffin and made into a stick for drawing.

CROCKET A decorative feature, usually shaped like a curling leaf, projecting at regular intervals from the angles of spires, PINNACLES, GABLES, etc. in Gothic architecture.

CROSS One of the most ancient symbolical and ornamental devices, found in many cultures from prehistoric times. In ancient Egypt a form of cross called an *ankh*, composed of a T surmounted by a loop, was the symbol of life. The *swastika*, a cross in which the arms are bent at right angles in the same relative direction, is of similarly ancient origin, notably in ancient India (supposedly a solar symbol). A cross became the main Christian symbol when it was adopted by the Roman emperor Constantine in the early fourth century, signifying 'Triumph over Death'. Crosses were used as liturgical objects to be set up beside (not on) the altar during services or carried in processions. There were two main types:

1. The *Latin Cross*, with a long vertical arm and a shorter horizontal one placed more than halfway up. This retained the 'triumphal' significance of early Constantinian crosses and was often elaborately worked and enriched with gold, gems, etc. and termed *crux gemmata* (9,2).

2. The *Greek Cross*, with equal arms fixed on a short handle, which signified the thaumaturgical power of Christ and was used for Benedictions.

Altar crosses – i.e. crosses intended to stand on the altar – were made from the ninth century in the Eastern Church and from the eleventh century in the Western Church. Early in the eleventh

century crosses began to be engraved or sculpted, either in relief or in the round, with the figure of Christ crucified, such crosses being termed *crucifixes*. They gradually replaced the *crux gemmata* and plain crosses. Altar crosses or crucifixes were abandoned by the Protestant Church after the Reformation and only returned in the nineteenth century. Various types of cross developed as symbols and ornaments include the Maltese Cross with wedge-shaped arms meeting at the centre.

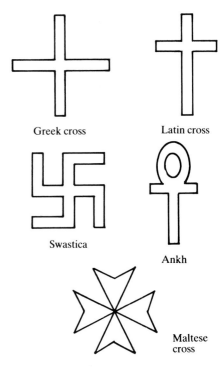

Greek cross Latin cross

Swastica Ankh

Maltese cross

CROSS-HATCHING A method of shading in drawings and ENGRAVINGS by superimposing HATCHING in opposite directions.

CROSSING The space at the intersection of the NAVE, CHOIR and TRANSEPTS of a church (13,15).

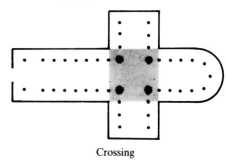

Crossing

CRUCIFIX, *see* CROSS.

CRUCIFORM Shaped like a CROSS, e.g. the PLAN of a church.

CRUX GEMMATA, *see* CROSS.

CRYPT A chamber or VAULT beneath the main floor of a church.

CUN (Ts'un) Chinese term for brush-strokes which indicate MODELLING and suggest texture within the outline or contour of a form – rocks, mountains, trees, etc., in landscape painting.

CUNEIFORM A script composed of nail-shaped wedges pressed into wet clay, the earliest known form of writing, developed in Sumerian Mesopotamia.

CUPOLA A dome, see VAULTING.

CURTAIN WALL The outer enclosing wall of a medieval castle or, especially with reference to twentieth-century architecture, a non-load-bearing wall applied to the exterior of a structure.

CYCLOPEAN MASONRY Masonry composed of very large irregular blocks (2,54).

D

DADO In Classical architecture, the portion of a PEDESTAL between the base and the CORNICE; but the word is more often used for the finishing of the lower part of an interior wall, from floor to waist height.

DAGABA or DAGOBA The name given to a STUPA in Sri Lanka (6,48).

DAGUERREOTYPE Photographic process invented by L.-J.-M. Daguerre (see pp. 666–7) and patented in 1839 for fixing positive images on silver-coated metal plates and widely used, especially for portraits, until the 1860s. Each daguerreotype is unique and the process was superseded by developments from the CALOTYPE process by which numerous PRINTS may be made from a single negative.

DEËSIS A representation of Christ enthroned in majesty between the Virgin and St John the Baptist, as found in Byzantine art.

DIAPER A pattern of small identical non-figurative, usually geometrical, units adopted either as a means of covering a surface or as a background for FIGURATIVE work.

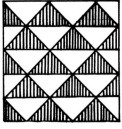

Diaper

DIORITE A hard, compact dark colored, black or gray stone used for sculpture, notably in ancient Mesopotamia and Egypt (2,11).

DIPTERAL TEMPLE A Classical temple with two rows of COLUMNS on each side.

DIPTYCH A picture or RELIEF on two hinged panels.

DIVISIONISM The technique of painting with small areas of unmixed PIGMENTS juxtaposed so that they combine optically when seen from a certain distance. Although employed empirically by several artists, notably Watteau, Delacroix and the Impressionists, it was first adopted as a stylistic term by Paul Signac and, independently, by the Italian Post-Impressionists in the 1880s, see pp. 722–3.

DOME, see VAULTING.

DORIC, see ORDERS.

DOUGONG Chinese term for a cluster of BRACKETS CANTILEVERED out from the top of a COLUMN to carry the rafters and overhanging eaves of a roof.

DOWELL In stone construction, a wooden or metal pin placed between blocks of different courses to prevent shifting. See also CRAMP.

DRUM A vertical wall supporting a DOME or CUPOLA. Also, one of the cylindrical blocks of stone that make up a COLUMN.

DRYPOINT Technique of PRINT-making by which the COPPER plate is scratched with a sharply pointed tool, often used in combination with other methods of ENGRAVING and ETCHING.

E

EARTH COLORS PIGMENTS made from materials in the soil, e.g. yellow ochre and umber.

EARTHWORK A large scale art-work for which the surface of the earth is the MEDIUM.

EASEL PAINTING A movable painting, usually on wood panel or CANVAS, as distinct from one on the surface of a wall or ceiling. Fixed ALTARPIECES are also normally excluded from this category.

ECLECTIC A term applied to works of art and especially nineteenth- and twentieth-century architecture combining elements from two or more historical styles. (The term 'eclecticism' with regard to Bolognese seventeenth-century painting is now obsolete.)

ELECTRUM A natural alloy of silver and gold.

ELEVATION An external face of a building, also a drawing of one made in projection on a vertical plane (11,59).

EMBRASURE A recess for a window, door, etc., or a small opening in the wall of a fortified building, usually splayed on the inside.

EMULSION TECHNIQUE A process of painting with mixed liquid PIGMENT in which one of the elements is suspended in minute drops.

ENAMEL A vitreous substance that can be fused to a metal surface under heat. *Champlevé* enamel is poured into grooves engraved on metal (9,61). *Cloisonné* enamel is poured into *cloisons* or compartments formed by a network of metal bands, the tops of which remain exposed, dividing one color area from another (9,17).

ENCAUSTIC An ancient technique of painting with PIGMENTED wax fused with the support by the application of hot irons.

ENGAGED COLUMN or SHAFT One that is attached to or sunk into a wall or PIER. An *engaged portico* is similarly one sunk into a FAÇADE which continues around and above it.

ENGRAVING An incised design, also a PRINT made from an engraved metal plate (10,56); see also ETCHING and WOODCUT.

ENTABLATURE, see ORDERS.

ENTASIS The slight convex curve in the shaft of a COLUMN, see p. 139.

ETCHING A PRINT from a metal plate on which the design has been etched or eaten away by acid (13,34).

ETUDE French term for a 'study': a painting, more rarely a sculpture, executed as a demonstration of technical ability but often from the early nineteenth century regarded as an independent work of art. It is distinct from a sketch made in the process of creating a larger work.

F

FAÇADE The architecturally emphasized front or face of a building.

FACETING The cutting of a round surface into a small flat areas at angles to one another as in a cut diamond; also, in Cubist painting, the representation of forms by small flat planes meeting at sharp angles, see p. 788.

FAIENCE Pottery with a tin-glaze (a GLAZE composed of oxides of lead and tin combined with silicate of potash) called in Italy *maiolica* (10,54); also a glassy substance made from powdered quartz in the ancient Near East and Aegean.

FENESTRATION The arrangement of windows in a building.

FERROCONCRETE A modern development of CONCRETE reinforced by the insertion of steel mesh or rods. Also called *reinforced concrete.*

FETISH An object to which magic power is attributed. The term *power figure* is nowadays preferred by students of African art.

FIGURATIVE ART Depictions of the visible world, not necessarily including human or animal figures.

FILIGREE Jewelry made from very fine threads and minute beads usually of GOLD or silver; by extension, large-scale carved decoration giving a similar effect of intricate delicacy.

FINIAL A formal ornament at the top of a canopy, PEDIMENT, spire, etc.

FLAMBOYANT The French Late Gothic style, characterized by window TRACERY with long wavy bars of stonework.

FLEUR DE LYS Stylized lily with three petals, as in the coat of arms of the French monarchy.

FLUTING Shallow concave grooves running vertically on the shaft of a COLUMN, PILASTER or other surface.

FLYING BUTTRESS, see BUTTRESS.

FLYING FAÇADE The continuation of the FAÇADE wall of a building above the roof-line, especially in Mayan architecture.

FONT A receptacle for the water used in the Christian rite of baptism (9,29).

FORESHORTENING PERSPECTIVE applied to a single form, e.g. a foot represented as pointing out of, not in line with, a pictorial plane (4,12; 4,14).

FORUM An open space surrounded by public buildings in an ancient Roman town, usually sited centrally; similar in function to the Greek AGORA.

FOUND IMAGES, MATERIALS or OBJECTS Those found in an everyday environment and APPROPRIATED for art-works, especially ASSEMBLAGES.

FRAME CONSTRUCTION A type of construction with walls and roof supported on a rigid framework of wooden or metal beams; the term covers that of both the timber-framed buildings in much vernacular architecture and modern metal and reinforced CONCRETE structures.

FRESCO Wall and ceiling painting on fresh (*fresco*) moist lime plaster with PIGMENTS ground in water so that they are absorbed into the plaster. Pigments added after the plaster has dried are said to be applied *a secco, see* p. 413 (9,80).

FRET A geometrical ornament of horizontal and vertical straight lines repeated to form a band.

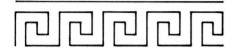

Fret

FRIEZE The middle division of an ENTABLATURE, *see* ORDERS, also loosely any sculptured or decorated horizontal band.

FUNCTIONALISM The theory that a building, piece of furniture or other object should be designed primarily to fulfil its material purpose and use and that its form should be determined exclusively by its function.

FUSUMA-E Japanese paintings of sliding screens.

G

GABLE A basically triangular portion of a wall at the end of a PITCHED ROOF.

GABLE ROOF, *see* HIPPED ROOF.

GALLERY In church architecture an upper story over an AISLE opening on to a NAVE (9,23), also an exterior feature with continuous open ARCADING in the upper part of the building. In domestic architecture a long room, sometimes used for the display of paintings, sculpture, etc. (hence the modern term 'art gallery').

GARGOYLE A waterspout projecting from a roof or the parapet of a wall carved into a grotesque human or animal figure.

GENRE PAINTING A picture of everyday life (13,47).

GENRES The various categories of painting, e.g. history, landscape, portrait, STILL LIFE etc.

GESSO A composition of gypsum or CHALK and SIZE sometimes with other materials. Applied to a panel it provides a smooth absorbent white GROUND for painting, usually in TEMPERA. It can also be modelled in RELIEF. The term gesso is sometimes used for *plaster of Paris*, a white gypsum powder that forms a paste when mixed with water and hardens into a solid, used by sculptors for molds and CASTS.

GILDING Coating with GOLD, GOLD LEAF or a gold colored substance. In medieval Europe panel paintings were often gilded, *see* GOLD GROUND. Similarly sculptures might be partly or wholly gilded. Various mechanical or chemical methods were used, notably for CERAMICS, metalwork and woodwork (e.g. for furniture). Today gold is usually applied to metalwork by electrolysis.

GLAZE On pottery a glossy waterproof surface produced by the vitrification of silica (present in most clays) with a flux, e.g. oxide of lead, tin, etc. In painting a transparent film of OIL PAINT which modifies the solid color over which it is applied.

GLORY A circular, oval or irregular flame-like area suggesting light surrounding the head or whole body of a sacred figure, e.g. the Buddha (6,89) or Christ and the Christian saints (9,30), also called a NIMBUS or AUREOLE.

GOLD The most precious of metals, found in various parts of the world either as veins in different types of rock, or alloyed with silver in electrum or as flakes, dust or nuggets. Its rarity combined with its unique ductility (a single grain may be drawn into a wire 500ft, 150m, long), malleability (it can be beaten very thin, *see* GOLD LEAF) and permanence (it will not oxidize or tarnish and is not corroded by naturally occurring substances) account for the great value placed on it and for the mystical properties attributed to it – hence its use on Buddhist images and Christian liturgical objects. In its pure state it is too soft and heavy for easy use so is usually alloyed with other metals (pure gold is of 24 carats, a half-and-half alloy is of 12 carats, the finest alloys nowadays being 18 or 22 carats). The color varies according to the alloy, COPPER giving a reddish, silver a pale greenish tinge while platinum makes it silvery. *See also* GILDING.

GOLD GROUND Medieval GILDING technique used for the backgrounds of panel paintings. GOLD LEAF is applied to the GESSO-coated panel with a glue SIZING, usually a dull red in color.

GOLD LEAF GOLD beaten very thin (down to three millionths of an inch, 0.000076mm).

GOLDEN SECTION or MEAN An irrational proportion, probably known to the ancient Greeks and much taken up by Renaissance art theorists. It may be defined as a line cut in such a way that the smaller section is to the greater as the greater is to the whole. This cannot be worked out mathematically, hence its fascination. Approximately it would be 5:8.

GOPURA Monumental gateway to a Hindu temple.

GOUACHE Opaque WATERCOLOR paint.

GRAPHIC ARTS The arts which depend on drawing rather than color but generally including all forms of PRINT-making.

GRAPHIC DESIGN The design of images and/or lettering to be printed on paper, fabrics, etc., usually for commercial purposes.

GRAPHITE A form of carbon, the 'lead' in a pencil.

GREEK CROSS, *see* CROSS.

GRISAILLE Painting in tones of gray, sometimes suggesting LOW RELIEF.

GROIN, *see* VAULT.

GROTESQUE Fanciful decoration similar to but distinct from ARABESQUE in that it includes human figures, animals and architectural elements.

GROUND The surface on which a painting is executed.

GROUND PLAN, *see* PLAN.

GUILLOCHE An ornamental pattern of curving interlaced bands resembling a plait of ribbons.

GUM PRINT A photographic PRINT on paper coated with light-sensitive gum arabic. In the process of fixing it tonalities may be controlled, detail removed, etc., differentiating prints made from the same negative. Gum prints were first exhibited in 1858 and were much favoured by art-photographers in the late nineteenth century.

GUTTAE, *see* ORDERS.

H

HALO A GLORY, usually restricted to the circular area behind a head.

HAPPENING An unscripted performance, usually in an ordinary open space (e.g. street or parking lot) in which one or more artists, using materials without fine art associations, encourage the spontaneous participation of spectators who condition its development; sometimes recorded by photography.

HATCHING Parallel lines indicating shadow in a drawing, ENGRAVING etc.

HAUNCH The part of an ARCH roughly midway between the SPRINGING LINE and the crown, where the lateral THRUST is strongest.

HERM A rectangular shaft terminating in a human head. *See also* TERM.

HEXASTYLE A PORTICO or other structure with six frontal COLUMNS.

HIEROGLYPHS The signs used in ancient Egyptian picture writing, representing either complete words or syllables forming part of a word.

HIGHLIGHT In a painting, a spot of the highest or lightest VALUE, usually white.

HIPPED ROOF A roof with all its surfaces sloped, as distinct from a *pitched* or *gable* roof which has vertical walls on two sides.

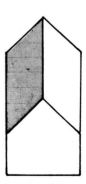 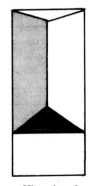

Pitched or gable roof   **Hipped roof**

HISTORIATED Ornament incorporating human or animal figures.

HISTORICISM The nineteenth-century revival of historical styles, as opposed to earlier revivals (e.g. Greek Revival). The term derives from the German *Historismus*, a pejorative term coined in the 1880s for the emphasis then given to history and later, by analogy, to the nineteenth-century philosophy of history (mainly Hegelian).

HISTORY PAINTING In European academic theory a FIGURATIVE painting of a scene from classical mythology, the Bible, the lives of saints or an historical event.

HOLOGRAPH A word, originally meaning 'writing in the hand of a single person', adopted in the 1960s to categorize the artistic development of *laser* technology to project colored three-dimensional images in space. Laser is an acronym for light amplification by stimulated emission of radiation.

HUA In Chinese roof construction a BRACKET, usually one of several comprising a DOUGONG.

HUE The property of COLOR that permits its location in the spectrum.

HYPOSTYLE HALL A large space over which the roof is supported by rows of COLUMNS.

I

ICON A small, portable panel painting of Christ, the Virgin and Child or the saints, produced for Greek or Russian Orthodox Christians from the sixth century to the present day.

ICONOCLASM The prohibition of sacred images. A decree by the emperor Leo III in AD 730 ordered the destruction of all images showing Christ, the Virgin Mary, saints or angels in human form. Repudiated by the Pope and Western Christendom, the prohibition was effective in the Orthodox Church until AD 843. *See* p. 323.

ICONOGRAPHY The study of the meaning of visual images whether conveyed directly or by symbols, allegories, etc.

ICONOLOGY The study of the meaning of visual images in relationship with their historical–cultural context.

ICONOSTASIS The screen separating the SANCTUARY from the NAVE of a Byzantine church, usually covered with ICONS.

ILLUMINATED MANUSCRIPT A manuscript decorated with drawings or paintings; *see also* MINIATURE PAINTING (7,45; 7,55; 7,56).

IMPASTO OIL PAINT thickly applied.

IMPOST BLOCK A block with splayed sides placed between ABACUS and CAPITAL.

INSTALLATION A designed environment set up as an art-work, usually multi-media, in a gallery or outdoor location, and always SITE SPECIFIC.

INSULA An ancient Roman apartment house or tenement block, of up to five stories (maximum height was about 70ft or 20m), with communal latrines, etc., and often VAULTED throughout with CONCRETE construction. *See* p. 194.

INTAGLIO A gem with incised carving, as distinct from a CAMEO.

INTARSIA Italian term for the flat decorations made from pieces of variously colored woods inlaid to form ornamental patterns, architectural perspectives, FIGURATIVE scenes, etc., on the panelled walls of rooms, choir-stalls, chests, etc.

INTENSITY The richness or saturation of COLOR.

INTERLACE Decoration formed of intertwined lines making knot-like patterns, notably in Celtic art, *see* pp. 329–32.

INTONACO The final layer of plaster to which *fresco* paint is applied.

INTRADOS The inner curve or underside of an ARCH.

IONIC, *see* ORDERS.

IRON A metal derived from ores found in many parts of the world, though the process of extracting it was not discovered until the second millennium BC in Anatolia. It can be wrought, hammered into form or CAST. Sculpture was cast in iron in China from at least as early as the fifteenth century AD but rarely in Europe before the nineteenth century. Wrought and/or welded iron has been used for sculpture in the West since the early twentieth century.

ITALIC The peoples of ancient Italy and their cultures, usually excluding Etruscan, Roman and colonial Greek.

IWAN In Near-Eastern architecture, a large porch or shallow hall with a pointed BARREL VAULT, as in the Sassanian palace at Ctesiphon (8,2) and many later Islamic buildings, where it may serve as an entrance (12,33) or face a courtyard (12,43).

J

JADE A mineralogically imprecise term covering several types of hard stone found mainly in Chinese Turkestan and Central America, ranging in color from very dark green to white, *see* pp. 117, 120.

JAMB The vertical face of an ARCH, doorway or window.

K

KAKEMONO Japanese painting mounted to be hung vertically. A PRINT made as a substitute is called a KAKEMONO-E.

KHANQAH In Islamic architecture, a hostel for Sufis, similar to a MADRASA.

KEYSTONE The central stone of an ARCH or RIB VAULT.

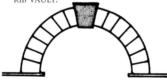

Keystone

KINETIC SCULPTURE A three-dimensional art-work that moves, usually by a mechanism.

KONDO The main hall of a Japanese Buddhist monastery (6,115).

KRATER Ancient Greek term for a large vessel used for mixing wine and water, of pottery (4,14) or metal (4,58).

KUFIC A formal type of Arabic CALLIGRAPHY, used decoratively on buildings, pottery, textiles, etc. (8,1; 8,27).

L

LACQUER A waterproof substance made from the sap of a Chinese tree (*Rhus verniciflua*) used mainly as a protective and decorative covering (p. 118 and 3,41). Large but light-weight sculptures made in China and Japan by the *dry lacquer* process are composed of pieces of hemp cloth soaked in lacquer and covered with further coats of lacquer, over a wooden

armature or clay core which could be removed to leave a hollow shell.

LANTERN In architecture a small circular or polygonal turret with windows all round, crowning a roof or dome.

LEKYTHOS Ancient Greek term for a small slender pottery container for oil, *see* pp. 54–5 (4,42).

LIERNE A tertiary RIB, i.e. one which does not spring either from one of the main springers or from a central boss.

LIFE-CLASS In an ACADEMY of art, a session devoted to drawing, painting or modelling from a living, usually nude, man or woman.

LINE The trace of a moving point, e.g. that of a pencil. In drawing, painting, ENGRAVING, etc., it may create a silhouette or define a CONTOUR, to represent MASS or VOLUME.

LINEAR STYLE Paintings in which forms are defined mainly by line, as distinct from those said to be PAINTERLY.

LINGA Phallic emblem of the Hindu god Shiva, usually a simple cylinder with rounded top (6,29).

LINO CUT A PRINT made from a piece of linoleum by the WOODCUT process.

LINTEL A horizontal beam or stone bridging an opening.

LITHOGRAPHY A process of PRINT-making from a drawing in oily CRAYON on stone, *see* p. 656 (15,18). Invented 1798.

LITURGICAL ORIENTATION, *see* ORIENTATION.

LOCAL COLOR An object's actual COLOR when seen close up in clear light, as distinct from the color it appears to have when seen from a distance, or takes on by reflection from other objects or from the atmosphere, e.g. at sunset.

LOGGIA A room or small building open on one or more sides, in Italian Renaissance architecture, with COLUMNS to support the roof.

LOST WAX, *see* CIRE PERDUE.

LOZENGE A flat rectilinear figure with four equal sides but two angles sharper than others.

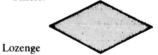

Lozenge

LUNETTE A semicircular shape.

LUSTRE On pottery, an iridescent metallic surface invented in the seventh–eighth centuries probably in Egypt, perfected in Baghdad in the ninth century, subsequently used widely in the Islamic world, notably Spain, and from the fifteenth century in Italy.

M

MADRASA Islamic college for teaching theology and canon law.

MAESTÀ Italian name for a painting of the Madonna and Child enthroned in majesty, i.e. surrounded by a celestial court of saints and angels (9,76).

MAGNA Trade name for a brand of ACRYLIC colors.

MAIDAN A term of Persian origin for an open space or square in or just outside a city, for ceremonies, military parades, etc.; a notable feature of urbanism in central Asia and Mughal India.

MAIOLICA, *see* FAIENCE.

MALANGGAN A ritual performed in New Ireland (Melanesia) and the objects used in it (18,14).

MANDALA A circular diagram of the cosmos used as an aid to meditation or as a magical or symbolical offering in Buddhist, Hindu and Jain religions. It may also provide the basis for the PLAN of a building, e.g. Borobudur (6,53).

MANDAPA A large open hall, especially one in a Hindu temple complex (12,59).

MANDORLA An upright almond shape, especially a GLORY of this form surrounding the figure of Christ in medieval art.

MARBLE A mineralogically imprecise term for hard metamorphic limestone that can be sawn into slabs and will take a high polish.

MARTYRIUM A church or other building erected over a site which bears witness to the Christian faith either by referring to an event in Christ's life or Passion, or by sheltering the grave of a martyr, a witness by virtue of having shed his or her blood. In Early Christian architecture, *martyria* were usually circular whereas churches were rectangular, *see* BASILICA.

MASS The three-dimensional bulk of an object, as distinct from the two-dimensional area it covers or the single plane of its surface.

MASTABA Superstructure of an ancient Egyptian tomb: a massive brick or stone mound with BATTERED walls on a rectangular PLAN.

Mastaba

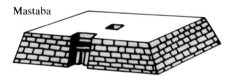

MAUSOLEUM An imposing tomb or building enclosing a tomb, named after that of Mausolus at Halicarnassos, c. 350 BC.

MBIS Carved wood memorial pole erected by the Asmat of New Guinea (18,11).

MEDAL A term originally applied to coins out of circulation; from the fifteenth century applied to small, coin-like metal RELIEFS, *see* pp. 440–1 (10,29; 10,30) and from the nineteenth century those awarded to soldiers, students etc.

MEDIUM The process or means used by an artist (e.g. FRESCO); also the binding agent that holds a PIGMENT together (e.g. oil in OIL PAINT, gum arabic in WATERCOLOR, egg-yolk in TEMPERA) which enables it to be applied evenly and fixes it to the GROUND.

MEGALITH A large piece of stone of irregular shape, roughly dressed or left as found (1,25).

MEGARON A 'large room' in Greek, the term is now used for a square or oblong room, usually with four COLUMNS supporting the roof, the lateral walls projecting to form a porch. Traditional in Greece since Mycenean times and sometimes thought to be the ancestor of the DORIC temple.

(see right)

MEMENTO MORI An image intended to serve as a reminder of death, usually a human skull.

METOPE, *see* ORDERS.

MEZZANINE A low story between two higher ones, mainly in Western architecture of the Renaissance and later.

MEZZOTINT A PRINT made from a copper plate on which an overall BURR has been raised and then smoothed in places which will carry less ink and record the image in a range of tones.

MIHRAB A niche or flat slab in the QUIBLA WALL of a MOSQUE.

MINARET A tall tower from which Muslims can be called to prayer, attached to a MOSQUE (8,13; 12,36).

MINBAR The high PULPIT from which an *imam* leads communal prayers and addresses the congregation in a MOSQUE.

MINIATURE PAINTING A painting with figures outlined in *minium* (a red PIGMENT), usually an ILLUMINATED MANUSCRIPT; by extension any manuscript illumination. More loosely, any very small painting, often a portrait head.

MOBILE A three-dimensional art-work, parts of which can be moved by a current of air, as distinct from KINETIC SCULPTURE with mechanically controlled movement.

MODELLING The process of fashioning such soft materials as clay or wax, and by extension (in painting, drawing, etc.) the indication of solid form by shading.

MODELLO A finished study for a painting or sculpture, in the latter case sometimes of clay or plaster and of the size of the finished work, to be executed in MARBLE with the aid of POINTING APPARATUS.

MODULE A unit of measurement used to regulate the proportions of a building.

MOLDING The CONTOUR given to projecting members in architecture.

MONASTERY A community of men or women (monks or nuns) who choose to follow a religious (Buddhist, Christian or Jain) rule of life isolated from worldly affairs.

MONOCHROME A painting in tones of a single COLOR, e.g. GRISAILLE.

MONOLITH A single stone, e.g. a COLUMN carved in one piece rather than assembled from blocks.

MONOTYPE A PRINT made from an image painted (not ENGRAVED) on a metal or glass plate. As the plate must be partly repainted each time it is used, each of the usually rather few prints made from it is unique.

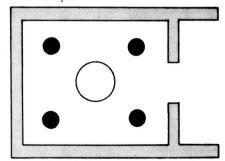

Megaron

MONSTRANCE A container, usually of precious metal, in which the host consecrated in Catholic ritual can be held and shown, as when carried in procession.

MONTAGE A picture composed of PRINTS, photographs, etc., cut out and mounted (20,16).

MOSAIC A pictorial composition made of small colored stones (*pebble mosaic*) (5,8) or cubes of stone, glass, etc., set in plaster (5,24; 7,28).

MOSQUE Islamic building for communal prayer, *see* pp. 844–56.

MUDRAS In Buddhist images, the gestures of the hands that convey clearly defined meanings.

MULLION A vertical post dividing an opening, usually a window, into lights.

MUQARNAS In Islamic architecture, ceiling ornaments formed by CORBELLED SQUINCHES of several layers of brick, scalloped and resembling natural stalactites.

MURAL A painting on a wall, usually but not necessarily in FRESCO.

N

NAMBAN A Japanese painting of foreigners, usually Europeans.

NAOS The walled sanctuary housing the cult image in an ancient Greek temple.

NARTHEX A porch or vestibule at the main entrance of a church.

NAVE The congregational area of a church, usually its western limb, flanked by AISLES.

Nave

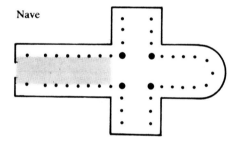

NIMBUS Alternative term for a HALO, especially one that is GILDED or in other ways brilliant.

O

OBELISK A tall tapering shaft of stone, usually granite, of square or rectangular section, and ending pyramidally. Prominently used in ancient Egypt, whence some were brought to Europe under the ancient Roman empire and again in the nineteenth century.

OCULUS A circular opening in a wall or DOME (5,50).

OGEE Double curved lines made up of a concave and convex part (S or inverted S), two such lines constituting an *ogee arch*.

Ogee arch

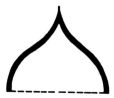

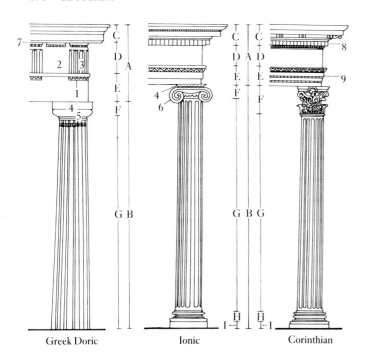
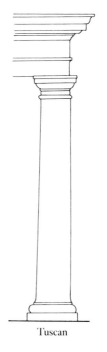
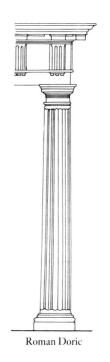
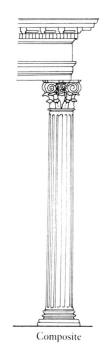

Greek Doric   Ionic   Corinthian   Tuscan   Roman Doric   Composite

Order

A Entablature	G Shaft	4 Abacus
B Column	H Base	5 Echinus
C Cornice	I Plinth	6 Volute
D Frieze	1 Guttae	7 Fluting
E Architrave	2 Metope	8 Dentils
F Capital	3 Triglyph	9 Fascia

OIL PAINT PIGMENT mixed with an oil (usually linseed) which hardens when dry into a transparent film. Oil paint is normally applied opaquely but it can be used as a colored translucent or semi-translucent film over opaque GROUND colors. It use was developed in the fifteenth century in Flanders and Italy and was soon taken up for EASEL PAINTINGS throughout Europe, see p. 430.

ORDERS In Classical architecture an order consists of a COLUMN with base (usually), shaft, CAPITAL and ENTABLATURE decorated and proportioned according to one of the six accepted models.

ORIENTATION or LITURGICAL ORIENTATION The relation of a Christian church to the points of the compass (west door, north and south TRANSEPTS, etc.) assuming that the main altar is at the east end, as it normally, but not invariably, is.

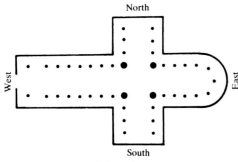

Orientation

ORTHOGONALS Lines running into space at right angles to the PICTURE PLANE in a painting or RELIEF, observing the laws of *linear perspective, see* p. 425.

ORTHOSTAT A slab of stone set upright at the base of a wall and sometimes carved in RELIEF, *see* pp. 92, 107.

P

PAGODA European name for a Far Eastern Buddhist temple tower, called in Chinese a *ta* (6,107), in Japanese a *shoro* if it serves as a bell-tower (6,119) or a *tahoto* if it has a single room with elaborate superstructure.

PAILOU A Chinese monumental gateway usually of stone.

PAINT PIGMENTS ground and mixed with a liquid vehicle, *see* ACRYLIC, FRESCO, GOUACHE, OIL PAINT, TEMPERA, WATERCOLOR.

PAINTERLY Characteristic of a painting in which forms are defined by tone rather than line.

PALETTE A slab on which PIGMENTS could be ground for cosmetics in ancient Egypt, *see* p. 63 (2,23); a wooden board on which painters arrange their colors ready for use and thus, figuratively, the range of colors used by an artist.

PANTOCRATOR Byzantine representation of Christ as universal ruler, usually in the DOME or APSE of a church (7,50).

PAPER A tissue of vegetable fibres used mainly for writing; made in China from the second century BC (if not earlier) and in Europe from the twelfth century AD. In the West it was preceded by PAPYRUS and PARCHMENT.

PAPIER COLLÉ A COLLAGE composed of pieces of variously colored paper glued to a GROUND.

PAPYRUS A substance somewhat similar to PAPER, made from dried and pressed strips of the stems of the marsh plant *Cyperus papyrus*, used as a GROUND for writing and painting in ancient Egypt from the third millenium BC and later in Greece and Rome. In Europe it was gradually superseded by PARCHMENT from the fourth century AD.

PARCEL GILT GILDED in parts.

PARCHMENT The skin of sheep, calf or other animal prepared by drying and stretching as a GROUND for writing from about the fifth century BC in Greece and by an improved process, said to have been invented at Pergamum, from the second century BC. It was used for ILLUMINATED MANUSCRIPTS throughout the European Middle Ages.

PARIETAL An anatomical term for interior surfaces, adopted for the painted or other decoration of similar surfaces, especially caves where there is no distinction between wall and ceiling, e.g. Chauvet, Lascaux, *see* pp. 37–41 (1,9).

PASTEL Dry powdered color mixed with a little gum as a binding agent.

PATINA The effect produced, either naturally or artificially, on BRONZE by oxidation; also LACQUERING applied to give a shiny brown or green surface to bronze. The term is also used figuratively for the surface texture of old objects.

PEBBLE MOSAIC, *see* MOSAIC.

PEDESTAL In Classical architecture, the base supporting a single COLUMN or COLONNADE; also, more loosely, the base for a statue, bust, vase or any superstructure.

PEDIMENT A low pitched GABLE over a PORTICO, door or window. When the CORNICE is discontinuous or broken, usually at the apex but sometimes at the base, it is called a *broken pediment.*

Pediment

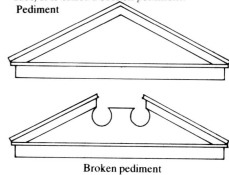

Broken pediment

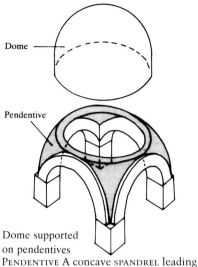

Dome

Pendentive

Dome supported
on pendentives

PENDENTIVE A concave SPANDREL leading from the angle of two walls to the base of a circular DOME (7,41).

PERFORMANCE ART The use of the artist's own body and its coverings as a medium for artistic expression in an action or event.

PERIPTERAL TEMPLE A temple surrounded by a single row of COLUMNS.

PERISTYLE A COLONNADE around the inside of a court or room, also the space surrounded by such a colonnade.

PERSPECTIVE Systems of representing objects in spatial recession, see pp. 19–22 and 425 (linear perspective) and p. 475 (aerial perspective).

PHOTOMONTAGE A term coined in Berlin c. 1918 for a COLLAGE composed of fragments of photographs, newsprint, etc., but later used also for a composite picture made by printing from several negatives on a single sheet.

PICTURE PLANE The flat surface of a picture. If painted according to Western ideas of PERSPECTIVE it is conceived as a transparent plane (or window) between the spectator and the pictorial space.

PIER A solid masonry support, as distinct from a COLUMN.

PIETÀ An image of the Virgin with the dead Christ on her lap.

PIGMENT The coloring substance, usually a powder, held together by a MEDIUM (e.g. oil for OIL PAINT, gum arabic for WATERCOLOR, egg-yolk for TEMPERA) which enables it to be applied evenly and fixes it to the GROUND.

PILASTER A shallow PIER projecting only slightly from a wall; in Classical architecture a rectangular COLUMN conforming to one of the ORDERS.

PILLAR A free-standing upright member, distinct from a COLUMN in that it need neither be cylindrical nor conform with any of the ORDERS.

PINNACLE A small termination to a spire, BUTTRESS, the angle of a parapet, etc., usually of steep pyramidal or conical shape and ornamented.

PITCHED ROOF, see HIPPED ROOF.

PIXELS The tiny points on a computer screen at the intersections of x and y axes.

PLAN The horizontal arrangement of one or more buildings or a single part of a building; or a diagram showing such an arrangement.

PLASTER OF PARIS, see GESSO.

PLEIN AIR PAINTING A painting executed out of doors rather than in a studio.

PLINTH The projecting base of a wall or COLUMN, see ORDERS.

PODIUM A continuous base or PLINTH supporting COLUMNS.

POINTILLISM, see DIVISIONISM.

POINTING APPARATUS A device for measuring volumetric proportions to enable carvers of marble and other stone (rarely wood) sculptures to make accurate copies, enlargements or reductions of models (usually in clay or plaster). The model is marked at its extremities with points and the distances between them and a plumb-line or wooden framework measured so that holes can be drilled at corresponding points to corresponding depths and a copy of the model thereby roughed out (0,2). Various instruments that can measure the relationship of any part of a model to three fixed points have been developed, e.g. the misleadingly named 'pointing machine' used in Europe from the early nineteenth century with one adjustable and three fixed points. (They are not to be confused with hydraulically or electrically operated carving machines developed since the mid-nineteenth century.)

POLYCHROMY The use of many colors in a painting, sculpture or building.

POLYPTYCH A painting or RELIEF, usually an ALTARPIECE on more than three panels, see TRIPTYCH.

PORCELAIN A scientifically imprecise term for several types of hard, dense, impermeable and translucent CERAMIC substance, usually applied to that made in China from about the eighth–ninth centuries and imitations of it made in Europe with different materials and processes from the late sixteenth century though mainly from the early eighteenth century onwards. In porcelain the body and GLAZE are homogeneous whereas in pottery (FAIENCE) the glaze is added to the body.

PORPHYRY Geologically a widespread type of igneous rock, but the term is used in the history of art to describe mainly that of a deep reddish-purple color incorporating large crystals, quarried in Egypt in antiquity. Under the Roman empire it was reserved for imperial use.

PORTICO A roofed space, open or partly enclosed, forming the entrance, and usually the centrepiece of the FAÇADE, of a temple, church or house.

POST AND LINTEL, see TRABEATED.

POTTERY Vessels or other objects made of baked clay, see FAIENCE.

POWER FIGURE The carving of a human being or animal which serves as a receptacle for substances with magic power, formerly called a FETISH (18,36).

PREDELLA The platform on which an altar is set or a small step at the back of an altar, often below an ALTARPIECE, also the paintings or carvings on either of these areas.

PRIMING A coating applied to a surface which is to be painted. A CANVAS for OIL PAINTING is usually coated with size (a thin solution of a gluey or resinous substance) and then primed with white lead.

PRINTS A generic term for all images made in multiple copies from woodblocks, metal plates, inked stone, photographic negatives, etc., see WOODCUT, ETCHING, ENGRAVING, LITHOGRAPHY, SILK-SCREEN.

PROCESS ART Art-works whose subject-matter is the process of their creation which the spectator is invited to reconstruct. Many were executed in the 1960s and 1970s.

PROGRAM The predetermined and often literary 'subject' of a work of art, e.g. the story illustrated in a narrative or HISTORY PAINTING, or the theme of an allegorical painting.

PROPYLAEUM Greek term for the entrance gateway to an enclosure, usually temple precincts, as on the Acropolis at Athens.

PROSCENIUM In a Greek or Roman theatre, the stage on which the action took place. In a modern theatre, the space between the curtain and the orchestra, sometimes including the arch and frontispiece facing the auditorium.

PSALTER A roll, CODEX or book of the Psalms of David, sometimes with a calendar indicating when each psalm was to be read in monastic religious services, and incorporating also hymns, prayers and a litany of saints. Manuscript examples of the eleventh–fourteenth centuries are often richly illuminated.

PULPIT An elevated stand surrounded by a parapet for a preacher or reader in a Christian place of worship, designed as an independent element often richly carved from the eleventh century (9,74) when it began to supersede the AMBO.

PURLIN A horizontal longitudinal timber in a roof.

PUTTO Italian for a male child, especially one shown naked in Renaissance and later art (10,55).

PYLON A pair of truncated pyramidal towers flanking a gateway in ancient Egyptian temple architecture (3,22).

Q

QIBLA WALL The wall of a MOSQUE facing Mecca to which Muslims must turn when praying.

QUINCUNX An arrangement of five verticals, with four at the angles of a rectangle and the fifth in the centre. The term is also applied to a Christian (usually Byzantine) church on a GREEK CROSS plan with a central DOME, four rectangular BAYS covered by BARREL VAULTS, and four smaller bays covered with domes in the angles of the cross.

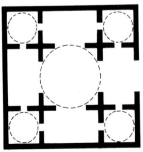

Quincunx or Greek cross church

QUOINS Dressed stones at the corners of a building, sometimes carved with RUSTICATION or otherwise made conspicuous by size or projection.

R

RADIOCARBON DATING A method of estimating the age of organic material (wood, bone, etc.) by measuring its residue of the radioactive isotope of carbon or C-14. C-14 is produced by nitrogen-14 in the atmosphere by cosmic radiation and taken into the compounds of all living matter. It was discovered in 1946 that when living matter dies its C-14 content begins to decay. Measurement of the radioactivity of a specimen gives an indication of the time that has elapsed since the death of its material with a 68% probability that this is within 130 years, plus or minus, a 95% probability that it is within 260 years, and a 99.5% probability that it is within 390 years. Pottery is not susceptible to radiocarbon dating but THERMOLUMINESCENCE tests (also based on radioactivity) indicate the lapse of time, plus or minus 10%, since the mineral crystals in the clay were last heated.

REINFORCED CONCRETE, see FERROCONCRETE.

RELIEF Sculpture with forms projecting from a GROUND, called *high relief* when they are at least half in the round, otherwise *low relief* or *bas-relief.*

RELIQUARY Receptacle for a sacred relic.

REPOUSSÉ RELIEF decoration on metal (mainly GOLD, silver and COPPER) produced by hammering from the underside (2,51).

REPOUSSOIR An object or figure placed in the foreground of a pictorial composition in order to direct the spectator's eye into the picture, usually placed towards the left- or right-hand edge.

REREDOS, see RETABLE.

RESIST The acid-resistant wax used to cover the copper plate for an ETCHING.

RESPOND A half-PIER bonded into a wall and carrying one end of an ARCH.

RETABLE The structure behind an altar (also called a *reredos*), especially one with carved figures in the CORPUS or central part, flanked by carved and/or painted wings (11,6).

RHYTON Ancient Greek term for a drinking vessel of conical form often elaborated into the likeness of an animal's head, see p. 79 (2,47).

RIB A projecting band on a ceiling or VAULT, usually structural but sometimes purely decorative, separating the cells of a groined vault.

RIDGE A horizontal longitudinal timber at the apex of a PITCHED ROOF supporting the ends of rafters.

ROOF COMB The ornamental extension of the rear wall above the roof level in a Mayan building (12,4).

ROSE WINDOW A large circular window in the FAÇADE of a Gothic church.

RUSTICATION Massive blocks of masonry with roughened surfaces and sunk joints, often simulated in plaster (10,20; 11,57).

S

SACRA CONVERSAZIONE The Virgin and Child with saints depicted in such a way that they occupy a single pictorial space, *see* p. 457 (10,49).

SALON French word for a formal room such as the Salon d'Apollon in the royal palace of the Louvre (Paris). Exhibitions of work by the Royal Academy of painters and sculptors were held there from the late seventeenth century and the word 'salon' thus acquired a special meaning. It was used in this sense for official exhibitions in other rooms in the Louvre and from the mid-nineteenth century to cover exhibitions held elsewhere in Paris.

SANCTUARY The area around the main altar of a church.

SAND PAINTING A technique of making designs with sands of different colors practised in many parts of the world, notably by Native Americans in North America.

SANGUINE A russety red CHALK used for drawing.

SARCOPHAGUS A stone or TERRACOTTA coffin: the term is derived from an ancient Greek word for a type of stone believed to have the property of consuming the flesh of a dead body.

SATURATION The relative brightness or dullness of a color, also called intensity.

SCROLL A long roll of PAPER, PAPYRUS, PARCHMENT or silk used for writing and/or painting, notably in China and Japan. In ancient Egypt and Europe scrolls were used as the GROUND for long texts until superseded by the CODEX in the fourth century AD.

SCUMBLE An upper layer of opaque or semi-opaque PIGMENT used in OIL PAINTING, applied irregularly so that areas of the color underneath remain visible, giving a broken or veiled effect, softening hard lines.

SCUOLA Venetian term for a religious confraternity of laymen and its premises, e.g. the Scuola di San Giorgio degli Schiavoni (10,53).

SECTION A diagrammatic drawing of a vertical plane cut through a building (5,49).

SERIGRAPHY, see SILK-SCREEN.

SFUMATO A soft, misty effect attained in OIL PAINTING mainly by the use of GLAZES to create delicate transitions of color and tone, see p. 475.

SHAFT GRAVE A deep narrow pit for burial of the dead.

SHAMAN A priest believed to have contact with and the ability to control good and evil spirits, especially in north-east Asian and north-west American cultures.

SHINGLES Wooden tiles for covering roofs, walls, etc.

SHORO, see PAGODA.

SIKHARA The spire or tower over the shrine of an Indian temple (6,40).

SILK-SCREEN A process of making PRINTS by squeezing paint through a piece of silk, parts of which have been masked, exploited by commercial artists since the 1930s. One impression can be made to differ from another by varying the density of paint. Also called *serigraphy.*

SILVER GELATIN PRINT A photographic PRINT on paper sensitized with silver salts in gelatin. Such paper first became available in the 1880s, was subsequently improved in quality and is still that commonly used for black-and-white photographs.

SILVER POINT A small silver rod with a pointed end for drawing on an abrasive surface (specially prepared PAPER or PARCHMENT or a PRIMED panel), first used in medieval Italy, elsewhere from the fifteenth century, but generally superseded by the GRAPHITE pencil in the seventeenth century.

SINOPIA A reddish brown PIGMENT. The under-drawing for a FRESCO, often made in this MEDIUM, is also called a *sinopia.*

SITE SPECIFIC A term used for an INSTALLATION, sculpture or other art-work designed for, and in reference to, a specific location.

SIZE, see PRIMING.

SLAB ROOF A flat roof composed either of single slabs stretching from one side of an enclosed space to another, or one of CONCRETE which has the appearance of a thick slab.

SLIP A mixture of fine clay and water used as a covering for vessels made from coarser and more porous clay, and fired together. Slip was often used decoratively.

SOCLE A base or PEDESTAL.

SOFFIT The underside of any architectural member, e.g. an ARCH.

SPANDREL A triangular area between the side of an ARCH, the horizontal drawn from its apex and the vertical from its SPRINGING, or that between two arches in an ARCADE, or that of a VAULT between RIBS.

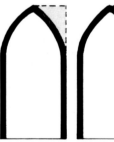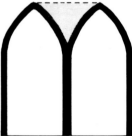

Spandrel

SPHINX A compound creature with a human head and lion's body, probably of ancient Egyptian origin, see p. 68 (2,30).

SPOLIA Materials removed from buildings of an earlier period than that in which they are incorporated, e.g. several RELIEFS on the Arch of Constantine, Rome (5,78), and the Roman COLUMNS in the Great Mosque, Córdoba (8,17).

SPRINGING LINE The level at which an ARCH springs from its supports. The bottom stone of an arch resting on an IMPOST BLOCK is called a *springer.*

SQUINCH An ARCH or system of concentrically wider and gradually projecting arches placed diagonally to support a polygonal or round superstructure on a square base.

STAFF-GOD Polynesian cult image of carved wood wrapped in cloth (18,5).

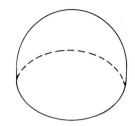

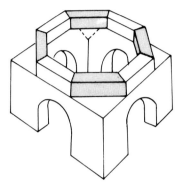

Dome supported on squinches

Squinch

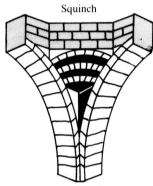

STATES A term used to distinguish groups of PRINTS, mainly ETCHINGS and DRYPOINTS, made from the same plate at different stages of its execution and re-working.

STEEL A metallurgically imprecise term for an alloy of IRON and carbon, generally applied to one that can be hardened and tempered.

STELE An upright slab with an inscription or RELIEF carving, usually commemorative (4,43).

STEREOTOMY The art of cutting stone into sections of geometric solids.

STILL LIFE A representation of such inanimate objects as flowers, fruit, dead animals or household articles.

STOA A covered COLONNADE in ancient Greek and Roman cities, flanking the AGORA or open market- and meeting-place.

STRING COURSE A continuous horizontal band in or more usually projecting from an exterior wall.

STUCCO Various types of plaster used as a protective and decorative covering for walls. A mixture including lime and powdered MARBLE has been extensively used for RELIEF decorations on ceilings and interior walls since the sixteenth century in Europe (14,15).

STUPA An Indian sacred mound, originally

sepulchral but later of a type erected by Buddhists to enshrine a relic or mark a holy site (6,6).

STYLOBATE The top step of the base of a Greek temple, but the term is also applied to the substructure on which a COLONNADE stands.

SURINOMO A Japanese presentation PRINT on special paper.

SUTRA A book of the Buddhist canon.

SWAG An ornamental motif resembling a piece of cloth draped over two supports.

SYMMETRY The correspondence of parts of an object or its decorations on either side of a real or imaginary central line. The PLAN of a building is said to be symmetrical when it has rooms of corresponding size, shape and disposition on either side of the centre, so that one half is the mirror image of the other. Symmetry is often no more than approximate, especially in pictorial compositions. But the term asymmetrical signifies a complete absence of symmetry.

SYNAESTHESIA The notion that an impression on one sense can be made by another, e.g. hearing by sight – the 'musical' effect of a painting – or vice-versa.

T

TA, see PAGODA.

TABERNACLE A canopied recess to contain an image; an ornamental receptacle for the consecrated host, usually in the form of a miniature building placed on an altar in a Catholic church; the portable shrine in which the Jewish Ark of the Covenant was housed.

TABLEAU-OBJET A term coined by the Cubists for a picture conceived as an independent construction rather than a representation – it means literally a 'picture-object'.

TAHOTO, see PAGODA.

TAOTIE Chinese term for the dragon mask on Shang dynasty BRONZE vessels (2,63; 2,64).

TELL Archeological term for a mound covering an ancient site in the Near East, e.g. Tell Halaf.

TEMPERA Painting with powdered PIGMENTS made workable (tempered) by egg-yolk and water, a technique practised in Europe from the early Middle Ages until the sixteenth century (9,71).

TERM A PEDESTAL tapering towards the base and usually supporting a bust; also a pedestal merging at the top into a human bust or animal figure and similarly tapering towards the base. See also HERM.

TERRACOTTA Baked or fired but unglazed clay, usually reddish-brown in color.

TESSERAE The small pieces of stone, glass or other material used to compose a MOSAIC.

THEATRE A place for viewing dramas or other spectacles, open-air in ancient Greece and Rome, see p. 156 (4,44; 5,69), usually covered in Europe since the sixteenth century.

THERMAE Ancient Roman buildings for public baths, sometimes of great splendour and incorporating also places

for sport, discussion, reading, etc., see pp. 217–8 (5,72; 5,73).

THERMOLUMINESCENCE, see RADIOCARBON DATING.

THOLOS Greek term for a building on a circular PLAN, usually a temple or tomb.

THRUST The outward force of an ARCH or VAULT, counterbalanced if necessary by BUTTRESSES.

TOKO-NO-MA The alcove in which a painting or print is hung and a flower vase placed in a Japanese house.

TONDO A painting or RELIEF of circular shape, e.g. Raphael's *Alba Madonna* (11,17).

TOPOGRAPHY The depiction of a particular locality as distinct from a wholly or partly imaginary landscape or townscape.

TORANA Indian gateway, especially one on the enclosure of a Buddhist STUPA (6,6).

TOTEM The emblem of an individual family or clan, usually an animal. The word is in origin Native American (Ojibwa) though used in a different sense.

TRABEATED Construction based mainly on upright members supporting horizontals, as in an ancient Greek temple. Also called *post and lintel*. To be distinguished from ARCUATED.

TRACERY Ornamental intersecting work in the upper part of a Gothic window, screen or panel, or on the surface of a VAULT. There are two main types: *plate tracery*, consisting of decoratively shaped openings cut through the solid stone infilling above an early Gothic window with two or more lights; *bar tracery*, consisting of ribwork made, as it were, by bending and interweaving the tops of the MULLIONS within the window frame.

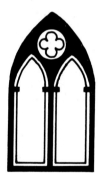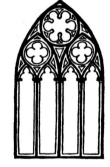

Plate tracery   Bar tracery

TRANSEPT The tranverse arms of a cross-shaped church.

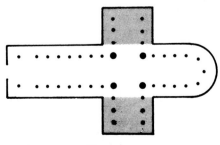

Transepts

TRANSVERSALS Lines parallel to the PICTURE PLANE in the system of linear

PERSPECTIVE, intersecting the ORTHOGONALS.

TRANSVERSE ARCH An ARCH separating one BAY of a VAULT from another in Romanesque and Gothic architecture.

TRIBHANGA Literally 'three bends', the sinuous pose in Indian art and dance (6,5).

TRIBUNE The APSE of a BASILICA or basilican church; also an alternative term for a GALLERY in a Romanesque or Gothic church.

TRIFORIUM An ARCADED wall passage facing on to the NAVE of a Romanesque or Gothic church, above the arcade and below the CLERESTORY.

TRIGLYPH, see ORDERS.

TRILITHON Two upright MEGALITHS supporting a horizontal one.

TRIPTYCH A painting on three panels.

TRIUMPHAL ARCH A free-standing monumental gateway of a type originated in Rome in the early second century BC (5,63). Also the TRANSVERSE ARCH at the east end of a medieval church, framing the altar and APSE and marking them off from the rest of the interior.

TROMPE L'OEIL An illusionistic painting intended to 'deceive the eye', see p. 189 (5,28).

TROPHY A carving or painting of a group of arms and armour such as were erected as memorials to victories by ancient Romans (5,57) and, by extension, similar groups of other objects.

TRUMEAU A stone MULLION supporting the middle of a TYMPANUM (9,28).

TRUSS A number of wooden or metal beams forming a rigid framework.

TYMPANUM The area between the LINTEL of a doorway and the ARCH above it (9,26); also the triangular or segmental space enclosed by the MOLDINGS of a PEDIMENT.

U

UKIYO-E Japanese representations of everyday life, usually PRINTS but also paintings (16,9).

UNDERPAINTING The initial layers of paint, especially in OIL PAINTING.

V

VALUE, see COLOR.

VANISHING POINT In an image observing the laws of linear PERSPECTIVE (see pp. 19–22 and 425), the point on which the lines defining horizontal parallels at right-angles to the pictorial surface would converge if continued, see ORTHOGONALS.

VANITAS An allegorical STILL LIFE often incorporating a skull as a reminder of mortal transience.

VARNISH A solution of resin applied as a protective coat over a painting, sometimes tinted to modify the colors of the PIGMENTS beneath it.

VAULTING A masonry roof or ceiling constructed on the principle of the ARCH. The simplest form is a tunnel or

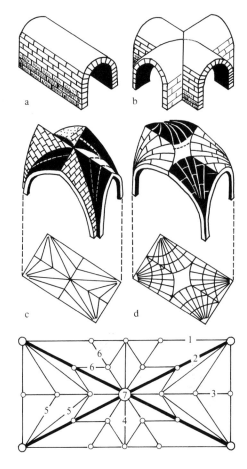

a Tunnel vault
b Groin vault
c Rib vault
d Fan vault

1 Transverse rib
2 Diagonal rib
3 Transverse ridge-rib
4 Longitudinal ridge-rib
5 Tiercerorns
6 Liernes
7 Boss

barrel vault of continuous semicircular or pointed SECTION unbroken by cross-vaults (9,23). The intersection of two tunnel vaults of identical shape produces a groin vault. A rib vault has a framework of arched diagonal RIBS between which the cells are filled with lighter stone (9,33). It is called quadripartite if each BAY is divided into four quarters or cells, sexpartite if divided transversely into two parts so that each bay has six compartments (9,34). A dome is a vault of even curvature on a circular PLAN and of segmental, semicircular, pointed or bulbous section. The simplest form is constructed by CORBELLING, see p. 83. If a dome is erected on a square base PENDENTIVES or SQUINCHES must be interpolated at the corners to mediate between square and circle.

VELLUM A fine type of PARCHMENT prepared from calf skin.

VIDEO RASTER GRAPHICS Computer generated and manipulated video images.

VIDEO SYNTHESIZER An instrument that enables video artists to manipulate electronic video information so that images can be stretched or shrunk, change color, break up, inset or merge with other images.

VIHARA Indian term for a Buddhist or Jain MONASTERY.

VILLA Latin word for a country-house, a villa urbana being one near a city, a villa rustica attached to a farm. Descriptions of both types influenced European architects from the sixteenth century, see p. 503.

VIMANA In a Hindu temple, the shrine and its superstructure.

VITRUVIAN SCROLL A band of repeated wave-like scrolls often used in FRIEZES in Classical architecture.

VOLUME Space enclosed by MASS, e.g. the interior of a building.

VOLUTE The spiral scroll on CAPITALS of the Ionic and, less prominently, Corinthian and Composite ORDERS.

VOUSSOIR A wedge-shaped brick or stone forming one of the units of an ARCH.

W

WASH An area of diluted ink or transparent WATERCOLOR spread evenly and showing no brush marks.

WATERCOLOR PIGMENTS mixed with a gum that dissolves in water providing a transparent stain for application to an absorbent surface, usually PAPER.

WENRENHUA Chinese term for the style of painting practised by literary men or scholar-artists, see pp. 280–3, 552–5 and 560–2.

WESTWORK The west end of a Carolingian or Romanesque church, crowned by a broad tower (sometimes flanked by turrets) with internally a large room opening on to a NAVE above a low entrance hall (9,4).

WOODCUT A print made from a block of wood from the surface of which all areas not intended to carry ink have been cut away (10,47; 10,55). The block is cut from a smoothed plank of fairly soft wood with the grain running parallel to the surface. A print made from a block of very hard wood cut across the grain and worked with a graving tool is called a wood engraving.

Y

YAKSHI Indian nature spirit (6,5).

YAMATO-E Japanese term for paintings in Japanese – as distinct from Chinese – styles (12,80).

Z

ZIGGURAT A rectangular mound built in stepped-back stages and crowned by a temple (2,13).

ZODIAC The band of the celestial sphere on either side of the apparent yearly path of the sun amongst the stars, divided since Babylonian times into twelve 'houses' each with its symbol.

ZOOMORPH Boulders carved by the Maya with animal and other forms, as distinct from the MEGALITHS (12,5) cut and carved into the form of STELAE.

FOR FURTHER READING

The following list is limited to books in English (only one place of publication usually being given, although most were published in both England and the USA. The date of first publication is given in brackets). For the most up-to-date bibliography, covering works in the European languages, see E. Arntzen and R. Rainwater, *Guide to the Literature of Art History*, Chicago, 1980. The 15-volume *Encyclopedia of World Art*, New York, 1959-68, presents an exceptionally full and well-illustrated world-wide survey, now partially superseded by J. S. Turner, ed., *The Dictionary of Art*, London/New York, 1996. Handy single-volume dictionaries of artistic terms with brief biographies of artists (mainly Western) include P. and L. Murray, *A Dictionary of Art and Artists* (1959), London, 1997; H. Read, rev. N. Stangos, *The Thames and Hudson Dictionary of Art and Artists* (1966), London, 1994; E. Lucie-Smith, *The Thames and Hudson Dictionary of Art Terms* (1984), London, 1988; J. Fleming, H. Honour and N. Pevsner, *The Penguin Dictionary of Architecture and Landscape Architecture* (1966), London/New York, 1998; J. Fleming and H. Honour, *Penguin Dictionary of Decorative Arts* (1977), London, 1995; I. Chilvers and H. Osborne, eds., *The Oxford Dictionary of Art* (1988), 1997.

Introduction

Art as craft
E. W. Anthony, *A History of Mosaics* (1935), New York, 1968
S. B. Butters, *The Triumph of Vulcan: Sculptors' Tools, Porphyry and the Prince in Ducal Florence*, Florence, 1997
C. Cennini, tr. D. V. Thompson, Jr., *The Craftsman's Handbook: The Italian 'Il Libro Dell'Arte'*, New Haven, 1933
N. Davey, *A History of Building Materials*, London, 1961
A. Geijer, *A History of Textile Art*, London/Totowa, NJ, 1979
A. M. Hind, *A History of Engraving and Etching* (1923), New York, 1963
W. M. Ivins, *Prints and Visual Communication* (1953), Cambridge, Mass., 1970
R. J. Mainstone, *Developments in Structural Form*, London (1968), 1975
A. H. Mayor, *Prints and People. A Social History of Printed Pictures*, New York, 1971
B. Newhall, *The History of Photography* (1937), New York, 1982
N. Penny, *The Materials of Sculpture*, New Haven, 1993
N. Rosenblum, *A World History of Photography* (1984), New York, 1997
W. Verhelst, *Sculpture: Tools, Materials, and Techniques* (1973), Englewood Cliffs, NJ, 1988
K. Whelte, *The Materials and Techniques of Painting* (1952), New York, 1975

Pictorial representation
J. Gage, *Color and Culture*, Boston, 1993
E. H. Gombrich, *Art and Illusion* (1960), London, 1977
M. Kemp, *The Science of Art*, New Haven, 1990
J. White, *The Birth and Rebirth of Pictorial Space* (1957), Boston, 1987

Style and the individual artist
E. H. Gombrich, *Norm and Form* (1966), Chicago, 1985
F. Lang, ed., *The Concept of Style*, Philadelphia, 1979
G. Wölfflin, *Principles of Art History* (1915), New York, 1950
H. Wollheim, *Painting as an Art*, Princeton/London, 1987

Context: function and meaning
J. Berger, *Ways of Seeing*, London, 1972
M. Baxandall, *Patterns of Intention: On the Historical Explanation of Pictures*, New Haven/London, 1985
A. Boime, *The Art of Exclusion*, Washington DC/London, 1990
J. Bryson, *Vision and Painting: The Logic of the Gaze*, London, 1983
L. Bugner, ed., *The Image of the Black in Western Art*, vols I, II and IV, Cambridge, Mass., 1976-89
J. Derrida, tr. G. Bennington & I. McLeod, *The Truth in Painting*, Chicago, 1987
A. Hauser, *The Social History of Art* (1951), New York, 1985
S. Kostof, *A History of Architecture: Settings and Rituals* (1986), rev. G. Castillo, New York/Oxford, 1995
S. Kostof, *The City Shaped, Urban Patterns and Meanings through History*, Boston/London, 1991
A. Locke, *The Negro in Art*, Washington DC, 1940
W. J. T. Mitchell, *Iconology: Image, Text and Ideology*, Chicago, 1986
C. Norberg-Schultz, *Meaning in Western Architecture*, New York, 1975
E. Panofsky, tr. J. J. S. Peake, *Idea: A Concept in Art Theory*, New York, 1968
E. Panofsky, *Meaning in the Visual Arts* (1955), Chicago, 1982
E. Panofsky, *Studies in Iconology* (1939), New York, 1972
E. W. Said, *Orientalism*, New York, 1978
E. B. Smith, *Architectural Symbolism of Imperial Rome and the Middle Ages* (1956), New York, 1978

Women artists
N. Broude & M. Garrard, eds., *Feminism and Art History: Questioning the Litany*, New York/London, 1982
N. Broude & M. D. Garrard, eds., *The Expanding Discourse: Feminism and Art History*, New York, 1992
W. Chadwick, *Women, Art and Society* (1990), London, 1996
P. Fister, *Japanese Women Artists*, Lawrence, Kans., 1988
D. Gaze, ed., *Dictionary of Women Artists*, London/Chicago, 1997
A. S. Harris & L. Nochlin, *Women Artists 1550–1950*, New York, 1976
L. Nochlin, *Women, Art and Power*, New York, 1988
R. Parker & G. Pollock, *Old Mistresses*, New York, 1981
K. Petersen & J. J. Wilson, *Women Artists: Recognition and Reappraisal from the Early Middle Ages to the Twentieth Century*, New York, 1976

G. Pollock, *Vision and Difference*, New York/London, 1988
N. Rosenblum, *A History of Women Photographers*, London, Paris and New York, 1994
M. Weidner *et al.*, *Views from the Jade Terrace: Chinese Women Artists 1300–1912*, Indianapolis, 1988
M. R. Witzling, ed., *Voicing Our Visions: Writings by Women Artists*, New York, 1991

The history of art
M. H. Abrams & J. Ackerman, *Theories of Criticism: Essays in Literature and Art*, Washington DC, 1984
J. Ackerman & R. Carpenter, *Art and Archeology*, Englewood Cliffs, NJ, 1963
L. S. Adams, *The Methodologies of Art: An Introduction*, New York, 1996
H. Belting, *The End of the History of Art?*, Chicago/London, 1987
N. Bryson, ed., *Calligram: Essays in New Art History from France*, Cambridge, 1988
D. Carrier, *Principles of Art History Writing*, University Park, Pa., 1991
P. Duro and M. Greenhalgh, *Essential Art History*, London, 1992
E. Fernie, *Art History and Its Methods: A Critical Anthology*, London, 1995
E. H. Gombrich, *Reflections on the History of Art: Views and Reviews*, Princeton/Oxford, 1987
F. Haskell, *History and its Images*, New Haven/London, 1993
A. Hauser, *The Philosophy of Art History*, London, 1959
M. A. Holly, *Past Looking: The Historical Imagination and the Rhetoric of the Image*, Ithaca/London, 1996
W. McA. Johnson, *Art History: Its Use and Abuse*, Toronto, 1988
W. E. Kleinbauer, *Modern Perspectives in Western Art History*, New York, 1971
D. Laing, *The Marxist Theory of Art*, Hassocks, Sussex, 1978
B. Lang & F. Williams, eds., *Marxism and Art: Writings in Aesthetics and Criticism*, New York, 1972.
V. H. Minor, *Art History's History*, Englewood Cliffs, NJ, 1994
R. S. Nelson & R. Shiff, eds., *Critical Terms for Art History*, Chicago, 1996
M. Podro, *The Critical Historians of Art*, New Haven/London, 1982
D. Preziosi, *Rethinking Art History: Meditations on a Coy Science*, New Haven/London, 1989
D. Preziosi, ed., *The Art of Art History: A Critical Anthology*, Oxford/New York, 1998
A. L. Rees & F. Borzello, eds., *The New Art History*, London, 1986
M. Roskill, *What is Art History* (1976), Amherst, Mass., 1989
L. Venturi, *History of Art Criticism* (1936), New York, 1964

1 Before history

C. L. Bruce, *The Stages of Human Evolution* (1968), Englewood Cliffs, NJ, 1979
J.-M. Chauvet *et al.*, *Chauvet Cave: The Discovery of the World's Oldest Paintings*, London, 1996

G. Clark, *World Prehistory in New Perspective* (1961), Cambridge, 1977

G. Daniel, *The Megalith Builders of Western Europe* (1958), Westport, Conn., 1985

J. D. Evans, *Prehistoric Antiquities of the Maltese Islands*, London, 1971

S. Giedion, *The Eternal Present: The Beginning of Art*, New York, 1962

M. Gimbutas, *The Civilization of the Goddess*, San Francisco, 1991

K. Helskog & B. Olsen, eds., *Perceiving Rock Art: Social and Political Perspectives*, Oslo, 1995

K. M. Kenyon, *Archaeology in the Holy Land* (1960), London, 1979

A. Leroi-Gourhan, *The Art of Prehistoric Man*, London, 1968

A. Leroi-Gourhan, *The Dawn of European Art*, New York/Cambridge, 1982

A. Marshak, *The Roots of Civilization*, London, 1971

J. Mellaart, *Catal Hüyük: A Neolithic Town in Anatolia*, London, 1967

J. Mellaart, *The Neolithic of the Near East*, New York, 1975

J. F. Pfeiffer, *The Creative Explosion: An Inquiry into the Origins of Art and Religion*, New York/London, 1982

P. Phillips, *The Prehistory of Europe*, London, 1980

C. Renfrew, *Before Civilization: The Radio-carbon Revolution and Prehistoric Europe* (1973), Harmondsworth, 1976

N. K. Sandars, *Prehistoric Art in Europe* (1968), Harmondsworth, 1985

P. Ucko & A. Rosenfeld, *Palaeolithic Cave Art*, London, 1967.

2   The early civilizations

3   Developments across the continents

Mesopotamia

G. Algaze, *The Uruk World System: The Dynamics of Expansion of Early Mesopotamian Civilization*, Chicago/New York, 1993

P. Amiet, *Art of the Ancient Near East*, New York, 1980

D. Collon, *Ancient Near Eastern Art*, London, 1995

H. Crawford, *Sumer and the Sumerians*, New York/Cambridge, 1991

J. E. Curtis, *Ancient Persia*, London, 1989

J. E. Curtis & J. E. Reade, eds., *Art and Empire: Treasures from Assyria in the British Museum*, London, 1995

H. Frankfort, *The Art and Architecture of the Ancient Orient* (1954), New Haven/London, 1996

R. Ghirshman, *Persia from the Origins to Alexander the Great*, London, 1964

H. A. Groenwegen-Frankfort, *Arrest and Movement* (1951), New York, 1978

S. A. A. Kubba, *Mesopotamian Architecture and Town Planning*, Oxford, 1987

A. Kuhrt, *The Ancient Near East, c. 3000–300 bc*, London/New York, 1995

S. Lloyd, *The Archaeology of Mesopotamia* (1978), London, 1984

S. A. Matheson, *Persia: An Archaeological Guide*, London, 1972

M. van de Mieroop, *The Ancient Mesopotamian City*, Oxford, 1997

A. Parrot, *Sumer and the Dawn of Art* and *The Arts of Assyria*, London, 1960–1

E. Porada & R. H. Dyson, *The Art of Ancient Iran*, New York, 1969

J. N. Postgate, *Early Mesopotamia: Society and Economy at the Dawn of History* (1992), London/New York, 1994

J. Reade, *Mesopotamia*, Cambridge, Mass./London, 1991

H. W. F. Saggs, *Babylonians*, London, 1995

Indus Valley

B. & R. Allchin, *The Rise of Civilization in India and Pakistan*, Cambridge, 1982

J. M. Kenoyer, *Ancient Cities of the Indus Valley*, New Delhi, forthcoming

E. J. H. Mackay, *Early Indus Civilization*, London, 1948

G. Possehl, ed., *A Harappan Civilization: A Contemporary Perspective*, Delhi, 1992

R. E. M. Wheeler, *The Indus Civilization*, Cambridge, 1968

Ancient Egypt

C. Aldred, *The Development of Ancient Egyptian Art from 3200 to 1315 bc*, 3 vols, London, 1973

D. Arnold, *Building in Egypt*, New York/Oxford, 1991

A. Badawy, *A History of Egyptian Architecture*, 3 vols, Berkeley, 1954-68

W. Davis, *The Canonical Tradition in Ancient Egyptian Art*, Cambridge, 1989

I. E. S. Edwards, *The Pyramids of Egypt* (1979), Harmondsworth, 1991

T. G. H. James, *An Introduction to Ancient Egypt*, London, 1979

G. Robins, *Proportion and Style in Ancient Egyptian Art*, London, 1994

G. Robins, *The Art of Ancient Egypt*, London, 1997

H. Schäfer, *Principles of Egyptian Art* (1918), Oxford, 1986

E. B. Smith, *Egyptian Architecture as Cultural Expression* (1938), New York, 1968

W. Stevenson Smith, *The Art and Architecture of Ancient Egypt* (1958), New Haven/London, 1980

J. A. Wilson, *The Burden of Egypt*, Chicago, 1951

Aegean

J. Boardman, *Pre-classical: From Crete to Archaic Greece* (1967), Harmondsworth, 1978

R. Castleden, *Minoans. Life in Bronze Age Crete*, New York/London, 1990

J. Chadwick, *The Mycenaean World*, New York/Cambridge, 1976

A. Cottrell, *The Minoan World*, London, 1979

O. Dickinson, *The Aegean Bronze Age*, Cambridge/New York, 1994

J. L. Fitton, *Cycladic Art*, London, 1989

R. Hampe & E. Simon, *The Birth of Greek Art: From the Mycenaean to the Archaic Period*, New York/London, 1981

S. Hood, *The Arts in Prehistoric Greece*, Harmondsworth, 1978

S. Marinatos & M. Hirmer, *Crete and Mycenae*, London, 1960 (Munich ed. 1973, includes Akrotiri)

S. P. Morris, *Daidalos and the Origins of Greek Art*, Princeton, 1992

C. Renfrew, *The Cycladic Spirit*, New York/London, 1991

E. T. Vermeule, *Greece in the Bronze Age*, Chicago, 1972

Hittites

E. Akurgal, *The Art of the Hittites*, London, 1962

China

G. L. Barnes, *China, Korea and Japan: The Rise of Civilization in East Asia*, London, 1993

Wen Fong, ed., *The Great Bronze Age of China*, New York, 1980

M. Loehr, *Ritual Vessels of Bronze Age China*, New York, 1968

Qian Hao et al., *Out of China's Earth. Archaeological Discoveries*, New York, 1981

M. J. Powers, *Art and Political Expression in Early China*, New Haven/London, 1991

J. Rawson, *Ancient China, Art and Archaeology*, London, 1980

J. Rawson, *Chinese Bronzes: Art and Ritual*, London, 1987

J. Rawson, *Chinese Jade from the Neolithic to the Qing*, London, 1995

J. Rawson, ed., *Mysteries of Ancient China: New Discoveries from the Early Dynasties*, London, 1996

W. Watson, *Ancient Chinese Bronze* (1962), London, 1977

W. Watson, *The Arts of China to ad 900*, New Haven/London, 1995

W. Willetts, *Chinese Art*, vol I, Harmondsworth, 1958

The Americas

M. Coe et al., *The Olmec World: Ritual and Rulership*, New York, 1995

G. Kubler, *The Art and Architecture of Ancient America* (1962), Harmondsworth, 1984

M. Miller & K. Taube, *The Gods and Symbols of Ancient Mexico and the Maya*, London, 1993

R. F. Townsend, ed., *The Ancient Americas: Art from Sacred Landscapes*, Chicago, 1992

Africa

E. Eyo & F. Willett, *Treasures of Ancient Nigeria*, New York, 1980

B. Fagg, *Nok Terracottas*, Lagos & London, 1977

P. Garlake, *The Hunter's Vision: Prehistoric Rock Art of Zimbabwe*, London, 1995

4   **The Greeks and their neighbours**

S. Adam, *The Technique of Greek Sculpture*, London, 1966

B. Ashmole, *Attic Red-Figure Vase-Painters* (1942), New York, 1984

J. D. Beazley, *The Development of Attic Black-Figure* (1951), Berkeley, 1986

J. Boardman, *Greek Art* (1984), London, 1996

J. Boardman, *The Greeks Overseas* (1964), London, 1980

J. Boardman, ed., *The Oxford History of Classical Art*, Oxford, 1993

R. Carpenter, *Greek Art*, Philadelphia, 1962

R. Carpenter, *Greek Sculpture. A Critical Review*, Chicago, 1971

R. Carpenter, *The Architects of the Parthenon*, Harmondsworth, 1970

R. Carpenter, *The Esthetic Basis of Greek Art* (1921), Bloomington, 1963

K. Clark, *The Nude* (1956), Harmondsworth, 1960

R. M. Cook, *Greek Art* (1972), London, 1991

W. B. Dinsmoor, *The Architecture of Ancient Greece* (1950), New York/London, 1975

I. D. Jenkins, *The Parthenon Frieze*, London, 1994

A. W. Lawrence, *Greek Architecture* (1957), New Haven/London, 1996

R. Osborne, *Archaic and Classical Greek Art*, Oxford, 1998

J. G. Pedley, *Greek Art and Archaeology* (1992), London, 1998

J. J. Pollitt, *Art and Experience in Classical Greece*, New York, 1972

J. J. Pollitt, *The Art of Ancient Greece Sources and Documents* (1965), Cambridge, 1990

T. Rasmussen & N. Spivey, eds., *Looking at Greek Vases*, Cambridge, 1991

G. Richter, *A Handbook of Greek Art* (1959), London, 1987

B. S. Ridgway, *Fifth Century Styles of Greek Sculpture*, Princeton, 1981

R. F. Rhodes, *Architecture and Meaning on the Athenian Acropolis*, Cambridge, 1995

M. Robertson, *A History of Greek Art*, Cambridge, 1975

V. Scully, *The Earth, the Temple and the Gods* (1962), New Haven/London, 1979

B. Sparkes, *Greek Pottery: An Introduction*, Manchester, 1991

B. A. Sparkes, *The Red and the Black: Studies in Greek Pottery*, London/New York, 1996

N. J. Spivey, *Understanding Greek Sculpture: Ancient Meanings, Modern Readings*, London, 1996

N. J. Spivey, *Greek Art*, London, 1997
A. Stewart, *Greek Sculpture, an Exploration* (1990), New Haven/London, 1993
A. Stewart, *Art, Desire and the Body in Ancient Greece*, Cambridge/New York, 1997

Scythian
E. C. Bunker, C. B. Chatwin & A. R. Farkas, *Animal Style Art from West to East*, New York, 1970
K. Jettmar, *Art of the Steppes*, London, 1967
B. Piotrovsky *et al.*, *Scythian Art*, Oxford, 1987

Celtic
B. Cunliffe, *The Ancient Celts*, Oxford, 1997
M. Green, *Celtic Art*, London, 1996
P. Jacobsthal, *Early Celtic Art*, Oxford, 1944
L. Laing & J. Laing, *Art of the Celts*, London, 1992
N. K. Sandars, *Prehistoric Art in Europe* (1968), Harmondsworth, 1985

Iberian
A. Arribas, *The Iberians*, London, 1964

Etruscan
G. Barker & T. Rasmussen, *The Etruscans*, Oxford, 1998
A. Boethius, *Etruscan and Early Roman Architecture* (1970), New Haven/London, 1979
O. J. Brendel, *Etruscan Art* (1978), New Haven/London, 1995
M. Cristofani, *The Etruscans: A New Investigation*, London, 1979
N. Spivey, *Etruscan Art*, London, 1997

5   Hellenistic and Roman art
See K. Clark, R. M. Cook, A. W. Lawrence & M. Robertson above
R. Bianchi Bandinelli, *Rome: the Centre of Power*, London, 1970
R. Bianchi Bandinelli, *Rome: the Late Empire*, London, 1971
M. Bieber, *The Sculpture of the Hellenistic Age*, New York, 1961
J. Boardman, *The Diffusion of Classical Art in Antiquity*, London, 1994
O. G. Brendel, *Prolegomena to the Study of Roman Art* (1953), New Haven/London, 1979
R. Brilliant, *Roman Art from the Republic to Constantine*, London, 1974
P. Brown, *The World of Late Antiquity*, London, 1971
A. Burford, *Craftsmen in Greek and Roman Society*, London, 1972
J. Charbonneaux, R. Martin & F. Villard, *Hellenistic Art*, London, 1973
J. R. Clarke, *The Houses of Roman Italy*, Berkeley/Oxford, 1991
E. D'Ambra, *Art and Identity in the Roman World* (US title: *Roman Art*), London, 1998 (US: New York, 1998)
G. Hanfmann, *Roman Art* (1964), New York, 1975
N. Hannestad, *Roman Art and Imperial Policy*, Aarhus, Denmark, 1986
C. M. Havelock, *Hellenistic Art* (1971), New York/London, 1981
D. E. E. Kleiner, *Roman Sculpture*, New Haven/London, 1992
R. Ling, *Roman Painting*, Cambridge, 1991
H. P. L'Orange, *The Roman Empire, Art Forms and Civic Life*, New York, 1985
M. Lyttelton, *Baroque Architecture in Classical Antiquity*, New York, 1974
W. L. MacDonald, *The Architecture of the Roman Empire*, vol I (1965) , London, 1982; vol II New Haven/London, 1986
W. L. MacDonald, *The Pantheon*, London, 1976
J. Onians, *Art and Thought in the Hellenistic Age*, London, 1979
E. D. Owens, *The City in the Greek and Roman World*, London, 1991
J. J. Pollitt, *Art in the Hellenistic Age*, Cambridge, 1986

J. J. Pollitt, *The Art of Rome c. 753 bc–ad 337: Sources and Documents* (1966), Cambridge, 1983
N. H. & A. Ramage, *The Cambridge Illustrated History of Roman Art*, Cambridge, 1991
N. H. & A. Ramage, *Roman Art* (1991), London, 1996
B. S. Ridgeway, *Hellenistic Sculpture*, Madison, 1990
R. R. R. Smith, *Hellenistic Sculpture*, London, 1991
D. E. Strong, *Roman Art* (1976), New Haven/London, 1988
C. V. Vermeule, *Roman Art, Early Republic to Late Empire*, Boston, 1979
A. Wallace-Hadrill, *Houses and Society in Pompeii and Herculaneum*, Princeton, 1994
J. B. Ward-Perkins, *Roman Imperial Architecture* (1970), New Haven/London, 1981

6   Buddhism and Far Eastern art
T. R. Blurton, *Hindu Art*, London, 1992
P. Brown, *Indian Architecture (Buddhist & Hindu)* (n.d.), Bombay, 1971
R. C. Craven, *Indian Art* (1976), London, 1997
J. Fontein, *The Sculpture of Indonesia*, New York/Washington DC, 1990
Wen C. Fong, *Beyond Representation: Chinese Painting and Calligraphy 8th–14th Century*, New Haven/London, 1992
J. C. Harle, *The Art and Architecture of the Indian Subcontinent* (1986), New Haven/London, 1994
S. L. Huntington, *The Art of Ancient India*, New York/Tokyo, 1985
S. Kramrisch, *The Art of India* (1955), London, 1965
S. Kramrisch, *The Hindu Temple*, Delhi, 1976
S. E. Lee, *A History of Far Eastern Art* (1964), New York, 1994
M. Loehr, *The Great Painters of China*, Oxford, 1980
G. Michell, *The Hindu Temple*, Chicago, 1977
J. Miksic, *Borobudur*, London/Singapore, 1990
D. Mitra, *Ajanta*, New Delhi, 1980
K. Nishikawa & E. J. Sano, *The Great Age of Japanese Buddhist Sculpture ad 600–1300*, Fort Worth, 1982
S. Noma, *The Arts of Japan*, Tokyo, 1978
R. T. Paine & A. Soper, *The Art and Architecture of Japan* (1955), New Haven/London, 1981
A. Paludan, *The Chinese Spirit Road: The Classical Tradition of Stone Tomb Statuary*, New Haven/London, 1991
J. Ramanaiah, *Temples of South India*, New Delhi, 1989
J. Rawson, ed., *The British Museum Book of Chinese Art*, London, 1992
B. Rowland, *The Evolution of the Buddha Image*, New York, 1963
S. Sickman & A. Soper, *The Art and Architecture of China* (1956), Harmondsworth, 1971
J. C. Singer & P. Denwood, eds., *Tibetan Art: Towards a Definition of Style*, London, 1997
J. Stanley-Baker, *Japanese Art*, London, 1984
P. C. Sturman, *Mi Fu: Style and the Art of Calligraphy in Northern Song China*, New Haven/London, 1997
M. Sullivan, *The Arts of China* (1967), Berkeley, 1984
M. Sullivan, *Symbols of Eternity*, Oxford, 1979
M. Tregear, *Chinese Art* (1980), London, 1997
W. Watson, *Style in the Arts of China*, Harmondsworth, 1974
P. Wheatley, *Pivot of the Four Corners*, Edinburgh, 1971
W. Willetts, *Chinese Calligraphy: Its History and Aesthetic Motivation*, Hong Kong, 1981
J. G. Williams, *The Art of Gupta India*, Princeton, 1982

H. R. Zimmer, *The Art of Indian Asia* (1955), Princeton, 1960

7   Early Christian and Byzantine art
D. Buckton, ed., *Byzantium*, London, 1994
R. Cormack, *Writing in Gold, Byzantine Society and its Icons*, London, 1985
R. Cormack, *Painting the Soul: Icons, Death Masks and Shrouds*, London, 1997
C. Davis-Weyer, *Early Medieval Art 300–1150: Sources and Documents*, Englewood Cliffs, NJ, 1971
A. Cutler, *The Hand of the Master: Craftsmanship, Ivory and Society in Byzantium (9th–11th Centuries)*, Princeton, 1994
J. Elsner, *Art and the Roman Viewer: The Transformation of Art from the Pagan World to Antiquity*, Cambridge, 1995
J. R. Elsner, *Imperial Rome and Christian Triumph*, Oxford, 1998
H. C. Evans & W. D. Wixom, eds., *The Glory of Byzantium*, New York, 1997
A. Grabar, *Christian Iconography*, Princeton, 1968
A. Grabar, *Early Christian Art*, London, 1968
A. Grabar & C. Nordenfalk, *Early Medieval Painting for the Fourth to the Eleventh Century*, New York, 1957
F. Henry, *Irish Art*, Ithaca, 1965–70
R. Hinks, *Carolingian Art* (1935), Ann Arbor, 1962
J. Hubert, *The Carolingian Renaissance*, London, 1970
L. James, *Light and Colour in Byzantine Art*, Oxford, 1996
E. Kitzinger, *Byzantine Art in the Making*, Cambridge, Mass./London, 1977
E. Kitzinger, *Early Medieval Art in the British Museum* (1940), London, 1983
R. Krautheimer, *Early Christian and Byzantine Architecture* (1965), New Haven/London, 1986
J. Lowden, *Early Christian and Byzantine Art*, London, 1997
R. J. Mainstone, *Hagia Sophia, Architecture, Structure and Liturgy*, London, 1988
C. Mango, *Byzantine Architecture* (1976), New York, 1985
C. Mango, *The Art of the Byzantine Empire 321–1453: Sources and Documents*, Englewood Cliffs, NJ, 1972
G. Mathew, *Byzantine Aesthetics*, London, 1963
T. F. Mathews, *The Clash of Gods: A Reinterpretation of Early Christian Art*, Princeton, 1993
T. F. Mathews, *The Art of Byzantium: Between Antiquity and the Renaissance* (US title: *Byzantium: From Antiquity to the Renaissance*), London, 1998 (US: New York, 1998)
R. Ousterhout & L. Brubaker, eds., *The Sacred Image East and West*, Urbana, Ill., 1995
A. L. Perkins, *The Art of Dura-Europos*, Oxford, 1973
L. Rodley, *Byzantine Art and Architecture*, Cambridge, 1994
S. Runciman, *Byzantine Style and Civilization*, Harmondsworth, 1975
K. Weitzman, *Ancient Book Illumination*, Cambridge, Mass., 1959
K. Weitzman, *Illustrations in Roll and Codex*, (1947), Princeton, 1970
K. Weitzmann, *Late Antique and Early Christian Book Illumination*, New York/London, 1977
K. Weitzmann & H. L. Kessler, *The Frescoes of the Dura Synagogue and Christian Art*, Washington DC, 1990
D. M. Wilson, *Anglo-Saxon Art*, London, 1984
D. M. Wilson & O. Klindt-Jensen, *Viking Art*, London (1966), London, 1980

8   Early Islamic art

J. Bloom & S. Blair, *Islamic Arts*, London, 1997

B. Brend, *Islamic Art*, Cambridge, Mass./London, 1991

K. A. C. Creswell, *Early Islamic Architecture* (1932–40), abridged ed., Harmondsworth, 1958, rev. ed., vol I (1969), Aldershot, 1989

J. D. Dodds., ed., *Al-Andalus: The Art of Islamic Spain*, New York, 1992

R. Ettinghausen, *Arab Painting* (1962), New York, 1977

R. Ettinghausen & O. Grabar, *The Art and Architecture of Islam, 650–1250*, Harmondsworth, 1987

O. Grabar, *The Formation of Islamic Art* (1973), New Haven/London, 1987

D. Hill, *Islamic Architecture and its Decoration ad 800–1500*, London, 1964

R. Hillenbrand, *Islamic Architecture: Form, Function and Meaning*, Edinburgh, 1994

R. Hillenbrand, *Islamic Art and Architecture*, London, 1999

J. D. Hoag, *Islamic Architecture* (1977), New York/London, 1987

S. H. Nasr, *Islamic Art and Spirituality*, New York, 1987

M. Rogers, *The Spread of Islam*, Oxford, 1976

A. Schimmel, *Calligraphy and Islamic Culture* (1984), New York/London, 1990

9   Medieval Christendom

J. J. G. Alexander, *Medieval Illuminators and their Methods of Work*, New Haven/London, 1992

J. Alexander & P. Binski, eds., *Age of Chivalry: Art in Plantagenet England 1200–1400*, London, 1987

J. Backhouse *et al.*, ed., *The Golden Age of Anglo-Saxon Art 966–1066*, London, 1984

H. Belting, *Likeness and Presence: A History of the Image Before the Era of Art*, Chicago, 1994

D. Bomford *et al.*, *Italian Painting Before 1400: Art in the Making*, London, 1989

J. Bony, *French Gothic Architecture of the 12th and 13th Centuries*, Los Angeles/London, 1983

E. Borsook, *The Mural Painters of Tuscany* (1960), Oxford, 1980

M. Camille, *Gothic Art*, London/New York, 1996

A. Chastel, *French Art: Prehistory to the Middle Ages*, Paris/New York, 1995

K. G. Conant, *Carolingian and Romanesque Architecture 800–1200* (1959), New Haven/London, 1990

O. Demus, *Byzantine Art and the West*, New York, 1970

C. R. Dodwell, *The Pictorial Arts of the West 800–1200*, New Haven/London, 1993

J. F. Fitchen, *The Construction of Gothic Cathedrals* (1961), London/Chicago, 1981

H. Focillon, *The Art of the West in the Middle Ages* (1938), London, 1980

P. Frankl, *Gothic Architecture*, Harmondsworth, 1962

T. G. Frisch, *Gothic Art 1140–1450: Sources and Documents*, Englewood Cliffs, NJ, 1971

J. Gimpel, *The Cathedral Builders*, New York, 1983

C. de Hamel, *A History of Illuminated Manuscripts* (1986), London, 1994

J. H. Harvey, *The Medieval Architect*, New York/London, 1972

G. Henderson, *Early Medieval* (1972), Harmondsworth, 1977

G. Henderson, *Gothic*, Harmondsworth, 1967

P. Hills, *The Light of Early Italian Painting*, New Haven/London, 1987

J. Huizinga, *The Waning of the Middle Ages* (1924), New York, 1988

H. Jantzen, *High Gothic* (1962), Princeton, 1984

A. Katzenellenbogen, *The Sculptural Programs of Chartres Cathedral* (1959), New York, 1964

P. Lasko, *Ars Sacra 800–1200* (1972), New Haven/London, 1994

E. Mâle, *Religious Art in France: The Twelfth Century* (1922), Princeton, 1978

E. Mâle, *Religious Art in France, XIII Century* (1898), Princeton, 1984

H. Mayr-Harting, *Ottonian Book Illumination: An Historical Study*, London, 1991

M. Meiss, *French Painting in the Time of Jean de Berry*, New York, 1967–74

M. Meiss, *Painting in Florence and Siena after the Black Death* (1951), New York, 1978

D. Norman, ed., *Siena, Florence and Padua: Art, Society and Religion 1280–1400*, New Haven/London, 1995

O. Pächt, *Book Illumination in the Middle Ages*, London, 1986

E. Panofsky, *Abbot Suger on the Abbey Church of St Denis* (1945), Princeton, 1979

E. Panofsky, *Renaissance and Renascences in Western Art* (1960), New York, 1972

A. Petzold, *Romanesque Art*, New York/London, 1995

J. Pope-Hennessy, *Italian Gothic Sculpture* (1955), London, 1996

C. M. Radding & W. W. Clark, *Medieval Architecture, Medieval Learning*, New Haven/London, 1992

W. Sauerländer, *Gothic Sculpture in France 1140–1270*, London, 1972

M. Schapiro, *Romanesque Art*, New York, 1977

O. G. von Simson, *The Gothic Cathedral* (1974), Princeton, 1988

J. Stayaert, *Late Gothic Sculpture: The Burgundian Netherlands*, Ghent, 1994

H. Swarzenski, *Monuments of Romanesque Art* (1954), Chicago, 1967

J. White, *Art and Architecture in Italy 1250–1400* (1966), New Haven/London, 1993

P. Williamson, *Gothic Sculpture 1140–1300*, New Haven/London, 1995

C. Wilson, *The Gothic Cathedral: The Architecture of the Great Church 1130–1530* (1990), London, 1992

G. Zarnecki, *Art of the Medieval World*, New York, 1975

G. Zarnecki, ed., *English Romanesque Art, 1066–1200*, London, 1984

G. Zarnecki, *Romanesque Art*, New York, 1989

10   The fifteenth century in Europe
11   The sixteenth century in Europe

J. Ackerman, *The Architecture of Michelangelo* (1961), Harmondsworth, 1970

F. Ames-Lewis & M. Rogers, eds., *Concepts of Beauty in Renaissance Art*, Aldershot/Brookfield, 1998

M. Baxandall, *Painting and Experience in Fifteenth-Century Italy* (1972), Oxford, 1988

M. Baxandall, *The Limewood Sculptors of Renaissance Germany*, New Haven/London, 1980

B. Berenson, *The Italian Painters of the Renaissance* (1894–1907), Oxford, 1980

O. Benesch, *The Art of the Renaissance in Northern Europe* (1945), Hamden, Conn., 1964

A. Blunt, *Artistic Theory in Italy 1450–1600* (1940), London, 1962

P. P. Bober & R. Rubinstein, *Renaissance Artists and Antique Sculpture*, London, 1986

E. Borsook & F. Superbi Gioffredi, eds., *Italian Altarpieces, 1250–1550: Function and Design*, Oxford, 1994

P. F. Brown, *Venetian Narrative Painting in the Age of Carpaccio*, New Haven, 1988

P. F. Brown, *Venice and Antiquity*, New Haven/London, 1996

P. F. Brown, *The Renaissance in Venice* (US title: *Art and Life in Renaissance Venice*), London, 1997 (US: New York, 1997)

J. C. Burckhardt, *The Civilization of the Renaissance in Italy* (1860), London, 1995

L. Campbell, *Renaissance Portraits*, New Haven/London, 1990

A. Chastel, *The Age of Humanism*, London, 1963

A. Chastel, *The Crisis of the Renaissance 1520–1600*, Geneva, 1968

A. Chastel, *French Art: The Renaissance, 1430–1620*, Paris, 1995

K. Clark, *Leonardo da Vinci* (1939), New York/London, 1988

A. Cole, *Art of the Italian Renaissance Courts: Virtue and Magnificence*, London/New York, 1995

C. Farago, ed., *Reframing the Renaissance: Visual Culture in Europe and Latin America, 1450–1650*, New Haven/London, 1995

S. J. Freedberg, *Painting in Italy 1500–1600* (1971), New Haven/London, 1993

S. J. Freedberg, *Paintings of the High Renaissance in Rome and Florence* (1961), New York, 1985

C. Gilbert, *History of Renaissance Art*, New York, 1973

C. Gilbert, *Italian Art, 1400–1500* (1980) Evanston, 1992

R. Goffen, *Piety and Patronage in Renaissance Venice*, New Haven/London, 1986

E. H. Gombrich, *Norm and Form: Studies in the Art of the Renaissance* (1966), London, 1985

E. H. Gombrich, *Symbolic Images* (1972), London, 1985

J. R. Hale, *The Civlization of Europe in the Renaissance*, London, 1993

E. C. Harbison, *The Art of the Northern Renaissance*, London, 1995

F. Hartt, *History of Italian Renaissance Art* (1969), rev. D. Wilkins, New York/London, 1994

T. Helton, ed., *The Renaissance, a Reconsideration of the Theories and Interpretations of the Age* (1961), Madison, 1964

L. H. Heydenreich, *Architecture in Italy 1400–1500* (1974), rev. P. Davies, New Haven/London, 1996

M. Hollingsworth, *Patronage in Renaissance Italy: From 1400 to the Early Sixteenth Century*, London, 1994

P. Humfrey, *The Altarpiece in Renaissance Venice*, New Haven/London, 1993

P. Humfrey, *Painting in Renaissance Venice*, New Haven/London, 1995

P. Humfrey & M. Kemp, eds., *The Altarpiece in the Renaissance*, Cambridge, 1990

N. Huse & W. Wolters, *The Art of Renaissance Venice*, Chicago, 1990

G. A. Johnson & S. F. M. Grieco, eds., *Picturing Women in Renaissance and Baroque Italy*, Cambridge, 1997

M. Kemp, *The Science of Art*, New Haven/London, 1990

M. Kemp, *Behind the Picture: Art and Evidence in the Italian Renaissance*, New Haven/London, 1997

R. Klein & H. Zerner, *Italian Art 1500–1600: Sources and Documents*, Englewood Cliffs, NJ, 1966

D. Landau & P. W. Parshall, *The Renaissance Print 1470–1550*, New Haven/London, 1994

M. A. Lavin, *The Place of Narrative, Mural Decoration in Italian Churches 431–1600*, Chicago/London, 1990

M. Levey, *High Renaissance*, Harmondsworth, 1975

M. Levey, *The Early Renaissance*, Harmondsworth, 1967

W. Lotz, *Architecture in Italy 1500–1600* (1974), intro. D. Howard, New Haven/London, 1995

T. Müller, *Sculpture in the Netherlands, Germany, France and Spain 1400–1500*, Harmondsworth, 1966

J. Onians, *Bearers of Meaning*, Princeton, 1988

G. von der Osten & H. Vey, *Painting and Sculpture in Germany and the Netherlands 1500–1600*, Harmondsworth, 1969

O. Pächt, *Van Eyck and the Founders of Early Netherlandish Painting*, ed. M. Schmidt-Dengler, London, 1994

E. Panofsky, *Early Netherlandish Painting* (1953), New York, 1971

E. Panofsky, *The Life and Art of Albrecht Dürer* (1943), Princeton, 1967

L. Partridge, *The Renaissance in Rome* (US title: *The Art of Renaissance Rome*), London, 1996 (US: New York, 1996)

J. Pope-Hennessy, *Italian High Renaissance and Baroque Sculpture* (1963), London, 1996

J. Pope-Hennessy, *Italian Renaissance Sculpture* (1958), London, 1996

D. Rosand, *Painting in Sixteenth-Century Venice* (1982), Cambridge, 1997

F. Saxl, *Heritage of Images*, Harmondsworth, 1970

F. Saxl, *Lectures*, London, 1957

S. K. Scher, ed., *The Currency of Fame: Portrait Medals of the Renaissance*, New York, 1994

J. Shearman, *Mannerism*, Harmondsworth, 1967

J. Snyder, *Northern Renaissance Art*, New York, 1985

W. Stechow, *Northern Renaissance Art 1400–1600: Sources and Documents*, Englewood Cliffs, NJ, 1966

C. L. Stinger, *The Renaissance in Rome*, Bloomington, 1985

D. Summers, *Michelangelo and the Language of Art*, Princeton, 1981

R. Tavernor, *Palladio and Palladianism*, New York/London, 1991

P. Tinagli, *Women in Italian Renaissance Art*, Manchester, 1997

A. R. Turner, *The Renaissance in Florence: The Birth of a New Art* (US title: *Renaissance Florence: The Invention of a New Art*), London, 1997 (US: New York, 1997)

G. Vasari (tr. A. B. Hinds, ed. W. Gaunt), *The Lives of the Painters, Sculptors and Architects*, New York/London, 1963

E. S. Welch, *Art and Authority in Renaissance Milan*, New Haven/London, 1995

E. S. Welch, *Art and Society in Italy 1350–1500*, Oxford/New York, 1997

J. Wilde, *Venetian Art from Bellini to Titian* (1974), Oxford, 1981

E. Wind, *Pagan Mysteries in the Renaissance* (1958), Harmondsworth, 1967

R. Wittkower, *Architectural Principles in the Age of Humanism* (1949), New York/London, 1988

12 The Americas, Africa and Asia

The Americas

K. Berrin, ed., *Feathered Serpents and Flowering Trees: Reconstructing the Murals of Teotihuacán*, San Francisco, 1988

K. Berrin & E. Pasztory, eds., *Teotihuacán: Art from the City of the Gods*, San Francisco/London, 1993

G. H. S. Bushnell & A. Digby, *Ancient American Pottery*, London, 1956

M. D. Coe & J. Kerr, *The Art of the Maya Scribe*, London, 1997

C. Donnan, *Ceramics of Ancient Peru*, Los Angeles, 1992

G. Kubler, *The Art and Architecture of Ancient America* (1962), New York, 1984

M. E. Miller, *The Art of Mesoamerica* (1986), London, 1996

M. E. Miller, *The Murals of Bonampak*, Princeton, 1986

E. Matos Moctezuma, *Teotihuacán, the City of the Gods*, Milan, 1990

E. Matos Moctezuma, *The Great Temple of the Aztecs*, London, 1988

E. Pasztory, *Pre-Columbian Art*, London/New York, 1998

D. Reents-Budet *et al.*, *Painting the Maya Universe: Royal Ceramics of the Classic Period*, Durham/London, 1994

J. A. Sabloff, *The Cities of Ancient Mexico* (1989), London, 1997

L. Schele & M. E. Miller, *The Blood of Kings, Dynasty and Ritual in Maya Art*, Fort Worth, 1986

R. Stone-Miller, ed., *To Weave for the Sun: Ancient Andean Textiles*, Boston, 1992

R. Stone-Miller, *Art of the Andes*, London, 1995

Africa

S. P. Blier, *Royal Arts of Africa*, London/New York, 1998

P. Ben-Amos, *The Art of Benin* (1980), London/Washington DC, 1995

P. J. C. Dark, *An Introduction to Benin Art and Technology*, Oxford, 1973

E. Eyo & F. Willett, *Treasures of Ancient Nigeria*, New York, 1980

K. Ezra, *Royal Art of Benin*, New York, 1992

W. Fagg, *Divine Kingship in Africa* (1970), London, 1978

W. Gillon, *A Short History of African Art*, Harmondsworth, 1984

T. N. Hoffman, *Symbols in Stone: Unravelling the Mystery of Great Zimbabwe*, Johannesberg, 1987

J. D. Lewis-Williams, *The Rock Art of Southern Africa*, Cambridge, 1983

T. Phillips, ed., *Africa: The Art of a Continent*, London/New York, 1995

M. N. & A. F. Roberts, eds., *Memory: Luba Art and the Making of History*, New York/Munich, 1996

T. Shaw, *Unearthing Igbo-Ukwu*, New York, 1977

F. Willett, *African Art: An Introduction* (1971), London, 1993

F. Willett, *Ife in the History of West African Sculpture*, London, 1967

The Islamic world and India

C. B. Asher, *Architecture of Mughal India*, Cambridge, 1992

C. B. Asher & T. R. Metcalf, eds., *Perceptions of South Asia's Visual Past*, New Delhi, 1994

O. Aslanapa, *Turkish Art and Architecture*, London, 1971

E. Atil, ed., *Turkish Art*, Washington DC/New York, 1980

P. L. Baker, *Islamic Textiles*, London, 1995

D. Barrett & B. Gray, *Painting in India* (1963), New York, 1978

M. C. Beach, *Mughal and Rajput Painting*, Cambridge, 1992

W. E. Begley & Z. A. Desai, *Taj Mahal*, Cambridge, Mass., 1989

S. S. Blair & J. M. Bloom, *The Art and Architecture of Islam 1250–1800*, New Haven/London, 1994

P. Brown, *Indian Architecture, The Islamic Period* (1942), Bombay, 1968

S. R. Canby, *Persian Painting*, London, 1993

J. Carswell, *Iznik Pottery*, London, 1998

V. Dehejia, *Indian Art*, London, 1997

F. W. Ferrier, ed., *The Arts of Persia*, New Haven/London, 1989

G. Goodwin, *A History of Ottoman Architecture*, London, 1971

O. Grabar, *The Alhambra*, Cambridge, Mass./London, 1978

B. Gray, *Persian Painting* (1961), New York/London, 1977

J. Guy & D. Swallow, eds., *Arts of India 1550–1900*, London, 1990

R. Irwin, *Islamic Art*, London/New York, 1997

E. Koch, *Mughal Architecture*, Munich, 1991

J. Levenson, ed., *Circa 1492: Art in the Age of Exploration*, Washington DC, 1991

G. Michell & A. Martinelli, *The Royal Palaces of India*, London, 1994

A. U. Pope, *Persian Architecture*, New York, 1965

V. Porter, *Islamic Tiles*, New York/London, 1995

J. M. Rogers, *Islamic Art and Design*, London, 1983

H. Soebadio, ed., *Pusaka: The Art of Indonesia*, Singapore, 1992

Sultan Süleyman the Magnificent, exh. cat., British Museum, London, 1988

C. Tadgell, *The History of Architecture in India*, London, 1990

R. Ward, *Islamic Metalwork*, New York/London, 1993

S. C. Welch, *India, Art and Culture 1300–1900*, New York, 1985

S. C. Welch, *Royal Persian Manuscripts*, New York/London, 1976

S. C. Welch, *The Art of Moghul India*, New York, 1965

See also works cited for Chapters 6 and 8.

China

R. M. Barnhart *et al.*, *Three Thousand Years of Chinese Painting*, New Haven/London, 1997

A. Boyd, *Chinese Architecture and Town Planning*, Chicago, 1962

J. Cahill, *Painting at the Shore, Chinese Painting of the Early and Middle Ming Dynasty 1368–1580*, New York, 1978

J. Cahill, *The Compelling Image*, Cambridge Mass./London, 1982

J. Cahill, *The Distant Mountains. Chinese Painting of the Late Ming Dynasty 1570–1644*, New York, 1982

C. Clunas, *Pictures and Visuality in Early Modern China*, London, 1997

C. Clunas, *Art in China*, Oxford/New York, 1997

Wen C. Fong, ed., *Possessing the Past: Treasures from the National Palace Museum, Taipei*, New York, 1996

R. Kerr, ed., *Chinese Art and Design*, London, 1991

M. Keswick, *The Chinese Garden*, London, 1978

L. G. Liu, *Chinese Architecture*, London, 1989

A. Murck & Wen Fong, *Chinese Poetry, Calligraphy and Painting*, New York/Princeton, 1991

N. S. Steinhardt, *Chinese Imperial City Planning*, Honolulu, 1990

S. J. Vainker, *Chinese Pottery and Porcelain from Prehistory to the Present*, London, 1991

M. Weidner *et al.*, *Views from the Jade Terrace: Chinese Women Artists 1300–1912*, Indianapolis, 1988

See also works cited for Chapter 6.

Japan

J. Earle, ed., *Japanese Art and Design*, London, 1986

J. Fontein & M. C. Hickman, eds., *Zen Painting and Calligraphy*, Greenwich, Conn., 1970

C. Guth, *Japanese Art of the Edo Period* (US title: *Art of Edo-Japan*), London, 1996 (US: New York, 1996)

M. L. Hickman, *Japan's Golden Age: Momoyama*, New Haven/London, 1996

S. E. Lee, *Japanese Decorative Style* (1961), New York, 1972

P. Mason, *History of Japanese Art*, New York, 1993

Y. Shimizu, ed., *Japan. The Shaping of Daimyo Culture 1185–1868*, New York, 1988

A. Yonemura *et al.*, *Twelve Centuries of Japanese Art from the Imperial Collections*, Washington DC/London, 1997

See also works cited for Chapter 6.

13 The seventeenth century in Europe

14 Enlightenment and liberty

B. Allen, ed., *Towards a Modern Art World*, New Haven/London, 1995

S. Alpers, *The Art of Describing: Dutch Art in the Seventeenth Century*, Chicago/London, 1983

S. Alpers, *Rembrandt's Enterprise, the Studio and the Market*, Chicago/London, 1988

J. Barrell, ed., *Painting and the Politics of Culture: New Essays on British Art 1700–1850*, Oxford/New York, 1992

A. Blunt, *Art and Architecture in France, 1500–1700* (1953), Harmondsworth, 1981

A. Blunt, ed., *Baroque and Rococo. Architecture and Decoration*, London, 1978

A. Boime, *Art in the Age of Revolution 1750–1800*, Chicago, 1987

B. Boucher, *Italian Baroque Sculpture*, London, 1998

A. Braham, *The Architecture of the French Enlightenment*, Berkeley/London, 1980

J. Brown, *The Golden Age of Painting in Spain*, New Haven, 1991

N. Bryson, *Word and Image: French Painting of the Ancien Régime*, Cambridge, 1981

J. Burke, *English Art 1714–1800*, Oxford, 1976

M. Craske, *Art in Europe, 1700–1830*, Oxford/New York, 1997

T. E. Crow, *Painters and Public Life in Eighteenth-Century Paris*, New Haven/London, 1985

T. DaCosta Kaufmann, *Court, Cloister and City: The Art and Culture of Central Europe 1450–1800*, London, 1995

L. Eitner, *Neoclassicism and Romanticism 1750–1850: Sources and Documents*, vol I, Englewood Cliffs, NJ, 1971

J. H. Elliott, *Spain and Its World 1500–1700*, New Haven/London, 1989

R. Enggass & J. Brown, *Italy and Spain 1600–1750: Sources and Documents*, Englewood Cliffs, NJ, 1970

W. E. Francis, *Paragons of Virtue: Women and Domesticity in Seventeenth Century Dutch Art*, Cambridge, 1993

M. Fried, *Absorption and Theatricality. Painting and Beholder in the Age of Diderot*, Berkeley, 1980

B. Haak, *The Golden Age: Dutch Painters of the Seventeenth Century*, New York/London, 1984

F. Haskell, *Patrons and Painters* (1963), New Haven, 1980

J. Held & D. Posner, *17th and 18th Century Art*, New York, 1974

E. Hempel, *Baroque Art and Architecture in Central Europe*, Harmondsworth, 1965

H.-R. Hitchcock, *Rococo Architecture in Southern Germany*, London, 1968

H. Honour, *Neoclassicism* (1968), Harmondsworth, 1977

W. von Kalnein, *Architecture in France in the Eighteenth Century*, New Haven/London, 1995

F. Kimball, *The Creation of the Rococo*, Philadelphia, 1943

G. A. Kubler & M. Soria, *Art and Architecture in Spain and Portugal and their American Dominions 1500–1800* (1959), Harmondsworth, 1984

R. W. Lee, *Ut Pictura Poesis: The Humanistic Theory of Painting*, New York, 1967

M. Levey, *Painting and Sculpture in France 1700–1789*, New Haven/London, 1993

M. Levey, *Painting in Eighteenth-Century Venice* (1959), New Haven/London, 1994

G. Luitjen et al., *Dawn of the Golden Age: Northern Netherlandish Art, 1580–1620*, Amsterdam, 1993

D. Mahon, *Studies in Seicento Art and Theory* (1947), Westport, Conn., 1971

J. R. Martin, *Baroque*, New York/London, 1977

A. Mérot, *French Painting in the Seventeenth Century*, New Haven/London, 1995

J. Montagu, *Roman Baroque Sculpture* (1989), New Haven/London, 1992

J. Montagu, *Gold, Silver and Bronze: Metal Sculpture of the Roman Baroque*, New Haven/London, 1996

M. North, *Art and Commerce in the Dutch Golden Age*, New Haven/London, 1997

R. Paulson, *Breaking and Remaking. Aesthetic Practice in England 1700–1820*, New Brunswick/London, 1989

R. Paulson, *Emblem and Expression*, London, 1975

N. Pevsner, *Academies of Art, Past and Present* (1940), New York, 1973

M. Pointon, *Hanging the Head: Portraiture and Social Formation in Eighteenth-Century England*, New Haven/London, 1993

H. H. Rhys, ed., *Seventeenth Century Science and the Arts*, Princeton, 1961

J. Rosenberg, S. Slive & E. H. ter Kuile, *Dutch Art and Architecture 1600–1800* (1966), New Haven/London, 1979

R. Rosenblum, *Transformations in Late Eighteenth Century Art* (1967), Princeton, 1970

S. Schama, *The Embarrassment of Riches. An Interpretation of Dutch Culture*, London, 1987

K. Scott, *The Rococo Interior: Decoration and Social Spaces in Early Eighteenth Century Paris*, New Haven/London, 1995

S. Slive, *Dutch Painting 1600–1800*, New Haven/London, 1995

D. H. Solkin, *Painting for Money: The Visual Arts and the Public Sphere in Eighteenth Century England*, New Haven/London, 1993

W. Stechow, *Dutch Landscape Painting in the Seventeenth Century* (1966), Oxford, 1981

J. Summerson, *Architecture in Britain 1530 to 1850* (1953), New Haven/London, 1993

P. C. Sutton, *Masters of 17th-century Dutch Genre Painting*, Philadelphia, 1984

P. C. Sutton et al., *Masters of 17th-century Dutch Landscape Painting*, Boston/London, 1987

P. Taylor, *Dutch Flower Painting 1600–1720*, New Haven/London, 1995

J. Tomlinson, *Painting in Spain: El Greco to Goya 1561–1828*, London/New York, 1997

J. Varriano, *Italian Baroque and Rococo Architecture*, New York/Oxford, 1986

M. Westermann, *The Art of the Dutch Republic 1585–1718* (US title: *A Wordly Art: The Dutch Republic, 1585–1718*), London, 1996 (US: New York, 1996)

M. Whinney & O. Millar, *English Art 1553–1625*, Oxford, 1957

R. Wittkower, *Art and Architecture in Italy 1600–1750* (1958), New Haven/London, 1982

15   Romanticism to Realism
17   Impressionism to Post-Impressionism

S. Adams, *The Barbizon School and the Origins of Impressionism*, London, 1994

K. Berger, *Japonisme in Western Painting*, Cambridge, 1992

A. Boime, *Art in an Age of Bonapartism 1800–1815*, Chicago, 1990

A. Boime, *The Academy and French Painting in the Nineteenth Century*, London, 1970

D. Bomford et al., *Impressionism: Art in the Making*, New Haven/London, 1991

N. Broude, *Impressionism: A Feminist Reading*, New Haven/London, 1991

D. Cherry, *Painting Women: Victorian Women Artists*, London/New York, 1993

T. J. Clark, *The Absolute Bourgeois*, London, 1973

T. J. Clark, *Image of the People*, London, 1973

T. J. Clark, *The Painting of Modern Life. Paris in the Art of Manet and his Followers*, New York, 1984

T. E. Crow, *Emulation: Making Artists for Revolutionary France*, New Haven/London, 1995

S. E. Eisenman et al., *Nineteenth Century Art: A Critical History*, New York/London, 1994

L. Eitner, *An Outline of 19th Century European Painting: From David through Cézanne*, New York/London, 1987–8

F. Frascina et al., *Modernity and Modernism: French Painting in the Nineteenth Century*, New Haven/London, 1993

P. Galassi, *Before Photography: Painting and the Invention of Photography*, New York, 1981

T. Garb, *Sisters of the Brush: Women's Artistic Culture in Late Nineteenth Century Paris*, New Haven/London, 1994

S. Giedion, *Mechanization takes Command* (1948), New York, 1955

S. Giedion, *Space, Time and Architecture* (1941), Cambridge, Mass., 1967

R. Goldwater, *Symbolism*, London, 1979

S. Greenough et al., eds., *On the Art of Fixing a Shadow. One Hundred and Fifty Years of Photography*, Washington DC, 1989

G. H. Hamilton, *Painting & Sculpture in Europe 1880–1940* (1967), New Haven/London, 1993

A. C. Hanson, *Manet and the Modern Tradition*, New Haven, 1977

R. Herbert, *Impressionism: Art, Leisure, and Parisian Society*, New Haven/London, 1988

H.-R. Hitchcock, *Architecture Nineteenth and Twentieth Centuries* (1958), New Haven/London, 1978

W. Hofmann, *The Earthly Paradise: Art in the Nineteenth Century*, London, 1961

H. Honour, *Romanticism* (1979), Harmondsworth, 1981

J. House et al., *Landscapes of France: Impressionism and Its Rivals*, London, 1995

J. Howard, *Art Nouveau: International and National Styles in Europe*, Manchester/New York, 1996

J. G. Hutton, *Neo-Impressionism and the Search for Solid Ground: Art, Science and Anarchism in Fin-de-Siècle France*, Baton Rouge/London, 1994

K. D. Kriz, *The Idea of the English Landscape Painter*, New Haven/London, 1997

S. Loevren, *The Genesis of Modernism* (1959), Bloomington, 1971

D. M. Lublin, *Picturing a Nation: Art and Social Change in Nineteenth-Century America*, New Haven/London, 1994

P. Mainardi, *Art and Politics of the Second Empire*, New Haven/London, 1987

J. Marsh & P. G. Nunn, *Women Artists and the Pre-Raphaelite Movement*, London, 1989

B. Newhall, *The History of Photography* (1937), New York, 1982

L. Nochlin, *Realism*, Harmondsworth, 1971

L. Nochlin, *Realism and Tradition in Art 1848–1900: Sources and Documents*, Englewood Cliffs, NJ, 1966

L. Nochlin, *Impressionism and Post-Impressionism 1874–1904: Sources and Documents*, Englewood Cliffs, NJ, 1966

L. Nochlin, *The Politics of Vision. Essays on Nineteenth Century Art and Society*, New York, 1989

B. Novak, *American Painting of the Nineteenth Century* (1969), New York/London, 1979

F. Novotny, *Painting and Sculpture in Europe 1780–1880* (1960), Harmondsworth, 1970

N. Pevsner, *Pioneers of Modern Design* (1936), Harmondsworth, 1975

J. Rewald, *Post-Impressionism from Van Gogh to Gauguin* (1957), New York/London, 1978

J. Rewald, *The History of Impressionism* (1946), New York, 1987

C. Rosen & H. Zerner, *Romanticism and Realism*, London, 1984

N. Rosenblum, *A World History of Photography* (1984), New York/London, 1989

R. Rosenblum & H. W. Janson, *19th Century Art*, New York, 1984

M. Schapiro, *Impressionism: Reflections and Perceptions*, New York, 1997

A. Scharf, *Art and Photography* (1968), London, 1974

D. L. Silverman, *Art Nouveau in Fin de Siècle France: Politics, Psychology and Style,*

Berkeley/Oxford, 1989
J. C. Sloane, *French Painting between the Past and the Present* (1951), Princeton, 1973
P. Smith, *Impressionism*, New York/London, 1995
J. Treuherz, *Victorian Painting*, London, 1993
W. H. Truettner, ed., *The West as America*, Washington DC/London, 1991
W. Vaughan, *German Romantic Painting* (1980), New Haven/London, 1994
P. C. Vitz & A. B. Glimcher, *Modern Art and Modern Science: The Parallel Analysis of Vision*, New York, 1984
G. P. Weisberg *et al.*, *Japonisme*, Cleveland, 1975
J. Wilmerding, *American Arts*, Harmondsworth, 1976
R. Wrigley, *The Origins of French Art Criticism*, Oxford, 1993

16 Eastern traditions
J. Cahill, *The Compelling Image: Nature and Style in Seventeenth-Century Chinese Painting*, Cambridge, Mass./London, 1982
R. A. Crichton, *The Floating World: Japanese Popular Prints 1700–1900*, London, 1973
J. Hillier, *The Japanese Print: A new Approach* (1960), Rutland, Vt., 1975
Zhu Jiajin, ed., *Treasures of the Forbidden City*, New York, 1986
Zu Zhuoyun, ed., *Palaces of the Forbidden City*, New York/London, 1984
R. D. Lane, *Masters of the Japanese Print*, London, 1962
For general studies of art in China and Japan, see works cited under Chapters 6 and 12.

18 Indigenous arts of Africa, the Americas, Australia and Oceania
R. Abiodun *et al.*, eds., *The Yoruba Artist: New Theoretical Perspectives on African Arts*, Washington DC/London, 1994
R. L. Anderson & K. L. Field, *Art in Small-Scale Societies: Contemporary Readings*, Englewood Cliffs, NJ, 1993
J. C. Berlo & L. A. Wilson, *Arts of Africa, Oceania, and the Americas*, Englewood Cliffs, NJ, 1993
F. Boas, *Primitive Art* (1927), Magnolia, 1962
A. Buehler, T. Barrow & C. P. Mountford, *The Art of the South Sea Islands*, New York, 1962
W. Caruana, *Aboriginal Art*, London, 1993
J. Clifford, *The Predicament of Culture*, Cambridge, Mass./London, 1988
R. T. Coe, *Sacred Circles*, exh. cat., Arts Council of Great Britain, London, 1976
J. Coote & A. Shelton, eds., *Anthropology, Art and Aesthetics*, Oxford, 1992
G. A. Corbin, *Native Arts of North America, Africa and the South Pacific*, New York/London, 1988
A. D'Alleva, *Art of the Pacific*, London/New York, 1998
P. J. C. Dark & R. G. Rose, eds., *Artistic Heritage in a Changing Pacific*, Honolulu, 1993
H. J. Drewal *et al.*, *Yoruba: Nine Centuries of African Art and Thought*, New York, 1989
P. Drucker, *Indians of the Northwest Coast* (1955), Garden City, NY, 1963
V. Ebin, *The Body Decorated*, London, 1979
W. Fagg *et al.*, *Yoruba: Sculpture of West Africa*, New York/London, 1982
C. F. Feest, *Native Arts of North America* (1980), London, 1992
D. Fraser, *Primitive Art*, Garden City, NY, 1962
P. Gathercole, A. L. Kaeppler & D. Newton, *The Art of the Pacific Islands*, exh. cat., Washington DC, 1979
W. Gillon, *A Short History of African Art*, Harmondsworth, 1984
I. Guiart, *The Arts of the South Pacific*, New

York, 1963
A. Hanson & L. Hanson, eds., *Art and Identity in Oceania*, Bathurst, NSW, 1993
E. W. Herbert, *Iron, Gender and Power: Rituals of Transformation in African Societies*, Bloomington, NY, 1993
I. Hessel, *Inuit Art: An Introduction*, London, 1998
J. C. H. King, *First Peoples, First Contacts: Native Peoples of North America*, London, 1998
P. Kopper, *The Smithsonian Book of North American Indians*, Washington DC, 1986
C. Lévi-Strauss, *The Savage Mind* (1962), London, 1976
B. Lüthi & G. Lee, *Aratjara: Art of the First Australians*, London, 1993
H. Morphy, *Australian Aboriginal Art*, London, 1998
J. Picton, ed., *The Arts of African Textiles*, London, 1995
S. Price, *Primitive Art in Civilised Places*, Chicago/London, 1989
C. Schmutz, *Oceanic Art*, New York, 1969
D. C. Starzecka, ed., *Maori: Art and Culture* (1996), London, 1998
N. Thomas, *Oceanic Arts*, London, 1995
R. F. Thompson, *African Art in Motion*, Los Angeles, 1974
R. F. Thompson, *Flash of the Spirit, African and Afro-American Art and Philosophy*, New York, 1983
E. L. Wade, ed., *The Arts of the North American Indian: Native Traditions in Evolution*, New York, 1986
F. Willett, *African Art: An Introduction*, London, 1971, rev. ed. 1994

19 Art from 1900 to 1919
N. H. Arnason, *History of Modern Art* (1968), rev. D. Wheeler, Englewood Cliffs, NJ, 1986
R. Banham, *Theory and Design in the First Machine Age*, Oxford, 1960
H. B. Chipp, *Theories of Modern Art*, Berkeley, 1968
P. Crowther, *The Language of Twentieth-Century Art: A Conceptual History*, New Haven/London, 1997
W. J. R. Curtis, *Modern Architecture since 1900* (1982), London, 1996
P. Daix and J. Rosselet, *Picasso: The Cubist Years*, London, 1979
J. Elderfield, *The Wild Beasts: Fauvism and its Affinities*, New York, 1976
B. Fer, *On Abstract Art*, New Haven/London, 1997
F. Frascina & J. Harris, eds., *Art in Modern Culture: An Anthology of Critical Texts*, New York/London, 1992
J. Freeman, *The Fauve Landscape*, New York, 1990
E. F. Fry, *Cubism*, New York/London, 1966
J. Golding, *Cubism* (1959), Cambridge, Mass./London, 1988
R. Goldwater, *Primitivism in Modern Art* (1938), Cambridge, Mass., 1986
E. D. Gordon, *Expressionism, Art and Idea* (1987), New Haven/London, 1991
C. Green, *Cubism and its Enemies*, New Haven, 1987
W. Haftmann, *Painting in the Twentieth Century* (1957), New York, 1980
G. H. Hamilton, *Painting and Sculpture in Europe 1880–1940* (1967), New Haven/London, 1993
C. Harrison & P. Wood, eds., *Art in Theory 1900–1990*, Cambridge, Mass./Oxford, 1992
C. Harrison *et al.*, *Primitivism, Cubism, Abstraction: The Early Twentieth Century*, New Haven/London, 1993
J. D. Herbert, *Fauve Painting: The Making of Cultural Politics*, New Haven/London, 1992
R. Hughes, *The Shock of the New* (1980), London, 1991

S. Hunter, *American Art of the Twentieth Century*, Englewood Cliffs, NJ, 1973
C. M. Joachimedes & N. Rosenthal, eds., *American Art in the 20th Century*, Munich/London, 1993
C. M. Joachimedes & N. Rosenthal, eds., *German Art in the 20th Century*, Munich, 1985
P. Kaplan & S. Manso, eds., *Major European Art Movements 1900–1945*, New York, 1977
J. Lloyd, *German Expressionism: Primitivism and Modernity*, New Haven/London, 1991
N. Lynton, *The Story of Modern Art* (1980), Oxford, 1989
M. W. Martin, *Futurist Art and Theory 1909–1915* (1968), New York, 1977
A. Moszynska, *Abstract Art*, London, 1990
J. F. O'Gorman, *Three American Architects, Richardson, Sullivan, and Wright 1865–1915*, Chicago/London, 1991
G. Perry, *Women Artists and the Parisian Avant-Garde*, Manchester/New York, 1995
C. Poggi, *In Defiance of Painting: Cubism, Futurism and the Invention of Collage*, New Haven/London, 1992
R. Poggioli, *The Theory of the Avant Garde*, Cambridge, Mass./London, 1981
C. Rhodes, *Primitivism and Modern Art*, London, 1994
R. Rosenblum, *Cubism and Twentieth Century Art* (1976), New York, 1982
W. Rubin, ed., *"Primitivism" in 20th Century Art*, New York, 1988
J. Russell, *The Meanings of Modern Art* (1981), London/New York, 1991
M. Schapiro, *Modern Art, 19th and 20th Centuries*, New York/London, 1978
L. Steinberg, *Other Criteria: Confrontations with Twentieth Century Art*, New York, 1972
W. Tucker, *The Language of Sculpture*, London, 1977
P. Vogt, *Expressionism: German Painting 1906–1920*, New York, 1980
J. Weiss, *The Popular Culture of Modern Art*, New Haven/London, 1994

20 Between the two world wars
D. Ades, *Dada and Surrealism Reviewed*, London, 1978
D. Ades, *Photomontage* (1976), London, 1986
D. Ades *et al.*, *Art and Power: Europe under the Dictators 1930–1945*, London, 1995
Y. A. Bois, *Painting as Model*, Cambridge, Mass., 1990
M. A. Caws, ed., *Surrealism and Women*, Cambridge, Mass., 1991
W. Chadwick, *Women Artists and the Surrealist Movement* (1985), London, 1991
H. B. Chipp, *Theories of Modern Art*, Berkeley, 1968
P. Collins, *Changing Ideals in Modern Architecture 1750–1950*, London, 1971
B. Fer *et al.*, *Realism, Rationalism, Surrealism*, New Haven/London, 1993
K. Frampton, *Modern Architecture: A Critical History* (1980), London, 1992
F. Frascina & J. Harris, eds., *Art in Modern Culture: An Anthology of Critical Texts*, New York/London, 1992
M. Gale, *Dada and Surrealism*, London, 1997
R. Golan, *Modernity and Nostalgia: Art and Politics in France Between the Wars*, New Haven/London, 1995
C. Gray, *The Russian Experiment in Art 1863–1922* (1971), rev. M. Burleigh-Motley, London, 1986
H. L. C. Jaffé, *De Stijl* (1971), Cambridge, Mass., 1986
L. R. Lippard, *Surrealists on Art*, Englewood Cliffs, NJ, 1970
C. Lodder, *Russian Constructivism*, New Haven/London, 1983
C. Robinson & R. Haag Bletter, *Skyscraper*

Style: Art Deco New York, New York, 1975
D. Rochfort, *Mexican Muralists*, London, 1993
B. Rose, *American Art Since 1900* (1967), New York, 1975
W. Rubin, *Dada and Surrealist Art*, New York, 1977
R. Short, *Dada and Surrealism*, London, 1994
K. E. Silver, *Esprit de Corps: The Art of the Parisian Avant-Garde and the First World War, 1914–1925*, Princeton, 1989
J. J. Spector, *The Education of the Surrealists*, New York, 1996
S. Stitch, *Anxious Visions: Surrealist Art*, Berkeley, Ca., 1990
D. Tashjian, *A Boatload of Madmen: Surrealism and the American Avant-Garde 1920–1950*, New York/London, 1994
R.-C. Washton Long, ed., *German Expressionism: Documents from the End of the Wilhelmine Empire to the Rise of National Socialism*, New York, 1993
H. M. Wingler, *The Bauhaus* (1968), Cambridge, Mass., 1978

21   Post-war to Post-Modern
M. Archer, *Art since 1960*, London, 1997
D. Ashton, *A Fable of Modern Art*, New York, 1980
D. Ashton, *American Art Since 1945*, New York, 1982
D. Ashton, *The New York School, A Cultural Reckoning*, New York, 1973
G. Battock, ed., *Minimal Art, A Critical Anthology*, New York, 1969
B. J. Beardsley, *Earthworks and Beyond* (1984), New York/London, 1998
B. Bognar, *Contemporary Japanese Architecture*, New York/London, 1985
N. Broude & M. D. Garrard, eds., *The Power of Feminist Art: The American Movement of the 1970s*, New York/London, 1994
A. Causey, *Sculpture since 1945*, Oxford/New York, 1998
H. B. Chipp, *Theories of Modern Art*, Berkeley, 1968
T. Crow, *The Rise of the Sixties: American and European Art in the Era of Dissent 1955–69*, London/New York, 1996
P. Crowther, *The Language of Twentieth-Century Art: A Conceptual History*, New Haven/London, 1997
W. J. R. Curtis, *Modern Architecture since 1900* (1982), London, 1996
A. C. Danto, *After the End of Art: Contemporary Art and the Pale of History*, Princeton, 1997
J. Fineberg, *Art Since 1940: Strategies of Being*, Englewood Cliffs, NJ, 1994
D. Ghirardo, *Architecture After Modernism*, London, 1996
A. E. Gibson, *Abstract Expressionism: Other Politics*, New Haven/London, 1997
E. Gillen, ed., *German Art from Beckmann to Richter*, Cologne, 1997
T. Godfrey, *Conceptual Art*, London, 1998
A. Goldstein & A. Rorimer, *Reconsidering the Object of Art, 1965–1975*, Los Angeles/Cambridge, Mass., 1995
C. Greenberg, *Art and Culture*, New York, 1973
A. Grundberg & K. McCarthy Gaussel, *Photography and Art, Interactions since 1945*, New York, 1987
J. Jacobus, *Twentieth Century Architecture, the Middle Years 1940–1964*, New York, 1966
C. Jencks, *Modern Movements in Architecture* (1973), Harmondsworth, 1985
C. Jencks, *What is Postmodernism?* (1987), London, 1996
J. Kastner, ed., *Land and Environmental Art*, London, 1998
R. E. Kraus, *The Optical Unconscious*, Cambridge, Mass., 1993
D. Kuspit, *The Cult of the Avant-Garde Artist*, New York, 1996
L. Leja, *Reframing Abstract Expressionism: Subjectivity and Painting in the 1940s*, New Haven/London, 1993
L. R. Lippard, *Dematerialization of the Art Object*, London, 1973
L. R. Lippard, *Pop Art* (1966), London, 1970
M. Livingstone, ed., *Pop Art: A Continuing History*, London, 1990
E. Lucie-Smith, *Art Today*, London, 1995
S. H. Madoff, ed., *Pop Art: A Critical History*, Berkeley, Ca./London, 1997
U. Meyer, *Conceptual Art*, New York, 1972
F. Morris, ed., *Paris Post War: Art and Existentialism*, London, 1993
S. Polkari, *Abstract Expressionism and Modern Experience*, Cambridge, 1991
C. Robins, *The Pluralist Era: American Art 1968–1981*, New York/London, 1984
I. Sandler, *The New York School: The Painters and Sculptors of the Fifties*, New York/London, 1978
I. Sandler, *The Triumph of American Painting: A History of Abstract Expressionism*, New York, 1970
I. Sandler, *Art of the Postmodern Era*, New York, 1996
A. Sonfist, ed., *Art in the Landscape, A Critical Anthology of Environmental Art*, New York, 1983
B. Taylor, *The Art of Today*, London/New York, 1995
D. Waldman, *Collage, Assemblage and the Found Object*, New York/London, 1992
M. Weaver, ed., *The Art of Photography 1939–1989*, New Haven/London, 1989
D. Wheeler, *Art Since Mid-Century*, New York/London, 1991
P. Wood et al., *Modernism in Dispute: Art since the Forties*, New Haven/London, 1993

22   Towards the third millennium
J. F. Andrews, *Painters and Politics in the People's Republic of China, 1949–1979*, Berkeley, Ca., Los Angeles and London, 1994
M. Archer et al., *Installation Art*, London/Washington DC, 1994
O. Bätschmann, *The Artist in the Modern World*, Cologne, 1997
N. Broude & D. Garrard, *The Power of Feminist Art*, New York, 1994
N. Broude & M. D. Garrard, eds., *The Power of Feminist Art: Emergence, Impact and Triumph of the American Feminist Movement*, London, 1995
C. Carr, *On Edge: Performance at the End of the Twentieth Century*, 1993
G. Clarke, *The Photograph*, Oxford, 1997
T. Clark, *Art and Propaganda in the Twentieth Century*, London/New York, 1997
J. L. Cohen, *The New Chinese Painting 1949–1986*, New York, 1987
T. Crow, *Modern Art in the Common Culture*, New Haven/London, 1996
A. C. Danto, *Beyond the Brillo Box*, New York, 1992
K. Deepwell, ed., *Women Artists and Modernism*, Manchester/New York, 1998
H. Foster, *The Return of the Real: The Avant-Garde at the End of the Century*, Cambridge, Mass./London, 1996
C. Goodman, *Digital Visions, Computers and Art*, New York, 1987
J. A. Isaak, *Feminism and Contemporary Art*, London/New York, 1996
T. Krens, M. Goven & J. Thompson, eds., *Refigured Painting: The German Image 1960–88*, Munich, 1989
D. Kuspit, *Idiosyncratic Identities: Artists at the End of the Avant-Garde*, Cambridge, 1996
L. R. Lippard, *Mixed Blessings, New Art in Multicultural America*, New York, 1990
M. Lovejoy, *Postmodern Currents, Art and*

New York, 1996

Artists in the Age of Electronic Media, Ann Arbor/London, 1989
E. Lucie-Smith, *Art in the Eighties*, New York/Oxford, 1990
E. Lucie-Smith, *Visual Arts in the Twentieth Century*, London, 1996
W. J. T. Mitchell, *Picture Theory: Essays on Verbal and Visual Presentation*, Chicago/London, 1994
P. Mortensen, *Art in the Social Order: The Making of the Modern Conception of Art*, Albany, NY, 1997
S. Nairne et al., *State of the Art, Ideas and Images in the 1980s*, London, 1987
C. Norris & A. Benjamin, *What is Deconstruction?*, New York/London, 1988
C. Owens, *Beyond Recognition*, Berkeley, Ca./Oxford, 1992
S. F. Patton, *African-American Art*, Oxford/New York, 1998
W. Pöhlmann, ed., *China Avant-Garde*, Berlin, 1993
F. Popper, *Art of the Electronic Age*, London, 1993
R. J. Powell, *Black Art and Culture in the Twentieth Century*, London/New York, 1997
H. Risatti, ed., *Postmodern Perspectives*, Englewood Cliffs, NJ, 1990
R. Rosen & C. Brawer, *Making Their Mark: Women Artists Move into the Mainstream*, New York, 1989
D. L. Schodek, *Structure in Sculpture*, Cambridge, Mass./London, 1993
H. J. Smagula, *Currents: Contemporary Directions in the Visual Arts*, London, 1983
N. Stangos, ed., *Concepts of Modern Art* (1974), London, 1994
K. Stiles & P. Selz, *Theories and Documents of Contemporary Art: A Sourcebook of Artists' Writings*, Berkeley, Ca./London, 1996
D. Sylvester, *About Modern Art: Critical Essays 1948–96*, London, 1996
B. Wallis, ed., *Art After Modernism: Rethinking Representation*, New York, 1984
M. Witzling, *Voicing Today's Visions: Writings by Contemporary Women Artists*, New York, 1994

CONCEPTS
Page 149
M. Robertson, *A History of Greek Art*, Cambridge 1975
E. Panofsky, *Idea: A Concept in Art Theory*, Columbia, S.C., 1968
Page 241
P. Acharaya, *Manasara Silpasastra*, Oxford, 1934
J. Mascarò, *The Bhagavad Gita*, Harmondsworth, 1962
G. Michell, *The Hindu Temple*, London, 1977
S. Kramrisch, *The Presence of Siva*, Princeton, 1981
Page 576
E. Panofsky, *Idea: A Concept in Art Theory*, Columbia, S.C., 1968
R. W. Lee, *Ut Pictura Poesis: The Humanistic Theory of Painting*, New York, 1967
Page 674
H. Osborne, *Aesthetics and Art Theory*, London, 1968
C. Baudelaire, *The Painter of Modern Life and Art in Paris, 1845–1862*, tr. and ed. J. Mayne, London, 1964–5
L. Nochlin, *Realism and Tradition in Art, 1848–1900*, Englewood Cliffs, 1966
M. C. Spencer, *The Art Criticism of Théophile Gautier*, Geneva, 1969
Page 845
M. Berman, *All that is Solid melts into Air: The Experience of Modernity*, 1983
C. Greenberg, *Art and Culture*, Boston, 1961
C. Greenberg, 'Modernist Painting', in *Art and Literature*, no. 4, Spring 1965

IN CONTEXT
Pages 44–5
A. Baring & J. Cashford, *The Myth of the Goddess. Evolution of an Image*, London, 1991

J. Mellaart, *Çatal Hüyük. A Neolithic Town in Anatolia*, London, 1967

M. Todd, *Çatal Hüyük in Perspective*, Menlo Park, 1976

Page 84
C. Doumas, *The Wall-Paintings of Thera*, Athens, 1992

H. L. Lorimer, *Homer and the Monuments*, London, 1950

Pages 96–7
N. Luomala, 'Matrilineal Reinterpretation of Some Ancient Egyptian Sacred Cows' in N. Broude & M. D. Garrard, eds., *Feminism and Art History: Questioning the Litany*, New York, 1982

G. Robins, *Women in Ancient Egypt*, London, 1993

J. Tyldesley, *Daughters of Isis: Women of Ancient Egypt*, London/New York, 1994

Page 123
R. L. Burger, *Chavin and the Origins of Andean Civilization*, London, 1992

Pages 144–5
F. Chamoux, *Fouilles de Delphes IV, Monuments figurés, 5, L'Aurige*, Paris, 1955

Page 187
U. Gehrig, *Hildesheimer Silberfund*, Berlin, 1967

D. B. Harden, *Glass of the Caesars*, Corning/London, 1987

Pages 208–9
H. P. L'Orange, *Apotheosis in Ancient Portraiture*, Oslo, 1947

H. P. L'Orange, *Art Forms and Civil Life in the late Roman Empire*, Princeton, 1965

C. B. Rose, *Dynastic Commemoration and Imperial Portraiture in the Julio-Claudian Period*, Cambridge/New York, 1997

S. Walker, *Greek and Roman Portraits*, London, 1995

A. N. Zadoks-Josephus Jitta, *Ancestral portraiture in Rome*, Amsterdam, 1932

Pages 230–1
R. Knox, *Amaravati. Buddhist Sculpture from the Great Stupa*, London, 1992

W. Zwalf, ed., *Buddhism. Art and Faith*, London, 1985

Page 245
H. Goetz, 'The Kailasa of Ellora', in *Artibus Asiae* xv (1952), pp. 84–107

S. L. Huntington, *The Art of Ancient India*, New York, 1985

Pages 266–7
M. J. Powers, *Art and Political Expression in early China*, New Haven/London, 1991

Pages 300–1
R. Bianchi-Bandinelli, *Rome. The Late Empire*, New York, 1971

E. Kitzinger, *Byzantine Art in the Making*, London, 1977

Pages 326–7
B. Brenk, *Die frühchristlichen Mosaiken in S. Maria Maggiore zu Rom*, Wiesbaden, 1975

R. Lane Fox, *Pagans and Christians*, Harmondsworth, 1986

M. Warner, *Alone of All Her Sex. The Myth and Cult of the Virgin Mary*, London, 1976

K. Weitzmann, *Late Antique and Early Christian Book Illumination*, London, 1997

Page 336
W. Braunfels, *Monasteries of Western Europe*, London/Princeton, 1972

Dom E. C. Butler, 'Monasticism' in H. M. Gwatkin & J. P. Whitney, eds., *The Cambridge Medieval History*, vol I (1924), Cambridge, 1957

Page 358
R. Hillenbrand in *The Encyclopedia of Islam*, vol V, Leiden, 1986, pp. 1123–55

Pages 386–7
E. Panofsky, *Abbot Suger on the Abbey Church of St.-Denis*, Princeton, 1979

R. Recht, ed., *Les Battisseurs des Cathédrales Gothiques*, Strasbourg, 1989

Pages 402–3
U. Nicolini, 'Chiara d'Assisi, santa' in *Dizionario Biografico degli Italiani*, vol XXIV, Rome, 1980

F. Todini, *La pittura in Italia. Il Duecento e Trecento*, Milan, 1988

Pages 432–3
E. Dhanens, *Van Eyck, The Ghent Altarpiece* (Art in Context), London, 1973

Page 460
P. F. Brown, *Venetian Narrative Painting in the Age of Carpaccio*, New Haven/London, 1988

Pages 478–9
J. Ackerman, *The Cortile del Belvedere*, Vatican City, 1954

H. W. Kruft, *A History of Architectural Theory. From Vitruvius to the present* (1985), London, 1994

R. Wittkower, *Architectural Principles in the Age of Humanism* (1949), New York, 1988

Pages 510–1
I. Buchanan, 'The collection of Niclaes Jongelinck' in *Burlington Magazine* CXXXII (1990), pp. 102–13, 541–50

Pages 546–7
S. C. Welch, *India: Art and Culture 1300–1900*, New York, 1985

R. Skelton, *The Shah Jahan Cup*, London, 1969

Pages 570–1
Yoshitomo Okamoto, *The Namban Art of Japan*, Tokyo, 1972

Namban ou de l'européisme japonais XVI–XVII siècles, exh. cat., Musée Cernuschi, Paris, 1980

Page 582
H. Honour, *The New Golden Land: European Images of America from the Present Time*, New York, 1975

E. van den Boogaart, ed., *Johan Maurits van Nassau-Siegen 1604–1679*, The Hague, 1979

Pages 602–3
M. D. Carroll, 'Rembrandt as Meditational Print-maker' in *Art Bulletin* LXIII (1981), pp. 585–610

C. White & K. C. Boon, *Rembrandt's Etchings*, Amsterdam, 1969

Pages 622–3
C. Duncan, 'Happy Mothers and other New Ideas in Eighteenth Century French Art' in N. Broude & M. D. Garrard, *Feminism and Art History. Questioning the Litany*, New York, 1982

J. Ingamells, *The Wallace Collection Catalogue of Pictures*, vol III, London, 1989

D. Posner, 'The Swinging Women of Watteau and Fragonard' in *Art Bulletin* LXIV (1982), pp. 75–88

Pages 662–3
A. Boime, *The Art of Exclusion*, Washington DC/London, 1990

H. Honour, *The Image of the Black in Western Art*, vol IV, Cambridge, Mass., 1989

Pages 684–5
H. Adams, 'A New Interpretation of Bingham's Fur Traders' in *Art Bulletin* LXV (1983), pp. 675–80

N. Rash, *The Paintings and Politics of George Caleb Bingham*, New Haven, 1991

W. H. Truettner, ed., *The West as America*, Washington DC/London, 1991

Page 695
S. E. Lee, 'Portraiture in Chinese and Japanese Art' in *Bulletin of the Cleveland Museum of Art*, April 1977

Pages 714–5
T. J. Clark, *The Painting of Modern Life. Paris in the Art of Manet and his Followers*, London/New York, 1985

T. Reff, *Manet: Olympia* (Art in Context), London, 1976

Pages 732–3
S. Giedion, *Space, Time and Architecture. The Growth of a New Tradition* (1941), Cambridge, Mass., 1967

R. Mainstone, *Developments in Structural Form*, London, 1975

M. Trachtenberg, *The Statue of Liberty* (Art in Context), New York/London, 1976

Page 754
F. Boas, *Primitive Art*, New York (1927), 1955

C. Lévi-Strauss, *Structural Anthropology*, Garden City, N.Y., 1967

J. C. H. King, *Portrait Masks from the Northwest Coast of America*, London, 1979

Pages 762–3
M. Kecskesi, *African Masterpieces from Munich*, New York, 1987

F. Kramer, *The Red Fez. Art and Spirit Possession in Africa* (1987), New York, 1993

J. Lips, *The Savage Hits Back* (1937), New York, 1966

Pages 776–7
W. Rubin et al., *Les Demoiselles d'Avignon*, New York, 1994

P. Leighton, 'The White Peril and L'Art nègre: Picasso, Primitivism and Anticolonialism' in *Art Bulletin* LXXII (1990), pp. 609–30

Pages 810–1
D. Rochfort, *Mexican Muralists*, London, 1991

P. Marnham, *Dreaming with his Eyes Open. A Life of Diego Rivera*, London, 1988

URBAN DEVELOPMENT
Pages 196–7
W. L. Macdonald, *The Architecture of the Roman empire*, vol II, New Haven, 1986

S. Kostof, *A History of Architecture: Settings and Rituals*, New York (1985), 1995

Pages 316–7
C. Mango, *Byzantine Architecture*, New York, 1976

T. F. Mathews, *The Art of Byzantium* (U.S. title: *Byzantium: From Antiquity to the Renaissance*) London, 1998 (US: New York, 1998)

Pages 492–3
W. Braunfels, *Urban Design in Western Europe*, Chicago, 1988

S. Kostof, *A History of Architecture. Settings and Rituals*, New York (1985), 1995

L. Partridge, *The Renaissance of Rome* (US title: *The Art of the Renaissance*), London, 1996 (US: New York, 1996)

Pages 540–1
S. S. Blair & J. M. Bloom, *The Art and Architecture of Islam 1250–1800*, NewHaven/London, 1994

H. Gaube, *Iranian Cities*, New York, 1979

R. Hillenbrand, 'Safavid Architecture' in *Cambridge History of Islam*, vol VI, Cambridge, 1986

R. Hillenbrand, *Islamic Architcture*, Edinburgh, 1994

Pages 644–5
G. R. Beveridge, *Frederick Law Olmsted. Designing the American Landscape*, New York, 1995

G. Chadwick, *The Park and the Town*, London 1966

H. Conway, *People's Parks: The Design and Development of Public Parks in Britain*, Cambridge, 1991

P. Lambert, ed., *Viewing Olmsted*, Cambridge, Mass., 1997

N. Pevsner, *A History of Building Types*, London, 1976

S. Pollard & J. Salt, eds., *Robert Owen. Prophet of the Poor*, London, 1971

Pages 828–9
R. Beever, *The Garden City Utopia. A Critical Biography of Ebenezer Howard*, London, 1988

W. Boesiger, ed., *Le Corbusier. Oeuvres complètes*, Zurich, 1970

W. Curtis, *Modern Architecture*, London (1982), 1996

R. Fishman, *Urban Utopias in the Twentieth Century*, New York, 1977

J. Lucan, ed., *Le Corbusier. Une encyclopédie*, Paris, 1987

D. MacFadyen, *Sir E. Howard and the Town Planning Movement*, London, 1933

F. L. Wright, *Architecture and Modern Life*, New York/London, 1939

F. L. Wright, *The Living City*, New York, 1958

INDEX

PICTURE CREDITS

Calmann & King Ltd, the authors and the picture researchers wish to thank the institutions and individuals who have kindly provided photographic material for use in this book.
Museum and gallery locations are given in the captions; other sources are listed below.

The following abbreviations have been used:

AAA: Ancient Art & Architecture Collection, Middlesex
Alinari: Alinari, Florence
Anderson: Anderson, Rome (Alinari, Florence)
ARS: Artists Rights Society, New York
Artothek: Artothek, Peissenberg, Germany
Bridgeman: The Bridgeman Art Library, London
CNMH: Caisse Nationale des Monuments Historiques et des Sites, Paris
DAI: Deutsches Archäologisches Institut
Fleming Honour: photographs by John Fleming and Hugh Honour
Forman: Werner Forman Archive, London
Fototeca Unione: Fototeca Unione of the American Academy in Rome
Giraudon: Giraudon, Paris
Halliday: Sonia Halliday, Weston Turville, UK
Harding: Robert Harding Picture Library, London
Hirmer: Fotoarchiv Hirmer, Munich
Kersting: A.F. Kersting, London
Marburg: Bildarchiv Marburg, Germany
MAS: Ampliaciones y Reproducciones MAS, Barcelona
Peerless: Ann & Bury Peerless, Birchington-on-Sea, UK
Powell: Josephine Powell, Rome
Prestel: Prestel Verlag, Munich
RMN: Réunion des Musées Nationaux, Paris
Scala: Scala, Florence
von Matt: Estate of Leonard von Matt, Buochs, Switzerland

frontispiece Achille Weider, Zürich
page 11 Christian Richters Fotograf, Münster

0,1;0,4;0,8 Alinari, Florence
0,2;0,14 Fleming Honour
0,3 DAI, Athens
0,5 © Paul M.R. Maeyaert, Mont de l'Enclus (Orroir), Belgium
0,9 © Giancarlo Costa, Milan

page 32 China Pictorial

1,3 RMN, Paris
1,4 Prestel
1,5 Achille Weider, Zurich Weider, Zurich
1,6;1,7;1,8 J. Clottes, Ministère de la Culture et de la Communication-Direction du Patrimoine-sous Direction de l'Archeologie
1,9 Colorphoto Hans Hinz, Allschwil, Switzerland
1,10 Institut Amatller D'Art Hispanic, Barcelona
1,11 Yan, Toulouse
1,14 Frobenius Institut, Frankfurt
1,15;1,22;1,23 Photo Resources, Canterbury
1,16 E. Böhm, Mainz
1,17;1,19 Anatolian Studies, (British Institute of Archaeolgy at Ankara), 1963 © James Mellaart
1,19 Jericho Excavation Fund, London
1,20 Arlette Mellaart, London
1,21 Powell
1,26 Kersting

2,1;2,32 RMN
2,2;2,12;2,23a+b;2,33;2,45;2,46;2,47;2,50;2,51;2,57 Hirmer
2,9;2,16;2,17;2,48;2,49 Scala
2,10;2,14 Gallimard, Paris
2,22;2,27;2,31 John Ross, Rome
2,24;2,35;2,37 Marburg
2,25;2,26 Fleming Honour
2,30 Kersting
2,43 Sonia Halliday
2,52 AAA

2,55 Estate of E. Boudot-Lamotte
2,58;2,59 from The Wallpaintings of Thera, 1992 Thera Foundation, London
2,61 China Pictorial

3,1 Halliday
3,3 Halliday/FHC Birch
3,2 Powell, Rome
3,6 John Ross, Rome
3,7;3,48 Forman
3,10 Griffith Institute, Ashmolean Museum, Oxford
3,11;3,44 Fleming Honour
3,12 Giraudon
3,15;3,16;3,17;3,28;3,29 Hirmer
3,18 Harding/John Ross
3,19;3,42 Harding
3,20 Metropolitan Museum of Art, New York (Egyptian Expedition)
3,22 Kersting
3,25 Institute of Archaeology Library, University of London
3,26 Giraudon
3,27 RMN
3,34;3,37;3,38 E. Boudot-Lamotte
3,35 ZEFA/Maroon
3,45 Gift of Gillett G. Griffin in honour of David W. Steadman Princeton Art Museum
3,49 John Hillelson Agency London/Dr Georg Gerster
3,50 South American Pictures/Tony Morrison, Suffolk
3,52;3,53;3,54 from Richard Burger, Chavin and the Origins of Andean Civilisation, Thames & Hudson 1992 page 158

4,1;4,3;4,8;4,10;4,12;4,13;4,14;4,20;4,24;4,29;4,30;4,33;4,34;4,37;4,42;4,73 Hirmer
4,6;4,15;4,19 Alison Frantz, Princeton, New Jersey
4,7 DAI, Athens
4,11 Forman
4,17 Calmann & King Archives, London/Ralph Liebermann
4,18 Douglas Dickins, London
4,23 Halliday
4,25 Professor Martin Robertson, Cambridge
4,28 Bildarchiv Preussicher Kulturbesitz, Berlin
4,35 Fotographia Foglia, Naples
4,36;4,70;4,74 Scala
4,38;4,40;4,43 Alinari
4,44 AAA
4,45 Marburg
4,47;4,52;4,53;4,55 Lee Boltin, Croton-on-Hudson, New York
4,57 Foto Furbock, Graz, Austria
4,58 Giraudon
4,61 RMN-Arnaudet
4,63;4,64 Anderson
4,67 Soprintendenza alle Antichità dell'Etruria Meridionale
4,68 DAI, Rome
4,71 von Matt

5,1;5,2;5,23 DAI, Istanbul
5,3;5,21 Hirmer
5,4;5,5 Anderson
5,6;5,15 RMN
5,7;5,8 Ekdotike Athenon, Athens
5,11;5,13;5,53;5,58;5,59;5,60;5,61;5,67;5,77 DAI, Rome
5,16;5,24;5,29;5,32;5,55 Scala
5,18;5,34;5,42;5,48;5,51;5,64;5,65;5,78 Alinari
5,20 ZEFA/Starphoto
5,25 Bildarchiv Preussicher Kulturbesitz, Berlin
5,27 Michael Larvey, Austin, Texas
5,28 Fotografica Foglia, Naples
5,31 Dr. Felbermeyer, Rome
5,35;5,40;5,46;5,66;5,69;5,74 Fototeca Unione of the American Academy in Rome
5,37 © Paul M.R. Maeyaert
5,41 Barnaby's Picture Library, London
5,43 Kersting
5,50 von Matt
5,52 © Araldo De Luca, Rome
5,53 Oscar Savio, Rome
5,56 R. Higginson, London
5,57 Photo Meyer, Vienna
5,62 © Studio Fotografico Quattrone, Florence
5,63 Kersting
5,68 Peter Clayton Associates, Hemel Hempstead, UK
5,70 G.E. Kiddersmith, New York
5,72 Istituto Centrale per il Catalogo e la Documentazione, Rome
5,75 Landesmuseum, Trier

page 222 Margaret Medley, London

6,1;6,26 India Office Library and Records, London
6,3 Soprintendenza alle Antichità delle Province di Napoli
6,5;6,10;6,27 Giraudon
6,6;6,21;6,50;6,51 Peerless
6,8;6,36 Archaeological Survey of India, New Delhi
6,12;6,32;6,55;6,63;6,66;6,73;6,75;6,107 Harding
6,13 John C. Huntington, Ohio State University
6,23;6,31;6,35;6,45;6,49;6,52;6,54;6,56;6,58;6,59;6,60;6,69;6,74;6,77;6,78;6,79;6,81;6,84;6,86;6,91;6,97;6,98;6,108;6,114;6,118 Fleming Honour

6,24;6,29;6,43 Dinodia, Bombay
6,25 Punjab Government/Numatullah Shah
6,28;6,34 E. Boudot-Lamotte
6,30 Macquitty International Collection, London
6,33;6,38;6,40;6,42 Kersting
6,41 Richard Lannoy, Bath
6,47 © Foto Wettstein & Kauf, Zurich
6,48 C.M. Dixon, Canterbury, Kent
6,57 Douglas Dickins, London
6,61 Rijksmuseum voor Volkenkunde, Leiden, Netherlands
6,65 RMN-John Goldings
6,67 Harding/G.A.Mather
6,68 École Française d'Extreme Orient
6,70 National Museum, Bangkok
6,71 Caroline Courtauld, Hong Kong
6,85;6,87;6,92 China Pictorial
6,88;6,94;6,119 Forman
6,96 G.&P. Corrigan/Biofotos, Farnham, Surrey
6,102 Thames & Hudson Ltd, London
6,103;6,124;6,126 The Zauho Press, Tokyo
6,110 RMN
6,111;6,113 Japan Information and Cultural Centre, London
6,115;6,122;6,123 Sakamoto Photo Research Laboratory, Tokyo
6,121 Asukaen, Nara, Japan
6,127 Orion Press, Tokyo

7,2;7,4;7,19;7,21;7,27;7,28;7,30;7,33;7,63;7,72 Scala
7,3;7,16;7,24;7,41 Hirmer
7,5 Yale University Art Gallery, New Haven, Conn (Dura Europos Collection)
7,6;7,8;7,9 Pontificia Commissione di Archeologia ed Arte Sacra, Rome
7,7 Foto Biblioteca Vaticana
7,11;7,14;7,25;7,49;7,51 Alinari
7,17;7,22 Fabbri, Milan
7,18 von Matt
7,20;7,74 © Giancarlo Costa, Milan
7,29 © Cameraphoto Arte, Venice
7,37;7,43 Halliday
7,40;7,62;7,67 Marburg
7,42;7,46 AAA
7,47 Giraudon
7,48 Dumbarton Oaks Center for Byzantine Studies, Washington, DC
7,50 Powell
7,61 Janet and Colin Bord, Montgomery, Powys
7,66 Roebild, Frankfurt
7,70 Meyer, Vienna

8,2 Giraudon
8,5 Halliday
8,6;8,24 Angelo Hornak, London
8,7;8,9;8,10 Editions d'Art Albert Skira, Geneva
8,8 Hugh Kennedy, University of St. Andrews
8,13 Aerofilms, Hertfordshire
8,14 Roger Wood, London
8,18 MAS
8,19 Raffaello Bencini, Florence
8,20;8,22 Powell
8,21;8,23 Prestel
8,27 Nasser D. Khalili Collection of Islamic Art (POT 1492), photograph © Nour Foundation
8,28 Scala
8,29 John Hillelson Agency London/Eric Lessing/Magnum

9,1;9,4 Rheinisches Bildarchiv, Cologne
9,2 Ann Münchow, Aachen
9,3 Forman
9,6;9,31;9,34;9,49;9,54;9,63 Marburg
9,8;9,35;9,61 Hirmer
9,10 © Studio Fotografico Quattrone, Florence
9,11;9,74;9,76;9,77;9,79;9,81;9,82;9,83;9,88 Scala
9,14 Harding/Rainbird Collection
9,16;9,17 © Cameraphoto Arte, Venice
9,18;9,84;9,87;9,89 Giraudon, Paris
9,19 Wim Swaan, London
9,20;9,21 Yan, Toulouse
9,26;9,27;9,28;9,29 © Paul M.R. Maeyaert
9,32 Kunstverlag Maria Laach, Maria Laach, Germany
9,33;9,47;9,51;9,52;9,58 Kersting
9,38;9,68 Fleming Honour
9,41 Angelo Hornak, London
9,43 James Austin, Cambridge
9,45;9,46 Halliday
9,48 Aerofilms Ltd, London
9,50 Roger-Viollet, Paris
9,53 Lauros-Giraudon/Bridgeman
9,55 Prestel
9,56 RMN
9,59 Conway Library, Courtauld Institute of Art, London
9,62 Helga Schmidt-Glassner, Stuttgart
9,64;9,65;9,71;9,72;9,73;9,75 Alinari
9,69 Powell
9,70 Dumbarton Oaks Center for Byzantine Studies, Washington, DC
9,80 Musei Civici Padova agli Eremitani/Studio Deganello, Padua
9,85 Osvaldo Böhm, Venice
9,90 Lauros/Giraudon